W9-CZT-804

NASA
FACTBOOK

NASA FACTBOOK

ALVIN RENETZKY, Ph.D.

Editor-in-Chief

BARBARA J. FLYNN, M.L.S.

Editor

and

**THE STAFF
OF
ACADEMIC MEDIA**

**Guide to National Aeronautics and
Space Administration Programs and Activities**

ACADEMIC MEDIA · ORANGE, NEW JERSEY

INTRODUCTION

CREATION AND AUTHORITY   The National Aeronautics and Space Administration was established by the National Aeronautics and Space Act of 1958 (72 Stat. 426; 42 U.S.C. 2451 et seq.), as amended.

PURPOSE   In carrying out the policy of Congress that activities in space should be devoted to peaceful purposes for the benefit of all mankind, the principal statutory functions of the NASA are:

1. Conduct research for the solution of problems of flight within and outside the earth's atmosphere, and develop, construct, test, and operate aeronautical and space vehicles.

2. Conduct activities required for the exploration of space with manned and unmanned vehicles.

3. Arrange for the most effective utilization of the scientific and engineering resources of the United States with other nations engaged in aeronautical and space activities for peaceful purposes.

4. Provide for the widest practicable and appropriate dissemination of information concerning NASA's activities and their results.

ORGANIZATION   The Administrator is charged with responsibility for all functions and authorities assigned to NASA. The Deputy Administrator is the Administrator's principal assistant acting under delegations of authority and assignments of responsibility from the Administrator. During the Administrator's absence the Deputy Administrator serves as Acting Administrator.

ASSOCIATE ADMINISTRATOR   Provides a focal point for developing, reviewing, and coordinating agency policy, programs, and plans, and participates with the Administrator in making major policy decisions. The Assistant Administrator for Policy reports to the Associate Administrator.

DEPUTY ASSOCIATE ADMINISTRATOR (PLANNING)   Provides central planning for the agency. Furnishes leadership and guidance to agency staff and program offices in all aspects of planning activity. Is responsible for formulating agency goals, objectives, and integrated plans.

ASSOCIATE DEPUTY ADMINISTRATOR   Is responsible for overall executive leadership of NASA's external relationships with other elements of government and with the general public. The Assistant Administrators for DOD and Interagency Affairs, International Affairs, Legislative Affairs, and Public Affairs report to the Associate Deputy Administrator.

ASSOCIATE ADMINISTRATOR FOR ORGANIZATION AND MANAGEMENT   Is primarily responsible for evaluating and strengthening agencywide management practices and policies relating to NASA's programs and activities that are carried out through NASA in-house, industrial, and university elements. He is responsible to the Administrator for leadership and supervision in the areas of Administration, Industry Affairs, Technology Utilization, University Affairs, Special

Contracts Negotiation and Review, and other offices on which NASA operations depend for effectiveness.

GENERAL COUNSEL   Reporting to the Administrator, provides legal review of NASA operations and general support and advice, based on his background of experience, to all NASA organizational elements.

ASSISTANT ADMINISTRATOR FOR MANAGEMENT DEVELOPMENT   Also reports to the Administrator and is responsible for assuring that NASA management procedures are documented for dissemination and use throughout NASA and for providing support and guidance on the effectiveness of NASA operations.

EXECUTIVE SECRETARIAT   Serves as the major communications system linking the Office of the Administrator with other Headquarters offices and organizational elements in the flow of decision-related documents and information needed for planning, coordination, and control. This office provides an overlay of communications on the normal structure of line and staff communication among the Headquarters offices and other organizational elements.

HEADQUARTERS PROGRAM OFFICES — FIELD INSTALLATIONS

Planning, coordination, and control of NASA programs are vested in Headquarters Directors of NASA's Field Centers and other installations are responsible for execution of NASA's programs, largely through contracts with research, development, and manufacturing enterprises. A broad range of research and development activities are conducted in NASA's Field Centers and installations by Government-employed scientists, engineers, and technicians to evaluate new concepts and phenomena and to maintain the competence required to manage contracts with private enterprises.

Four offices are headed by Associate Administrators who are responsible for planning and directing NASA's research and development programs. Three of these offices also provide overall management of assigned field installations. Although these field installations have a primary program responsibility to the Program Office to whom they report, they also conduct work for the other Program Offices. A brief description of the program responsibilities of these offices and of NASA's field installations follows:

OFFICE OF MANNED SPACE FLIGHT   Directs NASA's effort to develop and apply the manned space flight capability, including the development of the large launch vehicles and spacecraft, and the launch, operational, logistic, life support, and related systems required for man to perform missions in space.

Field installations primarily engaged in this part of NASA's program are:

John F. Kennedy Space Center: Provision of supporting activities for the major launchings; preparation and integration of space vehicles; collaboration with such elements of the Department of Defense as the Eastern Test Range and

Corps of Engineers to avoid unnecessary duplication of launch facilities, services, and capabilities.

Manned Spacecraft Center: Research and development of manned spacecraft, such as Apollo; development of life support systems; development and integration of experiments for assigned space flight activities; astronaut training; manned flight operations in space; and supporting scientific, engineering, and medical research.

George C. Marshall Space Flight Center: Research and development of launch vehicles and systems to launch manned and unmanned spacecraft; development and integration of experiments for assigned space flight activities; and supporting scientific and engineering research.

OFFICE OF SPACE SCIENCE AND APPLICATIONS Responsible for scientific explorations of space, the planets, the moon, and for peaceful applications of space systems technology such as communications and meteorology. Provides the focal point for NASA contacts with the Space Science Board of the National Academy of Sciences, and other advisory groups.

Field installations primarily engaged in space science and applications activities are:

Goddard Space Flight Center: Scientific research in space with unmanned satellites; research and development of meteorological and communications satellites; tracking and data acquisition operations.

Jet Propulsion Laboratory (Operated under contract by the California Institute of Technology): Deep space, lunar, and interplanetary scientific exploration; development of unmanned lunar and interplanetary spacecraft; operation of related tracking and data acquisition systems.

Wallops Station: Launch facilities and services for other NASA installations which conduct suborbital, orbital, and space probe experiments with vehicles ranging from small rockets to the Scout four-stage solid fuel rocket. Development of techniques for collection and processing of experimental data.

OFFICE OF ADVANCED RESEARCH AND TECHNOLOGY Responsible for NASA's program to provide technological knowledge for future aeronautical and space flight. Efforts include research and advanced technological development on aircraft, spacecraft, launch vehicles, nuclear and other propulsion systems, and electronics. This office coordinates the agency's total advanced research and development program to assure its overall adequacy and to avoid undesirable duplication.

Field installations primarily carrying out research and advanced technology work are:

Ames Research Center: Basic and applied research in space environmental physics, including simulation techniques; gas dynamics research at extreme speeds; configuration, stability, structures, and guidance and control of aeronautical and space vehicles; biomedical and biophysical research.

Flight Research Center: Research in extremely high performance aircraft and spacecraft, including flight operations and flight systems, and structural characteristics of aeronautical and space vehicles.

Langley Research Center: Aeronautical and space structures and materials, aerodynamics of re-entry vehicles, space environmental physics, life sciences, subsonic and supersonic flight.

Lewis Research Center: Power-plants and propulsion, high energy propellants, nuclear rockets, electric propulsion; management and procurement of medium launch vehicle programs.

Joint AEC-NASA Space Nuclear Propulsion Office: Research and development in conjunction with the Atomic Energy Commission, leading to nuclear rocket propulsion for space vehicles, including the nuclear reactor and non-reactor components of such systems.

OFFICE OF TRACKING AND DATA ACQUISITION Responsible for development, availability, and operation of tracking and data acquisition facilities, systems, equipment, and instrumentation necessary to acquire, record, process, and transmit technical and scientific data for NASA programs. It is also responsible for management of NASA's long line communication systems and for management and coordination of agencywide ADP requirements.

CONTENTS

CONTENTS

Part 1

NASA
IN REVIEW

Introduction

NASA's priority assignment for the 1960's—landing a man on the moon and returning him safely to earth—was successfully completed with the Apollo 11 mission. In 1970, only one launch took place in the Apollo program—Apollo 13. That mission was unsuccessful, and as a result, the scheduled Apollo 14 launch was postponed to January 1971, to allow time for spacecraft modifications that would assure the safety of the astronauts.

Consistent with new national goals established for the 1970's, NASA reviewed its priorities and redirected its activities in line with budgetary constraints. Steps were taken to develop a sound aeronautics and space program compatible with national resources and in keeping with the objective of maintaining our position of technological leadership.

In the Manned Space Flight area, in addition to Apollo, NASA was deeply engaged in work on the Skylab program, formerly known as Apollo Applications. Good progress was made in design, development, and testing for Skylab, and fabrication of flight hardware is underway. Space Shuttle and Space Station studies also moved ahead. For the shuttle, system characteristics were established and study contracts were let for both the vehicle and engine. For the space station, program definition studies were in the process of being completed.

NASA unmanned space programs for scientific investigations and space applications were also active. During 1970, previously launched orbiting observatories continued to make scientific discoveries, observations, surveys, and coordinated investigations. OAO–3, which carried a large telescope and other instruments, was launched November 30, but failed to go into orbit.

NASA also launched three Intelsat III commercial communications satellites for Comsat, and was preparing the first of the Intelsat IV series for launch. Applications Technology Satellites already in orbit were used experimentally for educational broadcasts, and for studies of the use of satellites for navigation and air traffic control.

This year, the 10th anniversary of the meteorological satellite flight program, the agency launched Nimbus 4 and Tiros–M, both highly sophisticated spacecraft. Tiros–M became operational as ITOS–1, the first of a new generation of Tiros spacecraft, and began support of the National Operational Meteorological Satellite System. In the earth resources survey program, aircraft were used in tests of remote sensing devices which are planned for use aboard spacecraft to obtain earth resources data from space. In addition, the Earth Resources Technology Satellite spacecraft design was completed and some parts were being fabricated.

The NASA advanced research and technology effort continued to investigate a very wide range of aeronautical and space problems. In one area of study, a theory was developed for predicting clear air turbulence under certain conditions; in another, progress was made in developing methods of improving control of general aviation aircraft; and in V/STOL research, the augmentor-wing concept looked promising as a means of developing jet transport aircraft with a good short-takeoff-and-landing capability.

Other research activities collected data on the behavior of groups in confined habitats (Tektite), on the ability of the balance control mechanism of the inner ear to adapt to sustained weightlessness; and on the feasibility of using optical techniques to give general aviation pilots warning of impending collisions.

Manned Space Flight

Apollo Program.—Two lunar landing missions were initially planned for 1970; however, after the unsuccessful Apollo 13 mission in April, the scheduled launch of Apollo 14 was changed from October 1970 to January 1971 in order to incorporate changes in the spacecraft to eliminate the problems encountered by Apollo 13.

In September, NASA reduced the number of remaining lunar missions from six to four. The elimination of two flights will permit their funding to be applied to future programs. This decision will give the space program some additional flexibility, providing Apollo hardware for possible use in future programs where manned operations or a heavy boost capability is required. It is now planned to complete the Apollo program in 1972.

Apollo 13.—The third intended lunar landing mission was successfully launched on schedule from Kennedy Space Center on April 11. Its major objective was to explore the Fra Mauro formation.

Launch, earth orbital insertion, and translunar trajectory insertion (TLI) all were satisfactory. Separation of the command and service modules (CSM), docking with the lunar module (LM), and extraction of the LM from the third propulsion stage (S–IVB), were also performed without difficulty. The S–IVB stage was then placed on a trajectory to impact the lunar surface near a seismometer left by the Apollo 12 crew nearly 5 months earlier. The recorded seismic impulse is contributing to an improved understanding of the subsurface lunar composition.

During the mission's third day while the spacecraft was still enroute to the moon, a failure in the service module oxygen system caused it to lose the ability to supply oxygen to the command module and to generate CSM electrical power and water with the fuel cells. It was decided to cancel the lunar landing. The command module, while still capable of supporting the crew for a short period, no longer contained enough consumables for the long journey around the moon and back to earth. It was therefore decided to retain the LM and use it as a "lifeboat," thereby conserving the command module and its limited consumables for reentry and splashdown. This required both flight and ground crews to modify the LM, intended only for two-man support, to a configuration that enabled it to support three men during more than 3 days of space flight.

Emergency systems were designed on earth and constructed by the astronauts from onboard materials; these systems supported them with no ill effects except discomfort caused by the cold and cramped quarters in the LM. These cold conditions were due to the necessity to power down equipment and heaters to conserve power. The astronauts returned to the command module shortly before reentry and jettisoned the LM. The command module then made nominal reentry and splashdown. Landing was within sight (about 4 miles) of the recovery ship U.S.S. *Iwo Jima,* and the astronauts were aboard the carrier within 45 minutes.

The actions taken to bring the spacecraft home safely under extremely adverse conditions demonstrated the inherent flexibility designed into the Apollo systems and operations. The spacecraft systems provided many different options from which a series of configurations were chosen to meet the varying requirements on the trip home. At the same time, the flight and ground crews demonstrated outstanding competence and the value of many hours of training in meeting a set of unusual circumstances.

A review board appointed by the NASA Administrator conducted an exhaustive investigation of the Apollo 13 mission. Its findings were conclusive: the anomaly was determined beyond a reasonable doubt to have been caused by the ignition of Teflon-coated wires inside the oxygen tank resulting in internal pressure which caused the tank to rupture. These wires were inadvertently damaged during prelaunch checkout at Cape Kennedy, although no evidence of the damaged wires was detected during the testing before the launch.

The recommendations of the Review Board are being carried out through changes in hardware and procedures for Apollo 14 and subsequent missions. A third oxygen tank will be installed in the service module. It will provide an adequate supply of oxygen for life support even if the other two oxygen tanks fail. Other modifications include removal of electric motors and fans from exposure to the high pressure oxygen atmosphere. Modifications have also been made to provide improved CSM return capability. These include adding a 400-ampere-hour battery for electrical power and additional stowage capability for potable water.

Lunar Exploration.—The Apollo 11 and Apollo 12 missions have made it possible to collect more data about our nearest neighbor in space than has been recorded since history began. The two missions returned a total of 123 pounds of lunar material. The scientific analysis of this material and of information obtained from experiments and observations is being carried out by experts in the United States and 16 foreign countries.

The data collected has been the basis for important conclusions about the moon. Lunar materials have been classified into four general categories: fine-grained and medium-grained igneous rocks, breccia (an accumulation of local material consolidated by temperature and pressure), and fines (small fragmented material, glass, and similar items). A very vigorous examination of near surface material has revealed no evidence of any viable organisms or fossil evidence of them on the moon. On remaining missions, deeper samples will be obtained for the same close examination.

Most lunar rocks are similar to the earth's volcanic rocks. A prime characteristic in the classification of such rocks is the silica content. An indication of the diversity of lunar rocks is the fact that rocks from the Apollo 12 site alone have a greater range of variation in silica content than is known for the rocks of the Hawaiian Islands. The average content of titanium, a refractory element in Apollo 12 rocks, is less than half that of Apollo 11 rocks. This element rarely exceeds 3 percent in terrestrial volcanic rocks but on the moon the range is primarily between 4 and 14 percent. Even larger differences are anticipated from samples to be brought back from the lunar highlands. It is expected that titanium will become a key parameter in the classification of lunar rocks. The moon's composition is heterogeneous, even at individual landing sites.

The present evidence indicates that the moon was formed around 4.5 billion years ago, approximately the same time as the earth and meteorites. The isotopic composition of lead in the samples is, however, distinct from that of the earth and meteorites indicating that three separate closed systems might have been formed. The moon must have been at least partially molten 500 million years to 1,000 million years after it was formed. Although there is no way of determining the percentage of melting or whether the melting was caused by meteorite impact or internal heat, it had to be on a large scale to accomplish the degree of differentiation found in the rocks. One obvious conclusion drawn from the studies is that events on the moon occurred over a long period of time and the moon can serve as a Rosetta Stone in unraveling the early history of the earth. Since no direct evidence older than 3.5 billion years is available for the earth, the possibility exists that the study of lunar rocks may yield information on the missing first billion years of history.

Passive Seismometer Experiments (PSE) were emplaced to detect vibrations of the lunar surface to determine its internal structure, physical state, and tectonic activity. The lunar seismic signals are different from those on earth and very complex. The PSE records an average of one moonquake a day. Although the source of these events could be shallow internal moonquakes, they are thought to be caused by meteorite impacts. The Apollo 13 spent S–IVB stage was impacted on the lunar surface 85 miles from the Apollo 12 site with an approximate force of 11.5 tons of TNT. The data from this well-calibrated signal indicate that the lunar material is fractured to depths of approximately 12 miles and shows no evidence of the major discontinuities which are a striking characteristic of the solid earth. More than 200 events of natural origin have been recorded by the seismometer during the first 8 months of operation. Fifty-eight of these events have been identified as moonquakes.

The moonquakes have been divided into nine different categories, i.e., nine zones producing seismic activity within a 200-mile radius of the passive seismometer. At least 26 are shallow moonquakes occurring within 3 days of the time when the moon comes closest to the earth (perigee) during its monthly orbit cycle. The source of these events is considered to be in the vicinity of Fra Mauro, to be visited on the Apollo 14 mission, about 125 miles from the PSE. This last group stands out as the most positive evidence of internal lunar activity. Otherwise the moon's outer shell appears very stable and cold in comparison with the earth's seismic activity.

A magnetometer was emplaced by the Apollo 12 crew to measure the magnetic field of the moon. Analysis of the data from this device showed the presence of a small magnetic field that measures approximately 38 gammas. The data indicates that this field is the result of a localized magnetic source near the Apollo 12 landing site rather than a uniform dipole associated with the whole moon. The origin of this field is considered highly significant by scientists.

It is also known, because of the remnant magnetism in some of the Apollo samples, that the moon's magnetic field was probably higher when the rocks solidified than it is now. Analyses of all the lunar magnetic data indicate that the moon may have a small central core of temperature near 800° to 1,000° C. This much heat in the lunar interior is still not sufficient to make the moon into a heat-engine resembling the earth, for no deep interior quakes have as yet been detected and there is no evidence of the kind of crustal movement and mountain building that is so important to earth's topography.

The Solar Wind Spectrometer measures the direct impact of the solar wind undeviated in any way in its path from the sun to the moon. The suprathermal ion detector records ionized particles near the lunar surface particularly at lunar sunrise. Large signals were also recorded at time of the S–IVB impact and at lunar perigee. These ionized particles do not occur in sufficiently large numbers or at low enough velocities to be chemically identified.

Efforts were made to measure the ambient lunar atmosphere with a Cold Cathode Gauge. Initial measurements made while the lunar module was still on the surface were inconclusive. The instrument stopped transmitting science data 14 hours after deployment. Through ground tests with similar equipment the failure has been identified, and an improved instrument will measure the lunar atmosphere on future missions.

The Solar Wind Composition Experiment exposes a strip of aluminum foil to the lunar environment to determine the elemental and isotopic composition of gases in the solar wind. Variations in isotopic ratios were found between Apollo 11 and Apollo 12. When compared with results obtained from lunar sample analyses, variations in the solar wind composition may be observed dating from antiquity.

The Laser Ranging Retroreflector (LR3) deployed at Tranquility Base by the Apollo 11 astronauts continues to perform as designed. It is serving as a target for point-to-point distance measurements from earth performed by recording the round trip travel time of short pulses of ruby laser radiation transmitted from a telescope, reflected from the LR3, and received approximately 2½ seconds later by the same telescope. Several measurements per week, with a precision of about 1 foot or less in the earth-moon distance, are being made on a routine basis by the McDonald Observatory staff. A continuing lunar ranging program has also been started by the Air Force Cambridge Research Laboratory. Additional Laser Ranging Retroreflectors will be deployed on the Apollo 14 and Apollo 15 missions to provide a network of instruments which will allow scientists to determine the dynamics of the earth-moon system. Measurements to date have been incorporated into the best numerical ephemeris of the moon to produce improvements in knowledge of lunar motion. The LR3 is available to any scientific observatory throughout the world which wishes to reflect signals from it.

The Apollo 12 astronauts visited the Surveyor III automated spacecraft during their second EVA on November 19, 1969. They returned to earth portions of the spacecraft which had been on the lunar surface and exposed to solar and cosmic radiation for 31 months. Engineers and scientists in the United States and Switzerland are evaluating the effects of space environment on the Surveyor parts. Most of the components, materials, optics, and other devices encountered had satisfactorily survived extremes of vacuum, radiation, and temperature well beyond design requirements. The detailed results can be used to reduce the uncertainties associated with the effects of operation and long storage in lunar and space environment, and to improve design and testing techniques for future missions.

Forthcoming Launches.—Two Apollo lunar landing missions are scheduled for 1971; Apollo 14 in January and Apollo 15 in July.

The landing site for Apollo 14 will be Fra Mauro, the intended site for Apollo 13. The Apollo 14 crew will deploy an Apollo Lunar Surface Experiments Package (ALSEP) similar to the one placed at the Ocean of Storms site by Apollo 12, and the Apollo 14 ALSEP will include several experiments which have been deployed on previous missions: the Passive Seismic Experiment, the Suprathermal Ion Detector, and the Cold Cathode Ionization Gauge. Two new experiments will be added to the package. One is an Active Seismic Experiment (ASE) to generate and monitor artificially stimulated seismic waves in the 3–250 Hz range in the lunar surface and near subsurface. It will also monitor natural events in the same frequency range. The other is a Low Energy Solar Wind Experiment to ascertain proton and electron flux data for evaluation of solar wind and cosmic rays.

Three other experiments will be independently deployed by the Apollo 14 astronauts on the lunar surface. A Laser Ranging Retroreflector (LR3) for precise earth-to-moon measurements will be the first leg of a planned LR3 network on the moon. A Solar Wind Composition Experiment to determine the isotopic composition of noble gases in the solar wind at the lunar surface will be retrieved at the end of EVA and returned to earth for analysis. And a portable magnetometer to measure the magnetic field of the moon at the Apollo 14 landing site will be deployed at the point of furthest traverse from the Lunar Module.

The magnetometer will be transported aboard the Mobile Equipment Transporter (MET), a lightweight two-wheel vehicle resembling a ricksha to be used on Apollo 14 only. The MET will also carry cameras, hand tools, and sample bags for use by the astronauts.

The Apollo 15 landing is planned at Hadley-Apennine, a site named for the meandering Hadley Rille and the nearby Apennine Mountains. It is hoped that the astronauts will be able to visit and collect samples both at the base of the mountains which rise over 8,000 feet, and at the rille which resembles a dry riverbed. Apollo 15 will be the first mission to carry a Lunar Roving Vehicle (LRV) to increase the range of travel for the astronauts on the lunar surface. The battery powered LRV, which will weigh approximately 500 pounds, will carry the astronauts and up to 170 pounds of equipment and lunar samples.

The last three Apollo missions, Apollo 15, 16 and 17, will have significantly increased capabilities for lunar exploration. The EVA's will be increased from two to three, providing 40 man hours per mission instead of 18; the landed scientific payload will be doubled (500 to 1,000 pounds); the LRV and suit mobility improvements will provide increased range and efficiency of surface operations; and each mission will carry an experiment package in the Service Module for use in lunar orbit to supplement the experiments deployed on the lunar surface. The intent is to maximize the scientific returns from the remaining Apollo missions.

Skylab Program.—The Skylab Program, formerly known as Apollo Applications, is designed to make important contributions to future manned space operations by contributing new knowledge in many fields —earth resources, environmental systems, oceanography, meteorology, solar and stellar astronomy, space physics, bioscience, space technology and engineering, zero "g" materials processing, measurements of the space environment, and the physiology of man in space.

The program objectives are: to determine and evaluate man's physiological responses and aptitudes in space under zero gravity conditions and his post mission adaptation to the terrestrial environment through a series of progressively longer missions; to develop and evaluate efficient techniques for utilizing man in sensor operation, discrimination, data selection and evaluation, manual control, maintenance and repair, assembly and installation of hardware components, and mobility involved in various operations; to develop techniques for increasing systems life, for long duration habitability and long duration mission control, and to investigate and develop techniques for in-flight test and qualification of advanced subsystems; to conduct astronomy and other science, technology, and applications experiments in which man's contribution is expected to improve the quality and/or yield of the results.

All program activities made good progress in design, development, and ground testing. Critical design reviews were completed by the third quarter and manufacture of hardware was underway on all flight articles in parallel with the final design phase.

A significant addition to the program was an Earth Resources Experiment Package (EREP). Carefully selected sensors will permit the astronauts to perform geological, geographical, hydrological, agricultural, forestry, oceanographic, and meteorologic studies of selected ground targets. The data acquired will be coordinated with other information obtained from airborne flights and from the Earth Resources Technology Satellite (ERTS) to demonstrate the potential usefulness of this technology in mapping, monitoring, and understanding phenomena which affect the environment.

NASA decided to utilize Launch Complex 39 at the Kennedy Space Center (KSC) for checkout and launching of Saturn IB as well as Saturn V launch vehicles to consolidate activities and economize on Skylab prelaunch test operations. The technical feasibility of launching Saturn IB's from LC–39 had been established in earlier studies by KSC, but action had been deferred because of schedule conflicts with Apollo. After the Skylab workshop was reconfigured to the so-called "dry" version, not requiring a mobile service structure, and schedule conflicts were resolved, the change was implemented. The decision will result in significant cost savings and more efficient launch operations at KSC.

Space Shuttle.—In keeping with space program objectives, NASA took steps to reduce the cost of future space operations and provide a capability for a balanced program of space activity by moving ahead with work on the Space Shuttle.

Space Shuttle system characteristics were established early in the year, and definition study contracts of 11 months duration were awarded in June. Each Shuttle is planned for 100 or more flights with payload transportation similar to commercial airline practice. The orbiting stage will contain a large compartment of about 10,000 cubic feet to accommodate a varying payload mix of satellites, passengers, and cargo. The Shuttle will be capable of being launched in any direction and on short notice—within 2 hours if necessary. With its low operating cost, flexibility, internal environment, and large payload capacity, applications such as placement or repositioning of satellites, satellite servicing, rescue operations, and space station support will be practical. Since the shirtsleeve environment within the Shuttle will be very much like that of an airplane, passengers will not require astronaut skills. The moderate acceleration loads will allow average people in good health to fly into space in comfort.

Two sets of study contracts were awarded and work is in progress. One set consists of two studies for the Shuttle vehicle, and the other comprises three studies for the engine. The fully reusable two-stage vehicle approach is being examined in detail. Basic definition objectives are to define the Shuttle system and the engine requirements, accomplish preliminary design, and predict the scope, schedule, and cost cf the program. In addition, other contractual studies of alternate vehicle concepts are also being conducted to insure that all approaches are fully explored.

In February, NASA and the Air Force signed an agreement establishing a Space Transportation System Committee which will ensure that objectives of both agencies in the field of space transportation will be fulfilled.

Concurrently with the definition effort, NASA also initiated other studies and analyses in areas such as payloads, economics, and mission traffic requirements. These efforts will provide better understanding of what the Shuttle will mean to payload designers, what its realistic value is as an economic investment, and how the projected missions will fit into a national traffic pattern.

Thermal protection systems were under study to determine the optimum high temperature structures for the Shuttle configuration. Technical studies proceeded in areas such as aerodynamic configurations, high pressure rocket engines, and integrated electronics systems.

NASA solicited international participation in the Shuttle effort in support of the President's policy of space cooperation. European representatives as well as Japanese officials were briefed on Shuttle opportunities, and talks were conducted with the European Space Research Organization, the European Launcher Development Organization, and with officials from a number of foreign countries.

Space Station.—NASA contractors were in the process of completing comprehensive program definition studies started in 1969 on two versions of a space station which could be launched on a Saturn–V-class vehicle. The designs are of a self-contained, general purpose laboratory whose facilities can be supplemented by attached or free-flying modules. The studies will provide operational, technical, and programmatic information on the station, its facilities, experiments, and modules for comparison with other station designs under consideration.

Program definition contractors were instructed to investigate modular space station designs which could provide the same facility capability but in a shuttle-compatible configuration. This approach would reduce early funding requirements and appears to offer a higher degree of flexibility from both technical and program implementation aspects. Most of the modular designs being considered require a cluster of modules, each of which would be delivered by a shuttle, to be assembled in orbit before commencing operations. While the modular stations generally have less initial capability than monolithic station concepts, similar capabilities can be achieved by the addition of modules in orbit. Also, the ease with which modules can be replaced would enhance program flexibility significantly.

In a parallel effort, equally applicable to either space station concept, potential station users were approached for help in determining facility characteristics, categorizing research activities, developing utilization management procedures, and generally making their requirements known at a very early design stage. Those approached included representatives of industry, government, and universities, both foreign and domestic.

Advanced Manned Missions.—Advanced Manned Missions activities continued the detailed examination of the NASA integrated plan with the goal of affirming that the projects in the plan would best serve national goals. Contracts initiated in 1969, which were directed toward specific requirements of the Space Station and Space Shuttle programs, were completed in 1970, and the results utilized to support the definition of those programs. Because the Space Station and Space Shuttle had progressed into the definition phase and therefore had independent status, the Advanced Manned Missions program focused its attention on integrated planning beyond these two programs. Conceptual studies were begun of the Space Tug, the Nuclear Shuttle, the Lunar Orbit Station, and the Lunar Base to provide NASA management with information about these projects and their role in the integrated planning concept. Additional studies considered safety and rescue aspects of the missions in the plan.

Space Science and Applications

Orbiting Observatories.—NASA's Orbiting Observatories continued to make major scientific contributions and to demonstrate their versatility and prolonged operating lifetimes. The Orbiting Astronomical Observatory–2 (OAO–2), launched in December 1968, discovered a great hydrogen cloud surrounding the bright comets Tago-Sago-Kosaka and Bennett. The cloud proved to be many times larger than ground observers had theorized. OAO–2 also made a series of observations of a nova (exploding star) in the Constellation Serpeus, which could not be seen from ground-based telescopes.

A third Orbiting Astronomical Observatory (OAO–3), carrying a 38-inch telescope and weighing 4,700 pounds, was launched November 30, but failed to achieve orbit. It was designed to measure ultraviolet radiation from selected celestial objects, and to point with an accuracy of one-arc second.

In 1970 the Orbiting Geophysical Observatory–5, orbited in March 1968, made a sky survey of Lyman-alpha radiation and observed the hydrogen cloud around the Comet Bennett. OGO–6, launched in June 1969, performed satisfactorily during the year, and achieved its mission objectives. Orbiting Solar Observatories–3, –4, –5, and –6 (launched between 1967 and 1969) were also utilized for investigations coordinated with other satellites and with observations from sounding rockets and ground-based instruments.

A bright fireball was optically tracked in January and three meteorite fragments from it were recovered near Lost City, Okla. This was the first time that recovered fragments could be correlated with a specific meteoroid coming from a known orbit. In March, scientists carried out an unprecedented study of a total solar eclipse, their observations involving complementary satellite, ground-based, and rocket-borne experiments.

Explorer and International Satellites.—NASA orbited its first Small Astronomy Satellite (SAS–A) in December. The SAS series of satellites (also designated Explorer) will investigate X-ray, gamma ray, ultraviolet, and infrared spectral regions of the electromagnetic spectrum. SAS–A was designed to develop a catalog of X-ray sources through systematic scanning of the celestial sphere, and in a single day it should transmit more data than through the total observation time of the X-ray instruments on all earlier satellites and rockets. This 320-pound spacecraft was launched into a 342-mile orbit by a Scout vehicle from the San Marco site operated by Italy off the coast of East Africa—the first American satellite to be launched outside the territorial limits of this country.

Explorer satellites still providing useful information included the University of Iowa satellite (Injun 5 launched in 1968) which detected trapped particles with masses greater than helium in the Van Allen radiation belts; Radio Explorer 1 (also orbited 1968) which continued to map the distribution of ionized hydrogen in the Milky Way; and Explorer 35 (IMP–E launched in 1967) which was mapping the magnetic field and providing support for the ALSEP experiments on the moon.

ISIS–1—largest of the international satellites and orbited in 1969—was continuing investigations of the upper ionosphere begun by Canadian-American spacecraft of the Alouette 1 and 2 series of 1962–65. Low energy particle detectors aboard the satellites have monitored a quite unexpected amount of low energy flux ranging from high to low latitudes.

Sounding Rockets and Balloons.—Almost 100 sounding rockets were launched to heights between 100 and 1,000 miles for studies in space physics and astronomy. Sixteen of these were launched from Wallops Island and three from the White Sands Missile Range during the solar eclipse; one of the 19 detected an unexpectedly high amount of neutral hydrogen streaming into the earth's upper atmosphere. Three launches were made from Woomera, Australia to obtain measurements from stars in the southern celestial sphere which cannot be seen from flights in the Northern Hemisphere. In addition, launches were made from Hawaii, Australia, Norway, Sweden, Brazil, Canada and India.

About 60 high-altitude balloons were launched for outer space observatories at altitudes as high as 150,000 feet, or above about 95 percent of the earth's atmosphere. One of these balloons carried Stratoscope 2, a 6,000-pound diffraction-limited, optical telescope 3 feet in diameter, remotely controlled from the ground.

Space Bioscience.—In research on the effects of altered gravity on living organisms, scientists at the University of California found that by increasing the force of gravity to three times that of the earth an extra amount of a "fat-regulating hormone" was forced from the hypothalamus and the pituitary gland. This hormone mobilizes fat from storage depots in the body, making it available for the production of energy

vital to life processes. It may also find applications in the search for a means of controlling obesity.

In a research project at Emory University to study the possible benefits of depressing body functions during prolonged space flight, a technique—differential hypothermia—was developed. The procedure consists of cooling most of a warm-blooded animal's body to a low temperature of 4° to 10° C. but keeping another part (a tumor) warmed to normal body temperature (37°). Hypothermic animals were able to tolerate very toxic or even lethal amounts of anti-cancer drugs with no ill effects. The reduced or depressed metabolic rate reduces the concentration of the drug in the cold tissues, focusing its effects on the malignant tissue or tumor only. The cooling process seemed to increase the metabolic rate of the warm tissues, making them more susceptible to the anti-cancer drug.

In research to discover ways by which earth's organisms might adapt themselves to the hostile environments of the planets such as Mars, scientists at the State University of New York in Buffalo have synthesized a living cell able to reproduce. In their experiments small, single-celled amoebae were dismembered and components from a number of them were put back together again to achieve the artificial synthesis.

Mariner Mars '71.—The two-Mariner spacecraft to be launched in May 1971 and to reach Mars in November, were fabricated and assembled and proof tests completed. The flight spacecraft were progressing toward final testing. For mission operations, planning was completed, training begun, and computer programs neared completion. Fabrication of the two Atlas/Centaur launch vehicles was finished, and they were being tested.

Mariner Venus-Mercury '73.—Another spacecraft of the Mariner class, to be launched sometime in October–November 1973, will pass Venus early in February 1974, and arrive at Mercury in late March. It is designed to investigate the environment, atmosphere, and body and surface characteristics of Mercury, and to obtain environmental and atmospheric data about Venus.

The Project Office at the Jet Propulsion Laboratory selected these experiments for the flight science payload: A charged particle telescope, dual magnetometers, a scanning electrostatic analyzer, and two TV cameras to provide wide- and narrow-angle pictures.

Viking.—In February, the Viking mission was rescheduled from 1973 to 1975 because of funding limitations. Viking is the program to investigate Mars by means of two spacecraft which will orbit the planet and send instrumented landers to the surface. The orbiters will map the planet and relay data from the landers to earth. Emphasis will be placed on collecting information relevant to the possibility of life on Mars.

During the year substantial progress was made in this project. Teams of scientists defined the experiments, developed instrument concepts, and helped NASA plan the mission. Baseline designs were prepared for the orbiter and the lander, and most planning and control documents were completed. Subcontractors began development of critical instruments and subsystems, and significant tests of spacecraft subsystems and instruments were conducted under simulated flight conditions. Model landing tests, wind tunnel tests, and laboratory tests were also conducted.

Pioneer.—Pioneer spacecraft F and G were in the planning and development stage. Spacecraft design was completed and engineering models of both spacecraft and scientific instruments were being assembled and tested. A radioisotope-thermal electric generator to supply electrical power for up to 5 years was designed for the AEC and is undergoing tests.

Pioneers 6 through 9—launched between 1965 and 1968—continued to provide data on the interplanetary medium, solar activity, and their influences on the earth's environment.

Helios.—The Federal Republic of Germany selected a prime contractor to build two instrumented spacecraft which will fly close to the sun between 1974 and and 1975. Scientific experiments for this cooperative NASA-West German project will transmit measurements on solar plasma, cosmic rays, magnetic fields, zodiacal light, and micrometeoroids as the spacecraft orbits the sun. A Titan-Centaur booster will be used for the launches.

Advanced Studies and Technology.—The mission design for a Grand Tour to the outer planets was completed, and a functional approach of the spacecraft for the mission was established. Conceptual design of key elements of the spacecraft was also established, with emphasis placed on the feasibility of an onboard Self-test and Repair (STAR) computer.

A conceptual design of a low-cost Delta-class spacecraft, able to serve as an orbiter or a delivery system for a multiple set of probes, was completed. This system is initially planned for use in exploring Venus.

NASA continued its studies of other possible future planetary missions.

Applications Technology Satellites.—Applications Technology Satellites (ATS) 1 and 3 (orbited in 1966 and 1967) were still being used in experiments in March 1970. The Corporation for Public Broadcasting carried out educational telecasts between Columbia, S.C. and Los Angeles, Calif., via ATS–3, and initial tests were made of an experiment which will employ the very high frequency transponder aboard ATS–1 for educational and public radio transmissions studies by Alaska.

In addition, signal acquisition and tracking tests for digital communications and ranging were performed by the L–band transponder of ATS–5. NASA selected a contractor for the ATS F and G spacecraft, and construction is scheduled to start in early 1971.

Navigation and Traffic Control Satellites.—ATS–1 and 3 demonstrated the feasibility of using satellites in geostationary orbit to fix the position of ships and aircraft in navigation and traffic control. The Federal Aviation Administration and the Coast Guard participated in the tests by providing the vehicles and by analyzing the data.

Joint technical studies by NASA and the European Space Research Organization of satellites for communications and independent surveillance of aircraft in the Atlantic Ocean region determined that a satellite system could meet technical aviation needs of the late 1970's.

Communication Satellites.—NASA launched three of the Intelsat III series commercial communications satellites for the Communications Satellite Corporation (Comsat) on a reimbursable basis in January, April, and July. The July (Intelsat III F–8) mission was unsuccessful as a result of a spacecraft failure. Five commercial communications satellites were in full operation in 1970—two in the Atlantic area, two in the Pacific area, and one over the Indian Ocean. A sixth satellite is available, on a contingency basis, for service in the Atlantic Ocean area.

The first of the Intelsat IV series was being prepared for a scheduled launch early in 1971. It will provide nominally 6,000 two-way channels compared to the 1,200 channels of Intelsat III. A maximum of 9000 two-way channels can be obtained by exclusively using regional rather than global beams. Intelsat IV will have a design life of 7 years as against 5 years for Intelsat III. An Atlas/Centaur launch vehicle will be used for the Intelsat IV program, and the launches will also be on a reimbursable basis.

NASA provided facilities and consulting services on a reimbursable basis to Comsat and advised the FCC and the OTP on Intelsat launchings and domestic satellites.

Geodetic Satellites.—GEOS–2, launched in January 1968, supported Air Force camera teams in geodetic observations; U.S. and French radar calibrations; Navy Tranet systems tests and calibration of the geoceiver doppler system; and the preliminary phase of the ISAGEX (*International SAtellite Geodesy EXperiment*) program. ISAGEX—sponsored by the International Committee of Space Research under

French project management—is supported by the U.S., France, Bulgaria, Hungary, Rumania, Czechoslavakia, U.S.S.R., West Germany, Italy, Japan, Australia, Switzerland, Latvia SSR, and Mongolia among others. The program will probably start in January 1971, and require that GEOS–2 be operated through most of that year.

In addition, GEOS–2 supported an experiment to determine the feasibility of using ground-based laser tracking equipment for more precise measurements of the motion of the earth's pole and for reducing the time for making the measurements from 5 days to less than 1 day.

Meteorological Satellites.—In support of the world weather program, the Nimbus spacecraft continued flight-testing sensors and techniques for quantitative measurements of global atmospheric structure and processes. Nimbus 3—after operating more than 17 months—suffered a failure of its aft scanner, which eventually caused most of the sensor data to be unusable. Nimbus 4, launched in April, carried nine experiments for measuring temperature structure, cloud cover and composition, emitted and reflected radiation from the ultraviolet to the infrared, composition of the atmosphere, solar energy variation, and wind velocities. Nimbus 4 made the first satellite measurement of vertical temperature soundings in the lower stratosphere which provides significant new data for long range weather forecasting. In addition, Nimbus achieved extremely precise stable spacecraft attitude control. The proof of this system has significance to the Earth Resources Technology Satellite which requires such stability for high resolution image taking. Nimbus E and F, with more sophisticated sensors, were being developed for launches in 1972 and 1973.

Tiros M—the operational prototype of the second generation of operational meteorological satellites—was launched in January. Redesignated ITOS–1 upon achieving orbit, it began supporting the National Operational Meteorological Satellite System (NOMSS) as the primary operational satellite for the National Oceanic and Atmospheric Administration (NOAA). The spacecraft, funded and developed by NASA to meet NOAA's requirements, is the first of an improved type to replace the two kinds of Tiros operational satellites operated earlier in the NOMSS.

ITOS–1 carries TV cameras to store global cloud-cover data for remote readout; Automatic Picture Transmission cameras for local readout of cloud-cover data; and newly developed scanning radiometers for global cloud data for remote and local readout, both day and night. The sensors are duplicated for reliability and designed with mutually complementary circuitry to extend their life if individual components fail. Since it can provide night coverage for the first time, ITOS–1 fully satisfies the primary objectives of NOMSS, that of obtaining global cloud-cover day and night.

As a secondary payload with the ITOS–1, NASA launched the Australis-Oscar (AO–5) radio amateur satellite. The first amateur spacecraft launched by the agency, and the fifth of the OSCAR satellites (*O*rbiting *S*atellites *C*arrying *A*mateur *R*adio), it was designed and built by students at Melbourne University, Australia. The 39-pound spacecraft carried beacon transmitters and was prepared and qualified for launch by the Radio Amateur Satellite Corporation, a Washington, D.C., organization of amateur radio operators.

The second satellite of the ITOS series (NOAA–1) was launched in December. Its sensors are identical to those of ITOS–1.

ESSA–8, after almost 2 years in orbit, continued to transmit local readout cloud-cover data and to support NOMSS by providing morning Automatic Picture Transmission (APT) coverage. ESSA–2, orbited in 1966, was converted to standby status in March and deactivated in October. ESSA–5 was deactivated in February; ESSA–7 in March; and ESSA–9 passed the 1-year-in-orbit mark in February.

Meteorological Sounding Rockets.—NASA launched 46 rockets of the Nike-Cajun class to obtain data on the structure and characteristics of the atmosphere at heights of between 20 and 60 miles. Techniques used for providing the vertical atmosphere profiles of wind, temperature, density, and ozone were acoustic grenades, pitot-static tubes, light reflecting vapor trails, luminous vapor trails, optical ozonesondes, and chemiluminescent ozone sensors. New instruments flown for the first time included a 31 grenade-payload, a second generation ozonesonde, and a transponder falling sphere. A series of ozone measurements was made using rocketborne optical techniques coincident with measurements from the backscatter ultraviolet ozone measuring instrument on Nimbus 4.

Wallops Station fired 204 boosted-Dart and Arcas-type meteorological sounding rockets in support of range operations, the sounding rocket development program, and national and international cooperative sounding programs. These soundings provided research and development data in conjunction with those cooperatively launched from other U.S. locations, and from Argentina, Brazil, and Spain. An experiment using nine research rockets (grenade, pitot-static tube, ozone, and falling sphere) and 11 Arcas and boosted-Dart rocketsondes was also conducted from this site before, during, and after the March 7 solar eclipse. New information was obtained about diurnal variations of ozone to an altitude of 40 miles, as was other meteorological data up to 75 miles altitude at the time of the eclipse.

The program of developing a cost-effective meteorological sounding rocket system continued—including a joint NASA–Army project to develop an efficient low cost meteorological rocket motor for routine probings up to 45 miles.

Earth Resources Survey Program.—In support of the program to develop the technology for remote sensing of earth resources data from space, three aircraft of the Earth Resources Survey Program, an aircraft of the University of Michigan, and support aircraft of other agencies completed over 50 missions.

Significant agricultural data were developed by aircraft flights as followups of the Apollo 9 multispectral photography experiment of 1969, and by surveys of blight made over the Corn Belt this year in cooperation with Purdue University. Surveys were also made of selected "census cities" to compare population and land use. A byproduct of this aircraft survey program was their use in various disaster surveys, such as hurricanes Camille and Celia and the Lubbock, Tex., tornado. International cooperation was marked by surveys following the Peruvian earthquake in August, and surveys of the Lake Ontario region in cooperation with the Canadian government.

The aircraft also carried out various sensing experiments for user agencies, such as the Department of Agriculture, Interior, Navy, and NOAA. Spectral coverages in the visible, infrared, near infrared, and microwave frequencies were providing data for the development of resources management methods in a wide range of user disciplines, such as agriculture, oceanography, fisheries, hydrology, geography, geology, and forestry.

During 1970 the prime contractor for the Earth Resources Technology Satellite (ERTS) was selected. Final design of the ERTS–A and –B spacecraft was completed, and certain components were in the fabrication stage. The first complete camera of the high resolution TV system underwent satisfactory tests, as did the mirror for the multispectral scanner. Several components of the wide band video tape recorder were also tested successfully.

Launch of ERTS–A is scheduled for March 1972 and ERTS–B a year later. An invitation was sent to all interested natural resources scientists here and abroad to participte in analyzing and interpreting the data from these two missions.

Earth Physics and Physical Oceanography.—A program was begun this year to apply geodetic satellite technology and associated precision tracking methods to studies of the motion of the earth's pole, variations in the rate of rotation of the earth, continental drift, and the general circulation of the world's oceans. These investigations should provide new data for geoscientists to use in preparing models for predicting major earthquakes, volcanic eruptions, changes in major ocean circulation patterns, and long term changes in earth's climate.

Significant progress was made in demonstrating the feasibility of using remote sensor techniques on aircraft and satellites to observe, monitor, or measure ocean surface and shallow water bottom features, sea surface temperature, ocean color, sea state conditions, sea ice, and pollutants. For example, aircraft flew over the ocean carrying a number of optical, microwave, and infrared remote sensor instruments to collect information; and data obtained by infrared sensors on Nimbus 4 and ITOS–1 were used in preparing ocean surface temperature maps.

Skylab Earth Resources Experiments Package (EREP).—The Skylab earth resources experiment sensors will include six bore-sighted cameras, an infrared spectrometer, a multispectral scanner, a 13.9 GHz radiometer/scatterometer, and 1.4 GHz radiometer. Several of the photographic bands and multispectral scanner bands correspond to the bands selected for the ERTS return beam vidicon and scanner. This correspondence will permit correlation of Skylab photographic and scanner data with the ERTS data.

The EREP sensors—along with associated tracking, control, and recording equipment—will be mounted in the Multiple Docking Adapter of Skylab and launched as part of the cluster. Skylab will be placed into a 50° inclination circular orbit at an altitude of 270 miles. Investigators will be given the opportunity to propose special observations or studies using EREP data.

Global Atmospheric Research Program.—NASA was also cooperating with other Government agencies and the scientific community in planning for U.S. participation in the Global Atmospheric Research Program (GARP). The program was set up as the result of a growing recognition by meteorologists of the possibility of long range weather predictions, and is expected to rely heavily on space technology in acquiring meteorological data on a global scale. In support of GARP, NASA will concentrate on improving data acquisition methods and planning for a Data Acquisition Test and the first GARP Global Experiment.

Launch Vehicle and Propulsion Programs.—The Scout launch vehicle successfuly launched the RAM C–C and OFO–A missions, a Defense Department navigation satellite, and the SAS–A spacecraft from the San Marco Range in Africa.

At the Western Test Range, the Air Force launch team was replaced by a contractor team under a NASA Scout system management contract. The development of an improved Scout first stage-motor continued with two successful motor firings.

Thor-Delta vehicles orbited the Intelsat III F–6, F–7, and F–8, ITOS–1, NATOSAT, SKYNET 2, and NOAA–1 satellites. The ITOS–1 launch was the first using more than three solid motors for thrust augmentation—six motors were used for the Thor booster. Also, the first Universal Boat Tail booster was delivered to NASA. It will be able to utilize three, six, or nine motors for thrust augmentation, as required by the mission. Other progress was made in adapting the Delta Inertial Guidance System.

Agreements were signed with the European Space Research Organization for the launching of the HEOS A–2 and TD–1 satellites on a Delta vehicle. In addition, preliminary discussions were held with Telesat Canada and the Italian Government concerning other missions using the vehicle.

Negotiations were completed with the Air Force for exclusive NASA use of Air Force Complex 41 at Cape Kennedy for launching the Titan-Centaur vehicle and for joint use of other Air Force support buildings and facilities associated with the assembly and checkout of the Titan boosters. Interface and launch complex details were defined and contract negotiations were initiated.

Advanced Research and Technology

High Strength Glass.—Research on glass resulted in the development of a stiff, high strength glass fiber 86 percent stiffer and over 60 percent stronger than that currently available. Composite materials containing the new fibers are expected to exhibit significant weight savings in advanced aerospace vehicles.

Improved Graphite.—A study of the behavior of graphite at high temperatures led to the invention of a boron-doped graphite having an electrical resistance nearly constant from room temperature to 5,000° F. Because the resistance of industrial graphite electrodes and resistors decreases as the temperature rises, such devices require costly controls to prevent burn out. The use of the boronated graphite should eliminate the need for special control devices and result in considerable savings.

Electrically Charged Polymers.—A new class of electrically charged polymers, called ionenes, synthesized for aerospace uses may have application in biomedical engineering. Heparin, a blood anticoagulant, can be bonded to these charged polymers, and they thus might have potential in the development of non-clotting tubing for blood transport in artificial kidney machines and in heart-lung assist devices. The ionenes are also bactericidal and may be useful in surgical sutures and similar applications where the growth of bacteria must be prevented.

High Temperature Polymers.—A new polyimide polymer with greatly improved high temperature mechanical properties was synthesized. It has a rigidity at room temperature twice that of commercially available polyimides, and even at 600° F. its stiffness exceeds that of the commercial materials at room temperature. Further research must be conducted to determine if these polyimides can be used in such aerospace applications as high temperature adhesives and foams.

Improved Electron Microscopy.—In surface physics research, investigators at the Ames Research Center discovered a new method of improving the resolution of the electron microscope. Use of the new technique made it possible to resolve discrete planes of atoms in extremely thin gold films and to make quantitative determination of the orientation of the films. The new method should enhance NASA capabilities in thin-film technology for electronic devices and in the control of surface behavior of materials for structural applications.

Structures.—The NASA sponsored comprehensive computer program for structural analysis—NASTRAN—was released in November for public use. The program tapes and documentation are available from the Computer Software Management and Information Center (COSMIC). Since its delivery to NASA last year, NASTRAN has been thoroughly evaluated and its capabilities confirmed.

Intensive research has shown that significant weight savings in spacecraft, space shuttle, and aircraft structures can be achieved with extensive applications of such composite materials as boron-aluminum, boron-epoxy, graphite-epoxy, and others. Test results are confirming the enhanced strength and stiffness properties of such structures. Work continued to define the design limits for these materials when subjected to the extreme environments associated with space vehicle and aircraft applications.

Space Shuttle Oscillation.—In studies of critical dynamic problems areas for the space shuttle, important progress was made in understanding the unusual dynamic conditions associated with shuttle-type configurations. Research determined the potentially critical nature of wind-induced oscillations on the launch pad and bi-wing interference flutter at transonic speeds during boost. Techniques for minimizing these problems are under development.

Fluid Dynamics.—Recent hypersonic research revealed what may be a fundamental aspect of high Mach number turbulent flow. Measurements made in a Mach 20 helium tunnel indicated that the pressure at the surface of a body may be two, or more times greater than the pressure at the outer edge of the boundary layer. This finding puts in question a pre-viously held assumption that pressure is nearly con-stant through the boundary layer. The increased pressure level experienced at the body surface could have an important effect on the loading of hypersonic vehicles and a strong influence on vehicle design.

A theory was developed for the prediction of clear air turbulence under certain conditions. Local gradi-ents in temperature and velocity are related to a para-meter called the Richardson number. When the Richardson number decreases to a certain level, turbu-lence can be expected. The newly obtained theory relates changes in Richardson number to topographical features such as mountains. Several instances of pilot-reported clear air turbulence have been successfully correlated with the theory.

A simple model was developed for predicting nitrogen oxide formation in turbojet combustors. This pollutant is a major ingredient in the photochemical process that results in the formation of smog. Nitrogen oxide is present in all hydrocarbon-air combustion processes and currently is much more significant for automobiles than for aircraft. However, the aircraft contribution is not negligible, and a model such as this one will contribute to the better understanding needed to reduce the nitrogen oxide emission to a minimum.

General Aviation Aircraft.—In research on improved control and display for general aviation aircraft, the Ames Research Center studied the use of aerodynamic spoilers on powered light aircraft. A spoiler system, similar to that used on gliders, was installed on a typical four-place single-engine general aviation air-plane. Preliminary results indicate marked improve-ments in the precision of flight path control and a reduction in touchdown point dispersion. The range of variation in the ratio of lift to drag (L/D) avail-able through the use of spoilers, in addition to pro-viding an effective "speed brake" for terminal area maneuvering, permits a threefold increase in usable aproach angles. Further studies will be conducted on control techniques and the effectiveness of this system when used differentially as a lateral control device.

V/STOL Aircraft.—Early in 1970, NASA decided to use a research aircraft to verify promising analytical results obtained on the augmentor-wing concept. In this concept, originated by a Canadian corporation, engine exhaust air is ejected into a channel formed by the upper and lower portions of a specially-designed flap system. Large-scale wind tunnel model tests con-ducted for several years indicated that significant in-creases in lift are attainable, compared with other concepts studied making possible the design of jet trans-port aircraft with attractive short-take-off-and-landing (STOL) capability. A contractor was selected to modify the NASA C–8A transport research aircraft

to incorporate an augmentor wing. NASA flight re-search with the modified aircraft is scheduled to begin in the spring of 1972. The vehicle will have the cap-ability of landing and taking off at speeds of about 75 m.p.h. and an associated capability of operating from fields of 1,500-foot length.

Tests, initiated in 1969, were completed this year to determine the effects of aeroelasticity, Mach number, and scale on the performance of tilt rotors. The concept appears promising for several military and civil appli-cations requiring a helicopter-like hover capability but higher cruise performance than that of a helicopter. In this joint program, use was made of the NASA 40- by 80-foot low-speed tunnel, the U.S. Army 7- by 10-foot low-speed tunnel, and the French ONERA 26-foot transonic tunnel. Both rigid and dynamically-scaled rotor models were tested, and reports comparing the experimentally-determined results with predicated values are in preparation.

To conduct studies of the many stability, control, and other problems associated with improvement of in-strument flight at very low airspeeds, NASA continued its V/STOL terminal-area flight-research program, which uses fundamentally different VTOL aircraft concepts and advanced VTOL cockpit-display con-cepts. This year, NASA flight tests were completed on the Air Force XC–142 transport, which utilizes the tilt-wing, deflected-slipstream concept. The investiga-tion identified major factors influencing the precision low-speed, instrument-approach task—as related to the tilt-wing concept specifically and to VTOL handling-quality and cockpit-display requirements in general. A similar, though more limited flight investigation was completed on the DO–31 transport which utilizes direct-lift jet engines to provide VTOL capability; the program was carried out by NASA pilots in the Federal Republic of Germany under an agreement with the builder of the aircraft. Related studies were continued using the NASA XV–5B fan-in-wing re-search aircraft; a variable stability helicopter having in-flight simulation capability; and ground-based simulators. A joint Navy-Air Force-NASA program was initiated to extend such studies through use of the Navy X–22 tilt ducted-fan variable stability research airplane.

Subsonic Aircraft.—The supercritical wing concept intended to permit efficient near-sonic cruise was suc-cessfully tested on wind tunnel models representing advanced transport configurations. A wing was constructed for flight test on an F–8 airplane to pro-vide initial validation of wind tunnel results. An alternate application, intended to permit structural weight savings on moderate speed subsonic aircraft by use of a thickened supercritical wing section, was tested successfully in flight.

Supersonic Aircraft.—NASA participated in the development of the Navy F–14 and the Air Force F–15 aircraft by providing technical consultations and over 5.200 hours of test time in various NASA wind tunnels. Design information was obtained in areas such as inlet system improvement, high-lift systems, nozzle-airframe interactions, spin and recovery characteristics, stability, control, and performance.

NASA–USAF YF–12 Flight Research Program.—Two YF–12 aircraft made 60 flights during 1970. The USAF aircraft carried out 40 flights at speeds up to the cruise mach number to obtain information pertinent to air defense studies. Before the mid-year grounding of the NASA aircraft for instrumentation overhaul and updating, 20 flights were completed and preliminary information was obtained on structural deformation, stability and control, and handling qualities criteria. The NASA phase of the program will continue to provide advanced design information for supersonic aircraft in such areas as aerothermoelastic effects on aircraft structures and on stability and control, inlet dynamics, airframe-propulsion systems interaction, and aerodynamic properties such as skin friction and heat transfer.

Hypersonic Research Engine.—The Langley Research Center began testing the first of two Hypersonic Research Engine models designed, developed, and fabricated to explore air-breathing propulsion systems capable of Mach 8 sustained flight. This model has a flight-weight, hydrogen regeneratively-cooled construction, and is being tested to demonstrate the integrity of a practical hypersonic structural design concept. The engine structure has been subjected to test conditions of 1,500 p.s.i.a. and 2,300° F. Another model being assembled has similar internal flow lines and will be used to study engine operation with hydrogen fuel and subsonic combustion at Mach numbers below 6, and supersonic combustion above Mach 6. Supersonic combustion is necessary at the higher Mach numbers to avoid excessively high internal temperatures and pressures. This aerothermodynamic model is water-cooled and is scheduled to be tested in mid-1971.

Runway Slipperiness.—The Langley Research Center developed a technique to provide pilots with knowledge of the slipperiness of wet runways in a practical and accurate manner. The technique uses an automobile, modified so the operator can apply brakes to one set of diagonal wheels with bald treads, while the opposite diagonal wheels with conventional treads continue rolling for directional control during the tests. The operator performs a locked-wheel skid from 60 m.p.h. The ratio of the distance it takes the car to stop on a wet pavement to the distance it takes to stop on a dry pavement measures the slipperiness. This ratio was found to be directly applicable to aircraft stopping ratios on the same pavement, thus giving the pilot and airport operators accurate knowledge of runway slipperiness and length required to stop under adverse conditions.

V/STOL Avionics.—NASA and the FAA have undertaken a joint program to implement and flight test terminal area avionics equipment and procedures which will allow efficient operation of V/STOL aircraft at crowded hub airports. The Ames Research Center is responsible for the airborne equipment and flight tests; Langley Research Center and FAA's National Aviation Facilities Experimental Center (NAFEC) will cooperate on system simulation of ATC situations; DOT's Transportation Systems Center will develop area navigation technology for Ames' use; and FAA will furnish microwave instrument landing systems and other ATC components for the flight tests. Results will guide design of V/STOL airport runways, traffic patterns at hub airports, navigation aids, and V/STOL navigation, guidance and flight control equipment. Equipment development is underway and flight tests are scheduled to commence in 1972.

Aircraft Noise.—Nacelle modifications intended to reduce fan compressor noise from a four-engine jet aircraft were fabricated and flight tested. Subjective reaction to the flyover noise following the nacelle modifications was assessed by asking a group to judge the acceptability of the sound of modified and unmodified aircraft as reproduced in an anechoic chamber, using the method of constant stimulus differences to assess pairs of stimuli. Each pair consisted of one recording from each aircraft, and sounds recorded outdoors and indoors were included. Operational conditions in the tests represented takeoff, reduced climb gradient, and landing approach thrusts at heights ranging from 500 to 2,500 feet. The installation of the modified nacelles produced improvements for all heights and thrusts investigated; improvements from 11 to 14 decibels of effective-perceived-noise level (EPNdB) for the landing-approach thrust condition; and a finding that the EPNdB noise-rating scale adequately assessed the improvement in acceptability.

Behavioral Research.—Tektite II, a marine sciences, biomedical, and behavioral studies project jointly conducted by the Navy, NASA, and the Department of the Interior, was carried out in an underwater habitat near the U.S. Virgin Islands. Teams of scientists, including one team of five females and one team of mixed nationals, lived and carried out research projects in this stressful environment for periods as long as 60 days. Their activities and responses to their confined habitat and close living conditions, typical of those likely to be obtained in future space stations, provided information on crew behavior and habitability as well as data on microbiology and hematology. NASA is presently analyzing the data.

Life Support Systems Testing.—A four-man 90-day closed-door test of a space vehicle cabin simulator was conducted for the Langley Research Center. This was the longest test in the United States utilizing a regenerative life support system. A space station type of system provided purified water and oxygen reclaimed from the crew's body wastes. The chamber was operated at 10 p.s.i.a. total pressure, with a partial pressure of oxygen equal to that at sea level. Potable water was reclaimed from urine and perspiration by a vacuum distillation-vapor filtration subsystem which used a radioisotope heat source. Separate equipment, containing filters, activated charcoal, and ion-exchange resins, recovered and purified the water used by the crew for washing. Oxygen was recovered from the carbon dioxide exhaled by the crew by the atmosphere purification and control subsystem, consisting of thermal control, carbon dioxide removal, and toxin control units, and by the atmosphere supply and pressurization subsystem containing a Sabatier reactor, water electrolysis unit and atmosphere supply control unit.

The 90-day run and earlier shorter runs indicated that successful long missions using regenerative life support systems will require the capability for onboard maintenance and repair. This will necessitate improved design for maintainability, ready access to operational and performance data, and appropriate crew training.

Orbiting Frog Otolith Experiment.—A 7-day space flight experiment using two bullfrogs as subjects provided information on the adaptability of the vestibule in the inner ear (which controls balance) to sustained weightlessness as well as its response to acceleration. The experiment was launched on a single Scout vehicle on November 9 from NASA Wallops Station, Wallops Island, Va. Excellent data were obtained on the electrical impulses from the otolith sensors and on the frogs' heart rates. Microelectrodes implanted in the vestibular nerves of the two bullfrogs furnished the first direct measures of the otolith sensor response during alternating periods of weightlessness and partial gravity.

Preliminary analysis of the data obtained suggests that adaptation occurred and that it extended to the sensor organ itself. If this preliminary finding is confirmed, it may mean that man can function in weightlessness for long periods without being incapacitated by vestibular influences on his balance, vision, digestive function, circulation, heart rate, and muscular coordination.

Lifting-Body Flight Research Program.—In the joint NASA-Air Force Lifting-Body Program, the NASA M2-F3 and HL-10, and the Air Force X-24A liftingbody research vehicles were flown 22 times during 1970, for a total of 77 flights to date. With its scheduled flight program essentially completed, the HL-10 made its most recent flights to evaluate powered approaches and landing. Both the X-24A and the M2-F3 were gradually flown at higher speeds and altitudes to study the problems and handling qualities associated with these vehicles. The pilots indicated that the handling qualities for the HL-10 were as good as, or better than, most current fighter aircraft.

Space Shuttle.—Approximately 10,000 hours of wind tunnel testing at Ames and Langley Research Centers were used in an aerothermodynamic study of space shuttle concepts.

Planetary Program.—The 5-year program of flight and wind tunnel testing to develop large parachutes capable of landing unmanned spacecraft on Mars was successfully concluded this year. In the flight test program, dummy payloads with various type parachutes up to 84 feet in diameter were propelled to test altitudes considerably over 100,000 feet. Following 18 test flights, the so-called disc-gap-band parachute was selected as the most suitable for the very low density and pressure conditions believed to exist near the surface of Mars. The unmanned Viking Mars lander scheduled for launch in 1975 will use a disc-gap-band parachute to help land a payload on Mars.

Significant improvements in the ability to predict spacecraft temperature during planetary entry resulted from the availability of a computing program to determine heating rates. As a consequence, the extremely high heating rates previously calculated for entry into the atmosphere of Jupiter have been reduced and will affect the future design of probes for a Jupiter exploration.

Planetary Approach Guidance.—From results of the Planetary Approach Guidance experiment which was on the Mariner VI spacecraft, it appears that this new technique is as good as presently used navigation systems at Mars distances and probably better at outer planetary distances. Earth-based navigation systems get progressively worse as the distance from earth increases while the planetary approach technique improves in accuracy as the target planet is approached. In this technique, a calibrated imaging tube on the spacecraft looks at the planet being approached and determines the spacecraft position by star sights on the limb of the planet itself or on its moons. The closer the spacecraft approaches, the more accurate the sightings become because all measurements are based on the position of the planet itself rather than radio signals from earth.

Planetary approach guidance is particularly important when gravity assisted flybys are used to change direction as is proposed for the longer outer planetary missions. In such cases, the distance from the planet at flyby is extremely critical in obtaining the proper trajectory to the next planet, and it is possible that only the planetary approach guidance technique can achieve the required accuracy.

Landing Radar.—Langley Research Center developed and flight tested an improved landing radar which is suitable for use by V/STOL aircraft or by planetary landers. The improvements were achieved by using a new modulation technique consisting of on-off continuous waves at higher altitudes and frequency modulation with carefully controlled modulation sidebands at lower altitudes. The control of these sidebands gives the radar especially good capability for measuring range and range rate at the lower altitudes including touchdown.

Magnetic Bearings.—Goddard Space Flight Center developed a magnetic bearing which eliminates essentially all the mechanical friction in an electric motor. The bearing with its electronic controls floats the rotating shaft within the bearing without mechanical or liquid support and thus permits the design of much more accurate control systems, aircraft instruments, and navigation devices.

Deep Space Unfurlable Antennas.—The Jet Propulsion Laboratory demonstrated the feasibility of constructing large, dish-type, deep-space communication antennas which can be folded for launch stowage. The antenna reflecting surface is a conic section of single curvature that makes it possible to maintain surface distortions within tolerable limits without extensive bracing. Use of the single curved surface was made possible by design of a special Gregorian-type subreflector which corrects beam distortion induced by the flat main reflecting surface. Further development of this technique will make it possible to design stowable antennas 50 feet or more in diameter to provide the communications capacity required for outer planet exploration missions.

Communications Channel Coding.—Research at Goddard Space Flight Center (GSFC) and Ames Research Center has produced telemetry coding techniques which significantly improve both information transmission rate and error reduction for space communication channels. Error correcting codes commonly operate by adding strategically located redundant bits to the data stream. Decoding of these redundant bits allows the correct identification of a limited number of data bits which may have been masked by channel noise. Since the added bits are themselves subject to noise induced error, current coding techniques require a compromise between the number of data bits and the number of redundant bits transmitted. GSFC developed a mathematical coding technique which avoids this compromise and approaches the theoretical maximum error correcting capability by suppressing all data bits and transmitting only properly coded error correcting bits from which the data bit stream is reconstructed. Error correcting codes are particularly applicable to such missions as Pioneer, Mariner, and outer planet exploration, as well as to earth survey or space station missions.

The complexity of hardware and computer operations required to implement error correcting codes has limited the rate at which information in coded form may be transmitted. The ARC research, which complements the GSFC effort, led to the development of a laboratory prototype coding device which provides a 15-fold increase in channel information rate.

High Volume Data Processing.—Research at GSFC in optical methods for data processing continued in an effort to apply lasers and coherent optics to the problem of handling and analysis of extremely large volumes of experimental data from spacecraft. A major impediment to their early employment has been the lack of an effective device for real time conversion of electrical signals to an optical form which can be handled by lenses. GSFC demonstrated that such a device is feasible and a test unit is being built.

Microprocessor Spacecraft Computer.—In research at GSFC, microcircuit techniques were developed which are applicable to the design of ultra low power, high performance, miniaturized spacecraft computing systems for both routine and complex data processing aboard aerospace vehicles. The microprocessor computers will relieve the burden on ground data processing facilities and increase performance in applications ranging from small scientific satellites to highly complex earth resources and space station missions.

Work by NASA and DOD on microcircuits has reduced circuit fabrication costs of complementary metal oxide semiconductor devices to the point where these devices are competitive in the commercial market for application in commercial and industrial systems.

Pilot Warning Indicator.—Flight tests were conducted to determine the feasibility of using optical techniques for providing general aviation pilots with early warning of impending mid-air collisions. All the equipment tested used a flashing xenon lamp on one aircraft to provide the warning signal which was then detected by an optical sensor on a second aircraft. Xenon lights are already installed on many aircraft for enhanced visibility and would require very little development to make them operational. The detectors would require further research to make them suitable for aircraft use. Two different sets of equipment were tested. Each detected other aircraft at ranges of 2–3 miles and warned the pilot of the approximate direction in which to look for further evaluation of the collision risk. Each device had an unacceptably high false alarm rate caused principally by the direct or reflected energy from the sun. Filter techniques may reduce this rate to an acceptable level, and other problems which were encountered, such as radiated electrical interference, can be easily solved. Both units are being redesigned and further flight tests will be conducted.

Optical Communication.—GSFC developed the equipment for and conducted the first experiment to measure the effect of the atmosphere on laser beams projected vertically to a near-stationary measuring platform. The measurements were made by a detector package carried to an altitude of about 18 miles by a large balloon. Two lasers on the ground operating at wavelengths of 10.6 and 0.5 microns were continuously pointed at the balloon package where the intensity of the beam was measured as a function of height, position in the beam, and weather conditions. Additional flights will be conducted in the summer of 1971 when weather conditions again permit balloon flights to add statistical credence to the first results and to conduct tests under a wider variety of weather conditions.

Electrophysics.—In research at Massachusetts Institute of Technology, ionized gas cells were placed in the path of a laser beam to control the wavelength of the laser. By varying the voltage applied across the cell, a point is reached where some of the excited gas molecules produce strong absorption characteristics over a very narrow bandwidth and at the laser frequency. If the laser radiation tends to deviate from its nominal frequency, it is pulled by this absorption line, called the "Lamb Dip," back to its original value. By this process the frequency of the laser oscillator can be precisely controlled, making it suitable for use as a frequency standard or for spectographic analysis.

Digital Blast Gage.—A maintenance-free, standby digital blast gage that is totally self-contained and capable of operating from $-40°$ to $+150°$ F. was developed by Marshall Space Flight Center to detect and record the magnitude of shock and blast fronts in the vicinity of test stands and launch pads. Explosion history is sensed, timed, digitized, and recorded on magnetic tape. Overpressures ranging from 0.1 to 1000 p.s.i. are detected by means of a quartz pressure transducer which initiates the recording of the impact and its storage in a memory bank. The system has the capability of initiating safety countermeasures.

Integrated Circuit Inspection Criteria.—NASA worked closely with the DOD to develop a standard for microcircuit inspection criteria. The criteria include drawings and photographs delineating defects and establishing reject criteria. The jointly developed military standard is now an accepted standard which microcircuit manufacturers are required to use on all DOD and NASA procurements of high reliability integrated circuits.

Nondestructive Weld Inspection.—A system developed by Ames Research Center for making and testing welded interconnections monitors such critical variables as temperature, pressure, and voltage waveform and maintains these variables within prescribed limits during the fabrication process. If any two of the three variables exceeds the prescribed limits, the device is rejected. Evaluation of the system on the production lines of two microcircuit manufacturers, including varying the process parameters to produce both good and bad welds, indicated that the system could successfully detect all bad welds.

Electronically Tuned Optical Filter.—A liquid-crystal-dye system was discovered in which the orientation of the molecular structure can be altered by applying an electric field, producing changes in the optical density of the material and consequently changing the color of light transmitted through the medium. The technique is being used to develop a series of filters which can produce a wide variety of colors. They may be used as color filters for aerial photography calling for films of various sensitivities and for information displays in which color can increase the efficiency with which information can be stored and/or read out by an observer.

Electrochemical Power.—Extended tests on rechargeable nickel cadmium cells and batteries showed that long cycle life can be attained by keeping the temperatures between $30°$ and $50°$ F. and by avoiding excessive overcharging. New battery-making procedures were developed and cell specifications written to assure greater uniformity and reliability of nickel-cadmium batteries. A novel inorganic separator appears to be of value for extending the usefulness of silver-zinc cells in space. Wet stand life was extended from a few weeks to well over 1 year, and active life of several hundred cycles was attained by putting each electrode in its own bag made of this separator material.

Solar Power.—A lightweight, 30 watts-per-pound solar array was ready for the technology stage. Lithium-doped cells with the same efficiency as conventional cells became available; preliminary data indicated about three times the radiation resistance under electron bombardment compared with normal cells. Exploratory work showed the feasibility of simultaneous multiple-cell connections and of the sandwiching of modules between Teflon covers. If these procedures prove to be practical, they will lower manufacturing costs and make safe and convenient storage of modules possible. The problems of high voltage solar arrays were being studied.

Electric Power Processing and Distribution.—In-house and contracted studies were concurrently examining the electric power processing and distribution needs of the space station, the space shuttle, and advanced aircraft in order to establish as high a degree of commonality among these vehicles as is practical. Maximum commonality will make it possible to conserve R. & D. resources, reduce logistics costs, and may improve performance significantly by concentrating R. & D. efforts on common problems.

Research and development activities related to advanced power systems for outer planet spacecraft demonstrated weight and volume reductions of 50–70 percent and reduction of piece parts and discrete interconnections by about 75 percent. The improvement was obtained through adaptation of hybrid thick film electronic circuit techniques on an alumina substrate, a combination with the essential characteristics of both high electrical insulation and high thermal conductivity.

Electric Propulsion.—The research aimed at providing the technological base required to realize the advantages of electric propulsion continued to progress. Interest in these devices is based on the fact that electric thrusters have the highest performance of all practical rocket engines known and may be able to sharply reduce the system mass and cost of high energy space missions.

The SERT II orbital test sought to demonstrate 4,383 hours operation in space of a 1-kilowatt mercury bombardment ion engine. Premature failure caused by erosion limited the test, and only 3,782 hours were accumulated on one engine and 2,011 hours on a second. Initial ground tests verified the design changes necessary to eliminate the erosion. The ground system technology program intended to demonstrate all the propulsion functions required on a solar-array-powered electrically propelled mission continued to progress toward an integrated system test planned for 1971. Data from the ground program and the SERT II flight results served as the basis for significant planning on a solar electric multimission space vehicle, considered the next logical step in the introduction of electric propulsion into mission use.

Thermoelectric Conversion.—The two SNAP–19 radioisotope thermoelectric generators (RTG's) aboard the Nimbus-3 satellite continued to deliver useful power to the spacecraft. The SNAP–27 RTG placed on the moon by the Apollo 12 crew also continued to supply power and heat to the Apollo Lunar Surface Experiments Package.

Work on prototype fueled RTG's for the Pioneer F Jupiter mission proceeded on schedule, and RTG development work for the Viking Mars Lander mission was underway. An advanced RTG for long duration outer planet missions was undergoing design and technology development.

Chemical Propulsion.—In the space shuttle propulsion area, main engine technology efforts were directed toward improving turbomachinery and developing the ability to calculate accurately combined chamber and nozzle performance. Turbomachinery work concentrated on propellant conditioning requirements at the pump inlet, amelioration of the effects of two-phase flow, feed system stability and dynamic interactions, and improved impeller fabrication. Combustion chamber work was investigating devices to observe local variations in mixture ratio in situ, combustion oscillation damping devices, improved injector configurations, and analytical procedures to define internal combustion and flow processes.

In the shuttle auxiliary propulsion technology area, studies were concerned with defining optimum systems and generating a technology base for the components of the systems. Experimental and analytical efforts were in progress to define thruster capabilities by exploring several alternate schemes for ignition, chamber cooling, injection of propellants, valves, and other items.

In work on spacecraft and upper stage propulsion, a hydrazine monopropellant attitude control system for long life outer planet spacecraft was designed. The design is based on thrusters of 50 to 100 millipound thrust, and initial tests of these thrusters indicated good performance for such very small devices.

The FLOX-Methane propellant combination is intended for large planetary orbiters and landers where higher thrust requirements suggest the need for pump-fed engine designs. A program to demonstrate the operational capability of a FLOX-Methane spacecraft propulsion system progressed towards testing a complete system in a simulated space environment. All parts for the propellant storage, pressurization, and feed subsystems were ordered, and a contract for the design, fabrication, test, and delivery of two 5,000-pound thrust pump-fed engines was awarded.

The technology program for the OF_2-Diborane propellant combination moved toward the demonstration of integrated system performance capability and operational readiness. Propellant storage, pressurization, and feed subsystem designs for a representative spacecraft propulsion system were frozen, and some parts were ordered. Several thrust chamber cooling techniques were being evaluated at the nominal 1,000-

pound thrust level and at a subscale 200-pound thrust level. They included regenerative cooling, cooling by means of the heat pipe concept, ablative cooling using carbon phenolic materials, and boundary-layer-assisted radiation cooling.

A solid rocket motor containing 2,800 pounds of high energy propellant was successfully ignited, burned for 34 seconds, then extinguished by injection of a small quantity of water. Only 13 pounds of water were required to drop the 9,000 pounds of thrust to essentially zero in 1 second. This is especially impressive since the propellant was a particularly "hot" composition, developing 10 percent more thrust per pound than those propellants currently in use. Later versions of this motor will be designed to allow reignition for a second burn, then a second quench. This stop-start motor is essentially two stages in one, giving the mission planner the ability to determine the duration of each pulse.

Solid rocket motors developing relatively low thrust for long durations were tested. They were designed to slow spacecraft gradually as they approach a planet, allowing a planetary orbit to be obtained. All 11 tests in this program were successful. In one test—the first that included a very large nozzle cone—a motor weighing 800 pounds (90 percent propellant by weight) was fired under simulated vacuum conditions. The burning time was over 2 minutes, roughly three times that normally attained in this motor shape. In three tests of a similar but smaller motor, "all carbon" nozzles performed successfully. The nozzles are made by a new process of wrapping carbon cloth and sequentially impregnating and charring the binder, and they operate at white heat without degradation. Since they can be very thin, there is considerable weight savings.

In sounding rocket research, the first dual thrust level, advanced state-of-the-art motor was fired, and performance was as predicted. This 2,700-pound unit is a full size prototype of a motor that could meet future NASA requirements in solar, physics and astronomy experiments and is a potential replacement for the aging Aerobee systems. The design included low cost construction, a new and very flexible propellant binder, and a one-piece molded nozzle.

In chemical propulsion technology, an igniter for gaseous hydrogen-gaseous oxygen thrusters based on heating of the gas by resonant phenomena was tested. Reliable ignition was obtained in 0.030 to 0.040 seconds after the flow was initiated. The advantage of this system is that it can be integrated with the propellant valves, and it requires no separate electrical system as does a spark igniter.

The regime of low density flows in small altitude control engines was investigated analytically and experimentally. Results from both the mathematical analyses and the sophisticated laboratory tests verified that for an optimum engine design, the low density flow

conditions (random loose molecular flow) must be accounted for. These results have also been of value in wind tunnel design.

Advances were made in the basic understanding of the nature of solid propellant polymer binders as part of an effort to develop the ability to make propellants with specific physical properties and predictable behavior. A binder which is essentially a pure compound was manufactured. It was used in propellant mixes, and the physical properties compared against various theories to check their validity.

New methods of measuring the exact burning rate of a solid propellant at any instant were found to be feasible. The new techniques involved microwave and ultrasonic devices which look through the motor case and propellant to the burning surface. Data collected by using these techniques will ultimately be used to select the best burning theories and to make possible more precise design of motors.

Nuclear Rocket Program.—The major objective of the joint NASA–AEC nuclear rocket program is to develop a 75,000-pound-thrust engine, NERVA, for space flight missions. Long range plans call for an engine which can be employed in a reusable nuclear stage as well as in a single-use application. The nuclear rocket program also includes a variety of supporting and advanced research and technology projects designed to extend the capability of solid-core nuclear rockets, to conduct research on advanced forms of nuclear propulsion, and to provide the base of information for the development of a nuclear stage.

Progress in NERVA Development.—The emphasis in NERVA development during 1970 was on the definition and preliminary design of the NERVA flight engine. Engine system and nonreactor development activities included the analysis of systems engineering results, the preparation of engine system and critical component specifications, and engine design. The systems engineering analyses sought to verify that the performance and reliability criteria established for the NERVA engine could be met through the materials and component design selections which evolved from the systems engineering NERVA trade studies. The analyses culminated in the preparation of engine system and component specifications for proceeding with the engine detailed design and the fabrication of hardware for development and qualification tests. In October, the preliminary design review of the engine was initiated to examine all engine design documentation, effect the review for adequacy to meet design compatability requirements and correct design deficiencies, and to officially approve the baseline engine configuration for proceeding with the next phase of engine development. These activities are expected to continue into the second quarter of 1971.

In addition to the NERVA design activities, important progress was achieved in other program areas. Procurement was initiated for certain engine critical components parts such as the turbopump and various valve parts. A turbopump bearing test program was started to examine the performance of high-speed, cryogenically-cooled bearing components under varying load conditions. Tests of materials for various high-stress cryogenic applications were continued in support of critical component detailed design activities. Work also was begun to procure, modify, and checkout the host of laboratory jigs, fixtures, and test equipment that will be required to test and evaluate engine components.

Facilities.—Preliminary planning and analyses aimed at the definition of Engine Test Stand No. 1 facility requirements for testing the NERVA engine were completed, and the preliminary design was initiated on the test stand modifications necessary to meet these requirements. Attention was focused on the hot-hydrogen exhaust and altitude simulation system, propellant storage system, and instrumentation and control system. Modification of the stand is scheduled to be completed by the latter half of 1974. A preliminary Engineering Report of Engine/Stage Test Stand No. 2 was completed, and performance and design requirements to support the test objectives for NERVA engine and stage development were established.

Nuclear Flight Stage Definition Studies.—The nuclear-powered stage definition studies were continued with primary emphasis on reusable stages. Potential uses treated in the studies included manned or unmanned transportation between earth orbit, lunar orbit, and geosynchronous orbit in a fully reusable mode, and the propulsion of payloads into deep space, employing the vehicle in either a reusable or expendable mode, depending on the mission objectives and vehicle size. The results of preliminary studies on stage concepts and program definition were published in May, and the study contracts were extended to May 1971 in order to attain a more complete assessment at the concept definition level of several types of reusable nuclear stages.

The two basic stage concepts under investigation were large single-tank configurations that could be launched by the Saturn V Intermediate–21 or by the space shuttle booster with an orbit insertion stage, and a multitank configuration in which the stage modules could be launched in the cargo bay of the space shuttle orbiter. Studies centered on operational requirements and systems definition, and the establishment of the manufacturing and facilities requirements necessary to define a total development program. Cost and cost-sensitivity factors were generated simultaneously with concept definition and will be used later in the studies to find ways in which both development and operational costs can be reduced without sacrifices in performance or reliability.

Preliminary study results indicated that both concepts were reasonably comparable in performance and cost effective for both logistic support of lunar exploration and high energy deep space missions. The preferred concept will not be selected until the size and configuration of the space shuttle have been determined and the direction of the future long range space program is more fully resolved.

Vehicle Technology.—This program provides technology to meet the requirements for the nuclear stage. Several technology programs started previously in support of the 33-foot diameter nuclear stage were completed during the year. One involved a small hydrogen reliquefier designed to reliquefy about 1 to 1½ lb./hr. out of a total of 3 lb./hr. of hydrogen vent gas. All components operated satisfactorily except for the piston seals; they are being redesigned. An experimental investigation was completed on the properties of colloidal hydrocarbon suspensions, and hydrocarbon gelling agents in liquid hydrogen. Of several hydrocarbons investigated, cyclopropane proved the most promising, in concentrations of about ½ percent by weight. Ethane proved to be the most effective gelling agent in liquid hydrogen, in minimum concentrations of 10 weight percent. These data will be useful for tailoring propellant properties to eliminate slush problems, to improve storage characteristics, and to allow effective use of slush hydrogen.

Advanced Nuclear Concepts.—Research was conducted on systems which offer high performance and/or significantly improved operating characteristics such as improved life, higher thrust-to-weight ratios, higher specific impulse, and reduced handling requirements. The cavity reactor (gas-core reactor) appears to offer the potential for the highest performance, but its development will require solving several formidable problems. The dust-bed reactor, on the other hand, appears to offer the potential for increased life, engine thrust-to-weight ratios of 10 or greater, and reduced operational problems. Research on the feasibility of such a system stresses three problems: the amount of power that can be expected without blowing the fuel particles out of the system; the amount of fuel required to make the reactor critical; and the highest temperature at which the system can be operated.

The research on gaseous-core reactors concentrated on propellant heating, the development of high-heat-flux radiant energy source, radiation damage, and fluid mechanics. Progress was made in all these areas.

Space Nuclear System Office.—In October, NASA and the Atomic Energy Commission (AEC) agreed to consolidate related NASA and AEC nuclear space power and power conversion technology activities under a single joint NASA-AEC office, the Nuclear Systems Office, by expanding the joint NASA–AEC Space Nuclear Propulsion Office.

Tracking and Data Acquisition

The NASA tracking and data acquisition networks supported over 50 ongoing space missions and some 20 new flight projects launched by NASA in 1970.

During the year, the networks established a new distance record for two-way deep space communications—250 million miles—and rendered outstanding support to the crippled Apollo 13 spacecraft. In addition, construction progressed on schedule for the 210-foot-diameter antennas being built in Spain and Australia.

Manned Space Flight Network.—The operations of the Manned Space Flight Network were highlighted by the safe return of Apollo 13. During that mission, the network demonstrated that it is, in fact, the astronauts' lifeline to the earth.

From the initial warning by the crew—"Houston, we've got a problem here"—until splashdown some 3½ days later, the network continuously received and transmitted data between the astronauts and the Mission Control Center (MCC) in Houston, Tex. The continuous stream of data carried by the network during this emergency period enabled ground personnel to evaluate the spacecraft systems and the condition of the astronauts and to simulate on the ground the problems experienced by Apollo 13. Ground-based scientific and engineering personnel were then able to explore alternate modes of operations for the astronauts and to send the necessary commands to the spacecraft via the network. The apparatus designed to purify the air in the lunar module was one example of such a ground-determined solution to an in-flight difficulty.

To assure maximum protection for spacecraft communications during Apollo 13's return to earth, NASA asked the Department of State to solicit international cooperation in avoiding radio operation in frequencies which might interfere with reception of the spacecraft transmissions.

The response was immediate and unanimously favorable, with many governments ordering suspension of all frequencies utilized by the spacecraft until after splashdown and recovery.

In addition to providing real-time voice communications between the astronauts and the MCC, the network continuously received and recorded telemetry from Apollo 13. Much of what occurred up to the time of the explosion went unseen and unheard but not unrecorded. Invaluable clues to the origin of the explosion, which were found through analyses of the telemetry data, gave the Apollo 13 Review Board the basis for its detailed investigations, and aided significantly in pinpointing the events that led to the explosion.

The network also supported seven unmanned spacecraft launched by NASA and 21 missions conducted by the Department of Defense. In addition, the network's tracking ship, the USNS *Vanguard,* was used in an ocean surface mapping expedition. The purpose of the expedition was to obtain accurate measurements of a huge depression in the ocean surface directly over the Atlantic's deepest spot—the 5-mile-deep Puerto Rico Trench. The *Vanguard,* together with the Department of Defense stations at Grand Bahama and Antigua, provided C-band radar tracking of the GEOS satellite to obtain triangulation data.

As the year ended, the network was undergoing mission simulation tests designed to insure network integrity and work reliability for the launch of Apollo 14.

Deep Space Network.—This network supported the the Mariners 6 and 7 spacecraft in the extended mission phase and the Apollo 13 mission. The network also continued to support the on-going Pioneer 6, 7, 8, and 9 missions. The network tracked Mariners 6 and 7 as they passed behind the sun at a distance of some 250 million miles from earth. The passage provided an opportunity to test Einstein's General Theory of Relativity and established a new distance record for two-way communications.

In the test of Einstein's Theory, radio signals were transmitted to the spacecraft along a path close to the sun. The effect of solar gravitation on the signals was determined by comparing the elapsed time for the signal to reach the spacecraft and return to earth along this path with the time required for a signal to be sent to the spacecraft and returned along a path outside the influence of the sun. Calculations based on the Einstein Theory indicate the time should be 200-millionths of a second slower due to the influence of the gravitational field of the sun. The data acquired thus far indicate verification of the Einstein Theory. However, to fully determine the effect of the solar gravity, extremely precise calculations derived from longer term tracking of the spacecraft are required. To obtain these data support will continue into 1971 to ensure that the orbits of the two Mariners have been precisely determined.

The network also provided vital support of the Apollo 13 mission, primarily through the 210-foot-diameter antenna at Goldstone, Calif. Original mission plans called for the 210-foot antenna to support only the close-in lunar phase of the mission. (This antenna allows about a sixfold increase in performance over the standard 85-foot antennas of the Manned Space Flight Network.) After the explosion aboard Apollo 13, the 210-foot antenna supported the mission until splashdown. Its added capability permitted voice communications with the astronauts in spite of the reduced spacecraft power during the emergency.

The four ongoing Pioneer spacecraft continued to furnish important solar particle data. Early in the year, Pioneers 6 and 7 were aligned in a manner which allowed the network to receive, for the first time, data simultaneously from two planetary spacecraft. The beamwidth of the 210-foot antenna which made this possible also made possible the collection of unprecedented scientific information on propagation of the higher energy particles from the sun.

The network also participated in several radio astronomy experiments. One was the successful demonstration of radar techniques at planetary distances in the X-band frequencies. The Goldstone 210-foot antenna worked jointly with the Lincoln Laboratory's 120-foot Haystack antenna (near Boston, Mass.) to conduct the experiment, using as radar targets the planets Mercury and Venus and the moons of Jupiter. The Haystack antenna transmitted radio frequency energy to the planets, and the Goldstone antenna received the returned signals. The results of the X-band performance may have applications in mission planning and spacecraft design of future planetary programs.

Construction work continued throughout the year on a second 210-foot antenna at Tidbinbilla, near Canberra, Australia, and in June, ground was broken about 40 miles west of Madrid, Spain, for construction of the network's third 210-foot antenna. Both antennas are essentially duplicates of the Goldstone antenna and are expected to become operational in 1973. Spaced at approximately equal distances around the earth, the three-antenna subnetwork will have the capability for continuous tracking of spacecraft billions of miles into space.

Satellite Network.—This network continued supporting an average daily workload of over 40 satellites, which in terms of total missions supported is the heaviest workload of all the NASA tracking and data acquisition facilities. In addition to supporting the majority of NASA's scientific and applications satellites, the network services a wide variety of space projects conducted by other Government agencies and foreign countries through cooperative international programs.

Among the major flight projects launched during the year and supported by the network are Tiros–M, SERT–2, Nimbus–4, and SAS–A.

The Tiros–M mission, now designated ITOS–1, was launched January 23, and represents the first in a series of second-generation operational meteorological satellites launched by NASA for the National Oceanic and Atmospheric Administration (NOAA). The network was responsible for all support activities of the spacecraft until it was completely checked out and ready for operational use. After some 5 months of extensive checkout, ITOS–1 was officially turned over to NOAA.

The Space Electric Rocket Test (SERT–2) had as its prime mission objective the evaluation of an ion engine in a space environment. Due to the presence of the active element onboard the spacecraft, the early postlaunch period of SERT–2 was extremely critical. To ensure maximum coverage for this period, supplemental support was obtained from the Department of Defense and the Manned Space Flight Network. The supplemental tracking facilities aided greatly in the rapid determination of the satellite's orbit and attitude. Once the spacecraft was verified to be gravity-gradient captured, the ion engines and other related experiments were activated. Both engines were operated and provided important new data on ion thruster performance in the space environment.

The Nimbus–4 mission was launched April 8. Its prime data acquisition stations are those at Rosman, N.C., and Fairbanks, Alaska. The network is participating in the Interrogation, Recording, and Location System experiment aboard the spacecraft. Weather balloons, launched from Christchurch, New Zealand, and Ascension Island, are interrogated by Nimbus–4 and transmit magnetic, meteorological, and oceanographic data for recording aboard the spacecraft. The data are later transmitted to the ground stations and relayed to the project control center at GSFC. From these data, balloon locations are calculated and the precise conditions existing at these points are determined. This information is furnished to the principal scientific investigators, including NOAA, the Smithsonian Institution, and the National Science Foundation.

International cooperative projects supported during the year included the first successful Japanese satellite, OHSUMI, and the DIAL–WIKA satellite, a joint development of France and Germany. In another type of international cooperation, arrangements were completed for mutual satellite tracking support by the French Centre National d'Etudes Spatiales (CNES) and NASA. Each agency will provide network support in tracking, data acquisition, and command activities when their respective workloads permit. The arrangement applies to support by the French stations in Canary Islands, Upper Volta, Congo, South Africa, French Guiana, and France. The NASA stations involved are in Australia, Madagascar, South Africa, Ecuador, Chile, England, and the United States.

SAS–A was successfully launched on December 12, 1970, from the San Marco platform, a modified oil rig in the Indian Ocean off Kenya. It was launched by Italian personnel, the first American satellite to be launched by scientists from another country. The Network is collecting data on X-ray sources in space from SAS–A.

International Affairs

NASA continued to develop international cooperative projects and to arrange for foreign support in the exploration of space. At the same time, the agency has undertaken a major effort to assure substantial participation by other nations in post-Apollo programs, with the United States sharing the costs as well as the benefits of future space activities. As part of this effort, principal potential overseas participants were briefed on NASA plans and provided with reports and other documents.

The European Space Conference (ESC) studied possibilities for substantive involvement with NASA, principally through groups such as the European Launcher Development Organization (ELDO) and the European Space Research Organization (ESRO). Both organizations now have full-time liaison personnel in Washington and have sent teams to visit NASA centers and contractor facilities. Special committees and panels were set up within ESC, ELDO, and ESRO management for preparatory studies by European industry. ESC voted several million dollars to support these studies, assigned observers to work with NASA in the area of supporting technology for the shuttle and space station, and formed working groups with the agency to coordinate European and American studies of space transportation systems and space stations.

In September, ESC ministers indicated that major participation in the U.S. space transportation system program would strain Europe's resources and probably mean an end to the Europa III launcher program. They were assured that the United States would make reimbursable launch services available for European payloads for peaceful purposes in exchange for their substantial participation in our program. Such participation was understood to mean at least 10 percent of the developmental costs of the space transportation system, or about $1 billion.

In a November ESC meeting, the results of the previous meeting were reviewed and a special committee was organized to formulate questions for further discussion with the United States. Also, Canada and Japan established special committees to assist their Governments in determining whether they should take part in the post-Apollo program.

In line with a 1969 Presidential pledge to share the benefits of earth resources survey techniques, the United States invited the Secretary General of the U.N., Member States, and Specialized Agencies to send representatives to an International Workshop on Earth Resources Survey Systems at the University of Michigan, May 3–14, 1971. Other activities included briefings for representatives of the United Nations Outer Space Committee and Secretariat and liaison with the Office of the U.N. Space Applications Expert.

Discussions were underway with Brazil, Canada, and Mexico on agreements to extend cooperation in the earth resources area. In addition, over 70 experimenters from 28 countries responded to a worldwide request for letters of intent to submit proposals to analyze data acquired by Earth Resources Technology Satellites.

Joint working group meetings were held in India and the United States on the Satellite Instructional Television Experiment planned for the ATS–F spacecraft. Work in the United States on the satellite and in India on the ground segment moved forward. The objective is to begin the 1-year experiment in early 1974.

NASA and the Agency for International Development began an 18-month experimental project with Korea in the applications of aerospace technology to Korean economic problems. The project, which involves visits by specialists of both countries, calls for the Korean Institute of Science and Technology to examine the technology utilization system and identify aerospace-generated technology potentially applicable to Korean industrial needs and then to adjust these techniques to Korean needs.

An agreement was made under which NASA and the Canadian Department of Industry, Trade, and Commerce are to study the "augmentor wing" concept and its possible application to STOL aircraft. An agreement was also concluded with the United Kingdom Ministry of Aviation Supply to test fly NASA's XH–51 rigid rotor helicopter in the U.K. and to share the resultant data.

NASA and the Netherlands Astronomy Satellite Program Authority agreed in June to the cooperative development and launching in 1974 of a small astronomical satellite (ANS), which will carry two Dutch and one U.S. experiment to investigate stellar UV and X-ray radiations. International cooperation in astronomy was also extended by an agreement with the Science Research Council in Great Britain to launch a British X-ray satellite (UK–5) in 1973. It will be the fifth in the Ariel series which began with Ariel I, the first international cooperative satellite. The Italians launched NASA's Small Astronomy Satellite (SAS–A) from the San Marco platform, and an agreement was concluded in June establishing the principles under which NASA will launch, on a reimbursable basis, the Italian satellite SIRIO which will study wave propagation and electron flows in the magnetosphere. Preliminary discussions between Indian and

NASA scientists took place in September on 13 experiments proposed by Indian scientists for inclusion in a cooperative scientific satellite, designated RS–2, to be launched on a NASA-supplied Scout vehicle.

An experiment to study stellar UV emissions for Skylab A was accepted from the French National Laboratory for Space Astronomy. An instrument developed by the French National Laboratory for Stellar and Planetary Physics will investigate the fine structure of the solar chromosphere from the OSO–1 spacecraft, scheduled for launching in 1972, and Britain's Jodrell Bank Observatory will assist in the planning activities of the radio science team for Project Viking, the Mars probe planned for 1975.

New sounding rocket agreements were signed with Australia, India, Spain, and Sweden, and negotiations with the French were nearing completion for cooperative upper-atmosphere sounding rocket launchings at Kourou, French Guiana. Under previous agreements, launchings took place in Argentina, Australia, Brazil, India, Norway, Pakistan, Spain, and Sweden.

Lunar material, returned by the Apollo 11 and 12 missions, is under study by 54 foreign principal investigators in 16 countries. They will present the results of their analyses at the Second Lunar Science Conference in January 1971.

Continuing efforts to expand U.S.-U.S.S.R. cooperation beyond the limited projects provided for in the Bilateral Space Agreement of 1962 led to preliminary technical discussions in October between representatives of NASA and the Soviet Academy of Sciences on possible compatible space docking arrangements. An agreement was reached on procedure and a schedule set for joint efforts to design compatible rendezvous and docking arrangements. Each nation will provide the other with supplementary technical information and a draft of technical requirements for those systems which it is judged should be made compatible. In March–April 1971, three joint working groups will meet to refine the requirements and attempt to develop a single set of requirements for compatibility. The two countries will then independently work out preliminary system designs, following which NASA and the Soviet Academy will jointly consider appropriate implementing action.

The BC–4 camera observations of the PAGEOS balloon satellite, under the National Geodetic Satellite Program were concluded. The observations were made under arrangements with 23 countries for the temporary stationing of Coast and Geodetic Survey and Army Map Service camera teams at 42 sites. The foreign sites provided the geographic distribution essential to the success of the observation program, whose objective is to increase man's knowledge of the size and shape of the earth.

Agreements for NASA tracking stations in Australia and the Malagasy Republic were extended, assuring continued support from these key locations. As a consequence of changed requirements, the manned flight tracking stations at Guaymas, Mexico, and Antigua and the scientific satellite station in Newfoundland were discontinued. The ATS transportable ground station, at Cooby Creek, Australia, was withdrawn and was being modified to support future ATS satellites. The transportable Apollo support facility at Grand Bahama Island was placed in caretaker status. An agreement was concluded between the United States and Canada concerning accommodation of U.S. sounding rocket and other scientific activities at Canada's Churchill Research Range. Since July the range was funded, operated, and maintained entirely as a Canadian venture following expiration of a 1965 agreement providing for joint United States-Canada funding.

Cooperation in the utilization of the tracking station capabilities of NASA and the space agencies of other countries increased. An agreement between NASA and the French space agency was completed in June for mutual tracking and data acquisition support from one agency's facilities to the others. Under the terms of this agreement and in accord with arrangements with agencies of the United Kingdom and Italy, NASA expects to receive support as necessary from tracking facilities of those agencies for the Small Astronomy Satellite. NASA facilities provided tracking assistance to support the successful Japanese satellite (OHSUMI) in February and also provided telemetry support to the German scientific satellite DIAL launched on a French DIAMANT–B vehicle from French Guiana in March.

Many offers of assistance in astronaut recovery were extended from nations around the world during Apollo 13. During the critical reentry period, the Parkes 210-foot-diameter antenna in Australia was voluntarily placed at NASA's service.

Mexico again hosted an astronaut training exercise in its Pinnacate area where the surface is similar to that of the moon.

Industry Affairs

Activities reported in this section are varied but industrially related. In each area, NASA efforts have been directed toward improvements in economy and efficiency of operations.

Inventions and Contributions.—The Inventions and Contributions Board completed action and made recommendations on 105 petitions for patent waiver received from NASA contractors during the year. The Board recommended the granting of monetary awards totaling approximately $85,000 for inventions and other scientific and technical contributions made by

NASA and NASA contractor employees. In September the Board held an oral hearing on the application for a monetary award for a scientific contribution submitted by a member of the general public. A comprehensive report summarizing the activities of NASA contractors granted patent waivers showed a 50-percent increase over 1969 in the number of inventions fully commercialized by NASA contractors or their licensees.

Research Grants.—The "Research Grant Handbook," incorporating all of NASA's regulations in this field, was published in January. With the distribution of the handbook, a new procedure was instituted to simplify and expedite the research grant process. Now the authority to award and administer grants is being delegated to each NASA field installation.

Procurement Processing.—In a step designed to streamline decision making, NASA established a Master Buy Plan procedure and a Simplified Procurement Plan procedure and began using them on a trial basis. The Master Buy Plan procedure is designed to enable management to focus its attention on a representative selection of high dollar value and sensitive procurement actions without compromising headquarters' visibility or control over essential management functions. It is also intended to reduce the number of procurements requiring headquarters review and approval, permit better planning of workload and better use of personnel resources, shorten the procurement review and approval cycle, and increase the delegation of procurement responsibility and authority to each field installation. The Simplified Procurement Plan procedure will reduce the number of offices reviewing procurement plans, simplify and reduce the contents of plans, and reduce the review time in the acquisition cycle.

Unanticipated Research and Development Clause.—NASA developed a new contract clause to provide for prompt administrative resolution of problems caused by a substantial amount of unexpected R & D work under fixed-price contracts for non-R & D projects considered at contracting time to be reasonably within the state of the art. The clause is expected to help prevent delays, extra costs, and other adverse program impacts.

Labor Relations.—The number of man-days lost due to strikes on all NASA contracts in 1970 decreased from 4,427 in 1969 to 3,627 in 1970. Man-days lost due to strikes at Kennedy Space Center in 1970 were reduced from 337 in 1969 to 90 in 1970. Over half the man-days lost were attributable to strikes during negotiations of labor agreements. The remaining man-days lost were the result of unresolved grievances over

the presence of nonunion contractors and working rules. They were of short duration and involved a minimum of lost time. Strikes by construction craft unions in 1970 accounted for 2,767 of the 3,627 man-days lost on all contracts. The Labor Relations Office worked with Center management to eliminate or minimize the impact of labor problems on NASA programs, and as a result, labor problems did not interfere with program schedules.

Reliability and Quality Assurance.—NASA developed a microelectronics reliability program which, through the cooperation of the Department of Defense, is reflected in a military specification and accompanying standards for the acquisition of high reliability microcircuits. NASA cooperated with the Education and Training Institute of the American Society for Quality Control by participating in five seminars to further industry and Government understanding of NASA reliability and quality assurance programs.

Technology Utilization

The NASA Technology Utilization Program has as a primary goal the expeditious transfer of technology from NASA's varied R & D programs to all sectors of the economy. To do this, the Technology Utilization Program seeks to identify and evaluate new technology and to actively assist in its transfer to other sectors.

New Technology Publications.—NASA continued its efforts to identify new technology resulting from ongoing R & D activities, selecting and reporting nearly 4,000 items this year. To facilitate the new technology identification process, prospective searching was emphasized. Over 700 "Tech Briefs" were published in 1970, and over 12,000 requests for backup material on the "Tech Briefs" and more than 7,000 requests for general information were received. Upward of 8,000 organizations routinely request "Tech Briefs". Technology utilization reports and surveys published during the year covered such topics as hydrogen leak detection, materials in fire safety, teleoperator systems, and new high-strength metal alloys.

Regional Dissemination.—The Centers continued to provide scientific and technical information services based on the NASA technical data system to industrial, academic, and Government users. Technical data bases in such areas as chemistry, engineering, electronics, plastics, and metallurgy were expanded.

The Computer Software Management and Information Center (COSMIC) program was aided by the Regional Dissemination Centers, as was the distribution of earth photography from space flights. The Centers also cooperated with the Small Business Administration, the Department of Commerce, and several State and local governmental units.

Technology and Biomedical Applications Teams.—A fourth Technology Applications Team was formed at a multidisciplinary research and consulting firm. This team is concentrating on transferring aerospace technology to urban planning and construction.

A fourth Biomedical Applications Team was created at the Stanford University Medical School in California. This and the other three teams continued to concentrate on seeking solutions to problems in clinical and medical research.

COSMIC.—The COSMIC continued to disseminate computer software from its expanding inventory of documented programs. The initial input of software developed under Department of Defense sponsorship was made this year. Announcement of software in the "Computer Pogram Abstracts"—a quarterly journal available through the Government Printing Office—and distribution through Regional Dissemination Centers contributed to the steadily increasing level of user interest and involvement.

Relationship with Other Government Agencies

Responsibility for coordinating NASA relationships with other Federal agencies engaged in aerospace activities is assigned to the Office of Department of Defense and Interagency Affairs.

The Aeronautics and Astronautics Coordinating Board, the principal formal organization for coordinating national space and aeronautics activities between NASA and DOD, considered the following subjects during the year: actions necessary to acquire new aeronautical facilities; on-going research in electronic components; development of data relay satellites; long term research leading to advanced aeronautical systems; areas where advance coordination and pooling of effort between NASA and DOD may be essential; current approaches used in funding the operation of R. & D. test facilities; air traffic control satellite issues; space transportation system status; and State Department views of international aeronautics and space cooperation.

The Office of DOD and Interagency Affairs continued to coordinate NASA research, design, development, test, and evaluation support of major DOD aeronautical systems, including the B–1, F–14, and F–15 aircraft.

The military services continued to collaborate with NASA in assigning military personnel to NASA for 2- to 3-year tours. In addition, arrangements were made with the Air Force Systems Command (AFSC)

for a USAF Research Associate Program at Ames Research Center (ARC). The program provides for 3-year assignments of up to three Air Force officers who will work in research areas agreeable to ARC and AFSC. NASA also made an agreement with the Department of the Army for increasing the number of Army personnel assigned to NASA aeronautical centers for joint participation in aeronautical technology work.

Additional agreements concluded between NASA and other Federal agencies covered such activities as the NASA-Air Force Committee to coordinate the space transportation system; the use of the NASA Mississippi test facility for the Coast Guard National Data Buoy Program and the Bureau of Commercial Fisheries Marine Resources Assessment and Harvesting Program; Air Force support for the NASA YF–12 aircraft and Applications Technology Satellite Programs; AEC support to the Pioneer program; Navy tracking and transportation support; NASA-DOD operation of the White Sands Test Facility; Navy extension of the F–8C aircraft loan; GSA operation of the NASA Central Motion Picture Film Depository; and NASA support of FAA's information systems.

NASA and DOD continued joint studies on ways and means of achieving economies in manpower and other resources in common endeavors. As a result, the two agencies consolidated additional activities at the Kennedy Space Center and the Air Force Eastern Test Range. Action to consolidate NASA and Air Force tracking stations in Hawaii was deferred.

This office continued to coordinate special reviews by the Astronautics and Space Engineering Board and the National Academy of Sciences of NASA's Space Transportation System Development and Life Sciences Programs, respectively. It also assumed chairmanship of the White Sands Task Force group which identified additional uses of NASA's White Sands Test Facility, thus allowing the facility to be maintained at a moderate level of effort rather than reduced to a caretaker status in 1971.

Communications activities included NASA support of the Department of Commerce investigation of communications satellites for Alaska. This looks toward expansion of a NASA study on broadcast satellites conducted under the auspices of the Office of Telecommunications Policy; studies of the problems of aeronautical satellites in conjunction with the FAA, Department of Transportation, Office of Telecommunications Management, and National Aeronautics and Space Council. NASA also continued liaison with the Department of Health, Education, and Welfare in connection with the possible use of communications satellites in education.

Also coordinated was NASA assistance to the U.S. Bureau of Standards in studies to determine the impact on the Nation of the increasing use of the metric system. As a result of this activity, NASA adopted a policy making the metric system the primary method of expressing measurements for the agency.

The NASA Safety Program

NASA continued to formalize and strengthen its system for the identification and control of hazards in space systems, aircraft operations, and facilities. New concepts in risk management and system safety were implemented and are being evaluated for effectiveness. A reorganization combining all elements of safety under one office increased the capability and effectiveness of the program.

Safety Management Approach.—A standardized safety contract clause was instituted as a firm requirement for all major contracts. This action makes contract safety requirements an agency position in contrast with the previous method of letting each Center set forth safety requirements in each contract awarded by the Center.

A scheduled safety review and evaluation of each major field installation was completed during the year. The results and recommendations for corrective action were sent to the appropriate field installation or headquarters office for resolution. The overall evaluation and review indicated a continuing improvement in safety practices at each installation and increased awareness of accident prevention through safety analysis and recognition of risk management techniques. The reviews have provided management with an appraisal of the safety efforts and highlighted areas for improvement and corrective action.

System Safety.—The System Safety approach, which includes identification and analysis of hazards, is stressed equally in manned and unmanned programs. Safety office personnel are colocated in all of the headquarters manned flight program offices, and a close working relationship is maintained with the unmanned programs. A training course in system safety technology was held at George Washington University and will be offered again in early 1971.

Industrial Safety.—NASA continued its reviews of each field installation in industrial accident prevention. Special emphasis was given to procurement plans to assure inclusion of the proper safety and fire protection requirements in plans and contracts, and to assure incorporation of proper safety and fire protection into the design and modification of NASA buildings and facilities. The Office of Facilities obtained funding for many safety and fire protection projects to correct existing deficiencies. The Safety Office cooperated in this effort by developing justification guidelines and priorities.

Fire protection seminars were held at two field centers to give supervisory and engineering personnel a better understanding of fire safety and its applications on NASA field installations. Four films on NASA fire safety program elements were provided to all field installations for orientation and training.

In a cooperative effort by the Manned Space Flight Tracking Network and the Goddard Space Flight Center's Health and Safety Engineering Office, a 5-week safety training course for instructors was held at GSFC's Network Training and Test Facility. Twenty contractor representatives, including at least one representative from each of the 15 MSFN stations, received broad safety training, and after return to their stations will train all other station personnel. All new employees for stations will be given this training at GSFC before assignment to tracking stations. The applicability of this program to the other tracking network is being investigated.

Aviation Safety.—Aviation Safety was expanded with the reorganization of the Safety Office, and the creation and filling of the position of Assistant Director for Aviation. The NASA Aviation Safety and Standardization Committee submitted a draft NASA Aircraft Operations Manual.

An aviation safety survey was made of each installation with aviation capabilities. Its purpose was to review and assess the effectiveness of aviation safety and accident prevention programs throughout NASA and to assist in developing NASA-wide standards for aviation operations. Safety programs have been improved, and NASA has had an aircraft flight accident-free year. Reports of the survey were sent to each installation, and a summary of observations and recommendations for all NASA segments was in preparation.

General Activities.—The 1970 NASA Safety and Risk Management Conference, held at Lewis Research Center in September, emphasized aviation and flight safety. Seventy NASA personnel in all safety disciplines and from all centers participated in a 2-day exchange of experiences, ideas, and new procedures in accident control, hazard identification, and risk management.

NASA sponsored a 2-day conference on "Materials for Improved Fire Safety" at Houston. A combined Government-industry review of NASA's technology developments that provide improved fire safety was presented for the 500 non-NASA people who attended. As a result of the conference, NASA has been asked to assist the International Association of Fire Fighters to design a universal fire suit and to assist both a major airline and the USAF in installing a noncombustible interior on one of their aircraft.

Action was taken to expand the Awareness Program to activities at all NASA Centers and their contractors to reduce human errors. The "Awareness" newsletter format was changed to reflect the agency's continuing concern with both safety and the morale of the Space Team. An Advisory Panel, comprised of agency and industry motivation representatives, began to identify mutual problems and take cooperative remedial actions. A program designed to call attention to the importance of Apollo 14 to the future of the Space Team was initiated and will be carried through to completion of the mission. Special posters were prepared for the Flight Crew Medical Director and for the "ZERO IN on Federal Safety" campaign due to begin January 1971. A number of Federal agencies have requested NASA permission to use these "ZERO IN" posters and arrangements have been made with the Department of Labor for printing and distribution throughout the Government.

A joint NASA–USAF Space Safety Escape, Rescue, and Recovery planning group was formed with the Assistant Director for Programs and Research Safety as a co-chairman with the representative of the USAF Space and Missile Systems Office.

The NASA Safety Office also participated in discussions concerning international rescue capabilities.

SOURCE: National Aeronautics and Space Council, "Aeronautics and Space Report of the President," 1971.

Part 2

NASA GRANTS AND RESEARCH CONTRACTS

REPORT FORMAT AND DATA CONTENT: GUIDANCE FOR USERS

Report Body: Format

(1)   (2)   (3)

NGR-01-002-045   University of Alabama   O. R. Ainsworth

(4)

A study of gyroscopic stability.

(5)	(6)	(7)	(8)
Proposal	FY	Agreement Period	Amount
−045	67	7/67 − 6/68	22880
−060	69	7/68 − 7/69	21688

(9)
Tech. Off.: THOMASON H

(10)
Funding Element: MSFC

(11)
CASE Code: 41

(12)
AWC: 933−35

_____

Legend

(1) Grant or Contract Number
(2) Performing Institution
(3) Principal Investigator at Performing Institution
(4) Brief Work Description
(5) NASA Control Number for Funded Proposal
(6) Fiscal Year of Program Funds
(7) Approximate Period of Performance
(8)   Funds Obligated for Period or no cost extension
(9) NASA Technical Officer
(10) NASA Funding Group
(11) Committee on Academic Science and Engineering government-wide fields
     of science and engineering classification
(12) Agency-Wide Fiscal Code; unique project and subprogram designator

Detailed Information Available from Legend

(1)   Grant or Contract Number

Prefix	Type	Negotiated By	Abbrev.
NAS1-	Contract	Langley Research Center	LARC
NAS2-	Contract	Ames Research Center	ARC
NAS3-	Contract	Lewis Research Center	LERC
NAS4-	Contract	Flight Research Center	FRC
NAS5-	Contract	Goddard Space Flight Center	GSFC
NAS6-	Contract	Wallops Station	WS
NAS7-	Contract	NASA Pasadena Office	NAPO
NAS8-	Contract	Marshall Space Flight Center	MSFC
NAS9-	Contract	Manned Spacecraft Center	MSC
NAS10	Contract	John F. Kennedy Space Center	KSC

Prefix	Type	Negotiated By	Abbrev.
NAS12-	Contract	Electronics Research Center	ERC
NGR	Research Grant	NASA Headquarters	HQ
NGL	Step Funded Research Grant	NASA Headquarters	HQ
NGT	Training Grant	NASA Headquarters	HQ
NGF	Facilities Grant	NASA Headquarters	HQ
NSR	Contract	NASA Headquarters	HQ
NASr-*	Contract	NASA Headquarters	HQ
NASw-*	Contract	NASA Headquarters	HQ
NsG-*	Research Grant	NASA Headquarters	HQ
NsG(T)-*	Training Grant	NASA Headquarters	HQ
NsG(F)-*	Facilities Grant	NASA Headquarters	HQ

*Discontinued for Educational Institutions.

Questions relating to the business administration of grants and contracts should be directed to the Contracts Division for NASA Headquarters or to the procuring office of the appropriate Field Installation.

Numeric suffixes for grants and "NSR" contracts, viz., 01-002-045 are interpreted as follows:

01 - Permanent identification number assigned to each state. ("52" indicates a foreign country)

002 - Permanent identification number for each university within a state.

045 - Unique identifier for a particular grant or contract.

(9)   NASA Technical Officer

Individual assigned by NASA to follow progress of work and serve as agency contact for principal investigator and others interested in technical aspects of the project. If not listed, name may be obtained from appropriate procuring activity. (See (1), "Grant or Contract Number," above).

Technical Officer is generally located in the NASA group which provided the funds. (See (10), below).

(10)   NASA Funding Group

Abbreviations are identified in (1), "Grant or Contract Number," above. Letters following "HQ" uniquely identify specific Headquarters offices.

(11)   C.A.S.E. Fields of Science and Engineering

NASA's university projects are classified by a system established by the Committee on Academic Science and Engineering of the Federal Council for Science and Technology. Codes are interpreted as follows:

PHYSICAL SCIENCES	MATHEMATICS	ENGINEERING	LIFE SCIENCES	SOCIAL SCIENCES
11 ASTRONOMY	21 ANY DISCIPLINE(S)	41 AERONAUTICAL	51 BIOLOGY	71 ANTHROPOLOGY
12 CHEMISTRY		42 ASTRONAUTICAL	52 CLINICAL MEDICAL	72 ECONOMICS
13 PHYSICS	**ENVIRONMENTAL**	43 CHEMICAL	59 LIFE SCIENCES,	73 HISTORY
19 PHYSICAL SCIENCES,	**SCIENCES**(*Terrestrial*	44 CIVIL	NEC*	74 LINGUISTICS
NEC*	*& extraterrestrial)*	45 ELECTRICAL		75 POLITICAL SCIENCE
		46 MECHANICAL	**PSYCHOLOGY**	76 SOCIOLOGY
	31 ATMOSPHERIC	47 METALLURGY AND		79 SOCIAL SCIENCE,
	SCIENCES	MATERIALS	61 BIOLOGICAL	NEC*
	32 GEOLOGICAL	49 ENGINEERING,	ASPECTS	
	SCIENCES	NEC*	62 SOCIAL ASPECTS	**OTHER SCIENCES****
	33 OCEANOGRAPHY		69 PSYCHOLOGICAL	
	39 ENVIRONMENTAL		SCIENCES, NEC*	99 ALL DISCIPLINES
	SCIENCES, NEC*			

Not Elsewhere Classified (Used for multidisciplinary projects and other projects for which a separate discipline name has not been assigned).

***Used for multidisciplinary and interdisciplinary projects which cannot be classified within any of the preceding main fields.*

ALABAMA

NGR-01-001-003   **Alabama A&M College**   **C. O. Lee**

Radiation effects in the metabolism of phospholipids in the central nervous system of albino rats.

Proposal	FY	Agreement Period	Amount
−004	67	7/67 − 6/68	15402
−004	67	7/68 − 6/69	NCE

Tech. Off.:   Funding Element: RB
CASE Code: 51   AWC: 127−49

NGR-01-001-006   **Alabama A&M College**   **R. H. Lee**

Study of NASA-oriented research capabilities of some developing institutions in Alabama and middle Tennessee.

Proposal	FY	Agreement Period	Amount
−006	68	7/68 −12/68	13790
		12/68 − 7/69	NCE

Tech. Off.:   REDDING E R   Funding Element: HQ−Y
CASE Code: 79   AWC: 183−00

NGR-01-001-007   **Alabama A&M College**   **M. C. George**

Development of a computer code for predicting the neutron reaction cross sections and gamma-ray spectrum in certain radiation shielding materials and also in nitrogen and oxygen.

Proposal	FY	Agreement Period	Amount
−007	67	6/69 − 6/70	22716

Tech. Off.:   MARR E G   Funding Element: HQ−Y
CASE Code: 21   AWC: 183−00

NGL-01-002-001   **University of Alabama (University)**
                                     R. Hermann, G. Croker

Research in the aerospace physical sciences.

Proposal	FY	Agreement Period	Amount
−029	66	3/66 − 2/69	475000
−041	67	3/67 − 2/70	425000
−054	68	3/69 − 2/71	150000

Tech. Off.:   QUINN H B   Funding Element: HQ−Y
CASE Code: 51   AWC: 183−00

NGR-01-002-063   **University of Alabama (Huntsville)**   **J. E. Rush**

Two-body strong interaction of elementary particles.

Proposal	FY	Agreement Period	Amount
−063	69	1/69 − 2/70	10000

Tech. Off.:   PARNELL T A   Funding Element: MSFC
CASE Code: 13   AWC: 124−09

NSR-01-002-033   **University of Alabama (University)**   **R. M. Hollub**

Contract for a summer institute in space-related engineering.

Proposal	FY	Agreement Period	Amount
−033	67	1/67 − 3/68	133900
−033	67	3/68 − 3/69	NCE
−062	69	3/69 − 3/70	131708

Tech. Off.:   CARTER E H   Funding Element: HQ−Y
CASE Code: 49   AWC: 181−00

NSR-01-002-057   **University of Alabama (Birmingham)**   **E. A. Sallin**

Support for a summer workshop conference.

Proposal	FY	Agreement Period	Amount
−057	68	8/68 − 8/69	15000

Tech. Off.:   ANDERSON L O   Funding Element: HQ−RB
CASE Code: 99   AWC: 127−49

NAS8-2585   **University of Alabama (Tuscaloosa)**   **R. A. Mann**

Investigation of surface ionization on metallic surfaces. Study of forces that interact between metal surface & the absorbed atom.

Proposal	FY	Agreement Period	Amount
		2/62 − 5/68	215000
	67	2/62 − 3/69	40000

Tech. Off.:   Funding Element: MSFC
CASE Code: 47   AWC: 124−09

NAS8-11202   **University of Alabama (University)**   **W. G. Moulton**

Study of the measurement of earth tremors, resulting from large rocket firings.

Proposal	FY	Agreement Period	Amount
		3/64 − 9/68	189000
	65	3/64 −10/69	50000

Tech. Off.:   DALINS I   Funding Element: MSFC
CASE Code: 32   AWC: 904−21

NAS8-20159   **University of Alabama (University)**   **R. A. Mann**

Study of cold welding in ultra high vacuum as a function of surface contamination.

Proposal	FY	Agreement Period	Amount
		6/65 − 6/68	117000
	67	6/65 − 7/69	25000

Tech. Off.:   DALINS I   Funding Element: MSFC
CASE Code: 46   AWC: 129−03

NAS8-20171   **University of Alabama (University)**   **J. F. Porter**

Determination of cesium distribution in porous tungsten.

Proposal	FY	Agreement Period	Amount
		6/65 − 6/68	93000
		7/68 − 4/70	25000

Tech. Off.:   Funding Element: MSFC
CASE Code: 47   AWC: 120−26

NAS8-20172   **University of Alabama (University)**   **M. A. Griffin**

Study and analysis of the FM/FM and SS/FM telemetry systems for the Saturn vehicle.

Proposal	FY	Agreement Period	Amount
		6/65 − 6/68	323000
	67	6/65 − 5/69	59000
		6/69 − 7/70	NCE

Tech. Off.:   FROST W   Funding Element: MSFC
CASE Code: 45   AWC: 150−22

ALABAMA (Cont'd.)

NAS8-21143   University of Alabama (University)   **H. R. Henry**
Two phase flow & heat transfer in porous beds under variable body forces.

Proposal	FY	Agreement Period	Amount
	68	5/67 – 1/69	100000
		2/69 – 5/69	74000

Tech. Off.: P R I C E   I   W   Funding Element: M S F C
CASE Code: 4 7   AWC: 9 3 2 – 4 0

NAS8-21321   University of Alabama (Huntsville)
                                        O. J. Christensen
Preparation of a program history of Project Saturn.

Proposal	FY	Agreement Period	Amount
	68	5/68 –11/70	100000
			M S F C

Tech. Off.:   Funding Element:
CASE Code: 9 9   AWC: 9 3 3 – 5 0

NAS8-21480   University of Alabama (University)   **T. E. Falgout**
Dynamic analysis of stability and deployment of inflatable shell structures.

Proposal	FY	Agreement Period	Amount
	68	6/68 – 6/69	25000
			M S F C

Tech. Off.:   Funding Element:
CASE Code: 4 6   AWC: 1 2 4 – 0 8

NAS8-23970   University of Alabama (Tuscaloosa)   **C. A. Gibson**
Development of dynamic gyro bearing monitor and analyzer.

Proposal	FY	Agreement Period	Amount
	69	3/69 – 3/70	21000

Tech. Off.:   Funding Element:
CASE Code: 4 6   AWC: 9 3 3 – 3 5

NAS8-30159   University of Alabama (Huntsville)   **C. C. Shih**
Scaling procedures needed to define Saturn ground winds and intense near-field acoustic design.

Proposal	FY	Agreement Period	Amount
	69	2/69 – 2/70	30000

Tech. Off.: R E E D   T   G   Funding Element: M S F C
CASE Code: 4 1   AWC: 9 3 3 – 5 0

NGT-01-002-002   University of Alabama (University)   **E. Rodgers**
Training of predoctoral graduate students in space-related science and technology.

No. Students	FY	Agreement Period	Amount
10	65	9/65 – 8/68	192000
12	66	9/66 – 8/69	230400
8	67	9/67 – 8/70	142200

Tech. Off.: H A N S I N G   F   D   Funding Element: H Q – Y
CASE Code: 9 9   AWC: 1 8 1 – 0 0

NGR-01-002-035   University of Alabama (Huntsville)   **E. W. Grohse**
Advanced electrochemical technology.

Proposal	FY	Agreement Period	Amount
–035	67	7/67 – 6/68	30000
–058	68	7/68 – 3/69	30000

Tech. Off.: GOODHUE W H   Funding Element: M S F C
CASE Code: 4 3   AWC: 1 2 0 – 3 4

NGR-01-003-008   Auburn University   **W. A. Shaw**
Computer techniques for multivariant function model generation, emphasizing programs applicable to space vehicle guidance.

Proposal	FY	Agreement Period	Amount
–029	68	3/68 – 3/69	27756
		3/69 –12/69	NCE

Tech. Off.: M I N E R   W   E   Funding Element: E R C
CASE Code: 1 3   AWC: 1 2 5 – 1 7

NGR-01-003-036   Auburn University   **P. M. Fitzpatrick**
A study of Hamilton-Jacobi theory for application to guidance related problems.

Proposal	FY	Agreement Period	Amount
–036	69	4/69 – 4/70	13147

Tech. Off.: CONCANNON P A   Funding Element: E R C
CASE Code: 4 9   AWC: 1 2 5 – 1 7

NSR-01-003-005   Auburn University   **R. I. Vachon**
A summer institute in space-related engineering.

Proposal	FY	Agreement Period	Amount
–033	68		111000
		4/65 – 3/70	251025

Tech. Off.: C A R T E R   C   H   Funding Element: H Q – Y
CASE Code: 9 9   AWC: 1 8 1 – 0 0

NSR-01-003-025   Auburn University   **R. I. Vachon**
A summer program in systems design engineering.

Proposal	FY	Agreement Period	Amount
–032	68	1/68 –12/68	100060
–032		12/69	NCE
–037	69	6/69 – 1/70	11047

Tech. Off.: C A R T E R   C   H   Funding Element: H Q – Y
CASE Code: 4 9   AWC: 1 8 1 – 0 0

NAS8-11184   Auburn University   **E. R. Graf**
Research telemetering, measuring & radio frequency systems.

Proposal	FY	Agreement Period	Amount
		3/64 – 6/68	736000
	68	3/64 – 6/69	30000

Tech. Off.: R E E D   B   R   Funding Element: M S F C
CASE Code: 4 5   AWC: 9 3 3 – 3 5

NAS8-11344   Auburn University   **M. A. Honnel**
Investigation of optimum design configurations for DC operational amplifiers.

Proposal	FY	Agreement Period	Amount
	68	1/65 – 3/69	32000

Tech. Off.: O W E N S   J   Funding Element: M S F C
CASE Code: 4 5   AWC: 9 3 3 – 3 5

ALABAMA (Cont'd.)

NAS8-20004 **Auburn University** J. L. Lowry
An investigation of the strapped-down inertial system.

Proposal	FY	Agreement Period	Amount
	66	1/65 – 2/69	40000
		3/69 – 6/69	NCE

Tech. Off.: KENNEL A F Funding Element: MSFC
CASE Code: 46 AWC: 125-17

NAS8-20104 **Auburn University** D. W. Russell
Analytical study of problems involving control of large space vehicles.

Proposal	FY	Agreement Period	Amount
	68	4/65 – 3/69	80000

Tech. Off.: BLANTOR J E Funding Element: MSFC
CASE Code: 42 AWC: 933-35

NAS8-20154 **Auburn University** E. R. Graf
Study of phase variation characteristics of very low frequency transmission.

Proposal	FY	Agreement Period	Amount
		10/65 – 4/68	263000
		5/68 – 8/69	4000

Tech. Off.: SAUNDERS E H Funding Element: MSFC
CASE Code: 45 AWC: 150-22

NAS8-20175 **Auburn University** J. Crenshaw
Study of orbital perturbing forces.

Proposal	FY	Agreement Period	Amount
	67	6/65 – 4/69	10000

Tech. Off.: HOLLAND R L Funding Element: MSFC
CASE Code: 42 AWC: 129-04

NAS8-20765 **Auburn University** M. A. Honnell
Studies concerning frequency modulated (FM) telemetry systems for 2.2 to 2.3 Gizahertz.

Proposal	FY	Agreement Period	Amount
		5/67 – 5/68	48000
	68	5/67 – 6/69	27000

Tech. Off.: STEPHENS J K Funding Element: MSFC
CASE Code: 45 AWC: 150-22

NAS8-21368 **Auburn University** C. L. Phillips
Sensitivity analysis of Saturn V elastic boosters.

Proposal	FY	Agreement Period	Amount
	68	6/68 – 6/69	17000
		7/68 – 6/70	16000
			MSFC

Tech. Off.: Funding Element:
CASE Code: 42 AWC: 124-08

NGT-01-003-001 **Auburn University** W. V. Parker
Training of predoctoral graduate students in space-related science and technology.

No. Students	FY	Agreement Period	Amount
12	66	9/66 – 8/69	225700
8	67	9/67 – 8/70	138200

Tech. Off.: HANSING F D Funding Element: HQ-Y
CASE Code: 99 AWC: 181-00

ALASKA

NGR-02-001-001 **University of Alaska**
S. Chapman, Syun-Ichi Akasofu
Theoretical study of the ring current and geomagnetic field phenomena.

Proposal	FY	Agreement Period	Amount
-052	68	1/68 – 12/68	50000
-057	69	1/69 – 1/70	30000

Tech. Off.: CHAPMAN S Funding Element: HQ-SG
CASE Code: 13 AWC: 188-36

NGR-02-001-063 **University of Alaska** R. B. Forbes
Geophysical and geochemical investigations of volcanic phenomena in the Katmai National Monument and contiguous areas, Alaska.

Proposal	FY	Agreement Period	Amount
-063	69	4/69 – 4/72	210200

Tech. Off.: FOSS T H Funding Element: MSC
CASE Code: 32 AWC: 914-50

NSR-02-001-025 **University of Alaska** K. B. Mather
Sounding rocket investigations of the auroral electrojet.

Proposal	FY	Agreement Period	Amount
-025	66	4/66 – 3/67	107554
-025	66	4/67 – 9/67	NCE
-025	66	10/67 – 6/68	NCE
-055	69	8/68 – 7/69	98968

Tech. Off.: DUBIN Funding Element: HQ-SG
CASE Code: 31 AWC: 879-10

NSR-02-001-035 **University of Alaska** K. B. Mather
Construct and operate image orthicon television systems to detect artificial auroras.

Proposal	FY	Agreement Period	Amount
-049	68	9/67 – 6/68	103055
-054	69	6/68 – 10/68	54218
-035	69	10/68 – 6/69	97275

Tech. Off.: Funding Element: GSFC
CASE Code: 31 AWC: 188-46

NAS9-8945 **University of Alaska**
Kotzebue-MacQuarie magnetometer stations.

Proposal	FY	Agreement Period	Amount
	69	12/68 – 12/69	10000

Tech. Off.: Funding Element:
CASE Code: 49 AWC: 914-40

ALASKA (Cont'd.)

NGT-02-001-007   University of Alaska   K. M. Rae

Training of predoctoral graduate students in space-related science and technology.

No. Students:	FY	Agreement Period	Amount
2	65	9/65 – 8/68	43200
3	66	9/66 – 8/69	55600
2	67	9/67 – 8/70	43200

Tech. Off.: HANSING F D   Funding Element: HQ-Y
CASE Code: 99   AWC: 181-00

ARIZONA

NAS8-21397   Arizona State University   N. S. Berman

Experimental measurements using the laser doppler velocity instrument.

Proposal	FY	Agreement Period	Amount
	68	4/68 – 4/69	10000

Tech. Off.: HUFFAKER   Funding Element: MSFC
CASE Code: 21   AWC: 124-07

NGL-03-001-001   Arizona State University   C. B. Moore

Investigate, develop, evaluate and improve procedures for sampling, characterizing, and classifying meteorite specimens.

Proposal	FY	Agreement Period	Amount
-045	68	3/68 – 2/71	35061
-050	69	3/69 – 3/72	17000

Tech. Off.:   Funding Element:
CASE Code: 32   AWC: 185-45

NGT-03-001-002   Arizona State University   W. J. Burke

Training of predoctoral graduate students in space-related science and technology.

No. Students:	FY	Agreement Period	Amount
8	65	9/65 – 8/68	141600
8	66	9/66 – 8/69	141600
4	67	9/67 – 8/70	61800

Tech. Off.: HANSING F D   Funding Element: HQ-Y
CASE Code: 99   AWC: 181-00

NGR-03-002-001   University of Arizona   R. W. G. Wyckoff

Generation and detection of ultralong-wavelength x-rays and quantitative studies of their interactions with matter.

Proposal	FY	Agreement Period	Amount
-067	66	5/65 – 4/68	50222
-103	67	5/66 – 4/69	49518
-129	68	5/67 – 4/70	49934

Tech. Off.: GLASER   Funding Element: HG-SG
CASE Code: 45   AWC: 188-38

NGL-03-002-002   University of Arizona   G. P. Kuiper

Selenodic and physical studies of lunar surface.

Proposal	FY	Agreement Period	Amount
-064	65	6/65 – 5/68	250000
-099	66	6/66 – 5/69	214500
-124	67	6/67 – 5/70	207131
-162	68	6/68 – 5/71	206891

Tech. Off.: BRUNK W E   Funding Element: HQ-SL
CASE Code: 42   AWC: 185-41

NGL-03-002-006   University of Arizona   L. E. Weaver

Research in the application of modern automatic control theory to nuclear rocket dynamics and control.

Proposal	FY	Agreement Period	Amount
-072	66	7/66 – 6/68	91877
-154	68	7/68 – 6/71	93661

Tech. Off.: MORRISSEY J   Funding Element: SNPO
CASE Code: 45   AWC: 122-28

NGR-03-002-011   University of Arizona   T. L. Vincent

Study of the calculus of variations, especially as related to aerospace engineering problems.

Proposal	FY	Agreement Period	Amount
-104	67	2/67 – 1/68	1528200
-104	67	1/68 – 6/68	NCE
-104	67	7/68 – 10/68	NCE
-161	69	10/68 – 1/70	17338

Tech. Off.: WILSON R   Funding Element: HQ-RR
CASE Code: 21   AWC: 129-04

NGR-03-002-017   University of Arizona   S. Bashkin

Studies in optical spectroscopy.

Proposal	FY	Agreement Period	Amount
-146	68	11/67 – 10/68	85000
-179	69	11/68 – 10/69	79996

Tech. Off.: ROMAN   Funding Element: HQ-SG
CASE Code: 11   AWC: 188-41

NGL-03-002-019   University of Arizona   S. A. Hoenig

Development of chemisorption detectors for specific components of planetary atmospheres.

Proposal	FY	Agreement Period	Amount
-065	65	6/65 – 5/68	30000
-105	67	6/66 – 8/69	40000
-140	68	9/67 – 8/70	29991
-172	69	9/68 – 8/69	29986

Tech. Off.: HIPSHER H F   Funding Element: HQ-SL
CASE Code: 31   AWC: 185-47

NGR-03-002-024   University of Arizona   G. A. Korn

Experimental and theoretical investigations of advanced hybrid (digital-analog) computing techniques and devices.

Proposal	FY	Agreement Period	Amount
-157	68	2/68 – 1/69	21747
-024	69	2/69 – 1/70	22959
-157		2/69 – 2/70	22959
-197	69	2/69 – 2/69	22000

Tech. Off.: CAMERON W   Funding Element: ARC
CASE Code: 21   AWC: 125-23

ARIZONA (Cont'd.)

NGR-03-002-032   University of Arizona   A. B. Meinel, W. G. Tifft
General studies related to photographic and photoelectric
signal detection in space.

Proposal	FY	Agreement Period	Amount
−156	68	2/68 − 3/69	125000
−186	69	4/69 − 3/70	96000

Tech. Off.: ROMAN   Funding Element: HG−SG
CASE Code: 42   AWC: 831−22

NGR-03-002-044   University of Arizona   D. B. Kececioglu
Methodology for designing specified reliabilities into mechanical components.

Proposal	FY	Agreement Period	Amount
−100	67	6/67 − 1/68	NCE
−181	69	2/68 − 3/69	18949

Tech. Off.:   Funding Element: ARC
CASE Code: 46   AWC: 120−27

NGR-03-002-068   University of Arizona   R. W. Lansing
Electrophysiological and performance measures of visual
excitability cycles in man.

Proposal	FY	Agreement Period	Amount
−143	68	11/67 −10/68	15524
		− 6/69	NCE

Tech. Off.: WEISSMAN N W   Funding Element: HQ−SB
CASE Code: 51   AWC: 189−52

NGR-03-002-071   University of Arizona   T. Bowen
Cosmic ray investigations of elementary particle phenomena at
very high energies.

Proposal	FY	Agreement Period	Amount
−148	68	2/68 − 1/69	110000
−183	69	2/69 − 2/70	120000

Tech. Off.: SCHARDT   Funding Element: HQ−SG
CASE Code: 11   AWC: 188−46

NGR-03-002-081   University of Arizona   A. M. J. Gehrels
Photometry and polarimetry of minor planets.

Proposal	FY	Agreement Period	Amount
−164	68	4/68 − 3/69	22264

Tech. Off.: DUBIN   Funding Element: HQ−SG
CASE Code: 11   AWC: 188−45

NGL-03-002-091   University of Arizona   H. D. Christensen
Multidisciplinary research program in space science and
technology.

Proposal	FY	Agreement Period	Amount
−091	66	5/66 − 5/69	400000
−125	67	5/67 − 4/70	200000

Tech. Off.:   Funding Element: HQ−Y
CASE Code: 99   AWC: 183−00

NGR-03-002-107   University of Arizona   C. Y. Fan
Basic research in astrophysics and space science.

Proposal	FY	Agreement Period	Amount
−107	68	9/67 − 8/68	45295
−173	69	9/68 − 8/69	40000

Tech. Off.: OPP   Funding Element: HQ−SG
CASE Code: 11   AWC: 188−46

NGR-03-002-115   University of Arizona   L. E. Weaver
State variable feedback design of guidance control systems
for aerospace vehicles.

Proposal	FY	Agreement Period	Amount
−152	68	2/68 − 6/69	26912

Tech. Off.: FREY K   Funding Element: LERC
CASE Code: 42   AWC: 125−19

NGR-03-002-116   University of Arizona   F. J. Low
Scanning and mapping the lunar surface at 20 microns.

Proposal	FY	Agreement Period	Amount
−116	67	1/67 −12/67	25991
		− 6/68	NCE
		12/67 − 1/69	NCE
−187	69	2/69 − 2/70	21527

Tech. Off.: BRUNK W E   Funding Element: HQ−SL
CASE Code: 42   AWC: 185−41

NGR-03-002-122   University of Arizona   E. Roemer
Astrometric and astrophysical investigations of comets, minor
planets, and satellites.

Proposal	FY	Agreement Period	Amount
−122	67	2/67 − 1/68	41080
−122	67	2/68 − 4/68	NCE
−165	68	5/68 − 4/69	24825
−192	69	5/69 − 4/70	21817

Tech. Off.: DUBIN   Funding Element: HQ−SG
CASE Code: 11   AWC: 185−41

NGR-03-002-153   University of Arizona   W. G. Tifft
Feasibility and preliminary design definition for a lunar surface
optical environment and experimental package.

Proposal	FY	Agreement Period	Amount
−153	68	6/68 − 5/69	50000

Tech. Off.:   Funding Element:
CASE Code: 11   AWC: 945−43

NGR-03-002-155   University of Arizona   B. M. Herman
Optimization of solutions of the equation of radiative transfer
for atmospheric processes including emission, absorption,
polarization, and multiple MIE scattering, and applications to
simulated satellite measurements.

Proposal	FY	Agreement Period	Amount
−155	68	5/68 − 4/69	50000
−196	69	5/69 − 5/70	50000

Tech. Off.:   Funding Element:
CASE Code: 21   AWC: 122−29

ARIZONA (Cont'd.)

NGR-03-002-169   University of Arizona   D. J. Hamilton
Integrated circuit synchrodyne receiver research.

Proposal	FY	Agreement Period	Amount
-169	68	7/68 - 6/69	36142
-169	69	1/69 - 6/69	3385

Tech. Off.:   Funding Element:
CASE Code: 45   AWC: 797-00

NGR-03-002-174   University of Arizona   G. P. Kuiper
LPL Surveyor evaluation program.

Proposal	FY	Agreement Period	Amount
-174	69	8/68 - 6/69	25000

Tech. Off.:   Funding Element:
CASE Code: 42   AWC: 383-10

NGR-03-002-180   University of Arizona   H. L. Johnson
Multicolor photoelectric photometry and interferometric (Fourier transform) infrared spectroscopy.

Proposal	FY	Agreement Period	Amount
-180	69	2/69 - 1/70	15000

Tech. Off.: LEVINE A L   Funding Element: GSFC
CASE Code: 13   AWC: 188-39

NGR-03-002-184   University of Arizona   H. L. Johnson
Multi-color basic photometry for stars brighter than 5.0 mag.

Proposal	FY	Agreement Period	Amount
-184	69	3/69 - 2/70	20276

Tech. Off.: RASKIN W H   Funding Element: GSFC
CASE Code: 31   AWC: 125-19

NGR-03-002-191   University of Arizona   G. P. Kuiper
Lunar surface and planetology.

Proposal	FY	Agreement Period	Amount
-191	69	6/69 - 6/72	155000

Tech. Off.: BRYSON R P   Funding Element: HQ-MA
CASE Code: 32   AWC: 195-42

NGR-03-002-193   University of Arizona   T. Gehrels
Photometry of planets, stars, and Seyfert galaxies (OAO-A2).

Proposal	FY	Agreement Period	Amount
-193	69	2/69 - 2/70	5877

Tech. Off.: ASHWORTH C D   Funding Element: HQ-SG
CASE Code: 11   AWC: 831-12

NGR-03-002-194   University of Arizona   W. G. Tifft
OAO-A2 observations of galaxies with photometrically abnormal nuclei.

Proposal	FY	Agreement Period	Amount
-194	69	3/69 - 3/70	1700

Tech. Off.: ASHWORTH C D   Funding Element: HQ-SG
CASE Code: 11   AWC: 831-12

NGR-03-102-171   University of Arizona   H. C. Urey
Analysis of carbonaceous meteorites.

Proposal	FY	Agreement Period	Amount
-171	69	10/68 - 9/69	50000

Tech. Off.:   Funding Element:
CASE Code: 32   AWC: 189-55

NASr-82   University of Arizona   G. P. Kuiper
(NSR-03-002-009) Construction of a 60-inch lunar and planetary telescope.

Proposal	FY	Agreement Period	Amount
2053	68	2/62 - 8/65	375000
		3/68 - 3/69	NCE

Tech. Off.: BRUNK W E   Funding Element: HQ-SL
CASE Code: 44   AWC: 185-41

NASr-138   University of Arizona   A. M. J. Gehrels
(NSR-03-002-010   Develop and test a prototype photopolarimeter suitable for use with balloons and space vehicles.

Proposal	FY	Agreement Period	Amount
-144	68	11/67 -10/68	49985
-182	69	11/68 -11/69	39970

Tech. Off.:   Funding Element:
CASE Code: 45   AWC: 185-41

NSR-03-002-048   University of Arizona   H. Johnson, A. Gehrels
Feasibility and design study of a prime experiment in stellar photometry and polarimetry in the ultraviolet, for the orbiting astronomical observatory.

Proposal	FY	Agreement Period	Amount
-090	66	5/66 - 4/67	795566
-132		6/68 - 9/68	NCE

Tech. Off.: ROMAN N G   Funding Element: HQ-SG
CASE Code: 11   AWC: 831-

NSR-03-002-163   University of Arizona   W. G. Tifft
Support study of manned space astronomy.

Proposal	FY	Agreement Period	Amount
-163	68	4/68 - 3/69	74660
		-10/69	NCE

Tech. Off.:   Funding Element:
CASE Code: 11   AWC: 945-84

NAS2-5167   University of Arizona   R. N. Carlile
Microwave measurement of the electron density and collision frequency profiles and the recombination rate in a supersonic arc jet.

Proposal	FY	Agreement Period	Amount
	69	11/68 - 6/69	6000

Tech. Off.:   Funding Element:
CASE Code: 41   AWC: 125-24

NAS5-11171   University of Arizona
Design and fabrication of 60-inch metal mirror telescope.

Proposal	FY	Agreement Period	Amount
	69	11/68 -11/69	120000

Tech. Off.:   Funding Element: GSFC
CASE Code: 32   AWC: 188-48

ARIZONA (Cont'd)

NAS8-21572   **University of Arizona**
Access to and use of Catalina Mountain Observatory.

Proposal	FY	Agreement Period	Amount
	69	4/69 – 4/70	3000

Tech. Off.:   Funding Element:
CASE Code: 1 1   AWC: 1 8 8 – 4 1

NAS8-23988   **University of Arizona**   **H. L. Johnson**
Infrared photometer.

Proposal	FY	Agreement Period	Amount
	68	9/68 – 6/69	15000

Tech. Off.:   Funding Element:
CASE Code: 1 1   AWC: 1 8 8 – 4 1

NAS9-7081   **University of Arizona**   **P. N. Slater**
System study of multi-spectral tracking.

Proposal	FY	Agreement Period	Amount
		9/61 –10/68	74000

Tech. Off.: K R A U S G   Funding Element: M S C
CASE Code: 4 2   AWC: 1 6 9 –

NAS9-8747   **University of Arizona**
Determine the presence or absence lipids, amino acids, and polymer-type organic matter in returned lunar samples.

Proposal	FY	Agreement Period	Amount
	69	8/68 – 8/69	90000

Tech. Off.:   Funding Element:
CASE Code: 5 1   AWC: 9 1 4 – 4 0

NGT-03-002-008   **University of Arizona**   **H. D. Rhodes**
Training of predoctoral graduate students in space-related science and technology.

No. Students	FY	Agreement Period	Amount
12	65	9/65 – 8/68	212400
12	66	9/66 – 8/69	212400
8	67	9/67 – 8/70	127500

Tech. Off.: H A N S I N G F D   Funding Element: H Q – Y
CASE Code: 9 9   AWC: 1 8 1 – 0 0

NGF-03-002-025   **University of Arizona**   **G. P. Kuiper**
Construction of a laboratory building housing the interdisciplinary Space Sciences Center.

Proposal	FY	Agreement Period	Amount
8096	64	8/64 – 2/67	1200000

Tech. Off.: H O L M E S D C   Funding Element: H Q – Y
CASE Code: 9 9   AWC: 1 8 2 – 0 0

ARKANSAS

NAS8-21179   **University of Arkansas**   **W. D. Dickinson**
Sunspots prediction methods.

Proposal	FY	Agreement Period	Amount
		6/67 – 6/68	15000

Tech. Off.:   Funding Element: M S F C
CASE Code: 3 1   AWC: 1 2 4 – 1 2

NGR-04-005-001   **Arkansas State University**   **J. L. Linnstaedter**
Applications of calculus of variations to multistage aerospace optimization problems.

Proposal	FY	Agreement Period	Amount
–001	69	1/69 –12/69	20000

Tech. Off.: L I S L E B J   Funding Element: E R C
CASE Code: 2 1   AWC: 1 2 5 – 1 7

NGR-04-001-029   **University of Arkansas**   **D. M. Scruggs**
The oxidation and agglomeration resistance of thin gage dispersion strengthened alloys.

Proposal	FY	Agreement Period	Amount
–029	69	2/69 – 2/70	23902

Tech. Off.: S T E I N B A   Funding Element: L A R C
CASE Code: 4 7   AWC: 1 2 9 – 0 3

NAS9-9433   **Harding College**   **H. D. Olree**
An evaluation of the Exergenie exerciser and the Collins pedal mode ergemeter for developing physical fitness.

Proposal	FY	Agreement Period	Amount
	69	4/69 – 5/70	44000

Tech. Off.: R U M M E L J A   Funding Element: M S C
CASE Code: 5 1   AWC: 9 4 8 – 6 0

CALIFORNIA

NGL-05-002-002   **California Institute of Technology**   **J. P. Liepmann**
Investigation of fluid mechanics of rarified gases by extending shock techniques into the low pressure regime.

Proposal	FY	Agreement Period	Amount
–048	66	2/66 – 1/69	130000
–082	67	2/67 – 1/70	65000
–101	68	2/68 – 1/71	60000
–139	69	2/69 – 2/72	50000

Tech. Off.: S C H W A R T Z R S   Funding Element: H Q – R R
CASE Code: 4 6   AWC: 1 2 9 – 0 1

NGR-05-002-003   **California Institute of Technology**   **H. Brown**
Investigation of problems in lunar and planetary exploration.

Proposal	FY	Agreement Period	Amount
–058	66	12/65 –11/68	140342
–079	67	12/66 –11/69	172206
–103	68	12/67 –11/70	157471
–128	69	12/68 –12/71	175000

Tech. Off.:   Funding Element:
CASE Code: 4 2   AWC: 1 8 5 – 4 2

CALIFORNIA (Cont'd.)

NGL-05-002-005   California Institute of Technology   W. G. Knauss
Experimental and theoretical research on failure criteria for viscoelastic materials typical of solid rocket propellants.

Proposal	FY	Agreement Period	Amount
-047	66	7/65 — 6/68	64600
-072	67	7/66 — 6/69	65000
-086	68	7/67 — 6/70	62230
-113	69	7/68 — 6/71	45000
Tech. Off.: Z I E M R W		Funding Element: HQ-RP	
CASE Code: 47		AWC: 128-32	

NGL-05-002-007   California Institute of Technology   R. B. Leighton
Space related research in selected fields of physics and astronomy, including cosmic rays, interplanetary magnetic fields, solar physics, theoretical astrophysics, planetary spectroscopy and infrared astronomy.

Proposal	FY	Agreement Period	Amount
-064	67	4/66 — 3/69	429500
-080	67	4/67 — 3/70	260006
-080	68	4/67 — 3/70	400600
-102	68	4/68 — 3/71	257232
-102	69	4/68 — 3/71	350000
-135	69	4/69 — 4/72	52621
Tech. Off.: ROMAN N G		Funding Element: HQ-SG	
CASE Code: 19		AWC: 185-48	

NGR-05-002-031   California Institute of Technology   F. Strunwasser
Neural control of hibernations in mammals.

Proposal	FY	Agreement Period	Amount
-057	66	9/65 — 8/68	57071
-089	68	9/67 — 8/68	55000
-119	69	9/68 — 8/69	44991
Tech. Off.: WEISSMAN N W		Funding Element: SG-SB	
CASE Code: 51		AWC: 189-52	

NGR-05-002-034   California Institute of Technology   H. Zirin
Research in solar flares and the solar atmosphere.

Proposal	FY	Agreement Period	Amount
-081	68	9/67 — 8/68	198740
		9/68 — 9/68	NCE
-081	69	9/68 — 8/69	200000
Tech. Off.: OERTEL G K		Funding Element: HQ-SG	
CASE Code: 31		AWC: 188-38	

NGR-05-002-092   California Institute of Technology   G. Neugebauer
X-ray astronomy observations from sounding rockets.

Proposal	FY	Agreement Period	Amount
-092	68	12/67 —11/68	75000
		9/68 — 5/69	NCE
Tech. Off.: ROMAN		Funding Element: HQ-SG	
CASE Code: 31		AWC: 879-10	

NGR-05-002-100   California Institute of Technology   M. A. Nicolet
Space charge effects in current transport.

Proposal	FY	Agreement Period	Amount
-100	68	4/68 — 3/69	22200
Tech. Off.: HOPKINS J		Funding Element: HQ-ER	
CASE Code: 11		AWC: 125-25	

NGR-05-002-105   California Institute of Technology   T. J. Ahrens
Shock effects in minerals.

Proposal	FY	Agreement Period	Amount
-105	68	6/68 — 3/69	72480
		— 6/69	NCE
Tech. Off.:		Funding Element:	
CASE Code: 47		AWC: 185-42	

NGR-05-002-114   California Institute of Technology D. O. Muhleman
Radio interferometry of Mars and Venus.

Proposal	FY	Agreement Period	Amount
-114	69	8/68 — 7/69	26390
Tech. Off.:		Funding Element:	
CASE Code: 31		AWC: 185-41	

NGR-05-002-116   California Institute of Technology   B. Murray
Infrared spectral reflectivity measurements from orbit to investigate composition of Martian frosts.

Proposal	FY	Agreement Period	Amount
-116	69	10/68 — 9/69	35235
Tech. Off.: DWORNIK S E		Funding Element: HQ-SL	
CASE Code: 11		AWC: 185-50	

NGR-05-002-117   California Institute of Technology   B. Murray
Approaches to photography from a Mercury/Venus flyby.

Proposal	FY	Agreement Period	Amount
-117	69	10/68 — 9/69	19016
Tech. Off.: DWORNIK S E		Funding Element: HQ-SL	
CASE Code: 49		AWC: 185-50	

NGR-05-002-118   California Institute of Technology   R. F. Scott
Analysis of surveyor surface sample data.

Proposal	FY	Agreement Period	Amount
-118	69	7/68 — 6/69	15855
Tech. Off.:		Funding Element:	
CASE Code: 31		AWC: 383-10	

NGR-05-002-121   California Institute of Technology N. H. Horowitz
A study of metabolism in neurospora crassa.

Proposal	FY	Agreement Period	Amount
-121	69	1/69 —12/69	16812
Tech. Off.: GEIB D S		Funding Element: HQ-SB	
CASE Code: 51		AWC: 189-55	

CALIFORNIA (Cont'd)

NGR-05-002-129   California Institute of Technology   D. L. Anderson
Development of performance criteria and functional specifications for a passive seismic experiment on Mars.

Proposal	FY	Agreement Period	Amount
-129	69	1/69 -12/70	94478

Tech. Off.: DWORNIK S E   Funding Element: HQ-SL
CASE Code: 32   AWC: 185-50

NGL-05-002-136   California Institute of Technology   W. D. Rannie
Research on turbomachines.

Proposal	FY	Agreement Period	Amount
-136	69	5/69 - 5/72	125325

Tech. Off.: EVVARD J C   Funding Element: LERC
CASE Code: 46   AWC: 126-15

NGR-05-002-138   California Institute of Technology   D. L. Anderson
Participation in the science steering group activity in planning for a 1973 Mars lander, and travel support for the seismometer team.

Proposal	FY	Agreement Period	Amount
-138	69	2/69 - 2/70	8296

Tech. Off.: MITZ M A   Funding Element: HQ-SL
CASE Code: 42   AWC: 815-20

NGR-05-002-140   California Institute of Technology   G. Munch
Research in planetary astronomy.

Proposal	FY	Agreement Period	Amount
-140	69	4/69 - 4/70	56300

Tech. Off.: BRUNK W E   Funding Element: HQ-SL
CASE Code: 11   AWC: 185-41

NGR-05-002-142   California Institute of Technology   R. B. Leighton
Support of research in solar physics.

Proposal	FY	Agreement Period	Amount
-142	69	4/69 -10/69	40000

Tech. Off.: OERTEL G K   Funding Element: HQ-SG
CASE Code: 31   AWC: 188-38

NSR-05-002-071   California Institute of Technology   H. Zirin
Feasibility study for large aperture solar telescope to fly on Apollo telescope mount (ATM) system.

Proposal	FY	Agreement Period	Amount
-106	68	4/68 - 4/69	49913
-127	69	4/69 - 6/70	124390

Tech. Off.: GLASER   Funding Element: HQ-SG
CASE Code: 42   AWC: 188-38

NSR-05-002-124   California Institute of Technology   J. N. Franklin
A summer program of NASA summer faculty fellowships.

Proposal	FY	Agreement Period	Amount
-124	68	3/69 - 3/70	84250

Tech. Off.: CARTER C H   Funding Element: HQ-Y
CASE Code: 99   AWC: 181-00

NSR-05-002-133   California Institute of Technology   Dr. Garmire
X-ray astronomy observations from sounding rockets.

Proposal	FY	Agreement Period	Amount
-133	69	3/69 - 3/70	107985

Tech. Off.: ROMAN N G   Funding Element: HQ-SG
CASE Code: 31   AWC: 879-11

NAS9-7963   California Institute of Technology   L. T. Silver
Determine lead isotopes, concentrations of u th pb and their occurrence in minerals.

Proposal	FY	Agreement Period	Amount
	68	6/68 - 7/69	88000

Tech. Off.:   Funding Element: MSC
CASE Code: 32   AWC: 914-40

NAS9-8074   California Institute of Technology   G. J. Wasserburg
Determine k ar rb sr and rare gas content.

Proposal	FY	Agreement Period	Amount
	68	6/68 - 6/69	194000

Tech. Off.:   Funding Element: MSC
CASE Code: 31   AWC: 914-40

NGT-05-002-009   California Institute of Technology   H. F. Bohnenblust
Training of predoctoral graduate students in space-related science and technology.

No. Students:	FY	Agreement Period	Amount
15	65	9/65 - 8/68	280100
15	66	9/66 - 8/69	289100
9	67	9/67 - 8/70	155900

Tech. Off.: HANSING F D   Funding Element: HQ-Y
CASE Code: 99   AWC: 181-00

NGR-05-013-010   California State College (Long Beach)   K. P. Luke
Application of electron diffraction and retarding potential techniques to the investigation of electron reflection properties of clean and gas-covered metal surfaces.

Proposal	FY	Agreement Period	Amount
-010	68	4/68 - 3/69	10106
-015	69	4/69 - 3/70	13077

Tech. Off.:   Funding Element: LERC
CASE Code: 11   AWC: 129-27

NGL-05-003-003   University of California (Berkeley)   M. Calvin
Studies of reflection spectra, meteorite analysis, paleobiochemistry, and biochemical evolution as bases for studying extra-terrestrial life.

Proposal	FY	Agreement Period	Amount
-258	68	11/67 -10/68	325000
-300	66	1/68 -10/70	325000
-310	69	11/68 -11/71	260000

Tech. Off.: GEIB D S   Funding Element: HQ-SB
CASE Code: 11   AWC: 185-55

CALIFORNIA (Cont'd.)

NGL-05-003-012   University of California (Berkeley)   S. Silver
Interdisciplinary space oriented research in the physical, biological, engineering, and social sciences.

Proposal	FY	Agreement Period	Amount
-262	68	2/68 - 1/71	420000
-281	64	2/68 - 8/68	67227
		9/68 -10/68	NCE
-317	66	2/69 - 2/72	200000

Tech. Off.:   Funding Element: HQ-Y
CASE Code: 99   AWC: 010-00

**NGL-05-003-016   University of California (Berkeley)   C. A. Desoer,
                                                    L. A. Zadek, E. Polak**
Advanced theoretical and experimental studies in automatic control and information systems.

Proposal	FY	Agreement Period	Amount
-267	68	1/68 -12/68	60000
-293	68	1/69 -12/70	60000
-315	69	1/69 -12/71	60000

Tech. Off.: JANOW C   Funding Element: HQ-RE
CASE Code: 49   AWC: 125-19

NGL-05-003-017   University of California (Berkeley)   K. A. Anderson
Study of high energy radiation associated with solar flares and Auroral zone phenomena.

Proposal	FY	Agreement Period	Amount
-157	66	2/66 - 1/69	86000
-175	67	2/66 - 1/69	36170
-221	67	2/67 - 1/70	88333
-268	68	2/68 - 1/70	128303
-323	69	2/69 - 1/72	175000

Tech. Off.: GAUGLER E A   Funding Element: HQ-SG
CASE Code: 31   AWC: 188-46

NGR-05-003-018   University of California (Berkeley)   N. Pace
Physiological mechanisms of hibernation in hibernators living at high altitudes.

Proposal	FY	Agreement Period	Amount
-111	65	8/65 - 7/68	90000
-187	67	8/66 - 7/68	75000
-284	68	8/68 - 7/69	60000

Tech. Off.: SAUNDERS J F   Funding Element: HQ-SB
CASE Code: 51   AWC: 189-54

NGR-05-003-019   Univensity of California (Berkeley)   H. Mark
Theoretical and experimental evaluation of inelastic neutron scattering and other neutron induced reactions for remote surface analysis.

Proposal	FY	Agreement Period	Amount
6105	63	4/63 - 4/65	36140
		- 3/69	NCE

Tech. Off.: BRYSON R   Funding Element:
CASE Code: 13   AWC: 185-42

NGR-05-003-020   University of California (Berkeley)   T. H. Jukes
Chemistry of living systems.

Proposal	FY	Agreement Period	Amount
-250	68	7/67 - 6/68	400000
-283	69	7/68 - 6/69	247000

Tech. Off.: JACOBS G F   Funding Element: HQ-SB
CASE Code: 51   AWC: 189-55

NGL-05-003-024   University of California (Berkeley)   N. Pace
Primate hemodynamics and metabolism under conditions of weightlessness, for the purpose of defining and verifying an experiment suitable for use in a bio-satellite.

Proposal	FY	Agreement Period	Amount
-255	68	8/67 - 7/68	250000
-255	68	8/68 - 7/70	250000
-313	69	8/68 - 8/71	220000

Tech. Off.: SAUNDERS J F   Funding Element: HQ-SB
CASE Code: 51   AWC: 189-54

NGL-05-003-050   University of California (Berkeley) A. K. Oppenheim
Gas-wave-dynamic studies of spray combustion.

Proposal	FY	Agreement Period	Amount
-110	65	6/65 - 5/68	140000
-215	67	1/67 -12/69	70000
		-12/72	NCE

Tech. Off.: DANBERG J E   Funding Element: HQ-RR
CASE Code: 43   AWC: 129-01

NGR-05-003-067   University of California (Berkeley)   W. B. N. Berry
Study of growth in recent and fossil invertebrate exoskeletons and its relationship to tidal cycles in the earth-moon system.

Proposal	FY	Agreement Period	Amount
-226	67	12/66 -11/67	11833
-226	67	11/67 - 6/68	NCE
-280	68	7/68 - 6/69	15000
-208	69	7/69 -11/69	12000

Tech. Off.: GEIB D S   Funding Element: HQ-SB
CASE Code: 51   AWC: 185-42

NGL-05-003-079   University of California (Berkeley)   A. D. McLaren
An investigation of enzyme assay techniques for life detection in extraterrestrial soils.

Proposal	FY	Agreement Period	Amount
-162	67	7/66 - 6/69	110000
-244	68	7/67 - 6/70	55000
-290	69	7/68 - 6/71	40000

Tech. Off.: GEIB D S   Funding Element: HQ-SB
CASE Code: 51   AWC: 189-55

NGR-05-003-089   University of California (Berkeley)   D. H. Calloway
Investigation of the nutritional properties of Hydro-genomonus eutropha.

Proposal	FY	Agreement Period	Amount
-271	68	1/68 -12/68	19737
-271		1/69 - 5/69	384000

Tech. Off.: SHAPIRA J   Funding Element: ARC
CASE Code: 51   AWC: 127-49

CALIFORNIA (Cont'd.)

NGR-05-003-125   University of California (Berkeley) C. W. Churchman
A study of technological and urban management, with particular emphasis on applying space technology and related technological knowledge to the solution of urban problems.

Proposal	FY	Agreement Period	Amount
−270	68	1/68 −12/68	50000
−322	68	1/69 − 9/69	40000

Tech. Off.: CARLSON J M   Funding Element: HQ−US
CASE Code: 76   AWC: 141−00

NGR-05-003-143   University of California (Berkeley) D. J. Sakrison, V. Algazi
Optimization of design of space experiment from the standpoint of data processing.

Proposal	FY	Agreement Period	Amount
−269	68	2/68 − 1/69	30000
−311	69	2/69 − 1/70	36000

Tech. Off.: FARR E H   Funding Element: ERC
CASE Code: 99   AWC: 125−23

NGR-05-003-220   University of California (Berkeley)   A. N. Kaufman
Plasma kinetic theory.

Proposal	FY	Agreement Period	Amount
−260	68	12/67 −11/68	20000
−314	69	2/69 − 1/70	15000

Tech. Off.: NORTHROP T   Funding Element: GSFC
CASE Code: 13   AWC: 188−46

NGR-05-003-228   University of California (Berkeley)   S. Margen
Calcium and magnesium metabolism as related to dietary protein intake.

Proposal	FY	Agreement Period	Amount
−228	66	12/67 − 5/68	NCE
−228	68	6/68 − 5/69	50000

Tech. Off.: WHEELER H O   Funding Element: MSC
CASE Code: 51   AWC: 949−10

NGR-05-003-230   University of California (Berkeley)   S. Silver
Structure of solar magnetic and velocity fields.

Proposal	FY	Agreement Period	Amount
−230	68	10/67 − 9/68	20000
−289	69	10/68 − 9/69	45000

Tech. Off.: GLASER   Funding Element: HQ−SG
CASE Code: 11   AWC: 188−38

NGR-05-003-243   University of California (Berkeley)   R. S. Muller
Field effect transistor stress transducers.

Proposal	FY	Agreement Period	Amount
−243	67	6/67 − 5/68	19200
−251	68	6/67 − 5/69	18000
−324	69	6/69 − 6/70	12000

Tech. Off.: PITTELLI E   Funding Element: ERC
CASE Code: 99   AWC: 125−25

NGR-05-003-256   University of California (Berkeley)   S. Silver
Properties of low altitude trapped protons at the geomagnetic equator.

Proposal	FY	Agreement Period	Amount
−256	68	7/68 − 6/69	79186

Tech. Off.:   Funding Element:
CASE Code: 11   AWC: 188−36

NGR-05-003-266   University of California (Berkeley)   S. Silver
Auroral data reduction.

Proposal	FY	Agreement Period	Amount
−266	68	5/68 − 4/69	20000

Tech. Off.: OPP A G   Funding Element: HQ−SG
CASE Code: 13   AWC: 879−10

NGL-05-003-272   University of California (Berkeley)   C. H. Townes
Research in radiation physics.

Proposal	FY	Agreement Period	Amount
−272	68	3/68 − 2/69	100000
−301	67	3/69 − 2/71	100000
−330	69	3/69 − 3/72	117475

Tech. Off.: JOHNSON P S   Funding Element: HQ−RR
CASE Code: 13   AWC: 129−02

NGR-05-003-273   University of California (Berkeley)   S. P. Siliberto
Satellite orbit study.

Proposal	FY	Agreement Period	Amount
−273	68	4/68 − 3/69	21800

Tech. Off.: PAYNE M   Funding Element: ERC
CASE Code: 41   AWC: 160−43

NGR-05-003-275   University of California (Berkeley)   H. P. Smith
Dynamical theory of low energy electron diffraction.

Proposal	FY	Agreement Period	Amount
−275	68	4/68 − 3/69	18672
−318	69	4/69 − 6/69	2139

Tech. Off.: FEINSTEIN L   Funding Element: ARC
CASE Code: 11   AWC: 129−03

NGR-05-003-278   University of California (Berkeley)   C. S. Bowyer
Study of x-ray emission from selected regions of the southern hemisphere sky.

Proposal	FY	Agreement Period	Amount
−278	68	1/68 − 7/68	39367
−278	69	8/68 −11/68	25133
−282	69	1/69 − 9/69	109000
−287	69	1/69 − 9/69	29675

Tech. Off.:   Funding Element:
CASE Code: 11   AWC: 879−11

NGR-05-003-285   University of California (Berkeley)   C. L. Tien
Phase I of research entitled "Investigation of Radiation and Conduction of Solids for Spacecraft Heat Transfer Applications —Phase I".

Proposal	FY	Agreement Period	Amount
−285	68	6/68 − 5/69	29700
−285		6/69 − 6/70	28600

Tech. Off.: STREED E   Funding Element: ARC
CASE Code: 99   AWC: 186−68

CALIFORNIA (Cont'd.)

NGL-05-003-286   University of California (Berkeley)   G. C. Pimentel
Infrared spectrometer development for an orbiting spacecraft, for terrestrial and for laboratory study of planetary atmospheres.

Proposal	FY	Agreement Period	Amount
-286	68	8/68 - 7/71	300000

Tech. Off.:   Funding Element:
CASE Code: 11   AWC: 185-47

NGR-05-003-297   University of California (Berkeley)   T. H. Pigford
Thermionic emission properties of rhenium in cesium.

Proposal	FY	Agreement Period	Amount
-297	69	8/68 - 7/69	35000

Tech. Off.:   Funding Element: LERC
CASE Code: 12   AWC: 120-27

NGR-05-003-302   University of California (Berkeley)   M. Calvin
Martian surface weathering studies.

Proposal	FY	Agreement Period	Amount
-302	69	8/68 - 8/69	60428

Tech. Off.: DWORNIK S E   Funding Element: HQ-SL
CASE Code: 32   AWC: 185-50

NGR-05-003-326   University of California (Berkeley)   H. Borsook
Erythropoietic stem cells in the blood: a new approach.

Proposal	FY	Agreement Period	Amount
-326	69	2/69 - 2/70	15000

Tech. Off.: LEON H A   Funding Element: ARC
CASE Code: 51   AWC: 127-49

NSR-05-003-100   University of California (Berkeley)   A. E. Whitford
Instrumentation for spectrophotometry of faint objects.

Proposal	FY	Agreement Period	Amount
-003	68	10/67 -11/68	85000
		11/68 - 4/69	NCE

Tech. Off.: ROMAN   Funding Element: GSFC
CASE Code: 11   AWC: 188-41

NSR-05-003-233   University of California (Berkeley)   N. Pace
A study to establish engineering design concepts for an automated primate research laboratory.

Proposal	FY	Agreement Period	Amount
-233	68	6/68 - 6/69	750000

Tech. Off.:   Funding Element:
CASE Code: 51   AWC: 945-82

NSR-05-003-287   University of California (Berkeley)   C. S. Bowyer
Study the x-ray emission from selected regions of the southern hemisphere sky.

Proposal	FY	Agreement Period	Amount
-287	69	3/68 -10/68	29675

Tech. Off.: OTT E J   Funding Element: HQ-SG
CASE Code: 19   AWC: 879-10

NAS2-4231   University of California (Berkeley)   N. Pace
Primate metabolic balance and body composition during 30-day biosatellite flight.

Proposal	FY	Agreement Period	Amount
	67	5/67 - 7/67	75000
	67	5/67 - 7/67	156000

Tech. Off.: CHRISTIANSEN R   Funding Element: ARC
CASE Code: 51   AWC: 883-12

NAS2-4915   University of California (Berkeley)
Investigate role of selenium in nutrition and physiology of neural tissues.

Proposal	FY	Agreement Period	Amount
	68	6/68 - 6/69	10000

Tech. Off.:   Funding Element: ARC
CASE Code: 51   AWC: 127-49

NAS5-9077   University of California (Berkeley)   K. A. Anderson
Energetic particle flux experiment.

Proposal	FY	Agreement Period	Amount
		1/65 - 6/68	381000

Tech. Off.: ANDERSON H   Funding Element: GSFC
CASE Code: 13   AWC: 861-22

NAS5-9091   University of California (Berkeley)   K. A. Anderson
Neher-type ion chamber experiment.

Proposal	FY	Agreement Period	Amount
	68	1/65 - 6/69	35000
			GSFC

Tech. Off.: ANDERSON H   Funding Element: GSFC
CASE Code: 13   AWC: 861-32

NAS5-9094   University of California (Berkeley)   K. A. Anderson
Instrumentation & associated equipment for energetic radiations from solar flares experiment for the OGO Programs, OGO-E Mission.

Proposal	FY	Agreement Period	Amount
	68	1/67 - 4/70	10000

Tech. Off.:   Funding Element: GSFC
CASE Code: 11   AWC: 841-12

NAS5-10362   University of California (Berkeley)   F. S. Mozer
Radiation measurement experiment for ATS-E.

Proposal	FY	Agreement Period	Amount
		5/67 - 6/69	512000
	68	5/67 - 6/69	11000
	69	5/67 - 6/69	42000

Tech. Off.: WAINSCOTT F   Funding Element: GSFC
CASE Code: 31   AWC: 630

NAS5-11038   University of California (Berkeley)   K. A. Anderson
IMP-I solar particles experiment.

Proposal	FY	Agreement Period	Amount
		6/67 -12/69	137000

Tech. Off.: BUTLER P   Funding Element: GSFC
CASE Code: 31   AWC: 861-52

CALIFORNIA (Cont'd.)

NAS8-11468   University of California (Berkeley)   W. H. Giedt
Study of heating by radiation from exhaust gases.

Proposal	FY	Agreement Period	Amount
	67	6/64 — 3/69	13000

Tech. Off.: HOPSON G   Funding Element: MSFC
CASE Code: 46   AWC: 124-10

NAS8-21407   University of California (Berkeley)
Asynptotic attitude study of orbiting vehicles.

Proposal	FY	Agreement Period	Amount
	68	5/68 — 3/69	75000

Tech. Off.:   Funding Element: MSFC
CASE Code: 32   AWC: 964-50

NAS8-21432   University of California (Berkeley)   J. R. Mitchell
Lunar surface engineering properties experiment definition.

Proposal	FY	Agreement Period	Amount
	68	6/68 — 7/69	99000

Tech. Off.: COSTES N C   Funding Element: MSFC
CASE Code: 31   AWC: 945-90

NAS9-5249   University of California (Berkeley)   S. Silver
Flight experiment to study trapped radiation study.

Proposal	FY	Agreement Period	Amount
		10/65 —12/67	404000

Tech. Off.:   Funding Element: MSC
CASE Code: 13   AWC: 942-91

NAS9-8806   University of California (Berkeley)
Search for magnetic monopoles in moon surface materials.

Proposal	FY	Agreement Period	Amount
	69	1/69 —12/69	283000

Tech. Off.:   Funding Element: MSC
CASE Code: 32   AWC: 914-40

NAS9-9348   University of California (Berkeley)
Identification and study of earth resources features in support of Apollo experiment S-065.

Proposal	FY	Agreement Period	Amount
	69	4/69 — 9/69	45000

Tech. Off.:   Funding Element: MSC
CASE Code: 32   AWC: 914-41

NAS9-9502   University of California (Berkeley)
Measurement of the world-wide ionospheric electric field on balloons.

Proposal	FY	Agreement Period	Amount
	69	05/69 —12/69	98000

Tech. Off.:   Funding Element: MSC
CASE Code: 19   AWC: 914-14

NAS9-9577   University of California (Berkeley)
Quantitative evaluation of multiband photographic techniques.

Proposal	FY	Agreement Period	Amount
	69	5/69 — 4/70	72000

Tech. Off.:   Funding Element: MSC
CASE Code: 49   AWC: 160-75

NGT-05-003-023   University of California (Berkeley)   S. S. Elberg
Training of predoctoral graduate students in space-related science and technology.

No. Students:	FY	Agreement Period	Amount
15	66	9/66 — 8/69	324000
9	67	9/67 — 8/70	178800

Tech. Off.: HANSING F D   Funding Element: HQ-Y
CASE Code: 99   AWC: 181-00

NGF-05-003-021   University of California (Berkeley)   S. Silver
Space sciences research facilities.

Proposal	FY	Agreement Period	Amount
3372	62	9/62 — 9/65	1990000

Tech. Off.: HOLMES D C   Funding Element: HQ-Y
CASE Code: 99   AWC: 182-00

NGR-05-004-008   University of California (Davis)   A. H. Smith, C. F. Kelly
Investigation of the physiological effects of chronic acceleration.

Proposal	FY	Agreement Period	Amount
-040	68	2/68 — 1/69	80000
-054	69	2/69 — 2/70	72864

Tech. Off.: SAUNDERS J F   Funding Element: HQ-SB
CASE Code: 51   AWC: 189-54

NGR-05-004-026   University of California (Davis)   L. D. Carlson
Peripheral volume measurements as indices of peripheral circulatory factors in the cardiovascular orthostatic response.

Proposal	FY	Agreement Period	Amount
-036	68	11/67 —10/68	46590
		4/69	NCE
-058	69	11/68 —10/69	39967

Tech. Off.:   Funding Element:
CASE Code: 52   AWC: 949-10

NGL-05-004-031   University of California (Davis)   L. D. Carlson
A systems analysis study of the properties of veins.

Proposal	FY	Agreement Period	Amount
-045	68	4/68 — 3/71	71273
-059	69	4/69 — 4/72	34000

Tech. Off.: SANDLER H   Funding Element: ARC
CASE Code: 52   AWC: 127-06

NGR-05-004-035   University of California (Davis)   R. E. Smith
The role of brown fat in the thermogenesis of animals and man.

Proposal	FY	Agreement Period	Amount
-035	68	9/67 — 8/68	40000
		9/68 —10/68	NCE
-052	69	11/68 —10/69	36535
-035		11/68 —10/69	36535

Tech. Off.: SAUNDERS J F   Funding Element: HQ-SB
CASE Code: 51   AWC: 189-54

CALIFORNIA (Cont'd.)

NGR-05-004-038   Unversity of California (Davis)   R. E. Smith
Circadian rhythms in primates as influenced by latitude, longitude, photoperiod and stress.

Proposal	FY	Agreement Period	Amount
−038	68	1/68 −12/68	40000
−055	69	1/69 − 6/69	9000

Tech. Off.: W I N G E T C   Funding Element: A R C
CASE Code: 5 1   AWC: 9 4 5 − 8 2

NGR-05-004-051   University of California (Davis)   M. A. Hoffman
Control power requirements of VTOL aircraft.

Proposal	FY	Agreement Period	Amount
−051	69	4/69 − 3/70	28881

Tech. Off.: R O B E R T S O N A   Funding Element: E R C
CASE Code: 4 1   AWC: 1 2 5 − 1 9

NGR-05-004-053   University of California (Davis)   R. Smith
Circadian variations in human and non-human cardiovascular regulations.

Proposal	FY	Agreement Period	Amount
−053	69	1/69 −12/70	45000

Tech. Off.: S A N D L E R H   Funding Element: A R C
CASE Code: 5 1   AWC: 1 2 7 − 4 9

NAS2-5245   University of California (Davis)   J. Beljan
Orbital flight effects on calcium kinetics and fracture healing repair studies.

Proposal	FY	Agreement Period	Amount
	69	1/69 − 2/70	230000

Tech. Off.:   Funding Element: A R C
CASE Code: 1 9   AWC: 7 0 8 − 1 2

NGL-05-007-002   University of California (Los Angeles)
G. J. F. MacDonald
Theoretical evaluation of internal structures and atmospheres of planets and moon.

Proposal	FY	Agreement Period	Amount
−040	66	1/66 −12/68	71847
−139	67	1/67 −12/68	10000
−239	69	1/69 − 1/72	30000

Tech. Off.:   Funding Element:
CASE Code: 3 1   AWC: 1 8 5 − 4 2

NGL-05-007-003   University of California (Los Angeles)   W. F. Libby
Interdisciplinary space oriented research in the physical, biological, and engineering sciences.

Proposal	FY	Agreement Period	Amount
−186	68	4/68 − 3/71	200000
−229	66	4/69 − 4/72	236000

Tech. Off.:   Funding Element: H Q − Y
CASE Code: 5 1   AWC: 1 8 3

NGR-05-007-004   University of California (Los Angeles) T. A. Farley,
W. F. Libby, P. J. Coleman
Theoretical and experimental investigations of particles and fields in space, including construction of prototype instrumentation.

Proposal	FY	Agreement Period	Amount
−064	65	7/65 − 9/68	220000
−112	67	10/66 − 9/69	183634
−162	68	10/67 − 9/69	110000
−223	69	10/69 − 9/70	210000

Tech. Off.: K A V A N A G H L D J R   Funding Element: H Q − S G
CASE Code: 3 1   AWC: 1 8 5 − 3 6

NGR-05-007-041   University of California (Los Angeles)   Z. Sekara
Feasibility studies of coordinated radiation experiments from meteorological satellites.

Proposal	FY	Agreement Period	Amount
−093	66	5/67 −10/67	20000
−093	66	11/67 − 4/68	NCE
−191	68	5/68 − 4/69	41480
−226	69	5/69 − 4/70	41536

Tech. Off.:   Funding Element: G S F C
CASE Code: 3 1   AWC: 1 6 0 − 4 4

NGR-05-007-046   University of California (Los Angeles)   L. H. Aller
Solar elements, their physical parameters and abundances.

Proposal	FY	Agreement Period	Amount
−117	67	1/67 −12/67	59987
−117	67	1/68 − 4/68	NCE
−180	68	5/68 − 4/69	69990
−241	69	3/69 − 3/70	80053
−248	69	5/69 − 5/72	64871

Tech. Off.: O E R T E L G K   Funding Element: H Q − S G
CASE Code: 3 1   AWC: 1 8 8 − 3 8

NGL-05-007-065   University of California (Los Angeles) P. J. Coleman
Reduction and analysis of data from Mariner IV magnetometer investigations.

Proposal	FY	Agreement Period	Amount
−178	68	4/68 − 3/69	99910
−209	64	4/69 − 3/71	99900

Tech. Off.: E A S T E R D P   Funding Element: H Q − S L
CASE Code: 2 1   AWC: 8 0 8 − 0 2

NGR-05-007-066   University of California (Los Angeles) A. Y. F. Wong
Investigation of interaction between ion beams and plasmas.

Proposal	FY	Agreement Period	Amount
−140	67	5/67 − 4/68	29768
−196	68	5/68 − 4/69	30000

Tech. Off.: M E N T Z E R R H   Funding Element: G S F C
CASE Code: 1 3   AWC: 1 8 8 − 3 6

NGR-05-007-091   University of California (Los Angeles)
Y. Mintz, A. Arakawa
Investigation of optimum meteorological satellite techniques by numerical simulation experiments.

Proposal	FY	Agreement Period	Amount
−165	68	1/68 −12/68	110000
−165		1/68 −12/68	19379
−222	69	1/69 −12/69	105000

Tech. Off.: C H A T T I N A M   Funding Element: G S F C
CASE Code: 1 1   AWC: 1 6 0 − 4 4

CALIFORNIA (Cont'd)

NGR-05-007-116   University of California (Los Angeles)   A. Banos
Theoretical study of non-linear waves and shock-like phenomena in hot plasmas.

Proposal	FY	Agreement Period	Amount
−188	68	12/67 − 2/69	29897
Tech. Off.: NORTHROP T		Funding Element: GSFC	
CASE Code: 13		AWC: 188−36	

NGR-05-007-122   University of California (Los Angeles)
A. V. Balakrishnan
Time domain analysis of system identification problems.

Proposal	FY	Agreement Period	Amount
−160	68	10/67 −11/68	28100
−228	69	12/68 −11/69	34100
Tech. Off.: TAYLOR L W		Funding Element: FRC	
CASE Code: 99		AWC: 125−19	

NGR-05-007-133   University of California (Los Angeles)   H. Sobel
Aging of biological systems in space missions.

Proposal	FY	Agreement Period	Amount
−133	68	6/68 − 5/70	23611
Tech. Off.:		Funding Element:	
CASE Code: 51		AWC: 189−54	

NGR-05-007-138   University of California (Los Angeles)   W. M. Kaula
Development of tidal theory and determination of tidal parameters from artificial satellite orbit perturbations.

Proposal	FY	Agreement Period	Amount
−138	67	6/67 − 2/68	24035
Tech. Off.: ROSENBERG J D		Funding Element: HQ−SA	
CASE Code: 42		AWC: 160−	

NGL-05-007-161   University of California (Los Angeles)   F. A. Haak
The application of far IR lasers to the investigation of the optical properties of materials.

Proposal	FY	Agreement Period	Amount
−161	68	11/67 −10/68	25000
−211	68	11/68 −10/70	25000
−240	69	11/68 −10/71	25000
Tech. Off.: HAAK F A		Funding Element: ERC	
CASE Code: 13		AWC: 125−22	

NGR-05-007-174   University of California (Los Angeles) K. C. Hamner
Studies on the Circadian leaf movements of pinto beans.

Proposal	FY	Agreement Period	Amount
−174	68	5/68 − 4/69	25450
Tech. Off.:		Funding Element:	
CASE Code: 51		AWC: 945−82	

NGR-05-007-187   University of California (Los Angeles)   J. J. Vidal
External scene acquisition and display in flight simulators.

Proposal	FY	Agreement Period	Amount
−187	68	2/68 − 1/69	29876
−237	69	2/69 − 1/70	29876
Tech. Off.: SMITH J P		Funding Element: FRC	
CASE Code: 99		AWC: 164−22	

NGR-05-007-190   University of California (Los Angeles)   C. F. Kennel
Theoretical space plasma physics.

Proposal	FY	Agreement Period	Amount
−190	68	2/68 − 1/69	33380
		− 7/69	NCE
Tech. Off.:		Funding Element:	
CASE Code: 13		AWC: 188−36	

NGL-05-007-195   University of California (Los Angeles)   J. D. French
Phenomena underlying behavior of complex living systems in space.

Proposal	FY	Agreement Period	Amount
−195	68	4/68 − 3/71	200000
Tech. Off.: WEISSMAN N W		Funding Element: HQ−SB	
CASE Code: 51		AWC: 189−52	

NGR-05-007-205   University of California (Los Angeles) F. S. Sjoatrand
An analysis of the circuitry of the visual pathway of the lateral eye of limulus.

Proposal	FY	Agreement Period	Amount
−205	69	4/69 − 3/70	24665
Tech. Off.: ALBUS J S		Funding Element: GSFC	
CASE Code: 51		AWC: 125−23	

NGR-05-007-215   University of California (Los Angeles)   W. F. Libby
Support of group for the analyses of carbon compounds in carbonaceous chrondites and anticipated returned lunar materials.

Proposal	FY	Agreement Period	Amount
−215	69	4/68 − 3/69	30000
Tech. Off.: GEIB D S		Funding Element: HQ−SB	
CASE Code: 12		AWC:	

NGR-05-007-235   University of California (Los Angeles)   R. E. Holzer
Data analysis on the first three OGO satellites.

Proposal	FY	Agreement Period	Amount
−235	69	1/69 − 6/69	50000
Tech. Off.: LEHAN J F JR		Funding Element: HQ−SG	
CASE Code: 42		AWC: 385−36	

NGR-05-010-044   University of California (Los Angeles)   H. P. Broida
Energy transfer in planetary atmospheres: optical spectroscopic studies.

Proposal	FY	Agreement Period	Amount
−044	69	6/69 − 6/70	28234
Tech. Off.: POPPOFF I G		Funding Element: ARC	
CASE Code: 31		AWC: 185−47	

NSR-05-007-083   University of California (Los Angeles)   W. M. Kaula
Lunar orbiter selenodesy studies.

Proposal	FY	Agreement Period	Amount
−083	66	7/66 − 6/68	31287
−199	68	7/68 − 6/69	20066
Tech. Off.: STRICKLAND A		Funding Element: HQ−MA	
CASE Code: 41		AWC: 814−12	

CALIFORNIA (Cont'd.)

NSR-05-007-089 University of California (Los Angeles) J. D. French
Summer Institute in Mammalian Physiological Functions in Space Environment.

Proposal	FY	Agreement Period	Amount
-182	68	12/67 -11/68	27600
		11/68 - 3/69	NCE
-227	69	3/69 - 3/70	37582

Tech. Off.: CARTER E H   Funding Element: HQ-Y
CASE Code: 51   AWC: 181-00

NSR-05-007-236 University of California (Los Angeles) R. A. Goodman
Workshop on dimensional analysis for design, development, and research executives.

Proposal	FY	Agreement Period	Amount
-236	69	3/69 - 9/69	6999

Tech. Off.: STEPHENS R E   Funding Element: HQ-Y
CASE Code: 79   AWC: 183-00

NAS2-2503 University of California (Los Angeles) W. R. Adey
Monitoring brain functions and performance in the primate under prolonged weightlessness: P-1001.

Proposal	FY	Agreement Period	Amount
	68	2/65 - 1/70	350000
	68	2/65 - 8/67	1052

Tech. Off.: CHRISTIANSEN R   Funding Element: ARC
CASE Code: 51   AWC: 883-12

NAS2-5311 University of California (Los Angeles) I. R. Kaplan
Isotopic analysis of natural and lab synthesized organic matter.

Proposal	FY	Agreement Period	Amount
	69	3/69 - 1/70	10000

Tech. Off.:   Funding Element:
CASE Code: 12   AWC: 914-40

NAS9-7282 University of California (Los Angeles) W. R. Adey
Data acquisition system.

Proposal	FY	Agreement Period	Amount
		6/67 - 2/68	48000

Tech. Off.: DELUCCI M R   Funding Element: MSC
CASE Code: 21   AWC: 949-10

NAS9-7882 University of California (Los Angeles)
Preparation and submission of reports for a biogeological study of lunar samples.

Proposal	FY	Agreement Period	Amount
	68	6/68 -12/69	56000

Tech. Off.:   Funding Element: MSC
CASE Code: 51   AWC: 914-40

NAS9-8095 University of California (Los Angeles)
Determine isotopes of rb sr r and pb by mass spectrometry.

Proposal	FY	Agreement Period	Amount
	68	6/68 -12/69	80000

Tech. Off.:   Funding Element: MSC
CASE Code: 12   AWC: 914-40

NAS9-8096 University of California (Los Angeles)
Preparation for chemical studies of returned lunar material.

Proposal	FY	Agreement Period	Amount
	68	6/68 -12/69	60000

Tech. Off.:   Funding Element: MSC
CASE Code: 32   AWC: 914-40

NAS12-2057 University of California (Los Angeles) L. McNamee
Prototype study and comp-aid sim of fm-to-am.

Proposal	FY	Agreement Period	Amount
	69	12/68 - 6/69	15000

Tech. Off.:   Funding Element:
CASE Code: 45   AWC: 125-25

NAS12-2104 University of California (Los Angeles)
Phototype construction of compiler for network analysis feasibility study.

Proposal	FY	Agreement Period	Amount
	69	5/69 - 4/70	45000

Tech. Off.:   Funding Element:
CASE Code: 45   AWC: 125-25

NAS12-2105 University of California (Los Angeles)
Stand. and qualification of comp. programs.

Proposal	FY	Agreement Period	Amount
	69	5/69 - 5/70	15000

Tech. Off.:   Funding Element:
CASE Code: 99   AWC: 125-25

NAS12-2138 University of California (Los Angeles)
Designer's maintenance manual for NASAP.

Proposal	FY	Agreement Period	Amount
	69	5/69 - 3/70	15000

Tech. Off.:   Funding Element: ERC
CASE Code: 99   AWC: 125-25

NGT-05-007-019 University of California (Los Angeles) W. F. Libby
Training of predoctoral graduate students in space-related science and technology.

No. Students:	FY	Agreement Period	Amount
15	65	9/65 - 8/68	288900
15	66	9/66 - 8/69	309100
9	67	9/67 - 8/70	177400

Tech. Off.: HANSING F D   Funding Element: HQ-Y
CASE Code: 99   AWC: 181-00

NGF-05-007-020 University of California (Los Angeles) W. F. Libby
Construction of a space science building connected with the geology and chemistry buildings on the campus at UCLA.

Proposal	FY	Agreement Period	Amount
3728	63	6/63 -12/65	2000000

Tech. Off.: HOLMES D C   Funding Element: HQ-Y
CASE Code: 99   AWC: 182-00

CALIFORNIA (Cont'd)

NGR-05-008-005   University of California (Riverside)   J. Callaway
Atomic scattering theory.

Proposal	FY	Agreement Period	Amount
-016	68	2/68 - 1/69	13000
-021	69	2/69 - 2/70	17000

Tech. Off.: TEMKIN A   Funding Element: GSFC
CASE Code: 13   AWC: 188-40

NGR-05-009-022   University of California (Riverside)   R. S. White
A proposal to measure neutrons from the sun.

Proposal	FY	Agreement Period	Amount
-022	69	7/69 - 7/70	50000

Tech. Off.: SCHARDT A W   Funding Element: HQ-SG
CASE Code: 31   AWC: 189-06

NGT-05-008-001   University of California (Riverside)   R. B. March
Training of predoctoral graduate students in space-related science and technology.

No. Students	FY	Agreement Period	Amount
4	65	9/65 - 8/68	77900
4	66	9/66 - 8/69	75800
2	67	9/67 - 8/70	39000

Tech. Off.: HANSING F D   Funding Element: HQ-Y
CASE Code: 99   AWC: 181-00

NGR-05-005-003   University of California (San Diego)   L. E. Peterson
Studies for x-ray and gamma ray astronomy.

Proposal	FY	Agreement Period	Amount
-024	66	12/65 -11/68	204000
-029	67	12/66 -11/69	130000
-034	68	12/67 -11/69	42000

Tech. Off.: ROMAN N G   Funding Element: HQ-SG
CASE Code: 11   AWC: 188-40

NGR-05-005-005   University of California (San Diego)   J. R. Arnold
Study of lunar gamma ray emission.

Proposal	FY	Agreement Period	Amount
-031	66	9/67 - 4/68	110000
-033	68	5/68 - 4/69	110242
-033		5/69 - 5/70	117000
-036	69	4/69 - 3/70	50000

Tech. Off.: BRYSON R   Funding Element: HQ-MAL
CASE Code: 11   AWC: 185-46

NGR-05-005-007   University of California (San Diego) C. E. McIlwain
Theoretical, analytical and experimental studies of geomagnetically trapped particles, by interpretation of Explorer and Injun satellite data, and by refinement and development of particle detectors, detector systems, and telemetered-data-processing equipment.

Proposal	FY	Agreement Period	Amount
-019	65	3/65 - 8/68	258000
-032	68	9/67 - 8/69	159000
-039		9/67 - 8/71	81000

Tech. Off.: SCHARDT   Funding Element: HQ-SG
CASE Code: 32   AWC: 188-46

NGR-05-009-002   University of California (San Diego)   G. Arrhenius
Study of the composition and structure of meteorites, including the use and refinement of x-ray microspectrometric and micro-diffraction techniques.

Proposal	FY	Agreement Period	Amount
-074	67	11/66 - 2/70	72000
-074	68	3/68 - 2/71	36000
-113		3/69 - 2/72	56000

Tech. Off.:   Funding Element:
CASE Code: 32   AWC: 185-45

NGR-05-009-004   University of California (San Diego)   J. R. Arnold
Investigation of the cosmogenci radioactivity and origin of meteorites, and the geochemistry of the solar nebula.

Proposal	FY	Agreement Period	Amount
-058	67	9/66 - 3/70	75000
-084	69	3/68 - 3/71	53000

Tech. Off.: WILMARTH V R   Funding Element: HQ-SL
CASE Code: 32   AWC: 185-45

NGL-05-009-005   University of California (San Diego)   H. E. Suess
Investigation of the cosmic abundances of the elements.

Proposal	FY	Agreement Period	Amount
-044	67	3/67 - 6/68	51998
-111	69	3/69 - 3/72	35000

Tech. Off.: BRYSON R   Funding Element: HQ-MA
CASE Code: 32   AWC: 185-45

NGR-05-009-025   University of California (San Diego)   P. A. Libby
Mass transfer in laminar hypersonic boundary layers.

Proposal	FY	Agreement Period	Amount
-051	67	1/67 -12/68	50571
-095	69	1/69 -12/67	25000
-120	69	1/69 - 1/72	25000

Tech. Off.: HOWE J T   Funding Element: HQ-RR
CASE Code: 99   AWC: 129-01

NGR-05-009-030   University of California (San Diego) R. H. Lovberg
Physical processes in the magneto-plasmadynamic arc.

Proposal	FY	Agreement Period	Amount
-030	66	2/66 - 1/68	160000
-085	68	2/68 - 1/70	154117

Tech. Off.: MULLIN J   Funding Element: HQ-RN
CASE Code: 13   AWC: 120-26

NGR-05-009-032   University of California (San Diego) S. L. Miller
Feasibility study on miniaturizing an automatic amino acid mission.

Proposal	FY	Agreement Period	Amount
-032	66	6/66 - 6/68	167445
-032	66	6/68 - 8/68	NCE
-090	68	6/68 - 8/70	164714
-108	68	8/68 - 8/70	30000
-108		8/68 - 8/70	48541

Tech. Off.: BRYSON R   Funding Element: HQ-MA
CASE Code: 46   AWC: 849-23

CALIFORNIA (Cont'd)

NGR-05-009-059 University of California (San Diego) B. Q. Duntley
Experimental techniques for analyzing visual detection probability of objects in space.

Proposal	FY	Agreement Period	Amount
-092	68	4/68 - 3/69	65000
		- 5/69	NCE

Tech. Off.: DUKE J A   Funding Element: ARC
CASE Code: 31   AWC: 127-51

NGR-05-009-062 University of California (San Diego) I. M. Jacobs
Coding studies for deep space communication.

Proposal	FY	Agreement Period	Amount
-082	68	4/68 - 3/69	16169
		- 6/69	NCE

Tech. Off.: STANTON O J   Funding Element: HQ-RE
CASE Code: 21   AWC: 125-21

NGR-05-009-076 University of California (San Diego) J. A. Fejer
Theory of wave propagation and wave-particle interaction in the earth's atmosphere.

Proposal	FY	Agreement Period	Amount
-076	68	10/67 - 9/68	40000
-101	69	10/68 - 9/69	40000

Tech. Off.: SCHMERLING E R   Funding Element: HQ-SG
CASE Code: 31   AWC: 188-39

NGR-05-009-081 University of California (San Diego) W. I. Axford
Theoretical studies of fields, particles and plasmas in space.

Proposal	FY	Agreement Period	Amount
-081	68	1/68 -12/68	60000
-107	69	1/69 -12/69	60000

Tech. Off.:   Funding Element:
CASE Code: 13   AWC: 188-36

NGR-05-009-083 University of California (San Diego) R. Galambos
Immunoneurological studies on the brain.

Proposal	FY	Agreement Period	Amount
-083	68	1/68 - 8/68	30840
-102	69	9/68 - 8/69	42219

Tech. Off.: WEISSMAN N W   Funding Element: HQ-SB
CASE Code: 51   AWC: 189-52

NGR-05-009-103 University of California (San Diego) N. A. Baily
Radiation measurement of radiological hazards in man and space.

Proposal	FY	Agreement Period	Amount
-103	69	10/68 - 9/69	59620

Tech. Off.: PETERSON S T   Funding Element: LARC
CASE Code: 19   AWC: 127-49

NGR-05-009-106 University of California (San Diego) A. M. Schneider
Theoretical studies on rendezvous.

Proposal	FY	Agreement Period	Amount
-106	69	3/69 -11/70	10000

Tech. Off.: KRAMER P C   Funding Element: MSC
CASE Code: 42   AWC: 924-23

NGR-05-009-109 University of California (San Diego) J. B. West
In-flight evaluation of weightlessness and gravity on cardiopulmonary function in man.

Proposal	FY	Agreement Period	Amount
-109	69	4/69 - 3/70	50000
-109		4/69 -10/69	100000

Tech. Off.: BILLINGHAM J   Funding Element: ARC
CASE Code: 51   AWC: 127-49

NGR-05-009-114 University of California (San Diego) H. C. Urey
Mars lander instrument team.

Proposal	FY	Agreement Period	Amount
-114	69	3/69 - 3/70	689

Tech. Off.: MITZ M A   Funding Element: HQ-SL
CASE Code: 42   AWC: 815-20

NSR-05-009-046 University of California (San Diego) C. E. McIlwain
Auroral particle experiment.

Proposal	FY	Agreement Period	Amount
-046	67	6/67 - 5/69	64448
-046	68	6/67 - 5/69	80381

Tech. Off.: SCHARDT   Funding Element: HQ-SB
CASE Code: 13   AWC: 879-10

NAS5-3177 University of California (San Diego) L. E. Peterson
X-ray experiment for solar satellite.

Proposal	FY	Agreement Period	Amount
	66	5/63 - 3/69	49000

Tech. Off.: OSTAFF W   Funding Element: GSFC
CASE Code: 31   AWC: 821-

NAS5-10364 University of California (San Diego) C. E. McIlwain
Experiment to study auroral electrons and protons with low energy detectors on ATS-E.

Proposal	FY	Agreement Period	Amount
		5/67 - 6/70	405000

Tech. Off.: WAINSCOTT F   Funding Element: GSFC
CASE Code: 11   AWC: 630-

NAS5-11080 University of California (San Diego) L. E. Peterson
Cosmic x-ray experiment OSO-H.

Proposal	FY	Agreement Period	Amount
	68	9/67 - 8/70	44000
	67	9/67 - 8/70	185000

Tech. Off.:   Funding Element: GSFC
CASE Code: 11   AWC: 821-22

NAS5-11081 University of California (San Diego)
Soft and hard solar x-ray experiment.

Proposal	FY	Agreement Period	Amount
	69	9/67 - 8/70	300000

Tech. Off.:   Funding Element:
CASE Code: 11   AWC: 821-22

CALIFORNIA (Cont'd)

NAS9-7891   **University of California (San Diego)   J. R. Arnold**
Determine cosmic ray and solar particle activation effects.

Proposal	FY	Agreement Period	Amount
	68	6/68 −10/69	59000

Tech. Off.:   Funding Element: MSC
CASE Code: 11   AWC: 914−40

NAS9-7892   **University of California (San Diego)   G. Arrhenius**
Determine microstructure characteristics and composition.

Proposal	FY	Agreement Period	Amount
	68	6/68 − 8/69	10000

Tech. Off.:   Funding Element: MSC
CASE Code: 51   AWC: 914−40

NAS9-8107   **University of California (San Diego)   H. C. Urey**
Isotopic abundance.

Proposal	FY	Agreement Period	Amount
	68	6/68 −10/69	16000

Tech. Off.:   Funding Element: MSC
CASE Code: 12   AWC: 914−40

NAS12-2119   **University of California (San Diego)**
Surface chlorophyll relating to marine research.

Proposal	FY	Agreement Period	Amount
	69	4/69 − 3/70	50000

Tech. Off.:   Funding Element: ERC
CASE Code: 33   AWC: 125−06

NAS12-2126   **University of California (San Diego)**
Atmospheric limit remote sensing sea surface.

Proposal	FY	Agreement Period	Amount
	69	4/69 − 6/70	90000

Tech. Off.:   Funding Element: ERC
CASE Code: 31   AWC: 160−75

NGT-05-009-008   **University of California (San Diego)   F. T. Wall**
Training of predoctoral graduate students in space-related
science and technology.

No. Students:	FY	Agreement Period	Amount
8	65	9/65 − 8/68	153300
10	66	9/66 − 8/69	188800
6	67	9/67 − 8/70	108100

Tech. Off.:   HANSING F D   Funding Element: HQ−Y
CASE Code: 99   AWC: 181−00

NGR-05-025-007   **University of California (San Francisco) L. E. Earley**
The role of systemic and renal hemodynamics as determinants
of sodium excretion and volume regulations.

Proposal	FY	Agreement Period	Amount
−007	68	6/68 − 5/69	71111
−010	69	6/69 − 6/70	65000

Tech. Off.:   Funding Element: MSC
CASE Code: 52   AWC: 127−49

NGR-05-025-008   **University of California (San Francisco)**
                                                        H. I. Maibach
Microbial ecology of anterior nares of man.

Proposal	FY	Agreement Period	Amount
−008	69	9/68 − 8/69	40000

Tech. Off.:   Funding Element: ARC
CASE Code: 51   AWC: 127−49

NGR-05-010-001   **University of California (Santa Barbara)**
                                                        W. C. Walker
Investigation of the optical parameters of certain solids in the
spectral region between 500 and 3000 Angstroms.

Proposal	FY	Agreement Period	Amount
−007	66	1/66 −12/68	35000
−022	68	1/68 −12/70	25000
		− 9/69	NCE

Tech. Off.:   ROMAN N G   Funding Element: HQ−SG
CASE Code: 13   AWC: 188−41

NGR-05-010-008   **University of California (Santa Barbara)   J. M. Sloss**
Elliptic differential equations.

Proposal	FY	Agreement Period	Amount
−017	68	8/67 − 8/68	20456
−030	69	8/68 − 8/69	21596

Tech. Off.:   WILSON R   Funding Element: HQ−RR
CASE Code: 21   AWC: 129−04

NGR-05-010-010   **University of California (Santa Barbara) W. C. Gogel**
Interrelations of perceived size and distance.

Proposal	FY	Agreement Period	Amount
−016	67	6/67 − 5/68	26168
−026	68	/ − /	27601
		− 9/69	NCE

Tech. Off.:   RANDLE R   Funding Element: ARC
CASE Code: 21   AWC: 127−51

NGR-05-010-019   **University of California (Santa Barbara)**
                                                        R. V. Fisher
Maar volcanoes and the role of water in their origins.

Proposal	FY	Agreement Period	Amount
−019	67	6/67 − 5/68	22435
−019	67	6/68 − 9/68	NCE
−027	69	10/69 − 9/70	25000

Tech. Off.:   BRYSON R   Funding Element: HQ−MA
CASE Code: 51   AWC: 185−42

NGR-05-010-020   **Unversity of California (Santa Barbara)**
                                                        T. P. Mitchell
Librational dynamics of deformable satellites.

Proposal	FY	Agreement Period	Amount
−020		11/67 −10/68	15215
		2/69	NCE
−032	69	2/69 − 1/70	15000

Tech. Off.:   MENTZER R H   Funding Element: GSFC
CASE Code: 41   AWC: 188−48

CALIFORNIA (Cont'd)

NGR-05-010-025   University of California (Santa Barbara)
                                                    H. H. Bossel

Investigation of near critical vortex flows.

Proposal	FY	Agreement Period	Amount
-025	69	11/68 -10/70	30368
			LARC

Tech. Off.:   Funding Element:
CASE Code: 4 1   AWC: 1 2 6 – 1 3

NGR-05-010-028   University of California (Santa Barbara) W. C. Kuby
Investigation of the turbulent mixing of the slightly under-expanded supersonic jet.

Proposal	FY	Agreement Period	Amount
-028	69	7/68 – 7/69	11327
			LARC

Tech. Off.:   Funding Element:
CASE Code: 4 9   AWC: 1 2 4 – 0 8

NGR-05-010-035   University of California (Santa Barbara) P. E. Cloud
Pre-Paleozoic biotas and environments.

Proposal	FY	Agreement Period	Amount
-035	69	8/68 – 7/69	35000

Tech. Off.:   G E I B D S   Funding Element: H Q – S B
CASE Code: 5 1   AWC: 1 8 9 – 5 5

NGR-05-010-041   University of California (Santa Barbara)
                                                    P. F. Ordung

Reliability studies in semiconductor fabrication.

Proposal	FY	Agreement Period	Amount
-041	69	4/69 – 4/70	14859

Tech. Off.:   S C H W A R T Z S   Funding Element: E R C
CASE Code: 4 7   AWC: 1 2 5 – 2 5

NSR-05-010-021   University of California (Santa Barbara)
                                                    W. T. Thomson

Space technology summer institute.

Proposal	FY	Agreement Period	Amount
-021	68	12/67 -11/68	53400
-033	69	11/68 -11/69	55369
-033	69	11/68 -11/69	43666

Tech. Off.:   C A R T E R E H   Funding Element: H Q – Y
CASE Code: 9 9   AWC: 1 8 1 – 0 0

NGT-05-010-005   University of California (Santa Barbara) A. Bruckner
Training of predoctoral graduate students in space-related science and technology.

No. Students	FY	Agreement Period	Amount
4	66	9/66 – 8/69	84800
2	67	9/67 – 8/70	37100

Tech. Off.:   H A N S I N G F D   Funding Element: H Q – Y
CASE Code: 9 9   AWC: 1 8 1 – 0 0

NGR-05-061-004   University of California (Santa Cruz)   E. M. Evleth
Geometrical influences on non-radioactive processes in organic molecules.

Proposal	FY	Agreement Period	Amount
-004	68	6/68 – 5/69	6500
-007		6/69 – 6/70	19774

Tech. Off.:   Funding Element: A R C
CASE Code: 1 3   AWC: 1 2 9 – 0 3

NGR-05-061-005   University of California (Santa Cruz)
                                                    W. M. McKeeman

A general purpose language interpreter.

Proposal	FY	Agreement Period	Amount
-005	69	7/69 – 7/70	50000

Tech. Off.:   U D I N D   Funding Element: E R C
CASE Code: 7 4   AWC: 1 2 5 – 0 6

NGR-05-061-006   University of California (Santa Cruz) E. J. Wampler
Cassegrain instrumentation for Lick Observatory 120-inch telescope.

Proposal	FY	Agreement Period	Amount
-006	69	5/69 – 5/70	79997

Tech. Off.:   O T T E J   Funding Element: H Q – S G
CASE Code: 1 1   AWC: 1 8 8 – 4 1

NGR-05-029-005   University of San Francisco   **A. Furst**
Advanced chemical food systems.

Proposal	FY	Agreement Period	Amount
-005	69	12/68 -11/69	16479

Tech. Off.:   S H A P I R A J   Funding Element: A R C
CASE Code: 1 2   AWC: 1 2 7 – 5 3

NGL-05-046-002   San Jose State College   **B. Clark**
Factors influencing the perception of angular acceleration in man.

Proposal	FY	Agreement Period	Amount
-002	68	9/67 – 8/68	40411
-004	68	9/68 – 8/70	40000
-004	69	9/67 – 8/68	4756
-003	69	9/68 – 8/71	40000
-004	69	9/68 – 8/71	4721

Tech. Off.:   C R O S S W A N E K   Funding Element: A R C
CASE Code: 5 1   AWC: 1 2 7 – 5 1

NGR-05-046-005   San Jose State College   **J. C. Thompson**
Study to assess the nature and magnitude of economic benefits of advances in meteorology.

Proposal	FY	Agreement Period	Amount
-005	68	9/68 – 8/69	17929

Tech. Off.:   S P R E E N W C   Funding Element: H Q – S A
CASE Code: 7 2   AWC:

NGR-05-017-013   University of Santa Clara   **D. A. Oliver**
Nonuniformities and instabilities in electrically conducting partially ionized gases in the presence of a magnetic field.

Proposal	FY	Agreement Period	Amount
-013	68	4/68 – 3/69	19000

Tech. Off.:   S T I N E H   Funding Element: A R C
CASE Code: 1 2   AWC: 1 2 9 – 0 1

CALIFORNIA (Cont'd)

NGR-05-017-017   University of Santa Clara   S. P. Chan
Research on the utilization of topological techniques for modelling of microcircuits.

Proposal	FY	Agreement Period	Amount
-017	68	6/68 - 5/69	10000

Tech. Off.:   Funding Element: ERC
CASE Code: 21   AWC: 125-25

NGR-05-018-001   University of Southern California   G. L. Weissler
Interactions of vacuum ultraviolet radiation with solid materials.

Proposal	FY	Agreement Period	Amount
-045	66	10/65 - 9/68	50000
-045	66	6/68 - 6/69	NCE

Tech. Off.:   Funding Element:
CASE Code: 13   AWC: 185-36

NGL-05-018-003   University of Southern California   J. P. Henry,
J. P. Meehan
Investigation of the role of experiences in the etiology of animal and human physiological and behavioral responses to situational stress in later life.

Proposal	FY	Agreement Period	Amount
-033	66	7/66 - 9/68	91980
-068	67	10/66 - 9/69	54948
-068	68	10/67 - 9/70	64266
-110	69	10/68 - 9/71	35534

Tech. Off.: WEISSMAN N W   Funding Element: HQ-SB
CASE Code: 51   AWC: 189-52

NGR-05-018-007   University of Southern California   D. L. Judge
Measurement of absolute photon flux using a superconducting bolometer.

Proposal	FY	Agreement Period	Amount
-050	66	2/66 - 1/67	29810
-050	66	1/67 - 7/67	NCE
-114	69	1/69 - 12/69	22561

Tech. Off.: BEAM B B   Funding Element: ARC
CASE Code: 13   AWC: 125-24

NGR-05-018-022   University of Southern California   G. A. Bekey
New techniques for analysis of manual control systems.

Proposal	FY	Agreement Period	Amount
-022	67	3/67 - 3/68	47443
-022	67	3/68 - 6/68	NCE
-102	68	7/68 - 6/69	44495

Tech. Off.: GOULD C H   Funding Element: HQ-RE
CASE Code: 99   AWC: 125-19

NGL-05-018-044   University of Southern California   H. Bichsel
Multidisciplinary research in the space-related engineering, physical, biological, and social sciences.

Proposal	FY	Agreement Period	Amount
-044	66	7/66 - 6/69	400000
-074	67	7/67 - 6/70	200000
-101	68	7/68 - 6/71	200000
-117	69	7/69 - 7/72	200000

Tech. Off.: QUINN H B   Funding Element: HQ-Y
CASE Code: 99   AWC: 183-00

NGR-05-018-065   University of Southern California   T. C. James
Investigation of molecules of interest in stellar and planetary atmospheres.

Proposal	FY	Agreement Period	Amount
-065	67	2/68 - 7/68	35000
-065	67	7/68 - 8/68	NCE
-107	69	9/68 - 8/69	24988

Tech. Off.: ROMAN N G   Funding Element: HQ-SG
CASE Code: 31   AWC: 188-40

NGR-05-018-079   University of Southern California   W. T. Kyner
Qualitative properties of the orbits of near earth satellites.

Proposal	FY	Agreement Period	Amount
-079	67	6/67 - 9/69	39539
-100	68	6/68 - 9/70	5000

Tech. Off.: PAYNE M   Funding Element: ERC
CASE Code: 41   AWC: 160-43

NGL-05-018-098   University of Southern California
Multidisciplinary research in management and administration with emphasis on large scale R & D public programs.

Proposal	FY	Agreement Period	Amount
-098	68	7/68 - 6/71	200000

Tech. Off.: CARTER C H   Funding Element: HQ-Y
CASE Code: 99   AWC: 183-00

NGR-05-018-104   University of Southern California R. M. Gagliardi
Study of synchronization techniques for optical communications systems.

Proposal	FY	Agreement Period	Amount
-104	69	12/68 - 11/69	25837
			ERC

Tech. Off.: KARP S   Funding Element: HQ-ER
CASE Code: 49   AWC: 125-22

NSR-05-018-087   University of Southern California   L. G. Goff
Observation of arterial blood pressure of the primate.

Proposal	FY	Agreement Period	Amount
-087	68	7/68 - 7/69	193000

Tech. Off.:   Funding Element:
CASE Code: 51   AWC: 945-82

NSR-05-018-119   University of Southern California   R. H. Edwards
A study of edge effects of a rocket which exhausts into a vacuum.

Proposal	FY	Agreement Period	Amount
-119	68	6/69 - 6/70	18926

Tech. Off.: SUDDRETH J A   Funding Element: HQ-RP
CASE Code: 49   AWC: 128-31

CALIFORNIA (Cont'd.)

NSR-05-018-120   University of Southern California
A study of condensation in rocket nozzles.

Proposal	FY	Agreement Period	Amount
–120	68	6/69 – 6/70	18998

Tech. Off.: SUDDRETH J A   Funding Element: HQ–RP
CASE Code: 41   AWC: 128–31

NAS2-2633   University of Southern California   J. P. Meehan
Monitoring cardiovascular function in the primate under prolonged weightlessness.

Proposal	FY	Agreement Period	Amount
	68	1/65 – 3/69	120000
	68	1/65 – 2/68	74000

Tech. Off.: HOFFMAN R   Funding Element: ARC
CASE Code: 51   AWC: 883–12

NGT-05-018-004   University of Southern California   M. C. Kloetzel
Training of predoctoral graduate students in space-related science and technology.

No. Students	FY	Agreement Period	Amount
12	65	9/65 – 8/68	230400
12	66	9/66 – 8/69	230400
8	67	9/67 – 8/70	139300

Tech. Off.: HANSING F D   Funding Element: HQ–Y
CASE Code: 99   AWC: 181–00

NGT-05-018-085   University of Southern California   R. E. Stephens
Training of predoctoral graduate students in space-related science and technology.

No. Students	FY	Agreement Period	Amount
5	67	9/67 – 8/70	10500

Tech. Off.: HANSING F D   Funding Element: HQ–Y
CASE Code: 99   AWC: 181–00

NGF-05-018-015   University of Southern California   J. P. Meehan
For construction and renovation of the human centrifuge facilities on the University of Southern California campus.

Proposal	FY	Agreement Period	Amount
6280	64	7/64 – 4/65	160000

Tech. Off.: HOLMES D C   Funding Element: HQ–Y
CASE Code: 59   AWC: 182–00

NGR-05-020-001   Stanford University   O. G. Villard
Electron content distribution and temporal variation in the ionosphere by means of scintillation and Faraday rotation of satellite radio transmissions, including consideration of latitudinal effects of magnetic storms.

Proposal	FY	Agreement Period	Amount
–270	68	1/68 – 8/68	50000
–317	69	8/68 – 8/69	55000

Tech. Off.: SCHMERLING   Funding Element: HQ–SG
CASE Code: 31   AWC: 150–22

NGR-05-020-004   Stanford University   J. Lederberg
Cytochemical studies of planetary microorganisms.

Proposal	FY	Agreement Period	Amount
–262	68	9/67 – 8/68	410000
–311	69	9/68 – 6/69	340000

Tech. Off.: GEIB D S   Funding Element: HQ–SB
CASE Code: 51   AWC: 189–55

NGR-05-020-007   Stanford University   R. H. Cannon, I. Flugge-Lotz
Basic studies on space vehicle attitude control systems.

Proposal	FY	Agreement Period	Amount
–246	68	9/67 – 8/68	80000
–316	69	9/68 – 9/70	130000

Tech. Off.: REMPFER P S   Funding Element: FRC
CASE Code: 46   AWC: 125–17

NGL-05-020-008   Stanford University   R. A. Helliwell
Investigation of experimental techniques for measurement of very-low-frequency electromagnetic phenomena in the ionosphere.

Proposal	FY	Agreement Period	Amount
–181	67	3/66 – 2/69	50000
–236	68	3/67 – 2/70	65067
–304	66	3/68 – 2/71	65000
–359		3/69 – 2/72	65000

Tech. Off.: SCHMERLING   Funding Element: HQ–SG
CASE Code: 31   AWC: 188–39

NGR-05-020-013   Stanford University   A. L. Schawlow
Spectroscopy and solid quantum electronics at optical and infrared wavelengths.

Proposal	FY	Agreement Period	Amount
–124	66	10/65 – 9/68	100000
–187	67	10/66 – 9/69	100000
–255	68	10/67 – 9/69	50000

Tech. Off.: JOHNSON P   Funding Element: HQ–RR
CASE Code: 13   AWC: 129–02

NGL-05-020-014   Stanford University   V. R. Eshleman
Theoretical experimental radio and radar studies of lunar and planetary ionospheres, atmospheres, and surfaces, the sun, and interplanetary medium.

Proposal	FY	Agreement Period	Amount
–144	66	10/65 – 9/68	200000
–188	67	10/66 – 9/69	200000
–239	68	10/67 – 9/70	220000
–302	69	10/68 – 9/71	220000

Tech. Off.: EASTER D P   Funding Element: HQ–SL
CASE Code: 31   AWC: 185–48

NGR-05-020-015   Stanford University   W. M. Fairbank
Gravitational and resonance experiments on very low-energy free electrons and positrons.

Proposal	FY	Agreement Period	Amount
–274	68	2/68 – 1/69	70000
–343		2/69 – 1/70	25000
–384	69	2/69 – 2/72	25000

Tech. Off.: TALKIN H   Funding Element: HQ–RR
CASE Code: 13   AWC: 129–02

CALIFORNIA (Cont'd.)

NGR-05-020-019 Stanford University R. H. Cannon, W. M. Fairbank, B. O. Lange

Investigations, theoretical and experimental analyses for a zero-g satellite development, and Schiff gyro test of the general theory of relativity.

Proposal	FY	Agreement Period	Amount
−261	68	4/68 − 9/68	180000
−325	69	10/68 − 9/69	139405

Tech. Off.: OTT E J   Funding Element: HQ−SG
CASE Code: 11   AWC: 188−40

NGR-05-020-039 Stanford University   A. S. Tetelman

The mechanism of strengthening and fracture in composite systems.

Proposal	FY	Agreement Period	Amount
−215	67	6/67 − 5/68	15000

Tech. Off.:   Funding Element:
CASE Code: 46   AWC: 129−03

NGR-05-020-043 Stanford University   G. L. Pearson

Fundamental studies of metallurgical, electrical and optical properties of Gallium phosphide.

Proposal	FY	Agreement Period	Amount
−298	69	2/69 − 1/70	34000
−365	69	2/69 − 2/72	34000
−113	66	2/66 − 1/69	150000

Tech. Off.: SMITHRICK J J   Funding Element: LERC
CASE Code: 12   AWC: 123−33

NGR-05-020-066 Stanford University   W. E. Spicer

Photoemission studies of solids.

Proposal	FY	Agreement Period	Amount
−222	68	5/67 − 4/68	43951
−279	69	5/68 − 4/69	32000
−342	69	5/69 − 5/70	32000

Tech. Off.: OTT E J   Funding Element: HQ−SG
CASE Code: 13   AWC: 188−41

NGR-05-020-073 Stanford University   R. E. Kalman

Research on stability and stochastic optimal control.

Proposal	FY	Agreement Period	Amount
−269	68	4/68 − 9/69	59998
−269		12/69	NCE

Tech. Off.: JANOW C   Funding Element: HQ−RE
CASE Code: 13   AWC: 125−19

NGR-05-020-077 Stanford University   F. W. Crawford

The nature and characteristics of space-related plasma resonance phenomena.

Proposal	FY	Agreement Period	Amount
−216	68	5/67 − 6/68	73816
−294	69	7/68 − 6/69	55000

Tech. Off.: OPP A G   Funding Element: HQ−SG
CASE Code: 13   AWC: 188−36

NGR-05-020-091 Stanford University   D. Bershader

Experimental and analytical studies of plasma transport properties.

Proposal	FY	Agreement Period	Amount
−221	67	6/67 − 5/68	60000
−283	68	6/68 − 5/69	50000

Tech. Off.: HOWE J   Funding Element: HQ−RR
CASE Code: 13   AWC: 129−01

NGR-05-020-102 Stanford University   K. Karamcheti

Theoretical studies of some nonlinear aspects of hypersonic panel flutter.

Proposal	FY	Agreement Period	Amount
−256	68	9/67 − 8/68	38888
−328	69	9/68 − 8/69	38337

Tech. Off.: GASPERS P A   Funding Element: ARC
CASE Code: 99   AWC: 126−04

NGR-05-020-103 Stanford University   S. H. Harris

Investigation of laser dynamics, modulation and control by means of intra-cavity time varying perturbation.

Proposal	FY	Agreement Period	Amount
−103	66	2/66 − 1/69	180000
−219	68	4/68 − 3/69	90000
−312	69	4/69 − 3/70	90000
−366		4/69 − 3/72	90000

Tech. Off.: MESON J K   Funding Element: HQ−RE
CASE Code: 49   AWC: 125−22

NGR-05-020-134 Stanford University   W. M. Kays

Mass transfer to a turbulent boundary layer with step changes in boundary conditions and variable free-stream velocity.

Proposal	FY	Agreement Period	Amount
−134	66	1/66 −12/68	55744
−322	69	1/69 −12/69	36554

Tech. Off.: MISER J W   Funding Element: LERC
CASE Code: 13   AWC: 129−01

NGR-05-020-137 Stanford University   L. Stryer, A. Kornberg

Structure and function of proteins and nucleic acids.

Proposal	FY	Agreement Period	Amount
−252	68	1/68 − 6/68	25000
−299	69	7/68 − 6/69	50000

Tech. Off.: JACOBS G   Funding Element: HQ−SB
CASE Code: 51   AWC: 189−57

NGR-05-020-165 Stanford University   M. Chodorow

Theoretical and experimental investigations of collective microwave phenomena in solids.

Proposal	FY	Agreement Period	Amount
−251	68	4/68 − 3/69	50000

Tech. Off.: GRAYZEL A I   Funding Element: ERC
CASE Code: 13   AWC: 125−21

CALIFORNIA (Cont'd.)

NGR-05-020-176   Stanford University   F. W. Crawford
Investigation of space-related "Whistler" propagation phenomena in laboratory plasmas.

Proposal	FY	Agreement Period	Amount
-235	68	6/67 - 6/68	59800
-235	69	7/68 - 6/69	55000
-297	69	7/68 - 6/69	55000

Tech. Off.: SCHMERLING   Funding Element: HQ-SG
CASE Code: 13   AWC: 188-39

NGL-05-020-177   Stanford University   R. E. Smith
Subcellular localization of pituitary enzymes.

Proposal	FY	Agreement Period	Amount
-240	68	9/67 - 8/68	21340
-309	68	9/68 - 8/70	21300

Tech. Off.: ELLIS S   Funding Element: ARC
CASE Code: 51   AWC: 127-49

NGR-05-020-209   Stanford University   T. R. Kane
Dynamics of the human body in free fall.

Proposal	FY	Agreement Period	Amount
-209	67	10/66 - 9/67	35148
-209	67	10/67 - 6/68	NCE
-278	68	7/68 - 6/69	35000

Tech. Off.: JONES J L   Funding Element: ARC
CASE Code: 51   AWC: 127-51

NGR-05-020-214   Stanford University   R. H. Bube
Mechanism of the photovoltaic effect in II-VI compounds.

Proposal	FY	Agreement Period	Amount
-214	67	4/67 - 3/69	46000
-284	69	4/69 - 3/70	25000
-367		4/69 - 3/72	25000

Tech. Off.: SMITHRICK J J   Funding Element: LERC
CASE Code: 45   AWC: 120-33

NGR-05-020-223   Stanford University   M. Anliker
Biomechanics within the field of cardiovascular physiology.

Proposal	FY	Agreement Period	Amount
-223	68	7/67 - 6/68	80000
-308	69	7/68 - 6/69	156190

Tech. Off.: OGDEN E   Funding Element: ARC
CASE Code: 52   AWC: 127-49

NGL-05-020-232   Stanford University   R. L. Kovach
Examination of lunar scientific objectives and evaluation and developmental studies for possible active seismic experiments during the post-Apollo period.

Proposal	FY	Agreement Period	Amount
-232	67	7/67 - 6/68	28130
-300	68	7/68 - 6/71	109338

Tech. Off.:   Funding Element:
CASE Code: 99   AWC: 185-42

NGR-05-020-234   Stanford University   A. E. Siegman
Study of laser frequency stability and spectral purity.

Proposal	FY	Agreement Period	Amount
-234	68	3/68 - 2/69	22500

Tech. Off.: MORREAL J A   Funding Element: ERC
CASE Code: 46   AWC: 125-21

NGR-05-020-242   Stanford University   I. Weinberg
Establishment of resident graduate research assistantships.

Proposal	FY	Agreement Period	Amount
-242	68	2/68 - 1/69	25000
-341	69	2/69 - 1/70	25021
-364		2/69 - 1/72	25000

Tech. Off.: WEINBERG I   Funding Element: HQ-RR
CASE Code: 12   AWC: 129-01

NGR-05-020-243   Stanford University   H. Ashley
Refined methods of aeroelastic analysis and optimization.

Proposal	FY	Agreement Period	Amount
-243	68	9/67 - 8/68	9868
-310	69	9/68 - 8/69	10162

Tech. Off.: RAINEY A G   Funding Element: LARC
CASE Code: 41   AWC: 126-14

NGR-05-020-244   Stanford University   R. C. Atkinson
Instructional strategies for optimizing the learning process.

Proposal	FY	Agreement Period	Amount
-244	68	1/68 -12/68	78731
-320	69	1/69 -12/69	80000

Tech. Off.: TANNER T   Funding Element: ARC
CASE Code: 62   AWC: 127-51

NGR-05-020-245   Stanford University   D. Baganoff
Experimental and analytical studies of reflecting shock waves in a real gas.

Proposal	FY	Agreement Period	Amount
-245	68	2/68 - 1/69	25000
-333	69	2/69 - 2/70	25000

Tech. Off.: HOWE J T   Funding Element: HQ-RR
CASE Code: 13   AWC: 129-01

NGL-05-020-250   Stanford University   J. D. Baldeschwieler
Study of abiogenic reaction mechanisms by cyclotron resonance spectroscopy.

Proposal	FY	Agreement Period	Amount
-250	68	8/67 - 7/68	24927
-303	64	8/68 - 7/70	25000
-323	69	8/68 - 7/71	24988

Tech. Off.: PONNAMPERUMA C   Funding Element: ARC
CASE Code: 51   AWC: 189-55

NGR-05-020-267   Stanford University   A. D. Howard
Investigation of lunar analogues of fluvial landscapes and possible implications.

Proposal	FY	Agreement Period	Amount
-267	68	3/68 - 2/70	36000

Tech. Off.:   Funding Element:
CASE Code: 32   AWC: 185-42

CALIFORNIA (Cont'd.)

NGR-05-020-272 Stanford University P. A. Sturrock
Theoretical study of the solar atmosphere and the structure of active regions.

Proposal	FY	Agreement Period	Amount
-272	68	7/68 -10/68	25000
-272	69	11/68 -10/69	75000
-291	69	11/68 -10/69	35000
-368		11/68 -10/71	111000

Tech. Off.: Funding Element:
CASE Code: 3 1 AWC: 1 8 8 - 3 8

NGL-05-020-275 Stanford University K. Karamcheti
A study of the fluid mechanics of edgetones.

Proposal	FY	Agreement Period	Amount
-275	68	1/68 -12/68	28443
-307	67	1/69 -12/70	30000
-350	69	1/69 -12/71	25000

Tech. Off.: SCHWARTZ I R Funding Element: HQ-RR
CASE Code: 1 3 AWC: 1 2 9 - 0 1

NGR-05-020-276 Stanford University V. R. Eshleman
Reduction and analysis of data from the Mariner V dual frequency receiver experiment.

Proposal	FY	Agreement Period	Amount
-287	68	10/67 - 4/69	66433

Tech. Off.: Funding Element:
CASE Code: 2 1 AWC: 8 1 7 - 4 7

NGR-05-020-277 Stanford University D. A. Dunn
Optical scattering methods in laboratory plasma diagnostics.

Proposal	FY	Agreement Period	Amount
-277	68	2/68 - 6/68	14000
-277	69	7/68 - 2/69	19044
-334	69	2/69 - 6/69	13000 ARC

Tech. Off.: Funding Element:
CASE Code: 1 3 AWC: 1 2 9 - 0 2

NGR-05-020-288 Stanford University R. A. Helliwell
Magnetosphere studies on satellite VLF/LF data acquired on OGO-I and OGO-II.

Proposal	FY	Agreement Period	Amount
-288	68	5/68 - 4/69	98568
-346		5/69 - 5/69	100000

Tech. Off.: Funding Element:
CASE Code: 3 1 AWC: 3 8 5 - 0 1

NGR-05-020-305 Stanford University D. C. Harrison
Evaluation of the cardiovascular system during various circulatory stresses.

Proposal	FY	Agreement Period	Amount
-305	69	9/68 - 8/69	92242

Tech. Off.: Funding Element: ARC
CASE Code: 5 1 AWC: 1 2 7 - 4 9

NGR-05-020-324 Stanford University L. A. Sapirstein
Measurement of cerebral blood flow in man by an isotopic technique employing external counting.

Proposal	FY	Agreement Period	Amount
-324	69	2/69 - 2/70	19000

Tech. Off.: CIFFONE D L Funding Element: ARC
CASE Code: 5 1 AWC: 1 2 9 - 0 1

NGR-05-020-326 Stanford University S. Levine
Influence of chronic and repeated stress on the pituitary adrenal system and behavior.

Proposal	FY	Agreement Period	Amount
-326	69	9/68 - 8/69	27781

Tech. Off.: VERNIKOS-DANELLIS Funding Element: ARC
CASE Code: 5 1 AWC: 1 2 7 - 4 9

NGR-05-020-330 Stanford University J. R. Spreiter
Dynamics of the solar wind and its interaction with bodies in the solar system.

Proposal	FY	Agreement Period	Amount
-330	69	4/69 - 4/70	30000

Tech. Off.: KAVANAGH L D JR Funding Element: HQ-SG
CASE Code: 3 1 AWC: 1 8 8 - 3 1

NGR-05-020-335 Stanford University A. C. Giese
Photochemical and photobiological effects of extreme ultraviolet radiation.

Proposal	FY	Agreement Period	Amount
-335	69	4/69 -10/69	11857

Tech. Off.: PONNAMPERUMA Funding Element: ARC
CASE Code: 1 9 AWC: 1 8 9 - 5 5

NGR-05-020-345 Stanford University J. L. Adams
Research in remote control.

Proposal	FY	Agreement Period	Amount
-345	69	7/69 - 7/70	20000

Tech. Off.: PALMER E Funding Element: ARC
CASE Code: 4 9 AWC: 1 2 7 - 5 1

NGR-05-020-348 Stanford University A. M. Peterson
The theory of parallel operations in digital systems.

Proposal	FY	Agreement Period	Amount
-348	69	7/69 - 9/70	85026

Tech. Off.: BRYSON R P Funding Element: HQ-MA
CASE Code: 2 1 AWC: 3 8 3 - 1 1

NGR-05-020-353 Stanford University V. R. Eshleman
Participation in the Mariner Mars 1973 radio team.

Proposal	FY	Agreement Period	Amount
-353	69	2/69 - 2/70	14130

Tech. Off.: MITZ M A Funding Element: HQ-SL
CASE Code: 4 2 AWC: 8 1 5 - 2 0

CALIFORNIA (Cont'd.)

NGR-05-020-354   Stanford University   J. Lederberg
Participation in development of active biology experiments for early Mars landers.

Proposal	FY	Agreement Period	Amount
-354	69	2/69 - 2/70	10603

Tech. Off.: MITZ M A   Funding Element: HQ-SL
CASE Code: 51   AWC: 815-20

NGR-05-020-386   Stanford University   W. A. Tiller
Investigation of the influence of environment on the nucleation and growth of fatigue cracks.

Proposal	FY	Agreement Period	Amount
-386	69	7/69 - 2/70	22405

Tech. Off.: SUMSION H T   Funding Element: ARC
CASE Code: 46   AWC: 129-03

NSR-05-020-088   Stanford University   M. Anliker
Summer institute in space-related engineering.

Proposal	FY	Agreement Period	Amount
-266	68	3/68 - 3/69	140000
-327	69	3/69 - 3/70	158412
-327	69	3/69 - 3/70	162412

Tech. Off.: CARTER C H   Funding Element: HQ-Y
CASE Code: 99   AWC: 181-00

NSR-05-020-151   Stanford University   W. Bollay
A summer program in systems design engineering.

Proposal	FY	Agreement Period	Amount
-271	68	6/68 - 8/68	85100
-332	69	12/68 -12/69	113246
-332	69	12/68 -12/69	111246

Tech. Off.:   Funding Element:
CASE Code: 49   AWC: 141-00

NAS2-3410   Stanford University   V. R. Eshlman
Radio propagation experiment for Project Pioneer.

Proposal	FY	Agreement Period	Amount
		2/66 - 6/69	710000
	66	2/66 - 6/69	8000

Tech. Off.: HALL C   Funding Element: ARC
CASE Code: 46   AWC: 811-12

NAS2-4671   Stanford University   T. Tomberlin
Pioneer C post-launch operations.

Proposal	FY	Agreement Period	Amount
	68	12/67 - 6/68	150000
	68	12/67 - 6/68	20000

Tech. Off.: HALL C   Funding Element: ARC
CASE Code: 99   AWC: 811-12

NAS2-4672   Stanford University   V. R. Eshlman
Pioneer C data analysis.

Proposal	FY	Agreement Period	Amount
	68	12/67 -12/68	67000

Tech. Off.: HALL C   Funding Element: ARC
CASE Code: 99   AWC: 811-12

NAS2-5355   Stanford University
Investigation of magnetospheric physics.

Proposal	FY	Agreement Period	Amount
	69	4/69 - 3/70	35000

Tech. Off.:   Funding Element:
CASE Code: 13   AWC: 129-02

NAS5-9309   Stanford University   R. A. Helliwell
VLF polarization experiment for the orbiting geophysical observatory, Mission F(OGO-F).

Proposal	FY	Agreement Period	Amount
		3/66 - 6/68	360000
	66	3/66 - 6/68	185000
	68	3/66 - 6/68	102000
	66	3/66 - 6/68	80000

Tech. Off.: MERCANTI E   Funding Element: GSFC
CASE Code: 11   AWC: 841-12

NAS5-9347   Stanford University   A. M. Peterson
Study of a computer-related training and education program.

Proposal	FY	Agreement Period	Amount
		6/66 - 1/69	55000
	68	6/66 - 6/69	25000

Tech. Off.:   Funding Element:
CASE Code: 21   AWC: 861-22

NAS5-10102   Stanford University   O. G. Villard
Radio propagation studies of the ionosphere.

Proposal	FY	Agreement Period	Amount
	68	6/66 - 2/69	85000

Tech. Off.:   Funding Element: GSFC
CASE Code: 11   AWC: 630-13

NAS9-5632   Stanford University   R. L. Kovach
Active seismic experiment for ALSEP.

Proposal	FY	Agreement Period	Amount
		2/66 - 2/69	325000

Tech. Off.: WEEKS E L   Funding Element: MSC
CASE Code: 99   AWC: 942-92

NAS9-7020   Stanford University   B. B. Lusignan
Preliminary study of atmospheric density measurements by means of satellites.

Proposal	FY	Agreement Period	Amount
		5/67 - 2/68	18000
	67	5/67 -11/68	25000

Tech. Off.: THOBEN B   Funding Element: MSC
CASE Code: 31   AWC: 160-44

CALIFORNIA (Cont'd.)

NAS9-7313   **Stanford University**   **R. J. Lyon**
Infrared spectrometry studies.

Proposal	FY	Agreement Period	Amount
		6/67 – 3/68	52000
	68	6/67 – 3/69	100000

Tech. Off.:   Funding Element: MSC
CASE Code: 12   AWC: 169–

NAS9-9439   **Stanford University**   **H. Halpern**
Measurement and analysis of lunar samples for porphyrins in
association with amino acid compounds.

Proposal	FY	Agreement Period	Amount
	69	5/69 –12/69	74000

Tech. Off.:   Funding Element:
CASE Code: 12   AWC: 914–40

NAS12-695   **Stanford University**
Design of a drag-free satellite applic. to geod.

Proposal	FY	Agreement Period	Amount
		5/68 – 5/69	40000

Tech. Off.:   Funding Element: ERC
CASE Code: 32   AWC: 160–43

NGT-05-020-228   **Stanford University**   **J. A. Vitale**
Training of predoctoral graduate students in space-related
science and technology.

No. Students:	FY	Agreement Period	Amount
	67	9/67 – 8/70	108000

Tech. Off.:   HANSING F D   Funding Element: HQ–Y
CASE Code: 99   AWC: 181–00

NGT-05-002-295   **Stanford University**   **J. M. Pettit**
Training grant in lasers and optics.

No. Students:	FY	Agreement Period	Amount
5	69	9/69 – 8/72	111000

Tech. Off.:   CARTER C H   Funding Element: HQ–Y
CASE Code: 13   AWC: 181–00

NGT-05-020-016   **Stanford University**   **H. Heffner**
Training of predoctoral graduate students in space-related
science and technology.

No. Students:	FY	Agreement Period	Amount
15	65	9/65 – 8/68	322200
15	66	9/66 – 8/69	324000
9	67	9/67 – 8/70	170400

Tech. Off.:   HANSING F D   Funding Element: HQ–Y
CASE Code: 99   AWC: 181–00

NGT-05-020-295   **Stanford University**   **J. M. Pettit**
Predoctoral traineeship of students in the fields of lasers and
optics.

No. Students:	FY	Agreement Period	Amount
5	68	9/68 – 8/71	111000

Tech. Off.:   HANSING F D   Funding Element: HQ–Y
CASE Code: 99   AWC: 181–00

NGT-05-020-361   **Stanford University**   **J. M. Pettit**
Predoctoral training of students in the field of aeronautics.

No. Students:	FY	Agreement Period	Amount
5	69	9/69 – 8/72	103500

Tech. Off.:   CARTER C H   Funding Element: HQ–Y
CASE Code: 41   AWC: 181–00

NGF-05-020-017   **Stanford University**   **J. Lederberg**
Biomedical instrumentation facilities.

Proposal	FY	Agreement Period	Amount
3363	62	9/62 – 3/65	535000
		10/64 –10/65	NCE
3363	66	11/65 – 6/66	NCE

Tech. Off.:   HOLMES D C   Funding Element: HQ–Y
CASE Code: 99   AWC: 182–00

NGF-05-020-092   **Stanford University**   **W. R. Rambo**
Construction of research laboratory facilities as a part of the Space
Engineering Building.

Proposal	FY	Agreement Period	Amount
–092	65	9/65 – 1/68	2080000

Tech. Off.:   HOLMES D C   Funding Element: HQ–Y
CASE Code: 49   AWC: 182–00

COLORADO

NGL–06-001-015   **Colorado School of Mines**   **L. T. Grose**
Applications of remote sensor data to geologic and economic
analysis of the Bonanza Test Site.

Proposal	FY	Agreement Period	Amount
–015	69	4/69 – 3/72	250000

Tech. Off.:   VITALE J A   Funding Element: HQ–Y
CASE Code: 99   AWC: 183–00

NAS8-30511   **Colorado School of Mines**
Research in phase change thermal control technology.

Proposal	FY	Agreement Period	Amount
	69	11/68 – 1/70	10000

Tech. Off.:   Funding Element:
CASE Code: 43   AWC: 124–09

NGT-06-001-001   **Colorado School of Mines**   **A. R. Jordan**
Training of predoctoral graduate students in space-related
science and technology.

No. Students:	FY	Agreement Period	Amount
4	65	9/65 – 8/68	54800
4	66	9/66 – 8/69	60300
2	67	9/67 – 8/70	35000

Tech. Off.:   HANSING F D   Funding Element: HQ–Y
CASE Code: 99   AWC: 181–00

COLORADO (Cont'd.)

NGR-06-002-018   Colorado State University   J. B. Best
Mechanisms of integration and behavior.

Proposal	FY	Agreement Period	Amount
-051	67	7/67 - 6/68	44533
-069	69	7/68 - 6/69	39249
	66	8/69	NCE

Tech. Off.:   Funding Element:
CASE Code: 99   AWC: 189-52

NGR-06-002-075   Colorado State University   J. P. Jordan
Metabolic effects of artificial environments.

Proposal	FY	Agreement Period	Amount
-075	69	11/68 -10/69	45000

Tech. Off.:   Funding Element:
CASE Code: 51   AWC: 189-54

NGR-06-002-084   Colorado State University   W. R. Mickelsen
Performance analysis, modelling, and critical tests of electric thruster systems.

Proposal	FY	Agreement Period	Amount
-084	69	4/69 - 4/70	15642

Tech. Off.:   ISLEY W C   Funding Element: GSFC
CASE Code: 49   AWC: 180-17

NGR-06-002-085   Colorado State University   C. B. Winn
Investigations of synchronous satellites for geodesy.

Proposal	FY	Agreement Period	Amount
-085	69	3/69 - 6/70	54982

Tech. Off.:   ROSENBERG J D   Funding Element: HQ-SA
CASE Code: 32   AWC: 160-43

NAS8-21049   Colorado State University   V. A. Sandborn
Crossed beam weather watch study.

Proposal	FY	Agreement Period	Amount
		3/67 - 3/68	95000
	68	3/67 - 6/68	8000

Tech. Off.:   KRAUSE F   Funding Element: MSFC
CASE Code: 31   AWC: 933-50

NGT-06-002-002   Colorado State University   W. H. Bragonier
Supporting the training of predoctoral graduate students in space-related science and technology.

No. Students	FY	Agreement Period	Amount
8	65	9/65 - 8/68	137400
8	66	9/66 - 8/69	146400
4	67	9/67 - 8/70	63900

Tech. Off.:   HANSING F D   Funding Element: HQ-Y
CASE Code: 99   AWC: 181-00

NGL-06-002-038   Colorado State University   R. Jensen
Multidisciplinary space-related research in the physical, engineering and life sciences.

Proposal	FY	Agreement Period	Amount
-038	66	9/66 - 8/69	200000
-049	67	9/67 - 8/70	100000
-076	68	9/68 - 8/69	19755

Tech. Off.:   QUINN H B   Funding Element: HQ-Y
CASE Code: 99   AWC: 183-00

NGR-06-002-053   Colorado State University   C. B. Winn
Theoretical investigation of an electrically propelled geodetic satellite.

Proposal	FY	Agreement Period	Amount
-065	68	7/68 - 1/69	21430
-072	68	9/68 - 3/69	3505

Tech. Off.:   PUCILLO G L   Funding Element: ERC
CASE Code: 13   AWC: 160-43

NGR-06-002-063   Colorado State University   F. W. Smith
Stress intensity factors for surface flawed fracture specimens.

Proposal	FY	Agreement Period	Amount
-063	69	1/69 -12/70	39735

Tech. Off.:   BOURKE E A   Funding Element: LERC
CASE Code: 13   AWC: 124-08

NGR-06-002-074   Colorado State University   D. R. Winder
Growth of crystals of the ternary sulfides.

Proposal	FY	Agreement Period	Amount
-074	69	2/69 - 1/70	20000

Tech. Off.:   HAAK F A   Funding Element: ERC
CASE Code: 13   AWC: 125-22

NAS5-11631   Colorado State University   W. E. Marlott
Atmospheric limitations to remote sensing study.

Proposal	FY	Agreement Period	Amount
	69	1/69 - 7/69	47000

Tech. Off.:   Funding Element:
CASE Code: 31   AWC: 160-44

NAS5-11666   Colorado State University   W. E. Marlott
Procurement, installation and operation of a multi-channel digital data acquisition system.

Proposal	FY	Agreement Period	Amount
	69	2/69 -12/69	90000

Tech. Off.:   REED H Z   Funding Element: GSFC
CASE Code: 31   AWC: 160-44

NGR-06-003-033   University of Colorado   A. Busemann
Optimal trajectories between elliptical orbits.

Proposal	FY	Agreement Period	Amount
-073	68	9/67 - 8/68	33000
		- 8/69	NCE

Tech. Off.:   WILSON R   Funding Element: HQ-RR
CASE Code: 13   AWC: 129-04

COLORADO (Cont'd.)

NGR-06-003-034   University of Colorado   W. A. Rense
Ultraviolet radiation research to support rocket and satellite solar ultraviolet experiments.

Proposal	FY	Agreement Period	Amount
−080		7/67 − 6/68	NCE
−034	66	7/67 − 9/67	NCE
−080	68	7/67 − 6/68	87936
		7/68 − 9/68	NCE

Tech. Off.: OERTEL G K   Funding Element: HQ−SG
CASE Code: 11   AWC: 188−38

NGL-06-003-052   University of Colorado   C. A. Barth
Theoretical and experimental research program in physics of planetary atmospheres.

Proposal	FY	Agreement Period	Amount
−052	66	7/66 − 6/69	300000
−070	67	7/67 − 6/70	342959
−094	68	7/68 − 6/71	537724

Tech. Off.: FELLOWS R F   Funding Element: HQ−SL
CASE Code: 13   AWC: 185−47

NGR-06-003-057   University of Colorado   R. H. Garstang
Basic research in solar physics.

Proposal	FY	Agreement Period	Amount
−057	68	9/67 − 8/68	57000
−091	69	9/68 − 8/69	82200

Tech. Off.: OERTEL G K   Funding Element: HQ−SG
CASE Code: 13   AWC: 188−38

NGR-06-003-064   University of Colorado   C. A. Barth
Rocket research program in the ultraviolet airglow and aurora of planetary atmospheres.

Proposal	FY	Agreement Period	Amount
−101	69	9/68 − 8/69	150000
−064	68	7/67 − 6/68	155000
−064	68	7/68 − 8/68	NCE

Tech. Off.: DUBIN   Funding Element: HQ−SG
CASE Code: 11   AWC: 879−10

NGR-06-003-069   University of Colorado   W. A. Rense
Solar physics research.

Proposal	FY	Agreement Period	Amount
−069	68	8/67 − 8/68	167524
−096	69	8/68 − 8/69	150000

Tech. Off.: OERTEL G K   Funding Element: HQ−SG
CASE Code: 31   AWC: 879−10

NGR-06-003-071   University of Colorado   R. Wolfgang
Chemical reactions in the electron-volt region.

Proposal	FY	Agreement Period	Amount
−071	68	9/67 − 8/69	87673

Tech. Off.: HIPSHER H F   Funding Element: HQ−SL
CASE Code: 12   AWC: 185−37

NGR-06-003-075   University of Colorado   A. Busemann
The feasibility of large sonic boom reductions.

Proposal	FY	Agreement Period	Amount
−075	68	7/67 − 6/68	37595
−075	68	6/68 − 6/69	NCE

Tech. Off.: DANBERG J E   Funding Element: HQ−RR
CASE Code: 41   AWC: 129−01

NGR-06-003-083   University of Colorado   I. Horowitz
Research in adaptive systems.

Proposal	FY	Agreement Period	Amount
−083	68	4/68 − 3/69	29275
−114	69	4/69 − 3/70	41648

Tech. Off.: TAYLOR L W   Funding Element: FRC
CASE Code: 99   AWC: 125−21

NGR-06-003-088   University of Colorado   R. E. Hayes
Nonreciprocal semiconductor millimeter wave devices.

Proposal	FY	Agreement Period	Amount
−088	68	3/68 − 2/69	21427
		− 6/69	NCE

Tech. Off.: HOLMSTROM R   Funding Element: ERC
CASE Code: 46   AWC: 125−21

NGR-06-003-092   University of Colorado   T. W. Speiser
Analysis of Imp-C data from magnetospheric tail.

Proposal	FY	Agreement Period	Amount
−092	69	11/68 −10/69	18000
−092		12/69	NCE

Tech. Off.: LEHAN J F JR   Funding Element: HQ−SG
CASE Code: 49   AWC:

NGR-06-003-120   University of Colorado   C. W. Hord
Participate in a science instrument team for the Mars lander.

Proposal	FY	Agreement Period	Amount
−120	69	2/69 − 2/70	9484

Tech. Off.: MITZ M A   Funding Element: HQ−SL
CASE Code: 42   AWC: 815−20

NAS5-3931   University of Colorado   W. A. Rense
Perform research on Orbiting Solar Observatory — E.

Proposal	FY	Agreement Period	Amount
		6/64 − 6/68	448000
	67	6/64 − 7/68	34000

Tech. Off.: BAILEY R   Funding Element: GSFC
CASE Code: 11   AWC: 821−22

NAS5-9327   University of Colorado   C. A. Barth
Ultraviolet photometer experiment for the Orbiting Geophysical Observatory Mission E.

Proposal	FY	Agreement Period	Amount
	66	3/66 − 9/67	63000
	69	3/66 − 6/69	140000

Tech. Off.:   Funding Element: GSFC
CASE Code: 11   AWC: 841−12

COLORADO (Cont'd)

NGT-06-003-004 University of Colorado   E. J. Archer
Supporting the training of predoctoral graduate students in space-related science and technology.

No. Students:	FY	Agreement Period	Amount
12	65	9/65 – 8/68	222100
12	66	9/66 – 8/69	250800
6	67	9/67 – 8/70	117700

Tech. Off.: HANSING F D   Funding Element: HQ–Y
CASE Code: 99   AWC: 181–00

NGF-06-003-005 University of Colorado   W. A. Rense
Construction of a building housing laboratories for atmospheric and space physics on the Boulder campus of the U. of Colorado.

Proposal	FY	Agreement Period	Amount
3254	63	6/63 –12/65	792000

Tech. Off.: HOLMES D C   Funding Element: HQ–Y
CASE Code: 99   AWC: 182–00

NGR-06-004-006 University of Denver   R. C. Amme
Study of atomic and molecular collision phenomena by high velocity atomic and molecular beams.

Proposal	FY	Agreement Period	Amount
–042	66	5/68 –10/68	NCE
–042	66	7/66 – 6/68	60000
		11/68 – 4/69	NCE

Tech. Off.: JOHNSON P   Funding Element: HQ–RR
CASE Code: 13   AWC: 129–01

NGL-06-004-007 University of Denver   S. A. Johnson
Multidisciplinary research in space-related science and engineering.

Proposal	FY	Agreement Period	Amount
–036	66	10/65 – 9/68	150000
–044	67	10/66 – 9/69	160000
–064	68	9/67 – 8/69	50000
–071	68	1/68 – 9/68	5000
–064		3/70	NCE

Tech. Off.: MARR E G   Funding Element: HQ–Y
CASE Code: 99   AWC: 181–00

NGR-06-004-058 University of Denver   V. L. Patel
Study of hydromagnetic disturbances in the geomagnetic field of satellite altitudes.

Proposal	FY	Agreement Period	Amount
–058	68	5/68 – 4/69	13000
–088	69	5/69 – 4/70	15000

Tech. Off.: KAVANAGH L D   Funding Element: HQ–SG
CASE Code: 11   AWC: 385–01

NGR-06-004-060 University of Denver   J. G. Roederer
Study of physical processes which govern the dynamics of geomagnetically trapped radiation.

Proposal	FY	Agreement Period	Amount
–060	68	6/68 – 5/69	20000
–094	69	6/69 – 6/70	21000

Tech. Off.:   Funding Element:
CASE Code: 32   AWC: 385–01

NGR-06-004-068 University of Denver   L. W. Ross
Effect of pulsed operation on the performance of life support system components.

Proposal	FY	Agreement Period	Amount
–068	68	12/67 –12/68	9277
–087	69	1/69 – 1/70	10135

Tech. Off.: SMITH W L   Funding Element: HQ–RB
CASE Code: 99   AWC: 127–53

NGL-06-004-078 University of Denver   A. A. Ezra
Program for the exploitation of unused NASA patents.

Proposal	FY	Agreement Period	Amount
–078	68	6/68 – 5/71	200000

Tech. Off.: VITALE J A   Funding Element: HQ–Y
CASE Code: 99   AWC: 183–00

NGR-06-004-082 University of Denver   C. W. Chiang
Basic research for a program of work entitled "Supersonic-Hypersonic Conical Flow of a Delta Wing".

Proposal	FY	Agreement Period	Amount
–082	69	12/68 –11/69	24750

Tech. Off.:   Funding Element: LARC
CASE Code: 41   AWC: 126–13

NSR-06-004-081 University of Denver   J. G. Milliken
Study of the transferability of "aerospace management technology".

Proposal	FY	Agreement Period	Amount
–081	67	1/69 – 4/70	49636

Tech. Off.: PHILIPS R J   Funding Element: HQ–UT
CASE Code: 79   AWC: 141–00

NAS1-7391 University of Denver   C. Lundin
A research and development study of the use of thermodynamic properties of metal-gas systems as partial pressure standards.

Proposal	FY	Agreement Period	Amount
		6/67 – 6/68	51000

Tech. Off.: KERN F A   Funding Element: LARC
CASE Code: 13   AWC: 125–24

NAS8-21436 University of Denver   J. Blizard
Long range solar flare prediction.

Proposal	FY	Agreement Period	Amount
	68	6/68 – 6/69	29000

Tech. Off.:   Funding Element: MSFC
CASE Code: 11   AWC: 933–50

NAS8-30179 University of Denver   D. G. Murcray
Development of high-response balloon-borne humidity and aerosol detection sensor.

Proposal	FY	Agreement Period	Amount
	69	3/69 – 3/70	30000

Tech. Off.: CAMP D W   Funding Element: LARC
CASE Code: 41   AWC: 125–24

COLORADO   (Cont'd.)

NAS-12-651   **Unversity of Denver**

Application of network analysis for system application program to the design of biomedical circuits.

Proposal	FY	Agreement Period	Amount
	68	4/68 – 6/69	10000

Tech. Off.:   Funding Element: E R C
CASE Code: 2 1   AWC: 1 2 5 – 2 5

NGT-06-004-008   **University of Denver**   **W. C. Miller**

Training of predoctoral graduate students in space-related science and technology.

No. Students	FY	Agreement Period	Amount
6	65	9/65 – 8/68	100800
6	66	9/66 – 8/69	108000
3	67	9/67 – 8/70	41200

Tech. Off.:   H A N S I N G   F   D   Funding Element: H Q – Y
CASE Code: 9 9   AWC: 1 8 1 – 0 0

NGF-06-004-024   **University of Denver**   **C. M. Alter**

Construction of a Space Sciences Laboratory.

Proposal	FY	Agreement Period	Amount
–024	65	9/65 – 9/67	900000

Tech. Off.:   H O L M E S   D   C   Funding Element: H Q – Y
CASE Code: 9 9   AWC: 1 8 2 – 0 0

NAS9-7566   **University of Denver**   **W. H. Mclain**

Real-time study of preignition and post-combustion reactions in hypergolic bipropellant rocket engine.

Proposal	FY	Agreement Period	Amount
		11/67 – 7/69	89000

Tech. Off.:   H O H M A N N   C   W   Funding Element: M S C
CASE Code: 4 9   AWC: 1 2 8 – 3 1

CONNECTICUT

NGL-07-002-002   **University of Connecticut**   **D. P. Lindorff**

Analytical and experimental research on reducing the sensitivity of control systems to parameter variations, and on the relative merits of various control system configurations.

Proposal	FY	Agreement Period	Amount
–021	66	9/65 – 8/68	42000
–026	68	9/67 – 8/69	45000
–038	68	9/67 – 8/70	23000
–039	69	9/68 – 8/71	36000

Tech. Off.:   J A N O W   J   Funding Element: H Q – R E
CASE Code: 9 9   AWC: 1 2 5 – 1 9

NSR-07-002-037   **University of Connecticut**   **S. W. Yost**

Operation of the New England Research Application Center regional dissemination.

Proposal	FY	Agreement Period	Amount
–037	68	4/68 – 3/69	260000

Tech. Off.:   Funding Element:
CASE Code: 7 9   AWC: 1 4 1 – 0 0

NGT-07-002-003   **University of Connecticut**   **N. L. Whetten**

Training of predoctoral graduate students in space-related science and technology.

No. Students	FY	Agreement Period	Amount
8	65	9/65 – 8/68	166400
8	66	9/66 – 8/69	168000
4	67	9/67 – 8/70	71500

Tech. Off.:   H A N S I N G   F   D   Funding Element: H Q – Y
CASE Code: 9 9   AWC: 1 8 1 – 0 0

NGR-07-010-002   **Fairfield University**   **J. H. McElaney**

Investigation of energy deposition processes in the upper atmosphere, and the interaction between the mesosphere and the thermosphere.

Proposal	FY	Agreement Period	Amount
–002	68	3/68 – 2/69	19800
		3/69 – 6/69	NCE

Tech. Off.:   Funding Element:
CASE Code: 1 1   AWC: 6 0 7 – 1 5

NGR-07-009-003   **Rensselaer Polytechnic Institute of Connecticut, Inc.**   **H. J. Schwarz**

Investigation of a quadrupole ultra-high vacuum ion pump.

Proposal	FY	Agreement Period	Amount
–003	69	9/68 – 8/69	20000

Tech. Off.:   Y E A G E R   P   R   Funding Element: L A R C
CASE Code: 4 9   AWC: 1 2 5 – 2 4

NGR-07-011-001   **St. Joseph College**   **M. T. J. Murphy**

Identification of aromatic hydrocarbons in spark discharge material and geological samples.

Proposal	FY	Agreement Period	Amount
–001	69	5/69 – 5/70	5500

Tech. Off.:   P O N N A M P E R U M A   Funding Element: A R C
CASE Code: 4 3   AWC: 9 1 4 – 4 9

NGR-07-006-004   **Wesleyan University**   **T. Page**

Ultraviolet energy distribution of galaxies.

Proposal	FY	Agreement Period	Amount
–004	69	4/69 – 4/70	8300

Tech. Off.:   A S H W O R T H   C   D   Funding Element: H Q – S G
CASE Code: 3 1   AWC: 8 3 1 – 1 2

NGR-07-006-005   **Wesleyan University**   **J. E. Faller**

To design and construct a laser ranging system to be used with a telescope at Lick Observatory for the transmission and detection of laser pulses to and from retroreflectors to be placed on the lunar surface.

Proposal	FY	Agreement Period	Amount
–005	68	4/69 –10/69	107000

Tech. Off.:   S T R I C K L A N D   A   T   Funding Element: H Q – M A
CASE Code: 1 1   AWC: 1 8 5 – 4 3

CONNECTICUT (Cont'd)

NGR-07-004-004　Yale University　　　　　R. Wildt

Steady-state interaction between radiation and matter in stellar atmospheres.

Proposal	FY	Agreement Period	Amount
2537	61	7/61 – 6/63	68621
	67	7/66 – 6/68	NCE
		– 6/70	NCE

Tech. Off.: ROMAN N G　　　Funding Element: HQ–SG
CASE Code: 31　　　　　　　AWC: 188–40

NGL-07-004-005　Yale University　　　　　R. C. Barker

Research on low-power, low-speed data storage and processing techniques.

Proposal	FY	Agreement Period	Amount
–099	68	1/68 –12/68	51900
–115		1/69 –12/71	52000

Tech. Off.: SCHAEFER D　　　Funding Element: GSFC
CASE Code: 45　　　　　　　AWC: 125–23

NGR-07-004-006　Yale University　　　　　V. W. Hughes

Theoretical research in relativity, cosmology, and nuclear astrophysics.

Proposal	FY	Agreement Period	Amount
–093	68	10/67 – 9/68	15000

Tech. Off.:　　　　　　　Funding Element:
CASE Code: 13　　　　　　AWC: 188–37

NGL-07-004-008　Yale University　　　　　S. R. Lipsky

Gas-chromatographic systems to analyze certain chemical constituents of surface of moon.

Proposal	FY	Agreement Period	Amount
–047	66	10/65 – 9/68	48305
–064	67	10/66 – 9/69	74980
–086	68	10/67 – 9/68	82145
–108	69	10/68 – 9/69	50000

Tech. Off.: EASTER D P　　　Funding Element: HQ–SL
CASE Code: 12　　　　　　　AWC: 185–37

NGR-07-004-009　Yale University　　　　　H. J. Morowitz

Determination and analysis of the properties and characteristics of extremely small free-living, self-replicating cells.

Proposal	FY	Agreement Period	Amount
–085	68	11/67 –10/68	20670
–110	69	11/68 –10/69	20700

Tech. Off.: YOUNG R S　　　Funding Element: HQ–SB
CASE Code: 51　　　　　　　AWC: 189–55

NGR-07-004-010　Yale University　　　　　R. Wildt

Studies of the constitution of planetary interiors, and mathematical techniques for planetary modeling.

Proposal	FY	Agreement Period	Amount
3867	63	10/62 – 9/65	117760
		– 9/70	NCE

Tech. Off.: BRUNK W E　　　Funding Element: HQ–SL
CASE Code: 21　　　　　　　AWC: 185–42

NGR-07-004-015　Yale University　　　　　M. M. Chen

An experimental and theoretical research on plasma sheaths and boundary layers around stagnation point electrodes.

Proposal	FY	Agreement Period	Amount
–063		6/67 – 5/68	31271
–063	67	6/67 – 5/68	34000
–104	69	6/68 – 5/69	10025

Tech. Off.: STINE H　　　Funding Element: ARC
CASE Code: 13　　　　　　AWC: 129–01

NGR-07-004-028　Yale University　　I. B. Bernstein, J. L. Hirshfield

Plasma physics in planetary and solar environments.

Proposal	FY	Agreement Period	Amount
–102	68	2/68 – 1/69	26000
	65	9/69	NCE

Tech. Off.: OPP　　　　　Funding Element: HQ–SG
CASE Code: 13　　　　　AWC: 188–36

NGR-07-004-029　Yale University　　　　　R. Wildt

Theoretical research in stellar and planetary astrophysics.

Proposal	FY	Agreement Period	Amount
–029	65	10/64 – 9/65	24499
	65	10/66 –09/67	NCE
–029	65	10/67 – 9/68	NCE
		– 9/70	NCE

Tech. Off.: QUINN H B　　　Funding Element: HQ–Y
CASE Code: 11　　　　　　　AWC: 183–00

NGR-07-004-034　Yale University　　C. MacClintock, A. L. McAlester

Study of relationship, through geologic time, of days per lunar month to growth increments in fossil and recent molluscan shells.

Proposal	FY	Agreement Period	Amount
–034	66	9/65 – 9/68	72000
–105	69	12/68 –11/69	25000

Tech. Off.: GIEB D S　　　Funding Element: HQ–SB
CASE Code: 51　　　　　　AWC: 189–55

NGR-07-004-035　Yale University　　　　　W. E. Lamb

Investigation of the basic foundations of masers and lasers.

Proposal	FY	Agreement Period	Amount
–091	68	1/68 –12/68	35000
–111	69	1/69 –12/69	30000

Tech. Off.: JOHNSON P S　　Funding Element: HQ–RR
CASE Code: 13　　　　　　AWC: 129–02

NGR-07-004-043　Yale University　　　　　R. Wolfgang

Chemical reactions in the electron-volt region.

Proposal	FY	Agreement Period	Amount
–043	66	10/65 – 9/68	61200
		10/68 – 9/69	NCE

Tech. Off.: HIPSHER H F　　Funding Element: HQ–SL
CASE Code: 45　　　　　　AWC: 185–37

CONNECTICUT (Cont'd.)

NGR-07-004-084   Yale University   R. A. Goldsby
Water metabolism as a life detection indicator.

Proposal	FY	Agreement Period	Amount
−084	68	1/68 −12/69	17930
−113	69	1/69 −12/69	17900

Tech. Off.: GIEB D S   Funding Element: HQ−SB
CASE Code: 51   AWC: 189−55

NGR-07-004-087   Yale University   F. B. Tuteur
Research in time and fuel optimal control systems.

Proposal	FY	Agreement Period	Amount
−087	68	9/67 − 8/68	14000
		9/68 − 6/69	NCE

Tech. Off.:   Funding Element:
CASE Code: 13   AWC: 129−04

NGR-07-004-090   Yale University   R. J. Wyman
Study of the role of proprioception in the coordination of locomotion.

Proposal	FY	Agreement Period	Amount
−090	68	1/68 −12/68	11401
−116		1/69 −12/69	11257

Tech. Off.:   Funding Element:
CASE Code: 51   AWC: 189−52

NGR-07-004-109   Yale University   E. B. Hooper
Ionospheric transport processes.

Proposal	FY	Agreement Period	Amount
−109	69	1/69 −12/69	28000

Tech. Off.: SCHMERLING E R   Funding Element: HQ−SG
CASE Code: 31   AWC: 188−39

NAS9-8032   Yale University   K. K. Turekian
Determine by neutron activation analysis those elements having half-lives greater than three days. Lunar sample analysis program.

Proposal	FY	Agreement Period	Amount
	68	5/68 −11/69	33000

Tech. Off.:   Funding Element: MSC
CASE Code: 32   AWC: 914−40

NAS9-8072   Yale University   S. R. Lipsky
Identification of certain organic compounds in lunar material.

Proposal	FY	Agreement Period	Amount
	68	6/68 −12/69	61000

Tech. Off.:   Funding Element: MSC
CASE Code: 32   AWC: 914−40

NAS9-8075   Yale University   B. J. Skinner
Examine returned lunar samples for condensed sublimates.

Proposal	FY	Agreement Period	Amount
	68	6/68 − 2/70	43000

Tech. Off.:   Funding Element: MSC
CASE Code: 32   AWC: 914−40

NGT-07-004-014   Yale University   J. P. Miller
Training of predoctoral graduate students in space-related science and technology.

No. Students	FY	Agreement Period	Amount
15	65	9/65 − 8/68	318000
15	66	9/66 − 8/69	324000
8	67	9/67 − 8/70	144800

Tech. Off.: HANSING F D   Funding Element: HQ−Y
CASE Code: 99   AWC: 181−00

DELAWARE

NGR-08-001-016   University of Delaware   E. J. Pellicciaro
A non-linear integral equation of the abel type arising from the theory of adsorption kinetics.

Proposal	FY	Agreement Period	Amount
−016	67	6/67 − 5/68	12286

Tech. Off.: WILSON R   Funding Element: HQ−RR
CASE Code: 21   AWC: 129−04

NGL-08-001-019   University of Delaware   T. W. F. Russell
Two-phase flow and boiling heat transfer problem in visco-elastic fluids.

Proposal	FY	Agreement Period	Amount
−019	68	5/68 − 4/71	50000

Tech. Off.: HOWE J T   Funding Element: HQ−RR
CASE Code: 13   AWC: 129−01

NAS1-8787   University of Delaware
Study of x-ray and electron damage of cadmium sulfide.

Proposal	FY	Agreement Period	Amount
	69	11/68 −11/69	15000

Tech. Off.:   Funding Element:
CASE Code: 47   AWC: 129−03

NGT-08-001-002   University of Delaware   C. E. Birchenall
Training of predoctoral graduate students in space-related science and technology.

No. Students	FY	Agreement Period	Amount
8	65	9/65 − 8/68	147900
8	66	9/66 − 8/69	150900
4	67	9/67 − 8/70	66400

Tech. Off.: HANSING F D   Funding Element: HQ−Y
CASE Code: 99   AWC: 181−00

DISTRICT OF COLUMBIA

NGR-09-003-014   American University   E. Callen
Studies of magnetic semiconductors.

Proposal	FY	Agreement Period	Amount
−014	69	4/69 − 3/70	30000

Tech. Off.: CHILDRESS J D   Funding Element: ERC
CASE Code: 47   AWC: 129−03

DISTRICT OF COLUMBIA (Cont'd)

NGR-09-005-008   Catholic University   R. E. Meijer

Theoretical and experimental studies of spin photon coupling effects in paramagnetic crystals.

Proposal	FY	Agreement Period	Amount
−036	66	11/66 −10/67	23280
−036	66	11/67 −10/68	NCE
		10/67 − 4/69	NCE
		− 8/69	NCE

Tech. Off.:   Funding Element:
CASE Code: 13   AWC: 129−02

NGR-09-005-014   Catholic University   T. Tanaka

Theoretical investigation of radiation damage in solar cells.

Proposal	FY	Agreement Period	Amount
−053	67	5/67 − 4/68	28000
−053	67	5/68 −10/68	NCE
		4/68 − 3/69	NCE

Tech. Off.:   FANG P H   Funding Element: GSFC
CASE Code: 11   AWC: 120−33

NGR-09-005-022   Catholic University   B. T. DeCicco

Genetic studies of hydrogen bacteria and their application to biological life support systems.

Proposal	FY	Agreement Period	Amount
−049	66	5/67 − 4/68	28164
−061	68	5/68 − 4/69	25598
−068	69	5/69 − 5/70	23146

Tech. Off.:   SAUNDERS J F   Funding Element: HQ−SB
CASE Code: 51   AWC: 189−54

NGR-09-005-025   Catholic University   C. C. Chang

Diagnostics of accelerating plasma.

Proposal	FY	Agreement Period	Amount
−058	68	12/67 −11/69	126146

Tech. Off.:   MULLIN J   Funding Element: HQ−RN
CASE Code: 13   AWC: 120−26

NGR-09-005-054   Catholic University   T. Tanaka

Theoretical investigation of microwave frequency doubling by means of magnetic non-linearity in antiferromagnetic crystals.

Proposal	FY	Agreement Period	Amount
−054	68	11/67 −10/68	21000

Tech. Off.:   CLEMENS D   Funding Element: GSFC
CASE Code: 13   AWC: 125−21

NGR-09-005-055   Catholic University   H. C. Khatri

Investigation of stability of distributed parameter systems.

Proposal	FY	Agreement Period	Amount
−055	68	5/68 − 4/69	17000
		− 8/70	NCE

Tech. Off.:   Funding Element:
CASE Code: 99   AWC: 129−04

NGR-09-005-063   Catholic University   Y. C. Whang

Interaction of the solar wind with the moon.

Proposal	FY	Agreement Period	Amount
−063	69	6/69 − 6/70	17000

Tech. Off.:   OPP A G   Funding Element: HQ−SG
CASE Code: 31   AWC: 385−36

NGR-09-005-067   Catholic University   S. C. Ling

Study of pulsatile blood flow under both normal and adverse environmental conditions.

Proposal	FY	Agreement Period	Amount
−067	69	4/69 − 4/70	14925

Tech. Off.:   HOWE J T   Funding Element: HQ−RR
CASE Code: 51   AWC: 129−01

NSR-09-005-059   Catholic University   B. T. Fang

A summer institute in space-related engineering.

Proposal	FY	Agreement Period	Amount
−059	68	2/68 − 1/69	99767
−066	68	1/69 − 1/70	90357
−066	69	2/69 − 2/70	87956

Tech. Off.:   CARTER C H   Funding Element: HQ−Y
CASE Code: 49   AWC: 181−00

NGT-09-005-006   Catholic University   J. P. O'Connor

Training of predoctoral graduate students in space-related science and technology.

No. Students	FY	Agreement Period	Amount
12	65	9/65 − 8/68	230400
12	66	9/66 − 8/69	230400
6	67	9/67 − 8/70	84400

Tech. Off.:   HANSING F D   Funding Element: HQ−Y
CASE Code: 99   AWC: 181−00

NGR-09-010-008   George Washington University   N. Filipescu

Synthesis and spectroscopic properties of rare earth chelates in solvents and polymers for optical masers.

Proposal	FY	Agreement Period	Amount
−037	67	5/67 − 6/68	31673
−047	68	7/68 − 6/69	25000

Tech. Off.:   AVOY M   Funding Element: GSFC
CASE Code: 32   AWC: 125−22

NGL-09-010-030   George Washington University   L. H. Mayo

Multidisciplinary program of policy studies in science and technology.

Proposal	FY	Agreement Period	Amount
−030	66	9/66 − 8/69	750000
−030	67	9/66 − 8/69	25000
−041	67	9/67 − 8/70	400000
−052	68	9/68 − 8/71	275000
−052	68	9/68 − 8/71	275000

Tech. Off.:   QUINN H B   Funding Element: HQ−Y
CASE Code: 99   AWC: 143−00

DISTRICT OF COLUMBIA (Cont'd)

NGR-09-010-053 George Washington University   H. Liebowitz
Research in space related areas in engineering and applied science.

Proposal	FY	Agreement Period	Amount
-053	69	12/68 -12/69	150000

Tech. Off.: DANBERG J E   Funding Element: LARC
CASE Code: 49   AWC:

NSR-09-010-027 George Washington University   C. W. Shilling
Scientific communication research in space biology.

Proposal	FY	Agreement Period	Amount
-039	68	7/67 -12/67	72341
-046	68	1/68 -12/68	165000
-039	68	1/68 -12/69	NCE
-049	68	6/68 -12/68	15000
-054	69	3/69 -12/69	232549

Tech. Off.: SCHMIDT R   Funding Element: HQ-SB
CASE Code: 45   AWC: 189-57

NSR-09-010-035 George Washington University   C. W. Shilling
Design and management of biomedical applications systems for NASA.

Proposal	FY	Agreement Period	Amount
-035	67	1/68 - 6/68	NCE
-048	68	1/67 - 5/69	98976

CASE Code: 51   AWC: 141-00
Tech. Off.: DUFFY R E   Funding Element: HQ-UT

NSR-09-010-057 George Washington University   C. W. Shilling
Support of the 1969 Summer Institute for Biomedical Research in Technology Utilization.

Proposal	FY	Agreement Period	Amount
-059	69	6/69 - 5/70	111580

Tech. Off.: PHILIPS R J   Funding Element: HQ-UT
CASE Code: 59   AWC: 141-00

NGT-09-010-003 George Washington University   A. E. Burns
Training of predoctoral graduate students in space-related science and technology.

No. Students	FY	Agreement Period	Amount
6	65	9/65 - 8/68	109800
6	66	9/66 - 8/69	109800
4	67	9/67 - 8/70	59700

Tech. Off.: HANSING F D   Funding Element: HQ-Y
CASE Code: 99   AWC: 181-00

NGR-09-009-024 Georgetown University   I. Gray
Study of multiple molecular forms of enzymes of leucocytes in infection, disease and stress.

Proposal	FY	Agreement Period	Amount
-024	68	7/68 - 6/69	15000

Tech. Off.: MANDEL A   Funding Element: ARC
CASE Code: 52   AWC: 120-49

NGR-09-009-025 Georgetown University   C. B. Ferster
The study of emotion and non-metabolic reinforcers in a multi-animal environment.

Proposal	FY	Agreement Period	Amount
-025	69	4/69 -10/70	22800

Tech. Off.: BELLEVILLE R E   Funding Element: HQ-SB
CASE Code: 59   AWC: 189-52

NGT-09-009-004 Georgetown University   J. B. Horigan
Training of predoctoral graduate students in space-related science and technology.

No. Students	FY	Agreement Period	Amount
8	65	9/65 - 8/68	141600
8	66	9/66 - 8/69	141600
4	67	9/67 - 8/70	70800

Tech. Off.: HANSING F D   Funding Element: HQ-Y
CASE Code: 99   AWC: 181-00

NGL-09-011-004 Howard University   H. Branson
Research in space sciences.

Proposal	FY	Agreement Period	Amount
-004	65	6/65 - 5/68	84000
-013	67	9/67 - 8/69	43000
-019		9/68 - 8/70	29000

Tech. Off.:   Funding Element: HQ-GSFC
CASE Code: 99   AWC: 125-24

NGR-09-011-006 Howard University   F. Senftle
Investigation of infra-red absorption and low angle x-ray scattering of tektites.

Proposal	FY	Agreement Period	Amount
-015	68	9/67 - 5/68	9998
-018	68	6/68 - 9/68	3000
-021	69	9/68 - 9/69	10000

Tech. Off.: SENPFLE   Funding Element: GSFC
CASE Code: 11   AWC: 185-42

NGT-09-011-001 Howard University   C. L. Miller
Training of predoctoral graduate students in space-related science and technology.

No. Students	FY	Agreement Period	Amount
5	65	9/65 - 8/68	104000
5	66	9/66 - 8/69	104200
3	67	9/67 - 8/70	62500

Tech. Off.: HANSING F D   Funding Element: HQ-Y
CASE Code: 99   AWC: 181-00

NGF-09-012-061 National Academy of Sciences   F. B. Seitz
Construction of a lunar science institute.

Proposal	FY	Agreement Period	Amount
-061	68	3/68 - 2/70	580000

Tech. Off.: HOLMES D C   Funding Element: HQ-Y
CASE Code: 32   AWC: 182-00

FLORIDA

NAS10-1255   **University of Florida**   **E. A. Farber**
Feasibility study on explosive effects of liquid propellants.

Proposal	FY	Agreement Period	Amount
		4/64 — 8/68	269000

Tech. Off.:   Funding Element: K S C
CASE Code: 1 2   AWC: 9 0 4 — 2 1

NAS10-5172   **Florida Institute of Technology**   **J. J. Frangie**
Apollo launch and support facilities.

Proposal	FY	Agreement Period	Amount
		9/67 — 9/69	38000

Tech. Off.: L I N D E M A N N R A   Funding Element: K S C
CASE Code: 9 9   AWC: 9 5 0 — 0 2

NGR-10-004-005   **Florida State University**   **L. Mandelkern**
Study of crystallization, crosslinking and dimensional changes during the crystal-liquid phase transition of oriented polymeric systems.

Proposal	FY	Agreement Period	Amount
—051	68	3/68 — 2/69	16994
		9/68 —10/69	NCE

Tech. Off.: A C H H A M M E R B G   Funding Element: H Q — R R
CASE Code: 1 3   AWC: 1 2 9 — 0 3

NGR-10-004-018   **Florida State University**   **H. Gaffron**
Photochemical transformation of acetate into algae cell material.

Proposal	FY	Agreement Period	Amount
—054	68	7/68 — 6/69	32500

Tech. Off.: G E I B D S   Funding Element: H Q — S B
CASE Code: 5 1   AWC: 1 8 9 — 5 5

NGR-10-004-029   **Florida State University**   **R. G. Cornell**
Space-related biostatistical studies, emphasizing microbiology and sterilization.

Proposal	FY	Agreement Period	Amount
—047	67	9/67 — 8/68	6400
—055	69	9/68 — 9/69	8800

Tech. Off.: H A L L L   Funding Element: H Q — S B
CASE Code: 5 1   AWC: 1 8 9 — 5 8

NGR-10-004-041   **Florida State University**   **W. Schwartz**
Microbial activity in non-aqueous systems.

Proposal	FY	Agreement Period	Amount
—041	68	9/67 — 8/68	26156
		9/68 — 5/69	NCE

Tech. Off.: S A U N D E R S J F   Funding Element: H Q — S B
CASE Code: 5 1   AWC: 1 8 9 — 5 4

NGR-10-004-056   **Florida State University**   **E. K. Plyler**
The infrared absorption from 0.8 to 1.5 microns of NH_3, CH_4 and CO_2.

Proposal	FY	Agreement Period	Amount
—056	69	2/69 — 1/70	42170

Tech. Off.: B R U N K W E   Funding Element: H Q — S L
CASE Code: 1 2   AWC: 1 8 5 — 4 1

NGR-10-004-058   **Florida State University**   **S. L. Hess**
Participation in the development of instruments for a Mars lander.

Proposal	FY	Agreement Period	Amount
—058	69	2/69 — 1/70	3350

Tech. Off.: M I T Z M A   Funding Element: H Q — S L
CASE Code: 4 2   AWC: 8 1 5 — 2 0

NGT-10-004-008   **Florida State University**   **R. J. Keirs**
Supporting the training of predoctoral graduate students in space-related science and technology.

No. Students	FY	Agreement Period	Amount
10	65	9/65 — 8/68	160900
10	66	9/66 — 8/69	166500
6	67	9/67 — 8/70	94400

Tech. Off.: H A N S I N G F D   Funding Element: H Q — Y
CASE Code: 9 9   AWC: 1 8 1 — 0 0

NGR-10-019-001   **Florida Technological University**   **H. N. Rexford**
The confinement and propagation of light beams.

Proposal	FY	Agreement Period	Amount
—001	68	3/68 — 2/69	12500

Tech. Off.:   Funding Element: G S F C
CASE Code: 1 1   AWC: 1 2 5 — 2 2

NGL-10-005-005   **University of Florida**   **L. E. Grinter**
Multidisciplinary program of research in space-related sciences and technology.

Proposal	FY	Agreement Period	Amount
—043	66	11/65 —10/68	335000
—067	67	11/66 —10/69	335000
—083	68	11/67 —10/70	125000

Tech. Off.:   Funding Element:
CASE Code: 9 9   AWC: 1 8 3 — 0 0

NGR-10-005-008   **University of Florida**   **A. E. S. Green**
Theoretical atmospheric physics.

Proposal	FY	Agreement Period	Amount
—051	66	5/66 — 4/68	64200
—094	68	5/68 — 4/70	50000

Tech. Off.: H O R O W I T Z R   Funding Element: H Q — S L
CASE Code: 1 1   AWC: 1 8 5 — 3 7

NGR-10-005-022   **University of Florida**   **R. D. Walker**
Gas solubilities and transport properties in fuel cell electrolytes.

Proposal	FY	Agreement Period	Amount
—022	66	9/65 — 8/68	92016
—100	69	9/68 — 8/69	34776

Tech. Off.: T O M A J   Funding Element: L E R C
CASE Code: 4 9   AWC: 1 2 3 — 3 4

FLORIDA   (Con't)

NGR-10-005-036   University of Florida   **G. E. Nevill**
Impact of shell type structures with continuous media.

Proposal	FY	Agreement Period	Amount
−036	66	4/66 − 3/68	43900
−036	66	3/68 − 9/68	NCE
−090	68	10/68 − 9/69	30000

Tech. Off.:   Funding Element:
CASE Code: 99   AWC: 124−08

NGL-10-005-039   University of Florida   **J. J. Hren**
Investigation of structure with the field ion microscope.

Proposal	FY	Agreement Period	Amount
−086	68	3/68 − 2/69	30000
−097	67	3/68 − 2/71	30000
−107	69	3/69 − 2/72	30000

Tech. Off.:   NASH R   Funding Element: HQ−RR
CASE Code: 46   AWC: 129−03

NGR-10-005-049   University of Florida   **R. T. Schneider**
Investigation of spectra in the vacuum UV and soft x-ray region.

Proposal	FY	Agreement Period	Amount
−093	68	3/68 − 2/69	19900
−105	69	3/69 − 2/70	26000

Tech. Off.:   OERTEL G K   Funding Element: HQ−SG
CASE Code: 13   AWC: 129−01

NGR-10-005-057   University of Florida   **W. B. Webb**
Studies of electroencephalographic patterns of sleep.

Proposal	FY	Agreement Period	Amount
−057	68	5/68 − 4/69	20000
−112	69	5/69 − 1/70	40000

Tech. Off.:   Funding Element:
CASE Code: 52   AWC: 189−52

NGR-10-005-080   University of Florida   **R. E. Hummel**
Electrotransport in thin films.

Proposal	FY	Agreement Period	Amount
−080	68	5/68 − 4/69	23273
−108	69	5/69 − 4/70	25000

Tech. Off.:   WEINBERG I   Funding Element: HQ−RR
CASE Code: 99   AWC: 129−03

NGL-10-005-082   University of Florida   **D. C. Goodman**
Dynamic interactions between cerebellum and primary vestibu-
lar neurons in the vestibular nuclear complex.

Proposal	FY	Agreement Period	Amount
−082	68	9/67 − 8/68	32275
−099	68	9/68 − 8/70	27000

Tech. Off.:   ANLIKER J   Funding Element: ERC
CASE Code: 52   AWC: 127−49

NGR-10-005-089   University of Florida   **R. T. Schneider**
Experimental investigation of a uranium plasma.

Proposal	FY	Agreement Period	Amount
−089	68	1/68 −12/68	62795
−109	69	1/69 −12/69	60000

Tech. Off.:   THOM K   Funding Element: HQ−RR
CASE Code: 13   AWC: 129−02

NSR-10-005-047   University of Florida   **H. Brown**
Analysis and synthesis of elastomers for use with liquid fluorine.

Proposal	FY	Agreement Period	Amount
−088		9/67 − 8/68	24999
−102	69	8/68 − 8/69	25000

Tech. Off.:   COMPITELLO F E   Funding Element: HQ−RP
CASE Code: 12   AWC: 128−31

NAS3-10412   University of Florida   **G. J. Schoessow**
Determination of triple point of carbon.

Proposal	FY	Agreement Period	Amount
		3/67 −12/67	31000

Tech. Off.:   Funding Element: LERC
CASE Code: 12   AWC: 122−28

NGT-10-005-006   University of Florida   **L. E. Grinter**
Supporting the training of predoctoral graduate students in
space-related science and technology.

No. Students	FY	Agreement Period	Amount
12	65	9/65 − 8/68	212400
12	66	9/66 − 8/69	217800

Tech. Off.:   HANSING F D   Funding Element: HQ−Y
CASE Code: 99   AWC: 181−00

NGF-10-005-024   University of Florida   **L. E. Grinter**
Construction of research laboratory facilities to be known as the
Space Sciences Building.

Proposal	FY	Agreement Period	Amount
−024	65	7/65 − 6/67	1190000

Tech. Off.:   HOLMES D C   Funding Element: HQ−Y
CASE Code: 99   AWC: 182−00

NGR-10-007-008   University of Miami   **S. W. Fox**
Space related biology, molecular evolution and aspects of
extraterrestrial environment.

Proposal	FY	Agreement Period	Amount
−063	68	10/67 − 9/68	166220
−071	69	10/68 − 9/69	160000

Tech. Off.:   GEIB D S   Funding Element: HQ−SB
CASE Code: 51   AWC: 185−

NGL-10-007-010   University of Miami   **E. H. Man**
Multidisciplinary research in Space Sciences.

Proposal	FY	Agreement Period	Amount
−010	66	11/66 −10/68	400000
−046	67	11/66 −10/69	200000
−060	68	11/67 −10/70	200000
−074	69	11/68 −10/71	200000

Tech. Off.:   REDDING F R   Funding Element: HQ−Y
CASE Code: 99   AWC: 183−00

FLORIDA (Cont'd.)

NGR-10-007-052   University of Miami   K. Harada
Study of optical activity in the context of pre-biological chemistry.

Proposal	FY	Agreement Period	Amount
-052	68	10/67 - 9/68	23040
-072	69	10/68 - 9/69	23000

Tech. Off.: GEIB D S   Funding Element: HQ-SB
CASE Code: 51   AWC: 189-55

NGR-10-007-054   University of Miami   G. Mueller
Comparative studies of the organic and inorganic chemistry, mineralogy and petrology of the earth's crust, the meteorites and lunar rocks.

Proposal	FY	Agreement Period	Amount
-054	68	10/67 - 9/68	10600
-073	69	10/68 - 9/69	10600

Tech. Off.: GEIB D S   Funding Element: HQ-SB
CASE Code: 12   AWC: 189-55

NGL-10-007-067   University of Miami   F. D. Kohler
The impact of Soviet and U.S. space and aeronautic programs and policies on societies and systems of the USSR and the U.S.

Proposal	FY	Agreement Period	Amount
-067	68	3/68 - 2/71	200000
-069	68	3/68 - 3/71	50000

Tech. Off.: PRYOR H E   Funding Element: HQ-KD
CASE Code: 76   AWC: 183-00

NGR-10-007-068   University of Miami   F. D. Kohler
The correlation of U.S. and Soviet space and oceanographic program.

Proposal	FY	Agreement Period	Amount
-068	68	5/68 - 4/71	120000

Tech. Off.: QUINN H B   Funding Element: HQ-Y
CASE Code: 33   AWC: 183-00

NSR-10-007-078   University of Miami   D. L. Harvey
Support to develop a comprehensive catalogue-index of available NASA in-house information resources for use by NASA management and by NASA research grantees, including the University of Miami, in understanding, evaluating and interpreting NASA programs.

Proposal	FY	Agreement Period	Amount
-078		6/69 -12/69	10499

Tech. Off.: GREENGLASS B   Funding Element: HQ-UB
CASE Code: 99   AWC: 636-01

NAS9-8101   University of Miami   S. Sox
Analysis of organic lunar samples for oc-amino acids and polymers thereof—lunar sample analysis program.

Proposal	FY	Agreement Period	Amount
	69	9/68 - 3/70	83000

Tech. Off.:   Funding Element:
CASE Code: 51   AWC: 914-40

NGT-10-007-006   University of Miami   J. A. Harrison
Training of predoctoral graduate students in space-related science and technology.

No. Students:	FY	Agreement Period	Amount
6	65	9/65 - 8/68	106200
6	66	9/66 - 8/69	106200
3	67	9/67 - 8/70	53100

Tech. Off.: HANSING F D   Funding Element: HQ-Y
CASE Code: 99   AWC: 181-00

NGR-10-007-070   University of Miami   M. L. Harvey
The U. S. Entry into the Space Age: an analytical accounting of the process of organizing and administering NASA 1961-1971, and the implications for U. S. national interests and purposes.

Proposal	FY	Agreement Period	Amount
-070	68	9/68 - 8/71	150000

Tech. Off.: STEPHENS R E   Funding Element: HQ-Y
CASE Code: 99   AWC: 183-00

NGR-10-008-005   University of South Florida   H. K. E. Wurmb
Mathematical techniques connected with problems in positional astronomy.

Proposal	FY	Agreement Period	Amount
-005	66	6/66 - 5/67	12800
-005	66	6/67 -12/67	NCE
-005	66	1/68 - 8/68	NCE
		- 4/69	NCE

Tech. Off.: WILSON R   Funding Element: RR
CASE Code: 21   AWC: 129-04

NGR-10-008-019   University of South Florida   H. K. Eichhorn
Use of geodetic satellites and techniques on astrometric investigations.

Proposal	FY	Agreement Period	Amount
-019	68	6/68 - 2/69	27500
		3/69 - 9/69	NCE
-023		6/69 - 5/70	15000

Tech. Off.: ROSENBERG J D   Funding Element: HQ-SA
CASE Code: 11   AWC: 160-43

NSR-10-008-021   University of South Florida   M. G. Kobasky
To hold a three-day conference on space food technology.

Proposal	FY	Agreement Period	Amount
-021	69	3/69 - 9/69	5597

Tech. Off.: PECORARO J N   Funding Element: HQ-RB
CASE Code: 59   AWC: 127-53

GEORGIA

NGR-11-001-009   Emory University   V. P. Popovic
Cardiovascular adaptation during long-term weightlessness.

Proposal	FY	Agreement Period	Amount
-020	67	5/67 - 4/68	50000
-027	68	5/68 - 4/69	50000

Tech. Off.: SAUNDERS J F   Funding Element: HQ-SB
CASE Code: 52   AWC: 189-54

GEORGIA (Cont'd.)

NGR-11-001-012   Emory University   B. W. Robinson
Control and analysis of primate behavior by brain telestimulation and telemetry.

Proposal	FY	Agreement Period	Amount
-018	68	8/67 - 7/68	85000
-029	69	8/68 - 7/69	47613

Tech. Off.: WEISSMAN N W   Funding Element: HQ-SB
CASE Code: 51   AWC: 189-52

NGR-11-001-016   Emory University   G. H. Bourne
Histopathological and histochemical study of sub-human primates.

Proposal	FY	Agreement Period	Amount
-028	68	12/67 -11/68	50000
-028	69	12/68 -11/69	78000

Tech. Off.: MASON E E   Funding Element: LARC
CASE Code: 52   AWC: 127-49

NGR-11-001-031   Emory University   S. W. Gray
The effects of weightlessness on the growth and orientation of roots and shoots of monocotyledenous seedlings.

Proposal	FY	Agreement Period	Amount
-031	69	3/69 - 2/70	62987

Tech. Off.: SAUNDERS J F   Funding Element: HQ-SB
CASE Code: 59   AWC: 189-54

NGT-11-001-005   Emory University   C. T. Lester
Training of predoctoral graduate students in space-related science and technology.

No. Students:	FY	Agreement Period	Amount
3	65	9/65 - 8/68	57600
4	66	9/66 - 8/69	76800
2	67	9/67 - 8/70	38400

Tech. Off.: HANSING F D   Funding Element: HQ-Y
CASE Code: 99   AWC: 181-00

NGR-11-002-004   Georgia Institute of Technology   H. D. Edwards
Theoretical and experimental studies of high altitude chemical release.

Proposal	FY	Agreement Period	Amount
-029	65	12/67 - 5/68	NCE
-077	68	6/68 - 5/69	40000

Tech. Off.: HOROWITZ R   Funding Element: HQ-SL
CASE Code: 31   AWC: 185-37

NGL-11-002-005   Georgia Institute of Technology   J. A. Knight
Chemical reactivity of hydrogen, nitrogen, and oxygen atoms at temperatures below 100°K.

Proposal	FY	Agreement Period	Amount
-058	66	1/66 -12/68	75000
-058	67	1/67 -12/69	40000
-079	68	1/68 -12/71	40000

Tech. Off.: HIPSHER H F   Funding Element: HQ-SL
CASE Code: 12   AWC: 185-37

NGL-11-002-018   Georgia Institute of Technology
K. Picha, V. Crawford
Multidisciplinary research in space sciences and technology.

Proposal	FY	Agreement Period	Amount
-046	66	3/66 - 3/69	300000
-057	67	3/67 - 2/70	300000
-075	68	3/68 - 3/71	100000

Tech. Off.: QUINN H B   Funding Element: HQ-Y
CASE Code: 99   AWC: 183-00

NGL-11-002-062   Georgia Institute of Technology   A. Ben Huang
Study of non-linear rarefied gas flows by the discrete ordinate method.

Proposal	FY	Agreement Period	Amount
-062	68	2/68 - 1/69	34836
-087	67	2/69 - 1/71	35000
-100	69	2/69 - 1/72	35000

Tech. Off.: SCHWARTZ I R •   Funding Element: HQ-RR
CASE Code: 13   AWC: 129-01

NGR-11-002-068   Georgia Institute of Technology   J. D. Clement
The attenuation of radiant energy in hot seeded hydrogen—an experimental study related to the gaseous core nuclear rocket.

Proposal	FY	Agreement Period	Amount
-068	68	9/67 - 8/68	58599
-086	69	9/68 - 8/69	57309

Tech. Off.: MASSER C C   Funding Element: LERC
CASE Code: 13   AWC: 122-28

NGR-11-002-081   Georgia Institute of Technology   V. Crawford
Phase II—predoctoral design training grant.

Proposal	FY	Agreement Period	Amount
-081	67	6/68 - 5/71	30948
-084	68	6/68 - 8/71	38200
-093		9/69 - 8/71	38200

Tech. Off.: VITALE J A   Funding Element: HQ-Y
CASE Code: 99   AWC: 183-00

NGR-11-002-083   Georgia Institute of Technology   B. T. Zinn
Application of the Galerkin method in the design of stable liquid rocket motors.

Proposal	FY	Agreement Period	Amount
-083	68	8/68 - 7/69	29604
			LERC

Tech. Off.: MARIANI T R   Funding Element: LERC
CASE Code: 46   AWC: 128-31

NGR-11-002-085   Georgia Institute of Technology   B. T. Zinn
Behavior of nozzles and acoustic liners in three-dimensional acoustic fields.

Proposal	FY	Agreement Period	Amount
-085	69	3/69 - 2/70	50000
-085	69	3/69 - 2/70	48980

Tech. Off.: STRONG J S   Funding Element: MSFC
CASE Code: 41   AWC: 128-31

GEORGIA (Con't)

NGR-11-002-096   Georgia Institute of Technology
Research on stability of large shells.

Proposal	FY	Agreement Period	Amount
−096	69	5/69 − 5/70	95000

Tech. Off.: PETERS R W   Funding Element: LARC
CASE Code: 46   AWC: 124−08

NGR-11-002-101   Georgia Institute of Technology   I. E. Perlin
Research in precision numerical integration methods.

Proposal	FY	Agreement Period	Amount
−101	69	4/69 − 4/70	10000

Tech. Off.: SCHMIEDER D H   Funding Element: ERC
CASE Code: 21   AWC: 129−04

NAS2-5016   Georgia Institute of Technology
Study for improved microwave cavities for polymer and biological ESR measurements.

Proposal	FY	Agreement Period	Amount
	68	6/68 − 6/69	23000

Tech. Off.:   Funding Element: ARC
CASE Code: 51   AWC: 129−03

NAS8-2473   Georgia Institute of Technology   J. L. Hammond
Development of new methods & applications to analog computations.

Proposal	FY	Agreement Period	Amount
	66	9/61 − 3/69	40000
	66	9/61 − 6/69	20000

Tech. Off.: POLSTORFF   Funding Element: MSFC
CASE Code: 21   AWC: 125−23

NGT-11-002-006   Georgia Institute of Technology   T. W. Jackson
Training of predoctoral graduate students in space-related science and technology.

No. Students	FY	Agreement Period	Amount
15	65	9/65 − 8/68	288000
15	66	9/66 − 8/69	272900
8	67	9/67 − 8/70	130000

Tech. Off.: HANSING F D   Funding Element: HQ−Y
CASE Code: 99   AWC: 181−00

NGT-11-002-064   Georgia Institute of Technology   J. A. Vitale
Supporting the training of predoctoral graduate students in the field of engineering design.

No. Students	FY	Agreement Period	Amount
	67	9/67 − 8/70	96000

Tech. Off.: HANSING F D   Funding Element: HQ−Y
CASE Code: 99   AWC: 181−00

NGF-11-002-012   Georgia Institute of Technology   K. G. Picha
Phase One of the construction of Space Sciences and Technology Center.

Proposal	FY	Agreement Period	Amount
8495	64	5/64 − 3/66	1000000
8495	66	3/66 − 9/66	NCE

Tech. Off.: HOLMES D C   Funding Element: HQ−Y
CASE Code: 49   AWC: 182−00

NGR-11-003-021   University of Georgia   D. R. Tompkins
A cosmic ray search for fast magnetic charges.

Proposal	FY	Agreement Period	Amount
−021	68	1/68 −12/68	20000
−025		6/69 − 5/70	20000

Tech. Off.:   Funding Element:
CASE Code: 13   AWC: 188−46

NGT-11-003-002   University of Georgia   G. B. Huff
Training of predoctoral graduate students in space-related science and technology.

No. Students	FY	Agreement Period	Amount
10	65	9/65 − 8/68	192000
10	66	9/66 − 8/69	192000
6	67	9/67 − 8/70	115200

Tech. Off.: HANSING F D   Funding Element: HQ−Y
CASE Code: 99   AWC: 181−00

HAWAII

NGR-12-001-002   University of Hawaii   K. Watanabe
Theoretical and experimental investigation of electron emission, conductivity and luminescence of selected solids under vacuum ultraviolet excitation.

Proposal	FY	Agreement Period	Amount
−037	68	9/67 − 8/68	25483
		−12/68	NCE
−058	69	1/69 −12/69	15000

Tech. Off.: OH E   Funding Element: HQ−SG
CASE Code: 13   AWC: 188−37

NGR-12-001-011   University of Hawaii   J. T. Jefferies
Research in coronal and chromospheric physics.

Proposal	FY	Agreement Period	Amount
−052	68	11/67 −10/68	397349
−060	69	11/68 −10/69	263961
−068	69	11/68 −10/71	270000

Tech. Off.: GLASER   Funding Element: HQ−SG
CASE Code: 13   AWC: 188−38

NGL-12-001-042   University of Hawaii   S. M. Siegel
The performance and capabilities of terrestrial organisms in extreme and unusual gaseous and liquid environments.

Proposal	FY	Agreement Period	Amount
−042	67	7/67 − 6/68	50685
−042	68	7/68 − 6/69	50823
−056	68	7/68 − 6/71	44870

Tech. Off.: SAUNDERS J F   Funding Element: HQ−SB
CASE Code: 51   AWC: 189−54

HAWAII (Cont'd.)

NGR-12-001-046   University of Hawaii   W. W. Peterson
Research in information transmission and processing.

Proposal	FY	Agreement Period	Amount
-046	68	1/68 -12/68	26981
			ERC

Tech. Off.: PRANGE E   Funding Element: ERC
CASE Code: 45   AWC: 125-21

NGR-12-001-053   University of Hawaii   S. M. Siegel
Role of gravitational stress in land plant evolution: the gravitational factor in lignification.

Proposal	FY	Agreement Period	Amount
-053	68	5/68 - 4/69	24847

Tech. Off.:   Funding Element:
CASE Code: 51   AWC: 945-82

NGR-12-001-057   University of Hawaii   J. T. Jefferies
Research in planetary studies.

Proposal	FY	Agreement Period	Amount
-057	68	7/68 - 6/69	201558

Tech. Off.:   Funding Element:
CASE Code: 11   AWC: 185-41

NASr-5   University of Hawaii   H. C. McAllister
(NSR-12-001-003) Design studies and experimental evaluations of a stigmatic spectrograph with nominal dispersion of 1A/mm and resolution of 0.01A, useful in the spectral range from 1000 A to 3000 A, and of sufficient compactness and speed to be suitable for use in a rocket vehicle.

Proposal	FY	Agreement Period	Amount
-051	68	9/67 - 8/68	248554
		8/68 -12/68	NCE
		12/68 - 2/69	NCE
		3/69	NCE
-063	69	4/69 -10/69	875152

Tech. Off.: GLASER   Funding Element: HQ-SG
CASE Code: 46   AWC: 188-38

NSR-12-001-019   University of Hawaii   J. T. Jefferies
Design, development, fabrication and installation of 84" telescope suitable for lunar, planetary and stellar observations.

Proposal	FY	Agreement Period	Amount
-039	67	7/67 - 6/68	320000
-040	67	7/67 - 6/68	500000
-040	67	6/68 - 6/69	NCE

Tech. Off.: BRUNK W E   Funding Element: HQ-SL
CASE Code: 46   AWC: 185-41

NSR-12-001-055   University of Hawaii   G. P. Woollard
Development of an interim global geometric system from a combination of satellite observations.

Proposal	FY	Agreement Period	Amount
-055	68	6/68 - 2/69	112704
	68	6/69	NCE

Tech. Off.:   Funding Element:
CASE Code: 46   AWC: 855-

NGT-12-001-005   University of Hawaii   W. Gorter
Supporting the training of predoctoral graduate students in space-related science and technology.

No. Students:	FY	Agreement Period	Amount
4	65	9/65 - 8/68	60000
5	66	9/66 - 8/69	76000
3	67	9/67 - 8/70	40700

Tech. Off.: HANSING F D   Funding Element: HQ-Y
CASE Code: 99   AWC: 181-00

IDAHO

NGT-13-001-001   University of Idaho   M. L. Jackson
Training of predoctoral graduate students in space-related science and technology.

No. Students:	FY	Agreement Period	Amount
4	65	9/65 - 8/68	70800
4	66	9/66 - 8/69	70800
2	67	9/67 - 8/70	36300

Tech. Off.: HANSING F D   Funding Element: HQ-Y
CASE Code: 99   AWC: 181-00

ILLINOIS

NGR-14-019-002   Bradley University   J. W. McNabb
Determination of test transients for the environmental testing of future spacecraft by comparison of flight data from the Lunar Orbiter series of flights with digital computer out-put for a multi-degree-of-freedom mathematical model for the Lunar Orbiter Spacecraft.

Proposal	FY	Agreement Period	Amount
-002	69	9/69 - 2/71	14945

Tech. Off.: HOWLETT J T   Funding Element: LARC
CASE Code: 41   AWC: 124-08

NAS2-5254   Bradley University
Study of phase estimate improvements for costas and conventional phase lock loops.

Proposal	FY	Agreement Period	Amount
	69	1/69 - 8/69	7000

Tech. Off.:   Funding Element: ARC
CASE Code: 99   AWC: 125-21

NGL-14-001-001   University of Chicago   E. N. Parker
Theoretical investigations of the effect of the solar wind in interplanetary space, and its association with terrestrial phenomena.

Proposal	FY	Agreement Period	Amount
-112	68	8/67 - 7/70	62609

Tech. Off.: GLASER   Funding Element: HQ-SG
CASE Code: 31   AWC: 185-38

ILLINOIS (Cont'd.)

NGR-14-001-005   **University of Chicago**   **P. Meyer**

Composition, energy spectrum and intensity of primary cosmic radiation.

Proposal	FY	Agreement Period	Amount
-069	66	11/65 -10/68	319556
-091	67	11/66 -10/69	252190
-114	68	11/66 -10/68	161000
-124	69	10/68 -10/69	319000

Tech. Off.: KAVANAGH L D JR   Funding Element: HQ-SG
CASE Code: 11   AWC: 188-46

NGL-14-001-006   **University of Chicago**   **J. A. Simpson**

Experimental and theoretical studies of energetic particles and electrodynamical processes in interplanetary space and in the vicinity of planets.

Proposal	FY	Agreement Period	Amount
-075	66	8/65 - 7/68	243188
-097	67	8/66 - 7/69	243188
-116	68	8/67 - 7/69	129000
-132	69	8/68 - 8/71	289000

Tech. Off.: SCHARDT A W   Funding Element: HQ-SG
CASE Code: 31   AWC: 185-46

NGR-14-001-008   **University of Chicago**   **T. Fujita**

Meteorological interpretation of satellite radiation data.

Proposal	FY	Agreement Period	Amount
-107	68	10/67 - 9/68	60000
-127	69	10/68 - 9/69	75000

Tech. Off.: BANDEEN W   Funding Element: GSFC
CASE Code: 31   AWC: 160-44

NGL-14-001-009   **University of Chicago**   **M. H. Cohen**

Theoretical and experimental investigations of superconductivity.

Proposal	FY	Agreement Period	Amount
-073	66	3/66 - 2/69	100000
-098	67	3/67 - 2/70	85000
-118	68	3/68 - 2/71	85000

Tech. Off.: JOHNSON P   Funding Element: HQ-RR
CASE Code: 99   AWC: 129-02

NGR-14-001-010   **University of Chicago**   **E. Anders**

Investigation of origin, age and composition of meteorites.

Proposal	FY	Agreement Period	Amount
-108	68	10/67 - 9/68	100000
-129	69	10/68 - 9/69	50000

Tech. Off.: BRYSON R P   Funding Element: HQ-MA
CASE Code: 32   AWC: 185-45

NGL-14-001-013   **University of Chicago**   **C. O. Hines**

An investigation of upper atmosphere dynamics.

Proposal	FY	Agreement Period	Amount
-057	64	7/65 - 6/68	83574
-111	67	1/68 -12/70	36823
-085	67	7/66 - 6/69	55522

Tech. Off.: HOROWITZ R   Funding Element: HQ-SL
CASE Code: 31   AWC: 185-47

NGR-14-001-054   **University of Chicago**   **W. A. Hiltner**

Variable polarization of the visible radiation from magnetic variable stars.

Proposal	FY	Agreement Period	Amount
-082	67	11/66 -10/67	20963
-054	65	11/66 -12/66	NCE
-082	67	11/67 -10/68	NCE
-119	69	11/68 -10/69	16503

Tech. Off.: ROMAN N G   Funding Element: HQ-SG
CASE Code: 11   AWC: 188-41

NGR-14-001-060   **University of Chicago**   **C. R. O'Dell**

Study of comet tails by photoelectric spectrophotometry.

Proposal	FY	Agreement Period	Amount
-120	68	6/68 - 8/69	18421

Tech. Off.: DUBIN M   Funding Element: HQ-SG
CASE Code: 12   AWC: 188-45

NGR-14-001-103   **University of Chicago**   **J. E. Lamport**

Advance technical development in support of scientific experiments in space.

Proposal	FY	Agreement Period	Amount
-103	68	1/68 -12/68	216794
		12/68 - 4/69	NCE

Tech. Off.:   Funding Element:
CASE Code: 99   AWC: 188-46

NGR-14-001-128   **University of Chicago**   **A. Turkevich**

Surveyor V, VI, and VII post mission data analysis.

Proposal	FY	Agreement Period	Amount
-128	69	8/68 - 6/69	106202

Tech. Off.: BRYSON R P   Funding Element: HQ-MA
CASE Code: 42   AWC: 383-10

NGR-14-001-135   **University of Chicago**   **A. L. Turkeviuh**

Feasibility of the alpha scattering technique for Martian survey analysis.

Proposal	FY	Agreement Period	Amount
-135	69	11/68 - 8/69	36008

Tech. Off.: DWORNIK S E   Funding Element: HQ-SL
CASE Code: 99   AWC: 185-50

NAS2-3876   **University of Chicago**   **J. A. Simpson**

Pioneer A & B post launch analysis.

Proposal	FY	Agreement Period	Amount
		8/66 - 9/68	257000

Tech. Off.: HALL C   Funding Element: MSC
CASE Code: 41   AWC: 811-12

NAS5-3095   **University of Chicago**   **J. A. Simpson**

Instrumentation & support for energetic particles experiment for S-50 observatory.

Proposal	FY	Agreement Period	Amount
		12/62 -12/68	826000
	65	11/62 -12/68	45000
	68	11/62 -12/68	50000
	66	11/62 -12/68	40000

Tech. Off.: MERCANTI E   Funding Element: GSFC
CASE Code: 11   AWC: 841-12

ILLINOIS (Cont'd.)

NAS5-9090   University of Chicago   J. A. Simpson
Solid state cosmic ray telescope experiment.

Proposal	FY	Agreement Period	Amount
		12/64 – 6/68	737000
	68	12/64 –12/68	21000
	68	12/64 –12/68	25000

Tech. Off.: BUTLER P   Funding Element: GSFC
CASE Code: 12   AWC: 861–22

NAS5-9096   University of Chicago   P. Meyer
Cosmic ray electron experiment, associated equipment and support.

Proposal	FY	Agreement Period	Amount
	67	11/64 – 4/70	80000

Tech. Off.:   Funding Element: GSFC
CASE Code: 12   AWC: 841–12

NAS5-9366   University of Chicago   J. A. Simpson
Low energy heavy cosmic ray particles experiment for OGO-E spacecraft.

Proposal	FY	Agreement Period	Amount
	66	6/66 – 4/70	52000
	68	6/66 – 4/70	74000

Tech. Off.: MERCANTI E   Funding Element: GSFC
CASE Code: 12   AWC: 841–12

NAS5-11037   University of Chicago   J. A. Simpson
IMP-I solar particles radiation experiment.

Proposal	FY	Agreement Period	Amount
		8/67 –12/69	193000

Tech. Off.: BUTLER P   Funding Element: GSFC
CASE Code: 31   AWC: 861–52

NAS8-21449   University of Chicago   P. Meyer
Definition of Experiment S-74—Primary Cosmic Ray Electrons.

Proposal	FY	Agreement Period	Amount
	68	6/68 – 2/69	99000

Tech. Off.:   Funding Element: MSFC
CASE Code: 11   AWC: 945–84

NAS9-7883   University of Chicago
Neutron activation analysis and measurements of intrinsic radioactivity.

Proposal	FY	Agreement Period	Amount
	68	6/68 –12/69	56000

Tech. Off.:   Funding Element: MSC
CASE Code: 11   AWC: 914–40

NAS9-7887   University of Chicago   A. Edward
Measurement and analysis of two types of trace elements.

Proposal	FY	Agreement Period	Amount
	68	6/68 – 7/69	79000

Tech. Off.:   Funding Element: MSC
CASE Code: 12   AWC: 914–40

NAS9-7888   University of Chicago
Determine stable isotope of oxygen study.

Proposal	FY	Agreement Period	Amount
	68	6/68 –12/69	19000

Tech. Off.:   Funding Element: MSC
CASE Code: 12   AWC: 914–40

NAS9-8080   University of Chicago
Measure oxidation state of iron radiation damage and al na and fe energy state in crystals.

Proposal	FY	Agreement Period	Amount
	68	6/68 –12/69	40000

Tech. Off.:   Funding Element: MSC
CASE Code: 32   AWC: 914–40

NAS9-8086   University of Chicago   J. V. Smith
Mineralogic-petrographic analysis using microprobe, x-ray diffraction and microscopic methods.

Proposal	FY	Agreement Period	Amount
	68	6/68 –12/69	30000

Tech. Off.:   Funding Element: MSC
CASE Code: 32   AWC: 914–40

NAS9-9103   University of Chicago   J. H. Rust
Study of irradiation.

Proposal	FY	Agreement Period	Amount
	69	2/69 – 2/70	35000

Tech. Off.: BARNES C M   Funding Element: MSC
CASE Code: 52   AWC: 914–50

NGT-14-001-015   University of Chicago   C. D. O'Connell
Training of predoctoral graduate students in space-related science and technology.

No. Students	FY	Agreement Period	Amount
15	65	9/65 – 8/68	310500
15	66	9/66 – 8/69	294700
9	67	9/67 – 8/70	175400

Tech. Off.: HANSING F D   Funding Element: HQ–Y
CASE Code: 99   AWC: 181–00

NGF-14-001-016   University of Chicago   J. A. Simson
Space science research facilities.

Proposal	FY	Agreement Period	Amount
3588	62	9/62 – 9/65	1749039

Tech. Off.: HOLMES D C   Funding Element: HQ–Y
CASE Code: 19   AWC: 182–00

NGR-14-004-028   Illinois Institute of Technology   Z. Lavan
Numerical solutions and visual display of flow over aerodynamic bodies.

Proposal	FY	Agreement Period	Amount
–028	68	9/67 – 8/68	29822
–028	68	7/68 –10/68	NCE
–038	69	10/68 – 9/69	29822

Tech. Off.: RAGSDALE R   Funding Element: LERC
CASE Code: 41   AWC: 122–28

ILLINOIS (Cont'd.)

NAS5-9590 Illinois Institute of Technology C. Vest
Vacuum test of instrument size gears.

Proposal	FY	Agreement Period	Amount
		6/65 – 4/68	88000

Tech. Off.: VEST C Funding Element: GSFC
CASE Code: 99 AWC: 125-23

NAS7-388 Illinois Institute of Technology
Study the completion of design data for pressurized gas systems. Follow-on to contract NAS7-105 with Stanford Research Institute.

Proposal	FY	Agreement Period	Amount
	67	6/65 – 7/68	25000
			WOO

Tech. Off.: Funding Element:
CASE Code: 46 AWC: 128-31

NAS9-7651 Illinois Institute of Technology
Suitability of glycol/water for use in Apollo electric power system.

Proposal	FY	Agreement Period	Amount
	68	1/68 – 6/68	45000

Tech. Off.: Funding Element: MSC
CASE Code: 45 AWC: 914-50

NAS-12-650 Illinois Institute of Technology
Application of network analysis for system application program to the design of communication circuits.

Proposal	FY	Agreement Period	Amount
	68	4/68 – 5/69	10000
			ERC

Tech. Off.: Funding Element:
CASE Code: 45 AWC: 125-25

NAS12-2064 Illinois Institute of Technology T. Webber
Designers manual for computer-aided design.

Proposal	FY	Agreement Period	Amount
	69	1/69 –11/69	15000

Tech. Off.: Funding Element:
CASE Code: 21 AWC: 125-25

NGT-14-004-002 Illinois Institute of Technology A. Grad
Training of predoctoral graduate students in space-related science and technology.

No. Students	FY	Agreement Period	Amount
12	65	9/65 – 8/68	250700
12	66	9/66 – 8/69	250800
6	67	9/67 – 8/70	108400

Tech. Off.: HANSING F D Funding Element: HQ-Y
CASE Code: 99 AWC: 181-00

NGR-14-012-004 University of Illinois (Chicago) J. H. Boyer
Nitrogen chemistry significant to primordial systems.

Proposal	FY	Agreement Period	Amount
-011	68	1/68 –12/68	60000
-015	69	1/69 –12/69	45000

Tech. Off.: GEIB D S Funding Element: HQ-SB
CASE Code: 51 AWC: 189-55

NGL-14-012-012 University of Illinois (Chicago) P. R. Nachtsheim
Turbulent mixing of chemically reacting nonequilibrium gases according to a simplified statistical description.

Proposal	FY	Agreement Period	Amount
-031	68	1/69 –12/70	40000
-019		1/69 –12/70	15000

Tech. Off.: NACHTSHEIM P R Funding Element: ARC
CASE Code: 12 AWC: 129-01

NGF-14-005-020 University of Illinois (Urbana) D. Alpert
Construction of research laboratory facilities housing space science research center at the University of Illinois.

Proposal	FY	Agreement Period	Amount
3381	64	8/64 – 8/66	1125000

Tech. Off.: HOLMES D C Funding Element: HQ-Y
CASE Code: 99 AWC: 182-00

NGR-14-005-002 University of Illinois (Urbana) E. C. Yeh
Theoretical and experimental studies of ionospheric electron control and irregularities.

Proposal	FY	Agreement Period	Amount
-113	68	7/67 – 6/68	100000
	69	7/68 – 6/69	75000

Tech. Off.: SCHMERLING E R Funding Element: HQ-SG
CASE Code: 31 AWC: 188-36

NGR-14-005-009 University of Illinois (Urbana) R. Mittra
A study of selected radiation and propagation problems related to antennas and probes in magneto-ionic media.

Proposal	FY	Agreement Period	Amount
-114	68	9/67 – 8/68	47871
-132	69	9/68 – 8/69	45000

Tech. Off.: SCHMERLING E R Funding Element: HQ-SG
CASE Code: 99 AWC: 188-39

NGR-14-005-013 University of Illinois (Urbana) S. A. Bowhill
Investigations and studies of electron density and collision frequency in the lower ionosphere (D and E regions).

Proposal	FY	Agreement Period	Amount
-122	68	8/67 – 7/68	230000
-135	69	8/68 – 7/69	250000

Tech. Off.: SCHMERLING E R Funding Element: HQ-SG
CASE Code: 11 AWC: 879-10

ILLINOIS (Cont'd.)

NGR-14-005-025   University of Illinois (Urbana)   J. D. Morrow

Study of the cause and significance of accelerated creep resulting from repeated stress reversals.

Proposal	FY	Agreement Period	Amount
-025	65	5/65 - 4/68	75231
		4/69	NCE
		- 8/70	NCE

Tech. Off.:   Funding Element: L E R C
CASE Code: 1 3   AWC: 7 2 0 - 0 3

NGL-14-005-074   University of Illinois (Urbana)   H. W. Ades

Physiological responses of central vestibular pathways and diffuse ascending systems to vestibular stimulation.

Proposal	FY	Agreement Period	Amount
-116	68	10/67 - 9/68	160000
-133	68	10/68 - 9/70	160000

Tech. Off.: A N D E R S O N L O   Funding Element: H Q - R B
CASE Code: 5 1   AWC: 1 2 7 - 4 9

NGR-14-005-088   University of Illinois (Urbana)   G. C. McVittie

Investigation of relativistic effects on space tracking data.

Proposal	FY	Agreement Period	Amount
-105	68	9/67 - 8/68	19274
		9/68 - 8/69	NCE

Tech. Off.: R O S E N B A U M B   Funding Element: G S F C
CASE Code: 2 1   AWC: 1 2 5 - 0 6

NGR-14-005-103   University of Illinois (Urbana)   J. C. Chato

Physiological and engineering study of advanced thermoregulatory systems for extravehicular space suits.

Proposal	FY	Agreement Period	Amount
-103	67	6/67 - 6/68	32985
-126	68	6/68 - 5/69	33735
-139	69	6/69 - 6/69	25000

Tech. Off.: B L A C K A B Y J R   Funding Element: A R C
CASE Code: 4 6   AWC: 1 2 7 - 5 3

NGR-14-005-111   University of Illinois (Urbana)   M. L. Babcock

A research program to study (1) relations between machine structure and syntactic relations of linguistic elements, and (2) the information bearing parameters displayed in time-domain speech signals.

Proposal	FY	Agreement Period	Amount
-111	68	7/67 - 6/68	80000
		6/68 - 1/69	NCE

Tech. Off.: L E A W   Funding Element: E R C
CASE Code: 1 3   AWC: 1 2 5 - 2 3

NGR-14-005-138   University of Illinois (Urbana)   A. M. Clausing

An analysis of film cooling as an alternate thermal protection system for spacecraft during atmospheric reentry.

Proposal	FY	Agreement Period	Amount
-138	69	2/69 - 1/70	22228

Tech. Off.: S W A N N R T   Funding Element: L A R C
CASE Code: 4 1   AWC: 1 2 4 - 0 8

NGR-14-005-140   University of Illinois (Urbana)   W. L. Chow

Research on fluid dynamic and heat transfer problems of modern air breathing propulsive systems.

Proposal	FY	Agreement Period	Amount
-140	69	6/69 - 6/70	39700

Tech. Off.: A N D E R S O N B H   Funding Element: L E R C
CASE Code: 4 9   AWC: 7 2 0 - 0 3

NAS8-21442   University of Illinois (Urbana)   D. D. Windlin

Study of an orbiting gyro experiment to measure gas density and base molecule surface interaction parameters.

Proposal	FY	Agreement Period	Amount
	68	6/68 - 6/69	29000
			MSFC

Tech. Off.:   Funding Element:
CASE Code: 3 1   AWC: 9 3 3 - 5 0

NGT-14-005-017   University of Illinois (Urbana)   D. Alpert

Training of predoctoral graduate students in space-related science and technology.

No. Students	FY	Agreement Period	Amount
15	65	9/65 - 8/68	310500
15	66	9/66 - 8/69	310500
9	67	9/67 - 8/70	168400

Tech. Off.: H A N S I N G F D   Funding Element: H Q - Y
CASE Code: 9 9   AWC: 1 8 1 - 0 0

NGR-14-007-011   Northwestern University   G. Herrmann

Stability nonconservative systems.

Proposal	FY	Agreement Period	Amount
-046	66	4/66 - 3/67	67111
-046	66	4/68 - 3/69	NCE
-046	66	4/67 - 3/68	NCE
		- 9/69	NCE

Tech. Off.: M A Y E R N   Funding Element: H Q - R V
CASE Code: 9 9   AWC: 1 2 4 - 0 8

NGR-14-007-016   Northwestern University   J. A. Hynek

Optical study and analysis of transient lunar phenomena.

Proposal	FY	Agreement Period	Amount
-066	67	6/67 - 5/68	77892
-076	68	6/68 - 5/69	70000
-079	68	6/68 - 5/71	70000
-083		6/69 - 5/72	71284

Tech. Off.: B R U N K W E   Funding Element: H Q - S L
CASE Code: 1 3   AWC: 1 8 5 - 4 1

NGR-14-007-027   Northwestern University   E. H. T. Whitten

Statistical evaluation of the chemistry, mineralogy, and rock types of selected test sites, and their relationship to remotely-sensed data.

Proposal	FY	Agreement Period	Amount
-040	66	8/65 - 7/68	125244
-040	66	8/68 - 7/69	NCE

Tech. Off.: R O S E N B E R G J D   Funding Element: H Q - S M
CASE Code: 2 1   AWC: 8 4 9 - 0 0

ILLINOIS (Cont'd.)

NGR-14-007-041   Northwestern University   S. S. Huang

Study of celestial objects of high angular moments.

Proposal	FY	Agreement Period	Amount
−061	67	1/68 − 4/68	NCE
−074	68	5/68 − 4/69	23000
−082	69	5/69 − 4/70	23016
−087		3/69 − 2/72	24000

Tech. Off.: ROMAN N G   Funding Element: HQ−SG
CASE Code: 1 1   AWC: 1 8 8 − 4 1

NGR-14-007-048   Northwestern University   K. G. Henize

Feasibility and design study of instrumentation for measuring sky brightness.

Proposal	FY	Agreement Period	Amount
−048	66	8/66 −12/67	68000
−080	69	7/68 − 6/69	35000

Tech. Off.: ROMAN N G   Funding Element: HQ−SG
CASE Code: 3 1   AWC: 1 8 8 − 4 1

NGL-14-007-058   Northwestern University   J. A. D. Copper

Research program in administration.

Proposal	FY	Agreement Period	Amount
−058	68	5/68 − 4/71	200000
−086		5/69 − 4/72	100000

Tech. Off.: STEPHENS R E   Funding Element: HQ−Y
CASE Code: 9 9   AWC: 1 8 3 − 0 0

NGR-14-007-062   Northwestern University   A. H. Rubenstein

Studies and analysis of the management of scientific research and development.

Proposal	FY	Agreement Period	Amount
−062	67	8/67 − 7/69	110000

Tech. Off.: BINGMAN C   Funding Element: HQ−EP
CASE Code: 9 9   AWC: 1 4 3 − 0 0

NGR-14-007-067   Northwestern University   G. Herrmann

Study of the dynamics of mechanical systems coupled to energy sources.

Proposal	FY	Agreement Period	Amount
−067	67	6/67 − 5/68	37220
−075	68	6/68 − 5/69	39391

Tech. Off.: REED W H   Funding Element: LARC
CASE Code: 9 9   AWC: 1 2 4 − 1 1

NGR-14-007-069   Northwestern University   K. G. Henize

Ultraviolet astronomical observations with an all-reflecting Schmidt telescope.

Proposal	FY	Agreement Period	Amount
−069	68	6/68 − 5/69	97418

Tech. Off.:   Funding Element:
CASE Code: 1 1   AWC: 9 4 5 − 8 4

NGR-14-007-071   Northwestern University   D. Mintzer

Microwave conductivity of slightly ionized gases.

Proposal	FY	Agreement Period	Amount
−071	69	1/69 −12/69	12056

Tech. Off.: KAHN D K   Funding Element: ERC
CASE Code: 1 3   AWC: 1 2 5 − 2 1

NGR-14-007-081   Northwestern University   J. T. Waber

Potential and charge distribution near a metal surface.

Proposal	FY	Agreement Period	Amount
−081		1/69 −12/69	25000

Tech. Off.: NASH R R   Funding Element: HQ−RR
CASE Code: 1 3   AWC: 1 2 9 − 0 3

NAS9-7222   Northwestern University   K. G. Henize

Apollo applications experiment development — Experiment SO19.

Proposal	FY	Agreement Period	Amount
	68	6/67 − 9/68	40000

Tech. Off.:   Funding Element: MSC
CASE Code: 2 1   AWC: 9 4 8 − 8 0

NGT-14-007-004   Northwestern University   R. H. Baker

Training of predoctoral graduate students in space-related science and technology.

No. Students	FY	Agreement Period	Amount
15	65	9/65 − 8/68	269 00
15	66	9/66 − 8/69	269 00
8	67	9/67 − 8/70	119800

Tech. Off.: HANSING F D   Funding Element: HQ−Y
CASE Code: 9 9   AWC: 1 8 1 − 0 0

NGR-14-008-002   Southern Illinois University   J. H. Lauchner

Study of advanced structural design concepts for future space missions.

Proposal	FY	Agreement Period	Amount
−010	66	4/66 − 3/69	85870
		− 1/70	NCE

Tech. Off.: MAYER N   Funding Element: HQ−RV
CASE Code: 4 6   AWC: 1 2 4 − 0 8

NGR-14-008-019   Southern Illinois University   P. K. Davis

Studies of the flow, bonding and damping characteristics of a squeeze film under dynamic conditions.

Proposal	FY	Agreement Period	Amount
−019	68	6/68 −10/69	19790

Tech. Off.:   Funding Element: LARC
CASE Code: 1 3   AWC: 1 2 4 − 0 8

NGT-14-008-008   Southern Illinois University   W. E. Simeone

Supporting the training of predoctoral graduate students in space-related science and technology.

No. Students	FY	Agreement Period	Amount
3	66	9/66 − 8/69	55800
2	67	9/67 − 8/70	37200

Tech. Off.: HANSING F D   Funding Element: HQ−Y
CASE Code: 9 9   AWC: 1 8 1 − 0 0

INDIANA

NGR-15-009-001   Ball State University   E. Montague
Study and analysis of space related developments in physical and biochemistry.

Proposal	FY	Agreement Period	Amount
-001	67	2/68 - 8/68	NCE
		8/68 -12/68	NCE
		-10/69	NCE

Tech. Off.: TUTTLE F B   Funding Element: HQ-FE
CASE Code: 51   AWC: 010-00

NGL-15-003-002   Indiana University   H. R. Johnson
A theoretical investigation of the steady-state interaction between radiation and matter in stellar atmospheres.

Proposal	FY	Agreement Period	Amount
-029	66	1/66 -12/68	81000
-042	67	1/67 -12/69	40500
-065	68	1/68 -12/70	40000
-080	69	1/69 -12/71	40000

Tech. Off.: BOGGESS N N   Funding Element: HQ-SG
CASE Code: 11   AWC: 188-41

NGR-15-003-007   Indiana University   W. D. Neff
An experimental investigation of the neurological correlates of information reception.

Proposal	FY	Agreement Period	Amount
-063	68	10/67 - 9/68	23750
-078	69	10/68 - 9/69	23735

Tech. Off.: WEISSMAN N W   Funding Element: HQ-SB
CASE Code: 51   AWC: 189-52

NGR-15-003-053   Indiana University   S. Mizell
Investigation of control mechanisms in physiological rhythms.

Proposal	FY	Agreement Period	Amount
-053	68	5/68 - 4/69	14076
-090		5/69 - 4/70	13875

Tech. Off.: SAUNDERS J F   Funding Element: HQ-SB
CASE Code: 51   AWC: 189-54

NGR-15-003-060   Indiana University   E. Hopf
Applications of functional and complex analysis to non-linear problems.

Proposal	FY	Agreement Period	Amount
-060	68	2/68 - 1/69	13000
-085		2/69 - 1/70	16342

Tech. Off.:   Funding Element:
CASE Code: 13   AWC: 129-04

NGR-15-003-064   Indiana University   J. R. Thompson
Application of mathematical statistics to digital data analysis.

Proposal	FY	Agreement Period	Amount
-064	68	6/68 - 5/69	15825

Tech. Off.: GRAHAM R L   Funding Element: MSFC
CASE Code: 21   AWC: 129-04

NGR-15-003-066   Indiana University   R. W. Campbell
Study of the impact of the space program on the Soviet economy.

Proposal	FY	Agreement Period	Amount
-066	68	2/68 - 1/69	30000
-084	69	1/69 - 6/69	23724

Tech. Off.: STEPHENS R F   Funding Element: HQ-Y
CASE Code: 72   AWC: 143-00

NGR-15-003-077   Indiana University   W. D. Neff
after exposure to sounds of high intensity.

Proposal	FY	Agreement Period	Amount
-077	68	7/68 - 6/69	30000

Tech. Off.: MERKIN A   Funding Element: HQ-RB
CASE Code: 13   AWC: 127-06

NSR-15-003-054   Indiana University   A. W. Weimer
An experiment in the decentralized reproduction and provision of hard-copy documents of aerospace generated technology contained in the NASA information resource.

Proposal	FY	Agreement Period	Amount
-054	67	4/67 - 3/68	42000
		4/68 - 5/69	NCE

Tech. Off.:   Funding Element:
CASE Code: 99   AWC: 141-00

NSR-15-003-067   Indiana University   L. Orr
An input-output analysis of the space program.

Proposal	FY	Agreement Period	Amount
-067	67	8/68 - 3/69	3906

Tech. Off.:   Funding Element:
CASE Code: 99   AWC: 143-00

NSR-15-003-069   Indiana University   G. W. Wilson
Preparing and conducting a graduate seminar entitled "The Economics of Technological Change".

Proposal	FY	Agreement Period	Amount
-069	67	9/68 - 8/69	12313

Tech. Off.: POLLARD J K   Funding Element: HQ-E
CASE Code: 79   AWC: 143-00

NSR-15-003-076   Indiana University
Continuation of regional dissemination center operation at the Aerospace Research Applications Center.

Proposal	FY	Agreement Period	Amount
-076	68	4/68 -12/70	105000

Tech. Off.: BARNES R J   Funding Element: HQ-UT
CASE Code: 41   AWC: 141-00

NAS9-8078   Indiana University
Research on visual parameters.

Proposal	FY	Agreement Period	Amount
	68	6/68 - 8/69	14000

Tech. Off.:   Funding Element: MSC
CASE Code: 13   AWC: 914-50

INDIANA (Con't)

NAS9-8224   **Indiana University**

Research on transparencies.

Proposal	FY	Agreement Period	Amount
	68	6/68 — 8/69	27000

Tech. Off.:   Funding Element: MSC
CASE Code: 1 3   AWC: 9 1 4 - 5 0

NGT-15-003-003 **Indiana University**   **R. B. Curtis**

Training of predoctoral graduate students in space-related science and technology.

No. Students:	FY	Agreement Period	Amount
12	65	9/65 — 8/68	246100
12	66	9/66 — 8/69	246600
6	67	9/67 — 8/70	100400

Tech. Off.: HANSING F D   Funding Element: HQ-Y
CASE Code: 9 9   AWC: 1 8 1 - 0 0

NGL-15-004-001 **University of Notre Dame**   **G. F. D'Alelio**

Synthesis of heat resistant polymers and directed polymerizations.

Proposal	FY	Agreement Period	Amount
-031	68	2/68 — 1/69	40000
-035	67	2/68 — 1/71	40000
-038	69	2/69 — 1/72	40000

Tech. Off.: REMBAUM A   Funding Element: HQ-RR
CASE Code: 4 7   AWC: 1 2 9 - 0 3

NGR-15-004-017 **University of Notre Dame**   **T. J. Starr**

Applications of the "germfree animal" to space ecology.

Proposal	FY	Agreement Period	Amount
-032	68	3/68 — 2/69	50000
-040		3/69 — 2/70	48576

Tech. Off.: SAUNDERS J F   Funding Element: HQ-UT
CASE Code: 5 1   AWC: 1 8 9 - 5 4

NGL-15-004-026 **University of Notre Dame**   **J. L. Massey**

Convolutional coding techniques for data protection.

Proposal	FY	Agreement Period	Amount
-026	68	9/67 — 9/68	25000
-036	68	9/68 — 9/70	25000
-037	68	9/68 — 9/71	27300

Tech. Off.: SCHAEFER D   Funding Element: GSFC
CASE Code: 2 1   AWC: 1 2 5 - 2 1

NGR-15-004-028 **University of Notre Dame**   **G. F. Dalelio**

Synthesis of polymers with high residues at high temperatures.

Proposal	FY	Agreement Period	Amount
-028	68	9/67 — 9/68	15000
		1/69	NCE
-028	68	/ — /	NCE
-039	69	2/69 — 1/70	15000
-041	69	2/69 — 2/72	15000

Tech. Off.: PARKER J A   Funding Element: ARC
CASE Code: 1 2   AWC: 1 2 9 - 0 3

NSR-15-004-029 **University of Notre Dame**   **T. J. Mueller**

Characteristics of separated flow regions within altitude compensating nozzles.

Proposal	FY	Agreement Period	Amount
-029	68	9/68 — 3/70	40000

Tech. Off.:   Funding Element:
CASE Code: 9 9   AWC: 1 2 8 - 3 1

NAS5-10454 **University of Notre Dame**   **J. D. Nicolaides**

Dynamic stability study for sounding rocket.

Proposal	FY	Agreement Period	Amount
		6/67 — 12/67	44000

Tech. Off.: SORGIT E   Funding Element: GSFC
CASE Code: 4 6   AWC: 8 7 9 - 3 0

NGT-15-004-002 **University of Notre Dame**   **P. E. Beichner**

Training of predoctoral graduate students in space-related science and technology.

No. Students:	FY	Agreement Period	Amount
10	65	9/65 — 8/68	192000
10	66	9/66 — 8/69	192000
6	67	9/67 — 9/70	103100

Tech. Off.: HANSING F D   Funding Element: HQ-Y
CASE Code: 9 9   AWC: 1 8 1 - 0 0

NGR-15-005-022 **Purdue University**   **R. Oldenburger**

Flow of single and two phase fluids in lines.

Proposal	FY	Agreement Period	Amount
-059	67	7/67 — 6/68	20000
-090	68	7/68 — 6/69	20000
-090		6/70	NCE

Tech. Off.: PINSON L D   Funding Element: LARC
CASE Code: 1 3   AWC: 1 2 4 - 1 1

NGR-15-005-003 **Purdue University**   **K. L. Andrew**

High precision spectroscopy with applications to the study of the atomic spectra of the carbon group and to the secondary standards in the vacuum ultraviolet and the development of computer methods of data analysis.

Proposal	FY	Agreement Period	Amount
-040	66	2/66 — 1/69	40000
-057	67	2/67 — 1/70	50000
-086	68	2/68 — 1/70	61000
-099	69	2/69 — 1/72	50000

Tech. Off.: OTT E J   Funding Element: HQ-SG
CASE Code: 1 2   AWC: 1 8 8 - 4 1

NGR-15-005-006 **Purdue University**   **J. C. Lindenlaub**

Theoretical and experimental studies of sub-optimal second and third generation self-adaptive binary communication systems.

Proposal	FY	Agreement Period	Amount
-051	67	1/67 — 12/68	15000
-082	68	1/68 — 12/68	28000
		— 6/69	NCE

Tech. Off.: STANTON O J   Funding Element: HQ-RE
CASE Code: 4 5   AWC: 1 2 5 - 2 2

INDIANA (Cont'd.)

NGR-15-005-021 Purdue University   **F. N. Andrews**

Multidisciplinary research in space-related science and engineering.

Proposal	FY	Agreement Period	Amount
-033	66	1/66 -12/68	300000
-049	67	1/67 -12/69	300000
-074	68	1/69 -12/70	100000

Tech. Off.: QUINN H B   Funding Element: HQ-Y
CASE Code: 99   AWC: 183-00

NGR-15-005-039 Purdue University   **W. Gautschi**

Numerical analysis of linear difference equations.

Proposal	FY	Agreement Period	Amount
-039	67	6/67 - 5/68	23252
-039	67	9/68 - 5/69	NCE

Tech. Off.: WILSON R   Funding Element: HQ-RR
CASE Code: 21   AWC: 129-04

NGR-15-005-058 Purdue University   **B. A. Reese**

Influence of high combustion pressure (4000 psia) upon performance, heat flux, and combustion stability.

Proposal	FY	Agreement Period	Amount
-058	67	7/67 - 6/68	69129
-058	68	7/68 - 6/69	66000
-108		7/69 - 6/70	58615

Tech. Off.: PRIEM R T   Funding Element: LERC
CASE Code: 13   AWC: 128-31

NGR-15-005-069 Purdue University   **J. Modrey**

Research in engineering design.

Proposal	FY	Agreement Period	Amount
-069	67	7/67 - 6/70	62000
-069	68	7/68 - 6/70	36500
-080	68	7/68 - 6/71	73692
-101	69	9/69 - 8/72	51348

Tech. Off.: VITALE J A   Funding Element: HQ-Y
CASE Code: 44   AWC: 183-00

NGR-15-005-077 Purdue University   **D. E. Abbott**

Transient boundary layer flow on shock tube splitter plates.

Proposal	FY	Agreement Period	Amount
-077		11/67 -10/68	11510
		-12/68	NCE
-104	69	1/69 - 1/70	15490

Tech. Off.: RUBESIN M R   Funding Element: ARC
CASE Code: 13   AWC: 189-01

NGR-15-005-085 Purdue University   **R. W. Stanley**

Atomic spectroscopy of rare gases.

Proposal	FY	Agreement Period	Amount
-085	68	7/68 - 6/69	25000

Tech. Off.:   Funding Element:
CASE Code: 12   AWC: 188-41

NGR-15-005-087 Purdue University

Analysis of spacecraft data systems.

Proposal	FY	Agreement Period	Amount
-087	68	5/68 - 4/69	19000
-105	69	5/69 - 1/70	19000

Tech. Off.:   Funding Element: GSFC
CASE Code: 21   AWC: 125-23

NGR-15-005-094 Purdue University   **J. G. Skifstad**

Aerodynamic problems related to jet-powered VTOL aircraft.

Proposal	FY	Agreement Period	Amount
-094	69	1/69 -12/70	31228

Tech. Off.: MARGASON R J   Funding Element: LARC
CASE Code: 41   AWC: 721-01

NGR-15-005-106 Purdue University   **P. A. Wintz**

Source encoding for 2-dimensional data.

Proposal	FY	Agreement Period	Amount
-106	69	7/69 - 7/70	39900

Tech. Off.: FARR E H   Funding Element: ERC
CASE Code: 21   AWC: 125-23

NSR-15-005-037 Purdue University   **Y. S. Touloukian**

Compilation and analysis of thermal radiative properties data.

Proposal	FY	Agreement Period	Amount
-060	67	6/67 - 5/68	86648
-092	68	6/68 - 6/69	81679

Tech. Off.: MOOK C P   Funding Element: HQ-RV
CASE Code: 21   AWC: 124-09

NAS9-8118   Purdue University   **E. R. Winter**

Radiant heat exchange study.

Proposal	FY	Agreement Period	Amount
	68	6/68 - 6/69	64000
			MSC

Tech. Off.:   Funding Element:
CASE Code: 13   AWC: 904-01

NGT-15-005-005 Purdue University   **F. N. Andrews**

Training of predoctoral graduate students in space-related science and technology.

No. Students	FY	Agreement Period	Amount
15	65	9/65 - 8/68	288000
15	66	9/66 - 8/69	288000
9	67	9/67 - 8/70	139500

Tech. Off.: HANSING F D   Funding Element: HQ-Y
CASE Code: 99   AWC: 181-00

NGT-15-005-061 Purdue University

Supporting the training of predoctoral graduate students in engineering design as related to aeronautical and space technology.

No. Students	FY	Agreement Period	Amount
5	67	9/67 - 8/70	111000
	67	9/68 - 8/71	111000
5	69	9/69 - 8/72	111000

Tech. Off.: VITALE J A   Funding Element: HQ-Y
CASE Code: 99   AWC: 181-00

INDIANA (Cont'd)

NGF-15-005-011   Purdue University   B. A. Reese

Construction of additional laboratory and rocket firing facilities at the Purdue University Jet Propulsion Center.

Proposal	FY	Agreement Period	Amount
8049	64	7/64 – 7/66	829380

Tech. Off.: HOLMES D C   Funding Element: HQ–Y

CASE Code: 49   AWC: 182–00

NGR-15-008-004   Rose Polytechnic Institute   H. A. Sabbagh

A theoretical analysis of static and dynamic behavior of some maser systems.

Proposal	FY	Agreement Period	Amount
–005	68	10/67 – 6/68	10000
		6/68 – 6/69	NCE

Tech. Off.: JOHNSON C C   Funding Element: GSFC

CASE Code: 13   AWC: 125–21

IOWA

NGR-16-002-005   Iowa State University   G. K. Serovy

Study and investigation of the application of blade-element techniques and performance prediction problems for axial-flow turbo-machinery.

Proposal	FY	Agreement Period	Amount
–014	67	3/67 – 2/69	61322
–020	68	3/69 – 2/71	30000
–023		3/69 – 2/72	45000

Tech. Off.: SUDDRETH J A   Funding Element: HQ–RP

CASE Code: 49   AWC: 128–31

NAS5-3097   Iowa State University   J. A. Van Allen

Instrumentation & support for galactic emission experiment for S-50 POGO satellite.

Proposal	FY	Agreement Period	Amount
		11/62 –12/68	526000
	66	11/62 – 6/68	90000

Tech. Off.: MERCANTI E   Funding Element: GSFC

CASE Code: 11   AWC: 841–12

NGT-16-002-002   Iowa State University   J. B. Page

Training of predoctoral graduate students in space-related science and technology.

No. Students	FY	Agreement Period	Amount
15	65	9/65 – 8/68	265500
15	66	9/66 – 8/69	288000
9	67	9/67 – 8/70	151200

Tech. Off.: HANSING F D   Funding Element: HQ–Y

CASE Code: 99   AWC: 181–00

NGL-16-001-002   University of Iowa   J. A. Van Allen

Theoretical and experimental studies related to the particles and fields associated with the major bodies of the solar system and with interplanetary space.

Proposal	FY	Agreement Period	Amount
–035	66	12/65 –11/68	300000
–053	67	12/66 –11/69	349600
–065	66	12/68 –11/70	200000

Tech. Off.: LEHAN J F   Funding Element: HQ–SG

CASE Code: 11   AWC: 188–46

NGR-16-001-031   University of Iowa   C. C. Wunder

Physiological and developmental changes resulting from reduced gravitational force with animals chronically adjusted to centrifugal fields.

Proposal	FY	Agreement Period	Amount
–031	68	8/67 – 7/68	15813
–031	69	7/68 – 6/69	16800

Tech. Off.: SAUNDERS J F   Funding Element: HQ–SB

CASE Code: 51   AWC: 189–54

NGR-16-001-043   University of Iowa   D. C. Montgomery & D. A. Gurnett

Waves in plasmas.

Proposal	FY	Agreement Period	Amount
–057	68	12/67 –11/68	49997
–067	69	12/68 –11/69	75000

Tech. Off.: SCHMERLING E R   Funding Element: HQ–SG

CASE Code: 13   AWC: 188–39

NSR-16-001-025   University of Iowa   D. A. Gurnett

A very-low-frequency radio noise experiment to be flown on a Javelin sounding rocket.

Proposal	FY	Agreement Period	Amount
–055	68	8/67 – 7/68	76095
–066	69	7/68 – 7/69	25127

Tech. Off.: SCHMERLING E R   Funding Element: HQ–SG

CASE Code: 31   AWC: 879–10

NAS1-8141   University of Iowa

Post-launch, experimenters' data reduction and analysis for

Proposal	FY	Agreement Period	Amount
	68	6/68 –11/70	94000

Tech. Off.:   Funding Element: LARC

CASE Code: 31   AWC: 863–11

NAS1-81446   University of Iowa

Acquisition of government facilities.

Proposal	FY	Agreement Period	Amount
	68	6/68 –12/70	91000

Tech. Off.:   Funding Element: LARC

CASE Code: 99   AWC: 863–11

NAS5-9076   University of Iowa   J. A. Van Allen

Electron & proton experiment.

Proposal	FY	Agreement Period	Amount
		12/64 – 6/68	407000
	68	12/64 – 6/68	23000

Tech. Off.: MARCOTTE P   Funding Element: GSFC

CASE Code: 13   AWC: 861–22

IOWA (Cont'd)

NAS5-10625   University of Iowa   J. A. Van Allen

Injun V spacecraft control and data acquisition.

Proposal	FY	Agreement Period	Amount
	68	6/68 −11/69	232000

Tech. Off.:   Funding Element: GSFC

CASE Code: 31   AWC: 311−07

NAS5-11039   University of Iowa

Imp-I low energy electron and proton experiment.

Proposal	FY	Agreement Period	Amount
	67	6/68 − 6/72	193000

Tech. Off.: BUTLER P   Funding Element: GSFC

CASE Code: 13   AWC: 861−52

	69	12/68 −12/69	30000

NGT-16-001-004   University of Iowa   D. C. Spriestersbach

Training of predoctoral graduate students in space-related science and technology.

No. Students:	FY	Agreement Period	Amount
15	65	9/65 − 8/68	264200
15	66	9/66 − 8/69	250200
8	67	9/67 − 8/70	119700

Tech. Off.: HANSING F D   Funding Element: HQ−Y

CASE Code: 99   AWC: 181−00

NGF-16-001-005   University of Iowa   J. A. Van Allen

Physics and astronomy research facilities.

Proposal	FY	Agreement Period	Amount
3517	62	9/62 − 9/65	610000

Tech. Off.: HOLMES D C   Funding Element: HQ−Y

CASE Code: 19   AWC: 182−00

KANSAS

NGL-17-001-005   Kansas State University   J. L. Brown

Multidisciplinary research in Space Related Science and Engineering.

Proposal	FY	Agreement Period	Amount
−021	66	9/65 − 8/68	75000
−029	67	9/66 − 8/69	75000

Tech. Off.: REDDING E R   Funding Element: HQ−Y

CASE Code: 99   AWC: 183−00

NGL-17-001-026   Kansas State University   D. Williams

Infrared laboratory studies of synthetic planetary atmosphere.

Proposal	FY	Agreement Period	Amount
−026	67	12/66 −11/68	44054
−035	68	12/68 −11/70	25000

Tech. Off.: HIPSHER H F   Funding Element: HQ−SL

CASE Code: 11   AWC: 185−47

NGR-17-001-034   Kansas State University   L. T. Fan

Investigate optimization of life support systems and their systems reliability.

Proposal	FY	Agreement Period	Amount
−034	68	6/68 − 5/69	30000
−036	69	6/69 − 6/70	30000

Tech. Off.: QUATTRONE P   Funding Element: ARC

CASE Code: 51   AWC: 127−53

NGT-17-001-002   Kansas State University   J. P. Noonan

Supporting the training of predoctoral graduate students in space-related science and technology.

No. Students:	FY	Agreement Period	Amount
10	65	9/65 − 8/68	177800
10	66	9/66 − 8/69	194000
6	67	9/67 − 8/70	104500

Tech. Off.: HANSING F D   Funding Element: HQ−Y

CASE Code: 99   AWC: 181−00

NGR-17-002-042   University of Kansas   R. H. Himes

Biochemical studies of thermophilic bacteria.

Proposal	FY	Agreement Period	Amount
−042	68	10/67 − 9/68	27626

Tech. Off.: SAUNDERS J F   Funding Element: HQ−SB

CASE Code: 51   AWC: 189−54

NGR-17-002-047   University of Kansas   K. H. Lenzen

Investigation of aeroelastic effects in aerospace vehicles.

Proposal	FY	Agreement Period	Amount
−047	67	6/67 − 5/68	9170
−056	68	6/68 − 5/69	10380

Tech. Off.: RAINEY R G   Funding Element: LARC

CASE Code: 41   AWC: 126−14

NGR-17-002-050   University of Kansas   E. J. Zeller

Production of organic compounds by proton and deuteron irradiation of inorganic solids.

Proposal	FY	Agreement Period	Amount
−050	68	7/68 − 6/69	27737

Tech. Off.:   Funding Element:

CASE Code: 12   AWC: 189−55

NGR-17-002-053   University of Kansas   G. L. Kelly

Study of optimum interpretability of digitized imagery.

Proposal	FY	Agreement Period	Amount
−053	68	7/68 − 9/69	20000

Tech. Off.: HILBORN E   Funding Element: ERC

CASE Code: 21   AWC: 127−51

NGR-17-004-019   University of Kansas   R. M. Haralick

Experimental evaluation of an adaptive pattern recognition system for earth applications data.

Proposal	FY	Agreement Period	Amount
−019	69	6/69 − 6/70	30000

Tech. Off.: DARLING E M JR   Funding Element: ERC

CASE Code: 39   AWC: 125−06

KANSAS (Cont'd.)

NAS9-7175   University of Kansas   R. K. Moore
Radar studies related to Earth Resources Program.

Proposal	FY	Agreement Period	Amount
		6/67 −12/67	160000

Tech. Off.: DYER B   Funding Element: MSC
CASE Code: 32   AWC: 169−

NGT-17-002-006   University of Kansas   W. P. Albrecht
Training of predoctoral graduate students in space-related science and technology.

No. Students:	FY	Agreement Period	Amount
10	65	9/65 − 8/68	178500
10	66	9/66 − 8/69	182800
6	67	9/67 − 8/70	96800

Tech. Off.: HANSING F D   Funding Element: HQ−Y
CASE Code: 99   AWC: 181−00

NGT-17-002-044   University of Kansas   W. P. Smith
Training of predoctoral graduate students in space-related science and technology.

No. Students:	FY	Agreement Period	Amount
4	67	9/67 − 8/70	88800

Tech. Off.: VITALE J A   Funding Element: HQ−Y
CASE Code: 99   AWC: 181−00

NGT-17-002-052   University of Kansas   J. A. Vitale
Training of predoctoral graduate students in space-related science and technology.

No. Students:	FY	Agreement Period	Amount
	68	5/68 − 4/71	45000

Tech. Off.: HANSING F D   Funding Element: HQ−Y
CASE Code: 99   AWC: 181−00

NGF-17-004-010   University of Kansas   B. G. Barr
Construction of a space research and technology laboratory at the University of Kansas.

Proposal	FY	Agreement Period	Amount
−010	66	4/67 − 5/69	1800000

Tech. Off.: HOLMES D C   Funding Element: HQ−Y
CASE Code: 99   AWC: 182−00

KENTUCKY

NGR-18-001-026   University of Kentucky   R. C. Birkebak
Thermal radiation characteristics and thermal conductivity of lunar material.

Proposal	FY	Agreement Period	Amount
−026	67	7/67 − 6/68	30000
		5/68 − 6/69	NCE

Tech. Off.: WILMARTH R   Funding Element: HQ−MAL
CASE Code: 13   AWC: 848−34

NGL-18-001-003   University of Kentucky   K. O. Lange
An investigation of gravity level preferences and the effects of gravitational forces on small animals and primates, and of techniques for related space flight experiments.

Proposal	FY	Agreement Period	Amount
−021	66	2/66 − 1/69	150000
−031	66	2/67 − 1/70	150000
−037	68	2/68 − 1/71	149963
−045		2/69 − 1/72	150000

Tech. Off.: WEISSMAN N W   Funding Element: HQ−SB
CASE Code: 51   AWC: 189−52

NGR-18-001-017   University of Kentucky   D. C. Leigh
Thermo-mechanical investigations of non-Newtonian fluids.

Proposal	FY	Agreement Period	Amount
−017	66	11/65 −10/68	31512
−034	68	11/68 −10/69	10000

Tech. Off.: HOWE J   Funding Element: HQ−RR
CASE Code: 13   AWC: 129−01

NGR-18-001-020   University of Kentucky   O. W. Dillon
Coupled thermo-mechanical effects in solids.

Proposal	FY	Agreement Period	Amount
−020	66	3/66 − 2/67	42477
−020	66	2/67 − 2/68	NCE
−020	66	3/68 − 2/69	NCE

Tech. Off.: MAYER N   Funding Element: HQ−RV
CASE Code: 13   AWC: 124−08

NGR-18-001-038   University of Kentucky   M. H. Leipold
Investigation of the interaction of cracks with microstructure in polycrystalline ceramics.

Proposal	FY	Agreement Period	Amount
−038	68	5/68 − 4/69	9305

Tech. Off.: GANGLER J   Funding Element: HQ−RR
CASE Code: 46   AWC: 129−03

NGR-18-001-042   University of Kentucky   M. H. Leipold
The role of anion impurities in mechanical failure of polycrystalline ceramics.

Proposal	FY	Agreement Period	Amount
−042	69	6/69 − 5/70	16606

Tech. Off.: LEIPOLD M H   Funding Element: HQ−RR
CASE Code: 47   AWC: 129−03

NAS9-8017   University of Kentucky
activation. Lunar sample analysis program.
Analysis of major rock forming elements by 14 mev neutron

Proposal	FY	Agreement Period	Amount
	68	5/68 −11/69	29000

Tech. Off.:   Funding Element: MSC
CASE Code: 32   AWC: 914−40

NAS9-8098   University of Kentucky
Thermal radiation characteristics and thermal conductivity of lunar materials.

Proposal	FY	Agreement Period	Amount
	68	6/68 −11/69	68000

Tech. Off.:   Funding Element: MSC
CASE Code: 32   AWC: 914−40

KENTUCKY (Con't)

NGT-18-001-005   University of Kentucky   L. W. Cochran
Supporting the training of predoctoral graduate students in space-related science and technology.

No. Students:	FY	Agreement Period	Amount
8	65	9/65 – 8/68	153600
8	66	9/66 – 8/69	153600
4	67	9/67 – 8/70	76800

Tech. Off.: HANSING F D   Funding Element: HQ-Y
CASE Code: 99   AWC: 181-00

NGL-18-002-005   University of Louisville   W. J. McGlothlin
Multidisciplinary space-related research in the physical, engineering and life sciences.

Proposal	FY	Agreement Period	Amount
-012	66	3/68 – 2/69	65000
-020	67	3/67 – 2/70	65000
-022	68	3/68 – 2/71	65000

Tech. Off.: QUINN H B   Funding Element: HQ-Y
CASE Code: 99   AWC: 183-00

NGR-18-002-008   University of Louisville   E. A. Alluisi
Performance measurements of intellectual functioning.

Proposal	FY	Agreement Period	Amount
-021	68	10/67 – 9/68	35929
-024	69	10/68 – 9/69	20000

Tech. Off.: PATTON R A   Funding Element: ARC
CASE Code: 51   AWC: 127-51

NGT-18-002-006   University of Louisville   J. A. Dillon
Training of predoctoral graduate students in space-related science and technology.

No. Students:	FY	Agreement Period	Amount
5	66	9/66 – 8/69	95400
3	67	9/67 – 8/70	55400

Tech. Off.: HANSING F D   Funding Element: HQ-Y
CASE Code: 99   AWC: 181-00

LOUISIANA

NAS9-8755   Centenary College
Development of a low energy/charge spectrometer.

Proposal	FY	Agreement Period	Amount
	69	8/68 – 5/69	37000

Tech. Off.:   Funding Element: MSC
CASE Code: 13   AWC: 914-40

NGR-19-003-003   Louisiana Polytechnic Institute   T. Williams
Multipath modeling and simulation studies for the Apollo s-band system.

Proposal	FY	Agreement Period	Amount
-003	69	6/69 – 5/70	28087

Tech. Off.: NOVOSAD S W   Funding Element:
CASE Code: 42   AWC: 921-30

NGR-19-001-012   Louisiana State University (Baton Rouge)
R. W. Huggett, K. Pinkau
Cosmic ray investigations utilizing an emulsion chamber-calorimeter combination.

Proposal	FY	Agreement Period	Amount
-052	68	1/68 – 12/68	120000
-063			140000

Tech. Off.: SCHARDT   Funding Element: HQ-SG
CASE Code: 11   AWC: 188-46

NGR-19-001-016   Louisiana State University (Baton Rouge) R. W. Pike
Evaluation of the energy transfer in the char-zone during ablation.

Proposal	FY	Agreement Period	Amount
-045	68	9/67 – 5/68	16000
-053	68	1/68 – 12/68	38814
		9/68 – 1/69	NCE
		4/69	NCE

Tech. Off.: SWANN R T   Funding Element: LARC
CASE Code: 47   AWC: 124-08

NGR-19-001-059   Louisiana State University (Baton Rouge) R. W. Pike
Analysis of the interaction of ablating protection systems and stagnation-region heating.

Proposal	FY	Agreement Period	Amount
-059	69	1/69 – 12/69	60000

Tech. Off.: SWANN R T   Funding Element: LARC
CASE Code: 46   AWC: 124-08

NGR-19-001-068   Louisiana State University (Baton Rouge)
E. J. Dantin
Special support of Saturn/Apollo utilizing Mississippi Test Facilities.

Proposal	FY	Agreement Period	Amount
-068	69	1/69 – 1/70	100000

Tech. Off.: FRITZ C G   Funding Element: MSFC
CASE Code: 99   AWC: 933-50

NAS1-8219   Louisiana State University (Baton Rouge)
Improvement of computer program for supersonic combustion.

Proposal	FY	Agreement Period	Amount
	68	6/68 – 8/69	17000

Tech. Off.:   Funding Element: LARC
CASE Code: 21   AWC: 126-15

NAS8-21116   Louisiana State University (Baton Rouge)
Ferroelectric memory.

Proposal	FY	Agreement Period	Amount
		4/67 – 4/68	22000

Tech. Off.: BAILEY G A   Funding Element: MSC
CASE Code: 21   AWC: 125-25

LOUISIANA (Cont'd)

NGT-19-001-001   Louisiana State University (Baton Rouge)

M. Goodrich

Training of predoctoral graduate students in space-related science and technology.

No. Students:	FY	Agreement Period	Amount
10	65	9/65 – 8/68	170 00
10	66	9/66 – 8/69	170000
6	67	9/67 – 8/70	98600

Tech. Off.: HANSING F D   Funding Element: HQ-Y
CASE Code: 99   AWC: 181-00

NGR-19-006-001   Northeast Louisiana State College   D. E. Dupree
Study of multivariate functional models by least squares techniques.

Proposal	FY	Agreement Period	Amount
-003	68	2/67 – 1/69	19950
-004	69	2/69 – 1/70	19269
-004	69	2/69 – 1/70	19269

Tech. Off.: MINER   Funding Element: ERC
CASE Code: 21   AWC: 129-04

NGR-19-002-027   Tulane University   A. M. Hermann
Electronic transport properties of molecular crystals.

Proposal	FY	Agreement Period	Amount
-027	69	2/69 – 1/70	17000
-028		2/69 – 1/72	17000

Tech. Off.: WEINBERG I   Funding Element: HQ-RR
CASE Code: 13   AWC: 129-03

NAS8-21484   Tulane University
Solution of systems of nonlinear equations.

Proposal	FY	Agreement Period	Amount
	68	6/68 – 8/69	24000

Tech. Off.:   Funding Element: MSFC
CASE Code: 21   AWC: 124-08

NAS12-2059   Tulane University   C. H. Beck
Designers manual for circuit design.

Proposal	FY	Agreement Period	Amount
	69	1/69 –11/69	15000

Tech. Off.:   Funding Element:
CASE Code: 49   AWC: 125-25

NGT-19-002-002   Tulane University   D. R. Deener
Training of predoctoral graduate students in space-related science and technology.

No. Students:	FY	Agreement Period	Amount
10	65	9/65 – 8/68	198000
10	66	9/66 – 8/69	198000
6	67	9/67 – 8/70	112000

Tech. Off.: HANSING F D   Funding Element: HQ-Y
CASE Code: 99   AWC: 181-00

MAINE

NGL-20-006-001   University of Maine (Orono)   T. H. Curry
Interdisciplinary studies in space-related science and technology.

Proposal	FY	Agreement Period	Amount
-008	66	2/66 – 1/69	75000
-012	68	2/68 – 1/71	75000

Tech. Off.: REDDING E R   Funding Element: HQ-Y
CASE Code: 99   AWC: 183-00

NGT-20-006-002   University of Maine (Orono)   F. P. Eggert
Training of predoctoral graduate students in space-related science and technology.

No. Students:	FY	Agreement Period	Amount
5	65	9/65 – 8/68	97400
5	66	9/66 – 8/69	94300
3	67	9/67 – 8/70	57300

Tech. Off.: HANSING F D   Funding Element: HQ-Y
CASE Code: 99   AWC: 181-00

MARYLAND

NGR-21-023-001   Columbia Union College   E. I. Mohr
Research in calibration techniques for radiometric devices.

Proposal	FY	Agreement Period	Amount
-001	68	4/68 – 9/68	6000
-002	69	10/68 – 6/69	4500

Tech. Off.:   Funding Element: GSFC
CASE Code: 45   AWC: 160-44

NGR-21-001-001   Johns Hopkins University   W. G. Fastie
Rocket and laboratory experiments and analysis on the ultraviolet spectra of the upper atmosphere.

Proposal	FY	Agreement Period	Amount
-053	68	7/67 – 7/68	276000
-054	68	7/67 – 7/68	30000
-061	68	7/68 – 3/69	70000
-066	69	7/68 – 7/69	250000

Tech. Off.: DUBIN M   Funding Element: HQ-SG
CASE Code: 31   AWC: 879-10

NGR-21-001-002   Johns Hopkins University   H. W. Moos
Theoretical and experimental investigation of the fundamental properties of rare earth crystals.

Proposal	FY	Agreement Period	Amount
-052	67	8/67 – 7/68	35000
-059	68	8/68 – 7/69	10000

Tech. Off.: JOHNSON P   Funding Element: HQ-RR
CASE Code: 32   AWC: 129-02

MARYLAND (Cont'd)

NGR-21-001-035   Johns Hopkins University   S. A. Weinstein
Behavioral regulation of gaseous environments.

Proposal	FY	Agreement Period	Amount
−056	68	10/67 − 9/68	29863
−068	69	10/68 − 9/69	20142

Tech. Off.: WEISSMAN N W   Funding Element: HQ−SB
CASE Code: 51   AWC: 189−52

NGR-21-001-037   Johns Hopkins University   H. P. Eugster
Ammonia and nitrogen in primitive atmospheres.

Proposal	FY	Agreement Period	Amount
−037	68	9/68 − 8/69	19886

Tech. Off.:   Funding Element:
CASE Code: 31   AWC: 189−55

NGR-21-001-043   Johns Hopkins University   H. H. Seliger
Excited state mechanisms in photobiology.

Proposal	FY	Agreement Period	Amount
−043	67	2/68 − 4/69	50000

Tech. Off.:   Funding Element: GSFC
CASE Code: 51   AWC: 189−55

NGR-21-001-069   Johns Hopkins University   J. F. Dardano
Research and development of fundamental performance information relevant to the behavior of organisms under conditions of space flight.

Proposal	FY	Agreement Period	Amount
−069	69	12/68 −11/69	59850

Tech. Off.: BELLEVILLE R E   Funding Element: HQ−SB
CASE Code: 51   AWC: 189−52

NGR-21-001-073   Johns Hopkins University   A. Chapanis
Effectiveness of man-man communication in order that the knowledge thus gained can be applied to man-computer communication.

Proposal	FY	Agreement Period	Amount
−073	69	5/69 − 5/70	32704

Tech. Off.: HILL J H   Funding Element: ERC
CASE Code: 99   AWC: 127−51

NSR-21-001-062   Johns Hopkins University   H. M. Crosswhite
Contract for wavelength tables of complex spectra.

Proposal	FY	Agreement Period	Amount
−062	69	9/68 − 8/69	15000

Tech. Off.: BOGGESS N W   Funding Element: HQ−SG
CASE Code: 19   AWC: 188−41

NGT-21-001-004   Johns Hopkins University   G. W. Shaffer
Training of predoctoral graduate students in space-related science and technology.

No. Students	FY	Agreement Period	Amount
12	65	9/65 − 8/68	224600
12	66	9/66 − 8/69	240000
6	67	9/67 − 8/70	103200

Tech. Off.: HANSING F D   Funding Element: HQ−Y
CASE Code: 99   AWC: 181−00

NGR-21-002-002   University of Maryland   H. Laster, E. Opik
Theoretical studies in atmospheric and space physics.

Proposal	FY	Agreement Period	Amount
−170	68	2/68 −10/68	55000
−194		10/68 − 9/69	55000

Tech. Off.: DUBIN   Funding Element: HQ−SG
CASE Code: 31   AWC: 185−47

NGR-21-002-003   University of Maryland   R. W. Krauss
Investigation of psychophysiology in controlled environments.

Proposal	FY	Agreement Period	Amount
−142	68	9/67 − 4/68	38112
−169	68	4/68 − 3/69	55000
−187	68	6/68 − 5/69	35575

Tech. Off.: JACKSON W L   Funding Element: ARC
CASE Code: 51   AWC: 189−54

NGR-21-002-005   Unversity of Maryland   D. A. Tidman
Theoretical investigations in dynamics of astrophysical plasmas including studies of the structure of plasma shock waves, solar corona, and their possible radio emission.

Proposal	FY	Agreement Period	Amount
−084	66	2/66 − 1/69	85000
−125	68	2/67 − 1/70	79000
−182	69	7/68 − 6/71	40000

Tech. Off.: OPP A G   Funding Element: HQ−SG
CASE Code: 11   AWC: 188−36

NGR-21-002-006   University of Maryland   T. D. Wilkerson
Studies of particle phenomena in the interplanetary plasma and of the excitation and ionization cross-sections of the hydrogen, helium, oxygen, and nitrogen atoms and molecular combinations.

Proposal	FY	Agreement Period	Amount
−133	68	6/67 − 5/68	85000
−192	69	11/68 −10/69	44000

Tech. Off.: OPP A G   Funding Element: HQ−SG
CASE Code: 11   AWC: 188−36

NGR-21-002-007   University of Maryland   T. D. Wilkerson
Research on measurement of atomic transition probabilities of high temperature gases.

Proposal	FY	Agreement Period	Amount
−071	67	11/66 −10/67	30000
−071	67	11/67 − 2/68	NCE
−071	67	6/68 −10/68	NCE
−200	69	11/68 −10/69	20000

Tech. Off.:   Funding Element:
CASE Code: .13   AWC: 188−41

NGL-21-002-008   University of Maryland   W. C. Rheinboldt
Multidisciplinary research on the application of high speed computers to space-related research problems.

Proposal	FY	Agreement Period	Amount
−083	66	3/66 − 2/69	365585
−123	67	3/67 − 2/70	35000
−163	68	3/68 − 2/71	120000

Tech. Off.: MARR E G   Funding Element: HQ−Y
CASE Code: 99   AWC: 183−00

MARYLAND (Cont'd)

NGR-21-002-010   University of Maryland   J. Weber
Study on theoretical and experimental research on gravitational radiation.

Proposal	FY	Agreement Period	Amount
−061	65	7/65 − 6/68	200000
−138	67	7/67 − 6/68	80193
−172	68	7/68 − 6/69	86610

Tech. Off.: BRUNK W E   Funding Element: HQ−SL
CASE Code: 13   AWC: 185−48

NGR-21-002-026   University of Maryland   R. G. Grenell
Neurobiological substrates of behavior.

Proposal	FY	Agreement Period	Amount
−140	68	9/67 − 6/68	90805
−177	69	7/68 − 6/69	125086

Tech. Off.: JACOBS G J   Funding Element: HQ−SB
CASE Code: 51   AWC: 189−52

NGR-21-002-029   University of Maryland   W. C. Erickson
Studies in the 11 meter range of radioastronomy.

Proposal	FY	Agreement Period	Amount
−162	68	10/67 − 9/68	65000
−162	68	10/67 − 9/68	15607
		9/68 − 3/69	NCE
−201	69	3/69 − 2/70	60000

Tech. Off.: ALEXANDER J   Funding Element: GSFC
CASE Code: 11   AWC: 188−39

NGL-21-002-033   University of Maryland   H. Laster
Theoretical & experimental studies in the space sciences, including consideration of rocket, probe, and satellites techniques.

Proposal	FY	Agreement Period	Amount
−063	65	6/65 − 5/68	175000
−100	66	6/66 − 5/69	332600
−100	67	6/67 − 5/70	196700
−137	68	6/68 − 5/70	80000
−185	66	6/68 − 5/71	122000

Tech. Off.: MERIDITH L   Funding Element: GSFC
CASE Code: 42   AWC: 188−38

NGR-21-002-040   University of Maryland   R. G. Grenell
Study of protein hydration in isolated cell surface structure.

Proposal	FY	Agreement Period	Amount
−161	68	11/67 −10/68	59112
−178	69	10/68 − 9/69	44000

Tech. Off.: JACOBS G J   Funding Element: HQ−SB
CASE Code: 51   AWC: 189−57

NGL-21-002-053   University of Maryland   R. B. Beckmann
Critical evaluation and compilation of viscosity and diffusivity data.

Proposal	FY	Agreement Period	Amount
−111	67	10/66 − 9/68	103300
−183	68	10/68 − 9/70	15000
−183	69	10/68 − 8/71	15000

Tech. Off.: SCHULMAN F   Funding Element: HQ−RN
CASE Code: 12   AWC: 120−27

NGR-21-002-057   University of Maryland   R. T. Bettinger
Ionospheric investigations with In Situ probes.

Proposal	FY	Agreement Period	Amount
−164	68	11/67 −10/68	50000
−202	69	11/68 −10/69	35000

Tech. Off.: SCHMERLING E R   Funding Element: HQ−SG
CASE Code: 31   AWC: 879−10

NGR-21-002-059   University of Maryland   E. R. Lippincott, Y. T. Pratt
Investigations on equilibrium and non-equilibrium systems in pre-biological atmospheres.

Proposal	FY	Agreement Period	Amount
−145	67	9/67 − 8/68	110001
−188	69	9/68 − 8/69	67000

Tech. Off.: JACOBS G J   Funding Element: HQ−SB
CASE Code: 51   AWC: 189−57

NGR-21-002-065   University of Maryland   A. M. Decker
Effect of environment on plant growth and development.

Proposal	FY	Agreement Period	Amount
−065	65	1/67 −12/67	NCE
−065	65	1/68 −12/68	NCE
		−12/69	NCE

Tech. Off.:   Funding Element: GSFC
CASE Code: 51   AWC: 189−55

NGR-21-002-066   University of Maryland   J. A. Earl
A study of primary cosmic ray electrons, utilizing balloon-borne experiments.

Proposal	FY	Agreement Period	Amount
−151	68	2/68 − 1/69	115000
	66	4/69	NCE
−210	69	5/69 − 5/70	85000

Tech. Off.: GANGLER F A   Funding Element: HQ−SG
CASE Code: 13   AWC: 188−46

NGR-21-002-073   University of Maryland   H. R. Griem
Experimental and theoretical investigation of plasma radiation.

Proposal	FY	Agreement Period	Amount
−168	68	3/68 − 2/69	70000
−204	69	3/69 − 2/70	69000

Tech. Off.: BOGGESS N W   Funding Element: HQ−SG
CASE Code: 13   AWC: 188−40

NGR-21-002-096   University of Maryland   R. T. Bettinger
Selected studies in atmospheric physics.

Proposal	FY	Agreement Period	Amount
−127	67	6/67 − 5/68	21000
−157	68	6/68 − 8/68	78369
−196	69	9/68 − 8/69	49900
−196	69	9/68 − 8/69	42900
−196	68	9/68 − 8/69	7000

Tech. Off.: BRACE   Funding Element: GSFC
CASE Code: 31   AWC: 872−13

MARYLAND   (Cont'd.)

NGR-21-002-109   **University of Maryland**   **C. O. Alley**

Feasibility studies and techniques for laser ranging to optical retro-reflection on the Moon.

Proposal	FY	Agreement Period	Amount
-154	68	4/67 – 6/68	50000
-109	69	7/68 – 6/69	70000
-109	69	7/68 – 9/69	200000
-199	69	2/69 –10/69	7893

Tech. Off.: STRICKLAND A T   Funding Element: HQ-MA
CASE Code: 11   AWC: 849-34

NGR-21-002-167   **University of Maryland**   **T. D. Wilkerson**

Optical absorption coefficients for uranium plasma.

Proposal	FY	Agreement Period	Amount
-167	68	1/68 –12/68	50408
-213		1/69 – 3/69	5000

Tech. Off.: FRANKLIN C   Funding Element: SNPO
CASE Code: 13   AWC: 122-28

NGR-21-002-175   **University of Maryland**   **W. J. Bailey**

Highly unsaturated sheet and ladder polymers with unusual electrical properties.

Proposal	FY	Agreement Period	Amount
-175	68	5/68 – 4/69	28000
			LARC

Tech. Off.:   Funding Element:
CASE Code: 12   AWC: 129-03

NGR-21-002-197   **University of Maryland**   **Y. Chu**

Analysis of data processing systems.

Proposal	FY	Agreement Period	Amount
-197	69	10/68 – 8/69	19000
			GSFC

Tech. Off.:   Funding Element:
CASE Code: 21   AWC: 150-22

NGR-21-002-206   **University of Maryland**   **Y. Chu**

A unified hardware-software design study.

Proposal	FY	Agreement Period	Amount
-206	69	3/69 – 2/70	50201

Tech. Off.: WANG G Y   Funding Element: ERC
CASE Code: 49   AWC: 125-06

NGR-21-002-211   **University of Maryland**   **S. K. Poultney**

Study of sub-nanosecond ranging possibilities of optical radar at the single photo electron level and with nanosecond pulses.

Proposal	FY	Agreement Period	Amount
-211	69	2/68 – 3/69	25892

Tech. Off.: BOZZI J W   Funding Element: GSFC
CASE Code: 13   AWC: 125-22

NGR-21-002-214   **University of Maryland**   **J. P. Richard**

Relativity effects on tracking data.

Proposal	FY	Agreement Period	Amount
-214	69	2/69 – 1/70	20000

Tech. Off.: VONBUN F O   Funding Element: GSFC
CASE Code: 49   AWC: 125-06

NGR-21-002-218   **University of Maryland**   **C. O. Alley**

The optical pumping of alkali atoms using coherent radiation from semi-conductor injection lasers.

Proposal	FY	Agreement Period	Amount
-218	69	1/69 –12/69	16000

Tech. Off.: BOZZI J W   Funding Element: GSFC
CASE Code: 43   AWC: 125-22

NGR-21-007-004   **University of Maryland**   **J. V. Brady**

Research and development of fundamental performance information relevant to the behavior of organisms under conditions of space flight.

Proposal	FY	Agreement Period	Amount
-150	68	8/67 – 7/70	22536

Tech. Off.:   Funding Element:
CASE Code: 51   AWC: 127-49

NSR-21-002-077   **University of Maryland**   **D. L. Matthews**

Wide-range energy spectra of electrons in the disturbed and undisturbed ionosphere.

Proposal	FY	Agreement Period	Amount
-144	68	10/67 –10/68	87000
-144	69	10/68 –10/69	85000

Tech. Off.: OPP A G   Funding Element: HQ-SG
CASE Code: 13   AWC: 879-10

NAS5-9217   **University of Maryland**   **H. Laster**

Data reduction services.

Proposal	FY	Agreement Period	Amount
	67	6/65e– 6/67	14000
	68	6/65 – 6/69	8000

Tech. Off.:   Funding Element: GSFC
CASE Code: 19   AWC: 188-46

NAS5-11063   **University of Maryland**   **H. Gloeckler**

Experiment to analyze ions and electrons for Imp-H&J.

Proposal	FY	Agreement Period	Amount
	69	6/68 – /	285000
	67	6/68 – 6/69	55000

Tech. Off.: MARCOTTE P   Funding Element: GSFC
CASE Code: 13   AWC: 861-42

NAS9-5886   **University of Maryland**   **J. Weber**

Lunar gravimeter experiment for ALSEP.

Proposal	FY	Agreement Period	Amount
		4/66 – 6/68	534000
	68	4/66 – 9/68	75000
	69	4/66 – 9/68	12000

Tech. Off.: SANDERS A   Funding Element: MSC
CASE Code: 42   AWC: 914-40

MARYLAND (Con't)

NAS9-7809   University of Maryland   C. V. Alley
Laser ranging retroreflector.

Proposal	FY	Agreement Period	Amount
	68	5/68 – 5/71	100000

Tech. Off.:   Funding Element: MSC
CASE Code: 31   AWC: 914-40

NGT-21-002-013   University of Maryland   M. J. Pelczar
Training of predoctoral graduate students in space-related science and technology.

No. Students	FY	Agreement Period	Amount
10	65	9/65 – 8/68	192000
12	66	9/66 – 8/69	209200
8	67	9/67 – 8/70	160000

Tech. Off.: HANSING F D   Funding Element: HQ-Y
CASE Code: 99   AWC: 181-00

NGF-21-002-016   University of Maryland   M. H. Martin
Construction of facilities to house laboratories for space-related sciences.

Proposal	FY	Agreement Period	Amount
7311	64	5/64 – 9/66	1500000

Tech. Off.: HOLMES D C   Funding Element: HQ-Y
CASE Code: 99   AWC: 182-00

NGR-21-025-001   Morgan State College
An appraisal of the capabilities of some developing institutions in Maryland, Delaware, the District of Columbia and Pennsylvania to participate in the university research program of NASA.

Proposal	FY	Agreement Period	Amount
-001	68	8/68 – 7/69	8400

Tech. Off.: QUINN H B   Funding Element: HQ-Y
CASE Code: 79   AWC: 183

NGR-21-012-001   Woodstock College   M. J. Bielefeld
Theoretical and experimental studies in planetary and atmospheric physics.

Proposal	FY	Agreement Period	Amount
-003	67	9/66 – 8/69	30000
-004	68	9/67 – 8/69	7000

Tech. Off.: O KEEFE J   Funding Element: GSFC
CASE Code: 31   AWC: 188-48

MASSACHUSETTS

NGT-22-003-001   Boston College   W. J. Feeney
Training of predoctoral graduate students in space-related science and technology.

No. Students	FY	Agreement Period	Amount
3	65	9/65 – 8/68	61200
3	66	9/66 – 8/69	61200
2	67	9/67 – 8/70	40800

Tech. Off.: HANSING F D   Funding Element: HQ-Y
CASE Code: 99   AWC: 181-00

NGR-22-004-018   Boston University   E. T. Angelakos
Ultrasonic measurement of heart volume.

Proposal	FY	Agreement Period	Amount
-018	68	3/68 – 2/69	25918
		2/69 – 8/69	NCE

Tech. Off.: ANLIKER J   Funding Element: ERC
CASE Code: 51   AWC: 127-49

NGT-22-004-003   Boston University   P. E. Kubzansky
Training of predoctoral graduate students in space-related science and technology.

No. Students	FY	Agreement Period	Amount
6	65	9/65 – 8/68	106200
6	66	9/66 – 8/69	106200
4	67	9/67 – 8/70	70800

Tech. Off.: HANSING F D   Funding Element: HQ-Y
CASE Code: 99   AWC: 181-00

NGR-22-005-001   Brandeis University   N. O. Kaplan
A comparative study of the evaluation of enzymes and nucleic acids.

Proposal	FY	Agreement Period	Amount
-024	68	2/68 – 1/69	39781
-027	69	2/69 – 1/70	25000

Tech. Off.: GEIB D S   Funding Element: HQ-SB
CASE Code: 12   AWC: 189-55

NGR-22-005-025   Brandeis University   J. W. Senders
Theoretical and analytical research of the attentional demand of complex perceptual tasks.

Proposal	FY	Agreement Period	Amount
-025	68	12/67 – 11/68	35000
-028	69	12/68 – 11/69	45475

Tech. Off.:   Funding Element: LARC
CASE Code: 51   AWC: 127-51

NGT-22-005-005   Brandeis University   H. Weisberg
Training of predoctoral graduate students in space-related science and technology.

No. Students	FY	Agreement Period	Amount
6	65	9/65 – 8/68	115200
6	66	9/66 – 8/69	107000
4	67	9/67 – 8/70	71500

Tech. Off.: HANSING F D   Funding Element: HQ-Y
CASE Code: 99   AWC: 181-00

NAS8-24392   Clark University   C. A. Coulter
Investigate applications of point set and algebraic topology to elementary particle physics.

Proposal	FY	Agreement Period	Amount
	69	5/69 – 6/70	15000

Tech. Off.:   Funding Element:
CASE Code: 13   AWC: 129-04

MASSACHUSETTS (Cont'd.)

NGT-22-006-001 Clark University D. E. Lee
Training of predoctoral graduate students in space-related science and technology.

No. Students:	FY	Agreement Period	Amount
3	65	9/65 – 8/68	43000
3	66	9/66 – 8/69	56100
2	67	9/67 – 8/70	37800

Tech. Off.: HANSING F D Funding Element: HQ-Y
CASE Code: 99 AWC: 181-00

NGR-22-007-003 Harvard University W. H. Sweet
Interdisciplinary studies of the effects of high energy protons on biologic systems, including participation in the nationwide cooperatve study on shielding materials as related to the Apollo Mission.

Proposal	FY	Agreement Period	Amount
-077	67	6/67 –12/67	NCE
-077	67	1/68 –12/68	NCE
		12/68 – 1/69	NCE
		–12/69	NCE

Tech. Off.: MALICH C Funding Element: ARC
CASE Code: 99 AWC: 127-49

NGL-22-007-006 Harvard University L. Goldberg
Theoretical and experimental studies in ultraviolet solar physics.

Proposal	FY	Agreement Period	Amount
-065	66	2/66 – 1/69	500000
-095	67	2/67 – 1/70	375000
-116	68	2/68 – 3/70	140236
-151	69	2/69 – 1/72	240000

Tech. Off.: GLASER Funding Element: HQ-SG
CASE Code: 11 AWC: 188-38

NGL-22-007-012 Harvard University B. Budiansky
Theoretical investigations in structural mechanics with particular emphasis on fracture mechanics and thin shell analysis.

Proposal	FY	Agreement Period	Amount
-052	66	7/65 – 6/68	48072
-080	67	7/66 – 6/69	57800
-107	68	7/67 – 6/70	77500
-132	69	7/68 – 6/71	77000

Tech. Off.: LEONARD R W Funding Element: LARC
CASE Code: 46 AWC: 124-11

NGR-22-007-019 Harvard University W. H. Abelman, L. E. Earley
Interrelations between systemic and regional blood volume, blood flow, and fluid and electrolyte balance.

Proposal	FY	Agreement Period	Amount
-085	67	1/67 – 6/68	72604
-127	68	7/68 – 6/69	58888

Tech. Off.: JOHNSON R L Funding Element: MSC
CASE Code: 51 AWC: 127-49

NGR-22-007-021 Harvard University G. R. Huguenin
Long wavelength extension of solar radio burst observations.

Proposal	FY	Agreement Period	Amount
-094	68	9/67 – 8/68	18942
-106	68	9/67 – 8/68	72755
-104	68	9/67 – 8/68	122563
-119	68	12/67 –10/68	119712
		11/68 – 6/69	NCE

Tech. Off.: GLASER Funding Element: HQ-SG
CASE Code: 31 AWC: 188-38

NGL-22-007-053 Harvard University W. A. Burgess
Study of space cabin atmospheres.

Proposal	FY	Agreement Period	Amount
-102	67	7/67 – 6/68	36194
-128	68	7/68 – 6/71	48000
-159	69	7/69 – 6/72	66491

Tech. Off.: LEAVITT W Z Funding Element: ERC
CASE Code: 31 AWC: 127-06

NGR-22-007-054 Harvard University N. F. Ramsey
Hydrogen maser studies of relativity.

Proposal	FY	Agreement Period	Amount
-054	65	9/67 – 3/68	NCE
-108	68	9/67 – 8/68	25144
-141	69	9/68 – 8/69	20000

Tech. Off.: OTT E Funding Element: SG
CASE Code: 13 AWC: 188-40

NGR-22-007-056 Harvard University R. W. P. King
Theoretical and experimental investigations of antennas and waves in plasma.

Proposal	FY	Agreement Period	Amount
-109	68	9/67 – 8/68	54306
-120	68	2/68 – 9/68	5000
-135	69	9/68 – 8/69	40000

Tech. Off.: CARON P D Funding Element: ERC
CASE Code: 13 AWC: 125-22

NGR-22-007-059 Harvard University K. R. Porter
The effects of stress on collagen biogenesis.

Proposal	FY	Agreement Period	Amount
-114	68	10/67 – 9/68	36038
-150	69	10/68 – 9/69	10591

Tech. Off.: Funding Element:
CASE Code: 51 AWC: 189-54

NGR-22-007-061 Harvard University L. Goldberg
Application of manned orbiting telescopes to solar observation.

Proposal	FY	Agreement Period	Amount
-061	65	4/66 – 3/67	16590
-061	65	3/67 – 1/68	NCE
		1/69	NCE

Tech. Off.: Funding Element:
CASE Code: 11 AWC: 981-10

MASSACHUSETTS (Cont'd.)

NGR-22-007-068   Harvard University   A. E. Bryson
Investigation of on-board computer techniques for space navigation.

Proposal	FY	Agreement Period	Amount
-118	68	1/68 -12/68	50000
-142	69	1/69 -12/69	20000

Tech. Off.: SCHMEIDER D H   Funding Element: ERC
CASE Code: 42   AWC: 125-17

NGL-22-007-069   Harvard University   E. S. Barghoorn
Infrared absorption spectrophotometry of organic extractives from precambrian sediments.

Proposal	FY	Agreement Period	Amount
-100	67	6/67 - 5/68	18013
-122	68	6/68 - 5/69	19875
-139	66	6/69 - 5/71	25000

Tech. Off.: YOUNG R   Funding Element: HQ-SB
CASE Code: 32   AWC: 189-55

NGR-22-007-070   Harvard University   R. A. McFarland
Human standards for Apollo, emphasizing environmental influences on performance.

Proposal	FY	Agreement Period	Amount
-088	67	11/66 -10/67	73799
-088	67	11/67 -10/68	NCE

Tech. Off.: BENJAMIN F   Funding Element: HQ-MM
CASE Code: 51   AWC: 904-01

NGR-22-007-096   Harvard University   F. R. Ervin
The estimation and prediction of mental alertness.

Proposal	FY	Agreement Period	Amount
-129	68	4/68 - 3/69	44478

Tech. Off.: MENGERL P H   Funding Element: ERC
CASE Code: 51   AWC: 127-49

NGL-22-007-101   Harvard University   D. M. Hegsted
Factors in bone formation and bone loss.

Proposal	FY	Agreement Period	Amount
-101	67	6/67 - 5/68	21924
-123	68	6/68 - 5/69	20000
-130	68	6/68 - 5/71	20000

Tech. Off.: YOUNG D   Funding Element: ARC
CASE Code: 51   AWC: 127-49

NGR-22-007-103   Harvard University   D. C. Noble
Geologic study of collapse calderas in the western United States.

Proposal	FY	Agreement Period	Amount
-103	69	3/69 - 2/72	30313

Tech. Off.: BRYSON R P   Funding Element: HQ-MA
CASE Code: 32   AWC: 195-42

NGR-22-007-117   Harvard University   N. Bloembergen
Investigation of the behavior of ultrashort light pulses of picosecond duration in optical media.

Proposal	FY	Agreement Period	Amount
-117	68	2/68 - 1/69	30000
-145	69	2/69 - 1/70	30000
-161		2/69 - 1/72	30000

Tech. Off.:   Funding Element:
CASE Code: 13   AWC: 129-02

NGR-22-007-124   Harvard University   R. A. Bauer
Nonlinear optics and quantum electronics.

Proposal	FY	Agreement Period	Amount
-124	68	2/68 - 8/68	24790
		-12/68	NCE
-149		12/68 -11/69	50000

Tech. Off.: HURON F H   Funding Element: ERC
CASE Code: 13   AWC: 125-06

NGR-22-007-126   Harvard University   P. S. Pershan
Raman scattering from solid materials.

Proposal	FY	Agreement Period	Amount
-126	68	11/67 -10/68	30000
		11/68 - 8/69	NCE
-162		9/68 - 8/71	51000

Tech. Off.:   Funding Element: ERC
CASE Code: 13   AWC: 125-22

NGR-22-007-136   Harvard University   A. Dalgarno
Theoretical atomic and molecular physics.

Proposal	FY	Agreement Period	Amount
-136	69	9/68 - 8/69	50000

Tech. Off.:   Funding Element:
CASE Code: 13   AWC: 188-38

NGR-22-007-137   Harvard University   R. T. Kelleher
Behavioral factors in the control of cardiovascular function.

Proposal	FY	Agreement Period	Amount
-137	69	3/69 - 2/70	19963

Tech. Off.: WEISSMAN N W   Funding Element: HQ-SB
CASE Code: 51   AWC: 189-52

NGR-22-007-138   Harvard University   R. J. Herrnstein
Concept formation in animals.

Proposal	FY	Agreement Period	Amount
-138	69	5/69 - 5/70	41898

Tech. Off.: BELLEVILLE R E   Funding Element: HQ-SB
CASE Code: 59   AWC: 189-52

NGR-22-007-143   Harvard University   Y. C. Ho
Application of pattern classication techniques to biosignal analysis.

Proposal	FY	Agreement Period	Amount
-143	69	4/69 - 3/70	25000
-143		4/69 - 4/72	24000

Tech. Off.: ANLIKER J   Funding Element: ERC
CASE Code: 51   AWC: 127-49

MASSACHUSETTS (Cont'd.)

NGR-22-007-154   **Harvard University**   **R. A. McFarland**

Systematic analysis of the effects of lunar metabolic loads and of ionizing radiation on human performance.

Proposal	FY	Agreement Period	Amount
-154	69	3/69 - 2/70	30164

Tech. Off.: ANDERSON L O   Funding Element: HQ-RB
CASE Code: 59   AWC: 127-49

NGR-22-007-163   **Harvard University**   **R. A. Bauer**

Research on the planning process.

Proposal	FY	Agreement Period	Amount
-163	69	5/69 - 8/69	39987

Tech. Off.: DEERWESTER J M   Funding Element: ARC
CASE Code: 59   AWC: 130-06

NSR-22-007-067   **Harvard University**   **L. Goldberg**

Investigation of center-to-limb variations in the far ultraviolet solar spectrum by means of a spectral scanning spectrometer flown aboard an Aerobee-Hi rocket.

Proposal	FY	Agreement Period	Amount
-110	68	7/67 - 1/68	71166
-121	69	9/68 - 6/69	205000

Tech. Off.: GLASER   Funding Element: HQ-SG
CASE Code: 11   AWC: 879-10

NSR-22-007-115   **Harvard University**   **L. Goldberg**

Contract for scientific, technical and staff support to the Astronomy Missions Board.

Proposal	FY	Agreement Period	Amount
-115	68	10/67 - 6/69	65831

Tech. Off.:   Funding Element:
CASE Code: 11   AWC: 188-48

NAS5-3949   **Harvard University**   **L. Goldberg**

Study and experiment for a high resolution ultraviolet telescope and spectrometer system.

Proposal	FY	Agreement Period	Amount
	68	1/65 - 6/67	600000
	68	1/65 - 6/67	851000

Tech. Off.:   Funding Element:
CASE Code: 11   AWC: 948-80

NAS5-9274   **Harvard University**   **L. Goldberg**

Pointed experiment for OSO-G Orbiting Solar Observatory.

Proposal	FY	Agreement Period	Amount
		6/66 - 7/69	2000000
	68	6/66 - 7/69	85000
	65	6/66 - 7/69	253000
	65	6/66 - 7/69	77000

Tech. Off.: OSTAFF W   Funding Element: GSFC
CASE Code: 11   AWC: 821-22

NAS9-8005   **Harvard University**

Use of cyclotron for calibration.

Proposal	FY	Agreement Period	Amount
	68	5/68 - 6/68	18000
			MSC

Tech. Off.:   Funding Element:
CASE Code: 13   AWC: 914-14

NAS9-8100   **Harvard University**

Research involving mineralogy and petrography of lunar material lunar sample analysis program.

Proposal	FY	Agreement Period	Amount
	69	8/68 - 1/69	81000

Tech. Off.:   Funding Element:
CASE Code: 32   AWC: 114-40

NGT-22-007-008   **Harvard University**   **R. A. McFarland**

Training of predoctoral graduate students in space-related science and technology.

No. Students:	FY	Agreement Period	Amount
3	65	9/65 - 8/67	71200
3	67	9/67 - 8/69	61800
	69	9/69 - 9/71	72800

Tech. Off.: HANSING F D   Funding Element: HQ-Y
CASE Code: 99   AWC: 181-00

NGF-22-007-009   **Harvard University**   **William H. Sweet**

Biomedical research facilities

Proposal	FY	Agreement Period	Amount
3220	62	11/62 - 11/63	182685

Tech. Off.: HOLMES D C   Funding Element: HQ-Y
CASE Code: 99   AWC: 182-00

NGR-22-091-002   **College of the Holy Cross**   **R. C. Gunter**

Investigation of the effect of space environment on replica gratings.

Proposal	FY	Agreement Period	Amount
-003	67	6/67 - 5/68	45000
-003	68	6/67 - 5/68	16250
-002	68	2/68 - 6/69	NCE
-002	68	6/68 - 5/69	4500
	68	6/70	NCE

Tech. Off.: STEIN J E   Funding Element: GSFC
CASE Code: 13   AWC: 188-38

NAS1-9016   **Lowell Technological Institute**

Furnishing diver acoustic homing and location equipment.

Proposal	FY	Agreement Period	Amount
	69	3/69 - 7/69	51000

Tech. Off.:   Funding Element:
CASE Code: 33   AWC: 124-07

NGT-22-018-002   **Lowell Technological Institute**   **E. L. Alexander**

Supporting the training of predoctoral graduate students in space-related science and technology.

No. Students:	FY	Agreement Period	Amount
2	66	9/66 - 8/69	40800

Tech. Off.: HANSING F D   Funding Element: HQ-Y
CASE Code: 99   AWC: 181-00

MASSACHUSETTS (Cont'd.)

NAS12-620   Lowell Technological Institute   J. R. Herman
HF duct-propagation data reduction and analysis.

Proposal	FY	Agreement Period	Amount
	68	3/68 — 3/69	27000

Tech. Off.:   Funding Element: ERC
CASE Code: 21   AWC: 188—39

NGR-22-009-002   Massachusetts Institute of Technology T. B. Sheridan
Study of the measurement and display of control information.

Proposal	FY	Agreement Period	Amount
—193	68	9/67 — 9/68	46560
—380	69	9/68 — 9/69	37000

Tech. Off.:   GOOLSBY L D   Funding Element: HQ—RE
CASE Code: 21   AWC: 125—19

NGL-22-009-003   Massachusetts Institute of Technology N. J. Grant
Research on mechanisms of alloy strengthening by fine particle dispersions, with particular emphasis on selective reduction of non-refractory oxides, stability of metal-metal oxide systems, and solid solution matrices in metal-metal oxide alloys.

Proposal	FY	Agreement Period	Amount
—292	68	1/68 — 1/69	84390
—400	69	1/69 — 1/72	87000

Tech. Off.:   MALTZ J   Funding Element: HQ—RR
CASE Code: 47   AWC: 129—03

NGR-22-009-005   Massachusetts Institute of Technology   K. Biemann
Detection and identification of life-related matter by mass spectroscopy.

Proposal	FY	Agreement Period	Amount
—313	68	12/67 — 1/69	75000

Tech. Off.:   GEIB D S   Funding Element: HQ—SB
CASE Code: 11   AWC: 185—55

NGR-22-009-007   Massachusetts Institute of Technology   J. Reintjes
Investigation of radar techniques and devices suitable for the exploration of the planet Venus.

Proposal	FY	Agreement Period	Amount
—306	68	11/67 —10/68	100000
—401	69	11/68 —10/69	55500

Tech. Off.:   BRUNK W E   Funding Element: HQ—SL
CASE Code: 11   AWC: 185—39

NGR-22-009-010   Massachusetts Institute of Technology W. R. Markey
Theoretical and experimental investigations to determine optimum guidance navigation and control system and instrumentation concepts and configuration for long term earth-orbiting and interplanetary spacecrafts.

Proposal	FY	Agreement Period	Amount
—273	68	1/68 —12/68	125000
—394	69	1/69 —12/70	80000
—349	69	1/69 —12/69	80000

Tech. Off.:   MICHAELS T S   Funding Element: HQ—RE
CASE Code: 42   AWC: 125—17

NGL-22-009-012   Massachusetts Institute of Technology   A. Javin
Research on properties of optical and infrared masers.

Proposal	FY	Agreement Period	Amount
—137	66	10/65 — 9/68	193000
—206	67	10/66 — 9/69	193000
—279	68	10/67 — 9/70	125000
—371	69	10/68 —10/71	125000

Tech. Off.:   JOHNSON P   Funding Element: HQ—RR
CASE Code: 13   AWC: 129—02

NGL-22-009-013   Massachusetts Institute of Technology

R. G. Gallager
Research on techniques of communication in the space environment.

Proposal	FY	Agreement Period	Amount
—285	68	11/67 —10/68	90000
—352	68	11/68 —10/70	90000
—370	69	11/68 —10/71	90000

Tech. Off.:   MESON J K   Funding Element: HQ—RE
CASE Code: 42   AWC: 125—21

NGR-22-009-014   Massachusetts Institute of Technology

H. H. Woodson, H. A. Haus, J. R. Melcher
Theoretical and experimental investigations in electrohydrodynamics (EHD) and wave-type magnetohydrodynamics (MHD).

Proposal	FY	Agreement Period	Amount
—287	68	2/68 — 1/69	55700
—342	67	2/68 — 1/71	56000
—402	69	2/69 — 1/72	56000

Tech. Off.:   SCHWARTZ R   Funding Element: HQ—RR
CASE Code: 13   AWC: 129—02

NGR-22-009-015   Massachusetts Institute of Technology H. S. Bridge
Theoretical and experimental investigations of the interplanetary medium and in gamma-ray astronomy.

Proposal	FY	Agreement Period	Amount
—128	66	1/66 —12/68	436500
—230	68	1/67 —12/70	357000
—320	68	1/68 —12/68	95000
—320	69	1/68 —12/70	300000

Tech. Off.:   OPP A G   Funding Element: HQ—SG
CASE Code: 13   AWC: 188—36

NGL-22-009-016   Massachusetts Institute of Technology A. H. Barrett
Electromagnetic investigations of planetary and solar atmospheres and the lunar surface.

Proposal	FY	Agreement Period	Amount
—103	65	5/65 — 4/68	230000
—175	66	5/66 — 4/69	184300
—236	67	5/67 — 4/70	184300
—322	68	5/68 — 4/71	167500
		5/71 — 4/72	NCE

Tech. Off.:   BRUNK W E   Funding Element: HQ—SL
CASE Code: 31   AWC: 185—39

MASSACHUSETTS (Cont'd.)

NGR-22-009-018   **Massachusetts Institute of Technology F. O. Schmitt**
Multidisciplinary studies in the neurosciences.

Proposal	FY	Agreement Period	Amount
−224	67	7/67 − 6/68	100000
−294	68	7/68 − 6/69	90000

Tech. Off.: WEISSMAN N W   Funding Element: HQ−RR
CASE Code: 51   AWC: 189−52

NGL-22-009-019   **Massachusetts Institute of Technology**
        J. V. Harrington
Multidisciplinary research in space-related physical, engineering, social and life sciences.

Proposal	FY	Agreement Period	Amount
−276	68	12/67 −11/70	300000
−379	69	12/68 − 3/69	400000
−379	69	12/68 −11/71	400000

Tech. Off.:   Funding Element:
CASE Code: 99   AWC: 123−33

NGR-22-009-059   **Massachusetts Institute of Technology**   **Z. M. Elias**
The use of stress functions in thin shell theory.

Proposal	FY	Agreement Period	Amount
−251	68	9/67 − 9/68	25212
		9/68 − 2/69	NCE
−251		8/69	NCE

Tech. Off.: WILSON R   Funding Element: HQ−RR
CASE Code: 46   AWC: 129−04

NGR-22-009-091   **Massachusetts Institute of Technology**
        R. E. Stickney
Study of transport properties of thermal plasmas.

Proposal	FY	Agreement Period	Amount
−263	67	11/67 −10/68	35000
−361	69	11/68 −10/69	30000

Tech. Off.: TOMA J   Funding Element: LERC
CASE Code: 13   AWC: 120−27

NGR-22-009-121   **Massachusetts Institute of Technology**   **L. Trilling**
Theoretical investigation of the processes of energy and momentum exchange at a gas-solid boundary.

Proposal	FY	Agreement Period	Amount
−121	65	11/65 −10/68	49375
−284	68	11/67 −10/68	17101
−367	69	11/68 −10/69	20000

Tech. Off.: SCHWARTZ I R   Funding Element: HQ−RR
CASE Code: 13   AWC: 129−01

NGR-22-009-123   **Massachusetts Institute of Technology**   **F. Press**
Experimental techniques in lunar passive seismography.

Proposal	FY	Agreement Period	Amount
−248	68	7/67 − 6/68	39500
−338	69	7/68 − 6/69	38400

Tech. Off.: ETTREDGE V   Funding Element: MSC
CASE Code: 32   AWC: 914−40

NGL-22-009-124   **Massachusetts Institute of Technology G. C. Newton**
Studies in control optimization, stabilization and computer algorithms.

Proposal	FY	Agreement Period	Amount
−278	68	9/67 − 8/68	50197
−341	68	9/68 − 8/70	50000
−364	69	9/69 − 8/71	50000

Tech. Off.: WOLOVICH W A   Funding Element: ERC
CASE Code: 21   AWC: 125−19

NGR-22-009-125   **Massachusetts Institute of Technology**   **H. C. Gatos**
Stuides on the relationship between crystalline structure and superconductivity.

Proposal	FY	Agreement Period	Amount
−244	67	4/67 − 4/68	47064
−307	68	4/68 − 3/69	35000

Tech. Off.: AUTLER S H   Funding Element: ERC
CASE Code: 47   AWC: 129−03

NGR-22-009-131   **Massachusetts Institute of Technology**   **G. Fiocco**
Sensing of meteorological variables by laser probe techniques.

Proposal	FY	Agreement Period	Amount
−255	67	8/67 − 7/68	48985
−255	67	5/68 − 6/69	NCE

Tech. Off.: GRAMS G W   Funding Element: ERC
CASE Code: 13   AWC: 160−44

NGL-22-009-156   **Massachusetts Institute of Technology**
        J. L. Meiry, Y. T. Li
Bio-physical evaluation of the human vestibular system.

Proposal	FY	Agreement Period	Amount
−281	68	1/68 −12/68	25082
−347	68	1/69 −12/70	25000
−391	69	1/69 −12/71	25000

Tech. Off.: ANDERSON L O   Funding Element: HQ−RR
CASE Code: 51   AWC: 127−49

NGL-22-009-163   **Massachusetts Institute of Technology R. P. Rafuse**
Investigation of solid state millimeter wave generation and amplification.

Proposal	FY	Agreement Period	Amount
−293	68	3/68 − 2/69	60000
−357	68	3/69 − 2/71	60000

Tech. Off.: VERONDA C M   Funding Element: ERC
CASE Code: 13   AWC: 125−21

NGR-22-009-167   **Massachusetts Institute of Technology G. R. Harrison**
Techniques for ruling improved large diffraction gratings.

Proposal	FY	Agreement Period	Amount
−298	68	3/68 − 2/69	72370
−298		8/69	NCE

Tech. Off.: GLASER   Funding Element: HQ−SG
CASE Code: 13   AWC: 188−38

MASSACHUSETTS (Cont'd.)

NGR-22-009-187   Massachusetts Institute of Technology   J. Watkins
Lunar geophysics as related to the Apollo Applications Program.

Proposal	FY	Agreement Period	Amount
-187	66	7/66 — 6/67	73782
-187	66	7/67 — 6/68	NCE
-187		6/69	NCE

Tech. Off.: WILMARTH R   Funding Element: HQ-MAL
CASE Code: 32   AWC: 849-

NGR-22-009-229   Massachusetts Institute of Technology
W. R. Markey
Problems in aircraft navigation.

Proposal	FY	Agreement Period	Amount
-291	68	9/67 — 9/68	77562
-382	68	9/68 — 9/69	60000

Tech. Off.: LIPTON A H   Funding Element: ERC
CASE Code: 41   AWC: 125-17

NGR-22-009-234   Massachusetts Institute of Technology
R. D. Thornton
Thermal interactions in semiconductor devices.

Proposal	FY	Agreement Period	Amount
-310	68	1/68 —12/68	34920
		— 6/69	NCE

Tech. Off.: BOWE J J   Funding Element: ERC
CASE Code: 13   AWC: 125-25

NGR-22-009-240   Massachusetts Institute of Technology   A. Javan
Spectroscope applications of optical and infrared masers.

Proposal	FY	Agreement Period	Amount
-318	68	12/67 —11/68	40000
-392	69	12/68 — 6/69	20000

Tech. Off.: KNABLE N   Funding Element: ERC
CASE Code: 13   AWC: 125-21

NGR-22-009-249   Massachusetts Institute of Technology
G. B. Benedek
High sensitivity magnets—optic modulator.

Proposal	FY	Agreement Period	Amount
-249	68	2/68 — 1/69	30000

Tech. Off.: MACRAKIS M   Funding Element: ERC
CASE Code: 13   AWC: 125-25

NGR-22-009-257   Massachusetts Institute of Technology
D. W. Strangway
The electrical resistivity of the Moon—the electrode problem.

Proposal	FY	Agreement Period	Amount
-257	66	5/67 — 4/68	30000
-257	68	5/68 — 4/69	75000

Tech. Off.:   Funding Element:
CASE Code: 32   AWC: 849-34

NGR-22-009-262   Massachusetts Institute of Technology W. R. Markey
Study of advanced geodetic applications and missions.

Proposal	FY	Agreement Period	Amount
-317	68	3/68 — 8/68	40000
		9/68 —11/68	NCE

Tech. Off.: PUCILLO G   Funding Element: ERC
CASE Code: 32   AWC: 160-43

NGR-22-009-269   Massachusetts Institute of Technology   J. A. Fay
Quasi-steady plasma acceleration.

Proposal	FY	Agreement Period	Amount
-269	68	9/67 — 9/68	36511
-362	69	9/68 — 9/69	29800

Tech. Off.: THOM K   Funding Element: HQ-RR
CASE Code: 13   AWC: 129-02

NGR-22-009-272   Massachusetts Institute of Technology R. J. Wurtman
Neuroendocrine rhythms: their control by environmental lighting.

Proposal	FY	Agreement Period	Amount
-272	68	12/67 —11/68	36885
-369	69	12/68 —11/69	64292

Tech. Off.: WEISSMAN N W   Funding Element: HQ-SB
CASE Code: 51   AWC: 189-52

NGR-22-009-277   Massachusetts Institute of Technology   A. Rich
The prebiotic synthesis of polynucleotides and polynucleotide, directed polypeptides.

Proposal	FY	Agreement Period	Amount
-277	68	10/67 — 9/68	44442

Tech. Off.: GEIB D S   Funding Element: HQ-SB
CASE Code: 51   AWC: 189-55

NGR-22-009-289   Massachusetts Institute of Technology   H. S. Bridge
Program of data reduction and analysis of data obtained from Mariner/Venus plasma probe.

Proposal	FY	Agreement Period	Amount
-289	68	3/68 — 2/70	95350

Tech. Off.:   Funding Element:
CASE Code: 42   AWC: 817-46

NGR-22-009-303   Massachusetts Institute of Technology   N. D. Ham
Investigation of rotor blade tip-vortex aerodynamics.

Proposal	FY	Agreement Period	Amount
-303	68	6/68 — 5/69	82991
-030		8/69	NCE

Tech. Off.:   Funding Element: LARC
CASE Code: 41   AWC: 721-02

NGL-22-009-304   Massachusetts Institute of Technology
H. J. Zimmerman
Research in the communication sciences.

Proposal	FY	Agreement Period	Amount
-304	67	12/67 —11/70	250000

Tech. Off.: GRABER P   Funding Element: HQ-SB
CASE Code: 45   AWC: 189-52

MASSACHUSETTS (Cont'd.)

NGL-22-009-308   Massachusetts Institute of Technology H. L. Teuber
Research in psychobiology.

Proposal	FY	Agreement Period	Amount
-308	68	12/67 -11/70	250000
Tech. Off.: BELLEVILLE R E		Funding Element: HQ-SB	
CASE Code: 51		AWC: 189-52	

NGL-22-009-309   Massachusetts Institute of Technology
Z. S. Zannetos
Research in integrated planning and control systems.

Proposal	FY	Agreement Period	Amount
-309	68	3/68 - 9/68	50000
-354	68	9/68 - 9/70	48000
-385	69	9/68 - 9/71	64000
Tech. Off.: HURON F H		Funding Element: ERC	
CASE Code: 49		AWC: 125-06	

NGR-22-009-311   Massachusetts Institute of Technology   J. P. Vinti
An improved representation of the earth's gravitational potential for use in geodetic studies.

Proposal	FY	Agreement Period	Amount
-311	68	4/68 - 3/69	19930
Tech. Off.: PAYNE M H		Funding Element: ERC	
CASE Code: 32		AWC: 160-43	

NGR-22-009-312   Massachusetts Institute of Technology   L. R. Young
Life support in unusual environments.

Proposal	FY	Agreement Period	Amount
-312	68	3/68 - 2/69	65000
-398	69	3/69 - 2/70	100000
Tech. Off.:		Funding Element:	
CASE Code: 51		AWC: 127-06	

NGR-22-009-329   Massachusetts Institute of Technology   F. Press
Study of lunar traverse geophysics.

Proposal	FY	Agreement Period	Amount
-329	68	7/68 - 6/69	78600
Tech. Off.: LINDSAY J M		Funding Element: MSC	
CASE Code: 32		AWC: 945-41	

NGR-22-009-334   Massachusetts Institute of Technology A. D. Pierce
Atmospheric effects on sonic boom pressure waveforms.

Proposal	FY	Agreement Period	Amount
-334	68	9/68 - 9/69	17000
Tech. Off.:		Funding Element: LARC	
CASE Code: 41		AWC: 126-61	

NGR-22-009-335   Massachusetts Institute of Technology M. O. Scully
The study of ultra-short laser pulses and their interaction with matter.

Proposal	FY	Agreement Period	Amount
-335	69	12/68 -11/69	28000
Tech. Off.: KNABLE N		Funding Element: ERC	
CASE Code: 13		AWC: 125-21	

NGR-22-009-337   Massachusetts Institute of Technology   P. Penfield
Avalanche diode devices for the generation of coherent radiation.

Proposal	FY	Agreement Period	Amount
-337	68	5/68 - 2/69	40000
Tech. Off.: HOLMSTROM R		Funding Element: ERC	
CASE Code: 45		AWC: 125-21	

NGR-22-009-339   Massachusetts Institute of Technology
E. A. Witmer
Investigation of concepts, methods of analysis and evaluation for containment/control of fragments from bursting turbine motors.

Proposal	FY	Agreement Period	Amount
-339	68	6/68 - 5/69	58635
-339		7/69	NCE
Tech. Off.: CHIARITO P T		Funding Element: LERC	
CASE Code: 46		AWC: 126-61	

NGR-22-009-350   Massachusetts Institute of Technology T. B. McCord
Spectral reflectance of planetary surfaces.

Proposal	FY	Agreement Period	Amount
-350	69	9/68 - 9/69	75700
Tech. Off.: BRYSON R P		Funding Element: HQ-MA	
CASE Code: 11		AWC: 195-52	

NGR-22-009-351   Massachusetts Institute of Technology
L. G. Bromwell
In situ mechanical properties of lunar soils.

Proposal	FY	Agreement Period	Amount
-351	69	7/68 - 7/69	52350
Tech. Off.: BRYSON R P		Funding Element: HQ-MA	
CASE Code: 32		AWC: 195-42	

NGR-22-009-359   Massachusetts Institute of Technology   R. Weiss
Laser frequency stabilization using a molecular beam.

Proposal	FY	Agreement Period	Amount
-359	69	2/69 - 9/69	23812
Tech. Off.: KNABLE N		Funding Element: ERC	
CASE Code: 13		AWC: 125-21	

NGR-22-009-372   Massachusetts Institute of Technology H. S. Bridge
Reduction and analysis of satellite data.

Proposal	FY	Agreement Period	Amount
-372	69	7/68 - 7/69	150000
Tech. Off.: OPP A G		Funding Element:	
CASE Code: 42		AWC: 353-36	

NGR-22-009-378   Massachusetts Institute of Technology
J. Fay, J. Keck
Production and dispersion of pollutants from jet aircraft.

Proposal	FY	Agreement Period	Amount
-378	69	2/69 - 1/70	70000
Tech. Off.: HOWE J T		Funding Element: HQ-RR	
CASE Code: 41		AWC: 129-01	

MASSACHUSETTS   (Cont'd)

NGR-22-009-383   Massachusetts Institute of Technology
                                                        J. L. Kerrebrock
Research in propulsion and power generation.

Proposal	FY	Agreement Period	Amount
-383	69	12/68 -11/69	65000

Tech. Off.: EVVARD J C   Funding Element: LERC
CASE Code: 45   AWC: 126-15

NGR-22-009-393   Massachusetts Institute of Technology   A. Evans
Research in extensible languages.

Proposal	FY	Agreement Period	Amount
-393	69	6/69 - 6/70	52325

Tech. Off.: UDIN D   Funding Element: ERC
CASE Code: 74   AWC: 125-06

NGL-22-009-418   Massachusetts Institute of Technology   D.J. Epstein
Semiconducting ferroelectrics.

Proposal	FY	Agreement Period	Amount
-418	69	6/69 - 6/72	50000

Tech. Off.: SAWYER D E   Funding Element: ERC
CASE Code: 47   AWC: 125-25

NGR-22-009-420   Massachusetts Institute of Technology
Participation in the science team for the Mars Lander.

Proposal	FY	Agreement Period	Amount
-420	69	2/69 - 2/70	10185

Tech. Off.: MITZ M A   Funding Element: HQ-SL
CASE Code: 42   AWC: 815-20

NGR-22-009-424   Massachusetts Institute of Technology   A. Rich
Detection of biological systems on Mars.

Proposal	FY	Agreement Period	Amount
-424	69	3/69 - 3/70	6581

Tech. Off.: MITZ M A   Funding Element: ERC
CASE Code: 59   AWC: 815-20

NSR-22-009-106   Massachusetts Institute of Technology P. B. Sebring
Radar and radiometric studies of the Lunar surface.

Proposal	FY	Agreement Period	Amount
-106	66	10/65 - 3/67	1173000
-106	66	9/67 -12/67	NCE

Tech. Off.: STRICKLAND A   Funding Element: HQ-SM
CASE Code: 11   AWC: 942-83

NSR-22-009-138   Massachusetts Institute of Technology   L. L. Sutro
Automatic object recognition for extraterrestrial life.

Proposal	FY	Agreement Period	Amount
-286	68	10/67 -10/68	150000
-373	69	10/68 -10/69	50000

Tech. Off.: YOUNG R S   Funding Element: HQ-SB
CASE Code: 31   AWC: 185-

NSR-22-009-288   Massachusetts Institute of Technology
                                                        W. S. Lewellen
Study of fluid dynamics of gaseous nuclear rockets.

Proposal	FY	Agreement Period	Amount
-288	68	4/68 - 3/70	40558
			SNPO

Tech. Off.: FRANKLIN C   Funding Element: NPO
CASE Code: 13   AWC: 122-28

NSR-22-009-321   Massachusetts Institute of Technology
                                                        H. W. Schnopper
Developmental study of a focussing X-ray spectrometer for manned space flight applications.

Proposal	FY	Agreement Period	Amount
-321	68	4/68 - 3/69	27396

Tech. Off.:   Funding Element:
CASE Code: 42   AWC: 188-41

NSR-22-009-404   Massachusetts Institute of Technology
                                                        J. V. Harrington
Review and redefinition of the Sunblazer mission objectives and system parameters.

Proposal	FY	Agreement Period	Amount
-404	69	1/69 - 6/69	359175

Tech. Off.: SCHMERLING E R   Funding Element: HQ-SG
CASE Code: 42   AWC: 856-10

NAS1-8423   Massachusetts Institute of Technology
An investigation of section characteristics of thin highly cambered aerodynamic surface.

Proposal	FY	Agreement Period	Amount
	68	6/68 - 6/69	27000

Tech. Off.:   Funding Element: LARC
CASE Code: 41   AWC: 124-07

NAS1-8658   Massachusetts Institute of Technology   C. Kelly
Continuation of studies and evaluation of a magnetic suspension system.

Proposal	FY	Agreement Period	Amount
	69	12/68 - 8/70	153000

Tech. Off.:   Funding Element:
CASE Code: 13   AWC: 126-13

NAS2-4919   Massachusetts Institute of Technology
Study on collisional energy transfer and chemical reaction in rapidly cooled gases.

Proposal	FY	Agreement Period	Amount
	68	6/68 - 9/69	40000

Tech. Off.:   Funding Element: ARC
CASE Code: 13   AWC: 129-01

NAS2-5043   Massachusetts Institute of Technology D. G. Fraser
Study of guidance and navigation requirements for unmanned flyby and swingby missions to the outer planets.

Proposal	FY	Agreement Period	Amount
	68	6/68 - 6/69	83000

Tech. Off.:   Funding Element:
CASE Code: 42   AWC: 130-06

MASSACHUSETTS (Cont'd.)

NAS5-3205   Massachusetts Institute of Technology   G. Garmire
Gamma ray detector for the S-57 solar satellite.

Proposal	FY	Agreement Period	Amount
		2/63 – 3/68	773000
	66	2/63 – 3/69	29000
	66	2/63 – 3/69	32000
	66	2/63 – 3/69	30000

Tech. Off.:   OSTAFF W   Funding Element: GSFC
CASE Code: 11   AWC: 821-

NAS5-9078   Massachusetts Institute of Technology   H. S. Bridge
Plasmaprobe experiment.

Proposal	FY	Agreement Period	Amount
		12/64 – 6/68	677000
	68	12/64 – 6/68	85000

Tech. Off.:   MARCOTTE P   Funding Element: GSFC
CASE Code: 13   AWC: 861-22

NAS5-11002   Massachusetts Institute of Technology   C. S. Draper
Inertial reference unit for OAO.

Proposal	FY	Agreement Period	Amount
		4/67 – 6/68	2962000
	68	4/67 – 6/68	162000
	69	4/67 – 6/68	500000

Tech. Off.:   MERCANTI E   Funding Element: GSFC
CASE Code: 11   AWC: 831-31

NAS5-11062   Massachusetts Institute of Technology   H. S. Bridge
Imp H&J plasma experiment.

Proposal	FY	Agreement Period	Amount
	67	6/64 – 5/68	50000

Tech. Off.:   MARCOTTE P   Funding Element: GSFC
CASE Code: 13   AWC: 861-42

NAS5-11082   Massachusetts Institute of Technology   G. Clark
Studies and design for a rotating wheel experiment to provide a two-color survey of the positions and time variations of cosmic x-ray sources.

Proposal	FY	Agreement Period	Amount
	68	12/67 – 8/70	132000
	68	12/67 – 8/70	50000

Tech. Off.:   Funding Element: GSFC
CASE Code: 11   AWC: 821-22

NAS8-2504   Massachusetts Institute of Technology
                                   S. H. Crandall
Establishment of guidelines for random and sinusoidal vibration correlation.

Proposal	FY	Agreement Period	Amount
		6/61 – 6/68	146000

Tech. Off.:   JEWELL R   Funding Element: MSFC
CASE Code: 13   AWC: 124-11

NAS8-21451   Massachusetts Institute of Technology   J. Hovorka
Investigation of physical basis for observed statistical correlations between solar activity and changes in planetary configurations.

Proposal	FY	Agreement Period	Amount
	68	6/68 – 4/69	35000
			MSFC

Tech. Off.:   Funding Element:
CASE Code: 11   AWC: 905-35

NAS8-24364   Massachusetts Institute of Technology
A study program of integration of NASA-sponsored studies on aluminum welding.

Proposal	FY	Agreement Period	Amount
	69	5/69 – 5/70	22000

Tech. Off.:   Funding Element:
CASE Code: 47   AWC: 908-10

NAS8-24365   Massachusetts Institute of Technology   K. Masubuchi
Analysis of thermal stresses and metal movement during welding.

Proposal	FY	Agreement Period	Amount
	69	5/69 –11/70	35000

Tech. Off.:   Funding Element:
CASE Code: 47   AWC: 933-50

NAS9-3079   Massachusetts Institute of Technology   P. Matthews
Gyroscope bearing improvement program.

Proposal	FY	Agreement Period	Amount
		6/64 – 3/68	742000
	67	6/64 – 3/68	73000

Tech. Off.:   JOHNSON R L   Funding Element: MSC
CASE Code: 46   AWC: 125-17

NAS9-4065   Massachusetts Institute of Technology   C. S. Draper
Apollo GM & LEM G & N systems design.

Proposal	FY	Agreement Period	Amount
		1/63 –12/67	43122000
	68	1/63 – 2/68	4000
	65	4/65 – 4/66	3213000
	67	4/65 – 4/66	8000
	66	1/63 – 2/68	1459000
	68	1/68 –12/68	8399406

Tech. Off.:   KELLY B   Funding Element: MSC
CASE Code: 42   AWC: 914-12

NAS9-4576   Massachusetts Institute of Technology
Apollo CM and LEM gas bearing study.

Proposal	FY	Agreement Period	Amount
		4/60 – 6/68	607000

Tech. Off.:   JONES M   Funding Element: MSC
CASE Code: 42   AWC: 908-40

MASSACHUSETTS (Cont'd.)

NAS9-6823   Massachusetts Institute of Technology C. S. Draper
Development & laboratory test of advanced manned mission
guidance and control techniques.

Proposal	FY	Agreement Period	Amount
		4/67 – 6/68	1285000
	68	4/67 – 2/69	770000

Tech. Off.: JONES M   Funding Element: MSC
CASE Code: 42   AWC: 905-02

NAS9-7183   Massachusetts Institute of Technology D. H. Staelin
Scientific support of experiment SO44C atmospheric temperatures from water microwave emission.

Proposal	FY	Agreement Period	Amount
		6/67 –12/67	44000

Tech. Off.:   Funding Element: MSC
CASE Code: 31   AWC: 945-81

NAS9-7382   Massachusetts Institute of Technology R. Biemann
Lunar receiving laboratory organic mass spectrometry development program.

Proposal	FY	Agreement Period	Amount
		9/67 – 6/68	254000

Tech. Off.: FLORY D   Funding Element: MSC
CASE Code: 13   AWC: 848-00

NAS9-7830   Massachusetts Institute of Technology J. V. Evans
Radar and radiometric lunar surface studies.

Proposal	FY	Agreement Period	Amount
	68	4/68 – 7/69	160000

Tech. Off.:   Funding Element: MSC
CASE Code: 32   AWC: 914-50

NAS9-8099   Massachusetts Institute of Technology
Mass spectrometric analysis in organic matter in lunar crust.

Proposal	FY	Agreement Period	Amount
	69	3/69 – 2/70	412000

Tech. Off.:   Funding Element:
CASE Code: 12   AWC: 914-40

NAS9-8102   Massachusetts Institute of Technology
Measurement of physical properties of lunar samples.

Proposal	FY	Agreement Period	Amount
	69	2/69 – 9/69	165000

Tech. Off.:   Funding Element:
CASE Code: 99   AWC: 914-40

NAS9-8241   Massachusetts Institute of Technology
Command module optical unit assembly.

Proposal	FY	Agreement Period	Amount
	68	6/68 –12/70	250000

Tech. Off.:   Funding Element: MSC
CASE Code: 42   AWC: 904-02

NAS9-8242   Massachusetts Institute of Technology
Strapdown inertial reference unit.

Proposal	FY	Agreement Period	Amount
	68	6/68 –12/70	344000
	68	6/68 –12/70	1000

Tech. Off.:   Funding Element: MSC
CASE Code: 42   AWC: 905-02

NAS9-8328   Massachusetts Institute of Technology   J. Hovorka
Study of the engineering and design of an EOTVOS experiment
in orbit and other gravitational experiments.

Proposal	FY	Agreement Period	Amount
	69	11/68 – 6/69	30000

Tech. Off.:   Funding Element:
CASE Code: 13   AWC: 914-40

NAS9-9024   Massachusetts Institute of Technology
Orbital navigation and guidance studies for long duration
orbital missions.

Proposal	FY	Agreement Period	Amount
	69	12/68 –12/69	143000

Tech. Off.:   Funding Element:
CASE Code: 42   AWC: 981-60

NAS12-102   Massachusetts Institute of Technology
                                              M. E. Connelly
Application of analog-digital computer techniques to guidance
and control problems.

Proposal	FY	Agreement Period	Amount
	68	2/66 – 8/68	10000

Tech. Off.: HAMILTON D   Funding Element: ERC
CASE Code: 21   AWC: 125-06

NAS12-514   Massachusetts Institute of Technology C. S. Draper
Calibrated detector ultraviolet measurements.

Proposal	FY	Agreement Period	Amount
		1/67 – 5/68	60000

Tech. Off.:   Funding Element: ERC
CASE Code: 31   AWC: 125-17

NAS12-569   Massachusetts Institute of Technology C. S. Draper
Develop improved gyroscopes & specifications for procurement.

Proposal	FY	Agreement Period	Amount
		6/67 – 8/70	1800000
	68	6/67 – 8/70	21000
	68	6/67 – 8/70	2000000

Tech. Off.: ELMS J   Funding Element: ERC
CASE Code: 46   AWC: 125-17

NAS12-640   Massachusetts Institute of Technology
Study of plated wire stack design.

Proposal	FY	Agreement Period	Amount
	68	4/68 – 6/69	55000

Tech. Off.:   Funding Element: ERC
CASE Code: 47   AWC: 180-17

MASSACHUSETTS (Cont'd)

NAS12-642   **Massachusetts Institute of Technology**
Design criteria monograph and survey.

Proposal	FY	Agreement Period	Amount
	68	4/68 – 4/69	65000

Tech. Off.:   Funding Element: ERC
CASE Code: 49   AWC: 124–12

NAS12-658   **Massachusetts Institute of Technology**
NASA Star Mapper investigations.

Proposal	FY	Agreement Period	Amount
	68	4/68 – 2/69	30000

Tech. Off.:   Funding Element: ERC
CASE Code: 11   AWC: 125–17

NAS12-668   **Massachusetts Institute of Technology**
Rel. test methods detect. gross leaks sld. dev.

Proposal	FY	Agreement Period	Amount
	68	5/68 – 3/69	33000

Tech. Off.:   Funding Element: ERC
CASE Code: 45   AWC: 125–25

NAS12-679   **Massachusetts Institute of Technology**
Research on charged particle sources for implantation.

Proposal	FY	Agreement Period	Amount
	68	7/68 – 8/69	25000

Tech. Off.:   Funding Element: ERC
CASE Code: 13   AWC: 125–25

NAS12-2111   **Massachusetts Institute of Technology**
Summer institute in dynamical astronomy.

Proposal	FY	Agreement Period	Amount
	69	5/69 – 6/70	44000

Tech. Off.:   Funding Element:
CASE Code: 11   AWC: 125–17

NGT-22-009-020   **Massachusetts Institute of Technology**   **H. L. Hazen**
Training of predoctoral graduate students in space-related science and technology.

No. Students:	FY	Agreement Period	Amount
15	65	9/65 – 8/68	315000
15	66	9/66 – 8/69	319200
9	67	9/67 – 8/70	163300

Tech. Off.:   HANSING F D   Funding Element: HQ–Y
CASE Code: 99   AWC: 181–00

NGF-22-009-021   **Massachusetts Institute of Technology**   **J. V. Harrington**
Construction of a center for space research.

Proposal	FY	Agreement Period	Amount
5399	63	6/63 – 6/66	3000000

Tech. Off.:   HOLMES D C   Funding Element: HQ–Y
CASE Code: 99   AWC: 182–00

NGR-22-010-012   **University of Massachusetts**   **R. V. Monopoli**
Control and estimation in systems with unknown parameter variations.

Proposal	FY	Agreement Period	Amount
–012	67	9/67 – 8/68	27558
–012	67	5/68 – 6/69	NCE

Tech. Off.:   FRISCH H   Funding Element: GSFC
CASE Code: 21   AWC: 125–19

NGR-22-010-018   **University of Massachusetts**   **R. V. Monopoli**
Pulse frequency modulation in control system.

Proposal	FY	Agreement Period	Amount
–032	68	2/68 – 1/69	15000
–046	69	2/69 – 1/70	8000

Tech. Off.:   BOZZI J W   Funding Element: GSFC
CASE Code: 13   AWC: 125–19

NGR-22-010-023   **University of Massachusetts**   **W. M. Irvine**
Theoretical studies of diffuse reflection and transmission of radiation in planetary atmospheres.

Proposal	FY	Agreement Period	Amount
–023	67	6/67 – 5/68	21661
–036	68	6/68 – 9/70	30271

Tech. Off.:   BRUNK W E   Funding Element: HQ–SL
CASE Code: 31   AWC: 185–41

NGL-22-010-029   **University of Massachusetts**   **J. F. Brandts**
Low temperature studies on proteins and certain organisms.

Proposal	FY	Agreement Period	Amount
–029	68	5/68 – 4/71	51440

Tech. Off.:   SAUNDERS J F   Funding Element: HQ–SB
CASE Code: 51   AWC: 189–54

NGR-22-010-039   **University of Massachusetts**   **G. R. Huguenin**
A research program in solar radio physics.

Proposal	FY	Agreement Period	Amount
–039	69	9/68 – 8/69	100000

Tech. Off.:   OERTEL G K   Funding Element: HQ–SG
CASE Code: 13   AWC: 188–38

NGR-22-010-041   **University of Massachusetts**   **J. R. Strong**
Spectroscopic and optical research in support of infrared balloon astronomy.

Proposal	FY	Agreement Period	Amount
–041	69	1/69 –12/70	7421

Tech. Off.:   INGRAO H C   Funding Element: ERC
CASE Code: 11   AWC: 125–22

NGR-22-010-042   **University of Massachusetts**   **J. Strong**
Long-path infrared absorption studies.

Proposal	FY	Agreement Period	Amount
–042	69	1/69 –12/69	17097

Tech. Off.:   HANST P L   Funding Element: FRC
CASE Code: 13   AWC: 160–44

MASSACHUSETTS (Cont'd)

NAS12-606 **University of Massachusetts** **R. E. McIntosh**
Information transmission study.

Proposal	FY	Agreement Period	Amount
	68	12/67 — 2/69	30000

Tech. Off.:   Funding Element: ERC
CASE Code: 21   AWC: 125-22

NGT-22-010-008 **University of Massachusetts** **E. C. Moore**
Training of predoctoral graduate students in space-related science and technology.

No. Students:	FY	Agreement Period	Amount
6	65	9/65 — 8/68	118100
6	66	9/66 — 8/69	105000
4	67	9/67 — 8/70	70000

Tech. Off.:   HANSING F D   Funding Element: HQ-Y
CASE Code: 99   AWC: 181-00

NGR-22-011-007 **Northeastern University W. B. Nowak, B. L. Cochrun**
Reliable solid-state circuits.

Proposal	FY	Agreement Period	Amount
-041	68	12/67 —11/68	40000
-047	69	12/68 —11/69	50000

Tech. Off.:   Funding Element: ERC
CASE Code: 45   AWC: 125-22

NGR-22-011-020 **Northeastern University** **J. Warga**
Optimization of trajectories by modern mathematical control theory and functional analysis.

Proposal	FY	Agreement Period	Amount
-028	68	9/67 — 9/68	30000
-044	69	9/68 — 9/69	20000

Tech. Off.:   MINER   Funding Element: ERC
CASE Code: 21   AWC: 129-04

NGL-22-011-024 **Northeastern University** **B. L. Cochrun**
Microminaturized devices for bioastronautical monitoring or analysis.

Proposal	FY	Agreement Period	Amount
-039	68	2/68 — 1/69	50000
-043	68	2/69 — 1/71	50000
-052	69	2/69 — 1/72	50000

Tech. Off.:   LAVERY A L   Funding Element: ERC
CASE Code: 51   AWC: 125-24

NGR-22-011-025 **Northeastern University** **K. Weiss**
Investigation of new systems for potential laser action.

Proposal	FY	Agreement Period	Amount
-038	68	3/68 —11/68	18000
-050	69	12/68 —11/69	20000

Tech. Off.:   KIM H H   Funding Element: ERC
CASE Code: 13   AWC: 125-21

NGR-22-011-042 **Northeastern University** **R. Madden**
A theoretical analysis of parachute deployment.

Proposal	FY	Agreement Period	Amount
-042	69	8/68 — 7/69	30000

Tech. Off.:   Funding Element: LARC
CASE Code: 41   AWC: 124-08

NGR-22-011-051 **Northeastern University** **C. H. Perry**
The study of optical properties and collective oscillations in new solid state materials as a function of temperature using infrared and Raman techniques.

Proposal	FY	Agreement Period	Amount
-051	69	5/69 — 5/70	20000

Tech. Off.:   HAAK F A   Funding Element: ERC
CASE Code: 12   AWC: 125-22

NSR-22-011-036 **Northeastern University** **C. G. Houtsma**
A program of NASA summer faculty fellowships.

Proposal	FY	Agreement Period	Amount
-036	68	1/68 —12/68	64885
-049	68	12/68 —12/69	75550
-049	68	12/68 —12/69	72296

Tech. Off.:   CARTER C H   Funding Element:
CASE Code: 99   AWC: 181-00

NAS12-2063 **Northeastern University**
Information dissemination in the state-of-the-art.

Proposal	FY	Agreement Period	Amount
	69	4/69 — 4/69	5000

Tech. Off.:   Funding Element:
CASE Code: 45   AWC: 125-25

NGT-22-011-003 **Northeastern University** **A. A. Vernon**
Training of predoctoral graduate students in space-related science and technology.

No. Students:	FY	Agreement Period	Amount
4	65	9/65 — 8/68	65500
5	66	9/66 — 8/69	78500
3	67	9/67 — 8/70	45900

Tech. Off.:   HANSING F D   Funding Element: HQ-Y
CASE Code: 99   AWC: 181-00

NGR-22-012-006 **Tufts University** **D. H. Spodick**
Investigation of atraumatic techniques for monitoring cardio-vascular conditioning.

Proposal	FY	Agreement Period	Amount
-014	68	4/68 — 3/69	26000

Tech. Off.:   ANLIKER J   Funding Element: ERC
CASE Code: 51   AWC: 127-06

NAS12-2128 **Tufts University**
Study of variable thermal impedance device.

Proposal	FY	Agreement Period	Amount
	69	5/69 — 6/70	11000

Tech. Off.:   Funding Element:
CASE Code: 46   AWC: 180-00

MASSACHUSETTS (Cont'd)

NGT-22-012-002   Tufts University   P. H. Flint
Training of predoctoral graduate students in space-related science and technology.

No. Students:	FY	Agreement Period	Amount
4	65	9/65 – 8/68	68800
4	66	9/66 – 8/69	68800
2	67	9/67 – 8/70	35300

Tech. Off.: HANSING F D   Funding Element: HQ-Y
CASE Code: 99   AWC: 181-00

NGR-22-017-006   Worcester Polytechnic Institute   I. Zwiebel
Environmental control for prolonged space voyages-adsorption/desorption of nitrogen oxides.

Proposal	FY	Agreement Period	Amount
-006	68	5/68 – 4/6?	20000
-012	69	5/69 – 4/70	20000
-041		5/69 – 4/72	20000

Tech. Off.: WYDEVEN T   Funding Element: ARC
CASE Code: 12   AWC: 127-53

NGR-22-017-008   Worcester Polytechnic Institute   A. H. Weiss
Study of the techniques feasible for food synthesis aboard a spacecraft.

Proposal	FY	Agreement Period	Amount
-008	68	2/68 – 1/69	28611
-010	69	2/69 – 1/70	30000

Tech. Off.: SHAPIRA J J   Funding Element: ARC
CASE Code: 51   AWC: 127-53

NGT-22-017-001   Worcester Polytechnic Institute   R. F. Morton
Training of predoctoral graduate students in space-related science and technology.

No. Students:	FY	Agreement Period	Amount
4	65	9/65 – 8/68	78000
4	66	9/66 – 8/69	80000
2	67	9/67 – 8/70	41000

Tech. Off.: HANSING F D   Funding Element: HQ-Y
CASE Code: 99   AWC: 181-00

MICHIGAN

NGR-23-002-001   University of Detroit   A. Szutka
Synthesis of morphine-like substances from simple precursors.

Proposal	FY	Agreement Period	Amount
-011	68	12/67 –11/68	23000
-012	69	12/68 –11/69	15000

Tech. Off.: GEIB D S   Funding Element: HQ-SB
CASE Code: 12   AWC: 189-55

NGR-23-004-001   Michigan State University   L. G. Augenstein
Selected studies of molecular organization and mental function.

Proposal	FY	Agreement Period	Amount
-053	68	8/67 – 7/68	9943

Tech. Off.: BELLEVILLE R E   Funding Element: HQ-SB
CASE Code: 51   AWC: 189-52

NGR-23-004-041   Michigan State University   C. Martin
Problems in interacting continua.

Proposal	FY	Agreement Period	Amount
-041	67	6/67 – 5/68	22454
-041	67	5/68 – 8/68	NCE
		-10/68	NCE
-059		9/68 – 6/70	16566

Tech. Off.: WILSON R   Funding Element: HQ-RR
CASE Code: 21   AWC: 129-04

NGR-23-004-056   Michigan State University   C. R. Gruhn
Research and development of lithium-drifted germanium for the detection of intermediate energy protons.

Proposal	FY	Agreement Period	Amount
-056	68	7/68 – 6/68	24126

Tech. Off.:   Funding Element: LERC
CASE Code: 13   AWC: 129-02

NGT-23-004-004   Michigan State University   J. Vinocur
Training of predoctoral graduate students in space-related science and technology.

No. Students:	FY	Agreement Period	Amount
12	65	9/65 – 8/68	230400
12	66	9/66 – 8/69	230400
6	67	9/67 – 8/70	95400

Tech. Off.: HANSING F D   Funding Element: HQ-Y
CASE Code: 99   AWC: 181-00

NGR-23-007-001   Michigan Technological University C. E. Work
Investigation of the influence of cyclic prestressing on fatigue of metals.

Proposal	FY	Agreement Period	Amount
-009	68	10/67 – 3/69	11752

Tech. Off.: ANGLIN A E JR   Funding Element: LERC
CASE Code: 47   AWC: 720-03

NGT-23-007-004   Michigan Technological University D. G. Yerg
Training of predoctoral graduate students in space-related science and technology.

No. Students:	FY	Agreement Period	Amount
3	66	9/66 – 8/69	56700
2	67	2/67 – 8/70	37800

Tech. Off.: HANSING F D   Funding Element: HQ-Y
CASE Code: 99   AWC: 181-00

MICHIGAN (Cont'd.)

NGR-23-005-001   University of Michigan   **F. J. Beutler**

Investigations in space communications theory, including topics related to random processes, filtering, telemetry, statistical methods, modulation, information transmission, and mathematical techniques.

Proposal	FY	Agreement Period	Amount
-180	66	4/66 - 3/69	40500
-265	68	4/68 - 3/69	24914

Tech. Off.: STANTON O J   Funding Element: HQ-RE
CASE Code: 21   AWC: 125-06

NGR-23-005-003   University of Michigan   **J. A. Nicholls**

Theoretical and experimental studies of the dynamics of reacting and charged particles in solid propellant rocket motor nozzles.

Proposal	FY	Agreement Period	Amount
-256	68	12/67 - 3/69	18000

Tech. Off.: ZIEM R W   Funding Element: HQ-RP
CASE Code: 43   AWC: 128-32

NGR-23-005-004   University of Michigan   **C. Kikuchi**

Investigation of the electromagnetic properties of materials for application to masers, lasers, and other solid state devices.

Proposal	FY	Agreement Period	Amount
-263	67	12/67 -11/68	34673
-263		7/70	NCE

Tech. Off.: JOHNSON P   Funding Element: HQ-RR
CASE Code: 13   AWC: 129-02

NGR-23-005-010   University of Michigan   **S. K. Clark**

Structural analysis of aircraft tires.

Proposal	FY	Agreement Period	Amount
-170	68	1/68 -12/68	38220
-331	69	1/69 - 1/70	36270

Tech. Off.: BATTERSON S A   Funding Element: LARC
CASE Code: 41   AWC: 126-14

NGR-23-005-015   University of Michigan   **A. Nagy**

Theoretical and experimental investigation of plasma waves, space vehicle plasma sheaths, and ionospheric electron temperatures.

Proposal	FY	Agreement Period	Amount
-259	68	9/67 - 8/68	80770
-313	69	7/68 - 6/69	80000

Tech. Off.: SCHMERLING   Funding Element: HQ-SG
CASE Code: 13   AWC: 879-10

NGR-23-005-017   University of Michigan   **F. T. Haddock**

Investigations of galactic and planetary radio astronomy.

Proposal	FY	Agreement Period	Amount
-191	67	10/65 - 9/68	150000
-315	69	10/68 - 9/69	70000

Tech. Off.: OTT E J   Funding Element: HQ-SG
CASE Code: 11   AWC: 185-38

NGR-23-005-041   University of Michigan   **H. C. Early**

Basic engineering studies of techniques for acceleration of a particle to hypervelocity by an electrically heated propellant plasma.

Proposal	FY	Agreement Period	Amount
-246	68	9/67 - 8/68	51847
		9/68 - 8/69	NCE

Tech. Off.: ALFARO E   Funding Element: LARC
CASE Code: 49   AWC: 124-09

NGR-23-005-062   University of Michigan   **J. E. Rowe**

Nonlinear interaction phenomena in the ionosphere.

Proposal	FY	Agreement Period	Amount
-250	68	10/67 - 9/68	40000
-322	69	10/68 - 9/69	20000

Tech. Off.: SCHMERLING E R   Funding Element: HQ-SG
CASE Code: 31   AWC: 188-39

NGR-23-005-094   University of Michigan   **V. C. Liu**

An investigation of plasma kinetics with emphasis on the interaction between rarefied plasmas and moving bodies.

Proposal	FY	Agreement Period	Amount
-177	66	5/66 - 4/68	43110
-282	68	5/68 - 4/69	35000

Tech. Off.: HOROWITZ R   Funding Element: HQ-SL
CASE Code: 13   AWC: 185-37

NGL-23-005-183   University of Michigan   **G. I. Haddad**
H. H. Woodson, H. A. Haus, J. R. Melcher

Theoretical and experimental investigations in electrohydrodynamics (EHD) and wave-type magnetohydrodynamics (MHD).

Proposal	FY	Agreement Period	Amount
-253	68	10/67 - 9/68	75000
-305	68	10/68 - 9/70	75000
-306	69	10/68 - 9/71	75000

Tech. Off.: KULKE B   Funding Element: ERC
CASE Code: 13   AWC: 125-21

NGR-23-005-185   University of Michigan   **J. R. P. French**

Investigate the application of new bioelectronics to cardiovascular stresses.

Proposal	FY	Agreement Period	Amount
-288	68	3/68 - 6/68	17983
-292	69	7/68 - 6/69	49771

Tech. Off.: ARNOLDI L B   Funding Element: HQ-BG
CASE Code: 51   AWC: 010-00

NGR-23-005-201   University of Michigan   **R. von Baumgarten**

Simulated weightlessness in fish and neurophysiological studies on memory in lower animals.

Proposal	FY	Agreement Period	Amount
-201	68	2/68 - 1/69	40000

Tech. Off.: BELLEVILLE R E   Funding Element: HQ-SB
CASE Code: 51   AWC: 189-52

MICHIGAN (Cont'd.)

NGR-23-005-275   University of Michigan   O. C. Mohler
Part I—Support for continuation of the solar research program of the McMath-Hulbert Observatory. Part II—Improvement of photoheliographic telescope.

Proposal	FY	Agreement Period	Amount
−275	68	4/68 − 3/69	55000
		4/69 −12/69	NCE
		12/69 − 1/70	NCE

Tech. Off.:   Funding Element:
CASE Code: 1 1   AWC: 1 8 8 − 3 8

NGR-23-005-285   University of Michigan   B. Arden
Digital computer simulation.

Proposal	FY	Agreement Period	Amount
−285	68	3/68 − 6/68	3333
−309	69	6/68 − 4/69	6200
			LARC

Tech. Off.:   Funding Element:
CASE Code: 2 1   AWC: 1 2 5 − 2 4

NGR-23-005-321   University of Michigan   F. T. Haddock
OGO-III data analysis: Dynamic spectra of radio bursts.

Proposal	FY	Agreement Period	Amount
−312	69	9/68 − 8/69	40000

Tech. Off.:   O T T E J   Funding Element: H Q − S G
CASE Code: AWC: 3 8 5 − 4 1

NGR-23-005-314   University of Michigan   F. T. Haddock
OGO-II data analysis: Satellite plasma wake study.

Proposal	FY	Agreement Period	Amount
−314	69	9/68 − 8/69	20000

Tech. Off.:   O T T E J   Funding Element: H Q − S G
CASE Code: 1 3   AWC: 1 8 8 − 4 1

NGR-23-005-320   University of Michigan   U. Samir
Theoretical and experimental studies of spacecraft-space-plasma interactions.

Proposal	FY	Agreement Period	Amount
−320	69	10/68 −10/69	22000

Tech. Off.:   S C H M E R L I N G E R   Funding Element: H Q − S G
CASE Code: 1 3   AWC: 1 8 8 − 3 9

NASr-54(05)   University of Michigan   L. M. Jones
(NSR-23-005-905) Survey measurements of upper air structure.

Proposal	FY	Agreement Period	Amount
−236	68	7/67 − 8/68	300000
−299	68	9/68 − 3/69	31210

Tech. Off.:   D U B I N   Funding Element: H Q − S G
CASE Code: 3 1   AWC: 8 7 9 − 1 0

NASr-54(06)   University of Michigan   R. W. Pew
(NSR-23-005-906) Development of on-line man-machine system performance measurement and display techniques.

Proposal	FY	Agreement Period	Amount
−237	68	7/67 − 6/68	140700
−325	69	6/68 − 6/69	100000

Tech. Off.:   W I N B L A D E R L   Funding Element: H Q − R E
CASE Code: 2 1   AWC: 1 2 5 − 1 9

NASr-54(11)   University of Michigan   L. M. Jones
(NSR-23-005-911) Develop grenade and sphere instrumentation.

Proposal	FY	Agreement Period	Amount
−261	68	1/68 − 6/68	30435
−324	68	7/68 −12/69	70000

Tech. Off.:   S M I T H W   Funding Element: GSFC
CASE Code: 4 6   AWC: 6 0 7 − 0 5

NAS5-3335   University of Michigan   G. R. Carigan
Atmospheric temperature and density measurement of the Earth's atmosphere.

Proposal	FY	Agreement Period	Amount
		6/63 − 5/68	1700000
	67	6/63 − 4/69	311000

Tech. Off.:   S M I T H W S   Funding Element: GSFC
CASE Code: 3 1   AWC: 6 0 7 −

NAS5-9113   University of Michigan   J. J. Horvath
Study of gas dynamics in an enclosed moving ion source.

Proposal	FY	Agreement Period	Amount
	65	12/64 − 3/69	300000
	68	12/64 − 3/69	77000
	68	12/64 − 3/69	100000
	68	12/64 − 3/69	5000

Tech. Off.:   T A Y L O R H   Funding Element: GSFC
CASE Code: 1 3   AWC: 8 7 2 − 1 2

NAS5-9306   University of Michigan   G. R. Carignan
Fabrication, instrumentation for electron temperature and density probe experiment for orbiting geophysical observatory Mission F (OGO-F).

Proposal	FY	Agreement Period	Amount
		3/66 − 6/68	148000
	67	3/66 − 6/68	10000
	67	3/66 − 6/68	12000

Tech. Off.:   M E R C A N T I E   Funding Element: GSFC
CASE Code: 4 2   AWC: 8 4 1 − 1 2

NAS5-9328   University of Michigan   G. R. Carignan
Neutral atmospheric composition experiment for orbiting geophysical observatory Mission F (OGO-F).

Proposal	FY	Agreement Period	Amount
		4/66 − 6/68	658000
	66	4/66 − 6/68	37000
	68	4/66 − 2/69	54000

Tech. Off.:   M E R C A N T I E   Funding Element: GSFC
CASE Code: 3 1   AWC: 8 4 1 − 1 2

MICHIGAN (Cont'd.)

NAS5-11073   **University of Michigan**   **G. R. Carignan**

Omegatron mass spectrometer system for the San Marco (C) satellite.

Proposal	FY	Agreement Period	Amount
		6/67 −12/69	155000

Tech. Off.: N E W T O N G   Funding Element: G S F C
CASE Code: 1 1   AWC: 8 9 4 − 1 2

NAS5-11174   **University of Michigan**   **F. T. Haddock**

Imp-I radio astronomy experiment.

Proposal	FY	Agreement Period	Amount
	69	5/69 −12/70	75000

Tech. Off.:   Funding Element:
CASE Code: 1 1   AWC: 8 6 1 − 5 2

NAS8-20228   **University of Michigan**   **J. A. Clark**

Investigation and study of transient heat transfer.

Proposal	FY	Agreement Period	Amount
		6/65 − 6/68	166000

Tech. Off.: B E D U E R F T I G   Funding Element: M S F C
CASE Code: 1 3   AWC: 9 3 3 − 3 3

NAS8-20312   **University of Michigan**   **V. L. Streeter**

Propellant line dynamics.

Proposal	FY	Agreement Period	Amount
		5/66 −12/67	57000

Tech. Off.:   Funding Element: M S F C
CASE Code: 4 3   AWC: 9 3 3 − 5 0

NAS8-20357   **University of Michigan**   **G. R. Carignan**

High altitude environment measurement study.

Proposal	FY	Agreement Period	Amount
		2/66 − 5/68	114000
	66	2/66 − 3/69	63000

Tech. Off.: S M I T H O E   Funding Element: M S F C
CASE Code: 3 1   AWC: 1 6 0 − 4 4

NAS8-21086   **University of Michigan**   **G. R. Carignan**

Space probe & test of an orbital density measuring instrument.

Proposal	FY	Agreement Period	Amount
		6/67 − 6/68	168000

Tech. Off.: S M I T H R   Funding Element: M S F C
CASE Code: 3 1   AWC: 9 3 3 − 5 0

NAS9-9304   **University of Michigan**

Multispectral facility maintenance and data collection

Proposal	FY	Agreement Period	Amount
	69	3/69 − 1/70	175000

Tech. Off.:   Funding Element:
CASE Code: 2 1   AWC: 6 4 0 − 0 2

NAS12-2117   **University of Michigan**

Earth resources survey atmospheric modeling.

Proposal	FY	Agreement Period	Amount
	69	5/69 − 3/70	60000

Tech. Off.:   Funding Element:
CASE Code: 3 9   AWC: 1 6 0 − 7 5

NGT-23-005-018   **University of Michigan**   **G. E. Hay**

Training of predoctoral graduate students in space-related science and technology.

No. Students	FY	Agreement Period	Amount
15	65	9/65 − 8/68	288000
15	66	9/66 − 8/69	262400
9	67	9/67 − 8/70	138000

Tech. Off.: H A N S I N G F D   Funding Element: H Q − Y
CASE Code: 9 9   AWC: 1 8 1 − 0 0

NGF-23-005-019   University of Michigan   **R. A. Sawyer**

Construction of a space research building on the North Campus of the University of Michigan.

Proposal	FY	Agreement Period	Amount
3516	63	6/63 − 6/65	1436000

Tech. Off.: H O L M E S D C   Funding Element: H Q − Y
CASE Code: 9 9   AWC: 1 8 2 − 0 0

NAS8-21267   **University of Michigan**   **J. C. Zorm**

Non-destructive examination of surfaces by neutral atom probes.

Proposal	FY	Agreement Period	Amount
	68	12/67 −12/68	15000

Tech. Off.:   Funding Element: M S F C
CASE Code: 1 3   AWC: 1 2 4 − 0 9

NGR-23-054-003   Oakland University   **J. E. Gibson**

Biosystems engineering research.

Proposal	FY	Agreement Period	Amount
−003	69	3/69 − 3/70	50000

Tech. Off.: M A R S E A S   Funding Element: E R C
CASE Code: 4 9   AWC: 1 2 5 − 1 0

NGR-23-006-047   Wayne State University   **C. N. DeSilva**

Theoretical research on the nonlinear responses of elastic shells to time-dependent loads and temperature fields.

Proposal	FY	Agreement Period	Amount
−047	67	2/67 − 1/68	16507
−047	67	2/68 − 7/68	NCE
−054	69	8/68 − 7/69	17301
−054		10/69	NCE

Tech. Off.: W I L S O N R   Funding Element: H Q − R R
CASE Code: 4 6   AWC: 1 2 9 − 0 4

NGT-23-006-001   Wayne State University   **J. E. Hill**

Training of predoctoral graduate students in space-related science and technology.

No. Students	FY	Agreement Period	Amount
6	65	9/65 − 8/68	95400
6	66	9/66 − 8/69	95400
3	67	9/67 − 8/70	47700

Tech. Off.: H A N S I N G F D   Funding Element: H Q − Y
CASE Code: 9 9   AWC: 1 8 1 − 0 0

MICHIGAN (Cont'd.)

NGR-23-010-004 Western Michigan University R. R. Hutchinson
Effects of noncontingent reinforcement and punishment.

Proposal	FY	Agreement Period	Amount
-004	68	2/68 – 1/69	10000
-004	69	2/69 – 1/70	16389

Tech. Off.:
CASE Code: 13
Funding Element:
AWC: 189-52

MINNESOTA

NGR-24-001-002 Concordia College H. R. Homann
Pentose and pentitol metabolism in hydrogenomonas species.

Proposal	FY	Agreement Period	Amount
-002	67	5/67 – 4/69	11419
-002	67	5/69 – 9/69	NCE

Tech. Off.:
CASE Code: 51
Funding Element: ARC
AWC: 189-54

NGL-24-005-008 University of Minnesota J. R. Winckler, E. P. Ney
Studies of cosmic rays, astrophysics, and energetic electrons in space, including balloon and rocket flight experiments.

Proposal	FY	Agreement Period	Amount
-085	66	7/65 – 6/68	460000
-115	67	7/66 – 6/69	409200
-139	68	7/67 – 6/69	143000
-166	66	7/68 – 6/70	267000
-157	69	7/68 – 6/71	460000

Tech. Off.: LEHAN J F
CASE Code: 11
Funding Element: HQ-SG
AWC: 188-46

NGL-24-005-009 University of Minnesota A. O. C. Nier
Experimental research on mass spectrometric techniques for study of planetary and upper atmosphere composition.

Proposal	FY	Agreement Period	Amount
-064	65	7/65 – 6/68	231743
-148	68	7/68 – 6/71	185600

Tech. Off.: HOROWITZ R
CASE Code: 11
Funding Element: HQ-SL
AWC: 185-47

NGR-24-005-050 University of Minnesota W. R. Webber, C. S. Waddington
Measurement of the gamma ray flux of various celestial point sources from high altitude balloons.

Proposal	FY	Agreement Period	Amount
-122	67	4/67 – 1/68	67395
-146	68	2/68 – 12/68	50000
-158	68	4/68 – 3/69	73149

Tech. Off.: ROMAN
CASE Code: 11
Funding Element: HQ-SG
AWC: 188-41

NGR-24-005-054 University of Minnesota F. M. Swain
Biochemical evaluation of pre-mesozoic carbohydrates.

Proposal	FY	Agreement Period	Amount
-054	66	9/65 – 8/68	47607
		8/68 – 12/68	NCE
-147	69	9/68 – 8/69	15000

Tech. Off.: YOUNG R S
CASE Code: 32
Funding Element: HQ-SB
AWC: 189-55

NGR-24-005-070 University of Minnesota C. C. Hsiao
Theoretical and experimental investigation of the mechanical strength of solids.

Proposal	FY	Agreement Period	Amount
-127	67	5/67 – 4/68	30000
-150	68	5/68 – 4/69	19842

Tech. Off.: WEINBERG T
CASE Code: 46
Funding Element: HQ-RR
AWC: 129-03

NGR-24-005-091 University of Minnesota R. J. Goldstein
Investigation of thermal convection in a horizontal layer of fluid when heated from below.

Proposal	FY	Agreement Period	Amount
-091	66	5/66 – 5/67	26350
-091	66	6/67 – 5/68	NCE
-091	66	6/68 – 5/69	NCE
		12/69	NCE

Tech. Off.:
CASE Code: 13
Funding Element:
AWC: 188-38

NGR-24-005-095 University of Minnesota R. Plunkett
Investigation of optimum structural design under dynamic loading.

Proposal	FY	Agreement Period	Amount
-131	67	6/67 – 6/68	18000
-156	68	6/68 – 6/69	10000
		6/70	NCE

Tech. Off.: RANEY J P
CASE Code: 46
Funding Element: LARC
AWC: 124-08

NGR-24-005-111 University of Minnesota J. R. Winckler
Electron radar technique as a probe of the trapped radiation belts.

Proposal	FY	Agreement Period	Amount
-111	67	8/66 – 7/68	128057
-161		8/68 – 8/69	108534

Tech. Off.: OPP A G
CASE Code: 11
Funding Element: HQ-SG
AWC: 879-10

NGR-24-005-176 University of Minnesota P. Kellogg
A measurement of decametric radio emission from Jupiter during a lunar occultation.

Proposal	FY	Agreement Period	Amount
-176	69	10/68 – 6/69	13579

Tech. Off.: BRUNK W E
CASE Code: 11
Funding Element: HQ-SL
AWC: 185-41

MINNESOTA (Cont'd.)

NGR-24-005-180   **University of Minnesota**   **L. J. Cahill**

Developing experiments and in analyzing and interpreting data from Explorer 14 and 26.

Proposal	FY	Agreement Period	Amount
-180	69	1/69 - 6/70	64283

Tech. Off.: LEHAN J F JR   Funding Element: HQ-SG
CASE Code: 42   AWC: 385-36

NGR-24-005-187   **University of Minnesota**   **A. O. C. Nier**

Planning of instruments for Mars lander program.

Proposal	FY	Agreement Period	Amount
-187	69	2/69 -12/69	4400

Tech. Off.: MITZ M A   Funding Element: HQ-SL
CASE Code: 42   AWC: 815-20

NASr-248   **University of Minnesota**   **A. O. C. Nier**

(NSR-24-005-025) Investigation of the neutral constituents of the atmosphere in the 100-200 km altitude range.

Proposal	FY	Agreement Period	Amount
-116	68	1/68 - 6/68	94119
-116	68	7/68 -12/68	NCE
-172		5/69 -12/69	68684

Tech. Off.: HOROWITZ R   Funding Element: HQ-SG
CASE Code: 31   AWC: 879-10

NSR-24-005-062   **University of Minnesota W. J. Luyten, J. E. Carroll**

Automatic proper motion survey of the stellar system.

Proposal	FY	Agreement Period	Amount
-121	67	11/66 - 6/68	72000
-121	68	11/66 - 6/68	118022
-062	65	6/65 - 6/68	276748

Tech. Off.:   Funding Element:
CASE Code: 31   AWC: 188-41

NAS2-2738   **University of Minnesota**   **F. Halberg**

Continuation of biosatellite project experiment P-1093—Spectra of Metabolic Rhythms in Rats.

Proposal	FY	Agreement Period	Amount
	68	12/64 - 6/68	28000
	65	12/64 - 6/68	40000

Tech. Off.: HARMOUNT T   Funding Element: ARC
CASE Code: 51   AWC: 883-12

NAS2-3360   **University of Minnesota**   **W. R. Webber**

Cosmic ray experiment for Pioneer Project.

Proposal	FY	Agreement Period	Amount
	68	12/65 -11/65	32000
		12/65 - 5/69	1356000

Tech. Off.: HALL C   Funding Element: ARC
CASE Code: 31   AWC: 811-12

NAS2-4629   **University of Minnesota**   **W. R. Webber**

Pioneer C pre- and post-launch data analysis.

Proposal	FY	Agreement Period	Amount
	68	12/67 -12/68	137000

Tech. Off.: HALL C   Funding Element: ARC
CASE Code: 19   AWC: 811-12

NAS3-7904   **University of Minnesota**   **E. R. Eckert**

Theory of film cooling for turbine blades.

Proposal	FY	Agreement Period	Amount
	68	6/65 - 3/69	39000

Tech. Off.:   Funding Element:
CASE Code: 41   AWC: 720-03

NAS5-3838   **University of Minnesota**   **E. P. Ney**

Zodiacal light experiment.

Proposal	FY	Agreement Period	Amount
	64	6/64 - 6/67	20000

Tech. Off.:   Funding Element: GSFC
CASE Code: 31   AWC: 821-00

NAS5-11060   **University of Minnesota**   **P. J. Kellogg**

Electromagnetic fields experiment for IMP-I.

Proposal	FY	Agreement Period	Amount
	67	3/68 -12/70	208000
			GSFC

Tech. Off.: BUTLER P   Funding Element: GSFC
CASE Code: 13   AWC: 861-52

NAS5-11687   **University of Minnesota**   **J. R. Winckler**

Study of particle acceleration mechanisms for the ATS-F.

Proposal	FY	Agreement Period	Amount
	69	5/69 - /	314000

Tech. Off.:   Funding Element:
CASE Code: 13   AWC: 630-22

NAS9-4500   **University of Minnesota**   **W. Kubicek**

Evaluation & development of an impedance plethysmographic system to measure cardiac output.

Proposal	FY	Agreement Period	Amount
		6/65 - 7/68	231000
	68	6/65 - 7/69	84000

Tech. Off.: JACKSON M   Funding Element: MSC
CASE Code: 51   AWC: 914-40

NAS9-8093   **University of Minnesota**   **R. O. Pepsin**

Measure the elemental and isotopic abundance of he, ne, ar, kr, and xe by mass spectrometer.

Proposal	FY	Agreement Period	Amount
	68	6/68 -12/69	33000

Tech. Off.:   Funding Element: MSC
CASE Code: 31   AWC: 914-40

MINNESOTA   (Cont'd)

NGT-24-005-012   University of Minnesota   **B. Crawford**
Training of predoctoral graduate students in space-related
science and technology.

No. Students:	FY	Agreement Period	Amount
15	65	9/65 – 8/68	288000
15	66	9/66 – 8/69	277700
9	67	9/67 – 8/70	157400

Tech. Off.: HANSING F D   Funding Element: HQ-Y
CASE Code: 99   AWC: 181-00

NGT-24-005-078   University of Minnesota   **G. W. Anderson**
Training of predoctoral graduate students in space-related
science and technology.

No. Students:	FY	Agreement Period	Amount
4	65	6/65 – 8/66	21600
	66	9/66 – 8/67	NCE
		6/69	NCE

Tech. Off.: HANSING F D   Funding Element: HQ-Y
CASE Code: 99   AWC: 181-00

NGF-24-005-011   University of Minnesota   **A. O. C. Nier**
Construction of additional physics research laboratories.

Proposal	FY	Agreement Period	Amount
3336	63	4/63 – 8/64	704000

Tech. Off.: HOLMES D C   Funding Element: HQ-Y
CASE Code: 99   AWC: 182-00

NGF-24-005-072   University of Minnesota   **W. B. Cheston**
Construction of research laboratory facilities housing the Space
Science Center.

Proposal	FY	Agreement Period	Amount
-072	65	6/65 –10/67	2500000

Tech. Off.: HOLMES D C   Funding Element: HQ-Y
CASE Code: 99   AWC: 182-00

MISSISSIPPI

NGR-25-001-004   Mississippi State University   **R. G. Tischer**
Influence of metabolic accumulation of products of Hydrogenomonas cells and their continued growth.

Proposal	FY	Agreement Period	Amount
-017	67	2/67 –12/68	22500
-018	67	2/67 –12/68	5775
		7/68 – 6/69	NCE

Tech. Off.: SAUNDERS J F   Funding Element: HQ-SB
CASE Code: 51   AWC: 189-54

NGR-25-001-008   Mississippi State University   **G. E. Jones**
Microwave spectroscopic identification of atmospheric contaminants.

Proposal	FY	Agreement Period	Amount
-023	68	10/67 – 9/68	42149
		– 3/69	NCE
		8/69	NCE

Tech. Off.: WHITE W R   Funding Element: LARC
CASE Code: 31   AWC: 127-53

NGL-25-001-028   Mississippi State University   **C. W. Bouchillon**
Multidisciplinary research on the environment and on energy
sources.

Proposal	FY	Agreement Period	Amount
-028	69	1/69 –12/72	200000
-028	69	1/69 –12/71	200000

Tech. Off.: QUINN H B   Funding Element: HQ-Y
CASE Code: 39   AWC: 183-00

NGR-25-001-032   Mississippi State University   **D. L. Murphree**
Special support for Saturn/Apollo.

Proposal	FY	Agreement Period	Amount
-032	69	2/69 – 1/70	100000

Tech. Off.:   Funding Element:
CASE Code: 42   AWC: 933-50

NAS1-7389   Mississippi State University   **P. S. Young**
Study of heavy primary cosmic radiation detected at low
altitudes.

Proposal	FY	Agreement Period	Amount
		5/67 – 5/68	30000

Tech. Off.: FOELSCHE R   Funding Element: LARC
CASE Code: 31   AWC: 720-04

NAS8-11334   Mississippi State University   **W. D. McCain**
Research study for determination of liquid surface profile in
a cryogenic tank during gas injection.

Proposal	FY	Agreement Period	Amount
		6/64 – 7/68	177000

Tech. Off.: CAMPBELL H   Funding Element: MSFC
CASE Code: 12   AWC: 933-50

NAS8-20284   Mississippi State University   **C. T. Carley**
Vibration effects on heat transfer in cryogenic systems.

Proposal	FY	Agreement Period	Amount
		6/66 – 7/68	106000

Tech. Off.: CAMPBELL H   Funding Element: MSFC
CASE Code: 43   AWC: 933-50

NAS8-21377   Mississippi State University   **W. L. McDaniel**
Investigation in adaptive sampling and optimum sampling
procedures.

Proposal	FY	Agreement Period	Amount
	68	5/68 – 5/69	34000

Tech. Off.:   Funding Element: MSFC
CASE Code: 21   AWC: 125-19

MISSISSIPPI (Cont'd.)

NGT-25-001-002   Mississippi State University   J. C. McKee

Training of predoctoral graduate students in space-related science and technology.

No. Students:	FY	Agreement Period	Amount
4	65	9/65 — 8/68	67200
4	66	9/66 — 8/69	67200
2	67	9/67 — 8/70	33600

Tech. Off.: HANSING F D   Funding Element: HQ-Y
CASE Code: 99   AWC: 181-0C

NGR-25-002-015   University of Mississippi   H. T. Milhorn

Conceptual idea of digital computer model of human respiratory system.

Proposal	FY	Agreement Period	Amount
-015	68	6/68 — 5/69	32118

Tech. Off.: LINEBARGER R   Funding Element: ARC
CASE Code: 51   AWC: 127-49

NGT-25-002-001   University of Mississippi   W. L. Nobles

Training of predoctoral graduate students in space-related science and technology.

No. Students:	FY	Agreement Period	Amount
4	65	9/65 — 8/68	76800
4	66	9/66 — 8/69	76800
2	67	9/67 — 8/70	38400

Tech. Off.: HANSING F D   Funding Element: HQ-Y
CASE Code: 99   AWC: 181-00

NGT-25-005-001   University of Southern Mississippi   R. S. Owings

Supporting the training of predoctoral graduate students in space-related science and technology.

No. Students:	FY	Agreement Period	Amount
2	65	9/65 — 8/68	38400
2	66	9/66 — 8/69	30700
2	67	9/67 — 8/70	31500

Tech. Off.: HANSING F D   Funding Element: HQ-Y
CASE Code: 99   AWC: 181-00

MISSOURI

NGR-26-003-023   University of Missouri (Rolla)   R. L. Wixon

Application of nitrogen metabolism in autotrophic bacteria to chemosynthetic bioregeneration in space missons.

Proposal	FY	Agreement Period	Amount
-023		10/67 — 9/68	20230
-043	69	10/68 — 9/69	18500

Tech. Off.: SAUNDERS J F   Funding Element: HQ-SB
CASE Code: 51   AWC: 189-54

NGL-26-004-003   University of Missouri (Columbia)   Ward J. Haas

Multidisciplinary research in space-related physical, engineering and life sciences.

Proposal	FY	Agreement Period	Amount
-023	66	2/66 — 1/69	150000
-034	67	2/67 — 1/70	150000
-048		2/68 — 1/71	50000

Tech. Off.: QUINN H B   Funding Element: HQ-Y
CASE Code: 99   AWC: 183-00

NGR-26-004-011   University of Missouri (Columbia)   C. W. Gehrke

Gas chromatographic techniques for the identification and study of nucleosides.

Proposal	FY	Agreement Period	Amount
-028	66	6/66 — 5/69	6000
-036	68	9/67 — 8/68	13000
-060	69	9/68 — 8/69	15000

Tech. Off.: PONNAMPERUMA C   Funding Element: ARC
CASE Code: 12   AWC: 189-54

NGL-26-004-021   University of Missouri (Columbia)   X. J. Musacchia

Effects of radiation on gastro-intestinal function and cyclic turnover of intestinal epithelium.

Proposal	FY	Agreement Period	Amount
-045	68	7/67 — 6/68	42341
-061	64	7/68 — 6/70	35000
-061	69	7/68 — 6/71	35000

Tech. Off.: SAUNDERS J F   Funding Element: HQ-SB
CASE Code: 51   AWC: 189-54

NGR-26-004-025   University of Missouri (Columbia)   F. E. Soutl

An Investigation of mammalian adaption to deep hypothermic and of hypothermia-hibernation relationships.

Proposal	FY	Agreement Period	Amount
-046	68	7/67 — 6/68	32500
-063	69	7/68 — 6/69	40000
-063	69	7/68 — 6/69	39850

Tech. Off.: SAUNDERS J F   Funding Element: HQ-SB
CASE Code: 51   AWC: 189-54

NAS9-9417   University of Missouri (Columbia)   C. Mengel

Study of effect of spacecraft atmospheres.

Proposal	FY	Agreement Period	Amount
	69	4/69 — 4/71	34000

Tech. Off.: FISHER C L   Funding Element: MSC
CASE Code: 42   AWC: 127-49

NGT-26-004-001   University of Missouri (Columbia)   C. E. Marshall

Supporting the training of predoctoral graduate students in space-related science and technology.

No. Students:	FY	Agreement Period	Amount
12	65	9/65 — 8/68	224400
12	66	9/66 — 8/69	212400
6	67	9/67 — 8/70	85700

Tech. Off.: HANSING F D   Funding Element: HQ-Y
CASE Code: 99   AWC: 181-00

MISSOURI (Cont'd.)

NGR-26-001-006   University of Missouri (Kansas City)   P. J. Bryant
Cohesion and binding energy relating to cold welding problems.

Proposal	FY	Agreement Period	Amount
-006	68	6/68 - 8/69	42870
			LARC

Tech. Off.: BRADFORD J M   Funding Element: LARC
CASE Code: 47   AWC: 124-09

NGR-26-003-026   University of Missouri (Rolla)   R. D. Rechtier
A study of the fluctuating pressure field in regions of indirect flow separation of supersonic speeds.

Proposal	FY	Agreement Period	Amount
-026	67	2/67 - 1/68	32502
-026	67	2/68 - 5/68	NCE
-026	68	6/68 - 5/69	35552

Tech. Off.: COE C F   Funding Element: ARC
CASE Code: 41   AWC: 124-11

NGR-26-003-037   University of Missouri (Rolla)   E. C. Bertnolli
Research on the impulse techniques for testing micro-circuits.

Proposal	FY	Agreement Period	Amount
-037	68	6/68 - 5/69	9942
		- 8/69	NCE
			ERC

Tech. Off.: SARKISIAN E   Funding Element: ERC
CASE Code: 45   AWC: 125-25

NGR-26-003-044   University of Missouri (Rolla)   T. L. Noack
Digital data detection study.

Proposal	FY	Agreement Period	Amount
-044	69	6/69 - 8/70	25000

Tech. Off.: SOS J Y   Funding Element: GSFC
CASE Code: 21   AWC: 150-22

NAS12-692   University of Missouri (Columbia)
Fault diagnosis for SSA electronic systems.

Proposal	FY	Agreement Period	Amount
	68	3/68 - 7/69	12000

Tech. Off.:   Funding Element: ERC
CASE Code: 45   AWC: 125-06

NGT-26-003-001   University of Missouri (Rolla)   W. Bosch
Training of predoctoral graduate students in space-related science and technology.

No. Students	FY	Agreement Period	Amount
6	65	9/65 - 8/68	115400
6	66	9/66 - 8/69	116600
4	67	9/67 - 8/70	69800

Tech. Off.: HANSING F D   Funding Element: HQ-Y
CASE Code: 99   AWC: 181-00

NGR-26-010-001   University of Missouri (St. Louis)   D. T. Haimo
Transforms related to generalized heat equations.

Proposal	FY	Agreement Period	Amount
-001	69	7/68 - 6/69	9917

Tech. Off.:   Funding Element:
CASE Code: 21   AWC: 129-04

NGL-26-006-016   St. Louis University   F. C. Bates
The structure and circulation of the lower martian troposphere.

Proposal	FY	Agreement Period	Amount
-016	67	2/67 - 1/69	41720
-025	68	2/69 - 1/72	50000

Tech. Off.: TOLEFSON H B   Funding Element: LARC
CASE Code: 31   AWC: 130-06

NGR-26-006-021   Saint Louis University   B. H. Ulrich Jr.
Computer method of redesign and non-linear analysis for a redundant complex structure.

Proposal	FY	Agreement Period	Amount
-021	69	2/69 - 2/70	36005

Tech. Off.: FULTON R E   Funding Element: LARC
CASE Code: 21   AWC: 126-14

NGR-26-006-024   Saint Louis University   D. S. Ousterhout
Study of the surface pressure distribution induced on bodies of revolution by a subsonic cold air jet exhausting normal to the surface and into a subsonic free-stream.

Proposal	FY	Agreement Period	Amount
-024	69	9/68 - 8/69	14150

Tech. Off.:   Funding Element: LARC
CASE Code: 19   AWC: 721-01

NGT-26-006-001   St. Louis University   H. Howe
Training of predoctoral graduate students in space-related science and technology.

No. Students	FY	Agreement Period	Amount
10	65	9/65 - 8/68	175500
10	66	9/66 - 8/69	175500
6	67	9/67 - 8/70	90900

Tech. Off.: HANSING F D   Funding Element: HQ-Y
CASE Code: 99   AWC: 181-00

NGR-26-008-001   Washington University (St. Louis)
J. Klarmann, M. W. Friedlander
Investigation of primary cosmic radiation using spark chambers and nuclear photographic emulsions.

Proposal	FY	Agreement Period	Amount
-047	68	2/68 - 1/69	59991
		- 9/69	NCE

Tech. Off.: KAVANAGH L K JR   Funding Element: HQ-SG
CASE Code: 11   AWC: 188-46

NGR-26-008-003   Washington University (St. Louis) M. L. Weidenbaum
Analyses of the impact of space activities on the national economy, and establishment of a methodology for determining space program effects on regional economic growth.

Proposal	FY	Agreement Period	Amount
-051	68	7/68 - 6/69	50000
		7/69 - 9/69	NCE

Tech. Off.:   Funding Element:
CASE Code: 76   AWC: 143-00

MISSOURI (Cont'd.)

NGR-26-008-006   **Washington University (St. Louis)**   **G. E. Pake**
University-wide research program in the space-related sciences
and engineering.

Proposal	FY	Agreement Period	Amount
−030	66	3/66 − 2/69	300000
−037	67	3/67 − 2/70	300000
−048	68	3/68 − 2/71	100000

Tech. Off.: MARR E G   Funding Element: HQ−Y
CASE Code: 99   AWC: 183−00

NGR-26-008-042   **Washington University (St. Louis)**   **J. Klarmann**
Gamma ray experiment based on spark chambers and nuclear
emulsions.

Proposal	FY	Agreement Period	Amount
−042	68	11/67 − 4/68	49683
−046	68	6/68 − 5/69	120741
−046		5/70	NCE

Tech. Off.: ROMAN N G   Funding Element: HQ−SG
CASE Code: 13   AWC: 188−41

NGR-26-008-043   **Washington University (St. Louis)**   **R. M. Walker**
Study of extremely heavy cosmic rays

Proposal	FY	Agreement Period	Amount
−043	68	9/67 − 8/68	25000
		8/68 − 2/69	NCE

Tech. Off.:   Funding Element:
CASE Code: 13   AWC: 188−46

NAS2-4151   **Washington University (St. Louis)**   **K. Hohenemser**
Studying of lifting rotor vibrations

Proposal	FY	Agreement Period	Amount
		1/67 − 8/68	39000
	65	1/67 − 8/68	2000
	67	1/67 − 7/69	27000

Tech. Off.:   Funding Element: ARC
CASE Code: 41   AWC: 126−

NAS9-8165   **Washington University (St. Louis)**   **R. W. Walker**
Measurement and analysis of the effect of cosmic radiation
on returned lunar samples.

Proposal	FY	Agreement Period	Amount
	68	6/68 −10/69	127000

Tech. Off.:   Funding Element: MSC
CASE Code: 13   AWC: 914−40

NAS9-8352   **Washington University (St. Louis)**   **R. W. Walker**
Study for the development and test of a plastic nuclear emulsion heavy ray detection system.

Proposal	FY	Agreement Period	Amount
	68	6/68 − 8/69	80000

Tech. Off.:   Funding Element: MSC
CASE Code: 42   AWC: 914−40

NGT-26-008-005   **Washington University (St. Louis)**   **G. E. Pake**
Training of predoctoral graduate students in space-related
science and technology.

No. Students	FY	Agreement Period	Amount
12	65	9/65 − 8/68	251400
12	66	9/66 − 8/69	249000
6	67	9/67 − 8/70	111800

Tech. Off.: HANSING F D   Funding Element: HQ−Y
CASE Code: 99   AWC: 181−00

NGF-26-008-009   **Washington University (St. Louis)**   **R. E. Norberg**
Construction of the 4th and 5th levels of research laboratory
facilities housing the Physics Laboratory.

Proposal	FY	Agreement Period	Amount
3738	64	4/64 − 2/66	600000

Tech. Off.: HOLMES D C   Funding Element: HQ−Y
CASE Code: 19   AWC: 182−00

MONTANA

NGR-27-001-001   **Montana State University**   **I. E. Dayton**
Multidisciplinary research in space science and engineering.

Proposal	FY	Agreement Period	Amount
−013	65	7/65 − 6/68	100000
−020	66	7/66 − 6/69	75000
−028	68	7/67 − 6/70	125000
−034	68	7/68 − 6/71	100000

Tech. Off.: QUINN H B   Funding Element: HQ−Y
CASE Code: 99   AWC: 183−00

NGR-27-001-035   **Montana State University**   **K. Nordtvedt**
Study and formulation of space experiments to test relativity
and gravitational theories.

Proposal	FY	Agreement Period	Amount
−035	69	2/69 − 5/70	22600

Tech. Off.: ROMAN N G   Funding Element: HQ−SG
CASE Code: 99   AWC: 188−41

NGT-27-001-003   **Montana State University**   **L. DS. Smith**
Training of predoctoral graduate students in space-related
science and technology.

No. Students	FY	Agreement Period	Amount
5	65	9/65 − 8/68	102300
6	66	9/66 − 8/69	122800
4	67	9/67 − 8/70	78100

Tech. Off.: HANSING F D   Funding Element: HQ−Y
CASE Code: 99   AWC: 181−00

NGT-27-002-001   **University of Montana**   **F. S. Honkala**
Training of predoctoral graduate students in space-related
science and technology.

No. Students	FY	Agreement Period	Amount
4	65	9/65 − 8/68	79200
4	66	9/66 − 8/69	79200
2	67	9/67 − 8/70	39600

Tech. Off.: HANSING F D   Funding Element: HQ−Y
CASE Code: 99   AWC: 181−00

NEBRASKA

NGT-28-004-001　University of Nebraska (Lincoln)　J. C. Olson

Training of predoctoral graduate students in space-related science and technology.

No. Students:	FY	Agreement Period	Amount
6	65	9/65 – 8/68	104400
6	66	9/66 – 8/69	104400
4	67	9/67 – 8/70	69600

Tech. Off.: HANSING F D　　　Funding Element: HQ–Y
CASE Code: 99　　　　　　　　AWC: 181–00

NEVADA

NGR-29-001-008　University of Nevada (Reno)　P. Atlick

Investigations of methods for the calculations of atomic photo-ionization cross sections.

Proposal	FY	Agreement Period	Amount
–028	68	9/67 – 8/68	25084

Tech. Off.: OERTEL G K　　　Funding Element: HQ–SG
CASE Code: 13　　　　　　　　AWC: 188–38

NGT-29-001-002　University of Nevada (Reno)　T. D. O'Brien

Training of predoctoral graduate students in space-related science and technology.

No. Students:	FY	Agreement Period	Amount
5	65	9/65 – 8/68	57000
5	66	9/66 – 8/69	56100
3	67	9/67 – 8/70	40700

Tech. Off.: HANSING F D　　　Funding Element: HQ–Y
CASE Code: 99　　　　　　　　AWC: 181–00

NEW HAMPSHIRE

NGR-30-001-001　Dartmouth College　C. J. Lyon

Investigation of the effects of plant growth hormones on plant development in the absence of gravitational effects.

Proposal	FY	Agreement Period	Amount
–016	68	9/67 – 8/68	31598
–025	69	9/68 – 8/70	16625

Tech. Off.: SAUNDERS J F　　　Funding Element: HQ–SB
CASE Code: 51　　　　　　　　AWC: 189–54

NGR-30-001-011　Dartmouth College　B. U. O. Sonnerup

Study of the structure of the magnetopause, utilizing satellite-obtained magnetometer data.

Proposal	FY	Agreement Period	Amount
–021	68	10/67 –10/68	20000
–026	69	10/68 –10/69	20000

Tech. Off.: KAVANAGH L D　　　Funding Element: HQ–SG
CASE Code: 31　　　　　　　　AWC: 188–36

NSR-30-001-018　Dartmouth College　T. Laaspere

Support of an existing network of Whistler ground stations to yield data for comparison with data from OGO-II, -D, and -F.

Proposal	FY	Agreement Period	Amount
–024	68	4/68 – 3/69	33915

Tech. Off.: SCHMERLING E R　　　Funding Element: HQ–SG
CASE Code: 31　　　　　　　　AWC: 841–12

NAS5-9305　Dartmouth College　T. Laaspere

Whistler-mode waves experiment for the Orbiting Geophysical Observatory, Mission F (OGO-F).

Proposal	FY	Agreement Period	Amount
		3/66 – 6/68	487000
	67	3/66 – 6/68	65000

Tech. Off.: MERCANTI E　　　Funding Element: GSFC
CASE Code: 11　　　　　　　　AWC: 841–12

NGT-30-001-003　Dartmouth College　J. F. Hornig

Training of predoctoral graduate students in space-related science and technology.

No. Students:	FY	Agreement Period	Amount
6	65	9/65 – 8/68	109800
6	66	9/66 – 8/69	109800
4	67	9/67 – 8/70	82100

Tech. Off.: HANSING F D　　　Funding Element: HQ–Y
CASE Code: 99　　　　　　　　AWC: 181–00

NGR-30-002-008　University of New Hampshire　R. E. Houston

Relationships between lower-ionospheric effects observed by VHF-absorption techniques, and cosmic-ray and geomagnetic activity.

Proposal	FY	Agreement Period	Amount
–037	68	10/67 – 9/68	16113
		9/68 – 1/69	NCE

Tech. Off.: SCHMERLING　　　Funding Element: HQ–SG
CASE Code: 31　　　　　　　　AWC: 188–39

NGR-30-002-010　University of New Hampshire　R. A. Kaufman

Studies and analyses of the magnetospheric boundary, the geomagnetic tail, and correlation with trapped particle measurements in the outer magnetosphere.

Proposal	FY	Agreement Period	Amount
–019	65	6/65 – 9/68	120819
–033	67	10/66 – 9/69	111626
–039	68	10/67 – 9/69	31195

Tech. Off.: GAUGLER　　　Funding Element: HQ–SG
CASE Code: 31　　　　　　　　AWC: 188–36

NGR-30-002-021　University of New Hampshire　E. L. Chupp

Investigation and development of techniques for solar neutron and gamma ray detection.

Proposal	FY	Agreement Period	Amount
–041	68	2/68 – 1/69	100000
–050	69	2/69 – 1/70	85000
–057	69	2/69 – 2/72	85000

Tech. Off.: LEHAN J F JR　　　Funding Element: HQ–SG
CASE Code: 11　　　　　　　　AWC: 188–46

NEW HAMPSHIRE (Cont'd)

NGR-30-002-028   University of New Hampshire   L. J. Cahill
Sounding rocket investigation of auroral displays.

Proposal	FY	Agreement Period	Amount
-028	67	5/67 - 4/68	91621
-028	68	5/68 - 4/69	91621

Tech. Off.: OPP A G	Funding Element: HQ-SG
CASE Code: 31	AWC: 879-10

NGR-30-002-056   University of New Hampshire   C. K. Taft
Research in control theory and application.

Proposal	FY	Agreement Period	Amount
-056	69	6/69 -12/70	60000

Tech. Off.: WOLOVICH W A	Funding Element: ERC
CASE Code: 99	AWC: 125-19

NASr-164   University of New Hampshire   J. A. Lockwood
(NSR-30-002-003) Measurement of neutron intensity in space.

Proposal	FY	Agreement Period	Amount
-036	68	9/67 - 9/68	130000
		7/68 - 1/69	NCE

Tech. Off.: CAHILL L J	Funding Element: HQ-SG
CASE Code: 11	AWC: 188-46

NSR-30-002-003   University of New Hampshire   J. A. Lockwood
Measurement of neutron intensity in space.

Proposal	FY	Agreement Period	Amount
-049	69	2/69 - 1/70	99999

Tech. Off.: KAVANAGH L D JR	Funding Element: HQ-SG
CASE Code: 31	AWC: 879-11

NAS2-5344   University of New Hampshire
Pioneer C, D and E data analysis.

Proposal	FY	Agreement Period	Amount
	69	4/69 - 6/69	11000

Tech. Off.:	Funding Element:
CASE Code: 42	AWC: 811-12

NAS5-11054   University of New Hampshire   E. L. Chupp
Study and design effort for rotating wheel experiment OSO-H.

Proposal	FY	Agreement Period	Amount
	68	8/67 - 9/70	100000
	67	8/67 - 9/70	270000

Tech. Off.:	Funding Element: GSFC
CASE Code: 11	AWC: 821-22

NAS5-11694   University of New Hampshire   R. L. Arnoldy
Low energy electron-proton experiment for ATS-F.

Proposal	FY	Agreement Period	Amount
	69	4/64 - 5/69	287000

Tech. Off.: WAINSCOTT F H II	Funding Element: GSFC
CASE Code: 13	AWC: 630-22

NAS12-2152   University of New Hampshire
Development of multi-spectral sensor arrays applications satellite.

Proposal	FY	Agreement Period	Amount
	69	5/69 - 5/70	25000

Tech. Off.:	Funding Element:
CASE Code: 42	AWC: 160-44

NGT-30-002-002   University of New Hampshire   W. H. Drew
Training of predoctoral graduate students in space-related science and technology.

No. Students	FY	Agreement Period	Amount
5	65	9/65 - 8/68	96500
6	66	9/66 - 8/69	114000
4	67	9/67 - 8/70	65500

Tech. Off.: HANSING F D	Funding Element: HQ-Y
CASE Code: 99	AWC: 181-00

NEW JERSEY

NGR-31-006-006   Fairleigh Dickinson University   K. D. Moeller
Improvements of spectroscopic devices in the far infrared.

Proposal	FY	Agreement Period	Amount
-006	69	1/69 -12/69	15000

Tech. Off.: HARD T M	Funding Element: ERC
CASE Code: 49	AWC: 125-24

NGR-31-011-002   New Jersey College of Medicine & Dentistry
Morphologic and functional effects of hepatic   **C. M. Leevy**
proton irradiation.

Proposal	FY	Agreement Period	Amount
-002	67	4/67 - 6/68	60216
-003	69	7/68 - 6/69	60000

Tech. Off.: DIETLEIN L F	Funding Element: MSC
CASE Code: 51	AWC: 914-50

NGR-31-009-004   Newark College of Engineering   P. Hrycak
Heat transfer from impinging jets.

Proposal	FY	Agreement Period	Amount
-004	67	6/67 - 5/68	21043
		- 9/68	NCE

Tech. Off.: BAZARKO V O	Funding Element: LERC
CASE Code: 46	AWC: 720-03

NAS8-21286   Newark College of Engineering   R. Misra
Chemical and structural analysis of second breakdown.

Proposal	FY	Agreement Period	Amount
	68	4/68 - 4/69	23000
			MSFC

Tech. Off.:	Funding Element:
CASE Code: 46	AWC: 905-31

NEW JERSEY (Cont'd.)

NAS12-2062   Newark College of Engineering   E. M. Rips
Designers manual for performance evaluation.

Proposal	FY	Agreement Period	Amount
	69	1/69 – 11/69	15000

Tech. Off.:   Funding Element:
CASE Code: 99   AWC: 1 2 5 – 2 5

NGR-31-001-001   Princeton University   M. Schwarzschild
Stratoscope II high altitude balloon telescope program.

Proposal	FY	Agreement Period	Amount
–118	68	2/68 – 6/68	400000
–118	68	2/68 – 5/68	100000
–154	69	10/68 – 6/69	100000

Tech. Off.: ROMAN   Funding Element: HQ-SG
CASE Code: 1 1   AWC: 1 8 8 – 4 1

NGL-31-001-007   Princeton University   L. Spitzer
Astrophysical ultraviolet studies.

Proposal	FY	Agreement Period	Amount
–069	66	4/66 – 3/69	301000
–101	67	4/67 – 3/70	102000
–126	66	4/68 – 3/71	134000
–160	69	4/69 – 3/72	120000

Tech. Off.: ROMAN   Funding Element: HQ-SG
CASE Code: 1 1   AWC: 1 8 8 – 4 1

NGR-31-001-025   Princeton University   W. R. Schowalter
Constitutive equations for nonviscometric flows.

Proposal	FY	Agreement Period	Amount
–053	65	7/65 – 6/68	36926
–070	66	7/66 – 6/68	21000
–131	68	7/68 – 6/69	15000

Tech. Off.: HOWE J   Funding Element: HQ-RR
CASE Code: 2 1   AWC: 1 2 9 – 0 1

NGR-31-001-044   Princeton University   L. Spitzer
Design study of manned orbiting telescope for an extended
Apollo system.

Proposal	FY	Agreement Period	Amount
–108	67	5/67 – 4/68	125000
–123	68	11/67 – 6/68	20000

Tech. Off.:   Funding Element:
CASE Code: 1 1   AWC: 6 8 5 – 1 0

NGR-31-001-059   Princeton University   E. Dowell
Investigation of non-linear problems and mathematical methods in aeroelasticity.

Proposal	FY	Agreement Period	Amount
–092	68	4/67 – 3/68	24320
–125	69	4/68 – 3/69	25917

Tech. Off.: WILSON R   Funding Element: HQ-RR
CASE Code: 2 1   AWC: 1 2 9 – 0 4

NGR-31-001-068   Princeton University   L. D. Davisson
Study of advanced communication techniques.

Proposal	FY	Agreement Period	Amount
–105	68	7/67 – 6/68	15000
–128	69	7/68 – 6/69	15361

Tech. Off.: KUTZ R   Funding Element: GSFC
CASE Code: 45   AWC: 1 6 0 – 4 4

NGR-31-001-074   Princeton University   C. L. Mellor
Investigation of turbulent boundary layers with suction, cross
flows and wall.

Proposal	FY	Agreement Period	Amount
–120	68	10/67 – 9/68	48010
–143	69	10/68 – 9/69	49940

Tech. Off.: LIEBLEIN S   Funding Element: LERC
CASE Code: 13   AWC: 7 2 1 – 0 3

NGR-31-001-093   Princeton University   R. B. Hargraves
Palemagnetic and petrographic investigation of possible meteorite impact structures in South Africa.

Proposal	FY	Agreement Period	Amount
–093	67	4/67 – 3/68	12498
–093	67	4/68 – 3/69	NCE

Tech. Off.: WILMARTH V R   Funding Element: HQ-SL
CASE Code: 32   AWC: 1 8 5 – 4 2

NGR-31-001-103   Princeton University   S. H. Lam
Studies in ionospheric aerodynamics.

Proposal	FY	Agreement Period	Amount
–103	67	7/67 – 8/68	25000
–103	68	7/67 – 8/68	66970
–141	69	9/68 – 8/69	30000

Tech. Off.: BRINTON H   Funding Element: GSFC
CASE Code: 31   AWC: 3 8 5 – 3 9

NGR-31-001-109   Princeton University   M. Summerfield
Design principles for predicting the ignition performance of solid
propellant rocket motors.

Proposal	FY	Agreement Period	Amount
–109	68	10/67 – 9/68	79478
–139	69	10/68 – 9/69	50000

Tech. Off.:   Funding Element: LARC
CASE Code: 43   AWC: 1 2 8 – 3 2

NGR-31-001-119   Princeton University   W. D. Hayes
Theoretical problems connected with sonic boom.

Proposal	FY	Agreement Period	Amount
–119	68	10/67 – 9/68	22790
–148	69	10/68 – 9/69	30000

Tech. Off.: SCHWARTZ I R   Funding Element: HQ-RR
CASE Code: 41   AWC: 1 2 9 – 0 1

NGR-31-001-129   Princeton University   I. Glassman
Combustion of metals.

Proposal	FY	Agreement Period	Amount
–129	68	4/68 – 9/68	30000
–153	69	10/68 – 9/69	45000

Tech. Off.:   Funding Element: LARC
CASE Code: 12   AWC: 1 2 8 – 3 2

NEW JERSEY (Cont'd.)

NGR-31-001-132   Princeton University   A. W. Lo
Impulse techniques for testing digital microcircuits.

Proposal	FY	Agreement Period	Amount
-132	68	7/68 - 6/69	9970
-132		9/69	NCE

Tech. Off.:   Funding Element: ERC
CASE Code: 21   AWC: 125-25

NGR-31-001-142   Princeton University   R. E. Danielson
Application of digital computer and optical analog techniques to rectification and enhancement of astronomical images.

Proposal	FY	Agreement Period	Amount
-142	69	12/68 -12/69	79500

Tech. Off.: SURES A H   Funding Element: HQ-SG
CASE Code: 42   AWC: 188-78

NGR-31-001-145   Princeton University   C. S. Pittendrigh
Circadian rhythms: an analysis under terrestrial conditions and in an orbiting biological satellite.

Proposal	FY	Agreement Period	Amount
-145	69	7/68 - 6/69	74627

Tech. Off.:   Funding Element:
CASE Code: 51   AWC: 189-52

NGR-31-001-146   Princeton University   E. H. Dowell
Boundary layer noise and panel flutter.

Proposal	FY	Agreement Period	Amount
-146	69	11/68 -10/69	34920

Tech. Off.:   Funding Element: LARC
CASE Code: 41   AWC: 126-14

NGR-31-001-151   Princeton University   A. J. Kelly
Molecular beam studies of inelastic neutral particle cross sections.

Proposal	FY	Agreement Period	Amount
-151	68	10/68 - 9/69	23993

Tech. Off.: HOWE J T   Funding Element: HQ-RR
CASE Code: 13   AWC: 129-01

NGR-31-001-155   Princeton University   D. T. Harrje
Non-linear aspects of combustion instability in liquid propellant rocket motors.

Proposal	FY	Agreement Period	Amount
-155	69	2/69 - 1/70	246000
-163	69	2/69 - 2/71	246000

Tech. Off.: HEIDMANN M F   Funding Element: LERC
CASE Code: 49   AWC: 128-31

NSR-31-001-104   Princeton University   E. Seckel
Investigation of the effect of turbulence on flying qualities.

Proposal	FY	Agreement Period	Amount
-104	68	6/68 - 5/69	49965

Tech. Off.:   Funding Element:
CASE Code: 41   AWC: 126-62

NSR-31-001-127   Princeton University   J. L. Lowrance
Evaluation and development of television tubes for space astronomy.

Proposal	FY	Agreement Period	Amount
-127	68	6/68 - 5/69	100000

Tech. Off.:   Funding Element:
CASE Code: 45   AWC: 188-41

NSR-31-001-150   Princeton University   J. P. Layton
Aerospace systems and mission analysis research.

Proposal	FY	Agreement Period	Amount
-150	69	9/68 -10/69	100000

Tech. Off.: HAUGHEY J W   Funding Element: HQ-SV
CASE Code: 42   AWC: 180-06

NSR-31-001-901   Princeton University   D. C. Morton
Ultraviolet spectrographic investigations by high altitude rocket flights.

Proposal	FY	Agreement Period	Amount
-091	67	2/67 - 9/68	433530
-134	68	9/68 - 6/69	100000

Tech. Off.: HOLTZ S R   Funding Element: HQ-SG
CASE Code: 31   AWC: 831-22

NSR-31-001-902   Princeton University   D. T. Harrje
Reference book on liquid propellant rocket combustion instability.

Proposal	FY	Agreement Period	Amount
-106	67	6/67 -11/68	76300
-106	68	9/68 -11/68	35000
		/ - 5/69	NCE

Tech. Off.: PRIEM R J   Funding Element: LERC
CASE Code: 43   AWC: 128-31

NAS1-7022   Princeton University   J. K. Gillham
Evaluation of the variables in the mechanical spectroscopy of pyrones.

Proposal	FY	Agreement Period	Amount
		1/67 - 4/68	14000
	67	1/67 - 5/69	30000

Tech. Off.: PEZDIRTZ G F   Funding Element: LARC
CASE Code: 32   AWC: 129-03

NAS2-5098   Princeton University   C. Pittendrigh
Biology experiments in support of applied flight experiment S-072 (Vinegar Gnat Clock) hardware definition.

Proposal	FY	Agreement Period	Amount
	68	8/68 - 2/69	27000

Tech. Off.:   Funding Element:
CASE Code: 51   AWC: 948-80

NEW JERSEY (Cont'd.)

NAS5-1810   **Princeton University**   **L. Spitzer**
Design, develop, fabricate & test orbiting astronomical observatory experiment.

Proposal	FY	Agreement Period	Amount
		6/62 –12/68	9890000
	68	6/62 –12/68	110000
	68	6/62 –12/68	200000
	68	6/62 –12/68	1049

Tech. Off.: STROUP R   Funding Element: GSFC
CASE Code: 11   AWC: 831–22

NAS9-7897   **Princeton University**   **H. H. Hess**
Determine pyroxene content by x-ray and optical methods.

Proposal	FY	Agreement Period	Amount
	68	6/68 –10/69	62000
			MSC

Tech. Off.:   Funding Element:
CASE Code: 32   AWC: 914–40

NGT-31-001-009 **Princeton University**   **C. S. Pittendrigh**
Training of predoctoral graduate students in space-related science and technology.

No. Students:	FY	Agreement Period	Amount
12	65	9/65 – 8/68	231300
15	66	9/66 – 8/69	324000
9	67	9/67 – 8/70	170500

Tech. Off.: HANSING F D   Funding Element: HQ–Y
CASE Code: 99   AWC: 181–00

NGF-31-001-011 **Princeton University**   **J. P. Layton**
Construction of a basic research laboratory wing of the Guggenheim Laboratories for the Aerospace Propulsion Sciences.

Proposal	FY	Agreement Period	Amount
5518	63	6/63 – 9/64	625000

Tech. Off.: HOLMES D C   Funding Element: HQ–Y
CASE Code: 49   AWC: 182–00

NAS5-9276   **Rutgers University**   **A. Rolly**
OSO-G experiment — determination for the brightness, polarization and ellipticity of the zodiacal light.

Proposal	FY	Agreement Period	Amount
	68	12/65 – 3/68	160000

Tech. Off.: OSTAFF W   Funding Element: GSFC
CASE Code: 31   AWC: 821–22

NGT-31-004-002 **Rutgers University**   **H. C. Torrey**
Supporting the training of predoctoral graduate students in space-related science and technology.

No. Students:	FY	Agreement Period	Amount
12	65	9/65 – 8/68	189600
12	66	9/66 – 8/69	178000
6	67	9/67 – 8/70	90600

Tech. Off.: HANSING F D   Funding Element: HQ–Y
CASE Code: 99   AWC: 181–00

NGR-31-003-014 **Stevens Institute of Technology**   **R. F. McAlevy**
Investigation of the flame spreading over the surface of ignited solid propellants.

Proposal	FY	Agreement Period	Amount
–058	68	10/67 –10/68	47000
–070	69	10/68 –10/69	47000

Tech. Off.: VANBANDINGHAM   Funding Element: LARC
CASE Code: 43   AWC: 128–32

NGL-31-003-020 **Stevens Institute of Technology**   **H. Meissner**
Proximity effects between superconducting and normal metals.

Proposal	FY	Agreement Period	Amount
–061	68	4/68 – 3/69	18900
–071	67	4/68 – 3/71	19000
–072	69	4/70 – 3/72	19000

Tech. Off.: JOHNSON P   Funding Element: HQ–RR
CASE Code: 12   AWC: 129–02

NGR-31-003-050 **Stevens Institute of Technology**   **G. J. Herskowitz**
Microcircuit models and diagnostic techniques for environmental failure mode prediction.

Proposal	FY	Agreement Period	Amount
–064	68	1/68 –12/68	15077
		– 6/69	NCE

Tech. Off.: CARPENTER R M   Funding Element: ERC
CASE Code: 45   AWC: 125–25

NGR-31-003-066 **Stevens Institute of Technology**   **E. C. Ney**
An investigation to develop computer techniques for fault identification in multi-terminal networks.

Proposal	FY	Agreement Period	Amount
–066	68	6/68 – 5/69	9993
			ERC

Tech. Off.: SARKISIAN   Funding Element: ERC
CASE Code: 21   AWC: 125–54

NAS1-8830   **Stevens Institute of Technology**   **S. Tsakongs**
Analytical study of airloads in rotar blades.

Proposal	FY	Agreement Period	Amount
	69	12/68 – 2/70	55000

Tech. Off.:   Funding Element:
CASE Code: 41   AWC: 721–01

NAS12-654   **Stevens Institute of Technology**
Analysis of nonlinear circuits by computer.

Proposal	FY	Agreement Period	Amount
	68	4/68 – 8/69	12000

Tech. Off.:   Funding Element: ERC
CASE Code: 21   AWC: 125–25

NAS12-2065   **Stevens Institute of Technology**   **G. J. Herskowitz**
Designers manual for computer-aided design.

Proposal	FY	Agreement Period	Amount
	69	1/69 –11/69	16000

Tech. Off.:   Funding Element:
CASE Code: 21   AWC: 125–25

NEW JERSEY (Cont'd)

NAS12-2101   **Stevens Institute of Technology**   **C. T. Brooth**
Application of dimensional analysis and similitude techniques.

Proposal	FY	Agreement Period	Amount
	69	3/69 – 2/70	16000

Tech. Off.:   Funding Element:
CASE Code: 49   AWC: 125-25

NGT-31-003-005   **Stevens Institute of Technology**   **R. A. Morgen**
Training of predoctoral graduate students in space-related science and technology.

No. Students	FY	Agreement Period	Amount
8	65	9/65 – 8/68	144000
8	66	9/66 – 8/69	144000
4	67	9/67 – 8/70	62500

Tech. Off.: HANSING F D   Funding Element: HQ-Y
CASE Code: 99   AWC: 181-00

NEW MEXICO

NGL-32-003-001   **New Mexico State University**   **C. W. Tombough**
Photographic, photoelectric and spectrographic observations and studies of the planets.

Proposal	FY	Agreement Period	Amount
-025	65	4/65 – 4/68	114955
-029	66	4/66 – 4/69	120673
-040	67	4/67 – 4/70	129948
-051	68	4/68 – 4/71	120000
-055		4/69 – 4/72	115000

Tech. Off.: BRUNK W E   Funding Element: HQ-SL
CASE Code: 11   AWC: 185-41

NGL-32-003-027   **New Mexico State University**   **J. E. Weiss**
Multidisciplinary research program in space science and engineering.

Proposal	FY	Agreement Period	Amount
-027	65	9/65 – 8/68	300000
-035	67	9/66 – 8/69	150000
-046	68	9/67 – 8/70	50000

Tech. Off.: MARR E G   Funding Element: HQ-Y
CASE Code: 99   AWC: 183-00

NAS5-10427   **New Mexico State University**   **R. A. Bumgarner**
Telemetry services and research and development.

Proposal	FY	Agreement Period	Amount
		6/67 – 6/69	558000
	68	6/67 – 6/69	502000
	68	6/67 – 6/69	470000

Tech. Off.: BISSELL E   Funding Element: GSFC
CASE Code: 49   AWC: 879-70

NAS5-10554   **New Mexico State University**   **R. B. Chavez**
Data reduction.

Proposal	FY	Agreement Period	Amount
		8/67 – 6/69	180000
	68	8/67 – 6/69	62000
	68	8/67 – 6/69	40000

Tech. Off.: OOSTERHAUT J   Funding Element: GSFC
CASE Code: 39   AWC: 311-01

NAS7-535   **New Mexico State University**   **R. A. Bumgarner**
Telemetry field services and research and development and technical operations support at the AF Eastern Test Range and AF Western Test Range.

Proposal	FY	Agreement Period	Amount
		12/66 – 12/68	425000

Tech. Off.: SHEPPARD D   Funding Element: GSFC
CASE Code: 49   AWC: 492-21

NAS7-716   **New Mexico State University**
Research and development and technical operations support at the AF Eastern Test Range, AF Western Test Range and other locations for temporary periods.

Proposal	FY	Agreement Period	Amount
	69	12/68 – 3/71	460000

Tech. Off.:   Funding Element:
CASE Code: 49   AWC: 492-21

NGT-32-003-004   **New Mexico State University**   **E. Walden**
Training of predoctoral graduate students in space-related science and technology.

No. Students	FY	Agreement Period	Amount
8	65	9/65 – 8/68	161800
8	66	9/66 – 8/69	161800
4	67	9/67 – 8/70	80900

Tech. Off.: HANSING F D   Funding Element: HQ-Y
CASE Code: 99   AWC: 181-00

NGR-32-004-026   **University of New Mexico**   **C. G. Richards**
Numerical study of the flow in the vortex rate sensor.

Proposal	FY	Agreement Period	Amount
-035	68	11/67 – 10/68	33416
		11/68 – 6/69	NCE

Tech. Off.: HELLBAUM R F   Funding Element: LARC
CASE Code: 21   AWC: 125-19

NGL-32-004-042   **University of New Mexico**   **W. W. Grannemann**
The proof-of-concept approach to the design and management of public policy programs.

Proposal	FY	Agreement Period	Amount
-042	68	2/68 – 1/71	300000
-056		2/69 – 1/72	150000

Tech. Off.: STEPHENS R E   Funding Element: HQ-Y
CASE Code: 79   AWC: 183-00

NEW MEXICO (Cont'd.)

NSR-32-004-049   University of New Mexico
Continuation of Regional Dissemination Center operation at the Technology Use Studies Center.

Proposal	FY	Agreement Period	Amount
−049	68	7/68 − 6/69	170000

Tech. Off.:   Funding Element:
CASE Code: 79   AWC: 141−00

NAS5-9275   University of New Mexico   C. P. Leavitt
Experiment for OSO—G entitled "High Energy Neutron Flux in Space".

Proposal	FY	Agreement Period	Amount
	68	12/65 − 6/68	81000

Tech. Off.:   OSTAFF W   Funding Element: GSFC
CASE Code: 11   AWC: 821−22

NAS5-9314   University of New Mexico   V. H. Regener
Solar ultraviolet energy survey experiment for the Orbiting Geophysical Observatories Program, OGO-F Mission.

Proposal	FY	Agreement Period	Amount
	68	3/66 − 6/68	66000
	66	3/66 − 6/66	15000
	68	3/66 − 6/68	19000

Tech. Off.:   MERCANTI E   Funding Element: GSFC
CASE Code: 11   AWC: 841−12

NAS9-9365   University of New Mexico   K. Keil
Study of lunar samples.

Proposal	FY	Agreement Period	Amount
	69	4/69 − 7/69	42000

Tech. Off.:   MC DAY D S   Funding Element:
CASE Code: 32   AWC: 914−40

NGR-32-004-001   University of New Mexico   A. Erteza
Investigate radar echoes from moon and planets, using methods and data from earth radar-return studies.

Proposal	FY	Agreement Period	Amount
−043	69	1/68 −12/68	19765
		− 9/69	NCE

Tech. Off.:   BRUNK W E   Funding Element: HQ−SL
CASE Code: 11   AWC: 185−39

NGR-32-004-002   University of New Mexico   W. W. Grannemann
Research on Hall effect for low voltage, high current DC and AC conversion.

Proposal	FY	Agreement Period	Amount
−041	68	1/68 −12/68	17323
		− 9/69	NCE

Tech. Off.:   SCHWARTZ F C   Funding Element: ERC
CASE Code: 13   AWC: 123−33

NGL-32-004-011   University of New Mexico   W. Elston
Comparative study of lunar craters and terrestrial volcano-tectonic depressions in rhyolite ash-flow plateaus.

Proposal	FY	Agreement Period	Amount
−034	67	8/67 − 7/68	25000

Tech. Off.:   Funding Element:
CASE Code: 32   AWC: 185−42

NGT-32-004-004   University of New Mexico   A. Steger
Training of predoctoral graduate students in space-related science and technology.

No. Students	FY	Agreement Period	Amount
8	65	9/65 − 8/68	149100
8	66	9/66 − 8/69	142600
4	67	9/67 − 8/70	68900

Tech. Off.:   HANSING F D   Funding Element: HQ−Y
CASE Code: 99   AWC: 181−00

NEW YORK

NGL-33-001-001   Adelphi University   R. Genberg
Multidisciplinary research in space-related sciences and technology.

Proposal	FY	Agreement Period	Amount
−011	66	3/66 − 2/69	80000
−017	67	3/67 − 2/70	80000

Tech. Off.:   MARR E G   Funding Element: HQ−Y
CASE Code: 99   AWC: 183−00

NGR-33-001-019   Adelphi University   R. Genberg
Cometary investigation during the total solar eclipse of 22 September 1968.

Proposal	FY	Agreement Period	Amount
−019	69	9/68 − 9/69	5000

Tech. Off.:   DUBIN M   Funding Element: HQ−SG
CASE Code: 11   AWC: 188−45

NGT-33-001-002   Adelphi University   M. V. B. Jennings
Training of predoctoral graduate students in space-related science and technology.

No. Students	FY	Agreement Period	Amount
4	65	9/65 − 8/68	79900
4	66	9/66 − 8/69	83200
2	67	9/67 − 8/70	41600

Tech. Off.:   HANSING F D   Funding Element: HQ−Y
CASE Code: 99   AWC: 181−00

NGT-33-002-002   Alfred University   E. E. Mueller
Training of predoctoral graduate students in space-related science and technology.

No. Students	FY	Agreement Period	Amount
2	65	9/65 − 8/68	26400
2	66	9/66 − 8/69	26400
1	67	9/67 − 8/70	18000

Tech. Off.:   HANSING F D   Funding Element: HQ−Y
CASE Code: 99   AWC: 181−00

NEW YORK (Cont'd.)

NGR-33-013-009   City College of New York   R. Shinner
Study of atomization of viscoelastic fluids.

Proposal	FY	Agreement Period	Amount
-009	65	9/65 – 8/67	49610
-009		9/66 –12/67	NCE
-009	65	1/68 – 4/68	NCE
-037	68	5/68 – 4/69	20000
-037		10/69	NCE

Tech. Off.: HOWE J   Funding Element: HQ-RR
CASE Code: 12   AWC: 129-01

NGR-33-013-017   City College of New York   M. Kolodney
Oxidation protection of columbium and tantalum.

Proposal	FY	Agreement Period	Amount
-028	67	9/67 – 8/68	10872
-028	67	9/68 – 8/69	NCE

Tech. Off.: OLDRIEVE R E   Funding Element: LERC
CASE Code: 12   AWC: 720-03

NGR-33-013-025   City College of New York
S. M. Chen
Analytical calibration of D. C. electromagnetic flowmeter.

Proposal	FY	Agreement Period	Amount
-025	67	2/67 –10/67	10944
-025	67	11/67 – 1/68	NCE
-042	69	2/69 – 1/70	11500

Tech. Off.:   Funding Element: LERC
CASE Code: 13   AWC: 120-27

NGR-33-013-029   City College of New York
R. Pfeffer
The effect of particle and fluid properties on the heat transfer coefficient and pressure drop of a dilute flowing gas-solid suspension.

Proposal	FY	Agreement Period	Amount
-029	68	10/67 – 9/69	23124

Tech. Off.: PUTRE H A   Funding Element: LERC
CASE Code: 13   AWC: 122-28

NGR-33-013-034   City College of New York
C. M. Tchen
Investigations of electromagnetics and statistical dynamics as applied to plasma propulsion.

Proposal	FY	Agreement Period	Amount
-034	68	4/68 – 3/71	32000
-044	69	4/69 – 4/72	16000

Tech. Off.:   Funding Element:
CASE Code: 13   AWC: 129-02

NGT-33-014-002   City University of New York   M. Rees
Training of predoctoral graduate students in space-related science and technology.

No. Students	FY	Agreement Period	Amount
6	65	9/65 – 8/68	118800
6	66	9/66 – 8/69	118800
4	67	9/67 – 8/70	76600

Tech. Off.: HANSING F D   Funding Element: HQ-Y
CASE Code: 99   AWC: 181-00

NGR-33-007-034   Clarkson College of Technology   L. C. Barrett
Effects on the motion of a body attracted by a rotating source.

Proposal	FY	Agreement Period	Amount
-034	67	6/67 – 5/68	18315
		5/68 – 9/68	NCE
-073	69	9/68 – 8/69	24675

Tech. Off.: WILSON R   Funding Element: HQ-RR
CASE Code: 13   AWC: 129-04

NGR-33-007-061   Clarkson College of Technology   C. W. Haines
Application of optimal control theory to the design of an autopilot for reduction of acceleration inputs to an aircraft in turbulent air.

Proposal	FY	Agreement Period	Amount
-061	68	2/68 – 5/69	12160

Tech. Off.:   Funding Element: LARC
CASE Code: 41   AWC: 125-17

NGR-33-007-074   Clarkson College of Technology   H. H. G. Jellinek
Photolysis of polymers in presence of NO_2, ozone, air and UV light and the influence of polymer morphology.

Proposal	FY	Agreement Period	Amount
-074	69	12/68 –11/69	20029

Tech. Off.:   Funding Element: ARC
CASE Code: 12   AWC: 129-03

NGL-33-007-075   Clarkson College of Technology   W. A. Thorton
Development of computer program for the minimum weight design of stiffened shells of revolution.

Proposal	FY	Agreement Period	Amount
-075	69	12/68 –11/71	36000

Tech. Off.: FULTON R E   Funding Element: LARC
CASE Code: 21   AWC: 124-08

NGT-33-007-001   Clarkson College of Technology   H. L. Shulman
Training of predoctoral graduate students in space-related science and technology.

No. Students	FY	Agreement Period	Amount
4	65	9/65 – 8/68	82800
4	66	9/66 – 8/69	82800
2	67	9/67 – 8/70	41400

Tech. Off.: HANSING F D   Funding Element: HQ-Y
CASE Code: 99   AWC: 181-00

NGR-33-008-009   Columbia University   R. Novick
Theoretical and experimental investigations of helium and lithium atoms and ions with emphasis on excited energy levels and the mechanism of energy transfer from metastable states.

Proposal	FY	Agreement Period	Amount
-101	68	1/68 –12/68	58000
-120	69	1/69 – 1/70	50000

Tech. Off.: THOM K   Funding Element: HQ-RR
CASE Code: 13   AWC: 129-02

NEW YORK (Cont'd.)

NGR-33-008-012   Columbia University

H. M. Foley, R. Novick, L. Woltjer, P. W. Gast

Theoretical and analytical studies of planetary and stellar structure, evolution and dynamical processes; and applicability of geophysical methods to such studies.

Proposal	FY	Agreement Period	Amount
-091	67	9/67 - 8/68	50000
-092	67	9/67 - 8/68	93000
-096	67	9/67 - 8/68	21000
-105	68	9/67 - 8/68	199253
-115	68	9/68 - 8/69	200000

Tech. Off.: LEVINE A   Funding Element: GSFC
CASE Code: 11   AWC: 160-44

NGR-33-008-061   Columbia University   P. W. Gast

Study of alkali metal, alkaline earth and lanthanide elements in lunar material.

Proposal	FY	Agreement Period	Amount
-094	67	5/67 - 4/68	39980

Tech. Off.: WILMARTH R   Funding Element: HQ-SL
CASE Code: 32   AWC: 848-00

NGR-33-008-090   Columbia University   C. C. Halkias

A systems approach to device-circuit interaction in electrical power processing.

Proposal	FY	Agreement Period	Amount
-090	67	6/67 - 5/68	62171
-108	68	6/68 - 5/69	75910

Tech. Off.: SCHWARTZ F C   Funding Element: ERC
CASE Code: 45   AWC: 120-33

NGR-33-008-098   Columbia University   M. B. Friedman

Research into the theory of the superboom.

Proposal	FY	Agreement Period	Amount
-098	68	8/67 - 7/68	30750
-110	69	8/68 - 7/69	37188

Tech. Off.: DANBERG J E   Funding Element: HQ-RR
CASE Code: 13   AWC: 129-01

NGR-33-008-102   Columbia University   E. J. Ott

Research in x-ray astronomy.

Proposal	FY	Agreement Period	Amount
-102	68	1/68 - 12/68	75000
-117	69	1/69 - 1/70	150000

Tech. Off.: ROMAN N G   Funding Element: HQ-SG
CASE Code: 11   AWC: 879-10

NGR-33-008-118   Columbia University   P. N. Borsky

Reactions of people to aircraft noise and sonic booms.

Proposal	FY	Agreement Period	Amount
-118	69	3/69 - 3/70	115415

Tech. Off.: CAWTHORN J M   Funding Element: LARC
CASE Code: 41   AWC: 127-49

NSR-33-008-069   Columbia University   W. A. Owens

Summer institute in space physics and in space science and engineering.

Proposal	FY	Agreement Period	Amount
-104	68	12/65 - 12/68	48640
-116	69	12/68 - 12/69	49480

Tech. Off.: CARTER C H   Funding Element: HQ-Y
CASE Code: 19   AWC: 181

NAS8-20331   Columbia University   C. M. Harris

Study of absorption of low audio frequency acoustic energy in the atmospheric media.

Proposal	FY	Agreement Period	Amount
		5/66 - 8/68	82000

Tech. Off.: JEWELL R   Funding Element: MSFC
CASE Code: 31   AWC: 124-10

NAS9-5957   Columbia University   G. Latham

Passive seismic experiment for ALSEP.

Proposal	FY	Agreement Period	Amount
		5/66 - 6/69	453000
	68	5/66 - 6/69	100000
	68	5/66 - 6/69	291000

Tech. Off.: LE CROIX B   Funding Element: MSC
CASE Code: 32   AWC: 914-40

NAS9-6037   Columbia University   M. Ewing

Heat flow experiment for ALSEP.

Proposal	FY	Agreement Period	Amount
		4/67 - 6/69	200000
	68	4/67 - 6/69	6000
	67	6/66 - 6/69	161000

Tech. Off.: MC COMB R   Funding Element: MSC
CASE Code: 13   AWC: 914-40

NAS9-7890   Columbia University   R. Anderson

Measurement of physical properties on returned lunar samples.

Proposal	FY	Agreement Period	Amount
	68	5/68 - 10/69	25000

Tech. Off.:   Funding Element: MSC
CASE Code: 32   AWC: 914-40

NAS9-7895   Columbia University   P. W. Gast

Determine concentration of the alkali alkaline earth and lanthanide elements by mass spectroscopy.

Proposal	FY	Agreement Period	Amount
	68	6/68 - 10/69	60000

Tech. Off.:   Funding Element: MSC
CASE Code: 32   AWC: 914-40

NGT-33-008-013   Columbia University   R. S. Halford

Training of predoctoral graduate students in space-related science and technology.

No. Students	FY	Agreement Period	Amount
15	65	9/65 - 8/68	275500
9	67	9/67 - 8/70	137700
15	66	9/66 - 8/69	275500

Tech. Off.: HANSING F D   Funding Element: HQ-Y
CASE Code: 99   AWC: 181-00

NEW YORK (Cont'd.)

NGR-33-010-013 Cornell University   **M. Alexander**
Paleobiochemistry of amino acids and polypeptides.

Proposal	FY	Agreement Period	Amount
-013	65	8/64 – 7/66	46880
-013	65	8/68 – 7/69	NCE

Tech. Off.: YOUNG R S   Funding Element: ARC
CASE Code: 51   AWC: 189-55

NGR-33-010-029 Cornell University   **L. H. Germer**
Adsorption and chemical reactions of atoms and molecules on the surface of crystals.

Proposal	FY	Agreement Period	Amount
-050	67	5/67 – 4/68	32000
-069	68	5/68 – 4/69	20000

Tech. Off.: NASH R   Funding Element: HQ-RR
CASE Code: 13   AWC: 129-03

NGR-33-010-039 Cornell University   **P. P. Van Riper**
Study of top level decision-making within the National Aeronautics and Space Administration.

Proposal	FY	Agreement Period	Amount
	67	7/66 – 6/67	26120
-039	67	7/67 – 6/68	NCE
		– 6/69	NCE

Tech. Off.: HALPERN I P   Funding Element: HQ-EP
CASE Code: 75   AWC: 039-00

NGR-33-010-042 Cornell University   **F. K. Moore**
Study of high temperature heat transfer.

Proposal	FY	Agreement Period	Amount
-053	68	7/67 – 6/68	50740
-076	69	7/68 – 6/69	49798

Tech. Off.: EWARD H C   Funding Element: LERC
CASE Code: 13   AWC: 122-28

NGL-33-010-047 Cornell University   **P. R. McIsaac**
Advanced concepts of microwave power amplification and generation utilizing linear beam devices.

Proposal	FY	Agreement Period	Amount
-062	68	11/67 – 10/68	30208
-077	68	11/68 – 10/70	30000
-085	69	11/68 – 10/71	30000

Tech. Off.: KULKE B   Funding Element: ERC
CASE Code: 13   AWC: 125-22

NGR-33-010-051 Cornell University   **C. L. Tang**
Theoretical and experimental studies of the ionized rare gas lasers.

Proposal	FY	Agreement Period	Amount
-068	68	2/68 – 1/69	25000

Tech. Off.: PAANANEN R A   Funding Element: ERC
CASE Code: 13   AWC: 125-21

NGL-33-010-054 Cornell University   **A. R. Seebass**
Sonic boom research.

Proposal	FY	Agreement Period	Amount
-054	68	9/67 – 8/70	58500
-086	69	9/68 – 8/71	30000

Tech. Off.: SCHART R   Funding Element: HQ-RR
CASE Code: 13   AWC: 129-01

NGR-33-010-064 Cornell University   **T. A. Cool**
Molecular energy transfer by fluid mixing.

Proposal	FY	Agreement Period	Amount
-064	68	1/68 – 12/70	40000
-095	69	1/69 – 12/71	40000

Tech. Off.: HOWE J T   Funding Element: HQ-RR
CASE Code: 13   AWC: 128-01

NGR-33-010-070 Cornell University   **R. H. Gallagher**
Finite element shell instability analysis.

Proposal	FY	Agreement Period	Amount
-070	69	11/68 – 10/70	67170

Tech. Off.: WILSON B M   Funding Element: LARC
CASE Code: 46   AWC: 126-14

NGR-33-010-071 Cornell University   **H. N. McManus**
Graduate engineering design program—Phase II.

Proposal	FY	Agreement Period	Amount
-071	67	7/68 – 6/70	29637
-083	68	9/68 – 8/71	74213
-089	69	9/69 – 8/72	46202

Tech. Off.: VITALE J A   Funding Element: HQ-Y
CASE Code: 49   AWC: 183-00

NGR-33-010-074 Cornell University   **F. D. McLeod**
Directional doppler flowmeter.

Proposal	FY	Agreement Period	Amount
-074	67	6/68 – 5/69	20790
			ERC

Tech. Off.: SULLIVAN P F   Funding Element: ERC
CASE Code: 13   AWC: 125-24

NGR-33-010-082 Cornell University   **C. Sagan**
Study of lunar and planetary surfaces and atmospheres.

Proposal	FY	Agreement Period	Amount
-082	69	9/68 – 8/69	46449

Tech. Off.:   Funding Element:
CASE Code: 32   AWC: 185-37

NGR-33-010-096 Cornell University   **C. Sagan**
Guest observations of the planets on OAO A2.

Proposal	FY	Agreement Period	Amount
-096	69	5/69 – 5/70	8411

Tech. Off.: ASHWORTH C D   Funding Element: HQ-SG
CASE Code: 42   AWC: 831-12

NEW YORK (Cont'd.)

NGR-33-010-098   Cornell University   C. Sagan
Participation in the Mars lander photointerpretation mission
definition study.

Proposal	FY	Agreement Period	Amount
-098	69	2/69 - 2/70	4677

Tech. Off.: MITZ M A   Funding Element: HQ-SL
CASE Code: 42   AWC: 815-20

NSR-33-010-055   Cornell University   M. F. Meserve
An investigation directed toward designing, developing and
testing the components of a total control lunar roving vehicle.

Proposal	FY	Agreement Period	Amount
-055	67	6/67 - 6/68	70311
-072	68	6/68 - 6/69	71070

Tech. Off.: KEE R   Funding Element: HQ-SL
CASE Code: 42   AWC: 186-68

NAS9-8018   Cornell University
Preparation of equipment and techniques for lunar sample
analysis.

Proposal	FY	Agreement Period	Amount
	68	6/68 -12/69	38000

Tech. Off.:   Funding Element: MSC
CASE Code: 32   AWC: 914-40

NAS9-9017   Cornell University
Fabrication of 1 working model of a close-up lunar surface
stereo camera.

Proposal	FY	Agreement Period	Amount
	69	12/68 - 3/69	10000

Tech. Off.:   Funding Element:
CASE Code: 42   AWC: 914-40

NGT-33-010-007   Cornell University   F. S. Erdman
Training of predoctoral graduate students in space-related
science and technology.

No. Students	FY	Agreement Period	Amount
15	65	9/65 - 8/68	279000
15	66	9/66 - 8/69	288000
9	67	9/67 - 8/70	175100

Tech. Off.: HANSING F D   Funding Element: HQ-Y
CASE Code: 99   AWC: 181-00

NGT-33-010-052   Cornell University   J. A. Vitale
Supporting the training of predoctoral graduate students in
engineering design as related to aeronautical and space technology.

No. Students	FY	Agreement Period	Amount
4	67	9/67 - 8/70	88000

Tech. Off.: HANSING F D   Funding Element: HQ-Y
CASE Code: 99   AWC: 181-00

NGF-33-010-010   Cornell University   T. Gold
Construction of laboratory facilities to house the Center for
Radiophysics and Space Research on the campus of Cornell
University.

Proposal	FY	Agreement Period	Amount
7698	64	7/64 - 5/67	1350000

Tech. Off.: HOLMES D C   Funding Element: HQ-Y
CASE Code: 99   AWC: 182-00

NGR-33-012-009   Fordham University   W. C. Corning
Central nervous system mechanisms and information processing in limulus.

Proposal	FY	Agreement Period	Amount
-009	68	7/68 - 6/70	6548

Tech. Off.: WEISSMAN N W   Funding Element: HQ-SB
CASE Code: 51   AWC: 189-52

NSR-33-012-006   Fordham University   J. Kubis
Time and motion study on astronauts' ground-based and in-
flight task performance.

Proposal	FY	Agreement Period	Amount
-006	66	7/67 - 6/68	25838
-006		6/67 - 6/68	6000

Tech. Off.: VINOGRAD S P   Funding Element: HQ-MM
CASE Code: 51   AWC: 949-10

NGT-33-012-002   Fordham University   J. F. Mulligan
Training of predoctoral graduate students in space-related
science and technology.

No. Students	FY	Agreement Period	Amount
4	65	9/65 - 8/68	70800
4	66	9/66 - 8/69	70800
2	67	9/67 - 8/70	35400

Tech. Off.: HANSING F D   Funding Element: HQ-Y
CASE Code: 99   AWC: 181-00

NAS9-9341   Long Island University   E. D. Yost
Field measurement and image collection in support of Apollo
experiment S-065.

Proposal	FY	Agreement Period	Amount
	69	4/69 - 9/69	25000

Tech. Off.:   Funding Element:
CASE Code: 32   AWC: 914-40

NGR-33-015-061   State University of New York (Buffalo) R. G. Hunt
Study of extra-contractual influences in government contracting.

Proposal	FY	Agreement Period	Amount
-061	67	6/67 - 5/68	71320
-061	67	6/68 - 8/68	NCE
-061	68	9/68 - 5/69	40000

Tech. Off.: VECCHIETTI G J   Funding Element: HQ-KD
CASE Code: 75   AWC: 039-00

NEW YORK (Cont'd.)

NGR-33-015-068   State University of New York (Stony Brook)
                                                    G. W. Stroke

Proposed novel techniques for interferometrically controlled ruling of improved large diffraction gratings.

Proposal	FY	Agreement Period	Amount
-068	68	10/67 - 9/68	84698
-068	69	7/68 - 9/68	28831
-090	69	10/68 - 9/68	29919
-090	69	10/68 - 7/69	60000

Tech. Off.: OERTEL G K   Funding Element: HQ-SG
CASE Code: 13   AWC: 188-38

NGR-33-015-082   State University of New York (Stony Brook)
                                                    O. A. Schaeffer

Study of high energy and relativistic astrophysics.

Proposal	FY	Agreement Period	Amount
-082	68	4/68 - 3/69	30000

Tech. Off.: JASTROW R   Funding Element: HQ-Y
CASE Code: 11   AWC: 183-00

NSR-33-015-077   State University of New York (Stony Brook)
                                                    O. A. Schaeffer

A summer program in observational and theoretical space sciences.

Proposal	FY	Agreement Period	Amount
-077	68	1/68 -12/68	29150
-096	69	12/68 -12/69	34640

Tech. Off.: CARTER C H   Funding Element: HQ-Y
CASE Code: 11   AWC: 181-00

NGT-33-015-099   State University of New York (Stony Brook)

Student internship program in engineering science.

No. Students:	FY	Agreement Period	Amount
	69	7/69 -10/69	9227

Tech. Off.: CARTER C H   Funding Element: HQ-Y
CASE Code: 49   AWC: 181-00

NGR-33-015-002   State University of New York (Buffalo) J. F. Danielli

Studies in cellular theory and molecular mechanisms.

Proposal	FY	Agreement Period	Amount
6347	63	8/63 - 7/66	201787
6347	66	8/66 - 6/69	NCE

Tech. Off.: JACOBS G J   Funding Element: HQ-SC
CASE Code: 13   AWC: 189-55

NGR-33-015-013   State University of New York (Stony Brook)
                                                    R. P. Tewarson

Product form of inverses of sparse matrices.

Proposal	FY	Agreement Period	Amount
-048	68	9/67 - 8/68	16588
-086		9/68 - 8/69	16822

Tech. Off.: WILSON R   Funding Element: HQ-RR
CASE Code: 21   AWC: 129-04

NGR-33-015-016   State University of New York (Buffalo)
                                                    J. Danielli

Multidisciplinary research in theoretical biology.

Proposal	FY	Agreement Period	Amount
-065	68	1/68 -12/68	100000
-091	69	1/69 -12/69	100000

Tech. Off.: JACOBS G J   Funding Element: HQ-SB
CASE Code: 59   AWC: 189-57

NAS9-8820   State University of New York (Albany)

Determine rare gas content by mass spectrometry—lunar sample analysis.

Proposal	FY	Agreement Period	Amount
	69	12/68 - 8/69	80000

Tech. Off.:   Funding Element:
CASE Code: 12   AWC: 914-40

NGT-33-015-004   State University of New York (Stony Brook)
                                                    R. Jordan

Training of predoctoral graduate students in space-related science and technology.

No. Students:	FY	Agreement Period	Amount
3	65	9/65 - 8/68	64600
4	66	9/66 - 8/69	86100
2	67	9/67 - 8/70	43100

Tech. Off.: HANSING F D   Funding Element: HQ-Y
CASE Code: 99   AWC: 181-00

NGT-33-015-027   State University of New York (Buffalo) A. W. Holt

Training of predoctoral graduate students in space-related science and technology.

No. Students:	FY	Agreement Period	Amount
6	66	9/66 - 8/69	106200
4	67	9/67 - 8/70	70800

Tech. Off.: HANSING F D   Funding Element: HQ-Y
CASE Code: 99   AWC: 181-00

NGL-33-015-035   State University of New York (Stony Brook)
                                                    L. L. Seigle

Investigation of thermodynamic properties of interstitial elements in the refractory metals.

Proposal	FY	Agreement Period	Amount
-059	67	6/67 - 5/68	25000
-081	68	6/68 - 5/69	23885
-089	67	6/69 - 5/70	25000
-103		6/69 - 5/72	21000

Tech. Off.: NASH R   Funding Element: HQ-RR
CASE Code: 47   AWC: 129-03

NGR-33-015-036   State University of New York (Stony Brook)
                                                    Y. H. Koa

Research in infrared astronomy.

Proposal	FY	Agreement Period	Amount
-067	68	12/67 -11/68	50000
-098		12/68 -11/69	20000

Tech. Off.: JASTROW R   Funding Element: HQ-Y
CASE Code: 11   AWC: 183-00

NEW YORK (Cont'd.)

NGR-33-015-085   State University of New York (Stony Brook)

F. F. Y. Wang

Dielectric studies of the cation substituted mixed crystals of niobates.

Proposal	FY	Agreement Period	Amount
-085	68	6/68 - 5/69	21592
-105	69	6/69 - 6/70	22731

Tech. Off.: KLEIN P   Funding Element: ERC
CASE Code: 13   AWC: 125-25

NGR-33-016-003   New York University

R. C. Sahni

Theoretical research in the fields of molecular quantum mechanics and transport properties of diatomic molecules.

Proposal	FY	Agreement Period	Amount
-094	66	5/66 - 4/68	90000
-132	68	5/68 - 4/69	60000
	68	4/70	NCE

Tech. Off.: TALKIN H   Funding Element: HQ-RR
CASE Code: 13   AWC: 129-01

NGL-33-016-013   New York University

J. E. Miller

Theoretical research on the properties of the atmospheres of the Earth and other planets and on the atmospheric effects of solar activity.

Proposal	FY	Agreement Period	Amount
-129	68	2/68 - 2/69	47938
-143	69	3/69 - 2/70	50000

Tech. Off.: ARKING A   Funding Element: GSFC
CASE Code: 31   AWC: 160-44

NGL-33-016-067   New York University

J. R. Ragazzini

Multidisciplinary research in space science and engineering.

Proposal	FY	Agreement Period	Amount
-067	66	9/65 - 8/68	600000
-103	67	9/66 - 8/69	300000
-122	68	9/67 - 8/70	100000

Tech. Off.: QUINN H B   Funding Element: HQ-Y
CASE Code: 99   AWC: 183-00

NGL-33-016-119   New York University

A. Ferri

Engine effect on sonic boom; unsteady engine inlet interaction.

Proposal	FY	Agreement Period	Amount
-119	67	6/67 - 5/68	64800
-123	68	6/67 - 5/68	29920
-135	67	8/68 - 7/70	30000
-140	69	8/68 - 7/71	55000

Tech. Off.: SCHWARTZ R   Funding Element: HQ-RR
CASE Code: 41   AWC: 129-01

NGR-33-016-128   New York University

L. Arnold

An investigation of jet noise and its abatement.

Proposal	FY	Agreement Period	Amount
-128	68	12/67 -11/68	50000
		12/68 - 3/69	NCE
		4/69 - 3/68	NCE
		3/69	NCE
		5/69	NCE
-128		6/69	NCE

Tech. Off.:   Funding Element: LARC
CASE Code: 13   AWC: 126-61

NGR-33-016-131   New York University

A. Ferri

Hypersonic engine airplane integration.

Proposal	FY	Agreement Period	Amount
-131	68	3/68 - 2/69	149780
-131		7/69	NCE

Tech. Off.:   Funding Element: LARC
CASE Code: 41   AWC: 722-01

NGR-33-016-141   New York University

J. Werner

Free-stream-jet interaction on VTOL aircraft.

Proposal	FY	Agreement Period	Amount
-141	69	2/69 - 1/70	26723

Tech. Off.: MARGASON R J   Funding Element: LARC
CASE Code: 41   AWC: 721-01

NGR-33-016-149   New York University

A. Ferri

Wind tunnel model study of dispersion of carbon monoxide in city streets.

Proposal	FY	Agreement Period	Amount
-149	69	3/69 - 3/70	30000
-155		3/69 - 2/72	30000

Tech. Off.: SCHWARTZ I R   Funding Element: HQ-RR
CASE Code: 39   AWC: 129-01

NGT-33-016-014   New York University

J. R. Ragazzini

Training of predoctoral graduate students in space-related science and technology.

No. Students	FY	Agreement Period	Amount
15	65	9/65 - 8/68	256000
15	66	9/66 - 8/69	260600
9	67	9/67 - 8/70	140100

Tech. Off.: HANSING F D   Funding Element: HQ-Y
CASE Code: 99   AWC: 181-00

NGF-33-016-034   New York University

A. Ferri

Construction of the Guggenheim Aerospace Laboratories.

Proposal	FY	Agreement Period	Amount
6956	64	11/64 - 6/66	582000

Tech. Off.: HOLMES D C   Funding Element: HQ-Y
CASE Code: 41   AWC: 182-00

NGR-33-016-102   New York University

J. Post

Biological effects of radiation: Metabolic and replication kinetics alterations.

Proposal	FY	Agreement Period	Amount
-102	67	7/67 - 6/68	25265
-102	68	7/68 - 6/69	24140

Tech. Off.: SAUNDERS J F   Funding Element: HQ-SB
CASE Code: 51   AWC: 189-54

NGR-33-006-007   Polytechnic Institute of Brooklyn   H. J. Juretschke

Theoretical and experimental studies of electronic properties of thin films.

Proposal	FY	Agreement Period	Amount
-034	67	5/67 - 4/68	50000
-048	68	5/68 - 4/69	35000

Tech. Off.: JOHNSON P S   Funding Element: HQ-RR
CASE Code: 13   AWC: 129-02

NEW YORK (Cont'd.)

NGR-33-006-020   Polytechnic Institute of Brooklyn   K. K. Clarke
A space communications study.

Proposal	FY	Agreement Period	Amount
−038	68	9/67 − 9/68	74953
−049	69	9/68 − 9/69	70000

Tech. Off.: GOLDSTEIN B S   Funding Element: ERC
CASE Code: 45   AWC: 125−21

NGR-33-006-040   Polytechnic Institute of Brooklyn   M. Schwartz
Digital techniques for signal processing.

Proposal	FY	Agreement Period	Amount
−040	68	1/68 −12/68	30000
−050	69	1/69 −12/69	30000

Tech. Off.: FARR E H   Funding Element: ERC
CASE Code: 21   AWC: 125−21

NGR-33-006-042   Polytechnic Institute of Brooklyn   J. J. Bongiorno
Minimum sensitivity design of attitude control systems.

Proposal	FY	Agreement Period	Amount
−042	68	3/68 − 2/69	24543

Tech. Off.: REDISCH W   Funding Element: GSFC
CASE Code: 42   AWC: 125−19

NGR-33-006-047   Polytechnc Institute of Brooklyn   S. Gross
Investigation of diffraction by planetary atmospheres.

Proposal	FY	Agreement Period	Amount
−047	68	4/68 − 3/69	14994
−051	69	4/69 − 3/70	19920

Tech. Off.: SCHMERLING E R   Funding Element: HQ−SG
CASE Code: 31   AWC: 188−39

NGR-33-006-053   Polytechnic Institute of Brooklyn   A. C. McKellar
Sequential decoding of convolutional codes.

Proposal	FY	Agreement Period	Amount
−053	69	6/69 −10/69	4985

Tech. Off.: BOZZI J W   Funding Element: GSFC
CASE Code: 21   AWC: 150−22

NGF-33-006-008   Polytechnic Institute of Brooklyn   M. H. Bloom
Construction of facilities housing the Aerodynamic Laboratory of the
Polytechnic Institute of Brooklyn.

Proposal	FY	Agreement Period	Amount
5915	64	11/64 −10/65	632000

Tech. Off.: HOLMES D C   Funding Element: HQ−Y
CASE Code: 49   AWC: 182−00

NGL-33-018-003   Rensselaer Polytechnic Institute   S. E. Wiberley
Interdisciplinary materials research.

Proposal	FY	Agreement Period	Amount
−044	65	5/65 − 4/68	300000
−058	66	5/66 − 4/69	300000
−080	67	5/67 − 4/70	300000
−100	68	5/68 − 4/71	300000

Tech. Off.: NASH R   Funding Element: HQ−RR
CASE Code: 99   AWC: 128−31

NGR-33-018-004   Rensselaer Polytechnic Institute   J. M. Greenberg
Theoretical research on interstellar dust and its interaction with
ultraviolet radiation.

Proposal	FY	Agreement Period	Amount
−064	66	3/66 − 2/69	38000
−081	67	3/67 − 2/70	38000
−128		3/69 − 2/72	25000

Tech. Off.: ROMAN   Funding Element: HQ−SG
CASE Code: 11   AWC: 188−41

NGL-33-018-007   Rensselaer Polytechnic Institute   P. Harteck
Chemistry of planetary atmospheres.

Proposal	FY	Agreement Period	Amount
−042	65	7/65 − 6/68	114000
−054	66	7/65 − 8/68	50000
−054	65	7/65 − 8/68	50000
−076	67	9/66 − 8/69	110000
−099	68	9/67 − 8/70	112000
−121	69	9/68 − 8/71	100000

Tech. Off.: HIPSHER H F   Funding Element: HQ−SL
CASE Code: 31   AWC: 185−37

NGL-33-018-053   Rensselaer Polytechnic Institute   F. A. White
Techniques for increasing the sensitivity of mass spectrometric
gas analyses, utilizing ion factors.

Proposal	FY	Agreement Period	Amount
−104	68	10/67 − 9/70	72000
−124		10/68 − 9/70	10000

Tech. Off.: WOOD G M JR   Funding Element: LARC
CASE Code: 12   AWC: 124−09

NGR-33-018-066   Rensselaer Polytechnic Institute   J. B. Hudson
A study of surface effects in gauges for ultrahigh vacuum
pressure measurements.

Proposal	FY	Agreement Period	Amount
−092	68	9/67 − 8/68	24980
−115	69	9/68 − 8/69	27700
−130		9/69 − 8/71	30000

Tech. Off.: OUTTAW R A   Funding Element: LARC
CASE Code: 13·   AWC: 125−24

NGR-33-018-075   Rensselaer Polytechnic Institute   E. Holt
Non-equilibrium properties of magnetoplasmas.

Proposal	FY	Agreement Period	Amount
−075	67	9/66 − 8/69	140000
−105	68	9/67 − 8/69	20000
−119	69	9/68 − 8/69	40000

Tech. Off.: THOM K   Funding Element: HQ−RR
CASE Code: 13   AWC: 129−01

NGR-33-018-086   Rensselaer Polytechnic Institute   P. Harteck
A study of the effect of surfaces on oxygen atom recombination
at low pressures.

Proposal	FY	Agreement Period	Amount
−086	67	5/67 − 4/68	35000
−113	68	5/68 − 4/69	30000
−127		2/69 − 4/69	8000

Tech. Off.: HOROWITZ R   Funding Element: HQ−SL
CASE Code: 31   AWC: 185−47

NEW YORK (Cont'd)

NAS8-21131   Rensselaer Polytechnic Institute   R. J. Roy
Advanced conventional control.

Proposal	FY	Agreement Period	Amount
		5/67 – 5/68	39000
	67	5/67 –11/68	19000

Tech. Off.: BORELLI M T   Funding Element: MSFC
CASE Code: 46   AWC: 905-14

NGT-33-018-010   Rensselaer Polytechnic Institute   S. E. Wiberley
Training of predoctoral graduate students in space-related
science and technology.

No. Students:	FY	Agreement Period	Amount
15	65	9/65 – 8/68	297500
9	67	9/67 – 8/70	154600
15	66	9/66 – 8/69	266500

Tech. Off.: HANSING F D   Funding Element: HQ-Y
CASE Code: 99   AWC: 181-00

NGF-33-018-011   Rensselaer Polytechnic Institute   S. E. Wiberly
Interdisciplinary materials research facilities.

Proposal	FY	Agreement Period	Amount
3341	62	9/62 – 9/65	1500000

Tech. Off.: HOLMES D C   Funding Element: HQ-Y
CASE Code: 99   AWC: 182-00

NGL-33-018-091   Rensselaer Polytechnic Institute   S. Yerazunis
Analysis and design of a capsule landing system and surface
vehicle control system for Mars exploration.

Proposal	FY	Agreement Period	Amount
-091	67	6/67 – 5/68	80000
-112	66	6/68 – 5/71	80000
-116	66	6/68 – 5/71	80000

Tech. Off.: KEE R M   Funding Element: HQ-SL
CASE Code: 42   AWC: 186-68

NGR-33-019-002   University of Rochester   W. Vishniac
Microbiological and chemical studies of planetary soils.

Proposal	FY	Agreement Period	Amount
-078	68	9/67 – 8/68	90000
-092	69	9/68 – 8/69	80000
-094	68	9/68 – 8/69	40000

Tech. Off.: YOUNG R S   Funding Element: HQ-SB
CASE Code: 32   AWC: 189-55

NGL-33-019-003   University of Rochester   P. W. Baumeister
Investigation of multilayer optical filters with particular
emphasis in the spectral region from 1200A to 2600A.

Proposal	FY	Agreement Period	Amount
-070	67	4/67 – 3/70	35000
-084	68	4/68 – 3/71	35000
-095	69	4/69 – 3/72	35000

Tech. Off.: OTT E J   Funding Element: HQ-SG
CASE Code: 13   AWC: 188-41

NGR-33-019-014   University of Rochester   E. Kinnen
A study of adaptive and non-linear control systems and
theory, applying the direct method of Lyapunov.

Proposal	FY	Agreement Period	Amount
7392	64	4/64 – 3/67	18000
		10/68 – 3/69	NCE

Tech. Off.: DOOLIN B   Funding Element: ARC
CASE Code: 21   AWC: 125-19

NGR-33-019-058   University of Rochester   G. Cohen
Investigation of computer aided circuit design.

Proposal	FY	Agreement Period	Amount
-058	67	9/66 – 8/68	50000
		9/68 – 8/69	NCE

Tech. Off.: MEISSNER C W   Funding Element: LARC
CASE Code: 21   AWC: 125-25

NGR-33-019-086   University of Rochester   D. H. Douglas
Interaction studies in superconductivity.

Proposal	FY	Agreement Period	Amount
-086	69	8/68 – 7/69	49492
-099	69	8/69 – 8/71	50000

Tech. Off.: JOHNSON P S   Funding Element: HQ-RR
CASE Code: 13   AWC:

NGR-33-019-087   University of Rochester   D. T. Blackstock
Laboratory model experiment to investigate the effect of
atmospheric distortion of sonic boom signatures.

Proposal	FY	Agreement Period	Amount
-087	69	6/69 –11/69	2488

Tech. Off.: CAWTHRON J M   Funding Element: LARC
CASE Code: 41   AWC: 126-61

NASr-14   University of Rochester   R. E. Hopkins
(NSR-33-019-007) Studies and investigations of optical systems.

Proposal	FY	Agreement Period	Amount
-073	68	12/67 –11/68	62330
-091	69	11/68 – 8/69	25000

Tech. Off.: HALLAN K   Funding Element: GSFC
CASE Code: 13   AWC: 188-41

NAS5-3178   University of Rochester   M. F. Kaplan
Research on cosmic ray charge & energy spectra.

Proposal	FY	Agreement Period	Amount
	69	2/63 – 3/69	49000

Tech. Off.:   Funding Element:
CASE Code: 11   AWC: 821-12

NGT-33-019-006   University of Rochester   R. G. Loewy
Training of predoctoral graduate students in space-related
science and technology.

No. Students:	FY	Agreement Period	Amount
10	65	9/65 – 8/68	186000
12	66	9/66 – 8/69	230400
8	67	9/67 – 8/70	149800

Tech. Off.: HANSING F D   Funding Element: HQ-Y
CASE Code: 99   AWC: 181-00

NEW YORK (Cont'd)

NGF-33-019-011   University of Rochester   W. O. Fenn

Construction of research laboratory facilities housing the Space Science Center.

Proposal	FY	Agreement Period	Amount
7084	65	8/65 – 9/67	1000000

Tech. Off.: HOLMES D C   Funding Element: HQ–Y

CASE Code: 99   AWC: 182–00

NGR-33-022-004   **Syracuse University**   D. V. Keller

Theoretical and experimental studies of adhesion of metals in high vaccum.

Proposal	FY	Agreement Period	Amount
–074	67	6/67 – 5/68	41150
–094	68	6/68 – 5/69	27825

Tech. Off.: MALTZ J   Funding Element: HQ–RR

CASE Code: 47   AWC: 129–03

NGR-33-022-023   Syracuse University   V. Weiss

Crack propagation in strain controlled fatigue.

Proposal	FY	Agreement Period	Amount
–087	68	9/67 – 8/68	32325
		7/68 –12/68	NCE
		– 3/69	NCE

Tech. Off.: ANGLIN A E JR   Funding Element: LERC

CASE Code: 46   AWC: 720–03

NGR-33-022-035   Syracuse University   M. E. Barzelay

Gas radiation and transport properties at high temperatures.

Proposal	FY	Agreement Period	Amount
–035	66	10/65 – 9/68	42720
–069	67	10/66 – 9/68	26000
–098	69	10/68 – 9/69	15000

Tech. Off.: SCHWARTZ R   Funding Element: HQ–RR

CASE Code: 13   AWC: 129–01

NGR-33-022-082   Syracuse University   D. S. Dosanjh

Noise generation from interacting high speed axisymmetric jet flows.

Proposal	FY	Agreement Period	Amount
–082	68	6/68 – 5/69	35000
			LARC

Tech. Off.: MAYES W H   Funding Element: LARC

CASE Code: 13   AWC: 126–61

NGL-33-022-090   Syracuse University   J. C. Honey

Multidisciplinary studies in management and development programs in the public sector.

Proposal	FY	Agreement Period	Amount
–090	68	1/68 –12/70	500000
–107	68	1/69 –12/70	12000
–112		1/69 –12/71	340000

Tech. Off.: BINGMAN C F   Funding Element: HQ–DX

CASE Code: 99   AWC: 183–00

NGR-33-022-091   Syracuse University   J. J. Zwislocki

Development of an acoustic coupler for earphone calibration.

Proposal	FY	Agreement Period	Amount
–091	68	5/68 – 4/69	15574
–100	69	5/69 – 4/70	15480

Tech. Off.: ANLIKER J   Funding Element: ERC

CASE Code: 13   AWC: 127–49

NGR-33-022-105   **Syracuse University**   V. Weiss

Crack initiation and propagation in fatigue.

Proposal	FY	Agreement Period	Amount
–105	69	3/69 – 9/69	17500

Tech. Off.: HIRSCHBERG M   Funding Element: LERC

CASE Code: 46   AWC: 720–07

NGT-33-022-005   Syracuse University   F. P. Piskor

Training of predoctoral graduate students in space-related science and technology.

No. Students	FY	Agreement Period	Amount
10	65	9/65 – 8/68	177000
10	66	9/66 – 8/69	192000
6	67	9/67 – 8/70	95700

Tech. Off.: HANSING F D   Funding Element: HQ–Y

CASE Code: 99   AWC: 181–00

NGT-33-022-097   Syracuse University   J. C. Honey

Training of predoctoral graduate students in public administration with emphasis on policy development, management, and administration of large scientific and technological programs.

No. Students	FY	Agreement Period	Amount
5	67	9/68 – 8/71	96000
5	69	9/69 – 8/72	105000

Tech. Off.: STEPHENS R F   Funding Element: HQ–Y

CASE Code: 99   AWC: 181–00

NGR-33-022-108   Syracuse University   D. V. Keller

Investigation of the effect of metallurgical structure and properties on the adhesion and friction behavior of cobalt alloys.

Proposal	FY	Agreement Period	Amount
–108	69	6/69 – 6/70	33440

Tech. Off.: JOHNSON R L   Funding Element: LERC

CASE Code: 47   AWC: 129–03

NGR-33-023-018   Yeshiva University   A. G. W. Cameron

Research in space physics.

Proposal	FY	Agreement Period	Amount
–029	68	7/67 – 6/68	75000
–033	69	7/68 – 6/69	75000

Tech. Off.: REDDING E R   Funding Element: HQ–Y

CASE Code: 11   AWC: 183–00

NGR-33-023-032   Yeshiva University   E. D. Weitzman

Study of the stability of sleep patterns in young adults for sequential nights over a three-week period.

Proposal	FY	Agreement Period	Amount
–032	68	6/68 – 6/70	117677
			MSC

Tech. Off.:   Funding Element:

CASE Code: 51   AWC: 945–60

NEW YORK   (Cont'd.)

NGT-33-023-003   Yeshiva University   A. Gelbart
Training of predoctoral graduate students in space-related science and technology.

No. Students:	FY	Agreement Period	Amount
6	65	9/65 – 8/68	106200
6	66	9/66 – 8/69	106200
4	67	9/67 – 8/70	70800

Tech. Off.:   HANSING F D   Funding Element: HQ–Y
CASE Code: 99   AWC: 181–00

NORTH CAROLINA

NGL-34-001-001   Duke University   T. G. Wilson
Research on satellite electrical power conversion systems and circuit protection.

Proposal	FY	Agreement Period	Amount
–028	68	2/68 – 1/69	69900
–030	68	2/69 – 1/71	70000
–034	69	2/69 – 1/72	70000

Tech. Off.:   YAGERHOFER F   Funding Element: GSFC
CASE Code: 42   AWC: 120–33

NGL-34-001-005   Duke University   J. B. Chaddock
Multidisciplinary space-related research in the physical, engineering, and life sciences.

Proposal	FY	Agreement Period	Amount
–022	67	2/67 – 1/70	100000
–027	68	2/68 – 1/71	100000

Tech. Off.:   QUINN H B   Funding Element: HQ–Y
CASE Code: 99   AWC: 183–00

NGR-34-001-019   Duke University   K. Schmidt-Koenig
Experimental analysis of animal orientation and related functions.

Proposal	FY	Agreement Period	Amount
–019	68	9/67 – 8/68	21369
		8/68 –11/68	NCE
–031	69	12/68 –11/69	19691

Tech. Off.:   WEISSMAN N W   Funding Element: HQ–SB
CASE Code: 51   AWC: 189–52

NSR-34-001-025   Duke University   T. D. Reynolds
Design and production of supplementary materials for teachers of high school mathematics.

Proposal	FY	Agreement Period	Amount
–025	67	7/67 –12/68	45631

Tech. Off.:   BERNARDO J V   Funding Element: HQ–FE
CASE Code: 71   AWC: 023–00

NGT-34-001-003   Duke University   R. L. Predmore
Training of predoctoral graduate students in space-related science and technology.

No. Students:	FY	Agreement Period	Amount
10	65	9/65 – 8/68	177000
10	66	9/66 – 8/69	177000
6	67	9/67 – 8/70	85400

Tech. Off.:   HANSING F D   Funding Element: HQ–Y
CASE Code: 99   AWC: 181–00

NAS1-7265   North Carolina State University
Assembling previous research results applicable to present-day, personal-type aircraft.

Proposal	FY	Agreement Period	Amount
	68	4/68 – 5/69	50000

Tech. Off.:   Funding Element: LARC
CASE Code: 41   AWC: 126–13

NGR-34-002-017   North Carolina State University   W. H. Bennett
Transverse instabilities of magnetically self-focusing streams in plasmas.

Proposal	FY	Agreement Period	Amount
–071	68	12/67 –11/68	17403
–093	69	1/69 –12/69	17520
–107	69	1/69 – 1/72	18000

Tech. Off.:   THOM K   Funding Element: HQ–RR
CASE Code: 13   AWC: 129–02

NGR-34-002-023   North Carolina State University   D. S. Grosch
Utilization of Habrobracon and Artemia as experimental materials in bioastronautic studies.

Proposal	FY	Agreement Period	Amount
–041	67	1/67 – 6/67	5049
–041	67	7/67 – 6/68	NCE

Tech. Off.:   SAUNDERS J F   Funding Element: HQ–SB
CASE Code: 13   AWC: 189–54

NGR-34-002-032   North Carolina State University   H. Sagan
Mathematical theory of optimal control.

Proposal	FY	Agreement Period	Amount
–036	68	9/67 – 9/69	40833
–104	69	9/67 – 9/71	20415

Tech. Off.:   BIRD J D   Funding Element: LARC
CASE Code: 21   AWC: 125–19

NGL-34-002-035   North Carolina State University   F. D. Hart
Research studies of statistical energy methods in sound and structural vibration analysis.

Proposal	FY	Agreement Period	Amount
–053	67	2/67 – 1/68	24799
–053	67	1/68 – 6/68	NCE
–080	68	6/68 – 5/71	52000
–099		6/69 – 5/72	29000

Tech. Off.:   FINDLEY D S   Funding Element: LARC
CASE Code: 13   AWC: 126–14

NORTH CAROLINA (Cont'd)

NGR-34-002-036   **North Carolina State University**   **F. O. Smetana**

An experimental investigation of the cryoentrainment pump.

Proposal	FY	Agreement Period	Amount
−063	68	11/67 −10/68	11365
−079	69	11/68 −10/69	19190

Tech. Off.: YEAGER P R   Funding Element: LARC

CASE Code: 46   AWC: 129−01

NGR-34-002-038   **North Carolina State University**   **F. J. Tischer**

A study of electro-optical data processing and reduction.

Proposal	FY	Agreement Period	Amount
−038	67	7/67 − 6/68	34631
		6/68 −12/68	NCE
		− 3/69	NCE

Tech. Off.:   Funding Element:

CASE Code: 21   AWC: 125−22

NGL-34-002-047   **North Carolina State University**   **F. J. Tischer**

Study of rectangular-guide-like structures for millimeter wave transmission.

Proposal	FY	Agreement Period	Amount
−047	67	7/67 − 6/68	39457
−074	68	7/68 − 6/71	49200
−083	68	7/68 − 6/71	50000

Tech. Off.: BROWN D   Funding Element: GSFC

CASE Code: 45   AWC: 125−21

NGR-34-002-048   **North Carolina State University**   **H. A. Hassan**

Theoretical investigation of surface interaction effects on plasma accelerators and MHD power generators.

Proposal	FY	Agreement Period	Amount
−048	67	2/67 − 1/70	50000
−070	68	2/68 − 1/70	10000
−092	69	2/69 − 1/70	15000

Tech. Off.: THOM K   Funding Element: HQ−RR

CASE Code: 13   AWC: 129−01

NGR-34-002-055   **North Carolina State University**   **R. G. Pearson**

Study of human factors aspects of noise.

Proposal	FY	Agreement Period	Amount
−055	67	2/67 − 1/68	32000
−055	67	1/68 − 5/68	NCE
−055	67	5/68 − 6/68	NCE
−077	68	7/68 − 6/69	38000
−103	69	7/68 − 7/71	35000

Tech. Off.: CAWTHORNE J M   Funding Element: LARC

CASE Code: 51   AWC: 127−49

NGL-34-002-061   **North Carolina State University**   **L. A. Jones**

Analysis of the total environment of closed ecological systems.

Proposal	FY	Agreement Period	Amount
−061	68	6/68 − 5/71	77500

Tech. Off.:   Funding Element: LARC

CASE Code: 62   AWC: 127−53

NGR-34-002-072   **North Carolina State University**   **L. A. Jones**

Studies in the oxidation and reduction of aromatic nitro compounds.

Proposal	FY	Agreement Period	Amount
−072	68	6/68 − 8/69	14176

Tech. Off.:   Funding Element: LARC

CASE Code: 12   AWC: 129−03

NGR-34-002-073   **North Carolina State University**   **M. A. Littlejohn**

The piezoresistive effect in electron irradiated silicon and its application to the improvement of semiconductor strain gages.

Proposal	FY	Agreement Period	Amount
−073	68	3/68 − 2/69	15000
		− 5/69	NCE

Tech. Off.:   Funding Element:

CASE Code: 45   AWC: 125−24

NGR-34-002-078   **North Carolina State University**   **F. O. Smetana**

Study experimentally the relationship between frequency and gas temperature in whistles capable of operation at high temperatures.

Proposal	FY	Agreement Period	Amount
−078	69	3/69 − 5/70	15752

Tech. Off.: GERMAIN E F   Funding Element: LARC

CASE Code: 49   AWC: 125−24

NGR-34-002-082   **North Carolina State University**   **N. F. J. Matthews**

Electrical and optical properties of cds.

Proposal	FY	Agreement Period	Amount
−082	69	12/68 −11/69	40120

Tech. Off.:   Funding Element: LARC

CASE Code: 49   AWC: 129−03

NGR-34-002-085   **North Carolina State University**   **J. S. Lee**

An analytical study of the relationship beteen frequency and gas temperature in whistles capable of operation at high temperatures.

Proposal	FY	Agreement Period	Amount
−085	69	3/69 − 2/70	8251

Tech. Off.: GERMAIN E F   Funding Element: LARC

CASE Code: 49   AWC: 125−24

NGR-34-002-086   **North Carolina State University**   **R. W. Truitt**

Conduct a research program in major systems design.

Proposal	FY	Agreement Period	Amount
−086	69	9/68 − 8/69	32353
−114	69	9/69 − 9/70	37062

Tech. Off.:   Funding Element: LARC

CASE Code: 49   AWC: 126−61

NGR-34-002-095   **North Carolina State University**   **R. G. Pearson**

Acoustic energy effects on sleep and human performance.

Proposal	FY	Agreement Period	Amount
−095	69	3/69 − 9/70	75000

Tech. Off.: CAWTHORN J M   Funding Element: LARC

CASE Code: 51   AWC: 127−49

NORTH CAROLINA (Cont'd.)

NGR-34-002-108   **North Carolina State University**   **C. R. Manning**
Development of high temperature materials for solid propellant rocket nozzle applications.

Proposal	FY	Agreement Period	Amount
–108	69	7/69 – 7/70	17003

Tech. Off.: BUCKLEY J D   Funding Element: LARC
CASE Code: 47   AWC: 180–32

NAS12-2096   **North Carolina State University**   **A. H. Shephard**
Testing procedures for integrated circuit development.

Proposal	FY	Agreement Period	Amount
	69	3/69 – 3/70	15000

Tech. Off.:   Funding Element:
CASE Code: 45   AWC: 125–25

NGT-34-002-003   **North Carolina State University**   **W. J. Peterson**
Training of predoctoral graduate students in space-related science and technology.

No. Students	FY	Agreement Period	Amount
12	65	9/65 – 8/68	212400
12	66	9/66 – 8/69	212400
6	67	9/67 – 8/70	92200

Tech. Off.: HANSING F D   Funding Element: HQ–Y
CASE Code: 99   AWC: 181–00

NGT-34-002-097   **North Carolina State University**   **F. D. Hart**
Graduate traineeship program in aerospace acoustics.

No. Students	FY	Agreement Period	Amount
	69	9/69 – 9/72	120000

Tech. Off.: CARTER C H   Funding Element: HQ–Y
CASE Code: 41   AWC: 181–00

NGR-34-003-021   **University of North Carolina (Chapel Hill)**
                          H. A. Tyroler
Study and assessment of community health factors near major aerospace installations.

Proposal	FY	Agreement Period	Amount
–033	67	7/67 – 6/68	41313

Tech. Off.: ARNOLDI L B   Funding Element: HQ–BG
CASE Code: 52   AWC: 010–00

NGR-34-003-026   **University of North Carolina (Chapel Hill)**
                          J. W. Hanson
The application of linear programming to functional approximation.

Proposal	FY	Agreement Period	Amount
–037	68	4/68 – 3/69	6440

Tech. Off.: MINER W E   Funding Element: ERC
CASE Code: 21   AWC: 125–17

NGR-34-003-040   **University of North Carolina (Chapel Hill)**
                          R. G. Faust
A study in interdisciplinary communication.

Proposal	FY	Agreement Period	Amount
–040	68	9/68 – 8/69	23000

Tech. Off.: REDDING E R   Funding Element: HQ–Y
CASE Code: 99   AWC: 183–00

NSR-34-003-039   **University of North Carolina (Chapel Hill)**
Partial support of symbolic mathematics by computer.

Proposal	FY	Agreement Period	Amount
–039	68	6/68 – 5/69	8400

Tech. Off.: REDDING E R   Funding Element: HQ–Y
CASE Code: 21   AWC: 181–00

NGT-34-003-001   **University of North Carolina (Chapel Hill)**
                          C. H. Holman
Training of predoctoral graduate students in space-related science and technology.

No. Students	FY	Agreement Period	Amount
12	65	9/65 – 8/68	230400
12	66	9/66 – 8/69	235800
6	67	9/67 – 8/70	90700

Tech. Off.: HANSING F D   Funding Element: HQ–Y
CASE Code: 99   AWC: 181–00

NORTH DAKOTA

NGT-35-001-001   **North Dakota State University**   **G. S. Smith**
Training of predoctoral graduate students in space-related science and technology.

No. Students	FY	Agreement Period	Amount
3	65	9/65 – 8/68	53100
3	66	9/66 – 8/69	53100
2	67	9/67 – 8/70	35500

Tech. Off.: HANSING F D   Funding Element: HQ–Y
CASE Code: 99   AWC: 181–00

NGT-35-002-004   **University of North Dakota**   **C. J. Hamre**
Training of predoctoral graduate students in space-related science and technology.

No. Students	FY	Agreement Period	Amount
2	66	9/66 – 8/69	42800
2	67	9/67 – 8/70	42700

Tech. Off.: HANSING F D   Funding Element: HQ–Y
CASE Code: 99   AWC: 181–00

OHIO

NGR-36-001-010   **University of Akron**   **R. Dubensky**
Analysis of fatigue crack growth experiments with 7075-T6 aluminum alloy sheet.

Proposal	FY	Agreement Period	Amount
–010	69	1/69 – 7/69	4000

Tech. Off.: HUDSON C M   Funding Element: LARC
CASE Code: 47   AWC: 126–14

OHIO (Cont'd.)

NGR-36-017-002   Bowling Green State University   I. I. Oster

Behavior of genetic material under space flight conditions.

Proposal	FY	Agreement Period	Amount
–002	69	2/69 – 1/70	34394

Tech. Off.: SAUNDERS J F   Funding Element: HQ–SB

CASE Code: 59   AWC: 189–54

NAS2-3528   Bowling Green State University   I. I. Oster

Biosatellite project experiment P-1160: Possible effects of zero-gravity on radiation induced somatic damage.

Proposal	FY	Agreement Period	Amount
	67	2/66 –12/68	85000

Tech. Off.: BOWMAN G   Funding Element: ARC

CASE Code: 51   AWC: 883–12

NGR-36-003-033   Case Western Reserve University   J. F. Wallace

An experimental investigation on modified eutectic alloys for high temperature service.

Proposal	FY	Agreement Period	Amount
–106	67	5/67 – 4/68	15000
–132	68	5/68 – 4/69	14964

Tech. Off.: MALTZ J   Funding Element: HQ–RR

CASE Code: 47   AWC: 129–03

NGR-36-003-042   Case Western Reserve University

B. Reswick and H. Mergler

Investigation of control in man-machine systems, with emphasis on problems of remote manipulations.

Proposal	FY	Agreement Period	Amount
–125	68	8/67 – 7/68	59897
–151	69	7/68 – 7/69	71755
–042	69	7/68 – 7/69	71755
–151		7/70	NCE

Tech. Off.: JOHNSEN E G   Funding Element: NPO

CASE Code: 51   AWC: 718–10

NGR-36-003-054   Case Western Reserve University   J. L. Koenig

Mechanical properties of polyethylene terephthalate under selected conditions and methods of preparation.

Proposal	FY	Agreement Period	Amount
–110	67	5/67 – 4/68	60000
–135	68	5/68 – 4/69	50000

Tech. Off.: ACHHAMMER B H   Funding Element: HQ–RR

CASE Code: 12   AWC: 129–03

NGR-36-003-064   Case Western Reserve University   S. Ostrach

Basic scientific research in fluid physics.

Proposal	FY	Agreement Period	Amount
–116	67	6/67 – 5/68	115000
–147	68	6/68 – 5/69	115000

Tech. Off.: EVVARD J C   Funding Element: LERC

CASE Code: 13   AWC: 129–01

NGR-36-003-079   Case Western Reserve University   W. H. Ko

Investigation of implantable multichannel biotelemetry systems.

Proposal	FY	Agreement Period	Amount
–133	68	3/68 – 2/69	48225
–155	69	3/69 – 6/70	50000

Tech. Off.: LAVERY A L   Funding Element: ERC

CASE Code: 45   AWC: 125–24

NGL-36-003-088   Case Western Reserve University   S. Ostrach

Investigation of biological fluid mechanics.

Proposal	FY	Agreement Period	Amount
–088	67	10/66 – 9/69	91500
–088	68	10/67 – 9/70	24000

Tech. Off.: HOWE J   Funding Element: HQ–RR

CASE Code: 51   AWC: 129–01

NGR-36-003-091   Case Western Reserve University   O. Ostrach

Theoretical and experimental studies of boiling in a swirling flow.

Proposal	FY	Agreement Period	Amount
–091	66	7/66 – 6/68	60000
–146	69	7/68 – 6/71	60000

Tech. Off.: KALTENSTEIN E R   Funding Element: LERC

CASE Code: 13   AWC: 120–27

NGR-36-003-094   Case Western Reserve University   L. Leonard

The effect of deformation on dispersion.

Proposal	FY	Agreement Period	Amount
–124	68	9/67 – 9/68	23750
		– 1/69	NCE
		6/69	NCE

Tech. Off.: WEETON S J   Funding Element: LERC

CASE Code: 46   AWC: 129–03

NGR-36-003-100   Case Western Reserve University   A. R. Cooper

Diffusive mixing as a tool for confirming the origin of tektites.

Proposal	FY	Agreement Period	Amount
–138	68	4/68 – 3/69	20000
–153	69	4/69 – 3/70	20000

Tech. Off.: OKEEFE J   Funding Element: GSFC

CASE Code: 32   AWC: 185–42

NSR-36-003-051   Case Western Reserve University

I. Greber, W. T. Olson

A summer institute in space-related engineering.

Proposal	FY	Agreement Period	Amount
–127	68	4/68 – 3/69	41655
–152	69	3/69 – 3/70	85830

Tech. Off.:   Funding Element:

CASE Code: 99   AWC: 181–00

NSR-36-003-092   Case Western Reserve University   G. M. Frye

Spark chamber detection of solar and cosmic gamma rays, and geomagnetically trapped radiation at low altitudes.

Proposal	FY	Agreement Period	Amount
–092	67	6/67 – 5/68	99800
–141	68	5/68 – 5/69	60000
–141		8/69	NCE

Tech. Off.: ROMAN   Funding Element: SG

CASE Code: 11   AWC: 188–41

OHIO (Cont'd.)

NGT-36-003-007   Case Western Reserve University   L. Gordon

Training of predoctoral graduate students in space-related science and technology.

No. Students:	FY	Agreement Period	Amount
12	65	9/65 – 8/68	258000
12	66	9/66 – 8/69	258800
8	67	9/67 – 8/70	155800

Tech. Off.: HANSING F D   Funding Element: HQ-Y
CASE Code: 99   AWC: 181-00

NGF-36-003-058   Case Western Reserve University   H. R. Nara

Construction of research facilities at Case Institute of Technology.

Proposal	FY	Agreement Period	Amount
-058	65	8/65 – 9/67	2226000
-058	65	10/67 – 3/69	NCE

Tech. Off.: HOLMES D C   Funding Element: HQ-Y
CASE Code: 99   AWC: 182-00

NGR-36-003-139   Case Western Reserve University   E. Reshotko

Investigation of fundamental phenomena relevent to the design of small pumps.

Proposal	FY	Agreement Period	Amount
-139	68	7/68 – 6/70	49945

Tech. Off.:   Funding Element:
CASE Code: 46   AWC: 128-31

NGR-36-027-001   Case Western Reserve University   E. L. Glaser

Specific aspects of computer-assisted software design.

Proposal	FY	Agreement Period	Amount
-001	69	6/69 – 6/70	100000

Tech. Off.: GREEN J   Funding Element: ERC
CASE Code: 49   AWC: 125-06

NGR-36-027-002   Case Western Reserve University   S. V. Radcliffe

The investigation of ductility and fracture phenomena in metals by high pressure techniques.

Proposal	FY	Agreement Period	Amount
-002	69	6/69 – 6/70	15000

Tech. Off.: RAFFO P L   Funding Element: LERC
CASE Code: 47   AWC: 129-03

NAS12-2107   Case Western Reserve University

Development of compiler-oriented tech. multiplier network.

Proposal	FY	Agreement Period	Amount
	69	4/69 – 3/70	10000

Tech. Off.:   Funding Element:
CASE Code: 45   AWC: 125-25

NGR-36-004-001   University of Cincinnati   P. Herget

Fundamental research in celestial mechanics.

Proposal	FY	Agreement Period	Amount
-425	60	10/59 – 9/62	178000
425	66	10/65 – 9/68	NCE
		10/68 – 3/69	NCE

Tech. Off.: BRUNK W E   Funding Element: HQ-SL
CASE Code: 11   AWC: 188-48

NGR-36-004-008   University of Cincinnati   Ti Yi Li, H. Oguro

Investigation of heat transfer and instability in two phase flow phenomena.

Proposal	FY	Agreement Period	Amount
-034	68	12/67 –11/68	71074
		12/68 – 8/69	NCE

Tech. Off.: DITTRICH R T   Funding Element: LERC
CASE Code: 13   AWC: 120-27

NGR-36-004-013   University of Cincinnati   R. J. Kroll

Investigation of the longitudinal vibration of liquid-fueled launch vehicle.

Proposal	FY	Agreement Period	Amount
-031	68	9/67 – 9/68	20500
		10/68 – 3/69	NCE

Tech. Off.: PINSON L D   Funding Element: LARC
CASE Code: 42   AWC: 124-11

NGL-36-004-014   University of Cincinnati   R. P. Harrington

Multidisciplinary space-related research in the physical, engineering, life and social sciences.

Proposal	FY	Agreement Period	Amount
-014	66	1/66 –12/68	300000
-025	67	1/67 –12/69	150000
-032	68	1/68 –12/71	50000

Tech. Off.: REDDING E R   Funding Element: HQ-Y
CASE Code: 99   AWC: 183-00

NGR-36-004-030   University of Cincinnati   L. Meirovitch

Dynamic characteristics of a variable-mass flexible missile.

Proposal	FY	Agreement Period	Amount
-030	68	9/67 – 8/68	29780
-036	69	9/68 – 8/69	25000

Tech. Off.: PIERCE H B   Funding Element: LARC
CASE Code: 46   AWC: 124-08

NGT-36-004-003   University of Cincinnati   C. Crockett

Supporting the training of predoctoral graduate students in space-related science and technology.

No. Students:	FY	Agreement Period	Amount
10	65	9/65 – 8/68	147000
10	66	9/66 – 8/69	145900
6	67	9/67 – 8/70	72200

Tech. Off.: HANSING F D   Funding Element: HQ-Y
CASE Code: 99   AWC: 181-00

OHIO (Cont'd)

NGR-36-025-001   Cleveland State University   K. J. Casper
Detection characteristics of germanium and silicon.

Proposal	FY	Agreement Period	Amount
-001	69	5/69 - 4/70	35000
-002	69	5/69 - 5/72	35000

Tech. Off.: BARILE S   Funding Element: LERC
CASE Code: 12   AWC: 120-27

NGR-36-019-001   Hiram College   L. B. Shaffer
Investigation of the effects of ion bombardment on single crystals.

Proposal	FY	Agreement Period	Amount
-001	66	6/66 - 5/69	119466
-001		12/69	NCE

Tech. Off.: HUNCZAK H R   Funding Element: LERC
CASE Code: 13   AWC: 120-26

NGR-36-006-003   John Carroll University   J. Trivisonno
High frequency ultrasonic attenuation studies in superconductors.

Proposal	FY	Agreement Period	Amount
-003	67	6/67 - 5/69	29240
		- 2/70	NCE

Tech. Off.: KALTENSTEIN F R   Funding Element: LERC
CASE Code: 13   AWC: 129-02

NGL-36-007-001   Kent State University   J. W. Reed
Theoretical and experimental studies of the magnetic and molecular properties of selected compounds, using neutron diffraction techniques.

Proposal	FY	Agreement Period	Amount
-022	68	7/68 - 6/70	47773

Tech. Off.: BEHRENDT D R   Funding Element: LERC
CASE Code: 13   AWC: 129-03

NGR-36-007-025   Kent State University   J. L. Fergason
Flexible display screens utilizing liquid crystal.

Proposal	FY	Agreement Period	Amount
-025	69	2/69 - 1/70	13908

Tech. Off.: LONG W C   Funding Element: LARC
CASE Code: 12   AWC: 125-19

NGT-36-007-002   Kent State University   J. White
Training of predoctoral graduate students in space-related science and technology.

No. Students	FY	Agreement Period	Amount
4	65	9/65 - 8/68	80900
4	66	9/66 - 8/69	86400
2	67	9/67 - 8/70	41000

Tech. Off.: HANSING F D   Funding Element: HQ-Y
CASE Code: 99   AWC: 181-00

NGR-36-022-001   Miami University   D. E. Cunningham
Study of NASA-university scientific relationships.

Proposal	FY	Agreement Period	Amount
-001	67	6/67 - 5/69	42210
		10/69	NCE

Tech. Off.: REDDING E R   Funding Element: HQ-Y
CASE Code: 76   AWC: 183-00

NGR-36-008-002   Ohio State University   C. A. Levis
Investigations and studies of detection and receiver techniques, at millimeter and submillimeter wavelengths.

Proposal	FY	Agreement Period	Amount
-100	68	10/67 - 9/68	25000
		10/68 - 3/69	NCE

Tech. Off.: MARANTZ H   Funding Element: ARC
CASE Code: 45   AWC: 125-21

NGR-36-008-004   Ohio State University   H. S. Weiss
Biological effects of prolonged exposure of small mammals to closed gaseous environments low in or free of nitrogen.

Proposal	FY	Agreement Period	Amount
-107	68	3/68 - 2/69	31986
-121	69	3/69 - 2/68	31000
-121	69	3/69 - 2/70	31000

Tech. Off.: LEON H   Funding Element: ARC
CASE Code: 51   AWC: 189-54

NGR-36-008-005   Ohio State University   C. Levis
Theoretical and experimental investigations of spacecraft antenna problems in the varied operational environments of far-out space and atmospheric re-entry, including considerations of immersion in a hot plasma sheath and of omni-directional coverage.

Proposal	FY	Agreement Period	Amount
-097	68	8/67 - 7/68	45000
-097	68	7/68 - 11/68	NCE
		- 5/69	NCE

Tech. Off.:   Funding Element: LARC
CASE Code: 42   AWC: 125-22

**NGR-36-008-041   Ohio State University   J. H. Dines,
                                                  L. B. Roberts**
Cardiovascular responses to environmental vibrations.

Proposal	FY	Agreement Period	Amount
-098	68	8/67 - 7/68	20000
		6/68 - 7/69	NCE

Tech. Off.: OTTEN E   Funding Element: ARC
CASE Code: 51   AWC: 127-49

NGL-36-008-051   Ohio State University   F. H. Beck
Stress corrosion cracking of titanium alloys.

Proposal	FY	Agreement Period	Amount
-051	66	7/66 - 6/69	78348
-111	67	7/69 - 6/71	26000
-111	69	7/69 - 6/72	26116

Tech. Off.: RARING R   Funding Element: HQ-RR
CASE Code: 47   AWC: 129-03

OHIO (Cont'd)

NGR-36-008-076   Ohio State University   H. Hemand
Techniques for generation of control and guidance signals derived from optical fields.

Proposal	FY	Agreement Period	Amount
−076	67	10/66 − 9/67	34994
−076	67	6/68 − 8/68	NCE
		9/68 −10/68	NCE
−113	69	11/68 −10/69	33593

Tech. Off.: WALSH T M   Funding Element: LARC
CASE Code: 13   AWC: 125−17

NGR-36-008-080   Ohio State University   C. A. Lewis
Millimeter-wavelength propagation studies.

Proposal	FY	Agreement Period	Amount
−080	67	12/66 −11/67	54000
−080	67	12/67 − 8/68	NCE
−080	69	9/68 − 8/69	50000

Tech. Off.: KING L   Funding Element: GSFC
CASE Code: 13   AWC: 164−22

NGR-36-008-093   Ohio State University   I. I. Mueller
Data analysis for the National Geodetic Satellite Program.

Proposal	FY	Agreement Period	Amount
−093	68	8/67 − 7/69	98700
−120	68	8/68 − 6/70	65243

Tech. Off.: ROSENBERG J D   Funding Element: HQ−SA
CASE Code: 32   AWC: 855−00

NGR-36-008-103   Ohio State University   W. W. Anderson
Electron beam pumped laser action in selenium and tellurium with applications for tunable backward wave para, etroc oscillations.

Proposal	FY	Agreement Period	Amount
−103	68	6/68 − 5/69	35000

Tech. Off.: HAAK F   Funding Element: ERC
CASE Code: 13   AWC: 125−22

NGL-36-008-106   Ohio State University   R. M. Nerem
Combined conductive and radiative end wall heat transfer behind reflected shock waves in air and nitrogen.

Proposal	FY	Agreement Period	Amount
−106	68	3/68 − 2/69	15000
−123	69	3/69 − 2/70	20000

Tech. Off.: HOWE J T   Funding Element: HQ−RR
CASE Code: 13   AWC: 129−01

NGR-36-008-109   Ohio State University   C. D. Bailey
Flutter of thermally stressed plates subjected to large deflections.

Proposal	FY	Agreement Period	Amount
−109	69	4/69 − 7/69	5000
−109	69	4/69 − 6/69	5000
−130		4/69 − 6/72	20000

Tech. Off.: TUOVILA W J   Funding Element: LARC
CASE Code: 46   AWC: 720−02

NGR-36-008-117   Ohio State University   R. M. Nerem
Fluid dynamic aspects of cardiovascular behavior during vibration.

Proposal	FY	Agreement Period	Amount
−117	69	11/68 −10/69	18300
−129		11/68 −10/71	18000

Tech. Off.: HOWE J T   Funding Element: HQ−RR
CASE Code: 51   AWC: 129−01

NGR-36-008-125   Ohio State University   S. K. Ghosh
Investigation into some of the problems of lunar orbiter photography system.

Proposal	FY	Agreement Period	Amount
−125	69	4/69 −10/70	29152

Tech. Off.: MORRIS J S   Funding Element: MSC
CASE Code: 42   AWC: 879−11

NGR-36-008-131   Ohio State University   B. E. Gatewood
Methods of solution of the integral equation for the foucault test.

Proposal	FY	Agreement Period	Amount
−131	69	7/69 − 9/69	5244

Tech. Off.: KATZOFF S   Funding Element: LARC
CASE Code: 21   AWC: 188−78

NSR-36-008-028   Ohio State University   A. W. Leissa
A study of continuum vibrations.

Proposal	FY	Agreement Period	Amount
−091	68	7/67 − 6/69	58865

Tech. Off.: MICHEL D   Funding Element: HQ−RV
CASE Code: 13   AWC: 124−11

NSR-36-008-108   Ohio State University   H. V. Ellington
Critical analysis and review of state-of-the-art in space medicine.

Proposal	FY	Agreement Period	Amount
−108	68	6/68 − 6/69	174411

Tech. Off.:   Funding Element:
CASE Code: 59   AWC: 904−01

NAS8-21317   Ohio State University   W. B. Campbell
Preparation of pigments for space-stable thermal control coatings.

Proposal	FY	Agreement Period	Amount
	68	6/68 − 6/69	20000

Tech. Off.:   Funding Element: MSFC
CASE Code: 47   AWC: 124−09

NAS9-6910   Ohio State University   C. Mengel
Effect of oxygen on red cells.

Proposal	FY	Agreement Period	Amount
		4/67 − 4/68	20000
	68	4/67 − 6/69	20000

Tech. Off.: FISHER C L   Funding Element: MSC
CASE Code: 51   AWC: 914−40

OHIO (Cont'd)

NAS9-7218   **Ohio State University**   **J. Shaw**

Infrared temperature sounding experiment SO43.

Proposal	FY	Agreement Period	Amount
		6/67 — 9/68	35000

Tech. Off.: HENSLEY B   Funding Element: MSC
CASE Code: 11   AWC: 945-81

NAS9-8379   **Ohio State University**   **C. Mengel**

MSF experiment definition.

Proposal	FY	Agreement Period	Amount
	68	6/68 — 7/70	32000

Tech. Off.:   Funding Element: MSC
CASE Code: 99   AWC: 945-60

NGT-36-008-006   **Ohio State University**   **W. M. Protheroe**

Training of predoctoral graduate students in space-related science and technology.

No. Students:	FY	Agreement Period	Amount
10	65	9/65 — 8/68	177000
12	66	9/66 — 8/69	212400
6	67	9/67 — 8/70	98300

Tech. Off.: HANSING F D   Funding Element: HQ-Y
CASE Code: 99   AWC: 181-00

NGT-36-008-007   **Ohio State University**   **F. H. Shillito**

Training of predoctoral graduate students in space-related science and technology.

No. Students:	FY	Agreement Period	Amount
3	66	7/66 — 6/68	76500
-101	68	7/68 — 6/70	86900

Tech. Off.: HANSING F D   Funding Element: HQ-Y
CASE Code: 99   AWC: 181-00

NGR-36-007-012   **Ohio University**   **W-K Chen**

Modelling and scaling procedures for electronic devices.

Proposal	FY	Agreement Period	Amount
-012	69	10/68 — 9/69	11875

Tech. Off.:   Funding Element: ERC
CASE Code: AWC: 125-25

NAS12-2082   **Ohio University**

Procedures for navigation and air traffic control.

Proposal	FY	Agreement Period	Amount
	69	3/69 — 3/70	15000

Tech. Off.:   Funding Element:
CASE Code: 41   AWC: 125-19

NGT-36-009-001   **Ohio University**   **T. Culbert**

Training of predoctoral graduate students in space-related science and technology.

No. Students:	FY	Agreement Period	Amount
3	65	9/65 — 8/68	44100
4	66	9/66 — 8/69	78400
2	67	9/67 — 8/70	36000

Tech. Off.: HANSING F D   Funding Element: HQ-Y
CASE Code: 99   AWC: 181-00

NGT-36-010-001   **University of Toledo**   **A. N. Solberg**

Training of predoctoral graduate students in space-related science and technology.

No. Students	FY	Agreement Period	Amount
5	65	9/65 — 8/68	75000
5	66	9/66 — 8/69	75000
3	67	9/67 — 8/70	42400

Tech. Off.: HANSING F D   Funding Element: HQ-Y
CASE Code: 99   AWC: 181-00

NGT-36-013-001   **Case Western Reserve University**   **W. M. Heston**

Training of predoctoral graduate students in space-related science and technology.

No. Students	FY	Agreement Period	Amount
10	65	9/65 — 8/68	192000
10	66	9/66 — 8/69	192000
6	67	9/67 — 8/70	107500

Tech. Off.: HANSING F D   Funding Element: HQ-Y
CASE Code: 99   AWC: 181-00

OKLAHOMA

NGL-37-002-011   **Oklahoma State University**   **V. S. Haneman**

Research in space-related sciences and engineering.

Proposal	FY	Agreement Period	Amount
-042	67	10/66 — 9/69	75000
-065	68	10/67 — 9/70	75000

Tech. Off.: REDDING E R   Funding Element: HQ-Y
CASE Code: 99   AWC: 183-00

NSR-37-002-045   **Oklahoma State University**   **K. A. McCollom**

A pilot program for selecting, editing and disseminating engineering and scientific educational subject matter from NASA technical reports.

Proposal	FY	Agreement Period	Amount
-060	67	6/66 — 8/68	99500
		8/68 — 11/68	NCE
-081	68	9/68 — 9/69	50000

Tech. Off.:   Funding Element:
CASE Code: 99   AWC: 141-00

NAS8-21391   **Oklahoma State University**   **F. E. Todd**

A study of dense aluminum plasma from hypervelocity impact and other sources.

Proposal	FY	Agreement Period	Amount
	68	5/68 — 3/69	35000

Tech. Off.: DUBIN   Funding Element: MSFC
CASE Code: 13   AWC: 188-45

NGT-37-002-002   **Oklahoma State University**   **M. T. Edmison**

Training of predoctoral graduate students in space-related science and technology.

No. Students:	FY	Agreement Period	Amount
10	65	9/65 — 8/68	165000
12	66	9/66 — 8/69	212400
6	67	9/67 — 8/70	88600

Tech. Off.: HANSING F D   Funding Element: HQ-Y
CASE Code: 99   AWC: 181-00

OKLAHOMA (Cont'd.)

NGL-37-003-026   University of Oklahoma   C. Riggs
Multidisciplinary research program in space science and engineering.

Proposal	FY	Agreement Period	Amount
−026	66	1/66 −12/68	200000
−036	67	1/67 −12/69	100000
−040	68	1/68 −12/70	100000

Tech. Off.: REDDING E R   Funding Element: HQ−Y
CASE Code: 99   AWC: 183−00

NGR-37-003-041   University of Oklahoma   D. M. Egle
The effect of end conditions on the dynamic response of aerospace vehicle components.

Proposal	FY	Agreement Period	Amount
−041	69	1/69 −12/69	15845

Tech. Off.: CLARY R R   Funding Element: LARC
CASE Code: 42   AWC: 124−08

NGR-37-003-043   University of Oklahoma   M. L. Rasmussen
Planar tumbling of bodies with non-zero aerodynamic trim during atmospheric entry.

Proposal	FY	Agreement Period	Amount
−043	69	2/69 − 2/70	4056

Tech. Off.: PETERSON V L   Funding Element: ARC
CASE Code: 41   AWC: 124−07

NAS8-30175   University of Oklahoma   E. F. Blick
Crossed beam spectrometer development (crossed beam spectroscopy in multi-component gas flows).

Proposal	FY	Agreement Period	Amount
	69	2/69 − 2/70	30000

Tech. Off.: KRAUSE F R   Funding Element: MSFC
CASE Code: 42   AWC: 125−24

NGT-37-003-001   University of Oklahoma   C. D. Riggs
Training of predoctoral graduate students in space-related science and technology.

No. Students	FY	Agreement Period	Amount
12	65	9/65 − 8/68	212400
12	66	9/66 − 8/69	212400
6	67	9/67 − 8/70	82800

Tech. Off.: HANSING F D   Funding Element: HQ−Y
CASE Code: 99   AWC: 181−00

NGT-37-003-044   University of Oklahoma   H. H. Blackshear
Three year residency training in aerospace medicine.

No. Students	FY	Agreement Period	Amount
−044	69	1/69 −12/71	54660
		9/68 − 8/71	NCE

Tech. Off.:   Funding Element:
CASE Code: 59   AWC: 127−49

NSR-37-004-008   Southeastern State College
Technology Use Studies Center special dissemination experiment.

Proposal	FY	Agreement Period	Amount
−008	68	4/68 − 3/69	85000
		− 5/69	NCE

Tech. Off.:   Funding Element:
CASE Code: 79   AWC: 141−00

OREGON

NGR-38-002-013   Oregon State University   H. C. Curl
Physiological ecology of cryophillic algae.

Proposal	FY	Agreement Period	Amount
−013	66	11/65 −10/67	48592
		6/68 − 8/68	NCE
		− 5/69	NCE
−030	69	9/68 − 8/69	26801

Tech. Off.: SAUNDERS J F   Funding Element: HQ−SB
CASE Code: 51   AWC: 189−54

NGR-38-002-017   Oregon State University   R. Y. Morita
Hydrostatic pressure-temperature, as environmental parameters, on growth, biochemistry and physiology of microorganisms.

Proposal	FY	Agreement Period	Amount
−017	67	1/67 −12/68	27710

Tech. Off.: SAUNDERS J F   Funding Element: HQ−SB
CASE Code: 51   AWC: 189−54

NGR-38-002-018   Oregon State University   S. E. Williamson
Development of a lexicon of space science terms for use of elementary school grades 4 through 6.

Proposal	FY	Agreement Period	Amount
−018	67	7/66 − 6/68	16050
		8/68 − 5/69	NCE

Tech. Off.: TUTTLE F B   Funding Element: HQ−FE
CASE Code: 73   AWC: 023−00

NGR-38-002-020   Oregon State University   R. A. Schmitt
Instrumental activation analysis of rare earths and other elements.

Proposal	FY	Agreement Period	Amount
−022	67	9/67 − 8/68	62140
−029		9/68 − 8/71	40000

Tech. Off.: BRYSON R   Funding Element: HQ−MA
CASE Code: 32   AWC: 185−45

NGL-38-002-032   Oregon State University   R. A. Schmitt
Determination of the concentrations of various chemical elements, vis., al, mg, na, mn, w, fe, si, o, etc., in extraterrestrial particles and in hypervelocity particles, viz., olivines, glass, metallic alloys, retained in impacted catchers of plastic or metallic composition.

Proposal	FY	Agreement Period	Amount
−032	69	7/69 − 6/72	20340

Tech. Off.: HIGH R W   Funding Element: MSC
CASE Code: 12   AWC: 124−09

OREGON (Cont'd)

NAS9-8097   **Oregon State University**   **R. A. Schmitt**
Activation analysis of lunar material.

Proposal	FY	Agreement Period	Amount
	68	6/68 −12/69	57000

Tech. Off.:   Funding Element: M S C
CASE Code: 3 2   AWC: 9 1 4 − 4 0

NGT-38-002-001   **Oregon State University**   **H. P. Hansen**
Training of predoctoral graduate students in space-related science and technology.

No. Students:	FY	Agreement Period	Amount
10	65	9/65 − 8/68	187200
10	66	9/66 − 8/69	187200
6	67	9/67 − 8/70	105200

Tech. Off.:   HANSING   F   D   Funding Element: HQ−Y
CASE Code: 9 9   AWC: 1 8 1 − 0 0

NGR-38-003-009   **University of Oregon**   **D. P. Weill**
Plagioclase thermometry of igneous rocks.

Proposal	FY	Agreement Period	Amount
−009	67	5/67 − 4/70	120000
−013	68	5/67 − 4/70	65000

Tech. Off.:   MC KAY D S   Funding Element: M S C
CASE Code: 3 1   AWC: 9 1 4 − 4 0

NGL-38-003-010   **University of Oregon**   **G. G. Goles**
The geochemistry of trace elements in meteorites and related materials.

Proposal	FY	Agreement Period	Amount
−010	67	9/67 − 8/70	70000

Tech. Off.:   BRYSON R   Funding Element: HQ−SL
CASE Code: 3 2   AWC: 1 8 5 − 4 5

NGR-38-003-012   **University of Oregon**   **A. R. McBirney**
Criteria for interpretation of volcanic depression in terrestrial and lunar environments.

Proposal	FY	Agreement Period	Amount
−012	67	5/67 − 4/69	99951
−017	69	5/69 − 4/71	65000

Tech. Off.:   FOSS T H   Funding Element: M S C
CASE Code: 3 2   AWC: 1 8 5 − 4 2

NGR-38-003-015   **University of Oregon**   **J. Roman**
Advanced studies of physiological responses to flight stresses.

Proposal	FY	Agreement Period	Amount
−015	68	7/68 −12/69	10050

Tech. Off.:   LEWIS C E   Funding Element: F R C
CASE Code: 6 1   AWC: ·1 2 7 − 4 9

NAS9-8071   **University of Oregon**
Determine temperature of rock formation by study of plagioclase properties.

Proposal	FY	Agreement Period	Amount
	68	6/68 −12/69	30000

Tech. Off.:   Funding Element:ᵇ   M S C
CASE Code: 3 2   AWC: 9 1 4 − 4 0

PENNSYLVANIA

NGR-39-018-002   **Bryn Mawr College**   **M. Yarczower**
The acquisition, long-term maintenance and extinction of stimulus control.

Proposal	FY	Agreement Period	Amount
−002	69	3/69 − 2/70	18298

Tech. Off.:   WEISSMAN N W   Funding Element: HQ−SB
CASE Code: 5 1   AWC: 1 8 9 − 5 2

NGR-39-002-011   **Carnegie-Mellon University**   **J. J. Wolken**
Microspectrophotometric techniques of studying. the constituents of living cells and organelles.

Proposal	FY	Agreement Period	Amount
−034	68	4/68 − 3/69	20000
−029	67	4/68 − 6/69	NCE
−034	69	7/69 − 6/70	20000

Tech. Off.:   GEIB D S   Funding Element: HQ−SB
CASE Code: 5 1   AWC: 1 8 9 − 5 5

NGR-39-002-023   **Carnegie-Mellon University**   **J. L. Swedlow**
Analysis of notches and cracks.

Proposal	FY	Agreement Period	Amount
−032	68	1/68 −12/68	37500
		− 4/69	NCE
−035	69	5/69 − 4/70	38000
−036	69	5/69 − 5/72	38000

Tech. Off.:   MC COMB H G   Funding Element: L A R C
CASE Code: 4 6   AWC: 1 2 6 − 1 4

NGT-39-002-002   **Carnegie-Mellon University**   **A. F. Strehler**
Training of predoctoral graduate students in space-related science and technology.

No. Students:	FY	Agreement Period	Amount
15	65	9/65 − 8/68	323200
15	66	9/66 − 8/69	323200
8	67	9/67 − 8/70	144800

Tech. Off.:   HANSING F D   Funding Element: HQ−Y
CASE Code: 9 9   AWC: 1 8 1 − 0 0

NGR-39-008-014   **Carnegie-Mellon University**   **E. G. Haney**
Investigation of stress corrosion cracking of titanium alloys.

Proposal	FY	Agreement Period	Amount
−017	68	8/67 − 7/68	40000
−019	69	8/68 − 7/69	40035

Tech. Off.:   BROWN W F   Funding Element: L E R C
CASE Code: 4 6   AWC: 1 2 9 − 0 3

NGR-39-087-001   **Carnegie-Mellon University**   **M. L. Renard**
Launch window analysis of highly eccentric orbits.

Proposal	FY	Agreement Period	Amount
−001	68	4/68 − 3/69	29882

Tech. Off.:   Funding Element: G S F C
CASE Code: 4 2   AWC: 8 6 1 − 5 1

PENNSYLVANIA (Cont'd)

NGR-39-087-002   Carnegie-Mellon University   A. G. Milnes

Study of semiconductor, heterojunctions of ZNSE, GAAS, and GE.

Proposal	FY	Agreement Period	Amount
-002	68	4/68 - 3/69	47500
-007	69	4/69 - 3/70	35000

Tech. Off.:   Funding Element: E R C
CASE Code: 1 3   AWC: 1 2 5 - 2 5

NGR-39-087-003   Carnegie-Mellon University   J. R. Low

Investigation of the effects of microstructure on the fracture toughness of high strength alloys.

Proposal	FY	Agreement Period	Amount
-003	68	4/68 - 3/69	29778
-008	69	4/69 - 4/70	29670

Tech. Off.: BROWN W F   Funding Element: L E R C
CASE Code: 4 6   AWC: 1 2 9 - 0 3

NAS1-8604   Carnegie-Mellon University

Light scattering studies of pyrrone prepolymers.

Proposal	FY	Agreement Period	Amount
	69	12/68 - 6/69	11000

Tech. Off.:   Funding Element:
CASE Code: 1 2   AWC: 1 2 9 - 0 3

NAS9-8073   Carnegie-Mellon University   T. Kohman

Determine isotope abundance of pb sr os tl nd ag by mass spectrometry.

Proposal	FY	Agreement Period	Amount
	68	6/68 - 10/69	38000

Tech. Off.:   Funding Element: M S C
CASE Code: 3 2   AWC: 9 1 4 - 4 0

NAS12-652   Carnegie-Mellon University

Tech. for parameter from experimental tests.

Proposal	FY	Agreement Period	Amount
	68	6/68 - 8/69	10000

Tech. Off.:   Funding Element: E R C
CASE Code: 4 5   AWC: 1 2 5 - 2 5

NGL-39-004-007   Drexel Institute of Technology   C. Gatlin

Multidisciplinary research in space science and technology.

Proposal	FY	Agreement Period	Amount
-007	66	6/66 - 5/69	200000
-014	67	6/67 - 5/70	100000
-018	68	6/68 - 5/71	100000

Tech. Off.: REDDING E R   Funding Element: HQ-Y
CASE Code: 9 9   AWC: 1 8 3 - 0 0

NGR-39-004-013   Drexel Institute of Technology   P. C. Chou

Transient responses of shell structures.

Proposal	FY	Agreement Period	Amount
-013	67	6/67 - 5/68	28000
		- 8/68	NCE

Tech. Off.: MIXON J S   Funding Element: LARC
CASE Code: 4 6   AWC: 1 2 4 - 1 1

NGL-39-004-015   Drexel Institute of Technology   M. M. Labes

Mechanisms for the effects of electric and magnetic fields on biological systems.

Proposal	FY	Agreement Period	Amount
-016	68	3/68 - 2/69	30000
-021	67	3/69 - 2/71	30000
-025	69	3/69 - 2/72	30000

Tech. Off.: NASH R   Funding Element: HQ-RR
CASE Code: 5 1   AWC: 1 2 9 - 0 3

NGL-39-004-020   Drexel Institute of Technology   W. Hagerty

Research and education in management of large-scale technical programs.

Proposal	FY	Agreement Period	Amount
-020	66	1/69 -12/72	234000

Tech. Off.: STEPHENS R E   Funding Element: HQ-Y
CASE Code: 9 9   AWC: 1 8 3 - 0 0

NGR-39-004-028   Drexel Institute of Technology   C. A. Silver

Human and linguistic aspects of oral communication with computers.

Proposal	FY	Agreement Period	Amount
-028	69	4/69 - 3/70	32057

Tech. Off.: HILL J H   Funding Element: E R C
CASE Code: 9 9   AWC: 1 2 7 - 5 1

NGT-39-004-005   Drexel Institute of Technology   O. W. Witzell

Supporting the training of predoctoral graduate students in space-related science and technology.

No. Students	FY	Agreement Period	Amount
4	66	9/66 - 8/69	76800
2	67	9/67 - 8/70	38400

Tech. Off.: HANSING F D   Funding Element: HQ-Y
CASE Code: 9 9   AWC: 1 8 1 - 0 0

NGT-39-019-002   Duquesne University   H. H. Petit

Training of predoctoral graduate students in space-related science and technology.

No. Students	FY	Agreement Period	Amount
2	65	9/65 - 8/68	31000
2	66	9/66 - 8/69	30800
2	67	9/67 - 8/70	38900

Tech. Off.: HANSING F D   Funding Element: HQ-Y
CASE Code: 9 9   AWC: 1 8 1 - 0 0

PENNSYLVANIA (Cont'd)

NGR-39-006-001 Haverford College   **L. C. Green**

Investigation of the solar ultraviolet spectrum of Fe II.

Proposal	FY	Agreement Period	Amount
-005	67	6/67 - 5/68	36104
-007	69	6/68 -11/69	29712
-008	69	6/68 - 6/71	30000

Tech. Off.: ROMAN N G   Funding Element: HQ-SG
CASE Code: 11   AWC: 188-41

NGR-39-007-007 Lehigh University   **R. W. Kraft**

Investigation of the solidification structure and properties of euctectic alloys, including consideration of properties control.

Proposal	FY	Agreement Period	Amount
-029	67	7/67 - 6/68	35000
-038	68	7/68 - 6/69	39605

Tech. Off.: MALTZ J   Funding Element: HQ-RR
CASE Code: 47   AWC: 126-14

NGR-39-007-011 Lehigh University   **F. Erdogan**

Investigation of fatigue crack propagation in thin plates and shells.

Proposal	FY	Agreement Period	Amount
-033	68	2/68 - 1/69	43465

Tech. Off.:   Funding Element:
CASE Code: 46   AWC: 126-14

NGR-39-007-017 Lehigh University   **A. Kalnins**

Analysis of large deformation of shells.

Proposal	FY	Agreement Period	Amount
-017	66	2/66 - 1/69	50000
-017	67	2/67 - 1/69	25600
		2/69 - 8/69	NCE

Tech. Off.: LEONARD R W   Funding Element: LARC
CASE Code: 46   AWC: 124-08

NGR-39-007-040 Lehigh University   **R. P. Wei**

Investigate the influence of temperature on fatigue crack growth.

Proposal	FY	Agreement Period	Amount
-040	69	9/68 - 8/69	29945

Tech. Off.:   Funding Element: LARC
CASE Code: 46   AWC: 129-03

NAS9-8084   Lehigh University

Using replication and thin section electron microscopy to determine the damage in minerals and rocks due to shock.

Proposal	FY	Agreement Period	Amount
	68	6/68 - 1/70	14000

Tech. Off.:   Funding Element: MSC
CASE Code: 32   AWC: 914-40

NGT-39-007-003 Lehigh University   **R. D. Stout**

Training of predoctoral graduate students in space-related science and technology.

No. Students:	FY	Agreement Period	Amount
10	65	9/65 - 8/68	192000
10	66	9/66 - 8/69	192000
6	67	9/67 - 8/70	101200

Tech. Off.: HANSING F D   Funding Element: HQ-Y
CASE Code: 99   AWC: 181-00

NGR-39-009-002 Pennsylvania State University   **W. J. Ross**

Ionospheric studies using beacon satellite transmissions.

Proposal	FY	Agreement Period	Amount
-101	68	10/67 - 9/68	55000
		9/68 - 9/69	NCE

Tech. Off.: SCHMERLING   Funding Element: HQ-SG
CASE Code: 31   AWC: 188-39

NGR-39-009-003 Pennsylvania State University   **J. S. Nisbet**

Theoretical and experimental research on electron densities in the upper ionosphere, including studies of a rocket and separating-capsule experimental technique.

Proposal	FY	Agreement Period	Amount
-059	66	3/66 - 2/69	158228
-091	67	3/67 -10/69	105000
-108	68	11/67 -10/69	50000
-131	69	11/68 -10/70	100000

Tech. Off.: SCHMERLING   Funding Element: HQ-SG
CASE Code: 31   AWC: 188-39

NGR-39-009-008 Pennsylvania State University   **E. C. Pollard**

Cellular biophysics: a study of the structure and function of living cells.

Proposal	FY	Agreement Period	Amount
-100	68	7/67 - 6/68	170000
-100	69	7/68 - 6/69	150434
-119	69	7/68 - 6/69	150434

Tech. Off.: JACOBS G F   Funding Element: HQ-SB
CASE Code: 51   AWC: 189-55

NGL-39-009-010 Pennsylvania State University   **D. P. Gold**

Study of structural and mineralogical signatures of meteorite impact sites including mineral paragenesis high pressure polymorphs, microfractures and quartz lamellae.

Proposal	FY	Agreement Period	Amount
4594	63	7/63 - 6/66	61563
-010	63	7/66 - 8/68	NCE

Tech. Off.:   Funding Element:
CASE Code: 32   AWC: 185-42

NGL-39-009-015 Pennsylvania State University   **P. Ebaugh**

Multidisciplinary space-related research.

Proposal	FY	Agreement Period	Amount
8399	65	9/65 - 8/68	600000
-073	66	9/66 - 8/69	300000
-098	68	9/67 - 8/70	100000
-124	66	9/68 - 9/71	200000

Tech. Off.: REDDING E R   Funding Element: HQ-Y
CASE Code: 99   AWC: 183-00

PENNSYLVANIA (Cont'd.)

NGR-39-009-023   Pennsylvania State University   J. L. Shearer
Research and development of on-board control systems and elements for aerospace vehicles.

Proposal	FY	Agreement Period	Amount
-103	68	10/67 - 9/68	57633
-130	69	10/68 - 9/69	59496

Tech. Off.: JANOW C   Funding Element: HQ-RE
CASE Code: 42   AWC: 125-19

NGR-39-009-032   Pennsylvania State University   B. R. F. Kendall
Evaluation of the constant-momentum mass spectrometer for ion analysis in the D and E regions of the ionosphere.

Proposal	FY	Agreement Period	Amount
-093	67	6/67 - 5/68	37040
-107	68	6/68 - 3/69	45000
-134	69	4/69 - 3/70	32699

Tech. Off.: SCHMERLING   Funding Element: HQ-SG
CASE Code: 31   AWC: 188-39

NGR-39-009-034   Pennsylvania State University   J. Marin
Low cycle fatigue under multiaxial strain cycling.

Proposal	FY	Agreement Period	Amount
-034	65	4/65 - 3/68	24971
-114	68	4/68 - 3/69	16000

Tech. Off.: HIRSCHBERG M H   Funding Element: LERC
CASE Code: 46   AWC: 720-03

NGR-39-009-077   Pennsylvania State University   G. M. Faeth
Investigation of near critical and supercritical burning of fuel droplets.

Proposal	FY	Agreement Period	Amount
-077	67	9/66 - 8/68	25345
-128	69	9/68 - 8/69	12158

Tech. Off.: PRIEM R J   Funding Element: LERC
CASE Code: 13   AWC: 128-31

NGR-39-009-095   Pennsylvania State University   R. G. Quinn
Cooperative ionospheric investigations.

Proposal	FY	Agreement Period	Amount
-095	68	3/68 - 2/71	30000

Tech. Off.:   Funding Element: GSFC
CASE Code: 31   AWC: 385-39

NGR-39-009-096   Pennsylvania State University
A theoretical and experimental investigation of the quantum mechanical effects on communication systems.

Proposal	FY	Agreement Period	Amount
-096	68	9/67 - 8/68	29664
-096	69	9/68 - 8/69	23116

Tech. Off.: ALDRIDGE M D   Funding Element: LARC
CASE Code: 21   AWC: 125-21

NGR-39-009-111   Pennsylvania State University   B. W. McCormick
Study of rotor-blade vortex interaction.

Proposal	FY	Agreement Period	Amount
-111	68	4/68 - 3/70	68379

Tech. Off.:   Funding Element: LARC
CASE Code: 41   AWC: 721-02

NGR-39-009-121   Pennsylvania State University   G. Reethof
Research in aircraft propulsion noise and its reduction.

Proposal	FY	Agreement Period	Amount
-121	69	1/69 -12/69	70000

Tech. Off.: FINDLEY D S   Funding Element: LARC
CASE Code: 41   AWC: 126-61

NGR-39-009-123   Pennsylvania State University   A. J. Engel
Cycled operation of water vapor electrolysis cell.

Proposal	FY	Agreement Period	Amount
-123	69	1/69 -12/69	14338
-123	69	1/69 -12/69	13621

Tech. Off.: WYDEVEN T   Funding Element: ARC
CASE Code: 13   AWC: 127-53

NGR-39-009-129   Pennsylvania State University   B. R. F. Kendall
Ion analyses in the D and E regions of the ionosphere using impulse mass spectrometers.

Proposal	FY	Agreement Period	Amount
-129	68	1/69 -12/69	40000

Tech. Off.: SCHMERLING E R   Funding Element: HQ-SG
CASE Code: 31   AWC: 188-39

NSR-39-009-129   Pennsylvania State University   B. R. F. Kendall
Ion analysis in the D and E regions of the ionospheres using impulse mass spectrometers.

Proposal	FY	Agreement Period	Amount
-129	69	1/69 -12/69	40000

Tech. Off.: SCHMERLING E R   Funding Element: HQ-SG
CASE Code: 31   AWC: 879-11

NAS8-21140   Pennsylvania State University   A. K. Blackadar
Investigation of the turbulent wind field below 500 feet altitude at the Eastern Test Range, Florida.

Proposal	FY	Agreement Period	Amount
		6/67 - 6/68	46000

Tech. Off.: FICHTL G   Funding Element: MSFC
CASE Code: 31   AWC: 124-11

NGT-39-009-011   Pennsylvania State University   M. N. McGeary
Training of predoctoral graduate students in space-related science and technology.

No. Students	FY	Agreement Period	Amount
15	65	9/65 - 8/68	310500
15	66	9/66 - 8/69	284800
8	67	9/67 - 8/70	162500

Tech. Off.: HANSING F D   Funding Element: HQ-Y
CASE Code: 99   AWC: 181-00

PENNSYLVANIA (Cont'd.)

NGT-39-009-141   Pennsylvania State University   G. Reethof

Predoctoral training of students in the field of acoustics as related to aeronautical and space technology.

No. Students:	FY	Agreement Period	Amount
6	69	9/69 – 9/72	133200

Tech. Off.: CARTER C H   Funding Element: HQ–Y
CASE Code: 49   AWC: 181–00

NGL-39-010-001   University of Pennsylvania   M. Altman

Research in the conversion of various forms of energy by unconventional techniques.

Proposal	FY	Agreement Period	Amount
–044	65	7/65 – 6/68	275000
–057	66	7/66 – 6/69	525000
–080	67	7/67 – 6/70	150000
–105		7/69 – 6/72	78000

Tech. Off.: COHN E M   Funding Element: GSFC
CASE Code: 13   AWC: 123–34

NGR-39-010-002   University of Pennsylvania   J. O'M. Bockris

Studies of the fundamental chemistry, properties, and behavior of fuel cells.

Proposal	FY	Agreement Period	Amount
–043	65	10/65 – 9/68	299915
–109	69	10/68 –10/71	200000

Tech. Off.: COHN E M   Funding Element: GSFC
CASE Code: 13   AWC: 123–34

NGR-39-010-087   University of Pennsylvania   F. Haber

An angle-measurement navigation satellite concepts study.

Proposal	FY	Agreement Period	Amount
–087	68	10/67 – 9/68	36531
–087	68	7/68 –12/68	NCE
–108	69	1/69 – 6/69	16000

Tech. Off.:   Funding Element:
CASE Code: 42   AWC: 160–18

NGL-39-010-097   University of Pennsylvenia   C. J. Lambertsen

Studies of acute acclimatization of subnormal PO₂ and PCO₂.

Proposal	FY	Agreement Period	Amount
–097	68	1/68 –12/68	50000
–103	68	1/69 –12/70	50000
–103	69	1/69 –12/71	33000

Tech. Off.: BILLINGHAM J   Funding Element: ARC
CASE Code: 51   AWC: 127–49

NGR-39-010-101   University of Pennsylvania   B. S. P. Shen

Calculations on spallation reactions in the upper atmosphere and in space.

Proposal	FY	Agreement Period	Amount
–101	69	9/68 – 8/70	19698

Tech. Off.:   Funding Element:
CASE Code: 31   AWC: 720–04

NGR-39-010-104   University of Pennsylvania   A. H. Brown

Effects of altered gravity and other factors on the growth and development of higher plants.

Proposal	FY	Agreement Period	Amount
–104	69	2/69 – 2/70	78465

Tech. Off.: SAUNDERS J F   Funding Element: HQ–SB
CASE Code: 59   AWC: 189–54

NSR-39-010-100   University of Pennsylvania   R. E. Forster

Support for symposium on chemistry and physiology.

Proposal	FY	Agreement Period	Amount
–100	68	7/68 – 6/69	12550

Tech. Off.:   Funding Element:
CASE Code: 51   AWC: 127–49

NAS1-8818   University of Pennsylvania   Z. Hashin

A research report on fiber reinforced materials.

Proposal	FY	Agreement Period	Amount
	69	12/68 – 9/69	17000

Tech. Off.:   Funding Element:
CASE Code: 47   AWC: 126–14

NAS5-14923   University of Pennsylvania

Tech. report for frequency assignment guideline for satellite radio links.

Proposal	FY	Agreement Period	Amount
	68	4/68 – 1/69	13000

Tech. Off.:   Funding Element: GSFC
CASE Code: 45   AWC: 150–22

NGT-39-010-007   University of Pennsylvania   A. N. Hixson

Training of predoctoral graduate students in space-related science and technology.

No. Students:	FY	Agreement Period	Amount
15	65	9/65 – 8/68	288000
15	66	9/66 – 8/69	293900
8	67	9/67 – 8/70	148900

Tech. Off.: HANSING F D   Funding Element: HQ–Y
CASE Code: 99   AWC: 181–00

NGL-39-011-002   University of Pittsburgh   D. Halliday

Interdisciplinary space-related research in the physical, life, and engineering sciences.

Proposal	FY	Agreement Period	Amount
–042	65	5/65 – 4/68	320000
–057	66	8/66 – 7/69	300000
–077	67	8/67 – 7/70	300000
–095	68	8/68 – 7/71	150000

Tech. Off.: MARR E G   Funding Element: HQ–Y
CASE Code: 99   AWC: 183–00

NGL-39-011-013   University of Pittsburgh   W. L. Fite

Investigation of airglow excitation mechanisms using atomic beam techniques.

Proposal	FY	Agreement Period	Amount
–092	66	2/68 – 1/71	40000
–104		2/69 – 1/72	45000

Tech. Off.: HOROWITZ R   Funding Element: HQ–SL
CASE Code: 31   AWC: 185–37

PENNSYLVANIA (Cont'd)

NGL-39-011-030   University of Pittsburgh   **E. C. Zipf**

Excitation in collisional deactivation of the measurable A³ state of nitrogen in the aurora and day airglow.

Proposal	FY	Agreement Period	Amount
−053	66	5/66 − 4/68	28622
−093	68	5/68 − 4/71	65000
−107		5/69 − 4/72	66000

Tech. Off.: HOROWITZ R   Funding Element: HQ−SL
CASE Code: 31   AWC: 185−37

NGR-39-011-035   University of Pittsburgh   **E. Gerjuoy**

New formulas for collision amplitudes and related quantities.

Proposal	FY	Agreement Period	Amount
−086	68	10/67 − 9/68	10000
−098	69	10/68 − 9/69	10290

Tech. Off.: MENTZER R H   Funding Element: GSFC
CASE Code: 13   AWC: 188−39

NGR-39-011-039   University of Pittsburgh   **W. G. Vogt**

Stability of solutions to partial differential equations.

Proposal	FY	Agreement Period	Amount
−084	68	11/67 −10/68	27950
−100	69	11/68 −10/69	31392

Tech. Off.: WILSON R   Funding Element: HQ−RR
CASE Code: 21   AWC: 129−04

NGR-39-011-067   University of Pittsburgh   **G. R. Fitterer**

The development of solids electrolyte techniques to determine the rate constants for the oxidation of metals and alloys.

Proposal	FY	Agreement Period	Amount
−067	68	9/67 − 8/68	22579
−067	68	6/68 − 3/69	NCE
−097	69	3/69 − 2/70	21549

Tech. Off.: OLDRIEVE R E   Funding Element: LERC
CASE Code: 47   AWC: 720−03

NGR-39-011-079   University of Pittsburgh   **R. S. Dougall**

Experimental determination of the heat-transfer and vapor-void characteristics of subcooled forced-convection boiling of Freon-113 at high pressures with emphasis on the bubble layer.

Proposal	FY	Agreement Period	Amount
−079	68	9/67 − 8/69	63038

Tech. Off.: HSU Y   Funding Element: LERC
CASE Code: 12   AWC: 122−29

NGL-39-011-080   University of Pittsburgh   **D. C. Stone**

Research program in public administration.

Proposal	FY	Agreement Period	Amount
−080	67	11/67 −11/70	103000
−101	69	11/68 −11/71	35000

Tech. Off.: STEPHENS R E   Funding Element: HQ−Y
CASE Code: 75   AWC: 183−00

NGR-39-011-083   University of Pittsburgh   **T. M. Donahue**

Photometer observations of auroral oxygen and nitrogen emissions.

Proposal	FY	Agreement Period	Amount
−083	68	10/67 − 9/68	7150

Tech. Off.: HAUGHNEY L C   Funding Element: ARC
CASE Code: 31   AWC: 188−45

NGR-39-011-085   University of Pittsburgh   **B. W. Hapke**

Studies relating to the surfaces of the moon and planets.

Proposal	FY	Agreement Period	Amount
−085	69	4/69 − 3/70	55954

Tech. Off.: BRYSON R P   Funding Element: HQ−MA
CASE Code: 39   AWC: 195−42

NGR-39-011-096   University of Pittsburgh   **E. J. Sternglass**

Microchemical surface analysis by electron spectroscopy.

Proposal	FY	Agreement Period	Amount
−096	69	1/69 − 6/69	35873
−096	69	1/69 − 6/69	38000
−096	69	7/69 −12/69	29320
−096	69	7/69 − 1/70	29320

Tech. Off.: FRIPP A L JR   Funding Element: LARC
CASE Code: 13   AWC: 125−25

NASr-169   University of Pittsburgh   **N. Wald**
(NSR-39-011-005) Automatic analysis of cytogenic material.

Proposal	FY	Agreement Period	Amount
−081	68	9/67 − 8/68	49965
−094	69	9/68 − 8/69	35000

Tech. Off.: JACOBS G F   Funding Element: HQ−SB
CASE Code: 13   AWC: 189−57

NASr-179   University of Pittsburgh   **T. M. Donahue**
(NSR-39-011-006) Helium geocorona and airglow investigations with sounding rockets.

Proposal	FY	Agreement Period	Amount
−062	67	4/67 − 3/68	170000
−088	69	3/68 − 9/69	180415
−088	69	3/68 − 9/69	50000

Tech. Off.: DUBIN   Funding Element: HQ−SG
CASE Code: 31   AWC: 879−10

NSR-39-001-064   University of Pittsburgh   **A. Kent**

Space technology information dissemination.

Proposal	FY	Agreement Period	Amount
−064	67	10/66 −10/67	19473
−064	67	10/67 −10/68	NCE

Tech. Off.:   Funding Element:
CASE Code: 42   AWC: 141−00

NSR-39-011-076   University of Pittsburgh   **J. Canter**

Special experimental projects involving information systems and technology utilization.

Proposal	FY	Agreement Period	Amount
−076	67	12/67 − 1/69	61968
		2/69 − 9/69	NCE

Tech. Off.: DUFFY R E   Funding Element: HQ−UT
CASE Code: 49   AWC: 141−00

PENNSYLVANIA (Cont'd)

NSR-39-011-078 **University of Pittsburgh** **G. McGee**

Experiment in direct provision of hard-copy documentation of aerospace generated technology to potential users.

Proposal	FY	Agreement Period	Amount
-078	66	7/67 − 6/68	28838
		7/68 − 2/69	NCE
		7/68 − 2/70	NCE

Tech. Off.: DUFFY R E Funding Element: HQ−UT
CASE Code: 76 AWC: 141−00

NSR-39-011-089 **University of Pittsburgh** **A. Kent**

Operation of a regional dissemination center program at the Knowledge Availability Systems Center.

Proposal	FY	Agreement Period	Amount
-089	68	3/68 − 2/69	195000
-089	68	4/69	NCE

Tech. Off.: Funding Element:
CASE Code: 76 AWC: 141−00

NSR-39-011-106 **University of Pittsburgh**

Support for the knowledge availability systems center, regional dissemination center.

Proposal	FY	Agreement Period	Amount
-106	68	3/69 − 2/70	64000

Tech. Off.: CARLSON J M Funding Element: HQ−UT
CASE Code: 79 AWC: 141−00

NAS5-11077 **University of Pittsburgh** **T. M. Donahue**

Sodium airglow experiment instrumentation ground support equipment and field support for the Orbiting Geophysical Observatory Mission F.

Proposal	FY	Agreement Period	Amount
		8/67 −12/68	96000
	67	8/67 −12/68	48000
			GSFC

Tech. Off.: MERCANTI E Funding Element: GSFC
CASE Code: 11 AWC: 841−12

NGT-39-011-003 **University of Pittsburgh** **P. F. Jones**

Training of predoctoral graduate students in space-related science and technology.

No. Students	FY	Agreement Period	Amount
15	65	9/65 − 8/68	272000
15	66	9/66 − 8/69	272000
8	67	9/67 − 8/70	136100

Tech. Off.: HANSING F D Funding Element: HQ−Y
CASE Code: 99 AWC: 181−00

NGT-39-011-075 **University of Pittsburgh** **D. C. Stone**

Training of predoctoral graduate students in administration and management with emphasis on policy development, management, and administration of large scientic and technological programs.

No. Students	FY	Agreement Period	Amount
5	67	9/67 − 8/70	90000
5	68	9/68 − 8/71	90000
5	69	9/69 − 8/72	105000

Tech. Off.: STEPHENS R E Funding Element: HQ−Y
CASE Code: 99 AWC: 181−00

NGF-39-011-004 **University of Pittsburgh** **D. Halliday**

Construction of a building housing the laboratories for a space research and coordination center on the campus of the University of Pittsburgh.

Proposal	FY	Agreement Period	Amount
5398	63	6/63 − 6/66	1496657

Tech. Off.: HOLMES D C Funding Element: HQ−Y
CASE Code: 99 AWC: 182−00

NAS1-7709 **Temple University** **C. S. Stokes**

The design, testing, fabrication, delivery, and launch support of a barium chemical release payload.

Proposal	FY	Agreement Period	Amount
		9/67 − 7/68	79000
	68	9/67 − 7/68	4000

Tech. Off.: JONES J L Funding Element: LARC
CASE Code: 31 AWC: 188−36

NAS5-9128 **Temple University** **J. L. Bohn**

Dust particle experiments.

Proposal	FY	Agreement Period	Amount
		2/65 − 6/68	545000
	67	12/64 − 6/68	18000

Tech. Off.: MARCOTTE P Funding Element: GSFC
CASE Code: 31 AWC: 861−22

NGT-39-012-007 **Temple University** **G. H. Huganir**

Training of predoctoral graduate students in space-related science and technology.

No. Students	FY	Agreement Period	Amount
4	66	9/66 − 8/69	74400
2	67	9/67 − 8/70	37000

Tech. Off.: HANSING F D Funding Element: HQ−Y
CASE Code: 99 AWC: 181−00

NGT-39-023-005 **Villanova University** **A. H. Buford**

Training of predoctoral graduate students in space-related science and technology.

No. Students	FY	Agreement Period	Amount
2	66	9/66 − 8/69	25000
1	67	9/67 − 8/70	13200

Tech. Off.: HANSING F D Funding Element: HQ−Y
CASE Code: 99 AWC: 181−00

RHODE ISLAND

NGL-40-002-009   Brown University   **P. T. Maeder**
Multidisciplinary space-related research program.

Proposal	FY	Agreement Period	Amount
8697	65	6/65 – 5/68	200000
–047	66	6/66 – 5/69	100000
–057	67	6/67 – 5/70	150000
		–11/70	NCE

Tech. Off.:   REDDING E R   Funding Element: HQ–Y
CASE Code: 99   AWC: 183–00

NGR-40-002-012   Brown University   **P. D. Richardson**
Variational methods for solving heat conduction problems.

Proposal	FY	Agreement Period	Amount
–067	68	4/67 – 4/68	11313
–067	68	4/68 –10/68	NCE
–067	11/68	– 4/69	NCE

Tech. Off.:   WILSON R   Funding Element: HQ–RR
CASE Code: 13   AWC: 129–04

NGL-40-002-015   Brown University   **J. P. LaSalle**
Theory of differential equations and their relationship to dynamical systems theory.

Proposal	FY	Agreement Period	Amount
–064	68	10/67 – 9/70	122412
–077	69	10/68 – 9/71	60000

Tech. Off.:   FREEDMAN M I   Funding Element: ERC
CASE Code: 21   AWC: 125–19

NGL-40-002-042   Brown University   **G. S. Heller**
Properties and application of solid state materials at submillimeter frequencies.

Proposal	FY	Agreement Period	Amount
–068	68	11/67 –10/68	30000
–076	68	11/68 –10/70	30000
–078	69	11/68 –10/71	30000

Tech. Off.:   CARSON J W   Funding Element: ERC
CASE Code: 45   AWC: 125–21

NGR-40-002-059   Brown University   **E. A. Mason**
Study of short-range intermolecular forces and high-temperature gas properties.

Proposal	FY	Agreement Period	Amount
–059	67	9/67 – 8/68	33000
–074	68	9/68 – 8/69	33000
–079	69	9/69 – 8/70	33000

Tech. Off.:   TALKIN R W   Funding Element: HQ–RR
CASE Code: 13   AWC: 129–01

NGR-40-002-080   Brown University   **C. Mylonas**
For studies of plasticity aspects of fracture mechanics analysis and testing.

Proposal	FY	Agreement Period	Amount
–080	69	3/69 – 2/70	35000

Tech. Off.:   BOURKE E A   Funding Element: LERC
CASE Code: 46   AWC: 124–08

NGR-40-002-081   Brown University   **T. A. Mutch**
Participation in Mars lander scientific instrument team.

Proposal	FY	Agreement Period	Amount
–081	69	2/69 – 1/70	12138

Tech. Off.:   MITZ M A   Funding Element: HQ–SL
CASE Code: 42   AWC: 815–20

NGR-40-002-082   Brown University   **J. E. Savage**
A study of decoders for error correction.

Proposal	FY	Agreement Period	Amount
–082	69	6/69 – 6/70	28000

Tech. Off.:   FARR E H   Funding Element: ERC
CASE Code: 45   AWC: 125–79

NAS12-2054   Brown University   **A. Wold**
Prep. & magnetic properties of some trans. metal co----.

Proposal	FY	Agreement Period	Amount
		12/68 –12/69	30000

Tech. Off.:   Funding Element: ERC
CASE Code: 19   AWC: 129–03

NGT-40-002-008   Brown University   **M. J. Brennan**
Training of predoctoral graduate students in space-related science and technology.

No. Students:	FY	Agreement Period	Amount
12	65	9/65 – 8/68	223200
12	66	9/66 – 8/69	223200
6	67	9/67 – 8/70	115200

Tech. Off.:   HANSING F D   Funding Element: HQ–Y
CASE Code: 99   AWC: 181–00

NGR-40-005-002   Providence College   **E. K. Gora**
Line shape theory research.

Proposal	FY	Agreement Period	Amount
–002	68	8/68 – 7/69	10000

Tech. Off.:   Funding Element: ERC
CASE Code: 49   AWC: 160–21

NGT-40-004-001   University of Rhode Island   **P. H. Nash**
Training of predoctoral graduate students in space-related science and technology.

No. Students:	FY	Agreement Period	Amount
4	65	9/65 – 8/68	70800
5	66	9/66 – 8/69	88500
3	67	9/67 – 8/70	48500

Tech. Off.:   HANSING F D   Funding Element: HQ–Y
CASE Code: 99   AWC: 181–00

SOUTH CAROLINA

NGR-41-001-016   Clemson University   **T. G. Proctor**
Studies on the existence of almost periodic solutions for certain differential and functional equations containing almost periodic members.

Proposal	FY	Agreement Period	Amount
–016	67	5/67 – 5/68	12720
–022	69	8/68 – 7/69	14174

Tech. Off.:   ARMSTRONG E S   Funding Element: LARC
CASE Code: 21   AWC: 125–17

SOUTH CAROLINA   (Cont'd)

NAS8-11259   Clemson University   C. V. Aucoin
Studies of statistical filter theory to selected problems of guidance control & navigation of space vehicle.

Proposal	FY	Agreement Period	Amount
	67	5/64 — 4/69	10000
	64	5/64 — 4/69	10000

Tech. Off.: HARDEN J W   Funding Element: MSFC
CASE Code: 42   AWC: 125-17

NGT-41-001-001   Clemson University   V. Hurst
Training of predoctoral graduate students in space-related science and technology.

No. Students:	FY	Agreement Period	Amount
6	65	9/65 — 8/68	117600
6	66	9/66 — 8/69	123300
3	67	9/67 — 8/70	58000

Tech. Off.: HANSING F D   Funding Element: HQ-Y
CASE Code: 99   AWC: 181-00

NGR-41-002-003   University of South Carolina   J. R. Durig
Infrared spectra of molecules and materials of astrophysical interest.

Proposal	FY	Agreement Period	Amount
-014	67	6/67 — 5/69	29922
-019	68	6/67 — 5/69	8000
-023	69	6/69 — 6/72	33327

Tech. Off.: HIPSHER H F   Funding Element: HQ-SL
CASE Code: 13   AWC: 185-47

NGR-41-002-024   University of South Carolina   D. L. Rohlfing
The effect of age on the catalytic activity of thermally prepared polyamino acids.

Proposal	FY	Agreement Period	Amount
-024	69	5/69 — 7/69	2545

Tech. Off.: GEIB D S   Funding Element: HQ-SB
CASE Code: 12   AWC: 125-79

NGT-41-002-002   University of South Carolina   J. A. Morris
Training of predoctoral graduate students in space-related science and technology.

No. Students:	FY	Agreement Period	Amount
6	65	9/65 — 8/68	118000
6	66	9/66 — 8/69	124300
3	67	9/67 — 8/70	62100

Tech. Off.: HANSING F D   Funding Element: HQ-Y
CASE Code: 99   AWC: 181-00

SOUTH DAKOTA

NGR-42-001-002   South Dakota School of Mines and Technology
C. L. Gruber
Experimental studies of the optically induced free carrier light modulation.

Proposal	FY	Agreement Period	Amount
-002	68	9/67 — 9/68	11313
-005	69	9/68 — 9/69	8176

Tech. Off.: BOZZI J W   Funding Element: GSFC
CASE Code: 13   AWC: 125-21

NGL-42-001-004   South Dakota School of Mines and Technology
R. A. Schleusener
Investigation of the application of aerospace technology to weather modification.

Proposal	FY	Agreement Period	Amount
-004	68	9/68 — 8/71	100000

Tech. Off.: QUINN H B   Funding Element: HQ-Y
CASE Code: 31   AWC: 183-00

NGT-42-002-001   University of South Dakota   W. W. Gutzman
Training of predoctoral graduate students in space-related science and technology.

No. Students:	FY	Agreement Period	Amount
3	65	9/65 — 8/68	62800
4	66	9/66 — 8/69	85200
2	67	9/67 — 8/70	42600

Tech. Off.: HANSING F D   Funding Element: HQ-Y
CASE Code: 99   AWC: 181-00

TENNESSEE

NGR-43-010-001   East Tennessee State University   H. D. Powell
An electron paramagnetic resonance study of magnesium and beryllium in silicon.

Proposal	FY	Agreement Period	Amount
-001	69	1/69 — 12/69	20350

Tech. Off.: KENIMER R L   Funding Element: LARC
CASE Code: 12   AWC: 124-09

NGR-43-003-007   Tennessee Technological University   R. Kinslow
Investigation of stress waves in laminated materials.

Proposal	FY	Agreement Period	Amount
-007	67	7/67 — 6/68	12616
-009	69	7/68 — 6/69	21000

Tech. Off.: PALAIRS B G   Funding Element: MSC
CASE Code: 47   AWC: 914-40

NGR-43-001-003   University of Tennessee   W. K. Stair
Theoretical and experimental studies of visco-type shaft seals.

Proposal	FY	Agreement Period	Amount
-046	67	4/67 — 4/68	38000
-061	68	4/68 — 3/69	27870
-076	69	4/69 — 4/70	29437

Tech. Off.: MALTZ J   Funding Element: HQ-RR
CASE Code: 47   AWC: 129-03

TENNESSEE (Cont'd)

NGL-43-001-006   University of Tennessee   N. M. Gailar
Theoretical and experimental very high resolution spectroscopic studies of line shapes of atmospheric gases and of absorption bands of inorganic solids.

Proposal	FY	Agreement Period	Amount
-045	67	10/66 - 9/69	101469
-006	68	10/67 - 9/70	101741
-033	66	10/65 - 9/68	103051
-078		10/68 - 9/69	107372

Tech. Off.: FELLOWS R F   Funding Element: HQ-SL
CASE Code: 13   AWC: 185-37

NGR-43-001-008   University of Tennessee   D. C. Bogue
Study of constitutive equations in two-dimensional accelerating flows.

Proposal	FY	Agreement Period	Amount
-019	65	9/65 - 8/68	8307
-030	66	9/66 - 8/68	7911
-051	67	9/67 - 8/69	14988

Tech. Off.: DANBERG J E   Funding Element: HQ-RR
CASE Code: 21   AWC: 129-01

NGL-43-001-021   University of Tennessee   C. O. Thomas
Multidisciplinary research program in space sciences and engineering.

Proposal	FY	Agreement Period	Amount
-021	66	1/66 -12/68	300000
-035	67	1/67 -12/69	250000
-069	68	1/68 -12/71	200000
-079		1/69 -12/71	238000

Tech. Off.: QUINN H B   Funding Element: HQ-Y
CASE Code: 99   AWC: 183-00

NGR-43-001-023   University of Tennessee   M. W. Milligan
Fundamental study in low-density gas dynamics.

Proposal	FY	Agreement Period	Amount
-044	67	5/67 - 4/68	32000
-062	68	5/68 - 6/69	33000
-077	69	7/69 - 7/70	26000

Tech. Off.: REAM L W   Funding Element: LERC
CASE Code: 13   AWC: 120-27

NGL-43-001-056   University of Tennessee   F. M. Shofner
Investigation of noise characteristics and amplitude stabilization of plasma lasers.

Proposal	FY	Agreement Period	Amount
-056	68	9/67 - 8/68	25000
-071	68	9/68 - 8/70	25000
-072	69	9/69 - 8/71	25000

Tech. Off.: MORREAL J A   Funding Element: ERC
CASE Code: 13   AWC: 125-21

NGR-43-001-075   University of Tennessee   H. D. Gruschka
Suppression of acoustic noise from jet propulsion engines by means of model tests.

Proposal	FY	Agreement Period	Amount
-075	69	1/69 -12/69	24000
-075	69	1/69 -12/69	23780

Tech. Off.: CAWTHORN J M   Funding Element: LARC
CASE Code: 41   AWC: 126-61

NAS8-11189   University of Tennessee   G. R. Shermann
Search for good algorithms for practical solutions to discrete optimization problems.

Proposal	FY	Agreement Period	Amount
	66	4/64 - 3/69	30000

Tech. Off.: ANDERSON A   Funding Element: MSFC
CASE Code: 21   AWC: 125-23

NGT-43-001-002   University of Tennessee   H. A. Smith
Training of predoctoral graduate students in space-related science and technology.

No. Students	FY	Agreement Period	Amount
12	65	9/65 - 8/68	212400
12	66	9/66 - 8/69	212400
6	67	9/67 - 8/70	97000

Tech. Off.: HANSING F D   Funding Element: HQ-Y
CASE Code: 99   AWC: 181-00

NGR-43-002-031   Vanderbilt University   C. E. Roos
Investigation of high energy radiation from a plasma focus.

Proposal	FY	Agreement Period	Amount
-031	69	2/69 - 9/69	23000
-031	69	2/69 - 8/69	23900

Tech. Off.: WOOD G P   Funding Element: LARC
CASE Code: 13   AWC: 129-02

NGR-43-002-032   Vanderbilt University   E. B. Shanks
Non-linear optimization techniques.

Proposal	FY	Agreement Period	Amount
-032	69	2/69 - 1/70	23400

Tech. Off.: ANDERSON A E   Funding Element: MSFC
CASE Code: 13   AWC: 129-04

NAS8-2559   Vanderbilt University   E. B. Shanks
Research on numerical integration of second order differential equations.

Proposal	FY	Agreement Period	Amount
		12/61 - 1/68	202000

Tech. Off.: ANDERSON A   Funding Element: MSFC
CASE Code: 21   AWC: 129-04

NGT-43-002-002   Vanderbilt University   R. T. Lagemann
Training of predoctoral graduate students in space-related science and technology.

No. Students	FY	Agreement Period	Amount
12	65	9/65 - 8/68	194400
12	66	9/66 - 8/69	228000
6	67	9/67 - 8/70	102500

Tech. Off.: HANSING F D   Funding Element: HQ-Y
CASE Code: 99   AWC: 181-00

TEXAS

NGR-44-003-001 Baylor University   P. Kellaway

Physiological mechanism of auditory masking and of correlations between physiological and psychological observations.

Proposal	FY	Agreement Period	Amount
−022	67	7/66 − 6/69	60503
−035	68	7/67 − 6/70	34853

Tech. Off.: WEISSMAN N W   Funding Element: HQ−SB
CASE Code: 61   AWC: 189−52

NGR-44-003-031 Baylor University   R. Roessler

Physiological correlates of optimal performance.

Proposal	FY	Agreement Period	Amount
−031	66	5/67 − 4/68	39964
−039	68	5/68 − 4/69	39911

Tech. Off.: DE LUCCI M R   Funding Element: MSC
CASE Code: 51   AWC: 949−10

NAS9-7237   Baylor University   P. Kellaway

Harness system.

Proposal	FY	Agreement Period	Amount
		6/67 − 5/68	24000
	68	6/67 − 3/69	19000

Tech. Off.: DE LUCCHI M R   Funding Element: MSC
CASE Code: 42   AWC: 949−10

NAS9-7280   Baylor University   P. C. Johnson

Cell life span.

Proposal	FY	Agreement Period	Amount
		6/67 − 7/68	46000
	68	6/67 − 7/69	35000

Tech. Off.: FISHER C L   Funding Element: MSC
CASE Code: 51   AWC: 949−10

NAS9-8109   Baylor University   W. C. Duncan

Evaluation of materials for space flight apparel.

Proposal	FY	Agreement Period	Amount
	68	6/68 −12/69	72000
			MSC

Tech. Off.:   Funding Element:
CASE Code: 47   AWC: 914−50

NAS9-8949   Baylor University   P. C. Johnson

Research study on reflex control of capillary fluid exchange in skeletal muscle and the maintenance of circulating blood volume.

Proposal	FY	Agreement Period	Amount
	69	12/68 −12/69	19000

Tech. Off.:   Funding Element:
CASE Code: 51   AWC: 914−50

NAS9-9418   Baylor University   J. D. Frost

EEG sleep analyzer.

Proposal	FY	Agreement Period	Amount
	69	5/69 − 3/70	41000

Tech. Off.:   Funding Element:
CASE Code: 51   AWC: 127−49

NGT-44-003-019 Baylor University   J. D. Bragg

Training of predoctoral graduate students in space-related science and technology.

No. Students:	FY	Agreement Period	Amount
2	66	9/66 − 8/69	35300
1	67	9/67 − 8/70	17700

Tech. Off.: HANSING F D   Funding Element: HQ−Y
CASE Code: 99   AWC: 181−00

NGR-44-005-002 University of Houston   J. Oro and A. Zlatkis

Studies in organic cosmochemistry, including compound formation under primitive earth conditions, and organic material in selected meteorites.

Proposal	FY	Agreement Period	Amount
−079	68	12/67 −11/68	40000
−093	69	12/68 −11/69	50000

Tech. Off.: GIEB D S   Funding Element: HQ−SB
CASE Code: 32   AWC: 185−55

NGL-44-005-021 University of Houston   J. R. Crump

Multidisciplinary space-related research.

Proposal	FY	Agreement Period	Amount
−021	66	3/66 − 2/69	150000
−063	67	3/67 − 2/70	125000

Tech. Off.: REDDING E R   Funding Element: HQ−Y
CASE Code: 99   AWC: 183−00

NGR-44-005-022 University of Houston   A. F. Hildebrant

Interactions of hydromagnetic wave energy with energetic plasmas, and other space-related scientific and technical investigations.

Proposal	FY	Agreement Period	Amount
−080	68	4/68 − 3/69	50000
		− 5/69	NCE
−080		8/69	NCE

Tech. Off.: DAVIS E L   Funding Element: MSC
CASE Code: 13   AWC: 914−50

NGR-44-005-041 University of Houston   C. Goodman

Study of solar flare particle events and related solar physics.

Proposal	FY	Agreement Period	Amount
−041	66	5/66 − 4/69	80000
−067	67	5/67 − 4/70	69536

Tech. Off.: MADISETTE J   Funding Element: MSC
CASE Code: 11   AWC: 914−40

TEXAS   (Cont'd)

NGR-44-005-065   **Universty of Houston**   **C. Dalton**
The hydrodynamic stability of pipe flow.

Proposal	FY	Agreement Period	Amount
–065	67	7/67 – 6/68	22967
–065	67	5/68 –12/68	NCE
		5/69	NCE

Tech. Off.: DAVIS E L   Funding Element: MSC
CASE Code: 46   AWC: 997–04

NGL-44-005-084   **University of Houston**   **C. J. Huang**
Hybrid computation research program.

Proposal	FY	Agreement Period	Amount
–084	68	8/68 – 7/71	150000

Tech. Off.: REDDING E R   Funding Element: HQ–Y
CASE Code: 21   AWC: 183–00

NGR-44-005-090   **University of Houston**   **C. J. Huang**
Establishment of resident graduate research assistantships.

Proposal	FY	Agreement Period	Amount
–090	69	7/69 – 7/70	44023

Tech. Off.: YOUNGBLOOD J L   Funding Element: MSC
CASE Code: AWC: 914–50

NGR-44-005-091   **University of Houston**   **R. S. Becker**
Spectroscopic and photochemical study of photochromic compounds.

Proposal	FY	Agreement Period	Amount
–091	69	2/69 – 1/70	50000

Tech. Off.: GEIB D S   Funding Element: HQ–SB
CASE Code: 12   AWC: 189–55

NGR-44-005-096   **University of Houston**   **M. Eisner**
Study of molecular collisions in the 10 to 100 ev energy range.

Proposal	FY	Agreement Period	Amount
–096	69	5/69 – 4/70	10992
–096	69	5/69 – 4/70	10991

Tech. Off.: DAVIS E L JR   Funding Element: MSC
CASE Code: 13   AWC: 997–82

NGR-44-005-098   **University of Houston**   **H. P. Decell**
Application and soluation of the matrix riccati equation.

Proposal	FY	Agreement Period	Amount
–098	69	6/69 – 5/70	20008

Tech. Off.: LEWALLEN J M   Funding Element: MSC
CASE Code: 21   AWC: 997–82

NGR-44-005-102   **University of Houston**   **J. Oro**
Participation in a science instrument team for the Mars lander.

Proposal	FY	Agreement Period	Amount
–102	69	2/69 – 1/70	2260

Tech. Off.: MITZ M A   Funding Element: HQ–SL
CASE Code: 42   AWC: 815–20

NSR-44-005-016   **University of Houston**   **C. J. Huang**
Summer institute in space-related engineering.

Proposal	FY	Agreement Period	Amount
–071	68	4/68 – 3/69	109700

Tech. Off.: CARTER C H   Funding Element: HQ–Y
CASE Code: 99   AWC: 181–00

NSR-44-005-059   **University of Houston**   **C. J. Huang**
A faculty space systems engineering institute.

Proposal	FY	Agreement Period	Amount
–074	68	6/68 – 8/68	109650
–089	69	12/68 –12/69	112699

Tech. Off.: CARTER E H   Funding Element: HQ–Y
CASE Code: 99   AWC: 181–00

NAS9-6331   **University of Houston**   **L. Swenson**
Chronologies of Projects Gemini and Apollo and a history of Project Gemini.

Proposal	FY	Agreement Period	Amount
		6/66 –12/68	97000
	68	6/66 – 6/69	3000
	69	6/66 – 6/69	17000

Tech. Off.: GRIMWOOD J   Funding Element: MSC
CASE Code: 73   AWC: 913–80

NAS9-8012   **University of Houston**
A comprehensive study of the carbonaceous and organogenic matter present in returned lunar samples.

Proposal	FY	Agreement Period	Amount
	68	6/68 –10/69	143000

Tech. Off.:   Funding Element: MSC
CASE Code: 32   AWC: 914–40

NAS9-8069   **University of Houston**
Measurement and analysis by petrographic microscope methods of shock effects on returned lunar samples.

Proposal	FY	Agreement Period	Amount
	68	6/68 –12/69	3000

Tech. Off.:   Funding Element: MSC
CASE Code: 32   AWC: 914–40

NAS9-8264   **University of Houston**
Development of LRL protocol.

Proposal	FY	Agreement Period	Amount
	68	6/68 – 8/69	30000

Tech. Off.:   Funding Element: MSC
CASE Code: 42   AWC: 914–50

NAS9-8869   **University of Houston**   **N. S. Kovar**
Contract for supporting studies for the coronagraph contamination experiment.

Proposal	FY	Agreement Period	Amount
	69	11/68 –10/70	30000

Tech. Off.:   Funding Element:
CASE Code: 19   AWC: 914–40

TEXAS (Cont'd)

NAS9-9104   **University of Houston**
Research and writing of the history of the Apollo spacecraft.

Proposal	FY	Agreement Period	Amount
	69	6/63 - 3/69	3000

Tech. Off.:   Funding Element:
CASE Code: 99   AWC: 914-80

NAS9-9184   **University of Houston**
Development of prototype task board.

Proposal	FY	Agreement Period	Amount
	69	2/69 - 8/69	27000

Tech. Off.:   Funding Element:
CASE Code: 99   AWC: 948-60

NAS9-9270   **University of Houston**
Parametric analysis.

Proposal	FY	Agreement Period	Amount
	69	3/69 - 4/70	27000

Tech. Off.:   Funding Element:
CASE Code: 19   AWC: 921-30

NGT-44-005-004   **University of Houston**   **J. C. Allred**
Training of predoctoral graduate students in space-related science and technology.

No. Students	FY	Agreement Period	Amount
10	65	9/65 - 8/68	177000
10	66	9/66 - 8/69	177000
6	67	9/67 - 8/70	93900

Tech. Off.: HANSING F D   Funding Element: HQ-Y
CASE Code: 99   AWC: 181-00

NAS9-8479   **North Texas State University**
Ecological study of bacteria as potential pathogens for experimental animals in simulated space environments.

Proposal	FY	Agreement Period	Amount
	68	7/68 -12/69	25000

Tech. Off.:   Funding Element:
CASE Code: 51   AWC: 127-49

NGR-44-033-001   **Prairie View A&M College**   **I. V. Nelson**
A research study of six developing institutions of higher education to identify and catalog their interests of NASA and its affiliates.

Proposal	FY	Agreement Period	Amount
-001	68	8/68 - 7/69	12890

Tech. Off.: QUINN H B   Funding Element: HQ-Y
CASE Code: 79   AWC:

NGL-44-006-001   **Rice University**   **F. R. Brotzen**
Research on the physics of solid materials, including study of the basic laws governing the behavior of solids at high temperatures.

Proposal	FY	Agreement Period	Amount
-027	65	7/65 - 6/68	200000
-046	66	7/66 - 6/69	300000
-069	67	7/67 - 6/70	200000
-079	68	7/68 - 6/71	300000
-097	69	7/69 - 6/72	250000
-097	69	7/69 - 6/72	250000

Tech. Off.: NASH R R   Funding Element: HQ-RR
CASE Code: 13   AWC: 129-03

NGR-44-006-012   **Rice University**   **F. C. Michel, A. J. Dessler**
An experimental investigation of the methodology and techniques for measuring the relative abundance of heavy ions in the solar wind.

Proposal	FY	Agreement Period	Amount
-074	68	10/67 - 9/68	140000
		9/68 -10/68	NCE
		- 9/69	NCE

Tech. Off.: OPP   Funding Element: HQ-SG
CASE Code: 13   AWC: 185-38

NGL-44-006-033   **Rice University**   **A. J. Chapman,**
Multidisciplinary space related research.

Proposal	FY	Agreement Period	Amount
-033	66	9/65 - 8/68	400000
-060	67	9/66 - 8/69	200000
-073	68	9/67 - 8/70	200000
-104		9/68 - 8/71	100000

Tech. Off.: REDDING E R   Funding Element: HQ-Y
CASE Code: 99   AWC: 183-00

NGR-44-006-065   **Rice University**   **F. J. Low**
Operate the Rice University flying infrared telescope.

Proposal	FY	Agreement Period	Amount
-065		5/69 - 3/70	80000

Tech. Off.: BRUNK W E   Funding Element: HQ-SL
CASE Code: 11   AWC: 188-41

NGR-44-006-088   **Rice University**   **R. B. McLellan**
Investigation of stress corrosion in titanium alloys and other metallic materials.

Proposal	FY	Agreement Period	Amount
-088	68	6/68 - 5/70	178940

Tech. Off.: JOHNSON R E   Funding Element: MSC
CASE Code: 47   AWC: 914-50

NGR-44-006-089   **Rice University**   **A. Miele**
Mathematical optimization techniques for aerospace applications.

Proposal	FY	Agreement Period	Amount
-089	68	6/68 - 5/69	30428
-109		6/69 - 5/70	29967
			MSC

Tech. Off.: LEWALLEN J M   Funding Element: MSC
CASE Code: 21   AWC: 997-82

TEXAS　(Cont'd)

NGR-44-006-105　　Rice University　　　　　　J. A. S. Adams

Potassium-argon dating of shocked rocks.

	Proposal	FY	Agreement Period	Amount
-105		3/69 - 3/70	28000
	Proposal	FY	Agreement Period	Amount

Tech. Off.: FOSS T H　　　　　Funding Element: MSC
CASE Code: 32　　　　　　　　　AWC: 914-40

NSR-44-006-023　　Rice University　　　　　　R. C. Haymes

Sounding rocket measurement of Sq current system.

Proposal	FY	Agreement Period	Amount
-053	67	8/66 - 9/67	98519
-053	67	10/67 -12/67	NCE
-086	69	4/69 - 4/70	25000

Tech. Off.: OPP　　　　　Funding Element: HQ-SG
CASE Code: 31　　　　　　AWC: 879-10

NSR-44-006-065　　Rice University　　　　　　E. J. Low

To construct and operate a flying infrared telescope.

Proposal	FY	Agreement Period	Amount
-090		3/68 - 3/69	79954

Tech. Off.: BRUNK W E　　　　Funding Element: SL
CASE Code: 11　　　　　　　　AWC: 185-41

NAS6-1061　　Rice University　　　　　　B. J. O'Brien

Design construction and use of two research satellites code named "Owl".

Proposal	FY	Agreement Period	Amount
		8/65 - 9/68	2776000
	67	8/65 - 9/68	425000
	67	8/65 - 9/68	500000

Tech. Off.: MAION C E　　　　Funding Element: WALL
CASE Code: 42　　　　　　　　AWC: 859-11

NAS9-5884　　Rice University

Charged-particle lunar environment experiment for ALSEP.

Proposal	FY	Agreement Period	Amount
		6/66 - 6/69	426000
	67	6/66 - 6/69	40000
	68	6/66 - 6/69	224000

Tech. Off.: CARAWAY A　　　　Funding Element: MSC
CASE Code: 31　　　　　　　　AWC: 914-40

NAS9-5911　　Rice University　　　　　　J. W. Freeman

Suprathermal ion detector experiment for ALSEP.

Proposal	FY	Agreement Period	Amount
		4/66 - 4/69	2854000
	68	4/66 - 4/69	150000
	68	4/66 - 4/69	200000
	68	4/66 - 4/69	250000
	68	4/66 - 4/69	250000
	67	4/66 - 4/69	239000

Tech. Off.: WEEKS E L　　　　Funding Element: MSC
CASE Code: 31　　　　　　　　AWC: 914-40

NAS9-7738　　Rice University　　　　　　H. R. Anderson

Electric field detector development.

Proposal	FY	Agreement Period	Amount
	66	2/68 -11/68	50000

Tech. Off.:　　　　　Funding Element: MSC
CASE Code: 31　　　　AWC: 849-34

NAS9-7899　　Rice University　　　　　　D. Heymann

Preparation for the performance of a program of research involving the measurement and analysis of rare gases and samples.

Proposal	FY	Agreement Period	Amount
	68	4/68 -10/69	42000
	68	4/68 -10/69	10000

Tech. Off.:　　　　　Funding Element: MSC
CASE Code: 32　　　　AWC: 914-40

NAS9-7969　　Rice University　　　　　　A. J. Chapman

Study of sublimation through a porous surface.

Proposal	FY	Agreement Period	Amount
	68	5/68 - 5/69	52000

Tech. Off.:　　　　　Funding Element: MSC
CASE Code: 13　　　　AWC: 904-01

NAS9-9003　　Rice University　　　　　　J. R. Sims

Courses attended by MSC employees at Rice University.

Proposal	FY	Agreement Period	Amount
	69	11/68 - 6/69	12000

Tech. Off.:　　　　　Funding Element:
CASE Code: 99　　　　AWC: 039-00

NGT-44-006-003　　Rice University　　　　　　W. E. Gordon

Training of predoctoral graduate students in space-related science and technology.

No. Students	FY	Agreement Period	Amount
15	65	9/65 - 8/68	288000
15	66	9/66 - 8/69	267400
9	67	9/67 - 8/70	159300

Tech. Off.: HANSING F D　　　Funding Element: HQ-Y
CASE Code: 99　　　　　　　　AWC: 181-00

NGF-44-006-008　　Rice University　　　　　　A. J. Dessler

For construction of a space science and technology building on the campus of Rice University.

Proposal	FY	Agreement Period	Amount
6752	64	5/64 - 3/66	1600000

Tech. Off.: HOLMES D C　　　Funding Element: HQ-Y
CASE Code: 99　　　　　　　　AWC: 182-00

NAS2-4849　　University of St. Thomas　　　　L. S. Browning

Biosatellite project experiment P-1159.

Proposal	FY	Agreement Period	Amount
	68	6/68 - 1/69	51000
	68	6/68 -12/68	24000

Tech. Off.:　　　　　Funding Element: ARC
CASE Code: 51　　　　AWC: 883-12

TEXAS (Cont'd)

NAS8-21292   **University of St. Thomas**   **J. L. Goldman**

Analysis of wind field conditions which adversely affect vehicle operations.

Proposal	FY	Agreement Period	Amount
	68	3/68 – 3/69	59000

Tech. Off.:   Funding Element: GSFC
CASE Code: 41   AWC: 904-21

NGR-44-007-004   **Southern Methodist University**   **H. A. Blum**

Heat transfers across surfaces in contact: practical effects of transient temperatures and pressure environments.

Proposal	FY	Agreement Period	Amount
-021	68	6/67 – 5/68	16226
-021	68	5/68 – 6/69	NCE
-041	66	2/69 – 2/72	100000

Tech. Off.: SCHOCKEN K   Funding Element: MSFC
CASE Code: 13   AWC: 124-09

NGL-44-007-006   **Southern Methodist University**   **J. C. Denton**

Multidisciplinary research in space-related science and technology.

Proposal	FY	Agreement Period	Amount
8712	65	5/65 – 4/68	200000
-017	66	2/66 – 1/69	100000
-023	67	2/67 – 1/70	100000
-032	68	2/68 – 1/71	100000

Tech. Off.: REDDING E R   Funding Element: HQ-Y
CASE Code: 99   AWC: 183-00

NGR-44-007-027   **Southern Methodist University**   **S. C. Gupta**

System analysis using topological structure and transform algorithms.

Proposal	FY	Agreement Period	Amount
-027	68	9/68 – 8/69	9818

Tech. Off.:   Funding Element: ERC
CASE Code: 21   AWC: 125-25

NGR-44-007-028   **Southern Methodist University**   **J. E. Walsh**

Efficient estimation of distribution for extreme observations in sample and nonsample cases.

Proposal	FY	Agreement Period	Amount
-028	68	1/68 –12/68	19000
		– 7/69	NCE

Tech. Off.:   Funding Element:
CASE Code: 21   AWC: 129-04

NGR-44-007-037   **Southern Methodist University**   **S. C. Gupta**

Digital phase locked techniques for aerospace communications.

Proposal	FY	Agreement Period	Amount
-037	69	9/69 – 8/70	39683

Tech. Off.: MILLER J E   Funding Element: GSFC
CASE Code: 49   AWC: 160-21

NGR-44-007-042   **Southern Methodist University**   **T. L. Chu**

Boron arsenide and boron phosphide for high temperature and luminescent devices.

Proposal	FY	Agreement Period	Amount
-042	69	7/69 – 7/70	29705

Tech. Off.: LOWEN J   Funding Element: ERC
CASE Code: 47   AWC: 125-25

NAS12-661   **Southern Methodist University**

Development of a computer program for the network analysis.

Proposal	FY	Agreement Period	Amount
	68	4/68 – 8/69	10000

Tech. Off.:   Funding Element: ERC
CASE Code: 21   AWC: 125-25

NAS12-2106   **Southern Methodist University**

Compiler logic for laplace transform opertn.

Proposal	FY	Agreement Period	Amount
	69	5/69 – 4/70	11000

Tech. Off.:   Funding Element:
CASE Code: 21   AWC: 125-25

NGT-44-007-002   **Southern Methodist University**   **C. C. Allbritton**

Training of predoctoral graduate students in space-related science and technology.

No. Students	FY	Agreement Period	Amount
4	65	9/65 – 8/68	72000
5	66	9/66 – 8/69	90000
3	67	9/67 – 8/70	54000

Tech. Off.: HANSING F D   Funding Element: HQ-Y
CASE Code: 99   AWC: 181-00

NGL-44-001-001   **Texas A & M University**   **H. E. Whitmore**

Interdisciplinary space-oriented research in the physical, life and engineering sciences.

Proposal	FY	Agreement Period	Amount
-041	66	2/66 – 1/69	150000
-049	67	2/67 – 1/70	100000
-062	68	2/67 – 1/70	9564
-068	68	2/68 – 1/71	100000

Tech. Off.: REDDING E R   Funding Element: HQ-Y
CASE Code: 99   AWC: 183-00

NGR-44-001-011   **Texas A & M University**   **A. E. Cronk**

Proposal	FY	Agreement Period	Amount
-075	69	4/68 – 3/69	79158
-075		9/69	NCE

Tech. Off.: HEYSON H H   Funding Element: LARC
CASE Code: 41   AWC: 721-03

NGR-44-001-031   **Texas A&M University**   **T. J. Kozik**

Analysis of structurally orthotropic shells by means of the compliance method.

Proposal	FY	Agreement Period	Amount
-069	68	12/67 –11/68	45000
		– 2/69	NCE

Tech. Off.: STEBBINS F J   Funding Element: MSC
CASE Code: 46   AWC: 124-08

TEXAS   (Cont'd)

NGR-44-001-036   **Texas A & M University**   **R. Thomas**
Study of the simulation of atmospheric processes in a wind tunnel.

Proposal	FY	Agreement Period	Amount
-065	68	6/67 – 9/68	61700
		9/68 – 6/69	NCE

Tech. Off.: RAINEY A G   Funding Element: LARC
CASE Code: 31   AWC: 124-11

NGL-44-001-044   **Texas A & M University**   **J. A. Stricklin**
The nonlinear static and dynamic analysis of shells of revolution with asymmetrical stiffness properties.

Proposal	FY	Agreement Period	Amount
-044	68	1/68 –12/68	49800
-044	68	1/68 –12/68	5000
-079	68	1/69 –12/70	50000
-082	68	1/69 –12/71	50000

Tech. Off.: STEBBINS F J   Funding Element: MSC
CASE Code: 46   AWC: 124-08

NGR-44-001-067   **Texas A&M University**   **R. E. Wainerdi**
Feasibility of fast neutron activation analysis as a nondestructive testing method for alpha phase titanium alloy.

Proposal	FY	Agreement Period	Amount
-067	68	1/68 – 6/68	19283
-080	68	6/68 –11/68	9906
		7/68 – 4/69	NCE
-067		9/69	NCE

Tech. Off.: ZUNKEL A D   Funding Element: MSC
CASE Code: 13   AWC: 914-50

NGR-44-001-071   **Texas A&M University**   **C. F. Kettleborough**
Study of Apollo water impact.

Proposal	FY	Agreement Period	Amount
-071	68	2/69 – 1/70	60623

Tech. Off.: STEBBINS F J   Funding Element: MSC
CASE Code: 49   AWC: 914-50

NGR-44-001-081   **Texas A&M University**   **J. R. Scoggins**
Relationships between stratospheric clear air turbulence and synoptic meteorological parameters.

Proposal	FY	Agreement Period	Amount
-081	69	9/68 – 8/69	19645

Tech. Off.: EHERNHERGER L J   Funding Element: FRC
CASE Code: 41   AWC: 126-61

NGR-44-001-097   **Texas A&M University**   **W. B. Smith**
Time series analysis with missing data.

Proposal	FY	Agreement Period	Amount
-097	69	6/69 – 6/70	10642

Tech. Off.: MICHELLI F A   Funding Element: MSC
CASE Code: 21   AWC: 914-50

NSR-44-001-053   **Texas A&M University**   **H. Monroe**
Design and production of supplementary materials for teachers of high school physics.

Proposal	FY	Agreement Period	Amount
-053	67	7/67 – 6/68	39866
-053	67	6/68 – 8/68	NCE
		8/68 – 5/69	NCE
-053		7/69	NCE

Tech. Off.: BERNARDO J V   Funding Element: HQ-FE
CASE Code: 19   AWC: 023-00

NAS8-21257   **Texas A & M University**   **N. E. Moyer**
Off the job training.

Proposal	FY	Agreement Period	Amount
	68	5/68 – 5/69	21000

Tech. Off.:   Funding Element: GSFC
CASE Code: 31   AWC: 933-50

NAS9-6812   **Texas A & M University**   **H. E. Whitmore**
Hypervelocity accelerations.

Proposal	FY	Agreement Period	Amount
		2/67 – 3/68	60000
	67	2/67 – 5/68	74000

Tech. Off.: HIGH R   Funding Element: MSC
CASE Code: 51   AWC: 124-09

NAS9-7951   **Texas A & M University**   **J. M. Prescott**
Effects of spacecraft environments on patterns in bacteria.

Proposal	FY	Agreement Period	Amount
	68	5/68 – 5/69	50000

Tech. Off.:   Funding Element: MSC
CASE Code: 51   AWC: 961-50

NAS9-9053   **Texas A&M University**   **D. Hightower**
Study on radiation effects control—eyes, skin.

Proposal	FY	Agreement Period	Amount
	69	12/68 –12/69	80000

Tech. Off.:   Funding Element:
CASE Code: 52   AWC: 914-50

NAS9-9285   **Texas A&M University**
Study of noise suppression system.

Proposal	FY	Agreement Period	Amount
	69	3/69 – 4/70	25000

Tech. Off.:   Funding Element:
CASE Code: 41   AWC: 921-30

NGT-44-001-003   **Texas A & M University**   **W. C. Hall**
Training of predoctoral graduate students in space-related science and technology.

No. Students	FY	Agreement Period	Amount
15	65	9/65 – 8/68	288000
15	66	9/66 – 8/69	274400
9	67	9/67 – 8/70	143400

Tech. Off.: HANSING F D   Funding Element: HQ-Y
CASE Code: 99   AWC: 181-00

TEXAS (Cont'd)

NGF-44-001-014   Texas A & M University   **R. E. Wainerdi**

Construction of research laboratory facilities housing the Texas A & M University's activation analysis research laboratory.

Proposal	FY	Agreement Period	Amount
5520	64	5/64 — 5/66	1000000

Tech. Off.: HOLMES D C   Funding Element: HQ-Y
CASE Code: 99   AWC: 182-00

NGR-44-009-008   Texas Christian University   **S. B. Sells**

Social structure and group behavior in extended duration space missions.

Proposal	FY	Agreement Period	Amount
-017	67	1/67 — 5/68	29941
-022	69	7/68 — 8/69	30000

Tech. Off.: SAUCER R T   Funding Element: LARC
CASE Code: 76   AWC: 127-49

NGR-44-009-018   Texas Christian University   **M. D. Arnoult**

Distance and rate judgments in simulated space.

Proposal	FY	Agreement Period	Amount
-018	68	9/67 — 8/68	27023
		8/68 —11/68	NCE
-024	69	11/68 —10/69	15000

Tech. Off.: PATTON R M   Funding Element: ARC
CASE Code: 51   AWC: 127-49

NAS8-21421   Texas Christian University

Radiative interactions of electrons with matter.

Proposal	FY	Agreement Period	Amount
	68	6/68 — 8/69	40000

Tech. Off.:   Funding Element: GSFC
CASE Code: 13   AWC: 124-09

NGT-44-009-002   Texas Christian University   **E. L. Secrest**

Training of predoctoral graduate students in space-related science and technology.

No. Students:	FY	Agreement Period	Amount
4	65	9/65 — 8/68	74800
5	66	9/66 — 8/69	93500
3	67	9/67 — 8/70	57600

Tech. Off.: HANSING F D   Funding Element: HQ-Y
CASE Code: 99   AWC: 181-00

NAS9-8795   Texas Southern University

Minority manpower resources study.

Proposal	FY	Agreement Period	Amount
	69	9/68 — 8/69	5000

Tech. Off.:   Funding Element:
CASE Code: 76   AWC: 039-00

NGR-44-011-026   Texas Technological College   **R. D. Shelton**

Performance improvement analysis for the Apollo unified S-band system.

Proposal	FY	Agreement Period	Amount
-026	69	9/68 — 8/69	27021

Tech. Off.: DAWSON C T   Funding Element: MSC
CASE Code: 45   AWC: 921-30

NGR-44-011-031   Texas Technological College   **H. F. Martz**

Investigation of an empirical Bayes filter for use in trajectory estimation.

Proposal	FY	Agreement Period	Amount
-031	69	6/69 — 5/70	18800

Tech. Off.: BARN G H   Funding Element: MSC
CASE Code: 42   AWC: 997-82

NAS9-8463   Texas Technological College

Effects of digital approximation in statistical estimation.

Proposal	FY	Agreement Period	Amount
	69	7/68 — 7/69	15000

Tech. Off.:   Funding Element:
CASE Code: 21   AWC: 997-00

NGL-44-012-006   University of Texas (Austin)   **A. E. Straiton**

Research on millimeter-wavelength radiation from solar bodies.

Proposal	FY	Agreement Period	Amount
-051	66	4/66 — 3/69	150000
-081	67	4/67 — 3/70	106800
-111	68	4/68 — 3/71	106800
-148		4/69 — 3/72	102200

Tech. Off.: BRUNK W E   Funding Element: HQ-SL
CASE Code: 11   AWC: 185-41

NGR-44-012-008   University of Texas (Austin)   **B. D. Tapley**

Study of theory and analysis of low-thrust guidance problems in deterministic linear control.

Proposal	FY	Agreement Period	Amount
-102	68	2/68 — 1/69	35010
-139	69	2/69 — 1/70	20000

Tech. Off.: PONTIOUS C E   Funding Element: HQ-RE
CASE Code: 13   AWC: 125-17

NGR-44-012-020   University of Texas (Austin)   **L. C. Reese**

Investigate soil modelling problems related to impact studies.

Proposal	FY	Agreement Period	Amount
-060	67	8/66 — 7/67	62000
-060	67	2/68 — 8/68	NCE
		9/68 — 5/69	NCE

Tech. Off.: FRANKLIN C   Funding Element: NPO
CASE Code: 32   AWC: 124-08

NGL-44-012-043   University of Texas (Austin)   **W. H. Hartwig**

Theoretical and experimental investigations in digital transducers.

Proposal	FY	Agreement Period	Amount
-043	66	7/66 — 6/68	50000
		7/68 — 8/68	NCE
-119	68	7/68 — 6/70	30000
-142	69	7/68 — 6/71	30000

Tech. Off.: RICHARDS R R   Funding Element: MSC
CASE Code: 21   AWC: 904-02

TEXAS   (Cont'd)

NGR-44-012-045   **University of Texas (Austin)**   **J. H. Mackin**
A study of ignimbrites in the cordilleran region as a basis for interpretation of lunar plains.

Proposal	FY	Agreement Period	Amount
-045	67	6/67 – 5/68	24984
		7/68 – 5/69	NCE

Tech. Off.: WILMARTH V R   Funding Element: HQ-SL
CASE Code: 32   AWC: 185-42

NGR-44-012-046   **University of Texas (Austin)**   **B. D. Tapley**
Investigation of methods for defining optimal open-loop control procedures for continuous powered space flight.

Proposal	FY	Agreement Period	Amount
-101	68	2/68 – 1/69	20460
-137	69	2/69 – 1/70	19979

Tech. Off.: MINER W F   Funding Element: ERC
CASE Code: 42   AWC: 125-17

NGR-44-012-055   **University of Texas (Austin)**   **J. N. Douglas**
Polarization and time structure of Jovian decametric radiation and the structure of interplanetary plasma.

Proposal	FY	Agreement Period	Amount
-086	67	5/67 – 4/68	108173
-116	68	5/68 – 4/69	85920
-149		5/69 – 4/70	89425

Tech. Off.: BRUNK W E   Funding Element: HQ-SL
CASE Code: 13   AWC: 185-41

NGR-44-012-088   **University of Texas (Austin)**   **B. Fruchter**
Investigation of multivariate techniques for biomedical analysis.

Proposal	FY	Agreement Period	Amount
-088	67	6/67 – 5/68	47990
-088	67	6/68 – 1/69	NCE
-088		2/68 – 8/69	NCE

Tech. Off.: MOSELEY E C   Funding Element: MSC
CASE Code: 51   AWC: 905-50

NGR-44-012-104   **University of Texas (Austin)**   **W. H. Hartwig**
A study of optical properties of materials at low temperatures and their application to optical detection.

Proposal	FY	Agreement Period	Amount
-104	68	6/68 – 5/69	35000

Tech. Off.: PACKARD R   Funding Element: ERC
CASE Code: 13   AWC: 125-17

NGR-44-012-132   **University of Texas (Austin)**   **V. Szebehely**
Applications of celestial mechanics to space research.

Proposal	FY	Agreement Period	Amount
-132	68	9/68 – 9/69	24900

Tech. Off.: CARPENTER L   Funding Element: GSFC
CASE Code: 11   AWC: 125-17

NGR-44-012-136   **University of Texas (Austin)**   **B. D. Tapley**
The application of regularization to the problem of computing optimal trajectories.

Proposal	FY	Agreement Period	Amount
-136	69	3/69 – 2/68	28541

Tech. Off.: LEWALLEN J M   Funding Element: MSC
CASE Code: 21   AWC: 997-82

NGR-44-012-144   **University of Texas (Austin)**   **C. V. Ramamoorthy**
Investigations in computer systems software.

Proposal	FY	Agreement Period	Amount
-144	69	6/69 – 5/70	50000

Tech. Off.: SNOW R M   Funding Element: ERC
CASE Code: 49   AWC: 125-06

NASr-242   **University of Texas (Austin)**   **H. Smith**
(NSR-44-012-025) Design, development, fabrication and installation at McDonald Observatory of 105-inch telescope suitable for lunar and planetary observations.

Proposal	FY	Agreement Period	Amount
-094	67	9/67 – 9/68	327000
-110	68	/ – 9/68	400000
-130	69	10/68 – 9/69	673000

Tech. Off.: BRUNK W E   Funding Element: HQ-SL
CASE Code: 11   AWC: 185-41

NAS5-10387   **University of Texas (Austin)**   **A. W. Straiton**
Boresight and alignment tests of radio telescope installation.

Proposal	FY	Agreement Period	Amount
	68	4/67 – 8/68	18000

Tech. Off.: RATLIFF R   Funding Element: GSFC
CASE Code: 11   AWC: 160-76

NAS8-18120   **University of Texas (Austin)**   **L. Clark**
Study of stability of guidance systems.

Proposal	FY	Agreement Period	Amount
		6/66 – 12/68	76000

Tech. Off.: DEARMAN C C   Funding Element: MSFC
CASE Code: 42   AWC: 125-17

NAS9-7153   **University of Texas (Austin)**   **B. A. Mitchell**
Hybrid computer development.

Proposal	FY	Agreement Period	Amount
		6/67 – 9/68	190000
	68	6/67 – 9/69	50000

Tech. Off.:   Funding Element: MSC
CASE Code: 21   AWC: 904-50

NAS9-7926   **University of Texas (Austin)**   **J. G. Thompson**
CRT display-light pen.

Proposal	FY	Agreement Period	Amount
	68	5/68 – 5/69	28000

Tech. Off.:   Funding Element: MSC
CASE Code: 21   AWC: 904-02

TEXAS (Cont'd)

NAS9-8122   **University of Texas (Austin)**   **S. E. Ritzmann**
Humoral and cellular aspects of man's immunity to manned space flight.

Proposal	FY	Agreement Period	Amount
	68	6/68 – 6/69	25000

Tech. Off.:   Funding Element: MSC
CASE Code: 51   AWC: 914-50

NAS9-8200   **University of Texas (Austin)**   **M. Wheatcroft**
Personal oral hygiene requirements for extended spaceflight.

Proposal	FY	Agreement Period	Amount
	68	6/68 – 8/69	35000

Tech. Off.:   Funding Element: MSC
CASE Code: 52   AWC: 914-50

NAS9-8258   **University of Texas (Austin)**   **S. E. Ritzmann**
Blood coagulation study.

Proposal	FY	Agreement Period	Amount
	68	6/68 – 6/69	35000

Tech. Off.:   Funding Element: MSC
CASE Code: 52   AWC: 945-60

NAS9-9266   **University of Texas (Galveston)**   **M. Guest**
Blood coagulation study.

Proposal	FY	Agreement Period	Amount
	69	5/69 – 4/70	14000

Tech. Off.:   Funding Element:
CASE Code: 51   AWC: 914-50

NGR-44-012-003   **University of Texas Southwestern Medical School**
P. O'B. Montgomery
Research on the influence of gravity on unicellular organisms, and optimization of the ultraviolet flying-spot microscope for living cell observations.

Proposal	FY	Agreement Period	Amount
-103	68	12/67 – 11/68	40000

Tech. Off.:   SAUNDERS J F   Funding Element: HQ-SB
CASE Code: 51   AWC: 189-54

NAS6-1296   **University of Texas (El Paso)**   **D. Stenstrom**
Data reduction for the meteorological rocket network program.

Proposal	FY	Agreement Period	Amount
		10/66 – 10/68	52000

Tech. Off.:   EVERTON E R   Funding Element: WALL
CASE Code: 31   AWC: 311-04

NGR-44-013-001   **Texas Woman's University**   **P. B. Mack**
An experimental investigation of skeletal mineral losses in humans and pigtail monkeys during immobilization.

Proposal	FY	Agreement Period	Amount
-007	67	4/66 – 3/69	35247
		– 6/69	NCE

Tech. Off.:   SAUNDERS J F   Funding Element: HQ-SB
CASE Code: 51   AWC: 189-54

NAS2-2711   **Texas Womans University**   **P. B. Mack**
Biosatellite experiment P-1062: investigation of bone density changes in various sites of the skeletal anatomy of primates for the purpose of defining and verifying an experiment suitable for use in a biosatellite.

Proposal	FY	Agreement Period	Amount
	66	3/65 – 2/69	36000
	65	3/65 – 2/69	5000

Tech. Off.:   CHRISTIANSEN R   Funding Element: ARC
CASE Code: 51   AWC: 883-12

NAS9-8246   **Texas Womans University**   **P. B. Mack**
Programmed exercise study.

Proposal	FY	Agreement Period	Amount
	68	6/68 – 6/69	45000

Tech. Off.:   Funding Element: MSC
CASE Code: 52   AWC: 948-60

NAS9-8888   **Texas Womans University**   **P. B. Mack**
Bone demineralization experiment.

Proposal	FY	Agreement Period	Amount
	69	11/68 – 3/69	27000

Tech. Off.:   Funding Element:
CASE Code: 51   AWC: 914-50

NAS9-9427   **Texas Womans University**   **P. B. Mack**
Study of bone density changes.

Proposal	FY	Agreement Period	Amount
	69	4/69 – 4/70	16000

Tech. Off.:   Funding Element:
CASE Code: 51   AWC: 127-49

UTAH

NGR-45-001-011   **Brigham Young University**   **D. E. Jones**
Analysis and interpretation of magnetic field measurements between Earth and Mars received from Mariner IV.

Proposal	FY	Agreement Period	Amount
-021	68	10/67 – 9/68	32530
-027	69	10/68 – 9/69	25000

Tech. Off.:   KAVANAGH L D JR   Funding Element: HQ-SG
CASE Code: 13   AWC: 808-02

NGR-45-001-026   **Brigham Young University**   **P. O. Berrett**
Study and development of a field emission ion source for a quadrupole mass spectrometer.

Proposal	FY	Agreement Period	Amount
-026	68	5/68 – 7/69	20000
-026		5/68 – 8/69	1000

Tech. Off.:   SHAPIRO H   Funding Element: GSFC
CASE Code: 13   AWC: 124-09

UTAH   (Cont'd)

NGT-45-001-002   Brigham Young University   W. P. Lloyd

Training of predoctoral graduate students in space-related science and technology.

No. Students:	FY	Agreement Period	Amount
6	65	9/65 – 8/68	61200
6	66	9/66 – 8/69	71100
3	67	9/67 – 8/70	37300

Tech. Off.: HANSING F D   Funding Element: HQ–Y
CASE Code: 99   AWC: 181–00

NGR-45-002-008   Utah State University   F. B. Salisbury

Response of higher plants to ultraviolet light and other stress factors.

Proposal	FY	Agreement Period	Amount
–008	68	9/67 – 8/68	36000
		8/68 –11/68	NCE
–012	69	9/68 – 8/69	31306

Tech. Off.: SAUNDERS J F   Funding Element: HQ–SB
CASE Code: 51   AWC: 189–54

NGR-45-002-014   Utah State University   E. W. Vendell

A theoretical study of Hall parameter measurements with an immersible three-coil conductivity-velocity plasma probe.

Proposal	FY	Agreement Period	Amount
–014	69	4/69 – 9/69	7340

Tech. Off.: JEDLICKA J R   Funding Element: ARC
CASE Code: 13   AWC: 125–24

NGT-45-002-001   Utah State University   E. J. Gardner

Training of predoctoral graduate students in space-related science and technology.

No. Students:	FY	Agreement Period	Amount
6	65	9/65 – 8/68	115200
6	66	9/66 – 8/69	115200
4	67	9/67 – 8/70	74000

Tech. Off.: HANSING F D   Funding Element: HQ–Y
CASE Code: 99   AWC: 181–00

NGL-45-003-019   University of Utah   N. W. Ryan

Investigation of the combustion chemistry of composite rocket propellants.

Proposal	FY	Agreement Period	Amount
–048	68	1/68 –12/68	32412
–055	68	1/69 –12/71	32000
–053	68	1/69 –12/71	32000

Tech. Off.: ZIEM R W   Funding Element: HQ–RP
CASE Code: 12   AWC: 128–32

NGL-45-003-025   University of Utah   F. L. Staffanson

Investigation of meteorological measurement techniques up to 100 kilometers.

Proposal	FY	Agreement Period	Amount
–047	68	12/67 –11/70	95000
–056	69	12/68 –11/71	95000

Tech. Off.: TOLEFSON H B   Funding Element: LARC
CASE Code: 31   AWC: 607–06

NGR-45-003-027   University of Utah   R. W. Grow

Theoretical and experimental investigation of solid state mechanisms for generating coherent radiation in the ultraviolet and x-ray regions.

Proposal	FY	Agreement Period	Amount
–049	68	5/68 – 4/69	25000

Tech. Off.: JOHNSON P   Funding Element: HQ–BR
CASE Code: 13   AWC: 129–02

NGR-45-003-037   University of Utah   M. L. Williams

Paramagnetic resonance effect in voscoelastic materials.

Proposal	FY	Agreement Period	Amount
–045	68	1/68 –12/68	31973
–057	69	1/69 –12/69	24234

Tech. Off.: ZIEM R W   Funding Element: HQ–RP
CASE Code: 12   AWC: 128–32

NGR-45-003-043   University of Utah   E. A. Shneour

Long term kinetics of brain macromolecular residues.

Proposal	FY	Agreement Period	Amount
–043	68	7/68 – 6/69	19994

Tech. Off.: JACOBS G   Funding Element: HQ–SB
CASE Code: 51   AWC: 189–57

NGR-45-003-050   University of Utah   G. A. Flandro

Optimum utilization of solar electric propulsion for unmanned interplanetary exploration.

Proposal	FY	Agreement Period	Amount
–050	68	9/68 – 8/69	24546

Tech. Off.:   Funding Element:
CASE Code: 13   AWC: 120–26

NGT-45-003-002   University of Utah   S. M. McMurrin

Training of predoctoral graduate students in space-related science and technology.

No. Students:	FY	Agreement Period	Amount
10	65	9/65 – 8/68	177000
10	66	9/66 – 8/69	177000
6	67	9/67 – 8/70	89800

Tech. Off.: HANSING F D   Funding Element: HQ–Y
CASE Code: 99   AWC: 181–00

NGR-45-003-038   University of Utah   W. J. Coles

Asymptotic behavior of solutions of second order ordinary differential equations.

Proposal	FY	Agreement Period	Amount
–038	67	6/67 – 6/68	24015
–038	67	7/68 – 9/68	NCE
		9/68 –12/68	NCE
		– 6/69	NCE

Tech. Off.: WILSON R   Funding Element: HQ–RR
CASE Code: 21   AWC: 129–04

VERMONT

NGL-46-001-008   University of Vermont   C. D. Cook
Multidisciplinary research program in space sciences and engineering, with particular emphasis on bio-engineering.

Proposal	FY	Agreement Period	Amount
−016	66	2/66 − 1/69	150000
−019	67	2/67 − 1/70	150000
−025	68	2/68 − 1/71	50000
−029		2/69 − 1/72	100000

Tech. Off.: REDDING E R   Funding Element: HQ−Y
CASE Code: 99   AWC: 183−00

NAS12-2142   University of Vermont
Measurement and analysis of biomedical signals.

Proposal	FY	Agreement Period	Amount
	69	5/69 − 3/70	24000

Tech. Off.:   Funding Element:
CASE Code: 59   AWC: 127−49

NGT-46-001-001   University of Vermont   W. H. Macmillan
Training of predoctoral graduate students in space-related science and technology.

No. Students:	FY	Agreement Period	Amount
5	65	9/65 − 8/68	93000
5	66	9/66 − 8/69	96000
3	67	9/67 − 8/70	54800

Tech. Off.: HANSING F D   Funding Element: HQ−Y
CASE Code: 99   AWC: 181−00

VIRGINIA

NGR-47-020-001   Hampton Institute   E. Kollmann
Exploration of ways in which developing institutions may contribute to the NASA program.

Proposal	FY	Agreement Period	Amount
−001	68	7/68 − 1/69	11125
		2/69 − 7/69	NCE

Tech. Off.: MARR E G   Funding Element: HQ−Y
CASE Code: 79   AWC: 183−00

NAS1-8311   Hampton Institute   L. C. Wyrett
Conversion of VGH flight records—FY'69.

Proposal	FY	Agreement Period	Amount
	69	7/68 − 6/69	57000

Tech. Off.:   Funding Element:
CASE Code: 73   AWC: 126−16

NGR-47-002-005   Virginia Commonwealth University   W. T. Ham
Radiation hazards to the eye.

Proposal	FY	Agreement Period	Amount
−017	68	7/67 − 6/68	49339
−021	69	7/68 − 6/69	37317

Tech. Off.: PETERSON S T   Funding Element: LARC
CASE Code: 51   AWC: 127−49

NGR-47-002-018   Virginia Commonwealth University S. W. Lippincott
Maximum permissable skin dose of penetrating electron radiation in the outer belt.

Proposal	FY	Agreement Period	Amount
−018	68	6/68 − 5/69	65000
−024	69	6/69 − 6/70	65000

Tech. Off.:   Funding Element: LARC
CASE Code: 51   AWC: 127−49

NGR-47-002-020   Virginia Commonwealth University   H. P. Dalton
Research on microbiological performance testing on the water management sub-system for a four man space capsule.

Proposal	FY	Agreement Period	Amount
−020	68	6/68 − 5/69	35440

Tech. Off.:   Funding Element: LARC
CASE Code: 51   AWC: 127−53

NGR-47-003-007   Old Dominion University   G. L. Goglia
A theoretical and experimental investigation of the vortex-sink rate sensor.

Proposal	FY	Agreement Period	Amount
−007	68	9/67 − 2/69	24000
		− 5/69	NCE
−019	69	6/69 − 6/70	35959

Tech. Off.: HELLBAUM R F   Funding Element: LARC
CASE Code: 13   AWC: 125−19

NGR-47-003-008   Old Dominion University   R. L. Williams
Studies in heterocyclic synthesis.

Proposal	FY	Agreement Period	Amount
−008	67	6/67 − 5/68	12102
−013	68	6/68 − 5/69	27799
−023		6/68 − 5/71	28000

Tech. Off.: JOHNSON N J   Funding Element: LARC
CASE Code: 12   AWC: 129−03

NGR-47-003-012   Old Dominion University   R. Y. K. Cheng
Investigation to establish a theoretical description of soil-tire interaction under moving wheel of aircraft.

Proposal	FY	Agreement Period	Amount
−012	68	6/68 − 5/69	31960
−021		6/69 − 5/72	72000

Tech. Off.:   Funding Element: LARC
CASE Code: 41   AWC: 126−61

NGR-47-003-015   Old Dominion University   W. D. Stanley
Doppler radar simulation studies.

Proposal	FY	Agreement Period	Amount
−015	69	2/69 − 5/70	19971

Tech. Off.: HARRINGTON R F   Funding Element: LARC
CASE Code: 44   AWC: 125−17

VIRGINIA   (Cont'd)

NSR-47-003-010   Old Dominion University   G. L. Goglia
ASEE-NASA summer faculty training program in systems engineering.

Proposal	FY	Agreement Period	Amount
−010	68	1/68 −12/68	97800
−010	68	1/68 −12/68	97800
−016	69	1/69 −12/69	78808
−016	69	1/69 −12/69	70483

Tech. Off.: CARTER C H   Funding Element: HQ−Y
CASE Code: 49   AWC: 181−00

NSR-47-003-011   Old Dominion University   G. L. Goglia
ASEE-NASA Summer Faculty Institute.

Proposal	FY	Agreement Period	Amount
−011	68	1/68 −12/68	116300
−017	69	12/68 −12/69	138533

Tech. Off.: CARTER C H   Funding Element: HQ−Y
CASE Code: 49   AWC: 181−00

NGL-47-004-006   Virginia Polytechnic Institute

F. W. Bull, J. A. Jacobs
Multidisciplinary, space-related research in engineering and the physical and life sciences.

Proposal	FY	Agreement Period	Amount
−021	66	3/66 − 8/69	175000
−027	67	9/66 − 8/69	50000
−027	67	9/67 − 8/70	36000
−035	68	9/67 − 8/70	80000

Tech. Off.:   Funding Element:
CASE Code: 99   AWC: 129−02

NGR-47-004-016   Virginia Polytechnic Institute   J. P. Wightman
The adsorption of gases on stainless steel in the pressure range 10^{-10} to 3^{-3} TORR.

Proposal	FY	Agreement Period	Amount
−016	67	6/67 − 6/68	26365
−038	68	6/68 − 5/69	19726
−049		6/69 − 6/70	12497

Tech. Off.: MUGLER J P   Funding Element: LARC
CASE Code: 12   AWC: 124−09

NGR-47-004-018   Virginia Polytechnic Institute   W. E. C. Moore
A study of techniques for determining the prescence of anaerobic bacteria.

Proposal	FY	Agreement Period	Amount
−028	67	1/67 − 6/68	24150
−028	67	6/68 − 6/69	NCE
−046	68	1/69 − 8/69	8500

Tech. Off.: FARMER F H   Funding Element: LARC
CASE Code: 51   AWC: 189−58

NGR-47-004-024   Virginia Polytechnic Institute   H. L. Wood
A study of the application of microwave techniques to the measurement of solid propellant burning rates.

Proposal	FY	Agreement Period	Amount
−024	67	9/66 − 8/67	44972
−037	68	9/67 − 8/68	41350
−024	67	5/68 − 6/69	NCE

Tech. Off.: HALE H J   Funding Element: LARC
CASE Code: 47   AWC: 128−32

NGR-47-004-030   Virginia Polytechnic Institute   R. A. Comparin
An analytical investigation of thrust vector control by secondary injection.

Proposal	FY	Agreement Period	Amount
−030	68	9/67 − 8/68	26519
		− 6/69	NCE

Tech. Off.: RIEBE J M   Funding Element: LARC
CASE Code: 21   AWC: 128−32

NGL-47-004-033   Virginia Polytechnic Institute   K. Gotow
Research in high energy nuclear physics.

Proposal	FY	Agreement Period	Amount
−033	68	7/67 − 6/68	100000
−033	68	7/67 − 6/70	100000
−045		7/68 − 6/71	40000

Tech. Off.:   Funding Element:
CASE Code: 13   AWC: 129−02

NGR-47-004-040   Virginia Polytechnic Institute   J. C. Schug
Electronic structure and spectra of organic compounds.

Proposal	FY	Agreement Period	Amount
−040	68	7/68 − 6/69	13810
			LARC

Tech. Off.:   Funding Element:
CASE Code: 12   AWC: 129−03

NGR-47-004-051   Virginia Polytechnic Institute   H. F. Brinson
Experimental and analytical investigation of the ductile fracture of polymers.

Proposal	FY	Agreement Period	Amount
−051	69	9/69 − 7/70	13425

Tech. Off.: WILLIAMS D P   Funding Element: ARC
CASE Code: 47   AWC: 129−02

NAS1-8145   Virginia Polytechnic Institute
Development of a small, lightweight gas detector.

Proposal	FY	Agreement Period	Amount
	68	6/68 − 6/69	25000
			LARC

Tech. Off.:   Funding Element:
CASE Code: 43   AWC: 124−09

NAS12-2134   Virginia Polytechnic Institute
Designer's manual for audiological devices.

Proposal	FY	Agreement Period	Amount
	69	5/69 − 3/70	15000

Tech. Off.:   Funding Element:
CASE Code: 51   AWC: 125−25

VIRGINIA (Cont'd)

NGT-47-004-001   Virginia Polytechnic Institute   F. W. Bull
Training of predoctoral graduate students in space-related science and technology.

No. Students:	FY	Agreement Period	Amount
12	65	9/65 – 8/68	212400
12	66	9/66 – 8/69	212400
8	67	9/67 – 8/70	117000

Tech. Off.: HANSING F D   Funding Element: HQ-Y
CASE Code: 99   AWC: 181-00

NGR-47-005-022   University of Virginia   J. W. Beams
Investigation to increase the accuracy of Newtonian gravitational constant, G.

Proposal	FY	Agreement Period	Amount
-092	68	9/67 – 8/68	40000
		9/68 – 9/69	NCE

Tech. Off.:   Funding Element:
CASE Code: 13   AWC: 185-48

NGR-47-005-026   University of Virginia   E. S. McVey, J. Moore
Investigation of systems and techniques for multi-component micro-force measurements on wind tunnel models.

Proposal	FY	Agreement Period	Amount
-074	67	6/67 – 6/68	49100
-100	68	6/68 – 5/69	43931

Tech. Off.: FOWKE J G   Funding Element: LARC
CASE Code: 41   AWC: 124-07

NGR-47-005-029   University of Virginia   H. M. Parker
Theoretical and experimental investigation of a three-dimensional magnetic-suspension balance for dynamic-stability research in wind tunnels.

Proposal	FY	Agreement Period	Amount
-073	67	9/66 – 9/68	199363
-104	68	9/68 – 8/69	165000

Tech. Off.: HAMLET I L   Funding Element: LARC
CASE Code: 41   AWC: 126-13

NGR-47-005-046   University of Virginia   S. S. Fisher
Research in the field of molecular collision phenomena using molecular beam techniques.

Proposal	FY	Agreement Period	Amount
-046	66	4/66 – 3/69	85000
-075	67	4/67 – 3/69	45000
-099	68	4/68 – 3/70	45000

Tech. Off.: SCHWARTZ R   Funding Element: HQ-RR
CASE Code: 13   AWC: 129-01

NGR-47-005-049   University of Virginia   F. R. Woods
An investigation in irreversible macroscopic phenomena.

Proposal	FY	Agreement Period	Amount
-076	67	6/67 – 5/68	18153
-105	69	6/68 – 5/69	18153

Tech. Off.: PETERSON J B JR   Funding Element: LARC
CASE Code: 13   AWC: 126-13

NGR-47-005-050   University of Virginia   E. J. Gunter
Investigation of the dynamic stability of the rigid body rotor.

Proposal	FY	Agreement Period	Amount
-078	67	6/67 – 5/68	22951
-103	68	6/68 – 8/69	42736

Tech. Off.: TRYON H B   Funding Element: LERC
CASE Code: 46   AWC: 120-27

NGR-47-005-059   University of Virginia   W. L. Duren
Global aspects of optimal control.

Proposal	FY	Agreement Period	Amount
-059	68	6/68 – 5/69	20000

Tech. Off.: SCHMEIDER D H   Funding Element: ERC
CASE Code: 42   AWC: 129-04

NGR-47-005-066   University of Virginia   L. W. Fredrick
Broad and specific studies in astronomy and in related scientific and engineering fields.

Proposal	FY	Agreement Period	Amount
-086	68	9/67 – 9/68	17537
-107	69	9/68 – 9/69	20000

Tech. Off.: ROMAN   Funding Element: HQ-SG
CASE Code: 11   AWC: 188-41

NGL-47-005-067   University of Virginia   N. Cabrera
Studies in high energy physics.

Proposal	FY	Agreement Period	Amount
-084	68	4/68 – 3/71	150000

Tech. Off.:   Funding Element:
CASE Code: 13   AWC: 129-02

NGR-47-005-077   University of Virginia   J. W. Boring
The interaction of oxygen atoms with solid surfaces at eV energies.

Proposal	FY	Agreement Period	Amount
-077	67	6/67 – 5/68	37918
-102	68	6/68 – 5/69	20000

Tech. Off.: HOROWITZ R   Funding Element: HQ-SL
CASE Code: 13   AWC: 185-47

NGR-47-005-085   University of Virginia   A. R. Saunders
Theoretical research on heterogeneous combustion.

Proposal	FY	Agreement Period	Amount
-085	68	10/67 -11/67	47000

Tech. Off.:   Funding Element:
CASE Code: 13   AWC: 128-32

NGR-47-005-093   University of Virginia   R. J. Mattauch
Investigation of the detectivity of radiation-produced defect levels in N- and P-type silicon and germanium.

Proposal	FY	Agreement Period	Amount
-093	68	2/68 – 1/69	23536
-093		6/69	NCE

Tech. Off.:   Funding Element: LARC
CASE Code: 13   AWC: 125-17

VIRGINIA (Cont'd)

NGL-47-005-098   University of Virginia   F. W. Barton

Study of numerical methodology for dynamic buckling of shell structures.

Proposal	FY	Agreement Period	Amount
-098	69	6/69 - 5/72	38398

Tech. Off.: WILSON B M   Funding Element: LARC
CASE Code: 21   AWC: 124-08

NGR-47-005-108   University of Virginia   J. K. Haviland

Topics in structural dynamics.

Proposal	FY	Agreement Period	Amount
-108	69	10/69 - 9/70	17000

Tech. Off.: RAINEY A G   Funding Element: LARC
CASE Code: 46   AWC: 126-14

NGR-47-005-110   University of Virginia   G. B. Matthews

Extension of the cold balance capabilities.

Proposal	FY	Agreement Period	Amount
-110	69	2/69 -10/69	15000

Tech. Off.: WILEY H G   Funding Element: LARC
CASE Code: 99   AWC: 126-49

NSR-47-005-070   University of Virginia   E. H. Hendricks

Conduct of a three-week bio-space technology training program at NASA Wallops Station.

Proposal	FY	Agreement Period	Amount
-090	68	1/68 -12/68	56476
-090	68	3/68 -12/68	1118

Tech. Off.: BOLTON V M   Funding Element: HQ-SB
CASE Code: 59   AWC: 189-74

NAS2-1554   University of Virginia   G. C. Pitts

Biosatellite project experiment P-1145, effect of weightlessness on gross body composition of the rat.

Proposal	FY	Agreement Period	Amount
	68	9/64 - 3/71	54000

Tech. Off.: HIGHTOWER W   Funding Element: ARC
CASE Code: 51   AWC: 883-12

NAS6-1616   University of Virginia

Graduate level course in theory of servomechanisms and feedback system.

Proposal	FY	Agreement Period	Amount
	69	1/69 - 5/69	7000

Tech. Off.:   Funding Element:
CASE Code: 46   AWC: 039-00

NGT-47-005-005   University of Virginia   E. Younger

Training of predoctoral graduate students in space-related science and technology.

No. Students:	FY	Agreement Period	Amount
12	65	9/65 - 8/68	196500
12	66	9/66 - 8/69	204000
8	67	9/67 - 8/70	115600

Tech. Off.: HANSING F D   Funding Element: HQ-Y
CASE Code: 99   AWC: 181-00

NGL-47-006-008   College of William and Mary   W. M. Jones

Multidisciplinary research in space sciences and technology.

Proposal	FY	Agreement Period	Amount
-036	68	10/67 - 9/70	100000
-043	66	10/68 - 9/71	100000

Tech. Off.:   Funding Element:
CASE Code: 99   AWC: 124-09

NGR-47-006-010   College of William & Mary   H. O. Funsten

An investigation of pion and muon beam transport systems.

Proposal	FY	Agreement Period	Amount
-033	67	6/67 - 5/68	12175
-042	68	6/68 - 5/69	15765
-042		2/70	NCE

Tech. Off.: SMITH D D   Funding Element: LARC
CASE Code: 13   AWC: 124-09

NGR-47-006-028   College of William and Mary   H. Friedman

Improving performance in absolute judgment tasks.

Proposal	FY	Agreement Period	Amount
-039		6/67 - 5/68	11000
		- 5/69	NCE

Tech. Off.: SAUCER R T   Funding Element: LARC
CASE Code: 21   AWC: 127-51

NGL-47-006-041   College of William and Mary   R. T. Siegel

Research in intermediate energy physics.

Proposal	FY	Agreement Period	Amount
-041	68	10/67 - 9/70	167000
-044	69	10/68 - 9/71	40000

Tech. Off.:   Funding Element: LARC
CASE Code: 13   AWC: 129-02

NGR-47-006-045   College of William and Mary   A. Sher

Temperature variation of the resistivity of metallic strain gauge materials.

Proposal	FY	Agreement Period	Amount
-045	69	6/69 -10/69	5951

Tech. Off.: GROSS C   Funding Element: LARC
CASE Code: 47   AWC: 125-24

NAS1-5700   College of William & Mary   R. T. Siegel

Management, EMT, operation and maintenance of the SREL.

Proposal	FY	Agreement Period	Amount
		1/66 - 6/70	1826000
	68	1/66 - 6/70	429000
	65	11/65 - 6/70	485000

Tech. Off.: MARTIN D   Funding Element: LARC
CASE Code: 49   AWC: 124-09

NGT-47-006-013   College of William and Mary   R. T. Siegel

Training of predoctoral graduate students in space-related science and technology.

No. Students:	FY	Agreement Period	Amount
2	65	9/65 - 8/68	39900
3	66	9/66 - 8/69	59900
2	67	9/67 - 9/70	40800

Tech. Off.: HANSING F D   Funding Element: HQ-Y
CASE Code: 99   AWC: 181-00

WASHINGTON

NGR-48-001-004   Washington State University   B. A. McFadden
Study of intermediary metabolic processes in hydrogenomonas facilis.

Proposal	FY	Agreement Period	Amount
-010	68	12/67 -11/68	18156
		6/68 - 6/69	NCE

Tech. Off.: SAUNDERS J F   Funding Element: HQ-SB
CASE Code: 51   AWC: 189-54

NGT-48-001-002   Washington State University   J. F. Short
Training of predoctoral graduate students in space-related science and technology.

No. Students	FY	Agreement Period	Amount
8	65	9/65 - 8/68	126400
8	66	9/66 - 8/69	133100
4	67	9/67 - 8/70	67400

Tech. Off.: HANSING F D   Funding Element: HQ-Y
CASE Code: 99   AWC: 181-00

NGR-48-002-003   University of Washington   R. J. H. Bollard
Analytical and experimental study, using photoelastic methods, to establish a stress analysis of a viscoelastic model subjected to transient temperature and time-dependent loading.

Proposal	FY	Agreement Period	Amount
-048	68	9/67 - 9/68	44325
-065	69	9/68 - 9/69	41675

Tech. Off.: WILLIAMS J G   Funding Element: LARC
CASE Code: 46   AWC: 124-08

NGL-48-002-004   University of Washington   J. I. Mueller
Multidisciplinary research activity in the materials sciences with emphasis on investigations of inorganic nonmetallic (ceramic) materials.

Proposal	FY	Agreement Period	Amount
8818	64	6/64 - 5/68	500000
-032	66	6/66 - 5/69	300000
-043	67	6/67 - 5/70	300000
-055	68	6/68 - 5/71	300000
-063	68	6/68 - 5/72	266170
-067	69	6/68 - 5/72	258170

Tech. Off.: GANGLER J   Funding Element: HQ-RR
CASE Code: 49   AWC: 129-03

NGR-48-002-009   University of Washington   J. K. Buettner
Spectrometric investigations of the emissivity of natural surface and materials, and feasibility studies of microwave experiments for future meteorological satellites.

Proposal	FY	Agreement Period	Amount
-049	68	9/67 - 8/68	25000
-068	69	10/68 - 9/69	11600

Tech. Off.:   Funding Element: GSFC
CASE Code: 31   AWC: 160-44

NGR-48-002-010   University of Washington   R. G. Joppa
Experimental and theoretical investigations of wind tunnel geometry, emphasizing factors pertinent to V/STOL vehicle testing.

Proposal	FY	Agreement Period	Amount
-036	67	9/66 - 9/67	43778
-036	67	9/67 - 9/68	NCE
-066	69	9/68 - 9/69	48970
-079		9/69 - 9/71	51000

Tech. Off.: ROGALLO F M   Funding Element: LARC
CASE Code: 41   AWC: 721-01

NGR-48-002-033   University of Washington   P. W. Hodge
Study of interplanetary dust.

Proposal	FY	Agreement Period	Amount
-050	68	12/67 -12/68	30000
		- 6/69	NCE

Tech. Off.: DUBIN   Funding Element: HQ-SG
CASE Code: 11   AWC: 188-45

NGR-48-002-035   University of Washington   W. H. Rae
An experimental investigation of wind tunnel test limits for V/STOL type vehicles in wind tunnels with curved walls.

Proposal	FY	Agreement Period	Amount
-035	67	7/67 - 4/68	NCE
		5/68 -12/68	NCE
-035		6/69	NCE

Tech. Off.: ROGALLO F M   Funding Element: LARC
CASE Code: 41   AWC: 721-01

NGL-48-002-044   University of Washington   A. Hertzberg
Generation of coherent radiation and the use of intense coherent radiation for the generation of plasmas.

Proposal	FY	Agreement Period	Amount
-044	67	11/66 -10/69	140000
-058	68	11/67 -10/70	70000
-071	69	11/68 -11/71	60000

Tech. Off.: HOWE J   Funding Element: HQ-RR
CASE Code: 13   AWC: 129-01

NGR-48-002-047   University of Washington   M. E. Childs
An investigation of the interaction of a shock wave and a turbulent boundary layer in axially symmetric internal flow.

Proposal	FY	Agreement Period	Amount
-047	68	9/67 -12/68	25710
-047		6/69	NCE

Tech. Off.: WATSON E C   Funding Element: ARC
CASE Code: 13   AWC: 126-15

NGL-48-002-057   University of Washington   A. Hertzberg
The study of fluid mechanical problems related to advanced concepts in aircraft.

Proposal	FY	Agreement Period	Amount
-057	68	11/67 -11/68	72380
-062	67	11/68 -11/70	73000

Tech. Off.:   Funding Element:
CASE Code: 41   AWC: 129-01

WASHINGTON (Cont'd.)

NGR-48-002-073   University of Washington   C. B. Leovy
Meteorology of Mars and Venus.

Proposal	FY	Agreement Period	Amount
-073	69	1/69 - 12/70	51900

Tech. Off.: FELLOWS R F   Funding Element: HQ-SL
CASE Code: 31   AWC: 185-47

NGR-48-002-074   University of Washington   J. Vagners
Investigations in the theory of lunar satellites.

Proposal	FY	Agreement Period	Amount
-074	69	6/69 - 5/70	19837

Tech. Off.: BORN G H   Funding Element: MSC
CASE Code: 42   AWC: 997-82

NGR-48-002-077   University of Washington   C. B. Leovy
Participation in the 1973 Mars lander project.

Proposal	FY	Agreement Period	Amount
-077	69	2/69 - 1/70	6120

Tech. Off.: MITZ M A   Funding Element: HQ-SL
CASE Code: 42   AWC: 815-20

NSR-48-002-054   University of Washington   H. G. Ahlstrom
Investigation of various areas of fluid dynamics.

Proposal	FY	Agreement Period	Amount
-054		9/67 - 9/68	22700
-054		6/69	NCE

Tech. Off.: HOWE J   Funding Element: HQ-RR
CASE Code: 13   AWC: 129-01

NGT-48-002-007   University of Washington   J. L. McCarthy
Training of predoctoral graduate students in space-related science and technology.

No. Students:	FY	Agreement Period	Amount
12	65	9/65 - 8/68	196300
12	66	9/66 - 8/69	217400
6	67	9/67 - 8/70	91800

Tech. Off.: HANSING F D   Funding Element: HQ-Y
CASE Code: 99   AWC: 181-00

NGF-48-002-031   University of Washington   J. H. Ballard
Construction of an Aerospace Research Laboratory.

Proposal	FY	Agreement Period	Amount
-031	66	9/66 - 3/69	1500000
	66	9/70	NCE

Tech. Off.: HOLMES D C   Funding Element: HQ-Y
CASE Code: 12   AWC: 182-00

WEST VIRGINIA

NGL-49-001-001   West Virginia University   J. C. Ludlum
Space-related studies in the physical, life, and engineering sciences.

Proposal	FY	Agreement Period	Amount
-017	66	10/65 - 9/68	50000
-021	67	10/66 - 9/69	50000
-033	68	10/67 - 9/70	50000
-037	68	10/68 - 9/71	150000

Tech. Off.: QUINN H B   Funding Element: HQ-Y
CASE Code: 99   AWC: 183-00

NGR-49-001-019   West Virginia University   W. H. Moran
The effect of changing gravity and weightlessness on vasopressin control systems.

Proposal	FY	Agreement Period	Amount
-036	68	2/68 - 1/69	20000
-019	69	2/69 - 2/70	20000
-038	69	2/69 - 2/70	20000

Tech. Off.: ANDERSON E   Funding Element: HQ-SG
CASE Code: 51   AWC: 127-49

NSR-49-001-039   University of West Virginia   E. J. Steinhardt
NASA-Langley Research Center-West Virginia University summer predoctoral fellowship program in engineering systems design.

Proposal	FY	Agreement Period	Amount
-039	69	1/69 - 12/69	61500

Tech. Off.: CARTER C H   Funding Element: HQ-Y
CASE Code: 49   AWC: 181-00

NGT-49-001-002   West Virginia University   J. Ludlum
Training of predoctoral graduate students in space-related science and technology.

No. Students:	FY	Agreement Period	Amount
10	65	9/65 - 8/68	189800
10	66	9/66 - 8/69	174000
6	67	9/67 - 8/70	87800

Tech. Off.: HANSING F D   Funding Element: HQ-Y
CASE Code: 99   AWC: 181-00

WISCONSIN

NGR-50-001-009   Marquette University   E. C. Foudriat
Study of problems relating to the precise determination of the attitude of a spin stabilized spacecraft.

Proposal	FY	Agreement Period	Amount
-009	68	4/68 - 3/69	29400
-011	69	4/69 - 3/70	30030
			LARC

Tech. Off.:   Funding Element:
CASE Code: 41   AWC: 125-17

WISCONSIN (Cont'd.)

NGR-50-001-010 Marquette University   W. Markowitz
Improved time capabilities for geodetic satellites.

Proposal	FY	Agreement Period	Amount
-010	69	1/69 -12/70	9668

Tech. Off.: ROSENBERG J D   Funding Element: HQ-SA
CASE Code: 42   AWC: 160-43

NGT-50-001-005 Marquette University   L. W. Friedrich
Training of predoctoral graduate students in space-related science and technology.

No. Students	FY	Agreement Period	Amount
2	66	9/66 - 8/69	35400
1	67	9/67 - 8/70	17700

Tech. Off.: HANSING F D   Funding Element: HQ-Y
CASE Code: 99   AWC: 181-00

NGL-50-002-001   University of Wisconsin (Madison)
J. O. Hirschfelder
A broad program of research in theoretical chemistry, particularly in molecular quantum and statistical mechanics, directed toward determination of the physical and chemical properties of materials, relation of these macroscopic properties of individual molecules, and determination of structure and properties of the individual molecules.

Proposal	FY	Agreement Period	Amount
-035	65	7/65 - 6/68	900000
-061	66	7/66 - 6/69	650000
-082	67	7/67 - 6/68	650000
-100	68	7/68 - 6/71	250000

Tech. Off.: QUINN H B   Funding Element: HQ-Y
CASE Code: 12   AWC: 183-00

NGR-50-002-002   University of Wisconsin (Madison) E. N. Cameron
Quantitative investigation of mineralogy and petrography of stone and iron meteorites.

Proposal	FY	Agreement Period	Amount
-056	66	7/66 - 6/69	15000
-062	66	7/66 - 6/69	23000
-062	68	7/67 - 6/69	1320
-123	69	7/69 - 7/70	4881

Tech. Off.: BRYSON R   Funding Element: HQ-MAL
CASE Code: 32   AWC: 185-45

NGL-50-002-013   University of Wisconsin (Madison)   A. D. Code
Investigations and studies of ultraviolet stellar spectra and associated instrumentation.

Proposal	FY	Agreement Period	Amount
-067	67	4/66 - 3/69	140000
-077	67	4/67 - 3/70	150000
-077	68	4/67 - 3/70	50000
-104	66	4/68 - 3/71	150000
-119	69	4/69 - 4/72	200000

Tech. Off.: OTT   Funding Element: HQ-SG
CASE Code: 11   AWC: 188-41

NGR-50-002-017   University of Wisconsin (Madison)   P. S. Myers
Research on oscillatory combustion and fuel vaporization.

Proposal	FY	Agreement Period	Amount
-057	66	6/66 - 5/68	40000
		- 5/69	NCE
-057	66	1/70	NCE

Tech. Off.: HOWE J   Funding Element: ARC
CASE Code: 43   AWC: 129-01

NGR-50-002-041   University of Wisconsin (Madison) L. A. Haskins
Neutron activation analysis for rare earths, lanthanides, and yttrium, on simulated lunar samples.

Proposal	FY	Agreement Period	Amount
-041	67	1/67 - 6/68	35000

Tech. Off.: WILMARTH R   Funding Element: HQ-MAL
CASE Code: 13   AWC: 848-00

NGR-50-002-044   University of Wisconsin (Madison) W. L. Krauschaar
Research in cosmic and solar physics.

Proposal	FY	Agreement Period	Amount
-091	68	1/68 -12/68	124214
-113	69	1/69 -12/69	138000
-126		1/69 -12/71	162000

Tech. Off.: ROMAN N G   Funding Element: HQ-SG
CASE Code: 11   AWC: 188-41

NGL-50-002-078   University of Wisconsin (Madison)   E. C. Dick
A study of methods to effect a more complete and rapid detection of human infectious agents.

Proposal	FY	Agreement Period	Amount
-078	67	6/67 - 5/68	26460
-098	68	6/68 - 5/69	28000
-107	68	6/68 - 5/71	26500

Tech. Off.: MANDEL A D   Funding Element: ARC
CASE Code: 52   AWC: 127-49

NGR-50-002-083   University of Wisconsin (Madison)   V. C. Rideout
Cardiovascular system study with computer modeling.

Proposal	FY	Agreement Period	Amount
-083	68	9/67 - 8/68	36378
-083	69	9/68 - 8/69	39409

Tech. Off.: LINEBARGER R N   Funding Element: ARC
CASE Code: 51   AWC: 127-49

NGR-50-002-086   University of Wisconsin (Madison)   D. O. Cliver
Stability of viruses in foods for space flights.

Proposal	FY	Agreement Period	Amount
-086	68	11/67 -10/68	31535
-086	68	11/67 -10/68	35000
		-11/68	NCE
-086	69	12/68 -11/69	20000

Tech. Off.: SMITH M   Funding Element: MSC
CASE Code: 52   AWC: 914-50

WISCONSIN (Cont'd)

NGR-50-002-114   University of Wisconsin (Madison)   V. E. Suomi
Multidisciplinary studies of the social, economic and political
impact resulting from recent advances in satellite meteorology.

Proposal	FY	Agreement Period	Amount
-114	69	1/69 -12/69	150000

Tech. Off.: MANDEVILLE R L   Funding Element: HQ-SA
CASE Code: 99   AWC: 160-76

NGR-50-002-116   University of Wisconsin (Madison)   R. W. Boom
A study or composite superconductors.

-116	69	7/69 - 6/70	39960

Tech. Off.: LAURENCE J C   Funding Element: LERC
CASE Code: 47   AWC: 129-03

NAS5-9677   University of Wisconsin (Madison)   V. E. Suomi
Flight model of a spin scan camera system.

Proposal	FY	Agreement Period	Amount
		9/65 -12/67	963000
	68	9/65 -12/67	60000
	68	9/65 -12/67	58000

Tech. Off.: SANDERLIN   Funding Element: GSFC
CASE Code: 42   AWC: 603-

NAS5-11068   University of Wisconsin (Madison)
Imp-H & P solar wind deuterium experiment.

Proposal	FY	Agreement Period	Amount
	67	5/68 - 8/72	243000

Tech. Off.: MARCOTTE P   Funding Element: GSFC
CASE Code: 31   AWC: 861-42

NAS5-11542   University of Wisconsin (Madison)
Meteorological measurements from satellite platforms.

Proposal	FY	Agreement Period	Amount
	68	6/68 - 6/69	185000

Tech. Off.:   Funding Element: GSFC
CASE Code: 31   AWC: 160-44

NAS8-21015   University of Wisconsin (Madison)
Development & construction of x-ray astronomy experiment
SO-27.

Proposal	FY	Agreement Period	Amount
		9/66 - 9/68	679000

Tech. Off.: PONDER T   Funding Element: MSFC
CASE Code: 11   AWC: 905-80

NAS9-7975   University of Wisconsin (Madison)   L. Haskin
Determine rare earth element by neutron activation analysis.

Proposal	FY	Agreement Period	Amount
	68	5/68 -11/69	33000

Tech. Off.:   Funding Element: MSC
CASE Code: 32   AWC: 914-40

NAS9-9300   University of Wisconsin (Madison)
Study to determine biocidal effects of silver.

Proposal	FY	Agreement Period	Amount
	69	3/69 - 1/70	45000

Tech. Off.:   Funding Element:
CASE Code: 51   AWC: 914-50

NGT-50-002-003   University of Wisconsin (Madison)   R. M. Bock
Training of predoctoral graduate students in space-related
science and technology.

No. Students	FY	Agreement Period	Amount
15	65	9/65 - 8/68	285800
15	66	9/66 - 8/69	292500
9	67	9/67 - 8/70	166200

Tech. Off.: HANSING F D   Funding Element: HQ-Y
CASE Code: 99   AWC: 181-00

NGF-50-002-004   University of Wisconsin (Madison)
                                              J. O. Hirschfelder
Construction of additional laboratory research facilities for the
Theoretical Chemistry Institute.

Proposal	FY	Agreement Period	Amount
	62	6/63 - 6/66	442760

Tech. Off.: HOLMES D C   Funding Element: HQ-Y
CASE Code: 99   AWC: 182-00

WYOMING

NGR-51-001-008   University of Wyoming   A. B. Denison
A study of the representatives of the group of canonical
transformations.

Proposal	FY	Agreement Period	Amount
-008	68	1/68 -12/68	14981
		- 6/69	NCE

Tech. Off.:   Funding Element:
CASE Code: 13   AWC: 129-04

NGR-51-001-010   University of Wyoming   E. A. Rinehart
Relative and absolute intensity measurement of microwave
spectral lines in pure and dilute gases.

Proposal	FY	Agreement Period	Amount
-010	67	1/67 -12/68	94907
-020	69	1/69 -12/69	34473

Tech. Off.: WHITE W F   Funding Element: LARC
CASE Code: 13   AWC: 127-53

NGR-51-001-019   University of Wyoming   J. N. Rosen
The simultaneous measurement of atmospheric dust by laser
and balloon sounding techniques.

Proposal	FY	Agreement Period	Amount
-019	69	11/68 -10/69	67731

Tech. Off.: LAWRENCE J D   Funding Element: LARC
CASE Code: 49   AWC: 126-61

WYOMING (Cont'd)

NGT-51-001-002   University of Wyoming   R. H. Bruce

Training of predoctoral graduate students in space-related science and technology.

No. Students:	FY	Agreement Period	Amount
4	65	9/65 – 8/68	72700
4	66	9/66 – 8/69	72100
2	67	9/67 – 8/70	36300

Tech. Off.: HANSING F D   Funding Element: HQ-Y
CASE Code: 99   AWC: 181-00

FOREIGN

NGR-52-042-004   University of Adelaide   E. G. Elford

Measurements of the orbits of shower and sporadic meteors in the southern hemisphere by a multi-station radio technique.

Proposal	FY	Agreement Period	Amount
–004	68	7/68 – 6/69	19970

Tech. Off.:   Funding Element:
CASE Code: 31   AWC: 188-45

NGR-52-119-001   University of Goteborg   H. Hyden

Study of biomedical and molecular changes in the brain.

Proposal	FY	Agreement Period	Amount
–001	68	2/68 – 1/69	8000

Tech. Off.:   Funding Element:
CASE Code: 51   AWC: 189-52

NGR-52-059-001   McMaster University   A. B. Kristofferson

A study of attention and psychological time.

Proposal	FY	Agreement Period	Amount
–003	68	9/67 – 8/68	30876

Tech. Off.: TANNER T A   Funding Element: ARC
CASE Code: 61   AWC: 125-19

NGR-52-093-001   University of Ottawa   H. Kozlowska

Role of surface oxide films in oxygen reduction and evolution.

Proposal	FY	Agreement Period	Amount
–001	68	7/68 – 6/69	8333

Tech. Off.: GILMAN S   Funding Element: ERC
CASE Code: 12   AWC: 120-34

NSR-52-112-001   Queen's University   F. J. Smith

Feasibility study of miniaturizing an automatic acid analyzer for use on an Apollo mission and a Mars Voyager mission.

Proposal	FY	Agreement Period	Amount
–001	67	7/66 – 6/67	8000

Tech. Off.: AHTYE W H   Funding Element: ARC
CASE Code: 42   AWC: 129-01

NSR-52-112-002   Queen's University   F. J. Smith

Calculations of higher order collision integrals for use in the determination of transport coefficients of high temperature gases.

Proposal	FY	Agreement Period	Amount
–002	68	4/68 – 3/69	8000

Tech. Off.:   Funding Element: ARC
CASE Code: 21   AWC: 129-01

NGR-52-025-003   University of Southampton   E. J. Richards

Investigation of building structure response to sonic boom.

Proposal	FY	Agreement Period	Amount
–003	66	6/66 – 5/68	62550
–004	69	6/68 – 5/70	42432

Tech. Off.: CAWTHORN J M   Funding Element: LARC
CASE Code: 44   AWC: 126-16

NGR-52-026-001   University of Toronto   J. B. French

Gas-surface interactions with satellite conditions.

Proposal	FY	Agreement Period	Amount
–014	66	3/66 – 2/69	63816
–025		3/69 – 2/70	23824

Tech. Off.: SCHWARTZ R   Funding Element: HQ-RR
CASE Code: 12   AWC: 129-01

NGR-52-026-011   University of Toronto   R. C. Tennyson

Buckling of circular cylindrical shells in axial compression.

Proposal	FY	Agreement Period	Amount
–021	67	7/67 – 6/69	16228

Tech. Off.: MC COMB H G   Funding Element: LARC
CASE Code: 46   AWC: 124-11

NGR-52-083-002   College of the Virgin Islands   F. B. Gray

Optimization of the separator subsystem for GC/MB life detection.

Proposal	FY	Agreement Period	Amount
–002	68	11/67 –10/68	34900
–005	69	11/68 –11/69	38520

Tech. Off.: EASTER D P   Funding Element: HQ-SL
CASE Code: 51   AWC: 185-37

NAS5-9980   University of The West Indies

GEOS minitract optical tracking system.

Proposal	FY	Agreement Period	Amount
	68	1/66 – 1/69	13000

Tech. Off.:   Funding Element:
CASE Code: 42   AWC: 311-01

NGR-52-134-001   York University   H. N. McFarland

The toxicity of the thermal degradation products of plastics and kindred materials.

Proposal	FY	Agreement Period	Amount
–001	69	7/69 – 6/70	70711

Tech. Off.: HARRIS E S   Funding Element: MSC
CASE Code: 47   AWC: 914-50

GRANTS AND CONTRACTS NUMERICALLY

NGR-01-001-003	Alabama A&M College	C. O. Lee	ALA
NGR-01-001-006	Alabama A&M College	R. H. Lee	ALA
NGR-01-001-007	Alabama A&M College	M. C. George	ALA
NGL-01-002-001	University of Alabama (University)		ALA
	R. Hermann, G. Croker		
NGR-01-002-035	University of Alabama (Huntsville)	E. W. Grohse	ALA
NGR-01-002-063	University of Alabama (Huntsville)	J. E. Rush	ALA
NGR-01-003-008	Auburn University	W. A. Shaw	ALA
NGR-01-003-036	Auburn University	P. M. Fitzpatrick	ALA
NGR-02-001-001	University of Alaska		
	S. Chapman, Syun-Ichi Akasofu		ALS
NGR-02-001-063	University of Alaska	R. B. Forbes	ALAS
NGL-03-001-001	Arizona State University	C. B. Moore	ARIZ
NGR-03-002-001	University of Arizona	R. W. G. Wyckoff	ARIZ
NGL-03-002-002	University of Arizona	G. P. Kuiper	ARIZ
NGL-03-002-006	University of Arizona	L. E. Weaver	ARIZ
NGR-03-002-011	University of Arizona	T. L. Vincent	ARIZ
NGR-03-002-017	University of Arizona	S. Bashkin	ARIZ
NGL-03-002-019	University of Arizona	S. A. Hoenig	ARIZ
NGR-03-002-024	University of Arizona	G. A. Korn	ARIZ
NGR-03-002-032	University of Arizona	A. B. Meinel, W. G. Tifft	ARIZ
NGR-03-002-044	University of Arizona	D. B. Kececioglu	ARIZ
NGR-03-002-068	University of Arizona	R. W. Lansing	ARIZ
NGR-03-002-071	University of Arizona	T. Bowen	ARIZ
NGR-03-002-081	University of Arizona	A. M. J. Gehrels	ARIZ
NGL-03-002-091	University of Arizona	H. D. Christensen	ARIZ
NGR-03-002-107	University of Arizona	C. Y. Fan	ARIZ
NGR-03-002-115	University of Arizona	L. E. Weaver	ARIZ
NGR-03-002-116	University of Arizona	F. J. Low	ARIZ
NGR-03-002-122	University of Arizona	E. Roemer	ARIZ
NGR-03-002-153	University of Arizona	W. G. Tifft	ARIZ
NGR-03-002-155	University of Arizona	B. M. Herman	ARIZ
NGR-03-002-169	University of Arizona	D. J. Hamilton	ARIZ
NGR-03-002-174	University of Arizona	G. P. Kuiper	ARIZ
NGR-03-002-180	University of Arizona	H. L. Johnson	ARIZ
NGR-03-002-184	University of Arizona	H. L. Johnson	ARIZ
NGR-03-002-191	University of Arizona	G. P. Kuiper	ARIZ
NGR-03-002-193	University of Arizona	T. Gehrels	ARIZ
NGR-03-002-194	University of Arizona	W. G. Tifft	ARIZ
NGR-03-102-171	University of Arizona	H. C. Urey	ARIZ
NGR-04-001-029	University of Arkansas	D. M. Scruggs	ARK
NGR-04-005-001	Arkansas State University	J. L. Linnstaedter	ARK
NGL-05-002-002	California Institute of Technology	J. P. Liepmann	CAL
NGR-05-002-003	California Institute of Technology	H. Brown	CAL
NGL-05-002-005	California Institute of Technology	W. G. Knauss	CAL
NGL-05-002-007	California Institute of Technology	R. B. Leighton	CAL
NGR-05-002-031	California Institute of Technology	F. Strunwasser	CAL
NGR-05-002-034	California Institute of Technology	H. Zirin	CAL
NGR-05-002-092	California Institute of Technology	G. Neugebauer	CAL
NGR-05-002-100	California Institute of Technology	M. A. Nicolet	CAL
NGR-05-002-105	California Institute of Technology	T. J. Ahrens	CAL
NGR-05-002-114	California Institute of Technology	D. O. Muhleman	CAL
NGR-05-002-116	California Institute of Technology	B. Murray	CAL
NGR-05-002-117	California Institute of Technology	B. Murray	CAL
NGR-05-002-118	California Institute of Technology	R. F. Scott	CAL
NGR-05-002-121	California Institute of Technology	N. H. Horowitz	CAL
NGR-05-002-129	California Institute of Technology	D. L. Anderson	CAL
NGL-05-002-136	California Institute of Technology	W. D. Rannie	CAL
NGR-05-002-138	California Institute of Technology	D. L. Anderson	CAL
NGR-05-002-140	California Institute of Technology	G. Munch	CAL
NGR-05-002-142	California Institute of Technology	R. B. Leighton	CAL
NGL-05-003-003	University of California (Berkeley)	M. Calvin	CAL
NGL-05-003-012	University of California (Berkeley)	S. Silver	CAL
NGL-05-003-016	University of California (Berkeley)	C. A. Desoer,	
	L. A. Zadek, E. Polak		CAL
NGL-05-003-017	University of California (Berkeley)	K. A. Anderson	CAL
NGR-05-003-018	University of California (Berkeley)	N. Pace	CAL
NGR-05-003-019	University of California (Berkeley)	H. Mark	CAL
NGR-05-003-020	University of California (Berkeley)	T. H. Jukes	CAL
NGL-05-003-024	University of California (Berkeley)	N. Pace	CAL
NGL-05-003-050	University of California (Berkeley)	A. K. Oppenheim	CAL
NGR-05-003-067	University of California (Berkeley)	W. B. N. Berry	CAL
NGL-05-003-079	University of California (Berkeley)	A. D. McLaren	CAL
NGR-05-003-089	University of California (Berkeley)	D. H. Calloway	CAL
NGR-05-003-125	University of California (Berkeley)	C. W. Churchman	CAL
NGR-05-003-143	University of California (Berkeley)	D. J. Sakrison,	CAL
	V. Algazi		
NGR-05-003-220	University of California (Berkeley)	A. N. Kaufman	CAL
NGR-05-003-228	University of California (Berkeley)	S. Margen	CAL
NGR-05-003-230	University of California (Berkeley)	S. Silver	CAL
NGR-05-003-243	University of California (Berkeley)	R. S. Muller	CAL
NGR-05-003-256	University of California (Berkeley)	S. Silver	CAL
NGR-05-003-266	University of California (Berkeley)	S. Silver	CAL
NGL-05-003-272	University of California (Berkeley)	C. H. Townes	CAL
NGR-05-003-273	University of California (Berkeley)	S. P. Siliberto	CAL
NGR-05-003-275	University of California (Berkeley)	H. P. Smith	CAL
NGR-05-003-278	University of California (Berkeley)	C. S. Bowyer	CAL
NGR-05-003-285	University of California (Berkeley)	C. L. Tien	CAL
NGL-05-003-286	University of California (Berkeley)	G. C. Pimentel	CAL
NGR-05-003-297	University of California (Berkeley)	T. H. Pigford	CAL
NGR-05-003-302	University of California (Berkeley)	M. Calvin	CAL
NGR-05-003-326	University of California (Berkeley)	H. Borsook	CAL
NGR-05-004-008	University of California (Davis)	A. H. Smith,	CAL
	C. F. Kelly		
NGR-05-004-026	University of California (Davis)	L. D. Carlson	CAL
NGL-05-004-031	University of California (Davis)	L. D. Carlson	CAL
NGR-05-004-035	University of California (Davis)	R. E. Smith	CAL
NGR-05-004-038	Unversity of California (Davis)	R. E. Smith	CAL
NGR-05-004-051	University of California (Davis)	M. A. Hoffman	CAL
NGR-05-004-053	University of California (Davis)	R. Smith	CAL
NGR-05-005-003	University of California (San Diego)	L. E. Peterson	CAL
NGR-05-005-005	University of California (San Diego)	J. R. Arnold	CAL
NGR-05-005-007	University of California (San Diego)	C. E. McIlwain	CAL
NGL-05-007-002	University of California (Los Angeles)		
	G. J. F. MacDonald		CAL
NGL-05-007-003	University of California (Los Angeles)	W. F. Libby	CAL
NGR-05-007-004	University of California (Los Angeles)	T. A. Farley,	
	W. F. Libby, P. J. Coleman		CAL
NGR-05-007-041	University of California (Los Angeles)	Z. Sekara	CAL
NGR-05-007-046	University of California (Los Angeles)	L. H. Aller	CAL
NGL-05-007-065	University of California (Los Angeles)	P. J. Coleman	CAL
NGR-05-007-066	University of California (Los Angeles)	A. Y. F. Wong	CAL

NGR-05-007-091	University of California (Los Angeles)		CAL
		Y. Mintz, A. Arakawa	
NGR-05-007-116	University of California (Los Angeles)	A. Banos	CAL
NGR-05-007-122	University of California (Los Angeles)		CAL
		A. V. Balakrishnan	
NGR-05-007-133	University of California (Los Angeles)	H. Sobel	CAL
NGR-05-007-138	University of California (Los Angeles)	W. M. Kaula	CAL
NGL-05-007-161	University of California (Los Angeles)	F. A. Haak	CAL
NGR-05-007-174	University of California (Los Angeles)	K. C. Hamner	CAL
NGR-05-007-187	University of California (Los Angeles)	J. J. Vidal	CAL
NGR-05-007-190	University of California (Los Angeles)	C. F. Kennel	CAL
NGL-05-007-195	University of California (Los Angeles)	J. D. French	CAL
NGR-05-007-205	University of California (Los Angeles)	F. S. Sjoatrand	CAL
NGR-05-007-215	University of California (Los Angeles)	W. F. Libby	CAL
NGR-05-007-235	University of California (Los Angeles)	R. E. Holzer	CAL
NGR-05-008-005	University of California (Riverside)	J. Callaway	CAL
NGR-05-009-002	University of California (San Diego)	G. Arrhenius	CAL
NGR-05-009-004	University of California (San Diego)	J. R. Arnold	CAL
NGL-05-009-005	University of California (San Diego)	H. E. Suess	CAL
NGR-05-009-022	University of California (Riverside)	R. S. White	CAL
NGR-05-009-025	University of California (San Diego)	P. A. Libby	CAL
NGR-05-009-030	University of California (San Diego)	R. H. Lovberg	CAL
NGR-05-009-032	University of California (San Diego)	S. L. Miller	CAL
NGR-05-009-059	University of California (San Diego)	B. Q. Duntley	CAL
NGR-05-009-062	University of California (San Diego)	I. M. Jacobs	CAL
NGR-05-009-076	University of California (San Diego)	J. A. Fejer	CAL
NGR-05-009-081	University of California (San Diego)	W. I. Axford	CAL
NGR-05-009-083	University of California (San Diego)	R. Galambos	CAL
NGR-05-009-103	University of California (San Diego)	N. A. Baily	CAL
NGR-05-009-106	University of California (San Diego)	A. M. Schneider	CAL
NGR-05-009-109	University of California (San Diego)	J. B. West	CAL
NGR-05-009-114	University of California (San Diego)	H. C. Urey	CAL
NGR-05-010-001	University of California (Santa Barbara)		CAL
		W. C. Walker	
NGR-05-010-008	University of California (Santa Barbara)	J. M. Sloss	CAL
NGR-05-010-010	University of California (Santa Barbara)	W. C. Gogel	CAL
NGR-05-010-019	University of California (Santa Barbara)		CAL
		R. V. Fisher	
NGR-05-010-020	Unversity of California (Santa Barbara)		CAL
		T. P. Mitchell	
NGR-05-010-025	University of California (Santa Barbara)		CAL
		H. H. Bossel	
NGR-05-010-028	University of California (Santa Barbara)	W. C. Kuby	CAL
NGR-05-010-035	University of California (Santa Barbara)	P. E. Cloud	CAL
NGR-05-010-041	University of California (Santa Barbara)		CAL
		P. F. Ordung	CAL
NGR-05-010-044	University of California (Los Angeles)	H. P. Broida	CAL
NGR-05-013-010	California State College (Long Beach)	K. P. Luke	CAL
NGR-05-017-013	University of Santa Clara	D. A. Oliver	CAL
NGR-05-017-017	University of Santa Clara	S. P. Chan	CAL
NGR-05-018-001	University of Southern California	G. L. Weissler	CAL
NGL-05-018-003	University of Southern California	J. P. Henry,	CAL
		J. P. Meehan	
NGR-05-018-007	University of Southern California	D. L. Judge	CAL
NGR-05-018-022	University of Southern California	G. A. Bekey	CAL
NGL-05-018-044	University of Southern California	H. Bichsel	CAL
NGR-05-018-065	University of Southern California	T. C. James	CAL
NGR-05-018-079	University of Southern California	W. T. Kyner	CAL
NGL-05-018-098	University of Southern California		CAL

NGR-05-018-104	University of Southern California	R. M. Gagliardi	CAL
NGR-05-020-001	Stanford University	O. G. Villard	CAL
NGR-05-020-004	Stanford University	J. Lederberg	CAL
NGR-05-020-007	Stanford University	R. H. Cannon, I. Flugge-Lotz	CAL
NGL-05-020-008	Stanford University	R. A. Helliwell	CAL
NGR-05-020-013	Stanford University	A. L. Schawlow	CAL
NGL-05-020-014	Stanford University	V. R. Eshleman	CAL
NGR-05-020-015	Stanford University	W. M. Fairbank	CAL
NGR-05-020-019	Stanford University	R. H. Cannon, W. M. Fairbank,	CAL
		B. O. Lange	
NGR-05-020-039	Stanford University	A. S. Tetelman	CAL
NGR-05-020-043	Stanford University	G. L. Pearson	CAL
NGR-05-020-066	Stanford University	W. E. Spicer	CAL
NGR-05-020-073	Stanford University	R. E. Kalman	CAL
NGR-05-020-077	Stanford University	F. W. Crawford	CAL
NGR-05-020-091	Stanford University	D. Bershader	CAL
NGR-05-020-102	Stanford University	K. Karamcheti	CAL
NGR-05-020-103	Stanford University	S. H. Harris	CAL
NGR-05-020-134	Stanford University	W. M. Kays	CAL
NGR-05-020-137	Stanford University	L. Stryer,	CAL
		A. Kornberg	
NGR-05-020-165	Stanford University	M. Chodorow	CAL
NGR-05-020-176	Stanford University	F. W. Crawford	CAL
NGL-05-020-177	Stanford University	R. E. Smith	CAL
NGR-05-020-209	Stanford University	T. R. Kane	CAL
NGR-05-020-214	Stanford University	R. H. Bube	CAL
NGR-05-020-223	Stanford University	M. Anliker	CAL
NGL-05-020-232	Stanford University	R. L. Kovach	CAL
NGR-05-020-234	Stanford University	A. E. Siegman	CAL
NGR-05-020-242	Stanford University	I. Weinberg	CAL
NGR-05-020-243	Stanford University	H. Ashley	CAL
NGR-05-020-244	Stanford University	R. C. Atkinson	CAL
NGR-05-020-245	Stanford University	D. Baganoff	CAL
NGL-05-020-250	Stanford University	J. D. Baldeschwieler	CAL
NGR-05-020-267	Stanford University	A. D. Howard	CAL
NGR-05-020-272	Stanford University	P. A. Sturrock	CAL
NGL-05-020-275	Stanford University	K. Karamcheti	CAL
NGR-05-020-276	Stanford University	V. R. Eshleman	CAL
NGR-05-020-277	Stanford University	D. A. Dunn	CAL
NGR-05-020-288	Stanford University	R. A. Helliwell	CAL
NGR-05-020-305	Stanford University	D. C. Harrison	CAL
NGR-05-020-324	Stanford University	L. A. Sapirstein	CAL
NGR-05-020-326	Stanford University	S. Levine	CAL
NGR-05-020-330	Stanford University	J. R. Spreiter	CAL
NGR-05-020-335	Stanford University	A. C. Giese	CAL
NGR-05-020-345	Stanford University	J. L. Adams	CAL
NGR-05-020-348	Stanford University	A. M. Peterson	CAL
NGR-05-020-353	Stanford University	V. R. Eshleman	CAL
NGR-05-020-354	Stanford University	J. Lederberg	CAL
NGR-05-020-386	Stanford University	W. A. Tiller	CAL
NGR-05-025-007	University of California (San Francisco)	L. E. Earley	CAL
NGR-05-025-008	University of California (San Francisco)		CAL
		H. I. Maibach	
NGR-05-029-005	University of San Francisco	A. Fúrst	CAL
NGL-05-046-002	San Jose State College	B. Clark	CAL
NGR-05-046-005	San Jose State College	J. C. Thompson	CAL
NGR-05-061-004	University of California (Santa Cruz)	E. M. Evleth	CAL
NGR-05-061-005	University of California (Santa Cruz)		
		W. M. McKeeman	CAL

NGR-05-061-006	University of California (Santa Cruz) E. J. Wampler	C A L
NGL—06-001-015	Colorado School of Mines	L. T. Grose	C O L O
NGR-06-002-018	Colorado State University	J. B. Best	C O L O
NGL-06-002-038	Colorado State University	R. Jensen	C O L O
NGR-06-002-053	Colorado State University	C. B. Winn	C O L O
NGR-06-002-063	Colorado State University	F. W. Smith	C O L O
NGR-06-002-074	Colorado State University	D. R. Winder	C O L O
NGR-06-002-075	Colorado State University	J. P. Jordan	C O L O
NGR-06-002-084	Colorado State University	W. R. Mickelsen	C O L O
NGR-06-002-085	Colorado State University	C. B. Winn	C O L O
NGR-06-003-033	University of Colorado	A. Busemann	C O L O
NGR-06-003-034	University of Colorado	W. A. Rense	C O L O
NGL-06-003-052	University of Colorado	C. A. Barth	C O L O
NGR-06-003-057	University of Colorado	R. H. Garstang	C O L O
NGR-06-003-064	University of Colorado	C. A. Barth	C O L O
NGR-06-003-069	University of Colorado	W. A. Rense	C O L O
NGR-06-003-071	University of Colorado	R. Wolfgang	C O L O
NGR-06-003-075	University of Colorado	A. Busemann	C O L O
NGR-06-003-083	University of Colorado	I. Horowitz	C O L O
NGR-06-003-088	University of Colorado	R. E. Hayes	C O L O
NGR-06-003-092	University of Colorado	T. W. Speiser	C O L O
NGR-06-003-120	University of Colorado	C. W. Hord	C O L O
NGR-06-004-006	University of Denver	R. C. Amme	C O L O
NGL-06-004-007	University of Denver	S. A. Johnson	C O L O
NGR-06-004-058	University of Denver	V. L. Patel	C O L O
NGR-06-004-060	University of Denver	J. G. Roederer	C O L O
NGR-06-004-068	University of Denver	L. W. Ross	C O L O
NGL-06-004-078	University of Denver	A. A. Ezra	C O L O
NGR-06-004-082	University of Denver	C. W. Chiang	C O L O
NGL-07-002-002	University of Connecticut	D. P. Lindorff	C O N N
NGR-07-004-004	Yale University	R. Wildt	C O N N
NGL-07-004-005	Yale University	R. C. Barker	C O N N
NGR-07-004-006	Yale University	V. W. Hughes	C O N N
NGL-07-004-008	Yale University	S. R. Lipsky	C O N N
NGR-07-004-009	Yale University	H. J. Morowitz	C O N N
NGR-07-004-010	Yale University	R. Wildt	C O N N
NGR-07-004-015	Yale University	M. M. Chen	C O N N
NGR-07-004-028	Yale University	I. B. Bernstein, J. L. Hirshfield	C O N N
NGR-07-004-029	Yale University	R. Wildt	C O N N
NGR-07-004-034	Yale University C. MacClintock, A. L. McAlester	C O N N
NGR-07-004-035	Yale University	W. E. Lamb	C O N N
NGR-07-004-043	Yale University	R. Wolfgang	C O N N
NGR-07-004-084	Yale University	R. A. Goldsby	C O N N
NGR-07-004-087	Yale University	F. B. Tuteur	C O N N
NGR-07-004-090	Yale University	R. J. Wyman	C O N N
NGR-07-004-109	Yale University	E. B. Hooper	C O N N
NGR-07-006-004	Wesleyan University	T. Page	C O N N
NGR-07-006-005	Wesleyan University	J. E. Faller	C O N N
NGR-07-009-003	Rensselaer Polytechnic Institute of Connecticut, C O N N Inc.	H. J. Schwarz
NGR-07-010-002	Fairfield University	J. H. McElaney	C O N N
NGR-07-011-001	St. Joseph College	M. T. J. Murphy	C O N N
NGR-08-001-016	University of Delaware	E. J. Pellicciaro	D E L
NGL-08-001-019	University of Delaware	T. W. F. Russell	D E L
NGR-09-003-014	American University	E. Callen	D C
NGR-09-005-008	Catholic University	R. E. Meijer	D C
NGR-09-005-014	Catholic University	T. Tanaka	D C
NGR-09-005-022	Catholic University	B. T. DeCicco	D C
NGR-09-005-025	Catholic University	C. C. Chang	D C

NGR-09-005-054	Catholic University	T. Tanaka	D C
NGR-09-005-055	Catholic University	H. C. Khatri	C A L
NGR-09-005-063	Catholic University	Y. C. Whang	D C
NGR-09-005-067	Catholic University	S. C. Ling	D C
NGR-09-009-024	Georgetown University	I. Gray	D C
NGR-09-009-025	Georgetown University	C. B. Ferster	D C
NGR-09-010-008	George Washington University	N. Filipescu	D C
NGL-09-010-030	George Washington University	L. H. Mayo	D C
NGR-09-010-053	George Washington University	H. Liebowitz	D C
NGL-09-011-004	Howard University	H. Branson	D C
NGR-09-011-006	Howard University	F. Senftle	D C
NGR-10-004-005	Florida State University	L. Mandelkern	F L A
NGR-10-004-018	Florida State University	H. Gaffron	F L A
NGR-10-004-029	Florida State University	R. G. Cornell	F L A
NGR-10-004-041	Florida State University	W. Schwartz	F L A
NGR-10-004-056	Florida State University	E. K. Plyler	F L A
NGR-10-004-058	Florida State University	S. L. Hess	F L A
NGL-10-005-005	University of Florida	L. E. Grinter	F L A
NGR-10-005-008	University of Florida	A. E. S. Green	F L A
NGR-10-005-022	University of Florida	R._ D. Walker	F L A
NGR-10-005-036	University of Florida	G. E. Nevill	F L A
NGL-10-005-039	University of Florida	J. J. Hren	F L A
NGR-10-005-049	University of Florida	R. T. Schneider	F L A
NGR-10-005-057	University of Florida	W. B. Webb	F L A
NGR-10-005-080	University of Florida	R. E. Hummel	F L A
NGL-10-005-082	University of Florida	D. C. Goodman	F L A
NGR-10-005-089	University of Florida	R. T. Schneider	F L A
NGR-10-007-008	University of Miami	S. W. Fox	F L A
NGL-10-007-010	University of Miami	E. H. Man	F L A
NGR-10-007-052	University of Miami	K. Harada	F L A
NGR-10-007-054	University of Miami	G. Mueller	F L A
NGL-10-007-067	University of Miami	F. D. Kohler	F L A
NGR-10-007-068	University of Miami	F. D. Kohler
NGR-10-007-070	University of Miami	M. L. Harvey	F L A
NGR-10-008-005	University of South Florida	H. K. E. Wurmb	F L A
NGR-10-008-019	University of South Florida	H. K. Eichhorn	F L A
NGR-10-019-001	Florida Technological University	H. N. Rexford	F L A
NGR-11-001-009	Emory University	V. P. Popovic	G A
NGR-11-001-012	Emory University	B. W. Robinson	G A
NGR-11-001-016	Emory University	G. H. Bourne	G A
NGR-11-001-031	Emory University	S. W. Gray	G A
NGR-11-002-004	Georgia Institute of Technology	H. D. Edwards	G A
NGL-11-002-005	Georgia Institute of Technology	J. A. Knight	G A
NGL-11-002-018	Georgia Institute of Technology	G A
		K. Picha, V. Crawford
NGL-11-002-062	Georgia Institute of Technology	A. Ben Huang	G A
NGR-11-002-068	Georgia Institute of Technology	J. D. Clement	G A
NGR-11-002-081	Georgia Institute of Technology	V. Crawford	G A
NGR-11-002-083	Georgia Institute of Technology	B. T. Zinn	G A
NGR-11-002-085	Georgia Institute of Technology	B. T. Zinn	G A
NGR-11-002-096	Georgia Institute of Technology	G A
NGR-11-002-101	Georgia Institute of Technology	I. E. Perlin	G A
NGR-11-003-021	University of Georgia	D. R. Tompkins	G A
NGR-12-001-002	University of Hawaii	K. Watanabe	H A W
NGR-12-001-011	University of Hawaii	J. T. Jefferies	H A W
NGL-12-001-042	University of Hawaii	S. M. Siegel	H A W
NGR-12-001-046	University of Hawaii	W. W. Peterson	H A W
NGR-12-001-053	University of Hawaii	S. M. Siegel	H A W
NGR-12-001-057	University of Hawaii	J. T. Jefferies	H A W

NGL-14-001-001	University of Chicago	E. N. Parker	I L L
NGR-14-001-005	University of Chicago	P. Meyer	I L L
NGL-14-001-006	University of Chicago	J. A. Simpson	I L L
NGR-14-001-008	University of Chicago	T. Fujita	I L L
NGL-14-001-009	University of Chicago	M. H. Cohen	I L L
NGR-14-001-010	University of Chicago	E. Anders	I L L
NGL-14-001-013	University of Chicago	C. O. Hines	I L L
NGR-14-001-054	University of Chicago	W. A. Hiltner	I L L
NGR-14-001-060	University of Chicago	C. R. O'Dell	I L L
NGR-14-001-103	University of Chicago	J. E. Lamport	I L L
NGR-14-001-128	University of Chicago	A. Turkevich	I L L
NGR-14-001-135	University of Chicago	A. L. Turkeviuh	I L L
NGR-14-004-028	Illinois Institute of Technology	Z. Lavan	I L L
NGR-14-005-002	University of Illinois (Urbana)	E. C. Yeh	I L L
NGR-14-005-009	University of Illinois (Urbana)	R. Mittra	I L L
NGR-14-005-013	University of Illinois (Urbana)	S. A. Bowhill	I L L
NGR-14-005-025	University of Illinois (Urbana)	J. D. Morrow	I L L
NGL-14-005-074	University of Illinois (Urbana)	H. W. Ades	I L L
NGR-14-005-088	University of Illinois (Urbana)	G. C. McVittie	I L L
NGR-14-005-103	University of Illinois (Urbana)	J. C. Chato	I L L
NGR-14-005-111	University of Illinois (Urbana)	M. L Babcock	I L L
NGR-14-005-138	University of Illinois (Urbana)	A. M. Clausing	I L L
NGR-14-005-140	University of Illinois (Urbana)	W. L. Chow	I L L
NGR-14-007-011	Northwestern University	G. Herrmann	I L L
NGR-14-007-016	Northwestern University	J. A. Hynek	I L L
NGR-14-007-027	Northwestern University	E. H. T. Whitten	I L L
NGR-14-007-041	Northwestern University	S. S. Huang	I L L
NGR-14-007-048	Northwestern University	K. G. Henize	I L L
NGL-14-007-058	Northwestern University	J. A. D. Copper	I L L
NGR-14-007-062	Northwestern University	A. H. Rubenstein	I L L
NGR-14-007-067	Northwestern University	G. Herrmann	I L L
NGR-14-007-069	Northwestern University	K. G. Henize	I L L
NGR-14-007-071	Northwestern University	D. Mintzer	I L L
NGR-14-007-081	Northwestern University	J. T. Waber	I L L
NGR-14-008-002	Southern Illinois University	J. H. Lauchner	I L L
NGR-14-008-019	Southern Illinois University	P. K. Davis	I L L
NGR-14-012-004	University of Illinois (Chicago)	J. H. Boyer	I L L
NGL-14-012-012	University of Illinois (Chicago)	P. R. Nachtsheim	I L L
NGR-14-019-002	Bradley University	J. W. McNabb	I L L
NGL-15-003-002	Indiana University	H. R. Johnson	I N D
NGR-15-003-007	Indiana University	W. D. Neff	I N D
NGR-15-003-053	Indiana University	S. Mizell	I N D
NGR-15-003-060	Indiana University	E. Hopf	I N D
NGR-15-003-064	Indiana University	J. R. Thompson	I N D
NGR-15-003-066	Indiana University	R. W. Campbell	I N D
NGR-15-003-077	Indiana University	W. D. Neff	I N D
NGL-15-004-001	University of Notre Dame	G. F. D'Alelio	I N D
NGR-15-004-017	University of Notre Dame	T. J. Starr	I N D
NGL-15-004-026	University of Notre Dame	J. L. Massey	I N D
NGR-15-004-028	University of Notre Dame	G. F. Dalelio	I N D
NGR-15-005-003	Purdue University	K. L. Andrew	I N D
NGR-15-005-006	Purdue University	J. C. Lindenlaub	I N D
NGR-15-005-021	Purdue University	F. N. Andrews	I N D
NGR-15-005-022	Purdue University	R. Oldenburger	I N D
NGR-15-005-039	Purdue University	W. Gautschi	I N D
NGR-15-005-058	Purdue University	B. A. Reese	I N D
NGR-15-005-069	Purdue University	J. Modrey	I N D
NGR-15-005-077	Purdue University	D. E. Abbott	I N D
NGR-15-005-085	Purdue University	R. W. Stanley	I N D
NGR-15-005-087	Purdue University		I N D
NGR-15-005-094	Purdue University	J. G. Skifstad	I N D
NGR-15-005-106	Purdue University	P. A. Wintz	I N D
NGR-15-008-004	Rose Polytechnic Institute	H. A. Sabbagh	I N D
NGR-15-009-001	Ball State University	E. Montague	I N D
NGL-16-001-002	University of Iowa	J. A. Van Allen	I O W A
NGR-16-001-031	University of Iowa	C. C. Wunder	I O W A
NGR-16-001-043	University of Iowa	D. C. Montgomery	I O W A
		& D. A. Gurnett	
NGR-16-002-005	Iowa State University	G. K. Serovy	I O W A
NGL-17-001-005	Kansas State University	J. L. Brown	K A N
NGL-17-001-026	Kansas State University	D. Williams	K A N
NGR-17-001-034	Kansas State University	L. T. Fan	K A N
NGR-17-002-042	University of Kansas	R. H. Himes	K A N
NGR-17-002-047	University of Kansas	K. H. Lenzen	K A N
NGR-17-002-050	University of Kansas	E. J. Zeller	K A N S
NGR-17-002-053	University of Kansas	G. L. Kelly	K A N
NGR-17-004-019	University of Kansas	R. M. Haralick	K A N
NGL-18-001-003	University of Kentucky	K. O. Lange	K Y
NGR-18-001-017	University of Kentucky	D. C. Leigh	K Y
NGR-18-001-020	University of Kentucky	O. W. Dillon	K Y
NGR-18-001-026	University of Kentucky	R. C. Birkebak	K Y
NGR-18-001-038	University of Kentucky	M. H. Leipold	K Y
NGR-18-001-042	University of Kentucky	M. H. Leipold	K Y
NGL-18-002-005	University of Louisville	W. J. McGlothlin	K Y
NGR-18-002-008	University of Louisville	E. A. Alluisi	K Y
NGR-19-001-012	Louisiana State University (Baton Rouge)		L A
		R. W. Huggett, K. Pinkau	
NGR-19-001-016	Louisiana State University (Baton Rouge)	R. W. Pike	L A
NGR-19-001-059	Louisiana State University (Baton Rouge)	R. W. Pike	L A
NGR-19-001-068	Louisiana State University (Baton Rouge)		L A
		E. J. Dantin	
NGR-19-002-027	Tulane University	A. M. Hermann	L A
NGR-19-003-003	Louisiana Polytechnic Institute	T. Williams	L A
NGR-19-006-001	Northeast Louisiana State College	D. E. Dupree	L A
NGL-20-006-001	University of Maine (Orono)	T. H. Curry	M E
NGR-21-001-001	Johns Hopkins University	W. G. Fastie	M D
NGR-21-001-002	Johns Hopkins University	H. W. Moos	M D
NGR-21-001-035	Johns Hopkins University	S. A. Weinstein	M D
NGR-21-001-037	Johns Hopkins University	H. P. Eugster	M D
NGR-21-001-043	Johns Hopkins University	H. H. Seliger	M D
NGR-21-001-069	Johns Hopkins University	J. F. Dardano	M D
NGR-21-001-073	Johns Hopkins University	A. Chapanis	M D
NGR-21-002-002	University of Maryland	H. Laster, E. Opik	M D
NGR-21-002-003	University of Maryland	R. W. Krauss	M D
NGR-21-002-005	Unversity of Maryland	D. A. Tidman	M D
NGR-21-002-006	University of Maryland	T. D. Wilkerson	M D
NGR-21-002-007	University of Maryland	T. D. Wilkerson	M D
NGL-21-002-008	University of Maryland	W. C. Rheinboldt	M D
NGR-21-002-010	University of Maryland	J. Weber	M D
NGR-21-002-026	University of Maryland	R. G. Grenell	M D
NGR-21-002-029	University of Maryland	W. C. Erickson	M D
NGL-21-002-033	University of Maryland	H. Laster	M D
NGR-21-002-040	University of Maryland	R. G. Grenell	M D
NGL-21-002-053	University of Maryland	R. B. Beckmann	M D
NGR-21-002-057	University of Maryland	R. T. Bettinger	M D
NGR-21-002-059	University of Maryland E. R. Lippincott, Y. T. Pratt		M D
NGR-21-002-065	University of Maryland	A. M. Decker	M D
NGR-21-002-066	University of Maryland	J. A. Earl	M D

NGR-21-002-073	University of Maryland	H. R. Griem	MD
NGR-21-002-096	University of Maryland	R. T. Bettinger	MD
NGR-21-002-109	University of Maryland	C. O. Alley	MD
NGR-21-002-167	University of Maryland	T. D. Wilkerson	MD
NGR-21-002-175	University of Maryland	W. J. Bailey	MD
NGR-21-002-197	University of Maryland	Y. Chu	MD
NGR-21-002-206	University of Maryland	Y. Chu	MD
NGR-21-002-211	University of Maryland	S. K. Poultney	MD
NGR-21-002-214	University of Maryland	J. P. Richard	MD
NGR-21-002-218	University of Maryland	C. O. Alley	MD
NGR-21-007-004	University of Maryland	J. V. Brady	MD
NGR-21-012-001	Woodstock College	M. J. Bielefeld	MD
NGR-21-023-001	Columbia Union College	E. I. Mohr	MD
NGR-21-025-001	Morgan State College		MD
NGR-22-004-018	Boston University	E. T. Angelakos	MASS
NGR-22-005-001	Brandeis University	N. O. Kaplan	MASS
NGR-22-005-025	Brandeis University	J. W. Senders	MASS
NGR-22-007-003	Harvard University	W. H. Sweet	MASS
NGL-22-007-006	Harvard University	L. Goldberg	MASS
NGL-22-007-012	Harvard University	B. Budiansky	MASS
NGR-22-007-019	Harvard University	W. H. Abelman, L. E. Earley	MASS
NGR-22-007-021	Harvard University	G. R. Huguenin	MASS
NGL-22-007-053	Harvard University	W. A. Burgess	MASS
NGR-22-007-054	Harvard University	N. F. Ramsey	MASS
NGR-22-007-056	Harvard University	R. W. P. King	MASS
NGR-22-007-059	Harvard University	K. R. Porter	MASS
NGR-22-007-061	Harvard University	L. Goldberg	MASS
NGR-22-007-068	Harvard University	A. E. Bryson	MASS
NGL-22-007-069	Harvard University	E. S. Barghoorn	MASS
NGR-22-007-070	Harvard University	R. A. McFarland	MASS
NGR-22-007-096	Harvard University	F. R. Ervin	MASS
NGL-22-007-101	Harvard University	D. M. Hegsted	MASS
NGR-22-007-103	Harvard University	D. C. Noble	MASS
NGR-22-007-117	Harvard University	N. Bloembergen	MASS
NGR-22-007-124	Harvard University	R. A. Bauer	MASS
NGR-22-007-126	Harvard University	P. S. Pershan	MASS
NGR-22-007-136	Harvard University	A. Dalgarno	MASS
NGR-22-007-137	Harvard University	R. T. Kelleher	MASS
NGR-22-007-138	Harvard University	R. J. Herrnstein	MASS
NGR-22-007-143	Harvard University	Y. C. Ho	MASS
NGR-22-007-154	Harvard University	R. A. McFarland	MASS
NGR-22-007-163	Harvard University	R. A. Bauer	MASS
NGR-22-009-002	Massachusetts Institute of Technology	T. B. Sheridan	MASS
NGL-22-009-003	Massachusetts Institute of Technology	N. J. Grant	MASS
NGR-22-009-005	Massachusetts Institute of Technology	K. Biemann	MASS
NGR-22-009-007	Massachusetts Institute of Technology	J. Reintjes	MASS
NGR-22-009-010	Massachusetts Institute of Technology	W. R. Markey	MASS
NGL-22-009-012	Massachusetts Institute of Technology	A. Javin	MASS
NGL-22-009-013	Massachusetts Institute of Technology	R. G. Gallager	MASS
NGR-22-009-014	Massachusetts Institute of Technology	H. H. Woodson, H. A. Haus, J. R. Melcher	MASS
NGR-22-009-015	Massachusetts Institute of Technology	H. S. Bridge	MASS
NGL-22-009-016	Massachusetts Institute of Technology	A. H. Barrett	MASS
NGR-22-009-018	Massachusetts Institute of Technology	F. O. Schmitt	MASS
NGL-22-009-019	Massachusetts Institute of Technology	J. V. Harrington	MASS
NGR-22-009-059	Massachusetts Institute of Technology	Z. M. Elias	MASS
NGR-22-009-091	Massachusetts Institute of Technology	R. E. Stickney	MASS
NGR-22-009-121	Massachusetts Institute of Technology	L. Trilling	MASS
NGR-22-009-123	Massachusetts Institute of Technology	F. Press	MASS
NGL-22-009-124	Massachusetts Institute of Technology	G. C. Newton	MASS
NGR-22-009-125	Massachusetts Institute of Technology	H. C. Gatos	MASS
NGR-22-009-131	Massachusetts Institute of Technology	G. Fiocco	MASS
NGL-22-009-156	Massachusetts Institute of Technology	J. L. Meiry, Y. T. Li	MASS
NGL-22-009-163	Massachusetts Institute of Technology	R. P. Rafuse	MASS
NGR-22-009-167	Massachusetts Institute of Technology	G. R. Harrison	MASS
NGR-22-009-187	Massachusetts Institute of Technology	J. Watkins	MASS
NGR-22-009-229	Massachusetts Institute of Technology	W. R. Markey	MASS
NGR-22-009-234	Massachusetts Institute of Technology	R. D. Thornton	MASS
NGR-22-009-240	Massachusetts Institute of Technology	A. Javan	MASS
NGR-22-009-249	Massachusetts Institute of Technology	G. B. Benedek	MASS
NGR-22-009-257	Massachusetts Institute of Technology	D. W. Strangway	MASS
NGR-22-009-262	Massachusetts Institute of Technology	W. R. Markey	MASS
NGR-22-009-269	Massachusetts Institute of Technology	J. A. Fay	MASS
NGR-22-009-272	Massachusetts Institute of Technology	R. J. Wurtman	MASS
NGR-22-009-277	Massachusetts Institute of Technology	A. Rich	MASS
NGR-22-009-289	Massachusetts Institute of Technology	H. S. Bridge	MASS
NGR-22-009-303	Massachusetts Institute of Technology	N. D. Ham	MASS
NGL-22-009-304	Massachusetts Institute of Technology	H. J. Zimmerman	MASS
NGL-22-009-308	Massachusetts Institute of Technology	H. L. Teuber	MASS
NGL-22-009-309	Massachusetts Institute of Technology	Z. S. Zannetos	MASS
NGR-22-009-311	Massachusetts Institute of Technology	J. P. Vinti	MASS
NGR-22-009-312	Massachusetts Institute of Technology	L. R. Young	MASS
NGR-22-009-329	Massachusetts Institute of Technology	F. Press	MASS
NGR-22-009-334	Massachusetts Institute of Technology	A. D. Pierce	MASS
NGR-22-009-335	Massachusetts Institute of Technology	M. O. Scully	MASS
NGR-22-009-337	Massachusetts Institute of Technology	P. Penfield	MASS
NGR-22-009-339	Massachusetts Institute of Technology	E. A. Witmer	MASS
NGR-22-009-350	Massachusetts Institute of Technology	T. B. McCord	MASS
NGR-22-009-351	Massachusetts Institute of Technology	L. G. Bromwell	MASS
NGR-22-009-359	Massachusetts Institute of Technology	R. Weiss	MASS
NGR-22-009-372	Massachusetts Institute of Technology	H. S. Bridge	MASS
NGR-22-009-378	Massachusetts Institute of Technology	J. Fay, J. Keck	MASS
NGR-22-009-383	Massachusetts Institute of Technology	J. L. Kerrebrock	MASS
NGR-22-009-393	Massachusetts Institute of Technology	A. Evans	MASS
NGL-22-009-418	Massachusetts Institute of Technology	D. J. Epstein	MASS
NGR-22-009-420	Massachusetts Institute of Technology		MASS
NGR-22-009-424	Massachusetts Institute of Technology	A. Rich	MASS
NGR-22-010-012	University of Massachusetts	R. V. Monopoli	MASS
NGR-22-010-018	University of Massachusetts	R. V. Monopoli	MASS
NGR-22-010-023	University of Massachusetts	W. M. Irvine	MASS
NGL-22-010-029	University of Massachusetts	J. F. Brandts	MASS
NGR-22-010-039	University of Massachusetts	G. R. Huguenin	MASS
NGR-22-010-041	University of Massachusetts	J. R. Strong	MASS

NGR-22-010-042	University of Massachusetts	J. Strong	MASS
NGR-22-011-007	Northeastern University W. B. Nowak, B. L. Cochrun		MASS
NGR-22-011-020	Northeastern University	J. Warga	MASS
NGL-22-011-024	Northeastern University	B. L. Cochrun	MASS
NGR-22-011-025	Northeastern University	K. Weiss	MASS
NGR-22-011-042	Northeastern University	R. Madden	MASS
NGR-22-011-051	Northeastern University	C. H. Perry	MASS
NGR-22-012-006	Tufts University	D. H. Spodick	MASS
NGR-22-017-006	Worcester Polytechnic Institute	I. Zwiebel	MASS
NGR-22-017-008	Worcester Polytechnic Institute	A. H. Weiss	MASS
NGR-22-091-002	College of the Holy Cross	R. C. Gunter	MASS
NGR-23-002-001	University of Detroit	A. Szutka	MICH
NGR-23-004-001	Michigan State University	L. G. Augenstein	MICH
NGR-23-004-041	Michigan State University	C. Martin	MICH
NGR-23-004-056	Michigan State University	C. R. Gruhn	MICH
NGR-23-005-001	University of Michigan	F. J. Beutler	MICH
NGR-23-005-003	University of Michigan	J. A. Nicholls	MICH
NGR-23-005-004	University of Michigan	C. Kikuchi	MICH
NGR-23-005-010	University of Michigan	S. K. Clark	MICH
NGR-23-005-015	University of Michigan	A. Nagy	MICH
NGR-23-005-017	University of Michigan	F. T. Haddock	MICH
NGR-23-005-041	University of Michigan	H. C. Early	MICH
NGR-23-005-062	University of Michigan	J. E. Rowe	MICH
NGR-23-005-094	University of Michigan	V. C. Liu	MICH
NGL-23-005-183	University of Michigan	G. I. Haddad	MICH
	H. H. Woodson, H. A. Haus, J. R. Melcher		
NGR-23-005-185	University of Michigan	J. R. P. French	MICH
NGR-23-005-201	University of Michigan	R. von Baumgarten	MICH
NGR-23-005-275	University of Michigan	O. C. Mohler	MICH
NGR-23-005-285	University of Michigan	B. Arden	MICH
NGR-23-005-321	University of Michigan	F. T. Haddock	MICH
NGR-23-005-314	University of Michigan	F. T. Haddock	MICH
NGR-23-005-320	University of Michigan	U. Samir	MICH
NGR-23-006-047	Wayne State University	C. N. DeSilva	MICH
NGR-23-007-001	Michigan Technological University	C. E. Work	MICH
NGR-23-010-004	Western Michigan University	R. R. Hutchinson	MICH
NGR-24-001-002	Concordia College	H. R. Homann	MINN
NGL-24-005-008	University of Minnesota	J. R. Winckler, E. P. Ney	MINN
NGL-24-005-009	University of Minnesota	A. O. C. Nier	MINN
NGR-24-005-050	University of Minnesota	W. R. Webber,	MINN
	C. S. Waddington		
NGR-24-005-054	University of Minnesota	F. M. Swain	MINN
NGR-24-005-070	University of Minnesota	C. C. Hsiao	MINN
NGR-24-005-091	University of Minnesota	R. J. Goldstein	MINN
NGR-24-005-095	University of Minnesota	R. Plunkett	MINN
NGR-24-005-111	University of Minnesota	J. R. Winckler	MINN
NGR-24-005-176	University of Minnesota	P. Kellogg	MINN
NGR-24-005-180	University of Minnesota	L. J. Cahill	MINN
NGR-24-005-187	University of Minnesota	A. O. C. Nier	MINN
NGR-25-001-004	Mississippi State University	R. G. Tischer	MISS
NGR-25-001-008	Mississippi State University	G. E. Jones	MISS
NGL-25-001-028	Mississippi State University	C. W. Bouchillon	MISS
NGR-25-001-032	Mississippi State University	D. L. Murphree	MISS
NGR-25-002-015	University of Mississippi	H. T. Milhorn	MISS
NGR-26-001-006	University of Missouri (Kansas City)	P. J. Bryant	MO
NGR-26-003-023	University of Missouri (Columbia)	R. L. Wixon	MO
NGR-26-003-026	University of Missouri (Rolla)	R. D. Rechtier	MO
NGR-26-003-037	University of Missouri (Rolla)	E. C. Bertnolli	MO
NGR-26-003-044	University of Missouri (Rolla)	T. L. Noack	MO
NGL-26-004-003	University of Missouri (Columbia)	Ward J. Haas	MO
NGR-26-004-011	University of Missouri (Columbia)	C. W. Gehrke	MO
NGL-26-004-021	University of Missouri (Columbia)	X. J. Musacchia	MO
NGR-26-004-025	University of Missouri (Columbia)	F. E. South	MO
NGL-26-006-016	St. Louis University	F. C. Bates	
NGR-26-006-021	Saint Louis University	B. H. Ulrich Jr.	MO
NGR-26-006-024	Saint Louis University	D. S. Ousterhout	MO
NGR-26-008-001	Washington University (St. Louis)		MO
	J. Klarmann, M. W. Friedlander		
NGR-26-008-003	Washington University (St. Louis) M. L. Weidenbaum		MO
NGR-26-008-006	Washington University (St. Louis)	G. E. Pake	MO
NGR-26-008-042	Washington University (St. Louis)	J. Klarmann	MO
NGR-26-008-043	Washington University (St. Louis)	R. M. Walker	MO
NGR-26-010-001	University of Missouri (St. Louis)	D. T. Haimo	MO
NGR-27-001-001	Montana State University	I. E. Dayton	MONT
NGR-27-001-035	Montana State University	K. Nordtvedt	MONT
NGR-29-001-008	University of Nevada (Reno)	P. Atlick	NEV
NGR-30-001-001	Dartmouth College	C. J. Lyon	N H
NGR-30-001-011	Dartmouth College	B. U. O. Sonnerup	N H
NGR-30-002-008	University of New Hampshire	R. E. Houston	N H
NGR-30-002-010	University of New Hampshire	R. A. Kaufman	N H
NGR-30-002-021	University of New Hampshire	E. L. Chupp	N H
NGR-30-002-028	University of New Hampshire	L. J. Cahill	N H
NGR-30-002-056	University of New Hampshire	C. K. Taft	N H
NGR-31-001-001	Princeton University	M. Schwarzschild	N J
NGL-31-001-007	Princeton University	L. Spitzer	N J
NGR-31-001-025	Princeton University	W. R. Schowalter	N J
NGR-31-001-044	Princeton University	L. Spitzer	N J
NGR-31-001-059	Princeton University	E. Dowell	N J
NGR-31-001-068	Princeton University	L. D. Davisson	N J
NGR-31-001-074	Princeton University	C. L. Mellor	N J
NGR-31-001-093	Princeton University	R. B. Hargraves	N J
NGR-31-001-103	Princeton University	S. H. Lam	N J
NGR-31-001-109	Princeton University	M. Summerfield	N J
NGR-31-001-119	Princeton University	W. D. Hayes	N J
NGR-31-001-129	Princeton University	I. Glassman	N J
NGR-31-001-132	Princeton University	A. W. Lo	N J
NGR-31-001-142	Princeton University	R. E. Danielson	N J
NGR-31-001-145	Princeton University	C. S. Pittendrigh	N J
NGR-31-001-146	Princeton University	E. H. Dowell	N J
NGR-31-001-151	Princeton University	A. J. Kelly	N J
NGR-31-001-155	Princeton University	D. T. Harrje	N J
NGR-31-003-014	Stevens Institute of Technology	R. F. McAlevy	N J
NGL-31-003-020	Stevens Institute of Technology	H. Meissner	N J
NGR-31-003-050	Stevens Institute of Technology	G. J. Herskowitz	N J
NGR-31-003-066	Stevens Institute of Technology	E. C. Ney	N J
NGR-31-006-006	Fairleigh Dickinson University	K. D. Moeller	N J
NGR-31-009-004	Newark College of Engineering	P. Hrycak	N J
NGR-31-011-002	New Jersey College of Medicine & Dentistry		N J
NGL-32-003-001	New Mexico State University	C. W. Tombough	NMEX
NGL-32-003-027	New Mexico State University	J. E. Weiss	NMEX
NGR-32-004-001	University of New Mexico	A. Erteza	NMEX
NGR-32-004-002	University of New Mexico	W. W. Grannemann	NMEX
NGL-32-004-011	University of New Mexico	W. Elston	NMEX
NGR-32-004-026	University of New Mexico	C. G. Richards	NMEX
NGL-32-004-042	University of New Mexico	W. W. Grannemann	NMEX
NGL-33-001-001	Adelphi University	R. Genberg	N Y
NGR-33-001-019	Adelphi University	R. Genberg	N Y
NGR-33-006-007	Polytechnic Institute of Brooklyn	H. J. Juretschke	N Y

NGR-33-006-020	Polytechnic Institute of Brooklyn	K. K. Clarke	N	Y
NGR-33-006-040	Polytechnic Institute of Brooklyn	M. Schwartz	N	Y
NGR-33-006-042	Polytechnic Institute of Brooklyn	J. J. Bongiorno	N	Y
NGR-33-006-047	Polytechnc Institute of Brooklyn	S. Gross	N	Y
NGR-33-006-053	Polytechnic Institute of Brooklyn	A. C. McKellar	N	Y
NGR-33-007-034	Clarkson College of Technology	L. C. Barrett	N	Y
NGR-33-007-061	Clarkson College of Technology	C. W. Haines	N	Y
NGR-33-007-074	Clarkson College of Technology	H. H. G. Jellinek	N	Y
NGL-33-007-075	Clarkson College of Technology	W. A. Thorton	N Y	
NGR-33-008-009	Columbia University	R. Novick	N	Y
NGR-33-008-012	Columbia University		N	Y
	H. M. Foley, R. Novick, L. Woltjer, P. W. Gast			
NGR-33-008-061	Columbia University	P. W. Gast	N	Y
NGR-33-008-090	Columbia University	C. C. Halkias	N	Y
NGR-33-008-098	Columbia University	M. B. Friedman	N	Y
NGR-33-008-102	Columbia University	E. J. Ott	N	Y
NGR-33-008-118	Columbia University	P. N. Borsky	N	Y
NGR-33-010-013	Cornell University	M. Alexander	N	Y
NGR-33-010-029	Cornell University	L. H. Germer	N	Y
NGR-33-010-039	Cornell University	P. P. Van Riper	N	Y
NGR-33-010-042	Cornell University	F. K. Moore	N	Y
NGL-33-010-047	Cornell University	P. R. McIsaac	N	Y
NGR-33-010-051	Cornell University	C. L. Tang	N	Y
NGL-33-010-054	Cornell University	A. R. Seebass	N	Y
NGR-33-010-064	Cornell University	T. A. Cool	N	Y
NGR-33-010-070	Cornell University	R. H. Gallagher	N	Y
NGR-33-010-071	Cornell University	H. N. McManus	N	Y
NGR-33-010-074	Cornell University	F. D. McLeod	N	Y
NGR-33-010-082	Cornell University	C. Sagan	N	Y
NGR-33-010-096	Cornell University	C. Sagan	N	Y
NGR-33-010-098	Cornell University	C. Sagan	N	Y
NGR-33-012-009	Fordham University	W. C. Corning	N	Y
NGR-33-013-009	City College of New York	R. Shinner	N	Y
NGR-33-013-017	City College of New York	M. Kolodney	N	Y
NGR-33-013-025	City College of New York		N	Y
	S. M. Chen			
NGR-33-013-029	City College of New York		N	Y
	R. Pfeffer			
NGR-33-013-034	City College of New York		N	Y
	C. M. Tchen			
NGR-33-015-002	State University of New York (Buffalo) J. F. Danielli		N	Y
NGR-33-015-013	State University of New York (Stony Brook)		N	Y
	R. P. Tewarson			
NGR-33-015-016	State University of New York (Buffalo)		N	Y
	J. Danielli			
NGL-33-015-035	State University of New York (Stony Brook)		N	Y
	L. L. Seigle			
NGR-33-015-036	State University of New York (Stony Brook)		N	Y
	Y. H. Koa			
NGR-33-015-061	State University of New York (Buffalo) R. G. Hunt		N	Y
NGR-33-015-068	State University of New York (Stony Brook)		N	Y
	G. W. Stroke			
NGR-33-015-082	State University of New York (Stony Brook)		N	Y
	O. A. Schaeffer			
NGR-33-015-085	State University of New York (Stony Brook)		N	Y
	F. F. Y. Wang			
NGR-33-016-003	New York University	R. C. Sahni	N	Y
NGL-33-016-013	New York University	J. E. Miller	N Y	
NGL-33-016-067	New York University	J. R. Ragazzini	N	Y

NGR-33-016-102	New York University	J. Post	N	Y
NGL-33-016-119	New York University	A. Ferri	N	Y
NGR-33-016-128	New York University	L. Arnold	N	Y
NGR-33-016-131	New York University	A. Ferri	N	Y
NGR-33-016-141	New York University	J. Werner	N	Y
NGR-33-016-149	New York University	A. Ferri	N	Y
NGL-33-018-003	Rensselaer Polytechnic Institute	S. E. Wiberley	N	Y
NGR-33-018-004	Rensselaer Polytechnic Institute	J. M. Greenberg	N	Y
NGL-33-018-007	Rensselaer Polytechnic Institute	P. Harteck	N	Y
NGL-33-018-053	Rensselaer Polytechnic Institute	F. A. White	N	Y
NGR-33-018-066	Rensselaer Polytechnic Institute	J. B. Hudson	N	Y
NGR-33-018-075	Rensselaer Polytechnic Institute	E. Holt	N	Y
NGR-33-018-086	Rensselaer Polytechnic Institute	P. Harteck	N	Y
NGL-33-018-091	Rensselaer Polytechnic Institute	S. Yerazunis	N	Y
NGR-33-019-002	University of Rochester	W. Vishniac	N	Y
NGL-33-019-003	University of Rochester	P. W. Baumeister	N	Y
NGR-33-019-014	University of Rochester	E. Kinnen	N	Y
NGR-33-019-058	University of Rochester	G. Cohen	N	Y
NGR-33-019-086	University of Rochester	D. H. Douglas	N	Y
NGR-33-019-087	University of Rochester	D. T. Blackstock	N	Y
NGR-33-022-004	Syracuse University	D. V. Keller	N	Y
NGR-33-022-023	Syracuse University	V. Weiss	N	Y
NGR-33-022-035	Syracuse University	M. E. Barzelay	N	Y
NGR-33-022-082	Syracuse University	D. S. Dosanjh	N	Y
NGL-33-022-090	Syracuse University	J. C. Honey	N	Y
NGR-33-022-091	Syracuse University	J. J. Zwislocki	N	Y
NGR-33-022-105	Syracuse University	V. Weiss	N	Y
NGR-33-022-108	Syracuse University	D. V. Keller	MASS	
NGR-33-023-018	Yeshiva University	A. G. W. Cameron	N	Y
NGR-33-023-032	Yeshiva University	E. D. Weitzman	N	Y
NGL-34-001-001	Duke University	T. G. Wilson	N	C
NGL-34-001-005	Duke University	J. B. Chaddock	N	C
NGR-34-001-019	Duke University	K. Schmidt-Koenig	N	C
NGR-34-002-017	North Carolina State University	W. H. Bennett	N	C
NGR-34-002-023	North Carolina State University	D. S. Grosch	N	C
NGR-34-002-032	North Carolina State University	H. Sagan	N	C
NGL-34-002-035	North Carolina State University	F. D. Hart	N	C
NGR-34-002-036	North Carolina State University	F. O. Smetana	N	C
NGR-34-002-038	North Carolina State University	F. J. Tischer	N	C
NGL-34-002-047	North Carolina State University	F. J. Tischer	N	C
NGR-34-002-048	North Carolina State University	H. A. Hassan	N	C
NGR-34-002-055	North Carolina State University	R. G. Pearson	N	C
NGL-34-002-061	North Carolina State University	L. A. Jones	N	C
NGR-34-002-072	North Carolina State University	L. A. Jones	N	C
NGR-34-002-073	North Carolina State University	M. A. Littlejohn	N	C
NGR-34-002-078	North Carolina State University	F. O. Smetana	N	C
NGR-34-002-082	North Carolina State University N. F. J. Matthews		N	C
NGR-34-002-085	North Carolina State University	J. S. Lee	N	C
NGR-34-002-086	North Carolina State University	R. W. Truitt	N	C
NGR-34-002-095	North Carolina State University	R. G. Pearson	N	C
NGR-34-002-108	North Carolina State University	C. R. Manning	N	C
NGR-34-003-021	University of North Carolina (Chapel Hill)		N	C
	H. A. Tyroler			
NGR-34-003-026	University of North Carolina (Chapel Hill)		N	C
	J. W. Hanson			
NGR-34-003-040	University of North Carolina (Chapel Hill)		N	C
	R. G. Faust			
NGR-36-001-010	University of Akron	R. Dubensky	OHIO	
NGR-36-003-033	Case Western Reserve University	J. F. Wallace	OHIO	

NGR-36-003-042	Case Western Reserve University		OHIO
	B. Reswick and H. Mergler		
NGR-36-003-054	Case Western Reserve University	J. L. Koenig	OHIO
NGR-36-003-064	Case Western Reserve University	S. Ostrach	OHIO
NGR-36-003-079	Case Western Reserve University	W. H. Ko	OHIO
NGL-36-003-088	Case Western Reserve University	S. Ostrach	OHIO
NGR-36-003-091	Case Western Reserve University	O. Ostrach	OHIO
NGR-36-003-094	Case Western Reserve University	L. Leonard	OHIO
NGR-36-003-100	Case Western Reserve University	A. R. Cooper	OHIO
NGR-36-003-139	Case Western Reserve University	E. Reshotko	OHIO
NGR-36-004-001	University of Cincinnati	P. Herget	OHIO
NGR-36-004-008	University of Cincinnati	Ti Yi Li H. Oguro	OHIO
NGR-36-004-013	University of Cincinnati	R. J. Kroll	OHIO
NGL-36-004-014	University of Cincinnati	R. P. Harrington	OHIO
NGR-36-004-030	University of Cincinnati	L. Meirovitch	OHIO
NGR-36-006-003	John Carroll University	J. Trivisonno	OHIO
NGL-36-007-001	Kent State University	J. W. Reed	OHIO
NGR-36-007-025	Kent State University	J. L. Fergason	OHIO
NGR-36-008-002	Ohio State University	C. A. Levis	OHIO
NGR-36-008-004	Ohio State University	H. S. Weiss	OHIO
NGR-36-008-005	Ohio State University	C. Levis	OHIO
NGR-36-008-041	Ohio State University	J. H. Dines,	OHIO
		L. B. Roberts	
NGL-36-008-051	Ohio State University	F. H. Beck	OHIO
NGR-36-008-076	Ohio State University	H. Hemand	OHIO
NGR-36-008-080	Ohio State University	C. A. Lewis	OHIO
NGR-36-008-093	Ohio State University	I. I. Mueller	OHIO
NGR-36-008-103	Ohio State University	W. W. Anderson	OHIO
NGL-36-008-106	Ohio State University	R. M. Nerem	OHIO
NGR-36-008-109	Ohio State University	C. D. Bailey	OHIO
NGR-36-008-117	Ohio State University	R. M. Nerem	OHIO
NGR-36-008-125	Ohio State University	S. K. Ghosh	OHIO
NGR-36-008-131	Ohio State University	B. E. Gatewood	OHIO
NGR-36-007-012	Ohio University	W-K Chen	OHIO
NGR-36-017-002	Bowling Green State University	I. I. Oster	OHIO
NGR-36-019-001	Hiram College	L. B. Shaffer	OHIO
NGR-36-022-001	Miami University	D. E. Cunningham	OHIO
NGR-36-025-001	Cleveland State University	K. J. Casper	OHIO
NGR-36-027-001	Case Western Reserve University	E. L. Glaser	OHIO
NGR-36-027-002	Case Western Reserve University	S. V. Radcliffe	OHIO
NGL-37-002-011	Oklahoma State University	V. S. Haneman	OKLA
NGL-37-003-026	University of Oklahoma	C. Riggs	OKLA
NGR-37-003-041	University of Oklahoma	D. M. Egle	OKLA
NGR-37-003-043	University of Oklahoma	M. L. Rasmussen	OKLA
NGR-38-002-013	Oregon State University	H. C. Curl	ORE
NGR-38-002-017	Oregon State University	R. Y. Morita	ORE
NGR-38-002-018	Oregon State University	S. E. Williamson	ORE
NGR-38-002-020	Oregon State University	R. A. Schmitt	ORE
NGL-38-002-032	Oregon State University	R. A. Schmitt	ORE
NGR-38-003-009	University of Oregon	D. P. Weill	ORE
NGL-38-003-010	University of Oregon	G. G. Goles	ORE
NGR-38-003-012	University of Oregon	A. R. McBirney	ORE
NGR-38-003-015	University of Oregon	J. Roman	ORE
NGR-39-002-011	Carnegie-Mellon University	J. J. Wolken	PA
NGR-39-002-023	Carnegie-Mellon University	J. L. Swedlow	PA
NGL-39-004-007	Drexel Institute of Technology	C. Gatlin	PA
NGR-39-004-013	Drexel Institute of Technology	P. C. Chou	PA
NGL-39-004-015	Drexel Institute of Technology	M. M. Labes	PA
NGL-39-004-020	Drexel Institute of Technology	W. Hagerty	PA
NGR-39-004-028	Drexel Institute of Technology	C. A. Silver	PA
NGR-39-006-001	Haverford College	L. C. Green	PA
NGR-39-007-007	Lehigh University	R. W. Kraft	PA
NGR-39-007-011	Lehigh University	F. Erdogan	PA
NGR-39-007-017	Lehigh University	A. Kalnins	PA
NGR-39-007-040	Lehigh University	R. P. Wei	PA
NGR-39-008-014	Carnegie-Mellon University	E. G. Haney	PA
NGR-39-009-002	Pennsylvania State University	W. J. Ross	PA
NGR-39-009-003	Pennsylvania State University	J. S. Nisbet	PA
NGR-39-009-008	Pennsylvania State University	E. C. Pollard	PA
NGL-39-009-010	Pennsylvania State University	D. P. Gold	PA
NGL-39-009-015	Pennsylvania State University	P. Ebaugh	PA
NGR-39-009-023	Pennsylvania State University	J. L. Shearer	PA
NGR-39-009-032	Pennsylvania State University	B. R. F. Kendall	PA
NGR-39-009-034	Pennsylvania State University	J. Marin	PA
NGR-39-009-077	Pennsylvania State University	G. M. Faeth	PA
NGR-39-009-095	Pennsylvania State University	R. G. Quinn	PA
NGR-39-009-111	Pennsylvania State University	B. W. McCormick	PA
NGR-39-009-121	Pennsylvania State University	G. Reethof	PA
NGR-39-009-123	Pennsylvania State University	A. J. Engel	PA
NGR-39-009-129	Pennsylvania State University	B. R. F. Kendall	PA
NGL-39-010-001	University of Pennsylvania	M. Altman	PA
NGR-39-010-002	University of Pennsylvania	J. O'M. Bockris	PA
NGR-39-010-087	University of Pennsylvania	F. Haber	PA
NGL-39-010-097	University of Pennsylvenia	C. J. Lambertsen	PA
NGR-39-010-101	University of Pennsylvania	B. S. P. Shen	PA
NGR-39-010-104	University of Pennsylvania	A. H. Brown	PA
NGL-39-011-002	University of Pittsburgh	D. Halliday	PA
NGL-39-011-013	University of Pittsburgh	W. L. Fite	PA
NGL-39-011-030	University of Pittsburgh	E. C. Zipf	PA
NGR-39-011-035	University of Pittsburgh	E. Gerjuoy	PA
NGR-39-011-039	University of Pittsburgh	W. G. Vogt	PA
NGR-39-011-067	University of Pittsburgh	G. R. Fitterer	PA
NGR-39-011-079	University of Pittsburgh	R. S. Dougall	PA
NGL-39-011-080	University of Pittsburgh	D. C. Stone	PA
NGR-39-011-083	University of Pittsburgh	T. M. Donahue	PA
NGR-39-011-085	University of Pittsburgh	B. W. Hapke	PA
NGR-39-011-096	University of Pittsburgh	E. J. Sternglass	PA
NGR-39-018-002	Bryn Mawr College	M. Yarczower	PA
NGR-39-087-001	Carnegie-Mellon University	M. L. Renard	PA
NGR-39-087-002	Carnegie-Mellon University	A. G. Milnes	PA
NGR-39-087-003	Carnegie-Mellon University	J. R. Low	PA
NGL-40-002-009	Brown University	P. T. Maeder	R I
NGR-40-002-012	Brown University	P. D. Richardson	R I
NGL-40-002-015	Brown University	J. P. LaSalle	R I
NGL-40-002-042	Brown University	G. S. Heller	R I
NGR-40-002-059	Brown University	E. A. Mason	R I
NGR-40-002-080	Brown University	C. Mylonas	R I
NGR-40-002-081	Brown University	T. A. Mutch	R I
NGR-40-002-082	Brown University	J. E. Savage	R I
NGR-40-005-002	Providence College	E. K. Gora	R I
NGR-41-001-016	Clemson University	T. G. Proctor	S C
NGR-41-002-003	University of South Carolina	J. R. Durig	S C
NGR-41-002-024	University of South Carolina	D. L. Rohlfing	S C
NGR-42-001-002	South Dakota School of Mines and Technology		S D
		C. L. Gruber	
NGL-42-001-004	South Dakota School of Mines and Technology		S D
NGR-43-001-003	University of Tennessee	W. K. Stair	TENN
NGL-43-001-006	University of Tennessee	N. M. Gailar	TENN

NGR-43-001-008	University of Tennessee	D. C. Bogue	TENN
NGL-43-001-021	University of Tennessee	C. O. Thomas	TENN
NGR-43-001-023	University of Tennessee	M. W. Milligan	TENN
NGL-43-001-056	University of Tennessee	F. M. Shofner	TENN
NGR-43-001-075	University of Tennessee	H. D. Gruschka	TENN
NGR-43-002-031	Vanderbilt University	C. E. Roos	TENN
NGR-43-002-032	Vanderbilt University	E. B. Shanks	TENN
NGR-43-003-007	Tennessee Technological University	R. Kinslow	TENN
NGR-43-010-001	East Tennessee State University	H. D. Powell	TENN
NGL-44-001-001	Texas A & M University	H. E. Whitmore	TEX
NGR-44-001-011	Texas A & M University	A. E. Cronk	TEX
NGR-44-001-031	Texas A&M University	T. J. Kozik	TEX
NGR-44-001-036	Texas A & M University	R. Thomas	TEX
NGL-44-001-044	Texas A & M University	J. A. Stricklin	TEX
NGR-44-001-067	Texas A&M University	R. E. Wainerdi	TEX
NGR-44-001-071	Texas A&M University	C. F. Kettleborough	TEX
NGR-44-001-081	Texas A&M University	J. R. Scoggins	TEX
NGR-44-001-097	Texas A&M University	W. B. Smith	TEX
NGR-44-003-001	Baylor University	P. Kellaway	TEX
NGR-44-003-031	Baylor University	R. Roessler	TEX
NGR-44-005-002	University of Houston	J. Oro and A. Zlatkis	TEX
NGL-44-005-021	University of Houston	J. R. Crump	TEX
NGR-44-005-022	University of Houston	A. F. Hildebrant	TEX
NGR-44-005-041	University of Houston	C. Goodman	TEX
NGR-44-005-065	Universty of Houston	C. Dalton	TEX
NGL-44-005-084	University of Houston	C. J. Huang	TEX
NGR-44-005-090	University of Houston	C. J. Huang	TEX
NGR-44-005-091	University of Houston	R. S. Becker	TEX
NGR-44-005-096	University of Houston	M. Eisner	TEX
NGR-44-005-098	University of Houston	H. P. Decell	TEX
NGR-44-005-102	University of Houston	J. Oro	TEX
NGL-44-006-001	Rice University	F. R. Brotzen	TEX
NGR-44-006-012	Rice University	F. C. Michel, A. J. Dessler	TEX
NGL-44-006-033	Rice University	A. J. Chapman,	TEX
NGR-44-006-065	Rice University	F. J. Low	TEX
NGR-44-006-088	Rice University	R. B. McLellan	TEX
NGR-44-006-089	Rice University	A. Miele	TEX
NGR-44-006-105	Rice University	J. A. S. Adams	TEX
NGR-44-007-004	Southern Methodist University	H. A. Blum	TEX
NGL-44-007-006	Southern Methodist University	J. C. Denton	TEX
NGR-44-007-027	Southern Methodist University	S. C. Gupta	TEX
NGR-44-007-028	Southern Methodist University	J. E. Walsh	TEX
NGR-44-007-037	Southern Methodist University	S. C. Gupta	TEX
NGR-44-007-042	Southern Methodist University	T. L. Chu	TEX
NGR-44-009-008	Texas Christian University	S. B. Sells	TEX
NGR-44-009-018	Texas Christian University	M. D. Arnoult	TEX
NGR-44-011-026	Texas Technological College	R. D. Shelton	TEX
NGR-44-011-031	Texas Technological College	H. F. Martz	TEX
NGR-44-012-003	University of Texas Southwestern Medical School		TEX
		P. O'B. Montgomery	
NGL-44-012-006	University of Texas (Austin)	A. E. Straiton	TEX
NGR-44-012-008	University of Texas (Austin)	B. D. Tapley	TEX
NGR-44-012-020	University of Texas (Austin)	L. C. Reese	TEX
NGL-44-012-043	University of Texas (Austin)	W. H. Hartwig	TEX
NGR-44-012-045	University of Texas (Austin)	J. H. Mackin	TEX
NGR-44-012-046	University of Texas (Austin)	B. D. Tapley	TEX
NGR-44-012-055	University of Texas (Austin)	J. N. Douglas	TEX
NGR-44-012-088	University of Texas (Austin)	B. Fruchter	TEX
NGR-44-012-104	University of Texas (Austin)	W. H. Hartwig	TEX
NGR-44-012-132	University of Texas (Austin)	V. Szebehely	TEX
NGR-44-012-136	University of Texas (Austin)	B. D. Tapley	TEX
NGR-44-012-144	University of Texas (Austin)	C. V. Ramamoorthy	TEX
NGR-44-013-001	Texas Woman's University	P. B. Mack	TEX
NGR-44-033-001	Prairie View A&M College	I. V. Nelson	TEX
NGR-45-001-011	Brigham Young University	D. E. Jones	UTAH
NGR-45-001-026	Brigham Young University	P. O. Berrett	UTAH
NGR-45-002-008	Utah State University	F. B. Salisbury	UTAH
NGR-45-002-014	Utah State University	E. W. Vendell	UTAH
NGL-45-003-019	University of Utah	N. W. Ryan	UTAH
NGL-45-003-025	University of Utah	F. L. Staffanson	UTAH
NGR-45-003-027	University of Utah	R. W. Grow	UTAH
NGR-45-003-037	University of Utah	M. L. Williams	UTAH
NGR-45-003-038	University of Utah	W. J. Coles	UTAH
NGR-45-003-043	University of Utah	E. A. Shneour	UTAH
NGR-45-003-050	University of Utah	G. A. Flandro	UTAH
NGL-46-001-008	University of Vermont	C. D. Cook	VT
NGR-47-002-005	Virginia Commonwealth University	W. T. Ham	VA
NGR-47-002-018	Virginia Commonwealth University	S. W. Lippincott	VA
NGR-47-002-020	Virginia Commonwealth University	H. P. Dalton	VA
NGR-47-003-007	Old Dominion University	G. L. Goglia	VA
NGR-47-003-008	Old Dominion University	R. L. Williams	VA
NGR-47-003-012	Old Dominion University	R. Y. K. Cheng	VA
NGR-47-003-015	Old Dominion University	W. D. Stanley	VA
NGL-47-004-006	Virginia Polytechnic Institute		VA
		F. W. Bull, J. A. Jacobs	
NGR-47-004-016	Virginia Polytechnic Institute	J. P. Wightman	VA
NGR-47-004-018	Virginia Polytechnic Institute	W. E. C. Moore	VA
NGR-47-004-024	Virginia Polytechnic Institute	H. L. Wood	VA
NGR-47-004-030	Virginia Polytechnic Institute	R. A. Comparin	VA
NGL-47-004-033	Virginia Polytechnic Institute	K. Gotow	VA
NGR-47-004-040	Virginia Polytechnic Institute	J. C. Schug	VA
NGR-47-004-051	Virginia Polytechnic Institute	H. F. Brinson	VA
NGR-47-005-022	University of Virginia	J. W. Beams	VA
NGR-47-005-026	University of Virginia	E. S. McVey, J. Moore	VA
NGR-47-005-029	University of Virginia	H. M. Parker	VA
NGR-47-005-046	University of Virginia	S. S. Fisher	VA
NGR-47-005-049	University of Virginia	F. R. Woods	VA
NGR-47-005-050	University of Virginia	E. J. Gunter	VA
NGR-47-005-059	University of Virginia	W. L. Duren	VA
NGR-47-005-066	University of Virginia	L. W. Fredrick	VA
NGL-47-005-067	University of Virginia	N. Cabrera	VA
NGR-47-005-077	University of Virginia	J. W. Boring	VA
NGR-47-005-085	University of Virginia	A. R. Saunders	VA
NGR-47-005-093	University of Virginia	R. J. Mattauch	VA
NGL-47-005-098	University of Virginia	F. W. Barton	VA
NGR-47-005-108	University of Virginia	J. K. Haviland	VA
NGR-47-005-110	University of Virginia	G. B. Matthews	VA
NGL-47-006-008	College of William and Mary	W. M. Jones	VA
NGR-47-006-010	College of William & Mary	H. O. Funsten	VA
NGR-47-006-028	College of William and Mary	H. Friedman	VA
NGL-47-006-041	College of William and Mary	R. T. Siegel	VA
NGR-47-006-045	College of William and Mary	A. Sher	VA
NGR-47-020-001	Hampton Institute	E. Kollmann	VA
NGR-48-001-004	Washington State University	B. A. McFadden	WASH
NGR-48-002-003	University of Washington	R. J. H. Bollard	WASH
NGL-48-002-004	University of Washington	J. I. Mueller	WASH
NGR-48-002-009	University of Washington	J. K. Buettner	WASH
NGR-48-002-010	University of Washington	R. G. Joppa	WASH

Grant No.	Institution	Investigator	State
NGR-48-002-033	University of Washington	P. W. Hodge	WASH
NGR-48-002-035	University of Washington	W. H. Rae	WASH
NGL-48-002-044	University of Washington	A. Hertzberg	WASH
NGR-48-002-047	University of Washington	M. E. Childs	WASH
NGL-48-002-057	University of Washington	A. Hertzberg	WASH
NGR-48-002-073	University of Washington	C. B. Leovy	WASH
NGR-48-002-074	University of Washington	J. Vagners	WASH
NGR-48-002-077	University of Washington	C. B. Leovy	WASH
NGL-49-001-001	West Virginia University	J. C. Ludlum	W VA
NGR-49-001-019	West Virginia University	W. H. Moran	W VA
NGR-50-001-009	Marquette University	E. C. Foudriat	WISC
NGR-50-001-010	Marquette University	W. Markowitz	WIS
NGL-50-002-001	University of Wisconsin (Madison)	J. O. Hirschfelder	WISC
NGR-50-002-002	University of Wisconsin (Madison)	E. N. Cameron	WISC
NGL-50-002-013	University of Wisconsin (Madison)	A. D. Code	WISC
NGR-50-002-017	University of Wisconsin (Madison)	P. S. Myers	WISC
NGR-50-002-041	University of Wisconsin (Madison)	L. A. Haskins	WISC
NGR-50-002-044	University of Wisconsin (Madison)	W. L. Krauschaar	WISC
NGL-50-002-078	University of Wisconsin (Madison)	E. C. Dick	WISC
NGR-50-002-083	University of Wisconsin (Madison)	V. C. Rideout	WISC
NGR-50-002-086	University of Wisconsin (Madison)	D. O. Cliver	WISC
NGR-50-002-114	University of Wisconsin (Madison)	V. E. Suomi	WISC
NGR-50-002-116	University of Wisconsin	R. W. Boom	WISC
NGR-51-001-008	University of Wyoming	A. B. Denison	WYO
NGR-51-001-010	University of Wyoming	E. A. Rinehart	WYO
NGR-51-001-019	University of Wyoming	J. N. Rosen	WYO
NGR-52-025-003	University of Southampton	E. J. Richards	FOR
NGR-52-026-001	University of Toronto	J. B. French	FOR
NGR-52-026-011	University of Toronto	R. C. Tennyson	FOR
NGR-52-042-004	University of Adelaide	E. G. Elford	FOR
NGR-52-059-001	McMaster University	A. B. Kristofferson	FOR
NGR-52-083-002	College of the Virgin Islands	F. B. Gray	FOR
NGR-52-093-001	University of Ottawa	H. Kozlowska	FOR
NGR-52-119-001	University of Goteborg	H. Hyden	FOR
NGR-52-134-001	York University	H. N. McFarland	FOR
NASr-5	University of Hawaii	H. C. McAllister	HAW
NASr-14	University of Rochester	R. E. Hopkins	N Y
NASr-54(05)	University of Michigan	L. M. Jones	MICH
NASr-54(06)	University of Michigan	R. W. Pew	MICH
NASr-54(11)	University of Michigan	L. M. Jones	MICH
NASr-82	University of Arizona	G. P. Kuiper	ARIZ
NASr-138	University of Arizona	A. M. J. Gehrels	ARIZ
NASr-164	University of New Hampshire	J. A. Lockwood	N H
NASr-169	University of Pittsburgh	N. Wald	PA
NASr-179	University of Pittsburgh	T. M. Donahue	PA
NASr-242	University of Texas (Austin)	H. Smith	TEX
NASr-248	University of Minnesota	A. O. C. Nier	MINN
NSR-01-002-033	University of Alabama (University)	R. M. Hollub	ALA
NSR-01-002-057	University of Alabama (Birmingham)	E. A. Sallin	ALA
NSR-01-003-005	Auburn University	R. I. Vachon	ALA
NSR-01-003-025	Auburn University	R. I. Vachon	ALA
NSR-02-001-025	University of Alaska	K. B. Mather	ALS
NSR-02-001-035	University of Alaska	K. B. Mather	ALS
NSR-03-002-048	University of Arizona	H. Johnson, A. Gehrels	ARIZ
NSR-03-002-163	University of Arizona	W. G. Tifft	ARIZ
NSR-05-002-071	California Institute of Technology	H. Zirin	CAL
NSR-05-002-124	California Institute of Technology	J. N. Franklin	CAL
NSR-05-002-133	California Institute of Technology	Dr. Garmire	CAL
NSR-05-003-100	University of California (Santa Cruz)	A. E. Whitford	CAL
NSR-05-003-233	University of California (Berkeley)	N. Pace	CAL
NSR-05-003-287	University of California (Berkeley)	C. S. Bowyer	CAL
NSR-05-007-083	University of California (Los Angeles)	W. M. Kaula	CAL
NSR-05-007-089	University of California (Los Angeles)	J. D. French	CAL
NSR-05-007-236	University of California (Los Angeles)	R. A. Goodman	CAL
NSR-05-009-046	University of California (San Diego)	C. E. McIlwain	CAL
NSR-05-010-021	University of California (Santa Barbara)	W. T. Thomson	CAL
NSR-05-018-087	University of Southern California	L. G. Goff	CAL
NSR-05-018-119	University of Southern California	R. H. Edwards	CAL
NSR-05-018-120	University of Southern California		CAL
NSR-05-020-088	Stanford University	M. Anliker	CAL
NSR-05-020-151	Stanford University	W. Bollay	CAL
NSR-06-004-081	University of Denver	J. G. Milliken	COLO
NSR-07-002-037	University of Connecticut	S. W. Yost	CONN
NSR-09-005-059	Catholic University	B. T. Fang	D C
NSR-09-010-027	George Washington University	C. W. Shilling	D C
NSR-09-010-035	George Washington University	C. W. Shilling	D C
NSR-09-010-057	George Washington University	C. W. Shilling	D C
NSR-10-005-047	University of Florida	H. Brown	FLA
NSR-10-007-078	University of Miami	D. L. Harvey	FLA
NSR-10-008-021	University of South Florida	M. G. Kobasky	FLA
NSR-12-001-019	University of Hawaii	J. T. Jefferies	HAW
NSR-12-001-055	University of Hawaii	G. P. Woollard	HAW
NSR-15-003-054	Indiana University	A. W. Weimer	IND
NSR-15-003-067	Indiana University	L. Orr	IND
NSR-15-003-069	Indiana University	G. W. Wilson	IND
NSR-15-003-076	Indiana University		IND
NSR-15-004-029	University of Notre Dame	T. J. Mueller	IND
NSR-15-005-037	Purdue University	Y. S. Touloukian	IND
NSR-16-001-025	University of Iowa	D. A. Gurnett	IOWA
NSR-21-001-062	Johns Hopkins University	H. M. Crosswhite	MD
NSR-21-002-077	University of Maryland	D. L. Matthews	MD
NSR-22-007-067	Harvard University	L. Goldberg	MASS
NSR-22-007-115	Harvard University	L. Goldberg	MASS
NSR-22-009-106	Massachusetts Institute of Technology	P. B. Sebring	MASS
NSR-22-009-138	Massachusetts Institute of Technology	L. L. Sutro	MASS
NSR-22-009-288	Massachusetts Institute of Technology	W. S. Lewellen	MASS
NSR-22-009-321	Massachusetts Institute of Technology	H. W. Schnopper	MASS
NSR-22-009-404	Massachusetts Institute of Technology	J. V. Harrington	MASS
NSR-22-011-036	Northeastern University	C. G. Houtsma	MASS
NSR-24-005-062	University of Minnesota	W. J. Luyten, J. E. Carroll	MINN
NSR-30-001-018	Dartmouth College	T. Laaspere	N H
NSR-30-002-003	University of New Hampshire	J. A. Lockwood	N H
NSR-31-001-104	Princeton University	E. Seckel	N J
NSR-31-001-127	Princeton University	J. L. Lowrance	N J
NSR-31-001-150	Princeton University	J. P. Layton	N J
NSR-31-001-901	Princeton University	D. C. Morton	N J
NSR-31-001-902	Princeton University	D. T. Harrje	N J
NSR-32-004-049	University of New Mexico		NMEX
NSR-33-008-069	Columbia University	W. A. Owens	N Y
NSR-33-010-055	Cornell University	M. F. Meserve	N Y
NSR-33-012-006	Fordham University	J. Kubis	N Y
NSR-33-015-077	State University of New York (Stony Brook)	O. A. Schaeffer	N Y

NSR-34-001-025	Duke University	T. D. Reynolds	N C
NSR-34-003-039	University of North Carolina (Chapel Hill)		N C
NSR-36-003-051	Case Western Reserve University		OHIO
		I. Greber, W. T. Olson	
NSR-36-003-092	Case Western Reserve University	G. M. Frye	OHIO
NSR-36-008-028	Ohio State University	A. W. Leissa	OHIO
NSR-36-008-108	Ohio State University	H. V. Ellington	OHIO
NSR-37-002-045	Oklahoma State University	K. A. McCollom	OKLA
NSR-37-004-008	Southeastern State College		OKLA
NSR-39-009-129	Pennsylvania State University	B. R. F. Kendall	PA
NSR-39-010-100	University of Pennsylvania	R. E. Forster	PA
NSR-39-001-064	University of Pittsburgh	A. Kent	PA
NSR-39-011-076	University of Pittsburgh	J. Canter	PA
NSR-39-011-078	University of Pittsburgh	G. McGee	PA
NSR-39-011-089	University of Pittsburgh	A. Kent	PA
NSR-39-011-106	University of Pittsburgh		PA
NSR-44-001-053	Texas A&M University	H. Monroe	TEX
NSR-44-005-016	University of Houston	C. J. Huang	TEX
NSR-44-005-059	University of Houston	C. J. Huang	TEX
NSR-44-006-023	Rice University	R. C. Haymes	TEX
NSR-44-006-065	Rice University	E. J. Low	TEX
NSR-47-003-010	Old Dominion University	G. L. Goglia	VA
NSR-47-003-011	Old Dominion University	G. L. Goglia	A
NSR-47-005-070	University of Virginia	E. H. Hendricks	VA
NSR-48-002-054	University of Washington	H. G. Ahlstrom	WASH
NSR-49-001-039	University of West Virginia	E. J. Steinhardt	W VA
NSR-52-112-001	Queen's University	F. J. Smith	FOR
NSR-52-112-002	Queen's University	F. J. Smith	FOR
NAS1-5700	College of William & Mary	R. T. Siegel	VA
NAS1-7022	Princeton University	J. K. Gillham	N J
NAS1-7265	North Carolina State University		N C
NAS1-7389	Mississippi State University	P. S. Young	MISS
NAS1-7391	University of Denver	C. Lundin	COLO
NAS1-7709	Temple University	C. S. Stokes	PA
NAS1-8141	University of Iowa		IOWA
NAS1-8145	Virginia Polytechnic Institute		VA
NAS1-8219	Louisiana State University (Baton Rouge)		LA
NAS1-8311	Hampton Institute	L. C. Wyrett	VA
NAS1-8423	Massachusetts Institute of Technology		MASS
NAS1-8604	Carnegie-Mellon University		PA
NAS1-8658	Massachusetts Institute of Technology	C. Kelly	MASS
NAS1-8787	University of Delaware		DEL
NAS1-8818	University of Pennsylvania	Z. Hashin	PA
NAS1-8830	Stevens Institute of Technology	S. Tsakongs	N J
NAS1-9016	Lowell Technological Institute		MASS
NAS1-81446	University of Iowa		IOWA
NAS2-1554	University of Virginia	G. C. Pitts	VA
NAS2-2503	University of California (Los Angeles)	W. R. Adey	CAL
NAS2-2633	University of Southern California	J. P. Meehan	CAL
NAS2-2711	Texas Womans University	P. B. Mack	TEX
NAS2-2738	University of Minnesota	F. Halberg	MINN
NAS2-3360	University of Minnesota	W. R. Webber	MINN
NAS2-3410	Stanford University	V. R. Eshlman	CAL
NAS2-3528	Bowling Green State University	I. I. Oster	OHIO
NAS2-3876	University of Chicago	J. A. Simpson	ILL
NAS2-4151	Washington University (St. Louis)	K. Hohenemser	MO
NAS2-4231	University of California (Berkeley)	N. Pace	CAL
NAS2-4629	University of Minnesota	W. R. Webber	MINN
NAS2-4671	Stanford University	T. Tomberlin	CAL
NAS2-4672	Stanford University	V. R. Eshlman	CAL
NAS2-4849	University of St. Thomas	L. S. Browning	TEX
NAS2-4915	University of California (Berkeley)		CAL
NAS2-4919	Massachusetts Institute of Technology		MASS
NAS2-5016	Georgia Institute of Technology		GA
NAS2-5043	Massachusetts Institute of Technology	D. G. Fraser	MASS
NAS2-5098	Princeton University	C. Pittendrigh	N J
NAS2-5167	University of Arizona	R. N. Carlile	ARIZ
NAS2-5245	University of California (Davis)	J. Beljan	CAL
NAS2-5254	Bradley University		ILL
NAS2-5311	University of California (Los Angeles)	I. R. Kaplan	CAL
NAS2-5344	University of New Hampshire		N H
NAS2-5355	Stanford University		CAL
NAS3-7904	University of Minnesota	E. R. Eckert	MINN
NAS3-10412	University of Florida	G. J. Schoessow	FLA
NAS5-1810	Princeton University	L. Spitzer	N J
NAS5-3095	University of Chicago	J. A. Simpson	ILL
NAS5-3097	Iowa State University	J. A. Van Allen	IOWA
NAS5-3177	University of California (San Diego)	L. E. Peterson	CAL
NAS5-3178	University of Rochester	M. F. Kaplan	N Y
NAS5-3205	Massachusetts Institute of Technology	G. Garmire	MASS
NAS5-3335	University of Michigan	G. R. Carigan	MICH
NAS5-3838	University of Minnesota	E. P. Ney	MINN
NAS5-3931	University of Colorado	W. A. Rense	COLO
NAS5-3949	Harvard University	L. Goldberg	MASS
NAS5-9076	University of Iowa	J. A. Van Allen	IOWA
NAS5-9077	University of California (Berkeley)	K. A. Anderson	CAL
NAS5-9078	Massachusetts Institute of Technology	H. S. Bridge	MASS
NAS5-9090	University of Chicago	J. A. Simpson	ILL
NAS5-9091	University of California (Berkeley)	K. A. Anderson	CAL
NAS5-9094	University of California (Berkeley)	K. A. Anderson	CAL
NAS5-9096	University of Chicago	P. Meyer	ILL
NAS5-9113	University of Michigan	J. J. Horvath	MICH
NAS5-9128	Temple University	J. L. Bohn	PA
NAS5-9217	University of Maryland	H. Laster	MD
NAS5-9274	Harvard University	L. Goldberg	MASS
NAS5-9275	University of New Mexico	C. P. Leavitt	NMEX
NAS5-9276	Rutgers University	A. Rolly	N J
NAS5-9305	Dartmouth College	T. Laaspere	N H
NAS5-9306	University of Michigan	G. R. Carignan	MICH
NAS5-9309	Stanford University	R. A. Helliwell	CAL
NAS5-9314	University of New Mexico	V. H. Regener	NMEX
NAS5-9327	University of Colorado	C. A. Barth	COLO
NAS5-9328	University of Michigan	G. R. Carignan	MICH
NAS5-9347	Stanford University	A. M. Peterson	CAL
NAS5-9366	University of Chicago	J. A. Simpson	ILL
NAS5-9590	Illinois Institute of Technology	C. Vest	ILL
NAS5-9677	University of Wisconsin (Madison)	V. E. Suomi	WISC
NAS5-9980	University of The West Indies		FOR
NAS5-10102	Stanford University	O. G. Villard	CAL
NAS5-10362	University of California (Berkeley)	F. S. Mozer	CAL
NAS5-10364	University of California (San Diego)	C. E. McIlwain	CAL
NAS5-10387	University of Texas (Austin)	A. W. Straiton	TEX
NAS5-10427	New Mexico State University	R. A. Bumgarner	NMEX
NAS5-10454	University of Notre Dame	J. D. Nicolaides	IND
NAS5-10554	New Mexico State University	R. B. Chavez	NMEX
NAS5-10625	University of Iowa	J. A. Van Allen	IOWA
NAS5-11002	Massachusetts Institute of Technology	C. S. Draper	MASS
NAS5-11037	University of Chicago	J. A. Simpson	ILL

NAS5-11038	University of California (Berkeley)	K. A. Anderson	CAL
NAS5-11039	University of Iowa		IOWA
NAS5-11054	University of New Hampshire	E. L. Chupp	N H
NAS5-11060	University of Minnesota	P. J. Kellogg	MINN
NAS5-11062	Massachusetts Institute of Technology	H. S. Bridge	MASS
NAS5-11063	University of Maryland	H. Gloeckler	MD
NAS5-11068	University of Wisconsin (Madison)		WISC
NAS5-11073	University of Michigan	G. R. Carignan	MICH
NAS5-11077	University of Pittsburgh	T. M. Donahue	PA
NAS5-11080	University of California (San Diego)	L. E. Peterson	CAL
NAS5-11081	University of California (San Diego)		CAL
NAS5-11082	Massachusetts Institute of Technology	G. Clark	MASS
NAS5-11171	University of Arizona		ARIZ
NAS5-11174	University of Michigan	F. T. Haddock	MICH
NAS5-11542	University of Wisconsin (Madison)		WISC
NAS5-11631	Colorado State University	W. E. Marlott	COLO
NAS5-11666	Colorado State University	W. E. Marlott	COLO
NAS5-11687	University of Minnesota	J. R. Winckler	MINN
NAS5-11694	University of New Hampshire	R. L. Arnoldy	N H
NAS5-14923	University of Pennsylvania		PA
NAS6-1061	Rice University	B. J. O'Brien	TEX
NAS6-1296	University of Texas (El Paso)	D. Stenstrom	TEX
NAS6-1616	University of Virginia		VA
NAS7-388	Illinois Institute of Technology		ILL
NAS7-535	New Mexico State University	R. A. Bumgarner	NMEX
NAS7-716	New Mexico State University		NMEX
NAS8-2473	Georgia Institute of Technology	J. L. Hammond	GA
NAS8-2504	Massachusetts Institute of Technology		MASS
		S. H. Crandall	
NAS8-2559	Vanderbilt University	E. B. Shanks	TENN
NAS8-2585	University of Alabama (Tuscaloosa)	R. A. Mann	ALA
NAS8-11184	Auburn University	E. R. Graf	ALA
NAS8-11189	University of Tennessee	G. R. Shermann	TENN
NAS8-11202	University of Alabama (University)	W. G. Moulton	ALA
NAS8-11259	Clemson University	C. V. Aucoin	S C
NAS8-11334	Mississippi State University	W. D. McCain	MISS
NAS8-11344	Auburn University	M. A. Honnel	ALA
NAS8-11468	University of California (Berkeley)	W. H. Giedt	CAL
NAS8-18120	University of Texas (Austin)	L. Clark	TEX
NAS8-20004	Auburn University	J. L. Lowry	ALA
NAS8-20104	Auburn University	D. W. Russell	ALA
NAS8-20154	Auburn University	E. R. Graf	ALA
NAS8-20159	University of Alabama (University)	R. A. Mann	ALA
NAS8-20171	University of Alabama (University)	J. F. Porter	ALA
NAS8-20172	University of Alabama (University)	M. A. Griffin	ALA
NAS8-20175	Auburn University	J. Crenshaw	ALA
NAS8-20228	University of Michigan	J. A. Clark	MICH
NAS8-20284	Mississippi State University	C. T. Carley	MISS
NAS8-20312	University of Michigan	V. L. Streeter	MICH
NAS8-20331	Columbia University	C. M. Harris	N Y
NAS8-20357	University of Michigan	G. R. Carignan	MICH
NAS8-20765	Auburn University	M. A. Honnell	ALA
NAS8-21015	University of Wisconsin (Madison)		WISC
NAS8-21049	Colorado State University	V. A. Sandborn	COLO
NAS8-21086	University of Michigan	G. R. Carignan	MICH
NAS8-21116	Louisiana State University (Baton Rouge)		LA
NAS8-21131	Rensselaer Polytechnic Institute	R. J. Roy	N Y
NAS8-21140	Pennsylvania State University	A. K. Blackadar	PA
NAS8-21143	University of Alabama (University)	H. R. Henry	ALA
NAS8-21179	University of Arkansas	W. D. Dickinson	ARK
NAS8-21257	Texas A & M University	N. E. Moyer	TEX
NAS8-21267	University of Michigan	J. C. Zorm	MICH
NAS8-21286	Newark College of Engineering	R. Misra	N J
NAS8-21292	University of St. Thomas	J. L. Goldman	TEX
NAS8-21317	Ohio State University	W. B. Campbell	OHIO
NAS8-21321	University of Alabama (Huntsville)		ALA
		O. J. Christensen	
NAS8-21368	Auburn University	C. L. Phillips	ALA
NAS8-21377	Mississippi State University	W. L. McDaniel	MISS
NAS8-21391	Oklahoma State University	F. E. Todd	OKLA
NAS8-21397	Arizona State University	N. S. Berman	ARIZ
NAS8-21407	University of California (Berkeley)		CAL
NAS8-21421	Texas Christian University		TEX
NAS8-21432	University of California (Berkeley)	J. R. Mitchell	CAL
NAS8-21436	University of Denver	J. Blizard	COLO
NAS8-21442	University of Illinois (Urbana)	D. D. Windlin	ILL
NAS8-21449	University of Chicago	P. Meyer	ILL
NAS8-21451	Massachusetts Institute of Technology	J. Hovorka	MASS
NAS8-21480	University of Alabama (University)	T. E. Falgout	ALA
NAS8-21484	Tulane University		LA
NAS8-21572	University of Arizona		ARIZ
NAS8-23970	University of Alabama (Tuscaloosa)	C. A. Gibson	ALA
NAS8-23988	University of Arizona	H. L. Johnson	ARIZ
NAS8-24364	Massachusetts Institute of Technology		MASS
NAS8-24365	Massachusetts Institute of Technology	K. Masubuchi	MASS
NAS8-24392	Clark University	C. A. Coulter	MASS
NAS8-30159	University of Alabama (Huntsville)	C. C. Shih	ALA
NAS8-30175	University of Oklahoma	E. F. Blick	OKLA
NAS8-30179	University of Denver	D. G. Murcray	COLO
NAS8-30511	Colorado School of Mines		COLO
NAS9-3079	Massachusetts Institute of Technology	P. Matthews	MASS
NAS9-4065	Massachusetts Institute of Technology	C. S. Draper	MASS
NAS9-4500	University of Minnesota	W. Kubicek	MINN
NAS9-4576	Massachusetts Institute of Technology		MASS
NAS9-5249	University of California (Berkeley	S. Silver	CAL
NAS9-5632	Stanford University	R. L. Kovach	CAL
NAS9-5884	Rice University		TEX
NAS9-5886	University of Maryland	J. Weber	MD
NAS9-5911	Rice University	J. W. Freeman	TEX
NAS9-5957	Columbia University	G. Latham	N Y
NAS9-6037	Columbia University	M. Ewing	N Y
NAS9-6331	University of Houston	L. Swenson	TEX
NAS9-6812	Texas A & M University	H. E. Whitmore	TEX
NAS9-6823	Massachusetts Institute of Technology	C. S. Draper	MASS
NAS9-6910	Ohio State University	C. Mengel	OHIO
NAS9-7020	Stanford University	B. B. Lusignan	CAL
NAS9-7081	University of Arizona	P. N. Slater	ARIZ
NAS9-7153	University of Texas (Austin)	B. A. Mitchell	TEX
NAS9-7175	University of Kansas	R. K. Moore	KAN
NAS9-7183	Massachusetts Institute of Technology	D. H. Staelin	MASS
NAS9-7218	Ohio State University	J. Shaw	OHIO
NAS9-7222	Northwestern University	K. G. Henize	ILL
NAS9-7237	Baylor University	P. Kellaway	TEX
NAS9-7280	Baylor University	P. C. Johnson	TEX
NAS9-7282	University of California (Los Angeles)	W. R. Adey	CAL
NAS9-7313	Stanford University	R. J. Lyon	CAL
NAS9-7382	Massachusetts Institute of Technology	R. Biemann	MASS
NAS9-7566	University of Denver	W. H. Mclain	COLO

NAS9-7651	Illinois Institute of Technology		ILL
NAS9-7738	Rice University	H. R. Anderson	TEX
NAS9-7809	University of Maryland	C. V. Alley	MD
NAS9-7830	Massachusetts Institute of Technology	J. V. Evans	MASS
NAS9-7882	University of California (Los Angeles)		CAL
NAS9-7883	University of Chicago		ILL
NAS9-7887	University of Chicago	A. Edward	ILL
NAS9-7888	University of Chicago		ILL
NAS9-7890	Columbia University	R. Anderson	N Y
NAS9-7891	University of California (San Diego)	J. R. Arnold	CAL
NAS9-7892	University of California (San Diego)	G. Arrhenius	CAL
NAS9-7895	Columbia University	P. W. Gast	N Y
NAS9-7897	Princeton University	H. H. Hess	N J
NAS9-7899	Rice University	D. Heymann	TEX
NAS9-7926	University of Texas (Austin)	J. G. Thompson	TEX
NAS9-7951	Texas A & M University	J. M. Prescott	TEX
NAS9-7963	California Institute of Technology	L. T. Silver	CAL
NAS9-7969	Rice University	A. J. Chapman	TEX
NAS9-7975	University of Wisconsin (Madison)	L. Haskin	WISC
NAS9-8005	Harvard University		MASS
NAS9-8012	University of Houston		TEX
NAS9-8017	University of Kentucky		KY
NAS9-8018	Cornell University		N Y
NAS9-8032	Yale University	K. K. Turekian	CONN
NAS9-8069	University of Houston		TEX
NAS9-8071	University of Oregon		ORE
NAS9-8072	Yale University	S. R. Lipsky	CONN
NAS9-8073	Carnegie-Mellon University	T. Kohman	PA
NAS9-8074	California Institute of Technology	G. J. Wasserburg	CAL
NAS9-8075	Yale University	B. J. Skinner	CONN
NAS9-8078	Indiana University		IND
NAS9-8080	University of Chicago		ILL
NAS9-8084	Lehigh University		PA
NAS9-8086	University of Chicago	J. V. Smith	ILL
NAS9-8093	University of Minnesota	R. O. Pepsin	MINN
NAS9-8095	University of California (Los Angeles)		CAL
NAS9-8096	University of California (Los Angeles)		CAL
NAS9-8097	Oregon State University	R. A. Schmitt	ORE
NAS9-8098	University of Kentucky		KY
NAS9-8099	Massachusetts Institute of Technology		MASS
NAS9-8100	Harvard University		MASS
NAS9-8101	University of Miami	S. Sox	FLA
NAS9-8102	Massachusetts Institute of Technology		MASS
NAS9-8107	University of California (San Diego)	H. C. Urey	CAL
NAS9-8109	Baylor University	W. C. Duncan	TEX
NAS9-8118	Purdue University	E. R. Winter	IND
NAS9-8122	University of Texas (Austin)	S. E. Ritzmann	TEX
NAS9-8165	Washington University (St. Louis)	R. W. Walker	MO
NAS9-8200	University of Texas (Austin)	M. Wheatcroft	TEX
NAS9-8224	Indiana University		IND
NAS9-8241	Massachusetts Institute of Technology		MASS
NAS9-8242	Massachusetts Institute of Technology		MASS
NAS9-8246	Texas Womans University	P. B. Mack	TEX
NAS9-8258	University of Texas (Austin)	S. E. Ritzmann	TEX
NAS9-8264	University of Houston		TEX
NAS9-8328	Massachusetts Institute of Technology	J. Hovorka	MASS
NAS9-8352	Washington University (St. Louis)	R. W. Walker	MO
NAS9-8379	Ohio State University	C. Mengel	OHIO
NAS9-8463	Texas Technological College		TEX
NAS9-8479	North Texas State University		TEX
NAS9-8747	University of Arizona		ARIZ
NAS9-8755	Centenary College		LA
NAS9-8795	Texas Southern University		TEX
NAS9-8806	University of California (Berkeley)		CAL
NAS9-8869	University of Houston	N. S. Kovar	TEX
NAS9-8888	Texas Womans University	P. B. Mack	TEX
NAS9-8945	University of Alaska		ALAS
NAS9-8949	Baylor University	P. C. Johnson	TEX
NAS9-9003	Rice University	J. R. Sims	TEX
NAS9-9017	Cornell University		N Y
NAS9-9024	Massachusetts Institute of Technology		MASS
NAS9-9053	Texas A&M University	D. Hightower	TEX
NAS9-9103	University of Chicago	J. H. Rust	ILL
NAS9-9104	University of Houston		TEX
NAS9-9184	University of Houston		TEX
NAS9-9266	University of Texas (Galveston)	M. Guest	TEX
NAS9-9270	University of Houston		TEX
NAS9-9285	Texas A&M University		TEX
NAS9-9300	University of Wisconsin (Madison)		WIS
NAS9-9304	University of Michigan		MICH
NAS9-9341	Long Island University	E. D. Yost	N Y
NAS9-9348	University of California (Berkeley)		CAL
NAS9-9365	University of New Mexico	K. Keil	NMEX
NAS9-9418	Baylor University	J. D. Frost	TEX
NAS9-9427	Texas Womans University	P. B. Mack	TEX
NAS9-9433	Harding College	H. D. Olree	ARK
NAS9-9439	Stanford University	H. Halpern	CAL
NAS9-9502	University of California (Berkeley)		CAL
NAS9-9577	University of California (Berkeley)		CAL
NAS10-1255	University of Florida	E. A. Farber	FLA
NAS10-5172	Florida Institute of Technology	J. J. Frangie	FLA
NAS12-102	Massachusetts Institute of Technology	M. E. Connelly	MASS
NAS12-514	Massachusetts Institute of Technology	C. S. Draper	MASS
NAS12-569	Massachusetts Institute of Technology	C. S. Draper	MASS
NAS12-606	University of Massachusetts	R. E. McIntosh	MASS
NAS12-620	Lowell Technological Institute	J. R. Herman	MASS
NAS12-640	Massachusetts Institute of Technology		MASS
NAS12-642	Massachusetts Institute of Technology		MASS
NAS-12-650	Illinois Institute of Technology		ILL
NAS-12-651	Unversity of Denver		COLO
NAS12-652	Carnegie-Mellon University		PA
NAS12-654	Stevens Institute of Technology		N J
NAS12-658	Massachusetts Institute of Technology		MASS
NAS12-661	Southern Methodist University		TEX
NAS12-668	Massachusetts Institute of Technology		MASS
NAS12-679	Massachusetts Institute of Technology		MASS
NAS12-692	University of Missouri (Columbia)		MO
NAS12-695	Stanford University		CAL
NAS12-2054	Brown University	A. Wold	R I
NAS12-2059	Tulane University	C. H. Beck	LA
NAS12-2063	Northeastern University		MASS
NAS12-2064	Illinois Institute of Technology	T. Webber	ILL
NAS12-2065	Stevens Institute of Technology	G. J. Herskowitz	N J
NAS12-2082	Ohio University		OHIO
NAS12-2096	North Carolina State University	A. H. Shephard	N C
NAS12-2101	Stevens Institute of Technology	C. T. Brooth	N J
NAS12-2104	University of California (Los Angeles)		CAL

NAS12-2105	University of California (Los Angeles)		CAL
NAS12-2106	Southern Methodist University		TEX
NAS12-2107	Case Western Reserve University		OHIO
NAS12-2111	Massachusetts Institute of Technology		MASS
NAS12-2117	University of Michigan		MICH
NAS12-2128	Tufts University		MASS
NAS12-2134	Virginia Polytechnic Institute		VA
NAS12-2138	University of California (Los Angeles)		CAL
NAS12-2142	University of Vermont		VT
NAS12-2152	University of New Hampshire		N H
NGT-01-002-002	University of Alabama (University)	E. Rodgers	ALA
NGT-01-003-001	Auburn University	W. V. Parker	ALA
NGT-02-001-007	University of Alaska	K. M. Rae	ALS
NGT-03-001-002	Arizona State University	W. J. Burke	ARIZ
NGT-03-002-008	University of Arizona	H. D. Rhodes	ARIZ
NGT-05-002-009	California Institute of Technology	H. F. Bohnenblust	CAL
NGT-05-002-295	Stanford University	J. M. Pettit	CAL
NGT-05-003-023	University of California (Berkeley)	S. S. Elberg	CAL
NGT-05-007-019	University of California (Los Angeles)	W. F. Libby	CAL
NGT-05-008-001	University of California (Riverside)	R. B. March	CAL
NGT-05-009-008	University of California (San Diego)	F. T. Wall	CAL
NGT-05-010-005	University of California (Santa Barbara)	A. Bruckner	CAL
NGT-05-018-004	University of Southern California	M. C. Kloetzel	CAL
NGT-05-018-085	University of Southern California	R. E. Stephens	CAL
NGT-05-020-016	Stanford University	H. Heffner	CAL
NGT-05-020-228	Stanford University	J. A. Vitale	CAL
NGT-05-020-295	Stanford University	J. M. Pettit	CAL
NGT-05-020-361	Stanford University	J. M. Pettit	CAL
NGT-06-001-001	Colorado School of Mines	A. R. Jordan	COLO
NGT-06-002-002	Colorado State University	W. H. Bragonier	COLO
NGT-06-003-004	University of Colorado	E. J. Archer	COLO
NGT-06-004-008	University of Denver	W. C. Miller	COLO
NGT-07-002-003	University of Connecticut	N. L. Whetten	CONN
NGT-07-004-014	Yale University	J. P. Miller	CONN
NGT-08-001-002	University of Delaware	C. E. Birchenall	DEL
NGT-09-005-006	Catholic University	J. P. O'Connor	D C
NGT-09-009-004	Georgetown University	J. B. Horigan	D C
NGT-09-010-003	George Washington University	A. E. Burns	D C
NGT-09-011-001	Howard University	C. L. Miller	D C
NGT-10-004-008	Florida State University	R. J. Keirs	FLA
NGT-10-005-006	University of Florida	L. E. Grinter	FLA
NGT-10-007-006	University of Miami	J. A. Harrison	FLA
NGT-11-001-005	Emory University	C. T. Lester	GA
NGT-11-002-006	Georgia Institute of Technology	T. W. Jackson	GA
NGT-11-002-064	Georgia Institute of Technology	J. A. Vitale	GA
NGT-11-003-002	University of Georgia	G. B. Huff	GA
NGT-12-001-005	University of Hawaii	W. Gorter	HAW
NGT-13-001-001	University of Idaho	M. L. Jackson	IDA
NGT-14-001-015	University of Chicago	C. D. O'Connell	ILL
NGT-14-004-002	Illinois Institute of Technology	A. Grad	ILL
NGT-14-005-017	University of Illinois (Urbana)	D. Alpert	ILL
NGT-14-007-004	Northwestern University	R. H. Baker	ILL
NGT-14-008-008	Southern Illinois University	W. E. Simeone	ILL
NGT-15-003-003	Indiana University	R. B. Curtis	IND
NGT-15-004-002	University of Notre Dame	P. E. Beichner	IND
NGT-15-005-005	Purdue University	F. N. Andrews	IND
NGT-15-005-061	Purdue University		IND
NGT-16-001-004	University of Iowa	D. C. Spriestersbach	IOWA
NGT-16-002-002	Iowa State University	J. B. Page	IOWA
NGT-17-001-002	Kansas State University	J. P. Noonan	KAN
NGT-17-002-006	University of Kansas	W. P. Albrecht	KAN
NGT-17-002-044	University of Kansas	W. P. Smith	KAN
NGT-17-002-052	University of Kansas	J. A. Vitale	KANS
NGT-18-001-005	University of Kentucky	L. W. Cochran	KY
NGT-18-002-006	University of Louisville	J. A. Dillon	KY
NGT-19-001-001	Louisiana State University (Baton Rouge)		LA
		M. Goodrich	
NGT-19-002-002	Tulane University	D. R. Deener	LA
NGT-20-006-002	University of Maine (Orono)	F. P. Eggert	ME
NGT-21-001-004	Johns Hopkins University	G. W. Shaffer	MD
NGT-21-002-013	University of Maryland	M. J. Pelczar	MD
NGT-22-003-001	Boston College	W. J. Feeney	MASS
NGT-22-004-003	Boston University	P. E. Kubzansky	MASS
NGT-22-005-005	Brandeis University	H. Weisberg	MASS
NGT-22-006-001	Clark University	D. E. Lee	MASS
NGT-22-007-008	Harvard University	R. A. McFarland	MASS
NGT-22-009-020	Massachusetts Institute of Technology	H. L. Hazen	MASS
NGT-22-010-008	University of Massachusetts	E. C. Moore	MASS
NGT-22-011-003	Northeastern University	A. A. Vernon	MASS
NGT-22-012-002	Tufts University	P. H. Flint	MASS
NGT-22-017-001	Worcester Polytechnic Institute	R. F. Morton	MASS
NGT-22-018-002	Lowell Technological Institute	E. L. Alexander	MASS
NGT-23-004-004	Michigan State University	J. Vinocur	MICH
NGT-23-005-018	University of Michigan	G. E. Hay	MICH
NGT-23-006-001	Wayne State University	J. E. Hill	MICH
NGT-23-007-004	Michigan Technological University	D. G. Yerg	MICH
NGT-24-005-012	University of Minnesota	B. Crawford	MINN
NGT-24-005-078	University of Minnesota	G. W. Anderson	MINN
NGT-25-001-002	Mississippi State University	J. C. McKee	MISS
NGT-25-002-001	University of Mississippi	W. L. Nobles	MISS
NGT-25-005-001	University of Southern Mississippi	R. S. Owings	MISS
NGT-26-003-001	University of Missouri (Rolla)	W. Bosch	MO
NGT-26-004-001	University of Missouri (Columbia)	C. E. Marshall	MO
NGT-26-006-001	St. Louis University	H. Howe	MO
NGT-26-008-005	Washington University (St. Louis)	G. E. Pake	MO
NGT-27-001-003	Montana State University	L. DS. Smith	MONT
NGT-27-002-001	University of Montana	F. S. Honkala	MONT
NGT-28-004-001	University of Nebraska (Lincoln)	J. C. Olson	NEB
NGT-29-001-002	University of Nevada (Reno)	T. D. O'Brien	NEV
NGT-30-001-003	Dartmouth College	J. F. Hornig	N H
NGT-30-002-002	University of New Hampshire	W. H. Drew	N H
NGT-31-001-009	Princeton University	C. S. Pittendrigh	N J
NGT-31-003-005	Stevens Institute of Technology	R. A. Morgen	N J
NGT-31-004-002	Rutgers University	H. C. Torrey	N J
NGT-32-003-004	New Mexico State University	E. Walden	NMEX
NGT-32-004-004	University of New Mexico	A. Steger	NMEX
NGT-33-001-002	Adelphi University	M. V. B. Jennings	N Y
NGT-33-002-002	Alfred University	E. E. Mueller	N Y
NGT-33-007-001	Clarkson College of Technology	H. L. Shulman	N Y
NGT-33-008-013	Columbia University	R. S. Halford	N Y
NGT-33-010-007	Cornell University	F. S. Erdman	N Y
NGT-33-010-052	Cornell University	J. A. Vitale	N Y
NGT-33-012-002	Fordham University	J. F. Mulligan	N Y
NGT-33-014-002	City University of New York	M. Rees	N Y
NGT-33-015-004	State University of New York (Stony Brook)		N Y
		R. Jordan	
NGT-33-015-027	State University of New York (Buffalo)	A. W. Holt	N Y
NGT-33-015-099	State University of New York (Stony Brook)		NY

NGT-33-016-014	New York University	J. R. Ragazzini	N Y
NGT-33-018-010	Rensselaer Polytechnic Institute	S. E. Wiberley	N Y
NGT-33-019-006	University of Rochester	R. G. Loewy	N Y
NGT-33-022-005	Syracuse University	F. P. Piskor	N Y
NGT-33-022-097	Syracuse University	J. C. Honey	N Y
NGT-33-023-003	Yeshiva University	A. Gelbart	N Y
NGT-34-001-003	Duke University	R. L. Predmore	N C
NGT-34-002-003	North Carolina State University	W. J. Peterson	N C
NGT-34-002-097	North Carolina State University	F. D. Hart	N C
NGT-34-003-001	University of North Carolina (Chapel Hill)		N C
		C. H. Holman	
NGT-35-001-001	North Dakota State University	G. S. Smith	N D
NGT-35-002-004	University of North Dakota	C. J. Hamre	N D
NGT-36-003-007	Case Western Reserve University	L. Gordon	OHIO
NGT-36-004-003	University of Cincinnati	C. Crockett	OHIO
NGT-36-007-002	Kent State University	J. White	OHIO
NGT-36-008-006	Ohio State University	W. M. Protheroe	OHIO
NGT-36-008-007	Ohio State University	F. H. Shillito	OHIO
NGT-36-009-001	Ohio University	T. Culbert	OHIO
NGT-36-010-001	University of Toledo	A. N. Solberg	OHIO
NGT-36-013-001	Case Reserve Western University	W. M. Heston	OHIO
NGT-37-002-002	Oklahoma State University	M. T. Edmison	OKLA
NGT-37-003-001	University of Oklahoma	C. D. Riggs	OKLA
NGT-38-002-001	Oregon State University	H. P. Hansen	ORE
NGT-39-002-002	Carnegie-Mellon University	A. F. Strehler	PA
NGT-39-004-005	Drexel Institute of Technology	O. W. Witzell	PA
NGT-39-007-003	Lehigh University	R. D. Stout	PA
NGT-39-009-011	Pennsylvania State University	M. N. McGeary	PA
NGT-39-009-141	Pennsylvania State University	G. Reethof	PA
NGT-39-010-007	University of Pennsylvania	A. N. Hixson	PA
NGT-39-011-003	University of Pittsburgh	P. F. Jones	PA
NGT-39-011-075	University of Pittsburgh	D. C. Stone	PA
NGT-39-012-007	Temple University	G. H. Huganir	PA
NGT-39-019-002	Duquesne University	H. H. Petit	PA
NGT-39-023-005	Villanova University	A. H. Buford	PA
NGT-40-002-008	Brown University	M. J. Brennan	R I
NGT-40-004-001	University of Rhode Island	P. H. Nash	R I
NGT-41-001-001	Clemson University	V. Hurst	S C
NGT-41-002-002	University of South Carolina	J. A. Morris	S C
NGT-42-002-001	University of South Dakota	W. W. Gutzman	S D
NGT-43-001-002	University of Tennessee	H. A. Smith	TENN
NGT-43-002-002	Vanderbilt University	R. T. Lagemann	TENN
NGT-44-001-003	Texas A & M University	W. C. Hall	TEX
NGT-44-003-019	Baylor University	J. D. Bragg	TEX
NGT-44-005-004	University of Houston	J. C. Allred	TEX
NGT-44-006-003	Rice University	W. E. Gordon	TEX
NGT-44-007-002	Southern Methodist University	C. C. Allbritton	TEX
NGT-44-009-002	Texas Christian University	E. L. Secrest	TEX
NGT-45-001-002	Brigham Young University	W. P. Lloyd	UTAH
NGT-45-002-001	Utah State University	E. J. Gardner	UTAH
NGT-45-003-002	University of Utah	S. M. McMurrin	UTAH
NGT-46-001-001	University of Vermont	W. H. Macmillan	VT
NGT-47-004-001	Virginia Polytechnic Institute	F. W. Bull	VA
NGT-47-005-005	University of Virginia	E. Younger	VA
NGT-47-006-013	College of William and Mary	R. T. Siegel	VA
NGT-48-001-002	Washington State University	J. F. Short	WASH
NGT-48-002-007	University of Washington	J. L. McCarthy	WASH
NGT-49-001-002	West Virginia University	J. Ludlum	W VA
NGT-50-001-005	Marquette University	L. W. Friedrich	WISC

NGT-50-002-003	University of Wisconsin (Madison)	R. M. Bock	WISC
NGT-51-001-002	University of Wyoming	R. H. Bruce	WYO
NGF-03-002-025	University of Arizona	G. P. Kuiper	ARIZ
NGF-05-003-021	University of California (Berkeley)	S. Silver	CAL
NGF-05-007-020	University of California (Los Angeles)	W. F. Libby	CAL
NGF-05-018-015	University of Southern California	J. P. Meeham	CAL
NGF-05-020-017	Stanford University	J. Lederberg	CAL
NGF-05-020-092	Stanford University	W. R. Rambo	CAL
NGF-06-003-005	University of Colorado	W. A. Rense	COLO
NGF-06-004-024	University of Denver	C. M. Alter	COLO
NGF-09-012-061	National Academy of Sciences	F. B. Seitz	DC
NGF-10-005-024	University of Florida	L. E. Grinter	FLA
NGF-11-002-012	Georgia Institute of Technology	K. G. Picha	GA
NGF-14-001-016	University of Chicago	J. A. Simson	ILL
NGF-14-005-020	University of Illinois (Urbana)	D. Alpert	ILL
NGF-15-005-011	Purdue University	B. A. Reese	IND
NGF-16-001-005	University of Iowa	J. A. Van Allen	IOWA
NGF-17-004-010	University of Kansas	B. G. Barr	KAN
NGF-21-002-016	University of Maryland	M. H. Martin	MD
NGF-22-007-009	Harvard University	William H. Sweet	MASS
NGF-22-009-021	Massachusetts Institute of Technology	J. V. Harrington	MASS
NGF-23-005-019	University of Michigan	R. A. Sawyer	MICH
NGF-24-005-011	University of Minnesota	A. O. C. Nier	MINN
NGF-24-005-072	University of Minnesota	W. B. Cheston	MINN
NGF-26-008-009	Washington University (St. Louis)	R. E. Norberg	MO
NGF-31-001-011	Princeton University	J. P. Layton	N J
NGF-33-006-008	Polytechnic Institute of Brooklyn	M. H. Bloom	N Y
NGF-33-010-010	Cornell University	T. Gold	N Y
NGF-33-016-034	New York University	A. Ferri	N Y
NGF-33-018-011	Rensselaer Polytechnic Institute	S. E. Wiberly	N Y
NGF-33-019-011	University of Rochester	W. O. Fenn	N Y
NGF-36-003-058	Case Western Reserve University	H. R. Nara	OHIO
NGF-39-011-004	University of Pittsburgh	D. Halliday	PA
NGF-44-001-014	Texas A & M University	R. E. Wainerdi	TEX
NGF-44-006-008	Rice University	A. J. Dessler	TEX
NGF-48-002-031	University of Washington	J. H. Ballard	WASH
NGF-50-002-004	University of Wisconsin (Madison)		WISC
		J. O. Hirschfelder	

CASE CATEGORIES

PHYSICAL SCIENCES

11 ASTRONOMY

NGR-03-002-017	University of Arizona	S. Bashkin	ARIZ
NGR-03-002-071	University of Arizona	T. Bowen	ARIZ
NGR-03-002-081	University of Arizona	A. M. J. Gehrels	ARIZ
NGR-03-002-107	University of Arizona	C. Y. Fan	ARIZ
NGR-03-002-122	University of Arizona	E. Roemer	ARIZ
NGR-03-002-153	University of Arizona	W. G. Tifft	ARIZ
NGR-03-002-193	University of Arizona	T. Gehrels	ARIZ
NGR-03-002-194	University of Arizona	W. G. Tifft	ARIZ
NGR-05-002-100	California Institute of Technology	M. A. Nicolet	CAL
NGR-05-002-116	California Institute of Technology	B. Murray	CAL
NGR-05-002-140	California Institute of Technology	G. Munch	CAL
NGL-05-003-003	University of California (Berkeley)	M. Calvin	CAL
NGR-05-003-230	University of California (Berkeley)	S. Silver	CAL
NGR-05-003-256	University of California (Berkeley)	S. Silver	CAL
NGR-05-003-275	University of California (Berkeley)	H. P. Smith	CAL
NGR-05-003-278	University of California (Berkeley)	C. S. Bowyer	CAL
NGL-05-003-286	University of California (Berkeley)	G. C. Pimentel	CAL
NGR-05-005-003	University of California (San Diego)	L. E. Peterson	CAL
NGR-05-005-005	University of California (San Diego)	J. R. Arnold	CAL
NGR-05-007-091	University of California (Los Angeles)		CAL
		Y. Mintz, A. Arakawa	CAL
NGR-05-013-010	California State College (Long Beach)	K. P. Luke	CAL
NGR-05-020-019	Stanford University R. H. Cannon, W. M. Fairbank,		CAL
		B. O. Lange	
NGR-05-061-006	University of California (Santa Cruz) E. J. Wampler		CAL
NGR-06-003-034	University of Colorado	W. A. Rense	COLO
NGR-06-003-064	University of Colorado	C. A. Barth	COLO
NGR-06-004-058	University of Denver	V. L. Patel	COLO
NGR-07-004-029	Yale University	R. Wildt	CONN
NGR-07-006-005	Wesleyan University	J. E. Faller	CONN
NGR-07-010-002	Fairfield University	J. H. McElaney	CONN
NGR-09-005-014	Catholic University	T. Tanaka	D C
NGR-09-011-006	Howard University	F. Senftle	D C
NGR-10-005-008	University of Florida	A. E. S. Green	FLA
NGR-10-008-019	University of South Florida	H. K. Eichhorn	FLA
NGR-10-019-001	Florida Technological University	H. N. Rexford	FLA
NGR-12-001-057	University of Hawaii	J. T. Jefferies	HAW
NGR-14-001-005	University of Chicago	P. Meyer	ILL
NGR-14-001-054	University of Chicago	W. A. Hiltner	ILL
NGR-14-005-013	University of Illinois (Urbana)	S. A. Bowhill	ILL
NGR-14-007-041	Northwestern University	S. S. Huang	ILL
NGR-14-007-069	Northwestern University	K. G. Henize	ILL
NGL-15-003-002	Indiana University	H. R. Johnson	IND
NGL-16-001-002	University of Iowa	J. A. Van Allen	IOWA
NGL-17-001-026	Kansas State University	D. Williams	KAN
NGR-19-001-012	Louisiana State University (Baton Rouge)		LA
		R. W. Huggett, K. Pinkau	
NGR-21-002-005	University of Maryland	D. A. Tidman	MD

NGR-21-002-006	University of Maryland	T. D. Wilkerson	MD
NGR-21-002-029	University of Maryland	W. C. Erickson	MD
NGR-21-002-109	University of Maryland	C. O. Alley	MD
NGL-22-007-006	Harvard University	L. Goldberg	MASS
NGR-22-007-061	Harvard University	L. Goldberg	MASS
NGR-22-009-005	Massachusetts Institute of Technology	K. Biemann	MASS
NGR-22-009-007	Massachusetts Institute of Technology	J. Reintjes	MASS
NGR-22-009-350	Massachusetts Institute of Technology	T. B. McCord	MASS
NGR-22-010-041	University of Massachusetts	J. R. Strong	MASS
NGR-23-005-017	University of Michigan	F. T. Haddock	MICH
NGR-23-005-275	University of Michigan	O. C. Mohler	MICH
NGR-23-005-321	University of Michigan	F. T. Haddock	MICH
NGL-24-005-008	University of Minnesota	J. R. Winckler, E. P. Ney	MINN
NGL-24-005-009	University of Minnesota	A. O. C. Nier	MINN
NGR-24-005-050	University of Minnesota	W. R. Webber,	MINN
		C. S. Waddington	
NGR-24-005-111	University of Minnesota	J. R. Winckler	MINN
NGR-24-005-176	University of Minnesota	P. Kellogg	MINN
NGR-26-008-001	Washington University (St. Louis)		MO
		J. Klarmann, M. W. Friedlander	
NGR-30-002-021	University of New Hampshire	E. L. Chupp	N H
NGR-31-001-001	Princeton University	M. Schwarzschild	N J
NGL-31-001-007	Princeton University	L. Spitzer	N J
NGR-31-001-044	Princeton University	L. Spitzer	N J
NGL-32-003-001	New Mexico State University	C. W. Tombough	NMEX
NGR-32-004-001	University of New Mexico	A. Erteza	NMEX
NGR-33-001-019	Adelphi University	R. Genberg	N Y
NGR-33-008-012	Columbia University		N Y
		H. M. Foley, R. Novick, L. Woltjer, P. W. Gast	
NGR-33-008-102	Columbia University	E. J. Ott	N Y
NGR-33-015-036	State University of New York (Stony Brook)		N Y
		Y. H. Koa	
NGR-33-015-082	State University of New York (Stony Brook)		N Y
		O. A. Schaeffer	
NGR-33-018-004	Rensselaer Polytechnic Institute	J. M. Greenberg	N Y
NGR-33-023-018	Yeshiva University	A. G. W. Cameron	N Y
NGR-36-004-001	University of Cincinnati	P. Herget	OHIO
NGR-39-006-001	Haverford College	L. C. Green	PA
NGR-44-005-041	University of Houston	C. Goodman	TEX
NGR-44-006-065	Rice University	F. J. Low	TEX
NGL-44-012-006	University of Texas (Austin)	A. E. Straiton	TEX
NGR-44-012-132	University of Texas (Austin)	V. Szebehely	TEX
NGR-47-005-066	University of Virginia	L. W. Fredrick	VA
NGR-48-002-033	University of Washington	P. W. Hodge	WASH
NGL-50-002-013	University of Wisconsin (Madison)	A. D. Code	WISC
NGR-50-002-044	University of Wisconsin (Madison) W. L. Krauschaar		WISC
NASr-164	University of New Hampshire	J. A. Lockwood	N H
NASr-242	University of Texas (Austin)	H. Smith	TEX
NSR-03-002-048	University of Arizona	H. Johnson, A. Gehrels	ARIZ
NSR-03-002-163	University of Arizona	W. G. Tifft	ARIZ
NSR-05-003-100	University of California (Santa Cruz) A. E. Whitford		CAL
NSR-22-007-067	Harvard University	L. Goldberg	MASS
NSR-22-007-115	Harvard University	L. Goldberg	MASS
NSR-22-009-106	Massachusetts Institute of Technology P. B. Sebring		MASS
NSR-33-015-077	State University of New York (Stony Brook)		N Y
		O. A. Schaeffer	

NSR-36-003-092	Case Western Reserve University	G. M. Frye	OHIO
NSR-44-006-065	Rice University	E. J. Low	TEX
NAS5-1810	Princeton University	L. Spitzer	N J
NAS5-3095	University of Chicago	J. A. Simpson	ILL
NAS5-3097	Iowa State University	J. A. Van Allen	IOWA
NAS5-3178	University of Rochester	M. F. Kaplan	N Y
NAS5-3205	Massachusetts Institute of Technology	G. Garmire	MASS
NAS5-3931	University of Colorado	W. A. Rense	COLO
NAS5-3949	Harvard University	L. Goldberg	MASS
NAS5-9094	University of California (Berkeley)	K. A. Anderson	CAL
NAS5-9274	Harvard University	L. Goldberg	MASS
NAS5-9275	University of New Mexico	C. P. Leavitt	NMEX
NAS5-9305	Dartmouth College	T. Laaspere	N H
NAS5-9309	Stanford University	R. A. Helliwell	CAL
NAS5-9314	University of New Mexico	V. H. Regener	NMEX
NAS5-9327	University of Colorado	C. A. Barth	COLO
NAS5-10102	Stanford University	O. G. Villard	CAL
NAS5-10364	University of California (San Diego)	C. E. McIlwain	CAL
NAS5-10387	University of Texas (Austin)	A. W. Straiton	TEX
NAS5-11002	Massachusetts Institute of Technology	C. S. Draper	MASS
NAS5-11054	University of New Hampshire	E. L. Chupp	N H
NAS5-11073	University of Michigan	G. R. Carignan	MICH
NAS5-11077	University of Pittsburgh	T. M. Donahue	PA
NAS5-11080	University of California (San Diego)	L. E. Peterson	CAL
NAS5-11081	University of California (San Diego)		CAL
NAS5-11082	Massachusetts Institute of Technology	G. Clark	MASS
NAS5-11174	University of Michigan	F. T. Haddock	MICH
NAS8-21015	University of Wisconsin (Madison)		WISC
NAS8-21436	University of Denver	J. Blizard	COLO
NAS8-21449	University of Chicago	P. Meyer	ILL
NAS8-21451	Massachusetts Institute of Technology	J. Hovorka	MASS
NAS8-21572	University of Arizona		ARIZ
NAS8-23988	University of Arizona	H. L. Johnson	ARIZ
NAS9-7218	Ohio State University	J. Shaw	OHIO
NAS9-7883	University of Chicago		ILL
NAS9-7891	University of California (San Diego)	J. R. Arnold	CAL
NAS12-658	Massachusetts Institute of Technology		MASS
NAS12-2111	Massachusetts Institute of Technology		MASS

12 CHEMISTRY

NGR-05-003-297	University of California (Berkeley)	T. H. Pigford	CAL
NGR-05-007-215	University of California (Los Angeles)	W. F. Libby	CAL
NGR-05-017-013	University of Santa Clara	D. A. Oliver	CAL
NGR-05-020-043	Stanford University	G. L. Pearson	CAL
NGR-05-020-242	Stanford University	I. Weinberg	CAL
NGR-05-029-005	University of San Francisco	A. Furst	CAL
NGR-06-003-071	University of Colorado	R. Wolfgang	COLO
NGL-07-004-008	Yale University	S. R. Lipsky	CONN
NGR-10-004-056	Florida State University	E. K. Plyler	FLA
NGR-10-007-054	University of Miami	G. Mueller	FLA
NGL-11-002-005	Georgia Institute of Technology	J. A. Knight	GA
NGR-14-001-060	University of Chicago	C. R. O'Dell	ILL
NGL-14-012-012	University of Illinois (Chicago)	P. R. Nachtsheim	ILL
NGR-15-004-028	University of Notre Dame	G. F. Dalelio	IND
NGR-15-005-003	Purdue University	K. L. Andrew	IND
NGR-15-005-085	Purdue University	R. W. Stanley	IND
NGR-17-002-050	University of Kansas	E. J. Zeller	KANS

NGL-21-002-053	University of Maryland	R. B. Beckmann	MD
NGR-21-002-175	University of Maryland	W. J. Bailey	MD
NGR-22-005-001	Brandeis University	N. O. Kaplan	MASS
NGR-22-011-051	Northeastern University	C. H. Perry	MASS
NGR-22-017-006	Worcester Polytechnic Institute	I. Zwiebel	MASS
NGR-23-002-001	University of Detroit	A. Szutka	MICH
NGR-26-004-011	University of Missouri (Columbia)	C. W. Gehrke	MO
NGR-31-001-129	Princeton University	I. Glassman	N J
NGL-31-003-020	Stevens Institute of Technology	H. Meissner	N J
NGR-33-007-074	Clarkson College of Technology	H. H. G. Jellinek	N Y
NGR-33-013-009	City College of New York	R. Shinner	N Y
NGR-33-013-017	City College of New York	M. Kolodney	N Y
NGL-33-018-053	Rensselaer Polytechnic Institute	F. A. White	N Y
NGR-34-002-072	North Carolina State University	L. A. Jones	N C
NGR-36-003-054	Case Western Reserve University	J. L. Koenig	OHIO
NGR-36-007-025	Kent State University	J. L. Fergason	OHIO
NGR-36-025-001	Cleveland State University	K. J. Casper	OHIO
NGL-38-002-032	Oregon State University	R. A. Schmitt	ORE
NGR-39-011-079	University of Pittsburgh	R. S. Dougall	PA
NGR-41-002-024	University of South Carolina	D. L Rohlfing	S C
NGR-43-010-001	East Tennessee State University	H. D. Powell	TENN
NGR-44-005-091	University of Houston	R. S. Becker	TEX
NGL-45-003-019	University of Utah	N. W. Ryan	UTAH
NGR-45-003-037	University of Utah	M. L. Williams	UTAH
NGR-47-003-008	Old Dominion University	R. L Williams	VA
NGR-47-004-016	Virginia Polytechnic Institute	J. P. Wightman	VA
NGR-47-004-040	Virginia Polytechnic Institute	J. C. Schug	VA
NGL-50-002-001	University of Wisconsin (Madison)		WISC
		J. O. Hirschfelder	
NGR-52-026-001	University of Toronto	J. B. French	FOR
NGR-52-093-001	University of Ottawa	H. Kozlowska	FOR
NSR-10-005-047	University of Florida	H. Brown	FLA
NAS1-8604	Carnegie-Mellon University		PA
NAS2-5311	University of California (Los Angeles)	I. R. Kaplan	CAL
NAS3-10412	University of Florida	G. J. Schoessow	FLA
NAS5-9090	University of Chicago	J. A. Simpson	ILL
NAS5-9096	University of Chicago	P. Meyer	ILL
NAS5-9366	University of Chicago	J. A. Simpson	ILL
NAS8-11334	Mississippi State University	W. D. McCain	MISS
NAS9-7313	Stanford University	R. J. Lyon	CAL
NAS9-7887	University of Chicago	A. Edward	ILL
NAS9-7888	University of Chicago		ILL
NAS9-8095	University of California (Los Angeles)		CAL
NAS9-8099	Massachusetts Institute of Technology		MASS
NAS9-8107	University of California (San Diego)	H. C. Urey	CAL
NAS9-9439	Stanford University	H. Halpern	CAL
NAS10-1255	University of Florida	E. A. Farber	FLA
NGF-48-002-031	University of Washington	J. H. Ballard	WASH

13 PHYSICS

NGR-01-002-063	University of Alabama (Huntsville)	J. E. Rush	ALA
NGR-01-003-008	Auburn University	W. A. Shaw	ALA
NGR-02-001-001	University of Alaska		
		S. Chapman, Syun-Ichi Akasofu	ALS
NGR-03-002-180	University of Arizona	H. L. Johnson	ARIZ
NGR-05-003-019	University of California (Berkeley)	H. Mark	CAL
NGR-05-003-220	University of California (Berkeley)	A. N. Kaufman	CAL

NGR-05-003-266	University of California (Berkeley)	S. Silver	CAL
NGL-05-003-272	University of California (Berkeley)	C. H. Townes	CAL
NGR-05-007-066	University of California (Los Angeles)	A. Y. F. Wong	CAL
NGR-05-007-116	University of California (Los Angeles)	A. Banos	CAL
NGL-05-007-161	University of California (Los Angeles)	F. A. Haak	CAL
NGR-05-007-190	University of California (Los Angeles)	C. F. Kennel	CAL
NGR-05-008-005	University of California (Riverside)	J. Callaway	CAL
NGR-05-009-030	University of California (San Diego)	R. H. Lovberg	CAL
NGR-05-009-081	University of California (San Diego)	W. I. Axford	CAL
NGR-05-010-001	University of California (Santa Barbara)		CAL
		W. C. Walker	CAL
NGR-05-018-001	University of Southern California	G. L. Weissler	CAL
NGR-05-018-007	University of Southern California	D. L. Judge	CAL
NGR-05-020-013	Stanford University	A. L. Schawlow	CAL
NGR-05-020-015	Stanford University	W. M. Fairbank	CAL
NGR-05-020-066	Stanford University	W. E. Spicer	CAL
NGR-05-020-073	Stanford University	R. E. Kalman	CAL
NGR-05-020-077	Stanford University	F. W. Crawford	CAL
NGR-05-020-091	Stanford University	D. Bershader	CAL
NGR-05-020-134	Stanford University	W. M. Kays	CAL
NGR-05-020-165	Stanford University	M. Chodorow	CAL
NGR-05-020-176	Stanford University	F. W. Crawford	CAL
NGR-05-020-245	Stanford University	D. Baganoff	CAL
NGL-05-020-275	Stanford University	K. Karamcheti	CAL
NGR-05-020-277	Stanford University	D. A. Dunn	CAL
NGR-05-061-004	University of California (Santa Cruz)	E. M. Evleth	CAL
NGR-06-002-053	Colorado State University	C. B. Winn	COLO
NGR-06-002-063	Colorado State University	F. W. Smith	COLO
NGR-06-002-074	Colorado State University	D. R. Winder	COLO
NGR-06-003-033	University of Colorado	A. Busemann	COLO
NGL-06-003-052	University of Colorado	C. A. Barth	COLO
NGR-06-003-057	University of Colorado	R. H. Garstang	COLO
NGR-06-004-006	University of Denver	R. C. Amme	COLO
NGR-07-004-006	Yale University	V. W. Hughes	CONN
NGR-07-004-015	Yale University	M. M. Chen	CONN
NGR-07-004-028	Yale University	I. B. Bernstein, J. L. Hirshfield	CONN
NGR-07-004-035	Yale University	W. E. Lamb	CONN
NGR-07-004-087	Yale University	F. B. Tuteur	CONN
NGL-08-001-019	University of Delaware	T. W. F. Russell	DEL
NGR-09-005-008	Catholic University	R. E. Meijer	D C
NGR-09-005-025	Catholic University	C. C. Chang	D C
NGR-09-005-054	Catholic University	T. Tanaka	D C
NGR-10-004-005	Florida State University	L. Mandelkern	FLA
NGR-10-005-049	University of Florida	R. T. Schneider	FLA
NGR-10-005-089	University of Florida	R. T. Schneider	FLA
NGL-11-002-062	Georgia Institute of Technology	A. Ben Huang	GA
NGR-11-002-068	Georgia Institute of Technology	J. D. Clement	GA
NGR-11-003-021	University of Georgia	D. R. Tompkins	GA
NGR-12-001-002	University of Hawaii	K. Watanabe	HAW
NGR-12-001-011	University of Hawaii	J. T. Jefferies	HAW
NGR-14-005-025	University of Illinois (Urbana)	J. D. Morrow	ILL
NGR-14-005-111	University of Illinois (Urbana)	M. L. Babcock	ILL
NGR-14-007-016	Northwestern University	J. A. Hynek	ILL
NGR-14-007-071	Northwestern University	D. Mintzer	ILL
NGR-14-007-081	Northwestern University	J. T. Waber	ILL
NGR-14-008-019	Southern Illinois University	P. K. Davis	ILL
NGR-15-003-060	Indiana University	E. Hopf	IND
NGR-15-003-077	Indiana University	W. D. Neff	IND
NGR-15-005-022	Purdue University	R. Oldenburger	IND
NGR-15-005-058	Purdue University	B. A. Reese	IND
NGR-15-005-077	Purdue University	D. E. Abbott	IND
NGR-15-008-004	Rose Polytechnic Institute	H. A. Sabbagh	IND
NGR-16-001-043	University of Iowa	D. C. Montgomery	IOWA
		& D. A. Gurnett	IOWA
NGR-18-001-017	University of Kentucky	D. C. Leigh	KY
NGR-18-001-020	University of Kentucky	O. W. Dillon	KY
NGR-18-001-026	University of Kentucky	R. C. Birkebak	KY
NGR-19-002-027	Tulane University	A. M. Hermann	LA
NGR-21-002-007	University of Maryland	T. D. Wilkerson	MD
NGR-21-002-010	University of Maryland	J. Weber	MD
NGR-21-002-010	University of Maryland	J. Weber	MD
NGR-21-002-073	University of Maryland	H. R. Griem	MD
NGR-21-002-167	University of Maryland	T. D. Wilkerson	MD
NGR-21-002-211	University of Maryland	S. K. Poultney	MD
NGR-22-007-054	Harvard University	N. F. Ramsey	MASS
NGR-22-007-056	Harvard University	R. W. P. King	MASS
NGR-22-007-117	Harvard University	N. Bloembergen	MASS
NGR-22-007-117	Harvard University	N. Bloembergen	MASS
NGR-22-007-126	Harvard University	P. S. Pershan	MASS
NGR-22-007-136	Harvard University	A. Dalgarno	MASS
NGL-22-009-012	Massachusetts Institute of Technology	A. Javin	MASS
NGR-22-009-014	Massachusetts Institute of Technology		MASS
		H. H. Woodson, H. A. Haus, J. R. Melcher	MASS
NGR-22-009-015	Massachusetts Institute of Technology	H. S. Bridge	MASS
NGR-22-009-091	Massachusetts Institute of Technology		MASS
		R. E. Stickney	
NGR-22-009-121	Massachusetts Institute of Technology	L. Trilling	MASS
NGR-22-009-131	Massachusetts Institute of Technology	G. Fiocco	MASS
NGL-22-009-163	Massachusetts Institute of Technology	R. P. Rafuse	MASS
NGR-22-009-167	Massachusetts Institute of Technology	G. R. Harrison	MASS
NGR-22-009-234	Massachusetts Institute of Technology		MASS
		R. D. Thornton	
NGR-22-009-240	Massachusetts Institute of Technology	A. Javan	MASS
NGR-22-009-249	Massachusetts Institute of Technology		MASS
		G. B. Benedek	
NGR-22-009-269	Massachusetts Institute of Technology	J. A. Fay	MASS
NGR-22-009-335	Massachusetts Institute of Technology	M. O. Scully	MASS
NGR-22-009-359	Massachusetts Institute of Technology	R. Weiss	MASS
NGR-22-010-018	University of Massachusetts	R. V. Monopoli	MASS
NGR-22-010-039	University of Massachusetts	G. R. Huguenin	MASS
NGR-22-010-042	University of Massachusetts	J. Strong	MASS
NGR-22-011-025	Northeastern University	K. Weiss	MASS
NGR-22-091-002	College of the Holy Cross	R. C. Gunter	MASS
NGR-23-004-056	Michigan State University	C. R. Gruhn	MICH
NGR-23-005-004	University of Michigan	C. Kikuchi	MICH
NGR-23-005-015	University of Michigan	A. Nagy	MICH
NGR-23-005-094	University of Michigan	V. C. Liu	MICH
NGL-23-005-183	University of Michigan	G. I. Haddad	MICH
		H. H. Woodson, H. A. Haus, J. R. Melcher	MICH
NGR-23-005-314	University of Michigan	F. T. Haddock	MICH
NGR-23-005-320	University of Michigan	U. Samir	MICH
NGR-23-010-004	Western Michigan University	R. R. Hutchinson	MICH
NGR-24-005-091	University of Minnesota	R. J. Goldstein	MINN
NGR-26-008-042	Washington University (St. Louis)	J. Klarmann	MO
NGR-26-008-043	Washington University (St. Louis)	R. M. Walker	MO
NGR-29-001-008	University of Nevada (Reno)	P. Atlick	NEV
NGR-31-001-074	Princeton University	C. L. Mellor	N J
NGR-31-001-151	Princeton University	A. J. Kelly	N J

Grant No.	Institution	Investigator	State
NGR-32-004-002	University of New Mexico	W. W. Grannemann	N MEX
NGR-33-006-007	Polytechnic Institute of Brooklyn	H. J. Juretschke	N Y
NGR-33-007-034	Clarkson College of Technology	L. C. Barrett	N Y
NGR-33-008-009	Columbia University	R. Novick	N Y
NGR-33-008-098	Columbia University	M. B. Friedman	N Y
NGR-33-010-029	Cornell University	L. H. Germer	N Y
NGR-33-010-042	Cornell University	F. K. Moore	N Y
NGL-33-010-047	Cornell University	P. R. McIsaac	N Y
NGR-33-010-051	Cornell University	C. L. Tang	N Y
NGL-33-010-054	Cornell University	A. R. Seebass	N Y
NGR-33-010-064	Cornell University	T. A. Cool	N Y
NGR-33-010-074	Cornell University	F. D. McLeod	N Y
NGR-33-013-025	City College of New York	S. M. Chen	N Y
NGR-33-013-029	City College of New York	R. Pfeffer	N Y
NGR-33-013-034	City College of New York	C. M. Tchen	N Y
NGR-33-015-002	State University of New York (Buffalo)	J. F. Danielli	N Y
NGR-33-015-068	State University of New York (Stony Brook)	G. W. Stroke	N Y
NGR-33-015-085	State University of New York (Stony Brook)	F. F. Y. Wang	N Y
NGR-33-016-003	New York University	R. C. Sahni	N Y
NGR-33-016-128	New York University	L. Arnold	N Y
NGR-33-018-066	Rensselaer Polytechnic Institute	J. B. Hudson	N Y
NGR-33-018-075	Rensselaer Polytechnic Institute	E. Holt	N Y
NGL-33-019-003	University of Rochester	P. W. Baumeister	N Y
NGR-33-019-086	University of Rochester	D. H. Douglas	N Y
NGR-33-022-035	Syracuse University	M. E. Barzelay	N Y
NGR-33-022-082	Syracuse University	D. S. Dosanjh	N Y
NGR-33-022-091	Syracuse University	J. J. Zwislocki	N Y
NGR-34-002-017	North Carolina State University	W. H. Bennett	N C
NGR-34-002-023	North Carolina State University	D. S. Grosch	N C
NGL-34-002-035	North Carolina State University	F. D. Hart	N C
NGR-34-002-048	North Carolina State University	H. A. Hassan	N C
NGR-36-003-064	Case Western Reserve University	S. Ostrach	OHIO
NGR-36-003-091	Case Western Reserve University	O. Ostrach	OHIO
NGR-36-004-008	University of Cincinnati	Ti Yi Li H Oguro	OHIO
NGR-36-006-003	John Carroll University	J. Trivisonno	OHIO
NGL-36-007-001	Kent State University	J. W. Reed	OHIO
NGR-36-008-076	Ohio State University	H. Hemand	OHIO
NGR-36-008-080	Ohio State University	C. A. Lewis	OHIO
NGR-36-008-103	Ohio State University	W. W. Anderson	OHIO
NGL-36-008-106	Ohio State University	R. M. Nerem	OHIO
NGR-36-019-001	Hiram College	L. B. Shaffer	OHIO
NGR-39-009-077	Pennsylvania State University	G. M. Faeth	PA
NGR-39-009-123	Pennsylvania State University	A. J. Engel	PA
NGL-39-010-001	University of Pennsylvania	M. Altman	PA
NGR-39-010-002	University of Pennsylvania	J. O'M. Bockris	PA
NGR-39-011-035	University of Pittsburgh	E. Gerjuoy	PA
NGR-39-011-096	University of Pittsburgh	E. J. Sternglass	PA
NGR-39-087-002	Carnegie-Mellon University	A. G. Milnes	PA
NGR-40-002-012	Brown University	P. D. Richardson	R I
NGR-40-002-059	Brown University	E. A. Mason	R I
NGR-41-002-003	University of South Carolina	J. R. Durig	S C
NGR-42-001-002	South Dakota School of Mines and Technology	C. L. Gruber	S D
NGL-43-001-006	University of Tennessee	N. M. Gailar	TENN
NGR-43-001-023	University of Tennessee	M. W. Milligan	TENN
NGL-43-001-056	University of Tennessee	F. M. Shofner	TENN
NGR-43-002-031	Vanderbilt University	C. E. Roos	TENN
NGR-43-002-032	Vanderbilt University	E. B. Shanks	TENN
NGR-44-001-067	Texas A&M University	R. E. Wainerdi	TEX
NGR-44-005-022	University of Houston	A. F. Hildebrant	TEX
NGR-44-005-096	University of Houston	M. Eisner	TEX
NGL-44-006-001	Rice University	F. R. Brotzen	TEX
NGR-44-006-012	Rice University	F. C. Michel, A. J. Dessler	TEX
NGR-44-007-004	Southern Methodist University	H. A. Blum	TEX
NGR-44-012-008	University of Texas (Austin)	B. D. Tapley	TEX
NGR-44-012-055	University of Texas (Austin)	J. N. Douglas	TEX
NGR-44-012-104	University of Texas (Austin)	W. H. Hartwig	TEX
NGR-45-001-011	Brigham Young University	D. E. Jones	UTAH
NGR-45-001-026	Brigham Young University	P. O. Berrett	UTAH
NGR-45-002-014	Utah State University	E. W. Vendell	UTAH
NGR-45-003-027	University of Utah	R. W. Grow	UTAH
NGR-45-003-050	University of Utah	G. A. Flandro	UTAH
NGR-47-003-007	Old Dominion University	G. L. Goglia	VA
NGL-47-004-033	Virginia Polytechnic Institute	K. Gotow	VA
NGR-47-005-022	University of Virginia	J. W. Beams	VA
NGR-47-005-046	University of Virginia	S. S. Fisher	VA
NGR-47-005-049	University of Virginia	F. R. Woods	VA
NGL-47-005-067	University of Virginia	N. Cabrera	VA
NGR-47-005-077	University of Virginia	J. W. Boring	VA
NGR-47-005-085	University of Virginia	A. R. Saunders	VA
NGR-47-005-093	University of Virginia	R. J. Mattauch	VA
NGR-47-006-010	College of William & Mary	H. O. Funsten	VA
NGL-47-006-041	College of William and Mary	R. T. Siegel	VA
NGL-48-002-044	University of Washington	A. Hertzberg	WASH
NGR-48-002-047	University of Washington	M. E. Childs	WASH
NGR-50-002-041	University of Wisconsin (Madison)	L. A. Haskins	WISC
NGR-51-001-008	University of Wyoming	A. B. Denison	WYO
NGR-51-001-010	University of Wyoming	E. A. Rinehart	WYO
NASr-14	University of Rochester	R. E. Hopkins	N Y
NASr-169	University of Pittsburgh	N. Wald	PA
NSR-05-009-046	University of California (San Diego)	C. E. McIlwain	CAL
NSR-21-002-077	University of Maryland	D. L. Matthews	MD
NSR-22-009-288	Massachusetts Institute of Technology	W. S. Lewellen	MASS
NSR-36-008-028	Ohio State University	A. W. Leissa	OHIO
NSR-48-002-054	University of Washington	H. G. Ahlstrom	WASH
NAS1-7391	University of Denver	C. Lundin	COLO
NAS1-8658	Massachusetts Institute of Technology	C. Kelly	MASS
NAS2-4919	Massachusetts Institute of Technology		MASS
NAS2-5355	Stanford University		CAL
NAS5-9076	University of Iowa	J. A. Van Allen	IOWA
NAS5-9077	University of California (Berkeley)	K. A. Anderson	CAL
NAS5-9078	Massachusetts Institute of Technology	H. S. Bridge	MASS
NAS5-9091	University of California (Berkeley)	K. A. Anderson	CAL
NAS5-9113	University of Michigan	J. J. Horvath	MICH
NAS5-11039	University of Iowa		IOWA
NAS5-11060	University of Minnesota	P. J. Kellogg	MINN
NAS5-11062	Massachusetts Institute of Technology	H. S. Bridge	MASS
NAS5-11063	University of Maryland	H. Gloeckler	MD
NAS5-11687	University of Minnesota	J. R. Winckler	MINN
NAS5-11694	University of New Hampshire	R. L. Arnoldy	N H
NAS8-2504	Massachusetts Institute of Technology	S. H. Crandall	MASS

NAS8-20228	University of Michigan	J. A. Clark	MICH
NAS8-21267	University of Michigan	J. C. Zorm	MICH
NAS8-21391	Oklahoma State University	F. E. Todd	OKLA
NAS8-21421	Texas Christian University		TEX
NAS8-24392	Clark University	C. A. Coulter	MASS
NAS9-5249	University of California (Berkeley	S. Silver	CAL
NAS9-6037	Columbia University	M. Ewing	N Y
NAS9-7382	Massachusetts Institute of Technology	R. Biemann	MASS
NAS9-7969	Rice University	A. J. Chapman	TEX
NAS9-8005	Harvard University		MASS
NAS9-8078	Indiana University		IND
NAS9-8118	Purdue University	E. R. Winter	IND
NAS9-8165	Washington University (St. Louis)	R. W. Walker	MO
NAS9-8224	Indiana University		IND
NAS9-8328	Massachusetts Institute of Technology	J. Hovorka	MASS
NAS9-8755	Centenary College		LA
NAS12-679	Massachusetts Institute of Technology		MASS
NGT-05-002-295	Stanford University	J. M. Pettit	CAL

19   PHYSICAL SCIENCES *(not elsewhere classified)*

NGL-05-002-007	California Institute of Technology	R. B. Leighton	CAL
NGR-05-009-103	University of California (San Diego)	N. A. Baily	CAL
NGR-05-020-335	Stanford University	A. C. Giese	CAL
NGR-26-006-024	Saint Louis University	D. S. Ousterhout	MO
NSR-05-003-287	University of California (Berkeley)	C. S. Bowyer	CAL
NSR-21-001-062	Johns Hopkins University	H. M. Crosswhite	MD
NSR-33-008-069	Columbia University	W. A. Owens	N Y
NSR-44-001-053	Texas A&M University	H. Monroe	TEX
NAS2-4629	University of Minnesota	W. R. Webber	MINN
NAS2-5245	University of California (Davis)	J. Beljan	CAL
NAS5-9217	University of Maryland	H. Laster	MD
NAS9-8869	University of Houston	N. S. Kovar	TEX
NAS9-9270	University of Houston		TEX
NAS9-9502	University of California (Berkeley)		CAL
NAS12-2054	Brown University	A. Wold	R I
NGF-14-001-016	University of Chicago	J. A. Simson	ILL
NGF-16-001-005	University of Iowa	J. A. Van Allen	IOWA
NGF-26-008-009	Washington University (St. Louis)	R. E. Norberg	MO

MATHEMATICS

21   ANY DISCIPLINE(S)

NGR-01-001-007	Alabama A&M College	M. C. George	ALA
NGR-03-002-011	University of Arizona	T. L. Vincent	ARIZ
NGR-03-002-024	University of Arizona	G. A. Korn	ARIZ
NGR-03-002-155	University of Arizona	B. M. Herman	ARIZ
NGR-04-005-001	Arkansas State University	J. L. Linnstaedter	ARK
NGL-05-007-065	University of California (Los Angeles)	P. J. Coleman	CAL
NGR-05-009-062	University of California (San Diego)	I. M. Jacobs	CAL
NGR-05-010-008	University of California (Santa Barbara)	J. M. Sloss	CAL
NGR-05-010-010	University of California (Santa Barbara)	W. C. Gogel	CAL
NGR-05-017-017	University of Santa Clara	S. P. Chan	CAL
NGR-05-020-276	Stanford University	V. R. Eshleman	CAL

NGR-05-020-348	Stanford University	A. M. Peterson	CAL
NGR-07-004-010	Yale University	R. Wildt	CONN
NGR-08-001-016	University of Delaware	E. J. Pellicciaro	DEL
NGR-10-008-005	University of South Florida	H. K. E. Wurmb	FLA
NGR-11-002-101	Georgia Institute of Technology	I. E. Perlin	GA
NGR-14-005-088	University of Illinois (Urbana)	G. C. McVittie	ILL
NGR-14-007-027	Northwestern University	E. H. T. Whitten	ILL
NGR-15-003-064	Indiana University	J. R. Thompson	IND
NGL-15-004-026	University of Notre Dame	J. L. Massey	IND
NGR-15-005-039	Purdue University	W. Gautschi	IND
NGR-15-005-087	Purdue University		IND
NGR-15-005-106	Purdue University	P. A. Wintz	IND
NGR-17-002-053	University of Kansas	G. L. Kelly	KAN
NGR-19-006-001	Northeast Louisiana State College	D. E. Dupree	LA
NGR-21-002-197	University of Maryland	Y. Chu	MD
NGR-22-009-002	Massachusetts Institute of Technology	T. B. Sheridan	MASS
NGL-22-009-124	Massachusetts Institute of Technology	G. C. Newton	MASS
NGR-22-010-012	University of Massachusetts	R. V. Monopoli	MASS
NGR-22-011-020	Northeastern University	J. Warga	MASS
NGR-23-004-041	Michigan State University	C. Martin	MICH
NGR-23-005-001	University of Michigan	F. J. Beutler	MICH
NGR-23-005-285	University of Michigan	B. Arden	MICH
NGR-26-003-044	University of Missouri (Rolla)	T. L. Noack	MO
NGR-26-006-021	Saint Louis University	B. H. Ulrich Jr.	MO
NGR-26-010-001	University of Missouri (St. Louis)	D. T. Haimo	MO
NGR-31-001-025	Princeton University	W. R. Schowalter	N J
NGR-31-001-059	Princeton University	E. Dowell	N J
NGR-31-001-132	Princeton University	A. W. Lo	N J
NGR-32-004-026	University of New Mexico	C. G. Richards	NMEX
NGR-33-006-040	Polytechnic Institute of Brooklyn	M. Schwartz	N Y
NGR-33-006-053	Polytechnic Institute of Brooklyn	A. C. McKellar	N Y
NGL-33-007-075	Clarkson College of Technology	W. A. Thorton	NY
NGR-33-015-013	State University of New York (Stony Brook)		N Y
		R. P. Tewarson	
NGR-33-019-014	University of Rochester	E. Kinnen	N Y
NGR-33-019-058	University of Rochester	G. Cohen	N Y
NGR-34-002-032	North Carolina State University	H. Sagan	N C
NGR-34-002-038	North Carolina State University	F. J. Tischer	N C
NGR-34-003-026	University of North Carolina (Chapel Hill)		N C
		J. W. Hanson	
NGR-36-008-131	Ohio State University	B. E. Gatewood	OHIO
NGR-39-011-039	University of Pittsburgh	W. G. Vogt	PA
NGL-40-002-015	Brown University	J. P. LaSalle	R I
NGR-41-001-016	Clemson University	T. G. Proctor	S C
NGR-43-001-008	University of Tennessee	D. C. Bogue	TENN
NGR-44-001-097	Texas A&M University	W. B. Smith	TEX
NGL-44-005-084	University of Houston	C. J. Huang	TEX
NGR-44-005-098	University of Houston	H. P. Decell	TEX
NGR-44-006-089	Rice University	A. Miele	TEX
NGR-44-007-027	Southern Methodist University	S. C. Gupta	TEX
NGR-44-007-028	Southern Methodist University	J. E. Walsh	TEX
NGL-44-012-043	University of Texas (Austin)	W. H. Hartwig	TEX
NGR-44-012-136	University of Texas (Austin)	B. D. Tapley	TEX
NGR-45-003-038	University of Utah	W. J. Coles	UTAH
NGR-47-004-030	Virginia Polytechnic Institute	R. A. Comparin	VA
NGL-47-005-098	University of Virginia	F. W. Barton	VA
NGR-47-006-028	College of William and Mary	H. Friedman	VA
NASr-54(06)	University of Michigan	R. W. Pew	MICH
NSR-15-005-037	Purdue University	Y. S. Touloukian	IND

NSR-34-003-039	University of North Carolina (Chapel Hill)		N C
NSR-52-112-002	Queen's University	F. J. Smith	FOR
NAS1-8219	Louisiana State University (Baton Rouge)		LA
NAS5-9347	Stanford University	A. M. Peterson	CAL
NAS8-2473	Georgia Institute of Technology	J. L. Hammond	GA
NAS8-2559	Vanderbilt University	E. B. Shanks	TENN
NAS8-11189	University of Tennessee	G. R. Shermann	TENN
NAS8-21116	Louisiana State University (Baton Rouge)		LA
NAS8-21377	Mississippi State University	W. L. McDaniel	MISS
NAS8-21397	Arizona State University	N. S. Berman	ARIZ
NAS8-21484	Tulane University		LA
NAS9-7153	University of Texas (Austin)	B. A. Mitchell	TEX
NAS9-7222	Northwestern University	K. G. Henize	ILL
NAS9-7282	University of California (Los Angeles)	W. R. Adey	CAL
NAS9-7926	University of Texas (Austin)	J. G. Thompson	TEX
NAS9-8463	Texas Technological College		TEX
NAS9-9304	University of Michigan		MICH
NAS12-102	Massachusetts Institute of Technology		MASS
		M. E. Connelly	
NAS12-606	University of Massachusetts	R. E. McIntosh	MASS
NAS12-620	Lowell Technological Institute	J. R. Herman	MASS
NAS-12-651	Unversity of Denver		COLO
NAS12-654	Stevens Institute of Technology		N J
NAS12-661	Southern Methodist University		TEX
NAS12-2064	Illinois Institute of Technology	T. Webber	ILL
NAS12-2065	Stevens Institute of Technology	G. J. Herskowitz	N J
NAS12-2106	Southern Methodist University		TEX
NGR-31-003-066	Stevens Institute of Technology	E. C. Ney	N J

ENVIRONMENTAL SCIENCES (Terrestrial & extraterrestrial)

31 ATMOSPHERIC SCIENCES

NGL-03-002-019	University of Arizona	S. A. Hoenig	ARIZ
NGR-03-002-184	University of Arizona	H. L. Johnson	ARIZ
NGR-05-002-034	California Institute of Technology	H. Zirin	CAL
NGR-05-002-092	California Institute of Technology	G. Neugebauer	CAL
NGR-05-002-114	California Institute of Technology	D. O. Muhleman	CAL
NGR-05-002-118	California Institute of Technology	R. F. Scott	CAL
NGR-05-002-142	California Institute of Technology	R. B. Leighton	CAL
NGL-05-003-017	University of California (Berkeley)	K. A. Anderson	CAL
NGL-05-007-002	University of California (Los Angeles)		CAL
		G. J. F. MacDonald	CAL
NGR-05-007-004	University of California (Los Angeles)	T. A. Farley,	CAL
		W. F. Libby, P. J. Coleman	CAL
NGR-05-007-041	University of California (Los Angeles)	Z. Sekara	CAL
NGR-05-007-046	University of California (Los Angeles)	L. H. Aller	CAL
NGR-05-009-022	University of California (Riverside)	R. S. White	CAL
NGR-05-009-059	University of California (San Diego)	B. Q. Duntley	CAL
NGR-05-009-076	University of California (San Diego)	J. A. Fejer	CAL
NGR-05-010-044	University of California (Los Angeles)	H. P. Broida	CAL
NGR-05-018-065	University of Southern California	T. C. James	CAL
NGR-05-020-001	Stanford University	O. G. Villard	CAL
NGL-05-020-008	Stanford University	R. A. Helliwell	CAL
NGL-05-020-014	Stanford University	V. R. Eshleman	CAL
NGR-05-020-272	Stanford University	P. A. Sturrock	CAL

NGR-05-020-288	Stanford University	R. A. Helliwell	CAL
NGR-05-020-330	Stanford University	J. R. Spreiter	CAL
NGR-06-003-069	University of Colorado	W. A. Rense	COLO
NGR-07-004-004	Yale University	R. Wildt	CONN
NGR-07-004-109	Yale University	E. B. Hooper	CONN
NGR-07-006-004	Wesleyan University	T. Page	CONN
NGR-09-005-063	Catholic University	Y. C. Whang	D C
NGR-11-002-004	Georgia Institute of Technology	H. D. Edwards	GA
NGL-14-001-001	University of Chicago	E. N. Parker	ILL
NGL-14-001-006	University of Chicago	J. A. Simpson	ILL
NGR-14-001-008	University of Chicago	T. Fujita	ILL
NGL-14-001-013	University of Chicago	C. O. Hines	ILL
NGR-14-005-002	University of Illinois (Urbana)	E. C. Yeh	ILL
NGR-14-007-048	Northwestern University	K. G. Henize	ILL
NGR-21-001-001	Johns Hopkins University	W. G. Fastie	MD
NGR-21-001-037	Johns Hopkins University	H. P. Eugster	MD
NGR-21-002-002	University of Maryland	H. Laster, E. Opik	MD
NGR-21-002-057	University of Maryland	R. T. Bettinger	MD
NGR-21-002-096	University of Maryland	R. T. Bettinger	MD
NGR-21-012-001	Woodstock College	M. J. Bielefeld	MD
NGR-22-007-021	Harvard University	G. R. Huguenin	MASS
NGL-22-007-053	Harvard University	W. A. Burgess	MASS
NGL-22-009-016	Massachusetts Institute of Technology	A. H. Barrett	MASS
NGR-22-010-023	University of Massachusetts	W. M. Irvine	MASS
NGR-23-005-062	University of Michigan	J. E. Rowe	MICH
NGR-25-001-008	Mississippi State University	G. E. Jones	MISS
NGL-26-006-016	St. Louis University	F. C. Bates	
NGR-30-001-011	Dartmouth College	B. U. O. Sonnerup	N H
NGR-30-002-008	University of New Hampshire	R. E. Houston	N H
NGR-30-002-010	University of New Hampshire	R. A. Kaufman	N H
NGR-30-002-028	University of New Hampshire	L. J. Cahill	N H
NGR-31-001-103	Princeton University	S. H. Lam	N J
NGR-33-006-047	Polytechnc Institute of Brooklyn	S. Gross	N Y
NGL-33-016-013	New York University	J. E. Miller	NY
NGL-33-018-007	Rensselaer Polytechnic Institute	P. Harteck	N Y
NGR-33-018-086	Rensselaer Polytechnic Institute	P. Harteck	N Y
NGR-38-003-009	University of Oregon	D. P. Weill	ORE
NGR-39-009-002	Pennsylvania State University	W. J. Ross	PA
NGR-39-009-003	Pennsylvania State University	J. S. Nisbet	PA
NGR-39-009-032	Pennsylvania State University	B. R. F. Kendall	PA
NGR-39-009-095	Pennsylvania State University	R. G. Quinn	PA
NGR-39-009-129	Pennsylvania State University	B. R. F. Kendall	PA
NGR-39-010-101	University of Pennsylvania	B. S. P. Shen	PA
NGL-39-011-013	University of Pittsburgh	W. L. Fite	PA
NGL-39-011-030	University of Pittsburgh	E. C. Zipf	PA
NGR-39-011-083	University of Pittsburgh	T. M. Donahue	PA
NGL-42-001-004	South Dakota School of Mines and Technology		S D
NGR-44-001-036	Texas A & M University	R. Thomas	TEX
NGL-45-003-025	University of Utah	F. L. Staffanson	UTAH
NGR-48-002-009	University of Washington	J. K. Buettner	WASH
NGR-48-002-073	University of Washington	C. B. Leovy	WASH
NGR-52-042-004	University of Adelaide	E. G. Elford	FOR
NASr-54(05)	University of Michigan	L. M. Jones	MICH
NASr-179	University of Pittsburgh	T. M. Donahue	PA
NASr-248	University of Minnesota	A. O. C. Nier	MINN
NSr-02-001-025	University of Alaska	K. B. Mather	ALS
NSR-02-001-035	University of Alaska	K. B. Mather	ALS
NSR-05-002-133	California Institute of Technology	Dr. Garmire	CAL
NSR-16-001-025	University of Iowa	D. A. Gurnett	IOWA

NSR-22-009-138	Massachusetts Institute of Technology	L. L. Sutro	MASS
NSR-24-005-062	University of Minnesota W. J. Luyten, J. E. Carroll		MINN
NSR-30-001-018	Dartmouth College	T. Laaspere	N H
NSR-30-002-003	University of New Hampshire	J. A. Lockwood	N H
NSR-31-001-901	Princeton University	D. C. Morton	N J
NSR-39-009-129	Pennsylvania State University	B. R. F. Kendall	PA
NSR-44-006-023	Rice University	R. C. Haymes	TEX
NAS1-7389	Mississippi State University	P. S. Young	MISS
NAS1-7709	Temple University	C. S. Stokes	PA
NAS1-8141	University of Iowa		IOWA
NAS2-3360	University of Minnesota	W. R. Webber	MINN
NAS5-3177	University of California (San Diego)	L. E. Peterson	CAL
NAS5-3335	University of Michigan	G. R. Carigan	MICH
NAS5-3838	University of Minnesota	E. P. Ney	MINN
NAS5-9128	Temple University	J. L. Bohn	PA
NAS5-9276	Rutgers University	A. Rolly	N J
NAS5-9328	University of Michigan	G. R. Carignan	MICH
NAS5-10362	University of California (Berkeley)	F. S. Mozer	CAL
NAS5-10625	University of Iowa	J. A. Van Allen	IOWA
NAS5-11037	University of Chicago	J. A. Simpson	ILL
NAS5-11038	University of California (Berkeley)	K. A. Anderson	CAL
NAS5-11068	University of Wisconsin (Madison)		WISC
NAS5-11542	University of Wisconsin (Madison)		WISC
NAS5-11631	Colorado State University	W. E. Marlott	COLO
NAS5-11666	Colorado State University	W. E. Marlott	COLO
NAS6-1296	University of Texas (El Paso)	D. Stenstrom	TEX
NAS8-20331	Columbia University	C. M. Harris	N Y
NAS8-20357	University of Michigan	G. R. Carignan	MICH
NAS8-21049	Colorado State University	V. A. Sandborn	COLO
NAS8-21086	University of Michigan	G. R. Carignan	MICH
NAS8-21140	Pennsylvania State University	A. K. Blackadar	PA
NAS8-21179	University of Arkansas	W. D. Dickinson	ARK
NAS8-21257	Texas A & M University	N. E. Moyer	TEX
NAS8-21432	University of California (Berkeley)	J. R. Mitchell	CAL
NAS8-21442	University of Illinois (Urbana)	D. D. Windlin	ILL
NAS9-5884	Rice University		TEX
NAS9-5911	Rice University	J. W. Freeman	TEX
NAS9-7020	Stanford University	B. B. Lusignan	CAL
NAS9-7183	Massachusetts Institute of Technology	D. H. Staelin	MASS
NAS9-7738	Rice University	H. R. Anderson	TEX
NAS9-7809	University of Maryland	C. V. Alley	MD
NAS9-8074	California Institute of Technology	G. J. Wasserburg	CAL
NAS9-8093	University of Minnesota	R. O. Pepsin	MINN
NAS12-514	Massachusetts Institute of Technology	C. S. Draper	MASS

32 GEOLOGICAL SCIENCES

NGR-02-001-063	University of Alaska	R. B. Forbes	ALAS
NGL-03-001-001	Arizona State University	C. B. Moore	ARIZ
NGR-03-002-191	University of Arizona	G. P. Kuiper	ARIZ
NGR-03-102-171	University of Arizona	H. C. Urey	ARIZ
NGR-05-002-129	California Institute of Technology	D. L. Anderson	CAL
NGR-05-003-302	University of California (Berkeley)	M. Calvin	CAL
NGR-05-005-007	University of California (San Diego)	C. E. McIlwain	CAL
NGR-05-009-002	University of California (San Diego)	G. Arrhenius	CAL
NGR-05-009-004	University of California (San Diego)	J. R. Arnold	CAL
NGL-05-009-005	University of California (San Diego)	H. E. Suess	CAL
NGR-05-020-267	Stanford University	A. D. Howard	CAL

NGR-06-002-085	Colorado State University	C. B. Winn	COLC
NGR-06-004-060	University of Denver	J. G. Roederer	COLO
NGR-09-010-008	George Washington University	N. Filipescu	D C
NGR-14-001-010	University of Chicago	E. Anders	ILL
NGR-21-001-002	Johns Hopkins University	H. W. Moos	MD
NGL-22-007-069	Harvard University	E. S. Barghoorn	MASS
NGR-22-007-103	Harvard University	D. C. Noble	MASS
NGR-22-009-123	Massachusetts Institute of Technology	F. Press	MASS
NGR-22-009-187	Massachusetts Institute of Technology	J. Watkins	MASS
NGR-22-009-257	Massachusetts Institute of Technology D. W. Strangway		MASS
NGR-22-009-262	Massachusetts Institute of Technology W. R. Markey		MASS
NGR-22-009-311	Massachusetts Institute of Technology	J. P. Vinti	MASS
NGR-22-009-329	Massachusetts Institute of Technology	F. Press	MASS
NGR-22-009-351	Massachusetts Institute of Technology L. G. Bromwell		MASS
NGR-24-005-054	University of Minnesota	F. M. Swain	MINN
NGR-31-001-093	Princeton University	R. B. Hargraves	N J
NGL-32-004-011	University of New Mexico	W. Elston	NMEX
NGR-33-008-061	Columbia University	P. W. Gast	N Y
NGR-33-010-082	Cornell University	C. Sagan	N Y
NGR-33-019-002	University of Rochester	W. Vishniac	N Y
NGR-36-003-100	Case Western Reserve University	A. R. Cooper	OHIO
NGR-36-008-093	Ohio State University	I. I. Mueller	OHIO
NGR-38-002-020	Oregon State University	R. A. Schmitt	ORE
NGL-38-003-010	University of Oregon	G. G. Goles	ORE
NGR-38-003-012	University of Oregon	A. R. McBirney	ORE
NGL-39-009-010	Pennsylvania State University	D. P. Gold	PA
NGR-44-005-002	University of Houston	J. Oro and A. Zlatkis	TEX
NGR-44-006-105	Rice University	J. A. S. Adams	TEX
NGR-44-012-020	University of Texas (Austin)	L. C. Reese	TEX
NGR-44-012-045	University of Texas (Austin)	J. H. Mackin	TEX
NGR-50-002-002	University of Wisconsin (Madison)	E. N. Cameron	WISC
NAS1-7022	Princeton University	J. K. Gillham	N J
NAS5-11171	University of Arizona		ARIZ
NAS8-11202	University of Alabama (University)	W. G. Moulton	ALA
NAS8-21407	University of California (Berkeley)		CAL
NAS9-5957	Columbia University	G. Latham	N Y
NAS9-7175	University of Kansas	R. K. Moore	KAN
NAS9-7830	Massachusetts Institute of Technology	J. V. Evans	MASS
NAS9-7890	Columbia University	R. Anderson	N Y
NAS9-7895	Columbia University	P. W. Gast	N Y
NAS9-7897	Princeton University	H. H. Hess	N J
NAS9-7899	Rice University	D. Heymann	TEX
NAS9-7963	California Institute of Technology	L. T. Silver	CAL
NAS9-7975	University of Wisconsin (Madison)	L. Haskin	WISC
NAS9-8012	University of Houston		TEX
NAS9-8017	University of Kentucky		KY
NAS9-8018	Cornell University		N Y
NAS9-8032	Yale University	K. K. Turekian	CONN
NAS9-8069	University of Houston		TEX
NAS9-8071	University of Oregon		ORE
NAS9-8072	Yale University	S. R. Lipsky	CONN
NAS9-8073	Carnegie-Mellon University	T. Kohman	PA
NAS9-8075	Yale University	B. J. Skinner	CONN
NAS9-8080	University of Chicago		ILL
NAS9-8084	Lehigh University		PA
NAS9-8086	University of Chicago	J. V. Smith	ILL
NAS9-8096	University of California (Los Angeles)		CAL

NAS9-8097	Oregon State University	R. A. Schmitt	ORE
NAS9-8098	University of Kentucky		KY
NAS9-8100	Harvard University		MASS
NAS9-8806	University of California (Berkeley)		CAL
NAS9-9341	Long Island University	E. D. Yost	N Y
NAS9-9348	University of California (Berkeley)		CAL
NAS9-9365	University of New Mexico	K. Keil	NMEX
NAS12-695	Stanford University		CAL

33   OCEANOGRAPHY

NGR-10-007-068	University of Miami	F. D. Kohler	FLA
NAS1-9016	Lowell Technological Institute		MASS

39   ENVIRONMENTAL SCIENCES *(not elsewhere classified)*

NGR-17-004-019	University of Kansas	R. M. Haralick	KAN
NGL-25-001-028	Mississippi State University	C. W. Bouchillon	MISS
NGR-33-016-149	New York University	A. Ferri	N Y
NGR-39-011-085	University of Pittsburgh	B. W. Hapke	PA
NAS5-10554	New Mexico State University	R. B. Chavez	NMEX
NAS12-2117	University of Michigan		MICH

ENGINEERING

41   AERONAUTICAL

NGR-05-003-273	University of California (Berkeley)	S. P. Siliberto	CAL
NGR-05-004-051	University of California (Davis)	M. A. Hoffman	CAL
NGR-05-010-020	Unversity of California (Santa Barbara)		CAL
		T. P. Mitchell	
NGR-05-010-025	University of California (Santa Barbara)		CAL
		H. H. Bossel	CAL
NGR-05-018-079	University of Southern California	W. T. Kyner	CAL
NGR-05-020-243	Stanford University	H. Ashley	CAL
NGR-06-003-075	University of Colorado	A. Busemann	COLO
NGR-06-004-082	University of Denver	C. W. Chiang	COLO
NGR-11-002-085	Georgia Institute of Technology	B. T. Zinn	GA
NGR-14-004-028	Illinois Institute of Technology	Z. Lavan	ILL
NGR-14-005-138	University of Illinois (Urbana)	A. M. Clausing	ILL
NGR-14-019-002	Bradley University	J. W. McNabb	ILL
NGR-15-005-094	Purdue University	J. G. Skifstad	IND
NGR-17-002-047	University of Kansas	K. H. Lenzen	KAN
NGR-22-009-229	Massachusetts Institute of Technology		MASS
		W. R. Markey	
NGR-22-009-303	Massachusetts Institute of Technology	N. D. Ham	MASS
NGR-22-009-334	Massachusetts Institute of Technology	A. D. Pierce	MASS
NGR-22-009-378	Massachusetts Institute of Technology		MASS
		J. Fay, J. Keck	MASS
NGR-22-011-042	Northeastern University	R. Madden	MASS
NGR-23-005-010	University of Michigan	S. K. Clark	MICH
NGR-26-003-026	University of Missouri (Rolla)	R. D. Rechtier	MO
NGR-31-001-119	Princeton University	W. D. Hayes	N J
NGR-31-001-146	Princeton University	E. H. Dowell	N J

NGR-33-007-061	Clarkson College of Technology	C. W. Haines	N Y
NGR-33-008-118	Columbia University	P. N. Borsky	N Y
NGL-33-016-119	New York University	A. Ferri	N Y
NGR-33-016-131	New York University	A. Ferri	N Y
NGR-33-016-141	New York University	J. Werner	N Y
NGR-33-019-087	University of Rochester	D. T. Blackstock	N Y
NGR-37-003-043	University of Oklahoma	M. L. Rasmussen	OKLA
NGR-39-009-111	Pennsylvania State University	B. W. McCormick	PA
NGR-39-009-121	Pennsylvania State University	G. Reethof	PA
NGR-43-001-075	University of Tennessee	H. D. Gruschka	TENN
NGR-44-001-011	Texas A & M University	A. E. Cronk	TEX
NGR-44-001-081	Texas A&M University	J. R. Scoggins	TEX
NGR-47-003-012	Old Dominion University	R. Y. K. Cheng	VA
NGR-47-005-026	University of Virginia	E. S. McVey, J. Moore	VA
NGR-47-005-029	University of Virginia	H. M. Parker	VA
NGR-48-002-010	University of Washington	R. G. Joppa	WASH
NGR-48-002-035	University of Washington	W. H. Rae	WASH
NGL-48-002-057	University of Washington	A. Hertzberg	WASH
NGR-50-001-009	Marquette University	E. C. Foudriat	WISC
NSR-05-007-083	University of California (Los Angeles)	W. M. Kaula	CAL
NSR-05-018-120	University of Southern California		CAL
NSR-15-003-076	Indiana University		IND
NSR-31-001-104	Princeton University	E. Seckel	N J
NAS1-7265	North Carolina State University		N C
NAS1-8423	Massachusetts Institute of Technology		MASS
NAS1-8830	Stevens Institute of Technology	S. Tsakongs	N J
NAS2-3876	University of Chicago	J. A. Simpson	ILL
NAS2-4151	Washington University (St. Louis)	K. Hohenemser	MO
NAS2-5167	University of Arizona	R. N. Carlile	ARIZ
NAS3-7904	University of Minnesota	E. R. Eckert	MINN
NAS8-21292	University of St. Thomas	J. L. Goldman	TEX
NAS8-30159	University of Alabama (Huntsville)	C. C. Shih	ALA
NAS8-30179	University of Denver	D. G. Murcray	COLO
NAS9-9285	Texas A&M University		TEX
NAS12-2082	Ohio University		OHIO
NGT-05-020-361	Stanford University	J. M. Pettit	CAL
NGT-34-002-097	North Carolina State University	F. D. Hart	N C
NGF-33-016-034	New York University	A. Ferri	N Y

42   ASTRONAUTICAL

NGL-03-002-002	University of Arizona	G. P. Kuiper	ARIZ
NGR-03-002-032	University of Arizona	A. B. Meinel, W. G. Tifft	ARIZ
NGR-03-002-115	University of Arizona	L. E. Weaver	ARIZ
NGR-03-002-116	University of Arizona	F. J. Low	ARIZ
NGR-03-002-174	University of Arizona	G. P. Kuiper	ARIZ
NGR-05-002-003	California Institute of Technology	H. Brown	CAL
NGR-05-002-138	California Institute of Technology	D. L. Anderson	CAL
NGR-05-007-138	University of California (Los Angeles)	W. M. Kaula	CAL
NGR-05-007-235	University of California (Los Angeles)	R. E. Holzer	CAL
NGR-05-009-106	University of California (San Diego)	A. M. Schneider	CAL
NGR-05-009-114	University of California (San Diego)	H. C. Urey	CAL
NGR-05-020-353	Stanford University	V. R. Eshleman	CAL
NGR-06-003-120	University of Colorado	C. W. Hord	COLO
NGR-10-004-058	Florida State University	S. L. Hess	FLA
NGR-14-001-128	University of Chicago	A. Turkevich	ILL
NGR-19-003-003	Louisiana Polytechnic Institute	T. Williams	LA
NGL-21-002-033	University of Maryland	H. Laster	MD

Grant No.	Institution	Investigator	State
NGR-22-007-068	Harvard University	A. E. Bryson	MASS
NGR-22-009-010	Massachusetts Institute of Technology	W. R. Markey	MASS
NGL-22-009-013	Massachusetts Institute of Technology		MASS
		R. G. Gallager	MASS
NGR-22-009-289	Massachusetts Institute of Technology	H. S. Bridge	MASS
NGR-22-009-372	Massachusetts Institute of Technology	H. S. Bridge	MASS
NGR-22-009-420	Massachusetts Institute of Technology		MASS
NGR-24-005-180	University of Minnesota	L. J. Cahill	MINN
NGR-24-005-187	University of Minnesota	A. O. C. Nier	MINN
NGR-25-001-032	Mississippi State University	D. L. Murphree	MISS
NGR-31-001-142	Princeton University	R. E. Danielson	N J
NGR-33-006-042	Polytechnic Institute of Brooklyn	J. J. Bongiorno	N Y
NGR-33-010-096	Cornell University	C. Sagan	N Y
NGR-33-010-098	Cornell University	C. Sagan	N Y
NGL-33-018-091	Rensselaer Polytechnic Institute	S. Yerazunis	N Y
NGL-34-001-001	Duke University	T. G. Wilson	N C
NGR-36-004-013	University of Cincinnati	R. J. Kroll	OHIO
NGR-36-008-005	Ohio State University	C. Levis	OHIO
NGR-36-008-125	Ohio State University	S. K. Ghosh	OHIO
NGR-37-003-041	University of Oklahoma	D. M. Egle	OKLA
NGR-39-009-023	Pennsylvania State University	J. L. Shearer	PA
NGR-39-010-087	University of Pennsylvania	F. Haber	PA
NGR-39-087-001	Carnegie-Mellon University	M. L. Renard	PA
NGR-40-002-081	Brown University	T. A. Mutch	R I
NGR-44-005-102	University of Houston	J. Oro	TEX
NGR-44-011-031	Texas Technological College	H. F. Martz	TEX
NGR-44-012-046	University of Texas (Austin)	B. D. Tapley	TEX
NGR-47-005-059	University of Virginia	W. L. Duren	VA
NGR-48-002-074	University of Washington	J. Vagners	WASH
NGR-48-002-077	University of Washington	C. B. Leovy	WASH
NGR-50-001-010	Marquette University	W. Markowitz	WIS
NSR-05-002-071	California Institute of Technology	H. Zirin	CAL
NSR-22-009-321	Massachusetts Institute of Technology		MASS
		H. W. Schnopper	
NSR-22-009-404	Massachusetts Institute of Technology		MASS
		J. V. Harrington	MASS
NSR-31-001-150	Princeton University	J. P. Layton	N J
NSR-33-010-055	Cornell University	M. F. Meserve	N Y
NSR-39-001-064	University of Pittsburgh	A. Kent	PA
NSR-52-112-001	Queen's University	F. J. Smith	FOR
NAS2-5043	Massachusetts Institute of Technology	D. G. Fraser	MASS
NAS2-5344	University of New Hampshire		N H
NAS5-9306	University of Michigan	G. R. Carignan	MICH
NAS5-9677	University of Wisconsin (Madison)	V. E. Suomi	WISC
NAS5-9980	University of The West Indies		FOR
NAS6-1061	Rice University	B. J. O'Brien	TEX
NAS8-11259	Clemson University	C. V. Aucoin	S C
NAS8-18120	University of Texas (Austin)	L. Clark	TEX
NAS8-20104	Auburn University	D. W. Russell	ALA
NAS8-20175	Auburn University	J. Crenshaw	ALA
NAS8-21368	Auburn University	C. L. Phillips	ALA
NAS8-30175	University of Oklahoma	E. F. Blick	OKLA
NAS9-4065	Massachusetts Institute of Technology	C. S. Draper	MASS
NAS9-4576	Massachusetts Institute of Technology		MASS
NAS9-5886	University of Maryland	J. Weber	MD
NAS9-6823	Massachusetts Institute of Technology	C. S. Draper	MASS
NAS9-7081	University of Arizona	P. N. Slater	ARIZ
NAS9-7237	Baylor University	P. Kellaway	TEX
NAS9-8241	Massachusetts Institute of Technology		MASS
NAS9-8242	Massachusetts Institute of Technology		MASS
NAS9-8264	University of Houston		TEX
NAS9-8352	Washington University (St. Louis)	R. W. Walker	MO
NAS9-9017	Cornell University		N Y
NAS9-9024	Massachusetts Institute of Technology		MASS
NAS12-2152	University of New Hampshire		N H

43 CHEMICAL

Grant No.	Institution	Investigator	State
NGR-01-002-035	University of Alabama (Huntsville)	E. W. Grohse	ALA
NGL-05-003-050	University of California (Berkeley)	A. K. Oppenheim	CAL
NGR-07-011-001	St. Joseph College	M. T. J. Murphy	CONN
NGR-21-002-218	University of Maryland	C. O. Alley	MD
NGR-23-005-003	University of Michigan	J. A. Nicholls	MICH
NGR-31-001-109	Princeton University	M. Summerfield	N J
NGR-31-003-014	Stevens Institute of Technology	R. F. McAlevy	N J
NGR-50-002-017	University of Wisconsin (Madison)	P. S. Myers	WISC
NSR-31-001-902	Princeton University	D. T. Harrje	N J
NAS1-8145	Virginia Polytechnic Institute		VA
NAS8-20284	Mississippi State University	C. T. Carley	MISS
NAS8-20312	University of Michigan	V. L. Streeter	MICH
NAS8-30511	Colorado School of Mines		COLO

44 CIVIL

Grant No.	Institution	Investigator	State
NGR-15-005-069	Purdue University	J. Modrey	IND
NGR-47-003-015	Old Dominion University	W. D. Stanley	VA
NGR-52-025-003	University of Southampton	E. J. Richards	FOR
NASr-82	University of Arizona	G. P. Kuiper	ARIZ

45 ELECTRICAL

Grant No.	Institution	Investigator	State
NGR-03-002-001	University of Arizona	R. W. G. Wyckoff	ARIZ
NGL-03-002-006	University of Arizona	L. E. Weaver	ARIZ
NGR-03-002-169	University of Arizona	D. J. Hamilton	ARIZ
NGR-05-020-214	Stanford University	R. H. Bube	CAL
NGL-07-004-005	Yale University	R. C. Barker	CONN
NGR-07-004-043	Yale University	R. Wolfgang	CONN
NGR-12-001-046	University of Hawaii	W. W. Peterson	HAW
NGR-15-005-006	Purdue University	J. C. Lindenlaub	IND
NGR-21-023-001	Columbia Union College	E. I. Mohr	MD
NGL-22-009-304	Massachusetts Institute of Technology		MASS
		H. J. Zimmerman	
NGR-22-009-337	Massachusetts Institute of Technology	P. Penfield	MASS
NGR-22-009-383	Massachusetts Institute of Technology		MASS
		J. L. Kerrebrock	MASS
NGR-22-011-007	Northeastern University	W. B. Nowak, B. L. Cochrun	MASS
NGR-26-003-037	University of Missouri (Rolla)	E. C. Bertnolli	MO
NGR-31-001-068	Princeton University	L. D. Davisson	N J
NGR-31-003-050	Stevens Institute of Technology	G. J. Herskowitz	N J
NGR-33-006-020	Polytechnic Institute of Brooklyn	K. K. Clarke	N Y
NGR-33-008-090	Columbia University	C. C. Halkias	N Y
NGL-34-002-047	North Carolina State University	F. J. Tischer	N C
NGR-34-002-073	North Carolina State University	M. A. Littlejohn	N C
NGR-36-003-079	Case Western Reserve University	W. H. Ko	OHIO
NGR-36-008-002	Ohio State University	C. A. Levis	OHIO

NGL-40-002-042	Brown University	G. S. Heller	R I
NGR-40-002-082	Brown University	J. E. Savage	R I
NGR-44-011-026	Texas Technological College	R. D. Shelton	TEX
NASr-138	University of Arizona	A. M. J. Gehrels	ARIZ
NSR-09-010-027	George Washington University	C. W. Shilling	D C
NSR-31-001-127	Princeton University	J. L. Lowrance	N J
NAS5-14923	University of Pennsylvania		PA
NAS8-11184	Auburn University	E. R. Graf	ALA
NAS8-11344	Auburn University	M. A. Honnel	ALA
NAS8-20154	Auburn University	E. R. Graf	ALA
NAS8-20172	University of Alabama (University)	M. A. Griffin	ALA
NAS8-20765	Auburn University	M. A. Honnell	ALA
NAS9-7651	Illinois Institute of Technology		ILL
NAS-12-650	Illinois Institute of Technology		ILL
NAS12-652	Carnegie-Mellon University		PA
NAS12-668	Massachusetts Institute of Technology		MASS
NAS12-692	University of Missouri (Columbia)		MO
NAS12-2063	Northeastern University		MASS
NAS12-2096	North Carolina State University	A. H. Shephard	N C
NAS12-2104	University of California (Los Angeles)		CAL
NAS12-2107	Case Western Reserve University		OHIO

46 MECHANICAL

NGR-03-002-044	University of Arizona	D. B. Kececioglu	ARIZ
NGL-05-002-002	California Institute of Technology	J. P. Liepmann	CAL
NGL-05-002-136	California Institute of Technology	W. D. Rannie	CAL
NGR-05-009-032	University of California (San Diego)	S. L. Miller	CAL
NGR-05-020-007	Stanford University	R. H. Cannon, I. Flugge-Lotz	CAL
NGR-05-020-039	Stanford University	A. S. Tetelman	CAL
NGR-05-020-234	Stanford University	A. E. Siegman	CAL
NGR-05-020-386	Stanford University	W. A. Tiller	CAL
NGR-06-003-088	University of Colorado	R. E. Hayes	COLO
NGL-10-005-039	University of Florida	J. J. Hren	FLA
NGR-11-002-083	Georgia Institute of Technology	B. T. Zinn	GA
NGR-11-002-096	Georgia Institute of Technology		GA
NGR-14-005-103	University of Illinois (Urbana)	J. C. Chato	ILL
NGR-14-008-002	Southern Illinois University	J. H. Lauchner	ILL
NGR-18-001-038	University of Kentucky	M. H. Leipold	KY
NGR-19-001-059	Louisiana State University (Baton Rouge)	R. W. Pike	LA
NGL-22-007-012	Harvard University	B. Budiansky	MASS
NGR-22-009-059	Massachusetts Institute of Technology	Z. M. Elias	MASS
NGR-22-009-339	Massachusetts Institute of Technology		MASS
		E. A. Witmer	
NGR-23-006-047	Wayne State University	C. N. DeSilva	MICH
NGR-24-005-070	University of Minnesota	C. C. Hsiao	MINN
NGR-24-005-095	University of Minnesota	R. Plunkett	MINN
NGR-31-009-004	Newark College of Engineering	P. Hrycak	N J
NGR-33-010-070	Cornell University	R. H. Gallagher	N Y
NGR-33-022-023	Syracuse University	V. Weiss	N Y
NGR-33-022-105	Syracuse University	V. Weiss	N Y
NGR-34-002-036	North Carolina State University	F. O. Smetana	N C
NGR-36-003-094	Case Western Reserve University	L. Leonard	OHIO
NGR-36-003-139	Case Western Reserve University	E. Reshotko	OHIO
NGR-36-004-030	University of Cincinnati	L. Meirovitch	OHIO
NGR-36-008-109	Ohio State University	C. D. Bailey	OHIO
NGR-39-002-023	Carnegie-Mellon University	J. L. Swedlow	PA
NGR-39-004-013	Drexel Institute of Technology	P. C. Chou	PA

NGR-39-007-011	Lehigh University	F. Erdogan	PA
NGR-39-007-017	Lehigh University	A. Kalnins	PA
NGR-39-007-040	Lehigh University	R. P. Wei	PA
NGR-39-008-014	Carnegie-Mellon University	E. G. Haney	PA
NGR-39-009-034	Pennsylvania State University	J. Marin	PA
NGR-39-087-003	Carnegie-Mellon University	J. R. Low	PA
NGR-40-002-080	Brown University	C. Mylonas	R I
NGR-44-001-031	Texas A&M University	T. J. Kozik	TEX
NGL-44-001-044	Texas A & M University	J. A. Stricklin	TEX
NGR-44-005-065	Universty of Houston	C. Dalton	TEX
NGR-47-005-050	University of Virginia	E. J. Gunter	VA
NGR-47-005-108	University of Virginia	J. K. Haviland	VA
NGR-48-002-003	University of Washington	R. J. H. Bollard	WASH
NGR-52-026-011	University of Toronto	R. C. Tennyson	FOR
NASr-5	University of Hawaii	H. C. McAllister	HAW
NASr-54(11)	University of Michigan	L. M. Jones	MICH
NSR-12-001-019	University of Hawaii	J. T. Jefferies	HAW
NSR-12-001-055	University of Hawaii	G. P. Woollard	HAW
NAS2-3410	Stanford University	V. R. Eshlman	CAL
NAS5-10454	University of Notre Dame	J. D. Nicolaides	IND
NAS6-1616	University of Virginia		VA
NAS7-388	Illinois Institute of Technology		ILL
NAS8-11468	University of California (Berkeley)	W. H. Giedt	CAL
NAS8-20004	Auburn University	J. L. Lowry	ALA
NAS8-20159	University of Alabama (University)	R. A. Mann	ALA
NAS8-21131	Rensselaer Polytechnic Institute	R. J. Roy	N Y
NAS8-21286	Newark College of Engineering	R. Misra	N J
NAS8-21480	University of Alabama (University)	T. E. Falgout	ALA
NAS8-23970	University of Alabama (Tuscaloosa)	C. A. Gibson	ALA
NAS9-3079	Massachusetts Institute of Technology	P. Matthews	MASS
NAS12-569	Massachusetts Institute of Technology	C. S. Draper	MASS
NAS12-2128	Tufts University		MASS

47 METALLURGY AND MATERIALS

NGR-04-001-029	University of Arkansas	D. M. Scruggs	ARK
NGL-05-002-005	California Institute of Technology	W. G. Knauss	CAL
NGR-05-002-105	California Institute of Technology	T. J. Ahrens	CAL
NGR-05-010-041	University of California (Santa Barbara)		CAL
		P. F. Ordung	CAL
NGR-09-003-014	American University	E. Callen	D C
NGL-15-004-001	University of Notre Dame	G. F. D'Alelio	IND
NGR-18-001-042	University of Kentucky	M. H. Leipold	KY
NGR-19-001-016	Louisiana State University (Baton Rouge)	R. W. Pike	LA
NGL-22-009-003	Massachusetts Institute of Technology	N. J. Grant	MASS
NGR-22-009-125	Massachusetts Institute of Technology	H. C. Gatos	MASS
NGL-22-009-418	Massachusetts Institute of Technology	D.J. Epstein	MASS
NGR-23-007-001	Michigan Technological University	C. E. Work	MICH
NGR-26-001-006	University of Missouri (Kansas City)	P. J. Bryant	MO
NGL-33-015-035	State University of New York (Stony Brook)		N Y
		L. L. Seigle	
NGR-33-022-004	Syracuse University	D. V. Keller	N Y
NGR-33-022-108	Syracuse University	D. V. Keller	MASS
NGR-34-002-108	North Carolina State University	C. R. Manning	N C
NGR-36-001-010	University of Akron	R. Dubensky	OHIO
NGR-36-003-033	Case Western Reserve University	J. F. Wallace	OHIO
NGL-36-008-051	Ohio State University	F. H. Beck	OHIO
NGR-36-027-002	Case Western Reserve University	S. V. Radcliffe	OHIO

NGR-39-007-007	Lehigh University	R. W. Kraft	PA
NGR-39-011-067	University of Pittsburgh	G. R. Fitterer	PA
NGR-43-001-003	University of Tennessee	W. K. Stair	TENN
NGR-43-003-007	Tennessee Technological University	R. Kinslow	TENN
NGR-44-006-088	Rice University	R. B. McLellan	TEX
NGR-44-007-042	Southern Methodist University	T. L. Chu	TEX
NGR-47-004-024	Virginia Polytechnic Institute	H. L. Wood	VA
NGR-47-004-051	Virginia Polytechnic Institute	H. F. Brinson	VA
NGR-47-006-045	College of William and Mary	A. Sher	VA
NGR-50-002-116	University of Wisconsin	R. W. Boom	WISC
NGR-52-134-001	York University	H. N. McFarland	FOR
NAS1-8787	University of Delaware		DEL
NAS1-8818	University of Pennsylvania	Z. Hashin	PA
NAS8-2585	University of Alabama (Tuscaloosa)	R. A. Mann	ALA
NAS8-20171	University of Alabama (University)	J. F. Porter	ALA
NAS8-21143	University of Alabama (University)	H. R. Henry	ALA
NAS8-21317	Ohio State University	W. B. Campbell	OHIO
NAS8-24364	Massachusetts Institute of Technology		MASS
NAS8-24365	Massachusetts Institute of Technology	K. Masubuchi	MASS
NAS9-8109	Baylor University	W. C. Duncan	TEX
NAS12-640	Massachusetts Institute of Technology		MASS

49 ENGINEERING *(not elsewhere classified)*

NGR-01-003-036	Auburn University	P. M. Fitzpatrick	ALA
NGR-05-002-117	California Institute of Technology	B. Murray	CAL
NGL-05-003-016	University of California (Berkeley)	C. A. Desoer, L. A. Zadek, E. Polak	CAL
NGR-05-010-028	University of California (Santa Barbara)	W. C. Kuby	CAL
NGR-05-018-104	University of Southern California	R. M. Gagliardi	CAL
NGR-05-020-103	Stanford University	S. H. Harris	CAL
NGR-05-020-345	Stanford University	J. L. Adams	CAL
NGR-06-002-084	Colorado State University	W. R. Mickelsen	COLO
NGR-06-003-092	University of Colorado	T. W. Speiser	COLO
NGR-07-009-003	Rensselaer Polytechnic Institute of Connecticut, Inc.	H. J. Schwarz	CONN CONN
NGR-09-010-053	George Washington University	H. Liebowitz	DC
NGR-10-005-022	University of Florida	R. D. Walker	FLA
NGR-14-005-140	University of Illinois (Urbana)	W. L. Chow	ILL
NGR-16-002-005	Iowa State University	G. K. Serovy	IOWA
NGR-21-002-206	University of Maryland	Y. Chu	MD
NGR-21-002-214	University of Maryland	J. P. Richard	MD
NGL-22-009-309	Massachusetts Institute of Technology	Z. S. Zannetos	MASS
NGR-23-005-041	University of Michigan	H. C. Early	MICH
NGR-31-001-155	Princeton University	D. T. Harrje	NJ
NGR-31-006-006	Fairleigh Dickinson University	K. D. Moeller	NJ
NGR-33-010-071	Cornell University	H. N. McManus	NY
NGR-34-002-078	North Carolina State University	F. O. Smetana	NC
NGR-34-002-082	North Carolina State University	N. F. J. Matthews	NC
NGR-34-002-085	North Carolina State University	J. S. Lee	NC
NGR-34-002-086	North Carolina State University	R. W. Truitt	NC
NGR-36-027-001	Case Western Reserve University	E. L. Glaser	OHIO
NGR-40-005-002	Providence College	E. K. Gora	RI
NGR-44-001-071	Texas A&M University	C. F. Kettleborough	TEX
NGR-44-007-037	Southern Methodist University	S. C. Gupta	TEX
NGR-44-012-144	University of Texas (Austin)	C. V. Ramamoorthy	TEX
NGL-48-002-004	University of Washington	J. I. Mueller	WASH

NGR-51-001-019	University of Wyoming	J. N. Rosen	WYO
NSR-01-002-033	University of Alabama (University)	R. M. Hollub	ALA
NSR-01-003-025	Auburn University	R. I. Vachon	ALA
NSR-05-018-119	University of Southern California	R. H. Edwards	CAL
NSR-05-020-151	Stanford University	W. Bollay	CAL
NSR-09-005-059	Catholic University	B. T. Fang	DC
NSR-39-011-076	University of Pittsburgh	J. Canter	PA
NSR-47-003-010	Old Dominion University	G. L. Goglia	VA
NSR-47-003-011	Old Dominion University	G. L. Goglia	A
NSR-49-001-039	University of West Virginia	E. J. Steinhardt	WVA
NAS1-5700	College of William & Mary	R. T. Siegel	VA
NAS5-10427	New Mexico State University	R. A. Bumgarner	NMEX
NAS7-535	New Mexico State University	R. A. Bumgarner	NMEX
NAS7-716	New Mexico State University		NMEX
NAS9-7566	University of Denver	W. H. Mclain	COLO
NAS9-8945	University of Alaska		ALAS
NAS9-9577	University of California (Berkeley)		CAL
NAS12-642	Massachusetts Institute of Technology		MASS
NAS12-2059	Tulane University	C. H. Beck	LA
NAS12-2101	Stevens Institute of Technology	C. T. Brooth	NJ
NGT-39-009-141	Pennsylvania State University	G. Reethof	PA
NGF-05-020-092	Stanford University	W. R. Rambo	CAL
NGF-11-002-012	Georgia Institute of Technology	K. G. Picha	GA

LIFE SCIENCES

51 BIOLOGY

NGR-01-001-003	Alabama A&M College	C. O. Lee	ALA
NGL-01-002-001	University of Alabama (University)	R. Hermann, G. Croker	ALA
NGR-03-002-068	University of Arizona	R. W. Lansing	ARIZ
NGR-05-002-031	California Institute of Technology	F. Strunwasser	CAL
NGR-05-002-121	California Institute of Technology	N. H. Horowitz	CAL
NGR-05-003-018	University of California (Berkeley)	N. Pace	CAL
NGR-05-003-020	University of California (Berkeley)	T. H. Jukes	CAL
NGL-05-003-024	University of California (Berkeley)	N. Pace	CAL
NGR-05-003-067	University of California (Berkeley)	W. B. N. Berry	CAL
NGL-05-003-079	University of California (Berkeley)	A. D. McLaren	CAL
NGR-05-003-089	University of California (Berkeley)	D. H. Calloway	CAL
NGR-05-003-228	University of California (Berkeley)	S. Margen	CAL
NGR-05-003-326	University of California (Berkeley)	H. Borsook	CAL
NGR-05-004-008	University of California (Davis)	A. H. Smith, C. F. Kelly	CAL
NGR-05-004-035	University of California (Davis)	R. E. Smith	CAL
NGR-05-004-038	Unversity of California (Davis)	R. E. Smith	CAL
NGR-05-004-053	University of California (Davis)	R. Smith	CAL
NGL-05-007-003	University of California (Los Angeles)	W. F. Libby	CAL
NGR-05-007-133	University of California (Los Angeles)	H. Sobel	CAL
NGR7-05-007-174	University of California (Los Angeles)	K. C. Hamner	CAL
NGL-05-007-195	University of California (Los Angeles)	J. D. French	CAL
NGR9-05-007-205	University of California (Los Angeles)	F. S. Sjoatrand	CAL
NGR-05-009-083	University of California (San Diego)	R. Galambos	CAL
NGR-05-009-109	University of California (San Diego)	J. B. West	CAL
NGR-05-010-019	University of California (Santa Barbara)	R. V. Fisher	CAL

NGR-05-010-035 University of California (Santa Barbara) P. E. Cloud CAL
NGL-05-018-003 University of Southern California   J. P. Henry, CAL
                                   J. P. Meehan
NGR-05-020-004 Stanford University   J. Lederberg CAL
NGR-05-020-137 Stanford University   L. Stryer, CAL
                                   A. Kornberg
NGL-05-020-177 Stanford University   R. E. Smith CAL
NGR-05-020-209 Stanford University   T. R. Kane CAL
NGL-05-020-250 Stanford University   J. D. Baldeschwieler CAL
NGR-05-020-305 Stanford University   D. C. Harrison CAL
NGR-05-020-324 Stanford University   L. A. Sapirstein CAL
NGR-05-020-326 Stanford University   S. Levine CAL
NGR-05-020-354 Stanford University   J. Lederberg CAL
NGR-05-025-008 University of California (San Francisco)   CAL
                                   H. I. Maibach
NGL-05-046-002 San Jose State College   B. Clark CAL
NGR-06-002-075 Colorado State University   J. P. Jordan COLO
NGR-07-004-009 Yale University   H. J. Morowitz CONN
NGR-07-004-034 Yale University   C. MacClintock, A. L. McAlester CONN
NGR-07-004-084 Yale University   R. A. Goldsby CONN
NGR-07-004-090 Yale University   R. J. Wyman CONN
NGR-09-005-022 Catholic University   B. T. DeCicco D C
NGR-09-005-067 Catholic University   S. C. Ling D C
NGR-10-004-018 Florida State University   H. Gaffron FLA
NGR-10-004-029 Florida State University   R. G. Cornell FLA
NGR-10-004-041 Florida State University   W. Schwartz FLA
NGR-10-007-008 University of Miami   S. W. Fox FLA
NGR-10-007-052 University of Miami   K. Harada FLA
NGR-11-001-012 Emory University   B. W. Robinson GA
NGL-12-001-042 University of Hawaii   S. M. Siegel HAW
NGR-12-001-053 University of Hawaii   S. M. Siegel HAW
NGL-14-005-074 University of Illinois (Urbana)   H. W. Ades ILL
NGR-14-012-004 University of Illinois (Chicago)   J. H. Boyer ILL
NGR-15-003-007 Indiana University   W. D. Neff IND
NGR-15-003-053 Indiana University   S. Mizell IND
NGR-15-004-017 University of Notre Dame   T. J. Starr IND
NGR-15-009-001 Ball State University   E. Montague IND
NGR-16-001-031 University of Iowa   C. C. Wunder IOWA
NGR-17-001-034 Kansas State University   L. T. Fan KAN
NGR-17-002-042 University of Kansas   R. H. Himes KAN
NGL-18-001-003 University of Kentucky   K. O. Lange KY
NGR-18-002-008 University of Louisville   E. A. Alluisi KY
NGR-21-001-035 Johns Hopkins University S. A. Weinstein MD
NGR-21-001-043 Johns Hopkins University   H. H. Seliger MD
NGR-21-001-069 Johns Hopkins University   J. F. Dardano MD
NGR-21-002-003 University of Maryland   R. W. Krauss MD
NGR-21-002-026 University of Maryland   R. G. Grenell MD
NGR-21-002-040 University of Maryland   R. G. Grenell MD
NGR-21-002-059 University of Maryland E. R. Lippincott, Y. T. Pratt MD
NGR-21-002-065 University of Maryland   A. M. Decker MD
NGR-21-007-004 University of Maryland   J. V. Brady MD
NGR-22-004-018 Boston University   E. T. Angelakos MASS
NGR-22-005-025 Brandeis University   J. W. Senders MASS
NGR-22-007-019 Harvard University W. H. Abelman, L. E. Earley MASS
NGR-22-007-059 Harvard University   K. R. Porter MASS
NGR-22-007-070 Harvard University   R. A. McFarland MASS
NGR-22-007-096 Harvard University   F. R. Ervin MASS
NGL-22-007-101 Harvard University   D. M. Hegsted MASS
NGR-22-007-137 Harvard University   R. T. Kelleher MASS

NGR-22-007-143 Harvard University   Y. C. Ho MASS
NGR-22-009-018 Massachusetts Institute of Technology F. O. Schmitt MASS
NGL-22-009-156 Massachusetts Institute of Technology   MASS
                          J. L. Meiry, Y. T. Li MASS
NGR-22-009-272 Massachusetts Institute of Technology R. J. Wurtman MASS
NGR-22-009-277 Massachusetts Institute of Technology   A. Rich MASS
NGL-22-009-308 Massachusetts Institute of Technology H. L. Teuber MASS
NGR-22-009-312 Massachusetts Institute of Technology L. R. Young MASS
NGL-22-010-029 University of Massachusetts   J. F. Brandts MASS
NGL-22-011-024 Northeastern University   B. L. Cochrun MASS
NGR-22-012-006 Tufts University   D. H. Spodick MASS
NGR-22-017-008 Worcester Polytechnic Institute   A. H. Weiss MASS
NGR-23-004-001 Michigan State University   L. G. Augenstein MICH
NGR-23-005-185 University of Michigan   J. R. P. French MICH
NGR-23-005-201 University of Michigan   R. von Baumgarten MICH
NGR-24-001-002 Concordia College   H. R. Homann MINN
NGR-25-001-004 Mississippi State University   R. G. Tischer MISS
NGR-25-002-015 University of Mississippi   H. T. Milhorn MISS
NGR-26-003-023 University of Missouri (Columbia) R. L. Wixon MO
NGL-26-004-021 University of Missouri (Columbia) X. J. Musacchia MO
NGR-26-004-025 University of Missouri (Columbia) F. E. South MO
NGR-30-001-001 Dartmouth College   C. J. Lyon N H
NGR-31-001-145 Princeton University   C. S. Pittendrigh N J
NGR-31-011-002 New Jersey College of Medicine & Dentistry   N J
NGR-33-010-013 Cornell University   M. Alexander N Y
NGR-33-012-009 Fordham University   W. C. Corning N Y
NGR-33-016-102 New York University   J. Post N Y
NGR-33-023-032 Yeshiva University   E. D. Weitzman N Y
NGR-34-001-019 Duke University   K. Schmidt-Koenig N C
NGR-34-002-055 North Carolina State University R. G. Pearson N C
NGR-34-002-095 North Carolina State University R. G. Pearson N C
NGR-36-003-042 Case Western Reserve University   OHIO
                      B. Reswick and H. Mergler
NGL-36-003-088 Case Western Reserve University   S. Ostrach OHIO
NGR-36-008-004 Ohio State University   H. S. Weiss OHIO
NGR-36-008-041 Ohio State University   J. H. Dines, OHIO
                              L. B. Roberts
NGR-36-008-117 Ohio State University   R. M. Nerem OHIO
NGR-36-007-012 Ohio University   W-K Chen OHIO
NGR-38-002-013 Oregon State University   H. C. Curl ORE
NGR-38-002-017 Oregon State University   R. Y. Morita ORE
NGR-39-002-011 Carnegie-Mellon University   J. J. Wolken PA
NGL-39-004-015 Drexel Institute of Technology   M. M. Labes PA
NGR-39-009-008 Pennsylvania State University   E. C. Pollard PA
NGL-39-010-097 University of Pennsylvania   C. J. Lambertsen PA
NGR-39-018-002 Bryn Mawr College   M. Yarczower PA
NGR-44-003-031 Baylor University   R. Roessler TEX
NGR-44-009-018 Texas Christian University   M. D. Arnoult TEX
NGR-44-012-003 University of Texas Southwestern Medical School   TEX
                          P. O'B. Montgomery TEX
NGR-44-012-088 University of Texas (Austin)   B. Fruchter TEX
NGR-44-013-001 Texas Woman's University   P. B. Mack TEX
NGR-45-002-008 Utah State University   F. B. Salisbury UTAH
NGR-45-003-043 University of Utah   E. A. Shneour UTAH
NGR-47-002-005 Virginia Commonwealth University W. T. Ham VA
NGR-47-002-018 Virginia Commonwealth University S. W. Lippincott VA
NGR-47-002-020 Virginia Commonwealth University H. P. Dalton VA
NGR-47-004-018 Virginia Polytechnic Institute   W. E. C. Moore VA
NGR-48-001-004 Washington State University   B. A. McFadden WASH

NGR-49-001-019	West Virginia University	W. H. Moran	W VA
NGR-50-002-083	University of Wisconsin (Madison)	V. C. Rideout	WISC
NGR-52-083-002	College of the Virgin Islands	F. B. Gray	FOR
NGR-52-119-001	University of Goteborg	H. Hyden	FOR
NSR-05-003-233	University of California (Berkeley)	N. Pace	CAL
NSR-05-007-089	University of California (Los Angeles)	J. D. French	CAL
NSR-05-018-087	University of Southern California	L. G. Goff	CAL
NSR-09-010-035	George Washington University	C. W. Shilling	D C
NSR-33-012-006	Fordham University	J. Kubis	N Y
NSR-39-010-100	University of Pennsylvania	R. E. Forster	PA
NAS2-1554	University of Virginia	G. C. Pitts	VA
NAS2-2503	University of California (Los Angeles)	W. R. Adey	CAL
NAS2-2633	University of Southern California	J. P. Meehan	CAL
NAS2-2711	Texas Womans University	P. B. Mack	TEX
NAS2-2738	University of Minnesota	F. Halberg	MINN
NAS2-3528	Bowling Green State University	I. I. Oster	OHIO
NAS2-4231	University of California (Berkeley)	N. Pace	CAL
NAS2-4849	University of St. Thomas	L. S. Browning	TEX
NAS2-4915	University of California (Berkeley)		CAL
NAS2-5016	Georgia Institute of Technology		GA
NAS2-5098	Princeton University	C. Pittendrigh	N J
NAS9-4500	University of Minnesota	W. Kubicek	MINN
NAS9-6812	Texas A & M University	H. E. Whitmore	TEX
NAS9-6910	Ohio State University	C. Mengel	OHIO
NAS9-7280	Baylor University	P. C. Johnson	TEX
NAS9-7882	University of California (Los Angeles)		CAL
NAS9-7892	University of California (San Diego)	G. Arrhenius	CAL
NAS9-7951	Texas A & M University	J. M. Prescott	TEX
NAS9-8101	University of Miami	S. Sox	FLA
NAS9-8122	University of Texas (Austin)	S. E. Ritzmann	TEX
NAS9-8479	North Texas State University		TEX
NAS9-8747	University of Arizona		ARIZ
NAS9-8888	Texas Womans University	P. B. Mack	TEX
NAS9-8949	Baylor University	P. C. Johnson	TEX
NAS9-9266	University of Texas (Galveston)	M. Guest	TEX
NAS9-9300	University of Wisconsin (Madison)		WIS
NAS9-9418	Baylor University	J. D. Frost	TEX
NAS9-9427	Texas Womans University	P. B. Mack	TEX
NAS9-9433	Harding College	H. D. Olree	ARK
NAS12-2134	Virginia Polytechnic Institute		VA

52 CLINICAL MEDICAL

NGR-05-004-026	University of California (Davis)	L. D. Carlson	CAL
NGL-05-004-031	University of California (Davis)	L. D. Carlson	CAL
NGR-05-020-223	Stanford University	M. Anliker	CAL
NGR-05-025-007	University of California (San Francisco)	L. E. Earley	CAL
NGR-09-009-024	Georgetown University	I. Gray	D C
NGR-10-005-057	University of Florida	W. B. Webb	FLA
NGL-10-005-082	University of Florida	D. C. Goodman	FLA
NGR-11-001-009	Emory University	V. P. Popovic	GA
NGR-11-001-016	Emory University	G. H. Bourne	GA
NGR-34-003-021	University of North Carolina (Chapel Hill)		N C
		H. A. Tyroler	
NGL-50-002-078	University of Wisconsin (Madison)	E. C. Dick	WISC
NGR-50-002-086	University of Wisconsin (Madison)	D. O. Cliver	WISC
NAS9-8200	University of Texas (Austin)	M. Wheatcroft	TEX
NAS9-8246	Texas Womans University	P. B. Mack	TEX

NAS9-8258	University of Texas (Austin)	S. E. Ritzmann	TEX
NAS9-9053	Texas A&M University	D. Hightower	TEX
NAS9-9103	University of Chicago	J. H. Rust	ILL

59 LIFE SCIENCES *(not elsewhere classified)*

NGR-09-009-025	Georgetown University	C. B. Ferster	D C
NGR-11-001-031	Emory University	S. W. Gray	GA
NGR-22-007-138	Harvard University	R. J. Herrnstein	MASS
NGR-22-007-154	Harvard University	R. A. McFarland	MASS
NGR-22-007-163	Harvard University	R. A. Bauer	MASS
NGR-22-009-424	Massachusetts Institute of Technology	A. Rich	MASS
NGR-33-015-016	State University of New York (Buffalo)		N Y
		J. Danielli	
NGR-36-017-002	Bowling Green State University	I. I. Oster	OHIO
NGR-39-010-104	University of Pennsylvania	A. H. Brown	PA
NSR-09-010-057	George Washington University	C. W. Shilling	D C
NSR-10-008-021	University of South Florida	M. G. Kobasky	FLA
NSR-36-008-108	Ohio State University	H. V. Ellington	OHIO
NSR-47-005-070	University of Virginia	E. H. Hendricks	VA
NAS12-2142	University of Vermont		VT

PSYCHOLOGY

61 BIOLOGICAL ASPECTS

NGR-38-003-015	University of Oregon	J. Roman	ORE
NGR-44-003-001	Baylor University	P. Kellaway	TEX
NGR-52-059-001	McMaster University	A. B. Kristofferson	FOR

62 SOCIAL ASPECTS

NGR-05-020-244	Stanford University	R. C. Atkinson	CAL
NGL-34-002-061	North Carolina State University	L. A. Jones	N C

SOCIAL SCIENCES

71 ANTHROPOLOGY

NSR-34-001-025	Duke University	T. D. Reynolds	N C

72 ECONOMICS

NGR-05-046-005	San Jose State College	J. C. Thompson	CAL
NGR-15-003-066	Indiana University	R. W. Campbell	IND

208   *NASA Grants and Research Contracts*

73 HISTORY

NGR-38-002-018	Oregon State University	S. E. Williamson	ORE
NAS1-8311	Hampton Institute	L. C. Wyrett	VA
NAS9-6331	University of Houston	L. Swenson	TEX
NGR-05-061-005	University of California (Santa Cruz)		CAL
		W. M. McKeeman	CAL
NGR-22-009-393	Massachusetts Institute of Technology	A. Evans	MASS

75 POLITICAL SCIENCE

NGR-33-010-039	Cornell University	P. P. Van Riper	N Y
NGR-33-015-061	State University of New York (Buffalo)	R. G. Hunt	N Y
NGL-39-011-080	University of Pittsburgh	D. C. Stone	PA

76 SOCIOLOGY

NGR-05-003-125	University of California (Berkeley)	C. W. Churchman	CAL
NGL-10-007-067	University of Miami	F. D. Kohler	FLA
NGR-26-008-003	Washington University (St. Louis)	M. L. Weidenbaum	MO
NGR-36-022-001	Miami University	D. E. Cunningham	OHIO
NGR-44-009-008	Texas Christian University	S. B. Sells	TEX
NSR-39-011-078	University of Pittsburgh	G. McGee	PA
NSR-39-011-089	University of Pittsburgh	A. Kent	PA
NAS9-8795	Texas Southern University		TEX

79 SOCIAL SCIENCES *(not elsewhere classified)*

NGR-01-001-006	Alabama A&M College	R. H. Lee	ALA
NGR-21-025-001	Morgan State College		MD
NGL-32-004-042	University of New Mexico	W. W. Grannemann	NMEX
NGR-44-033-001	Prairie View A&M College	I. V. Nelson	TEX
NGR-47-020-001	Hampton Institute	E. Kollmann	VA
NSR-05-007-236	University of California (Los Angeles)	R. A. Goodman	CAL
NSR-06-004-081	University of Denver	J. G. Milliken	COLO
NSR-07-002-037	University of Connecticut	S. W. Yost	CONN
NSR-15-003-069	Indiana University	G. W. Wilson	IND
NSR-32-004-049	University of New Mexico		NMEX
NSR-37-004-008	Southeastern State College		OKLA
NSR-39-011-106	University of Pittsburgh		PA

OTHER SCIENCES

99 ALL DISCIPLINES

NGL-03-002-091	University of Arizona	H. D. Christensen	ARIZ
NGL-05-003-012	University of California (Berkeley)	S. Silver	CAL
NGR-05-003-143	University of California (Berkeley)	D. J. Sakrison,	CAL
		Y. Algazi	
NGR-05-003-243	University of California (Berkeley)	R. S. Muller	CAL
NGR-05-003-285	University of California (Berkeley)	C. L. Tien	CAL
NGR-05-007-122	University of California (Los Angeles)		CAL
		A. V. Balakrishnan	CAL

NGR-05-007-187	University of California (Los Angeles)	J. J. Vidal	CAL
NGR-05-009-025	University of California (San Diego)	P. A. Libby	CAL
NGR-05-018-022	University of Southern California	G. A. Bekey	CAL
NGL-05-018-044	University of Southern California	H. Bichsel	CAL
NGL-05-018-098	University of Southern California		CAL
NGR-05-020-102	Stanford University	K. Karamcheti	CAL
NGL-05-020-232	Stanford University	R. L. Kovach	CAL
NGL-06-001-015	Colorado School of Mines	L. T. Grose	COLO
NGR-06-002-018	Colorado State University	J. B. Best	COLO
NGL-06-002-038	Colorado State University	R. Jensen	COLO
NGR-06-003-083	University of Colorado	I. Horowitz	COLO
NGL-06-004-007	University of Denver	S. A. Johnson	COLO
NGR-06-004-068	University of Denver	L. W. Ross	COLO
NGL-06-004-078	University of Denver	A. A. Ezra	COLO
NGL-07-002-002	University of Connecticut	D. P. Lindorff	CONN
NGR-09-005-055	Catholic University	H. C. Khatri	CAL
NGL-09-010-030	George Washington University	L. H. Mayo	D C
NGL-09-011-004	Howard University	H. Branson	D C
NGL-10-005-005	University of Florida	L. E. Grinter	FLA
NGR-10-005-036	University of Florida	G. E. Nevill	FLA
NGR-10-005-080	University of Florida	R. E. Hummel	FLA
NGL-10-007-010	University of Miami	E. H. Man	FLA
NGR-10-007-070	University of Miami	M. L. Harvey	FLA
NGL-11-002-018	Georgia Institute of Technology		GA
		K. Picha, V. Crawford	GA
NGR-11-002-081	Georgia Institute of Technology	V. Crawford	GA
NGL-14-001-009	University of Chicago	M. H. Cohen	ILL
NGR-14-001-103	University of Chicago	J. E. Lamport	ILL
NGR-14-001-135	University of Chicago	A. L. Turkeviuh	ILL
NGR-14-005-009	University of Illinois (Urbana)	R. Mittra	ILL
NGR-14-007-011	Northwestern University	G. Herrmann	ILL
NGL-14-007-058	Northwestern University	J. A. D. Copper	ILL
NGR-14-007-062	Northwestern University	A. H. Rubenstein	ILL
NGR-14-007-067	Northwestern University	G. Herrmann	ILL
NGR-15-005-021	Purdue University	F. N. Andrews	IND
NGL-17-001-005	Kansas State University	J. L. Brown	KAN
NGL-18-002-005	University of Louisville	W. J. McGlothlin	KY
NGR-19-001-068	Louisiana State University (Baton Rouge)		LA
		E. J. Dantin	
NGL-20-006-001	University of Maine (Orono)	T. H. Curry	ME
NGR-21-001-073	Johns Hopkins University	A. Chapanis	MD
NGL-21-002-008	University of Maryland	W. C. Rheinboldt	MD
NGR-22-007-003	Harvard University	W. H. Sweet	MASS
NGL-22-009-019	Massachusetts Institute of Technology		MASS
		J. V. Harrington	MASS
NGL-26-004-003	University of Missouri (Columbia)	Ward J. Haas	MO
NGR-26-008-006	Washington University (St. Louis)	G. E. Pake	MO
NGR-27-001-001	Montana State University	I. E. Dayton	MONT
NGR-27-001-035	Montana State University	K. Nordtvedt	MONT
NGR-30-002-056	University of New Hampshire	C. K. Taft	N H
NGL-32-003-027	New Mexico State University	J. E. Weiss	NMEX
NGL-33-001-001	Adelphi University	R. Genberg	N Y
NGL-33-016-067	New York University	J. R. Ragazzini	N Y
NGL-33-018-003	Rensselaer Polytechnic Institute	S. E. Wiberley	N Y
NGL-33-022-090	Syracuse University	J. C. Honey	N Y
NGL-34-001-005	Duke University	J. B. Chaddock	N C
NGR-34-003-040	University of North Carolina (Chapel Hill)		N C
		R. G. Faust	
NGL-36-004-014	University of Cincinnati	R. P. Harrington	OHIO

NGL-37-002-011	Oklahoma State University	V. S. Haneman	OKLA
NGL-37-003-026	University of Oklahoma	C. Riggs	OKLA
NGL-39-004-007	Drexel Institute of Technology	C. Gatlin	PA
NGL-39-004-020	Drexel Institute of Technology	W. Hagerty	PA
NGR-39-004-028	Drexel Institute of Technology	C. A. Silver	PA
NGL-39-009-015	Pennsylvania State University	P. Ebaugh	PA
NGL-39-011-002	University of Pittsburgh	D. Halliday	PA
NGL-40-002-009	Brown University	P. T. Maeder	R I
NGL-43-001-021	University of Tennessee	C. O. Thomas	TENN
NGL-44-001-001	Texas A & M University	H. E. Whitmore	TEX
NGL-44-005-021	University of Houston	J. R. Crump	TEX
NGR-44-005-090	University of Houston	C. J. Huang	TEX
NGL-44-006-033	Rice University	A. J. Chapman,	TEX
NGL-44-007-006	Southern Methodist University	J. C. Denton	TEX
NGL-46-001-008	University of Vermont	C. D. Cook	VT
NGL-47-004-006	Virginia Polytechnic Institute		VA
		F. W. Bull, J. A. Jacobs	
NGR-47-005-110	University of Virginia	G. B. Matthews	VA
NGL-47-006-008	College of William and Mary	W. M. Jones	VA
NGL-49-001-001	West Virginia University	J. C. Ludlum	W VA
NGR-50-002-114	University of Wisconsin (Madison)	V. E. Suomi	WISC
NSR-01-002-057	University of Alabama (Birmingham)	E. A. Sallin	ALA
NSR-01-003-005	Auburn University	R. I. Vachon	ALA
NSR-05-002-124	California Institute of Technology	J. N. Franklin	CAL
NSR-05-010-021	University of California (Santa Barbara)		CAL
		W. T. Thomson	
NSR-05-020-088	Stanford University	M. Anliker	CAL
NSR-10-007-078	University of Miami	D. L. Harvey	FLA
NSR-15-003-054	Indiana University	A. W. Weimer	IND
NSR-15-003-067	Indiana University	L. Orr	IND
NSR-15-004-029	University of Notre Dame	T. J. Mueller	IND
NSR-22-011-036	Northeastern University	C. G. Houtsma	MASS
NSR-36-003-051	Case Western Reserve University		OHIO
		I. Greber, W. T. Olson	
NSR-37-002-045	Oklahoma State University	K. A. McCollom	OKLA
NSR-44-005-016	University of Houston	C. J. Huang	TEX
NSR-44-005-059	University of Houston	C. J. Huang	TEX
NAS1-81446	University of Iowa		IOWA
NAS2-4671	Stanford University	T. Tomberlin	CAL
NAS2-4672	Stanford University	V. R. Eshlman	CAL
NAS2-5254	Bradley University		ILL
NAS5-9590	Illinois Institute of Technology	C. Vest	ILL
NAS8-21321	University of Alabama (Huntsville)		ALA
		O. J. Christensen	
NAS9-5632	Stanford University	R. L. Kovach	CAL
NAS9-8102	Massachusetts Institute of Technology		MASS
NAS9-8379	Ohio State University	C. Mengel	OHIO
NAS9-9003	Rice University	J. R. Sims	TEX
NAS9-9104	University of Houston		TEX
NAS9-9184	University of Houston		TEX
NAS10-5172	Florida Institute of Technology	J. J. Frangie	FLA
NAS12-2105	University of California (Los Angeles)		CAL
NAS12-2138	University of California (Los Angeles)		CAL
NGT-01-002-002	University of Alabama (University)	E. Rodgers	ALA
NGT-01-003-001	Auburn University	W. V. Parker	ALA
NGT-02-001-007	University of Alaska	K. M. Rae	ALS
NGT-03-001-002	Arizona State University	W. J. Burke	ARIZ
NGT-03-002-008	University of Arizona	H. D. Rhodes	ARIZ
NGT-05-002-009	California Institute of Technology	H. F. Bohnenblust	CAL

NGT-05-003-023	University of California (Berkeley)	S. S. Elberg	CAL
NGT-05-007-019	University of California (Los Angeles)	W. F. Libby	CAL
NGT-05-008-001	University of California (Riverside)	R. B. March	CAL
NGT-05-009-008	University of California (San Diego)	F. T. Wall	CAL
NGT-05-010-005	University of California (Santa Barbara)	A. Bruckner	CAL
NGT-05-018-004	University of Southern California	M. C. Kloetzel	CAL
NGT-05-018-085	University of Southern California	R. E. Stephens	CAL
NGT-05-020-016	Stanford University	H. Heffner	CAL
NGT-05-020-228	Stanford University	J. A. Vitale	CAL
NGT-05-020-295	Stanford University	J. M. Pettit	CAL
NGT-06-001-001	Colorado School of Mines	A. R. Jordan	COLO
NGT-06-002-002	Colorado State University	W. H. Bragonier	COLO
NGT-06-003-004	University of Colorado	E. J. Archer	COLO
NGT-06-004-008	University of Denver	W. C. Miller	COLO
NGT-07-002-003	University of Connecticut	N. L. Whetten	CONN
NGT-07-004-014	Yale University	J. P. Miller	CONN
NGT-08-001-002	University of Delaware	C. E. Birchenall	DEL
NGT-09-005-006	Catholic University	J. P. O'Connor	D C
NGT-09-009-004	Georgetown University	J. B. Horigan	D C
NGT-09-010-003	George Washington University	A. E. Burns	D C
NGT-09-011-001	Howard University	C. L. Miller	D C
NGT-10-004-008	Florida State University	R. J. Keirs	FLA
NGT-10-005-006	University of Florida	L. E. Grinter	FLA
NGT-10-007-006	University of Miami	J. A. Harrison	FLA
NGT-11-001-005	Emory University	C. T. Lester	GA
NGT-11-002-006	Georgia Institute of Technology	T. W. Jackson	GA
NGT-11-002-064	Georgia Institute of Technology	J. A. Vitale	GA
NGT-11-003-002	University of Georgia	G. B. Huff	GA
NGT-12-001-005	University of Hawaii	W. Gorter	HAW
NGT-13-001-001	University of Idaho	M. L. Jackson	IDA
NGT-14-001-015	University of Chicago	C. D. O'Connell	ILL
NGT-14-004-002	Illinois Institute of Technology	A. Grad	ILL
NGT-14-005-017	University of Illinois (Urbana)	D. Alpert	ILL
NGT-14-007-004	Northwestern University	R. H. Baker	ILL
NGT-14-008-008	Southern Illinois University	W. E. Simeone	ILL
NGT-15-003-003	Indiana University	R. B. Curtis	IND
NGT-15-004-002	University of Notre Dame	P. E. Beichner	IND
NGT-15-005-005	Purdue University	F. N. Andrews	IND
NGT-15-005-061	Purdue University		IND
NGT-16-001-004	University of Iowa	D. C. Spriestersbach	IOWA
NGT-16-002-002	Iowa State University	J. B. Page	IOWA
NGT-17-001-002	Kansas State University	J. P. Noonan	KAN
NGT-17-002-006	University of Kansas	W. P. Albrecht	KAN
NGT-17-002-044	University of Kansas	W. P. Smith	KAN
NGT-17-002-052	University of Kansas	J. A. Vitale	KANS
NGT-18-001-005	University of Kentucky	L. W. Cochran	KY
NGT-18-002-006	University of Louisville	J. A. Dillon	KY
NGT-19-001-001	Louisiana State University (Baton Rouge)		LA
		M. Goodrich	
NGT-19-002-002	Tulane University	D. R. Deener	LA
NGT-20-006-002	University of Maine (Orono)	F. P. Eggert	ME
NGT-21-001-004	Johns Hopkins University	G. W. Shaffer	MD
NGT-21-002-013	University of Maryland	M. J. Pelczar	MD
NGT-22-003-001	Boston College	W. J. Feeney	MASS
NGT-22-004-003	Boston University	P. E. Kubzansky	MASS
NGT-22-005-005	Brandeis University	H. Weisberg	MASS
NGT-22-006-001	Clark University	D. E. Lee	MASS
NGT-22-007-008	Harvard University	R. A. McFarland	MASS
NGT-22-009-020	Massachusetts Institute of Technology	H. L. Hazen	MASS

NGT-22-010-008	University of Massachusetts	E. C. Moore	MASS
NGT-22-011-003	Northeastern University	A. A. Vernon	MASS
NGT-22-012-002	Tufts University	P. H. Flint	MASS
NGT-22-017-001	Worcester Polytechnic Institute	R. F. Morton	MASS
NGT-22-018-002	Lowell Technological Institute	E. L. Alexander	MASS
NGT-23-004-004	Michigan State University	J. Vinocur	MICH
NGT-23-005-018	University of Michigan	G. E. Hay	MICH
NGT-23-006-001	Wayne State University	J. E. Hill	MICH
NGT-23-007-004	Michigan Technological University	D. G. Yerg	MICH
NGT-24-005-012	University of Minnesota	B. Crawford	MINN
NGT-24-005-078	University of Minnesota	G. W. Anderson	MINN
NGT-25-001-002	Mississippi State University	J. C. McKee	MISS
NGT-25-002-001	University of Mississippi	W. L. Nobles	MISS
NGT-25-005-001	University of Southern Mississippi	R. S. Owings	MISS
NGT-26-003-001	University of Missouri (Rolla)	W. Bosch	MO
NGT-26-004-001	University of Missouri (Columbia)	C. E. Marshall	MO
NGT-26-006-001	St. Louis University	H. Howe	MO
NGT-26-008-005	Washington University (St. Louis)	G. E. Pake	MO
NGT-27-001-003	Montana State University	L. DS. Smith	MONT
NGT-27-002-001	University of Montana	F. S. Honkala	MONT
NGT-28-004-001	University of Nebraska (Lincoln)	J. C. Olson	NEB
NGT-29-001-002	University of Nevada (Reno)	T. D. O'Brien	NEV
NGT-30-001-003	Dartmouth College	J. F. Hornig	N H
NGT-30-002-002	University of New Hampshire	W. H. Drew	N H
NGT-31-001-009	Princeton University	C. S. Pittendrigh	N J
NGT-31-003-005	Stevens Institute of Technology	R. A. Morgen	N J
NGT-31-004-002	Rutgers University	H. C. Torrey	N J
NGT-32-003-004	New Mexico State University	E. Walden	NMEX
NGT-32-004-004	University of New Mexico	A. Steger	NMEX
NGT-33-001-002	Adelphi University	M. V. B. Jennings	N Y
NGT-33-002-002	Alfred University	E. E. Mueller	N Y
NGT-33-007-001	Clarkson College of Technology	H. L. Shulman	N Y
NGT-33-008-013	Columbia University	R. S. Halford	N Y
NGT-33-010-007	Cornell University	F. S. Erdman	N Y
NGT-33-010-052	Cornell University	J. A. Vitale	N Y
NGT-33-012-002	Fordham University	J. F. Mulligan	N Y
NGT-33-014-002	City University of New York	M. Rees	N Y
NGT-33-015-004	State University of New York (Stony Brook)		N Y
		R. Jordan	N Y
NGT-33-015-027	State University of New York (Buffalo)	A. W. Holt	N Y
NGT-33-015-099	State University of New York (Stony Brook)		N Y
NGT-33-016-014	New York University	J. R. Ragazzini	N Y
NGT-33-018-010	Rensselaer Polytechnic Institute	S. E. Wiberley	N Y
NGT-33-019-006	University of Rochester	R. G. Loewy	N Y
NGT-33-022-005	Syracuse University	F. P. Piskor	N Y
NGT-33-022-097	Syracuse University	J. C. Honey	N Y
NGT-33-023-003	Yeshiva University	A. Gelbart	N Y
NGT-34-001-003	Duke University	R. L Predmore	N C
NGT-34-002-003	North Carolina State University	W. J. Peterson	N C
NGT-34-003-001	University of North Carolina (Chapel Hill)		N C
		C. H. Holman	N C
NGT-35-001-001	North Dakota State University	G. S. Smith	N D
NGT-35-002-004	University of North Dakota	C. J. Hamre	N D
NGT-36-003-007	Case Western Reserve University	L. Gordon	OHIO
NGT-36-004-003	University of Cincinnati	C. Crockett	OHIO
NGT-36-007-002	Kent State University	J. White	OHIO
NGT-36-008-006	Ohio State University	W. M. Protheroe	OHIO
NGT-36-008-007	Ohio State University	F. H. Shillito	OHIO
NGT-36-009-001	Ohio University	T. Culbert	OHIO
NGT-36-010-001	University of Toledo	A. N. Solberg	OHIO
NGT-36-013-001	Case Reserve Western University	W. M. Heston	OHIO
NGT-37-002-002	Oklahoma State University	M. T. Edmison	OKLA
NGT-37-003-001	University of Oklahoma	C. D. Riggs	OKLA
NGT-38-002-001	Oregon State University	H. P. Hansen	ORE
NGT-39-002-002	Carnegie-Mellon University	A. F. Strehler	PA
NGT-39-004-005	Drexel Institute of Technology	O. W. Witzell	PA
NGT-39-007-003	Lehigh University	R. D. Stout	PA
NGT-39-009-011	Pennsylvania State University	M. N. McGeary	PA
NGT-39-010-007	University of Pennsylvania	A. N. Hixson	PA
NGT-39-011-003	University of Pittsburgh	P. F. Jones	PA
NGT-39-011-075	University of Pittsburgh	D. C. Stone	PA
NGT-39-012-007	Temple University	G. H. Huganir	PA
NGT-39-019-002	Duquesne University	H. H. Petit	PA
NGT-39-023-005	Villanova University	A. H. Buford	PA
NGT-40-002-008	Brown University	M. J. Brennan	R I
NGT-40-004-001	University of Rhode Island	P. H. Nash	R I
NGT-41-001-001	Clemson University	V. Hurst	S C
NGT-41-002-002	University of South Carolina	J. A. Morris	S C
NGT-42-002-001	University of South Dakota	W. W. Gutzman	S D
NGT-43-001-002	University of Tennessee	H. A. Smith	TENN
NGT-43-002-002	Vanderbilt University	R. T. Lagemann	TENN
NGT-44-001-003	Texas A & M University	W. C. Hall	TEX
NGT-44-003-019	Baylor University	J. D. Bragg	TEX
NGT-44-005-004	University of Houston	J. C. Allred	TEX
NGT-44-006-003	Rice University	W. E. Gordon	TEX
NGT-44-007-002	Southern Methodist University	C. C. Allbritton	TEX
NGT-44-009-002	Texas Christian University	E. L. Secrest	TEX
NGT-45-001-002	Brigham Young University	W. P. Lloyd	UTAH
NGT-45-002-001	Utah State University	E. J. Gardner	UTAH
NGT-45-003-002	University of Utah	S. M. McMurrin	UTAH
NGT-46-001-001	University of Vermont	W. H. Macmillan	VT
NGT-47-004-001	Virginia Polytechnic Institute	F. W. Bull	VA
NGT-47-005-005	University of Virginia	E. Younger	VA
NGT-47-006-013	College of William and Mary	R. T. Siegel	VA
NGT-48-001-002	Washington State University	J. F. Short	WASH
NGT-48-002-007	University of Washington	J. L. McCarthy	WASH
NGT-49-001-002	West Virginia University	J. Ludlum	W VA
NGT-50-001-005	Marquette University	L. W. Friedrich	WISC
NGT-50-002-003	University of Wisconsin (Madison)	R. M. Bock	WISC
NGT-51-001-002	University of Wyoming	R. H. Bruce	WYO
NGF-03-002-025	University of Arizona	G. P. Kuiper	ARIZ
NGF-05-003-021	University of California (Berkeley)	S. Silver	CAL
NGF-05-007-020	University of California (Los Angeles)	W. F. Libby	CAL
NGF-05-018-015	University of Southern California	J. P. Meeham	CAL
NGF-05-020-017	Stanford University	J. Lederberg	CAL
NGF-06-003-005	University of Colorado	W. A. Rense	COLO
NGF-06-004-024	University of Denver	C. M. Alter	COLO
NGF-09-012-061	National Academy of Sciences	F. B. Seitz	DC
NGF-10-005-024	University of Florida	L. E. Grinter	FLA
NGF-14-005-020	University of Illinois (Urbana)	D. Alpert	ILL
NGF-15-005-011	Purdue University	B. A. Reese	IND
NGF-17-004-010	University of Kansas	B. G. Barr	KAN
NGF-21-002-016	University of Maryland	M. H. Martin	MD
NGF-22-007-009	Harvard University	William H. Sweet	MASS
NGF-22-009-021	Massachusetts Institute of Technology	J. V. Harrington	MASS
NGF-23-005-019	University of Michigan	R. A. Sawyer	MICH
NGF-24-005-011	University of Minnesota	A. O. C. Nier	MINN
NGF-24-005-072	University of Minnesota	W. B. Cheston	MINN

NGF-31-001-011	Princeton University	J. P. Layton	N J
NGF-33-006-008	Polytechnic Institute of Brooklyn	M. H. Bloom	N Y
NGF-33-010-010	Cornell University	T. Gold	N Y
NGF-33-018-011	Rensselaer Polytechnic Institute	S. E. Wiberly	N Y
NGF-33-019-011	University of Rochester	W. O. Fenn	N Y

NGF-36-003-058	Case Western Reserve University	H. R. Nara	OHIO
NGF-39-011-004	University of Pittsburgh	D. Halliday	PA
NGF-44-001-014	Texas A & M University	R. E. Wainerdi	TEX
NGF-44-006-008	Rice University	A. J. Dessler	TEX
NGF-50-002-004	University of Wisconsin (Madison)		WISC
		J. O. Hirschfelder	

MAJOR NASA PROGRAM AREAS

OFFICE OF PUBLIC AFFAIRS

NGR-15-009-001	Ball State University	E. Montague	IND
NGR-33-015-061	State University of New York (Buffalo)	R. G. Hunt	N Y
NGR-38-002-018	Oregon State University	S. E. Williamson	ORE
NSR-34-001-025	Duke University	T. D. Reynolds	N C
NSR-44-001-053	Texas A&M University	H. Monroe	TEX

OFFICE OF INDUSTRY AFFAIRS

NGL-05-007-003	University of California (Los Angeles)	W. F. Libby	CAL
NSR-33-008-069	Columbia University	W. A. Owens	N Y

OCCUPATIONAL HEALTH DIVISION

NGR-23-005-185	University of Michigan	J. R. P. French	MICH
NGR-34-003-021	University of North Carolina (Chapel Hill)		N C
		H. A. Tyroler	

OFFICE OF ADVANCED RESEARCH & TECHNOLOGY

NGR-01-001-003	Alabama A&M College	C. O. Lee	ALA
NGR-03-002-011	University of Arizona	T. L. Vincent	ARIZ
NGR-03-002-024	University of Arizona	G. A. Korn	ARIZ
NGL-05-002-002	California Institute of Technology	J. P. Liepmann	CAL
NGL-05-002-005	California Institute of Technology	W. G. Knauss	CAL
NGL-05-003-016	University of California (Berkeley)	C. A. Desoer, L. A. Zadek, E. Polak	CAL
NGL-05-003-050	University of California (Berkeley)	A. K. Oppenheim	CAL
NGL-05-003-272	University of California (Berkeley)	C. H. Townes	CAL
NGR-05-003-275	University of California (Berkeley)	H. P. Smith	CAL
NGL-05-004-031	University of California (Davis)	L. D. Carlson	CAL
NGR-05-009-025	University of California (San Diego)	P. A. Libby	CAL
NGR-05-009-030	University of California (San Diego)	R. H. Lovberg	CAL
NGR-05-009-062	University of California (San Diego)	I. M. Jacobs	CAL
NGR-05-010-008	University of California (Santa Barbara)	J. M. Sloss	CAL
NGR-05-018-007	University of Southern California	D. L. Judge	CAL
NGR-05-018-022	University of Southern California	G. A. Bekey	CAL
NGR-05-020-007	Stanford University	R. H. Cannon, I. Flugge-Lotz	CAL
NGR-05-020-013	Stanford University	A. L. Schawlow	CAL
NGR-05-020-015	Stanford University	W. M. Fairbank	CAL
NGR-05-020-039	Stanford University	A. S. Tetelman	CAL
NGR-05-020-073	Stanford University	R. E. Kalman	CAL
NGR-05-020-091	Stanford University	D. Bershader	CAL
NGR-05-020-103	Stanford University	S. H. Harris	CAL
NGR-05-020-242	Stanford University	I. Weinberg	CAL
NGR-05-020-245	Stanford University	D. Baganoff	CAL
NGL-05-020-275	Stanford University	K. Karamcheti	CAL
NGR-06-003-033	University of Colorado	A. Busemann	COLO
NGR-06-003-075	University of Colorado	A. Busemann	COLO
NGR-06-004-006	University of Denver	R. C. Amme	COLO
NGR-06-004-068	University of Denver	L. W. Ross	COLO

NGL-07-002-002	University of Connecticut	D. P. Lindorff	CONN
NGR-07-004-035	Yale University	W. E. Lamb	CONN
NGR-07-004-087	Yale University	F. B. Tuteur	CONN
NGR-08-001-016	University of Delaware	E. J. Pellicciaro	DEL
NGL-08-001-019	University of Delaware	T. W. F. Russell	DEL
NGR-09-005-008	Catholic University	R. E. Meijer	D C
NGR-09-005-025	Catholic University	C. C. Chang	D C
NGR-09-005-055	Catholic University	H. C. Khatri	CAL
NGR-09-005-067	Catholic University	S. C. Ling	D C
NGR-10-004-005	Florida State University	L Mandelkern	FLA
NGR-10-005-036	University of Florida	G. E. Nevill	FLA
NGL-10-005-039	University of Florida	J. J. Hren	FLA
NGR-10-005-080	University of Florida	R. E. Hummel	FLA
NGL-10-005-082	University of Florida	D. C. Goodman	FLA
NGR-10-005-089	University of Florida	R. T. Schneider	FLA
NGR-10-008-005	University of South Florida	H. K. E. Wurmb	FLA
NGR-11-001-016	Emory University	G. H. Bourne	GA
NGL-11-002-062	Georgia Institute of Technology	A. Ben Huang	GA
NGL-14-001-009	University of Chicago	M. H. Cohen	ILL
NGL-14-005-074	University of Illinois (Urbana)	H. W. Ades	ILL
NGR-14-007-011	Northwestern University	G. Herrmann	ILL
NGR-14-007-081	Northwestern University	J. T. Waber	ILL
NGR-14-008-002	Southern Illinois University	J. H. Lauchner	ILL
NGR-15-003-060	Indiana University	E. Hopf	IND
NGR-15-003-077	Indiana University	W. D. Neff	IND
NGL-15-004-001	University of Notre Dame	G. F. D'Alelio	IND
NGR-15-004-028	University of Notre Dame	G. F. Dalelio	IND
NGR-15-005-006	Purdue University	J. C. Lindenlaub	IND
NGR-15-005-039	Purdue University	W. Gautschi	IND
NGR-15-005-058	Purdue University	B. A. Reese	IND
NGR-16-002-005	Iowa State University	G. K. Serovy	IOWA
NGR-18-001-017	University of Kentucky	D. C. Leigh	KY
NGR-18-001-020	University of Kentucky	O. W. Dillon	KY
NGR-18-001-038	University of Kentucky	M. H. Leipold	KY
NGR-18-001-042	University of Kentucky	M. H. Leipold	KY
NGR-19-002-027	Tulane University	A. M. Hermann	LA
NGR-21-001-002	Johns Hopkins University	H. W. Moos	MD
NGL-21-002-053	University of Maryland	R. B. Beckmann	MD
NGR-21-007-004	University of Maryland	J. V. Brady	MD
NGR-22-007-003	Harvard University	W. H. Sweet	MASS
NGL-22-007-012	Harvard University	B. Budiansky	MASS
NGL-22-007-101	Harvard University	D. M. Hegsted	MASS
NGR-22-007-117	Harvard University	N. Bloembergen	MASS
NGR-22-007-154	Harvard University	R. A. McFarland	MASS
NGR-22-009-002	Massachusetts Institute of Technology	T. B. Sheridan	MASS
NGL-22-009-003	Massachusetts Institute of Technology	N. J. Grant	MASS
NGR-22-009-010	Massachusetts Institute of Technology	W. R. Markey	MASS
NGL-22-009-012	Massachusetts Institute of Technology	A. Javin	MASS
NGL-22-009-013	Massachusetts Institute of Technology	R. G. Gallager	MASS
NGR-22-009-014	Massachusetts Institute of Technology	H. H. Woodson, H. A. Haus, J. R. Melcher	MASS
NGL-22-009-019	Massachusetts Institute of Technology	J. V. Harrington	MASS
NGR-22-009-059	Massachusetts Institute of Technology	Z. M. Elias	MASS
NGR-22-009-121	Massachusetts Institute of Technology	L. Trilling	MASS

NGR-22-009-125	Massachusetts Institute of Technology	H. C. Gatos	MASS
NGL-22-009-156	Massachusetts Institute of Technology		MASS
		J. L. Meiry, Y. T. Li	
NGR-22-009-269	Massachusetts Institute of Technology	J. A. Fay	MASS
NGR-22-009-312	Massachusetts Institute of Technology	L. R. Young	MASS
NGR-22-009-378	Massachusetts Institute of Technology		MASS
		J. Fay, J. Keck	
NGR-22-011-007	Northeastern University W. B. Nowak, B. L. Cochrun		MASS
NGR-23-004-041	Michigan State University	C. Martin	MICH
NGR-23-005-001	University of Michigan	F. J. Beutler	MICH
NGR-23-005-003	University of Michigan	J. A. Nicholls	MICH
NGR-23-005-004	University of Michigan	C. Kikuchi	MICH
NGR-23-005-010	University of Michigan	S. K. Clark	MICH
NGR-23-006-047	Wayne State University	C. N. DeSilva	MICH
NGR-24-005-070	University of Minnesota	C. C. Hsiao	MINN
NGR-26-010-001	University of Missouri (St. Louis)	D. T. Haimo	MO
NGR-31-001-025	Princeton University	W. R. Schowalter	N J
NGR-31-001-059	Princeton University	E. Dowell	N J
NGR-31-001-119	Princeton University	W. D. Hayes	N J
NGR-31-001-151	Princeton University	A. J. Kelly	N J
NGR-31-003-014	Stevens Institute of Technology	R. F. McAlevy	N J
NGL-31-003-020	Stevens Institute of Technology	H. Meissner	N J
NGR-32-004-002	University of New Mexico W. W. Grannemann		NMEX
NGR-33-006-007	Polytechnic Institute of Brooklyn	H. J. Juretschke	N Y
NGR-33-007-034	Clarkson College of Technology	L. C. Barrett	N Y
NGR-33-008-009	Columbia University	R. Novick	N Y
NGR-33-008-098	Columbia University	M. B. Friedman	N Y
NGR-33-010-029	Cornell University	L. H. Germer	N Y
NGL-33-010-054	Cornell University	A. R. Seebass	N Y
NGR-33-010-064	Cornell University	T. A. Cool	N Y
NGR-33-013-009	City College of New York	R. Shinner	N Y
NGR-33-013-034	City College of New York		N Y
		C. M. Tchen	
NGR-33-015-013	State University of New York (Stony Brook)		N Y
		R. P. Tewarson	
NGL-33-015-035	State University of New York (Stony Brook)		N Y
		L. L. Seigle	
NGR-33-016-003	New York University	R. C. Sahni	N Y
NGL-33-016-119	New York University	A. Ferri	N Y
NGR-33-016-149	New York University	A. Ferri	N Y
NGL-33-018-003	Rensselaer Polytechnic Institute	S. E. Wiberley	N Y
NGR-33-018-075	Rensselaer Polytechnic Institute	E. Holt	N Y
NGR-33-019-014	University of Rochester	E. Kinnen	N Y
NGR-33-019-086	University of Rochester	D. H. Douglas	N Y
NGR-33-022-004	Syracuse University	D. V. Keller	N Y
NGR-33-022-035	Syracuse University	M. E. Barzelay	N Y
NGR-34-002-017	North Carolina State University	W. H. Bennett	N C
NGR-34-002-048	North Carolina State University	H. A. Hassan	N C
NGR-36-003-033	Case Western Reserve University	J. F. Wallace	OHIO
NGR-36-003-054	Case Western Reserve University	J. L. Koenig	OHIO
NGL-36-003-088	Case Western Reserve University	S. Ostrach	OHIO
NGR-36-003-094	Case Western Reserve University	L. Leonard	OHIO
NGR-36-003-139	Case Western Reserve University	E. Reshotko	OHIO
NGR-36-008-002	Ohio State University	C. A. Levis	OHIO
NGL-36-008-051	Ohio State University	F. H. Beck	OHIO
NGL-36-008-106	Ohio State University	R. M. Nerem	OHIO
NGR-36-008-117	Ohio State University	R. M. Nerem	OHIO
NGL-39-004-015	Drexel Institute of Technology	M. M. Labes	PA
NGR-39-007-007	Lehigh University	R. W. Kraft	PA

NGR-39-007-011	Lehigh University	F. Erdogan	PA
NGR-39-008-014	Carnegie-Mellon University	E. G. Haney	PA
NGR-39-009-023	Pennsylvania State University	J. L. Shearer	PA
NGR-39-009-077	Pennsylvania State University	G. M. Faeth	PA
NGL-39-010-001	University of Pennsylvania	M. Altman	PA
NGR-39-010-002	University of Pennsylvania	J. O'M. Bockris	PA
NGR-39-011-039	University of Pittsburgh	W. G. Vogt	PA
NGR-39-087-003	Carnegie-Mellon University	J. R. Low	PA
NGR-40-002-012	Brown University	P. D. Richardson	R I
NGL-40-002-015	Brown University	J. P. LaSalle	R I
NGR-40-002-059	Brown University	E. A. Mason	R I
NGR-43-001-003	University of Tennessee	W. K. Stair	TENN
NGR-43-001-008	University of Tennessee	D. C. Bogue	TENN
NGL-44-006-001	Rice University	F. R. Brotzen	TEX
NGR-44-007-004	Southern Methodist University	H. A. Blum	TEX
NGR-44-007-028	Southern Methodist University	J. E. Walsh	TEX
NGR-44-012-008	University of Texas (Austin)	B. D. Tapley	TEX
NGL-45-003-019	University of Utah	N. W. Ryan	UTAH
NGR-45-003-027	University of Utah	R. W. Grow	UTAH
NGR-45-003-037	University of Utah	M. L. Williams	UTAH
NGR-45-003-038	University of Utah	W. J. Coles	UTAH
NGR-45-003-050	University of Utah	G. A. Flandro	UTAH
NGL-47-004-006	Virginia Polytechnic Institute		VA
		F. W. Bull, J. A. Jacobs	
NGL-47-004-033	Virginia Polytechnic Institute	K. Gotow	VA
NGR-47-005-046	University of Virginia	S. S. Fisher	VA
NGL-47-005-067	University of Virginia	N. Cabrera	VA
NGR-48-002-003	University of Washington	R. J. H. Bollard	WASH
NGL-48-002-004	University of Washington	J. I. Mueller	WASH
NGL-48-002-044	University of Washington	A. Hertzberg	WASH
NGL-48-002-057	University of Washington	A. Hertzberg	WASH
NGR-49-001-019	West Virginia University	W. H. Moran	W VA
NGR-50-002-017	University of Wisconsin (Madison)	P. S. Myers	WISC
NGR-51-001-008	University of Wyoming	A. B. Denison	WYO
NGR-52-026-001	University of Toronto	J. B. French	FOR
NASr-54(06)	University of Michigan	R. W. Pew	MICH
NSR-01-002-057	University of Alabama (Birmingham)	E. A. Sallin	ALA
NSR-05-018-119	University of Southern California	R. H. Edwards	CAL
NSR-05-018-120	University of Southern California		CAL
NSR-10-005-047	University of Florida	H. Brown	FLA
NSR-10-008-021	University of South Florida	M. G. Kobasky	FLA
NSR-15-004-029	University of Notre Dame	T. J. Mueller	IND
NSR-15-005-037	Purdue University	Y. S. Touloukian	IND
NSR-31-001-104	Princeton University	E. Seckel	N J
NSR-31-001-902	Princeton University	D. T. Harrje	N J
NSR-36-008-028	Ohio State University	A. W. Leissa	OHIO
NSR-39-010-100	University of Pennsylvania	R. E. Forster	PA
NSR-48-002-054	University of Washington	H. G. Ahlstrom	WASH
NAS7-388	Illinois Institute of Technology		ILL

OFFICE OF SPACE SCIENCES & APPLICATIONS

NGR-02-001-001	University of Alaska		
		S. Chapman, Syun-Ichi Akasofu	ALS
NGL-03-001-001	Arizona State University	C. B. Moore	ARIZ
NGR-03-002-001	University of Arizona	R. W. G. Wyckoff	ARIZ

Grant No.	Institution	Investigator	State
NGL-03-002-002	University of Arizona	G. P. Kuiper	ARIZ
NGR-03-002-017	University of Arizona	S. Bashkin	ARIZ
NGL-03-002-019	University of Arizona	S. A. Hoenig	ARIZ
NGR-03-002-032	University of Arizona	A. B. Meinel, W. G. Tifft	ARIZ
NGR-03-002-068	University of Arizona	R. W. Lansing	ARIZ
NGR-03-002-071	University of Arizona	T. Bowen	ARIZ
NGR-03-002-081	University of Arizona	A. M. J. Gehrels	ARIZ
NGR-03-002-107	University of Arizona	C. Y. Fan	ARIZ
NGR-03-002-116	University of Arizona	F. J. Low	ARIZ
NGR-03-002-122	University of Arizona	E. Roemer	ARIZ
NGR-03-002-155	University of Arizona	B. M. Herman	ARIZ
NGR-03-002-174	University of Arizona	G. P. Kuiper	ARIZ
NGR-03-002-191	University of Arizona	G. P. Kuiper	ARIZ
NGR-03-002-193	University of Arizona	T. Gehrels	ARIZ
NGR-03-002-194	University of Arizona	W. G. Tifft	ARIZ
NGR-03-102-171	University of Arizona	H. C. Urey	ARIZ
NGR-05-002-003	California Institute of Technology	H. Brown	CAL
NGL-05-002-007	California Institute of Technology	R. B. Leighton	CAL
NGR-05-002-031	California Institute of Technology	F. Strunwasser	CAL
NGR-05-002-034	California Institute of Technology	H. Zirin	CAL
NGR-05-002-092	California Institute of Technology	G. Neugebauer	CAL
NGR-05-002-105	California Institute of Technology	T. J. Ahrens	CAL
NGR-05-002-114	California Institute of Technology	D. O. Muhleman	CAL
NGR-05-002-116	California Institute of Technology	B. Murray	CAL
NGR-05-002-117	California Institute of Technology	B. Murray	CAL
NGR-05-002-118	California Institute of Technology	R. F. Scott	CAL
NGR-05-002-121	California Institute of Technology	N. H. Horowitz	CAL
NGR-05-002-129	California Institute of Technology	D. L. Anderson	CAL
NGR-05-002-138	California Institute of Technology	D. L. Anderson	CAL
NGR-05-002-140	California Institute of Technology	G. Munch	CAL
NGR-05-002-142	California Institute of Technology	R. B. Leighton	CAL
NGL-05-003-003	University of California (Berkeley)	M. Calvin	CAL
NGL-05-003-017	University of California (Berkeley)	K. A. Anderson	CAL
NGR-05-003-018	University of California (Berkeley)	N. Pace	CAL
NGR-05-003-019	Unversity of California (Berkeley)	H. Mark	CAL
NGR-05-003-020	University of California (Berkeley)	T. H. Jukes	CAL
NGL-05-003-024	University of California (Berkeley)	N. Pace	CAL
NGR-05-003-067	University of California (Berkeley)	W. B. N. Berry	CAL
NGL-05-003-079	University of California (Berkeley)	A. D. McLaren	CAL
NGR-05-003-230	University of California (Berkeley)	S. Silver	CAL
NGR-05-003-266	University of California (Berkeley)	S. Silver	CAL
NGR-05-003-278	University of California (Berkeley)	C. S. Bowyer	CAL
NGL-05-003-286	University of California (Berkeley)	G. C. Pimentel	CAL
NGR-05-003-302	University of California (Berkeley)	M. Calvin	CAL
NGR-05-004-008	University of California (Davis)	A. H. Smith, C. F. Kelly	CAL
NGR-05-004-035	University of California (Davis)	R. E. Smith	CAL
NGR-05-005-003	University of California (San Diego)	L. E. Peterson	CAL
NGR-05-005-005	University of California (San Diego)	J. R. Arnold	CAL
NGR-05-005-007	University of California (San Diego)	C. E. McIlwain	CAL
NGL-05-007-002	University of California (Los Angeles)	G. J. F. MacDonald	CAL
NGR-05-007-004	University of California (Los Angeles)	T. A. Farley, W. F. Libby, P. J. Coleman	CAL
NGR-05-007-046	University of California (Los Angeles)	L. H. Aller	CAL
NGL-05-007-065	University of California (Los Angeles)	P. J. Coleman	CAL
NGR-05-007-133	University of California (Los Angeles)	H. Sobel	CAL
NGR-05-007-138	University of California (Los Angeles)	W. M. Kaula	CAL
NGR-05-007-190	University of California (Los Angeles)	C. F. Kennel	CAL
NGL-05-007-195	University of California (Los Angeles)	J. D. French	CAL
NGR-05-007-215	University of California (Los Angeles)	W. F. Libby	CAL
NGR-05-007-235	University of California (Los Angeles)	R. E. Holzer	CAL
NGR-05-009-002	University of California (San Diego)	G. Arrhenius	CAL
NGR-05-009-004	University of California (San Diego)	J. R. Arnold	CAL
NGL-05-009-005	University of California (San Diego)	H. E. Suess	CAL
NGR-05-009-022	University of California (Riverside)	R. S. White	CAL
NGR-05-009-032	University of California (San Diego)	S. L. Miller	CAL
NGR-05-009-076	University of California (San Diego)	J. A. Fejer	CAL
NGR-05-009-081	University of California (San Diego)	W. I. Axford	CAL
NGR-05-009-083	University of California (San Diego)	R. Galambos	CAL
NGR-05-009-114	University of California (San Diego)	H. C. Urey	CAL
NGR-05-010-001	University of California (Santa Barbara)	W. C. Walker	CAL
NGR-05-010-019	University of California (Santa Barbara)	R. V. Fisher	CAL
NGR-05-010-035	University of California (Santa Barbara)	P. E. Cloud	CAL
NGR-05-018-001	University of Southern California	G. L. Weissler	CAL
NGL-05-018-003	University of Southern California	J. P. Henry, J. P. Meehan	CAL
NGR-05-018-065	University of Southern California	T. C. James	CAL
NGR-05-020-004	Stanford University	J. Lederberg	CAL
NGL-05-020-008	Stanford University	R. A. Helliwell	CAL
NGL-05-020-014	Stanford University	V. R. Eshleman	CAL
NGR-05-020-019	Stanford University	R. H. Cannon, W. M. Fairbank, B. O. Lange	CAL
NGR-05-020-066	Stanford University	W. E. Spicer	CAL
NGR-05-020-077	Stanford University	F. W. Crawford	CAL
NGR-05-020-137	Stanford University	L. Stryer, A. Kornberg	CAL
NGR-05-020-176	Stanford University	F. W. Crawford	CAL
NGL-05-020-232	Stanford University	R. L. Kovach	CAL
NGR-05-020-267	Stanford University	A. D. Howard	CAL
NGR-05-020-272	Stanford University	P. A. Sturrock	CAL
NGR-05-020-276	Stanford University	V. R. Eshleman	CAL
NGR-05-020-288	Stanford University	R. A. Helliwell	CAL
NGR-05-020-330	Stanford University	J. R. Spreiter	CAL
NGR-05-020-348	Stanford University	A. M. Peterson	CAL
NGR-05-020-353	Stanford University	V. R. Eshleman	CAL
NGR-05-020-354	Stanford University	J. Lederberg	CAL
NGR-05-046-005	San Jose State College	J. C. Thompson	CAL
NGR-05-061-006	University of California (Santa Cruz)	E. J. Wampler	CAL
NGR-06-002-018	Colorado State University	J. B. Best	COLO
NGR-06-002-075	Colorado State University	J. P. Jordan	COLO
NGR-06-002-085	Colorado State University	C. B. Winn	COLO
NGR-06-003-034	University of Colorado	W. A. Rense	COLO
NGL-06-003-052	University of Colorado	C. A. Barth	COLO
NGR-06-003-057	University of Colorado	R. H. Garstang	COLO
NGR-06-003-064	University of Colorado	C. A. Barth	COLO
NGR-06-003-069	University of Colorado	W. A. Rense	COLO
NGR-06-003-071	University of Colorado	R. Wolfgang	COLO
NGR-06-003-092	University of Colorado	T. W. Speiser	COLO
NGR-06-003-120	University of Colorado	C. W. Hord	COLO
NGR-06-004-058	University of Denver	V. L. Patel	COLO
NGR-06-004-060	University of Denver	J. G. Roederer	COLO
NGR-07-004-004	Yale University	R. Wildt	CONN
NGR-07-004-006	Yale University	V. W. Hughes	CONN
NGL-07-004-008	Yale University	S. R. Lipsky	CONN
NGR-07-004-009	Yale University	H. J. Morowitz	CONN

NGR-07-004-010	Yale University	R. Wildt	CONN
NGR-07-004-028	Yale University	I. B. Bernstein, J. L. Hirshfield	CONN
NGR-07-004-034	Yale University	C. MacClintock, A. L. McAlester	CONN
NGR-07-004-043	Yale University	R. Wolfgang	CONN
NGR-07-004-084	Yale University	R. A. Goldsby	CONN
NGR-07-004-090	Yale University	R. J. Wyman	CONN
NGR-07-004-109	Yale University	E. B. Hooper	CONN
NGR-07-006-004	Wesleyan University	T. Page	CONN
NGR-07-006-005	Wesleyan University	J. E. Faller	CONN
NGR-09-005-022	Catholic University	B. T. DeCicco	D C
NGR-09-005-063	Catholic University	Y. C. Whang	D C
NGR-09-009-025	Georgetown University	C. B. Ferster	D C
NGR-09-011-006	Howard University	F. Senftle	D C
NGR-10-004-018	Florida State University	H. Gaffron	FLA
NGR-10-004-029	Florida State University	R. G. Cornell	FLA
NGR-10-004-041	Florida State University	W. Schwartz	FLA
NGR-10-004-056	Florida State University	E. K. Plyler	FLA
NGR-10-004-058	Florida State University	S. L. Hess	FLA
NGR-10-005-008	University of Florida	A. E. S. Green	FLA
NGR-10-005-057	University of Florida	W. B. Webb	FLA
NGR-10-007-008	University of Miami	S. W. Fox	FLA
NGR-10-007-052	University of Miami	K. Harada	FLA
NGR-10-007-054	University of Miami	G. Mueller	FLA
NGR-10-008-019	University of South Florida	H. K. Eichhorn	FLA
NGR-11-001-009	Emory University	V. P. Popovic	GA
NGR-11-001-012	Emory University	B. W. Robinson	GA
NGR-11-001-031	Emory University	S. W. Gray	GA
NGR-11-002-004	Georgia Institute of Technology	H. D. Edwards	GA
NGL-11-002-005	Georgia Institute of Technology	J. A. Knight	GA
NGR-11-003-021	University of Georgia	D. R. Tompkins	GA
NGR-12-001-002	University of Hawaii	K. Watanabe	HAW
NGR-12-001-011	University of Hawaii	J. T. Jefferies	HAW
NGL-12-001-042	University of Hawaii	S. M. Siegel	HAW
NGR-12-001-057	University of Hawaii	J. T. Jefferies	HAW
NGL-14-001-001	University of Chicago	E. N. Parker	ILL
NGR-14-001-005	University of Chicago	P. Meyer	ILL
NGL-14-001-006	University of Chicago	J. A. Simpson	ILL
NGR-14-001-010	University of Chicago	E. Anders	ILL
NGL-14-001-013	University of Chicago	C. O. Hines	ILL
NGR-14-001-054	University of Chicago	W. A. Hiltner	ILL
NGR-14-001-060	University of Chicago	C. R. O'Dell	ILL
NGR-14-001-103	University of Chicago	J. E. Lamport	ILL
NGR-14-001-128	University of Chicago	A. Turkevich	ILL
NGR-14-001-135	University of Chicago	A. L. Turkeviuh	ILL
NGR-14-005-002	University of Illinois (Urbana)	E. C. Yeh	ILL
NGR-14-005-009	University of Illinois (Urbana)	R. Mittra	ILL
NGR-14-005-013	University of Illinois (Urbana)	S. A. Bowhill	ILL
NGR-14-007-016	Northwestern University	J. A. Hynek	ILL
NGR-14-007-027	Northwestern University	E. H. T. Whitten	ILL
NGR-14-007-041	Northwestern University	S. S. Huang	ILL
NGR-14-007-048	Northwestern University	K. G. Henize	ILL
NGR-14-012-004	University of Illinois (Chicago)	J. H. Boyer	ILL
NGL-15-003-002	Indiana University	H. R. Johnson	IND
NGR-15-003-007	Indiana University	W. D. Neff	IND
NGR-15-003-053	Indiana University	S. Mizell	IND
NGR-15-004-017	University of Notre Dame	T. J. Starr	IND
NGR-15-005-003	Purdue University	K. L. Andrew	IND
NGR-15-005-085	Purdue University	R. W. Stanley	IND
NGL-16-001-002	University of Iowa	J. A. Van Allen	IOWA
NGR-16-001-031	University of Iowa	C. C. Wunder	IOWA
NGR-16-001-043	University of Iowa	D. C. Montgomery & D. A. Gurnett	IOWA
NGL-17-001-026	Kansas State University	D. Williams	KAN
NGR-17-002-042	University of Kansas	R. H. Himes	KAN
NGR-17-002-050	University of Kansas	E. J. Zeller	KANS
NGL-18-001-003	University of Kentucky	K. O. Lange	KY
NGR-18-001-026	University of Kentucky	R. C. Birkebak	KY
NGR-19-001-012	Louisiana State University (Baton Rouge)	R. W. Huggett, K. Pinkau	LA
NGR-21-001-001	Johns Hopkins University	W. G. Fastie	MD
NGR-21-001-035	Johns Hopkins University	S. A. Weinstein	MD
NGR-21-001-037	Johns Hopkins University	H. P. Eugster	MD
NGR-21-001-069	Johns Hopkins University	J. F. Dardano	MD
NGR-21-002-002	University of Maryland	H. Laster, E. Opik	MD
NGR-21-002-003	University of Maryland	R. W. Krauss	MD
NGR-21-002-005	Unversity of Maryland	D. A. Tidman	MD
NGR-21-002-006	University of Maryland	T. D. Wilkerson	MD
NGR-21-002-007	University of Maryland	T. D. Wilkerson	MD
NGR-21-002-010	University of Maryland	J. Weber	MD
NGR-21-002-026	University of Maryland	R. G. Grenell	MD
NGR-21-002-040	University of Maryland	R. G. Grenell	MD
NGR-21-002-057	University of Maryland	R. T. Bettinger	MD
NGR-21-002-059	University of Maryland	E. R. Lippincott, Y. T. Pratt	MD
NGR-21-002-066	University of Maryland	J. A. Earl	MD
NGR-21-002-073	University of Maryland	H. R. Griem	MD
NGR-21-002-109	University of Maryland	C. O. Alley	MD
NGR-21-012-001	Woodstock College	M. J. Bielefeld	MD
NGR-22-005-001	Brandeis University	N. O. Kaplan	MASS
NGL-22-007-006	Harvard University	L. Goldberg	MASS
NGR-22-007-021	Harvard University	G. R. Huguenin	MASS
NGR-22-007-054	Harvard University	N. F. Ramsey	MASS
NGR-22-007-059	Harvard University	K. R. Porter	MASS
NGL-22-007-069	Harvard University	E. S. Barghoorn	MASS
NGR-22-007-103	Harvard University	D. C. Noble	MASS
NGR-22-007-136	Harvard University	A. Dalgarno	MASS
NGR-22-007-137	Harvard University	R. T. Kelleher	MASS
NGR-22-007-138	Harvard University	R. J. Herrnstein	MASS
NGR-22-009-005	Massachusetts Institute of Technology	K. Biemann	MASS
NGR-22-009-007	Massachusetts Institute of Technology	J. Reintjes	MASS
NGR-22-009-015	Massachusetts Institute of Technology	H. S. Bridge	MASS
NGL-22-009-016	Massachusetts Institute of Technology	A. H. Barrett	MASS
NGR-22-009-018	Massachusetts Institute of Technology	F. O. Schmitt	MASS
NGR-22-009-167	Massachusetts Institute of Technology	G. R. Harrison	MASS
NGR-22-009-187	Massachusetts Institute of Technology	J. Watkins	MASS
NGR-22-009-257	Massachusetts Institute of Technology	D. W. Strangway	MASS
NGR-22-009-272	Massachusetts Institute of Technology	R. J. Wurtman	MASS
NGR-22-009-277	Massachusetts Institute of Technology	A. Rich	MASS
NGR-22-009-289	Massachusetts Institute of Technology	H. S. Bridge	MASS
NGL-22-009-304	Massachusetts Institute of Technology	H. J. Zimmerman	MASS
NGL-22-009-308	Massachusetts Institute of Technology	H. L. Teuber	MASS
NGR-22-009-350	Massachusetts Institute of Technology	T. B. McCord	MASS
NGR-22-009-351	Massachusetts Institute of Technology	L. G. Bromwell	MASS
NGR-22-009-372	Massachusetts Institute of Technology	H. S. Bridge	MASS
NGR-22-009-420	Massachusetts Institute of Technology		MASS
NGR-22-009-424	Massachusetts Institute of Technology	A. Rich	MASS

NGR-22-010-023	University of Massachusetts	W. M. Irvine	MASS
NGL-22-010-029	University of Massachusetts	J. F. Brandts	MASS
NGR-22-010-039	University of Massachusetts	G. R. Huguenin	MASS
NGR-23-002-001	University of Detroit	A. Szutka	MICH
NGR-23-004-001	Michigan State University	L. G. Augenstein	MICH
NGR-23-005-015	University of Michigan	A. Nagy	MICH
NGR-23-005-017	University of Michigan	F. T. Haddock	MICH
NGR-23-005-062	University of Michigan	J. E. Rowe	MICH
NGR-23-005-094	University of Michigan	V. C. Liu	MICH
NGR-23-005-201	University of Michigan	R. von Baumgarten	MICH
NGR-23-005-275	University of Michigan	O. C. Mohler	MICH
NGR-23-005-321	University of Michigan	F. T. Haddock	MICH
NGR-23-005-314	University of Michigan	F. T. Haddock	MICH
NGR-23-005-320	University of Michigan	U. Samir	MICH
NGR-23-010-004	Western Michigan University	R. R. Hutchinson	MICH
NGR-24-001-002	Concordia College	H. R. Homann	MINN
NGL-24-005-008	University of Minnesota	J. R. Winckler, E. P. Ney	MINN
NGL-24-005-009	University of Minnesota	A. O. C. Nier	MINN
NGR-24-005-050	University of Minnesota	W. R. Webber, C. S. Waddington	MINN
NGR-24-005-054	University of Minnesota	F. M. Swain	MINN
NGR-24-005-091	University of Minnesota	R. J. Goldstein	MINN
NGR-24-005-111	University of Minnesota	J. R. Winckler	MINN
NGR-24-005-176	University of Minnesota	P. Kellogg	MINN
NGR-24-005-180	University of Minnesota	L. J. Cahill	MINN
NGR-24-005-187	University of Minnesota	A. O. C. Nier	MINN
NGR-25-001-004	Mississippi State University	R. G. Tischer	MISS
NGR-26-003-023	University of Missouri (Columbia)	R. L. Wixon	MO
NGL-26-004-021	University of Missouri (Columbia)	X. J. Musacchia	MO
NGR-26-004-025	University of Missouri (Columbia)	F. E. South	MO
NGR-26-008-001	Washington University (St. Louis)	J. Klarmann, M. W. Friedlander	MO
NGR-26-008-042	Washington University (St. Louis)	J. Klarmann	MO
NGR-26-008-043	Washington University (St. Louis)	R. M. Walker	MO
NGR-27-001-035	Montana State University	K. Nordtvedt	MONT
NGR-29-001-008	University of Nevada (Reno)	P. Atlick	NEV
NGR-30-001-001	Dartmouth College	C. J. Lyon	N H
NGR-30-001-011	Dartmouth College	B. U. O. Sonnerup	N H
NGR-30-002-008	University of New Hampshire	R. E. Houston	N H
NGR-30-002-010	University of New Hampshire	R. A. Kaufman	N H
NGR-30-002-021	University of New Hampshire	E. L. Chupp	N H
NGR-30-002-028	University of New Hampshire	L. J. Cahill	N H
NGR-31-001-001	Princeton University	M. Schwarzschild	N J
NGL-31-001-007	Princeton University	L. Spitzer	N J
NGR-31-001-044	Princeton University	L. Spitzer	N J
NGR-31-001-093	Princeton University	R. B. Hargraves	N J
NGR-31-001-142	Princeton University	R. E. Danielson	N J
NGR-31-001-145	Princeton University	C. S. Pittendrigh	N J
NGL-32-003-001	New Mexico State University	C. W. Tombough	NMEX
NGR-32-004-001	University of New Mexico	A. Erteza	NMEX
NGL-32-004-011	University of New Mexico	W. Elston	NMEX
NGR-33-001-019	Adelphi University	R. Genberg	N Y
NGR-33-006-047	Polytechnc Institute of Brooklyn	S. Gross	N Y
NGR-33-008-061	Columbia University	P. W. Gast	N Y
NGR-33-008-102	Columbia University	E. J. Ott	N Y
NGR-33-010-013	Cornell University	M. Alexander	N Y
NGR-33-010-082	Cornell University	C. Sagan	N Y
NGR-33-010-096	Cornell University	C. Sagan	N Y
NGR-33-010-098	Cornell University	C. Sagan	N Y
NGR-33-012-009	Fordham University	W. C. Corning	N Y
NGR-33-015-002	State University of New York (Buffalo)	J. F. Danielli	N Y
NGR-33-015-016	State University of New York (Buffalo)	J. Danielli	N Y
NGR-33-015-068	State University of New York (Stony Brook)	G. W. Stroke	N Y
NGR-33-016-102	New York University	J. Post	N Y
NGR-33-018-004	Rensselaer Polytechnic Institute	J. M. Greenberg	N Y
NGL-33-018-007	Rensselaer Polytechnic Institute	P. Harteck	N Y
NGR-33-018-086	Rensselaer Polytechnic Institute	P. Harteck	N Y
NGL-33-018-091	Rensselaer Polytechnic Institute	S. Yerazunis	N Y
NGR-33-019-002	University of Rochester	W. Vishniac	N Y
NGL-33-019-003	University of Rochester	P. W. Baumeister	N Y
NGR-34-001-019	Duke University	K. Schmidt-Koenig	N C
NGR-34-002-023	North Carolina State University	D. S. Grosch	N C
NGR-36-004-001	University of Cincinnati	P. Herget	OHIO
NGR-36-008-004	Ohio State University	H. S. Weiss	OHIO
NGR-36-008-093	Ohio State University	I. I. Mueller	OHIO
NGR-36-008-125	Ohio State University	S. K. Ghosh	OHIO
NGR-36-017-002	Bowling Green State University	I. I. Oster	OHIO
NGR-38-002-013	Oregon State University	H. C. Curl	ORE
NGR-38-002-017	Oregon State University	R. Y. Morita	ORE
NGR-38-002-020	Oregon State University	R. A. Schmitt	ORE
NGL-38-003-010	University of Oregon	G. G. Goles	ORE
NGR-39-002-011	Carnegie-Mellon University	J. J. Wolken	PA
NGR-39-006-001	Haverford College	L. C. Green	PA
NGR-39-009-002	Pennsylvania State University	W. J. Ross	PA
NGR-39-009-003	Pennsylvania State University	J. S. Nisbet	PA
NGR-39-009-008	Pennsylvania State University	E. C. Pollard	PA
NGL-39-009-010	Pennsylvania State University	D. P. Gold	PA
NGR-39-009-032	Pennsylvania State University	B. R. F. Kendall	PA
NGR-39-009-129	Pennsylvania State University	B. R. F. Kendall	PA
NGR-39-010-087	University of Pennsylvania	F. Haber	PA
NGR-39-010-104	University of Pennsylvania	A. H. Brown	PA
NGL-39-011-013	University of Pittsburgh	W. L. Fite	PA
NGL-39-011-030	University of Pittsburgh	E. C. Zipf	PA
NGR-39-011-085	University of Pittsburgh	B. W. Hapke	PA
NGR-39-018-002	Bryn Mawr College	M. Yarczower	PA
NGR-40-002-081	Brown University	T. A. Mutch	R I
NGR-41-002-003	University of South Carolina	J. R. Durig	S C
NGL-43-001-006	University of Tennessee	N. M. Gailar	TENN
NGR-44-003-001	Baylor University	P. Kellaway	TEX
NGR-44-005-002	University of Houston	J. Oro and A. Zlatkis	TEX
NGR-44-005-091	University of Houston	R. S. Becker	TEX
NGR-44-005-102	University of Houston	J. Oro	TEX
NGR-44-006-012	Rice University	F. C. Michel, A. J. Dessler	TEX
NGR-44-006-065	Rice University	F. J. Low	TEX
NGR-44-012-003	University of Texas Southwestern Medical School	P. O'B. Montgomery	TEX
NGL-44-012-006	University of Texas (Austin)	A. E. Straiton	TEX
NGR-44-012-045	University of Texas (Austin)	J. H. Mackin	TEX
NGR-44-012-055	University of Texas (Austin)	J. N. Douglas	TEX
NGR-44-013-001	Texas Woman's University	P. B. Mack	TEX
NGR-45-001-011	Brigham Young University	D. E. Jones	UTAH
NGR-45-002-008	Utah State University	F. B. Salisbury	UTAH
NGR-45-003-043	University of Utah	E. A. Shneour	UTAH
NGR-47-005-022	University of Virginia	J. W. Beams	VA
NGR-47-005-066	University of Virginia	L. W. Fredrick	VA
NGR-47-005-077	University of Virginia	J. W. Boring	VA

Grant	Institution	PI	State
NGR-47-020-001	Hampton Institute	E. Kollmann	VA
NGR-48-001-004	Washington State University	B. A. McFadden	WASH
NGR-48-002-033	University of Washington	P. W. Hodge	WASH
NGR-48-002-073	University of Washington	C. B. Leovy	WASH
NGR-48-002-077	University of Washington	C. B. Leovy	WASH
NGR-50-001-010	Marquette University	W. Markowitz	WIS
NGR-50-002-002	University of Wisconsin (Madison)	E. N. Cameron	WISC
NGL-50-002-013	University of Wisconsin (Madison)	A. D. Code	WISC
NGR-50-002-041	University of Wisconsin (Madison)	L. A. Haskins	WISC
NGR-50-002-044	University of Wisconsin (Madison)	W. L. Krauschaar	WISC
NGR-50-002-114	University of Wisconsin (Madison)	V. E. Suomi	WISC
NGR-52-042-004	University of Adelaide	E. G. Elford	FOR
NGR-52-083-002	College of the Virgin Islands	F. B. Gray	FOR
NGR-52-119-001	University of Goteborg	H. Hyden	FOR
NASr-5	University of Hawaii	H. C. McAllister	HAW
NASr-54(05)	University of Michigan	L. M. Jones	MICH
NASr-82	University of Arizona	G. P. Kuiper	ARIZ
NASr-138	University of Arizona	A. M. J. Gehrels	ARIZ
NASr-164	University of New Hampshire	J. A. Lockwood	NH
NASr-169	University of Pittsburgh	N. Wald	PA
NASr-179	University of Pittsburgh	T. M. Donahue	PA
NASr-242	University of Texas (Austin)	H. Smith	TEX
NASr-248	University of Minnesota	A. O. C. Nier	MINN
NSR-02-001-025	University of Alaska	K. B. Mather	ALS
NSR-03-002-048	University of Arizona	H. Johnson, A. Gehrels	ARIZ
NSR-05-002-071	California Institute of Technology	H. Zirin	CAL
NSR-05-002-133	California Institute of Technology	Dr. Garmire	CAL
NSR-05-003-100	University of California (Santa Cruz)	A. E. Whitford	CAL
NSR-05-003-287	University of California (Berkeley)	C. S. Bowyer	CAL
NSR-05-007-083	University of California (Los Angeles)	W. M. Kaula	CAL
NSR-05-009-046	University of California (San Diego)	C. E. McIlwain	CAL
NSR-09-010-027	George Washington University	C. W. Shilling	DC
NSR-10-007-078	University of Miami	D. L. Harvey	FLA
NSR-12-001-019	University of Hawaii	J. T. Jefferies	HAW
NSR-12-001-055	University of Hawaii	G. P. Woollard	HAW
NSR-16-001-025	University of Iowa	D. A. Gurnett	IOWA
NSR-21-001-062	Johns Hopkins University	H. M. Crosswhite	MD
NSR-21-002-077	University of Maryland	D. L. Matthews	MD
NSR-22-007-067	Harvard University	L. Goldberg	MASS
NSR-22-007-115	Harvard University	L. Goldberg	MASS
NSR-22-009-138	Massachusetts Institute of Technology	L. L. Sutro	MASS
NSR-22-009-321	Massachusetts Institute of Technology	H. W. Schnopper	MASS
NSR-22-009-404	Massachusetts Institute of Technology	J. V. Harrington	MASS
NSR-24-005-062	University of Minnesota	W. J. Luyten, J. E. Carroll	MINN
NSR-30-001-018	Dartmouth College	T. Laaspere	NH
NSR-30-002-003	University of New Hampshire	J. A. Lockwood	NH
NSR-31-001-127	Princeton University	J. L. Lowrance	NJ
NSR-31-001-150	Princeton University	J. P. Layton	NJ
NSR-31-001-901	Princeton University	D. C. Morton	NJ
NSR-33-010-055	Cornell University	M. F. Meserve	NY
NSR-36-003-092	Case Western Reserve University	G. M. Frye	OHIO
NSR-39-009-129	Pennsylvania State University	B. R. F. Kendall	PA
NSR-44-006-023	Rice University	R. C. Haymes	TEX
NSR-44-006-065	Rice University	E. J. Low	TEX
NSR-47-005-070	University of Virginia	E. H. Hendricks	VA

OFFICE OF MANNED SPACE FLIGHT

Grant	Institution	PI	State
NGR-03-002-153	University of Arizona	W. G. Tifft	ARIZ
NGR-05-003-256	University of California (Berkeley)	S. Silver	CAL
NGR-05-004-026	University of California (Davis)	L. D. Carlson	CAL
NGR-05-007-174	University of California (Los Angeles)	K. C. Hamner	CAL
NGR-12-001-053	University of Hawaii	S. M. Siegel	HAW
NGR-14-007-069	Northwestern University	K. G. Henize	ILL
NGR-22-007-061	Harvard University	L. Goldberg	MASS
NGR-22-007-070	Harvard University	R. A. McFarland	MASS
NGR-22-009-329	Massachusetts Institute of Technology	F. Press	MASS
NSR-03-002-163	University of Arizona	W. G. Tifft	ARIZ
NSR-05-003-233	University of California (Berkeley)	N. Pace	CAL
NSR-05-018-087	University of Southern California	L. G. Goff	CAL
NSR-22-009-106	Massachusetts Institute of Technology	P. B. Sebring	MASS
NSR-33-012-006	Fordham University	J. Kubis	NY
NSR-36-008-108	Ohio State University	H. V. Ellington	OHIO

OFFICE OF UNIVERSITY AFFAIRS

Grant	Institution	PI	State
NGR-01-001-006	Alabama A&M College	R. H. Lee	ALA
NGR-01-001-007	Alabama A&M College	M. C. George	ALA
NGL-01-002-001	University of Alabama (University)	R. Hermann, G. Croker	ALA
NGL-03-002-091	University of Arizona	H. D. Christensen	ARIZ
NGL-05-018-044	University of Southern California	H. Bichsel	CAL
NGL-05-018-098	University of Southern California		CAL
NGL-06-001-015	Colorado School of Mines	L. T. Grose	COLO
NGL-06-002-038	Colorado State University	R. Jensen	COLO
NGL-06-004-007	University of Denver	S. A. Johnson	COLO
NGL-06-004-078	University of Denver	A. A. Ezra	COLO
NGR-07-004-029	Yale University	R. Wildt	CONN
NGL-10-005-005	University of Florida	L. E. Grinter	FLA
NGL-10-007-010	University of Miami	E. H. Man	FLA
NGL-10-007-067	University of Miami	F. D. Kohler	FLA
NGR-10-007-068	University of Miami	F. D. Kohler	FLA
NGR-10-007-070	University of Miami	M. L. Harvey	FLA
NGL-11-002-018	Georgia Institute of Technology	K. Picha, V. Crawford	GA
NGR-11-002-081	Georgia Institute of Technology	V. Crawford	GA
NGL-14-007-058	Northwestern University	J. A. D. Copper	ILL
NGR-15-005-021	Purdue University	F. N. Andrews	IND
NGR-15-005-069	Purdue University	J. Modrey	IND
NGL-17-001-005	Kansas State University	J. L. Brown	KAN
NGL-18-002-005	University of Louisville	W. J. McGlothlin	KY
NGL-20-006-001	University of Maine (Orono)	T. H. Curry	ME
NGL-21-002-008	University of Maryland	W. C. Rheinboldt	MD
NGR-21-025-001	Morgan State College		MD
NGL-25-001-028	Mississippi State University	C. W. Bouchillon	MISS
NGL-26-004-003	University of Missouri (Columbia)	Ward J. Haas	MO
NGR-26-008-006	Washington University (St. Louis)	G. E. Pake	MO
NGR-27-001-001	Montana State University	I. E. Dayton	MONT
NGL-32-003-027	New Mexico State University	J. E. Weiss	NMEX
NGL-32-004-042	University of New Mexico	W. W. Grannemann	NMEX
NGL-33-001-001	Adelphi University	R. Genberg	NY

NGR-33-010-071	Cornell University	H. N. McManus	N Y
NGR-33-015-036	State University of New York (Stony Brook)		N Y
		Y. H. Koa	
NGR-33-015-082	State University of New York (Stony Brook)		N Y
		O. A. Schaeffer	
NGL-33-016-067	New York University	J. R. Ragazzini	N Y
NGL-33-022-090	Syracuse University	J. C. Honey	N Y
NGR-33-023-018	Yeshiva University	A. G. W. Cameron	N Y
NGL-34-001-005	Duke University	J. B. Chaddock	N C
NGR-34-003-040	University of North Carolina (Chapel Hill)		N C
		R. G. Faust	
NGL-36-004-014	University of Cincinnati	R. P. Harrington	OHIO
NGR-36-022-001	Miami University	D. E. Cunningham	OHIO
NGL-37-002-011	Oklahoma State University	V. S. Haneman	OKLA
NGL-37-003-026	University of Oklahoma	C. Riggs	OKLA
NGL-39-004-007	Drexel Institute of Technology	C. Gatlin	PA
NGL-39-004-020	Drexel Institute of Technology	W. Hagerty	PA
NGL-39-009-015	Pennsylvania State University	P. Ebaugh	PA
NGL-39-011-002	University of Pittsburgh	D. Halliday	PA
NGL-39-011-080	University of Pittsburgh	D. C. Stone	PA
NGL-40-002-009	Brown University	P. T. Maeder	R I
NGL-42-001-004	South Dakota School of Mines and Technology		S D
NGL-43-001-021	University of Tennessee	C. O. Thomas	TENN
NGL-44-001-001	Texas A & M University	H. E. Whitmore	TEX
NGL-44-005-021	University of Houston	J. R. Crump	TEX
NGL-44-005-084	University of Houston	C. J. Huang	TEX
NGL-44-006-033	Rice University	A. J. Chapman,	TEX
NGL-44-007-006	Southern Methodist University	J. C. Denton	TEX
NGR-44-033-001	Prairie View A&M College	I. V. Nelson	TEX
NGL-46-001-008	University of Vermont	C. D. Cook	VT
NGL-49-001-001	West Virginia University	J. C. Ludlum	W VA
NGL-50-002-001	University of Wisconsin (Madison)		WISC
		J. O. Hirschfelder	
NSR-01-002-033	University of Alabama (University)	R. M. Hollub	ALA
NSR-01-003-005	Auburn University	R. I. Vachon	ALA
NSR-01-003-025	Auburn University	R. I. Vachon	ALA
NSR-05-002-124	California Institute of Technology	J. N. Franklin	CAL
NSR-05-007-089	University of California (Los Angeles)	J. D. French	CAL
NSR-05-007-236	University of California (Los Angeles)	R. A. Goodman	CAL
NSR-05-010-021	University of California (Santa Barbara)		CAL
		W. T. Thomson	
NSR-05-020-088	Stanford University	M. Anliker	CAL
NSR-09-005-059	Catholic University	B. T. Fang	D C
NSR-22-011-036	Northeastern University	C. G. Houtsma	MASS
NSR-33-015-077	State University of New York (Stony Brook)		N Y
		O. A. Schaeffer	
NSR-34-003-039	University of North Carolina (Chapel Hill)		N C
NSR-36-003-051	Case Western Reserve University		OHIO
		I. Greber, W. T. Olson	
NSR-44-005-016	University of Houston	C. J. Huang	TEX
NSR-44-005-059	University of Houston	C. J. Huang	TEX
NSR-47-003-010	Old Dominion University	G. L. Goglia	VA
NSR-47-003-011	Old Dominion University	G. L. Goglia	A
NSR-49-001-039	University of West Virginia	E. J. Steinhardt	W VA
NGT-01-002-002	University of Alabama (University)	E. Rodgers	ALA
NGT-01-003-001	Auburn University	W. V. Parker	ALA
NGT-02-001-007	University of Alaska	K. M. Rae	ALS
NGT-03-001-002	Arizona State University	W. J. Burke	ARIZ
NGT-03-002-008	University of Arizona	H. D. Rhodes	ARIZ

NGT-05-002-009	California Institute of Technology	H. F. Bohnenblust	CAL
NGT-05-002-295	Stanford University	J. M. Pettit	CAL
NGT-05-003-023	University of California (Berkeley)	S. S. Elberg	CAL
NGT-05-007-019	University of California (Los Angeles)	W. F. Libby	CAL
NGT-05-008-001	University of California (Riverside)	R. B. March	CAL
NGT-05-009-008	University of California (San Diego)	F. T. Wall	CAL
NGT-05-010-005	University of California (Santa Barbara)	A. Bruckner	CAL
NGT-05-018-004	University of Southern California	M. C. Kloetzel	CAL
NGT-05-018-085	University of Southern California	R. E. Stephens	CAL
NGT-05-020-016	Stanford University	H. Heffner	CAL
NGT-05-020-228	Stanford University	J. A. Vitale	CAL
NGT-05-020-295	Stanford University	J. M. Pettit	CAL
NGT-05-020-361	Stanford University	J. M. Pettit	CAL
NGT-06-001-001	Colorado School of Mines	A. R. Jordan	COLO
NGT-06-002-002	Colorado State University	W. H. Bragonier	COLO
NGT-06-003-004	University of Colorado	E. J. Archer	COLO
NGT-06-004-008	University of Denver	W. C. Miller	COLO
NGT-07-002-003	University of Connecticut	N. L. Whetten	CONN
NGT-07-004-014	Yale University	J. P. Miller	CONN
NGT-08-001-002	University of Delaware	C. E. Birchenall	DEL
NGT-09-005-006	Catholic University	J. P. O'Connor	D C
NGT-09-009-004	Georgetown University	J. B. Horigan	D C
NGT-09-010-003	George Washington University	A. E. Burns	D C
NGT-09-011-001	Howard University	C. L. Miller	D C
NGT-10-004-008	Florida State University	R. J. Keirs	FLA
NGT-10-005-006	University of Florida	L. E. Grinter	FLA
NGT-10-007-006	University of Miami	J. A. Harrison	FLA
NGT-11-001-005	Emory University	C. T. Lester	GA
NGT-11-002-006	Georgia Institute of Technology	T. W. Jackson	GA
NGT-11-002-064	Georgia Institute of Technology	J. A. Vitale	GA
NGT-11-003-002	University of Georgia	G. B. Huff	GA
NGT-12-001-005	University of Hawaii	W. Gorter	HAW
NGT-13-001-001	University of Idaho	M. L. Jackson	IDA
NGT-14-001-015	University of Chicago	C. D. O'Connell	ILL
NGT-14-004-002	Illinois Institute of Technology	A. Grad	ILL
NGT-14-005-017	University of Illinois (Urbana)	D. Alpert	ILL
NGT-14-007-004	Northwestern University	R. H. Baker	ILL
NGT-14-008-008	Southern Illinois University	W. E. Simeone	ILL
NGT-15-003-003	Indiana University	R. B. Curtis	IND
NGT-15-004-002	University of Notre Dame	P. E. Beichner	IND
NGT-15-005-005	Purdue University	F. N. Andrews	IND
NGT-15-005-061	Purdue University		IND
NGT-16-001-004	University of Iowa	D. C. Spriestersbach	IOWA
NGT-16-002-002	Iowa State University	J. B. Page	IOWA
NGT-17-001-002	Kansas State University	J. P. Noonan	KAN
NGT-17-002-006	University of Kansas	W. P. Albrecht	KAN
NGT-17-002-044	University of Kansas	W. P. Smith	KAN
NGT-17-002-052	University of Kansas	J. A. Vitale	KANS
NGT-18-001-005	University of Kentucky	L. W. Cochran	KY
NGT-18-002-006	University of Louisville	J. A. Dillon	KY
NGT-19-001-001	Louisiana State University (Baton Rouge)		LA
		M. Goodrich	
NGT-19-002-002	Tulane University	D. R. Deener	LA
NGT-20-006-002	University of Maine (Orono)	F. P. Eggert	ME
NGT-21-001-004	Johns Hopkins University	G. W. Shaffer	MD
NGT-21-002-013	University of Maryland	M. J. Pelczar	MD
NGT-22-003-001	Boston College	W. J. Feeney	MASS
NGT-22-004-003	Boston University	P. E. Kubzansky	MASS
NGT-22-005-005	Brandeis University	H. Weisberg	MASS

NGT-22-006-001	Clark University	D. E. Lee	MASS
NGT-22-007-008	Harvard University	R. A. McFarland	MASS
NGT-22-009-020	Massachusetts Institute of Technology	H. L. Hazen	MASS
NGT-22-010-008	University of Massachusetts	E. C. Moore	MASS
NGT-22-011-003	Northeastern University	A. A. Vernon	MASS
NGT-22-012-002	Tufts University	P. H. Flint	MASS
NGT-22-017-001	Worcester Polytechnic Institute	R. F. Morton	MASS
NGT-22-018-002	Lowell Technological Institute	E. L. Alexander	MASS
NGT-23-004-004	Michigan State University	J. Vinocur	MICH
NGT-23-005-018	University of Michigan	G. E. Hay	MICH
NGT-23-006-001	Wayne State University	J. E. Hill	MICH
NGT-23-007-004	Michigan Technological University	D. G. Yerg	MICH
NGT-24-005-012	University of Minnesota	B. Crawford	MINN
NGT-24-005-078	University of Minnesota	G. W. Anderson	MINN
NGT-25-001-002	Mississippi State University	J. C. McKee	MISS
NGT-25-002-001	University of Mississippi	W. L. Nobles	MISS
NGT-25-005-001	University of Southern Mississippi	R. S. Owings	MISS
NGT-26-003-001	University of Missouri (Rolla)	W. Bosch	MO
NGT-26-004-001	University of Missouri (Columbia)	C. E. Marshall	MO
NGT-26-006-001	St. Louis University	H. Howe	MO
NGT-26-008-005	Washington University (St. Louis)	G. E. Pake	MO
NGT-27-001-003	Montana State University	L. DS. Smith	MONT
NGT-27-002-001	University of Montana	F. S. Honkala	MONT
NGT-28-004-001	University of Nebraska (Lincoln)	J. C. Olson	NEB
NGT-29-001-002	University of Nevada (Reno)	T. D. O'Brien	NEV
NGT-30-001-003	Dartmouth College	J. F. Hornig	NH
NGT-30-002-002	University of New Hampshire	W. H. Drew	NH
NGT-31-001-009	Princeton University	C. S. Pittendrigh	NJ
NGT-31-003-005	Stevens Institute of Technology	R. A. Morgen	NJ
NGT-31-004-002	Rutgers University	H. C. Torrey	NJ
NGT-32-003-004	New Mexico State University	E. Walden	NMEX
NGT-32-004-004	University of New Mexico	A. Steger	NMEX
NGT-33-001-002	Adelphi University	M. V. B. Jennings	NY
NGT-33-002-002	Alfred University	E. E. Mueller	NY
NGT-33-007-001	Clarkson College of Technology	H. L. Shulman	NY
NGT-33-008-013	Columbia University	R. S. Halford	NY
NGT-33-010-007	Cornell University	F. S. Erdman	NY
NGT-33-010-052	Cornell University	J. A. Vitale	NY
NGT-33-012-002	Fordham University	J. F. Mulligan	NY
NGT-33-014-002	City University of New York	M. Rees	NY
NGT-33-015-004	State University of New York (Stony Brook)		NY
		R. Jordan	
NGT-33-015-027	State University of New York (Buffalo)	A. W. Holt	NY
NGT-33-015-099	State University of New York (Stony Brook)		NY
NGT-33-016-014	New York University	J. R. Ragazzini	NY
NGT-33-018-010	Rensselaer Polytechnic Institute	S. E. Wiberley	NY
NGT-33-019-006	University of Rochester	R. G. Loewy	NY
NGT-33-022-005	Syracuse University	F. P. Piskor	NY
NGT-33-022-097	Syracuse University	J. C. Honey	NY
NGT-33-023-003	Yeshiva University	A. Gelbart	NY
NGT-34-001-003	Duke University	R. L. Predmore	NC
NGT-34-002-003	North Carolina State University	W. J. Peterson	NC
NGT-34-002-097	North Carolina State University	F. D. Hart	NC
NGT-34-003-001	University of North Carolina (Chapel Hill)		NC
		C. H. Holman	
NGT-35-001-001	North Dakota State University	G. S. Smith	ND
NGT-35-002-004	University of North Dakota	C. J. Hamre	ND
NGT-36-003-007	Case Western Reserve University	L. Gordon	OHIO
NGT-36-004-003	University of Cincinnati	C. Crockett	OHIO
NGT-36-007-002	Kent State University	J. White	OHIO
NGT-36-008-006	Ohio State University	W. M. Protheroe	OHIO
NGT-36-008-007	Ohio State University	F. H. Shillito	OHIO
NGT-36-009-001	Ohio University	T. Culbert	OHIO
NGT-36-010-001	University of Toledo	A. N. Solberg	OHIO
NGT-36-013-001	Case Reserve Western University	W. M. Heston	OHIO
NGT-37-002-002	Oklahoma State University	M. T. Edmison	OKLA
NGT-37-003-001	University of Oklahoma	C. D. Riggs	OKLA
NGT-38-002-001	Oregon State University	H. P. Hansen	ORE
NGT-39-002-002	Carnegie-Mellon University	A. F. Strehler	PA
NGT-39-004-005	Drexel Institute of Technology	O. W. Witzell	PA
NGT-39-007-003	Lehigh University	R. D. Stout	PA
NGT-39-009-011	Pennsylvania State University	M. N. McGeary	PA
NGT-39-009-141	Pennsylvania State University	G. Reethof	PA
NGT-39-010-007	University of Pennsylvania	A. N. Hixson	PA
NGT-39-011-003	University of Pittsburgh	P. F. Jones	PA
NGT-39-011-075	University of Pittsburgh	D. C. Stone	PA
NGT-39-012-007	Temple University	G. H. Huganir	PA
NGT-39-019-002	Duquesne University	H. H. Petit	PA
NGT-39-023-005	Villanova University	A. H. Buford	PA
NGT-40-002-008	Brown University	M. J. Brennan	RI
NGT-40-004-001	University of Rhode Island	P. H. Nash	RI
NGT-41-001-001	Clemson University	V. Hurst	SC
NGT-41-002-002	University of South Carolina	J. A. Morris	SC
NGT-42-002-001	University of South Dakota	W. W. Gutzman	SD
NGT-43-001-002	University of Tennessee	H. A. Smith	TENN
NGT-43-002-002	Vanderbilt University	R. T. Lagemann	TENN
NGT-44-001-003	Texas A & M University	W. C. Hall	TEX
NGT-44-003-019	Baylor University	J. D. Bragg	TEX
NGT-44-005-004	University of Houston	J. C. Allred	TEX
NGT-44-006-003	Rice University	W. E. Gordon	TEX
NGT-44-007-002	Southern Methodist University	C. C. Allbritton	TEX
NGT-44-009-002	Texas Christian University	E. L. Secrest	TEX
NGT-45-001-002	Brigham Young University	W. P. Lloyd	UTAH
NGT-45-002-001	Utah State University	E. J. Gardner	UTAH
NGT-45-003-002	University of Utah	S. M. McMurrin	UTAH
NGT-46-001-001	University of Vermont	W. H. Macmillan	VT
NGT-47-004-001	Virginia Polytechnic Institute	F. W. Bull	VA
NGT-47-005-005	University of Virginia	E. Younger	VA
NGT-47-006-013	College of William and Mary	R. T. Siegel	VA
NGT-48-001-002	Washington State University	J. F. Short	WASH
NGT-48-002-007	University of Washington	J. L. McCarthy	WASH
NGT-49-001-002	West Virginia University	J. Ludlum	WVA
NGT-50-001-005	Marquette University	L. W. Friedrich	WISC
NGT-50-002-003	University of Wisconsin (Madison)	R. M. Bock	WISC
NGT-51-001-002	University of Wyoming	R. H. Bruce	WYO
NGF-03-002-025	University of Arizona	G. P. Kuiper	ARIZ
NGF-05-003-021	University of California (Berkeley)	S. Silver	CAL
NGF-05-007-020	University of California (Los Angeles)	W. F. Libby	CAL
NGF-05-018-015	University of Southern California	J. P. Meeham	CAL
NGF-05-020-017	Stanford University	J. Lederberg	CAL
NGF-05-020-092	Stanford University	W. R. Rambo	CAL
NGF-06-003-005	University of Colorado	W. A. Rense	COLO
NGF-06-004-024	University of Denver	C. M. Alter	COLO
NGF-09-012-061	National Academy of Sciences	F. B. Seitz	DC
NGF-10-005-024	University of Florida	L. E. Grinter	FLA
NGF-11-002-012	Georgia Institute of Technology	K. G. Picha	GA
NGF-14-001-016	University of Chicago	J. A. Simson	ILL
NGF-14-005-020	University of Illinois (Urbana)	D. Alpert	ILL

NGF-15-005-011	Purdue University	B. A. Reese	IND
NGF-16-001-005	University of Iowa	J. A. Van Allen	IOWA
NGF-17-004-010	University of Kansas	B. G. Barr	KAN
NGF-21-002-016	University of Maryland	M. H. Martin	MD
NGF-22-007-009	Harvard University	William H. Sweet	MASS
NGF-22-009-021	Massachusetts Institute of Technology	J. V. Harrington	MASS
NGF-23-005-019	University of Michigan	R. A. Sawyer	MICH
NGF-24-005-011	University of Minnesota	A. O. C. Nier	MINN
NGF-24-005-072	University of Minnesota	W. B. Cheston	MINN
NGF-26-008-009	Washington University (St. Louis)	R. E. Norberg	MO
NGF-31-001-011	Princeton University	J. P. Layton	NJ
NGF-33-006-008	Polytechnic Institute of Brooklyn	M. H. Bloom	NY
NGF-33-010-010	Cornell University	T. Gold	NY
NGF-33-016-034	New York University	A. Ferri	NY
NGF-33-018-011	Rensselaer Polytechnic Institute	S. E. Wiberly	NY
NGF-33-019-011	University of Rochester	W. O. Fenn	NY
NGF-36-003-058	Case Western Reserve University	H. R. Nara	OHIO
NGF-39-011-004	University of Pittsburgh	D. Halliday	PA
NGF-44-001-014	Texas A & M University	R. E. Wainerdi	TEX
NGF-44-006-008	Rice University	A. J. Dessler	TEX
NGF-48-002-031	University of Washington	J. H. Ballard	WASH
NGF-50-002-004	University of Wisconsin (Madison)		WISC
		J. O. Hirschfelder	

OFFICE OF TECHNOLOGY UTILIZATION

NGR-05-003-125	University of California (Berkeley)	C. W. Churchman	CAL
NGL-09-010-030	George Washington University	L. H. Mayo	DC
NGR-14-007-062	Northwestern University	A. H. Rubenstein	ILL
NGR-15-003-066	Indiana University	R. W. Campbell	IND
NGR-26-008-003	Washington University (St. Louis)	M. L. Weidenbaum	MO
NSR-05-020-151	Stanford University	W. Bollay	CAL
NSR-06-004-081	University of Denver	J. G. Milliken	COLO
NSR-07-002-037	University of Connecticut	S. W. Yost	CONN
NSR-09-010-035	George Washington University	C. W. Shilling	DC
NSR-09-010-057	George Washington University	C. W. Shilling	DC
NSR-15-003-054	Indiana University	A. W. Weimer	IND
NSR-15-003-067	Indiana University	L. Orr	IND
NSR-15-003-069	Indiana University	G. W. Wilson	IND
NSR-15-003-076	Indiana University		IND
NSR-32-004-049	University of New Mexico		NMEX
NSR-37-002-045	Oklahoma State University	K. A. McCollom	OKLA
NSR-37-004-008	Southeastern State College		OKLA
NSR-39-001-064	University of Pittsburgh	A. Kent	PA
NSR-39-011-076	University of Pittsburgh	J. Canter	PA
NSR-39-011-078	University of Pittsburgh	G. McGee	PA
NSR-39-011-089	University of Pittsburgh	A. Kent	PA
NSR-39-011-106	University of Pittsburgh		PA

OFFICE OF TRACKING AND DATA ACQUISITION

NGR-05-020-001	Stanford University	O. G. Villard	CAL

CENTERS

AMES RESEARCH CENTER

NGR-03-002-169	University of Arizona	D. J. Hamilton	ARIZ
NGR-05-003-089	University of California (Berkeley)	D. H. Calloway	CAL
NGR-05-003-285	University of California (Berkeley)	C. L. Tien	CAL
NGR-05-003-326	University of California (Berkeley)	H. Borsook	CAL
NGR-05-004-038	Unversity of California (Davis)	R. E. Smith	CAL
NGR-05-004-053	University of California (Davis)	R. Smith	CAL
NGR-05-009-059	University of California (San Diego)	B. Q. Duntley	CAL
NGR-05-009-109	University of California (San Diego)	J. B. West	CAL
NGR-05-010-010	University of California (Santa Barbara)	W. C. Gogel	CAL
NGR-05-017-013	University of Santa Clara	D. A. Oliver	CAL
NGR-05-020-102	Stanford University	K. Karamcheti	CAL
NGL-05-020-177	Stanford University	R. E. Smith	CAL
NGR-05-020-209	Stanford University	T. R. Kane	CAL
NGR-05-020-223	Stanford University	M. Anliker	CAL
NGR-05-020-244	Stanford University	R. C. Atkinson	CAL
NGL-05-020-250	Stanford University	J. D. Baldeschwieler	CAL
NGR-05-020-277	Stanford University	D. A. Dunn	CAL
NGR-05-020-305	Stanford University	D. C. Harrison	CAL
NGR-05-020-324	Stanford University	L. A. Sapirstein	CAL
NGR-05-020-326	Stanford University	S. Levine	CAL
NGR-05-020-335	Stanford University	A. C. Giese	CAL
NGR-05-020-345	Stanford University	J. L. Adams	CAL
NGR-05-020-386	Stanford University	W. A. Tiller	CAL
NGR-05-025-008	University of California (San Francisco)		CAL
		H. I. Maibach	
NGR-05-029-005	University of San Francisco	A. Furst	CAL
NGL-05-046-002	San Jose State College	B. Clark	CAL
NGR-05-061-004	University of California (Santa Cruz)	E. M. Evleth	CAL
NGR-07-004-015	Yale University	M. M. Chen	CONN
NGR-07-011-001	St. Joseph College	M. T. J. Murphy	CONN
NGR-09-009-024	Georgetown University	I. Gray	DC
NGR-14-005-103	University of Illinois (Urbana)	J. C. Chato	ILL
NGL-14-012-012	University of Illinois (Chicago)	P. R. Nachtsheim	ILL
NGR-15-005-077	Purdue University	D. E. Abbott	IND
NGR-17-001-034	Kansas State University	L. T. Fan	KAN
NGR-18-002-008	University of Louisville	E. A. Alluisi	KY
NGR-22-007-163	Harvard University	R. A. Bauer	MASS
NGR-22-017-006	Worcester Polytechnic Institute	I. Zwiebel	MASS
NGR-22-017-008	Worcester Polytechnic Institute	A. H. Weiss	MASS
NGR-25-002-015	University of Mississippi	H. T. Milhorn	MISS
NGR-26-003-026	University of Missouri (Rolla)	R. D. Rechtier	MO
NGR-26-004-011	University of Missouri (Columbia)	C. W. Gehrke	MO
NGR-33-007-074	Clarkson College of Technology	H. H. G. Jellinek	NY
NGR-36-008-041	Ohio State University	J. H. Dines,	OHIO
		L. B. Roberts	
NGR-37-003-043	University of Oklahoma	M. L. Rasmussen	OKLA
NGR-39-009-123	Pennsylvania State University	A. J. Engel	PA

NGL-39-010-097	University of Pennsylvenia	C. J. Lambertsen	PA
NGR-39-011-067	University of Pittsburgh	G. R. Fitterer	PA
NGR-39-011-083	University of Pittsburgh	T. M. Donahue	PA
NGR-44-009-018	Texas Christian University	M. D. Arnoult	TEX
NGR-45-002-014	Utah State University	E. W. Vendell	UTAH
NGR-47-004-051	Virginia Polytechnic Institute	H. F. Brinson	VA
NGR-48-002-047	University of Washington	M. E. Childs	WASH
NGL-50-002-078	University of Wisconsin (Madison)	E. C. Dick	WISC
NGR-50-002-083	University of Wisconsin (Madison)	V. C. Rideout	WISC
NGR-52-059-001	McMaster University	A. B. Kristofferson	FOR
NSR-52-112-001	Queen's University	F. J. Smith	FOR
NSR-52-112-002	Queen's University	F. J. Smith	FOR
NAS2-1554	University of Virginia	G. C. Pitts	VA
NAS2-2503	University of California (Los Angeles)	W. R. Adey	CAL
NAS2-2633	University of Southern California	J. P. Meehan	CAL
NAS2-2711	Texas Womans University	P. B. Mack	TEX
NAS2-2738	University of Minnesota	F. Halberg	MINN
NAS2-3360	University of Minnesota	W. R. Webber	MINN
NAS2-3410	Stanford University	V. R. Eshlman	CAL
NAS2-3528	Bowling Green State University	I. I. Oster	OHIO
NAS2-3876	University of Chicago	J. A. Simpson	ILL
NAS2-4151	Washington University (St. Louis)	K. Hohenemser	MO
NAS2-4231	University of California (Berkeley)	N. Pace	CAL
NAS2-4629	University of Minnesota	W. R. Webber	MINN
NAS2-4671	Stanford University	T. Tomberlin	CAL
NAS2-4672	Stanford University	V. R. Eshlman	CAL
NAS2-4849	University of St. Thomas	L. S. Browning	TEX
NAS2-4915	University of California (Berkeley)		CAL
NAS2-4919	Massachusetts Institute of Technology		MASS
NAS2-5016	Georgia Institute of Technology		GA
NAS2-5043	Massachusetts Institute of Technology	D. G. Fraser	MASS
NAS2-5098	Princeton University	C. Pittendrigh	NJ
NAS2-5167	University of Arizona	R. N. Carlile	ARIZ
NAS2-5245	University of California (Davis)	J. Beljan	CAL
NAS2-5254	Bradley University		ILL
NAS2-5311	University of California (Los Angeles)	I. R. Kaplan	CAL
NAS2-5344	University of New Hampshire		NH
NAS2-5355	Stanford University		CAL

ELECTRONICS RESEARCH CENTER

NGR-01-003-008	Auburn University	W. A. Shaw	ALA
NGR-01-003-036	Auburn University	P. M. Fitzpatrick	ALA
NGR-04-005-001	Arkansas State University	J. L. Linnstaedter	ARK
NGR-05-002-100	California Institute of Technology	M. A. Nicolet	CAL
NGR-05-003-143	University of California (Berkeley)	D J. Sakrison, V. Algazi	CAL
NGR-05-003-243	University of California (Berkeley)	R. S. Muller	CAL
NGR-05-003-273	University of California (Berkeley)	S. P. Siliberto	CAL
NGR-05-004-051	University of California (Davis)	M. A. Hoffman	CAL
NGL-05-007-161	University of California (Los Angeles)	F. A. Haak	CAL
NGR-05-010-041	University of California (Santa Barbara)	P. F. Ordung	CAL
NGR-05-010-044	University of California (Los Angeles)	H. P. Broida	CAL
NGR-05-017-017	University of Santa Clara	S. P. Chan	CAL
NGR-05-018-079	University of Southern California	W. T. Kyner	CAL

NGR-05-018-104	University of Southern California	R. M. Gagliardi	CAL
NGR-05-020-165	Stanford University	M. Chodorow	CAL
NGR-05-020-234	Stanford University	A. E. Siegman	CAL
NGR-05-061-005	University of California (Santa Cruz)	W. M. McKeeman	CAL
NGR-06-002-053	Colorado State University	C. B. Winn	COLO
NGR-06-002-074	Colorado State University	D. R. Winder	COLO
NGR-06-003-088	University of Colorado	R. E. Hayes	COLO
NGR-09-003-014	American University	E. Callen	DC
NGR-11-002-101	Georgia Institute of Technology	I. E. Perlin	GA
NGR-12-001-046	University of Hawaii	W. W. Peterson	HAW
NGR-14-005-111	University of Illinois (Urbana)	M. L. Babcock	ILL
NGR-14-007-071	Northwestern University	D. Mintzer	ILL
NGR-15-005-106	Purdue University	P. A. Wintz	IND
NGR-17-002-053	University of Kansas	G. L. Kelly	KAN
NGR-17-004-019	University of Kansas	R. M. Haralick	KAN
NGR-19-006-001	Northeast Louisiana State College	D. E. Dupree	LA
NGR-21-001-073	Johns Hopkins University	A. Chapanis	MD
NGR-21-002-206	University of Maryland	Y. Chu	MD
NGL-22-007-053	Harvard University	W. A. Burgess	MASS
NGR-22-007-056	Harvard University	R. W. P. King	MASS
NGR-22-007-068	Harvard University	A. E. Bryson	MASS
NGR-22-007-096	Harvard University	F. R. Ervin	MASS
NGR-22-007-124	Harvard University	R. A. Bauer	MASS
NGR-22-007-126	Harvard University	P. S. Pershan	MASS
NGR-22-007-143	Harvard University	Y. C. Ho	MASS
NGL-22-009-124	Massachusetts Institute of Technology	G. C. Newton	MASS
NGR-22-009-131	Massachusetts Institute of Technology	G. Fiocco	MASS
NGL-22-009-163	Massachusetts Institute of Technology	R. P. Rafuse	MASS
NGR-22-009-229	Massachusetts Institute of Technology	W. R. Markey	MASS
NGR-22-009-234	Massachusetts Institute of Technology	R. D. Thornton	MASS
NGR-22-009-240	Massachusetts Institute of Technology	A. Javan	MASS
NGR-22-009-249	Massachusetts Institute of Technology	G. B. Benedek	MASS
NGR-22-009-262	Massachusetts Institute of Technology	W. R. Markey	MASS
NGL-22-009-309	Massachusetts Institute of Technology	Z. S. Zannetos	MASS
NGR-22-009-311	Massachusetts Institute of Technology	J. P. Vinti	MASS
NGR-22-009-335	Massachusetts Institute of Technology	M. O. Scully	MASS
NGR-22-009-337	Massachusetts Institute of Technology	P. Penfield	MASS
NGR-22-009-359	Massachusetts Institute of Technology	R. Weiss	MASS
NGR-22-009-393	Massachusetts Institute of Technology	A. Evans	MASS
NGL-22-009-418	Massachusetts Institute of Technology	D.J. Epstein	MASS
NGR-22-010-041	University of Massachusetts	J. R. Strong	MASS
NGR-22-010-042	University of Massachusetts	J. Strong	MASS
NGR-22-011-020	Northeastern University	J. Warga	MASS
NGL-22-011-024	Northeastern University	B. L. Cochrun	MASS
NGR-22-011-025	Northeastern University	K. Weiss	MASS
NGR-22-011-051	Northeastern University	C. H. Perry	MASS
NGR-22-012-006	Tufts University	D. H. Spodick	MASS
NGL-23-005-183	University of Michigan	G. I. Haddad, H. H. Woodson, H. A. Haus, J. R. Melcher	MICH
NGR-26-003-037	University of Missouri (Rolla)	E. C. Bertnolli	MO
NGR-30-002-056	University of New Hampshire	C. K. Taft	NH
NGR-31-001-109	Princeton University	M. Summerfield	NJ
NGR-31-001-132	Princeton University	A. W. Lo	NJ
NGR-31-003-050	Stevens Institute of Technology	G. J. Herskowitz	NJ

NGR-31-003-066	Stevens Institute of Technology	E. C. Ney	N J
NGR-31-006-006	Fairleigh Dickinson University	K. D. Moeller	N J
NGR-33-006-020	Polytechnic Institute of Brooklyn	K. K. Clarke	N Y
NGR-33-006-040	Polytechnic Institute of Brooklyn	M. Schwartz	N Y
NGR-33-008-090	Columbia University	C. C. Halkias	N Y
NGL-33-010-047	Cornell University	P. R. McIsaac	N Y
NGR-33-010-051	Cornell University	C. L. Tang	N Y
NGR-33-010-074	Cornell University	F. D. McLeod	N Y
NGR-33-015-085	State University of New York (Stony Brook)		N Y
		F. F. Y. Wang	
NGR-33-022-091	Syracuse University	J. J. Zwislocki	N Y
NGR-34-003-026	University of North Carolina (Chapel Hill)		N C
		J. W. Hanson	
NGR-36-003-079	Case Western Reserve University	W. H. Ko	OHIO
NGR-36-008-103	Ohio State University	W. W. Anderson	OHIO
NGR-36-007-012	Ohio University	W-K Chen	OHIO
NGR-36-027-001	Case Western Reserve University	E. L. Glaser	OHIO
NGR-39-004-028	Drexel Institute of Technology	C. A. Silver	PA
NGR-39-087-002	Carnegie-Mellon University	A. G. Milnes	PA
NGL-40-002-042	Brown University	G. S. Heller	R I
NGR-40-002-082	Brown University	J. E. Savage	R I
NGR-40-005-002	Providence College	E. K. Gora	R I
NGR-41-002-024	University of South Carolina	D. L. Rohlfing	S C
NGL-43-001-056	University of Tennessee	F. M. Shofner	TENN
NGR-44-007-027	Southern Methodist University	S. C. Gupta	TEX
NGR-44-007-042	Southern Methodist University	T. L. Chu	TEX
NGR-44-012-046	University of Texas (Austin)	B. D. Tapley	TEX
NGR-44-012-104	University of Texas (Austin)	W. H. Hartwig	TEX
NGR-44-012-144	University of Texas (Austin)	C. V. Ramamoorthy	TEX
NGR-47-005-059	University of Virginia	W. L. Duren	VA
NGR-52-093-001	University of Ottawa	H. Kozlowska	FOR
NAS1-5700	College of William & Mary	R. T. Siegel	VA
NAS1-7022	Princeton University	J. K. Gillham	N J
NAS1-7389	Mississippi State University	P. S. Young	MISS
NAS1-7391	University of Denver	C. Lundin	COLO
NAS1-7709	Temple University	C. S. Stokes	PA
NAS12-102	Massachusetts Institute of Technology		MASS
		M. E. Connelly	
NAS12-514	Massachusetts Institute of Technology	C. S. Draper	MASS
NAS12-569	Massachusetts Institute of Technology	C. S. Draper	MASS
NAS12-606	University of Massachusetts	R. E. McIntosh	MASS
NAS12-620	Lowell Technological Institute	J. R. Herman	MASS
NAS12-640	Massachusetts Institute of Technology		MASS
NAS12-642	Massachusetts Institute of Technology		MASS
NAS-12-650	Illinois Institute of Technology		ILL
NAS-12-651	University of Denver		COLO
NAS12-652	Carnegie-Mellon University		PA
NAS12-654	Stevens Institute of Technology		N J
NAS12-658	Massachusetts Institute of Technology		MASS
NAS12-661	Southern Methodist University		TEX
NAS12-668	Massachusetts Institute of Technology		MASS
NAS12-679	Massachusetts Institute of Technology		MASS
NAS12-692	University of Missouri (Columbia)		MO
NAS12-695	Stanford University		CAL
NAS12-2054	Brown University	A. Wold	R I
NAS12-2059	Tulane University	C. H. Beck	LA
NAS12-2063	Northeastern University		MASS
NAS12-2064	Illinois Institute of Technology	T. Webber	ILL
NAS12-2065	Stevens Institute of Technology	G. J. Herskowitz	N J

NAS12-2082	Ohio University		OHIO
NAS12-2096	North Carolina State University	A. H. Shephard	N C
NAS12-2101	Stevens Institute of Technology	C. T. Brooth	N J
NAS12-2104	University of California (Los Angeles)		CAL
NAS12-2105	University of California (Los Angeles)		CAL
NAS12-2106	Southern Methodist University		TEX
NAS12-2107	Case Western Reserve University		OHIO
NAS12-2111	Massachusetts Institute of Technology		MASS
NAS12-2117	University of Michigan		MICH
NAS12-2128	Tufts University		MASS
NAS12-2134	Virginia Polytechnic Institute		VA
NAS12-2138	University of California (Los Angeles)		CAL
NAS12-2142	University of Vermont		VT
NAS12-2152	University of New Hampshire		N H

FLIGHT RESEARCH CENTER

NGR-05-007-122	University of California (Los Angeles)		CAL
		A. V. Balakrishnan	
NGR-05-007-187	University of California (Los Angeles)	J. J. Vidal	CAL
NGR-06-003-083	University of Colorado	I. Horowitz	COLO
NGR-38-003-015	University of Oregon	J. Roman	ORE
NGR-44-001-081	Texas A&M University	J. R. Scoggins	TEX

GODDARD SPACE FLIGHT CENTER

NGR-03-002-180	University of Arizona	H. L. Johnson	ARIZ
NGR-03-002-184	University of Arizona	H. L. Johnson	ARIZ
NGR-05-003-220	University of California (Berkeley)	A. N. Kaufman	CAL
NGR-05-007-041	University of California (Los Angeles)	Z. Sekara	CAL
NGR-05-007-066	University of California (Los Angeles)	A. Y. F. Wong	CAL
NGR-05-007-091	University of California (Los Angeles)		CAL
		Y. Mintz, A. Arakawa	
NGR-05-007-116	University of California (Los Angeles)	A. Banos	CAL
NGR-05-007-205	University of California (Los Angeles)	F. S. Sjoatrand	CAL
NGR-05-008-005	University of California (Riverside)	J. Callaway	CAL
NGR-05-010-020	University of California (Santa Barbara)		CAL
		T. P. Mitchell	
NGR-06-002-084	Colorado State University	W. R. Mickelsen	COLO
NGL-07-004-005	Yale University	R. C. Barker	CONN
NGR-07-010-002	Fairfield University	J. H. McElaney	CONN
NGR-09-005-014	Catholic University	T. Tanaka	D C
NGR-09-005-054	Catholic University	T. Tanaka	D C
NGR-09-010-008	George Washington University	N. Filipescu	D C
NGL-09-011-004	Howard University	H. Branson	D C
NGR-10-019-001	Florida Technological University	H. N. Rexford	FLA
NGR-14-001-008	University of Chicago	T. Fujita	ILL
NGR-14-005-088	University of Illinois (Urbana)	G. C. McVittie	ILL
NGL-15-004-026	University of Notre Dame	J. L. Massey	IND
NGR-15-005-087	Purdue University		IND
NGR-15-008-004	Rose Polytechnic Institute	H. A. Sabbagh	IND
NGR-21-001-043	Johns Hopkins University	H. H. Seliger	MD
NGR-21-002-029	University of Maryland	W. C. Erickson	MD

NGL-21-002-033	University of Maryland	H. Laster	MD
NGR-21-002-065	University of Maryland	A. M. Decker	MD
NGR-21-002-096	University of Maryland	R. T. Bettinger	MD
NGR-21-002-197	University of Maryland	Y. Chu	MD
NGR-21-002-211	University of Maryland	S. K. Poultney	MD
NGR-21-002-214	University of Maryland	J. P. Richard	MD
NGR-21-002-218	University of Maryland	C. O. Alley	MD
NGR-21-023-001	Columbia Union College	E. I. Mohr	MD
NGR-22-010-012	University of Massachusetts	R. V. Monopoli	MASS
NGR-22-010-018	University of Massachusetts	R. V. Monopoli	MASS
NGR-22-091-002	College of the Holy Cross	R. C. Gunter	MASS
NGR-26-003-044	University of Missouri (Rolla)	T. L. Noack	MO
NGR-31-001-068	Princeton University	L. D. Davisson	N J
NGR-31-001-103	Princeton University	S. H. Lam	N J
NGR-33-006-042	Polytechnic Institute of Brooklyn	J. J. Bongiorno	N Y
NGR-33-006-053	Polytechnic Institute of Brooklyn	A. C. McKellar	N Y
NGR-33-008-012	Columbia University		N Y
	H. M. Foley, R. Novick, L. Woltjer, P. W. Gast		
NGL-33-016-013	New York University	J. E. Miller	NY
NGL-34-001-001	Duke University	T. G. Wilson	N C
NGR-34-002-038	North Carolina State University	F. J. Tischer	N C
NGL-34-002-047	North Carolina State University	F. J. Tischer	N C
NGR-36-003-100	Case Western Reserve University	A. R. Cooper	OHIO
NGR-36-008-080	Ohio State University	C. A. Lewis	OHIO
NGR-39-009-095	Pennsylvania State University	R. G. Quinn	PA
NGR-39-011-035	University of Pittsburgh	E. Gerjuoy	PA
NGR-39-087-001	Carnegie-Mellon University	M. L. Renard	PA
NGR-42-001-002	South Dakota School of Mines and Technology		S D
	C. L. Gruber		
NGR-44-007-037	Southern Methodist University	S. C. Gupta	TEX
NGR-44-012-132	University of Texas (Austin)	V. Szebehely	TEX
NGR-45-001-026	Brigham Young University	P. O. Berrett	UTAH
NASr-14	University of Rochester	R. E. Hopkins	N Y
NASr-54(11)	University of Michigan	L. M. Jones	MICH
NSR-02-001-035	University of Alaska	K. B. Mather	ALS
NAS5-1810	Princeton University	L. Spitzer	N J
NAS5-3095	University of Chicago	J. A. Simpson	ILL
NAS5-3097	Iowa State University	J. A. Van Allen	IOWA
NAS5-3177	University of California (San Diego)	L. E. Peterson	CAL
NAS5-3178	University of Rochester	M. F. Kaplan	N Y
NAS5-3205	Massachusetts Institute of Technology	G. Garmire	MASS
NAS5-3335	University of Michigan	G. R. Carigan	MICH
NAS5-3838	University of Minnesota	E. P. Ney	MINN
NAS5-3931	University of Colorado	W. A. Rense	COLO
NAS5-9076	University of Iowa	J. A. Van Allen	IOWA
NAS5-9077	University of California (Berkeley)	K. A. Anderson	CAL
NAS5-9078	Massachusetts Institute of Technology	H. S. Bridge	MASS
NAS5-9090	University of Chicago	J. A. Simpson	ILL
NAS5-9091	University of California (Berkeley)	K. A. Anderson	CAL
NAS5-9094	University of California (Berkeley)	K. A. Anderson	CAL
NAS5-9096	University of Chicago	P. Meyer	ILL
NAS5-9113	University of Michigan	J. J. Horvath	MICH
NAS5-9128	Temple University	J. L. Bohn	PA
NAS5-9217	University of Maryland	H. Laster	MD
NAS5-9274	Harvard University	L. Goldberg	MASS
NAS5-9275	University of New Mexico	C. P. Leavitt	NMEX
NAS5-9276	Rutgers University	A. Rolly	N J
NAS5-9305	Dartmouth College	T. Laaspere	N H
NAS5-9306	University of Michigan	G. R. Carignan	MICH

NAS5-9309	Stanford University	R. A. Helliwell	CAL
NAS5-9314	University of New Mexico	V. H. Regener	NMEX
NAS5-9327	University of Colorado	C. A. Barth	COLO
NAS5-9328	University of Michigan	G. R. Carignan	MICH
NAS5-9347	Stanford University	A. M. Peterson	CAL
NAS5-9366	University of Chicago	J. A. Simpson	ILL
NAS5-9590	Illinois Institute of Technology	C. Vest	ILL
NAS5-9677	University of Wisconsin (Madison)	V. E. Suomi	WISC
NAS5-9980	University of The West Indies		FOR
NAS5-10102	Stanford University	O. G. Villard	CAL
NAS5-10362	University of California (Berkeley)	F. S. Mozer	CAL
NAS5-10364	University of California (San Diego)	C. E. McIlwain	CAL
NAS5-10387	University of Texas (Austin)	A. W. Straiton	TEX
NAS5-10427	New Mexico State University	R. A. Bumgarner	NMEX
NAS5-10454	University of Notre Dame	J. D. Nicolaides	IND
NAS5-10554	New Mexico State University	R. B. Chavez	NMEX
NAS5-10625	University of Iowa	J. A. Van Allen	IOWA
NAS5-11002	Massachusetts Institute of Technology	C. S. Draper	MASS
NAS5-11037	University of Chicago	J. A. Simpson	ILL
NAS5-11038	University of California (Berkeley)	K. A. Anderson	CAL
NAS5-11039	University of Iowa		IOWA
NAS5-11054	University of New Hampshire	E. L. Chupp	N H
NAS5-11060	University of Minnesota	P. J. Kellogg	MINN
NAS5-11062	Massachusetts Institute of Technology	H. S. Bridge	MASS
NAS5-11063	University of Maryland	H. Gloeckler	MD
NAS5-11068	University of Wisconsin (Madison)		WISC
NAS5-11073	University of Michigan	G. R. Carignan	MICH
NAS5-11077	University of Pittsburgh	T. M. Donahue	PA
NAS5-11080	University of California (San Diego)	L. E. Peterson	CAL
NAS5-11081	University of California (San Diego)		CAL
NAS5-11082	Massachusetts Institute of Technology	G. Clark	MASS
NAS5-11171	University of Arizona		ARIZ
NAS5-11174	University of Michigan	F. T. Haddock	MICH
NAS5-11542	University of Wisconsin (Madison)		WISC
NAS5-11631	Colorado State University	W. E. Marlott	COLO
NAS5-11666	Colorado State University	W. E. Marlott	COLO
NAS5-11687	University of Minnesota	J. R. Winckler	MINN
NAS5-11694	University of New Hampshire	R. L. Arnoldy	N H
NAS5-14923	University of Pennsylvania		PA

KENNEDY SPACE CENTER

NAS7-535	New Mexico State University	R. A. Bumgarner	NMEX
NAS7-716	New Mexico State University		NMEX
NAS10-1255	University of Florida	E. A. Farber	FLA
NAS10-5172	Florida Institute of Technology	J. J. Frangie	FLA

LANGLEY RESEARCH CENTER

NGR-04-001-029	University of Arkansas	D. M. Scruggs	ARK
NGR-05-009-103	University of California (San Diego)	N. A. Baily	CAL
NGR-05-010-025	University of California (Santa Barbara)		CAL
		H. H. Bossel	
NGR-05-010-028	University of California (Santa Barbara)	W. C. Kuby	CAL

Grant Number	Institution	Investigator	State
NGR-05-020-243	Stanford University	H. Ashley	CAL
NGR-06-004-082	University of Denver	C. W. Chiang	COLO
NGR-07-009-003	Rensselaer Polytechnic Institute of Connecticut, Inc.	H. J. Schwarz	CONN
NGR-09-010-053	George Washington University	H. Liebowitz	D C
NGR-10-005-049	University of Florida	R. T. Schneider	FLA
NGR-11-002-096	Georgia Institute of Technology		GA
NGR-14-005-138	University of Illinois (Urbana)	A. M. Clausing	ILL
NGR-14-007-067	Northwestern University	G. Herrmann	ILL
NGR-14-008-019	Southern Illinois University	P. K. Davis	ILL
NGR-14-019-002	Bradley University	J. W. McNabb	ILL
NGR-15-005-022	Purdue University	R. Oldenburger	IND
NGR-15-005-094	Purdue University	J. G. Skifstad	IND
NGR-17-002-047	University of Kansas	K. H. Lenzen	KAN
NGR-19-001-016	Louisiana State University (Baton Rouge)	R. W. Pike	LA
NGR-19-001-059	Louisiana State University (Baton Rouge)	R. W. Pike	LA
NGR-21-002-175	University of Maryland	W. J. Bailey	MD
NGR-22-005-025	Brandeis University	J. W. Senders	MASS
NGR-22-009-303	Massachusetts Institute of Technology	N. D. Ham	MASS
NGR-22-009-334	Massachusetts Institute of Technology	A. D. Pierce	MASS
NGR-22-011-042	Northeastern University	R. Madden	MASS
NGR-23-005-041	University of Michigan	H. C. Early	MICH
NGR-23-005-285	University of Michigan	B. Arden	MICH
NGR-24-005-095	University of Minnesota	R. Plunkett	MINN
NGR-25-001-008	Mississippi State University	G. E. Jones	MISS
NGR-26-001-006	University of Missouri (Kansas City)	P. J. Bryant	MO
NGL-26-006-016	St. Louis University	F. C. Bates	
NGR-26-006-021	Saint Louis University	B. H. Ulrich Jr.	MO
NGR-26-006-024	Saint Louis University	D. S. Ousterhout	MO
NGR-31-001-129	Princeton University	I. Glassman	N J
NGR-31-001-146	Princeton University	E. H. Dowell	N J
NGR-32-004-026	University of New Mexico	C. G. Richards	NMEX
NGR-33-007-061	Clarkson College of Technology	C. W. Haines	N Y
NGL-33-007-075	Clarkson College of Technology	W. A. Thorton	NY
NGR-33-008-118	Columbia University	P. N. Borsky	N Y
NGR-33-010-070	Cornell University	R. H. Gallagher	N Y
NGR-33-016-128	New York University	L. Arnold	N Y
NGR-33-016-131	New York University	A. Ferri	N Y
NGR-33-016-141	New York University	J. Werner	N Y
NGL-33-018-053	Rensselaer Polytechnic Institute	F. A. White	N Y
NGR-33-018-066	Rensselaer Polytechnic Institute	J. B. Hudson	N Y
NGR-33-019-058	University of Rochester	G. Cohen	N Y
NGR-33-019-087	University of Rochester	D. T. Blackstock	N Y
NGR-33-022-082	Syracuse University	D. S. Dosanjh	N Y
NGR-34-002-032	North Carolina State University	H. Sagan	N C
NGL-34-002-035	North Carolina State University	F. D. Hart	N C
NGR-34-002-036	North Carolina State University	F. O. Smetana	N C
NGR-34-002-055	North Carolina State University	R. G. Pearson	N C
NGL-34-002-061	North Carolina State University	L. A. Jones	N C
NGR-34-002-072	North Carolina State University	L. A. Jones	N C
NGR-34-002-073	North Carolina State University	M. A. Littlejohn	N C
NGR-34-002-078	North Carolina State University	F. O. Smetana	N C
NGR-34-002-082	North Carolina State University	N. F. J. Matthews	N C
NGR-34-002-085	North Carolina State University	J. S. Lee	N C
NGR-34-002-086	North Carolina State University	R. W. Truitt	N C
NGR-34-002-095	North Carolina State University	R. G. Pearson	N C
NGR-34-002-108	North Carolina State University	C. R. Manning	N C
NGR-36-001-010	University of Akron	R. Dubensky	OHIO
NGR-36-004-013	University of Cincinnati	R. J. Kroll	OHIO
NGR-36-004-030	University of Cincinnati	L. Meirovitch	OHIO
NGR-36-007-025	Kent State University	J. L. Fergason	OHIO
NGR-36-008-005	Ohio State University	C. Levis	OHIO
NGR-36-008-076	Ohio State University	H. Hemand	OHIO
NGR-36-008-109	Ohio State University	C. D. Bailey	OHIO
NGR-36-008-131	Ohio State University	B. E. Gatewood	OHIO
NGR-37-003-041	University of Oklahoma	D. M. Egle	OKLA
NGR-39-002-023	Carnegie-Mellon University	J. L. Swedlow	PA
NGR-39-004-013	Drexel Institute of Technology	P. C. Chou	PA
NGR-39-007-017	Lehigh University	A. Kalnins	PA
NGR-39-007-040	Lehigh University	R. P. Wei	PA
NGR-39-009-111	Pennsylvania State University	B. W. McCormick	PA
NGR-39-009-121	Pennsylvania State University	G. Reethof	PA
NGR-39-010-101	University of Pennsylvania	B. S. P. Shen	PA
NGR-39-011-096	University of Pittsburgh	E. J. Sternglass	PA
NGR-41-001-016	Clemson University	T. G. Proctor	S C
NGR-43-001-075	University of Tennessee	H. D. Gruschka	TENN
NGR-43-002-031	Vanderbilt University	C. E. Roos	TENN
NGR-43-010-001	East Tennessee State University	H. D. Powell	TENN
NGR-44-001-011	Texas A & M University	A. E. Cronk	TEX
NGR-44-001-036	Texas A & M University	R. Thomas	TEX
NGR-44-009-008	Texas Christian University	S. B. Sells	TEX
NGR-44-012-020	University of Texas (Austin)	L. C. Reese	TEX
NGL-45-003-025	University of Utah	F. L. Staffanson	UTAH
NGR-47-002-005	Virginia Commonwealth University	W. T. Ham	VA
NGR-47-002-018	Virginia Commonwealth University	S. W. Lippincott	VA
NGR-47-002-020	Virginia Commonwealth University	H. P. Dalton	VA
NGR-47-003-007	Old Dominion University	G. L. Goglia	VA
NGR-47-003-008	Old Dominion University	R. L. Williams	VA
NGR-47-003-012	Old Dominion University	R. Y. K. Cheng	VA
NGR-47-003-015	Old Dominion University	W. D. Stanley	VA
NGR-47-004-016	Virginia Polytechnic Institute	J. P. Wightman	VA
NGR-47-004-018	Virginia Polytechnic Institute	W. E. C. Moore	VA
NGR-47-004-024	Virginia Polytechnic Institute	H. L. Wood	VA
NGR-47-004-030	Virginia Polytechnic Institute	R. A. Comparin	VA
NGR-47-004-040	Virginia Polytechnic Institute	J. C. Schug	VA
NGR-47-005-026	University of Virginia	E. S. McVey, J. Moore	VA
NGR-47-005-029	University of Virginia	H. M. Parker	VA
NGR-47-005-049	University of Virginia	F. R. Woods	VA
NGR-47-005-085	University of Virginia	A. R. Saunders	VA
NGR-47-005-093	University of Virginia	R. J. Mattauch	VA
NGL-47-005-098	University of Virginia	F. W. Barton	VA
NGR-47-005-108	University of Virginia	J. K. Haviland	VA
NGR-47-005-110	University of Virginia	G. B. Matthews	VA
NGL-47-006-008	College of William and Mary	W. M. Jones	VA
NGR-47-006-010	College of William & Mary	H. O. Funsten	VA
NGR-47-006-028	College of William and Mary	H. Friedman	VA
NGL-47-006-041	College of William and Mary	R. T. Siegel	VA
NGR-47-006-045	College of William and Mary	A. Sher	VA
NGR-48-002-010	University of Washington	R. G. Joppa	WASH
NGR-48-002-035	University of Washington	W. H. Rae	WASH
NGR-50-001-009	Marquette University	E. C. Foudriat	WISC
NGR-51-001-010	University of Wyoming	E. A. Rinehart	WYO
NGR-51-001-019	University of Wyoming	J. N. Rosen	WYO
NGR-52-025-003	University of Southampton	E. J. Richards	FOR
NGR-52-026-011	University of Toronto	R. C. Tennyson	FOR
NAS1-7265	North Carolina State University		N C
NAS1-8141	University of Iowa		IOWA
NAS1-8145	Virginia Polytechnic Institute		VA

NAS1-8219	Louisiana State University (Baton Rouge)		LA
NAS1-8311	Hampton Institute	L. C. Wyrett	VA
NAS1-8423	Massachusetts Institute of Technology		MASS
NAS1-8604	Carnegie-Mellon University		PA
NAS1-8658	Massachusetts Institute of Technology	C. Kelly	MASS
NAS1-8787	University of Delaware		DEL
NAS1-8818	University of Pennsylvania	Z. Hashin	PA
NAS1-8830	Stevens Institute of Technology	S. Tsakongs	N J
NAS1-9016	Lowell Technological Institute		MASS
NAS1-81446	University of Iowa		IOWA

LEWIS RESEARCH CENTER

NGR-03-002-115	University of Arizona	L. E. Weaver	ARIZ
NGL-05-002-136	California Institute of Technology	W. D. Rannie	CAL
NGR-05-003-297	University of California (Berkeley)	T. H. Pigford	CAL
NGR-05-013-010	California State College (Long Beach)	K. P. Luke	CAL
NGR-05-020-043	Stanford University	G. L. Pearson	CAL
NGR-05-020-134	Stanford University	W. M. Kays	CAL
NGR-05-020-214	Stanford University	R. H. Bube	CAL
NGR-06-002-063	Colorado State University	F. W. Smith	COLO
NGR-10-005-022	University of Florida	R. D. Walker	FLA
NGR-11-002-068	Georgia Institute of Technology	J. D. Clement	GA
NGR-11-002-083	Georgia Institute of Technology	B. T. Zinn	GA
NGR-14-004-028	Illinois Institute of Technology	Z. Lavan	ILL
NGR-14-005-025	University of Illinois (Urbana)	J. D. Morrow	ILL
NGR-14-005-140	University of Illinois (Urbana)	W. L. Chow	ILL
NGR-22-004-018	Boston University	E. T. Angelakos	MASS
NGR-22-009-091	Massachusetts Institute of Technology		MASS
		R. E. Stickney	
NGR-22-009-339	Massachusetts Institute of Technology		MASS
		E. A. Witmer	
NGR-22-009-383	Massachusetts Institute of Technology		MASS
		J. L. Kerrebrock	
NGR-23-004-056	Michigan State University	C. R. Gruhn	MICH
NGR-23-007-001	Michigan Technological University	C. E. Work	MICH
NGR-31-001-074	Princeton University	C. L. Mellor	N J
NGR-31-001-155	Princeton University	D. T. Harrje	N J
NGR-31-009-004	Newark College of Engineering	P. Hrycak	N J
NGR-33-010-042	Cornell University	F. K. Moore	N Y
NGR-33-013-017	City College of New York	M. Kolodney	N Y
NGR-33-013-025	City College of New York		N Y
NGR-33-013-029	City College of New York		N Y
		R. Pfeffer	
NGR-33-022-023	Syracuse University	V. Weiss	N Y
NGR-33-022-105	Syracuse University	V. Weiss	N Y
NGR-33-022-108	Syracuse University	D. V. Keller	MASS
NGR-36-003-064	Case Western Reserve University	S. Ostrach	OHIO
NGR-36-003-091	Case Western Reserve University	O. Ostrach	OHIO
NGR-36-004-008	University of Cincinnati	Ti Yi Li, H. Oguro	OHIO
NGR-36-006-003	John Carroll University	J. Trivisonno	OHIO
NGL-36-007-001	Kent State University	J. W. Reed	OHIO
NGR-36-019-001	Hiram College	L. B. Shaffer	OHIO
NGR-36-025-001	Cleveland State University	K. J. Casper	OHIO
NGR-36-027-002	Case Western Reserve University	S. V. Radcliffe	OHIO
NGR-39-009-034	Pennsylvania State University	J. Marin	PA

NGR-39-011-079	University of Pittsburgh	R. S. Dougall	PA
NGR-40-002-080	Brown University	C. Mylonas	R I.
NGR-43-001-023	University of Tennessee	M. W. Milligan	TENN
NGR-47-005-050	University of Virginia	E. J. Gunter	VA
NGR-50-002-116	University of Wisconsin	R. W. Boom	WISC
NAS3-7904	University of Minnesota	E. R. Eckert	MINN
NAS3-10412	University of Florida	G. J. Schoessow	FLA

MANNED SPACECRAFT CENTER

NGR-02-001-063	University of Alaska	R. B. Forbes	ALAS
NGR-05-003-228	University of California (Berkeley)	S. Margen	CAL
NGR-05-009-106	University of California (San Diego)	A. M. Schneider	CAL
NGR-05-025-007	University of California (San Francisco)	L. E. Earley	CAL
NGR-19-003-003	Louisiana Polytechnic Institute	T. Williams	LA
NGR-22-007-019	Harvard University	W. H. Abelman, L. E. Earley	MASS
NGR-22-009-123	Massachusetts Institute of Technology	F. Press	MASS
NGR-31-011-002	New Jersey College of Medicine & Dentistry		N J
NGR-33-023-032	Yeshiva University	E. D. Weitzman	N Y
NGL-38-002-032	Oregon State University	R. A. Schmitt	ORE
NGR-38-003-009	University of Oregon	D. P. Weill	ORE
NGR-38-003-012	University of Oregon	A. R. McBirney	ORE
NGR-43-003-007	Tennessee Technological University	R. Kinslow	TENN
NGR-44-001-031	Texas A&M University	T. J. Kozik	TEX
NGL-44-001-044	Texas A & M University	J. A. Stricklin	TEX
NGR-44-001-067	Texas A&M University	R. E. Wainerdi	TEX
NGR-44-001-071	Texas A&M University	C. F. Kettleborough	TEX
NGR-44-001-097	Texas A&M University	W. B. Smith	TEX
NGR-44-003-031	Baylor University	R. Roessler	TEX
NGR-44-005-022	University of Houston	A. F. Hildebrant	TEX
NGR-44-005-041	University of Houston	C. Goodman	TEX
NGR-44-005-065	Universty of Houston	C. Dalton	TEX
NGR-44-005-090	University of Houston	C. J. Huang	TEX
NGR-44-005-096	University of Houston	M. Eisner	TEX
NGR-44-005-098	University of Houston	H. P. Decell	TEX
NGR-44-006-088	Rice University	R. B. McLellan	TEX
NGR-44-006-089	Rice University	A. Miele	TEX
NGR-44-006-105	Rice University	J. A. S. Adams	TEX
NGR-44-011-026	Texas Technological College	R. D. Shelton	TEX
NGR-44-011-031	Texas Technological College	H. F. Martz	TEX
NGL-44-012-043	University of Texas (Austin)	W. H. Hartwig	TEX
NGR-44-012-088	University of Texas (Austin)	B. Fruchter	TEX
NGR-44-012-136	University of Texas (Austin)	B. D. Tapley	TEX
NGR-48-002-074	University of Washington	J. Vagners	WASH
NGR-50-002-086	University of Wisconsin (Madison)	D. O. Cliver	WISC
NGR-52-134-001	York University	H. N. McFarland	FOR
NAS9-3079	Massachusetts Institute of Technology	P. Matthews	MASS
NAS9-4065	Massachusetts Institute of Technology	C. S. Draper	MASS
NAS9-4500	University of Minnesota	W. Kubicek	MINN
NAS9-4576	Massachusetts Institute of Technology		MASS
NAS9-5249	University of California (Berkeley	S. Silver	CAL
NAS9-5632	Stanford University	R. L. Kovach	CAL
NAS9-5884	Rice University		TEX
NAS9-5886	University of Maryland	J. Weber	MD
NAS9-5911	Rice University	J. W. Freeman	TEX
NAS9-5957	Columbia University	G. Latham	N Y

NAS9-6037	Columbia University	M. Ewing	N Y
NAS9-6331	University of Houston	L. Swenson	TEX
NAS9-6812	Texas A & M University	H. E. Whitmore	TEX
NAS9-6823	Massachusetts Institute of Technology	C. S. Draper	MASS
NAS9-6910	Ohio State University	C. Mengel	OHIO
NAS9-7020	Stanford University	B. B. Lusignan	CAL
NAS9-7081	University of Arizona	P. N. Slater	ARIZ
NAS9-7153	University of Texas (Austin)	B. A. Mitchell	TEX
NAS9-7175	University of Kansas	R. K. Moore	KAN
NAS9-7183	Massachusetts Institute of Technology	D. H. Staelin	MASS
NAS9-7218	Ohio State University	J. Shaw	OHIO
NAS9-7222	Northwestern University	K. G. Henize	ILL
NAS9-7237	Baylor University	P. Kellaway	TEX
NAS9-7280	Baylor University	P. C. Johnson	TEX
NAS9-7282	University of California (Los Angeles)	W. R. Adey	CAL
NAS9-7313	Stanford University	R. J. Lyon	CAL
NAS9-7382	Massachusetts Institute of Technology	R. Biemann	MASS
NAS9-7566	University of Denver	W. H. Mclain	COLO
NAS9-7651	Illinois Institute of Technology		ILL
NAS9-7738	Rice University	H. R. Anderson	TEX
NAS9-7809	University of Maryland	C. V. Alley	MD
NAS9-7830	Massachusetts Institute of Technology	J. V. Evans	MASS
NAS9-7882	University of California (Los Angeles)		CAL
NAS9-7883	University of Chicago		ILL
NAS9-7887	University of Chicago	A. Edward	ILL
NAS9-7888	University of Chicago		ILL.
NAS9-7890	Columbia University	R. Anderson	N Y
NAS9-7891	University of California (San Diego)	J. R. Arnold	CAL
NAS9-7892	University of California (San Diego)	G. Arrhenius	CAL
NAS9-7895	Columbia University	P. W. Gast	N Y
NAS9-7897	Princeton University	H. H. Hess	N J
NAS9-7899	Rice University	D. Heymann	TEX
NAS9-7926	University of Texas (Austin)	J. G. Thompson	TEX
NAS9-7951	Texas A & M University	J. M. Prescott	TEX
NAS9-7963	California Institute of Technology	L. T. Silver	CAL
NAS9-7969	Rice University	A. J. Chapman	TEX
NAS9-7975	University of Wisconsin (Madison)	L. Haskin	WISC
NAS9-8005	Harvard University		MASS
NAS9-8012	University of Houston		TEX
NAS9-8017	University of Kentucky		KY
NAS9-8018	Cornell University		N Y
NAS9-8032	Yale University	K. K. Turekian	CONN
NAS9-8069	University of Houston		TEX
NAS9-8071	University of Oregon		ORE
NAS9-8072	Yale University	S. R. Lipsky	CONN
NAS9-8073	Carnegie-Mellon University	T. Kohman	PA
NAS9-8074	California Institute of Technology	G. J. Wasserburg	CAL
NAS9-8075	Yale University	B. J. Skinner	CONN
NAS9-8078	Indiana University		IND
NAS9-8080	University of Chicago		ILL
NAS9-8084	Lehigh University		PA
NAS9-8086	University of Chicago	J. V. Smith	ILL
NAS9-8093	University of Minnesota	R. O. Pepsin	MINN
NAS9-8095	University of California (Los Angeles)		CAL
NAS9-8096	University of California (Los Angeles)		CAL
NAS9-8097	Oregon State University	R. A. Schmitt	ORE
NAS9-8098	University of Kentucky		KY
NAS9-8099	Massachusetts Institute of Technology		MASS
NAS9-8100	Harvard University		MASS

NAS9-8101	University of Miami	S. Sox	FLA
NAS9-8102	Massachusetts Institute of Technology		MASS
NAS9-8107	University of California (San Diego)	H. C. Urey	CAL
NAS9-8109	Baylor University	W. C. Duncan	TEX
NAS9-8118	Purdue University	E. R. Winter	IND
NAS9-8122	University of Texas (Austin)	S. E. Ritzmann	TEX
NAS9-8165	Washington University (St. Louis)	R. W. Walker	MO
NAS9-8200	University of Texas (Austin)	M. Wheatcroft	TEX
NAS9-8224	Indiana University		IND
NAS9-8241	Massachusetts Institute of Technology		MASS
NAS9-8242	Massachusetts Institute of Technology		MASS
NAS9-8246	Texas Womans University	P. B. Mack	TEX
NAS9-8258	University of Texas (Austin)	S. E. Ritzmann	TEX
NAS9-8264	University of Houston		TEX
NAS9-8328	Massachusetts Institute of Technology	J. Hovorka	MASS
NAS9-8352	Washington University (St. Louis)	R. W. Walker	MO
NAS9-8379	Ohio State University	C. Mengel	OHIO
NAS9-8463	Texas Technological College		TEX
NAS9-8479	North Texas State University		TEX
NAS9-8747	University of Arizona		ARIZ
NAS9-8755	Centenary College		LA
NAS9-8795	Texas Southern University		TEX
NAS9-8806	University of California (Berkeley)		CAL
NAS9-8869	University of Houston	N. S. Kovar	TEX
NAS9-8888	Texas Womans University	P. B. Mack	TEX
NAS9-8945	University of Alaska		ALAS
NAS9-8949	Baylor University	P. C. Johnson	TEX
NAS9-9003	Rice University	J. R. Sims	TEX
NAS9-9017	Cornell University		N Y
NAS9-9024	Massachusetts Institute of Technology		MASS
NAS9-9053	Texas A&M University	D. Hightower	TEX
NAS9-9103	University of Chicago	J. H. Rust	ILL
NAS9-9104	University of Houston		TEX
NAS9-9184	University of Houston		TEX
NAS9-9266	University of Texas (Galveston)	M. Guest	TEX
NAS9-9270	University of Houston		TEX
NAS9-9285	Texas A&M University		TEX
NAS9-9300	University of Wisconsin (Madison)		WIS
NAS9-9304	University of Michigan		MICH
NAS9-9341	Long Island University	E. D. Yost	N Y
NAS9-9348	University of California (Berkeley)		CAL
NAS9-9365	University of New Mexico	K. Keil	NMEX
NAS9-9418	Baylor University	J. D. Frost	TEX
NAS9-9427	Texas Womans University	P. B. Mack	TEX
NAS9-9433	Harding College	H. D. Olree	ARK
NAS9-9439	Stanford University	H. Halpern	CAL
NAS9-9502	University of California (Berkeley)		CAL
NAS9-9577	University of California (Berkeley)		CAL

MARSHALL SPACE FLIGHT CENTER

NGR-01-002-035	University of Alabama (Huntsville)	E. W. Grohse	ALA
NGR-01-002-063	University of Alabama (Huntsville)	J. E. Rush	ALA
NGR-11-002-085	Georgia Institute of Technology	B. T. Zinn	GA
NGR-15-003-064	Indiana University	J. R. Thompson	IND

NGR-19-001-068	Louisiana State University (Baton Rouge)		LA
		E. J. Dantin	
NGR-25-001-032	Mississippi State University	D. L. Murphree	MISS
NGR-43-002-032	Vanderbilt University	E. B. Shanks	TENN
NGR-48-002-009	University of Washington	J. K. Buettner	WASH
NAS5-3949	Harvard University	L. Goldberg	MASS
NAS8-2473	Georgia Institute of Technology	J. L. Hammond	GA
NAS8-2504	Massachusetts Institute of Technology		MASS
		S. H. Crandall	
NAS8-2559	Vanderbilt University	E. B. Shanks	TENN
NAS8-2585	University of Alabama (Tuscaloosa)	R. A. Mann	ALA
NAS8-11184	Auburn University	E. R. Graf	ALA
NAS8-11189	University of Tennessee	G. R. Shermann	TENN
NAS8-11202	University of Alabama (University)	W. G. Moulton	ALA
NAS8-11259	Clemson University	C. V. Aucoin	SC
NAS8-11334	Mississippi State University	W. D. McCain	MISS
NAS8-11344	Auburn University	M. A. Honnel	ALA
NAS8-11468	University of California (Berkeley)	W. H. Giedt	CAL
NAS8-18120	University of Texas (Austin)	L. Clark	TEX
NAS8-20004	Auburn University	J. L. Lowry	ALA
NAS8-20104	Auburn University	D. W. Russell	ALA
NAS8-20154	Auburn University	E. R. Graf	ALA
NAS8-20159	University of Alabama (University)	R. A. Mann	ALA
NAS8-20171	University of Alabama (University)	J. F. Porter	ALA
NAS8-20172	University of Alabama (University)	M. A. Griffin	ALA
NAS8-20175	Auburn University	J. Crenshaw	ALA
NAS8-20228	University of Michigan	J. A. Clark	MICH
NAS8-20284	Mississippi State University	C. T. Carley	MISS
NAS8-20312	University of Michigan	V. L. Streeter	MICH
NAS8-20331	Columbia University	C. M. Harris	NY
NAS8-20357	University of Michigan	G. R. Carignan	MICH
NAS8-20765	Auburn University	M. A. Honnell	ALA
NAS8-21015	University of Wisconsin (Madison)		WISC
NAS8-21049	Colorado State University	V. A. Sandborn	COLO
NAS8-21086	University of Michigan	G. R. Carignan	MICH
NAS8-21116	Louisiana State University (Baton Rouge)		LA
NAS8-21131	Rensselaer Polytechnic Institute	R. J. Roy	NY
NAS8-21140	Pennsylvania State University	A. K. Blackadar	PA
NAS8-21143	University of Alabama (University)	H. R. Henry	ALA
NAS8-21179	University of Arkansas	W. D. Dickinson	ARK
NAS8-21257	Texas A & M University	N. E. Moyer	TEX
NAS8-21267	University of Michigan	J. C. Zorm	MICH
NAS8-21286	Newark College of Engineering	R. Misra	NJ
NAS8-21292	University of St. Thomas	J. L. Goldman	TEX
NAS8-21317	Ohio State University	W. B. Campbell	OHIO
NAS8-21321	University of Alabama (Huntsville)		ALA
		O. J. Christensen	
NAS8-21368	Auburn University	C. L. Phillips	ALA
NAS8-21377	Mississippi State University	W. L. McDaniel	MISS
NAS8-21391	Oklahoma State University	F. E. Todd	OKLA
NAS8-21397	Arizona State University	N. S. Berman	ARIZ
NAS8-21407	University of California (Berkeley)		CAL
NAS8-21421	Texas Christian University		TEX
NAS8-21432	University of California (Berkeley)	J. R. Mitchell	CAL
NAS8-21436	University of Denver	J. Blizard	COLO
NAS8-21442	University of Illinois (Urbana)	D. D. Windlin	ILL
NAS8-21449	University of Chicago	P. Meyer	ILL
NAS8-21451	Massachusetts Institute of Technology	J. Hovorka	MASS
NAS8-21480	University of Alabama (University)	T. E. Falgout	ALA
NAS8-21484	Tulane University		LA
NAS8-21572	University of Arizona		ARIZ
NAS8-23970	University of Alabama (Tuscaloosa)	C. A. Gibson	ALA
NAS8-23988	University of Arizona	H. L. Johnson	ARIZ
NAS8-24364	Massachusetts Institute of Technology		MASS
NAS8-24365	Massachusetts Institute of Technology	K. Masubuchi	MASS
NAS8-24392	Clark University	C. A. Coulter	MASS
NAS8-30159	University of Alabama (Huntsville)	C. C. Shih	ALA
NAS8-30175	University of Oklahoma	E. F. Blick	OKLA
NAS8-30179	University of Denver	D. G. Murcray	COLO
NAS8-30511	Colorado School of Mines		COLO

SPACE NUCLEAR PROPULSION OFFICE

NGL-03-002-006	University of Arizona	L. E. Weaver	ARIZ
NGR-21-002-167	University of Maryland	T. D. Wilkerson	MD
NGR-36-003-042	Case Western Reserve University		OHIO
		B. Reswick and H. Mergler	
NSR-22-009-288	Massachusetts Institute of Technology		MASS
		W. S. Lewellen	
NAS6-1061	Rice University	B. J. O'Brien	TEX
NAS6-1296	University of Texas (El Paso)	D. Stenstrom	TEX
NAS6-1616	University of Virginia		VA

SOURCE: NASA, "NASA'S University Program," 1970.

Part 3

NASA PERSONNEL AND FACILITIES

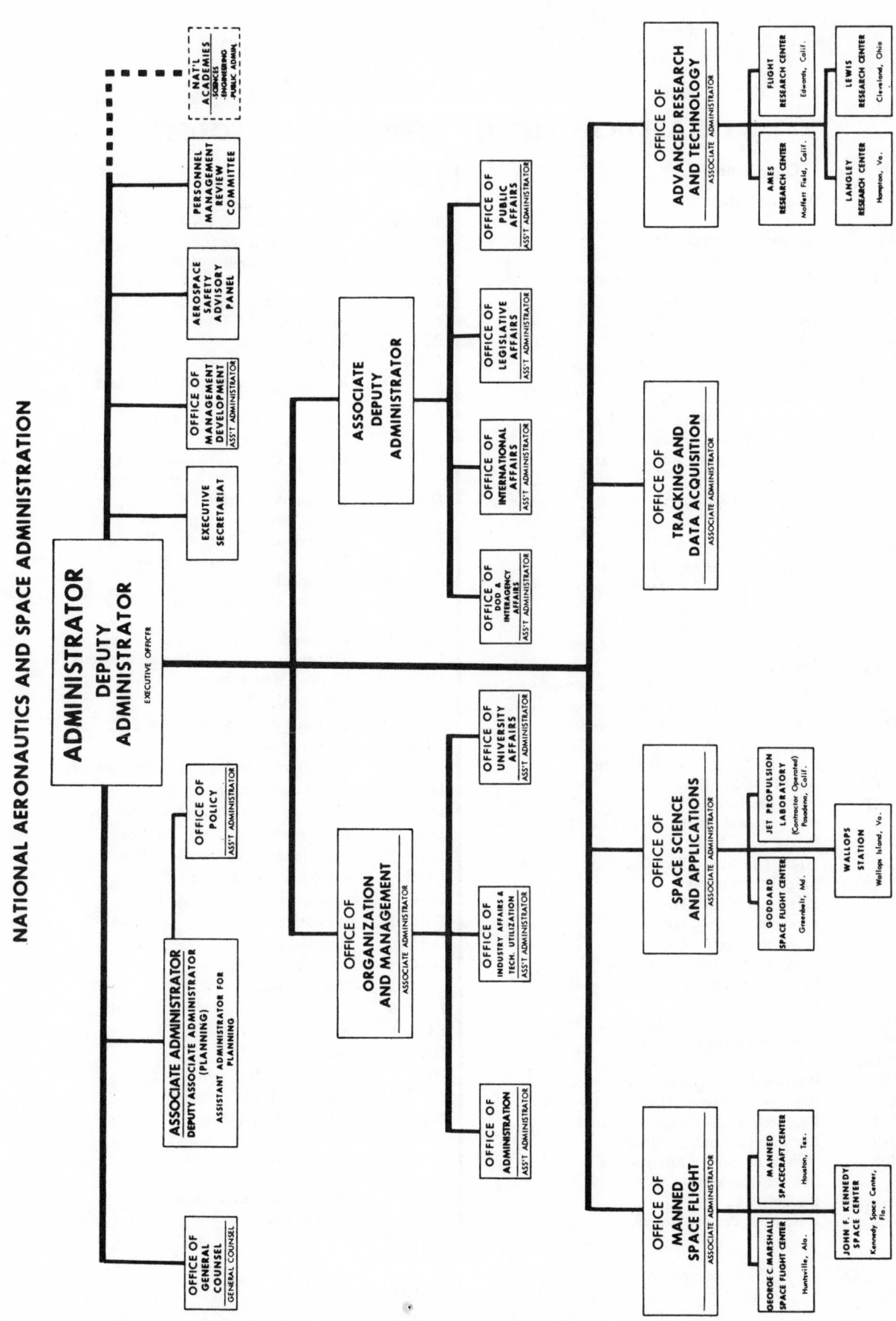

ALPHABETICAL LIST OF OFFICIAL MAIL CODES

Code	Organization	Code	Organization
A	Administrator	BX	Office of Facilities
		BX–MR	MSF Facilities Office
AA	Associate Administrator	BX–RM	OART Facilities Office
		BX–SP	SSA/TDA Facilities Office
AAD	Deputy Associate Administrator	BXA	Facilities Planning
AAD–1	Asst. Admin. for Planning	BXB	Programs & Engineering
AAD–1D	Deputy Admin. for Planning	BXC	Maintenance & Operations
AAD–2	Office of Long Range Plans	BXC–1	Transportation
AAD–3	Office of Analysis & Eval.	BXD	Real Estate
AAD–4	Office of Plans Integration	BXE	Industrial Facilities & Cryogenics
ABA	Board of Contract Appeals		
ABB	Contract Adjustment Board	C	Office of Legislative Affairs
AD	Deputy Administrator		
ADA	Associate Deputy Administrator	D	Office of Organization and Management
B	Office of Adminstration	DH	HQ Administration Office
		DHA	Administrative Services Div.
B–1	Asst. to the Asst. Administrator	DHA–1	Administrative Standards Branch
BD	Property and Supply Division	DHA–2	Buildings Management Branch
BDC	Cataloging and Standardization	DHA–3	Printing Branch
BDM	Property Management	DHA–31	Printing (Plant) Section
BDU	Utilization and Disposal	DHA–4	Logistics Branch
BF	Financial Management Division	DHA–42	Publications Distribution Section
BF–1	Technical Assistant	DHA–5	Transportation and Communications Branch
BFA	Agency Accounts and Reports Branch	DHA–50	Central Mailroom Section
BFC	Contractor Finance & Accounting Branch	DHA–501	Distribution Unit
BFG	General Financial Systems Branch	DHA–51	Teletype & Datafax Center
BFH	Headquarters Accounting Branch	DHA–52	Travel Section
BFP	Program Eval. & Assist. Branch	DHA–53	Transportation & Duty Office Section
BF–RM	OART Co-location	DHA–6	Visual Aids Branch
BF–SP	OSSA Co-location	DHA–7	Management Issuances & Info. Br.
BG	Occupational Medicine &.Env. Health Div.	DHA–71	Management Issuances Section
BG–1	Nurse	DHA–72	Headquarters Information Center
BG–2	Stress Lab Study Physician	DHB	Headquarters Budget Officer
BP	Office of Personnel	DHC	Headquarters Contracts Div.
BP–1	Personnel Mgmt. Group 1	DHC–1	Support Staff
BP–2	Personnel Mgmt. Group 2	DHC–3	Negotiation Branch
BP–3	Personnel Mgmt. Group 3	DHC–4	Negotiation Branch
BPA	Manpower Analysis Division	DHC–5	Negotiation Branch
BPC	Occupational & Salary Analysis Div.	DHC–6	Contract Administration Branch
BPE	Executive Staff	DHE	Emergency Planning
BPL	Labor-Management Relations Div.	DHZ	Security Division
BPM	Personnel Admin. Div.	DI	Inspections Division
BPM–2	Emp oyment Assistance Ctr.	DU	Audit Division
BPT	Personnel Development Div.	DY	NASA Safety Office
BR	Resources Analysis Division		
BR–1	Research & Development Branch	E	Office of Policy
BR–2	Installation Analysis Branch		
BR–3	Cost & Economic Analysis Br.	EH	NASA Historical Staff
BT	Budget Operations Division	EP	Policy Staff
BT–1	Budget Branch		
BT–2	Resources Project Branch		

Code	Organization
F	Office of Public Affairs
F–2	Special Assistant/Community Rel.
F–3	Resources Management Officer
FA	Planning & Media Development
FAD	Distribution Branch
FAE	Exhibits Production & Operations Br.
FAM	Audio-Visual Br.
FAP	Publications Production Branch
FD	Deputy Assistant Administrator
FE	Educational Programs
FG	Public Services
FGA	Activities Branch
FGC	Communications Branch
FGE	Exhibits Branch
FGM	Public Inquiries & Reports Br.
FP	Public Information Division
FPT	Radio/TV Programs
G	Office of General Counsel
GK	Asst. Gen. Counsel for Procurement Matters
GL	Law Library
GP	Asst. Gen. Counsel for Patent Matters
I	Office of International Affairs
K	Office of Industry Affairs
KB	Inventions and Contributions Board
KD	Procurement Office
KD–2	Procurement Operations, Director
KD–3	Policy & Administration, Director
KD–4	Small Business Advisor (Industry Assistance)
KDA	Asst. Dir. Administration
KDA–1	Surveys Division
KDA–2	Inquiries Division
KDA–3	Staff Operations Division
KDA–31	Administrative Officer
KDM	Asst. Director, Manned Programs
KDM-MA	Apollo Procurement Division
KDM-ML	Advanced Manned Space Programs Div.
KDP	Asst. Dir. Policy
KDP–1	Policy & Regulations Div.
KDP–2	Pricing Division
KDP–3	Contract Admin. Div.
KDR	Asst. Director, Contract Review
KDS	Asst. Dir. Science Tech. & Track. Prog.
KDS-RM	OART Programs
KDS-SP	OSSA Programs
KDS-TC	OTDA Programs
KL	Industrial Relations Office
KM	Management Systems Office
KM–1	Project Manager
KMA	Systems Applications Div.
KMB	ADP Systems Operations Div.
KMB–1	Operations Supervisor
KMC	Systems Integration & Control Div.
KME	Systems Technology Div.

Code	Organization
KMF	Systems Design Div.
KR	Reliability and Quality Assurance Office
KS	Scientific & Technical Info. Div.
KSA	Program Coordination Div.
KSB	Systems Development Div.
KSI	Acquisition & Dissemination Div.
KSP	Technical Publications Div.
KSS	Information Services Div.
KSS–10	Headquarters Library
KT	Technology Utilization Office
L	Office of Management Development
M	Office of Manned Space Flight.
M–1	Executive Assistant
MA	Apollo Program
MA–1	Executive Assistant
MAB	Asst. Div. Mgr. (Boeing)
MAE	Engineering
MAG	Washington Office (G.E.)
MAL	Apollo Lunar Exploration
MAO	Operations
MAP	Prog. Budget & Control
MAQ	Reliability, Quality & Safety
MAS	Systems Engr. (Bellcomm)
MB	Budget & Program Analysis
MB–1	Executive Assistant
MBB	Budget Director
MBD	Deputy Director
MBM	Management Center
MBP	Program Analysis
ME	Engineering & Operations
MED	Deputy Director
MF	Space Station Task Force
MF–1	Special Assistant
MFB	Program Budget & Control
MFI	Program Integration
MH	Space Shuttle Program
MH–1	Executive Assistant
MHD	Deputy Director
MLA	Project Integration
MLB	Program Budget & Control
MLD	Deputy Director
MLE	Engineering
MLO	Operations
MLQ	Reliability, Quality & Safety
MLS	System Engr. (Bellcomm)
MM	Life Sciences
MMC	Program Planning & Control
MMD	Deputy Director
MME	Bioengineering
MMR	Bioresearch
MMS	Space Medicine
MMV	Bioenvironmental Systems
M–N	Public Affairs Officer
MQ	Reliability, Quality & Safety
MQD	Deputy Director

Code	Organization	Code	Organization
MR	Administration	RR	Research Council
MRD	Deputy Director	RRT	Technical Assistant
MRO	Field Center Operations	RS	Shuttle Technologies Office
MRS	Organization Support	RSD	Deputy Director
MT	Advanced Missions	RT	Supercritical Tech. Office
MT-1	Executive Asst. (Tektite II)	RV	Entry Technology Office
MT-2	Staff Scientist	RW	Materials & Structures Div.
MT-3	Special Assistant	RWM	Materials Branch
MTA	Economic Analysis	RWS	Structures Branch
MTE	Program Studies	RX	Advanced Concepts & Mission Div.
MTG	Advanced Development	RY	Safety & Operating Systems Office
MTL	Payload Planning		
MTS	Systems Engr. (Bellcomm)	S	Office of Space Science and Applications
MX	Executive Staff		
		SA	Deputy Associate Administrator (Applications)
NS	Space Nuclear Systems Office	SAA	Special Assistant
NS-1	Deputy Director	SC	Communications Programs
NS-2	Asst. Mgr. for NERVA Develop. (Germantown, Md.)	SCC	Communications Satellite Program
		SCD	Deputy Director
NS-2	Space Nuclear Systems Office (Germantown, Md.)	SCE	Systems Branch
		SCF	Advanced Programs & Technology Programs
		SCG	Geodetic Satellites Program
OE	Executive Officer	SCN	Navigation & Traffic Control Program
OSP	Aerospace Safety Advisory Panel	SCO	Operational Systems Support Program
OY	Special Assistant to the Administrator	SCP	Program Review & Resources Management
		SCS	Applications Technology Satellites Program
R	Office of Advanced Research and Technology	SD	Deputy Associate Administrator for Space Science and Applications
R-1	Senior Research Associate	SF	Advanced Programs
R-2	Public Affairs Officer	SG	Physics and Astronomy Programs
RA	Aerodynamics & Vehicle Systems Div.	SL	Planetary Programs
RAA	Aerodynamics & Fluid Mech. Br.	SN	Public Affairs Officer
RAL	Loads & Flight Dynamics Br.	SP	Program Review and Resources Management
RAS	High-Speed Aircraft Br.	SPA	Administrative Operations
RAV	Low-Speed Aircraft Br.	SPI	Institutional Planning & Development
RB	Aero. Life Sciences Div.	SPP	Program Review
RBT	Technical Assistant	SPR	Resources Management
RD-A	Deputy Associate Administrator (Aeronautics)	SR	Earth Observations Programs
		SRA	Assistant Director
RD-M	Deputy Associate Administrator (Management)	SRB	Earth Resources Survey Flights Program
		SRD	Deputy Director & Director of Meteorology
RD-S	Deputy	SRE	Deputy Director, Flight Programs
RE	Guidance, Control & Info. Systems Div.	SRF	Advanced Programs & Technology Programs
REG	Guidance & Optics Br.	SRG	Earth Physics & Phys. Ocean Prog.
RET	Information Systems Br.	SRM	Meteorology & Sounding Rockets
RF	Technology Applications Office	SRN	Nimbus Program
RFE	Flight Exper. Br.	SRO	Operational Meteorology Satellites Program
RFP	Flight Project Br.	SRP	Program Review & Resources Management
RFS	Technology Program Mgr.	SRR	Earth Resources Survey Disciplines Program
RJ	Short Takeoff & Landing Technology Office	SRS	Earth Res. Exp. Pkg. Programs
RL	Aeronautical Propulsion Div.	SRW	Global Atmospheric Res. Programs
RLC	Propulsion Components Br.	SS	Deputy Assoc. Admin. (Sciences)
RLS	Propulsion Systems Br.	SV	Launch Vehicle and Propulsion Programs
RM	Resources & Institutional Mgmt. Div.		
RMI	Institutional Mgmt. Br.	T	Office of Tracking and Data Acquisition
RMR	R&D Programs Br.		
RMS	Mgmt. Systems & Administration Br.	TA	Advanced Systems
RO	Aeronautical Operating Systems Div.	TC	Program Review & Resources Mgmt.
ROA	Air Traffic Systems Br.	TD	Deputy Associate Administrator
ROO	Operating Factors Br.		
RP	Space Prop. & Power Div.		
RPD	Deputy Director		

Code	Organization	Code	Organization
TN	Operations, Communications & ADP	XC	Communications Division
TS	Network Development & Engineering	XP	Program and Special Reports Division
W	Office of DoD & Interagency Affairs	XS	Secretariat Support Division
WX	Technical Assistant	Y	Office of University Affairs
X	Executive Secretary	Z	GAO Representatives

IMPORTANT DIRECTORY INFORMATION

The prefix letter to room numbers identifies the appropriate building, as follows:

B Federal Office Building 10B, 600 Independence Ave. SW, Washington, D.C.

E Atomic Energy Commission Building, Germantown, Maryland

F Federal Office Building 6, Maryland Ave. & 4th Street SW, Washington, D.C.

L L'Enfant Plaza North, Washington, D.C.

R Reporters Building, 300 7th Street SW, Washington, D.C.

W NASA Warehouse, 1411 S. Fern Street, Arlington, Virginia

Dialing instructions:

1. If the number listed in the EXT column is a five digit number, dial (202)-96 plus the extension number [e.g. 27149; dial (202)-962-7149].

2. If the number listed in the EXT column is a seven digit number starting with 119, dial (301)-973 plus the last four digits [e.g. 119-3774; dial (301)-973-3774].

3. If the number listed in the EXT column is a seven digit number and the first digit is 2 through 9, dial (202) plus the full seven digit number [e.g. 484-7888; dial (202)-484-7888].

CLASSIFIED DIRECTORY

ORGANIZATION	CODE	EXT	NAME	ROOM
ADMINISTRATOR	A	21271	Dr. James Fletcher	F7137
Secretary		25077	Nina Scrivener	F7137
DEPUTY ADMINISTRATOR	AD	21271	Dr. George M. Low	F7137
Secretary		25077	Nina Scrivener	F7137
ASSOCIATE ADMINISTRATOR	AA	26602	Dr. Homer E. Newell	F7137
Secretary		26602	Elvira W. Haas	F7137
ASSOCIATE DEPUTY ADMINISTRATOR	ADA	24715	Willis H. Shapley	F7137
Secretary		24715	Alice O. McGilvra	F7137
DEPUTY ASSOCIATE ADMINISTRATOR	AAD	24938	Dr. Wernher von Braun	F7137
Secretary		24938	Julia E. Kertes	F7137
BOARD OF CONTRACT APPEALS	ABA			
Chairman		24405	Ernest W. Brackett	F6075
Recorder		24405	Marilyn Sholtis	F6075
CONTRACT ADJUSTMENT BOARD	ABB			
Chairman		21457	E. M. Shafer	F7057
ASSISTANT ASSOCIATE ADMINISTRATOR	AA	37919	David Williamson Jr	F6147
SPECIAL ASSISTANT TO THE ADMINISTRATOR	OY	23802	Jacob E. Smart	F7109
EXECUTIVE OFFICER	OE	21426	Clare F. Farley	F7137
EXECUTIVE SECRETARY	X	21426	Clare F. Farley (Act.)	F7137
Asst. Executive Secretary		24023	George P. Chandler	F7137
Asst. Executive Secretary		24024	Dr. Dudley G. McConnell	F7137
Asst. Executive Secretary		36934	Martin F. Sedlazek	F7137
Asst. Executive Secretary		24075	Francis T. Hoban	F7137
PROGRAMS & SPECIAL REPORTS DIV. DIR	XP	37293	Lawrence J. Filippelli	F7127
Program Reviews & Reports Chf		37293	Lawrence J. Filippelli (Act.)	F7127
Mgmt. Presentation Chf		24825	James T. Futch (Act.)	F7121
Review Center Receptionist		24631	Mary Jane Behney	F7002
SECRETARIAT SUPPORT DIV. DIR	XS	24946	William H. Banks	F6075
COMMUNICATIONS DIV. DIR	XC	20321	Elaine B. Beran (Act.)	F7118
AEROSPACE SAFETY ADVISORY PANEL				
Special Assistant	OSP	27934	Gilbert L. Roth	F6083
DEPUTY ASSOCIATE ADMINISTRATOR (PLANNING)	AAD	24938	Dr. Wernher von Braun	F7137
Assistant Administrator for Planning	AAD-1	37297	Dr. DeMarquis D. Wyatt	F6147
Deputy Assistant Administrator for Planning	AAD-1D	24710	J. N. Foster	F6147
Office of Long-Range Plans, Director	AAD-2	37278	Dr. J. Ian Dodds	F6147
Deputy Director	AAD-2	37278	Dr. J. Ian Dodds (Act.)	F6147
Office of Analysis and Evaluation, Director	AAD-3	36914	Francis L. Williams	F6011
Deputy Director	AAD-3	37275	William A. Fleming	F6011
Office of Plans Integration, Director	AAD-4	24710	J. N. Foster (Act.)	F6147
Planning Center Receptionist		28421	Diane E. Terrill	F6011

SEE PRECEDING PAGE FOR IMPORTANT DIRECTORY INFORMATION

ORGANIZATION	CODE	EXT	NAME	ROOM

OFFICE OF GENERAL COUNSEL

GENERAL COUNSEL	G	21191	Spencer M. Beresford	F7065
Deputy General Counsel		21246	S. Neil Hosenball	F7065
Associate General Counsel		21457	E. M. Shafer	F7057
Asst. General Counsel		21456	Arthur D. Holzman	F7057
Asst. General Counsel for Procurement Matters	GK	21325	John A. Whitney	B225
Asst General Counsel for Patent Matters	GP	24391	Leonard Rawicz	F7045
Administrative Officer		28018	Margaret F. Nelson	F7062

OFFICE OF MANAGEMENT DEVELOPMENT

ASSISTANT ADMINISTRATOR	L	33748	Charles E. Weakley	F6137

OFFICE OF POLICY

ASSISTANT ADMINISTRATOR	E	34188	(Vacant)	F6141
POLICY STAFF DIR	EP	24805	Willis B. Foster	F6141
NASA HISTORICAL STAFF DIR	EH	37371	Dr. Eugene M. Emme	R706

OFFICE OF DOD AND INTERAGENCY AFFAIRS

ASSISTANT ADMINISTRATOR	W	23802	Jacob E. Smart	F7109
Technical Asst		23804	William R. Coupland	F7109
Senior Scientist		24413	Milton W. Rosen	F7109
Tech. Coord./Communications		24583	Walter A. Radius	F7101
Tech. Coord./Interagency Affairs		23978	John C. Damon	F7101
Tech. Coord./DOD Affairs		24583	John M. Coulter	F7101
Tech. Coord./Interagency Affairs		24205	Raymond W. Thompson	F7101
Tech. Coord./Survey Applications	WX	24707	Myron W. Krueger	F7112
Tech. Asst./Special Programs		24707	Floyd J. Sweet	F7112

OFFICE OF INTERNATIONAL AFFAIRS

ASSISTANT ADMINISTRATOR	I	21187	Arnold W. Frutkin	F7077
Deputy Asst. Administrator		21253	Donald R. Morris	F7077
Int'l Program Policy, Dir		22281	Dr. O. E. Anderson, Jr	F7077
Int'l Planning & Programs, Dir		33164	William Cohen	F7077
Deputy Dir		21213	Richard J. H. Barnes	F7087
Int'l Program Support, Dir		21253	Donald R. Morris, Act	F7077
Operations Support		21236	Carl N. Jones	F7089
International Technology Affairs		35975	Karl F. Mautner	F7089
Personnel Exchanges Officer		21543	Thomas E. R. Stribling	F7090
Public Information Officer		21337	Richard Friedman	F7090
Executive Assistant		21993	Ruth Thomas	F7090

OFFICE OF LEGISLATIVE AFFAIRS

ASSISTANT ADMINISTRATOR	C	21717	H. Dale Grubb	F6065
Congressional Liaison Director		21841	Gerald J. Mossinghoff	F6061
Legislative Affairs Officer (OMSF)		21841	Jack V. Cramer	F6061
Legislative Affairs Officer (OART, OTDA)		21841	Clarence E. Kresin	F6061
Legislative Affairs Officer (OSSA)		21841	William L. Sturdevant, Jr	F6061
Legislation Director		22726	James J. Laux (Act.)	F6069
Congressional Inquiries Director		34265	Bertram A. Mulcahy	F6069

OFFICE OF PUBLIC AFFAIRS

ASSISTANT ADMINISTRATOR	F	35302	Julian Scheer	F7019
Spec. Asst./Community Relations	F-2	22368	O. B. Lloyd, Jr	F7025
Resources Management Officer	F-3	24286	John A. Broadhurst	F6053
Public Affairs Off., OMSF	M-N	20666	William J. O'Donnell	B456
Public Affairs Off., OART	R-2	23865	William W. Pomeroy	B656
Public Affairs Off., OSSA	SN	21176	Richard T. Mittauer	F5017

ORGANIZATION	CODE	EXT	NAME	ROOM
Public Affairs Officer OIA/TU	K	27387	Mary G. Fitzpatrick	F5011
Public Affairs Officer, OTDA	TN	20117	Joseph A. Stein	B526
Public Affairs Officer, OIA	I	21337	Richard Friedman	F7090
EDUCATIONAL PROGRAMS DIR	FE	33532	Dr. Fred B. Tuttle	R801
Deputy Dir		33125	Everett Collin	R801
Research & Analysis		33532	Dr. Fred B. Tuttle (Act.)	R805
Teacher Services & Spacemobile Program		22562	Dr. William B. Rich	R805
Instructional Resources		22429	Myrl Ahrendt	R805
Counseling & Career Program		22654	Dr. Paul Gardner	R805
Vocational and Technical Guidance		22722	Robert S. Tiemann	R805
Special Activities		22560	Muriel Thorne	R805
PUBLIC INFORMATION DIR	FP	21736	Alfred P. Alibrando	F6047
Associate Dir		21737	Walter A. Pennino	F6047
Asst. to Dir		24222	Jack Maher	F6038
News Chief		36925	Ralph E. Gibson	F6043
News Audio-Visual Chief		21721	Les Gaver	F6035
Radio/TV Programs	FPT	34086	Joseph Headlee	F6102
PUBLIC SERVICES DIR	FG	21571	Wade St. Clair	F6107
Deputy Dir		24440	James M. Funkhouser	F6107
Associate Director		37636	Harris B. Hull	F6103
Exhibits Br. Chf	FGE	27306	Mack R. Herring	F6052
Public Inq. & Reports Br. Chf	FGM	28041	George DeGennaro	F6021
Activities Br. Chf	FGA	24351	Eugene A. Marianetti	F6093
Communications Br. Chf	FGC	33349	Jefferson D. Bates	F6103
PLANNING & MEDIA DEVELOPMENT DIR	FA	22161	Edward A. Pierce, Jr.	R802
Deputy		23477	James Dean	R802
Associate Dir		20331	Alex P. Nagy	R806
Exhibits Production & Operations Br	FAE	20331	James Dean (Act.)	R802
Exhibit Operations		33642	Maurice Peter	R806
Design & Construction		34904	Frank Fisher	R808
Audio-Visual Br	FAM	22516	Clayton Edwards (Act.)	R811
Production		22752	James Etheredge	R811
Distribution	FAD	24341	William Detrich (Act.)	W–Bldg.
Publications Production Br	FAP	22867	George Gardner	R812

OFFICE OF ORGANIZATION AND MANAGEMENT

ORGANIZATION	CODE	EXT	NAME	ROOM
ASSOCIATE ADMINISTRATOR	D	34783	Richard C. McCurdy	F5137
Deputy Associate Admin		24463	Bernard Moritz	F5137
Executive Assistant		28127	William J. Pendleton	F5137
Special Assistant		37517	Raymond A. Kline	F5137
Special Assistant		33241	Raymond Einhorn	F5137
Special Assistant		33242	Walter C. Shupe	F5137
HDQRS. ADMINISTRATION, DIR	DH	24513	Lawrence W. Vogel	F5001
ADMINISTRATIVE SERVICES DIV. DIR	DHA	24506	Albert A. Clagett	B168
Assistant Director		24506	Nathan C. Haines	B168
Special Asst		24506	Pierre D. Bynum	B168
Administrative Standards Br. Chf	DHA–1	24831	Sidney F. Musselman	B168
Buildings Management Br. Chf	DHA–2	24281	Richard P. Burgess	B150
Printing Br. Chf	DHA–3	24445	Herman S. Nader	B146
Printing (Plant) Section	DHA–31	23910	Arthur F. Hood	BC Lev.
Logistics Branch, Chf	DHA–4	22305	David M. King	W–Bldg.
Procurement Section		22305	James T. Campbell	W–Bldg.
Property Mgmt. & Transport Section		22305	Dwight E. Conrad	W–Bldg.
Transportation & Communications Br. Chf	DHA–5	21469	James W. Poland	BB Lev.
Central Mailroom Section	DHA–50	21446	Joseph W. McKenney (Act.)	BA19
Distribution Unit	DHA–501	24033	Norman Morris	BA24

ORGANIZATION	CODE	EXT	NAME	ROOM
Teletype & Datafax Center	DHA-51	21618	Warren R. Whitley	BA25
Travel Section	DHA-52	36616	Martha M. Platt	BA26
Transportation & Duty Office Sec	DHA-53	24442	Charles E. Freeman	BB Lev.
Visual Aids Branch, Chf	DHA-6	21918	Stephen A. Saliga	BA56
Mgmt. Issuances & Info. Br. Chf	DHA-7	22225	Eleanor G. Borella	B154
Mgmt. Issuances Section Chf	DHA-71	33602	Angela M. Murphy	B154
Headquarters Information Center	DHA-72	34956	Dema S. Nappier	B126
HDQRS. BUDGET OFFICER	DHB	25091	T. C. Crabe	R814
HDQRS. CONTRACTS DIV. DIR	DHC	28645	William M. Collins, Jr	R721
Deputy Director	DHC	28646	Herbert S. Snyder	R721
Support Staff, Chf	DHC-1	23605	Dorothy E. Shackelford	R721
Negotiation Br. Chf	DHC-3	21411	J. Ronald Jeshow	R721
Negotiation Br. Chf	DHC-4	23703	William Quintrell	R721
Negotiation Br. Chf	DHC-5	21327	James B. Phillips, Jr	R721
Contract Administration Br. Chf	DHC-6	21149	Joseph T. Davis	R721
EMERGENCY PLANNING	DHE	37620	Donald H. Lichty	F7071
SECURITY DIVISION DIR	DHZ	21532	Bartley A. Fugler	R424
Deputy Director		21532	Edwin H. Stevens	R424
Physical & Industrial Security Br		23965	Arnold W. Garrett	R424
Visit Clearance		21795	Nannie L. Parker	R424
Personnel Security & Investigation Br		22155	Francis B. Dukes	R424
Classification Management		21532	Howard G. Maires	R424
INSPECTIONS DIV. DIR	DI	24325	Ralph F. Winte	F7071
Inspector		24325	A. W. Sanders	F7071
Inspector		24325	Robert L. Lagassey	F7071
Inspector		24325	Robert L. McCulloch	F7071
AUDIT DIV. DIR	DU	22375	Martin Sacks	R511
Assistant Director		23236	James D. McNamara	R505
Assistant Director		22464	Eugene T. Nettles	R505
Special Assistant		22445	Earl E. McGinty	R507
Special Assistant		22464	Bernard F. Carey	R505
Audit Manager		22445	Robert S. Rollin	R507
NASA SAFETY OFFICE	DY	20514	Jerome F. Lederer	F6089
Asst. Dir., Industrial Safety		35364	Daniel F. Hayes, Sr	F6089
Asst. Dir., Safety Prog. & Res		25438	Philip H. Bolger	F6089
Asst. Dir., Aviation		24608	Reuben P. Prichard	F6143

OFFICE OF ADMINISTRATION

ORGANIZATION	CODE	EXT	NAME	ROOM
ASSISTANT ADMINISTRATOR	B	28113	William E. Lilly	F6127
Dept. Asst. Administrator	B	28806	Boyd C. Myers	F6127
Asst. to the Asst. Administrator	B	28146	Albert P. Little	F6127
Special Assistant	B	28107	Ralph E. Cushman	F6127
FINANCIAL MANAGEMENT DIV. DIR	BF	22811	H. Frank Hann	R624
Deputy Director	BF	22813	Louis N. Lushina	R624
Technical Asst	BF-1	26773	Julia C. Bruce	R624
OSSA Co-location	BF-SP	24843	Henry A. DeGolyer	F5122C
OART Co-location	BF-RM	26162	Francis J. Sullivan	B644
Program Evaluation & Assistance Br. Chf	BFP	24801	John N. Buynitzky (Act.)	R628
General Financial Systems Br. Chf	BFG	37767	William M. Thompson	R628
Agency Accounts & Reports Br. Chf	BFA	26085	John R. Harbison	R623
Contractor Finance & Accounting Br. Chf	BFC	25935	J. Howard Kelly	R627
HDTRS Accounting Br. Chf	BFH	35427	Herbert F. Brooks	R609
Cashier		22010	Selden Wicks	R606
Travel Authorizations			(See Support Services)	
Payroll Unit		26053	Mildred V. Morris	R611
BUDGET OPERATIONS DIV. DIR	BT	20669	Charles M. Hochberg	F6015
Budget Br. Chf	BT-1	24146	Frederick L. Dunlap	F6015
Deputy		24145	George R. West	F6012A

ORGANIZATION	CODE	EXT	NAME	ROOM
Budget Oper. Sec. Chf		24145	William R. Leaman	F6012C
Budget Formulation Sec. Chf		24145	Charles W. Kelley	F6012D
Resources Proj. Br. Chf	BT-2	37167	Irving Summit	F6015
OCCUPATIONAL MEDICINE & ENVIRON-MENTAL HEALTH DIV. DIR.	BG	27432	Louis B. Arnoldi, M.D.	BA36
Occupational Medicine Br. Chf		27432	Lousi B. Arnoldi, M.D. (Act.)	BA36
Environmental Health Br. Chf		24774	Rudloph M. Marrazzo	BA36
Radiological Health		22850	Robert E. Alexander	BA36
Medical Management Br. Chf		35306	D. D. Limoncelli (Act.)	BA36
Statistical Assistant		27839	Jean C. Mockbee	BA36
OFFICE OF PERSONNEL DIR	BP	27582	Grove Webster	R526
Deputy Dir		27582	Madison B. Smith	R526
Asst. Dir. (Fed. Labor-Mgmt. Rel.)	BPL	23601	Patrick A. Gavin	R522
Asst. Dir. (Operations)	BPM	21368	Owen P. Gallagher	R421
Executive Personnel Staff:				
Executive Salary Admin	BPE	28044	Howard N. Braithwaite	R526
Executive Staffing	BPE	23481	Francis S. Miceli	R526
Program Evaluation & Planning Staff:				
Program Management	BP	24034	Kathryn C. Walker	R526
Program Evaluation	BP	24034	Rufus C. Unruh	R526
Manpower Analysis Div. Chf	BPA	21771	John F. Duggan	R527
Occupational & Salary Anal. Div. Chf	BPC	28072	Samuel O. Holdsambeck	R519
Labor-Mgmt. Relations Div. Chf	BPL	23601	Patrick A. Gavin	R522
Personnel Admin. Div. Chf	BPM	23168	Owen P. Gallagher	R421
Personnel Devel. Div. Chf. (Act.)	BPT	20640	Walter S. Hixon	R524
Personnel Mgmt. Group 1	BP-1	20894	Charles R. Row	F6058
Personnel Mgmt. Group 2	BP-2	21203	Rufus C. Unruh	B656
Personnel Mgmt. Group 3	BP-3	20234	Robert T. O'Neil	B356
Employment Assistance Ctr	BPM-2	28696	Bernard A. Neuman	R602
Hdqrs. EEO Officer	BPM	23168	Owen P. Gallagher	R421
PROPERTY & SUPPLY DIV. DIR	BD	26484	Leonard T. Witczak (Act.)	R701
Cataloging & Standardization, Chf	BDC	26484	Julian H. Schlaudecker	R701
Property Mgmt. Chf	BDM	26484	Leonard T. Witczak (Act.)	R701
Utilization & Disposal Chf	BDU	26484	Leonard T. Witczak	R701
OFFICE OF FACILITIES, DIR	BX	21855	R. H. Curtin	B300
Deputy Director		20583	R. H. Curtin (Act.)	B300
Facilities Planning	BXA	33660	Lawrence Jacobsen	B300
MSF Facilities Office, Chf	BX-MR	23551	Louis M. Tierney (Act.)	B340
ART Facilities Office, Chf	BX-RM	20154	John F. Madden	B636
SSA/TDA Facilities Office, Chf	BX-SP	21030	James F. Weir, Jr	F5122
Programs & Engineering, Dir	BXB	33666	James M. Bayne	B300
Maintenance & Operations, Dir	BXC	33905	Gerald P. Gaffney	B326
Real Estate, Dir	BXD	24466	R. L. Barber	B326
Industrial Fac & Cryogenics, Dir	BXE	24467	Roy L. Bullock	B326
RESOURCES ANALYSIS DIV. DIR	BR	35752	Joseph F. Malaga	F6031
Deputy Director	BR	35752	Charles T. Newman	F6031
Research & Development Br. Chf	BR-1	28483	Godfrey E. Barber	F6119
Installation Analysis Br. Chf	BR-2	37164	Otis F. Redfield	F6113
Cost & Economic Analysis Br. Chf	BR-3	36046	Thomas Campbell	F6025

OFFICE OF INDUSTRY AFFAIRS AND TECHNOLOGY UTILIZATION

ORGANIZATION	CODE	EXT	NAME	ROOM
ASSISTANT ADMINISTRATOR	K	36937	Daniel J. Harnett	F5011
Deputy Asst. Admin., Industry Affairs		36937	George J. Vecchietti	F5011
Executive Assistant		27591	Donald B. Smith	F5011
Asst. to Asst. Admin		36206	Robert J. Shafer	F5011
Sp. Asst. to Asst. Admin		36206	Jeffrey T. Hamilton	F5011
Administrative Officer		36206	James R. Ciaravino	F5011
Public Affairs Officer		27386	Mary Fitzpatrick	F5006

ORGANIZATION	CODE	EXT	NAME	ROOM
INVENTIONS & CONTRIBUTIONS BOARD				
Chairman	KB	24004	Ernest W. Brackett	R601
Director of the Staff		24001	Francis W. Kemmett	R601
PROCUREMENT OFFICE				
Director	KD	20697	George J. Vecchietti	B101
Executive Assistant	KD	20570	Philip H. Sload	B111
Special Projects	KD	24193	Raymond Staley	B101
Small Business Advisor (Ind. Asst.)	KD-4	24025	Kenneth J. Kier	B129
Policy & Administration, Dir	KD-3	28057	William P. Risso	B101
Asst. Dir., Policy	KDP	20557	A. G. Carretta	B101
Policy & Reg. Div., Chf	KDP-1	21876	Harry E. Tetirick	B125
Pricing Division, Chf	KDP-2	25086	Joseph Garcia (Act.)	B136
Contract Admin. Div., Chf	KDP-3	34818	William J. Wilken	B111
Assistant Director, Administration	KDA	26898	Harvey M. Kennedy	B111
Surveys Division, Chf	KDA-1	22468	Owen F. Karstad	B136
Inquiries Division, Chf	KDA-2	24757	Brian T. Kildee	B136
Staff Oper. Div., Chf	KDA-3	24717	Harold E. Pryor	BA1I
Administrative Officer	KDA-31	20246	Frankie L. Wallace	B133
Procurement Operations, Dir	KD-2	24193	Richard J. Keegan	B101
Asst. Director, Contract Review	KDR	24705	William E. Stuckmeyer	B112
Asst. Director, Manned Programs	KDM	20526	Sidney A. Cariski	B100
Apollo Procurement Div., Chf	KDM-MA	20531	George H. Wood	L5073
Adv. Manned Space Prog. Div. Chf	KDM-ML	37987	Peter D. Koutsandreas	B216
Asst. Dir., Science Tech. & Track. Prog	KDS	26584	Edmond J. Golden	B100
OART Programs, Chf	KDS-RM	27531	William W. Hudson	B656
OTDA Programs, Chf	KDS-TC	20117	James M. Tompkins	B526
OSSA Programs, Chf	KDS-SP	21269	Herbert D. Broman	F5128
INDUSTRIAL RELATIONS OFFICE				
Director	KL	20138	Robert E. King	B137
Deputy Director		20138	Ralph W. Tyner	B137
Contractor Equal Opportunity Prog., Dir		35304	Joseph M. Hogan	B145
MGMT SYSTEMS OFFICE, DIR	KM	23351	S. P. Lejko (Act)	R401
Asst. Dir. Plans & Sys. Integr		20260	Gail F. Sedgwick	R401
Asst. Dir. Mgmt. Engineering		20074	Wallace E. Velander	R401
Systems Applications Div. Chf	KMA	23453	R. J. Affholder	R401
ADP Systems Operations Div. Chf	KMB	24765	Norman J. Edwards	R405
Sys. Integration & Control Div Chf	KMC	35281	William J. Hynes	R411
Systems Design Div. Chf	KMF	24765	Joseph D. Walker	R405
Systems Technology Div. Chf	KME	20820	Charles G. Lokey (Act)	R502
REL. & QUALITY ASSURANCE OFFICE				
Director	KR	37281	Dr. John E. Condon	B155
Deputy Director	KR	24933	Howard M. Weiss	B155
Prin. Spec., Eval. & Analysis	KR	24931	Abraham I. Moskovitz	B155
Prin. Spec., Gov. Rel. & Quality Assur	KR	24932	Daniel E. Negola	B155
SCIENTIFIC & TECHNICAL INFO. OFFICE DIR	KS	23648	John F. Stearns	R822
Deputy Director		24638	Peppino N. Vlannes	R822
Administrative Officer		24679	Shirley H. Kerze	R822
Program Coordination Division Chf	KSA	23521	Ivan G. Rice	R824
Systems Development Division Chf	KSB	24796	Van A. Wente	R825
Acquisition & Dissemination Division Chf	KSI	26150	F. George Drobka	R823
Technical Publications Division Chf	KSP	25185	Frank Rowsome, Jr	R829
Information Services Division Chf	KSS	26156	Paul S. Feinstein	R827
Headquarters Library	KSS-10	37327	Alfred C. String	BA39
TECHNOLOGY UTILIZATION OFFICE DIR	KT	37925	Ronald J. Philips	R402
Special Asst. to the Dir		27947	D. W. Orrick, Jr	R406
Identification and Publication Div. Chf		26798	Leonard A. Ault	R410
Resources and Reports Div. Chf	KT	24336	Edward T. Sullivan	R414

ORGANIZATION	CODE	EXT	NAME	ROOM
Dissem. & Program Eval. Div. Chf		20297	Roland J. Philips (Act.)	R402
Technology Applications Div. Chf		24701	James T. Richards, Jr	R402
HQ Technology Utilization Officer		24336	Herbert L. Holley	R410

OFFICE OF UNIVERSITY AFFAIRS

ASSISTANT ADMINISTRATOR	Y	26596	Francis B. Smith	B200
Executive Assistant		23960	Jurgen G. Pohly	B200
SUSTAINING UNIVERSITY PROG. DIV. DIR		23119	Dr. Frank D. Hansing	B200
Research Br. Chf		24365	Herbert B. Quinn	B200
Engineering Sys. Design Br. Chf		23310	Joseph A. Vitale	B200
Management & Admin. Br. Chf		23119	Dr. Frank D. Hansing (Act.)	B200
Special Training Br. Chf		23110	Charles H. Carter	B200
UNIVERSITY PROG. COORD. DIV. DIR		25045	Edward M. James, Jr	B200
Deputy Director		23952	Donald C. Holmes	B200
Programs Branch, Chf		23952	Donald C. Holmes (Act.)	B200
Proposal Control		23808	Doris Goodwin (Act.)	B212
Coordination Branch, Chf		23104	William A. Greene	B200

OFFICE OF TRACKING AND DATA ACQUISITION

ASSOCIATE ADMINISTRATOR	T	24703	Gerald M. Truszynski	B500
Deputy Associate Administrator	TD	20088	H. R. Brockett	B500
ADVANCED SYSTEMS DIR	TA	20114	Frederick B. Bryant	B521
PROG. REVIEW & RESOURCES MGMT. DIR	TC	20117	Thomas V. Lucas	B526
OPER., COMM. & ADP DIR	TN	20011	Charles A. Taylor	B500
Network Operations Chf		20002	James C. Bavely	B512
Comm. & Frequency Mgmt. Chf		20131	Paul A. Price	B521
ADP Management Chief		20774	Kenneth R. Webster	B512
NETWORK DEVEL & ENG DIR	TS	20062	Norman Pozinsky	B507
PUBLIC INFORMATION OFFICER	TN	20117	Joseph A. Stein	B526

OFFICE OF MANNED SPACE FLIGHT

ASSOCIATE ADMINISTRATOR	M	20224	Dale D. Myers	B468
Deputy Assoc. Admin	MD	20614	Charles W. Mathews	B468
Deputy Assoc. Admin (Management)	MD-M	20303	Harry H. Gorman	B468
Deputy Assoc. Admin (Technical)	MD-T	24975	Charles J. Donlan	B468
Exec. Asst. to the Assoc. Admin	M-1	20226	Robert C. Littlefield	B468
Special Assistant	M-X	27215	Robert F. Freitag	B456
Special Assistant	M-X	27216	V. John Lyle	B456
Special Assistant	M-X	20671	Norman Rafel	B456
ADMINISTRATION DIR	MR	20661	M. Keith Wible	B368
Deputy Director	MRD	37413	James Costantino	B368
Organization Support Dir	MRS	34514	S. D. Cianella	B336
Field Center Operations Dir	MRO	20242	Edward P. O'Rourke	B350
MSF EXPERIMENTS BOARD		23582	Abraham S. Bass	B431
ADVANCED MISSIONS DIR	MT	20317	Philip E. Culbertson	B440
Special Asst	MT-3	20031	Merle G. Waugh	B440
Staff Scientist	MT-2	24860	Dr. Harvey Hall	B440
Exec Asst & Tektite II Mgr	MT-1	20077	Richard H. Sprince	B440
Advanced Development Dir	MTG	20295	Eldon W. Hall	B440
Payload Planning Dir	MTL	20426	William O. Armstrong	B431
Program Studies Dir	MTE	20315	Dr. Jack W. Wild	B431
Economic Analysis Dir	MTA	20317	Philip E. Culbertson (Act.)	B440
Systems Engineering (Bellcomm)	MTS [1]	484-7888	J. W. Timco	L8094

ORGANIZATION	CODE	EXT	NAME	ROOM
APOLLO PROGRAM DIR	MA	36244	Dr. Rocco A. Petrone	L5043
Mission Dir	MA	20203	Chester M. Lee	L5047
Exec Asst	MA-1	20523	John R. Schaibley	L5042
Asst for Rel., Quality, & Safety	MAQ	33085	Willis J. Willoughby	L5067
Program Budget and Control Dir	MAP	24311	John S. Potate	L5044
Engineering Dir	MAE	37348	William E. Stoney	L5039
Asst Dir Special Projects	MAE	37291	Benjamin Milwitzky	L5041
Asst Dir Test Engineering	MAE	36475	Charles H. King, Jr	L5009
Operations Dir	MAO	20643	John K. Holcomb	L5046
Apollo Lunar Exploration Dir	MAL	34882	Lee R. Scherer	L5084
Asst Dir, Flight Sys. Dev	MAL	28138	William T. O'Bryant	L5085
Asst Dir, Lunar Science	MAL	35367	Dr. R. J. Allenby	L5081
Asst Dir, Lunar Sample	MAL	37831	Dr. John Pomeroy	L5087
Sys Eng Dir (Bellcomm)	MAS [1]	484-7625	Robert L. Wagner	L7035
Asst Div Mgr (Boeing)	MAB [2]	484-2037	Robert L. Campbell	L4705
Washington Office (G.E.)	MAG [3]	37965	Jack E. Vessely	L1501
BUDGET AND PROGRAM ANALYSIS DIR	MB	20303	Harry H. Gorman (Acting)	B468
Deputy Director	MBD	20326	Bernard L. Johnson	B400
Exec Asst	MB-1	20681	Thomas P. Thiringer	B400
Budget Dir	MBB	24496	Charles E. Koenig	B412
Program Analysis Dir	MBP	20676	William J. Little, Jr	B412
Management Center, Chf	MBM	20686	Peter L. Robinson, Jr	B426
ENGINEERING AND OPERATIONS DIR	ME	20258	Robert N. Lindley	B400
Deputy Director	MED	20596	John D. Stevenson	B400
NASA DIR. FOR LIFE SCIENCES	MM	20111	James W. Humphreys, Jr., M.D.	B300
Deputy Director	MMD	20016	Walton L. Jones, M.D	B300
Dir. Prog. Planning & Control	MMC	20418	Herbert S. Brownstein	B300
Assoc. NASA Dir., Bioenvironmental Systems	MMV	20436	Joseph N. Pecoraro	B300
Assoc. NASA Dir., Bioresearch	MMR	26011	Sherman P. Vinograd, M.D	B409
Assoc. NASA Dir., Bioengineering	MME	26002	Dr. Stanley Deutsch	B415
Assoc. NASA Dir., Space Medicine	MMS	36323	Col. Rufus R. Hessberg, USAF, MC	B330
PUBLIC AFFAIRS OFFICER	M-N	20666	William J. O'Donnell	B419
RELIABILITY, QUALITY AND SAFETY				
Director	MQ	20411	Haggai Cohen	B247
Deputy Director	MQD	20408	George C. White, Jr	L5066
SKYLAB PROGRAM DIR	ML	20633	William C. Schneider	B268
Deputy Director	MLD	34345	John H. Disher	B268
Spec. Asst. for Missions	MLD-1	35347	B. Porter Brown	B268
Exec. Asst	ML-1	23250	William T. Ashley	B268
Asst. for Rel., Quality, & Safety	MLQ	20411	Haggai Cohen (Acting)	B247
Program Budget and Control Dir	MLB	36161	J. Pemble Field, Jr	B236
Project Integration Dir	MLA	20391	Thomas E. Hanes	B256
Engineering Dir	MLE	22071	Melvyn Savage	B243
Operations Dir	MLO	35256	Wyendell B. Evans	B246
Systems Eng. Dir. (Bellcomm)	MLS [1]	484-7654	Donald R. Hagner	L7033
SPACE SHUTTLE PROGRAM DIR	MH	23812	Charles J. Donlan (Act.)	B368
Deputy Director	MHD	25104	LeRoy E. Day	B368
Spec. Asst	MH	37343	William F. Moore	B347
Exec. Asst	MH-1	24975	Carl H. Dry	B347
Vehicle Development Dir		20431	William A. Summerfelt	B347
Systems Engineering Dir		23113	Clarence C. Gay, Jr	B347
Program Management Dir		27588	Richard J. Allen	B347

[1] For Bellcomm personnel not listed, call 484-7500.
[2] For Boeing personnel not listed, call 484-2121.
[3] For G.E. personnel not listed, call 963-7965.

ORGANIZATION	CODE	EXT	NAME	ROOM
SPACE STATION TASK FORCE DIR	MF	36181	Douglas R. Lord	B325
Spec. Asst.	MF-1	36181	Samuel H. Hubbard	B325
Program Integration Dir	MFI	22861	Robert L. Lohman	B325
Program Budget and Control Dir	MFB	25777	William J. Hamon	B325
Operations Group	MF	34462	Robert O. Aller	B325
Experiment Payloads Group	MF	28991	Dr. Rodney W. Johnson	B325

OFFICE OF SPACE SCIENCE AND APPLICATIONS

ORGANIZATION	CODE	EXT	NAME	ROOM
ASSOCIATE ADMINISTRATOR	S	21158	Dr. John E. Naugle	F5131
Deputy Assoc. Admin.	SD	21156	Vincent L. Johnson	F5131
Deputy Assoc. Admin. (Science)	SS	35886	Dr. Henry J. Smith	F5131
Deputy Assoc. Admin. (Applications)	SA	37344	Leonard Jaffe	F5131
Special Assistant	SAA	27695	Louis B. Fong	F5065
ADVANCED PROGRAMS DIR	SF	26812	Dr. Robert G. Wilson	F5129
Deputy Director		26296	George Duncan	F5129
Tech. Asst.		24086	Robert J. Gutheim	F5129
PUBLIC AFFAIRS OFFICER	SN	21176	Richard T. Mittauer	F5017
PROGRAM REVIEW & RESOURCES MGMT. DIR.	SP	21125	Eldon D. Taylor	F5123
Deputy Director		24511	Richard L. Daniels	F5123
Special Asst. to the Dir		24403	John R. Biggs	F5123
Program Review Chf	SPP	36230	John W. Rosenberry (Act.)	F5119
Resources Mgmt. Chf	SPR	37152	Charles E. Wash	F5122D
Admin. Oper. Chf	SPA	24842	Donald W. Tomayko	F5122C
Instit. Plan & Dev. Chf	SPI	36230	John W. Rosenberry	F5119
COMMUNICATIONS PROGRAMS DIR	SC	20888	Dr. R. B. Marsten	F5081
Deputy Director	SCD	33361	Jerome D. Rosenberg	F5081
Program Rev. & Resources Mgmt Chf	SCP	22110	Albert A. Jenkel	F5081
Advanced Programs & Tech. Prog. Mgr	SCF	22110	Samuel W. Fordyce	F5081
Systems Prog. Chf	SCE	37346	Donald Silverman	F5081
Applic. Tech. Satellites Prog. Mgr	SCS	20581	Joseph R. Burke	F5081
Geodetic Satellites Prog. Mgr	SCG	33361	Jerome D. Rosenberg (Act.)	F5081
Communications Satellite Prog. Chf	SCC	22389	A. M. Greg Andrus	F5081
Navigation and Traffic Control Prog. Chf	SCN	22388	Eugene Ehrlich	F5081
EARTH OBSERVATIONS PROGRAMS DIR	SR	20891	Dr. John M. DeNoyer	F5065
Dep. Dir. & Dir. of Meteor.	SRD	36521	Dr. Morris Tepper	F5065
Deputy Dir. Flight Prog.	SRE	20891	Pitt G. Thome	F5065
Program Rev. & Resources Mgmt. Chf	SRP	36975	Richard T. Hibbard	F5065
Earth Res. Survey Flights Prog. Mgr	SRB	20574	Theodore A. George	F5065
Adv. Prog. & Tech. Prog. Mgr	SRF	24563	Dr. Robert A. Summers	F5065
Adv. Instru. & Sensor Eng. Prog. Mgr	SRF	24563	Jules Lehmann	F5065
Earth Physics & Phys. Ocean. Prog. Chf	SRG	36523	Dr. Martin J. Swetnick (Act.)	F5065
Meteorology & Sounding Rockets Chf	SRM	37497	William C. Spreen	F5065
Nimbus Program Mgr	SRN	34335	Bruton B. Schardt	F5065
Oper. Meteor. Satellites Prog. Mgr	SRO	34291	Michael L. Garbacz	F5065
Earth Res. Survey Prog. Chf	SRR	36523	Dr. Arch B. Park	F5065
Earth Resources Exp. Pkg. Prog. Mgr	SRS	28318	Thomas L. Fischetti	B268
Global Atmos. Res. Prog. (GARP) Mgr	SRW	24563	Norman L. Durocher	F5065
LAUNCH VEHICLE & PROP. PROG. DIR	SV	24531	Joseph B. Mahon	F5111
Prog. Rev. & Res. Mgmt. Chf		24533	Edward J. Kunec	F5113
Medium Launch Vehicle Prog. Mgr		24534	T. B. Norris	F5109
Improved Centaur Mgr		24534	W. L. Lovejoy	F5109
Atlas Centaur Mgr		24534	F. R. Schmidt	F5109
Titan III Mgr		24534	T. B. Norris (Act.)	F5109

ORGANIZATION	CODE	EXT	NAME	ROOM
Small Launch Veh. & Inter. Prog. Mgr.		24534	R. W. Manville	F5109
Agena Mgr.		24534	R. W. Manville (Act.)	F5109
Delta Mgr.		24534	I. T. Gillam, IV	F5109
Scout Mgr.		24534	Paul E. Goozh	F5109
Adv. Prog. & Tech. Prog. Mgr.		24553	Joseph E. McGolrick	F5113
PLANETARY PROGRAMS DIR.	SL	24581	Robert S. Kraemer (Act.)	F5093
Deputy Director		24581	Robert S. Kraemer	F5093
Prog. Rev. & Res. Mgt. Chf.		24580	Peter K. Hatt	F5093
Advanced Programs & Technology Mgr.		36985	Daniel H. Herman	F5086
Pioneer Program Mgr.		24557	Fred D. Kochendorfer	F5103
Mariner Mercury '73 Mgr.		24585	N. William Cunningham	F5103
Mariner Mars '71 Mgr.		36985	Earl W. Glahn	F5086
Viking Program Mgr.		25618	Walter Jakobowski	F5091
Planetary Astronomy Chf.		21216	Dr. William Brunk	F5103
Planetary Atmospheres Chf.		21861	Dr. Robert Fellows	F5103
Planetology Chf.		21151	Stephen E. Dwornik	F5103
Advanced Science Planning Chf.		21384	Dr. Milton A. Mitz	F5093
Exobiology Chief		24965	Dr. Richard S. Young	F5055
Planetary Quarantine Chief		34341	Lawrence B. Hall	F5038
PHYSICS & ASTRONOMY PROGRAMS DIR.	SG	21653	Jesse L. Mitchell	F5035
Deputy Dir.		21987	Dr. Alois W. Schardt	F5035
Prog. Rev. & Res. Mgmt.		20147	Herbert B. Chisholm	F5030
Advanced Programs & Technology Mgr.		21983	Marcel J. Aucremanne	F5029
Astronomy Chf.		22989	Dr. Nancy G. Roman	F5023
High Energy Astrophysics Chf.		21987	Dr. Thomas L. Cline (Act.)	F5045
Interplan Dust & Comet. Physics Spec. Proj. Chf.		22847	Maurice Dubin	F5023
Magnetospheric Physics Chf.		21973	Dr. E. R. Schmerling	F5041
Solar Physics Chf.		20157	Dr. Goetz K. Oertel (Act.)	F5029
Obser Mgr.		20146	C. Dixon Ashworth	F5030
ATM Mgr.		35347	Dixon L. Forsythe	B268
High Energy Astronomy Observatory		21987	Richard E. Halpern (Act.)	F5045
Explorers & Sounding Rockets Mgr.		23825	John R. Holtz	F5041

OFFICE OF ADVANCED RESEARCH AND TECHNOLOGY

ORGANIZATION	CODE	EXT	NAME	ROOM
ASSOCIATE ADMINISTRATOR	R	34445	Roy P. Jackson	B668
Deputy Associate Admin. (Aeronautics)	RD-A	20166	Neil A. Armstrong	B668
Deputy Associate Admin. (Management)	RD-M	28511	Edwin C. Kilgore	B647
Asst. Associate Administrator	RC	20937	John L. Sloop	B647
Senior Research Assistant	R-1	20211	Milton B. Ames, Jr.	B568
Public Affairs Officer	R-2	23865	William W. Pomeroy	B656
ADVANCED CONCEPTS & MISSION DIV DIR	RX	23363	Richard J. Wisniewski	B656
Deputy Director		⁴ 2679	David H. Dennis	
Aero. Missions & Tech. Br. Chf.		⁴ 2120	Richard H. Petersen	
Space Missions Br. Chf.		⁴ 2131	Dr. Paul R. Swan	
Propulsion Systems Br. Chf.		⁴ 2130	Dr. Federico G. Casal	
Special Project Br. Chf.		⁴ 2125	Harold Hornby	
AERONAUTICAL OPERATING SYSTEMS DIV DIR.	RO	20018	George W. Cherry	B626
Deputy Director		27253	Charles H. Gould (Act.)	B626
Air Traffic Systems Br. Chf.	ROA	27253	Lee D. Goolsby	B626
Operating Factors Br. Chf.	ROO	27253	William A. McGowan	B626
AERONAUTICAL PROPULSION DIV. DIR.	RL	20151	Harry W. Johnson	B612
Deputy Director		20183	Nelson F. Rekos (Act.)	B612
Propulsion Components Br. Chf.	RLC	20183	Nelson F. Rekos	B612
Propulsion Systems Br. Chf.	RLS	20151	Robert W. Ziem	B612

⁴ 415-961-(plus extension shown).

ORGANIZATION	CODE	EXT	NAME	ROOM
AERODYNAMICS & VEHICLE SYSTEMS DIV. DIR.	RA	20176	Albert J. Evans	B600
Deputy Director		20213	William S. Aiken, Jr	B600
Staff Assistant		20069	Benson E. Gammon	B600
Aerodynamics & Fluid Mechanics Br. Chf	RAA	28607	Alfred Gessow	B600
Loads & Flt. Dynamics Br. Chf	RAL	20066	Thomas V. Cooney	B600
Low-Speed Aircraft Br. Chf	RAV	20213	Ralph W. May, Jr	B600
High-Speed Aircraft Br. Chf	RAS	25747	Leonard Sternfield	B600
SUPERCRITICAL TECHNOLOGY OFFICE DIR	RT	37335	Gerald G. Kayten	B621
SHORT TAKEOFF & LANDING TECHNOLOGY OFFICE DIR.	RJ	37335	Gerald G. Kayten (Act.)	B621
GUIDANCE, CONTROL & INFO SYS. DIV. DIR	RE	20106	Frank J. Sullivan	B607
Deputy Director		20141	Charles E. Pontious	B607
Technical Assistant		27294	Jules I. Kanter	B607
Guidance & Optics Br. Chf	REG	27335	Henry L. Anderton	B607
Information Systems Br. Chf	RET	27427	John L. East	B607
AERONAUTICAL LIFE SCIENCES DIV. DIR	RB	20033	Dr. Leo Fox	B626
Technical Assistant	RBT	20313	Roy Whitten	B626
ENTRY TECHNOLOGY OFFICE DIR	RV	20036	Frederick J. DeMeritte	B621
MATERIALS & STRUCTURES DIV. DIR	RW	35815	George C. Deutsch	B647
Materials Br. Chf	RWM	20271	James J. Gangler	B647
Structures Br. Chf	RWS	20263	Melvin G. Rosche	B647
RESEARCH COUNCIL	RR	20028	Dr. H. H. Kurzweg	B568
Technical Assistant	RRT	20286	Werner C. Steinle	B568
SAFETY & OPERATING SYSTEMS OFFICE DIR	RY	26891	H. Kurt Strass	B556
SHUTTLE TECHNOLOGIES OFFICE DIR	RS	22521	Adelbert O. Tischler	B541
Deputy Director	RSD	24601	Ernest O. Pearson, Jr	B541
SPACE NUCLEAR SYSTEMS OFFICE MGR	NS–2	119–3027	Milton Klein	EE456
Deputy Mgr	NS–2	119–4118	David S. Gabriel	EE468
Executive Officer	NS–2	119–3036	Edward H. Schnieder	EE468
SPACE PROP. & POWER DIV. DIR	RP	20021	William H. Woodward	B568
Deputy Director	RPD	20022	Don A. Hart, Jr	B568
Staff Assistant		20026	John H. Walker	B568
TECHNOLOGY APPLICATIONS OFFICE DIR	RF	20006	R. D. Ginter	B525
Deputy Director		20006	Bernard Maggin	B525
Staff Assistant		20006	R. L. Schrunk	B525
Application Manager	RFS	20051	L. F. Gilchrist	B525
Application Manager	RFS	20051	R. I. LaRock	B525
Application Manager	RFS	20051	K. W. Heising	B525
Flight Proj. Br. Chf	RFP	23597	W. A. Guild	B525
Flight Exper. Br. Chf	RFE	22817	David Novik	B525
RESOURCES & INSTITUTIONAL MGMT. DIV. DIR.	RM	20281	Paul E. Cotton	B656
Deputy Director	RMD	27327	Floyd D. Brandon	B656
Mgmt. Systems & Administration Br. Chf	RMS	27531	Richard G. Mulligan	B656
Institutional Mgmt. Br. Chf	RMI	36586	Ronald S. Schwartz	B656
R&D Programs Br. Chf	RMR	36586	Ronald S. Schwartz (Act.)	B656
Co-located Personnel:				
ART Facilities Office, Chf	BX–RM	20154	John F. Madden	B656
Financial Management	BF–RM	26152	Francis J. Sullivan	B656
Procurement (OART Programs) Chf	KDS–RM	27531	W. W. Hudson	B656

ORGANIZATION	CODE	EXT	NAME	ROOM
TECHNOLOGY APPLICATIONS OFFICE DIR	RF	20006	R. D. Ginter	B525
Deputy Director		20006	Bernard Maggin	B525
Staff Assistant		20006	R. L. Schrunk	B525
Application Manager	RFS	20051	L. F. Gilchrist	B525
Application Manager	RFS	20051	R. I. LaRock	B525
Application Manager	RFS	20051	K. W. Heising	B525
Flight Proj. Br. Chf	RFP	23597	W. A. Guild	B525
Flight Exper. Br. Chf	RFE	22817	David Novik	B525

ALPHABETICAL TELEPHONE DIRECTORY

NAME	EXT	ROOM	CODE
A			
ABDO, Frances S	36457	R611	BFH
ABERNETHY, Leo X	20682	B412	MBB-1
ACHAMMER, Bernard G	20271	B647	RWM
ADAMS, Carmeen P	20222	B456	MC
ADAMSON, William E	26484	R701	BDM
AFFHOLDER, Richard J	23453	R401	KMA
AGEE, Emma, L	26481	R527	BPA
AHMAJAN, A. Michael, Col. USA	36523	F5065	SRR
AHRENDT, Myrl H	22429	R805	FE
AIKEN, Mavis L	21462	B125	KDP-1
AIKEN, William S	23055	B600	RA
ALBERT, M. Eileen	37275	F6011	AAD-3
ALBERT, Thomas J	20270	B440	MT
ALBRIGHT, Jean V	28044	R526	BPE
ALEXANDER, Carolyn E	20154	B656	BX-RM
ALEXANDER, Robert E	22850	BA36	BG
ALIBRANDO, Alfred P	20666	B456	M-N
ALLAWAY, Howard G	20666	B419	M-N
ALLEN, Barbara D	21297	R721	DHC-5
ALLEN, Mildred E	24933	B155	KR
ALLEN, Richard J., Dr	27588	B347	MHB
ALLEN, William	20561	BA1F	KDP-3
ALLEN, William H	22516	R811	FAP
ALLENBY, Richard J., Dr	35367	L5081	MAL
ALLER, Robert O	34462	B325	MF
ALLISON, Gary B	37164	F6113	BR-2
ALLMAN, James	20457	L5023	MAE
ALSTON, Valerie A	20774	B512	TN
ALTON, Mark J	21347	B112	KDR
AMBROSE, Mary S	25046	B125	KDP-1
AMES, Milton B., Jr	20211	B568	R-1
ANDERBERG, Virginia I	25045	B200	Y
ANDERSON, Alan A., Jr	23453	R405	KMA
ANDERSON, Carolyn L	22432	F7025	F-2
ANDERSON, Frank W., Jr., Dr.	35494	R706	EH
ANDERSON, Lowell O	20312	B626	RB
ANDERSON, Mary E	37327	BA39	KSS-10
ANDERSON, Oscar E., Jr., Dr.	22281	F7077	I
ANDERSON, Paul H	22155	R424	DHZ
ANDERSON, Roberta B	36997	B326	BXB
ANDERSON, Virgil W	36997	B326	BXB
ANDERTON, Henry L	27335	B607	REG

NAME	EXT	ROOM	CODE
ANDREWS, E. Sherrell	21537	F7084	I
ANDREWS, Edward P	36341	B256	MLA
ANDRUS, A. M. Greg	22389	F5081	SCC
ANGELL, Roy S	27884	B236	MRR-ML
AQUILINO, Rose Ann	25618	F5091	SL
AQUILINO, Toni M	24365	B200	Y
ARCHBOLD, William F	21379	R721	DHC-3
ARCHER, Catherine L	24802	R625	BFP
ARMSTRONG, Betty M	22445	R507	DU
ARMSTRONG, Neil A	20166	B668	RD-A
ARMSTRONG, William O	20426	B431	MTL
ARNESON, Henry K., Jr	33656	F5122C	SPA
ARNETT, Guy	20506	B145	KL
ARNEY, Hope S	20435	B300	MMV
ARNOLDI, Louis B., Dr	27432	BA36	BG
ASBERRY, Lula R	24223	F7094	I
ASCH, Milton M	25086	B136	KDP-2
ASHBY, Marjorie B	36586	B656	RMI
ASHLEY, Francine F	24311	L5044	MAP
ASHLEY, William T	23250	B268	ML-1
ASHWORTH, C. Dixon	20146	F5030	SG
ATCHESON, Margaret M	24557	F5103	SL
ATCHISON, Kenneth C	20666	B419	M-N
ATKINSON, Kathleen	26265	B125	KDP-1
ATWELL, Lawrence A	23522	R824	KSA
AUCREMANNE, Marcel J	21983	F5029	SG
AULT, Leonard A	26798	R410	KT
B			
BAILEY, Marion J	21983	F5029	SG
BAINBRIDGE, Catherine C	20321	F7118	XC
BAKER, Lucille L	24842	F5122C	SPA
BALES, Bobby C	24356	R609	BFH
BALKO, Ellen S	21405	R721	DHC-3
BALL, Janis M	34086	F6102	FPT
BALTAS, Milton M	20581	F5081	SCS
BANKS, William H	24946	F6075	XS
BARBER, Godfrey E	28483	F6119	BR-1
BARBER, R. L	24466	B326	BXD
BARBER, Thomas A	20121	B547	RNT
BARGELOH, Sylvia H	24187	R612	BFH
BARNES, Geneva B	21571	F6107	FG
BARNES, Nancy S	20546	B336	MRS
BARNES, Richard J. H	21213	F7087	I
BARNES, Virginia	36245	L5043	MA

NAME	EXT	ROOM	CODE	NAME	EXT	ROOM	CODE
BARNO, Barbara	23429	R721	DHC-1	BOWIE, Donald W	21537	F7087	I
BARR, Earl W	20238	B350	MRO	BOWLER, Virginia L	35884	B137	KL
BARRETT, James C	22305	W-Bldg.	DHA-4	BOYD, Rebecca L	34447	B356	MRO
BARRITT, Paul F	20126	B521	TA	BOYES, William W., Jr	28711	F6086	DY
BARRY, Thomas W	26063	R628	BFG	BRACKETT, Ernest W	24405	F6075	ABA
BASS, Abraham S	23582	B431	MTX	BRADLEY, Audrey O	35426	R609	BFH
BASS, Alvin S	26611	F7032	GP	BRADLEY, Frank D	34341	F5038	SL
BATES, Jefferson D	33349	F6103	FGC	BRADY, Henry W	37987	B216	KDM-ML
BATTLE, Althea M	20321	F7118	XC				
BAUGUESS, Rita A	22388	F5081	SCC	BRADY, Jeanette L	20147	F5030	SG
BAVELY, James C	20002	B512	TN	BRAITHWAITE, Howard N	28044	R526	BPE
BAYER, Philip J	24887	L5035	MAO	BRANDON, Floyd D	27327	B656	RMD
BAYNE, James M	33666	B300	BXB	BRAZILL, Edward J	23582	B431	MTX
BEACH, Madolyn E	20683	B421	MBB-2	BREDT, James H., Dr	23582	B431	MTX
BEATTIE, Donald A	26628	L5001	MAL	BRERETON, Roy G., Dr	21967	L5078	MAL
BECK, Alice J	26924	R612	BFH	BREWER, Jack D	25748	B600	RAV
BECK, Donald E., Lt. Comdr. USN.	24887	L5035	MAO	BREWER, John H	34341	F5038	SL
				BRICKWEDDE, Louetta A	20411	B247	MLQ
BECKER, Donald J	26859	B225	GK	BRIER, Barbara R	26478	R612	BFH
BEHMER, Robert E	119-4567	EE459	NS-2	BROADHURST, John A	24286	F6053	F-3
BEHNEY, Mary Jane	24631	F7002	XP	BROCKETT, H. R	20088	B500	TD
BEHUN, Michael	35305	B368	MHE	BROCKMAN, Paul R	35983	F6137	L
BEICHER, Joseph R	20131	B521	TN	BROGAN, Raymond F	23453	R405	KMA
BEISER, Claire	24707	F7112	WX	BROMAN, Ann	20321	F7118	XC
BELCHER, Arnold C	20002	B512	TN	BROMAN, Herbert D	21269	F5128	KDS-SP
BELL, Robert L	20574	F5065	SRF	BRONSON, Carolyn M	21727	L5055	MAP-1
BELLAMY, Lewis	27531	B625T	RMS	BROOKE, Doris L	25091	R814	DHB
BELLEVILLE, Richard E., Dr.	26023	B409	MMR	BROOKS, Herbert F	35427	R609	BFH
				BROUNS, Robert C	119-4547	EE471	NS-2
BELTON, James C	24825	F7121	XP	BROWER, Dorothy W	21703	B568	RPL
BENDER, Elizabeth A	23113	B347	MHO	BROWN, B Porter	35347	B268	MLD-1
BENJAMIN, Jacqueline	24139	F6069	C	BROWN, Bonnie S	35691	B326	BXC
BERAN, Elaine B	20321	F7118	XC	BROWN, C. Lynne	27253	B626	RO
BERESFORD, Spencer M	21191	F7065	G	BROWN, Deborah S	26387	F6052	FGE
BERKAN, Joseph J	20593	BA1I	KDA-3	BROWN, Joseph D	26923	R607	BFH
BERMAN, Robert	26839	B225	GK	BROWN, Martha P	20888	F5081	SC
BERRY, Gwynne R	22947	R522	BPL	BROWN, Thomas C., Jr., Lt. Col. USAF.	21523	B347	MH
BESSETTE, Denis E	20534	B236	MLB				
BEST, Nancy C	24530	F5111	SV	BROWNSTEIN, Herbert S	20418	B300	MMC
BIGGS, John R	24403	F5123	SP	BRUCE, Julia C	26773	R624	BF-1
BINKLEY, Maurice E	20061	B507	TS	BRUNING, Susan	22780	F6073	C
BIVINS, Royal G	24701	R406	KT	BRUNK, William E., Dr	21216	F5103	SL
BLANDFORD, Janatta	24413	F7109	W	BRUNSON, Shirley V	35367	L5081	MAL
BLANK, Walter E	27561	B356	MRO	BRYANT, Frederick B	20114	B521	TA
BLAYLOCK, Michelle	24717	BA1I	KDA-3	BRYSON, Doris D	37831	L5087	MAL
BOARDMAN, William E	28041	F6051	FGM	BRYSON, Robert P	35367	L5075	MAL
BOGERT, Hazel W	24003	R605	KB	BUCKLEY, Edward C	27427	B607	RET
BOGGESS, Nancy W., Dr	35997	F5023	SG	BUCKMASTER, Mary K	20281	B656	RM
BOHLING, Raymond F	20083	B612	RVA	BULLOCK, Roy L	24467	B326	BXE
BOKELMAN, Donald J	26063	R628	BFG	BUMGARDNER, Oliver T	36086	B243	MLE
BOLCE, William J., Jr	36018	B400	MCS	BURCHER, Eugene S	23825	F5041	SG
BOLD, Thomas P	37278	F6147	AAD-4	BURDETTE, Eleanor M	37327	BA39	KSS-10
BOLDEN, Harry M	24852	R608	BFH	BURDETTE, Harold E., Sr	22155	R424	DHZ
BOLGER, Philip H	25438	F6091	DY	BURDULIS, Helen M	34265	F6069	C
BOND, Kathleen A	28127	F5137	D	BURGESS, Ada C	26909	R608	BFH
BOOZE, Cynthia J	23561	B668	RMS	BURGESS, Albert	22305	W-Bldg.	DHA-4
BORDNER, Eldyne E	20226	B468	M-1	BURGESS, Richard P	24281	B150	DHA-2
BORELLA, Eleanor G	33602	B154	DHA-7	BURKE, John R	21831	B431	MTE
BORS, Ruth R	24513	F5001	DH	BURKE, Joseph R	20581	F5081	SCS
BOSMAJIAN, Charles P	20131	B521	TN	BURL, Elizabeth J	20041	B568	RPE
BOSTICK, Linda L	27531	B656	RMS	BURLINGAME, Charles W	20774	B512	TN
BOUR, Lawrence J	23965	R424	DHZ	BURNHAM, Robert M	21877	B125	KDP-1

NAME	EXT	ROOM	CODE	NAME	EXT	ROOM	CODE
BURNS, Ramona G.	28607	B612	RAA	CHRISTIAN, Peggy P.	22328	B568	R-1
BURRELL, Carl	20688	B426	MBM	CHRISTIANSON, Edward L.	33114	B256	MLA
BUTLER, Mary-Margaret	20593	BA1H	KDA-3	CHRISTIANSON, Mary E.	20636	B246	MLO
BUTLER, Richard E.	22305	W-Bldg.	DHA-4	CIANELLA, S. D.	34514	B336	MRS
BUYNITZKY, John N.	24802	R625	BFP	CIARAVINO, James R.	36206	F5011	K
BYNUM, Pierre D.	24506	B168	DHA	CIRCOSTA, Robert S.	24286	F6053	F-3
BYRNES, Olive F.	24831	B168	DHA-1	CLAGETT, Albert A.	24506	B168	DHA
				CLARK, E. Katheryn, RN	20268	BA36	BG

C

NAME	EXT	ROOM	CODE	NAME	EXT	ROOM	CODE
				CLINE, Jack S.	24946	F6075	XS
CADISAL, Jose	24844	F7137	XS	CLINE, Ray C.	25935	R627	BFC
CAGIWA, Clara G.	22281	F7077	I	CLINE, Thomas L., Dr.	21987	F5045	SG
CALABRESE, Rosemarie T.	28146	F6127	B	COBURN, Kenneth R., Dr.	26023	B409	MMR
CALAHAN, Hubert D.	20146	F5030	SG	COFIELD, William B., Col. USAF.	20411	B247	MLQ
CALLEY, Ellen	22161	R802	FA				
CALLIS, William A.	20561	BA1F	KDP-3	COHEN, Haggai	20411	B247	MQ
CAMLOH, Bernadette M.	20891	F5065	SR	COHEN, Nathaniel B.	24038	F6141	E
CAMPBELL, James T., Jr.	22305	W-Bldg.	DHA-4	COHEN, William	33164	F7077	I
CAMPBELL, Margaret A.	33349	F6103	FGC	COHN, Ernst M.	20121	B568	RPP
CAMPBELL, Thomas	36046	F6025	BR-3	COLE, Kathleen M.	27427	B607	RET
CANNETTI, Anthony R.	27561	B350	MRO	COLEMAN, A. Marie	21158	F5131	S
CANNETTI, Frances I.	28511	B668	RD-M	COLEMAN, George W.	20561	BA1F	KDP-3
CAREY, Bernard F.	22464	R505	DU	COLEMAN, Lillian C.	20126	B521	TA
CARISKI, Sidney A.	20526	B100	KDM	COLES, Victor L.	22127	R827	KSS
CARLEY, Richard R.	24073	B368	MHE	COLEY, Estella V.	34968	R519	BPC
CARLSON, Joseph M.	20297	R402	KT	COLLIN, Everett E.	33125	R801	FE
CARLTON, Juanita M.	24825	F7121	XP	COLLINS, William M., Jr.	28645	R721	DHC
CARRETTA, Anthony G.	20557	B101	KDP	COMBERIATE, Michael B.	20081	B612	RLC
CARRICO, Beverly S.	27588	B347	MHB	COMPITELLO, Frank E.	21703	B625	RPL
CARSON, Joseph H.	23910	BC-Lev.	DHA-31	CONDON, John E., Dr.	37281	B155	KR
CARTER, Charles H.	23110	B200	Y	CONNERS, Robert C.	36586	B656	RMI
CARTER, Elizabeth A.	21738	F7026	GP	CONRAD, Dwight E.	22305	W-Bldg.	DHA-4
CARTER, Elma C.	21337	F7090	I	CONRAD, Jeanette B.	24024	F7137	X
CARTER, Rosemary L.	22375	R511	DU	CONVERSANO, Andrew., Jr.	20228	B356	MR
CARULLI, Leonard	24021	F6137	L	CONWAY, Emmett G.	21877	B125	KDP-1
CASE, Edward N.	24336	R410	KT	CONWAY, Iris D.	23860	B212	Y
CASEY, Leland J.	27441	L5014	MAE	COOCH, Linda J.	24563	F5065	SRF
CAST, James G.	34086	F6102	FPT	COOKRO, James A.	37152	F5122D	SPR
CATLOTH, Mary M.	36181	B325	MF	COONEY, Thomas V.	20066	B600	RAL
CATRON, Dora B.	20117	B526	TC	COOPER, James L.	34462	B325	MF
CAVALLINI, Joyce A.	21405	R721	DHC-3	CORBIN, Joann M.	26481	R527	BPA
CAVANAUGH, Joan E.	33602	B154	DHA-71	COSTAGLIOLA, Agnes	20269	BA40	BG-1
CENTERS, Charles D.	20576	F5065	SRB	COSTANTINO, James	37413	B368	MRD
CEOPHAS, Jacqueline V.	36456	R611	BFH	COTTON, Paul E.	20281	B656	RM
CERRETA, Peter A.	20058	B621	RV	COULTER, John M.	24583	F7101	W
CHACONAS, Stephanie S.	23602	R522	BPL	COUNTS, Edwina G.	20418	B300	MMC
CHADWICK, Christina A.	25777	B325	MF	COUPLAND, William R.	23804	F7109	W
CHAMBERS, Lawrence P.	36943	B247	MLQ	COVER, Joseph W.	20506	L5002	MOP
CHANDLER, George P.	24023	F7137	X	COVERT, Elizabeth R.	33943	F7137	A
CHANDLER, Russell L.	21987	F5045	SG	COWLEY, Mary L.	21918	BA56	DHA-6
CHANG, Yu Ta	24844	F7137	XS	COX, Marilyn	21426	F7137	X
CHARAK, Mason T.	35835	B626	ROO	COYA, Albert	36586	B656	RMI
CHASE, Pamela S.	25935	R627	BFC	CRABE, Thomas C.	25091	R814	DHB
CHASE, Roland H.	21983	F5029	SG	CRAIN, Doris J.	20111	B300	MM
CHEATHAM, Diane C.	21737	F6043	FP	CRAMER, Jack V.	21841	F6061	C
CHERRICK, Irwin L.	36943	B247	MLQ	CRAMER, Karen A.	21717	F6065	C
CHERRY, George W.	20018	B626	RO	CRANFORD, Marie K.	20557	B101	KD
CHILDS, Charles W.	21942	F6088	DY	CRAVEN, Robert P.	20537	B211	KDM-ML
CHISHOLM, Herbert B.	20147	F5030	SG				
CHOP, Albert M.	22782	F6088	DY	CRAWFORD, Vera P.	27432	BA36	BG
CHRISTENSEN, Elmer M.	35367	L5074	MAL	CRICKENBERGER, Frances L.	27977	F7065	G
CHRISTENSEN, Paul W.	33642	R806	FAE				

NAME	EXT	ROOM	CODE	NAME	EXT	ROOM	CODE
CROBAUGH, Albert O	36914	F6011	AAD-3	DESIMONE, A. A.	26270	R821	KSI
CROCKER, J. Allen	25097	F7137	AA	DETRICH, Harry W., Jr.	24341	W-Bldg.	FAD
CROMWELL, Robert D	20654	L5063	MAR	DEUTSCH, George C.	35815	B647	RW
CROSBY, Recille M	37236	R512	Z	DEUTSCH, Stanley., Dr.	26002	B421	MME
CROSIER, W. Raymond	22149	R421	BPM	DEVEREAUX, Linda C.	22468	B136	KDA-1
CROSS, Julia S	20561	BA1F	KDP-3	DEVOL, Ina B	21253	F7077	I
CRUMB, Ealise	23630	R721	DHC-4	DIAMOND, Anthony T.	36046	F6025	BR-3
CRUZ, Juan T	24844	F7137	XS	DIBELLA, Josephine	34445	B668	R
CUFFEY, Mary M	24091	L5011	MAL	DICHTEL, Anne M	36523	F5065	SRR
CUFFEY, Teresa C	21379	R721	DHC-3	DICK, Louise	36925	F6043	FP
CULBERTSON, Philip E	20317	B440	MT	DIFABIO, Janet M.	21537	F7087	I
CUNNINGHAM, Dennis	23481	R526	BPE	DILLARD, Audrey C.	20102	B421	BPM
CUNNINGHAM, Lillian V.	20506	B145	KL	DILLER, Dick S.	20475	L5029	MAE
CUNNINGHAM, Newton W.	24585	F5103	SL	DIMAGGIO, Jo Marie	21694	R414	BPM
CURD, Annie M	35364	F6089	DY	DIMAGGIO, Samuel S., Jr.	21967	L5076	MAL
CURD, Laura F	20593	BA1H	KDA-3	DIMOPOULLOS, Joan E.	20034	B626	RB
CURRAN, Robert H	24442	BB-Lev.	DHA-53	DISHER, John H.	34345	B268	MLD
CURTIN, Robert H	21855	B300	BX	DITTMER, Daniel G., Dr.	20401	B300	MMC
CUSHMAN, Ralph E	28107	F6127	B	DOCKERY, Judy L.	119-3182	ED-402	NS-2

D

				DODDS, J. Ian., Dr.	37278	F6147	AAD-2
D'AIUTOLO, Charles T.	20068	B612	RV-1	DODSON, Quinton A.	34773	F7120	DHA-50
D'ALESSIO, Anna M	34581	R406	KT	DOLBY, William R.	36904	F5122C	SPA
DADE, Earl W	24831	B154	DHA-1	DONDEY, Leon	23825	F5041	SG
DAISEY, Roy L	27531	B656	RMS	DONLAN, Charles J.	23812	B468	MD-T
DALLOW, Thomas P	24557	F5103	SL	DONOFRIO, Gus A.	22440	B243	MLE
DALTON, Ella M	20458	L5025	MAE	DORFMAN, Martin S.	28064	F7054	G
DAMON, John C	23978	F7101	W	DORN, Robert J.	25086	B136	KDP-2
DANGLE, Eugene E	20201	B525	RAV	DOTSON, Mary L.	24917	R824	KSA
DANIEL, Charligna C.	27217	R608	BFH	DOUGLAS, Eugene F.	24281	B150	DHA-2
DANIEL, Peggy C	27207	R612	BFH	DOUGLAS, Mary A.	33601	B300	BXA
DANIELS, Richard L	24511	F5123	SP	DOUVARJO, Dennis A.	22493	R721	DHC-4
DANIELS, Walter M	22946	R522	BPL	DOWLING, Leona M.	23978	F7101	W
DANTLEY, Rita F	37348	L5042	MAE	DOWNS, Celland R., Capt., USAF	20636	B246	MLO
DARDEN, Elwyn J	21347	B112	KD				
DARGAN, Evera	24146	F6124C	BT-1	DOYLE, Gladys	35838	F6124C	BT-1
DARON, Alma D	36937	F5011	K	DOYLE, Sharon A.	20141	B607	REE
DAUE, Arnold K	23965	R424	DHZ	DRAPER, Cecil N.	20117	B526	TC
DAVIDS, Irving	20566	B243	MLE	DREHER, Martha E.	20263	B647	RWS
DAVIN, Edward M	26628	L5003	MAL	DROBKA, F. George	26150	R823	KSI
DAVIS, Dorothy A	34462	B325	MF	DRY, Carl H.	24975	B368	MH-1
DAVIS, Dorothy C	21571	F6107	FG	DUBBS, Elizabeth M.	20401	B300	MM
DAVIS, Dorothy M	22155	R424	DHZ	DUBIN, Maurice	22847	F5023	SG
DAVIS, Evelyn H	20224	B468	M	DUGGAN, John F.	21771	R527	BPA
DAVIS, Joseph T	21149	R721	DHC-6	DUKES, Francis B.	22155	R424	DHZ
DAVIS, Mary E	33242	F5137	D	DUNCAN, George H.	26296	F5129	SF
DAVIS, Paul D	21380	F6088	DY	DUNFEE, Paul V.	20238	B350	MRO
DAVIS, Yolonda Y	24356	R609	BFH	DUNKIN, Patricia B.	36230	F5119	SPI
DAWSON, Doris L	24635	R822	KS	DUNLAP, Frederick L.	24145	F6015	BT-1
DAY, Leroy E	25104	B368	MHD	DUNN, Donald W.	24765	R411	KMC
DEAN, Hilliard R., Sr.	21918	BA56	DHA-6	DUNN, Jean C.	36994	B326	BXD
DEAN, James D	23477	R802	FA	DUNNING, Robert W.	22568	B300	MMC
DECKER, Ralph S	119-4335	EE479	NS-2	DUROCHER, Norman L.	24563	F5065	SRW
				DWORNIK, Stephen E.	21151	F5103	SL
DEFIBAUGH, Sharron L.	20894	F6058	BP-1				
DEGENNARO, George B.	28041	F6051	FGM				
DEGOYLER, Henry A.	24843	F5122C	BF-SP				
DELANEY, Charles J.	27343	F7049	G	EAKIN, Birch	28421	F6147	AAD-4
DELANO, Miles M	24442	BB-Lev.	DHA-53	EAST, John L.	27427	B607	RET
DEMERITTE, Frederick J.	20036	B621	RV	EASTWOOD, Charles R.	24336	R410	KT
DENNY, James E	21715	F7033	GP	EBBERTS, Ruth L.	119-4547	EE477	NS-2
DENOYER, John M., Dr.	20891	F5065	SR	EBERT, Nancy L.	25160	R829	KSP

E

NAME	EXT	ROOM	CODE	NAME	EXT	ROOM	CODE
EDDY, Mary Ann	22814	R624	BF	FISHER, Frank E	34904	R808	FAE
EDGE, Walter L	26048	R624	BFP	FITZPATRICK, Mary G	27387	F5006	K
EDWARDS, Clayton L	22516	R811	FAM	FLAKOWICZ, Irene H	23027	R421	BPM
EDWARDS, Norman J	24765	R405	KMB	FLANAGAN, Robert B	26387	F6052	FGE
EGLIN, Catherine C	23478	R802	FA	FLATTERY, Matthew M	20543	L5071	MRR-MA
EHRLICH, Eugene	22388	F5081	SCF-2	FLECK, Robert L., M.D	20284	BA36	BG-1
EICHMANN, Annette A	20157	F5029	SG	FLEMING, William A	37275	F6011	AAD-3
EJNHORN, Raymond	33241	F5137	D	FLETCHER, James	21271	F7137	A
ELAM, Frank E., Jr	20646	B300	BXB	FLING, Mary E	24628	F7117	XP
ELIEFF, Alexander T	36974	F5128	KDS-SP	FOLSOM, William L	20126	B521	TA
ELLINGTON, Tony L	21618	BA25	DHA-51	FONG, Louis B	27695	F5065	SAA
ELLIOTT, James R	24021	F6137	L	FORD, Naomi C	33126	R801	FE
ELLIOTT, Margaret L	20583	B300	BX	FORDYCE, Samuel W	22110	F5081	SCF
ELLIOTT, Rosalie D	24553	F5113	SV	FORSBERG, James H	37236	R512	Z
ELLIS, John H	22475	R721	DHC-5	FORSYTHE, Dixon L	35347	B268	MLA
ELLIS, Norman L., Maj., USAF	20471	L5053	MAP-7	FOSQUE, Hugh S	20126	B521	TA
ELLIS, Ruth	33114	B256	MLA	FOSTER, J. N	24710	F6147	AAD-1D
EMBER, William N	119-4335	EE476	NS-2	FOSTER, Willis B	24805	F6141	E
				FOX, Donald G., Dr	34341	F5038	SL
EMME, Eugene M., Dr	37371	R706	EH	FOX, Kathryn A	34967	R521	BPM
ENO, Dale	24827	F7121	XP	FOX, Leo., Dr	20033	B626	RB
ERICKSON, Todd L	24488	W-Bldg.	DHA-42	FRANDSEN, Niels P	23093	B243	MLE
ERIKSEN, George A	36264	L5068	MAR	FRANK, Frederick A	35983	F6137	L
ERSKINE, Robin W	24461	B347	MHB	FRANKLIN, Charles E	119-4547	EE469	NS-2
ESENWEIN, George F., Jr	20495	L5005	MAL	FREEMAN, Charles E	24442	B B-LEV	DHA-53
ETHELL, Louise E	20612	R421	BPM	FREIBAUM, Jerome	36478	F5081	SCF-3
ETHEREDGE, James B	22752	R811	FAM	FREITAG, Robert F	27215	B456	M-X
EUBANK, Dorothy O	33602	B154	DHA-71	FRENZEN, Donald W	26849	B225	GK
EVANS, Albert J	20176	B600	RA	FRIEDMAN, Richard	21337	F7090	I
EVANS, Vera E	27934	F6083	OSP	FRISINA, John	22121	W-Bldg.	DHA-4
EVANS, W. B	35256	B246	MLO	FRUTKIN, Arnold W	21187	F7077	I
EWELL, Howard	34773	F7020	XS	FUGLER, Bartley A	21532	R424	DHZ
EY, Nancy B	21861	F5103	SL	FULKS, John W	20531	L5073	KDM-MA
F				FUNKHOUSER, James M	24440	F6107	FG
				FUTCH, James T	24825	F7121	XP
FALCONE, Guy	21918	BA56	DHA-6	FYOCK, Janice R	23812	B368	MH
FALKENHAYN, Edward, Jr	26475	B236	MLB	**G**			
FALL, Anthony J	20646	B300	BXB	GABRIEL, David S	119-4118	EE468	NS-2
FALTESEK, Dorothy S	23028	R421	BPM	GAETANO, Frank W	36929	F5047	SG
FARFEL, Martin I	119-4347	EE480	NS-2	GAFFIELD, Sue A	27448	R421	BPM
FARLEY, Clare F	21426	F7137	OE	GAFFNEY, Gerald P	33905	B326	BXC
FARRELL, Richard M Lt., USAF.	20464	B300	MMS	GAGLIARDI, Lydia M	21454	B112	KDR
FAULK, Barbara E	35886	F5131	SS	GALLAGHER, Owen P	23168	R421	BPM
FEINSTEIN, Paul S	26156	R827	KSS	GALLAGHER, Suzanne	34341	F5038	SL
FELLNER, Mary Jo	27561	B350	MRO	GALVIN, W. Corlett	20061	B507	TS
FELLOWS, Robert F., Dr	21861	F5103	SL	GAMMON, Benson E	20069	B600	RA
FERGUSON, C. Guy	26481	R527	BPA	GANGLER, James J	20271	B647	RWM
FERGUSON, Rosemary	24336	R410	KT	GARBACZ, Michael L	34291	F5065	SRO
FERRELL, Ruby J	20049	B625	RPX	GARBER, Linda M	21715	F7032	GP
FESSLER, Josephine M	21717	F6065	C	GARCIA, Joseph	25086	B136	KDP-2
FESSLER, Richard E	21030	F5122C	BX-SP	GARDNER, George N	22891	R812	FAP
FETHEROLF, Martin D., Jr	34849	F6090	DY	GARDNER, Paul L., Dr	22654	R805	FE
FETTERS, Pamela K	22042	R624	BF	GARNER, Annie L	22761	B347	MH
FIELD, J. Pemble., Jr	36161	B236	MLB	GARNER, Suzanne S. T	26053	R628	BFG
FIELD, Lucille W	21819	F6067	C	GARRETT, Arnold W	23965	R424	DHZ
FIELD, M. Arlene	22861	B325	MF	GARRETT, David W	23865	B656	R-2
FILIPPELLI, Lawrence J	37293	F7121	XP	GARRISON, John C., Jr	35691	B326	BXC
FILLMORE, William C	36046	F6025	BR-3	GARZIGLIA, Bernard J	20674	B421	MBB-2
FINCH, Larry	28421	F6147	AAD-4	GASKINS, Mary Ann	24581	F5093	SL
FISCHETTI, Thomas L	28318	B268	MLA	GASKINS, Mary G	24511	F5123	SP

NAME	EXT	ROOM	CODE
GAVER, Les	21721	F6035	FP
GAVIGAN, Francis X	119–4335	EE479	NS-2
GAVIN, Patrick A	23601	R522	BPL
GAY, Clarence C., Jr	23113	B347	MHO
GEIB, Donna S	24965	F5050	SL
GEORGE, Theodore A	20574	F5065	SRB
GERBER, Roberta V	119–4567	EE463	NS-2
GERSCHANECK, Susan M	25046	B125	KDP-1
GERSTEIN, Norman J	119–4567	EE461	NS-2
GESELL, Ralph T	21721	F6035	FP
GESSOW, Alfred	28607	B600	RAA
GEVARTER, William B., Dr	24038	F6141	EP
GIBSON, Ralph E	36925	F6043	FP
GILBREATH, Stephen W	20894	F6050	BP-1
GILCHRIST, Laurence F	20051	B525	RFS
GILL, Jocelyn R., Dr	22848	F5023	SG
GILLAM, Isaac T., IV	24534	F5109	SV
GILLEN, Richard J	20894	F6058	BP-1
GILLOOLY, John T	36943	B247	MLQ
GILSTAD, Douglas A	20263	B647	RWS
GINTER, R. D	20006	B525	RF
GLAHN, Earl W	36985	F5086	SL
GLASCOCK, Diane E	20002	B512	TN
GLASGOW, Gloria J	20091	B547	NS-1
GLASSMAN, Steven J., Dr	24336	R414	KT
GOBER, Jeanne B	24440	F6107	FG
GOETZ, Barbara A	21537	F7090	I
GOFF, Loyal G	24961	F5038	SL
GOLDEN, Edmond J	26584	B100	KDS
GOLDEN, Howard S	22867	R812	FAP
GOODWIN, Doris	23808	B212	Y
GOOLSBY, Lee D	27253	B626	ROA
GOOZH, Paul E	24534	F5109	SV
GORDON, Ida C	20495	L5005	MAL
GORELICK, Albert P	21454	B112	KDR
GORMAN, Harry H	20303	B468	MD-M
GOSHORN, Gretta T	20214	B600	RAV
GOULD, Charles H	27253	B626	RO
GOWERS, D. Carmen	21187	F7077	I
GRABER, Margaret M	24227	F5129	SS
GRADE, George T	24831	B154	DHA-1
GRAHAM, A. Diane	20506	B145	KL
GREEN, Elma D	24710	F6147	AAD-1D
GREEN, Johanna N	20894	F6058	BP-1
GREEN, Plummer W	21446	BA19	DHA-50
GREEN, Renee S	37413	B368	MRD
GREEN, William D., Jr	21961	B256	MLA
GREENE, John E	20057	B617	RV
GREENE, William A	23104	B200	Y
GRIFFIN, John J	20651	B421G	BXC-1
GRIMM, Frank K	22757	R811	FAM
GRIVAS, Spiro J	24893	F6147	AAD-4
GROSS, Barbara R	119–4335	EE477	NS-2
GROUNDS, Sharon K	20618	F6003	AAD-4
GROVES, Sandra	24946	F6075	XS
GRUBB, H. Dale	21717	F6065	C
GRUBER, Michael	119–3774	EE461	NS-2
GRUHL, Werner M	36046	F6025	BR-3
GRYBOSKI, Charles N	26356	R621	BFA
GUILD, Warren A	23597	B525	RFP
GUTHEIM, Robert J	24086	F5129	SF

NAME	EXT	ROOM	CODE
H			
HAAS, Elvira W	26602	F7137	AA
HABER, Gitta G	21855	B300	BX
HABER, Wolf	21686	F7051	G
HABERMAN, William L., Dr	21831	B431	MTE
HADEN, Elmo E	22468	B136	KDA-1
HAGLER, Thomas	21484	B431	MTE
HAINES, Nathan C	24506	B168	DHA
HALL, C. Robert	26268	R621	BFA
HALL, Eldon W	20295	B440	MTG
HALL, Harvey, Dr	24860	B440	MT-2
HALL, Inez P	23093	B243	MLE
HALL, Lawrence B	34341	F5038	SL
HALL, Susanne	24805	F6141	E
HALLENBECK, David R	21987	F5047	SG
HALPERN, Richard E	21987	F5045	SG
HAMBY, William H	37313	B246	MLO
HAMILTON, George N	21618	BA25	DHA-51
HAMILTON, Jeffrey T	36206	F5011	K
HAMM, Nellie F	20937	B647	RC
HAMMACK, Alvin C	23956	B425	M
HAMMANN, Harry W	26356	R621	BFA
HAMMERSMITH, John L	23582	B431	MTX
HAMON, William J	25777	B325	MF
HAMPTON, Catharina T	27595	F5065	SRM
HANBURY, William L	34740	F6080	DY
HAND, Elizabeth P	755–4347	B626	RO
HANES, Thomas E	20391	B256	MLA
HANLEY, John B., Dr	26628	L5004	MAL
HANN, H. Frank	22811	R624	BF
HANSING, Frank D., Dr	23119	B200	Y
HANSSTON, Knute G	28483	F6119	BR-1
HARBISON, John R	26085	R623	BFA
HARDESTY, Ann	20259	B400	ME
HARDY, Alice C	27392	R421	BPM
HARGRAVE, Charles W	22126	R827	KSS
HARKLEROAD, Edgar L	20636	B246	MLO
HARMAN, Patricia M	20431	B368	MHE
HARNETT, Daniel J	36937	F5011	K
HARPER, John W., Sr	23910	B C-Lev.	DHA-31
HARRIS, Brenda C	20593	BA11	KDA-3
HARRIS, Hortense N	37636	F6103	FG
HARRIS, John L	24855	R608	BFH
HARRIS, John P	22305	W–BLDG	DHA-4
HARRISON, Carolyn L	20091	B547	RPM
HARRISON, Edward K	21819	F6069	C
HARRISON, Harry, Dr	119–4347	EE477	NS-2
HART, Delores C	21708	F7137	A
HART, Don A, Jr	20022	B568	RPD
HARTKE, Martin J	36991	B326	BXE
HARTMAN, Orvis B	28991	B325	MF
HARTMAN, Pierre M	26855	B225	GK
HARTMAN, Richard A., Capt., USAF	36323	B300	MMS
HARWOOD, William R., Jr	36991	B326	BXE
HATT, Peter K	24580	F5093	SL
HAUGHEY, Joseph W	24553	F5113	SV
HAUTIER, M. Kay	21655	R421	BPM
HAWKINS, Carlton R	21446	BA19	DHA-50
HAWKINS, Charles, Jr	21446	BA19	DHA-50

NAME	EXT	ROOM	CODE	NAME	EXT	ROOM	CODE
HAWLEY, Edith M_____	28023	R721	DHC-6	HOUGHTEN, Robert L_____	37497	F5065	SRM
HAWTHORNE, Randolph___	25882	F6099	FGC	HOUSER, Constance L_____	26011	B409	MMR
HAYDEN, Lila L_____	20021	B568	RP	HOWARD, William J_____	35838	F6124C	BT-1
HAYDEN, William G_____	21918	BA56	DHA-6	HUBBARD, Samuel H_____	36181	B325	MF
HAYES, Daniel F., Sr_____	35364	F6089	DY	HUDELSON, Jeanne K_____	21925	F7084	I
HAYMAN, Harry_____	27427	B607	RET	HUDOCK, Doris A_____	24860	B440	MT-2
HEADLEE, Joseph L_____	34086	F6102	FPT	HUDSON, William W_____	27531	B656	KDS-RM
HEATER, Gerald D_____	27561	B350	MRO	HUFF, Vearl N_____	21321	B431	MTE
HEBERLE, Elizabeth_____	24925	F6075	XS	HUGHES, Jacob W_____	26481	R527	BPA
HECHLER, Theodore, Jr____	36523	F5054	SRR	HULL, Harris B_____	37636	F6103	FG
HECKEL, Richard D_____	20002	B512	TN	HUMPHREYS, J. W.,	20111	B300	MM
HEINE, Frank L_____	36283	BA1F	KDP-3	Jr., M.D.			
HEISING, Kenneth W_____	20051	B525	RFS	HUNGERFORD,	23440	R721	DHC-4
HELMS, Ira L_____ 119-4567		EE461	NS-2	Beverly J.			
HENDERICKSON, Mary Lou	35302	F7019	F	HUNT, Mary B_____	21213	F7087	I
HENDERSON, Charles F___	21454	B112	KDR	HUNT, Robert E_____	36992	B326	BXE
HENDRICKSON, Charles S_	25083	BA26	DHA-52	HUSAR, Mary E_____	34188	F6141	E
HENRY, Edith I_____	20321	F7118	XC	HUSSA, Lillian E_____	26270	R821	KSI
HENRY, Wood T_____	21347	B100	KDS	HYNES, William J_____	35281	R411	KMC
HENSLEY, Reece V_____	28231	B541	RS				
HERING, Walter_____	21721	F6035	FP	**I**			
HERMAN, Daniel H_____	36985	F5086	SL				
HERMAN, Dorothy M_____	20646	B300	BXB	IAQUINTA, Jacqueline E____	20131	B521	TN
HERNDON, W. Joy_____	20058	B621	RV	INGELFINGER, A. Layton_	20437	B300	MMV
HERRING, Mack R_____	27306	F6052	FGE	IRELAND, Delbert H.,	20651	B-415	BXA
HESSBERG, Rufus R., Col.	36323	B300	MMS	Lt. Comdr., USN.			
USAF MC.				**J**			
HIBBARD, Richard T_____	36975	F5065	SRP				
HICKS, Margaret M_____	22891	R812	FAP	JACKSON, Bettie L_____	21176	F5017	SN
HIETT, Stephen C_____	37152	F5122D	SPR	JACKSON, Dianne E_____	35366	F6088	DY
HILL, Sylvia A_____	20682	B412	MBB-1	JACKSON, Dorothy J_____	21738	F7026	GP
HINGER, Alfred F_____	20238	B350	MRO	JACKSON, Frank W_____	21446	BA19	DHA-50
HIPSHER, Harold F_____	36985	F5086	SL	JACKSON, Juanita S_____	22681	R805	FE
HIPSHER, Mildred H_____	34783	F5137	D	JACKSON, Roy P_____	34445	B668	R
HIXON, S. Walter, Jr_____	20640	R524	BPT	JACOBS, George J., Dr_____	24944	F5055	SRR
HLASS, I. Jerry_____	33669	B326	BXB	JACOBS, Robert J_____	22044	R623	BFA
HOBAN, Francis T_____	24075	F7137	X	JACOBSEN, Lawrence_____	33660	B300	BX
HOCHBERG, Charles M____	20669	F6015	BT	JAFFE, Leonard_____	37344	F5131	SA
HODGES, Donna J_____	23597	B536	RFP	JAKOBOWSKI, Walter_____	25618	F5091	SL
HOFFMAN, Judith M_____	23104	B200	Y	JAMES, Edward M., Jr_____	25045	B200	Y
HOFMANN, Glenn E_____	34969	R519	BPC	JAMES, Wilson, Jr_____	36994	B326	BXD
HOGAN, Joseph M_____	35304	B145	KL	JANOW, Carl_____	27335	B607	REG
HOLCOMB, John K_____	20643	L5046	MAO	JENKEL, Albert A_____	22110	F5081	SCP
HOLDSAMBECK, Samuel O.	28072	R519	BPC	JENKINS, Patricia A_____	24155	F6043	FP
HOLLAND, Dolores A_____	24056	B200	Y	JENSEN, Sally A_____	37393	BA50	KSS-10
HOLLAND, Harold_____	26475	B236	MLB	JESHOW, J. Ronald_____	21411	R721	DHC-3
HOLLEY, Herbert_____	24336	R410	KT	JOHNS, Trevor_____	20883	B440	MTG
HOLMES, Donald C_____	23952	B200	Y	JOHNSEN, Edwin G_____ 119-3353		EE480	NS-2
HOLMES, Jay E_____	20222	B456	MC	JOHNSON, Barbara J_____	21380	F6088	DY
HOLMES, Norman F_____	24488	W-Bldg.	DHA-42	JOHNSON, Bernard L_____	20326	B400	MBD
HOLMES, Yvonne S_____	34763	L6137	L	JOHNSON, Bettie A_____	23582	B431	MTX
HOLT, Patricia M_____	36987	F5086	SL	JOHNSON, Collis H_____	23910	B C-Lev.	DHA-31
HOLTZ, John R_____	23825	F5041	SG	JOHNSON, George P., Maj.,	20155	B656	BX-RM
HOLZMAN, Arthur D_____	21456	F7057	G	USA.			
HONEYCUTT, Mary H_____	20091	B547	NS-1	JOHNSON, Harry W_____	20151	B612	RL
HOOD, Arthur F_____	23910	B C-Lev.	DHA-31	JOHNSON, Joseph F_____	21088	R607	BFH
HOOD, James C_____	21918	BA56	DHA-6	JOHNSON, Karin I_____	24391	F7045	GP
HORNESTAY, David H____	37164	F6113	BR-2	JOHNSON, Laverne Y_____	21325	B225	GK
HOROWITZ, Dorothy M____	21759	R421	BPM	JOHNSON, Malinda H_____	37807	F5117	SPI
HORVATH, John E_____	21297	R721	DHC-5	JOHNSON, Mary E_____	21819	F6067	C
HOSE, Patricia A_____	20388	B431	MTE	JOHNSON, Moses_____	34773	F7018	XS
HOSENBALL, S. Neil_____	21246	F7065	G	JOHNSON, Natalie M_____	23769	B336	MRT-2
				JOHNSON, Paul G_____ 119-4547		EE471	NS-2

NAME	EXT	ROOM	CODE
JOHNSON, Rodney W., Dr..	28991	B325	MF
JOHNSON, Shirley J.	28725	F6141	E
JOHNSON, Shirley T.	23351	R401	KM
JOHNSON, Vincent L.	21156	F5131	SD
JOHNSON, Virginia V.	21841	F6061	C
JOHNSON, William H.	119–4347	EE480	NS-2
JOHNSTON, Robert L.	24717	BA1F	KDA-3
JONES, Carl N.	21236	F7089	I
JONES, Larry	21446	BA19	DHA-50
JONES, Lloyd E., Jr.	21213	F7087	I
JONES, Marie A.	22752	R811	FAM
JONES, Patricia R.	28113	F6127	B
JONES, Ruth E.	24075	F7137	X
JONES, V. C. Pat	36930	F6103	FGC
JONES, Walton L., Dr.	20016	B300	MMD
JORDAN, Alfred	21918	BA56	DHA-6
JORDAN, Michael J.	23796	FSB042	BG
JOSEPH, Kenneth R.	20774	B512	TN

K

NAME	EXT	ROOM	CODE
KAFKA, Egon E.	22393	B243	MLE
KAHN, Arlene B. M.	24286	F6053	F-3
KAISER, Harriette H.	36086	B243	MLE
KANTER, Jules I.	27294	B607	REP
KAREGEANNES, Carrie E.	35493	R706	EH
KARNES, Anita R.	24463	F5137	D
KARSTAD, Owen F.	22468	B136	KDA-1
KAVANAGH, Lawrence D., Jr., Dr.	21987	F5045	SG
KAYTEN, Gerald G.	37335	B621	RT
KAZIMER, Katherine D.	24946	F6075	XS
KEANY, John P.	24155	F6043	FP
KEEGAN, Edna L.	24773	F5137	D
KEEGAN, Richard J.	24193	B101	KD-2
KEEGAN, Thomas A.	22117	B431	MTE
KEEHN, Shirley M.	21841	F6061	C
KEEN, Beverly H.	34345	B268	MLD
KEIGHER, Donald J.	34740	F6088	DY
KEITH, Ernest L.	20636	B246	MLO
KELLER, J. Warren	25468	F5091	SL
KELLEY, Charles W.	24145	F6012D	BT-1
KELLY, Donald J.	37167	F6015	BT-2
KELLY, Francis W.	20561	BA1F	KDP-3
KELLY, J. Howard	25935	R627	BFC
KELLY, John J., Jr.	20446	L5057	MAP-7
KEMMETT, Francis W.	24001	R601	KB
KENNEDY, Barbara E.	24705	B112	KDR
KENNEDY, Harvey M.	26898	B111	KDA
KENNEDY, Robert A.	25618	F5091	SL
KENNEY, Harry S., Jr.	26484	R701	BD
KERNEN, Madeline R.	24703	B500	T
KERR, Thomas B.	20054	B556	RYN
KERRIGAN, Edward J.	34058	B500	TN
KERSHAW, Albert F.	20874	B350	MRO
KERTES, Julia E.	24938	F7137	AAD
KERZE, Shirley H.	24679	R822	KS
KEULER, Leroy A.	20601	L5069	MRR-MA
KIDWELL, Joseph D.	24351	F6093	FGA
KIER, Kenneth J.	24025	B129	KD-4
KIESSLING, Carole A.	36991	B326	BXE

NAME	EXT	ROOM	CODE
KILDEE, Brian T.	24757	B136	KDA-2
KILGORE, Edwin C.	28511	B668	RD-M
KILLIAM, Lydia Joyce	20117	B526	TC
KING, Charles H., Jr.	36475	L5009	MAE
KING, David M.	22305	W-Bldg.	DHA-4
KING, Easter L.	27531	B656	BP-2
KING, J. David	26904	B136	KDA-1
KING, Robert E.	20138	B137	KL
KISTLE, James I.	37117	L5013	MAE
KLEIN, Milton	119–3027	EE456	NS-2
KLEIN, Vickie	20874	B350	MRO
KLEY, John A.	24155	F6043	FP
KLINE, Raymond A.	37517	F5137	D
KNAGGS, Vincent L.	20061	B507	TS
KNOTTS, Allen S.	26908	R608	BFH
KOCEN, Mina J.	24089	R721	DHC-1
KOCHENDORFER, Fred D.	24557	F5103	SL
KOENIG, Charles E.	24496	B412	MBB
KOKOSKI, Dorothy J.	20614 ·	B468	MD
KONKEL, Ronald M.	36046	F6025	BR-3
KONOPKA, Arthur F.	21685	F7058	G
KOSOFSKY, Leon J.	20495	L5006	MAL
KOUTSANDREAS, John D.	20576	F5065	SRB
KOUTSANDREAS, Peter D.	37987	B216	KDM-ML
KOWALSKI, Andrew	34447	B356	MRO
KRAEMER, Robert S.	24581	F5091	SL
KRAETZ, Oliver	25920	B125	KDP-1
KRAMER, Milton J.	24892	F6147	AAD-4
KRASNICAN, Milan J.	26984	B656	RX
KRAVETZ, Agnes B.	26053	R611	BFH
KRESIN, Clarence E.	21841	F6061	C
KRUEGER, Myron W.	24707	F7112	WX
KUGLER, Virginia M.	24391	F7045	GP
KUNEC, Edward J.	24533	F5113	SV
KUPPERMAN, Helen S.	33063	F7056	G
KURZWEG, Hermann H., Dr.	20028	B568	RR

L

NAME	EXT	ROOM	CODE
LABOWSKI, Joseph	24002	R605	KB
LACY, John P.	26831	B225	GK
LAGASSEY, Robert L.	24325	F7071	DI
LAM, B. C.	24553	F5113	SV
LAMB, Constance L.	37343	B347	MHL
LAMB, Neil F.	24717	BA1I	KDA-3
LAND, Elwood W., Jr.	24887	L5037	MAO
LANDIS, Orville O.	23453	R405	KMA
LANE, John J.	119–4335	EE479	NS-2
LANG, Robert H., Col. USAF, MC.	20464	B300	MMS
LANGFORD, James E.	20546	B336	MRS
LANGHORNE, E. Larry	24281	B150	DHA-2
LAROCK, Ralph I.	20051	B525	RFS
LATHAM, Ann M.	20581	F5081	SCS
LAUX, James J.	22727	F6069	C
LAVERY, Beatrice H.	24369	W-Bldg.	FAD
LAVIGNE, Adeline M.	22522	B541	RS
LAWSON, Mickey J.	28057	B101	KD-3
LAZAR, James	20041	B547	RPE
LAZOR, Trudy J.	34969	R519	BPC
LEAMAN, William R.	24145	F6012C	BT-1

NAME	EXT	ROOM	CODE	NAME	EXT	ROOM	CODE
LEBERT-FRANCIS, Brian	24920	F5137	D	LOTTMANN, Robert V	21715	F7035	GP
LECOMPTE, Jean P	21156	F5131	SD	LOVEJOY, William L	24534	F5109	SV
LECKEY, Donna Jean	20653	B414	BXC-1	LOVELACE, Barbara A	37344	F5131	SA
LECTKA, Janet E	21987	F5045	SG	LOVELACE, Rose M	20303	B468	MD-M
LECTKA, Joan F	36975	F5065	SRP	LOVELETT, Robert F	22861	B325	MF
LEDERER, Jerome F	20514	F6089	DY	LOW, George M., Dr	21271	F7137	AD
LEE, Beverly A	27215	B456	MC	LOWE, Brinda K	25083	BA26	DHA-52
LEE, Beverly Ann	25438	F6089	DY	LOZUPONE, Louis A	24442	B B-Lev.	DHA-53
LEE, Chester M	20203	L5047	MA	LUCAS, Jennie E	26946	B656	BP-2
LEE, W. Mildred	24757	B136	KDA-2	LUCAS, Thomas V	20117	B526	TC
LEE, William L	33046	R519	BPC	LUCAS, William A	20876	B243	MLE
LEEFER, Bernard I	20121	B568	RPA	LUCKRITZ, Margaret E	20593	BA1H	KDA-3
LEES, Frederick J	26611	F7033	GP	LUNDHOLM, Joseph G., Dr	33114	B256	MLA
LEHMANN, Jules	24563	F5065	SRF	LUSHINA, Louis N	22813	R624	BF
LEISTNER, Kathleen M	22464	R505	DU	LUTTER, Wilma K	24831	B154	DHA-1
LEJKO, Stephen P	23351	R401	KM	LYLE, V. John	27216	B456	M-X
LESLIE, Betty	21272	F7137	AD	LYLES, Alfreda D	25083	BA26	DHA-52
LEVINE, Jack	23597	B536	RFP	LYMAN, Alexander S	20587	L5051	MAP
LEVINE, Robert S., Dr	21703	B625	RPL	LYNCH, James J	20091	B547	NS-1
LEVY, Gertrude	26475	B236	MLB	LYNN, Samuel	20506	B145	KL
LEVY, Lillian R	35650	F6099	FGC	LYONS, Bonnie	20561	BALF	KDP-3
LEW, John D	35591	B300	BXA				
LEWELLYN, Jack R	20774	B512	TN	**M**			
LEWIS, Erva R	20011	B500	TN				
LEWIS, Herbert J	26475	B236	MLB	MACK, Addie S	26860	B225	GK
LEWIS, James G	24145	F6124B	BT-1	MACLEAN, Ruth Ann	35347	B268	MLD-1
LEWIS, Shirley A	21918	BA56	DHA-6	MACRAE, Maryanne E	26150	R823	KSI
LIBERMAN, David S	24933	B155	KR	MADDEN, John F	20154	B656	BX-RM
LICCARDI, Anthony L	22861	B325	MF	MADDEN, Sandra A	36904	F5122C	SPA
LICCINI, Luke L	37275	F6011	AAD-3	MAGGIN, Bernard	20006	B536	RF
LICHTY, Donald H	37620	F7071	DHE	MAHER, John C	24222	F6038	FP
LIEBERMANN, Carl R	21727	L5055	MAP-1	MAHON, Joseph B	24531	F5111	SV
LIEVENS, Edward J., Jr	20248	B409	MCL	MAINES, Howard G	21532	R424	DHZ
LILLY, William E	28113	F6127	B	MALAGA, Joseph F	35752	F6031	BR
LIMONCELLI, Donald D	35306	BA36	BG	MALAGA, Sandra W	20224	B468	M
LINCOLN, Marie B	21973	F5041	SG	MALAMENT, Jerome C	23315	B440	MTG
LINDLEY, Robert N	20258	B400	ME	MALAMENT, Seline Z	26628	L5001	MAL
LINDSEY, Audrey M	22989	F5023	SG	MALAMUT, Martin	37117	L5015	MAE
LINDSEY, Theodore L	21918	BA56	DHA-6	MALLOY, Daniel J	36283	BA1F	KDP-3
LIPKEY, George L	28483	F6119	BR-1	MALONE, Annie S	36904	F5122C	SPA
LIPPOLIS, Mary R	25097	F7137	AA	MALTARICH, Jean M	36904	F5122C	SPA
LITTLE, Albert P	28146	F6127	B	MALTZ, Joseph	20271	B647	RWM
LITTLE, William J	20676	B412	MBP	MANAHAN, Richard R.,	33601	B300	BXA
LITTLEFIELD, Robert C	20226	B468	M-1	Maj. USA.			
LITTLEJOHN, James H	20687	B426	MBM	MANNHEIMER, Harry	36341	B256	MLA
LIVINGSTON, Richard C	23315	B440	MTG	MANNING, John R	21738	F7030	GP
LLOYD, Janice M	23253	R524	BPT	MANSON, Simon V	20091	B547	NS-1
LLOYD, O. B., Jr	22432	F7025	F-2	MANUEL, Linda D	20526	B100	KDM
LOCKLEY, Gwendolyn	27884	B244	MRR-ML	MANVILLE, Robert W	24534	F5109	SV
LOGAN, Prince S	21113	F7096	I	MAPP, Richard C., Jr	20446	L5053	MAP-7
LOHMAN, Robert L	22861	B325	MF	MARIANETTI, Eugene A	24351	F6093	FGA
LOHR, Josephine T	21967	L5079	MAL	MARINARI, Randie M	24701	R406	KT
LOKEY, Charles G	20820	R502	KME	MARK, Ann	34235	F6052	FGE
LONG, Joseph E	25747	B600	RAS	MARKEY, Melvin F	23315	B440	MTG
LONGENETTE, Gladys M	34904	R806	FAE	MARLL, Florence	20643	L5046	MAO
LOOKABILL, Sylvia E	26812	F5129	SF	MARPLE, George C	24825	F7121	XP
LORD, Douglas R	36181	B325	MF	MARR, E. Gene	24365	B200	Y
LORENSON, Louis E	20674	B421	MBB-2	MARRAZZO, Rudolph M	24774	BA36	BG
LORIA, John C	35370	B556	RY	MARSH, John	20876	B243	MLE
LOSEE, Madeleine W	26194	R824	KSA	MARSHALL, Rosemarie H	23703	R721	DHC-4
LOSS, Bessie G	35428	R609	BFH	MARSTEN, Richard B., Dr	20888	F5081	SC
				MARTIN, James A	24738	B600	RAB

NAME	EXT	ROOM	CODE	NAME	EXT	ROOM	CODE
MARTIN, Joseph	27884	B244	MRR-ML	MERKIN, Allan	20311	B621	RB
MARTIN, Thomas S., Jr	24357	R609	BFH	MESON, John K	27335	B607	REG
MARUSZEWSKI, Eugene T	37987	B216	KDM-ML	MESSINA, Peggy E	37281	B155	KR
				METCALFE, Rayburn A	20640	R524	BPT
MASRI, Sidney G	26878	B225	GK	MEYERS, Edward J	20618	F6147	AAD-4
MATHEWS, Charles W	20614	B468	MD	MICELI, Francis S	23481	R526	BPE
MATHEWSON, Vicki L	36943	B247	ML	MICHAELS, Theodore S	27335	B607	REG
MATTHEWS, Rex O	25094	R829	KSP	MICHEL, Douglas	37404	B647	RWS
MATTOS, Marie E	20028	B568	RR	MICHELSEN, Martin A	24145	F6124B	BT-1
MAUTNER, Karl F	21236	F7089	I	MIDGETT, Richard W	37278	F6147	AAD-2
MAXWELL, Preston T	20041	B547	RPM	MILBOURN, Clarence C	25086	B136	KDP-2
MAY, Ralph W	20213	B600	RAV	MILFORD, L. Arlene	36914	F6011	AAD-3
MAYER, Norman J	34779	B647	RWS	MILLER, Aurianne B	20514	F6089	DY
McBEAN, Carole P	20101	R421	BPM	MILLER, David J	119-4547	EE469	NS-2
McCABE, Norman H	25680	R824	KSI	MILLER, Nancy C	27947	R402	KT
McCLANAHAN, Jack T	20491	L5045	MAO	MILLER, Paul R	20091	B547	NS-1
McCOLLOM, James C	24506	B168	DHA	MILLER, Raymond	23825	F5041	SG
McCOLLUM, Kirby L	21155	R721	DHC-6	MILLER, Stella R	22568	B300	MMS
McCOMBS, Mary J	20166	B668	RD-A	MILLER, Wayne	24461	B347	MHB
McCONNELL, Dudley G., Dr.	24024	F7137	X	MILLER, William E., Jr	34462	B325	MF
				MILLS, Rodney A	25618	F5091	SL
McCONNELL, Linda M	24608	F6143	DY	MILWITZKY, Benjamin	37291	L5041	MAE
McCOY, Garland T	24391	F7045	GP	MINER, Richard J	24701	R406	KT
McCOY, Melvin	22257	R712	DHA-50	MIRACLE, Herbert B	23965	R424	DHZ
McCULLOCH, Robert L	24325	F7071	DI	MISCHEL, David S	35263	R421	BPM
McCURDY, Richard C	34783	F5137	D	MISENER, Garland C., Jr	24540	F5119	SPP
McCURDY, W. Doris	34968	R519	BPC	MITCHELL, Jesse L	21653	F5035	SG
McDANIEL, Belva K	24583	F7101	W	MITCHELL, Richard E	24765	R411	KMF
McDONALD, John E	26226	BA1I	KDA-3	MITCHELL, Wilfred F	24831	B154	DHA-1
McDONALD, John J	21250	R721	DHC-5	MITTAUER, Richard T	21176	F5017	SN
McDONALD, Michael E	20147	F5030	SG	MITZ, Milton A., Dr	21384	F5091	SL
McELROY, James B	20131	B521	TN	MIXSON, Meryle W	34335	F5065	SRN
McENANEY, John D	27531	B656	RMS	MIZE, Robert F	20618	F6147	AAD-4
McGARRY, Elizabeth K	24139	F6069	C	MOCKBEE, Jean C	27839	BA36	BG
McGHEE, Wendeth E	20543	L5071	MRR-MA	MOGAVERO, Louis N	21484	B431	MTE
				MOLLENBERG, Ernst F	25995	L5021	MAE
McGILVERY, Rita L	22445	R507	DU	MOLLOY, James C	37767	R628	BFG
McGILVRA, Alice O	24715	F7137	ADA	MOLLOY, Martin W., Dr	21967	L5077	MAL
McGINTY, Earl E	22445	R507	DU	MONFALCONE, Delores A	36475	L5025	MAE
McGOLRICK, Joseph E	24553	F5113	SV	MONROE, Roscoe	24351	F6093	FGA
McGOWAN, William A	27253	B626	ROO	MOONEY, Mary C	24025	B129	KD-4
McGRATH, Mary-Ellen	34320	F6137	L	MOORE, Charles W	37236	R512	Z
McGRATH, Patricia L	25091	R814	DHB	MOORE, Diane A	25749	B600	RA
McGRAW, Lenore M	20661	B368	MR	MOORE, Gwen	22847	F5023	SG
McGUIRE, Charles W	36847	F6091	DY	MOORE, William F	37343	B347	MHL
McJENNETT, John F., Jr	37441	F6057	FGM	MOREHOUSE, Helen H	34296	F7137	XS
McKAY, Anne E	21088	R612	BFH	MORGAN, Winnie M	26165	R821	KSI
McKENNEY, Joseph W	21446	BA19	DHA-50	MORITZ, Bernard	24463	F5137	D
McKINNEY, Vernor L., Maj., USAF	26001	B415	MME	MORONEY, John J	23253	R524	BPT
				MORRIS, Annabel O	35347	B268	MLA
McLAUGHLIN, Edward J., Dr.	20464	B300	MMS	MORRIS, Donald R	21253	F7077	I
				MORRIS, Dorothea A	23521	R824	KSA
McNAMARA, James D	23236	R505	DU	MORRIS, Elliot, Dr	24559	F5103	SL
McROBERTS, Joseph J	21176	F5017	SN	MORRIS, Jerome D	23300	B200	Y
McVICKER, Sandra T	28064	F7052	G	MORRIS, Mildred V	26053	R611	BFH
MEARS, David F	22476	R721	DHC-3	MORRIS, Norman E	24033	BA24	DHA-501
MEDWAY, Lawrence E	27377	F6069	C	MORRISON, James R	21213	F7087	I
MEEK, Diane M	23038	F7090	I	MORRISSEY, John E	119-4547	EE471	NS-2
MELESKI, Benjamin J	37152	F5122D	SPR	MOSKOVITZ, Abraham I	24931	B155	KR
MENDES, Gabriella	20117	B526	TC	MOSSINGHOFF, Gerald J	21841	F6061	C
MERKER, June	24812	F7137	AA	MOWRY, Shirley A	23363	B656	RX

NAME	EXT	ROOM	CODE	NAME	EXT	ROOM	CODE
MULCAHY, Bertram A.	34265	F6069	C	OERTEL, Goetz K., Dr.	20157	F5029	SG
MULLEN, Arthur R.	26484	R701	BD	OLINGER, Margaret K.	25160	R829	KSP
MULLEN, Donald E.	36086	B243	MLE	O'NEIL, Robert T.	20234	B356	BP-3
MULLIGAN, Richard G.	27531	B656	RMS	O'ROURKE, Edward P.	20242	B350	MRO
MULLIN, Jerome P.	20041	B547	RPE	ORRICK, Decourcy W., Jr.	27947	R406	KT
MURAD, Ronald V.	22861	B325	MF	ORTZMAN, Philip	22155	R424	DHZ
MURPHY, Angela M.	33602	B154	DHA-71	OTT, Ernest J.	35996	F5023	SG
MURPHY, Joseph L.	24932	B155	KR	OURAM, John E.	36283	BA1F	KDP-3
MUSAR, Linda J.	20271	B647	RWN	OWEN, Nancy C.	24534	F5109	SV
MUSSELMAN, Sidney F.	24831	B168	DHA-1	OWENS, James J.	27448	R421	BPM
MYERS, Boyd C., II	28806	F6127	B	OWENS, Lynda F.	22493	R721	DHC-4
MYERS, Dale D.	20224	B468	M	OWENS, Rome K.	24215	B146	DHA-3
MYERS, Herbert B.	26806	B347	MHB				
MYLES, Margy K.	23965	R424	DHZ				

N

P

NAME	EXT	ROOM	CODE	NAME	EXT	ROOM	CODE
				PAGLIUSO, Michael A.	35691	B326	BXC
				PAIR, Harmon E., Jr.	21446	BA19	DHA-50
NADER, Herman S.	24445	B146	DHA-3	PALMER, Marcella C.	20391	B256	MLA
NAGURNEY, Myron C.	22124	R827	KSS	PARK, Arch B., Dr.	36523	F5065	SRR
NAGY, Alex P.	20331	R806	FA	PARKER, Gayle	24391	F7039	GP
NANCE, John A.	24215	B146	DHA-3	PARKER, Nannie L.	21795	R424	DHZ
NAPPIER, Dema S.	34956	B126	DHA-72	PARKS, Elmo B.	24917	R824	KSA
NASH, Ralph R., Dr.	20187	B647	RWM	PARR, Martha V.	24222	F6038	FP
NAUGLE, John E., Dr.	21158	F5131	S	PATON, Albert E., Jr.	24187	R612	BFH
NEILL, Arthur H., Capt., USPHS	34341	F5038	SL	PATRICK, Kathleen F.	21411	R721	DHC-3
				PAUL, Carl F., Jr.	26828	B225	GK
NELSON, Alfred M.	24891	F6147	AAD-4	PAULIN, Juanita B.	24325	F7071	DI
NELSON, Helen G.	20633	B268	ML	PEARCY, Audrey A.	20317	B440	MT
NELSON, Margaret F.	28018	F7062	G	PEARSON, Ernest O.	22521	B541	RS
NELSON, William D.	37380	BA39	KSS-10	PEARSON, Sally F.	26611	F7032	GP
NETTLES, Eugene T.	22464	R505	DU	PECORARO, Joseph N.	20436	B300	MMV
NEUMAN, Bernard A.	28696	R602	BPM-2	PEERY, Julia E.	23802	F7109	W
NEWBERRY, A. W.	24563	F5054	SRG	PEIGARE, Shirley C.	24351	F6093	FGA
NEWCOMB, Wallace D., Jr.	24891	F6147	AAD-4	PEIL, Norman G.	35935	B368	MHE
NEWCOMER, Gordon M.	35366	F6082	DY	PEKICH, Sarah B.	26831	B225	GK
NEWCOMER, Patricia S.	28216	F5026	XP	PENARANDA, Frank E.	33614	B656	RX
NEWELL, Homer E., Dr.	26602	F7137	AA	PENDLETON, William J.	28127	F5137	D
NEWKIRK, Ivey S.	28107	F6127	B	PENNINO, Walter	21737	F6047	FP
NEWMAN, Abraham D.	23236	R505	DU	PEPER, Craig K.	37152	F5122D	SPR
NEWMAN, Charles T.	35752	F6031	BR	PERRON, Edward J.	22947	R522	BPL
NEWTON, Mary E.	22149	R421	BPM	PERRY, John F., II	20066	B600	RAB
NEY, Michael S.	20238	B356	MRI-1	PERRYGO, Louis W.	23630	R721	DHC-4
NICHOL, Marianna J.	23860	B212	Y	PETER, Maurice A.	33642	R806	FAE
NICHOLS, Joanne S.	36974	F5128	SP	PETERS, Dorothy D.	27582	R526	BP
NICHOLSON, Robert E.	21877	B125	KDP-1	PETERSON, Mechthild E.	24023	F7137	X
NOBLITT, Bobby G.	22861	B325	MF	PETERSON, Robert A.	37238	R512	Z
NOLAN, Bernard T.	36523	F5054	SRR	PETIT, William H., Jr.	20038	F5108	SPI
NOLAN, James P., Jr.	24021	F6137	L	PETRONE, Rocco, A., Dr.	36244	L5043	MA
NORDIN, Edna	36264	L5068	MAR	PETTIGREW, Sandra A.	25086	B136	KDP-2
NORRIS, Theodrick B.	24534	F5109	SV	PETTIT, John L.	24488	W-Bldg.	DHA-42
NOVIK, David	22817	B525	RFE	PHILIPS, Ronald J.	37925	R402	KT
NUMBERS, Frank E.	33012	R519	BPC	PHILLIPS, A. Felder., Jr.	27441	L5019	MAE
NUNLEY, Emma E.	20151	B612	RL	PHILLIPS, James B., Jr.	21327	R721	DHC-5
NUTWELL, James J.	37767	R628	BFG	PICKENS, Fern Lee	28696	R602	BPM-2
				PICKERING, Nancy S.	21333	F7065	G

O

NAME	EXT	ROOM	CODE	NAME	EXT	ROOM	CODE
				PIERCE, Edward A., Jr.	22161	R802	FA
				PILGER, Carl F.	25995	L5021	MAE
OAKES, Walter F., Jr.	24831	B154	DHA-1	PINKLER, Donald G.	37152	F5122D	SPR
O'BRIEN, Patrick F.	25935	R627	BFC	PIRKLE, James J.	28188	B656	RMR
O'BRYANT, William T.	28138	L5085	MAL	PITT, Patricia M.	20636	B246	MLO
O'DONNELL, Therese M.	34235	F6052	FGE	PLATT, Martha J.	36616	BA26	DHA-52
O'DONNELL, William J.	20666	B419	M-N	POE, Synethia A.	22780	F6073	C

NAME	EXT	ROOM	CODE	NAME	EXT	ROOM	CODE
POHLY, Jurgen G.	23960	B200	Y	RICHARDS, James T.	24701	R402	KT
POLAND, James W.	21469	BB-LEV	DHA-5	RICHARDS, Robert	23796	FSB 042	BG
POLIZZI, Dominick C.	36996	B326	BXD	RICHARDSON, Juanita W.	28188	B656	RMR
POLKING, Urban H.	24887	L5033	MAO	RICKERT, Willis H., Jr.	36360	B146	DHA-3
POLKOWSKI, Francis J.	37236	R512	Z	RICKS, Nancy J.	20676	B412	MBP
POMEROY, John H., Dr.	37831	L5087	MAL	RIEDER, Richard W.	35951	B336	MRS
POMEROY, William W.	23865	B656	R-2	RILEY, Consuello G.	22159	R608	BFH
PONTIOUS, Charles E.	20141	B607	RE	RISSO, William P.	28057	B101	KD-3
POSTELLE, Arnold W.	20546	B336	MRS	RITCHIE, Mary E.	21667	R421	BPM
POTATE, John S.	24311	L5044	MAP	ROACHE, Carol A.	37293	F7121	XP
POWERS, James E., Jr.	26475	B236	MLB	ROBENOLT, Darla A.	34304	R611	BFH
POZINSKY, Norman	20062	B507	TS	ROBERSON, Floyd I.	20495	L5007	MAL
PREBLE, Barbara S.	27206	R612	BFH	ROBERTS, Betty S.	24468	F7071	D-2
PRETE, Anna Marie	26484	R701	BD	ROBERTS, Cecelia E.	36046	F6025	BR-3
PRICE, Alcine F.	23027	R421	BPM	ROBERTS, David G.	20874	B350	MRO
PRICE, Helen L.	24391	F7032	GP	ROBERTS, Frederick S.	20534	B236	MLE
PRICE, Joyce Z. L.	37177	F7120	XP	ROBERTS, James L.	20883	B440	MTG
PRICE, Paul A.	20131	B521	TN	ROBERTS, John E., Jr.	20651	B421	BXC-1
PRICHARD, Reuben P., Jr.	24608	F6143	DY	ROBERTSON, Donald D.	26048	R624	BFP
PRIDGEN, Hope Y.	24854	R608	BFH	ROBERTSON, Francis E.	779-2121	R824	KSA
PRYOR, Harold E.	24717	BA1I	KDA-3	ROBINSON, Lorne M.	20061	B507	TS
PUDER, Albert, Jr.	22155	R424	DHZ	ROBINSON, Peter L., Jr.	20686	B426	MBM
PULLMAN, Lillian S.	26866	F7133	XP	ROBINSON, Ralph H.	35876	F5122C	SPA
PUMPHREY, Cheryl L.	28138	L5085	MAL	ROBINSON, Virginia F.	28041	F6051	FGM
PURINTON, Janet C.	25920	B125	KDP-1	ROCHEN, Herbert D.	20151	B612	RLC
PYLES, Joseph L.	21087	R612	BFH	ROCKELLI, Gerald H.	24145	F6124D	BT-1
				ROCKHOLD, B. Merle	27695	F5065	SRA
Q				ROGERS, Donald P.	37347	F5081	SCF-1
				ROGERS, Tiyette N.	24356	R609	BFH
QUINN, Herbert B.	24365	B200	Y	ROLLIN, Robert S.	22445	R507	DU
QUINTRELL, William	23703	R721	DHC-4	ROLLINS, Robert H., II	35854	B656	RX
				ROMAN, Nancy G., Dr.	22989	F5023	SG
R				ROSCHE, Melvin G.	20263	B647	RWS
				ROSE, Edward L.	21819	F6067	C
RADIUS, Walter A., Dr.	24583	F7101	W	ROSE, Walter H.	21359	R721	DHC-3
RAFEL, Norman	20671	B456	M-X	ROSEMAN, Howard M.	26806	B347	MHB
RAGSDALE, Milton M.	33883	L5065	MAR	ROSEN, Eugene D.	20531	L5072	KDM-MA
RALETICH, Edward	24827	F7121	XP				
RANDALL, William T.	34988	F7118	XC	ROSEN, Milton W.	24413	F7109	W
RANSOM, Brenda	35984	F6137	L	ROSENBERG, Frank T.	25777	B325	MF
RAPP, Robert A.	20061	B507	TS	ROSENBERG, Jerome D.	33361	F5085	SCD
RARING, Richard H.	35604	B647	RWN	ROSENBERRY, John W.	36230	F5119	SPI
RAU, Donald C.	28483	F6119	BR-1	ROSENBURGH, Arthur	36283	BA1F	KDP-3
RAWICZ, Leonard	24391	F7045	GP	ROSENFELD, Samuel A.	27427	B607	RET
RAY, Thomas W.	37371	R706	EH	ROTH, Gilbert L.	27934	F6083	OSP
RAYMOND, W. Jean	23253	R524	BPT	ROUCK, Barbara A.	20326	B400	MBD
REDDING, Edward R.	24365	B200	Y	ROUDEBUSH, William H., Dr.	28608	B600	RAA
REDFIELD, Marvin	20883	B440	MTG				
REDFIELD, Otis F.	37164	F6113	BR 2	ROUNSAVILLE, William R.	119-4347	EE476	NS-2
REECER, Robert L.	24796	R825	KSB				
REED, Judith D.	36985	F5086	SL	ROW, Charles R.	20894	F6058	BP-1
REED, Mary J.	26481	R527	BPT	ROWSOME, Frank H., Jr.	25185	R829	KSP
REEDER, Grace B.	37327	BA39	KSS-10	RUBIN, Bernard, Dr.	20141	B607	REE
REETZ, Arthur., Jr.	35854	B656	RX	RUBINSTEIN, Vivian T.	21537	F7087	I
REGALA, Susan J.	20446	L5057	MAP-7	RUDA, Mildred G.	37353	BA39	KSS-10
REKOS, Nelson F.	20183	B612	RLC	RUPERT, Gayle P.	21327	R721	DHC-5
RENFROW, Sandra H.	23074	R421	BPM	RYAN, Alfred L., Sr.	36943	B247	MLQ
RENIERE, Emile R.	20131	B521	TN	RYAN, Donald A.	26806	B347	MHB
RESPESS, Patricia A.	36206	F5011	K	RYAN, John F.	36995	B326	BXD
REYNOLDS, Minnie S.	119-4118	EE468	NS-2	RYAN, Thomas J.	36991	B326	BXE
RHODES, Hoyt M.	21523	B347	MHO	RYNEX, Charles D.	35691	B326	BXE
RICE, Ivan G.	23521	R824	KSA				
RICH, William B., Dr.	22562	R805	FE				

NAME	EXT	ROOM	CODE
S			
SACKS, Martin	22375	R511	DU
SAEGESSER, Lee D	37371	R706	EH
SAKSS, Uidis J	28079	F7090	I
SALIGA, Stephen A	21918	BA56	DHA-6
SALMANSON, Jay A	34045	F5086	SL
SALTERS, Theresa T	23703	R721	DHC-4
SANCHEZ, Edmund L	28188	B656	RMR
SANDERS, Angus W	24325	F7071	DI
SANDERS, June N	23074	R421	BPM
SANDY, Judith A	23027	R421	BPM
SANFORD, Heidemarie A	20106	B607	RE
SAUNDERS, James F., Jr	20457	L5017	MAE
SAUNDERS, Joseph F., Dr	26012	B409	MMR
SAUNDERS, Mary	41876	B125	KDP-1
SAUNDERS, Morris R	21313	B440	MRR-MT
SAVAGE, Melvyn	22071	B243	MLE
SAWMELLE, Stanley A	20593	BA1I	KDA-3
SAWYER, Gail M	33164	F7077	I
SCAFFIDI, Sandra J	25079	R829	KSP
SCALDAFERRI, Olga E	26270	R821	KSI
SCHAEFER, Herbert	21321	B431	MTE
SCHAIBLEY, John R	20523	L5042	MA
SCHANK, Wallace J	26357	R621	BFA
SCHARDT, Alois W., Dr	21731	F5035	SG
SCHARDT, Bruton B	34335	F5065	SRN
SCHEER, Julian	35302	F7019	F
SCHEIB, Walter S	119-3774	EE459	NS-2
SCHELLER, John A	23093	B243	MLE
SCHERER, Lee R	34882	L5084	MAL
SCHLAUDECKER, Julian H.	26484	R701	BDC
SCHMAHL, Antoinette B	20088	B500	TD
SCHMERLING, Erwin R., Dr.	21973	F5041	SG
SCHMID, Richard C	20418	B300	MMC
SCHMIDT, Carolyn A	21717	F6065	C
SCHMIDT, F. Robert	24534	F5109	SV
SCHNEIDER, Edward H	119-3036	EE468	NS-2
SCHNEIDER, William C	20633	B268	ML
SCHNYER, Arnold D	20388	B431	MTE
SCHOLZE, Anita L	24887	L5046	MAO
SCHRADER, Margaret	24336	R410	KT
SCHROCK, Paul D	23093	B243	MLE
SCHRUEFER, Norbert J	37152	F5122D	SPR
SCHRUNK, Raymond L	20006	B525	RF
SCHULHERR, Kay H	27377	F6069	C
SCHULHERR, Richard M	28696	R602	BPM-2
SCHULMAN, Fred, Dr	20091	B547	NS-1
SCHWARTZ, Ira R	20213	B600	RAS
SCHWARTZ, Ronald S	36586	B656	RMI
SCHWARTZ, Seymour	119-3774	EE459	NS-2
SCHWARZKOPF, Alexander J.	20587	L5058	MAP-1
SCHWENK, Francis C	119-4547	EE467	NS-2
SCOTT, Frank A	23910	B C-Lev.	DHA-31
SCOTT, Maxine E	37353	BA39	KSS-10
SCOTT, Russell S	23910	B C-Lev.	DHA-31
SCRIVENER, Nina	25077	F7137	AD
SEARS, Andrew F	24003	R605	KB
SEATON, Donald F., Jr	24891	F6147	AAD-4
SEDGWICK, Gail F	20260	R401	KM
SEDLAZEK, Martin F	36934	F7137	X
SEGAL, Jacques H	24281	B150	DHA-2
SEIGLE, Victor	22867	R812	FAP
SELLERS, Lana G	23825	F5041	SG
SEMANCIK, Mary J	20061	B507	TS
SENICH, Donald, Col	21967	L5079	MAL
SERICE, Dan S	20126	B521	TA
SETAGORD, Thomas	22195	R612	BFH
SEWELL, Lavonne P	23028	F7090	I
SHACKELFORD, Dorothy E.	23605	R721	DHC-1
SHADE, Anna M	35429	F6057	FGM
SHAFER, Edward M	21457	F7057	G
SHAFER, Robert J	36206	F5011	K
SHAFFER, Shirley M	24496	B412	MBR
SHAHEEN, Janie E	20061	B507	TS
SHANE, Donald M	21618	BA25	DHA-51
SHAPLEY, Willis H	24715	F137	ADA
SHAUKLAS, Victor F	26260	R824	KSA
SHAW, James R	20270	B440	MT
SHAW, Morton	34462	B325	MF
SHEAHAN, John P	27885	B242	MRR-ML
SHELDON, Lucille E	20183	B612	RL
SHERIDAN, Robert B	24887	L5031	MAO
SHILLITO, Thomas B	426-8889	B626	RO
SHIMEL, Wilbur H	25772	B426	MBP-2
SHIRLEY, William H	24091	L5008	MAL
SHIRO, Ethel L	24145	F6012B	BT-1
SHIVELY, Gloria L	20531	L5073	KDM-MA
SHOLTIS, Marilyn	24405	F6075	ABA
SHRUM, Karen B	24540	F5117	SPI
SHUPE, Peggy D	119-3036	EE468	NPO
SHUPE, Walter C	33242	F5137	D
SIGEL, Toby A	20464	B300	MMS
SILVERMAN, Donald	37346	F5081	SCE
SIMMONS, Ellsworth B	27247	B425	MBM
SIMPKINS, Sonya R	21236	F7089	I
SIMPSON, John P	21225	R721	DHC-5
SIPPEL, Joseph T	23253	R524	BPT
SKIDMORE, Donna J	20203	L5046	MA
SLACK, Vivian M	35983	F6137	L
SLIGH, Mary L	26918	R608	BFH
SLIVKA, William R	119-4567	EE463A	NS-2
SLOAD, Philip H	20570	B111	KD-5
SLOOP, John L	20937	B647	RC
SLUDER, Pamela H	25016	R825	KSB
SMART, Jacob E	23802	F7109	W
SMIALEK, Robert A	35691	D326	BXC
SMITH, Arcille	26167	R821	KSI
SMITH, Carol S	36934	F7137	X
SMITH, Donald B	27591	F5011	K
SMITH, Earl A	20566	B243	MLE
SMITH, F. Louise	35815	B647	RW
SMITH, Francis B	26596	B200	Y
SMITH, George C	26356	R621	BFA

NAME	EXT	ROOM	CODE	NAME	EXT	ROOM	CODE
SMITH, Henry J., Dr_____	35886	F5131	SS	STRASS, M. Kurt_____	26891	B556	RY
SMITH, Joan A_____	27884	B236	MRR–	STRIBLING, Thomas E. R.__	21543	F7090	I
			ML	STRICKLAND, Arthur T.___	24091	L5011	MAL
SMITH, Madison B_____	27582	R526	BP	STRING, Alfred C., Jr_____	37377	BA39	KSS–10
SMITH, Sandra I_____	21721	F6035	FP	STROBEL, Guenter K_____	24585	F5103	SL
SMITH, Saundra R_____	37167	F6015	BT–2	STROTHER, David H_____	21537	F7084	I
SMITH, Sheila K_____	26918	R608	BFH	STUCKMEYER, William E_	24705	B112	KDR
SMITH, William L_____	20435	B300	MMV	STUHRMANN, Robert H___	34447	B356	MRO
SMOLENSKY, Stanley M___	26529	F6141	E	STUMPF, John C_____	34773	F7018	XS
SMULL, Thomas L. K_____	20068	B600	RAA	STURDEVANT, William L.,	21841	F6061	C
SNOUFFER, F. Delma_____	119–3027	EE456	NS–2	Jr.			
SNYDER, David C_____	24631	F7121	XP	STURDIVANT, Ellen P_____	24853	R608	BFH
SNYDER, Herbert S_____	28646	R721	DHC	STURGILL, C. Quentin_____	20874	B350	MRO
SNYDER, Mary F._____	24965	F5055	SL	SUDDRETH, Jack A_____	20081	B612	RLC
SNYDER, Samuel_____ 119–3182	ED402		NS–2	SUIT, Marlene A_____	20242	B356	MRT
SOMEGUESTAVA, June E__	26611	F7032	GP	SULLIVAN, Edward T_____	24336	R410	KT
SONDHEIMER, Jo A_____	26484	R701	BD	SULLIVAN, Francis J_____	26162	B656	BF–RM
SOPER, Josephine A_____	36925	F6043	FP	SULLIVAN, Frank J_____	20106	B607	RE
SOUTHARD, John B_____	24442	B B-Lev.	DHA–53	SULLIVAN, Patricia A_____	24635	R822	KS
SOUTHER, Sharon A_____	20596	B400	MED	SULLIVAN, Walter B_____	22568	B300	MMC
SOWARD, Margaret C____ 119–3353	EE480		NS–2	SUMMERFELT, William A_	20431	B368	MHE
SPADE, Joan P_____	24701	R406	KT	SUMMERS, Garth E_____	35591	B326	BXB
SPAN, Florence_____	34882	L5084	MAL	SUMMERS, Robert A., Dr_	24563	F5065	SRF
SPANN, Charolette B_____	24079	R721	DHC–4	SUMMIT, Irving_____	37167	F6015	BT–2
SPARGO, Robert A_____	26904	B136	KDA–1	SURES, Allan H_____	21983	F5029	SG
SPARGUR, Jean B_____	21841	F6061	C	SUTHERLAND, Franklin P_	33046	R519	BPC
SPEAKE, Edwin R_____	25935	R627	BFC	SUTTER, Allan_____	22305	W-Bldg.	DHA–4
SPENCER, James K_____	37236	R512	Z	SWEENEY, Carol A_____	24496	B412	MRD
SPENCER, Paulette L_____	26002	B421	MME	SWEET, Floyd J_____	24707	F7112	WX
SPERRY, Harry C_____	26268	R621	BFA	SWETNICK, Martin J., Dr__	36523	F5065	SRG
SPERRY, John W., Jr_____	36086	B243	MLE	SWILLING, Nora_____	24089	R721	DHC–1
SPREEN, William C_____	37497	F5065	SRM	SWORD, Norma J_____	20674	B421	MBB–2
SPRIGGS, Barbara T_____	23602	R522	BPL	SYLVIA, Francis R_____	24496	B412	MBB–1
SPRINCE, Richard H_____	20077	B440	MT–1	SYLVIA, Jane G_____	20674	B421	MBB–2
ST CLAIR, Wade_____	21571	F6107	FG				
STALEY, Raymond M_____	24193	B101	KD			**T**	
STALEY, Shirley_____ 426–3253	10A 327		BG–1				
STANFORD, Robert J_____	24145	F6124D	BT–1	TALTAVULL, Linda M_____	34967	R519	BPC
STANTON, Charles I_____	21710	B347	MHO	TARVER, Paul_____	36985	F5086	SL
STARR, Gloria F_____	21877	B125	KDP–1	TATE, Franklin G_____	37807	F5117	SPI
STARUCH, Mary_____	21682	F7057	G	TAUB, William P_____	21721	F6035	FP
STAUGHTON, Harry_____	37164	F6113	BR–2	TAVARES, Ronald J_____	34904	R808	FAE
STEADMON, Curtis_____	23910	B C-Lev.	DHA–31	TAYLOR, Arthur S_____	36283	BA1F	KDP–3
STEARNS, John F_____	23648	R822	KS	TAYLOR, Bernice M_____	35302	F7019	F
STEELE, Evelyn B_____	20426	B431	MTX	TAYLOR, Charles A_____	20011	B500	TN
STEELE, Stella M_____	37177	F7120	XP	TAYLOR, Eldon D_____	21125	F5123	SP
STEIN, Joseph A_____	20117	B526	TN	TAYMAN, Susan M_____	37518	F5137	D
STEINLE, Werner C_____	20286	B568	RRT	TEMPLETON, Edna F_____	20213	B600	RVD
STEINMETZ, Carl F_____	24765	R405	KMB	TENNYSON, George P., Jr__	34335	F5065	SRN
STEPHENS, Robert R_____	20061	B507	TS	TEPPER, Morris, Dr_____	36521	F5065	SRD
STEPHENSON, Frank W.,	20048	B625	RPX	TERRELL, Vivian D_____	20506	B145	KL
Jr.				TERRILL, Diane E_____	24891	F6147	AAD–4
STERNFIELD, Leonard_____	25747	B600	RAS	TERWILLIGER, Richard G._	33841	F5065	SRO
STEVEN, Fred R_____	37277	F6011	AAD–3	TESCH, Gary L_____	26844	B225	GK
STEVENS, Edwin H_____	21532	R424	DHZ	TETIRICK, Harry E_____	24728	B125	KDP–1
STEVENSON, Geneva J_____	22392	F6031	BR	THACKER, Ellen S_____	20246	B133	KDA–31
STEVENSON, John D_____	20596	B400	MED	THEISEN, Roland W_____	20117	B526	TC
STEWART, Frank S_____	20688	B426	MBM	THIBIDEAU, Philip A_____	21925	F7077	I
STOCK, Richard L_____	20117	B526	TC	THIRINGER, Thomas P____	20681	B400	MB–1
STOCKWELL, Ephriam J___	20002	B512	TN	THOM, Karlheinz Dr_____ 119–4347	EE477		NS–2
STONEY, William E., Jr____	37348	L5039	MAE	THOMAS, Ruth_____	21993	F7090	I
STORM, Richard E_____	36943	B247	MLQ	THOME, Pitt G_____	20891	F5065	SRE

NAME	EXT	ROOM	CODE
THOMPSON, David W_____	26481	R527	BPA
THOMPSON, Dolores O_____	20295	B440	MTG
THOMPSON, John F_____	20969	R502	KME
THOMPSON, Pearl B_____	23453	R401	KMA
THOMPSON, Raymond W., Jr.	24205	F7101	W
THOMPSON, William M____	37767	R628	BFG
THOMSON, Patricia I_____	37347	F5081	SCF
THORNE, Muriel M_____	22560	R805	FE
THORNE, Victoria R_____	33361	F5081	SCD
THORPE, Cynthia M_____	35767	R506	BPM
THWEATT, Frank M., Jr___	23481	R526	BPE
TIEMANN, Robert S_____	22722	R805	FE
TIERNEY, Louis M_____	20874	B340	RX–MR
TILLING, Robert I., Dr_____	37831	L5088	MAL
TISCHLER, Adelbert O_____	22521	B541	RS
TODD, Gloria L_____	24351	F6093	FGA
TOLIAFERRO, Gloria T____	37371	R706	EH
TOMAYKO, Donald W_____	24842	F5122C	SPA
TOMPKINS, James M_____	20117	B526	KDS–TC
TOMPKINS, Lizzie S_____	24089	R721	DHC–1
TOMS, Ronald_____	34045	F5086	SL
TORREY, Volta W_____	25070	R829	KSP
TRAVAGLIA, Mary M_____	22313	R424	DHZ
TRAVIS, Linda M_____	27591	F5005	K
TREXLER, May B_____	27367	BA36	BG–1
TRUNK, Mary V_____	24532	F5113	SV
TRUSZYNSKI, Gerald M___	24703	B500	T
TSACOUMIS, Theofolus P___	20141	B607	REE
TULIP, Charles, Jr_____	37164	F6113	BR–2
TURNER, Don N_____	22861	B325	MF
TUTTLE, Frederick B., Dr___	33532	R801	FE
TYNER, Ralph W_____	20138	B137	KL

U

NAME	EXT	ROOM	CODE
ULMER, Ralph E_____	24145	F6124B	BT–1
UNGER, Bernard_____	21586	R421	BPM
UNRUH, Rufus C_____	21203	B656	BP–2

V

NAME	EXT	ROOM	CODE
VACCA, Gene A_____	22393	B243	MLE
VACTOR, Margaret A_____	37278	F6147	AAD–2
VAN SCHAACK, Phyllis J___	37987	B216	KDM–ML
VANDEVENTER, Nancy M_	35370	B556	RY
VEATER, John H_____	36586	B656	RMI
VECCHIETTI, George J____	20697	B101	KD
VELANDER, Wallace E_____	20074	R401	KM
VINCE, Rebekah A_____	28188	B656	RMR
VINOGRAD, Sherman P., M.D.	26011	B409	MMR
VINSON, Norman_____	26869	B112	KDR
VIRGIL, Adelaide K_____	20315	B431	MTE
VIRGIL, Lloyd B_____	24185	B212	Y
VITAGLIANO, James_____	33669	B326	BXB
VITALE, Joseph A_____	23310	B200	Y
VLANNES, Peppino N_____	24638	R822	KS
VOELKER, Donald E_____	23253	R524	BPT
VOGEL, Lawrence W_____	24513	F5001	DH
VOGLEWEDE, Kay E_____	25036	R829	KSP

NAME	EXT	ROOM	CODE
VOGT, Rebecca Ann_____	20408	L5066	MAR
VON BRAUN, Wernher, Dr__	24938	F7137	AAD
VONSAUNDER, Raymond O.	20534	B236	MLB

W

NAME	EXT	ROOM	CODE
WACHTER, Marcia G_____	27582	R526	BP
WADDELL, Dorothy A_____	24002	R605	KB
WADE, Margaret E_____	25935	B347	MH
WADLIN, Kenneth L_____	36985	F5086	SL
WAGGONER, Miles M_____	36926	F6043	FP
WAGNER, Charles L_____	26484	R701	BD
WALKER, Ann L_____	22071	B243	MLE
WALKER, Betty B_____	20017	B300	MMD
WALKER, Delores Y_____	22475	R721	DHC–5
WALKER, John H_____	20026	B568	RPR
WALKER, John W_____	24281	B150	DHA–2
WALKER, Joseph D_____	24765	R405	KMF
WALKER, Kathryn C_____	24034	R526	BPR
WALKER, Kathryn K_____	20546	B336	MRS
WALKER, Louisa_____	24636	F5011	K
WALLACE, Dorothy L. M___	20666	B419	M–N
WALLACE, Frankie L_____	20246	B133	KDA–31
WALLACE, Kathy R_____	22305	W-Bldg.	DHA–4
WALLACE, William M_____	24887	L5031	MAO
WALLER, Forrest E_____	37413	B356	MRI
WALLIS, Marvin G_____	35281	R411	KMC
WALLS, Linwood_____	34773	F7018	XS
WALSH, Francis_____	37167	F6015	BT–2
WARD, Molly K_____	20131	B521	TN
WARDEN, John H_____	21738	F7037	GP
WARE, Margaret S_____	21721	F6035	FP
WARREN, Barbara A_____	24145	F6012B	BT–1
WARREN, Lawrence E_____	27700	BA19	DHA–50
WASEL, Robert A_____	21808	B625	RPX
WASH, Charles E_____	37152	F5122D	SPR
WASHINGTON, Althea R___	26054	R611	BFH
WASICKO, Richard J_____	20067	B600	RAL
WATERS, Arrell B_____	21653	F5035	SG
WATERS, William R_____	21891	R625	BFP
WATKINS-BULL, June_____	24001	R601	KB
WATSON, Claudia M_____	26960	B112	KDR
WATSON, James M_____	779–2121	R823	KSI
WATTS, Lenore B_____	20051	B536	RFS
WAUGH, Merle G_____	20031	B440	MT–3
WAVRO, Paula J_____	27884	B244	MRR–ML
WEAKLEY, Charles E_____	33748	F6137	L
WEAVER, Arell E_____	20874	B350	MRO
WEAVER, Joenne K_____	119–4347	EE480	NS–2
WEBER, Sally H_____	23429	R721	DHC–1
WEBER, Shirley B_____	23363	B656	RMD
WEBER, William J_____	20774	B512	TN
WEBSTER, Grove_____	27582	R526	BP
WEBSTER, Kenneth R_____	20774	B512	TN
WEEKS, Robert A_____	21967	L5076	MAL
WEINBERG, Irving, Dr____	20187	B647	RWM
WEINGARTEN, Sylvia R___	26919	R608	BFH
WEINLEY, Doris C_____	28023	R721	DHC–6
WEIR, James F., Jr_____	21030	F5122C	BX–SP

NAME	EXT	ROOM	CODE
WEISE, Janet M.	21457	F7057	G
WEISS, Howard M.	24933	B155	KR
WEISSMAN, Norman W., Dr.	26024	B409	MMR
WELCH, Lawrence W.	24827	F7121	XP
WELDON, James M.	20157	F5029	SG
WENTE, Van A.	24796	R825	KSB
WERNER, Leo N., Dr.	24474	B256	MLA
WEST, George R.	24145	F6012A	BT-1
WESTFALL, Dale S.	36161	B236	MLB
WESTFALL, Judy A.	20214	B600	RAV
WETHERINGTON, Ryndal L.	26201	B368	MHE
WETZEL, Paul F.	20201	B541	RS
WEXLER, Lewis	20061	B507	TS
WHEELER, Roger E.	20131	B521	TN
WHETZEL, Judith A.	26849	B225	GK
WHITE, Annie R.	20669	F6015	BT
WHITE, George C., Jr.	20408	L5066	MQD
WHITE, Geraldine F.	20146	F5030	SG
WHITE, Helen M.	24728	B125	KDP-1
WHITE, Pearl C.	28072	R519	BPC
WHITE, Richard P.	25086	B136	KDP-2
WHITE, Stanley C., Col., USAF, MC	20401	B300	MMS
WHITFIELD, Shirley A.	23253	R524	BPT
WHITLEY, Susan K.	20894	F6050	BP-1
WHITLEY, Warren R.	21618	BA25	DHA-51
WHITNEY, John A.	21325	B225	GK
WHITTEN, Raymond P.	20313	B626	RBT
WIBLE, M. Keith	20661	B368	MR
WICKS, Selden	22010	R606	BFH
WILBUR, Stafford W.	20081	B612	RLC
WILCOX, Ward W.	20047	B625	RPX
WILD, Jack W., Dr.	20315	B431	MTE
WILHELM, John R.	22861	B325	MF
WILKEN, William J.	34818	B111	KDP-3
WILKENS, Charles S.	21609	F5128	KDS-SP
WILLIAMS, Charles	28483	F6119	BR-1
WILLIAMS, Francis L.	36914	F6011	AAD-3
WILLIAMS, Inez C.	20687	B426	MBM
WILLIAMS, Jane P.	20697	B101	KD
WILLIAMS, Manning H.	23702	F6099	FG
WILLIAMS, Richard W.	26475	B236	MLB
WILLIAMS, Rose K.	20242	B350	MRO
WILLIAMS, William E., Jr.	20002	B512	TN
WILLIAMS, Wynell	24774	BA36	BG
WILLIAMS, Yvonne H.	21700	F7062	GL
WILLIAMSON, C. Imogene	26470	F6093	FGA
WILLIAMSON, David, Jr.	37919	F6147	AA
WILLIS, Norman J.	35592	B326	BXB
WILLOUGHBY, Willis J.	33805	L5067	MAQ
WILSON, James H.	25086	B136	KDP-2
WILSON, Phyllis A.	20176	B600	RA
WILSON, Robert G., Dr.	26812	F5129	SF
WILSON, Wilbur A.	20531	L5073	KDM-MA
WINBLADE, Roger L.	25747	B600	RAV
WINES, Harriette B.	24506	B168	DHA
WING, Mildred D.	22727	F6069	C
WINSBORO, Robert B.	37808	F5117	SPP
WINSLOW, Diana S.	37987	B216	KDM-ML
WINTE, Ralph F.	24325	F7071	DI
WINTERHALTER, David, L.	20495	L5009	MAL
WISE, Candice	23073	R421	BPM
WISNIEWSKI, Richard J.	23363	B656	RX
WITCZAK, Leonard T.	26484	R701	BDU
WOJTAL, Robert J.	26860	B225	GK
WOLF, Richard N.	21683	B225	GK
WONG, Henry P.	20566	B243	MLE
WOOD, Charles P.	33754	L5061	MAR
WOOD, Clotaire	755-4347	B626	RO
WOOD, E. Darlene	24286	F6053	F-3
WOOD, George H.	20531	L5073	KDM-MA
WOODS, Clifford L., Jr.	21618	BA25	DHA-51
WOODS, James S.	20674	B421	MBB-2
WOODWARD, William H.	20021	B568	RP
WORKMAN, Joseph D.	23453	R405	KMA
WOYTOVICH, Paul	20774	B512	TN
WRIGHT, Dorothy M.	22726	F6069	C
WYATT, Demarquis D., Dr.	37297	F6147	AAD-1

Y

NAME	EXT	ROOM	CODE
YANCEY, Zenobia R.	37393	BA50	KSS-10
YATES, Joyce A.	20006	B536	RF
YEICH, Helga S.	20234	B356	BP-3
YETTER, Charles R.	20537	B211	KDM-ML
YOUNG, Gifford A.	26139	R821	KSI
YOUNG, Judith A.	119-3036	EE468	NS-2
YOUNG, Richard S., Dr.	24965	F5055	SL
YOUNGER, Anna M.	24357	R609	BFH

Z

NAME	EXT	ROOM	CODE
ZEBRASKY, Helen R.	25468	F5091	SL
ZIEM, Robert W.	20151	B612	RLS
ZIMMERMAN, Bonnie J.	35752	F6031	BR
ZISELBERGER, August R.	119-4347	EE476	NS-2
ZITO, Albert P.	23956	B425	MBM
ZIVKOVICH, George	25777	B325	MF
ZUCCARDY, Charles A.	25046	B125	KDP-1
ZYLSTRA, Donald L.	20331	R808	FAE

LOCATION OF NASA MAJOR AND COMPONENT INSTALLATIONS

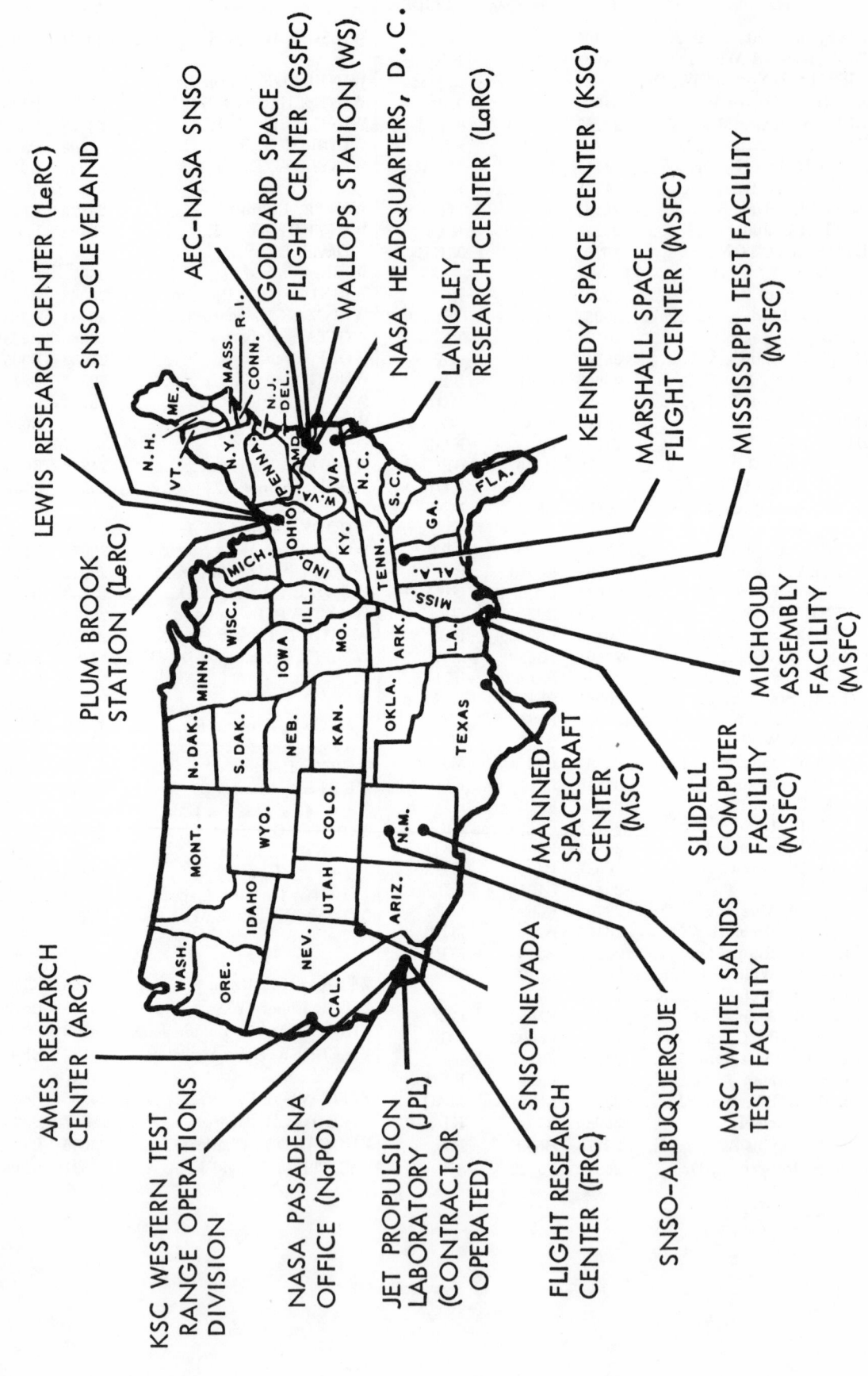

OFFICIAL INSTALLATION ADDRESSES

	Installation	Installation Telephone Information Number
HEADQUARTERS_____	National Aeronautics and Space Administration_____ (Note: No street address is to be used) Washington, D.C. 20546	202–963–7101
ARC_____	Ames Research Center_____ National Aeronautics and Space Administration Moffett Field, Calif. 94035 Director: Dr. Hans M. Mark	415–961–1111
FRC_____	Flight Research Center_____ National Aeronautics and Space Administration P.O. Box 273 Edwards, Calif. 93523 Director: Mr. Paul F. Bikle	805–258–3311
GSFC_____	Goddard Space Flight Center_____ National Aeronautics and Space Administration Greenbelt, Md. 20771 Director: Dr. John F. Clark	301–982–5042
GI FOR SS_____	Goddard Institute For Space Studies_____ National Aeronautics and Space Administration 2880 Broadway New York: N.Y. 10025 Director: Dr. Robert Jastrow	212–866–3600
JPL_____	Jet Propulsion Laboratory_____ 4800 Oak Grove Dr. Pasadena, Calif. 91103 Director: Dr. William H. Pickering	213–354–4321
KSC_____	John F. Kennedy Space Center_____ National Aeronautics and Space Administration Kennedy Space Center, Fla. 32899 Director: Dr. Kurt H. Debus	305–867–7113
KSC–WTROD_____	KSC Western Test Range Operations Division_____ National Aeronautics and Space Administration P.O. Box 425 Lompoc, Calif. 93436 Chief: Mr. H. R. Van Goey	805–866–1611
LaRC_____	Langley Research Center_____ National Aeronautics and Space Administration Langley Station Hampton, Va. 23365 Director: Mr. Edgar M. Cortright	703–827–1110

OFFICIAL INSTALLATION ADDRESSES—Continued

Installation		Installation Telephone Information Number
LeRC	Lewis Research Center National Aeronautics and Space Administration 21000 Brookpark Rd. Cleveland, Ohio 44135 Director: Mr. Bruce T. Lundin	216–433–4000
MSC	Manned Spacecraft Center National Aeronautics and Space Administration Houston, Texas 77058 Director: Dr. Robert R. Gilruth	713–483–3111
MSFC	George C. Marshall Space Flight Center National Aeronautics and Space Administration Marshall Space Flight Center, Ala. 35812 Director: Dr. Eberhard Rees	205–453–2121
MICHOUD	Michoud Assembly Facility National Aeronautics and Space Administration P.O. Box 29300 New Orleans, La. 70129 Manager: Mr. James L. Stamy (Act.)	504–255–3311
MISSISSIPPI	Mississippi Test Facility National Aeronautics and Space Administration Bay St. Louis, Miss. 39520 Manager: Mr. Jackson M. Balch	601–688–2211
NaPO	NASA Pasadena Office 4800 Oak Grove Dr. Pasadena, Calif. 91103 Director: Mr. Earle J. Sample	213–354–4321
SNSO Germantown	AEC–NASA Space Nuclear Systems Office U.S. Atomic Energy Commission Washington, D.C. 20545 Manager: Mr. Milton Klein	301–973–1000
PLUM BROOK	Plum Brook Station National Aeronautics and Space Administration Sandusky, Ohio 44871 Director: Mr. Alan D. Johnson	419–625–1123
SNPO: ALBUQUERQUE	Space Nuclear Systems Office—Albuquerque National Aeronautics ad Space Administration P.O. Box 5400 Albuquerque, N. Mex. 87115 Chief: Mr. Jack F. Cully	505–264–7221
CLEVELAND	Space Nuclear Systems Office—Cleveland National Aeronautics and Space Administration Lewis Research Center 21000 Brookpark Road Cleveland, Ohio 44135 Chief: Mr. Robert W. Schroeder	216–433–6286

OFFICIAL INSTALLATION ADDRESSES—Continued

	Installation	Installation Telephone Information Number
NEVADA	Space Nuclear Systems Office—Nevada National Aeronautics and Space Administration Nuclear Rocket Development Station P.O. Box 1 Jackass Flats, Nev. 89023 Chief: Mr. John P. Jewett	702–986–5721
WALLOPS	Wallops Station National Aeronautics and Space Administration Wallops Island, Va. 23337 Director: Mr. Robert L. Krieger	703–824–3411
White Sands	MSC White Sands Test Facility National Aeronautics and Space Administration P.O. Drawer MM Las Cruces, N. Mex. 88001 Manager: Mr. Kenneth B. Gilbreath	505–524–5011
Australian Representative	NASA Senior Scientific Representative in Australia NASA Canberra Office c/o Department of Supply Canberra, A.C.T. 2600 Australia Mr. Willson H. Hunter	
European Representative	NASA European Representative c/o American Embassy APO. N.Y., New York 09777 Mr. Robert E. Bernier	
Spanish Representative	NASA Representative in Spain Madrid Space Station INTA–NASA Oficina Central Orense, 11, 5°A Madrid 20, Spain Mr. Henry Schultz	

OFFICIAL INSTALLATION ADDRESSES—Continued

NASA Regional Audit Offices

Address	Telephone	NASA Audit Manager
NASA Audit Office Ames Research Center Mail Stop 237-7 Moffett Field, Calif. 94035	415–961–2043	Mr. Michio Nakajima
NASA Audit Office Post Office Box 2500 Daytona Beach, Fla. 32015	904–258–4447	Mr. William Norwalk
NASA Regional Audit Office Goddard Space Flight Center Code 200.1 Greenbelt, Md. 20771	301-982-5561	Mr. Samuel Regal
NASA Regional Audit Office John F. Kennedy Space Center (Code AUD) Kennedy Space Center, Fla. 32899	305–867–4664	Mr. Gerald Greenway
NASA Regional Audit Office Mail Stop 450, Bldg. 1149T Langley Research Center Hampton, Va. 23365	703-827-1110	Mr. Searcy Smith
NASA Regional Audit Office Lewis Research Center, MS 500–311 21000 Brookpark Road Cleveland, Ohio 44135	216–433–6683	Mr. D. Thomas Smith
NASA Regional Audit Office Manned Spacecraft Center Houston, Tex. 77058	713–483–3151	Mr. Claude Lynch
NASA Regional Audit Office, MSFC Room 343, Bldg. 4202, MDU–MSFC Marshall Space Flight Center, Ala. 35812	205–453–3620	Mr. Samuel Huffstetler
NASA Audit Office Michoud Assembly Facility, Bldg. 101 Post Office Box 29300 New Orleans, La. 70129	504–255–3465	Mr. Fred Schmitt
NASA Western Regional Audit Office Federal Building, Room 13113 11000 Wilshire Boulevard Los Angeles, Calif. 90024	213–824–7555	Mr. Earle Smith

OFFICIAL INSTALLATION ADDRESSES—Continued

NASA Regional Inspectors

Address	Telephone	NASA Regional Inspector
Southern Regional Inspections Office Room 3342, KSC Headquarters Building John F. Kennedy Space Center/NASA Kennedy Space Center, Florida 32815	305–867–4714	Roy E. Wood
Southern Regional Inspections Office Room 329, Building 4202 George C. Marshall Space Flight Center/NASA Marshall Space Flight Center, Alabama 35812	205–453–4123	Francis X. Kane
Western Regional Inspections Office Mail Stop 237–4 Ames Research Center Moffett Field, California 94035	415–961–2892	William J. Hurley
Southwestern Regional Inspections Office Room 963, Building 2 Manned Spacecraft Center Houston, Texas 77058	713–483–3960	Glenn L. McAvoy

NASA Liaison Personnel With the National Aeronautics and Space Council [1]

Aeronautics Staff	John H. Enders	3562
	Joseph Stickle	3562
Space Staff	Jack Posner	3526
	John E. Morrissey	3562
	Lester K. Fero	3593
Mail Stop: 28	P.O. Address: National Aeronautics and Space Council, Executive Office of the President, Washington, D.C. 20502	

[1] 395 plus extension.

SOURCE: NASA, "NASA Headquarters Telephone Directory," 1971.

ADDRESSES

Station Name - TWX Designation

ASCENSION ISLAND   GACN

Attention: Station Director
NASA-Devil's Ashpit Station
P. O. Box 4187, Ascension AAF
Patrick AFB, Florida 32925

BERMUDA   GBDA

Attention: Station Director
NASA Station (Bermuda)
Box 7015
FPO N.Y., N.Y.   09560

CANBERRA (PRIME SITE MSFN)   AHSK

Attention: Station Director
Honeysuckle Creek Tracking Station
P. O. Box 369
Manuka
Australian Capital Territory
Australia 2603

CANBERRA (MSFN WING)   ANBE

Attention: Station Director
DSS 42 (MSFN WING) Tidbinbilla
P. O. Box 350
Kingston, Australian Capital Territory
Australia 2604

CARNARVON   ACRO

Attention: Station Director
Tracking Station
P. O. Box 348
Carnarvon, Western Australia, 6701
Australia

Air Parcel Post or First Class Airmail Packages:

The Manager
Stores and Transport Branch
Department of Supply
Box 4052, G.P.O.
Sydney,
New South Wales
Australia 2001
(For Carnarvon Tracking Station, W. A.)

CORPUS CHRISTI, TEXAS   GTEX

Attention: Station Director
NASA Manned Space Flight Tracking Station
P. O. Box 8289
Corpus Christi, Texas 78412

GOLDSTONE   GGDS

Attention: Station Director
NASA/MSFN Tracking Station
P. O. Box 789
Barstow, California 92311

GRAND BAHAMA ISLAND   GGBM

Attention: Station Director
NASA/MSFN Tracking Station
Grand Bahama Island (GBM)
P. O. Box 4187
PAFB, Florida 32925

CANARY ISLAND   LCYI

Attention: Station Director
NASA/MSFN Station
Apartado 48
Las Palmas, Grand Canary Is., Spain

GUAM   PGWM

Attention: Station Director
NASA Tracking Station
DanDan, Guam 96910

HAWAII   PHAW

Attention: Station Director
NASA/MSFN Station
P.O. Box 538
Waimea, Kauai, Hawaii 96796
M/F STADIR

MADRID   LMAD

Attention: Station Director
NASA/INTA (MSFN)
Attn: (Title of Individual or Section)
Apartado 50860
Madrid, Spain

MERRITT ISLAND   GMIL

Attention: Station Director
NASA Tracking Station
P. O. Box 1947
Titusville, Florida 32980

MSFN VANGUARD   MVAN

Attention: Station Director
NASA-Vanguard Tracking Station
P. O. Box 96
Cape Canaveral, Florida 32920
                              or
(when ship is away for extended periods)
Attention: Station Director
NASA Vanguard Tracking Station
c/o USNS Vanguard (T-AGN-19)
Fleet Post Office
New York, New York 09501

NASA STADAN STATION ADDRESSES

Station Name – TWX Designation

ORRORAL (CANBERRA), AUSTRALIA   AORR

Attention: Station Director
STADAN Facility
Orroral Valley
P. O. Box 585
Canberra City, A.C.T. Australia 2604

FAIRBANKS, ALASKA   GULA

NASA STADAN Station
P. O. Box 1307
Fairbanks, Alaska   99701

FORT MYERS, FLORIDA   GYRS

NASA STADAN Station
Daniels Road
Route 3, Box 20
Fort Myers, Florida   33901

JOHANNESBURG, SOUTH AFRICA   GBUR

The Director
National Institute for Telecommunications Research
    (Attention: NASA STADAN Station:
                Johannesburg)
P. O. Box 3718
Johannesburg
TRANSVAAL
Republic of South Africa

MOJAVE, CALIFORNIA   GAVE

NASA STADAN Station, Mojave
P. O. Box 727
Barstow, California   92311

QUITO, ECUADOR   CQUI

NASA STADAN Station
U. S. Embassy
Quito, Ecuador

ROSMAN, NORTH CAROLINA   GROS

NASA STADAN Station
Rosman, North Carolina   28772

SANTIAGO, CHILE   GAGO

NASA Director
Santiago, Chile - Embassy
c/o Department of State
Washington, D.C. 20521
Mark: "VIA AIR MAIL"

TANANARIVE, MADAGASCAR   LTAN

NASA Station Director
Tananarive, Madagascar
c/o Department of State
Washington, D.C. 20521
Mark: "VIA AIR MAIL"

WINKFIELD, ENGLAND   LWNK

S.R.C. Station Director
NASA STADAN Station
Winkfield Field Station, S.R.C.
Pigeonhouse Lane
Winkfield
Berkshire, England
(Station Matters)

The Director
Radio & Space Research Station, S.R.C.
Ditton Park
Slough Bucks, England
(Policy Matters)

NASA SWITCHING CENTERS ADDRESSES

Station Name - TWX Designation

HONOLULU, HAWAII PHON

Attention: Station Manager
NASA Switching Center
P. O. Box 2200
Honolulu, Hawaii   96805

LONDON, ENGLAND LLDN

Attention: Station Manager
NASA Communications Switching Center
Room 1A, Electra House
Victoria Embankment
London W.C. 2, England

Parcel Post Address:

NASA Communications Switching Center
Box 74
c/o FPO N.Y., N.Y.   09510

MADRID, SPAIN   LROB

Attention: Station Director
NASCOM Switching Center
NASA-INTA
APARTADO 50719
Madrid, Spain

Parcel Post Address:

NASCOM Switching Center
NASA-INTA
APARTADO 50719
Madrid, Spain

DEAKIN A.C.T., AUSTRALIA   ACSW

Officer in Charge
NASCOM Switching Centre
Deakin Telephone Exchange Building
Kent Street
Deakin A.C.T.
Australia,   2600

Air Parcel Post Address:
The Manager
Stores and Transport Branch
Department of Supply
Box 4052 G.P.O.
Sydney
New South Wales
Australia,   2001
(For NASCOM Switching Centre
    Deakin A.C.T.)

SOURCE: NASA, "Goddard Space Flight Center Telephone Directory," 1971.

Part 4

NASA STATISTICS

UNITED STATES SPACECRAFT RECORD

Year	Earth orbit		Earth escape		Year	Earth orbit		Earth escape	
	Success	Failure	Success	Failure		Success	Failure	Success	Failure
1957.	0	1	0	0	1965.	94	8	3	0
1958.	5	8	0	4	1966.	95	12	5	[1] 1
1959.	9	9	1	2	1967.	77	4	10	0
1960.	16	12	1	2	1968.	61	15	3	0
1961.	35	12	0	0	1969.	58	1	8	1
1962.	54	12	4	1	1970.	36	1	3	0
1963.	60	11	0	0					
1964.	69	8	4	0	Total.	669	114	42	11

[1] This earth escape failure did attain earth orbit and therefore is included in the earth-orbit success totals.

Notes: The criterion of success or failure used is the attainment of earth orbit or earth escape rather than a judgment of mission success.

This tabulation includes spacecraft from cooperating countries which were launched by U.S. launch vehicles.

SOURCE: National Aeronautics and Space Council, "Aeronautics and Space Report of the President," 1971.

WORLD RECORD OF SPACE LAUNCHINGS SUCCESSFUL IN ATTAINING EARTH ORBIT OR BEYOND

Year	United States	U.S.S.R.	France	Italy	Australia	Japan	Red China
1957.		2					
1958.	5	1					
1959.	10	3					
1960.	16	3					
1961.	29	.6					
1962.	52	20					
1963.	38	17					
1964.	57	30					
1965.	63	48	1				
1966.	73	44	1				
1967.	57	66	2	1	1		
1968.	45	74					
1969.	40	70					
1970.	28	81	2	[1] 1		1	1
Total.	513	465	6	2	1	1	1

[1] Includes foreign launchings of U.S. spacecraft.

Note: This tabulation enumerates launchings rather than spacecraft. Some launches did successfully orbit multiple spacecraft.

SOURCE: National Aeronautics and Space Council, "Aeronautics and Space Report of the President," 1971.

SUCCESSFUL UNITED STATES LAUNCHES: 1969

Launch date (Gmt) Spacecraft name Cospar designation Launch vehicle	Spacecraft data	Apogee and Perigee (in statute miles)— Period (minutes)— Inclination to Equator (degrees)	Remarks
Jan. 22 OSO–V Thor-Delta	Objective: To obtain high-spectral resolution data from pointed experiments from approximately 1 to 1,250 Angstrom during at least 1 solar rotation period including roster scans of the solar disk in selected wave lengths; to obtain extended observation data from the nonpointed experiments of single lines and solar flares. Spacecraft: Revolving 9-sided polyhedron 44-in. diameter and 15-in. high with sun-pointing 22-in. radius semicircular sail; spin stabilized; 26-watt solar cell power supply; weight: 636 lbs.	353 338 95.8 33.0	Continues OSO I, II, III and IV investigations of the Sun. Spacecraft carried 8 experiments. All functioned normally.
Jan. 22 Defense 7A Titan IIIB/Agena	Objective: Development of space flight techniques and technologies. Spacecraft: Not announced.	672.5 92.0 96.9 106.1	Decayed Feb. 3, 1969.
Jan. 30 ISIS–I 9A Thrust-augmented Thor-Delta	Objective: To obtain information about the ionosphere in the region above the F-layer maximum; the distribution of free electrons and the various species of ions as a function of time and position; the composition and fluxes of the energetic particles which interact with the ionosphere; and the velocity distribution of thermal electrons and ions. Spacecraft: 8-sided oblate spheroid with diameter of 50-in and height of 42-in.; spin stabilized; 90 watt solar cell power supply; weight: 520 lbs.	2,186 356 128.3 88.4	This is the third in a series of 5 spacecraft in a joint United States-Canadian ionospheric research program. Nine of ten experiments functioned normally; 10th experiment functioned partially. Mission judged successful.
Feb. 5 Defense 10A Thor/Agena	Objective: Development of space flight techniques and technology. Spacecraft: Not announced.	171.0 91.7 88.7 81.6	Decayed Feb. 24, 1969.
Feb. 5 Defense 10B Thor/Agena	Objective: Development of space flight techniques and technology. Spacecraft: Not announced.	894.9 866.4 114.1 80.4	Still in orbit.
Feb. 6 Intelsat III (F–3) 11A Thrust-augmented Thor-Delta	Objective: To provide equivalent of 1,200 two-way voice circuits or 4 color TV channels to carry commercial communications traffic between the United States, Hawaii, and the Western Pacific. Spacecraft: Cylindrical 56-in. diameter and 78-in. high; spin-stabilized; 300-watt solar cell power supply; weight: 303 lbs.	22,200 22,190 1,436.4 1.3	Launched by NASA for Comsat Corp., the manager of Intelsat. F–3 spacecraft initially positioned over Pacific. Component failure reduced capacity. After F–4 was launched. F–3 was moved to Indian Ocean to carry lighter traffic load. Currently operating satisfactorily.
Feb. 9 Tacsat I 13A Titan IIIC	Objectives: To explore and demonstrate the feasibility of using a spaceborne repeater to satisfy selected communications needs of the DOD mobile tactical forces. Spacecraft: Weight 1,600 lbs.	22,387 22,332 1,446.6 00.6	Still in orbit.
Feb. 25 Mariner-Mars VI 14A Atlas Centaur	Objective: To conduct a 1,800-mile Mars fly-by mission to make exploratory investigations of Mars which will set the basis for future experiments, particularly those relevant to search for extraterrestrial life. Spacecraft: Octagonal boxshape structure 54-in. wide and 18-in. high, 4 extended solar cell panels; overall width 19 feet; cold gas jet stabilization; solar cell power supply—800 watts near Earth and 449 watts near Mars; weight: 908 lbs.	In heliocentric orbit	Successfully passed by Mars at 2,130 miles on July 31. Transmitted 74 television pictures and investigated Martian atmosphere.

SUCCESSFUL UNITED STATES LAUNCHES: 1969 (Continued)

Launch date (Gmt) Spacecraft name Cospar designation Launch vehicle	Spacecraft data	Apogee and Perigee (in statute miles)— Period (minutes)— Inclination to Equator (degrees)	Remarks
Feb. 26 ESSA IX 16A Thor-Delta	Objective: To operate two advanced vidicon camera systems in a sun-synchronous orbit having a local equator crossing time between 2:15 and 2:35 p.m. local time so that daily AVCS cloud cover pictures of the entire globe can be obtained regularly and dependably; and to make measurements of net radiation of the earth from which the heat balance of the atmospere can be derived. Spacecraft: Cylindrical 42-in. diameter and 22.5 in. high; spin stabilized, solar cell power supply; weight: 347 lbs.	997 935 115. 2 101. 71	All systems functioning normally.

Mar. 3 Apollo 9 18A command module 18C lunar module Saturn V	Objective: To demonstrate crew/space vehicle/ mission support facilities performance during a manned Saturn V mission with service module (CSM) and lunar module (LM); to demonstrate LM/crew performance; to assess consumables; to demonstrate performance of nominal and selected backup lunar orbit rendezvous mission activities, including:
	    Transposition, docking, LM withdrawal,
	    Intervehicular crew transfer,
	    Extravehicular capability,
	    Service propulsion and descent propulsion system burns, and
	    LM active rendezvous and docking.
	Spacecraft: Carried full lunar landing configuration, including command module (CM), service module, and lunar module. Three 31-cell, Bacon-type, hydrogen-oxygen fuel cells plus batteries in command module and 6 batteries in the LM. Total weight at initial earth orbit insertion: 289,970 lbs.
		Varied.	Crew consisted of J. A. McDivitt, commander; D. R. Scott, command module pilot; and R. L. Schweickart, lunar module pilot. All objectives of the flight successfully accomplished. Length of flight: 241 hours, 01 minute. Also 46 minutes EVA by Schweickart.

Mar. 4 Defense 19A Titan IIIB	Objective: Development of space flight techniques and technology. Spacecraft: Not announced.	279. 6 96. 3 90. 3 92. 0	Decayed Mar. 18, 1969.
Mar. 18 OV 1–17 25A Atlas	Objective: To perform 12 solar radiation experiments. Spacecraft: Weight 312 lbs.	287. 7 246. 7 93. 1 99. 1	Still in orbit.
Mar. 18 OV 1–18 25B Atlas	Objective: To gather information on the ionosphere, radio interference, electrical fields and radiation. Spacecraft: Weight 275 lbs.	362. 3 288. 3 95. 0 98. 8	Still in orbit.
Mar. 18 OV 1–19 25C Atlas	Objective: To perform 7 experiments studying trapped radiation and 5 studying radiation hazards. Spacecraft: Weight 273 lbs.	3, 592. 9 288. 0 153. 5 104. 7	Still in orbit.
Mar. 18 OV 1–17A 25D Atlas	Objective: To operate 2 radio beacons mounted on the OV 1–17 propulsion module. Spacecraft: Weight 487 lbs.	233. 0 106. 9 89. 8 99. 0	Decayed Mar. 24, 1969.
Mar. 19 Defense 26A Thor-Agena	Objective: Development of space flight techniques and technology. Spacecraft: Not announced.	156. 6 102 5 86. 6 82. 9	Decayed Mar. 24, 1969.

SUCCESSFUL UNITED STATES LAUNCHES: 1969 (Continued)

Launch date (Gmt) Spacecraft name Cospar designation Launch vehicle	Spacecraft data	Apogee and Perigee (in statute miles)— Period (minutes)— Inclination to Equator (degrees)	Remarks
Mar. 19 Defense 26B Thor-Agena	Objective: Development of space flight techniques and technology. Spacecraft: Not announced.	318. 8 312. 8 94. 7 83. 0	Still in orbit.
Mar. 27 Mariner-Mars VII 30A Atlas Centaur	Objective: To conduct a 1,800-mile Mars fly-by mission to make exploratory investigations of Mars which will set the basis for future experiments, particularly those relevant to search for extraterrestrial life. Spacecraft: Octagonal boxshape structure 54 in. wide and 18 in. high, 4 extended solar cell panels; overall width 19 ft.; cold gas jet stabilization; solar cell power supply—800 watts near earth and 449 watts near Mars; weight: 908 lbs.	In heliocentric orbit	Successfully passed by Mars at 2,190 miles on Aug 5. Transmitted 91 TV pictures to Earth and investigated Mars atmosphere. Mariner VI and VII made following preliminary observations: Nothing new to encourage existence of earthlike life, but does not preclude unknown forms which may have evolved in the Martian environment; night temperature: −150 to −190° F; day temperature: −60 to +60° F; atmospheric pressure 4 to 7 millibars, silica or silicates (sand) in equatorial regions; terrain varied from crater, featureless, to chaotic.
Apr. 13 Defense 36A Atlas-Agena	Objective: Development of space flight techniques and technology. Spacecraft: Not announced.	24, 391 20, 302 1, 436. 0 10. 2	Still in orbit.
Apr. 14 Nimbus III 37A Thorad-Agena	Objective: to make IR measurements from which a vertical temperature profile of the atmosphere can be determined; to conduct global mapping of radiative energy balance of earth atmosphere; to demonstrate feasibility of surface pressure and tropospheric wind measurements, to conduct global mapping of the earth and its cloud cover day and night; and to demonstrate SNAP 19 power supply. Spacecraft: Torus ring structure 56-in. diameter with pyramidal frame structure 120-in. high. Active 3 axis stabilization; 415 watt solar cell plus two 25-watt SNAP–19 power supply; weight: 1,360 lbs.	704 667 107. 3	The following experiments were carried out: high resolution IR radiometer; image dissector camera; monitor of UV solar energy; IR interferometer spectrometer; interrogation recording, and location subsystem; and two SNAP 19 radioisotope thermoelectric generators.
Apr. 14 Secor XIII 37B Thorad-Agena	Objective: To continue geodetic measurements program. Spacecraft: Rectangular box-shaped structure 9 in. by 11 in. by 13 in.; solar cell power supply; weight: 46 lbs.	704 667 107. 3 99. 9	Launched by NASA for the Department of Defense (Army) as a secondary payload. Spacecraft functioning normally.
Apr. 15 Defense 39A Titan IIIB/Agena	Objective: Development of space flight techniques and technology. Spacecraft: Not announced.	292. 7 78. 9 89. 9 108. 7	Decayed Apr. 20, 1969.
May 2 Defense 41A Thor-Agena	Objective: Development of space flight techniques and technology. Spacecraft: Not announced.	202. 1 104. 6 89. 5 64. 9	Decayed May 23, 1969.

SUCCESSFUL UNITED STATES LAUNCHES: 1969 (Continued)

Launch date (Gmt) Spacecraft name Cospar designation Launch vehicle	Spacecraft data	Apogee and Perigee (in statute miles)— Period (minutes)— Inclination to Equator (degrees)	Remarks
May 2 Defense 41B Thor-Agena	Objective: Development of space flight techniques and technology. Spacecraft: Not announced.	283. 2 255. 9 93. 2 65. 7	Still in orbit.
May 18 Apollo 10 43A command module 43C lunar module Saturn V	Objective: To demonstrate crew/space vehicle/ mission support facilities performance during a manned lunar mission with the command service module and the lunar module; to evaluate the lunar module performance in the cis-lunar and lunar environment. Spacecraft: Carried full lunar landing configuration, including command module, service module, and lunar module. Three 31-cell, Bacon-type, hydrogen-oxygen fuel cells plus batteries in command module and 6 batteries in the LM. Total weight at initial Earth orbit insertion: 289,970 lbs.		Crew consisted of E. A. Cernan, commander; J. W. Young, command module pilot; and T. P. Stafford, lunar module pilot. The lunar module successfully made two 47,000-foot, low-altitude passes over the prospective Apollo 11 landing area. Length of flight: 192 hours and 3 minutes.
May 22 Intelsat III (F–4) 45A Thrust-augmented Thor-Delta	Objective: To provide equivalent of 1,200 2-way voice circuits or 4 color TV channels to carry commercial communications traffic between the United States, Hawaii, and the Western Pacific. Spacecraft: Cylindrical 56-in. diameter and 78-in. high; spin-stabilized; 300-watt solar cell power supply; weight: 303 lbs.	22, 205 22, 190 1, 436. 0 . 54	Launched by NASA for Comsat Corp., the manager of Intelsat. Stationed at 170° east longitude. Spacecraft operating normally.
May 23 OV 5–5 46A Titan IIIC	Objective: To measure the power spectrum of magnetic and electrical field fluctuations at the magnetospheric boundary. Spacecraft: 11-in. side octahedral research satellite weighing 25 lbs.	69, 427 10, 480 3, 119. 6 32. 9	Still in orbit.
May 23 OV 5–6 46B Titan IIIC	Objective: To provide research data about the solar processes which influence the near Earth environment. Spacecraft: 11-in. side octahedral research satellite weighing 25 lbs.	69, 427 10, 480 3, 119. 6 32. 9	Still in orbit.
May 23 OV 5–9 46C Titan IIIC	Objective: To measure the energetic particles emitted by the Sun and study the trapped electrons and protons at near-synchronous altitude. Spacecraft: 11-in. side octahedral research satellite weighing 25 lbs.	69, 427 10, 480 3, 119. 6 32. 9	Still in orbit.
May 23 Vela 9 46D Titan IIIC	Objective: To orbit nuclear detection sensors capable of monitoring X-ray, gamma ray, neutron, optical, electromagnetic pulse, and air fluorescence emissions. Spacecraft: Weight: 571 lbs.	69, 387 68, 653 6, 718. 5 32. 7	Still in orbit.
May 23 Vela 10 46E Titan IIIC	Objective: Same as Vela 9 located in similar orbit, satellites separated by 180°. Spacecraft: Weight: 571 lbs.	69, 614 68, 774 6, 707. 6 32. 8	Still in orbit.
June 3 Defense 50A Titan IIIB/Agena	Objective: Development of space flight techniques and technology. Spacecraft: Not announced.	265. 3 86. 4 89. 8 110. 0	Decayed June 14, 1969.

SUCCESSFUL UNITED STATES LAUNCHES: 1969 (Continued)

Launch date (Gmt) Spacecraft name Cospar designation Launch vehicle	Spacecraft data	Apogee and Perigee (in statute miles)—Period (minutes)—Inclination to Equator (degrees)	Remarks
June 5 OGO VI 51A Thorad-Agena D	Objective: To make detailed measurements near solar maximum of the near-Earth environment, including the global composition and density of the neutral atmosphere; the composition and structure of the ionosphere: the solar radiation producing ionization; the auroral and polar cap phenomena of the polar regions; the structure and variability of terrestrial fields, the propagation and form of VLF emissions; the trapping and precipitation of particles; and air glow emissions related to photochemical dissociative or recombination interactions. Spacecraft: Rectangular boxlike structure 67 in. by 32 in. by 31 in. with 2 shaft-mounted rotatable solar cell arrays, 2 22-ft.-long booms, and 4 4-ft. booms; active 3 axis and spin stabilization; 560-watt solar cell power supply; weight 1,394 lbs.	682 246 99. 8 82. 0	Spacecraft and experiments are functioning normally.
June 21 Explorer XLI (IMP–G) 53A Thrust-augmented Thor-Delta	Objective: To obtain measurements of plasma and energetic particle during period of solar maximum at distances of 100,000 miles and at an angle in excess of 80° to the equator. Spacecraft: Octagonal box structure 27 in. wide and 10 in. high with 4 solar cell paddles and 2 6-ft. booms for magnetometer and balance; spin stabilized; 70-watt solar cell power supply; weight: 174 lbs.	130, 640 210 4, 906 87	This is the seventh of a series of 10 Interplanetary Monitoring Platform spacecraft. Carries 12 experiments. All functioned normally.
June 29 Bios-III 56A Thor-Delta	Objective: To make detailed measurements on a 14-lb pigtailed monkey during a 30-day orbiting flight, to include measurements of wave patterns from 10 areas in the brain; record heart action and respiration; take measurements at 4 circulatory system sites; make 3 urinary measurements; and provide observation of performance on 2 selected behavioral tasks. Spacecraft: Combined a blunt nose cone reentry capsule mounted on cylindrical section. Total length 84 in.; maximum diameter 57 in. 135-watt hydrogen/oxygen fuel cell plus batteries power. Active stabilization. Weight: 1,536 lbs.	245 224 92. 1 33. 6	Flight was terminated after 8 days. Monkey successfully recovered but died about a day later from apparent heart failure. Results are still being analyzed.
July 16 Apollo 11 59A Command Module 59C Lunar Module Saturn V	Objective: To perform a manned lunar landing in the southwest corner of the Sea of Tranquility, to conduct limited geological exploration in the vicinity of the touchdown point, deploy passive seismic experiment, laser ranging retroreflector, and solar wind experiment, and return to earth. Spacecraft: Carried full lunar landing configuration including command module, service module, and lunar module. Three 31-cell Bacon-type hydrogen-oxygen fuel cells plus batteries in command module and 6 batteries in the LM. Total weight at initial Earth orbit insertion: 292,865 lbs.	N.A.	Crew consisted of Neil A. Armstrong, commander; Michael Collins, command module pilot; Edwin E. Aldrin, Jr., lunar module pilot. The mission was successfully accomplished. Touchdown occurred at 20:17:43 Gmt, July 20 and Armstrong stepped on to the lunar surface at 02:56:15 and Aldrin at 04:11:00 Gmt on July 21. The Lunar Module lifted off from the lunar surface 17:50:00 Gmt, July 21, for a total stay time of 21 hours, 36 minutes, 17 seconds. Total flight time: 195 hours, 19 minutes.
July 23 Defense 62A Thor/Burner II	Objective: Development of space flight techniques and technology. Spacecraft: Not announced.	531. 5 488. 4 101. 3 98. 8	Still in orbit.

SUCCESSFUL UNITED STATES LAUNCHES: 1969 (Continued)

Launch date (Gmt) Spacecraft name Cospar designation Launch vehicle	Spacecraft data	Apogee and Perigee (in statute miles)— Period (minutes)— Inclination to Equator (degrees)	Remarks
July 24 Defense 63A Thor-Agena	Objective: Development of space flight techniques and technology. Spacecraft: Not announced.	136. 1 110. 6 88. 4 74. 9	Decayed Aug. 23, 1969.
July 26 Intelsat III (F–5) 64A Thor-Delta	Objective: To provide equivalent of 1,200 2-way voice circuits or 4 color TV channels to carry commercial communications traffic between North America, Europe, South America, and Africa. Spacecraft: Cylindrical 56-in. diameter and 78 in. high; spin stabilized; 300-watt solar cell power supply; weight: 303 lbs.	3, 325 168 146. 2 30. 2	Intended as replacement for F–2 launched in December 1968 which was having antenna difficulties. Due to third-stage failure, the spacecraft did not achieve a usable orbit. F–2 appears to have overcome its difficulties.
July 31 Defense 65A Thor-Agena	Objective: Development of space flight techniques and technology. Spacecraft: Not announced.	333. 1 288. 9 94. 6 75. 0	Still in orbit.
Aug 9 OSO–VI 68A Thrust-augmented Thor-Delta	Objective: To obtain high spectral resolution data within the range of 10 to 20 Kev and 1–1,300 Angstrom; to detect the zodiacal light, hard solar X-rays, and the Earth's x-ray albedo, high energy neutron fluxes, and solar helium emissions. Spacecraft: Revolving 9-sided polyhedron 44-in. diameter, and 22-in. radius semicircular sail; spin stabilized; 26-watt solar cell power supply; weight: 610 lbs.	348 308 95. 2 33. 0	To continue OSO I, II, III, IV, and V investigations of the Sun. All experiments are functioning normally.
Aug 9 PAC 68B Thrust-augmented Thor-Delta	Objective: To test an experimental spacecraft control system which can be used to convert the 3d stage of the Thor-Delta to a 3-axis Earth stabilized platform for various future piggyback payloads. Spacecraft: Not applicable.	340 300 94. 2 32. 9	Experiment functioned as planned.
Aug. 12 ATS–5 69A	Objectives: To conduct a carefully instrumented gravity gradient orientation experiment directed toward providing the basic design information for stabilization and control of long-lived spacecraft in synchronous orbit, to conduct millimeter wave and L-band aeronautical communications experiments, and to make environmental measurements. Spacecraft: Cylindrical 56-in. diameter and 72-in. long; gravity gradient stabilization; 148-watt solar all power supply; weight: 951 lbs.	23, 500 23, 500 1, 435. 9 2. 5	The spacecraft arrived at a synchronous geostationary orbit but with an abnormally high spin rate about the yaw axis. This prevented the principal spacecraft experiments to function and therefore the mission is assessed as a failure.
Aug. 23 DEFENSE 74A Titan IIIB/Agena	Objective: Development of space flight techniques and technology. Spacecraft: Not announced.	234. 3 85. 8 89. 6 108. 1	Decayed Sep. 7, 1969.
Sep. 22 Defense 79A Thor-Agena	Objective: Development of space flight techniques and technology. Spacecraft: Not announced.	157. 2 110. 0 88. 7 85. 0	Decayed Oct. 12, 1969.
Sep. 22 Defense 79B Thor-Agena	Objective: Development of space flight techniques and technology. Spacecraft: Not announced.	308. 2 305. 1 94. 4 85. 1	Still in orbit.

SUCCESSFUL UNITED STATES LAUNCHES: 1969 (Continued)

Launch date (Gmt) Spacecraft name Cospar designation Launch vehicle	Spacecraft data	Apogee and Perigee (in statute miles)— Period (minutes)— Inclination to Equator (degrees)	Remarks
Sep. 30 Defense 82A Thor-Agena	Objective: Development of space flight techniques and technology. Spacecraft: Not applicable.	303. 2 299. 5 93. 8 69. 6	Still in orbit.
Sep. 30 Defense 82B Thor-Agena	Objective: Development of space flight techniques and technology. Spacecraft: Not announced.	586. 0 574. 8 103. 7 70. 7	Still in orbit.
Oct. 1 ESRO-1B (Borealis) 83A Scout	Objective: To perform an integrated study of high latitude ionosphere and particles and associated effects. Spacecraft: Cylindrical 30-in. diameter and 40-in. high; spin stabilized; 23-watt solar cell power supply; weight 189 lbs.	237 181 91. 2 85. 1	All experiments functioned normally.
Oct. 24 Defense 95A Titan IIIB/Agena	Objective: Development of space flight techniques and technology. Spacecraft: Not announced.	395. 8 78. 3 92. 1 108. 1	Decayed Nov. 8, 1969.
Nov. 8 Azur (GRS–A) 97A Scout	Objective: To make measurements of the inner Van Allen belt, the auroral zones of the Northern Hemisphere, and the spectral variations of solar particles versus time during solar flares. Spacecraft: Cylindrical section with conical top, 30-in. diameter and 44-in. high. Spin stabilized, 29-watt solar cell power supply; weight: 159 lbs.	1, 952 239 121. 6 103. 0	This is the first of a series of cooperative missions between the German Ministry for Scientific Research and NASA under a memorandum of understanding dated 17 July 1965. Seven scientific experiments are carried. All experiments functioning normally.
Nov. 14 Apollo 12 99A command module 99C lunar module Saturn V	Objective: To perform a manned lunar landing in the Ocean of Storms, to develop techniques for a point landing capability, to perform selenological inspection, survey, and sampling in a mare area, to deploy and activate an Apollo lunar surface experiments package, to develop man's capability to work in lunar environment, and obtain photographs of candidate exploration sites. Spacecraft: Carried full lunar landing configuration, including command module, service module, and lunar module. Three 31-cell, Bacon-type, hydrogen-oxygen fuel cells plus batteries in command module and 6 batteries in the LM. Total weight at initial Earth orbit insertion: 289,970 lbs.	N.A.	Crew consisted of Charles Conrad, Jr., commander; Richard F. Gordon, command module pilot, and Alan L. Bean, lunar module pilot. All mission objectives were successfully accomplished. Lunar module landed at 06:54:35 (Gmt) on Nov. 19 and lifted off again at 14:26:00 (Gmt) on Nov. 20. Total lunar stay time: 31 hours, 31 minutes. Total flight time: 244 hours, 36 minutes, 25 seconds.
Nov. 22 Skynet A 101A Thrust-augmented Thor-Delta	Objective: To place into synchronous orbit over the Indian Ocean a United Kingdom communications spacecraft as part of the initial defense communications satellite program (augmented) in response to a United States/United Kingdom agreement. Spacecraft: Cylinder 54-in. diameter and 32-in. high; spin stabilized; solar cell power supply; weight: 535 lbs.	22, 777 20, 546 1, 431. 0 2. 4	Spacecraft is functioning normally.
Dec. 4 Defense 105A Thor-Agena	Objective: Development of space flight techniques and technology. Spacecraft: Not announced.	155. 3 105. 6 88. 4 81. 4	Still in orbit.

SOURCE: National Aeronautics and Space Council, "Aeronautics and Space Report of the President," 1970.

SUCCESSFUL UNITED STATES LAUNCHES: 1970

Launch date (Gmt) Spacecraft name Cospar designation Launch vehicle	Spacecraft data	Apogee and Perigee (in statute miles)— Period (minutes)— Inclination to Equator (degrees)	Remarks
Jan. 14 Defense 2A Titan IIIB-Agena	Objective: Development of space flight techniques and technology. Spacecraft: Not announced.	253 78 89. 8 109. 9	Decayed Feb. 1, 1970.
Jan. 15 Intelsat III (F–6) 3A Thrust-augmented Thor-Delta	Objective: To provide equivalent of 1,200 2-way voice circuits or 4-Color TV channels to carry communications traffic between the United States, Latin America, Europe, and the Middle East. Spacecraft: Cylindrical 56-in. diameter and 78 in. high; spin stabilized; 5-year lifetime electrical power system provides 130 watts generated by 10,720 solar cells; rechargeable 20-cell nickel-cadmium battery; weight 334 lbs.	22, 259 22, 243 1, 437. 2 0. 9	Launched by NASA for Comsat Corp., the manager of Intelsat. Stationed in synchronous orbit at 24° west longitude. Replaced Intelsat III F–2 over Atlantic. Spacecraft operating normally; began full-time commercial services Feb. 1, 1970.
Jan. 23 ITOS 1 (Tiros M) 8A Thrust-augmented Thor-Delta (2 stage)	Objective: To flight qualify the prototype spacecraft, thereby obtaining the engineering data required for the evaluation of a single momentum wheel stabilization system for an earth-oriented, stabilized platform. To evaluate the use of the stabilized platform for operational methodology by performing cloud-cover observations in both direct readout and stored modes of operation. Spacecraft: Rectangular, box-shaped spacecraft with a deployable 3-panel solar array. 3-axis stabilized, earth-oriented satellite carries 2 Advanced Vidicon Camera System (AVCS) and 2 Automatic Picture Transmission (APT) camera subsystems which provide daytime coverage, and 2 Scanning Radiometer (SR) Subsystems (infrared) which furnish nighttime coverage. Solar panels measure 3 ft. by 5 ft. each and total 48 sq. ft. Spacecraft measures 14 ft. with panels deployed. Thermal control system. 4 antennas. 10,000-n-on-p solar cells produce 250 watts average power. Weight: 675 lbs.	925 887 115. 0 101. 9	Second generation operational meteorological satellite placed in a circular, near-polar, sun-synchronous orbit. First launch of Delta with 6 strap-ons. Provides first daily global day-night cloud cover data; also furnishes both remote and local readout. All systems functioning normally.
Jan. 23 Oscar 5 (Australis) 8B Thrust-augmented Thor-Delta	Objective: To transmit low-power signals on 2 amateur bands to be used by radio amateurs world-wide for training in the art of tracking and for experiments useful to NASA in radio propagation. Spacecraft: Carries 20 lbs. of batteries and transmits at 29.45 mhz in 10-m band and 144.05 mhz in the 2-meter band; weight: 39 lbs.	921 891 115. 0 101. 9	Built at the University of Melbourne in Australia and launched by NASA as secondary payload for the Radio Amateur Satellite Corporation. Spacecraft is functioning normally.
Feb. 4 SERT–II 9A Thrust-augmented Thor-Agena	Objective: To accumulate 6 months (4382 hours) of satisfactory operation on an electric ion thruster system in space. Spacecraft: Cylindrical 21-in. long and 59-in. diameter is supported by same size Spacecraft Support Unit (SSU) which is attached to 21.5 ft. long and 5 ft. diameter Agena D second stage. Two 5 ft. by 19 ft. solar arrays attach-to Agena D stage measure 187.5 sq. ft. total and contain total of 33,300 solar cells for power total of 1471 watts. Spacecraft contains 21 kw ion thrusters each powered by 29 lbs. of mercury propellant. Thermal control system. Weight in orbit is approximately 3,330 lbs. of which 1100 lbs. is spacecraft and SSU weight.	627 620 105. 1 99. 1	First orbital test of electron-bombardment ion engines. Spacecraft's solar arrays are largest ever flown on NASA satellite. No. 1 engine shut down July 23 after successful operation for 3782 hours. No. 2 engine shut down Oct. 17 after 2,011 hours of operation.

SUCCESSFUL UNITED STATES LAUNCHES: 1970 (Continued)

Launch date (Gmt) Spacecraft name Cospar designation Launch vehicle	Spacecraft data	Apogee and Perigee (in statute miles)— Period (minutes)— Inclination to Equator (degrees)	Remarks
Feb. 11 Defense 12A Thor-Burner II	Objective: Development of space flight techniques and technology. Spacecraft: Not announced.	542 480 101. 3 98. 6	Still in orbit.
Mar. 4 Defense 16A Thor-Agena	Objective: Development of space flight technqiues and technology. Spacecraft: Not announced.	141. 0 139. 7 88. 4 88. 4	Decayed Mar. 26, 1970
Mar. 4 Defense 16B Thor-Agena	Objective: Development of space flight techniques and technology. Spacecraft: Not announced.	315 273 94. 0 88. 1	Still in orbit.
Mar. 20 NATO I 21A Thor-Delta	Objective: The NATO I is a military communications satellite placed in geostationary orbit over the mid-Atlantic Ocean. It will be used for command and control of NATO military forces with the U.S. terminal located at Norfolk, Va. (SACLANT). Spacecraft: Weight 285 lbs.	22, 548 21, 258 1, 440 2. 8	Still in orbit.
Apr. 8 Nimbus-IV 25A Thrust-augmented Thor-Agena	Objective: To acquire a sufficient number of global samples of atmospheric radiation measurements for the purpose of comparing vertical temperature, water vapor, and ozone profiles, and of providing a basis for comparing the merits of the several instrument approaches. Comparative data are to be obtained from the successful operation of at least three of the five spectrometric experiments: The Satellite Infrared Spectrometer (SIRS), the Infrared Interferometer Spectrometer (IRIS), the Filter Wedge Spectrometer (FWS), the Selective Chopper Radiometer (SCR), or the Backscatter Ultraviolet (BUV) Spectrometer, or from successful operation of either the FWS or SCR, plus either the SIRS or IRIS. Spacecraft: 120-in. high and 132-in. wide spacecraft. Torus ring base structure 56-in. diameter with pyramidal frame structure and two 3-ft. by 5-ft. solar paddles. Active three-axis stabilization. Solar cells provide 465 watts of power and eight nickel-cadmium batteries average 255 watts. Weight: 1,488 lbs.	684 679 107. 1 99. 8	Spacecraft and sensors operating successfully except for FWS, which failed June 7, 1970. Primary objectives achieved and flight a success.
Apr. 8 TOPO–1 25B Thor-Agena	Objective: This Army tactical satellite survey system is a SECOR type satellite and is used through triangulation for ground tactical positioning. Spacecraft: Weight 48 lbs.	667 667 107 99	Still in orbit.
Apr. 8 Vela 11 27A Titan III C	Objective: To orbit nuclear detection sensors capable of monitoring X-ray, gamma ray, neutron, optical, electromagnetic pulse, and air fluorescence emissions. Spacecraft: weight 770 lbs.	68, 478. 4 68, 810. 3 6, 695 37. 7	Still in orbit.
Apr. 8 Vela 12 27B Titan III C	Objective: Same as Vela 11. Located in similar orbit; satellites separated by 180.° Spacecraft: weight 770 lbs.	69, 281. 8 69, 041. 2 6, 699 32. 9	Still in orbit.

SUCCESSFUL UNITED STATES LAUNCHES: 1970 (Continued)

Launch date (Gmt) Spacecraft name Cospar designation Launch vehicle	Spacecraft data	Apogee and Perigee (in statute miles)— Period (minutes)— Inclination to Equator (degrees)	Remarks
Apr. 11 Apollo 13 (CSM 104) 29A Saturn V	Objective: To perform selenological inspection, survey, and sampling of materials in a preselected region of the Fra Mauro Formation; to deploy and activate an Apollo Lunar Surface Experiments Package (ALSEP); to develop man's capability to work in the lunar environment; to obtain photographs of candidate exploration sites. Spacecraft: Carried full lunar landing configuration including command module, service module, and lunar module. Three 31-cell Bacon-type hydrogen-oxygen fuel cells plus batteries in command module and six batteries in LM. Total weight at initial earth orbit insertion: 296,463 lbs.; at translunar injection: 110,210 lbs.; command and service modules: 61,453 lbs. CSM: 34 ft. long, 12.8 ft. diam.	Circumlunar	Aborted after 56 hours. GET due to loss of pressure in liquid oxygen in Service Module and failure of fuel cells 1 & 3. Preflight damage to wiring insulation in tank caused electrical short circuits which initiated combustion in oxygen tank No. 2. Astronauts were James H. Lovell, Jr., Fred Haise, Jr., and John L. Swigert, Jr. Splashdown in Pacific Ocean after total flight time of 142 hrs. 54 min. 44 sec., April 17, 1970.
Apr. 11 Saturn IVB (AS 508) 29B Saturn V	Objective: To bring payload to lunar transfer injection; then to fly independently to impact the moon in further seismic tests to be detected by Apollo 12 ALSEP instruments. Spacecraft: A cylinder about 61.3 ft. long by 21.7 ft. in diam. Total weight at impact, about 28,665 lbs.	Lunar strike	Crashed on moon April 15, 1970 about 88 miles from Apollo 12 landing site with a force equal to 11 tons of TNT, setitng up signals for 4 hours.
Apr. 11 Lunar Excursion Module (LM 7) 29C Saturn V	Objective: To support lunar landing and takeoff for return to lunar orbit in support of tasks named above. Spacecraft: Combined descent and ascent stages about 13.5 ft. high, 12.3 ft. wide, and 10.3 ft. deep. Total weight about 34,067 lbs.	Circumlunar	After explosion in service module, the lunar module was used as a lifeboat by the astronauts for the flight around the moon and back toward earth; jettisoned just prior to reentry. Decayed in earth's atmosphere April 17, 1970.
Apr. 15 Defense 31A Titan III B-Agena	Objective: Development of spaceflight echnique and technology. Spacecraft: Not announced.	240 85 89. 7 110. 9	Decayed May 6, 1970.
Apr. 23 Intelsat III (F–7) 32A Thrust-augmented Thor-Delta	Objective: To provide equivalent of 1,200 two-way voice circuits or four color TV channels to carry communications traffic between the United States, Europe, North Africa, and the Middle East. Spacecraft: Cylindrical 56-in. diameter and 78-in. high; spin stabilized; 5 year lifetime electrical power system provides 130 watts generated by 10.720 solar cells; rechargeable 20-cell nickel-cadmium battery; weight: 334 lbs.	21, 902 21, 891 1, 408. 1 0. 3	Launched by NASA for Comsat Corp., the manage of Intelsat. Launch vehicle underperformed and onboard hydrazine thrusters pushed satellite into desired synchronous orbit 19° west longitude over Atlantic. Remaining fuel expected to maintain satellite in proper orbit for five years. Began commercial service May 8, 1970.
May 20 Defense 40A Thor-Agena	Objective: Development of spacecraft techniques and technology. Spacecraft: Not announced.	147 111 88. 6 83. 0	Decayed June 17, 1970.
May 20 Defense 40B Thor-Agena	Objective: Development of spaceflight techniques and technology. Spacecraft: Not announced.	313 304 94. 5 83. 1	Still in orbit.
Jun. 19 Defense 46A Atlas-Agena	Objective: Development of spaceflight techniques and technology. Spacecraft: Not announced.	22, 270 22, 240 1, 426. 5 0. 1	Still in orbit.

SUCCESSFUL UNITED STATES LAUNCHES: 1970 (Continued)

Launch date (Gmt) Spacecraft name Cospar designation Launch vehicle	Spacecraft data	Apogee and Perigee (in statute miles)— Period (minutes)— Inclination to Equator (degrees)	Remarks
Jun. 25 Defense 48A Titan III B-Agena	Objective: Development of spaceflight techniques and technology. Spacecraft: Not announced.	255 73. 9 89. 8 108. 8	Decayed July 6, 1970.
Jul. 23 Defense 54A Titan III B-Agena	Objective: Development of spaceflight techniques and technology. Spacecraft: Not announced.	251 73. 9 90. 1 59. 9	Decayed Aug. 19, 1970.
Jul. 23 Intelsat III(F–8) 55A Thrust-augmented Thor-Delta	Objective: To provide equivalent of 1,200 two-way voice circuits of four color TV channels to carry communications traffic between the United States, Hawaii, and the Western Pacific. Spacecraft: Cylindrical 56-in. diameter and 78-in. high; spin stabilized; five year lifetime electrical power system provides 130 watts generated by 10,720 solar cells; rechargeable 20-cell nickel-cadmium battery; weight: 334 lbs.	22, 553 175 642. 7 28. 0	Launched successfully into transfer orbit by NASA for Comsat Corp., the manager of Intelsat. Comsat-controlled apogee motor began scheduled 27 second burn at 27 hours GET to place satellite into planned synchronous orbit at 128° east longitude over Western Pacific, but motor cut off after burning 14.5 seconds and contact lost. Last of Intelsat III series.
Aug. 18 Defense 61A Titan III B-Agena	Objective: Development of spaceflight techniques and technology. Spacecraft: Not announced.	246 94 89. 9 110. 9	Decayed Sept. 3, 1970.
Aug. 19 SKYNET II 62A Thor-Delta	Objective: The Skynet II is the second and final military communications satellite launched for the United Kingdom. The satellite was to be placed in geostationary orbit over the Indian Ocean where it was to support communications of British forces. Spacecraft: Weight 285 lbs.		Orbit undetermined. Status unknown, contact lost during apogee boost motor firing.
Aug. 26 Defense 66A Thor-Agena	Objective: Development of spaceflight technique and technology. Spacecraft: Not announced.	313 301 94. 4 74. 9	Still in orbit.
Aug. 27 Defense 67A Scout	Objective: To provide a navigation satellite. Spacecraft: Not announced.	757 595 106. 9 90. 0	Still in orbit.
Sept. 1 Defense 69A Atlas-Agena	Objective: Development of spaceflight techniques and technology. Spacecraft: Not announced.	24, 750 19, 830 1, 441. 9 10. 3	Still in orbit.
Sept. 3 Defense 70A Thor-Burner II	Objective: Development of spaceflight techniques and technology. Spacecraft: Not announced.	542 475 101. 2 98. 7	Still in orbit.
Oct. 23 Defense 90A Titan III B–Agena	Objective: Development of spaceflight techniques and technology. Spacecraft: Not announced.	248 81 89. 8 111. 0	Decayed Nov. 11, 1970.
Nov. 6 Defense 93A Titan III C	Objective: Development of spaceflight techniques and technology. Spacecraft: Not announced.	22, 299 16, 186 1, 197. 1 7. 8	Still in orbit.

SUCCESSFUL UNITED STATES LAUNCHES: 1970 (Continued)

Launch date (Gmt) Spacecraft name Cospar designation Launch vehicle	Spacecraft data	Apogee and Perigee (in statute miles)— Period (minutes)— Inclination to Equator (degrees)	Remarks
Nov. 9 Orbiting Frog Otolith (OFO) 94A Scout	Objective: To obtain information on the functioning and adaptability in weightlessness of the portion of the inner ear which controls balance. Also to obtain data on the acceleration of .001 g or less at the otolith during weightlessness, and on water environment temperature. Spacecraft: Truncated cone with spherical top affixed to octogonal platform; 47-in. long and 30-in. diameter. Two 9-cell battery packs deliver 28 volts; five antennas; four booms extend 78-in. from side of spacecraft; yoyo despin assembly. 91 lb. Frog Otolith Experiment Package (FOEP) contains two bullfrogs and encased in pressure-tight 18-in. diameter and 18-in. long container. Total weight: 292 lbs.	328. 0 186. 4 92. 8 37. 4	6 day flight met all research objectives and considered a success. Frogs adapted to zero gravity of space after three days in orbit. Demonstrated that sense organ of man rather than central nervous system makes the adjustments.
Nov. 9 Radiation/ Meteroid (R/M) 94B Scout	Objective: Radiation—to demonstrate the feasibility and accuracy of an advanced dosimeter concept in a real time mode of the space environment; Meteoroid—to verify, in flight, the proper operation of instrumentation (including sensor materials) to be used on long duration flight experiments for future study of the meteoroid population of the solar system. Spacecraft: Cylindrical 30-in. diameter and 28-in. high attached to Scout 4th stage (FW–4); spin stabilized; total length (including FW–4) 67-in.; 7 sq. ft. of solar cells provide 25 watts of power; 2 nickel-cadmium batteries; R/M weight: 46 lbs.	328. 0 186. 4 92. 8 37. 4	Spacecraft launched as secondary payload, operating satisfactorily.
Nov. 18 Defense 98 A Thor-Agena	Objective: Development of space flight techniques and technology. Spacecraft: Not announced.	140. 4 110. 0 88. 5 82. 9	Decayed Dec. 11, 1970.
Nov. 18 Defense 98B Thor-Agena	Objective: Development of space flight techniques and technology. Spacecraft: Not announced.	317. 5 302. 0 94. 5 83. 1	Still in orbit.
Dec. 11 NOAA–I 106A Long-Tank, Thrust-Augmented, Thor-Delta	Objective: To place spacecraft in a sun-synchronous orbit having a local equator crossing time between 3:00 pm and 3:20 pm, and conduct in-orbit engineering evaluation so that daytime and nighttime cloudcover observations can be obtained regularly and dependably in both direct readout and stored modes of operation. Spacecraft: Rectangular, box-shaped spacecraft with a deployable 3-panel solar array. Three-axis stabilized, earth-oriented satellite carries 2 Advanced Vidicon Camera Subsystems (AVCS) and 2 Automatic Picture Transmission (APT) Camera Subsystems which provide daytime coverage, and 2 Scanning Radiometer (SR) Subsystems (infrared) which furnish nighttime coverage. Solar panels measure 3 ft. by 5 ft. each and total 48 sq. ft. Spacecraft measures 14 ft. with panels deployed. Thermal control system. 4 antennas. 10,000 n-on-p solar cells produce 250 watts average power. Weight: 675 lbs.	914. 8 884. 0 114. 8 101. 95	First operational spacecraft of Improved TIROS Operational System (ITOS) series. Spacecraft is functioning normally.

SUCCESSFUL UNITED STATES LAUNCHES: 1970 (Continued)

Launch date (Gmt) Spacecraft name Cospar designation Launch vehicle	Spacecraft data	Apogee and Perigee (in statute miles)— Period (minutes)— Inclination to Equator (degrees)	Remarks
Dec. 11 CEP 106B Long-Tank, Thrust-Augmented, Thor-Delta	Objective: To obtain information on electron density, temperature, and ion current in the ionosphere during a 2-orbit lifetime. Spacecraft: 5 lb. experiment which carries its own small analog computer; permanently attached to second stage of Delta launch vehicle.	916. 6 885. 7 114. 9 101. 9	Spacecraft launched as secondary payload. Obtained useful information during 2-orbit lifetime which may aid in reducing ground data processing.
Dec. 12 Explorer XLII (SAS–A) 107A Scout	Objective: To develop a catalog of celestial x-ray sources by systematic scanning of the celestial sphere in the energy range from 2–20 KEV. Spacecraft: Cylindrical 22-in. diameter and 20-in. high; 4 solar paddles (10-in. by 53-in.) with solar cells on both sides, hinged to outer shell and measure about 13 ft. tip-to-tip. One nickel-cadmium battery provides 27 watts average power; thermal control system; carries advanced x-ray instruments; spin stabilized; weight: 315 lbs.	355. 4 329. 9 95. 7 3. 04	First launch of an American spacecraft by a crew of another country (Italy). Launched as part of San Marco project from mobile seaborne equatorial facility off coast of Kenya. All spacecraft systems operating normally.

SOURCE: National Aeronautics and Space Council, "Aeronautics and Space Report of the President," 1971.

AERONAUTICAL EVENTS: 1969

Jan. 8 —— U.S.S.R.'s supersonic transport, the Tu 144, successfully made its second test flight.

Jan. 10 —— Japan approved a licensing agreement with a U.S. company to produce 104 F–4E jet fighters in Japan by fiscal year 1977.

Jan. 15 —— A new SST configuration was submitted to the FAA for approval. The new design incorporated a delta wing platform with a horizontal tail.

Feb. 4 —— The U.S. Navy announced the award of a $40,000,000 contract for the engineering development phase of the F–14A supersonic fighter.

Feb. 7 —— The XB–70 research airplane was flown from the NASA's Flight Research Center, Edwards, Calif., to Wright Patterson AFB, Ohio, to be placed in the Air Force Museum.

Feb. 9 —— The 747 Jumbo Jet made its successful 1 hour and 15 minute maiden flight from Paine Field, Everett, Wash.

Feb. 9 —— NASA announced that it would flight test the Whitcomb-designed supercritical wing on a U.S. Navy F–8 fighter at NASA's Flight Research Center.

Feb. 10 —— President Nixon appointed a 12-member interdepartmental ad hoc committee to review the supersonic transport program.

Mar. 2 —— The Anglo-French supersonic transport aircraft, the Concorde, made its successful maiden flight from Toulouse-Blagnac Airport, France.

Apr. 17 —— NASA's X–24A lifting body research vehicle successfully completed its first glide flight, launched from a B–52 carrier aircraft at 45,000 feet over Rogers Dry Lake, Calif.

Apr. 27 —— NASA announced the retirement of the 2 remaining active X–15 research aircraft to the Smithsonian Institution and the Air Force Museum.

May 9 —— The NASA HL–10 lifting body vehicle made its first supersonic flight, reaching 54,000 feet and mach 1.1, after a 45,000-foot air launch from a B–52.

May 21 —— U.S.S.R. publicly demonstrated its TU–144 supersonic airliner in a 90-minute test flight from Sheremetyevo Airport.

May 23 —— FAA announced allocations of nearly $35,000,000 to construct and improve 177 U.S. airports under the fiscal year 1970 Federal aid to airports plan.

May 29 —— The 28th Salon Internationale de l'Aeronautique et de l'Espace (Paris Air Show) opened, featuring nearly 550 exhibitors from 14 nations. In the United States, the C–5A "Galaxy" took off at a gross weight of 728,000 pounds, the heaviest airplane ever flown.

June 5 —— U.S.S.R.'s TU–144 supersonic airliner exceeded mach 1 for the first time during flight tests.

Sept. 23 —— President Nixon recommended proceeding with the construction of 2 U.S. supersonic transport prototypes, asking Congress for $96,000,000 to finance the program in fiscal year 1970.

Oct. 8 —— The Air Force received its first new bomber in almost a decade with the delivery of the first FB–111 to the Strategic Air Command.

Nov. 3 —— The Air Force issued requests for proposals to airframe and engine manufacturers asking for their plans for the development of the B–1 strategic bomber.

Nov. 12 —— A regulation was announced by FAA which established noise standards and maximum noise levels for all new subsonic transport turbojet airplanes.

Nov. 28 —— Japan successfully flew its first VTOL research test bed vehicle.

SOURCE: National Aeronautics and Space Council, "Aeronautics and Space Report of the President," 1970.

AERONAUTICAL EVENTS: 1970

Jan. 21 ...... The Boeing 747 (the first jumbo jet, type certificated on Dec. 30, 1969) made its first flight in commercial airline operations.

Feb. 18 ...... The rocket-powered HL–10 lifting body research vehicle achieved a new speed record for lifting body flight vehicles of Mach 1.86 (1,224 mph).

Apr. 10 ...... A notice of proposed rulemaking banning flights by civil aircraft in the United States at speeds producing sonic booms capable of reaching the ground (except in designated flight test areas) was issued by FAA. (Final rule-making action was expected early in 1971.)

May 21 ...... Landmark legislation (Public Law 91–258, of which title I is the Airport and Airway Development Act of 1970 and title II is the Airport and Airway Revenue Act of 1970) was signed into law by President Nixon, solving the longstanding problem of adequate funding for airport and airway development by establishing an Airport and Airway Trust Fund based on aviation-user taxes.

June 2 ...... The M2–F3 lifting body research vehicle made its first unpowered glide flight.

June 6 ...... The C–5A was introducted to the first operational squadron at Charleston AFB.

June 22 .... The President issued a policy statement on international air transportation.

July 1 ...... Neil Armstrong, former NASA test pilot and Apollo 11 astronaut was appointed NASA's Deputy Associate Administrator for Aeronautics.

Aug. 29 ..... The Douglas DC–10 "airbus" made its first flight. The DC–10 is a large-capacity jet designed for medium- and long-haul operations.

Sept. 11 .... President Nixon announced a 5-point program to deal with the problem of air piracy. The program included the placing of specially trained, armed U.S. Government personnel on flights of U.S. commercial airliners.

Oct. 20 ...... A full-scale hypersonic research engine was tested for the first time in the 8-foot, high-temperature structures tunnel at Langley at a Mach No. of 7.4 reaching temperatures of 2,000° F.

Oct. 24 ...... The X–24 lifting-body research vehicle, having first flown earlier this year, made its first supersonic flight, reaching 760 m.p.h.

Nov. 4 ...... The Anglo-French Concorde 001 flew at the speed of mach 2 at 50,000 ft.

Nov. 14 .... The joint Army-Navy-Marine Corps Heavy Lift Helicopter request for proposals was issued to industry. This aircraft will have a payload of 22.5 tons, double the existing free world capability.

Nov. 16 .... The Lockheed L–1011 "airbus" completed its maiden flight. The L–1011 is also a large-capacity jet designed for medium- and long-haul operations.

Nov. 24 ..... In a joint Navy-NASA flight program, a modified T–2–C aircraft made its first flight with a thick supercritical wing.

Dec. 21 ...... The F–14A Tomcat, Navy air superiority fighter, successfully flew for the first time at Calverton, N.Y.

SOURCE: National Aeronautics and Space Council, "Aeronautics and Space Report of the President," 1971.

UNITED STATES APPLICATIONS SATELLITES, 1958-70

GEODESY

Date	Name	Launch vehicle	Remarks
Oct. 31, 1962	Anna 1B	Thor-Able Star	Used 3 independent measuring techniques: Doppler frequency shift, flashing lights, and radio triangulation.
Jan. 11, 1964	Secor I	Thor-Agena D	Uses radio triangulation and trilateration.
Oct. 10, 1964	Beacon-Explorer XXII	Scout	Conducted reflecting-light geodetic measurements.
Mar. 9, 1965	Secor III	Thor-Agena D	
Mar. 11, 1965	Secor II	Thor-Able Star	
Apr. 3, 1965	Secor IV	Atlas-Agena D	
Apr. 29, 1965	Beacon-Explorer XXVII	Scout	
Aug. 10, 1965	Secor V	Scout	
Nov. 6, 1965	GEOS–I Explorer XXIX	Thor-Delta	
June 9, 1966	Secor VI	Atlas-Agena D	
June 23, 1966	Pageos I	Thor-Agena D	Spacecraft is a 100-foot-diameter balloon used as a photographic target to make geodetic measurements.
Aug. 19, 1966	Secor VII	Atlas-Agena D	
Oct. 5, 1966	Secor VIII	Atlas-Agena D	
June 29, 1967	Secor IX	Thor-Burner II	
Jan. 11, 1968	GEOS II	Thor-Delta	
Apr. 14, 1969	Secor XIII	Thor-Agena D	
Apr. 8, 1970	Topo I	Thor-Agena D	

COMMUNICATIONS

Date	Name	Launch vehicle	Remarks
Dec. 18, 1958	Score	Atlas B	First Comsat, carried taped messages.
Aug. 12, 1960	Echo I	Thor-Delta	100-foot balloon served as first passive Comsat, relayed voice and TV signals.
Oct. 4, 1960	Courier 1B	Thor-Able Star	First active-repeater Comsat.
Mar. 30, 1961	Lofti I	Thor-Able Star	Low-frequency experiment; failed to separate from rest of payload.
Oct. 21, 1961	Westford I	Atlas-Agena B	First attempt to establish filament belt around earth; failed to disperse as planned.
Dec. 12, 1961	Oscar I	Thor-Agena B	First amateur radio "ham" satellite.
June 2, 1962	Oscar II	Thor-Agena B	
July 10, 1962	Telstar I	Thor-Delta	Industry-furnished spacecraft in near-earth orbit.
Dec. 13, 1962	Relay I	Thor-Delta	Active-repeater Comsat.
Feb. 14, 1963	Syncom I	Thor-Delta	Successfully injected into near-synchronous orbit but communication system failed at orbital injection.
May 7, 1963	Telstar II	Thor-Delta	
May 9, 1963	Westford II	Atlas-Agena B	Filaments formed reflective belt around earth as planned for emergency communications experiment.
July 26, 1963	Syncom II	Thor-Delta	First successful synchronous orbit active-repeater Comsat. After experimental phase, used operationally by DOD.
Jan. 21, 1964	Relay II	Thor-Delta	
Jan. 25, 1964	Echo II	Thor-Agena B	135-foot balloon, passive Comsat, first joint use by United States and U.S.S.R.
Aug. 19, 1964	Syncom III	Thor-Delta	Synchronous-orbit Comsat; after experimental phase, used operationally by DOD.
Feb. 11, 1965	LES I	Titan IIIA	Experimental payload did not reach intended apogee.
Mar. 9, 1965	Oscar III	Thor-Agena D	
Apr. 6, 1965	Intelsat I (Early Bird)	Thor-Delta	First Intelsat (Comsat Corporation) spacecraft, 240 2-way voice circuits; commercial transatlantic communication service initiated June 28, 1965.
May 6, 1965	LES II	Titan IIIA	All solid state advanced experiment.
Dec. 21, 1965	LES III	Titan IIIC	All solid state, UHF signal generator.
	LES IV		All solid state SHF or X band experiment.
	Oscar IV		
June 16, 1966	IDCSP 1–7	Titan IIIC	Initial defense communication satellites program (IDCSP)- Active-repeater spacecraft in near-synchronous orbit, random. spaced.

UNITED STATES APPLICATIONS SATELLITES, 1958-70 (Continued)

COMMUNICATIONS—Continued

Date	Name	Launch vehicle	Remarks
Oct. 26, 1966	Intelsat II–F1	Thor-Delta(TAT)	First in Intelsat II series spacecraft; 240 2-way voice circuits or 1 color TV channel. Orbit achieved not adequate for commercial operation.
Nov. 3, 1966	OV 4–1T OV 4–IR	Titan IIIC	Transmitter and receiver for low-power satellite-to-satellite F layer experiments.
Dec. 7, 1966	ATS I	Atlas-Agena D	Multipurpose, including VHF exchange of signals with aircraft.
Jan. 11, 1967	Intelsat II–F2	Thor-Delta(TAT)	Transpacific commercial communication service initiated Jan. 11, 1967.
Jan. 18, 1967	IDCSP 8–15	Titan IIIC	
Mar. 22, 1967	Intelsat II–F3	Thor-Delta(TAT)	Positioned to carry transatlantic commercial communication traffic.
Apr. 6, 1967	ATS II	Atlas-Agena D	Multipurpose, but did not attain planned orbit.
July 1, 1967	IDCSP 16–18 LES V DATS DODGE	Titan IIIC	Tactical military communications tests with aircraft, ships, and mobile land stations from near synchronous orbit. Electronically despun antenna experiment. Multipurpose, gravity stabilized.
Sept. 27, 1967	Intelsat II–F4	Thor-Delta(TAT)	Positioned to carry commercial transpacific communication traffic.
Nov. 5, 1967	ATS III	Atlas-Agena D	Multipurpose including communications.
June 13, 1968	IDCSP 19–26	Titan IIIC	
Aug. 10, 1968	ATS IV	Atlas-Centaur	Multipurpose; failed to separate from Centaur, did not reach planned orbit.
Sept. 26, 1968	LES 6	Titan IIIC	Continued military tactical communications experiments.
Dec. 18, 1968	Intelsat III (F–2)	Thor-Delta(TAT)	First in Intelsat III series of spacecraft, 1,200 2-way voice circuits or 4 color TV channels. Positioned over Atlantic to carry traffic between North America, South America, Africa, and Europe. Entered commercial service on Dec. 24, 1968.
Feb. 6, 1969	Intelsat III(F–3)	Thor-Delta (TAT)	Stationed over Pacific to carry commercial traffic between the United States, Far East, and Australia.
Feb. 9, 1969	Tacsat I	Titan IIIC	Demonstrated feasibility of using a spaceborne repeater to satisfy selected communications needs of DOD mobile forces.
May 22, 1969	Intelsat III(F–4)	Thor-Delta(TAT)	Stationed over Pacific to replace F–3 which was moved westward to the Indian Ocean. Completes global coverage.
July 26, 1969	Intelsat III(F–5)	Thor-Delta(TAT)	Spacecraft failed to achieve the proper orbit. Not usable.
August 12, 1969	ATS V	Atlas Centaur	Multipurpose; for millimeter and L band communications; entered flat spin.
Nov. 22, 1969	Skynet I (IDCSP–A)	Thor-Delta(TAT)	Launched for the United Kingdom in response to an agreement to augment the IDCSP program.
Jan. 15, 1970	Intelsat III(F–6)	Thor-Delta(TAT)	Stationed over Atlantic to carry commercial traffic between the United States, Europe, Latin America, and the Middle East.
Jan. 23, 1970	Oscar V (Australis)	Thor-Delta(TAT)	Ham radio satellite built by amateur radio operators at Melbourne University, Melbourne, Australia.
Mar. 20, 1970	NATOSAT–I (NATO–A)	Thor-Delta (TAT)	First NATO satellite, stationed over Atlantic to carry military traffic between the United States and other NATO countries.
Apr. 23, 1970	Intelsat III (F–7)	Thor-Delta (TAT)	Stationed over Atlantic to carry commercial traffic between the United States, Europe, North Africa, and the Middle East.
Jul. 23, 1970	Intelsat III (F–8)	Thor-Delta (TAT)	Spacecraft failed to achieve the proper orbit. Not usable. Last launch of Intelsat III series.
Aug. 22, 1970	Skynet II (IDCSP–B)	Thor-Delta (TAT)	Launched for the United Kingdom in response to an agreement to augment the IDCSP program. Spacecraft failed to achieve the proper orbit.

NAVIGATION

Date	Name	Launch vehicle	Remarks
Apr. 13, 1960	Transit 1B	Thor-Able Star	First navigation satellite. Used Doppler frequency shift for position determination.
June 22, 1960	Transit 2A	Thor-Able Star	
Feb. 21, 1961	Transit 3B	Thor-Able Star	
June 29, 1961	Transit 4A	Thor-Able Star	Used the first spacecraft nuclear SNAP–3 as a secondary power supply.
Nov. 15, 1961	Tranist 4B	Thor-Able Star	
Dec. 18, 1962	Transit 5A	Scout	Operational prototype, power failed during first day.
June 15, 1963	NavSat	Scout	Used gravity-gradient stabilization system.

UNITED STATES APPLICATIONS SATELLITES, 1958-70   (Continued)

NAVIGATION—Continued

Date	Name	Launch vehicle	Remarks
Sept. 28, 1963	NavSat	Thor-Able Star	Used first nuclear SNAP–9A as primary power supply.
Dec. 5, 1963	NavSat	Thor-Able Star	
June 4, 1964	NavSat	Scout	
Oct. 6, 1964	NavSat	Thor-Able Star	
Dec. 13, 1964	NavSat	Thor-Able Star	
Mar. 11, 1965	NavSat	Thor-Able Star	
June 24, 1965	NavSat	Thor-Able Star	
Aug. 13, 1965	NavSat	Thor-Able Star	
Dec. 22, 1965	NavSat	Scout	
Jan. 28, 1966	NavSat	Scout	
Mar. 25, 1966	NavSat	Scout	
May 19, 1966	NavSat	Scout	
Aug. 18, 1966	NavSat	Scout	
Apr. 13, 1967	NavSat	Scout	
May 18, 1967	NavSat	Scout	
Sept. 25, 1967	NavSat	Scout	
Mar. 1, 1968	NavSat	Scout	
Aug. 27, 1970	NavSat	Scout	

WEATHER OBSERVATION

Date	Name	Launch vehicle	Remarks
Apr. 1, 1960	Tiros I	Thor-Able	First weather satellite providing cloud-cover photography.
Nov. 23, 1960	Tiros II	Thor-Delta	
July 12, 1961	Tiros III	Thor-Delta	
Feb. 8, 1962	Tiros IV	Thor-Delta	
June 19, 1962	Tiros V	Thor-Delta	
Sept. 18, 1962	Tiros VI	Thor-Delta	
June 19, 1963	Tiros VII	Thor-Delta	
Dec. 21, 1963	Tiros VIII	Thor-Delta	First weather satellite designed to transmit continuously local cloud conditions to ground stations equipped with APT receivers.
Aug. 28, 1964	Nimbus I	Thor-Agena B	Carried advanced videcon camera system, APT, and a high resolution infrared radiometer for night pictures.
Jan. 22, 1965	Tiros IX	Thor-Delta	First weather satellite in a sun-synchronous orbit.
July 2, 1965	Tiros X	Thor-Delta	
Feb. 3, 1966	ESSA 1	Thor-Delta	First operational weather satellite; carried 2 wide-angle TV camera systems.
Feb. 28, 1966	ESSA 2	Thor-Delta	Complemented ESSA I with 2 wide-angle APT cameras.
May 15, 1966	Nimbus II	Thor-Agena B	
Oct. 2, 1966	ESSA 3	Thor-Delta	Odd-numbered ESSA spacecraft carry 2 advanced videcon camera systems. Even-numbered spacecraft carry 2 automatic picture transmission camera systems.
Dec. 6, 1966	ATS–1	Atlas-Agena D	Provided continuous black-and-white cloud-cover pictures from a synchronous orbit, using a Suomi camera system.
Jan. 26, 1967	ESSA 4	Thora-Delta	
Apr. 20, 1967	ESSA 5	Thor-Delta	
Nov. 5, 1967	ATS–3	Atlas-Agena	Provided continuous color cloud-cover pictures from a synchronous orbit, using 3 Suomi camera systems.
Nov. 10, 1967	ESSA 6	Thor-Delta	
Aug. 16, 1968	ESSA 7	Thor-Delta	
Dec. 15, 1968	ESSA 8	Thor-Delta	
Feb. 26, 1969	ESSA 9	Thor-Delta	
Apr. 14, 1969	Nimbus III	Thor-Agena	Provided first vertical temperature profile on a global basis of the atmosphere from the spacecraft to the Earth's surface.
Jan. 23, 1970	ITOS I (Tiros M)	Thor-Delta	Second generation operational meteorological satellite.
Apr. 8, 1970	Nimbus IV	Thor-Agena	Fifth in a series of 7 advanced research and development weather satellites.
Dec. 11, 1970	NOAA–1 (ITOS-A)	Thor-Delta	Second generation operational meteorological satellite

SOURCE: National Aeronautics and Space Council, "Aeronautics and Space Report of the President," 1971.

HISTORY OF UNITED STATES AND SOVIET MANNED SPACE FLIGHTS

Spacecraft	Launch date	Crew	Flight time	Highlights
Vostok 1	Apr. 12, 1961	Yuri A. Gagarin	1 hr. 48 mins.	First manned flight.
Mercury-Redstone 3	May 5, 1961	Alan N. Shepard, Jr.	15 mins.	First U.S. flight; suborbital.
Mercury-Redstone 4	July 21, 1961	Virgil I. Grissom	16 mins.	Suborbital; capsule sank after landing.
Vostok 2	Aug. 6, 1961	Gherman S. Titov	25 hrs. 18 mins.	First flight exceeding 24 hrs.
Mercury-Atlas 6	Feb. 20, 1962	John H. Glenn, Jr.	4 hrs. 55 mins.	First American to orbit.
Mercury-Atlas 7	May 24, 1962	M. Scott Carpenter	4 hrs. 56 mins.	Landed 250 mi. from target.
Vostok 3	Aug. 11, 1962	Andrian G. Nikolayev	94 hrs. 22 mins.	First dual mission (with Vostok 4)
Vostok 4	Aug. 12, 1962	Pavel R. Popovich	70 hrs. 57 mins.	Came within 4 mi. of Vostok 3.
Mercury-Atlas 8	Oct. 3, 1962	Walter M. Schirra, Jr.	9 hrs. 13 mins.	Landed 5 mi. from target.
Mercury-Atlas 9	May 15, 1963	L. Gordon Cooper, Jr.	34 hrs. 20 mins.	First long U.S. flight.
Vostok 5	June 14, 1963	Valery F. Bykovsky	119 hrs. 6 mins.	Second dual mission (with Vostok 6).
Vostok 6	June 16, 1963	Valentina V. Tereshkova	70 hrs. 50 mins.	First woman in space; within 3 mi. of Vostok 5.
Voskhod 1	Oct. 12, 1964	Vladimir M. Komarov Konstantin P. Feoktistov Dr. Boris G. Yegorov	24 hrs. 17 mins.	First 3-man crew.
Voskhod 2	Mar. 18, 1965	Aleksei A. Leonov Pavel I. Belyayev	26 hrs. 2 mins.	First extravehicular activity (Leonov, 10 mins.).
Gemini 3	Mar. 23, 1965	Virgil I. Grissom John W. Young	4 hrs. 53 mins.	First U.S. 2-man flight; first manual maneuvers in orbit.
Gemini 4	June 3, 1965	James A. McDivitt Edward H. White, 2d	97 hrs. 56 mins.	21-minute extravehicular activity (White).
Gemini 5	Aug. 21, 1965	L. Gordon Cooper, Jr. Charles Conrad, Jr.	190 hrs. 55 mins.	Longest-duration manned flight to date.
Gemini 7	Dec. 4, 1965	Frank Borman James A. Lovell, Jr.	330 hrs. 36 mins.	Longest-duration manned flight.
Gemini 6–A	Dec. 15, 1965	Walter M. Schirra, Jr. Thomas P. Stafford	25 hrs. 51 mins.	Rendezvous within 1 foot of Gemini 7.
Gemini 8	Mar. 16, 1966	Neil A. Armstrong David R. Scott	10 hrs. 41 mins.	First docking of 2 orbiting space craft (Gemini 8 with Agena target rocket).
Gemini 9–A	June 3, 1966	Thomas P. Stafford Eugene A. Cernan	72 hrs. 21 mins.	Extravehicular activity; rendezvous.
Gemini 10	July 18, 1966	John W. Young Michael Collins	70 hrs. 47 mins.	First dual rendezvous (Gemini 10 with Agena 10, then Agena 8.).
Gemini 11	Sept. 12, 1966	Charles Conrad, Jr. Richard F. Gordon, Jr.	71 hrs. 17 mins.	First initial-orbit rendezvous; first tethered flight; highest Earth-orbit altitude (853 miles).
Gemini 12	Nov. 11, 1966	James A. Lovell, Jr. Edwin E. Aldrin, Jr.	94 hrs. 35 mins.	Longest extravehicular activity (Aldrin, 5 hours 37 minutes).
Soyuz 1	Apr. 23, 1967	Vladimir M. Komarov	26 hrs. 40 mins.	Cosmonaut killed in reentry accident.
Apollo 7	Oct. 11, 1968	Walter M. Schirra, Jr. Donn F. Eisele R. Walter Cunningham	260 hrs. 8 mins.	First U.S. 3-man mission.
Soyuz 3	Oct. 26, 1968	Georgi Beregovoy	94 hrs. 51 mins.	Maneuvered near unmanned Soyuz 2.
Apollo 8	Dec. 21, 1968	Frank Borman James A. Lovell, Jr. William A. Anders	147 hrs.	First manned orbit(s) of moon; first manned departure from earth's sphere of influence; highest speed ever attained in manned flight.
Soyuz 4	Jan. 14, 1969	Vladimir Shatalov	71 hrs. 22 mins.	Soyuz 4 and 5 docked and transferred 2 Cosmonauts from Soyuz 5 to Soyuz 4.
Soyuz 5	Jan. 15, 1969	Boris Volynov Alecksey Yeliseyev Yevgeniv Khrunov	72 hrs. 40 mins.	
Apollo 9	Mar. 3, 1969	James A. McDivitt David R. Scott Russell L. Schweickart	241 hrs. 1 min.	Successfully simulated in earth orbit operation of lunar module to landing and takeoff from lunar surface and rejoining with command module.
Apollo 10	May 18, 1969	Thomas P. Stafford John W. Young Eugene A. Cernan	192 hrs. 3 mins.	Successfully demonstrated complete system, including lunar module descent to 47,000 ft. from the lunar surface.
Apollo 11	July 16, 1969	Neil A. Armstrong Michael Collins Edwin E. Aldrin, Jr.	195 hrs. 19 mins.	First manned landing on lunar surface and safe return to earth. First return of rock and soil samples to earth, and manned deployment of experiments on lunar surface.

HISTORY OF UNITED STATES AND SOVIET MANNED SPACE FLIGHTS   (Continued)

Spacecraft	Launch date	Crew	Flight time	Highlights
Soyuz 6	Oct. 11, 1969	Georgiy Shonin Valeriy Kubasov	118 hrs. 21 mins.	Soyuz 6, 7 and 8 operated as a group flight without actually docking. Each conducted certain experiments, including welding and earth and celestial observations.
Soyuz 7	Oct. 12, 1969	Anatoliy Filipchencko Vladislav Volkov Viktor Gorbatko	118 hrs. 43 mins.	
Soyuz 8	Oct. 13, 1969	Vladimir Shatalov Aleksey Yeliseyev	118 hrs. 51 mins.	
Apollo 12	Nov. 14, 1969	Charles Conrad, Jr. Richard F. Gordon, Jr. Alan L. Bean	244 hrs. 36 mins.	Second manned lunar landing. Continued manned exploration and retrieved parts of Surveyor III spacecraft which landed in Ocean of Storms on Apr. 19, 1967.
Apollo 13	Apr. 11, 1970	James A. Lovell, Jr. Fred W. Haise, Jr. John L. Swigert, Jr.	142 hrs. 55 mins.	Mission aborted due to explosion in the service module. Ship circled moon, with crew using LEM as "lifeboat" until just prior to reentry.
Soyuz 9	Jun. 1, 1970	Andrian G. Nikolayev Vitaliy I. Sevastianov	424 hrs. 59 mins.	Longest manned space flight lasting 17 days 16 hrs. 59 mins.

SOURCE: National Aeronautics and Space Council, "Aeronautics and Space Report of the President," 1971.

UNITED STATES SPACE LAUNCH VEHICLES

Vehicle	Stages	Propellant [4]	Thrust (in thousands of pounds)	Max. dia. (feet)	Height spacecraft (feet)	Payload (pounds) 300 NM orbit	Escape	First launch
Scout	1. Algol (IIB)	Solid	100.9	3.3	64.4	320	50	[1] 1965 (60)
	2. Castor II	Solid	60.7					
	3. Antares II	Solid	20.9					
	4. Altair III or FW4	Solid	5.9					
Thrust-augmented Thorad-Delta.	1. Thor (SLV-2J) plus	LOX/RP	170	11	92	2,000	525	1968 (60)
	three TX 354-5	Solid	[2] 52					
	2. Delta (DSV-3)	IRFNA/UDMH	7.8					
	3. FW-4D/TE 364	Solid	5.9/10.0					
Thrust-augmented Thorad-Agena.	1. Thor (SLV-2H) plus	LOX/RP	170	11	90	2,900	....	1966 (60)
	three TX 354-5	Solid	[2] 52					
	2. Agena	IRFNA/UDMH	16					
Atlas-Burner II	1. Atlas booster and sustainer (SLV-3A).	LOX/RP	400	'10	84	4,950	700	1968
	2. Burner II	Solid	10					
Atlas-Agena	1. Atlas booster and sustainer (SLV-3A).	LOX/RP	[6] 465	10	100	7,500	1,430	1968 (60)
	2. Agena	IRFNA/UDMH	16					
Titan IIIB-Agena	1. LR-87	N₂O₄/Aerozine	440	10	113	8,000	1,550	1966
	2. LR-91	N₂O₄/Aerozine	100					
	3. Agena	IRFNA/UDMH	16					
Titan IIIC	1. Two 5-segment 120" diameter.	Solid	2,400	10x30	107	25,000	5,500	1965
	2. LR-87	N₂O₄/Aerozine	[5] 527					
	3. LR-91	N₂O₄/Aerozine	100					
	4. Transtage	N₂O₄/Aerozine	16					
Titan-Centaur	1. Two 5-segment 120" diameter.	Solid	2,400	10x30	209.5	[7] 32,000	11,000	1974 (est.)
	2. LR-87	N₂O₄/Aerozine	440					
	3. LR-91	N₂O₄/Aerozine	110					
	4. Centaur (Two RL-10).	LOX/LH	30					
Atlas-Centaur	1. Atlas booster and sustainer.	LOX/RP	400	10	103	9,100	2,700	1967 (62)
	2. Centaur (Two RL-10).	LOX/LH	30					

See footnotes at end of table.

UNITED STATES SPACE LAUNCH VEHICLES   (Continued)

Vehicle	Stages	Propellant [4]	Thrust (in thousands of pounds)	Max. dia. (feet)	Height spacecraft (feet)	Payload (pounds) 300 NM orbit	Escape	First launch
Uprated Saturn IB..	1. S–IB (Eight H–1).	LOX/RP.........	1,600	21.6	142	40,000@ 105 NM	....	1966
	2. S–IVB (One J–2).	LOX/LH........	200					
Saturn V.........	1. S–IC (Five F–1)..	LOX/RP.........	7,570	33	[3] 281	285,000@ 105 NM	100,000	1967
	2. S–II (Five J–2)...	LOX/LH........	1,150					
	3. S–IVB (One J–2).	LOX/LH........	230					

[1] The date of first launch applies to this latest modification with a date in parentheses for the initial version.

[2] Each motor.

[3] 363 feet, including Apollo modules and Launch Escape System.

[4] Propellant abbreviations used are as follows: Liquid Oxygen and a modified Kerosene—LOX/RP; Solid propellant combining in a single mixture both fuel and oxidizer—Solid;

Inhibited Red Fuming Nitric Acid and Unsymmetrical Dimethylhydrazine—IRFNA/UDMH; Nitrogen Tetroxide and 50% UDMH and 50% Hydrazine (N_2H_4)—N_2O_4/Aerozine; Liquid Oxygen and Liquid Hydrogen—LOX/LH.

[5] Vacuum thrust; stage 1 is ignited at altitude.

[6] Thrust at sea level.

[7] Structural weight limitation currently 12,000 lbs.

SOURCE: National Aeronautics and Space Council, "Aeronautics and Space Report of the President," 1971.

UNITED STATES SUCCESSFUL LAUNCHES TO EARTH ORBIT OR BEYOND BY LAUNCH VEHICLE, 1958-70

Launch vehicle	Subtotals	Launch vehicle	Subtotals
Thor-Able........................	3	Titan IIIB Agena.............................	29
Thor-Able Star....................	14	Titan IIIC...................................	14
Thor-Delta........................	76		
Thor-Agena........................	155	TITAN total.............................	57
Thor-Altair.......................	5	SCOUT total.............................	43
Thor-Burner II....................	10		
		Saturn I....................................	6
THOR total.........................	263	Saturn IB....................................	3
Atlas.............................	16	SATURN I total.........................	9
Atlas-Agena.......................	90	SATURN V total.........................	8
Atlas-Centaur.....................	17	REDSTONE total.........................	3
		JUPITER total............................	4
ATLAS total.........................	123	VANGUARD total........................	3
Titan II....................................	11	Grand total..........................	513
Titan IIIA..................................	3		

SOURCE: National Aeronautics and Space Council, "Aeronautics and Space Report of the President," 1971.

NUCLEAR POWER SYSTEMS FOR SPACE APPLICATION

Designation	Application	Status
SNAP–3	Navigation satellites (DOD)	Units launched in June and November 1961. Unit still operating at reduced power levels.
SNAP–9A	Navigation satellites (DOD)	Units launched in September and December 1963. Units still operating at reduced power level. Third satellite failed to orbit in April 1964.
SNAP–19	Nimbus B weather satellite (NASA)	First Nimbus B launch aborted; Pu-238 fuel recovered from offshore waters. Replacement unit launched in April 1969 and has operated continuously at gradually reducing power levels since that time.
SNAP–27	Apollo lunar surface experiment package (NASA)	First SNAP–27 placed on lunar surface by Apollo 12 astronaut in November 1969. System is supplying total power for ALSEP.
SNAP–10A	Unmanned missions	Tested in orbit in 1965.
Transit [1]	Navigation satellites (DOD)	Development program underway.
Pioneer [1]	Jupiter flyby mission (NASA)	Modified SNAP–19 generator system will be used.
Viking [1]	Mars unmanned lander mission (NASA)	Modified SNAP–19 generator system will be used.

[1] Planned missions.

SOURCE: National Aeronautics and Space Council, "Aeronautics and Space Report of the President," 1971.

SPACE ACTIVITIES OF THE UNITED STATES GOVERNMENT

10-Year Summary and 1972 Budget Recommendations, January 1971—New Obligational Authority

[In millions of dollars (may not add due to rounding)]

	NASA		Department of Defense	AEC	Commerce	Interior	Agriculture	NSF	Total space
	Total	Space [1]							
1959..............	305. 4	235. 4	489. 5	34. 3	....			...	759. 2
1960..............	523. 6	461. 5	560. 9	43. 3	....			. 1	1, 065. 8
1961..............	964. 0	926. 0	813. 9	67. 7	....			. 6	1, 808. 2
1962..............	1, 824. 9	1, 796. 8	1, 298. 2	147. 8	50. 7	....		1. 3	3, 294. 8
1963..............	3, 673. 0	3, 626. 0	1, 549. 9	213. 9	43. 2	....		1. 5	5, 434. 5
1964..............	5, 099. 7	5, 046. 3	1, 599. 3	210. 0	2. 8	....		3. 0	6, 861. 4
1965..............	5, 249. 7	5, 167. 6	1, 573. 9	228. 6	12. 2	....		3. 2	6, 985. 5
1966..............	5, 174. 9	5, 094. 5	1, 688. 8	186. 8	26. 5	4. 1	....	3. 2	7, 003. 9
1967..............	4, 967. 6	4, 862. 2	1, 663. 6	183. 6	29. 3	3. 0	....	2. 8	6, 744. 5
1968..............	4, 588. 8	4, 452. 5	1, 921. 8	145. 1	28. 1	2. 0	0. 5	3. 2	6, 553. 2
1969..............	3, 990. 9	3, 822. 0	2, 013. 0	118. 0	20. 0	2. 0	0. 7	1. 9	5, 977. 6
1970..............	3, 745. 8	3, 547. 0	1, 678. 4	102. 8	8. 0	2. 0	0. 8	2. 4	5, 341. 4
1972 budget									
1971.............	3, 297. 0	3, 101. 4	1, 553. 1	94. 5	25. 0	3. 0	1. 1	2. 2	4, 780. 3
1972.............	3, 270. 0	3, 055. 4	1, 552. 6	56. 2	32. 0	7. 0	1. 5	2. 0	4, 706. 7

[1] Excludes amounts for aviation technology.   Source: Office of Management and Budget.

SOURCE: National Aeronautics and Space Council, "Aeronautics and Space Report of the President," 1971.

UNITED STATES SPACE BUDGET: NEW OBLIGATIONAL AUTHORITY

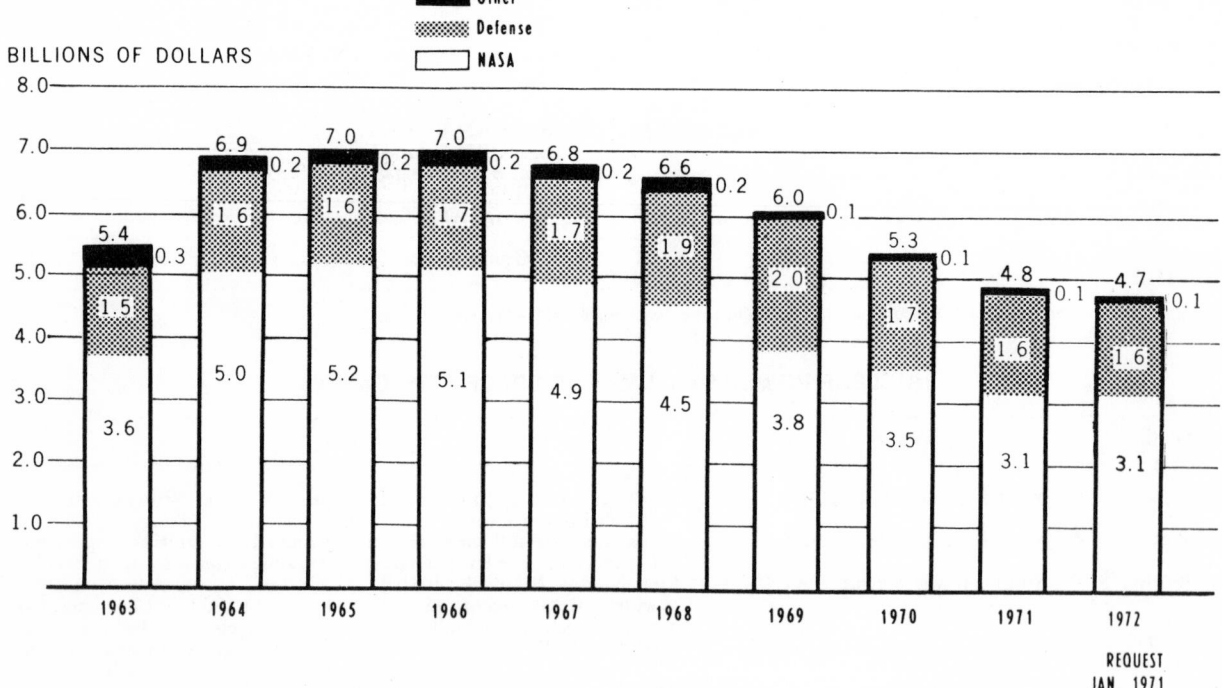

SOURCE: National Aeronautics and Space Council, "Aeronautics and Space Report of the President," 1971.

SPACE ACTIVITIES BUDGET

[In millions of dollars]

	New obligational authority			Expenditures		
	1970 actual	1971 estimate	1972 estimate	1970 actual	1971 estimate	1972 estimate
Federal space programs:						
NASA [1]	3,547.0	3,101.4	3,055.4	3,565.2	3,185.2	2,957.6
Defense	1,678.4	1,553.1	1,552.6	1,756.1	1,577.0	1,574.8
AEC	102.8	94.5	56.2	102.6	96.5	62.3
Commerce	8.0	25.0	32.0	24.0	23.0	29.0
Interior	2.0	3.0	7.0	2.0	3.0	6.0
NSF	2.4	2.2	2.0	2.3	2.1	2.0
Agriculture	0.8	1.1	1.5	1.0	1.1	1.5
Total	5,341.4	4,780.3	4,706.7	5,453.2	4,887.9	4,633.2
NASA:						
Manned space flight	2,262.5	1,770.2	1,637.6	2,209.2	1,887.3	1,662.2
Space science and applications	637.1	693.2	889.8	569.4	631.1	727.2
Space technology	288.4	278.2	208.0	328.1	286.1	234.6
Aviation technology	198.8	195.6	214.6	187.9	183.7	194.8
Supporting activities	364.9	373.1	333.4	460.2	392.6	345.6
Less receipts	—5.9	—13.3	—13.4	—5.9	—13.3	—13.4
Total NASA	3,745.8	3,297.0	3,270.0	3,748.9	3,367.5	3,151.0

[1] Excludes amounts for aviation technology.

SOURCE: National Aeronautics and Space Council, "Aeronautics and Space Report of the President," 1971.

AERONAUTICS BUDGET

[In millions of dollars]

	New obligational authority		
	1970	1971 estimate	1972 estimate
Federal aeronautics programs:			
NASA [1]	198.8	195.6	214.6
Department of Defense [2]	1,640.9	1,642.8	1,975.4
Department of Transportation	41.8	70.0	81.5
Total	1,881.5	1,908.4	2,271.5

[1] R. & D., R. & P.M., C. of F.
[2] R.D.T. & E. aircraft and related equipment.

SOURCE: National Aeronautics and Space Council, "Aeronautics and Space Report of the President," 1971.

FEDERAL FUNDS FOR SPACE RESEARCH AND TECHNOLOGY

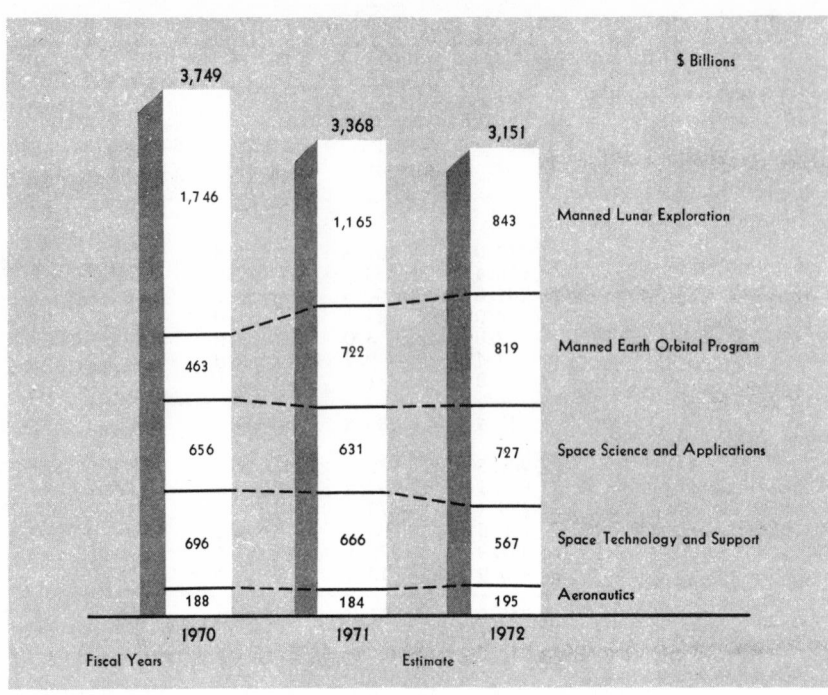

[In millions of dollars]

Program	Outlays			Recommended budget authority for 1972 [1]
	1970 actual	1971 estimate	1972 estimate	
Manned space flight:				
Lunar program	1,746	1,165	843	726
Earth orbital program	463	722	819	912
Space science and applications	656	631	727	890
Space technology	328	286	234	208
Aircraft technology	188	184	195	215
Supporting space activities [2]	374	393	347	333
Deductions for offsetting receipts:				
Proprietary receipts from the public	−6	−13	−13	−13
Total	**3,749**	**3,368**	**3,151**	**3,270**

[1] Compares with budget authority for 1970 and 1971, as follows:
  1970 total, $3,746 million.
  1971 total, $3,297 million.

[2] Includes both Federal funds and trust funds.

SOURCE: Office of Management and Budget, "The Budget of the United States Government, Fiscal Year 1972."

FEDERAL FUNDS FOR SPACE RESEARCH AND TECHNOLOGY (Continued)

NATIONAL AERONAUTICS AND SPACE ADMINISTRATION

(in thousands of dollars)

		1970 enacted	1971 estimate	1972 estimate	Increase or decrease (−)	Explanation
Federal Funds						
General and special funds:						
Research and development:	NOA	**2,992,954**	**2,555,000**	[2] **2,517,700**	**−37,300**	Requirements for the Apollo lunar exploration program are reduced due to the prior cancellation of Apollo 18 and 19. Other decreases result from reduction of the NERVA nuclear rocket program, reduction of supporting activities, and the completion of certain science and applications projects. These decreases are partially offset by increases for Skylab experimental space station, engine development for a space shuttle, Viking unmanned Mars lander, the outer planets Grand Tour program, and space applications projects.
	Exp.	2,991,634	2,610,000	2,411,000	−199,000	
(Manned space flight)	NOA	**(1,912,694)**	**(1,431,100)**	**(1,286,475)**	**(−144,625)**	
	Exp.	(1,856,990)	(1,543,000)	(1,317,000)	(−226,000)	
(Space science and applications)	NOA	**(519,179)**	**(563,300)**	**(749,200)**	**(185,900)**	
	Exp.	(530,896)	(502,600)	(597,800)	(95,200)	
(Space technology)	NOA	**(175,396)**	**(164,600)**	**(104,025)**	**(−60,575)**	
	Exp.	(201,376)	(176,500)	(128,000)	(−48,500)	
(Aircraft technology)	NOA	**(95,685)**	**(102,000)**	**(110,000)**	**(8,000)**	
	Exp.	(83,995)	(85,900)	(91,700)	(5,800)	
(Supporting space activities)	NOA	**(290,000)**	**(294,000)**	**(268,000)**	**(−26,000)**	
	Exp.	(318,377)	(302,000)	(276,500)	(−25,500)	
Construction of facilities:	NOA	**53,233**	**24,950**	[2] **56,300**	**31,350**	Increases in manned space flight reflect requirements for the space shuttle program. Increase in space science and applications reflects launch pad modifications for improved launch vehicles. The balance of the request provides for wind tunnel improvements, tracking station modification, and laboratory facilities and design.
	Exp.	54,297	50,000	43,000	−7,000	
(Manned space flight)	NOA	**(14,250)**	**(570)**	**(20,000)**	**(19,430)**	
	Exp.	(14,490)	(9,100)	(13,700)	(4,600)	
(Space science and applications)	NOA	**(1,170)**	**(2,580)**	**(15,200)**	**(12,620)**	
	Exp.	(7,629)	(2,400)	(3,800)	(1,400)	
(Space technology)	NOA	----------	**(1,250)**	----------	**(−1,250)**	
	Exp.	(12,965)	(1,300)	(500)	(−800)	
(Aircraft technology)	NOA	**(4,767)**	----------	**(6,500)**	**(6,500)**	
	Exp.	(4,859)	(5,100)	(4,800)	(−300)	
(Supporting space activities)	NOA	**(33,046)**	**(20,550)**	**(14,600)**	**(−5,950)**	
	Exp.	(14,354)	(32,100)	(20,200)	(−11,900)	
Research and program management.	NOA	**702,555**	688,579 } [1] 29,854 }	[2] **697,350**	**−21,083**	Increased costs of research and program management at Government laboratories are more than offset by a reduction in personnel.
	Exp.	707,210	708,930	698,350	−10,580	
(Manned space flight)	NOA	**(335,571)**	(324,424) } [1] (14,066) }	**(331,100)**	**(−7,390)**	
	Exp.	(337,794)	(335,191)	(331,500)	(−3,691)	
(Space science and applications)	NOA	**(116,761)**	(122,060) } [1] (5,292) }	**(125,400)**	**(−1,952)**	
	Exp.	(117,535)	(126,110)	(125,600)	(−510)	
(Space technology)	NOA	**(113,011)**	(104,349) } [1] (4,525) }	**(104,000)**	**(−4,874)**	
	Exp.	(113,760)	(107,812)	(105,150)	(−2,662)	
(Aircraft technology)	NOA	**(98,392)**	(89,736) } [1] (3,890) }	**(98,150)**	**(4,524)**	
	Exp.	(99,044)	(92,714)	(98,300)	(5,586)	
(Supporting space activities)	NOA	**(38,820)**	(48,010) } [1] (2,081) }	**(38,700)**	**(−11,391)**	
	Exp.	(39,077)	(47,103)	(37,800)	(−9,303)	
Total Federal funds National Aeronautics and Space Administration.	NOA	**3,748,742**	**3,298,383**	**3,271,350**	**−27,033**	
	Exp.	3,753,141	3,368,930	3,152,350	−216,580	
Trust Funds						
Miscellaneous trust funds (permanent, indefinite)	NOA	**3,028**	**11,870**	**12,050**	**180**	Provides for purchase of materials and services for the European Space Research Organization and the Telesat Canada Corporation.
	Exp.	1,712	11,870	12,050	180	

[1] Proposed for separate transmittal, civilian pay act supplemental.
[2] Recommended to carry out authorizing legislation to be proposed.

This tabulation shows, for each appropriation and fund account, information on new obligational authority (NOA), and expenditures (Exp.)

SOURCE: Office of Management and Budget, "The Budget of the United States Government, Fiscal Year 1972."

FEDERAL FUNDS FOR SPACE RESEARCH AND TECHNOLOGY (Continued)

NATIONAL AERONAUTICS AND SPACE ADMINISTRATION —Continued

(in thousands of dollars)

		1970 enacted	1971 estimate	1972 estimate	Increase or decrease (—)
SUMMARY					
Federal funds:					
(As shown in detail above)	NOA	3,748,742	3,298,383	3,271,350	—27,033
	Exp.	3,753,141	3,368,930	3,152,350	—216,580
Deductions for offsetting receipts: Proprietary receipts from the public	NOA } Exp.	—2,898	—1,429	—1,349	80
	NOA } Exp.	—1	—1	—1	----------
Total Federal funds	NOA	3,745,843	3,296,953	3,270,000	—26,953
	Exp.	3,750,242	3,367,500	3,151,000	—216,500
Trust funds:					
(As shown in detail above)	NOA	3,028	11,870	12,050	180
	Exp.	1,712	11,870	12,050	180
Deductions for offsetting receipts: Proprietary receipts from the public	NOA } Exp.	—3,028	—11,870	—12,050	—180
Total trust funds	Exp	—1,316	----------	----------	----------
Total National Aeronautics and Space Administration:‡					
Total budget authority___	NOA	3,745,844	3,296,953	3,270,000	—26,953
Total outlays_____	Exp.	3,748,926	3,367,500	3,151,000	—216,500

‡Totals for the agency are distributed as follows:

	1971		1972	
	NOA	*Exp.*	*NOA*	*Exp.*
Federal funds:				
Enacted/transmitted_____	3,268,529	3,340,530	3,271,350	3,150,896
Separate transmittal:				
(D) Civilian pay_____	29,854	28,400	----------	1,454
Deductions for offsetting receipts_____	—1,430	—1,430	—1,350	—1,350
Total Federal funds_____	3,296,953	3,367,500	3,270,000	3,151,000
Trust funds:				
Enacted/transmitted_____	11,870	11,870	12,050	12,050
Deductions for offsetting receipts_____	—11,870	—11,870	—12,050	—12,050
Total trust funds_____	----------	----------	----------	----------
Total National Aeronautics and Space Administration_____	3,296,953	3,367,500	3,270,000	3,151,000

NATIONAL AERONAUTICS AND SPACE COUNCIL

(in thousands of dollars)

		1970 enacted	1971 estimate	1972 estimate	Increase or decrease (—)	Explanation
Federal Funds						
General and special funds:						
Salaries and expenses	NOA	549	500	485	—15	The Council advises and assists the President on policies, plans, and programs in aeronautical and space activities.
	Exp.	538	495	501	6	

SOURCE: Office of Management and Budget, "The Budget of the United States Government, Fiscal Year 1972."

Part 5

NASA LEGISLATION

TITLE 42.–THE PUBLIC HEALTH AND WELFARE
Chapter 26.–NATIONAL SPACE PROGRAM

SUBCHAPTER I.—GENERAL PROVISIONS

§ 2451. Congressional declaration of policy and purpose.

(a) The Congress declares that it is the policy of the United States that activities in space should be devoted to peaceful purposes for the benefit of all mankind.

(b) The Congress declares that the general welfare and security of the United States require that adequate provisions be made for aeronautical and space activities. The Congress further declares that such activities shall be the responsibility of, and shall be directed by, a civilian agency exercising control over aeronautical and space activities sponsored by the United States, except that activities peculiar to or primarily associated with the development of weapons systems, military operations, or the defense of the United States (including the research and development necessary to make effective provision for the defense of the United States) shall be the responsibility of, and shall be directed by, the Department of Defense; and that determination as to which such agency has responsibility for and direction of any such activity shall be made by the President in conformity with section 2471 (c) of this title.

(c) The aeronautical and space activities of the United States shall be conducted so as to contribute materially to one or more of the following objectives:

(1) The expansion of human knowledge of phenomena in the atmosphere and space;

(2) The improvement of the usefulness, performance, speed, safety, and efficiency of aeronautical and space vehicles;

(3) The development and operation of vehicles capable of carrying instruments, equipment, supplies, and living organisms through space;

(4) The establishment of long-range studies of the potential benefits to be gained from, the opportunities for, and the problems involved in the utilization of aeronautical and space activities for peaceful and scientific purposes;

(5) The preservation of the role of the United States as a leader in aeronautical and space science and technology and in the application thereof to the conduct of peaceful activities within and outside the atmosphere;

(6) The making available to agencies directly concerned with national defense of discoveries that have military value or significance, and the furnishing by such agencies, to the civilian agency established to direct and control nonmilitary aeronautical and space activities, of information as to discoveries which have value or significance to that agency;

(7) Cooperation by the United States with other nations and groups of nations in work done pursuant to this chapter and in the peaceful application of the results thereof; and

(8) The most effective utilization of the scientific and engineering resources of the United States, with close cooperation among all interested agencies of the United States in order to avoid unnecessary duplication of effort, facilities, and equipment.

(d) It is the purpose of this chapter to carry out and effectuate the policies declared in subsections (a), (b), and (c) of this section. (Pub. L. 85–568, title I, § 102, July 29, 1958, 72 Stat. 426.)

REFERENCES IN TEXT

"This chapter", referred to in the text, was in the original "this Act", meaning Pub. L. 85–568, which is classified to this chapter, section 22–1 of Title 5, Executive Departments and Government Officers and Employees, sections 2302 and 2303 of Title 10, Armed Forces, sections 799 and 1114 of Title 18, Crimes and Criminal Procedure, and sections 511—513 and 515 of Title 50, War and National Defense, and as notes under sections 2451 and 2472 of this title and section 2302 of Title 10.

SHORT TITLE

Section 101 of Pub. L. 85–568, which is classified to this chapter, section 22–1 of Title 5, Executive Departments and Government Officers and Employees, sections 2302 and 2303 of Title 10, Armed Forces, sections 799 and 1114 of Title 18, Crimes and Criminal Procedure, and sections 511—513 and 515 of Title 50, War and National Defense, and as notes under sections 2451 and 2472 of this title and section 2302 of Title 10, should be popularly known as the "National Aeronautics and Space Act of 1958".

Ex. Ord. No. 10946. Labor Disputes at Missile and Space Sites

Ex. Ord. No. 10946, May 26, 1961, 26 F.R. 4629, provided:

WHEREAS a successful missile program is vital to our national security, and a successful space program is vital to the national interest, therefore uninterrupted and economical operations at missile and space sites are imperative; and

WHEREAS manufacturers, construction concerns and labor unions involved in the missile and space programs have pledged their cooperation in avoiding uneconomical operations and work stoppages at missile and space sites; and

WHEREAS the Government has the clear responsibility for encouraging such cooperation and providing a proper framework for its effective operation:

NOW THEREFORE, by virtue of the authority vested in me as President of the United States, it is ordered as follows:

SECTION 1. For the purpose of developing policies, procedures, and methods of adjustment for labor problems at missile and space sites, there is hereby established a Missile Sites Labor Commission composed of: the Secretary of Labor, hereby designated as Chairman; the Director of the Federal Mediation and Conciliation Service, hereby designated as Vice-chairman; three representatives of the public, three representatives drawn from labor and three representatives drawn from management, as designated by the President.

Alternates may be designated by each member of the Commission.

In carrying out its duties the Commission shall consult fully with the Secretary of Defense, the Administrator of the National Aeronautics and Space Administration, and the Chairman and the General Counsel of the National Labor Relations Board, and such officers and the officers of other Government agencies concerned shall cooperate fully with the Commission.

The Commission is hereby empowered to employ an Executive Secretary and to delegate such powers to its Chairman, Vice-chairman and Executive Secretary as it may deem appropriate. Subject to the provisions of Section 9 of this order, the Commission may employ such staff as may be necessary and may incur other necessary expenditures.

SEC. 2. The Commission shall arrange for the establishment at each missile or space site of appropriate Missile Site Labor Relations Committees. Such Committees shall be composed of representatives of manufacturers and construction concerns, labor organizations, contracting agencies and a Mediator assigned by the Federal Mediation and Conciliation Service. These Committees will be so constituted and instructed as to take account of any necessary and appropriate distinctions in representational interests. It shall be the primary functions of such Committees to anticipate impending problems and to arrange for proper disposition of them prior to the time that such problems become acute, utilizing fully all voluntary settlement procedures already in existence, and encouraging establishment of adequate grievances and jurisdictional procedures where such procedures do not now exist, to the end of preventing any interruptions of efficient performance of work. The Commission will take such steps as are necessary to assure that labor organizations will assign appropriate international union representatives to missile sites on which their members are working for the purpose of obtaining the full cooperation of each such international union.

SEC. 3. The Commission shall establish procedures whereby it will be advised of any labor relations problem at any missile or space site which it appears cannot be settled by the voluntary settlement procedures already in existence or by action instituted by the local Missile Site Labor Relations Committee. In such event the Commission shall establish such procedures as appear to it necessary and appropriate to produce a satisfactory settlement of such problem, relying in the first instance on presently established private or governmental procedures, including available legal proceedings, so far as these will be effective.

SEC. 4. The Commission is authorized to establish special panels, composed of members of the Commission or others (as designated by the Chairman of the Commission), to hold hearings in disputed matters over which the Commission has jurisdiction, to make findings of fact, to make recommendations for the settlement of such disputes, to obtain agreement for final and binding arbitration of such disputes, to mediate such disputes, to issue such directives and to take such other action as the Commission may direct. These panels will be so constituted as to take account of any necessary and appropriate distinctions in representational interests, and in the event of conflict between manufacturing and construction groups of either industry or labor the panel shall be composed of public members only.

SEC. 5. The Commission shall develop with the federal contracting agencies and with the parties programs for obtaining, in collective bargaining contracts or other agreements or arrangements covering work at missile and space sites, the inclusion of effective commitments that there will be no lockouts or work stoppages at such sites, with adequate procedures being established for the expeditious resolution of grievances and labor problems at such sites.

SEC. 6. The commission shall take such other action as will promote the policies of this order, and shall make recommendations to government agencies, labor organizations or other authorized employee representatives and employers to assure efficient and economical completion of missile programs.

SEC. 7. Contracting agencies shall make appropriate assignments of labor relations representatives to each missile or space site on which they are operating and issue instructions and directives to insure that the policies and purposes of this Order are fully understood and will be carried out by the persons responsible for the progress of work on day-to-day basis.

SEC. 8. The National Labor Relations Board and the General Counsel of the Board are requested to establish accelerated procedures for dealing with matters at missile and space sites within the Board's jurisdiction, in accordance with law, and to make such assignment of personnel as is necessary to this end; provided that voluntary procedures for the adjustment of such matters shall continue to be used wherever available, appropriate and effective but the provisions of this Order shall not affect the authority of the Board under the National Labor Relations Act, as amended [section 151 et seq. of Title 29, Labor].

SEC. 9. The matter referred to in this Order is hereby found to constitute an emergency affecting the national interest within the meaning of the provisions appearing under the heading "Emergency Fund for the President—National Defense" in Title 1 of the General Government Matters Appropriation Act, 1961 (Public Law 86–642), approved July 12, 1960. During the fiscal year 1961 the expenditures of the commission may be paid out of an allotment made by the President from the appropriation made under the aforesaid heading "Emergency Fund for the President—National Defense"; and during the fiscal year 1962, to the extent permitted by law, such expenditures may be similarly paid from any corresponding or like appropriation made available for such fiscal year. Such payments may be made without regard to the provisions of (a) section 3681 of the Revised Statutes (31 U.S.C. 672), (b) section 9 of the act of March 4, 1909, 35 Stat. 1027 (31 U.S.C. 673), and (c) such other provisions of law as the President may hereafter specify. Members, and employees of the Commission and panel members appointed under this Order, shall, if not otherwise compensated, receive such compensation and allowances as the President shall hereafter fix, in a manner to be hereafter determined.

JOHN F. KENNEDY

§ 2452. Definitions.

As used in this chapter—

(1) the term "aeronautical and space activities" means (A) research into, and the solution of, problems of flight within and outside the earth's atmosphere, (B) the development, construction, testing, and operation for research purposes of aeronautical and space vehicles, and (C) such other activities as may be required for the exploration of space; and

(2) the term "aeronautical and space vehicles" means aircraft, missiles, satellites, and other space vehicles, manned and unmanned, together with related equipment, devices, components, and parts.

(Pub. L. 85–568, title I, § 103, July 29, 1958, 72 Stat. 427.)

REFERENCES IN TEXT

"This chapter", referred to in the text, was in the original "this Act", meaning Pub. L. 85–568, which is classified to this chapter, section 22–1 of Title 5, Executive Departments and Government Officers and Employees, sections 2302 and 2303 of Title 10, Armed Forces, sections 799 and 1114 of Title 18, Crimes and Criminal Procedure, and sections 511—513 and 515 of Title 50, War and National Defense, and as notes under sections 2451 and 2472 of this title and section 2302 of Title 10.

§ 2453. Transfer of related functions to Administration; reports to the Congress.

(a) Subject to the provisions of this section, the President, for a period of four years after July 29, 1958, may transfer to the Administration any functions (including powers, duties, activities, facilities, and parts of functions) of any other department or agency of the United States, or of any officer or organizational entity thereof, which relate primarily to the functions, powers, and duties of the Administration as prescribed by section 2473 of this title. In connection with any such transfer, the President may, under this section or other applicable authority, provide for appropriate transfers of records, property, civilian personnel, and funds.

(b) Whenever any such transfer is made before January 1, 1959, the President shall transmit to the Speaker of the House of Representatives and the President pro tempore of the Senate a full and complete report concerning the nature and effect of such transfer.

(c) After December 31, 1958, no transfer shall be made under this section until (1) a full and complete report concerning the nature and effect of such proposed transfer has been transmitted by the President to the Congress, and (2) the first period of sixty calendar days of regular session of the Congress following the date of receipt of such report by the Congress has expired without the adoption by the Congress of a concurrent resolution stating that the Congress does not favor such transfer. (Pub. L. 85–568, title III, § 302, July 29, 1958, 72 Stat. 433.)

EX. ORD. NO. 10783. TRANSFER OF FUNCTIONS FROM DEPARTMENT OF DEFENSE TO NATIONAL AERONAUTICS AND SPACE ADMINISTRATION

Ex. Ord. No. 10783, Oct. 1, 1958, 23 F. R. 7643, provided:

SECTION 1. All functions (including powers, duties, activities, and parts of functions) of the Department of Defense, or of any officer or organizational entity of the Department of Defense, with respect to the following are hereby transferred to the National Aeronautics and Space Administration:

(a) The United States scientific satellite project (Project VANGUARD).

(b) Specific projects of the Advanced Research Projects Agency and of the Department of the Air Force which relate to space activities (including lunar probes, scientific satellites and superthrust boosters) within the scope of the functions devolving upon the National Aeronautics and Space Administration under the provisions of the National Aeronautics and Space Act of 1958 [this chapter], and which shall be more particularly described in one or more supplementary Executive orders hereafter issued.

SEC. 2. (a) The Secretary of the Treasury shall immediately transfer to the appropriation of the National Aeronautics and Space Administration for "Research and Development", from such appropriations of the Department of Defense as the Secretary of Defense shall designate, the following amounts:

(1) In connection with the transfer of functions provided for in section 1 (a) hereof, such amounts as shall be determined by the Director of the Bureau of the Budget pursuant to section 202 (b) of the Budget and Accounting Procedures Act of 1950 [section 581c (b) of Title 31] and section 1 (k) of Executive Order No. 10530 of May 11, 1954 [section 301 note of Title 3].

(2) In connection with the transfer of functions of the Advanced Research Projects Agency provided for in section 1 (b) hereof, $59,200,000.

(3) In connection with the transfer of functions of the Department of the Air Force provided for in section 1 (b) hereof, $57,800,000.

(b) In connection with the transfer of functions provided for in section 1, appropriate transfers of records, property, facilities, and civilian personnel shall be carried out as may be agreed upon from time to time by the National Aeronautics and Space Administration and the Department of Defense.

DWIGHT D. EISENHOWER

EX. ORD. NO. 10793. TRANSFER OF· CERTAIN FUNCTIONS FROM DEPARTMENT OF DEFENSE TO NATIONAL AERONAUTICS AND SPACE ADMINISTRATION

Ex. Ord. No. 10793, Dec. 3, 1958, 23 F.R. 9405, provided:

By virtue of the authority vested in me by the National Aeronautics and Space Act of 1958 (Public Law 85–568; 72 Stat. 426) [this chapter] and section 202 (b) of the Budget and Accounting Procedures Act of 1950 (31 U. S. C. 581c (b)), and as President of the United States, it is ordered as follows:

SECTION 1. Those functions (including powers, duties, activities, and parts of functions) of the Department of the Army or of any officer or organizational entity thereof which are now being performed at the Jet Propulsion Laboratory of the California Institute of Technology, near Pasadena, California (hereinafter referred to as the Laboratory), except so much thereof as relates primarily to military operations and weapon system development programs, are hereby transferred to the National Aeronautics and Space Administration.

SEC. 2. In connection with the transfer of functions provided for in section 1 of this order, there is hereby transferred to the National Aeronautics and Space Administration custody, possession, and control of the Government-owned property occupied or utilized by the Laboratory except those items of equipment therein which relate primarily to military operations and weapon system development programs of the Department of the Army.

SEC. 3. The Department of Defense and the National Aeronautics and Space Administration shall effect necessary administrative arrangements, including appropriate transfer of records, in connection with the transfers of functions and property provided for in sections 1 and 2 hereof. In order to provide for the most effective utilization of scientific and engineering resources, the National Aeronautics and Space Administration shall to the extent permitted by its own programs and facilities provide research and development support at the Laboratory in respect of military matters to the Department of Defense.

SEC. 4. The Secretary of the Treasury shall immediately transfer from such appropriations of the Department of Defense pertinent to the functions transferred by section 1 of this order as the Secretary of Defense shall designate, to such appropriations of the National Aeronautics and Space Administration as the Administrator of the National Aeronautics and Space Administration shall specify, the amount of $4,078,250.

DWIGHT D. EISENHOWER

TRANSFER PLAN
Mar. 15, 1960, 25 F.R. 2151

Transmitted by the President and delivered to the Congress January 14, 1960, pursuant to the provisions of section 302 of the National Aeronautics and Space Act of 1958 (72 Stat. 433) [this section]

MAKING CERTAIN TRANSFERS FROM THE DEPARTMENT OF DEFENSE TO THE NATIONAL AERONAUTICS AND SPACE ADMINISTRATION

SECTION 1. Those functions (including powers, duties, activities, and parts of functions) of the Department of Defense, or of any officer or organizational entity thereof, relating to the development of space vehicle systems (excluding ballistic missiles) and research connected therewith, which are being performed by the Army Ballistic Missile Agency of the Department of the Army, or by any officer or organizational entity of the said Agency, are transferred to the National Aeronautics and Space Administration.

Sec. 2. (a) The following shall be transferred to the National Aeronautics and Space Administration, pursuant to authority conferred by the provisions of section 302(a) of the National Aeronautics and Space Act of 1958 [this section] and other applicable authority, at such time or times as may be appropriate:

(1) So much of the unexpended balances of appropriations, allocations, and other funds of the Department of Defense, available or to be made available, as the Director of the Bureau of the Budget shall determine to relate to the functions transferred by the provisions of section 1 of this transfer plan and to be needed by the National Aeronautics and Space Administration in connection with those functions.

(2) To the extent needed by the National Aeronautics and Space Administration in connection with the aforesaid transferred functions, (i) civilian personnel employed in the Development Operations Division of the Army Ballistic Missile Agency, and other civilian personnel employed in the Department of the Army for administrative and technical support of the Development Operations Division, together with their respective positions, and (ii) records and property of the Department of Defense (including those of any organizational entity of the Department of Defense) relating to the said transferred functions. The Secretary of Defense and the Administrator of the National Aeronautics and Space Administration, jointly, or, to any extent that they shall fail to agree, the Director of the Bureau of the Budget, shall (A) determine the number of employees to be so transferred and the identity of the particular employees who are to be transferred, (B) designate the specific records and property to be transferred, and (C) fix the date or dates of these transfers.

(b) Without limiting the foregoing provisions of this transfer plan, the functions transferred to the National Aeronautics and Space Administration by the provisions of section 1 of this transfer plan shall include so much of the functions of the Department of Defense, or of any officer or organizational entity thereof, as relate to the appointment and pay of civilian personnel employed in the Development Operations Division of the Army Ballistic Missile Agency, including authority to continue certain transferred positions in grades 16, 17, and 18 of the General Schedule of the Classification Act of 1949, as amended, pursuant to the provisions of section 1, of Public Law 86–377 [section 1105 of Title 5, Executive Departments and Government Officers and Employees], and authority to continue certain transferred positions requiring the services of specially qualified scientists or professional personnel pursuant to the provisions of section 2 of Public Law 86–377 [section 1581 of Title 10, Armed Forces].

(c) Such further measures and dispositions as the Director of the Bureau of the Budget shall deem to be necessary in order to effectuate transfers under the foregoing provisions of this section shall be carried out in such manner as he shall direct and by such agencies as he shall designate.

Sec. 3. The provisions of this transfer plan shall become effective upon the expiration of the first period of sixty calendar days of regular session of the Congress following the date stated in the heading hereof unless the Congress has during that period adopted a concurrent resolution stating that Congress does not favor this transfer plan. Thereafter, as promptly as may be, this transfer plan shall be published in the Federal Register.

§ 2454. Access to information.

Information obtained or developed by the Administrator in the performance of his functions under this chapter shall be made available for public inspection, except (A) information authorized or required by Federal statute to be withheld, and (B) information classified to protect the national security: *Provided,* That nothing in this chapter shall

authorize the withholding of information by the Administrator from the duly authorized committees of the Congress. (Pub. L. 85–568, title III, § 303, July 29, 1958, 72 Stat. 433.)

References in Text

"This chapter", referred to in the text, was in the original "this Act", meaning Pub. L. 85–568, which is classified to this chapter, section 22–1, of Title 5, Executive Departments and Government Officers and Employees, sections 2302 and 2303 of Title 10, Armed Forces, sections 799 and 1114 of Title 18, Crimes and Criminal Procedure, and sections 511—513 and 515 of Title 50, War and National Defense, and as notes under sections 2451 and 2472 of this title and section 2302 of Title 10.

§ 2455. Security requirements.

(a) Establishment; investigations; referral to Federal Bureau of Investigation.

The Administrator shall establish such security requirements, restrictions, and safeguards as he deems necessary in the interest of the national security. The Administrator may arrange with the Civil Service Commission for the conduct of such security or other personnel investigations of the Administration's officers, employees, and consultants, and its contractors and subcontractors and their officers and employees, actual or prospective, as he deems appropriate; and if any such investigation develops any data reflecting that the individual who is the subject thereof is of questionable loyalty the matter shall be referred to the Federal Bureau of Investigation for the conduct of a full field investigation, the results of which shall be furnished to the Administrator.

(b) Access to Restricted Data of Atomic Energy Commission.

The Atomic Energy Commission may authorize any of its employees, or employees of any contractor, prospective contractor, licensee, or prospective licensee of the Atomic Energy Commission or any other person authorized to have access to Restricted Data by the Atomic Energy Commission under 2165 (b) of this title, to permit any member, officer, or employee of the Council, or the Administrator, or any officer, employee, member of an advisory committee, contractor, subcontractor, or officer or employee of a contractor or subcontractor of the Administration, to have access to Restricted Data relating to aeronautical and space activities which is required in the performance of his duties and so certified by the Council or the Administrator, as the case may be, but only if (1) the Council or Administrator or designee thereof has determined, in accordance with the established personnel security procedures and standards of the Council or Administration, that permitting such individual to have access to such Restricted Data will not endanger the common defense and security, and (2) the Council or Administrator or designee thereof finds that the established personnel and other security procedures and standards of the Council or Administration are adequate and in reasonable conformity to the standards established by the Atomic Energy Commission under section 2165 of this title. Any individual granted access to such Restricted Data pursuant to this subsection may exchange such Data with any individual who (A) is an officer or employee of the Department of Defense, or any department or agency thereof, or a member of the armed forces, or a contractor or subcontractor of any such department, agency, or armed force, or an officer or employee of any such contractor or subcontractor, and (B) has been authorized to have access to Restricted Data under the provisions of section 2163 of this title. (Pub. L. 85–568, title III, § 304 (a), (b), July 29, 1958, 72 Stat. 433.)

CODIFICATION

Section is comprised of subsec. (a) and (b) of section 304 of Pub. L. 85–568. Subsecs. (c) and (d) of section 304 are classified to sections 799 and 1114, respectively, of Title 18, Crimes and Criminal Procedure. Subsec. (e) of section 304 is classified to section 2456 of this title.

§ 2456. Permission to use firearms.

The Administrator may direct such of the officers and employees of the Administration as he deems necessary in the public interest to carry firearms while in the conduct of their official duties. The Administrator may also authorize such of those employees of the contractors and subcontractors of the Administration engaged in the protection of property owned by the United States and located at facilities owned by or contracted to the United States as he deems necessary in the public interest, to carry firearms while in the conduct of their official duties. (Pub. L. 85–568, title III, § 304 (e), July 29, 1958, 72 Stat. 435.)

CODIFICATION

Section constitutes subsec. (e) of section 304 of Pub. L. 85–568. Subsecs. (a) and (b) of section 304 are classified to section 2455 of this title. Subsecs. (c) and (d) of section 304 are classified to sections 799 and 1114, respectively, of Title 18, Crimes and Criminal Procedure.

§ 2457. Property rights in inventions.

(a) Exclusive property of United States; issuance of patent.

Whenever any invention is made in the performance of any work under any contract of the Administration, and the Administrator determines that—

(1) the person who made the invention was employed or assigned to perform research, development, or exploration work and the invention is related to the work he was employed or assigned to perform, or that it was within the scope of his employment duties, whether or not it was made during working hours, or with a contribution by the Government of the use of Government facilities, equipment, materials, allocated funds, information proprietary to the Government, or services of Government employees during working hours; or

(2) the person who made the invention was not employed or assigned to perform research, development, or exploration work, but the invention is nevertheless related to the contract, or to the work or duties he was employed or assigned to perform, and was made during working hours, or with a contribution from the Government of the sort referred to in clause (1),

such invention shall be the exclusive property of the United States, and if such invention is patentable a patent therefor shall be issued to the United States upon application made by the Administrator, unless the Administrator waives all or any part of the

rights of the United States to such invention in conformity with the provisions of subsection (f) of this section.

(b) Contract provisions for furnishing reports of inventions, discoveries, improvements, or innovations.

Each contract entered into by the Administrator with any party for the performance of any work shall contain effective provisions under which such party shall furnish promptly to the Administrator a written report containing full and complete technical information concerning any invention, discovery, improvement, or innovation which may be made in the performance of any such work.

(c) Patent application.

No patent may be issued to any applicant other than the Administrator for any invention which appears to the Commissioner of Patents to have significant utility in the conduct of aeronautical and space activities unless the applicant files with the Commissioner, with the application or within thirty days after request therefor by the Commissioner, a written statement executed under oath setting forth the full facts concerning the circumstances under which such invention was made and stating the relationship (if any) of such invention to the performance of any work under any contract of the Administration. Copies of each such statement and the application to which it relates shall be transmitted forthwith by the Commissioner to the Administrator.

(d) Issuance of patent to applicant; request by Administrator; notice; hearing; determination; review.

Upon any application as to which any such statement has been transmitted to the Administrator, the Commissioner may, if the invention is patentable, issue a patent to the applicant unless the Administrator, within ninety days after receipt of such application and statement, requests that such patent be issued to him on behalf of the United States. If, within such time, the Administrator files such a request with the Commissioner, the Commissioner shall transmit notice thereof to the applicant, and shall issue such patent to the Administrator unless the applicant within thirty days after receipt of such notice requests a hearing before a Board of Patent Interferences on the question whether the Administrator is entitled under this section to receive such patent. The Board may hear and determine, in accordance with rules and procedures established for interference cases, the question so presented, and its determination shall be subject to appeal by the applicant or by the Administrator to the Court of Customs and Patent Appeals in accordance with procedures governing appeals from decisions of the Board of Patent Interferences in other proceedings.

(e) False representations; request for transfer of title to patent; notice; hearing; determination; review.

Whenever any patent has been issued to any applicant in conformity with subsection (d) of this section, and the Administrator thereafter has reason to believe that the statement filed by the applicant in connection therewith contained any false representation of any material fact, the Administrator within five years after the date of issuance of such patent may file with the Commissioner a request for the transfer to the Administrator of title to such patent on the records of the Commissioner. Notice of any such request shall be transmitted by the Commissioner to the owner of record of such patent, and title to such patent shall be so transferred to the Administrator unless within thirty days after receipt of such notice such owner of record requests a hearing before a Board of Patent Interferences on the question whether any such false representation was contained in such statement. Such question shall be heard and determined, and determination thereof shall be subject to review, in the manner prescribed by subsection (d) of this section for questions arising thereunder. No request made by the Administrator under this subsection for the transfer of title to any patent, and no prosecution for the violation of any criminal statute, shall be barred by any failure of the Administrator to make a request under subsection (d) of this section for the issuance of such patent to him, or by any notice previously given by the Administrator stating that he had no objection to the issuance of such patent to the applicant therefor.

(f) Waiver of rights to inventions; Inventions and Contributions Board.

Under such regulations in conformity with this subsection as the Administrator shall prescribe, he may waive all or any part of the rights of the United States under this section with respect to any invention or class of inventions made or which may be made by any person or class of persons in the performance of any work required by any contract of the Administration if the Administrator determines that the interests of the United States will be served thereby. Any such waiver may be made upon such terms and under such conditions as the Administrator shall determine to be required for the protection of the interests of the United States. Each such waiver made with respect to any invention shall be subject to the reservation by the Administrator of an irrevocable, nonexclusive, nontransferrable, royalty-free license for the practice of such invention throughout the world by or on behalf of the United States or any foreign government pursuant to any treaty or agreement with the United States. Each proposal for any waiver under this subsection shall be referred to an Inventions and Contributions Board which shall be established by the Administrator within the Administration. Such Board shall accord to each interested party an opportunity for hearing, and shall transmit to the Administrator its findings of fact with respect to such proposal and its recommendations for action to be taken with respect thereto.

(g) License regulations.

The Administrator shall determine, and promulgate regulations specifying, the terms and conditions upon which licenses will be granted by the Administration for the practice by any person (other than an agency of the United States) of any invention for which the Administrator holds a patent on behalf of the United States.

(h) Protection of title.

The Administrator is authorized to take all suitable and necessary steps to protect any invention or discovery to which he has title, and to require that contractors or persons who retain title to inventions or discoveries under this section protect the inventions or discoveries to which the Administration has or may acquire a license of use.

(i) Administration as defense agency.

The Administration shall be considered a defense agency of the United States for the purpose of chapter 17 of Title 35.

(j) Definitions.

As used in this section—

(1) the term "person" means any individual, partnership, corporation, association, institution, or other entity;

(2) the term "contract" means any actual or proposed contract, agreement, understanding, or other arrangement, and includes any assignment, substitution of parties, or subcontract executed or entered into thereunder; and

(3) the term "made", when used in relation to any invention, means the conception or first actual reduction to practice of such invention.

(Pub. L. 85–568, title III, § 305, July 29, 1958, 72 Stat. 435.)

§ 2458. Contributions awards.

(a) Applications; referral to Board; hearing; recommendations; determination by Administrator.

Subject to the provisions of this section, the Administrator is authorized, upon his own initiative or upon application of any person, to make a monetary award, in such amount and upon such terms as he shall determine to be warranted, to any person (as defined by section 2457 of this title) for any scientific or technical contribution to the Administration which is determined by the Administrator to have significant value in the conduct of aeronautical and space activities. Each application made for any such award shall be referred to the Inventions and Contributions Board established under section 2457 of this title. Such Board shall accord to each such applicant an opportunity for hearing upon such application, and shall transmit to the Administrator its recommendation as to the terms of the award, if any, to be made to such applicant for such contribution. In determining the terms and conditions of any award the Administrator shall take into account—

(1) the value of the contribution to the United States;

(2) the aggregate amount of any sums which have been expended by the applicant for the development of such contribution;

(3) the amount of any compensation (other than salary received for services rendered as an officer or employee of the Government) previously received by the applicant for or on account of the use of such contribution by the United States; and

(4) such other factors as the Administrator shall determine to be material.

(b) **Apportionment of awards; surrender of claims to compensation; limitation on amount; reports to Congressional Committees.**

If more than one applicant under subsection (a) of this section claims an interest in the same contribution, the Administrator shall ascertain and determine the respective interests of such applicants, and shall apportion any award to be made with respect to such contribution among such applicants in such proportions as he shall determine to be equitable. No award may be made under subsection (a) of this section with respect to any contribution—

(1) unless the applicant surrenders, by such means as the Administrator shall determine to be effective, all claims which such applicant may have to receive any compensation (other than the award made under this section) for the use of such contribution or any element thereof at any time by or on behalf of the United States, or by or on behalf of any foreign government pursuant to any treaty or agreement with the United States, within the United States or at any other place;

(2) in any amount exceeding $100,000, unless the Administrator has transmitted to the appropriate committees of the Congress a full and complete report concerning the amount and terms of, and the basis for, such proposed award, and thirty calendar days of regular session of the Congress have expired after receipt of such report by such committees.

(Pub. L. 85–568, title III, § 306, July 29, 1958, 72 Stat. 437.)

§ 2459. Appropriations; authorizations; availability and use; termination.

(a) There are authorized to be appropriated such sums as may be necessary to carry out this chapter, except that nothing in this chapter shall authorize the appropriation of any amount for (1) the acquisition or condemnation of any real property, or (2) any other item of a capital nature (such as plant or facility acquisition, construction, or expansion) which exceeds $250,000. Sums appropriated pursuant to this subsection for the construction of facilities, or for research and development activities, shall remain available until expended.

(b) Any funds appropriated for the construction of facilities may be used for emergency repairs of existing facilities when such existing facilities are made inoperative by major breakdown, accident, or other circumstances and such repairs are deemed by the Administrator to be of greater urgency than the construction of new facilities.

(c) Notwithstanding any other provision of law, the authorization of any appropriation to the Administration shall expire (unless an earlier expiration is specifically provided) at the close of the third fiscal year following the fiscal year in which the authorization was enacted, to the extent that such appropriation has not theretofore actually been made. (Pub. L. 85–568, title III, § 307, July 29, 1958, 72 Stat. 438; Pub. L. 88–113, § 6, Sept. 6, 1963, 77 Stat. 144.)

References in Text

"This chapter", referred to in the text, was in the original "this Act", meaning Pub. L. 85–568, which is classified to this chapter, section 22–1 of Title 5, Executive Departments and Government Officers and Employees, sections 2302 and 2303 of Title 10, Armed Forces, sections 799 and 1114 of Title 18, Crimes and Criminal Procedure, and sections 511—513 and 515 of Title 50, War and National Defense, and as notes under sections 2451 and 2472 of this title and section 2302 of Title 10.

Amendments

1963—Subsec. (c). Pub. L. 88–113 added subsec. (c).

Appropriations for Any Period Prior to June 30, 1960

Sections 701 of Pub. L. 85–766, title VII, Aug. 27, 1958, 72 Stat. 873, provided in part that: "No appropriation may be made to the National Aeronautics and Space Administration for any period prior to June 30, 1960, unless previously authorized by legislation hereafter enacted by the Congress."

§ 2460. Appropriations; prior authorization by Congress.

Notwithstanding the provisions of any other law, no appropriation may be made to the National Aeronautics and Space Administration unless previously authorized by legislation hereafter enacted by the Congress. (Pub. L. 86–45, § 4, June 15, 1959, 73 Stat. 75.)

Codification

Section was not enacted as part of the National Aeronautics and Space Act of 1958, which is classified principally to this chapter.

Subchapter II.—Coordination of Aeronautical and Space Activities

§ 2471. National Aeronautics and Space Council.

(a) **Establishment; membership.**

There is established, in the Executive Office of the President, the National Aeronautics and Space Council (hereinafter called the "Council") which shall be composed of—

(1) the Vice President, who shall be Chairman of the Council;

(2) the Secretary of State;

(3) the Secretary of Defense;

(4) the Administrator of the National Aeronautics and Space Administration; and

(5) the Chairman of the Atomic Energy Commission.

(b) **Alternate presiding officer.**

The President shall from time to time designate one of the members of the Council to preside over meetings of the Council during the absence, disability, or unavailability of the Chairman.

(c) **Alternate members.**

Each member of the Council may designate another officer of his department or agency to serve on the Council as his alternate in his unavoidable absence.

(d) **Designations by and with advice and consent of Senate.**

Each alternate member designated under subsection (c) of this section shall be designated to serve as such by and with the advice and consent of the Senate unless at the time of his designation he holds an office in the Federal Government to which he was appointed by and with the advice and consent of the Senate.

(e) **Functions.**

It shall be the function of the Council to advise and assist the President, as he may request, with respect to the performance of functions in the aeronautics and space field, including the following function:

(1) survey all significant aeronautical and space activities, including the policies, plans, programs, and accomplishments of all departments and agencies of the United States engaged in such activities;

(2) develop a comprehensive program of aeronautical and space activities to be conducted by departments and agencies of the United States;

(3) designate and fix responsibility for the direction of major aeronautical and space activities;

(4) provide for effective cooperation among all departments and agencies of the United States engaged in aeronautical and space activities, and specify, in any case in which primary responsibility for any category of aeronautical and space activities has been assigned to any department or agency, which of those activities may be carried on concurrently by other departments or agencies; and

(5) resolve differences arising among departments and agencies of the United States with respect to aeronautical and space activities under this chapter, including differences as to whether a particular project is an aeronautical and space activity.

(f) Employment of personnel; executive secretary; security check; other applicable employment provisions.

The Council may employ a staff to be headed by a civilian executive secretary who shall be appointed by the President by and with the advice and consent of the Senate. The executive secretary, subject to the direction of the Council, is authorized to appoint and fix the compensation of such personnel, including not more than seven persons who may be appointed without regard to the civil service laws or the Classification Act of 1949 and compensated at not to exceed the highest rate of grade 18 of the General Schedule of the Classification Act of 1949, as amended, as may be necessary to perform such duties as may be prescribed by the Council in connection with the performance of its functions. Each appointment under this subsection shall be subject to the same security requirements as those established for personnel of the National Aeronautics and Space Administration appointed under section 2473 (b)(2) of this title. Other provisions of law or regulations relating to Government employment (except those relating to pay and retirement) shall apply to council employees reporting directly to the chairman to the extent that such provisions are applicable to employees in the office of the Vice President.

(g) Repealed. Pub. L. 87–26, §1(b), Apr. 25, 1961, 75 Stat. 47.

(Pub. L. 85–568, title I, § 201, July 29, 1958, 72 Stat. 427; Pub. L. 87–26, § 1, Apr. 25, 1961, 75 Stat. 46; Pub. L. 87–367, title II, § 207, Oct. 4, 1961, 75 Stat. 792; Pub. L. 87–584, § 7, Aug. 14, 1962, 76 Stat. 385; Pub. L. 88–426, title III, §§ 305(13)(A), 306(c), Aug. 14, 1964, 78 Stat. 423, 428.)

REFERENCES IN TEXT

"This chapter", referred to in the text, was in the original "this Act", meaning Pub. L. 85–568, which is classified to this chapter, section 22–1 of Title 5, Executive Departments and Government Officers and Employees, sections 2302 and 2303 of Title 10, Armed Forces, sections 799 and 1114 of Title 18, Crimes and Criminal Procedure, and sections 511—513 and 515 of Title 50, War and National Defense, and as notes under sections 2451 and 2472 of this title and section 2302 of Title 10.

The civil service laws, referred to in subsec. (f), are classified generally to Title 5, Executive Departments and Government Officers and Employees.

The Classification Act of 1949, referred to in subsec. (f), is classified to chapter 21 of Title 5.

AMENDMENTS

1964—Subsec. (f). Pub. L. 88–426 repealed provisions which prescribed the compensation of the executive secretary, and substituted "compensated at not to exceed the highest rate of grade 18 of the General Schedule of the Classification Act of 1949, as amended" for "compensated at the rate of not more than $19,000 a year." See section 2211 of Title 5, Executive Departments and Government Officers and Employees.

1962—Subsec. (f). Pub. L. 87–584 provided for the application of other provisions of law or regulations relating to Government employment to council employees reporting directly to the chairman.

1961—Subsec. (a). Pub. L. 87–26, § 1(a), placed the Council in the Executive Office of the President, replaced the President as the presiding officer of Council meetings with the Vice President as Chairman of the Council, and eliminated from membership one additional Government member and three distinguished civilians, appointed by the President.

Subsec. (b). Pub. L. 87–26, § 1(a), added subsec. (b). Former subsec. (b) redesignated (c).

Subsec. (c). Pub. L. 87–26, § 1(a), redesignated former subsec. (b) as (c) and eliminated therefrom "from a department or agency of the Federal Government" following "of the Council." Former subsec. (c) redesignated (d).

Subsec. (d). Pub. L. 87–26, § 1(a), redesignated former subsec. (c) as (d), eliminated therefrom introductory words "Each member of the Council appointed or designated under paragraphs (6) and (7) of subsection (a) of this section, and" references to appointment, and substituted "subsection (c)" for "subsection (b)". Former subsec. (d) incorporated in subsec. (e).

Subsec. (e). Pub. L. 87–26 § 1(a), consolidated the provisions of former subsecs. (d) and (e) requiring the Council to advise the President with respect to performance of prescribed duties of the Executive and enumeration of such duties, modified such former provisions by requiring the Council to advise and assist the President, as he may request, with respect to performance of functions in the aeronautics and space field, by making the prescribed duties of the President the functions of the Council and amending the same to include references to departments in pars. (1) and (2) and to provide for cooperation among all departments and agencies of the United States engaged in aeronautical and space activities and for concurrent effort instead of only between the Administration and the Department of Defense and the concurrent effort of such agencies in par. (4).

Subsec. (f). Pub. L. 87–367 authorized the executive secretary of the National Aeronautics and Space Council to increase the number of employees employed at $19,000 per annum from three to seven.

Subsec. (g). Pub. L. 87–26, § 1(b), repealed subsec. (g) provisions relating to compensation of members.

EFFECTIVE DATE OF 1964 AMENDMENT

Amendment of section by Pub. L. 88–426 effective on the first day of the first pay period which begins on or after July 1, 1964, except to the extent provided in section 501(c) of Pub. L. 88–426, see section 501 of Pub. L. 88–426, set out as a note under section 1113 of Title 5, Executive Departments and Government Officers and Employees.

§ 2472. National Aeronautics and Space Administration.

(a) Establishment; appointment and duties of Administrator.

There is established the National Aeronautics and Space Administration (hereinafter called the "Administration"). The Administration shall be headed by an Administrator, who shall be appointed from civilian life by the President by and with the advice and consent of the Senate. Under the supervision and direction of the President, the Administrator shall be responsible for the exercise of all powers and the discharge of all duties of the Administration, and shall have authority and control over all personnel and activities thereof.

(b) Deputy Administrator; appointment and duties.

There shall be in the Administration a Deputy Administrator, who shall be appointed from civilian life by the President by and with the advice and consent of the Senate and shall perform such duties and exercise such powers as the Administrator may prescribe. The Deputy Administrator shall act for, and exercise the powers of, the Administrator during his absence or disability.

(c) Restriction on engaging in any other business, vocation, or employment.

The Administrator and the Deputy Administrator shall not engage in any other business, vocation, or employment while serving as such. (Pub. L. 85–568, title II, § 202, July 29, 1958, 72 Stat. 429; Pub. L. 88–426, title III, § 305(12), Aug. 14, 1964, 78 Stat. 423.)

AMENDMENTS

1964—Subsec. (a). Pub. L. 88–426, § 305(12)(A), repealed provisions which prescribed the compensation of the Administrator.

Subsec. (b). Pub. L. 88–426, § 305(12)(B), repealed provisions which prescribed the compensation of the Deputy Administrator.

EFFECTIVE DATE OF 1964 AMENDMENT

Amendment of section by Pub. L. 88–426 effective on the first day of the first pay period which begins on or after July 1, 1964, except to the extent provided in section 501(c) of Pub. L. 88–426, see section 501 of Pub. L. 88–426, set out as a note under section 1113 of Title 5, Executive Departments and Government Officers and Employees.

EMERGENCY PREPAREDNESS FUNCTIONS

Ex. Ord. No. 11095, Feb. 26, 1963, 28 F.R. 1859, directed the Administrator of the National Aeronautics and Space Administration to prepare national emergency plans and develop preparedness programs covering functions assigned to him by the Executive Order, designed to develop a state of readiness with respect to all conditions of national emergency, including attack upon the United States.

TERMINATION OF NATIONAL ADVISORY COMMITTEE FOR AERONAUTICS; TRANSFER OF FUNCTIONS

Section 301(a) of Pub. L. 85–568 provided that: "The National Advisory Committee for Aeronautics, on the effective date of this section [see note under section 2302 of Title 10, Armed Forces], shall cease to exist. On such date all functions, powers, duties, and obligations, and all real and personal property, personnel (other than members of the Committee), funds, and records of that organization, shall be transferred to the Administration."

EX. ORD. NO. 10849. ESTABLISHMENT OF SEAL FOR NATIONAL AERONAUTICS AND SPACE ADMINISTRATION

Ex. Ord. No. 10849, Nov. 27, 1959, 24 F.R. 9559, as amended by Ex. Ord. No. 10942, May 19, 1961, 26 F.R. 4419, provided:

WHEREAS the Administrator of the National Aeronautics and Space Administration has caused to be made, and has recommended that I approve, a seal for the National Aeronautics and Space Administration, the design of which accompanies and is hereby made a part of this order, and which is described as follows:

On a disc of the blue sky strewn with white stars, to dexter a larger yellow sphere bearing a red flight symbol apex in upper sinister and wings enveloping and casting a brown shadow upon the sphere, all partially encircled with a horizontal white orbit, in sinister a small light-blue sphere; circumscribing the disc a white band edged gold inscribed "National Aeronautics and Space Administration U.S.A." in red letters.

AND WHEREAS it appears that such seal is of suitable design and appropriate for establishment as the official seal of the National Aeronautics and Space Administration:

NOW, THEREFORE, by virtue of the authority vested in me as President of the United States, I hereby approve such seal as the official seal of the National Aeronautics and Space Administration.

DWIGHT D. EISENHOWER

CROSS REFERENCES

Compensation of Administrator and Deputy Administrator, see section 2211 of Title 5, Executive Departments and Government Officers and Employees.

§ 2473. Functions of the Administration.

(a) The Administration, in order to carry out the purpose of this chapter, shall—

(1) plan, direct, and conduct aeronautical and space activities;

(2) arrange for participation by the scientific community in planning scientific measurements and observations to be made through use of aeronautical and space vehicles, and conduct or arrange for the conduct of such measurements and observations; and

(3) provide for the widest practicable and appropriate dissemination of information concerning its activities and the results thereof.

(b) In the performance of its functions the Administration is authorized—

(1) to make, promulgate, issue, rescind, and amend rules and regulations governing the manner of its operations and the exercise of the powers vested in it by law;

(2) to appoint and fix the compensation of such officers and employees as may be necessary to carry out such functions. Such officers and employees shall be appointed in accordance with the civil-service laws and their compensation fixed

in accordance with the Classification Act of 1949, except that (A) to the extent the Administrator deems such action necessary to the discharge of his responsibilities, he may appoint not more than four hundred and twenty-five of the scientific, engineering, and administrative personnel of the Administration without regard to such laws, and may fix the compensation of such personnel not in excess of the highest rate of grade 18 of the General Schedule of the Classification Act of 1949, as amended, and (B) to the extent the Administrator deems such action necessary to recruit specially qualified scientific and engineering talent, he may establish the entrance grade for scientific and engineering personnel without previous service in the Federal Government at a level up to two grades higher than the grade provided for such personnel under the General Schedule established by the Classification Act of 1949, and fix their compensation accordingly;

(3) to acquire (by purchase, lease, condemnation, or otherwise), construct, improve, repair, operate, and maintain laboratories, research and testing sites and facilities, aeronautical and space vehicles, quarters and related accommodations for employees and dependents of employees of the Administration, and such other real and personal property (including patents), or any interest therein, as the Administration deems necessary within and outside the continental United States; to acquire by lease or otherwise, through the Administrator of General Services, buildings or parts of buildings in the District of Columbia for the use of the Administration for a period not to exceed ten years without regard to section 34 of Title 40; to lease to others such real and personal property; to sell and otherwise dispose of real and personal property (including patents and rights thereunder) in accordance with the provisions of the Federal Property and Administrative Services Act of 1949, as amended; and to provide by contract or otherwise for cafeterias and other necessary facilities for the welfare of employees of the Administration at its installations and purchase and maintain equipment therefor;

(4) to accept unconditional gifts or donations of services, money, or property, real, personal, or mixed, tangible or intangible;

(5) without regard to section 529 of Title 31, to enter into and perform such contracts, leases, cooperative agreements, or other transactions as may be necessary in the conduct of its work and on such terms as it may deem appropriate, with any agency or instrumentality of the United States, or with any State, Territory, or possession, or with any political subdivision thereof, or with any person, firm, association, corporation, or educational institution. To the maximum extent practicable and consistent with the accomplishment of the purpose of this chapter, such contracts, leases, agreements, and other transactions shall be allocated by the Administrator in a manner which will enable small-business concerns to participate equitably and proportionately in the conduct of the work of the Administration;

(6) to use, with their consent, the services, equipment, personnel, and facilities of Federal and other agencies with or without reimbursement, and on a similar basis to cooperate with other public and private agencies and instrumentalities in the use of services, equipment, and facilities. Each department and agency of the Federal Government shall cooperate fully with the Administration in making its services, equipment, personnel, and facilities available to the Administration, and any such department or agency is authorized, notwithstanding any other provision of law, to transfer to or to receive from the Administration, without reimbursement, aeronautical and space vehicles, and supplies and equipment other than administrative supplies or equipment;

(7) to appoint such advisory committees as may be appropriate for purposes of consultation and advice to the Administration in the performance of its functions;

(8) to establish within the Administration such offices and procedures as may be appropriate to provide for the greatest possible coordination of its activities under this chapter with related scientific and other activities being carried on by other public and private agencies and organizations;

(9) to obtain services as authorized by section 55a of Title 5, at rates not to exceed $100 per diem for individuals;

(10) when determined by the Administrator to be necessary, and subject to such security investigations as he may determine to be appropriate, to employ aliens without regard to statutory provisions prohibiting payment of compensation to aliens;

(11) Repealed. Pub. L. 88–448, title IV, § 402 (a)(34), Aug. 19, 1964, 78 Stat. 495.

(12) with the approval of the President, to enter into cooperative agreements under which members of the Army, Navy, Air Force, and Marine Corps may be detailed by the appropriate Secretary for services in the performance of functions under this chapter to the same extent as that to which they might be lawfully assigned in the Department of Defense; and

(13) (A) to consider, ascertain, adjust, determine, settle, and pay, on behalf of the United States, in full satisfaction thereof, any claim for $5,000 or less against the United States for bodily injury, death, or damage to or loss of real or personal property resulting from the conduct of the Administration's functions as specified in subsection (a) of this section, where such claim is presented to the Administration in writing within two years after the accident or incident out of which the claim arises; and

(B) if the Administration considers that a claim in excess of $5,000 is meritorious and would otherwise be covered by this paragraph, to report the facts and circumstances thereof to the Congress for its consideration.

(14) to reimburse, to the extent determined by the Administrator or his designee to be fair and reasonable, the owners and tenants of land and interests in land acquired on or after November

1, 1961, by the United States for use by the Administration by purchase, condemnation, or otherwise for expenses and losses and damages incurred by such owners and tenants as a direct result of moving themselves, their families, and their possessions because of said acquisition. Such reimbursement shall be in addition to, but not in duplication of, any payments that may otherwise be authorized by law to be made to such owners and tenants. The total of any such reimbursement to any owner or tenant shall in no event exceed 25 per centum of the fair value, as determined by the Administrator, of the parcel of land or interest in land to which the reimbursement is related. No payment under this paragraph shall be made unless application therefor, supported by an itemized statement of the expenses, losses, and damages incurred, is submitted to the Administrator within one year from (a) the date upon which the parcel of land or interest in land is to be vacated under agreement with the Government by the owner or tenant or pursuant to law, including but not limited to, an order of a court, or (b) the date upon which the parcel of land or interest in the land involved is vacated, whichever first occurs. The Administrator may perform any and all acts and make such rules and regulations as he deems necessary and proper for the purpose of carrying out this paragraph. All functions performed under this paragraph shall be exempt from the operation of sections 1001—1011 of Title 5, except as to the requirements of section 1002 of Title 5. Funds available to the Administration for the acquisition of real property or interests therein shall also be available for carrying out this paragraph.

(Pub. L. 85–568, title II, § 203, July 29, 1958, 72 Stat. 429; Pub. L. 86–20, May 13, 1959, 73 Stat. 21; Pub. L. 86–481, § 5, June 1, 1960, 74 Stat. 153; Pub. L. 87–367, title II, § 206(a), Oct. 4, 1961, 75 Stat. 791; Pub. L. 87–584, § 6, Aug. 14, 1962, 76 Stat. 384; Pub. L. 87–793, § 1001(f), Oct. 11, 1962, 76 Stat. 864; Pub. L. 88–426, title III, § 306(d), Aug. 14, 1964, 78 Stat. 429; Pub. L. 88–448, title IV, § 402(a)(34), Aug. 19, 1964, 78 Stat. 495.)

REFERENCES IN TEXT

"This chapter", referred to in the text, was in the original "this Act", meaning Pub. L. 85–568, which is classified to this chapter, section 22–1 of Title 5, Executive Departments and Government Officers and Employees, sections 2302 and 2303 of Title 10, Armed Forces, sections 799 and 1114 of Title 18, Crimes and Criminal Procedure, and sections 511—513 and 515 of Title 50, War and National Defense, and as notes under sections 2451 and 2472 of this title and section 2302 of Title 10.

The civil service laws, referred to in subsec. (b), are classified generally to Title 5, Executive Departments and Government Officers and Employees.

The Classification Act of 1949, referred to in subsec. (b), is classified to chapter 21 of Title 5.

The Federal Property and Administrative Services Act of 1949, as amended, referred to in subsec. (b) (3), is classified to chapter 11C of Title 5, Executive Departments and Government Officers and Employees, chapter 10 of Title 40, Public Buildings, Property and Works, section 5 and chapter 4 of Title 41, Public Contracts, and chapter 11 of Title 44, Public Printing and Documents.

AMENDMENTS

1964—Subsec. (b)(2). Pub. L. 88–426 eliminated provisions from cl. (A) which permitted the Administrator to fix compensation at not more than $21,000 for a maximum of thirty positions and provisions which related to the filling of positions prior to Mar. 1, 1962, and July 1, 1962.

Subsec. (b)(11). Pub. L. 88–448 repealed former subsec. (b)(11) which authorized the employment of retired commissioned officers. See section 3101 et seq. of Title 5, Executive Departments and Government Officers and Employees.

1962—Subsec. (b). Pub. L. 87–793 substituted "(at not to exceed the highest rate of grade 18 of the General Schedule of the Classification Act of 1949, as amended, or for a maximum of thirty positions, not to exceed $21,000 a year) of" for "(up to a limit of $19,000 a year, or up to a limit of $21,000 a year for a maximum of thirty positions) of ", in par (2).

Pub. L. 87–584 added par (14).

1961—Subsec. (b)(2). Pub. L. 87–367 substituted "thirty" for "thirteen" and "four hundred and twenty-five (of which not to exceed three hundred and fifty-five may be filled prior to March 1, 1962 and not to exceed three hundred and ninety may be filed prior to July 1, 1962)" for "two hundred and ninety."

1960—Subsec. (b)(2). Pub. L. 86–481 substituted "thirteen" for "ten" and "two hundred and ninety" for "two hundred and sixty."

1959—Subsec. (b)(3). Pub. L. 86–20 authorized the Administration to acquire, by lease or otherwise, buildings or parts of buildings in the District of Columbia for a period of not more than 10 years.

EFFECTIVE DATE OF 1964 AMENDMENTS

Amendment of section by Pub. L. 88–448 effective on the first day of the first month which begins later than the ninetieth day following Aug. 19, 1964, see section 403 of Pub. L. 88–448, set out as a note under section 3101 of Title 5, Executive Departments and Government Officers and Employees.

Amendment of section by Pub. L. 88–426 effective on the first day of the first pay period which begins on or after July 1, 1964, except to the extent provided in section 501(c) of Pub. L. 88–426, see section 501 of Pub. L. 88–426, set out as a note under section 1113 of Title 5, Executive Departments and Government Officers and Employees.

EFFECTIVE DATE OF 1962 AMENDMENT

Amendment of section by Pub. L. 87–793 effective on the first day of the first pay period which begins on or after Oct. 11, 1962, see section 1008 of Pub. L. 87–793, set out as a note under section 1161 of Title 5, Executive Departments and Government Officers and Employees.

§ 2473a. Reports to Congress; confidential information.

(1) The Administrator of the National Aeronautics and Space Administration shall submit to the Congress not later than forty-five days after the close of each fiscal year a report which sets forth, as of the close of such fiscal year—

(A) the number of positions established under section 2473(b)(2) of this title;

(B) the name, rate of compensation, and description of the qualifications of each incumbent of each position established under such section 2473(b)(2), together with the position title and a statement of the duties and responsibilities performed by each such incumbent;

(C) the position or positions in or outside the Federal Government held by each such incumbent, and his rate or rates of compensation, during the five-year period immediately preceding the date of appointment of such incumbent to such position; and

(D) such other information as the Administrator may deem appropriate or which may be required by the Congress or a committee thereof.

Nothing contained in this subsection shall require the resubmission of any information required under subparagraphs (B) and (C) of this subsection which has been reported pursuant to this subsection and remains unchanged.

(2) In any instance in which the Administrator may find full public disclosure of any or all of the matter covered by paragraph (1) of this subsection to be detrimental to the national security, the Administrator is authorized—

(A) to omit in such report those matters with respect to which full public disclosure is found to be detrimental to the national security;

(B) to inform the Congress of such omission; and

(C) at the request of any congressional committee to which such report is referred, to present all information concerning such matters. (Pub. L. 87–367, title II, § 206(b), Oct. 4, 1961, 75 Stat. 791.)

CODIFICATION

Section was not enacted as a part of the Federal National Aeronautics and Space Act of 1958, which comprises this chapter.

§ 2474. Civilian-Military Liaison Committee.

(a) Establishment; membership.

There shall be a Civilian-Military Liaison Committee consisting of—

(1) a Chairman, who shall be the head thereof and who shall be appointed by the President, shall serve at the pleasure of the President;

(2) one or more representatives from the Department of Defense, and one or more representatives from each of the Departments of the Army, Navy, and Air Force, to be assigned by the Secretary of Defense to serve on the Committee without additional compensation; and

(3) representatives from the Administration, to be assigned by the Administrator to serve on the Committee without additional compensation, equal in number to the number of representatives assigned to serve on the Committee under paragraph (2).

(b) Duties.

The Administration and the Department of Defense, through the Liaison Committee, shall advise and consult with each other on all matters within their respective jurisdictions relating to aeronautical and space activities and shall keep each other fully and currently informed with respect to such activities.

(c) Referral to President.

If the Secretary of Defense concludes that any request, action, proposed action, or failure to act on the part of the Administrator is adverse to the responsibilities of the Department of Defense, or the Administrator concludes that any request, action, proposed action, or failure to act on the part of the Department of Defense is adverse to the responsibilities of the Administration, and the Administrator and the Secretary of Defense are unable to reach an agreement with respect thereto, either the Administrator or the Secretary of Defense may refer the matter to the President for his decision (which shall be final) as provided in section 2471 (e) of this title.

(d) Chairman.

Notwithstanding the provisions of any other law, any active or retired officer of the Army, Navy, or Air Force may serve as Chairman of the Liaison Committee without prejudice to his active or retired status as such officer. Any such active officer serving as Chairman of the Liaison Committee shall receive, in addition to his pay and allowances, including special and incentive pays, an amount equal to the difference between such pay and allowances, including special and incentive pays, and the compensation fixed by subsection (a)(1) of this section for such Chairman. Any such retired officer serving as Chairman of the Liaison Committee shall receive the compensation fixed by subsection (a)(1) of this section for such Chairman and his retired pay, subject to section 3102 of Title 5. (Pub. L. 85–568, title II, § 204, July 29, 1958, 72 Stat. 431; Pub. L. 88–426, title III, § 305(13)(B), Aug. 14, 1964, 78 Stat. 423; Pub. L. 88–448, title IV, § 401(g), Aug. 19, 1964, 78 Stat. 490.)

AMENDMENTS

1964—Subsec. (a). Pub. L. 88–426 repealed provisions which prescribed the compensation of the Chairman of the Committee formerly contained in cl. (1). See section 2211 of Title 5, Executive Departments and Government Officers and Employees.

Subsec. (d). Pub. L. 88–448 substituted provisions permitting a retired officer serving as Chairman of the Liaison Committee to receive the compensation fixed by subsection (a)(1) of this section for such Chairman and his retired pay, subject to section 3102 of title 5, for provisions which permitted a retired officer to receive an amount equal to the amount (if any) by which the compensation fixed by subsection (a)(1) of this section for such Chairman exceeds his retired pay.

Pub. L. 88–426 repealed words "fixed by subsection (a)(1)" which followed "the compensation."

EFFECTIVE DATE OF 1964 AMENDMENTS

Amendment of section by Pub. L. 88–448 effective on the first day of the first month which begins later than the ninetieth day following Aug. 19, 1964, see section 403 of Pub. L. 88–448, set out as a note under section 3101 of Title 5, Executive Departments and Government Officers and Employees.

Amendment of section by Pub. L. 88–426 effective on the first day of the first pay period which begins on or after July 1, 1964, except to the extent provided in section 501(c) of Pub. L. 88–426, see section 501 of Pub. L. 88–426, set out as a note under section 1113 of Title 5, Executive Departments and Government Officers and Employees.

CROSS REFERENCES

Compensation of Chairman, see section 2211 of Title 5, Executive Departments and Government Officers and Employees.

§ 2475. International cooperation.

The Administration, under the foreign policy guidance of the President, may engage in a program of international cooperation in work done pursuant to this chapter, and in the peaceful application of the results thereof, pursuant to agreements made by the President with the advice and consent of the Senate. (Pub. L. 85–568, title II, § 205, July 29, 1958, 72 Stat. 432.)

REFERENCES IN TEXT

"This chapter", referred to in the text, was in the original "this Act", meaning Pub. L. 85–568, which is classified to this chapter, section 22–1 of Title 5, Executive Departments and Government Officers and Employees, sections 2302 and 2303 of Title 10, Armed

Forces, sections 799 and 1114 of Title 18, Crimes and Criminal Procedure, and sections 511–513 and 515 of Title 50, War and National Defense, and as notes under sections 2451 and 2472 of this title and section 2302 of Title 10.

§ 2476. Reports to the Congress.

(a) Submission to the President.

The Administration shall submit to the President for transmittal to the Congress, semiannually and at such other times as it deems desirable, a report of its activities and accomplishments.

(b) Presidential report; transmittal.

The President shall transmit to the Congress in January of each year a report, which shall include (1) a comprehensive description of the programed activities and the accomplishments of all agencies of the United States in the field of aeronautics and space activities during the preceding calendar year,

SOURCE: United States Code, 1964 Edition. 1965.

and (2) an evaluation of such activities and accomplishments in terms of the attainment of, or the failure to attain, the objectives described in section 2451 (c) of this title.

(c) Recommendations for additional legislation.

Any report made under this section shall contain such recommendations for additional legislation as the Administrator or the President may consider necessary or desirable for the attainment of the objectives described in section 2451 (c) of this title.

(d) Classified information.

No information which has been classified for reasons of national security shall be included in any report made under this section, unless such information has been declassified by, or pursuant to authorization given by, the President. (Pub. L. 85–568, title II, § 206, July 29, 1958, 72 Stat. 432.)

TITLE 42.–THE PUBLIC HEALTH AND WELFARE
Chapter 26.–NATIONAL SPACE PROGRAM
(Supplement)

SUBCHAPTER I.—GENERAL PROVISIONS

SUBCHAPTER I.—GENERAL PROVISIONS

§ 2451. Congressional declaration of policy and purpose.

EXECUTIVE ORDER No. 10946

Ex. Ord. No. 10946, May 26, 1961, 26 F.R. 4629, set out as a note under this section, which related to labor disputes at missile and space sites, was revoked by Ex. Ord. No. 11374, Oct. 11, 1967, 32 F.R. 14199, set out as a note under this section.

EX. ORD. No. 11374. ABOLITION OF MISSILE SITES LABOR COMMISSION

Ex. Ord. No. 11374, Oct. 11, 1967, 32 F.R. 14199, provided:

By virtue of the authority vested in me as President of the United States, it is ordered as follows:

SECTION 1. The Missile Sites Labor Commission is hereby abolished, and its functions and responsibilities are transferred to the Federal Mediation and Conciliation Service.

SEC. 2. The Director of the Federal Mediation and Conciliation Service shall establish within the Federal Mediation and Conciliation Service such procedures as may be necessary to provide for continued priority for resolution of labor disputes or potential labor disputes at missile and space sites, and shall seek the continued cooperation of manufacturers, contractors, construction concerns, and labor unions in avoiding uneconomical operations and work stoppages at missile and space sites.

SEC. 3. The Department of Defense, the National Aeronautics and Space Administration, and other appropriate government departments and agencies shall continue to cooperate in the avoidance of uneconomical operations and work stoppages at missile and space sites. They shall also assist the Federal Mediation and Conciliation Service in the discharge of its responsibilities under this order.

SEC. 4. All records and property of the Missile Sites Labor Commission are hereby transferred to the Federal Mediation and Conciliation Service.

SEC. 5. Any disputes now before the Missile Sites Labor Commission shall be resolved by the personnel now serving as members of the Missile Sites Labor Commissions under special assignment for such purposes by the Director of the Federal Mediation and Conciliation Service.

SEC. 6. Executive Order No. 10946 of May 26, 1961, is hereby revoked.

LYNDON B. JOHNSON.

§ 2459. Appropriations; authorizations; availability and use; termination.

GEOGRAPHICAL DISTRIBUTION OF FUNDS

Pub. L. 91–119, § 5, Nov. 18, 1969, 83 Stat. 198, provided that: "It is the sense of the Congress that it is in the national interest that consideration be given to geographical distribution of Federal research funds whenever feasible, and that the National Aeronautics and Space Administration should explore ways and means of distributing its research and development funds whenever feasible."

Similar provisions were contained in the following prior Appropriation Acts:

1968—Pub. L. 90–373, § 6, July 3, 1968, 82 Stat. 283.
1967—Pub. L. 90–67, § 5, Aug. 21, 1967, 81 Stat. 170.
1966—Pub. L. 89–528, § 5, Aug. 5, 1966, 80 Stat. 339.
1965—Pub. L. 89–53, § 5, June 28, 1965, 79 Stat. 194.

§ 2461. Congressional Space Medal of Honor; appropriations.

The President may award, and present in the name of Congress, a medal of appropriate design, which shall be known as the Congressional Space Medal of Honor, to any astronaut who in the performance of his duties has distinguished himself by exceptionally meritorious efforts and contributions to the welfare of the Nation and of mankind.

There is authorized to be appropriated from time to time such sums of money as may be necessary to carry out the purposes of this section. (Pub. L. 91–76, §§ 1, 2, Sept. 29, 1969, 83 Stat. 124.)

CODIFICATION

Section was not enacted as part of the National Aeronautics and Space Act of 1958, which is classified principally to this chapter.

The first and second pars. of this section are comprised of section 1 and 2 of Pub. L. 91–76, respectively.

§ 2462. Reporting requirements.

(a) Definitions.

As used in this section—

(1) The term "aerospace contractor" means any individual, firm, corporation, partnership, association, or other legal entity, which provides services and materials to or for the National Aeronautics and Space Administration in connection with any aerospace system.

(2) The term "services and materials" means either services or materials or services and materials which are provided as a part of or in connection with any aerospace system.

(3) The term "aerospace system" includes, but is not limited to, any rocket, launch vehicle, rocket engine, propellant, spacecraft, command module, service module, landing module, tracking device, communications device, or any part or component thereof, which is used in either manned or unmanned spaceflight operations.

(b) Former employees of the Administration.

Any former employee of the National Aeronautics and Space Administration who at any time during the five-year period immediately preceding his termination of employment with the National Aeronautics and Space Administration was directly engaged in the procurement of any aerospace system or directly engaged in the negotiation, renegotiation, approval, or disapproval of any contract for the procurement of services or materials for or in connection with any aerospace system; or who served during the five-year period immediately preceding his termination of employment with the National Aeronautics and Space Administration at the factory or plant of an aerospace contractor in connection with work performed by such contractor or any aerospace system; or who was employed by the National Aeronautics and Space Administration during the five-year period preceding the termina-

tion of his employment at an annual salary rate of GS–15 or higher; and who

(1) was employed for any period of time during any calendar year by an aerospace contractor,

(2) represented any aerospace contractor during any calendar year at any hearing, trial, appeal, or other action in which the United States was a party and which involved services and materials provided or to be provided to the United States by such contractor, or

(3) represented any such contractor in any transaction with the National Aeronautics and Space Administration involving services or materials provided or to be provided by such contractor to the National Aeronautics and Space Administration,

shall file with the Administrator, in such form and manner as the Administrator may prescribe, not later than March 1 of the next succeeding calendar year, a report containing the following information:

(1) His name and address.

(2) The name and address of the aerospace contractor by whom he was employed or whom he represented.

(3) The title of the position held by him with the aerospace contractor.

(4) A brief description of his duties with the aerospace contractor.

(5) A brief description of his duties while employed by the National Aeronautics and Space Administration during the three-year period immediately preceding his termination of employment.

(6) A description of any work performed by him in connection with any aerospace system while employed by the National Aeronautics and Space Administration, if the aerospace contractor by whom he is employed is providing substantial services or materials for such aerospace system, or is negotiating or bidding to provide substantial services or materials for such aerospace system.

(7) The date of the termination of his employment with the National Aeronautics and Space Administration, and the date on which his employment with the aerospace contractor began and, if no longer employed by such aerospace contractor, the date on which his employment with such aerospace contractor terminated.

(8) Such other pertinent information as the Administrator may require.

(c) Employees of the Administration formerly employed by aerospace contractors.

Any employee of the National Aeronautics and Space Administration who was previously employed by an aerospace contractor in any calendar year and—

(1) who is directly engaged in the procurement of any aerospace system or is directly engaged in the negotiation, renegotiation, approval, or disapproval of any contract for the procurement of services or materials for or in connection with any aerospace system, or

(2) who is serving or has served as a representative of the National Aeronautics and Space Administration at the factory or plant of an aero-

space contractor in connection with work being performed by such contractor on any aerospace system,

shall file with the Administrator, in such form and manner as the Administrator may prescribe, not later than March 1 of the next succeeding calendar year, a report containing the following information:

(1) His name and address.

(2) The title of his position with the National Aeronautics and Space Administration.

(3) A brief description of his duties with the National Aeronautics and Space Administration.

(4) The name and address of the aerospace contractor by whom he was employed.

(5) The title of his position with such aerospace contractor.

(6) A brief description of his duties at the time he was employed by such aerospace contractor.

(7) A description of any work performed by him in connection with any aerospace system while he was employed by the aerospace contractor or while performing any legal services for such contractor, if such contractor is providing substantial services or materials for such aerospace system or is negotiating or bidding to provide substantial services or materials for such aerospace system.

(8) The date on which his employment with such contractor terminated and the date on which his employement with the National Aeronautics and Space Administration began thereafter.

(9) Such other pertinent information as the Administrator may require.

(d) Exceptions.

(1) No former employee of the National Aeronautics and Space Administration shall be required to file a report under this section for any year in which he was employed by an aerospace contractor if the total cost to the United States of services and materials provided the United States by such contractor during such year was less than $10,000,000; and no employee of the National Aeronautics and Space Administration shall be required to file a report under this section if the total cost to the United States of services and materials provided the United States by the aerospace contractor by whom such employee was employed was less than $10,000,000 in each of the applicable calendar years that he was employed by such contractor.

(2) No former National Aeronautics and Space Administration employee shall be required to file a report under this section for any calendar year on account of employment with the National Aeronautics and Space Administration if such active duty or employment was terminated three years or more prior to the beginning of such calendar year; and no employee of the National Aeronautics and Space Administration shall be required to file a report under this section for any calendar year on account of employment with or services performed for an aerospace contractor if such employment was terminated or such services were performed three years or more prior to the beginning of such calendar year.

(e) Reports to Congress.

The Administrator shall, not later than May 1 of each year, file with the President of the Senate and the Speaker of the House of Representatives a report containing a list of the names of persons who have filed reports with him for the preceding calendar year pursuant to subsections (b) and (c) of this section. The Administrator shall include after each name so much information as he deems appropriate, and shall list the names of such persons under the aerospace contractor for whom they worked or for whom they performed services.

(f) Termination of employment; filing reports under subsection (b) or (c).

Any former employee of the National Aeronautics and Space Administration whose employment with an aerospace contractor terminated during any calendar year shall be required to file a report pursuant to subsection (b) of this section for such year if he would otherwise be required to file under such subsection; and any person whose employment with the National Aeronautics and Space Administration terminated during any calendar year shall be required to file a report pursuant to subsection (c) of this section for such year if he would otherwise be required to file under such subsection.

(g) Recordkeeping; availability of information.

The Administrator shall maintain a file containing the information filed with him pursuant to subsections (b) and (c) of this section and such file shall be open for public inspection at all times during the regular workday.

(h) Penalties.

Any person who fails to comply with the filing requirements of this section shall be guilty of a misdemeanor and shall, upon conviction thereof, be punished by not more than six months in prison or a fine of not more than $1,000, or both.

(i) Commencement date.

No person shall be required to file a report pursuant to this section for any year prior to the calendar year 1970. (Pub. L. 91–119, § 6, Nov. 18, 1969, 83 Stat. 199.)

CODIFICATION

Section was not enacted as part of the National Aeronautics and Space Act of 1958, which is classified principally to this chapter.

SUBCHAPTER II.—COORDINATION OF AERONAUTICAL AND SPACE ACTIVITIES

§ 2472. National Aeronautics and Space Administration.

EMERGENCY PREPAREDNESS FUNCTIONS

For assignment of certain emergency preparedness functions to the Administrator of the National Aeronautics and Space Administration, see Parts 1, 22, and 30 of Ex. Ord. No. 11490, Oct. 28, 1969, 34 F.R. 17567, set out as a note under section 2292 of Title 50, Appendix, War and National Defense.

§ 2473. Functions of the Administration.

SECTION REFERRED TO IN OTHER SECTIONS

This section is referred to in title 5 section 5532.

§ 2474. Civilian-Military Liaison Committee.

ABOLITION OF CIVILIAN-MILITARY LIAISON COMMITTEE

The Civilian-Military Liaison Committee was abolished and its functions, together with the functions of its chairman and other officers, were transferred to the President of the United States by sections 1(e) and 3(a) of Reorg. Plan No. 4 of 1965, eff. July 27, 1965, 30 F.R. 9353, 79 Stat. 1321, set out in the Appendix to Title 5, Government Organization and Employees.

§ 2477. Aerospace Safety Advisory Panel; membership; appointment; term; powers and duties of Panel; Chairman; compensation, travel and other necessary expenses; NASA membership restriction.

There is hereby established an Aerospace Safety Advisory Panel consisting of a maximum of nine members who shall be appointed by the Administrator for terms of six years each. The Panel shall review safety studies and operations plans referred to it and shall make reports thereon, shall advice the Administrator with respect to the hazards of proposed or existing facilities and proposed operations and with respect to the adequacy of proposed or existing safety standards and shall perform such other duties as the Administrator may request. One member shall be designated by the Panel as its Chairman. Members of the Panel who are officers or employees of the Federal Government shall receive no compensation for their services as such, but shall be allowed necessary travel expenses (or in the alternative, mileage for use of privately owned vehicles and a per diem in lieu of subsistence not to exceed the rates prescribed in sections 5702, 5704 of Title 5), and other necessary expenses incurred by them in the performance of duties vested in the Panel, without regard to the provisions of subchapter I, chapter 57 of Title 5, the Standardized Government Travel Regulations, or section 5731 of Title 5. Members of the Panel appointed from outside the Federal Government shall each receive compensation at the rate of $100 for each day such member is engaged in the actual performance of duties vested in the Panel in addition to reimbursement for travel, subsistence, and other necessary expenses in accordance with the provisions of the foregoing sentence. Not more than four such members shall be chosen from among the officers and employees of the National Aeronautics and Space Administration. (Pub. L. 90–67, § 6, Aug. 21, 1967, 81 Stat. 170.)

SOURCE: United States Code, 1964 Edition, Supplement V. 1970.

Part 6

NASA
PATENT
INFORMATION

NASA DOMESTIC PATENT LICENSING PROGRAM

Several thousand inventions result each year from the aeronautical and space research supported by the National Aeronautics and Space Administration. These inventions cover practically all fields of technology and include many that have useful and valuable commercial application.

The inventions having important use in Government programs or significant commercial potential are patented by NASA. In order to encourage the widest possible commercial use of these inventions, NASA makes its patents and applications for patent available for commercial licensing in accordance with the NASA Patent Licensing Regulations, Title 14 Code of Federal Regulations Section 1245.200 et seq.

NASA will grant nonexclusive, royalty-free licenses for inventions covered by patents and applications for patent for the term of the patent unless subsequently revoked or terminated by either party pursuant to agreed upon conditions. If commercial use of an invention has not occured by the end of the second year after the issue date of the patent, an exclusive, royalty-free license may be granted by NASA to a qualified applicant thereby adding the incentive of exclusivity to encourage the commercial development of the invention.

ADDRESS

Inquiries and all applications for licenses should be addressed to:

> Assistant General Counsel for Patent Matters
> National Aeronautics and Space Administration
> Washington, D.C. 20546

APPLICATION FOR LICENSE

An application for a patent license shall include:

1. Identification of invention for which license is desired:
   Title of invention
   U.S. Patent No. or Application No. (if known)
   NASA Tech Brief No. (if applicable)
   Other identification of invention (if any)
2. Name and address of company or organization applying for license
3. Name and address of representative or applicant to whom correspondence should be sent
4. Nature and type of applicant's business
5. Number of employees
6. Identification of source of information about the availability of a license on this invention
7. Purpose for which license is desired.

An application for exclusive license shall also include:

8. Applicant's status, if any, in any one or more of the following categories: (a) small business firms; (b) location in a surplus labor area; (c) location in a low income urban area; and (d) location in an area designated by the Government as economically despressed.

9. A description of applicant's capability to undertake the industrial marketing and development required to achieve the practical application of the invention.

10. The time and expenditure which the applicant estimates to be required to develop the invention to the point of practical application and the applicant's intention to invest that sum of money in development of the invention if the license is granted.

11. Whether the applicant would be willing to accept an exclusive license in a limited field of use or for any geographic portion less than the entirety of the United States of America, its territories and possessions, and if so, define the geographic portion or limited field.

12. Any other facts which the applicant believes to show it to be in the interests of the United States of America for the Administration to grant an exclusive license rather than a nonexclusive license and that such an exclusive license should be granted to the applicant.

Listed below are the U.S. patents available for royalty-free licensing from the National Aeronautics and Space Administration. Copies of the patents may be purchased directly from the U.S. Patent Office, Washington, D.C., for fifty cents a copy. Any NASA patent more than two years old and not in commercial use may be available for exclusive licensing. The patents marked with an asterisk (*) are believed to have good commercial potential use without much further development. Those marked with a double asterisk (**) have good potential, but may require further development for commercial use.

Patent No.	Date	Title
2,837,706	6-3-58	Line Following Servosystem
2,898,889	8-11-59	Mechanically-Limited Electrically Operated Hydraulic Valve System for Aircraft Controls
2,903,307	9-8-59	Two Component Bearing
2,926,123	2-23-60	Temperature Reducing Coating for Metals Subject to Flame Exposure
2,934,331	4-26-60	Apparatus for Making a Metal Slurry Product
2,940,259	6-14-60	Rocket Propellant Injector
2,944,316	7-12-60	Process of Casting Heavy Slips
2,945,667	7-19-60	Flexible Seal for Valves
2,956,772	10-18-60	Liquid-Spray Cooling Method
2,971,837	2-14-61	High Temperature Nickel-Base Alloy
2,971,838	2-14-61	High Temperature Nickel-Base Alloy
2,974,925	3-14-61	External Liquid-Spray Cooling of Turbine Blades
2,984,735	5-16-61	Runway Light
2,991,671	7-11-61	Wire Grid Forming Apparatus
2,991,961	7-11-61	Jet Aircraft Configuration
2,996,212	8-15-61	Self Supporting Space Vehicle
2,997,274	8-22-61	Turbo-Machine Blade Vibration Damper
3,001,363	9-26-61	Spherical Solid-Propellant Rocket Motor
3,001,395	9-26-61	Air Frame Drag Balance
3,001,739	9-26-61	Aerial Capsule Emergency Separation Device
3,004,735	10-17-61	Particle Detection Apparatus
3,005,081	10-17-61	High Intensity Heat and Light Unit
3,005,339	10-24-61	Wind Tunnel Airstream Oscillating Apparatus
3,008,229	11-14-61	Process for Applying a Protective Coating for Salt Bath Brazing
3,010,372	11-28-61	Folding Apparatus
3,011,760	12-5-61	Transportation Cooled Turbine Blade Manufactured from Wires
3,012,400	12-21-61	Nozzle
3,012,407	12-21-61	Insulating Structure
3,016,693	1-16-62	Electro-Thermal Rocket
3,016,863	1-16-62	Hydrofoil
3,022,672	2-27-62	Differential Pressure Cell
3,024,659	3-13-62	Magnetically Centered Liquid Column Float
3,028,122	4-3-62	Landing Arrangement for Aerial Vehicles
3,028,126	4-3-62	Three Axis Controller
3,028,128	4-3-62	Reentry Vehicle Leading Edge
3,038,077	6-5-62	Infrared Scanner
3,038,175	6-12-62	Survival Couch
3,041,587	6-26-62	Angular Measurement System
3,041,924	7-3-62	Motion Picture Camera for Optical Pyrometry
3,045,424	7-24-62	Method for Continuous Variation of Propellant Flow and Thrust in Propulsive Devices

Patent No.	Date	Title
3,049,876	8-21-62	Annular Rocket Motor and Nozzle Configuration
3,053,484	9-11-62	Variable Sweep Wing Configuration
3,057,597	10-9-62	Modification and Improvements to Cooled Blades
3,059,220	10-16-62	Apparatus for Coupling a Plurality of Ungrounded Circuits to a Gounded Circuit
3,063,291	11-13-62	High Vacuum Condenser Tank for Ion Rocket Engines
3,064,928	11-20-62	Variable Sweep Wing Aircraft
3,067,573	12-11-62	Telescoping-Spike Supersonic Inlet for Aircraft Engines
3,068,658	12-18-62	Venting Vapor Apparatus
3,069,123	12-18-62	Instrument Support with Precise Lateral Adjustment
3,070,330	12-25-62	Attitude and Propellant Flow Control System and Method
3,070,349	12-25-62	Multistage Multiple-Reentry Turbine
3,070,407	12-25-62	Air Bearing
3,072,574	1-8-63	Gas Lubricant Compositions
3,076,065	1-29-63	High-Speed Low-Level Electrical Stepping Switch
3,077,599	2-12-63	Collapsible Loop Antenna for Space Vehicle
3,079,113	2-26-63	Vehicle Parachute and Equipment Jettison System
3,080,711	3-12-63	Penshape Exhaust Nozzle for Super-sonic Engine
3,083,611	4-2-63	Multi-Lobar SCAN Horizon Sensor
3,084,421	4-9-63	Reinforced Metallic Composites
3,085,165	4-9-63	Ultra-Long Monostable Multivibrator Employing Bistable Semiconductor Switch to Allow Charging or Timing Circuit
3,087,692	4-30-63	Variable-Span Aircraft
3,088,441	5-7-63	Valve Actuator
**3,090,212	5-21-63	Sandwich Panel Construction
3,090,580	5-21-63	Space and Atmospheric Reentry Vehicle
3,093,000	6-11-63	Check Valve Assembly for a Probe
3,093,346	6-11-63	Space Capsule
3,098,630	7-23-63	Annular Supersonic Decelerator or Drogue
**3,100,294	8-6-63	Time-Division Multiplexer
3,100,990	8-20-63	Two-Plane Balance
3,102,948	9-3-63	Electric Arc Welding
3,104,079	9-17-63	Variable-Geometry Winged Reentry Vehicle
**3,104,082	9-17-63	Variable Sweep Aircraft Wing
3,105,515	10-1-63	Pressure Regulating System
**3,106,603	10-8-63	High Voltage Cable
3,108,171	10-22-63	Radiant Heater Having Formed Filaments

Patent No.	Date	Title	Patent No.	Date	Title
3,110,318	11-12-63	Slosh Suppressing Device and Method	**3,160,950	12-15-64	Method and Apparatus for Shock Protection
3,112,672	12-3-63	Umbilical Separator for Rockets	3,162,012	12-22-64	Formed Metal Ribbon Wrap
3,115,630	12-24-63	Reflector Space Satellite	**3,163,935	1-5-65	Mechanical Coordinate Converter
3,118,100	1-14-64	Electric Battery and Method of Operating the Same	3,164,222	1-5-65	Non-Reusable Kinetic Energy Absorber
3,119,232	1-28-64	Rocket Engine	3,164,369	1-5-65	Multistage Multiple-Reentry Turbine
3,120,101	2-4-64	Channel Type Shell Construction for Rocket Engine and the Like	3,165,356	1-12-65	Shock Absorbing Support and Restraint Means
3,120,361	2-4-64	Landing Arrangement for Aerospace Vehicle	3,166,834	1-26-65	Catalyst Bed Removing Tool
3,120,738	2-11-64	Ignition System for Monopropellant Combustion Devices	3,167,426	1-26-65	Nickel-Base Alloy
3,121,309	2-18-64	Spherically Shaped Rocket Motor	3,168,827	2-9-65	Airplane Take-off Performance Indicator
3,122,000	2-25-64	Apparatus for Transferring Cryogenic Liquids	*3,169,001	2-9-65	Aircraft Wheel Spray Drag Alleviator
3,122,098	2-25-64	Apparatus and Method for Control of a Solid Fueled Rocket Vehicle	**3,169,613	2-16-65	Elastic Universal Joint
			**3,169,725	2-16-65	Erectable Modular Space Station
3,122,885	3-3-64	Injector for Bipropellant Rocket Engines	3,170,286	2-23-65	Injector Valve Device
3,123,248	3-3-64	Expulsion Bladder Equipped Storage Tank Structure	3,170,290	2-23-65	Liquid Rocket System
			3,170,295	2-23-65	Propellant Tank Pressurization System
**3,127,157	3-31-64	Multiple Belleville Spring Assembly	3,170,324	2-23-65	Aerodynamic Measuring Device
3,128,389	4-7-64	Variable Frequency Magnetic Multivibrator	**3,170,471	2-23-65	Inflatable Honeycomb
3,128,845	4-14-64	Despin Weight Release	3,170,486	2-23-65	Two-Component Valve Assembly
3,130,940	4-28-64	Heat Shield	3,170,605	2-23-65	Ejection Valve
3,132,342	5-5-64	Antenna System Using Parasitic Elements and Two Driven Elements at 90° Angle Fed 180° Out of Phase	3,170,657	2-23-65	Landing Arrangement for Aerial Vehicle
			3,170,660	2-23-65	Parachute Glider
			3,170,773	2-23-65	Reinforced Metallic Composites
3,132,476	5-12-64	Thrust Vector Control Apparatus	3,171,060	2-23-65	Plasma Accelerator
3,132,479	5-12-64	Universal Restrainer and Joint	3,171,081	2-23-65	Ionization Vacuum Gauge
**3,132,903	5-12-64	Slit Regulated Gas Journal Bearing	3,172,097	3-2-65	Binary to Binary-Coded-Decimal Converter
3,135,089	6-2-64	Decomposition Unit			
3,135,090	6-2-64	Rocket Motor System	3,173,246	3-16-65	Colloid Propulsion Method and Apparatus
3,136,123	6-9-64	Rocket Engine Injector			
3,138,837	6-30-64	Method of Making Fiber Reinforced Metallic Composites	3,173,251	3-16-65	Apparatus for Igniting Solid Propellants
			3,174,278	3-23-65	Continuously Operating Induction Plasma
3,139,725	7-7-64	Steerable Solid Propellant Rocket Motor	3,174,279	3-23-65	Rocket Thrust Chamber
**3,140,728	7-14-64	High Pressure Four-Way Valve	3,174,827	3-23-65	Production of High Purity Silicon Carbide
3,141,340	7-21-64	Gravity Device			
3,141,769	7-21-64	Method of Producing Porous Tungsten Ionizers for Ion Rocket Engines	3,175,789	3-30-65	Landing Pad Assembly for Aerospace Vehicles
3,141,932	7-21-64	Switching Mechanism with Energy Storage Means	3,176,222	3-30-65	Apparatus Having Coaxial Capacitor Structure for Measuring Fluid Density
**3,143,321	8-4-64	Frangible Tube Energy Dissipation	3,176,499	4-6-65	High Temperature Testing Apparatus
3,143,651	8-4-64	X-Ray Reflection Collimator Adapted For Focus X-Radiation Directly On A Detector	3,176,933	4-6-65	Thermal Control of Space Vehicles
			*3,177,933	4-13-65	Thermal Switch
			3,178,883	4-20-65	Attitude Control for Spacecraft
3,144,219	8-11-64	Manned Space Station	3,180,264	4-27-65	Coupling for Linear Shaped Charge
3,144,999	8-18-64	Propellant Blade Loading Control	3,180,587	4-27-65	Attitude Orientation of Spin-Stablized Space Vehicles
3,145,874	8-18-64	Means For Controlling Repture Of Shock Tube Diaphrams	3,181,821	5-4-65	Spacecraft Soft Landing System
3,147,422	9-1-64	Electronic Motor Control System	3,182,496	5-11-65	Electric Arc Driven Wind Tunnel
3,149,897	9-22-64	Printed Cable Connector	3,183,506	5-11-65	Radar Ranging Receiver
3,150,329	9-22-64	Variable Frequency Magnetic Coupled Multivibrator	3,185,023	5-25-65	Optical Inspection Apparatus
			3,187,583	6-8-65	Space Simulator
**3,150,387	9-29-64	Foam Generator	3,188,472	6-8-65	Method and Apparatus for Determining Satellite Orientation Utilizing Spatial Energy Sources
*3,152,344	10-13-64	Life Preserver			
3,155,992	11-10-64	Life Raft			
3,156,090	11-10-64	Ion Rocket	3,188,844	6-15-65	Electrical Discharge Apparatus for Forming
3,157,529	11-17-64	Bonded Solid Lubricant Coating			
3,158,172	11-24-64	High-Temperature, High-Pressure Spherical Segment Valve	3,189,299	6-15-65	Dynamic Precession Damper for Spin Stabilized Vehicles
3,158,336	11-24-64	Assembly for Recovering a Capsule	**3,189,535	6-15-65	Means and Method of Depositing Thin Films on Substrates
**3,158,764	11-24-64	Two-Fluid Magnethydrodynamic System and Method for Thermal-Electric Power Conversion	3,189,726	6-15-65	High Temperature Heat Source
			3,189,794	6-15-65	Relay Binary Circuit
3,159,967	12-8-64	Variable Thrust Ion Engine Utilizing Thermally Decomposable Solid Fuel	3,189,864	6-15-65	Electrical Connector for Flat Cables
**3,160,825	12-8-64	Temperature Compensating Means for Cavity Resonator of Amplifier	3,191,316	6-29-65	Lunar Landing Flight Research Vehicle
			3,191,379	6-29-65	Propellant Grain for Rocket Motors

Patent No.	Date	Title
3,191,907	6-29-65	Conical Valve Plug
3,192,730	7-6-65	Helium Refining by Superfluidity
3,193,883	7-13-65	Mandrel for Shaping Solid Propellant Rocket Fuel into a Motor Casing
3,194,060	7-13-65	Seismic Displacement Transducer
3,194,525	7-13-65	Supporting and Protecting Device
3,194,951	7-13-65	Logarithmic Converter
3,196,261	7-20-65	Full Binary Adder
3,196,362	7-20-65	Temperature Compensated Solid State Differential
3,196,557	7-27-65	Centrifuge Mounted Motion Simulator
3,196,558	7-27-65	Means for Visually Indicating Flight Paths of Vehicles Between the Earth
3,196,598	7-27-65	Inlet Deflector for Jet Engines
3,196,675	7-27-65	Optical Torquemeter
3,196,690	7-27-65	Impact Simulator
3,197,616	7-27-65	Temperature Regulation Circuit
3,198,955	8-3-65	Binary Magnetic Memory Device
3,199,340	8-10-65	Accelerometer with F.M. Output
3,199,343	8-10-65	Electric Propulsion Engine Test Chamber
3,199,931	8-10-65	Externally Pressurized Fluid Bearing
3,200,706	8-17-65	Gas Actuated Bolt Disconnect
3,201,560	8-17-65	Electric-Arc Heater
3,201,635	8-17-65	Method and Apparatus for Producing a Plasma
3,201,980	8-24-65	Thrust Dynamometer
3,202,381	8-24-65	Recoverable Rocket Vehicle
3,202,398	8-24-65	Locking Device for Turbine Rotor Blades
3,202,844	8-24-65	Energy Conversion Apparatus
3,202,915	8-24-65	Particle Beam Measurement Apparatus Using Beam Kinetic Energy to Change the Heat Sensitive Resistance of the Detection Probe
**3,202,998	8-24-65	Flexible Foam Erectable Space Structure
3,204,447	9-7-65	Enthalphy and Stagnation Temperature Determination of a High Temperature Laminar Flow Gas Stream
3,204,889	9-7-65	Space Vehicle Electrical System
3,205,361	9-7-65	Light Sensitive Digital Aspect Sensor
3,205,362	9-7-65	Photosensitive Device to Detect Bearing Deviation
3,205,381	9-7-65	Ionospheric Battery
3,206,141	9-14-65	Space Vehicle Attitude Control
3,208,215	9-28-65	Gimbaled, Partially Submerged Rocket Nozzle
3,208,272	9-28-65	Surface Roughness Detector
3,208,694	9-28-65	Nose Gear Steering System for Vehicle with Main Skid
3,208,707	9-28-65	Pivotal Shock Absorbing Pad Assembly
3,209,360	9-28-65	Antenna Beam-Shaping Apparatus
3,209,361	9-28-65	Cassegrainian Antenna Subreflector Flange for Supressing Ground Noise
3,210,927	10-12-65	Electro-Thermal Rockets Having Improved Heat Exchangers
3,211,169	10-12-65	Shrink-fit Gas Valve
3,211,414	10-12-65	Thermally Operated Valve
3,212,096	10-12-65	Parabolic Reflector Horn Feed With Spillover Correction
3,212,259	10-15-65	Tertiary Flow Injection Thrust Vectoring System
3,212,325	10-12-65	Force Measuring Instrument
3,212,564	10-19-65	Heat Conductive Resiliently Compressible Structure for Space Electronic Package Modules
3,215,572	11-02-65	Low Viscosity Magnetic Fluid Obtained by the Colloidal Suspension of Magnetic Particles
*3,215,842	11-02-65	Optical Communication System
3,216,007	11-02-65	Analog-to-Digital Conversion System
**3,217,624	11-16-65	Electrically-operated Rotary Shutter
3,218,479	11-16-65	Phase Detector Assembly
3,218,547	11-16-65	Flux Sensing Device Using a Tubular Core with Toroidal Gating Coil and Solenoidal Output Coil
3,218,850	11-23-65	Thermo-protective Device for Balances
3,219,250	11-23-65	Flexible Back-up Bar
3,219,365	11-23-65	Spherical Shield
3,219,828	11-23-65	Vibrating Reticle Star Tracker
3,220,004	11-23-65	Passive Communication Satellite
3,221,547	12-7-65	Apparatus for Absorbing and Measuring Power
**3,221,549	12-7-65	Aircraft Instrument
*3,223,374	12-14-65	Miniature Vibration Isolator
3,224,001	12-14-65	Inflatable Radar Reflector Unit
3,224,173	12-21-65	Liquid-gas Separator System
3,224,263	12-21-65	Null-type Vacuum Microbalance
3,224,336	12-21-65	Missile Launch Release System
3,228,492	1-11-66	Double-Acting Shock Absorber
3,228,558	1-11-66	Measuring Device
3,229,099	1-11-66	Electro-Optical Alignment Control System
3,229,102	1-11-66	Radiation Direction Detector Including Means for Compensating for Photocell Aging
3,229,139	1-11-66	High Temperature Spark Plug
3,229,155	1-11-66	Electric Arc Device for Heating Gases
3,229,463	1-18-66	Trajectory-correction Propulsion System
3,229,568	1-18-66	Concave Grating Spectrometer
3,229,636	1-18-66	Missile Stage Separation Indicator and Stage Initiator
3,229,682	1-18-66	Device for Directionally Controlling Electromagnetic Radiation
3,229,689	1-18-66	Resuscitation Apparatus
3,229,884	1-18-66	Segmented Back-up Bar
3,229,930	1-18-66	Stretch Yo-Yo De-spin Mechanism
**3,230,053	1-18-66	Apparatus for Producing High Purity Silicon Carbide Crystals
3,230,377	1-18-66	Self-stablized Theodolite for Manual Tracking Using Photosensitive Stablizing Means
3,236,066	2-22-66	Energy Absorption Device
3,237,253	3-1-66	Method of Making Screen by Casting
3,238,345	3-1-66	Hypersonic Test Facility
3,238,413	3-1-66	Magnetically Controlled Plasma Accelerator
3,238,715	3-8-66	Electrostatic Ion Engine Having a Permanent Magnetic Circuit
3,238,730	3-8-66	Anti-backlash Circuit for Hydraulic Drive System
3,238,774	3-8-66	Pressurized Cell Micrometeroroid Detector
*3,238,777	3-8-66	Differential Temperature Transducer
3,239,660	3-8-66	Illumination System Including a Virtual Light Source
3,242,716	3-29-66	Apparatus for Measuring Thermal Conductivity
3,243,154	3-29-66	Vibration Damping System
3,243,791	3-29-66	Bi-carrier Demodulator with Modulation
3,249,012	5-3-66	Umbilical Disconnect
**3,249,013	5-3-66	Remote Controlled Tubular Disconnect
3,251,053	5-10-66	Analog to Digital Converter
3,252,100	5-17-66	Pulse Generating Circuit
3,254,395	6-7-66	Method for Making a Rocket Motor Casing
3,254,487	6-7-66	Rocket Motor Casing
3,257,780	6-28-66	Zero Gravity Separator
3,258,582	6-28-66	Energy Management System for Glider Type Vehicle
3,258,687	6-28-66	Wide Range Linear Fluxgate Magnetometer
3,258,831	7-5-66	Method of Making a Molded Connector

Patent No.	Date	Title	Patent No.	Date	Title
3,258,912	7-5-66	Method of Igniting Solid Propellants	3,274,304	9-20-66	Method of Making Impurity-Type Semi-conductor Electrical Contacts
3,258,918	7-5-66	Fluid Dispensing Apparatus and Method			
**3,260,055	7-12-66	Automatic Thermal Switch	*3,276,251	10-4-66	Test Unit Free-Flight Suspension System
3,260,204	7-12-66	Velocity Package			
3,260,326	7-12-66	Wind-tunnel Microphone Structure	3,276,376	10-4-66	Thrust and Direction Control Apparatus
3,261,210	7-19-66	Superconductive Accelerometer	3,276,602	10-4-66	Cable Arrangement for Rigid Tethering
3,262,186	7-26-66	Method of Improving the Reliability of a Rolling Element System	3,276,679	10-4-66	Separator
			3,276,722	10-4-66	Flight Craft
3,262,262	7-26-66	Electrostatic Ion Rocket Engine	3,276,726	10-4-66	Inflation System for Balloon Type Satellites
3,262,351	7-26-66	Separation Nut			
3,262,365	7-26-66	Space Capsule Ejection Assembly	3,276,865	10-4-66	High Temperature Cobalt-Base Alloy
3,262,395	7-26-66	Hydraulic Transformer	3,276,866	10-4-66	Nickel-Base Alloy Containing Mo-W-Al-Cr-Ta-Zr-C-Nb-B
3,262,518	7-26-66	Emergency Escape System			
3,262,655	7-26-66	Alleviation of Divergence During Rocket Launch	3,276,946	10-4-66	Low Friction Magnetic Recording Tape
			3,277,314	10-4-66	High-Efficiency Multivibrator
3,263,016	7-26-66	Black-body Furnance	3,277,366	10-4-66	Insertion Loss Measuring Apparatus Having Transformer Means Connected Across a Pair of Bolometers
3,263,171	7-26-66	Micro Current Measuring Device Using Plural Logarthmic Response Heated Gilamentrary Type Diodes			
			3,277,373	10-4-66	Serrodyne Frequency Converter Re-entrant Amplifier System
3,263,610	8-2-66	Quick-Release Connector			
**3,264,135	8-2-66	Method of Coating Carbonaceous Base To Prevent Oxidation Destruction and Coated Base	3,277,375	10-4-66	Reentry Communication by Material Addition
			3,277,458	10-4-66	Condition and Condition Duration Indicator
3,270,441	9-6-66	Reduced Gravity Similator			
3,270,499	9-6-66	Injector Assembly for Liquid Fueled Rocket Engines	3,277,486	10-4-66	Method and Means for Damping Nutation in a Satellite
3,270,501	9-6-66	Aerodynamic Spike Nozzle	3,279,193	10-18-66	Method and Construction for Protecting Heat Sensitive Bodies From Thermal Radiation and Convective Heat
3,270,503	9-6-66	Ablation Structures			
3,270,504	9-6-66	Automatically Deploying Nozzle Exit Cone Extension			
			3,281,963	11-01-66	Training Vehicle for Controlling Attitude
3,270,505	9-6-66	Control System for Rocket Vehicles	3,281,964	11-01-66	Rotating Space Station Simulator
**3,270,512	9-6-66	Intermittent Type Silica gel Absorption Refrigerator	**3,281,965	11-01-66	Controlled Visibility Device for an Aircraft
			3,282,035	11-01-66	Molecular Beam Velocity Selector
3,270,565	9-6-66	Omnidirectional Acceleration Device	3,282,091	11-01-66	Instrument for Measuring Torsional Creep and Recovery
3,270,756	9-6-66	Fluid Flow Control Valve			
3,270,802	9-6-66	Method and Apparatus for Varying Thermal Conductivity	3,282,532	11-01-66	Stabilization of Gravity Oriented Satellites
3,270,835	9-6-66	Device for Suppressing Sound and Heat Produced by High-velocity Exhaust Jets	3,282,541	11-01-66	Attitude Control System for Sounding Rockets
			3,282,739	11-01-66	Non-magnetic Battery Case
3,270,908	9-6-66	Space Capsule	**3,282,740	11-01-66	Sealed Battery Gas Manifold Construction
3,270,985	9-6-66	Reactance Control System	3,283,088	11-01-66	Multiple Circuit Switch Apparatus With Improved Pivot Actuator Structure
3,270,986	9-6-66	Hand-held Self-maneuvering Unit			
3,270,988	9-6-66	Minimum Induced Drag Airfoil Body	3,283,175	11-01-66	AC Logic Flip-Flop Circuits
**3,270,989	9-6-66	Variable Sweep Aircraft	3,283,241	11-01-66	Apparatus for Field Strength Measurement of a Space Vehicle
3,270,990	9-6-66	Absorptive Splitter for Closely Spaced Supersonic Engine Air Inlets			
			3,286,274	11-22-66	Pressure suit tie-down mechanism
3,271,140	9-6-66	High Temperature Cobalt-Base Alloy	3,286,531	11-22-66	Omni-Directional Anisotropic Molecular Trap
**3,271,181	9-6-66	Method of Coating Carbonaceous Base To Prevent Oxidation Destruction and Coated Base			
			3,286,629	11-22-66	Multi-mission module
			3,286,630	11-22-66	Spacecraft separation system for spinning vehicles and/or payloads
3,271,532	9-6-66	Three-axis Finger Tip Controller for Switches			
			3,286,882	11-22-66	Booster tank system
3,271,558	9-6-66	Spectral Method for Monitoring Atmospheric Contamination of Inert-gas Welding Shields	3,286,953	11-22-66	Roll attitude star sensor system
			3,286,957	11-22-66	Flexible wing deployment device
			3,287,031	11-22-66	Indexed Keyed Connection
3,271,594	9-6-66	Transient Augmentation Circuit for Pulse Amplifiers	3,287,174	11-22-66	Prevention of pressure build-up in electrochemical cells
**3,271,620	9-6-66	Starting Circuit for Vapor Lamps and the Like	3,287,496	11-22-66	Digital television camera control system
			3,287,582	11-22-66	Apparatus for increasing ion engine beam density
3,271,637	9-6-66	Gas Solar Detector Using Manganese as a Doping Agent			
3,271,649	9-6-66	Regenerative Braking System	3,287,640	11-22-66	Pulse Counting circuit which simultaneously indicates the occurrence of the Nth pulse
3,273,094	9-13-66	Superconducting Magnet			
3,273,355	9-20-66	Heat Protective Apparatus			
3,273,381	9-20-66	Means and Method of Measuring Visco-elastic Strain	**3,287,660	11-22-66	Solid State chemical source for ammonia beam maser
			3,287,725	11-22-66	Phase-locked loop with a sideband rejecting properties
3,273,388	9-20-66	Apparatus for Measuring Electric Field Strength on the Surface of a Model Vehicle			
			3,289,205	11-29-66	Method & Apparatus for determining Electromagnetic characteristics of Large Surface Area Passive Reflectors
3,273,392	9-20-66	Hot Wire Liquid Level Detector for Cryogenic Fluids			
3,273,399	9-20-66	Traversing Probe			

Patent No.	Date	Title
3,295,360	01-03-67	Dynamic sensor
*3,295,366	01-03-67	Support apparatus for dynamic testing
3,295,377	01-03-67	Angular accelerometer
3,295,386	01-03-67	Three axis controller
3,295,512	01-03-67	Foldable solar concentrator
3,295,545	01-03-67	Liquid storage tank venting device for zero gravity environment
3,295,556	01-03-67	Foldable conduit
**3,295,684	01-03-67	High pressure filter
3,295,699	01-03-67	Folding boom assembly
3,295,782	01-03-67	Endless tape cartridge
3,295,790	01-03-67	Recoverable single stage spacecraft booster
3,295,791	01-03-67	Storage container mounting for space vehicles
3,295,798	01-03-67	Landing gear
**3,295,808	01-03-67	Parallel motion suspension device
3,296,060	01-03-67	Unrefined-ceramic flame resistant insulation and method of making the same
3,296,526	01-03-67	Micrometeroid velocity measuring device
3,296,531	01-03-67	Electrostatic plasma modulator for space vehicle re-entry communication
3,298,175	01-17-67	Method and device for cooling
3,298,182	01-17-67	Ignition means for monopropellant
3,298,221	01-17-67	Densitometer
3,298,285	01-17-67	Reinforcing means for diaphragms
3,298,362	01-17-67	Instrument for use in performing a controller Valsalva Maneuver
3,298,582	01-17-67	Camera film feed having a detent means
*3,299,364	01-17-67	Folded traveling wave maser structure
3,299,431	01-17-67	Unfurlable structure including coiled strips thrust launched upon tension release
3,299,913	01-24-67	Adjustable Tension Wire Guide
3,300,162	01-24-67	Radial module space station
3,300,717	01-24-67	Method & Apparatus for measuring potentials in plasmas
3,300,721	01-24-67	Means for communication through a layer of ionized gases
3,300,847	01-31-67	Portable alignment tool
3,300,949	01-31-67	Liquid-gas separator for zero gravity environment
3,300,981	01-31-67	Zero gravity starting means for liquid propellant motors
3,301,046	01-37-67	Method of obtaining permanent record of surface flow phenomena
3,301,315	01-31-67	Thermal conductive connection and method of making same
3,301,507	01-31-67	Hypersonic Re-entry Vehicle
3,301,511	01-31-67	Wing Deployment Method and Apparatus
3,301,578	01-31-67	Cryogenic connector for vacuum use
3,302,023	01-31-67	Apparatus for producing three dimensional recordings of fluorescense spectra
3,302,040	01-31-67	Linear sawtooth voltage-wave generator employing transistor timing circuit having capacitor-zener diode combination feedback
3,302,569	02-07-67	Quick release separation mechanism
3,302,633	02-07-67	Universal pilot restraint suit and body support therefor
*3,302,662	02-07-67	Antiflutter ball check valve
3,302,960	02-07-67	Locking device with rolling detents
3,303,304	02-07-67	Discrete Local Altitude Sensing Device
3,304,028	02-14-67	Attitude control for spacecraft
3,304,718	02-21-67	Double optic system for ion engine
3,304,724	02-21-67	Tank construction for space vehicles
3,304,729	02-21-67	Cryogenic Storage System
*3,304,768	02-21-67	Fatigue testing device
3,304,773	02-21-67	Force transducer
3,304,799	02-21-67	Proportional controller
3,304,865	02-21-67	Self-sealing, unbonded, rocket motor nozzle closure
3,305,415	02-21-67	Process for preparing sterile solid propellants
3,305,636	02-21-67	Phase-shift data transmission system having a pseudo-noise sync code modulated with the data in a single channel
**3,305,801	02-21-67	Variable time constant smoothing circuit
**3,305,810	02-21-67	Solenoid construction
3,305,861	02-21-67	Closed Loop Ranging System
3,305,870	02-21-67	Dual Mode Horn Antenna
3,307,407	03-07-67	Micro-particle impact sensing apparatus
3,308,848	03-14-67	Fluid power transmission
3,309,012	03-14-67	Thermal pump-compressor for space use
3,309,961	03-21-67	Hermetically sealed explosive release mechanism
*3,310,054	03-21-67	File card marker
*3,310,138	03-21-67	Viscous-pendulum damper
3,310,256	03-21-67	Aerodynamic protection for space flight vehicles
3,310,258	03-21-67	Technique for control of free-flight rocket vehicles
3,310,261	03-21-67	Control for flexible parawing
3,310,262	03-21-67	Supersonic Aircraft
3,310,443	03-21-67	Method of forming thin window drifted silicon charged particle detector
3,310,978	03-28-67	Fiber optic vibration transducer and analyzer
3,310,980	03-28-67	Hydraulic support for dynamic testing
**3,311,315	03-28-67	Endless tape transport mechanism
3,311,502	03-28-67	Didymium hydrate additive to nickel hydroxide electrodes
3,311,510	03-28-67	Method of making a silicon semiconductor device
3,311,748	03-28-67	Sun tracker with rotatable plane-parallel plate and two photocells
**3,311,772	03-28-67	Focussing system for an ion source having apertured electrodes
3,311,832	03-28-67	Multiple Input Radio Receiver
3,312,101	04-04-67	Gas Analyzer for Bi-gaseous mixtures
3,316,716	05-02-67	Composite Powerplant and Shroud Therefor
3,316,752	05-02-67	Method and Apparatus for detection and location of microleaks
*3,316,991	05-02-67	Automatic Force measuring system
3,317,180	05-02-67	High Pressure regulator valve
3,317,341	05-02-67	Metallic film diffusion for boundary lubrication
3,317,352	05-02-67	Method for determining the state of charge of batteries by the use of tracers
3,317,641	05-02-67	Method For Molding Compounds
3,317,731	05-02-67	Canopus Detector Including Automative Gain Control of Photomultiplier Tube
3,317,751	05-02-67	Reversible Ring Counter Employing Cascaded Single SCR Stages
3,317,797	05-02-67	Microelectronic Module Package
3,317,825	05-02-67	Three-Wire Ground Type Electrical Receptacle Tester
3,317,832	05-02-67	Single or Joint Amplitude Distrubution Analyzer
3,317,846	05-02-67	Linear Accelerator for Micrometeoroids Having a Variable Voltage Source
3,318,093	05-09-67	Hydraulic Drive Mechanism
3,318,096	05-09-67	Purge Device for Thrust Engines
3,318,343	05-09-67	Tool Attachment for Spreading Loose Elements Away From Work
*3,318,622	05-09-67	All-Directional Fastener
3,319,175	05-09-67	Electronic Amplifier With Power Supply Switching
3,319,979	05-16-67	Quick Attach and Release Fluid Coupling Assembly
3,320,669	05-23-67	Line Cutter
3,321,034	05-23-67	Sample Collecting Impact Bit

Patent No.	Date	Title
3,321,154	05-23-67	Transpirationally Cooled Heat Ablation System
3,321,157	05-23-67	Double-Hinged Flap
3,321,159	05-23-67	Techniques for Insulating Cryogenic Fuel Containers
*3,321,570	05-23-67	Printed circuit board with bellows rivet connection
3,321,628	05-23-67	Baseline stabilization system for ionization detector
**3,321,645	05-23-67	Switching circuit employing regeneratively connected complementary transistors
3,321,922	05-30-67	Small Rocket Engine
3,323,356	06-06-67	Apparatus for Positioning and Loading a test specimen
3,323,362	06-06-67	Positive Displacement Flowmeter
3,323,370	06-06-67	Mass measuring system
**3,323,386	06-06-67	Two-axis controller
3,323,408	06-06-67	Optical alignment system
3,323,484	06-06-67	Liquid Flow Sight Assembly
**3,323,967	06-06-67	Masking Device
3,324,370	06-06-67	Electronic Beam Switching Commutator
3,324,388	06-06-67	Meteoroid sensing apparatus having a coincidence network connected to a pair of capacitors
**3,324,423	06-06-67	Dual waveguide mode source having control means for adjusting the relative amplitudes of two modes
3,324,659	06-13-67	Electrostatic Thrustor with Improved Insulators
3,325,229	06-13-67	Air Bearing
3,325,723	06-13-67	Voltage-current characteristic simulator
3,325,749	06-13-67	Variable Frequency Oscillator with Temperature Compensation
3,326,043	06-20-67	Inductive Liquid Level Detection System
3,326,407	06-20-67	Thin-walled pressure vessel
3,327,298	06-20-67	System for recording and reproducing pulse code modulated data
*3,327,991	06-27-67	Valve seat with Resilient Support Member
3,328,624	06-27-67	High efficiency ionizer assembly
3,329,375	07-04-67	Attitude Control and damping system for spacecraft
3,329,918	07-04-67	High voltage divider system
3,330,052	07-11-67	Subgravity Simulator
**3,330,082	07-11-67	Central sparand module joint
3,330,510	07-11-67	Orbital Escape Device
3,330,549	07-11-67	Shock Absorber
3,331,071	07-11-67	Satellite Communication System
3,331,246	07-18-67	Hypersonic test facility
3,331,255	07-18-67	Non-magnetic, explosive actuated indexing device
3,331,404	07-18-67	Apparatus for purging systems handling
3,331,951	07-18-67	Trigonometric Vehicle Guidance Assembly which aligns the three perpendicular axes of two-axes systems
**3,333,152	07-25-67	Self-repeating plasma accelerator
3,333,788	08-01-67	Artificial gravity spin deployment system
3,336,725	08-22-67	Canister closing device
3,336,748	08-22-67	Plasma Device Feed System
3,337,004	08-22-67	Impact energy absorber
3,337,279	08-22-67	Gas purged dry box glove
3,337,315	08-22-67	Method for Fiberizing Ceramic Materials
3,337,337	08-22-67	Method for producing fiber reinforced metallic composites
**3,337,790	08-22-67	Mercury capillary interrupter
3,337,812	08-22-67	Circulator having quarter wavelength resonant post and parametric amplifier circuits utilizing the same
3,339,404	09-05-67	Lunar Penetrometer
3,339,863	09-05-67	Solar vane actuator
3,340,099	09-05-67	Bonded elastomeric seal for electrochemical cells
3,340,395	09-05-67	Time-of-flight mass spectrometer with feed-back means from the detector to the low sources and a specific counter
3,340,397	09-05-67	Multiple environment materials test chamber having a multiple port X-ray tube for irradiating a plurality of samples
**3,340,430	09-05-67	Diode and protection fuse unit
3,340,532	09-05-67	Tracking receiver
3,340,599	09-12-67	Simple method of making photovoltaic junctions
3,340,713	09-12-67	Spin forming tubular elbows
3,340,727	09-12-67	Ablation Probe
3,340,732	09-12-67	Meteorological Balloon
3,341,151	09-12-67	Apparatus providing a directive field pattern and attitude sensing of a spin stabilized satellite
3,341,169	09-12-67	Filler Valve
3,341,708	09-12-67	Amplitude modulated laser transmitter
3,341,778	09-12-67	Optimum pre-detection diversity receiving system
**3,341,977	09-19-67	Conforming Polisher for aspheric surfaces of revolution
3,342,055	09-19-67	Protective device for machine and metalworking tools
3,342,066	09-19-67	Model launcher for wind tunnels
*3,342,653	09-19-67	Method of making inflatable honeycomb
*3,343,180	09-26-67	Stretcher
3,343,189	09-26-67	Rescue litter floatation assembly
3,344,340	09-26-67	Regulated power supply
3,344,425	09-26-67	Monopulse Tracking System
3,345,820	10-10-67	Electron Bombardment Ion Engine
3,345,822	10-10-67	Burning rate control of solid propellants
3,345,840	10-10-67	Tube Dimpling Tool
*3,345,866	10-10-67	Multilegged Support System
3,346,419	10-10-67	Solar cell mounting
3,346,515	10-10-67	Method of producing alternating ether-siloxane copolymers
3,346,724	10-10-67	Random Function Tracer
3,346,806	10-10-67	Pressure monitoring with a plurality of ionization gauges controlled at a central location
3,346,929	10-17-67	Latching Mechanism
3,347,046	10-17-67	Control of transverse instability in rocket combustors
3,347,057	10-17-67	Rapid cooling method and apparatus
3,347,309	10-17-67	Self Adjusting Multi-Segment, Deployable Natural Circulation Radiator
3,347,465	10-17-67	Prestressed refractor structure
3,347,466	10-17-67	Nacelle Afterbody for jet engines
3,347,531	10-17-67	Stirring apparatus for plural test tubes
3,347,665	10-17-67	Low temperature aluminum alloy
3,348,048	10-17-67	Horizon sensor with a plurality of fixedly-positioned radiation-compensated radiation sensitive detector
3,348,053	10-17-67	Amplifier Clamping Circuit for horizon scanner
3,348,152	10-17-67	Diversity receiving system
3,349,814	10-31-67	Method and apparatus for making a heat insulating and ablative structure
3,350,033	10-31-67	Reaction wheel scanner
3,350,034	10-31-67	Satellite appendage tie-down cord
3,350,643	10-31-67	Signal-to-noise ratio estimated by taking ratio of mean and standard deviation of integrated signal samples
**3,350,671	10-31-67	High power-high voltage waterload
**3,350,926	11-07-67	Miniature Stress Transducer
3,352,157	11-14-67	Inertia diaphragm pressure transducer
*3,352,192	11-14-67	Split nut separation system
3,353,359	11-21-67	Multislot film cooled pyrolytic graphite rocket nozzle
3,354,098	11-21-67	Elastomeric Silazane polymers and process for preparing the same
3,354,320	11-21-67	Light position locating system

Patent No.	Date	Title
3,354,462	11-21-67	Event Recorder
3,355,861	12-05-67	Mixture Separation Cell
3,355,948	12-05-67	Spherical Tank Gauge
3,356,320	12-05-67	Device for Separating Occupant from an ejection seat
*3,356,549	12-05-67	Method and apparatus for bonding a plastics sleeve onto a metallic body
3,356,885	12-05-67	Small plasma probe
3,357,024	12-05-67	Method of recording a gas flow pattern
*3,357,093	12-12-67	Soldering with solder flux which leaves corrosion-resistant coating
3,357,237	12-12-67	Ablation Sensor
3,357,862	12-12-67	Combined Electrolysis device and fuel cell and method of operation
3,358,145	12-12-67	Radiation detector readout system
*3,358,264	12-12-67	Coaxial Cable Connector
3,359,046	12-19-67	Bismuth-lead coatings for gas bearings used in atmospheric environments and vacuum chambers
3,359,132	12-19-67	Method of coating circuit paths on printed circuit boards with solder
3,359,409	12-19-67	Correlation function apparatus
**3,359,435	12-19-67	Holder for crystal resonators
3,359,555	12-19-67	Polarization diversity monopulse tracking receiver
*3,359,819	12-26-67	Bidirectional step torque filter with zero backlash characteristic
*3,359,855	12-26-67	Optical projector system
3,360,798	12-26-67	Collapsible reflector
3,360,864	01-02-68	Internal flare angle gauge
**3,360,972	01-02-68	Magnetomotive metal working device
3,360,980	01-02-68	Vapor pressure measuring system and method
3,360,988	01-02-68	Electric arc apparatus
3,361,045	01-02-68	Fast-opening diaphragm
**3,361,067	01-02-68	Piezoelectric pump
3,361,400	01-02-68	Clamping assembly for components inertial
*3,361,666	01-02-68	Inorganic solid film lubricants
3,361,985	01-02-68	Signal detection and tracking apparatus
3,364,311	01-16-68	Elimination of frequency shift in a multiplex communication system
3,364,366	01-16-68	Multiple Slope Sweep Generator
*3,364,578	01-23-68	Ellipsograph for Pantograph
3,364,631	01-23-68	Inflatable Support Structure
3,364,777	01-23-68	Null Device for Hand Controller
3,364,813	01-23-68	Self-Calibrating displacement transducer
3,365,580	01-23-68	Film reader with transparent capstan and U-shaped light conducting rod
3,365,657	01-23-68	Power Supply
3,365,665	01-23-68	Hall current measuring apparatus having a series resistor for temperature compensation
3,365,897	01-30-68	Cryogenic Thermal Insulation
3,365,930	01-30-68	Thermal shock apparatus
3,365,941	01-30-68	Precision thrust gage
3,366,886	01-30-68	Linear accelerator frequency control system
3,366,894	01-30-68	Variable duration pulse integrator
3,367,114	02-06-68	Construction and Method of Arranging a Plurality of Ion Engines
**3,367,121	02-06-68	Refrigeration device
3,367,182	02-06-68	Heat Flux System
3,367,224	02-06-68	Aligning and Positioning Device
3,367,271	02-06-68	Automatic Pump
3,367,308	02-06-68	Exposure system for animals
*3,367,445	02-06-68	Fluid Lubricant System
3,368,486	02-13-68	Single Action Separation Mechanism
3,369,222	02-13-68	Data Compressor
3,369,223	02-13-68	Incremental tape recorder and data rate converter
3,369,564	02-20-68	Transfer Valve
3,370,039	02-20-68	Process for Preparation of High-Molecular-Weight Polyaryloxysilanes
3,372,588	03-12-68	Constant temperature heat sink for calorimeters
*3,373,069	03-12-68	Method of Making an Inflatable Panel
3,373,404	03-12-68	Error-Correcting Method and Apparatus
3,373,430	03-12-68	Omnidirectional Microwave Spacecraft Antenna
3,373,431	03-12-68	Low Noise Single Aperture Multimode Monopulse Antenna Feed System
3,373,640	03-19-68	Apparatus for Machining Geometric Cones
3,373,914	03-19-68	Automatic Welding Speed Controller
3,374,339	3-19-68	Counter and Shift-Register
3,374,366	03-19-68	Complementary Regenerative Switch
**3,374,830	02-26-68	Thermal Control Panel
3,374,966	03-26-68	Control System
3,375,451	03-26-68	Adaptive Tracking Notch Filter System
3,375,479	03-26-68	Continuous Turning Slip Ring Assembly
3,376,730	04-09-68	Friction Measuring Apparatus
3,377,208	04-09-68	Thermocouple Assembly
3,377,845	04-16-68	Moment of Inertia Test Fixture
3,378,315	04-16-68	Hybrid Lubrication System and Bearing
3,378,851	04-23-68	Soft Frame Adjustable Eyeglasses
*3,378,892	04-23-68	Quick Attach Mechanism
3,379,064	04-23-68	Automatic Recording McLeod Gauge
3,379,330	04-23-68	Cryogenic Insulation System
3,379,885	04-23-68	Sight Switch Using an Infrared Source and Sensor
3,379,974	04-23-68	Particle Detection Apparatus Including a Ballistic Pendulum
3,380,042	04-23-68	Digital Telemetry System
3,380,049	04-23-68	Method of Resolving Clock Synchronization Error and Means Therefor
*3,381,339	05-07-68	Hydraulic Casting of Liquid Polymers
3,381,517	05-07-68	Rotary Bead Dropper and Selector For Testing Micrometeorite Detectors
3,381,527	05-07-68	Tension Measurement Device
3,381,569	05-17-68	Attitude Sensor For Space Vehicles
3,381,778	05-07-68	Energy Absorbing Device
**3,382,082	05-07-68	Foamed-In-Place Ceramic Refractory Insulating Material
3,382,105	05-17-68	Ion-Exchange Membrane and Electrode Assembly
3,382,107	05-17-68	Sealing Device For An Electrochemical Cell
3,382,714	05-14-68	Heat Sensing Instrument
3,383,461	05-14-68	Reduced Bandwidth Video Communication System Utilizing Sampling Technique
3,383,524	05-14-68	Solid State Pulse Generator With Constant Output Width, For Variable Input Width, In Nanosecond Range
3,383,903	05-21-68	Pressure Transducer Calibrator
3,383,922	05-21-68	Linear Differential Pressure Sensor
3,384,016	05-21-68	Lateral Displacement System For Separated Rocket Stages
3,384,075	05-21-68	Thermal Control Wall Panel
3,384,111	05-21-68	Positive Locking Check Valve
**3,384,324	05-21-68	Thermal Control Wall Panel
*3,384,820	05-21-68	Vibrating Element Electrometer With Output Signal Magnified Over Input Signal By A Function Of The Mechanical Q Of The Vibrating Element
3,384,895	05-21-68	Portable Superclean Air Column Device
3,385,036	05-28-68	Portable Superclean Air Column Device
3,386,337	06-04-68	Portable Milling Tool
**3,386,685	06-04-68	Spacecraft Airlock
3,386,686	06-04-68	Station Keeping Of A Gravity-Gradient Stabilized Satellite
3,387,149	06-04-68	Phonocardiograph Transducer
3,388,258	06-11-68	Fluid Flow Meter With Comparator Reference Means

Patent No.	Date	Title	Patent No.	Date	Title
**3,388,387	06-11-68	Drive Circuit Utilizing Two Cores	3,407,304	10-22-68	Micrometeoroid Penetration Measuring Device
**3,388,590	06-18-68	Connector Internal Force Gauge	3,408,816	11-05-68	Rocket Engine Injector
3,389,017	06-18-68	Sealing Member And Combination Thereof And Method Of Producing Said Sealing Member	3,408,861	11-05-68	Rocket Engine Thrust Vector Deviation Measurement Device
3,389,260	06-18-68	Solar Sensor Having Coarse And Fine Sensing With Matched Preirradiated Cells and Method of Selecting Cells	3,408,870	11-05-68	Zero Gravity Apparatus
			3,409,247	11-05-68	Solid State Thermal Control Polymer Coating
3,389,346	06-18-68	Compensating Bandwidth Switching Transients In An Amplifier Circuit	3,409,252	11-05-68	Controllers
3,389,877	06-25-68	Inflatable Tether	3,409,554	11-05-68	Gd or Sm Doped Silicon Semi-Conductor Composition
3,390,017	06-25-68	Sealed Electrochemical Cell Provided With A Flexible Casing	3,409,730	11-05-68	Thermal Radiation Shielding
			*3,411,356	11-19-68	Zeta Potential Flow Meter
3,390,020	06-25-68	Semiconductor Material And Method Of Making Same	3,412,559	11-26-68	Ion Engine Casing Construction And Method of Making Same
3,390,282	06-25-68	Passive Synchronized Spike Generator With High Input Impedance And Low Output Impedance And Capacitor Power Supply	3,412,598	11-26-68	Impact Testing Machine
			*3,412,729	11-26-68	Method And Apparatus For Continuously Monitoring Blood Oxygenation, Blood Pressure, Pulse Rate and The Pressure Pulse Curve Utilizing An Ear Oximeter As Transducer
**3,390,378	06-25-68	Comparator For The Comparison Of Two Binary Numbers			
3,391,080	07-02-68	Metallic Film Diffusion For Boundary Lubrication	3,412,961	11-26-68	Means For Suppressing Or Attenuating Bending Motion Of Elastic Bodies
3,392,403	07-09-68	Measurement Of Time Differences Between Luminous Events	*3,413,115	11-26-68	Brazing Alloy
3,392,586	07-16-68	Device For Measuring Pressure	3,413,510	11-26-68	Electronic Cathode Having A Brush-Like Structure And A Relatively Thick Oxide Emissive Coating
3,392,864	07-16-68	Insulation System			
3,392,865	07-16-68	Filament-Wound Container	3,413,536	11-26-68	Automatic Battery Charger
3,392,936	07-16-68	Leading Edge Curvature Based On Convective Heating	3,414,012	12-03-68	Dual Latching Solenoid Valve
			3,414,358	12-03-68	Optical Monitor Panel
**3,393,059	07-16-68	Decontamination of Petroleum Products	3,415,032	12-10-68	Evacuation Port Seal
3,393,330	07-16-68	Thermionic Converter With Current Augmented By Self-Induced Magnetic Field	3,415,069	12-10-68	High Pressure Helium Purifier
			3,415,116	12-10-68	Floating Two-Force-Component Measuring Device
3,393,332	07-16-68	Superconducting Alternator	3,415,126	12-10-68	Azimuth Laying System
3,393,380	07-16-68	Phase Locked Phase Modulator Including A Voltage Controlled Oscillator	3,415,156	12-10-68	Controlled Release Device
			*3,415,556	12-10-68	Ceramic-To-Metal Seal And Method Of Making Same
3,393,347	07-16-68	Power Supply Circuit	3,415,643	12-10-68	High Temperature Ferromagnetic Cobalt-Base
3,393,384	07-16-68	Radio Frequency Coaxial High Pass Filter			
3,394,359	07-23-68	Digital Memory Sense Amplifying Means	3,415,992	12-10-68	Extended Area Semiconductor Radiation Detectors And A Novel Readout Arrangement
3,394,975	07-30-68	Petzval Type Objective Including Field Shaping Lens			
**3,395,053	07-30-68	Thermal Control Coating	3,416,106	12-10-68	Broadband Microwave Waveguide Window
3,396,057	08-06-68	Method Of Electrolytically Binding A Layer of Semiconductors Together	3,416,274	12-17-68	Flexibly Connected Support And Skin
			**3,416,939	12-17-68	Alkali-Metal Silicate Protective Coating
3,396,184	08-06-68	Trialkyl-Dihalotantalum And Niobium Compounds	3,416,975	12-17-68	Etching Of Aluminum For Bonding
			3,416,988	12-17-68	Traveling Sealer For Contoured Table
3,396,303	08-06-68	ARC Electrode Of Graphite With Ball Tip	3,417,247	12-17-68	Radiant Energy Intensity Measurement System
3,396,584	08-13-68	Space Simulation And Radiative Property Testing System and Method			
3,396,920	08-13-68	Apparatus For Changing The Orientation And Velocity Of A Spinning Body Traversing A Path	3,417,266	12-17-68	Pulse Modulator Providing Fast Rise And Fall Times
			3,417,298	12-17-68	Polarity Sensitive Circuit
			3,417,316	12-17-68	Sidereal Frequency Generator
**3,397,094	08-13-68	Method Of Changing The Conductivity Of Vapor Deposited Gallium Arsenide By The Introduction Of Water Into The Vapor Deposition Atmosphere	3,417,321	12-17-68	Increasing Efficiency Switching-Type Regulator Circuits
			3,417,332	12-17-68	Frequency Shift Keying Apparatus
			3,417,399	12-17-68	Millimeter-Wave Radiometer For Radio-Astronomy
*3,397,117	08-13-68	Compact Solar Still			
3,397,318	08-13-68	Ablation Sensor	3,417,400	12-17-68	Triaxial Antenna
3,397,512	08-20-68	Vapor-Liquid Separator	*3,419,329	12-31-68	Combined Optical Attitude And Altitude Indicating Instrument
3,397,932	08-20-68	Semi-Linear Ball Bearing			
3,399,299	08-27-68	Apparatus For Phase Stability Determination	3,419,363	12-31-68	Self-Lubricating Fluoride-Metal Composite Materials
3,399,574	09-03-68	Method For Leakage Testing of Tanks	3,419,433	12-31-68	Solar Cell And Circuit Array And Process For Nullifying Magnetic Fields
3,404,348	10-01-68	Low Level Signal Limiter			
3,405,406	10-15-68	Hard Space Suit	**3,419,537	12-31-68	Dicyanoacetylene Polymers
3,405,887	10-15-68	Ring Wing Tension Vehicle	*3,419,827	12-31-68	Indexing Microwave Switch
3,406,336	10-15-68	RC Rate Generator For Slow Speed Measurement	3,419,964	01-07-69	Apparatus For Measuring Swelling Characteristics of Membranes
*3,406,742	10-22-68	Automatic Fatigue Test Temperature Programmer	3,420,069	01-07-69	Condenser-Separator

Patent No.	Date	Title
*3,420,223	01-07-69	Electrode For Biological Recording
3,420,225	01-07-69	Balanced Bellows Spirometer
3,420,338	01-07-69	Hermetic Sealed Vibration Damper
3,420,704	01-07-69	Depositing Semiconductor Films Utilizing A Thermal Gradient
3,420,945	01-07-69	Electrode and Insulator With Shielded Dielectric Junction
**3,420,978	01-07-69	Pretreatment Method For Anti-Wettable Materials
3,421,004	01-07-69	Solar Optical Telescope Dome Control System
3,421,053	01-07-69	Tumbler System To Provide Random Motion
3,421,056	01-07-69	Thin Window Drifted Silicon, Charged Particle Detector
3,421,105	01-07-69	Automatic Acquisition System For Phase-Lock Loop
*3,421,134	01-07-69	Electrical Connector
3,421,363	01-14-69	Harness For Vertically Supporting Slender Bodies For Vibration Testing
3,421,506	01-14-69	Relief Container
3,421,541	01-14-69	Relief Valve
3,421,549	01-14-69	Pneumatic System For Controlling And Actuating Pneumatic Cyclic Devices
*3,421,591	01-14-69	Rock Drill For Recovering Samples
3,421,700	01-14-69	Electromechanical Actuator
3,421,768	01-14-69	Foil Seal
**3,421,864	01-14-69	Multilayer Porous Ionizer
**3,421,948	01-14-69	Method Of Making Membranes
3,422,019	01-14-69	Method For Processing Ferrite Cores
3,422,213	01-14-69	Connector Strips
3,422,278	01-14-69	Signal Generator
**3,422,291	01-14-69	Magnetohydrodynamic Induction Machine
*3,422,324	01-14-69	Pressure Variable Capacitor
3,422,352	01-14-69	Apparatus For Measuring Current Flow
**3,422,354	01-14-69	Test Fixture For Pellet-Like Electrical Elements
3,422,390	01-14-69	Coupling Device
3,422,403	01-14-69	Data Compression System
3,422,440	01-14-69	Plural Recorder System
3,423,179	01-21-69	Catalyst For Growth Of Boron Carbide Crystal Whiskers
3,423,290	01-21-69	Lyophilized Reaction Mixtures
*3,423,579	01-21-69	Electronic Divider And Multiplier Using Photocells
3,423,608	01-21-69	Nonmagnetic Thermal Motor For A Magnetometer
3,424,966	01-28-69	Synchronous Servo Loop Control System
3,425,131	02-04-69	Extensometer
3,425,486	02-04-69	Garments For Controlling The Temperature Of The Body
3,425,487	02-04-69	Space Suit Heat Exchanger
*3,426,230	02-04-69	Direct Radiation Cooling Of The Collector Of Linear Beam Tubes
**3,426,263	02-04-69	Method And Apparatus For Battery Charge Control
**3,426,272	02-04-69	Device For Determining The Accuracy Of The Flare On A Flared Tube
3,426,746	02-11-69	Method And Apparatus For Attaching Physiological Monitoring Electrodes
3,427,089	02-11-69	Ultraviolet Filter
3,427,097	02-11-69	Pneumatic Mirror Support System
3,427,205	02-11-69	Spacecraft Battery Seals
3,427,525	02-11-69	Regulated D.C. to D.C. Converter
3,428,761	02-18-69	Excitation And Detection Circuitry For A Flux Responsive Magnetic Head
3,428,812	02-18-69	Optical Spin Compensator
3,428,910	02-18-69	Automatic Gain Control System
3,428,919	02-18-69	Signal Multiplexer
3,428,923	02-18-69	Broadband Choke For Antenna Structure
3,429,477	02-25-69	Apparatus for Ejection Of An Instrument Cover
3,429,529	02-25-69	Control Devices For Flexible Wing Aircraft
3,430,115	02-25-69	Apparatus For Ballasting High Frequency Transistors
3,430,182	02-25-69	Electrical Feed-Through Connection For Printed Circuit Boards And Printed Cables
3,430,237	02-25-69	Time Division Multiplex System
3,430,909	03-04-69	Device For Handling Heavy Loads
3,432,730	03-11-69	Semiconductor P-N Junction Stress And Strain Sensor
3,433,015	03-18-69	Gas Turbine Combustion Apparatus
*3,433,953	03-18-69	Compensating Radiometer
3,433,960	03-18-69	Retrodirective Optical System
3,433,961	03-18-69	Scanning Aspect Sensor Employing An Apertured Disc And A Commutator
3,434,037	03-18-69	Multiple Varactor Frequency Doubler
3,434,050	03-18-69	High Impedance Measuring Apparatus
3,434,064	03-18-69	Amplifier Drift Tester
3,434,885	03-25-69	Method Of Making Electrical Contact On Silicon Solar Cell And Resultant Product
3,435,246	03-25-69	Light Radiation Direction Indicator With A Baffle Of Two Parallel Grids
3,437,527	04-08-69	Method For Producing A Solar Cell Having An Integral Protective Covering
3,437,560	04-08-69	Use Of The Enzyme Hexokinase For The Reduction Of Inherent Light Levels
3,437,832	04-08-69	Ring Counter
3,437,874	04-08-69	Display For Binary Characters
3,437,903	04-08-69	Protection For Energy Conversion Systems
3,437,919	04-08-69	Cryogenic Apparatus For Measuring The Intensity Of Magnetic Fields
3,437,935	04-08-69	Varactor High Level Mixer
3,437,959	04-08-69	Helical Coaxial Resonator RF Filter
3,438,044	04-08-69	Monopulse System With An Electronic Scanner
3,438,263	04-15-69	Fluid Sample Collector
3,439,886	04-22-69	Visual Target For Retrofire Attitude Control
3,443,208	05-06-69	Optically Pumped Resonance Magnetometer For Determining Vectroral Components In A Spatial Coordinate System
3,444,380	05-13-69	Electronic Background Suppression Method And Apparatus For A Field Scanning Sensor
3,446,387	05-27-69	Piping Arrangement Through A Double Wall Chamber
3,446,676	05-27-69	Solar Battery With Interconnecting Means For Plural Cells
3,446,960	05-27-69	Device For Measuring Electron-Beam Intensities And For Subjecting Materials To Electron Irradiation In An Electron Microscrope
3,446,992	05-27-69	Bus Voltage Compensation Circuit For Controlling Direct Current Motor
3,446,998	05-27-69	Bimetallic Power Controlled Actuator
3,447,015	05-27-69	Ion Thruster Cathode
3,447,071	05-27-69	Probes Having Guard Ring and Primary Sensor At Same Potential To Prevent Collection Of Stray Wall Currents In Ionized Gases
3,447,154	05-27-69	Cooperative Doppler Radar System
3,447,155	05-27-69	Ranging System
3,447,233	06-03-69	Bonding Thermoelectric Elements To Nonmagnetic Refractory Metal Electrodes
3,477,774	06-03-69	High Pressure Air Valve
3,448,346	06-03-69	Extensible Cable Support
3,448,273	06-03-69	Plurality of Photosensitive Cells On A Pyramidical Base For Planetary Trackers
3,448,290	06-03-69	Variable-Width Pulse Integrator
3,448,341	06-03-69	Electrical Load Protection Device

Patent No.	Date	Title	Patent No.	Date	Title
3,447,850	06-03-69	Sealed Cabinetry	3,460,378	08-12-69	Strain Gauge Measuring Techniques
3,450,878	06-17-69	Dosimeter For High Levels of Absorbed Radiation	3,460,759	08-12-69	Combustion Chamber
			3,460,379	08-12-69	Tensile Strength Testing Device
3,450,842	06-17-69	Doppler Frequency Spread Correction Device For Multiplex Transmissions	3,461,437	08-12-69	Digital Memory In Which the Driving Of Each Word Location Is Controlled By A Switch Core
3,450,946	06-17-69	Protective Circuit of the Spark Gap Type			
3,452,976	07-01-69	Printed Circuit Soldering Aid	3,460,397	08-12-69	Mechanical Actuator
3,452,872	07-01-69	Shock-Layer Radiation Measurement	3,461,393	08-12-69	Cascaded Complementary Pair Broad-band Transistor Amplifiers
3,453,172	07-01-69	Bonding Graphite With Fused Silver Chloride	3,461,290	08-12-69	Conically Shaped Cavity Radiometer With a Dual Purpose Cone Winding
3,452,423	07-01-69	Segmenting Lead Telluride-Silicon Germanium Thermoelements	3,461,721	08-19-69	Flow Field Simulation
			3,461,855	08-19-69	Conditioning Suit
3,458,313	07-29-69	High Resolution Developing of Photo-sensitive Resists	3,463,563	08-26-69	Swivel Support For Gas Bearings
			3,464,049	08-26-69	Load Cell Protection Device
3,458,833	07-29-69	Frequency Control Network For a Current Feedback Oscillator	3,463,939	08-26-69	Pulsed Differential Comparator Circuit
			3,464,051	08-26-69	Electrical Spot Terminal Assembly
3,458,104	07-29-69	Weld Control System Using Thermocouple Wire	3,464,012	08-26-69	Automatic Signal Range Selector For Metering Devices
3,458,162	07-29-69	Control Devices for Flexible Wing Aircraft	3,463,001	08-26-69	Thrust Dynamometer
			3,464,016	08-26-69	Demodulation System
3,456,112	07-15-69	Temperature Sensitive Capacitor Device	3,463,673	08-26-69	Electrochemical Coulometer and Method of Forming
3,456,193	07-15-69	Phase Quadrature-Plural Channel Data Transmission System	3,464,018	08-26-69	Digitally Controlled Frequency Synthesizer
3,458,702	07-29-69	Telespectrograph			
3,458,651	07-29-69	Television Simulation For Aircraft and Space Flight	3,464,652	09-02-69	Control Devices For Flexible Wing Aircraft
3,458,726	07-29-69	Power Control Circuit	3,466,243	09-09-69	Alloys for Bearings
3,453,462	07-01-69	Slug Flow Magnetohydrodynamic Generator	3,465,482	09-09-69	Spacecraft Radiator Cover
			3,466,198	09-09-69	Solar Cell Matrix
3,453,546	07-01-69	Telemeter Adaptable for Implanting In An Animal	3,466,085	09-09-69	Articulated Multiple Couch Assembly
**3,454,410	07-08-69	Alkali-Metal Silicate Protective Coating	3,466,459	09-09-69	Current Steering Switch
3,455,171	07-15-69	Inertial Reference Apparatus	3,466,570	09-09-69	Inverter With Means For Base Current Shaping For Sweeping Charge Carriers From Base Region
3,456,201	07-15-69	System For Monitoring Signal Amplitude Ranges			
3,458,851	07-29-69	Electrical Connector Pin With Wiping Action	3,465,986	09-09-69	Satellite Despin Device
			3,466,484	09-09-69	Ionization-Vacuum Gauge With All But The End of the Ion-collector Shielded
3,458,217	07-29-69	Tubular Coupling Having Low Profile Band Segments With Means for Preventing Relative Rotation	3,466,424	09-09-69	Evaporant Source for Vapor Deposition
			3,466,052	09-09-69	Foil Seal
3,455,121	07-15-69	Water Separating System	3,465,567	09-09-69	Method of Making Tubes
*3,459,391	08-05-69	Interconnection of Solar Cells	3,465,569	09-09-69	Low Temperature Flexure Fatigue Cryostat
3,460,995	08-12-69	Method and Device for Determining Battery State of Charge			
			3,465,747	09-09-69	Ballistocardiograph
3,460,381	08-12-69	Balance Torquemeter	3,466,418	09-09-69	Determination of Spot Weld Quality
3,460,781	08-12-69	Tape Recorder	3,466,560	09-09-69	Stable Amplifier Having A Stable Quiescent Point
3,460,784	08-12-69	Control Devices for Flexible Wing Aircraft			

SOURCE: NASA, "U.S. Patents for NASA Inventions."

Appendix A

Glossary of Terms Used in the Exploration of Space

A

Aberration—1. In astronomy, the apparent displacement of the position of a celestial body in the direction of motion of the observer, caused by the combination of the velocity of the observer and the velocity of light. 2. In optics, a deviation from perfect imagery as, for example, distortion.

Ablating Material—A material designed to dissipate heat by vaporizing or melting.

Ablating materials are used on the surfaces of some reentry vehicles. Ablating materials absorbs heat by increase in temperature and change in chemical or physical state. The heat is carried away from the surface by a loss of mass (liquid or vapor). The departing mass also blocks part of the convective heat transfer to the remaining material.

Ablation—The removal of surface material from a body by vaporization, melting, or other process; specifically the intentional removal of material from a nosecone or spacecraft during high-speed movement through a planetary atmosphere to provide thermal protection to the underlying structure. See **Ablating Material**.

Abort—To cancel or cut short a flight.

Absolute Altitude—Altitude above the actual surface of a planet or natural satellite, either land or water.

Absolute Pressure—In engineering literature, a term used to indicate pressure above the absolute zero value corresponding to empty space as distinguished from "gage pressure".

In vacuum technology, "pressure" always corresponds to absolute pressure, and therefore the term "absolute pressure" is not required.

Absolute Temperature—Temperature value relative to absolute zero.

Absolute Zero—The theoretical temperature at which all molecular motion ceases.

"Absolute zero" may be interpreted as the temperature at which the volume of a perfect gas vanishes, or more generally as the temperature of the cold source which would render a Carnot cycle 100 percent efficient. The value of absolute zero is now estimated to be $-273.16°$ Celsius (Centigrade), $-459.69°$ Fahrenheit, $0°$ Rankine.

Absorption—The process in which incident electromagnetic radiation is retained by a substance. A further process always results from absorption: that is, the irreversible conversion of the absorbed radiation into some other form of energy within and according to the nature of the absorbing medium. The absorbing medium itself may emit radiation, but only after an energy conversion has occurred.

Acceleration—The rate of change of velocity.

Decrease in velocity is sometimes called "negative acceleration."

Accelerometer—An instrument which measures acceleration or gravitational forces capable of imparting acceleration.

An accelerometer usually uses a concentrated mass (seismic mass) which resists movement because of its inertia. The displacement of the seismic mass relative to its supporting frame or container is used as a measure of acceleration.

Acceptance—The act of an authorized representative of the Government by which the Government assents to ownership by it of existing and identified articles, or approves specific services rendered as partial or complete performance of the contract.

Access Time—Of a computer, the time required under specified conditions to transfer information to or from storage, including the time required to communicate with the storage location.

Accumulator—A device or apparatus that accumulates or stores up, as: 1. A contrivance in a hydraulic system that stores fluid under pressure. 2. A device sometimes incorporated in the fuel system of a gas-turbine engine to store up and release fuel under pressure as an aid in starting.

Acoustic Excitation—Process of inducing vibration in a structure by exposure to sound waves.

Acoustic Generator—Transducer which converts electric, mechanical, or other forms of energy into sound.

Acoustic Velocity—The speed of propagation of sound waves. Also called "speed of sound."

Acquisition—1. The process of locating the orbit of a satellite or trajectory of a space probe so that tracking or telemetry data can be gathered. 2. The process of pointing an antenna or telescope so that it is properly oriented to allow gathering of tracking or telemetry data from a satellite or space probe.

Actinic—Pertaining to electromagnetic radiation capable of initiating photochemical reactions, as in photography or the fading of pigments.

Because of the particularly strong action of ultraviolet radiation on photochemical processes, the term has come to be almost synonymous with ultraviolet, as in "actinic rays".

Active—Transmitting a signal, as "active satellite," in contrast to "passive".

Adiabatic—Without gain or loss of heat.

Adsorption—The adhesion of a thin film of liquid or gas to the surface of a solid substance. The solid does not combine chemically with the adsorbed substance.

Aerobiology—The study of the distribution of living organisms freely suspended in the atmosphere.

Aeroduct—A ramjet type of engine designed to scoop up ions and electrons freely available in the outer reaches of the atmosphere or in the atmospheres of other spatial bodies, and by a chemical process within the duct of this engine, expel particles derived from the ions and electrons as a propulsive jet stream.

Aerodynamic Heating—The heating of a body produced by passage of air or other gases over the body, significant chiefly at high speeds, caused by friction and by compression processes.

Aerodynamics—The science that treats of the motion of air and other gaseous fluids, and of the forces acting on bodies when the bodies move through such fluids, or when such fluids move against or around the bodies, as "his research in aerodynamics".

Aerodynamic Vehicle—A device, such as an airplane, glider, etc., capable of flight only within a sensible atmosphere and relying on aerodynamic forces to maintain flight.

This term is used when the context calls for discrimination from "space vehicle."

Aeroelasticity—The study of the effect of aerodynamic forces on elastic bodies.

Aerolite—A meteorite composed principally of stony material.

Aeronomy—1. The study of the upper regions of the atmosphere where physical and chemical reactions due to solar radiation take place. 2. Science dealing with theories of planetary atmospheres.

Aeropause—A region of indeterminate limits in the upper atmosphere, considered as a boundary or transition region between the denser portion of the atmosphere and space.

From a functional point of view, it is considered to be that region in which the atmosphere is so tenuous as to have a negligible, or almost negligible, effect on men and aircraft, and in which the physiological requirements of man become increasingly important in the design of aircraft and auxiliary equipment.

Aerospace—(From *aeronautics* and *space*.) Of or pertaining to both the earth's atmosphere and space, as in "aerospace industries".

Aerothermodynamic Border—An altitude at about 100 miles, above which the atmosphere is so rarefied that the motion of an object through it at high speeds generates no significant surface heat.

Aerothermodynamics—The study of the aerodynamics and thermodynamic problems connected with aerodynamic heating.

Afterbody—1. A companion body that trails a satellite. 2. A section or piece of a rocket or missile that reenters the atmosphere unprotected behind the nosecone or other body that is protected for reentry. 3. The aft part of a vehicle.

Agena—A second stage rocket which burns liquid oxygen and kerosene, often used with an ATLAS first stage by the United States for satellite and spacecraft launchings.

Agravic—Of or pertaining to a condition of no gravitation. See **Weightlessness**.

Airglow—The quasi-steady radiant emission from the upper atmosphere as distinguished from the sporadic emission of the aurorae.

Airglow is a chemiluminescence due primarily to the emission of the molecules O_2 and N_2, the radical OH, and the atoms O and Na. It may be due to released latent energy from energy stored during daylight. Emissions observed in airglow could arise from 3-body atom collisions forming molecules, from 2-body reactions between atoms and molecules, or from recombination of ions.

Historically "airglow" has referred to visual radiation. Some recent studies use "airglow" to refer to radiation outside the visual range.

Air Shower—A grouping of cosmic-ray particles observed in the atmosphere.

Primary cosmic rays slowed down in the atmosphere emit bremsstrahlung photons of high energy. Each of these photons produces secondary electrons which generate more photons and the process continues until the available energy is absorbed.

Air Sounding—The act of measuring atmospheric phenomena or determining atmospheric conditions at altitude, especially by means of apparatus carried by balloons or rockets.

Albedo—The ratio of the amount of electromagnetic radiation reflected by a body to the amount incident upon it, commonly expressed as a percentage. Compare Bond albedo.

The albedo is to be distinguished from the reflectivity, which refers to one specific wavelength (monochromatic radiation).

Usage varies somewhat with regard to the exact wavelength interval implied in albedo figures; sometimes just the visible portion of the spectrum is considered, sometimes the totality of wavelengths in the solar spectrum.

Alpha Particle—(Symbol $_2He^4$.) A positively charged particle emitted from the nuclei of certain atoms during radioactive disintegration. The alpha particle has an atomic weight of 4 and a positive charge equal in magnitude to 2 electronic charges hence it is essentially a helium nucleus (helium atom stripped of its two planetary electrons).

Alpha particles are important in atmospheric electricity as one of the agents responsible for atmospheric ionization. Minute quantities of radioactive materials such as radium, present in almost all soils and rocks, emit alpha particles and those which enter the surface air layer produce large numbers of ions along their short air paths. Alpha particles of average energy have a range of only a few centimeters in air, so radioactive matter in the earth cannot directly ionize the air above a height of a fraction of a meter. On the other hand, certain radioactive gases, such as radon and thoron, may be carried to heights of several kilometers (after initial formation during a radioactive disintegration of atoms of soil or rock matter) before emitting characteristic alpha particles which can there ionize air in the free atmosphere. The high density of ion pairs produced along the track of an alpha particle favors very rapid recombination (columnar recombination) that greatly reduces the effective ionization produced by these particles.

Ambient—Specifically, pertaining to the environment about a flying aircraft or other body but undisturbed or unaffected by it, as in "ambient air", or "ambient temperature."

Amplidyne—A special type of dc generator used as a power amplifier, in which the output voltage responds to changes in field excitation; used extensively in servo systems.

Analog Computer—A computing machine that works on the principle of measuring, as distinguished from counting, which the input data are made analogous to a measurement continuum, such as voltages, linear lengths, resistances, light intensities, etc., which can be manipulated by the computer.

Analog computers range from the relatively simple devices of the slide rule or airspeed indicator to complicated electrical machines used for solving mathematical problems.

Angel—A radar echo caused by a physical phenomenon not discernible to the eye.

Angstrom (Å)—A unit of length, used chiefly in expressing short wavelengths. Ten billion angstroms equal one meter.

Anomaly—1. In general, a deviation from the norm. 2. In geodesy, a deviation of an observed value from a theoretical value, due to an abnormality in the observed quantity. 3. In celestial mechanics, the angle between the radius vector to an orbiting body from its primary (the focus of the orbital ellipse) and the line of apsides of the orbit, measured to the direction of travel, from the point of closest approach to the primary (perifocus).

The term defined above is usually called "true anomaly", v, to distinguish it from the eccentric anomaly, E, which is measured at the center of the orbital ellipse, or from the mean anomaly, M, which is what the true anomaly would become if the orbiting body had a uniform angular motion.

Anomalistic Period—The interval between two successive perigee passes of a satellite in orbit about a primary. Also called "perigee-to-perigee period."

Anoxia—A complete lack of oxygen available for physiological use within the body. Compare hypoxia.

"Anoxia" is popularly used as a synonym for "hypoxia." This usage should be avoided.

Antigravity—A hypothetical effect that would arise from some energy field's cancellation of the effect of the gravitational field of the earth or other body.

Aphelion—That orbital point farthest from the sun when the sun is the center of attraction. That point nearest the sun is called "perihelion."

The aphelion of the earth is 1.520 x 10^{13} cm from the sun.

Apogee—In an orbit about the earth, the point at which the satellite is farthest from the earth; the highest altitude reached by a sounding rocket.

Apogee Rocket—A rocket attached to a satellite or spacecraft designed to fire when the craft is at apogee, the point farthest from the earth in orbit. The effect of the apogee rocket is to establish a new orbit farther from the earth or to allow the craft to escape from earth orbit.

Apollo—United States program with the objective of earth-orbiting a space laboratory, launching astronauts to the vicinity of the moon, and landing a man on the moon, and returning him to earth.

Arago Point—One of the three commonly detectable points along the vertical circle through the sun at which the degree of polarization of skylight goes to zero; a neutral point.

The Arago point, so named for its discoverer, is customarily located at about 20° above the antisolar point; but it lies at higher elevations in turbid air. The latter property makes the Arago distance a useful measure of atmospheric turbidity. Measurements of the location of this neutral point are typically more easily carried out than measurements of the Babinet point and the Brewster point, both of which lie so close to the sun (about 20° above and below the sun, respectively) that glare problems become serious.

Arc-Jet Engine—A type of electrical rocket engine in which the propellant gas is heated by passing through an electric arc.

Artifical Antenna—A device which has the equivalent impedance characteristics of an antenna and the necessary power-handling capabilities, but which does not radiate or intercept radiofrequency energy. Also called "dummy antenna."

Artificial Gravity—A simulated gravity established within a space vehicle, as by rotating a cabin about an axis of a spacecraft, the centrifugal force generated being similar to the force of gravity.

Assembly—An element of a component consisting of parts and/or subassemblies which performs functions necessary to the operation of the component as a whole. Examples are: pulsing networks, gyro assembly, oscillator assembly, etc.

Asteriod—One of the many small celestial bodies revolving around the sun, most of the orbits being between those of Mars and Jupiter. Also called "planetoid," "minor planet." See **Planet**.

The term "minor planet" is preferred by many astronomers but "asteriod" continues to be used in astronomical literature, especially attributively, as in "asteriod belt."

Astro—A prefix meaning "star" or "stars" and, by extension, sometimes used as the equivalent of "celestial," as in *astro*nautics.

Astroballistics—The study of the phenomena arising out of the motion of a solid through a gas at speeds high enough to cause ablation; for example, the interaction of a meteoroid with the atmosphere.

Astroballistics uses the data and methods of astronomy, aerodynamics, ballistics, and physical chemistry.

Astrobiology—The study of living organisms on celestial bodies other than the earth.

Astrodynamics—The practical application of celestial mechanics, astroballistics, propulsion theory, and allied fields to the problem of planning and directing the trajectories of space vehicles.

Astronaut—1. A person who occupies a space vehicle. 2. Specifically one of the test pilots selected to participate in Project Mercury, the first United States program for manned space flight.

Astronautics—1. The art, skill, or activity of operating space vehicles. 2. In a broader sense, the science of space flight.

Astronomical Unit (abbr AU)—In the astronomical system of measures, a unit of length usually defined as the distance from the Earth to the Sun, approximately 92,900,000 statute miles or 14,960,000 kilometers. It is more precisely defined as the unit of distance in terms of which, in Kepler's Third Law, $n^2a^3 = k^2(1 + m)$, the semimajor axis a of an elliptical orbit must be expressed in order that the numerical value of the Gaussian constant, k, may be exactly 0.01720209895 when the unit of time is the ephemeris day.

In astronomical units, the mean distance of the Earth from the Sun, calculated by Kepler's law from the observed mean motion n and adopted mass m, is 1.00000003.

Atlas—An intercontinental ballistic missile which a total THRUST of about 360,000 pounds, frequently used as a first stage for satellite and spacecraft launchings by the United States. It is a liquid-fueled rocket, burning liquid oxygen and kerosene.

Atmosphere—The envelope of air surrounding the earth; also the body of gases surrounding or comprising any planet or other celestial body.

Atmospheric Drag—The retarding force produced on a satellite by its passage through the gas of the high atmosphere. It drops off exponentially with height, and has a small effect on satellites whose PERIGEE is higher than a few hundred kilometers.

Atomic Clock—A precision clock that depends for its operation on an electrical oscillator (as a quartz crystal) regulated by the natural vibration frequencies of an atomic system (as a beam of cesium atoms or ammonia molecules).

Attenuation—In physics, any process in which the flux density (or power, amplitude, intensity, illuminance, etc.) of a "parallel beam" of energy decreases with increasing distance from the energy source. Attenuation is always due to the action of the transmitting medium itself (mainly by absorption and scattering). It should not be applied to the divergence of flux due to distance alone, as described by the inverse-square law. See **Absorption.**

The space rate of attenuation of electromagnetic radiation is described by Bouguer's law.

In meteorological optics, the attenuation of light is customarily termed "extinction." (The latter is sometimes used with regard to any electromagnetic radiation.)

Attitude—The position or orientation of an aircraft, spacecraft, etc., either in motion or at rest, as determined by the relationship between its axes and some reference line or plane such as the horizon.

Auger Shower—A very large cosmic-ray shower. Also called "extensive air-shower."

Augmentation—The apparently larger semi-diameter of a celestial body, when seen against the horizon, as compared to its apparent decrease in size with increased altitude.

The term is used principally in reference to the moon.

Aurora—The sporadic visible emission from the upper atmosphere over middle and high latitudes. Also called "northern lights."

Aurora Australia—The aurora of the Southern Hemisphere. See **Aurora.**

Aurora Borealis—The aurora of northern latitudes. Also called "aurora polaris," "northern lights." See **Aurora.**

Axis—(pl. axes) 1. A straight line about which a body rotates, or around which a plane figure may rotate to produce a solid; a line of symmetry. 2. One of a set of reference lines for certain systems of coordinates.

Azimuth—1. Horizontal direction or bearing. Compare azimuth angle, bearing. 2. In navigation, the horizontal direction of a celestial point from a terrestrial point, expressed as the angular distance from a reference direction, usually measured from 000° at the reference direction clockwise through 360°.

Azusa—A short range tracking system which gives space position and velocity of the object being tracked.

B

Backout—An undoing of things already done during a countdown, usually in reverse order.

Backup—1. An item kept available to replace an item which fails to perform satisfactorily. 2. An item under development intended to perform the same general function performed by another item also under development.

Baker-Nunn Camera—A large camera used in tracking satellites.

Balance—1. The equilibrium attained by an aircraft, rocket, or the like when forces and moments are acting upon it so as to produce steady flight, especially without rotation about its axes; also used with reference to equilibrium about any specified axis, as, an airplane in balance about its longitudinal axis. 2. A weight that counterbalances something, especially, on an aircraft control surface, a weight installed forward of the hinge axis to counterbalance the surface aft of the hinge axis.

Ballistics—The science that deals with the motion, behavior, and effects of projectiles, especially bullets, aerial bombs, rockets, or the like; the science or art of designing and hurling projectiles so as to achieve a desired performance.

Ballistic Trajectory—The trajectory followed by a body being acted upon only by gravitational forces and the resistance of the medium through which it passes.

A rocket without lifting surfaces is in a ballistic trajectory after its engines cease operating.

Balloon-type Rocket—A rocket, such as Atlas, that requires the pressure of its propellants (or other gases) within it to give it structural integrity.

Bar—Unit of pressure equal to 10^6 dyne per cm^2 (10^6 barye) 1000 millibars, 29.53 in. of Hg.

Barye—Something used by British to denote pressure unit of the cgs system of physical units, equal to one dyne per cm^2 (0.001 millibar). See **Microbar.**

Beam—1. A ray or collection of focused rays of radiated energy. See beam width, radiation pattern. 2. = electron beam. 3. A beam (sense 1) of radio waves used as a navigation aid.

Binary Notation—A system of positional notation in which the digits are coefficients of powers of the base 2 in the same way as the digits in the conventional decimal system are coefficients of powers of the base 10.

Binary notation employs only two digits, 1 and 0, therefore is used extensively in computers where the "on" and "off" positions of a switch or storage device can represent the two digits.

In decimal notation $111 = (1 \times 10^2) + (1 \times 10^1) + (1 \times 10^0) = 100 + 10 + 1 = $ *one hundred and eleven.*

In binary notation $111 = (1 \times 2^2) + (1 \times 2^1) \times (1 \times 2^0) = 4 + 2 + 1 = $ *seven.*

Bionics—The study of systems which function after the manner of, or in a manner characteristic of, or resembling, living systems.

Bipropellant—A rocket propellant consisting of two unmixed or uncombined chemicals (fuel and oxidizer) fed to the combustion chamber separately.

Bird—A colloquial term for a rocket, satellite, or spacecraft.

Bit—(From *binary digit.*) A unit of information.

Black Body (abbr b).—1. A hypothetical "body" which absorbs all of the electromagnetic radiation striking it; that is, one which neither reflects nor transmits any of the incident radiation.

No actual substance behaves as a true black body, although platinum black and other soots rather closely approximate this ideal. However, one does speak of a black body with respect to a particular wavelength interval. This concept is fundamental to all of the radiation laws, and is to be compared with the similarly idealized concepts of the white body and the gray body. In accordance with Kirchoff's law, a black body not only absorbs all wavelengths, but emits at all wavelengths and does so with maximum possible intensity for any given temperature.

Black Box—Colloquially, any unit, usually an electronic device such as an amplifier, which can be mounted in a rocket, spacecraft, or the like as a single package. See **Component.**

Blackout—1. A fadeout of radio communications due to environmental factors such as ionospheric disturbances, or a plasma sheath surrounding a reentry vehicle. 2. A condition in which vision is temporarily obscured by a blackness, accompanied by a dullness of certain of the other senses, brought on by decreased blood pressure in the head and a consequent lack of oxygen, as may occur in pulling out of a high-speed dive in an airplane.

Blockhouse—(Also written "block house"). A reinforced concrete structure, often built underground or partly underground, and sometimes dome-shaped, to provide protection against blast, heat, or explosion during rocket launchings or related activities; specifically, such a structure at a launch site that houses electronic control instruments used in launching a rocket.

Boilerplate—As in "boilerplate capsule," a metal copy of the flight model, the structure or components of which are heavier than the flight model.

Boiloff—The vaporization of a cold propellant such as liquid oxygen or liquid hydrogen, as the temperature of the propellant mass rises as in the tank of a rocket being readied for launch.

"Bola" Concept—Concept of a manned nuclear vehicle in which a long cable separates the manned platform from the reactor power system, with consequent reduction of biological hazard and the need for heavy shielding.

Boltzmann's Constant—The ratio of the universal gas constant to Avogadro's number; equal to 1.3804 x 10^{-16} ergs per degree K. Sometimes called "gas constant per molecule," "Boltzmann's universal conversion factor."

Bond Albedo—The ratio of the amount of light reflected from a sphere exposed to parallel light to the amount of light incident upon it. Sometimes shortened to "albedo."

The Bond albedo is used in planetary astronomy.

Booster—Short for "booster engine" or "booster rocket."

Booster Engine—An engine, especially a booster rocket, that adds its thrust to the sustainer engine.

Booster Rocket—1. A rocket engine, either solid or liquid fuel, that assists the normal propulsive system or sustainer engine of a rocket or aeronautical vehicle in some phase of its flight. 2. A rocket used to set a missile vehicle in motion before another engine takes over.

In sense 2 the term "launch vehicle" is more commonly used.

Boostglide Vehicle—A vehicle (half aircraft, half spacecraft) designed to fly to the limits of the sensible atmosphere, then be boosted by rockets into the space above, returning to earth by gliding under aerodynamic control.

Bouguer's Law—A relationship describing the rate of decrease of a flux density of a plane-parallel beam of monochromatic radiation as it penetrates a medium which both scatters and absorbs at that wavelength.

Braking Ellipses—A series of ellipses, decreasing in size due to aerodynamic drag, followed by a spacecraft in entering a planetary atmosphere.

In theory, this maneuver will allow a spacecraft to dissipate energy through aerodynamic heating without burning up.

Breakoff Phenomenon—The feeling which sometimes occurs during high-altitude flight of being totally separated and detached from the earth and human society. Also called the "breakaway phenomenon."

Bremsstrahlung Effect—The emission of electromagnetic radiation as a consequence of the acceleration of charged elementary particles, such as electrons, under the influence of the attractive or repulsive force—fields of atomic nuclei near which the ambient, charged particle moves.

In cosmic-ray shower production, bremsstrahlung (in German, "braking radiation") effects give rise to emission of gamma rays as electrons encounter atmospheric nuclei. The emission of radiation in the bremsstrahlung effect is merely one instance of the general rule that electromagnetic radiation is emitted only when electric charges undergo acceleration.

British Thermal Unit (Btu)—The amount of heat required to raise 1 pound of water at 60°F, 1°F. General usage makes 1 Btu equal 252 calories.

Buffer—In computers: 1. An isolating circuit used to avoid reaction of a driven circuit on the corresponding driving circuit. 2. A storage device used to compensate for a difference in rate of flow of information or time on occurrence of events when transmitting information from one device to another.

Burn—A period during which a rocket engine is firing, as in "second burn" the second period during a flight in which the engine is firing.

Burning Rate (abbr r).—Velocity at which a solid propellant in a rocket is consumed, measured in a direction normal to the propellant surface and is usually expressed in inches per second.

Burnout—1. An act or instance of the end of fuel and oxidizer burning in a rocket; the time at which this burnout occurs. Compare cutoff. 2. An act or instance of something burning out or of overheating; specifically, an act or instance of a rocket combustion chamber, nozzle, or other part overheating so as to result in damage or destruction.

Burst—1. A single pulse of radio energy; specifically such a pulse at radar frequencies. 2. Solar radio burst. 3. Cosmic ray burst.

C

Calorie—Originally amount of heat required to raise temperature of one gram of water through one degree centigrade (the gram-calorie), but a more precise expression is that a 15° gram-calorie (cal $_{15}$) is the amount of heat required to raise the temperature of one gram of water from 14.5°C to 15.5°C and is equal to 4.1855 joules.

Capacity—In computer operations: 1. The largest quantity which can be stored, processed, or transferred. 2. The largest number of digits or characters which may be regularly processed. 3. The upper and lower limits of the quantities which may be processed.

Capsule—1. A boxlike component or unit, often sealed. 2. A small, sealed, pressurized cabin with an internal environment which will support life in a man or animal during extremely high altitude flight, space flight, or emergency escape.
   The term, "spacecraft," is preferred to capsule for any man-carrying vehicle.

Cascade Shower—A group occurrence of cosmic rays. Also called "air shower."

Cavitation—The turbulent formation of bubbles in a fluid, occurring whenever the static pressure at any point in the fluid flow becomes less than the fluid vapor pressure.

Celestial Mechanics—The study of the theory of the motions of celestial bodies under the influence of gravitational fields.

Celestial Sphere—An imaginary sphere of infinite radius concentric with the earth, on which all celestial bodies except the earth are assumed to be projected.

Centrifuge—A mechanical device which applies centifugal force to the test specimen by means of a long rotating arm to simulate very closely the prolonged accelerations encountered in high-performance aircraft, rockets, and spacecraft.
   The simulated acceleration of centrifugal force produced is proportional to the distance from the center of rotation and the square of the rotational velocity.

Characteristic—Any dimensional, visual, functional, mechanical, electrical, chemical, physical, or material feature or property; and any process-control element which describes and establishes the design, fabrication, and operating requirements of an article.

Chase Pilot—A pilot who flies in an escort apirlane advising a pilot who is making a check, training, or research flight in another craft.

Checkout—1. A sequence of actions taken to test or examine a thing as to its readiness for incorporation into a new phase of use, or for the performance of its intended function. 2. The sequence of steps taken to familiarize a person with the operation of an airplane or other piece of equipment.
   In sense 1, a checkout is usually taken at a transition point between one phase of action and another. To shorten the time of checkout, automation is frequently employed.

Cheese Antenna—A cylindrical parabolic reflector enclosed by two plates perpendicular to the cylinder, so spaced as to permit the propagation of more than one mode in the desired direction of polarization. It is fed on the focal line.

Chemical Fuel—1. A fuel that depends upon an oxidizer for combustion or for development of thrust, such as liquid or solid rocket fuel or internal-combustion-engine fuel; distinguished from nuclear fuel. 2. A fuel that uses special chemicals, such as a boron-based fuel.

Chemical Rocket—A rocket using chemical fuel, fuel which requires an oxidizer for combustion, such as liquid or solid rocket fuel.

Chemosphere—The vaguely defined region of the upper atmosphere in which photochemical reactions take place. It is generally considered to include the stratosphere (or the top thereof) and the mesosphere, and sometimes the lower part of the thermosphere.
   This entire region is the seat of a number of important photochemical reactions involving atomic oxygen 0, molecular oxygen O_2, ozone O_3, hydroxyl OH, nitrogen N_2, sodium Na, and other constituents to a lesser degree.

Chromosphere—A thin layer of relatively transparent gases above the PHOTOSPHERE of the sun. It is most easily observed during a total solar eclipse.

Chokes—Pain and irritation in the chest and throat as a result of reduced ambient pressure.

Chugging—A form of combustion instability, especially in a liquid-propellant rocket engine, characterized by a pulsing operation at a fairly low frequency, sometimes defined as occurring between particular frequency limits; the noise made in this kind of combustion. Also called "chuffing."

Cislunar—(Latin cis "on this side".) Of or pertaining to phenomena, projects, or activity in the space between the earth and moon, or between the earth and the moon's orbit.

Closed Ecological System—A system that provides for the maintenance of life in an isolated living chamber such as a spacecraft cabin by means of a cycle wherein exhaled carbon dioxide, urine, and other waste matter are converted chemically or by photosynthesis into oxygen, water, and food.

Coherent—Of electromagnetic radiation, being in phase so that waves at various points in space act in unison.

Cold-flow Test—A test of a liquid rocket without firing it to check or verify the efficiency of a propulsion subsystem, providing for the conditioning and flow of propellants (including tank pressurization, propellant loading, and propellant feeding.)

Comet—A luminous member of the solar system composed of a head or coma at the center of which a presumably solid nucleus is sometimes situated, and often with a spectacular gaseous tail extending a great distance from the head.

Command—A signal which initiates or triggers an action in the device which receives the signal.

The orbits of comets are highly elliptical.

Communications Satellite—A satellite designed to reflect or relay radio or other communications waves.

Companion Body—A nose cone, last-stage rocket, or other body that orbits along with an earth satellite.

Complex—Entire area of launch site facilities. This includes blockhouse, launch pad, gantry, etc. Also referred to as a "launch complex."

Component—A self-contained combination of parts and/or assemblies within a subsystem performing a function necessary to the subsystem's operation. Examples are: receivers, transmitters, modulators, etc.

Composite Materials—Structural materials of metal alloys or plastics with built-in strengthening agents which may be in the form of filaments, foils, or flakes of a strong material.

Composite Propellant—A solid rocket propellant consisting of a fuel and an oxidizer.

Computer—A machine for carrying out calculations and performing specified transformations on information.

Configuration—A particular type of a specified aircraft, rocket, etc., which differs from others of the same model by virtue of the arrangement of its components or by the addition or omission of auxiliary equipment as "long-range configuration," "cargo configuration."

Conic—A conic section.

Conic Section—A curve formed by the intersection of a plane and a right circular cone. Usually called "conic."

The conic sections are the ellipse, the parabola, and the hyperbola; curves that are used to describe the paths of bodies moving in space.

The circle is a special case of the ellipse, an ellipse with an eccentricity of zero.

Console—An array of controls and indicators for the monitoring and control of a particular sequence of actions, as in the checkout of a rocket, a countdown action, or a launch procedure.

A console is usually designed around desklike arrays. It permits the operator to monitor and control different activating instruments, data recording instruments, or event sequencers.

Constellation—Originally a conspicuous configuration of stars; now a region of the celestial sphere marked by arbitrary boundary lines.

Contractor—The individual(s) or concern(s) who enter(s) into a prime contract with the Government.

Contravane—A vane that reverses or neutralizes a rotation of a flow. Also called a "countervane."

Control—Specifically, to direct the movements of an aircraft, rocket, or spacecraft with particular reference to changes in altitude and speed. Contrast guidance.

Control Rocket—A vernier engine, retrorocket, or other such rocket, used to guide or make small changes in the velocity of a rocket, spacecraft, or the like.

Coriolis Acceleration—An acceleration of a particle moving in a (moving) relative coordinate system. The total acceleration of the particle, as measured in an internal coordinate system, may be expressed as the sum of the acceleration within the relative system, the acceleration of the relative system itself, and the coriolis acceleration.

In the case of the earth, moving with angular velocity Ω, a particle moving relative to the earth with velocity V has the coriolis acceleration 2Ω x V. If Newton's laws are to be applied in the relative system, the coriolis acceleration and the acceleration of the relative system must be treated as forces. See **Gravity**.

Corona—1. The faintly luminous outer envelope of the sun. Also called "solar corona."

The corona can be observed at the earth's surface only at solar eclipse or with the coronagraph, a photographic instrument which artificially blocks out the image of the body of the sun.

2. Discharge of electricity which occurs at the surface of a conductor under high voltage. The phenomenon is dependent or ambient pressure of the gas surrounding the conductor.

Since phenomenon is enhanced by reduced pressure, tests must be conducted to verify that no significant corona exists within the spacecraft or its components under anticipated conditions.

Cosmic Dust—Small meteoroids of a size similar to dust.

Cosmic Rays—The aggregate of extremely high energy subatomic particles which bombard the atmosphere from outer space. Cosmic-ray primaries seem to be mostly protons, hydrogen nuclei, but also comprise heavier nuclei. On colliding with atmospheric particles they produce many different kinds of lower-energy secondary cosmic radiation (see **Cascade Shower.**) Also called "cosmic radiation."

The maximum flux of cosmic rays, both primary and secondary, is at an altitude of 20 km, and below this the absorption of the atmosphere reduces the flux, though the rays are still readily detectable at sea level. Intensity of cosmic ray showers has also been observed to vary with latitude, being more intense at the poles.

COSPAR—Abbreviation for "Committee on Space Research," International Council of Scientific Unions.

Countdown—The time period in which a sequence of events is carried out to launch a rocket; the sequence of events.

Cryogenic Propellant—A rocket fuel, oxidizer, or propulsion fluid which is liquid only at very low temperatures.

Cryogenic Temperature—In general, a temperature range below about —50°C; more particularly, temperatures within a few degrees of absolute zero.

Cutoff—An act or instance of shutting something off; specifically in rocketry, an act of instance of shutting off the propellant flow in a rocket, or of stopping the combustion of the propellant.

D

Data Reduction—Transformation of observed values into useful, ordered, or simplified information.

Debug—1. To isolate and remove malfunctions from a device, or mistakes from a computer routine or program. 2. Specifically, in electronic manufacturing, to operate equipment under specified environmental and test conditions in order to eliminate early failures and to stabilize equipment prior to actual use.

Deceleration—1. The act or process of moving, or of causing to move, with decreasing speed; the state of so moving. 2. A force causing deceleration; also, inertial forces sometimes called "negative acceleration".

Deep Space Net—A combination of three radar and communications stations in the United States, Australia, and South Africa so located as to keep a spacecraft in deep space under observation at all times.

Deep Space Probes—Spacecraft designed for exploring space to the vicinity of the moon and beyond. Deep space probes with specific missions may be referred to as "lunar probe," "Mars probe," "solar probe," etc.

Degradation—Gradual deterioration in performance.

Delay—The time (or equivalent distance) displacement of some characteristic of a wave relative to the same characteristics of a reference wave; that is, the difference in phase between the two waves. Compare lag.

In one-way radio propagation, for instance, the phase delay of the reflected wave over the direct wave is a measure of the extra distance traveled by the reflected wave in reaching the same receiver.

Design Engineering Tests—Environmental tests having the purpose of trying certain design features prior to finalizing design for Design Qualification Tests. For instance the structural model of the spacecraft is subjected to certain environmental exposures or Design Engineering Tests up to design qualification level in order to establish confidence in its structural design.

Design Qualification Tests—Series of environmental and other tests applied to prototype spacecraft, subsystems, components, or experiments to determine if design meets requirements for launch and flight of spacecraft. These tests are planned to subject spacecraft to considerably greater rigors of environment than expected during launch and flight in order to achieve maximum design reliability.

Destruct—The deliberate action of destroying a rocket vehicle after it has been launched, but before it has completed its course.

Destructs are executed when the rocket gets off its plotted course or functions in a way so as to become a hazard.

Deviation—1. In NASA quality control, specific authorization, granted before the fact, to depart from a particular requirement of specifications or related documents. 2. In statistics, the difference between two numbers. Also called "departure." It is commonly applied to the difference of a variable from its mean, or to the difference of an observed value from a theoretical value.

Digital Computer—A computer which operates on the principle of counting as opposed to measuring. See **Analog Computer.**

Diplexer—A device permitting an antenna system to be used simultaneously or separately by two transmitters. Compare with duplexer.

Dish—A parabolic type of radio or radar antenna, roughly the shape of a soup bowl.

Display—The graphic presentation of the output data of a device or system as, for example, a radar scope.

Docking—The process of bringing two spacecraft together while in space.

Doppler Shift—The change in frequency with which energy reaches a receiver when the source of radiation or a reflector of the radiation and the receiver are in motion relative to each other. The Doppler shift is used in many tracking and navigation systems.

Dosimeter—A device, worn by persons working around radioactive material, which indicates the amount (dose) of radiation to which they have been exposed.

Dovap—From Doppler, velocity and position, a tracking system which uses the Doppler shift caused by a target moving relative to a ground transmitter to obtain velocity and position information.

Drogue Parachute—A type of parachute attached to a body, used to slow it down; also called "deceleration parachute," or "drag parachute."

Duplexer—A device which permits a single antenna system to be used for both transmitting and receiving.

"Duplexer" should not be confused with "diplexer," a device permitting an antenna system to be used simultaneously or separately by two transmitters.

Dynamic Pressure—Symbol q. 1. The pressure exerted by a fluid, such as air, by virtue of its motion, equal to one half the fluid density times the fluid velocity square $\frac{1}{2}\rho V^2$.

2. The pressure exerted on a body, by virtue of its motion through a fluid, for example, the pressure exerted on a rocket moving through the atmosphere.

Dyne (abbr d)—That unbalanced force which acting for 1 second on body of 1 gram mass produces a velocity change of 1 cm/sec.
The dyne is the unit of force in the cgs system.

Dysbarism—A general term which includes a complex group of a wide variety of symptoms within the body caused by changes in ambient pressure, exclusive of hypoxia.

E

Ebullism—The formation of bubbles, with particular reference to water vapor bubbles in biological fluids, caused by reduced ambient pressure.

Eccentric—Not having the same center; varying from a circle, as in "eccentric orbit."

Echo—A large plastic balloon with a diameter of 30 meters and weight of 50 kilograms launched on August 12, 1960 by the United States and inflated in orbit. It was launched as a passive communications satellite, to reflect microwaves from a transmitter to a receiver beyond the horizon.

Ecliptic—The apparent annual path of the sun among the stars; the intersection of the plane of the earth's orbit with the celestial sphere.

This is a great circle of the celestial sphere inclined at an angle of about 23°27' to the celestial equator.

Ecological System—A habitable environment, either created articially, such as in a manned space vehicle, or occurring naturally, such as the enviroment on the surface of the earth, in which man, animals, or other organisms can live in mutual relationship with each other.

Ideally, the environment furnishes the sustenance for life, and the resulting waste products revert or cycle back into the environment to be used again for the continuous support of life.

Effective Atmosphere—1. That part of the atmosphere which effectively influences a particular process or motion, its outer limits varying according to the terms of the process or motion considered.

For example, an earth satellite orbiting at 250 miles altitude remains within the ionosphere, but because the air particles are so rare at this altitude as to cause no appreciable friction or deflection, the satellite may be considered to be outside the effective atmosphere. For movement of air vehicles the effective atmosphere ends at the aerospause (which see.)

Ejection Capsule—1. In an aircraft or manned spacecraft, a detachable compartment serving as a cockpit or cabin, which may be ejected as a unit and parachuted to the ground. 2. In an artificial satellite, probe, or unmanned spacecraft, a boxlike unit usually containing recording instruments or records of observed data, which may be ejected and returned to earth by a parachute or other deceleration device.

Elasticizer—An elastic substance or fuel used in a solid rocket propellant to prevent cracking of the propellant grain and to bind it to the combustion-chamber case.

Electric Propulsion—The generation of thrust for a rocket engine involving acceleration of a propellant by some electrical device such as an arc jet, ion engine, or magnetohydrodynamic accelerator.

Electromagnetic Radiation—Energy propagated through space or through material media in the form of an advancing disturbance in electrical and magnetic fields existing in space or in the media. Also called simply "radiation."

Electron—The subatomic particle that possesses the smallest possible electric charge.

The term "electron" is usually reversed for the orbital particle whereas the term "beta particle" refers to a particle of the same electric charge inside the nucleus of the atom.

Electron Volt—A unit of energy equal to 1.601×10^{-16} erg. It is defined as the kinetic energy gained by an electron which is accelerated through a potential difference of one volt.

Electronic Data Processing—The use of electronic devices and systems in the processing of data so as to interpret the data and put it into usable form.

Ellipse—A plane curve constituting the locus of all points the sum of whose distances from two fixed point called "foci" is constant; an elongated circle.

The orbits of planets, satellites, planetoids, and comets are ellipses; center of attraction is at one focus.

Emissivity—1. The ratio of the emittance of a given surface at a specified wavelength and emitting temperature to the emittance of an ideal black body at the same wavelength and temperature. Sometimes called "emissive power."

The greatest value that an emissivity may have is unity, the least value zero. It is a corollary of Kirchhoff's law that the emissivity of any surface at a specified temperature and wavelength is exactly equal to the absorptivity of that surface at the same temperature and wavelength. The spectral emissivity is for a definite wavelength. The total emissivity is for all wavelengths.

2. (abbr ε) Specifically, the ratio of the flux emitted by a clean, perfectly polished surface of the material to the flux that would have been emitted by a black body at the same temperature.

Environment—An external condition or the sum of such conditions, in which a piece of equipment or a system operates, as in "temperature environment," "vibration environment," or "space environment."

Environments are usually specified by a range of values, and may be either natural or artificial.

Epoch—A particular instant for which certain data are valid.

Escape Velocity—The radial speed which a particle or larger body must attain in order to escape from the gravitational field of a planet or star.

The escape velocity from Earth is approximately 7 miles per sec.; from Mars, 3.2 miles per sec.; and from the Sun, 390 miles per sec. In order for a celestial body to retain an atmosphere for astronomically long periods of time, the mean velocity of the atmospheric molecules must be considerably below the escape velocity.

Exhaust Velocity—The speed at which the exhaust gases are expelled from the nozzle of a rocket. It depends upon the propellant-burning characteristics, and the over-all engine efficiency. Present exhaust velocities using liquid oxygen and kerosene are of the order of 8000 feet per second, about half the theoretical maximum for chemical propellants.

Exobiology—The study of living organisms existing on celestial bodies other than the earth.

Exosphere—The outermost, or topmost portion of the atmosphere.

In the exosphere, the air density is so low that the mean free path of individual particles depends upon their direction with respect to the local vertical, being greatest for upward moving particles. It is only from the exosphere that atmospheric gases can, to any appreciable extent, escape into outer space.

Exotic Fuel—Any fuel considered to be unusual, as a boron-based fuel.

Experiment—A combination of two or more components, including both the sensor and associated electronics, designed for acquisition of data for space research.

Explosive Bolt—A bolt incorporating an explosive which can be detonated on command, thus destroying the bolt. Explosive bolts are used, for example, in separating a satellite from a rocket.

Extraterrestrial—From outside the earth.

Extraterrestrial Radiation—In general, solar radiation received outside the earth's atmosphere.

Eyeballs In, Eyeballs Out—Terminology used by test pilots to describe the acceleration experienced by the person being accelerated. Thus the acceleration experienced by an astronaut at lift-off is "eyeballs in" (positive g in terms of vehicle acceleration), and the acceleration experienced when retrorockets fire is "eyeballs out" (negative g in terms of vehicle acceleration.)

F

Fallaway Section—A section of a rocket vehicle that is cast off and separates from the vehicle during flight, especially such a section that falls back to the earth.

Fatigue—A weakening or deterioration of metal or other material, or of a member, occurring under load, especially under repeated, cyclic, or continued loading.

Field—A region of space at each point of which a given physical quantity has some definite value, thus a "gravitational field," an "electric field," a "magnetic field," etc.

Film Cooling—The cooling of a body or surface, such as the inner surface of a rocket combustion chamber, by maintaining a thin fluid layer over the affected area.

Fixed Satellite—An earth satellite that orbits from west to east at such a speed as to remain constantly over a given place on the earth's equator.

Flare—A bright eruption from the sun's chromosphere.

Flares may appear within minutes and fade within an hour. They cover a wide range of intensity and size, and they tend to occur between sunspots.

Flares are related to radio fadeouts and terrestrial magnetic disturbances.

Flashback—A reversal of flame propagation in a system, counter to the usual flow of the combustible mixture.

Flight—Describes or pertains to travel of spacecraft or stages after liftoff. Thus, in testing, designates spacecraft or element thereof which is to be launched as distinct from structural model and prototype spacecraft which are test specimens only.

Flight Acceptance Tests—The environmental and other tests which spacecraft, subsystems, components, or experiments scheduled for flight must pass before launch. These tests are planned to approximate expected environmental conditions and have the purpose of detecting flaws in material and workmanship.

Flight Unit—Spacecraft which is undergoing or has passed Flight Acceptance Tests (environmental and other tests) which qualify it for launch and space flight.

Flux—The rate of flow of some quantity, often used in reference to the flow of some form of energy. Also called "transport." 2. In nuclear physics generally, the number of radioactive particles per unit volume times their mean velocity.

Flux Density—The flux (rate of flow) of any quantity, usually a form of energy, through a unit area of specified surface. (Note that this is not a volumetric density like radiant density.) Compare luminous density.

The flux density of electromagnetic radiation in general often is preferably specified as "radiant flux density" or "irradiance" in order to distinguish it from the slightest different concept of luminous flux density or illuminance. In radar, flux density commonly is referred to as power density. It is essential to understand that the flux density of radiation is in no sense a vector quantity, because it is the sum of the flux corresponding to all ray directions incident upon one "side" of the unit area.

Forbush Decrease—The observed decrease in COSMIC RAY activity about a day after a SOLAR FLARE. It is now believed to be caused by a shielding effect produced by magnetic fields contained in the PLASMA cloud emitted from the sun at the time of a flare.

Flying Test Bed—An aircraft, rocket, or other flying vehicle used to carry objects or devices being flight tested.

Free Fall—1. The fall or drop of a body, such as a rocket not guided, nor under thrust, and not retarded by a parachute or other braking device. 2. Weightlessness.

G

g or G—An acceleration equal to the acceleration of gravity, approximately 32.2 feet per second per second at sea level; used as a unit of stress measurement for bodies undergoing acceleration.

GSE—See Ground Support Equipment.

Gamma Ray—A quantum of electromagnetic radiation emitted by a nucleus, each such photon being emitted as the result of a quantum transition between two energy levels of the nucleus. Gamma rays have energies usually between 10 kev and 10 Mev, with correspondingly short wavelengths and high frequencies. Also called "gamma radiation."

Gantry—A frame structure that spans over something, as an elevated platform that runs astride a work area, supported by wheels on each side; specifically, short for "gantry crane" or "gantry scaffold."

Gantry Scaffold—A massive scaffolding structure mounted on a bridge or platform supported by a pair of towers or trestles that normally run back and forth on parallel tracks, used to assemble and service a large rocket on its launching pad. Often shortened to "gantry." Also called "service tower."

This structure is a latticed arrangement of girders, tubing, platforms, cranes, elevators, instruments, wiring, floodlights, cables, and ladders—all used to attend the rocket.

Garbage—Miscellaneous objects in orbit, usually material ejected or broken away from a launch vehicle or satellite.

Gas Cap—The gas immediately in front of a meteoroid or reentry body as it travels through the atmosphere; the leading portion of a meteor. This gas is compressed and adiabatically heated to incandescence.

Generation—In any technical or technological development, as of a missile, jet engine, or the like, a stage or period that is marked by features or performances not marked, or existent, in a previous period of development or production, as in "second generation rocket."

Geo—A prefix meaning "earth," as in "geology," "geophysics."

Most writers used the established terms such as "geology" to refer to the same concept on other bodies of the solar system, as "the geology of Mars," rather than "areology" or "marsology," "geology of the moon," rather than "selenology."

Geocentric—Relative to the earth as a center; measured from the center of the earth.

Geodetic—Pertaining to geodesy, the science which deals with the size and shape of the earth.

Geoid—The equipotential surface which most nearly approximates the mean sea level of the earth.

Geomagnetism—The magnetic phenomena, collectively considered, exhibited by the earth and its atmosphere; by extension, the magnetic phenomena in interplanetary space.

Geophysics—The physics of the earth and its environment, i.e., earth, air, and (by extension), space.

Classically, geophysics is concerned with the nature of physical occurrences at and below the surface of the earth including, therefore, geology, oceanography, geodesy, seismology, hydrology, etc. The trend is to extend the scope of geophysics to include meteorology, geomagnetism, astrophysics, and other sciences concerned with the physical nature of the universe.

Geopotential—The potential energy of a unit mass relative to sea level, numerically equal to the work that would be done in lifting the unit mass from sea level to the height at which the mass is located; commonly expressed in terms of dynamic height or geopotential height.

Geoprobe—A rocket vehicle designed to explore space near the earth at a distance of more than 4,000 miles from the earth's surface. Rocket vehicles operating lower than 4,000 miles are termed "sounding rockets."

Giga—A prefix meaning multiplied by one billion.

Gimbal—1. A device with two mutually perpendicular and intersecting axes of rotation, thus giving free angular movement in two directions, on which an engine or other object may be mounted. 2. In a gyro, a support which provides the spin axis with a degree-of-freedom.

Gnotobiotics—The study of germ-free animals.

Gox—Gaseous oxygen.

Grain—An elongated molding or extrusion of solid propellant for a rocket, regardless of size.

Gravitation—The acceleration produced by the mutual attraction of two masses, directed along the line joining their centers of mass, and of magnitude inversely proportional to the square of the distance between the two centers of mass.

Gravity—The force imparted by the earth to a mass on, or close to the earth. Since the earth is rotating, the force observed as gravity is the resultant of the force of gravitation and the centrifugal force arising from this rotation.

Ground Support Equipment (GSE)—Any ground-based equipment used for launch, checkout, or in-flight support of a space project.

g-suit or G-Suit—A suit that exerts pressure on the abdomen and lower parts of the body to prevent or retard the collection of blood below the chest under positive acceleration.

G-Tolerance—A tolerance in a person or other animal, or in a piece of equipment, to an acceleration of a particular value.

Guidance—The process of directing the movements of an aeronautical vehicle or space vehicle, with particular reference to the selection of a flight path. See **Control.**

In preset guidance a predetermined path is set into the guidance mechanism and not altered, in inertial guidance accelerations are measured and integrated within the craft, in command guidance the craft responds to information received from an outside source. Beam-rider guidance utilizes a beam, terrestrial-reference guidance some influence of the earth, celestial guidance the celestial bodies and particularly the stars, and homing guidance information from the destination. In active homing guidance the information is in response to transmissions from the craft, in semiactive homing guidance the transmissions are from a source other than the craft, and in passive homing guidance natural radiations from the destination are utilized. Midcourse guidance extends from the end of the launching phase to an arbitrary point enroute and terminal guidance extends from this point to the destination.

Gyro—A device which utilizes the angular momentum of a spinning rotor to sense angular motion of its base about one or two axes at right angles to the spin axis. Also called "gyroscope."

H

Hall Effect—The electrical polarization of a horizontal conducting sheet of limited extent, when that sheet moves laterally through a magnetic field having a component vertical to the sheet.

The Hall effect is important in determining the behavior of the electrical currents generated by winds in the lower ionosphere, since these winds advect the ionized layers across the earth's magnetic field and produce a complex electrical current system in the ionosphere. This current system in turn produces small changes in the earth's magnetic field as measured at the surface.

Hardness—Of X-rays and other radiation of high energy, a measure of penetrating power. Radiation which will penetrate a 10-centimeter thickness of lead is considered "hard radiation."

Heat Exchanger—A device for transferring heat from one fluid to another without intermixing the fluids. A regenerator is an example.

Heat Shield—Any device that protects something from heat.

Heat Sink—1. In thermodynamic theory, a means by which heat is stored, or is dissipated or transferred from the system under consideration. 2. A place toward which the heat moves in a system. 3. A material capable of absorbing heat; a device utilizing such a material and used as a thermal protection device on a spacecraft or reentry vehicle. 4. In nuclear propulsion, any thermodynamic device, such as a radiator or condenser, that is designed to absorb the excess heat energy of the working fluid. Also called "heat dump."

Heterosphere—The upper portion of a two-part division of the atmosphere according to the general homogeneity of atmospheric composition; the layer above the homosphere. The heterosphere is characterized by variation in composition, and mean molecular weight of constituent gases.

This region starts at 80 to 100 km above the earth, and therefore closely coincides with the ionosphere and the thermosphere.

Hold—During a countdown: To halt the sequence of events until an impediment has been removed so that the countdown can be resumed, as in "T minus 40 and holding."

Homosphere—The lower portion of a two-part division of the atmosphere according to general homogeneity of atmospheric composition; opposed to the heterosphere. The region in which there is no gross change in atmospheric composition, that is, all of the atmosphere from the earth's surface to about 80 or 100 km.

The homosphere is about equivalent to the neutrosphere, and includes the troposphere, stratosphere, and mesosphere, and also the ozonosphere and at least part of the chemosphere.

Hot Test—A propulsion system test conducted by actually firing the propellants.

Human Engineering—The art or science of designing, building, or equipping mechanical devices or artificial environments to the anthropometric, physiological, or psychological requirements of the men who will use them.

Hunting—Fluctuation about a midpoint due to instability, as oscillations of the needle of an instrument about a median value.

Hydromagnetics—See Magnetohydrodynamics.

Hypersonic—1. Pertaining to hypersonic flow. 2. Pertaining to speeds of Mach 5 or greater.

Hypersonic Flow—In aerodynamics, flow of a fluid over a body at speeds much greater than the speed of sound and in which the shock waves start at a finite distance from the surface of the body.

Hypoxia—Oxygen deficiency in the blood, cells, or tissues of the body in such degree as to cause psychological and physiological disturbances.

Hypoxia may result from a scarcity of oxygen in the air being breathed, or from an inability of the body tissues to absorb oxygen under conditions of low ambient pressure. In the latter case, water vapors from body fluids increase in the sacs of the lungs, crowding out the oxygen.

I

Igniter—Any device used to begin combustion, such as a spark plug in the combustion chamber of a jet engine, or a squib used to ignite fuel in a rocket.

Impact Area—The area in which a rocket strikes the earth's surface.

Used specifically in reference to the "impact area" of a rocket range.

Impact Bag—An inflatable bag attached to a spacecraft or reentry capsule to absorb part of the shock of landing.

Inertial Guidance—Guidance by means of acceleration measured and integrated within the craft.

Infrared—Infrared radiation; electromagnetic radiation in the wavelength interval from the red end of the visible spectrum on the lower limit to microwaves used in radar on the upper limit.

Infrared Radiation (abbr IR)—Electromagnetic radiation lying in the wavelength interval from about 0.8 microns to an indefinite upper boundary sometimes arbitrarily set at 1,000 microns (0.01 cm). Also called "black light," "long wave radiation."

At the lower limit of this interval, the infrared radiation spectrum is bounded by visible radiation, while on its upper limit it is bounded by microwave radiation of the type important in radar technology.

Whereas visible radiation is generated primarily by intra-atomic processes, infrared radiation is generated almost wholly by larger-scale intra-molecular processes, chiefly molecular rotations and internal vibrations of many types. Electrically symmetric molecules, such as the nitrogen and oxygen molecules which comprise most of the earth's atmosphere, are not capable of absorbing or emitting infrared radiation, but several of the triatomic gases, such as water vapor, carbon doxide, and ozone are infrared-active and play important roles in the propagation of infrared radiation in the atmosphere.

Since a black body at terrestrial temperature radiates with maximum intensity in the spectrum (near 10 microns), there exists a complex system of infrared radiation currents within our atmosphere.

Injection—1. The introduction of fuel, fuel and air, fuel and oxidizer, water, or other substance into an engine induction system or combustion chamber. 2. The process of putting an artificial satellite into orbit. 3. The time following launching when non-gravitational forces (thrust, lift, and drag) become negligible in their effect on the trajectory of a space vehicle.

More than one injection is possible in a single flight if engines are stopped and restarted.

Insertion—The process of putting an artificial satellite into orbit. Also the time of such action.

Intensity—1. In general, the degree or amount, usually expressed by the elemental time rate or spatial distribution, of some condition or physical quantity, such as electric field, sound, magnetism, etc.

2. With respect to electromagnetic radiation, a measure of the radiant flux per unit solid angle emanating from some source. Frequently, it is desirable to specify this as radiant intensity in order to clearly distinguish it from luminous intensity.

Interface—The junction points or the points within or between systems or subsystems where matching or accommodation must be properly achieved in order to make their operation compatible with the successful operation of all other functional entities in the space vehicle and its ground support.

International Geophysical Year (abbr IGY)—By international agreement, a period during which greatly increased observation of world-wide geophysical phenomena is undertaken through the cooperative effort of participating nations. July 1957-December 1958 was the first such "year"; however, precedent was set by the International Polar Years of 1882 and 1921.

International Year of the Quiet Sun (abbr IQSY)—The international program for maximum observation and research in connection with expected period of low solar activity between April 1964 and December 1965.

Ion—An atom or molecularly bound group of atoms having an electric charge. Sometimes also a free electron or other charged subatomic particle.

Ionic Propulsion (electrostatic propulsion)—Rocket propulsion using the THRUST furnished by electrically accelerated ions. Much higher SPECIFIC IMPULSES and EXHAUST VELOCITIES may be obtained than with chemical propulsion, but current laboratory versions of the ionic rocket are capable of furnishing a total thrust of only a few ounces.

Ionosphere—The atmospheric shell characterized by a high ion density. Its base is at about 70 or 80 km and it extends to an indefinite height.

The ionosphere is classically subdivided into "layers." Each "layer," except the D-layer, is supposedly characterized by a more or less regular maximum of electron density.

D-layer.—The D-layer exists only in the daytime. It is not strictly a layer at all, since it does not exhibit a peak of electron or ion density, but is rather a region of increasing electron and ion density, starting at about 70 to 80 km and merging with the bottom of the E-layer.

The lowest clearly defined layer is the E-layer, occurring between 100 and 120 km. The F_1-layer and F_2-layer occur in the general region between 150 and 300 km, the F_2-layer being always present and having the higher electron density. The existence of a G-layer has been suggested, but is questionable. The portions of the ionosphere in which these "layers" tend to form are known as ionospheric "regions," as in "D-region," "E-region," "F-region," "G-region."

Sudden increases in ionization are referred to as "sporadic," as in "sporadic E" or "sporadic D."

The above assumption that the ionosphere is stratified in the vertical into discrete layers is currently under serious question. Some evidence supports a belief that ion clouds are the basic elements of the ionosphere. Other investigations appear to reveal the ionosphere as a generally ionized region characterized by more or less random fluctuations of electron density.

Isotropic—In general, pertaining to a state which a quantity or spatial derivatives thereof are independent of direction.

IQSY—See International Year of the Quiet Sun.

J

Jerk—A vector that specifies the time rate of change of an acceleration; the third derivative of displacement with respect to time.

Joule's Constant—The ratio between heat and work units from experiments based on the first law of thermodynamics: 4.186 x 10⁷ ergs/cal. Also called "mechanical equivalent of heat."

K

Kelvin Temperature Scale (abbr K)—An absolute temperature scale independent of the thermometric properties of the working substance. On this scale, the difference between two temperatures T_1 and T_2 is proportional to the heat converted into mechanical work by a Carnot engine operating between the isotherms and adiabats through T_1 and T_2. Also called "absolute temperature scale," "thermodynamic temperature scale."

For convenience the Kelvin degree is identified with the Celsius degree. The ice point in the Kelvin scale is 273.16°K. See **Absolute Zero.**

Kepler's Laws—The three empirical laws describing the motions of planets in their orbits, discovered by Johannes Kepler (1571-1630). These are: (1) The orbits of the planets are ellipses, with the sun at a common focus. (2) As a planet moves in its orbit, the line joining the planet and sun sweeps over equal areas in equal intervals of time. Also called "law of equal areas." (3) The squares of the periods of revolution of any two planets are proportional to the cubes of their mean distances from the sun.

Kev—A unit of energy, one thousand electron volts.

Kirchhoff's Law—The radiation law which states that at a given temperature the ratio of the emissivity to the absorptivity for a given wavelength is the same for all bodies and is equal to the emissivity of an ideal black body at that temperature and wavelength.

Loosely put, this important law asserts that good absorbers of a given wavelength are also good emitters of that wavelength. It is essential to note that Kirchhoff's law relates absorption and emission at the same wavelength and at the same temperature. Also called "Kirchhoff's radiation law."

L

Laser—(From light amplification by stimulated emission of radiation.) A device for producing light by emission of energy stored in a molecular or atomic system when simulated by an input signal.

Launch Pad—The load-bearing base or platform from which a rocket vehicle is launched. Usually called "pad."

Launch Ring—The metal ring on the launch pad on which a missile stands before launch.

Launch Vehicle—Any device which propels and guides a spacecraft into orbit about the earth or into a trajectory to another celestial body: Often called "booster."

Launch Window—An interval of time during which a rocket can be launched to accomplish a particular purpose as "lift-off occurred 5 minutes after the beginning of the 82-minute launch window."

Libration—A real or apparent oscillatory motion, particularly the apparent oscillation of the moon.

Because of libration, more than half of the moon's surface is revealed to an observer on the earth, even though the same side of the moon is always toward the earth because the moon's periods of rotation and revolution are the same.

Lift-off—The action of a rocket vehicle as it separates from its launch pad in a vertical ascent.

A lift-off is applicable only to vertical ascent; a take-off is applicable to ascent at any angle. A lift-off is action performed by a rocket; a launch is action performed upon a rocket or upon a satellite or spaceship carried by a rocket.

Light Year—The distance light travels in one year at rate of 186,000 miles per second (300,000 kilometers per second.) Equal to 5.9×10^{12} miles. See PARSEC.)

Line of Position—In navigation, a line representing all possible locations of a craft at a given instant.

In space this concept can be extended to "sphere of position," "plane of position," etc.

Liquid-Propellant Rocket Engine—A rocket engine fueled with propellant or propellants in liquid form. Also called "liquid-propellant rocket."

Rocket engines of this kind vary somewhat in complexity, but they consist essentially of one or more combustion chambers together with the necessary pipes, values, pumps, injectors, etc.

Local Vertical—At a particular point, the direction in which the force of gravity acts.

Longitudinal Axis—The fore-and-aft line through the center of gravity of a craft.

Longitudinal Vibration—Vibration in which the direction of motion of the particles is the same as the direction of advance of the vibratory motion.

This is in contrast with transverse vibration, in which the direction of motion is pependicular to that of advance.

Lox—1. Liquid oxygen. Used attributively as in "lox tank," "lox unit." Also called "loxygen." 2. To load the fuel tanks of a rocket vehicle with liquid oxygen. Hence, "loxing."

Lunar Atmospheric Tide—An atmospheric tide due to the gravitational attraction of the moon. The only detectable components are the 12-lunar-hour or semidiurnal, as in the oceanic tides, and two others of very nearly the same period. The amplitude of this atmospheric tide is so small that it is detected only by careful statistical analysis of a long record, being about 0.06 mb in the tropics and 0.02 mb in the middle latitudes.

Lyman Alpha Radiation—Ultraviolet radiation at a wavelength of 1216 Å emitted by atomic hydrogen when it passes from its first excited electronic state to its ground state. Light of this short wavelength is not transmitted by the earth's atmosphere, and a study of this extremely important line in the sun's spectrum was made only with the advent of rocket and satellite astronomy. The Lyman alpha transition is the longest wavelength member of the Lyman series of atomic hydrogen, and the strongest ultraviolet line emitted by the sun.

M

Mach Number—(After Ernst Mach (1838-1916), Austrian scientist.) A number expressing the ratio of the speed of a body or of a point on a body with respect to the surrounding air or other fluid, or the speed of a flow, to the speed of sound in the medium; the speed represented by this number.

If the Mach number is less than one, the flow is called "subsonic" and local disturbances can propagate ahead of the flow. If the Mach number is greater than one, the flow is called "supersonic" and disturbance cannot propagate ahead of the flow, with the result that shock waves form.

Magnetic Storm—A worldwide disturbance of the earth's magnetic field.

Magnetic storms are frequently characterized by a sudden onset, in which the magnetic field undergoes marked changes in the course of an hour or less, followed by a very gradual return to normality, which may take several days. Magnetic storms are caused by solar disturbances, though the exact nature of the link between the solar and terrestrial disturbances is not understood. Sometimes a magnetic storm can be linked to a particular solar disturbance. In these cases, the time between solar flare and onset of the magnetic storm is about one or two days, suggesting that the disturbance is carried to the earth by a cloud of particles thrown out by the sun.

Magnetohydrodynamics—The study of the interaction that exists between a magnetic field and an electrically conducting fluid. Also called "magnetoplasmadynamics," "magnetogasdynamics," "hydromagnetics," "MHD."

Magnetometer—An instrument used in the study of geomagnetism for measuring any magnetic element.

Magnetosphere—That part of the earth's atmosphere which exists by virtue of the earth's magnetic field. The magnetosphere consists of trapped particles, mainly electrons and protons, which spiral about the magnetic lines of force from pole to pole, and gradually precess eastward or westward, depending on their charge. Particles are lost by the magnetosphere when they descend into the atmosphere at high latitudes. It is believed that particles are fed into the magnetosphere by effects associated with the arrival of PLASMA clouds ejected during SOLAR FLARES as well as from the beta decay of neutrons produced by COSMIC RAYS striking the upper atmosphere. Particles may also be injected into the magnetosphere by high altitude nuclear explosions. (See VAN ALLEN BELTS.)

Magnitude—Relative brightness of a celestial body. The smaller the magnitude number, the brighter the body.

Decrease of light by a factor of 100 increases the stellar magnitude by 5.00; hence the brightest objects have negative magnitudes. (Sun: −26.8; mean full moon; −12.5; Venus at brightest: −4.3; Jupiter at opposition: −2.3; Sirius: −1.6; Vega: +0.2; Polaris: +2.1). The faintest stars visible to the Naked eye on a clear dark night are of about the sixth magnitude.

Main Bang—Within a radar system, the transmitted pulse.

Main Stage—1. In a multistage rocket, the stage that develops the greatest amount of thrust, with or without booster engines. 2. In a single-stage rocket vehicle powered by one or more engines, the period when full thrust (at or above 90 percent) is attained. 3. A sustainer engine, considered as a stage after booster engines have fallen away, as in "the main stage of the Atlas."

Manometer—An instrument for measuring pressure of gases and vapors both above and below atmospheric pressure.

Maria—The large, darker areas, of generally circular outline on the lunar surface. It has been suggested that they are caused by lava flow following the impact of large meteorites during the last stages of formation of the moon.

Mariner—The initial unmanned exploration of the planets is being conducted in the United States under the Mariner program. Mariner 2, launched August 26, 1962, passed within 21,000 miles of Venus on December 14, 1962, and radioed to earth information concerning the infrared and microwave emission of the planet, and the strength of the planet's magnetic field. Future flyby missions to both Venus and Mars are planned.

Mars I— An instrumented spacecraft launched by the Soviet Union on November 1, 1962, designed to investigate the interplanetary medium and transmit photographs of Mars to the earth. It is programmed to pass the planet in June, 1963, when it will be at a distance of 150 million miles.

Maser—An amplifier utilizing the principle of microwave amplification by stimulated emission of radiation. Emission of energy stored in a molecular or atomic system by a microwave power supply is stimulated by the input signal.

Mass—The measure of the amount of matter in a body, thus its inertia.

The weight of a body is the force with which it is attracted by the earth.

Mass-Energy Equivalence—The equivalence of a quantity of mass m and a quantity of energy E, the two quantities being related by the mass-energy relation, $E = mc^2$, where c = the speed of light.

Mass Ratio—The ratio of the mass of the propellant charge of a rocket to the total mass of the rocket charged with the propellant.

Mate—To fit together two major components of a system.

Mean Free Path—Of any particle, the average distance that a particle travels between successive collisions with the other particles of an ensemble.

Mechanoreceptor—A nerve ending that reacts to mechanical stimuli, as touch, tension, and acceleration.

Mega—A prefix meaning multiplied by one million as in "megacycles."

Memory—The component of a computer, control system, guidance system, instrumented satellite, or the like designed to provide ready access to data or instructions previously recorded so as to make them bear upon an immediate problem, such as the guidance of a physical object, or the analysis and reduction of data.

Mercury—The initial man-in-space program of the United States. The first manned sub-orbital flight took place on April 23, 1961, and the first orbital mission on February 20, 1962. Two others followed on May 24, 1962 and October 3, 1962. An 18 orbit flight is scheduled for April, 1963.

Mesosphere—1. The atmospheric shell between about 20 km and about 70 or 80 km, extending from the top of the stratosphere to the upper temperature minimum (the mesopause.) It is characterized by a broad temperature maximum (the mesopeak) at about 50 km, except possibly over the winter polar regions.

2. The atmospheric shell between the top of the ionosphere (the top of this region has never been clearly defined) and the bottom of the exosphere. (This definition has not gained general acceptance.)

Meteor—In particular, the light phenomenon which results from the entry into the earth's atmosphere of a solid particle from space: more generally, any physical object or phenomenon associated with such an event.

Meteoric—Of or pertaining to meteors, or meteoroids.

Meteorite—A meteoroid which has reached the surface of the earth without being completely vaporized.

Meteorid—A solid object moving in interplanetary space, of a size considerably smaller than an asteroid and considerably larger than an atom or molecule.

Meteorological Rocket—A rocket designed primarily for routine upper-air observation (as opposed to research) in the lower 250,000 feet of the atmosphere, especially that portion inaccessible to balloons, i.e., above 100,000 feet. Also called "rocketsonde."

MEV—A unit of energy, one million electron volts.

Micro—1. A prefix meaning divided by one million. 2. A prefix meaning very small as in "micrometeorite."

Microbar (abbr μb)—The unit of pressure in the c.g.s. system and equal to one dyne per square centimeter.

Micrometeorite—A very small meteorite or meteoritic particle with a diameter in general less than a millimeter.

Micron—One millionth of a meter, abbreviated μ.

Microwave Region—Commonly, that region of the radio spectrum between approximately 1000 Mc and 300,000 Mc.

Corresponding wavelengths are 30 cm to 1 mm.
The limits of the microwave region are not clearly defined but in general it is considered to be the region in which radar operates.

Millibar—A unit of pressure equal to 1,000 dynes per square centimeter, or 1/1,000 of a bar.

The millibar is used as a unit of measure of atmospheric pressure, a standard atmosphere being equal to 1,013.25 millibars or 29.92 inches of mercury.

Mini.—A contraction of "minitaure" used in combination, as in "minicomponent," "miniradio," "minitransistor."

Miniaturize—To construct a functioning miniature of a part or instrument. Said of telemetering instruments or parts used in an earth satellite or rocket vehicle, where room is at a premium. Hence, "miniaturized," "miniaturization."

Minimum Ionizing Speed—The speed with which a free electron must move through a given gas to be able to ionize gas atoms or molecules by collision. In air at standard conditions, this speed is about 10^7 cm/sec.

Minitrack—A satellite tracking system consisting of a field of separate antennas and associated receiving equipment interconnected so as to form interferometers which track a transmitting beacon in the satellite itself.

Missile—Any object thrown, dropped, fired, launched, or otherwise projected with the purpose of striking a target. Short for "ballistic missile," "guided missile."

Missile is loosely used as a synonym for "rocket" or "spacecraft" by some careless writers.

Mock-Up—A full-sized replica or dummy of something, such as a spacecraft, often made of some substitute material, such as wood, and sometimes incorporating functioning pieces of equipment, such as engines.

Mode of Propagation—In transmission, a form of propagation of guided waves that is characterized by a particular field pattern in a plane transversed to the direction of propagation, which field pattern is independent of position along the axis of the waveguide.

In the case of uniconductor waveguides the field pattern of a particular mode of propagation is also independent of frequency.

Mode of Vibration—In a system undergoing vibration, a characteristic pattern assumed by the system, in which the motion of every particle is simple harmonic with the same frequency.

Two or more modes of vibration may exist concurrently in a multiple-degree-of-freedom system.

Modulation—Specifically, vibration of some characteristic of a radio wave, called the "carrier wave," in accordance with instantaneous values of another wave, called the "modulating wave."

Variation of amplitude is amplitude modulation, variation of frequency is frequency modulation, and variation of phase is phase modulation. The formation of very short bursts of a carrier wave, separated by relatively long periods during which no carrier wave is transmitted, is pulse modulation.

Module—1. A self-contained unit of a launch vehicle or spacecraft which serves as a building block for the overall structure. The module is usually designated by its primary function as "command module," "lunar landing module," etc. 2. A one-package assembly of functionally associated electronic parts; usually a plug-in unit.

Module—An aggregate of two or more atoms of a substance that exists as a unit.

Molecule—An aggregate of two or more atoms of a substance that exists as a unit.

Moment (abbr M)—A tendency to cause rotation about a point or axis, as of a control surface about its hinge or of an airplane about its center of gravity; the measure of this tendency, equal to the product of the force and the perpendicular distance between the point of axis of rotation and the line of action of the force.

Moment of Inertia (abbr I)—Of a body about an axis, the Σmr^2, where m is the mass of a particle of the body and r its distance from the axis.

Momentum—Quantity of motion.

Linear momentum is the quantity obtained by multiplying the mass of a body by its linear speed. Angular momentum is the quantity obtained by multiplying the moment of inertia of a body by its angular speed.

The momentum of a system of particles is given by the sum of the moments of the individual particles which make up the system, or by the product of the total mass of the system and the velocity of the center of gravity of the system.

The momentum of a continuous medium is given by the integral of the velocity over the mass of the medium, or by the product of the total mass of the medium and the velocity of the center of gravity of the medium.

Monopropellant—A rocket propellant consisting of a single substance, especially a liquid, capable of producing a heated jet without the addition of a second substance.

M-Region—Name given to a region of activity on the sun when the nature of that activity cannot be determined.

The M-region used in accounting for recurrent magnetic storms with a period the same as the period of solar rotation relative to the earth, 27.3 days. See **Magnetic Storms.**

Multiplexer—A mechanical or electrical device for sharing of a circuit by two or more coincident signals.

Multiplexing—The simultaneous transmission of two or more signals within a single channel.

The three basic methods of multiplexing involve the separation of signals by time division, frequency division, and phase division.

Multipropellant—A rocket propellant consisting of two or more substances fed separately to the combustion chamber.

Multistage Rocket—A vehicle having two or more rocket units, each unit firing after the one in back of it has exhausted its propellant. Normally, each unit, or stage, is jettisoned after completing its firing. Also called a "multiple-stage rocket" or, infrequently, a "step rocket."

Musa Antenna—A "multiple-unit steerable antenna" consisting of a number of stationary antennas, the composite major lobe of which is electrically steerable.

N

NACA (abbr)—National Advisory Committee of Aeronautics.

Nano—A prefix meaning divided by one billion, as in "nanosecond," one billionth of a second.

Nanosecond (abbr nsec)—10^{-9} second. Also called "millimicrosecond."

NASA (abbr)—National Aeronautics and Space Administration.

NASC (abbr)—National Aeronautics and Space Council.

Natural Frequency—1. The frequency of free oscillation of a system. For a multiple-degree-of-freedom system, the natural frequencies are the frequencies of the normal modes of vibration. 2. The undamped resonant frequency of the rotor gimbal and its elastic restraint. It is expressed in cycles per unit time. 3. Specifically, of a gyro.

Nautical Mile—A unit of distance used principally in navigation. For practical navigation it is usually considered the length of one minute of any great circle of the earth, the meridian being the great circle most commonly used. Also called "sea mile." By international agreement of 1 July 1959, U.S., Great Britain and nearly all maritime nations established the International Nautical Mile, equal to exactly 1852 meters. Using the yard-meter conversion factor effective July 1, 1959, the International Nautical Mile is equivalent to 6,076.11549 international feet.

NASA's Designated Representative—A representative of the NASA installation stationed at supplier's plant or a representative of the inspection agency to whom quality assurance functions have been delegated.

NASA Installation—A major organization unit of the NASA; includes Headquarters and field installations. Field installations are assigned specific missions in the NASA space program.

Neutron—A subatomic particle with no electric charge, and with a mass slightly more than the mass of the proton.

Protons and neutrons comprise atomic nuclei; and they are both classed as nucleons.

Neutrosphere—The atmospheric shell from the earth's surface upward in which the atmospheric constituents are for the most part un-ionized, i.e., electrically neutral.

The region of transition between the neutrosphere and the ionosphere is somewhere between 70 and 90 km, depending on latitude and season.

Newton's laws of motion—A set of three fundamental postulates forming the basis of the mechanics of rigid bodies, formulated by Newton in 1687.

The first law is concerned with the principle of inertia and states that if a body in motion is not acted upon by an external force, its momentum remains constant (law of conservation of momentum.) The second law asserts that the rate of change of momentum of a body is proportional to the force acting upon the body and is the direction of the applied force. A familiar statement of this is the equation

$$F = ma$$

Where F is vector sum of the applied forces, m the mass, and a the vector acceleration of the body. The third law is the principle of action and reaction, stating that for every force acting upon a body there exists a corresponding force of the same magnitude exerted by the body in the opposite direction.

Noctilucent Clouds—Rarely observed clouds of unknown composition which occur at great height. Photometric measurements have located them between 75 and 90 km. They resemble thin cirrus, but usually with a bluish or silverish color, although sometimes orange to red, standing out against a dark night sky. Sometimes called "luminous clouds."

Node—1. One of the two points of intersection of the orbit of a planet, planetoid, or comet with the ecliptic, or of the orbit of a satellite with the plane of the orbit of its primary. Also called "nodal point."

That point at which the body crosses to the north side of the reference plane is called the ascending node; the other, the descending node. The line connecting the nodes is called line of nodes.

2. A point, line, or surface in a standing wave where some characteristic of the wave has essentially zero amplitude.

The appropriate modifier should be used before the word "node" to signify the type that is intended; e.g., displacement node, velocity node, pressure node.

3. A terminal of any branch of a network or a terminal common to two or more branches of a network. Also called "junction point," "branch point," or "vertex."

Noise—1. Any undesired sound. By extension, noise is any unwanted disturbance within a useful frequency band, such as undesired electric waves in a transmission channel or device. When caused by natural electrical discharges in the atmosphere noise may be called "static."

2. An erratic, intermittent, or statistically random oscillation.

If ambiguity exists as to the nature of the noise, a phrase such as "acoustic noise" or "electric noise" should be used.

Since the above definitions are not mutually exclusive, it is usually necessary to depend upon context for distinction.

Nonrelativistic Particles—Particles which possess a velocity small with respect to that of light, which is 186,000 miles/second or 3×10^{10} centimeters per second. (See RELATIVISTIC PARTICLES.)

Nonthermal Radiation—Electromagnetic radiation emitted by accelerated charged particles not in thermal equilibrium. The distribution of energy with frequency of nonthermal radiation usually differs from that of blackbody or THERMAL RADIATION. CYCLOTRON and SYNCHROTRON RADIATION of charged particles in magnetic fields are examples of nonthermal radiation, as is the light from a fluorescent lamp or the AURORA.

Normal Mode of Vibration—A mode of free vibration of an undamped system. In general, any composite motion of a vibrating system is analyzable into a summation of its normal modes, also called natural mode, "characteristic mode," and "eigen mode."

Normal Shock Wave—A shock wave perpendicular, or substantially so, to the direction of flow in a supersonic flow field. Sometimes shortened to "normal shock."

Nosecone—The cone-shaped leading end of a rocket vehicle, consisting of (a) a chamber or chambers in which a satellite, instruments, animals, plants, or auxiliary equipment may be carried, and (b) an outer surface built to withstand high temperatures generated by aerodynamic heating.

In a satellite vehicle, the nosecone may become the satellite itself after separating from the final stage of the rocket or it may be used to shield the satellite until orbital speed is accomplished, then separating from the satellite. See **Shroud.**

Nozzle—Specifically, the part of a rocket thrust chamber assembly in which the gases produced in the chamber are accelerated to high velocities.

Nuclear Fuel—Fissionable material of reasonably long life, used or usable in producing energy in a nuclear reactor.

Nuclear Radiation—The emission of neutrons and other particles from an atomic nucleus as the result of nuclear fission or nuclear fusion.

Nuclear Reactor—An apparatus in which nuclear fission may be sustained in self-supporting chain reaction. Commonly called "reactor."

Nucleosynthesis—The production of the various elements occurring in nature out of hydrogen nuclei or protons. Examples of nucleosynthesis are: thermonuclear reactions in stars and interactions involving fast, charged particles (COSMIC RAYS) near stars or in the interstellar medium.

Nucleus—The positively charged core of an atom with which is associated practically the whole mass of the atom but only a minute part of its volume.

A nucleus is composed of one or more protons and an approximately equal number of neutrons.

O

OAO—The Orbiting Astronomical Observatory which will make possible telescopic observations in the infrared, visible, ultraviolet, and x-ray regions from a stabilized platform above the obscuring effects of the earth's atmosphere. The first OAO will be launched using an ATLAS-AGENA by the United States late in 1963 or early in 1964, with successive flights at six-month intervals.

Occultation—The disappearance of a body behind another body of larger apparent size.

When the moon passes between the observer and a star, the star is said to be occulted.

Octave—The interval between any two frequencies having the ratio of 1:2.

The interval in octaves between any two frequencies is the logarithm to the base 2 (or 3.322 times the logarithm to the base 10) of the frequency ratio.

Oculogravic Illusion—The apparent displacement of an object in space caused by the difference which may exist between the direction of the vertical and that of resultant g.

Oculogyral Illusion—The apparent movement of an object in the same direction as that in which one seems to be turning when the semicircular canals of the inner ear are stimulated.

OGO—The Orbiting Geophysical Observatory will be a standardized satellite designed to undertake a large variety of geophysical experiments, including investigations of the MAGNETOSPHERE, the earth's magnetic field, MICROMETEORITES, and radio propagation. The first launching using an ATLAS-AGENA is scheduled by the United States for 1963, the following for 1964.

Orbit—1. The path of a body or particle under the influence of a gravitational or other force. For instance, the orbit of a celestial body is its path relative to another body around which it revolves. 2. To go around the earth or other body in an orbit.

Orbital Elements—A set of 7 parameters defining the orbit of a satellite.

Orbital Period—The interval between successive passages of a satellite.

Orbital Velocity—1. The average velocity at which an earth satellite or other orbiting body travels around its primary. 2. The velocity of such a body at any given point in its orbit, as in "its orbital velocity at the apogee is less than at the perigee."

Order of Magnitude—A factor of 10.

Two quantities of the same kind which differ by less than a factor of 10 are said to be of the same order of magnitude. "Order of magnitude" is used loosely by many writers to mean a pronounced difference in quantity but with the difference much less or much more than a factor of 10.

Orthogonal—At right angles.

OSO—The Orbiting Solar Observatory. OSO I was launched by the United States on March 7, 1962. It is designed in particular to gather information on the emission by the sun of x and y rays, ultraviolet light, neutrons, protons, and electrons which cannot be obtained from the earth's surface. A second similar OSO will be launched in 1963, with improved versions following.

Otolith—A small calcareous concretion located in the inner ear which plays a part in the mechanism of orientation.

Outgassing—The evolution of gas from a solid in a vacuum.

Oxidizer—Specifically, a substance (not necessarily containing oxygen) that supports the combustion of a fuel or propellant.

OZONE—The molecule O_3. It is produced in the upper STRATOSPHERE by the PHOTODISSOCIATION of O_2 and subsequent union of O and O_2. Ozone absorbs ultraviolet strongly in the wavelength region from 2000 to 3000 Å.

Ozonosphere—The general stratum of the upper atmosphere in which there is an appreciable ozone concentration and in which ozone plays an important part in the radiative balance of the atmosphere. This region lies roughly between 10 and 50 km, with maximum ozone concentration at about 20 to 25 km. Also called 'ozone layer.'

P

Pad = Launch Pad.

Paraglider—A flexible-winged, kite-like vehicle designed for use in a recovery system for launch vehicles or as a reentry vehicle.

Parameter—1. In general, any quantity of a problem that is not an independent variable. More specifically, the term is often used to distinguish, from dependent variables, quantities which may be more or less arbitrarily assigned values for purposes of the problem at hand. 2. In statistical terminology, any numerical constant derived from a population or a probability distribution. Specifically, it is an arbitrary constant in the mathematical expression of a probability distribution.

Parsec—A unit of distance commonly used to measure interstellar dimensions. It is the distance at which an ASTRONOMICAL UNIT, the mean distance of the earth from the sun, would subtend an angle of one second of an arc. A parsec equals 3.26 LIGHT YEARS.

Part—An element of a component, assembly or subassembly which is not normally subject to further subdivision or disassembly or maintenance purposes. Examples are: resistors, transformers, electron tubes, relays, etc.

Passive—Reflecting a signal without transmission, as "Echo is a passive satellite." Contrasted with "active."

Payload—1. Originally, the revenue-producing portion of an aircraft's load, e.g., passengers, cargo, mail, etc. 2. By extension, that which an aircraft, rocket, or the like carries over and above what is necessary for the operation of the vehicle during its flight.

Peri—A prefix meaning near, as in "perigee."

Perigee—That orbital point nearest the earth when the earth is the center of attraction.

That orbital point farthest from the earth is called "apogee." Perigee and apogee are used by many writers in referring to orbits of satellites, especially artificial satellites, around any planet or satellite, thus avoiding coinage of new terms for each planet and moon.

Perihelion—For an elliptic orbit about the sun, the point closest to the sun.

Pencil-Beam Antenna.—A unidirectional antenna, so designed that cross sections of the major lobe by planes perpendicular to the direction of maximum radiation are approximately circular.

Perihelion—That orbital point nearest the sun when the sun is the center of attraction.

That orbital point farthest from the sun is called "aphelion." The term "perihelion" should not be confused with "parhelion," a form of halo.

Period—The interval needed to complete a cycle. Often used in reference to time of complete orbit.

Perturbation—Specifically, a disturbance in the regular motion of a celestial body, the result of a force additional to those which cause the regular motion.

Photodissociation—The removal of one or more atoms from a molecule by the absorption of a quantum of electromagnetic or photon energy. The energy of the photon absorbed by a system such as an atom or molecule increases in direct proportion to the frequency of the radiation. Simple molecules such as O_2, N_2, CO_2, H_2O which are the primary molecular constituents of the atmosphere can only be photodissociated by ultraviolet or higher frequency (shorter wavelength) light. They are not dissociated by visible light. (See PHOTOIONIZATION.)

Photoionization—The removal of one or more electrons from an atom or molecule by the absorption of a photon. As with PHOTODISSOCIATION, ultraviolet or shorter wavelength light is required to photoionize simple molecules.

Photon—According to the quantum theory of radiation, the elementary quantity, or "quantum" of radiant energy. It is regarded as a discrete quantity having a mass equal to hv/c^2, where h is Planck's constant, v the frequency of radiation, and c the speed of light in a vacuum.

Photon Engine—A projected type of reaction engine in which thrust would be obtained from a stream of electromagnetic radiation.

Although the thrust of this engine would be minute, it may be possible to apply it for extended periods of time. Theoretically, in space, where no resistance is offered by air particles, very high speeds may be built up.

Photosphere—The intensely bright portion of the sun visible to the unaided eye. The photosphere is that portion of the sun's atmosphere which emits the continuous radiation upon which the Fraunhofer lines are superimposed. In one sun model, the photosphere is thought to be below the reversing layer in which Fraunhofer absorption takes place. In another model, all strata are considered equally effective in producing continuous emissions and line absorption.

Physiological acceleration—The acceleration experienced by a human or an animal test subject in an accelerating vehicle.

Pickoff—A sensing device, used in combination with a gyroscope in an automatic pilot or other automatic or robot apparatus, that responds to angular movement to create a signal or to effect some type of control.

Pickup—1. A device that converts a sound, scene, or other form of intelligence into corresponding electric signals (e.g., a microphone, a television camera, or a phonograph pickup.) 2. The minimum current, voltage, power, or other value at which a relay will complete its intended function. 3. Interference from a nearby circuit or system.

Pico—A prefix meaning divided by one million million.

Pioneer—A series of DEEP SPACE PROBES designed to investigate the interplanetary medium. Pioneer I, launched October 11, 1959, determined the radial extent of the earth's MAGNETOSPHERE, and made the first determination of the density of MICROMETEORITES in space. Pioneer 5, launched March 11, 1960 made the first measurements of the effects of a SOLAR FLARE far from the earth's magnetic field, and established a record of radio communication of 22.5 million miles, since exceeded only by MARINER 2.

Pip—Signal indication on the scope of an electronic instrument, produced by a short, sharply peaked pulse of voltage. Also called "blip."

Pitchover—The programed turn from the vertical that a rocket under power takes as it describes an arc and points in a direction other than vertical.

Plages—Clouds of calcium or hydrogen vapor that show up as bright patches on the visible surface of the sun.

Planck's Constant (abbr h)—A constant, usually designated h, of dimensions mass x length^2 x time $-^1$ equal to 6.6252 x 10^{-27} erg sec. It scales the energy of electromagnetic radiation of frequency v such that the radiation appears only in quanta nhv, n being an integer.

Planck's Law—An expression for the variation of monochromatic emittance (emissive power) as a function of wavelength of black-body radiation at a given temperature; it is the most fundamental of the radiation laws.

Planet—A celestial body of the solar system, revolving around the sun in a nearly circular orbit, or a similar body revolving around a star.

The larger of such bodies are sometimes called "principal planets" to distinguish them from asteroids, planetoids, or minor planets, which are comparatively very small.

An inferior planet has an orbit smaller than that of the earth; a superior planet has an orbit larger than that of the earth. The four planets nearest the sun are called "inner planets"; the others, "outer planets." The four largest planets are called "major planets." The world "planet" is of Greek origin meaning, literally, wanderer, applied because the planets appear to move relative to the stars.

Plasma—An electrically conductive gas comprised of neutral particles, ionized particles, and free electrons but which, taken as a whole, is electrically neutral.

A plasma is further characterized by relatively large intermolecular distances, large amounts of energy stored in the internal energy levels of the particles and by the presence of a plasma sheath at all boundaries of the plasma.

Plasmas are sometimes referred to as a fourth state of matter.

Plasma Engine—A reaction engine using magnetically accelerated plasma as propellant.

A plasma engine is a type of electrical engine.

Plasma Jet—A magnetohydrodynamic rocket engine in which the ejection of plasma generates thrust.

Plasma Sheath—1. The boundary layer of charged particles between a plasma and its surrounding walls, electrodes, or other plasmas.

The sheath is generated by the interaction of the plasma with the boundary material. Current flow may be in only one direction across the sheath (single sheath), in both directions across the sheath (double sheath), or when the plasma is immersed in a magnetic field, may flow along the sheath surface at right angles to the magnetic field (magnetic current sheath.)

2. An envelope of ionized gas that surrounds a body moving through an atmosphere at hypersonic velocities.

The plasma sheath affects transmission, reception, and diffraction of radio waves; thus is important in operational problems of spacecraft, especially during reentry.

Pod—An enclosure, housing, or detachable container of some kind, as: (a) an engine pod, (b) an ejection capsule.

Polarization—1. The state of electromagnetic radiation when transverse vibrations take place in some regular manner, e.g., all in one plane, in a circle, in an ellipse, or in some other definite curve.

Radiation may become polarized because of the nature of its emitting source, as is the case with many types of radar antennas, or because of some processes to which it is subjected after leaving its source, as that which results from the scattering of solar radiation as it passes through the earth's atmosphere.

Posigrade Rocket—An auxiliary rocket which fires in the direction in which the vehicle is pointed, used for example in separating two stages of a vehicle.

Pound (abbr lb)—1. A unit of weight equal in the United States to 0.45359237 kilograms. 2. Specifically, a unit of measurement for the thrust or force of a reaction engine representing the weight the engine can move, with 100,000 pounds of thrust.

Precession—Change in the direction of the axis of rotation of a spinning body, as a gyroscope, when acted upon by a torque.

The direction of motion of the axis is such that it causes the direction of spin of the gyroscope to tend to coincide with that of the impressed torque. The horizontal component of precession is called "drift," and the vertical component is called "topple."

Precession of the Equinoxes—The conical motion of the earth's axis about the vertical to the plane of the ecliptic, caused by the attractive force of the sun, moon, and other planets on the equatorial protuberance of the earth.

Pressure (abbr p)—As measured in a vacuum system, the quantity measured at a specified time by a so-

called vacuum gage, whose sensing element is located in a cavity (gage tube) with an opening oriented in a specified direction at a specified point within the system, assuming a specified calibration factor.

The sensitivity of the sensing element is in general not the same for all molecular species, but the gage reading is frequently reported using the calibration factor for air regardless of the composition of the gas. The opening to the gage tube is often carelessly oriented with respect to mass-flow vectors in the gas (which is seldom at rest), and errors due to variations in wall temperatures of tube and system are frequently neglected. The actual total pressure in a high-vacuum system cannot usually be measured by a single gage, but in vacuum technology the term "total pressure" is sometimes used to refer to the reading of a single untrapped gage which responds to condensable vapors as well as permanent gases.

Pressure Suit—A garment designed to provide the human body an environment above ambient pressure so that respiratory and circulatory functions may continue normally, or nearly so, under low-pressure conditions, such as occur at high altitudes or in space without benefit of a pressurized cabin.

Pressurized—Containing air, or other gas, at a pressure that is higher than the pressure outside the container.

Prestage—A step in the action of igniting a large liquid rocket taken prior to the ignition of the full flow, and consisting of igniting a partial flow of propellants into the thrust chamber.

Primary—1. Short for "primary body." 2. Short for "primary cosmic ray."

Primary Body—The spatial body about which a satellite or other body orbits, or from which it is escaping, or towards which it is falling.

The primary body of the moon is the earth; the primary body of the earth is the sun.

Primary Cosmic Rays—High energy particles originating outside the earth's atmosphere.

Primary cosmic rays appear to come from all directions in space. Their energy appears to range from 10^9 to more than 10^{17} electron volts.

Probable Error (abbr pe)—In statistics, that value e_p for which there exists an even probability (0.5) that the actual error exceeds e_p. The probable error e_p is 0.6745 times the standard deviation σ.

The probable error is not "probable" in the normal sense of the word.

Probability—The chance that a prescribed event will occur, represented as a number greater than zero but less than one. The probability of an impossible event is zero, and that of an inevitable event is one.

Probe—Any device inserted in an environment for the purpose of obtaining information about the environment. Specifically, an instrumented vehicle moving through the upper atmosphere or space or landing upon another celestial body in order to obtain information about the specific environment.

Almost any instrumented spacecraft can be considered a probe. However, earth satellites are not usually referred to as "probes." Also, almost any instrumented rocket can be considered a probe. In practice, rockets which attain an altitude of less than one earth radius (4000 miles) are called "sounding rockets," those which attain an altitude of more than one earth radius are called "probes" or "space probes." Spacecraft which enter into orbit around the sun are called "deep-space probes." Spacecraft which enter into orbit around the sun are called "deep-space probes." Spacecraft designed to pass near or land on another celestial body are often designated "lunar probe," "Martian probe," "Venus probe," etc.

Prominence—A filament-like protuberance from the chromosphere of the sun.

Prominences can be observed (optically) whenever the sun's disk is masked, as during an eclipse or using a coronagraph; and can be observed instrumentally by filtering in certain wavelengths, as with a spectroheliograph. A typical prominence is 6,000 to 12,000 km thick, 60,000 km high, and 200,000 km long.

Propellant—Short for "rocket propellant."

Prospector—The successor to the Surveyor program with the mission of obtaining detailed photographs of the lunar surface, SOFT-LANDING mobile, automated laboratories on the moon, and returning lunar soil samples to the earth for analysis.

Proton—A positively-charged subatomic particle having a mass slightly less than that of a neutron but about 1847 times greater than that of an electron. Essentially, the proton is the nucleus of the hydrogen isotope $_1H^1$ (ordinary hydrogen stripped of its orbital electron.) Its electric charge ($+4.8025 \times 10^{-10}$ esu) is numerically equal, but opposite in sign, to that of the electron.

Protons and neutrons comprise atomic nuclei; they are both classed as "nucleons."

Prototype—Spacecraft or element thereof which is undergoing or has passed environmental and other tests which qualify design for fabrication of flight units or elements thereof.

Proving Stand—A test stand for reaction engines, especially rocket engines.

Purge—To rid a line or tank of residual fluid, especially of fuel or oxygen in the tanks or lines of a rocket after a test firing or simulated test firing.

Q

q = **Dynamic Pressure.**

Quantization—The process of converting from continuous values of information to a finite number of discrete values.

Quantum theory—The theory (first stated by Max Planck before the Physical Society of Berlin on December 14, 1900) that all electromagnetic radiation is emitted and absorbed in "quanta" each of magnitude $h\nu$, h being Planck's constant and ν the frequency of the radiation.

Quiet Sun—See "Year of the Quiet Sun."

R

Radar Astronomy—The development of powerful radar transmitters, large antennas, and very sensitive receivers allows the detection of high frequency radio waves (radar) reflected off the nearby members of the solar system. Signals reflected from the moon were first detected in 1945, while the first signals from Venus were unambiguously received in 1961. A careful analysis of the reflected signal gives information as to the distance, velocity of approach or recession, surface roughness, rate of rotation, and dielectric constant of the planet. A large antenna with an aperture of 1000 feet under construction in Puerto Rico should allow radar detection of Mercury, Mars, some of the asteroids, the satellites of Jupiter, and the planet Jupiter itself, if the dense Jovian atmosphere does not absorb all of the incident radar signal.

Radiation—Short for "electromagnetic radiation," "nuclear radiation."

Radiation Belts—See VAN ALLEN BELTS, MAGNETOSPHERE.

Radiation Pressure (abbr Pr)—Pressure exerted upon any material body when electromagnetic radiation is incident upon body.

This pressure is manifested whenever the electromagnetic momentum in a radiation field is changed, and is exactly twice as great when the radiation is reflected at normal incidence as it is when the radiation is entirely absorbed at normal incidence. The magnitude of any radiation pressure effect is directly proportional to the intensity of the radiation, and is very small by most standards.

On a perfectly reflecting surface Pr = v/3 where v = radiation density the amount of radiative energy per unit volume in the space above the surface. Radiation pressure has perceptible effect on the orbit of earth satellites, especially those with a large reflecting surface such as Echo.

Radiation Shield—1. A device used on certain types of instruments to prevent unwanted radiation from biasing the measurement of a quantity. 2. A device used to protect bodies from the harmful effects of nuclear radiation, cosmic radiation, or the like.

Radiator—1. Any source of radiant energy, especially electromagnetic radiation. 2. A device that dissipates heat from something, as from water or oil, not necessarily by radiation only.

Generally, the application of the terms "radiator" (in sense 2) or "heat exchanger" to a particular apparatus depends upon the point of view: If the emphasis is upon merely getting rid of heat, "radiator" is most often used, or sometimes "cooler"; if the emphasis is upon transferring heat, "heat exchanger" is used—but these distinctions do not always hold true.

Radio Astronomy—The earth's atmosphere is transparent to electromagnetic radiation in only two frequency bands, or "windows". The familiar "optical window" lies in the wavelength interval from 3000 Å to a few MICRONS. Practically all astronomy and astrophysics prior to thirty years ago was based on the information received through this window. Since that time, the development of sensitive electronic receivers and the construction of large antennas has allowed the detection of radio waves from astronomical sources which pass through the atmosphere in the "radio window," from a wavelength of a few millimeters to a few tens of meters. Radio astronomy has furnished information about the moon, the planets, the sun, the interstellar medium (in particular the distribution of atomic hydrogen), supernova fragments, and the structure of galaxies.

Radiometer—A device used to measure some property of electromagnetic radiation. In the visible and ultraviolet regions of the spectrum, a photocell or photographic plate may be thought of as a radiometer. In the infrared, solid state detectors such as photoconductors, lead sulfide cells and thermocouples are used, while in the radio and microwave regions, vacuum tube receivers, often with parametric or maser preamplifiers, are the most sensitive detectors of electromagnetic radiation.

Radio Meteor—A meteor detected by the reflection of a radio signal from the meteor trail of relatively high ion density (ion column).

Such an ion column is left behind a meteoroid when it reaches the region of the upper atmosphere between about 80 and 120 km, although occasionally radio meteors are detected at higher altitudes.

Radiosonde—A balloon-borne instrument for the simultaneous measurement and transmission of meteorological data.

Radio Telescope—A device for receiving, amplifying, and measuring the intensity of radio waves originating outside the earth's atmosphere.

Ranger—The initial United States program for the investigation of the moon, and the region between the moon and the earth. Early versions of the Ranger are designed to provide closeup television photographs of the lunar surface, and to rough-land seismographs on the moon.

Rarefied Gas Dynamics—The study of the phenomena related to the molecular or noncontinuum nature of gas flow at low densities.

Rayleigh-Jeans Law—An approximation to PLANCK'S LAW for blackbody radiation valid in the limit of long wavelengths. It is almost always of sufficient accuracy in the radio and microwave regions of the spectrum.

Reaction Control System—A system of controlling the attitude of a craft when outside the atmosphere by using jets of gas in lieu of aerodynamic control surfaces.

Reaction Engine—An engine that develops thrust by its reaction to ejection of a substance from it; specifically, such an engine that ejects a jet or stream of gases created by the burning of fuel within the engine.

A reaction engine operates in accordance with Newton's third law of motion, i.e., to every action (force) there is an equal and opposite reaction. Both rocket engines and jet engines are reaction engines.

Readout—1. The action of a radio transmitter transmitting data either instantaneously with the acquisition of the data or by play of a magnetic tape upon which the data have been recorded. 2. In computer operations to extract information from storage.

Readout Station—A recording or receiving radio station at which data are received from a transmitter in a probe, satellite, or other spacecraft.

Real Time—Time in which reporting on events or recording of events is simultaneous with the events.

For example, the real time of a satellite is that time in which it simultaneously reports its environment as it encounters it; the real time of a computer is that time during which it is accepting data.

Recombination—The process by which a positive and a negative ion join to form a neutral molecule or other neutral particle.

Recovery—The procedure or action that obtains when the whole of a satellite, or a satellite instrumentation package, or other part of a rocket vehicle is recovered after a launch; the result of this procedure.

Recycle—In a countdown: To stop the count and to return to an earlier point in the countdown, as in "we have recycled, now at T minus 80 and counting." Compare hold. In testing: to repeat a group or series of tests.

Red Shift—In astronomy, the displacement of observed spectral lines toward the longer wavelengths of the red end of the spectrum. Compare **space reddening.**

The "red shift" in the spectrum of distant galaxies has been interpreted as evidence that the universe is expanding.

Reentry—The event occurring when a spacecraft or other object comes back into the sensible atmosphere after being rocketed to altitudes above the sensible atmosphere; the action involved in this event.

Reentry Vehicle—A space vehicle designed to return with its payload to earth through the sensible atmosphere.

Reentry Window—The area at the limits of the earth's atmosphere through which a spacecraft in a given trajectory can pass to accomplish a successful reentry.

Regenerative Cooling—The cooling of a part of an engine by the propellant being delivered to the combustion chamber; specifically, the cooling of a rocket—engine combustion chamber or nozzle by circulating the fuel or oxidizer, or both, around the part to be cooled.

Regenerator—A device used in a thermodynamic process for capturing and returning to the process heat that would otherwise be lost. Also called "a heat exchanger".

Relative Humidity (abbr rh)—The (dimensionless) ratio of the actual vapor pressure of the air to the saturation vapor pressure.

Relativistic Particles—In general, pertaining to material, as a subatomic particle, moving at speeds which are an appreciable fraction of the speed of light.

Relativity—A principle that postulates the equivalence of the description of the universe, in terms of physical laws, by various observers, or for various frames of reference.

Rendezvous—The event of two or more objects meeting at a preconceived time and place.

A rendezvous would be involved, for example, in servicing or resupplying a space station.

Resonance—1. The phenomenon of amplification of a free wave or oscillation of a system by a forced wave or oscillation of exactly equal period. The forced wave may arise from an impressed force upon the system or from a boundary condition. The growth of the resonant amplitude is characteristically linear in time. 2. Of a system in forced oscillation, the condition which exists when any change, however small, in the frequency of excitation causes a decrease in the response of the system.

Resonance Frequency—A frequency at which resonance exists. Also called "resonant frequency."

In case of possible confusion, the type of resonance must be indicated; as "velocity resonance frequency."

Retrorocket—(From 'retroacting'.) A rocket fitted on or in a spacecraft, satellite, or the like to produce thrust opposed to forward motion.

Revolution—Motion of a celestial body in its orbit; circular motion about an axis usually external to the body.

In some contexts the terms "revolution" and "rotation" are used interchangeably; but with reference to the motions of a celestial body, "revolution" refers to the motion in an orbit or about an axis external to the body, while "rotation" refers to motion about an axis within the body. Thus, the earth revolves about the sun annually and rotates about its axis daily.

Rills—Narrow, sharply-defined features that extend across the surfaces of the lunar MARIA. They may be cracks or wrinkles in the lava beds.

Rocket—1. A projectile, pyrotechnic device, or flying vehicle propelled by a rocket engine. 2. A rocket engine.

Rocket Engine—A reaction engine that contains within itself, or carries along with itself, all the substances necessary for its operation or for the consumption or combustion of its fuel, not requiring intake of any outside substance and hence capable of operation in outer space. Also called **"Rocket Motor."**

Rocket Propellant—Any agent used for consumption or combustion in a rocket and from which the rocket derives its thrust, such as a fuel, oxidizer, additive, catalyst, or any compound or mixture of these. "Rocket propellant" is often shortened to "propellant."

Rocketsonde—Meteorological rocket.

Rockoon—A high-altitude sounding system consisting of a small solid-propellant research rocket launched from a large plastic balloon.

The rocket is fired near the maximum altitude of the balloon flight. It is a relatively mobile rocket-sounding system, and has been used extensively from shipboard.

Roentgen—That amount of x or gamma radiation sufficient to produce ions carrying one electrostatic unit of charge in one cm³ of air. The term is loosely used to signify that amount of any ionizing radiation which produces the same effect as one roentgen of gamma rays. The average person receives about 0.1 roentgen per year of total body radiation from COSMIC RAYS and the radioactivity of the earth. Five hundred roentgens of full body radiation is fatal to most people.

Roll—The rotational or oscillatory movement of an aircraft or similar body which takes place about a longitudinal axis through the body—called "roll" for any amount of such rotation.

Rotation—Turning of a body about an axis within the body, as the daily rotation of the earth. See **Revolution.**

Rumble—A form of combustion instability, especially in a liquid-propellant rocket engine, characterized by a low-pitched, low-frequency rumbling noise; the noise made in this kind of combustion.

S

Satellite—1. An attendant body that revolves about another body, the primary; especially in the solar system, a secondary body, or moon, that revolves about a planet. 2. A man made object that revolves about a spatial body, such as Explorer I orbiting about the earth.

Scale Height—A measure of the relationship between density and temperature at any point in an atmosphere; the thickness of a homogeneous atmosphere which would give the observed temperature or pressure.

Schlieren—(German, "streaks," "striae.") 1. Regions of different density in a fluid, especially as shown by special apparatus. 2. A method or apparatus for visualizing or photographing regions of varying density in a field of flow.

Screaming—A form of combustion instability, especially in a liquid-propellant rocket engine, of relatively high frequency and characterized by a high-pitched noise.

Scrub—To cancel a scheduled rocket firing, either before or during countdown.

Secondary Cosmic Rays—Secondary emission in the atmosphere stimulated by primary cosmic rays.

Seeing—A blanket term long used by astronomers for the disturbing effects produced by the atmosphere upon the image quality of an observed astronomical body.

Selenocentric—Relating to the center of the moon; referring to the moon as a center.

Selenographic—1. Of or pertaining to the physical geography of the moon. 2. Specifically, referring to positions on the moon measured in latitude from the moon's equator and in longitude from a reference meridian.

Semicircular Canals—Tubes located in the inner ear which play a part in the mechanism of balance and orientation.

Sensible Atmosphere—That part of the atmosphere that offers resistance to a body passing through it. See **Effective Atmosphere.**

Sensor—The component of an instrument that converts an input signal into a quantity which is measured by another part of the instrument. Also called "sensing element."

Service Tower—Gantry Scaffold.

Shadowgraph—A picture or image in which steep density gradients in the flow about a body are made visible, the body itself being presented in silhouette.

Shaker—An electromagnetic device capable of imparting known, and/or controlled vibratory acceleration to a given object.

Shield—Short for "radiation shield"; "heat shield."

Shock Tube—A relatively long tube or pipe in which very brief high-speed gas flows are produced by the sudden release of gas at very high pressure into a low-pressure portion of the tube; the high-speed flow moves into the region of low pressure behind a shock wave.

The shock tube is used as a tool in the study of gases or as a kind of intermittent wind tunnel.

Shock Waves—The phenomena in compressible fluid flow where a positive pressure disturbance propagates and eventually steepens into a shock front. In the limit of a perfect fluid conductor, such variables as velocity, pressure density, temperature, and magnetic field can change discontinuously across a shock front. A high-velocity shock can be driven by passing a large electric current through a highly ionized PLASMA. Highly ionized shocks which propagate through a magnetic field are called MAGNETOHYDRODYNAMIC (MHD) shock waves.

Shoran—(From "short range navigation.") A precision electronic position fixing system using a pulse transmitter and receiver and two transponder beacons at fixed points.

Shot—An act or instance of firing a rocket, especially for the earth's surface, as "the shot carried the rocket 200 miles."

Shroud—The nosecone of a space vehicle when it is used only as a shield for passage through the atmosphere from launch to orbit. It is usually jettisoned when orbital speed is achieved.

Sidereal—Of or pertaining to the stars.

Sloshing—The back-and-forth splashing of a liquid fuel in its tank, creating problems of stability and control in the vehicle.

Slug—A unit of mass; the mass of a free body which if acted upon by a force of 1 pound would experience an acceleration of 1 foot per second per second.

Slurry—A suspension of fine solid particles in a liquid.

Soft Radiation—Radiation which is absorbed by an absorber equivalent to 10 centimeters of lead or less. Radiation which can penetrate more than 10 centimeters of lead is termed "hard radiation."

Solar Atmospheric Tide—Vertical motion of the atmosphere due to thermal or gravitational action of the sun.

Solar Cell—A photovoltaic device that converts sunlight directly into electrical energy.

Solar Constant—The rate at which solar radiation is received on a surface perpendicular to the incident radiation and at the earth's mean distance from the sun, but outside the earth's atmosphere.

Solar Cycle—The observed fluctuation from maximum to minimum of the incidence of SUNSPOTS, and the activity of SOLAR FLARES and prominences, with a mean period of 11.2 years. There is also evidence that the overall magnetic field of the sun fluctuates with the same period.

Solar Flare—Sudden local increase in the intensity of the light of hydrogen on the sun. Some solar flares are associated with the expulsion of charged particles and the production of radio bursts.

Solar Plasma—See **Solar Wind**.

Solar Radiation—The total electromagnetic radiation emitted by the sun.

Solar Wind—A stream of protons constantly moving outward from the sun. Synonymous with solar plasma.

Solid Propellant—Specifically, a rocket propellant in solid form, usually containing both fuel and oxidizer combined or mixed and formed into a monolithic (not powdered or granulated) grain. See **Rocket Propellant** and **Grain**.

Solid-Propellant Rocket Engine—A rocket engine using a solid propellant. Such engines consist essentially of a combustion chamber containing the propellant, and a nozzle for the exhaust jet, although they often contain other components, as grids, liners, etc. See **Rocket Engine** and **Solid Propellant**.

Sonic—1. Aerodynamics: Of or pertaining to the speed of sound; that moves at the speed of sound, as in "sonic flow"; designed to operate or perform at the speed of sound, as in "sonic leading edge." 2. Of or pertaining to sound, as in "sonic amplifier".

Sonic Boom—A noise caused by the shock wave that emanates from an aircraft or other object traveling in the atmosphere at or above the speed of sound.

Sonic Speed—The speed of sound; by extension, the speed of a body traveling at Mach 1.

Sound travels at different speeds through different mediums and at different speeds through any given medium under different conditions of temperature, etc. In the standard atmosphere at sea level, sonic speed is approximately 760 miles per hour.

Sounding—1. In geophysics, any penetration of the natural enviroment for scientific observation. 2. In meteorology, same as upper-air observation. However, a common connotation is that of a single complete radiosonde observation.

Sounding Rocket—A rocket designed to explore the atmosphere within 4,000 miles of the earth's surface.

Space—1. Specifically, the part of the universe lying outside the limits of the earth's atmosphere. 2. More generally, the volume in which all spatial bodies, including the earth, move.

Space-Air Vehicle—A vehicle that may be operated either within or above the sensible atmosphere.

Spacecraft—Devices, manned or unmanned, which are designed to be placed into an orbit about the earth or into a trajectory to another celestial body.

Space Equivalent—A condition within the earth's atmosphere that is virtually identical, in terms of a particular function, with a condition in outer space.

For example, at 50,000 feet the low air pressure and the scarcity of oxygen create a condition, so far as respiration is concerned, that is equivalent to a condition in outer space where no appreciable oxygen is present; thus, a physiological space equivalent is present in the atmosphere.

Space Medicine—A branch of aerospace medicine concerned specifically with the health of persons who make, or expect to make, flights into space beyond the sensible atmosphere.

Space Probe—See **Probe**.

Space Reddening—The observed reddening, or absorption of shorter wavelengths, of the light from distant celestial bodies caused by scattering by small particles in interstellar space. Compare **red shift**.

Space Simulator—A device which simulates some condition or conditions existing in space and used for testing equipment, or in training programs.

Space System—A system consisting of launch vehicle(s), spacecraft and ground support equipment.

Space Vehicle—A launch vehicle and its associated spacecraft.

Spatial—Pertaining to space.

Spatio—A combining form meaning "space."

Specific Impulse—A performance parameter of a rocket propellant, expressed in seconds, and equal to thrust (in pounds) divided by weight flow rate (in pounds per second). See **Thrust**.

Spectrometer—An instrument which measures some characteristics such as intensity, of electromagnetic radiation as a function of wavelength or frequency.

Spectrum—1. In physics, any series of energies arranged according to wavelength (or frequency); specifically, the series of images produced when a beam of radiant energy, such as sunlight, is dispersed by a prism or a reflecting grating. 2. Short for "electromagnetic spectrum" or for any part of it used for a specific purpose as the 'radio spectrum' (10 kilocycles to 300,000 megacycles).

Sputtering—Dislocation of surface atoms of a material bombarded by high-energy atomic particles.

Stage—A propulsion unit of a rocket, especially one unit of a multistage rocket, including its own fuel and tanks.

Stage-and-a-Half—A liquid-rocket propulsion unit of which only part falls away from the rocket vehicle during flight, as in the case of booster rockets falling away to leave the sustainer engine to consume remaining fuel.

Standard Atmosphere—1. A hypothetical vertical distribution of atmospheric temperature, pressure, and density which, by agreement, is taken to be representative of the atmosphere for purposes of pressure altimeter calibrations, aircraft performance calculations, aircraft and rocket design, ballistic tables, etc. 2. A standard unit of atmospheric pressure exerted by a 760 mm column of mercury at gravity (980.665 cm/sec²) at temperature 0°C.

One standard atmosphere = 760 mm Hg
= 29.9213 in. Hg
= 1013.250 mb

Stationary Orbit—An orbit in which an equatorial satellite revolves about the primary at the same angular rate as the primary rotates on its axis. From the primary, the satellite thus appears to be stationary over a point on the primary.

Stefan-Boltzmann Law—One of the radiation laws which states that the amount of energy radiated per unit time from a unit surface area of an ideal black body is proportional to the fourth power of the absolute temperature of the black body.

Stoichiometric—Of a combustible mixture, have the exact proportions required for complete combustion.

Stratosphere—The region of the atmosphere lying on the average between about 12 and 60 kilometers; it has a temperature which is either constant or increases with altitude, and is therefore stable against convection. The upper part of the stratosphere is at a temperature of about 260°K, and is heated by the absorption of ultraviolet light by OZONE.

Subassembly—An assembly within a larger assembly.

Subatomic Particle—A component of an atom, such as an electron, a proton, a meson, etc.

Subsonic—In aerodynamics, dealing with speeds less than the speed of sound (see sonic speed), as in "subsonic aerodynamics."

Subsystem—A functioning entity within a major system (launch vehicle, spacecraft, etc.) of a space system such as propulsion subsystem of a launch vehicle or attitude control subsystem of a spacecraft. Also considered a system.

Sudden Ionospheric Disturbance—(Often abbreviated SID). A complex combination of sudden changes in the condition of the ionosphere, and the effects of these changes.

Sunspot—A relatively dark area on the surface of the sun, consisting of a dark central umbra surrounded by a penumbra which is intermediate in brightness between the umbra and the surrounding photosphere.

Sunspots usually occur in pairs with opposite magnetic polarities. They have a lifetime ranging from a few days to several months. Their occurrence exhibits approximately an eleven year period (the sunspot cycle).

Sunspot Cycle—A cycle with an average length of 11.1 years, but varying between about 7 and 17 years, in the number and area of sunspots, as given by the relative sunspot number. This number rises from a minimum of 0-10 to a maximum of 50-140 about four years later, and then declines more slowly.

An approximate 11-year cycle has been found or suggested in geomagnetism, frequency of aurora, and other ionospheric characteristics.

Eleven-year cycles have been suggested for various tropospheric phenomena, but none of these has been substantiated.

Supersonic—Pertaining to speeds greater than the speed of sound. Compare **ultrasonic.**

Surveyor—The United States program for the scientific exploration of the surface and subsurface of the moon, following the RANGER program. Surveyor A, designed to make SOFT LANDINGS on the moon, will explore the physical, chemical, and mineralogical properties of the moon at the landing site. It is expected to be launched using an ATLAS-Centaur in the last half of 1964. Surveyor B will be placed in a stable orbit about 60 miles above the lunar surface. It will allow a scan by television of the visible and hidden faces of the moon, and will be used for a preliminary selection of APOLLO landing sites, as well as permit studies of radiation near the lunar surface, and the gravity and mass distribution of the moon. The launching of a total of seven Surveyor A's and 5 Surveyor B's is currently planned.

Sustainer Engine—An engine that maintains the velocity of a missile rocket vehicle once it has achieved its programmed velocity by use of booster or other engine.

This term is applied, for example, to the remaining engine of the Atlas after the two booster engines have been jettisoned. The term is also applied to a rocket engine used on an orbital glider to provide the small amount of thrust now and then required to compensate for the drag imparted by air particles in the upper atmosphere.

Sweep—The motion of the visible dot across the face of a cathode-ray tube, as a result of scanning deflection of the electron beam.

Synchronous Rotation—Rotation of a planet or satellite about its axis with the same period as its revolution about a parent body, with the axis of rotation assumed perpendicular to the plane of the orbit. A consequence of this type of rotation is that the planet or satellite always presents the same side or face to the parent body. The moon rotates synchronously with respect to the earth, and Mercury with respect to the sun. There is some evidence that Venus also rotates synchronously with respect to the sun, or at least has a day comparable in length to its year. Synchronous rotation is usually assumed to be caused by TIDAL DRAG acting during the planet's past.

Synchrotron Radiation—Electromagnetic radiation generated by the acceleration of charged relativistic particles (usually electrons) in a magnetic field. Radiation of this kind was first encountered in the particle accelerator called the synchrotron. It is an important mechanism for the generation of nonthermal, continuous radio waves in supernova fragments and galactic halos.

Synchronous Satellite—An equatorial west-to-east satellite orbiting the earth at an altitude of 22,300 statute miles at which altitude it makes one revolution in 24 hours, synchronous with the earth's rotation.

Synergic Curve—A curve plotted for the ascent of a rocket, space-air vehicle, or space vehicle calculated to give the vehicle an optimum economy in fuel with an optimum velocity.

This curve, plotted to minimize air resistance, starts off vertically, but bends towards the horizontal between 20 and 60 miles altitude.

System—1. An organized arrangement in which the operational results of two or more functioning entities can be predicted.

2. Used in term, space system, to mean the launch vehicle, spacecraft and ground support used in a space launch and flight.

3. One of major subdivisions of a space system, such as launch vehicle, spacecraft, or ground support system.

4. One of major functioning entities within a major subdivision of a space system, such as the guidance system of a launch vehicle or the attitude control system of a spacecraft.

In sense 4, synonymous with subsystem.

Systems Intergration—The management process by which the systems of a project (for example, the launch vehicle, the spacecraft, and its supporting ground equipment and operational procedures) are made compatible, in order to achieve the purpose of the project or the given flight mission.

T

Tektite—A small glassy body containing no crystals, probably of meteoritic origin, and bearing no antecedent relation to the geological formation in which it occurs.

Tektites are found in certain large areas called "strewn fields." They are named as minerals with the suffix "ite," as "australite," found in Australia; "billitonite," "indochinite," and "rizalite," found in Southeast Asia; "bediasite" from Texas, and "moldavite" from Bohemia and Moravia.

Telemetry—The science of measuring a quantity or quantities, transmitting the measured value to a distant station, and there interpreting, indicating, or recording the quantities measured.

Terminator—The line separating illuminated and dark portions of a nonluminous body, as the moon.

Terrestrial—Pertaining to the earth.

Thermal Radiation—The electromagnetic radiation emitted by a hot blackbody, such as the filament of a lamp. The distribution of energy with frequency of thermal radiation is given by PLANCK'S LAW. The sun radiates approximately as a blackbody with a temperature of about 5700°K. (See NONTHERMAL RADIATION.)

Thermocouple—A temperature-sensing element which converts thermal energy directly into electrical energy. In its basic form it consists of two dissimilar metallic electrical conductors connected in a closed loop. Each junction forms a thermocouple.

If one thermocouple is maintained at a temperature different from that of the other, an electrical current proportional to this temperature difference will flow in the circuit; the value of this proportionality varies with materials used. For meteorological purposes, couples of copper and constantan are frequently used which generate approximately 40 microvolts per °C of couple temperature difference.

Thermodynamic—Pertaining to the flow of heat or to thermodynamics.

Thermodynamics—The study of the relationships between heat and mechanical energy.

Thermonuclear—Pertaining to a nuclear reaction that is triggered by particles of high thermal energy.

Thermosphere—The region of the atmosphere, above the MESOSPHERE, in which there is strong heating and increasing temperature, resulting from the PHOTO-DISSOCIATION of O_2 and the PHOTOIONIZATION of N, N_2 and O. It extends roughly from an altitude of 90 to 600 kilometers.

Thrust—1. The pushing force developed by an aircraft engine or a rocket engine. 2. Specifically, in rocketry, the product of propellant mass flow rate and exhaust velocity relative to the vehicle.

Thrust-to-Weight Ratio—The ratio of the engine THRUST of a rocket to the total vehicle weight. This ratio must be greater than one to lift the vehicle off the ground.

Tidal Drag—The damping of a planet or satellite's rotation produced by frictional losses associated with tides raised either in the solid body of the planet or satellite, or in seas upon its surface. (See SYNCHRONOUS ROTATION.)

Tiros—A series of United States meteorological satellites designed to observe the cloud coverage of the earth and measure the heat radiation emitted by the earth in the infrared.

Topside Sounder—A satellite designed to measure ion concentration in the ionosphere from above the ionosphere.

Tore or Torus—In geometry the surface described by a conic section, especially a circle, rotating about a straight line in its own plane or the solid of revolution enclosed by such a surface. Hence, the extended sections of a manned space laboratory, having a generally circular configuration and rotating around a stationary central section.

Torr. (From Torricelli)—Suggested international standard term to replace the English term "millimeter of mercury" and its abbreviation "mm of Hg" (or the French "mm de Hg").

Both "Tor" and "Torr" have been used in Germany, the latter spelling being more common and the one officially adopted by the German Standards Association. The "Torr" is defined as 1/760 of a standard atmosphere or 1,013,250/760 dynes per square centimeter. This is equivalent to defining the "Torr" as 1333.22 microbars and differs by only one part in seven million from the International Standard millimeter of mercury. It is recommended that "Torr" not be abbreviated. However, the abbreviation τ has been used. The prefixes "milli" and "micro" are attached without hyphenation.

Tracking—The process of following the movement of a satellite or rocket by radar, radio, and photographic observations.

Trajectory—In general, the path traced by any body, as a rocket, moving as a result of externally applied forces.

Trajectory is loosely used to mean "flight path" or "orbit."

Transducer—A device capable of being actuated by energy from one or more transmission systems or media, as a microphone, a thermocouple, etc.

Transfer Orbit—In interplanetary travel an elliptical trajectory tangent to the orbits of both the departure planet and the target planet.

Transit—1. The passage of a celestial body across a celestial meridian; usually called "meridian transit." 2. The apparent passage of a celestial body across the face of another celestial body or across any point, area, or line.

Translunar—Of or pertaining to space outside the moon's orbit about the earth.

Transponder—A combined receiver and transmitter whose function is to transmit signals automatically when triggered by an interrogating signal.

Transponder Beacon—A beacon having a transponder.

T-Time—Any specific time, minus or plus, as referenced to "zero," or "launch" time, during a countdown sequence that is intended to result in the firing of a rocket propulsion unit that launches a rocket vehicle or missile.

Troposphere—That portion of the atmosphere from the earth's surface to the tropopause; that is, the lowest 10 to 20 km of the atmosphere. The troposphere is characterized by decreasing temperature with height, appreciable vertical wind motion, appreciable water vapor content, and weather. Dynamically, the troposphere can be divided into the following layers: surface boundary layer, Ekman layer, and free atmosphere.

U

Ullage—The amount that a container, such as a fuel tank, lacks of being full.

Ultrasonic—Of or pertaining to frequencies above those that affect the human ear, i.e., more than 20,000 vibrations per second.

The term "ultrasonic" may be used as a modifier to indicate a device or system intended to operate at an ultrasonic frequency.

Although "supersonic" was formerly used in acoustics synonymously with "ultrasonic," this usage is now rare.

Ultraviolet Radiation—Electromagnetic radiation shorter in wavelength than visible radiation but longer than X-rays; roughly, radiation in the wavelength interval between 10 and 4000 angstroms.

Ultraviolet radiation from the sun is responsible for many complex photochemical reactions characteristic of the upper atmosphere, e.g., the formation of the ozone layer through ultraviolet dissociation of oxygen molecules followed by recombination to form ozone.

Umbilical Cord—Any of the servicing electrical or fluid lines between the ground or a tower and an upright rocket missile or vehicle before the launch. Often shortened to 'umbilical'.

Upper-Air Observation—A measurement of atmospheric conditions aloft, above the effective range of a surface weather observation. Also called "sounding," "upper-air sounding."

V

Van Allen Belt, Van Allen Radiation Belt—[For James A. Van Allen, 1915-.] The zone of high-intensity radiation surrounding the earth beginning at altitudes of approximately 1000 kilometers.

The radiation of the Van Allen belt is composed of protons and electrons temporarily trapped in the earth's magnetic field. The intensity of radiation varies with the distance from the earth, thus the Van Allen belt is often considered as two belts or zones, with maxima of intensity at approximately 3600 kilometers and 16,000 kilometers.

Vehicle—Specifically, a structure, machine, or device, such as an aircraft or rocket, designed to carry a burden through air or space; more restrictively, a rocket craft.

This word has acquired its specific meaning owing to the need for a term to embrace all flying craft, including aircraft and rockets.

Vehicle Control System—A system, incorporating control surfaces or other devices, which adjusts and maintains the altitude and heading, and sometimes speed, of the vehicle in accordance with signals received from a guidance system.

The essential difference between a control system and a guidance system is that the control system points the vehicle and the guidance system gives the commands which tell the control system where to point. However, the control system maintains the instantaneous orientation of the vehicle without specific commands from the guidance system.

Vernier Engine—A rocket engine of small thrust used primarily to obtain a fine adjustment in the velocity and trajectory of a ballistic missile or space vehicle just after the thrust cutoff of the last propulsion engine, and used secondarily to add thrust to a booster or sustainer engine. Also called 'vernier rocket'.

Vertical—The direction in which the force of gravity acts.

Visible Radiation—Electromagnetic radiation lying within the wavelength interval to which the human eye is sensitive, which is from approximately 0.4 to 0.7 micron (4000 to 7000 angstroms). This portion of the electromagnetic spectrum is bounded on the shortwavelength end by ultraviolet radiation, and on the longwavelength end by infrared radiation.

Voyager—A series of spacecraft which will be launched by the United States as a successor to the MARINER program. Voyager craft, launched using the Saturn, will be directed into stable orbits around Mars and Venus, and will attempt to SOFT-LAND instrumented payloads on both these planets. Others may be used for flyby studies of Mercury and Jupiter.

W

Waveguide—A system of material boundaries capable of guiding electromagnetic waves.

SOURCE: NASA, "What's Up There."

Weight—The force with which an earth-bound body is attracted toward the earth.

Weightlessness—A condition in which no acceleration, whether of gravity or other force, can be detected by an observer within the system in question.

Any object falling freely in a vacuum is weightless, thus an unaccelerated satellite orbiting the earth is "weightless" although gravity affects its orbit. Weightlessness can be produced within the atmosphere in aircraft flying a parabolic flight path.

Waiver—Granted use or acceptance of an article which does not meet specified requirements.

Whistler—A radio-frequency electromagnetic signal sometimes generated by lightning discharges.

This signal apparently propagates along a geomagnetic line of force, and often "bounces" several times between the Northern and Southern Hemispheres. Its name derives from the sound heard on radio receivers.

X

X-Ray—Electromagnetic radiation of very short wavelength, lying within the wavelength interval of 0.1 to 100 angstroms (between gamma rays and ultraviolet radiation', 'Roentgen ray).

X-rays penetrate various thickness of all solids and they act upon photographic plates in the same manner as light. Secondary X-rays are produced whenever X-rays are absorbed by a substance, in the case of absorption by a gas, this results in ionization.

Y

Yaw—1. The lateral rotational or oscillatory movement of an aircraft, rocket, or the like about a transverse axis. 2. The amount of this movement, i.e., the angle of yaw.

Year of the Quiet Sun—Eleven year low period in solar activity which is expected between April, 1964 and December, 1965. The international program for maximum observation and research in this interval is termed International Year of the Quiet Sun (IQSY).

Z

Zenith—That point of the celestial sphere vertically overhead. The point 180° from the zenith is called the "nadir."

Zero G = Weightlessness.

Appendix B

Aeronautics and Space Activities of Other Agencies

National Aeronautics and Space Council

Introduction

The National Aeronautics and Space Council was established by the National Aeronautics and Space Act of 1958 to advise and assist the President on matters pertaining to aeronautics and space activities conducted by the departments and agencies of the United States. That same Act also established the National Aeronautics and Space Administration.

The Vice President of the United States is the Chairman of the Council; its members are the Secretary of State, the Secretary of Defense, the Secretary of Transportation, the Administrator of the National Aeronautics and Space Administration, and the Chairman of the Atomic Energy Commission. The Secretary of Transportation was added to the Council on September 23, 1970, with the enactment of an amendment to the National Aeronautics and Space Act of 1958.

Formal meetings of the Council are held to review and assess policies, plans, programs, and accomplishments of aeronautics and space activities, and to decide issues or to make recommendations to the President. Council members frequently meet to consider important issues which do not require the involvement of the Chairman or all members. Much of the Council's business is conducted through the Council staff.

The Executive Secretary is a member of two National Security Council subcommittees which review and recommend programs and projects involving U.S. international space cooperation. Staff activity throughout the year has supported his contributions to these committees.

Specific Activities

During 1970, the Council was concerned with and involved in many important aeronautics and space activities. Among these were:

Supersonic Transport (SST).—The Council members and staff strongly supported the SST program because it can contribute materially to the maintenance of U.S. world leadership in civil aviation. The advanced technology being applied in the design and construction of this aircraft will provide higher speed, greater capacity, and resulting higher productivity to compete effectively with the Anglo-French Concorde and Russian TU–144 aircraft which are flying today. The current SST program is to build and test two prototype aircraft. Data from the flight test program are essential for decisions regarding production. Properly instrumented flights of the prototype SST and other aircraft will also provide important data which can be used to help resolve the environmental issues. The Council staff has been actively reviewing the progress of government and industry sponsored programs to reduce jet aircraft noise and smoke. In particular, consider-

able activity has been focused on planning for comprehensive research programs to reduce sideline noise.

Short Haul Air Transportation.—The Council approved a study by the staff to examine short haul air transportation to determine its potential role in the national transportation system. In aviation, short haul concerns flights of 500 miles or less. New short take-off and landing (STOL) aircraft promise more economical operations, less noise, and less congestion on and around airports. The Council staff has served as a focus working with federal agencies, airlines, and aerospace manufacturers and a continuing dialogue on STOL technology has been established. In addition, joint coordination meetings have been held among airlines, federal agencies, and the Council staff to address common requirements for STOL vehicles. Interagency cooperation on environmental issues is excellent and has led to additional research and development on quieter jet engines. Coordination is also excellent in other vital aspects of the program, such as STOL ports and air traffic control. In addition, there are indications that new regional developments can be accomplished through an improved short haul air transportation system.

Civil Aviation Research and Development (CARD) Policy Study.—The CARD Policy Study was undertaken jointly by NASA and DOT, as recommended by Senate Report 957, to determine the criteria for federal involvement in civil aviation research and development. The specific objectives of the CARD Policy Study are to identify significant policy issues, to recommend courses of action relative to these issues, to identify CARD areas of emphasis and the criteria for setting levels of effort in these areas, and to assess the benefits which will accrue to the nation from this research and development.

Aeronautical and Marine Services Satellites.—The Council reviewed the policy implications of aeronautical and marine services satellites for civil, military, and international users. To assist, the Council staff undertook to identify the principal national and international organizations, both public and private, which have responsibilities for or an interest in surveillance, navigation position fixing, air traffic control, aeronautical and maritime communications, emergency location and rescue operations, and similar functions which could be facilitated by aeronautical and marine services satellites. The most pressing near-term need which aeronautical services satellites can satisfy appears to be reliable communications with aircraft operating in oceanic areas. The Council staff participated in an Executive Office working group chaired by the Office of Telecommunications Policy (OTP) to examine the communications segment of the aeronautical services satellite.

Earth Resources Survey Program.—Another issue addressed by the Council was the national earth resources survey program which employs devices located on the earth's surface, in aircraft, and in spacecraft to sense remotely and record data relating to earth resources and the condition of the environment. The Executive Secretary convened an ad hoc interagency group to identify relationships between the existing experimental Earth Resources Survey Program and a future operational program as well as the roles and responsibilities of government agencies in both phases. In addition, the group was requested to determine alternatives for interagency coordination and for management of the program.

An in-depth examination of the program was made in management, data acquisition, data handling, and user requirements. The study was based on past and current activities both from an experimental and operational viewpoint, and was aimed at determining the direction and schedule for future activity. A preliminary summary report was furnished to the Office of Management and Budget to support the fiscal year 1972 budget deliberations and the full report will be completed in early 1971.

Communications Satellites.—Assistance was given in defining the government's role in developing commercial domestic satellite systems, and also in establishing guidance on the use of satellites for broadcast purposes for the U.S. delegation to the United Nations Committee on the Peaceful Uses for Outer Space.

Geodetic Data Policies.—Because of increased scientific interest, both national and international, in advanced theories of continental drift coupled with the high precision measurement made possible by the use of lasers and orbiting satellites, the Council called for a review of the U.S. policies on the release of geodetic data. New policies were established which will permit NASA to assume the U.S. leadership in an international cooperative program which is intended to make precise geodetic measurements under the auspices of COSPAR.

Review and Approval Procedures for Use of Radioisotopes in Space.—A guide for the use of small radioisotope sources in space was approved by the Council members in July. It had been prepared by the Council staff with the guidance and assistance of the principal agencies involved.

International Cooperation in the Post-Apollo Program.—The Council members and the staff have been active in the area of international cooperation to insure that the benefits of space are shared with all mankind. Cooperation in aeronautical, navigation, communications, and earth resources satellites continues both bilaterally and multilaterally with other nations. The space shuttle and space station are subjects of serious discussions with the European community; definitive proposals from Europe are anticipated. Based on these discussions, the European countries will decide whether or not to develop an independent large booster capability, or to rely on the purchase of U.S. boosters. If the latter course is followed, European funds will be available for use in post-Apollo cooperative ventures.

Department of Defense

Introduction

The Department of Defense concluded 1970 with a growing list of achievements in space and aeronautics. During the year, the space efforts of the DOD encompassed communications, nuclear detection, navigation, geophysics, solar radiation monitoring, and efforts in numerous areas of space technology. Testing of terminal equipment and the development of operational procedures, doctrine, and multiple access techniques advanced satellite communications capabilities. The sixth pair of Vela nuclear detection satellites were successfully launched from Cape Kennedy by a Titan IIIC space booster on April 8. These spacecraft provide an extended capability to view surface and low altitude detonations while still maintaining a constant monitoring of deep space. Continued operational use was made of the Transit navigation satellite system. An improved satellite (SOLRAD) for monitoring electromagnetic and particle emissions from the sun was prepared for launch. Data from a SOLRAD satellite in orbit since 1968 was monitored throughout 1970 and passed to other users in support of military communications operations and research, scientific research efforts, and the Apollo program.

During 1970, significant progress was made toward fulfilling the country's need for modern military aircraft. Engineering development of the advanced carrier-based fighter (F–14) produced a test version which has made its first flight. The new engine for an improved tactical antisubmarine warfare aircraft (S–3A) was readied for in-flight evaluation. Fabrica-tion of evaluation models of key avionics systems began, and early in 1970 a highly successful mockup review of the aircraft was held. Continued development of carrier-based aircraft with sophisticated electronic warfare capabilities (EA–6B) and with the capability of an improved airborne early warning system (E–2C) is leading to an improved readiness of the fleet to operate in any warfare environment. Many hours of operational flight experience during 1970 by Marine Corps pilots utilizing British Harrier (AV–8A) close-support aircraft has laid the essential groundwork for systematically adding this aircraft and the V/STOL concept of operations to our fleet capability during the upcoming year. The Air Force's F–15 successfully completed its aircraft preliminary design review in September and is proceeding on schedule. The F–15 will be a twin-engine fighter optimized for air superiority. Contracts were awarded in June for development of a new Air Force bomber, the B–1. This aircraft will take advantage of the many advances that have been made in airframe and engine technology during the past few years. The Air Force completed a feasibility demonstration of the radar techniques to be employed on the AWACS aircraft. That aircraft will provide command and control for interceptor forces as well as sustaining air operations such as counterair interdiction, close air support, rescue, airlift, etc. Recent flight tests of the Army's Cheyenne helicopter have shown none of the technical problems that plagued earlier development efforts. In firing tests all Cheyenne weapons subsystems have demonstrated excellent accuracy.

Space Activities

DOD Communications Satellite Program.—The DOD communications satellite program is currently divided into two broad categories, long distance and tactical. The long distance systems are characterized by communications involving a controlled network and are an integral part of the Defense Communications System. Tactical satellite communications networks provide multiple access service to many small terminal users such as airplanes, ships, and mobile land vehicles operating in a relatively undisciplined communications environment.

Defense Satellite Communications System.—The long distance satellite communications capability is provided by the Defense Satellite Communications System (DSCS). The mission of the DSCS is to provide secure communications in support of critical command, control, intelligence, warning, presidential, and other special user requirements.

Phase I of the program, the Initial Defense Satellite Communications System, has continued to perform satisfactorily during the past year. The Phase I DSCS now consists of 23 operational satellites and 29 earth terminals. Phase I DSCS satellites have a low power capability and limited bandwidth and operate in near synchronous orbits. They are designed for automatic turnoff during the time frame 1972–74.

Operational use of the Phase I DSCS continues to satisfy unique and vital communications requirements in accordance with the DSCS mission. One of these requirements being provided by the Phase I DSCS is the transmission of high resolution photographs.

Acquisition of Phase II of the DSCS, an improvement of the initial system, has proceeded satisfactorily during the past year. This effort was started in early 1969 with the award of a contract for procurement of six high-power geostationary satellites equipped with both earth coverage and steerable narrow beam antennas. The initial launch of two satellites, on a Titan IIIC space booster, is scheduled for mid-1971. The Phase II satellites will have significantly higher power and bandwidth capability permitting the provision of many additional channels of communications. Further improvement in satellite communications service will result from positioning Phase II satellites in synchronous equatorial orbit. The Phase I terminals will be modified to capitalize on the greatly increased capability of the Phase II satellites. Improved terminal performance and the full-time availability of a synchronous satellite will provide significant improvement in satellite communications service.

New Phase II ground and shipboard terminals including more efficient modulation equipment are now being developed by the Army and the Navy respectively. The new terminals will be much more reliable and have large communications capacity.

The numbers of Phase II satellites and new terminals to be initially deployed are now being studied. Other Government agencies and certain allied governments will also be provided service through the Phase II satellites using their own earth terminals.

Tactical Satellite Communication Program.—The initial phase of this experimental program was to investigate the use of spaceborne communication repeaters to satisfy selected communication needs of our mobile forces. The effort involved the Lincoln Experimental Satellite No. 6 (LES–6), the TACSAT I satellite, and 65 terminals installed in aircraft, jeeps, trucks, ships, and submarines. Operational testing will continue. The data obtained during the test program is being analyzed to determine the design of future operational systems. The orbital performance of LES–6 and TACSAT I has been satisfactory. LES–6 is located over the mid-Atlantic in a geostationary orbit. TACSAT I is being moved to a new position. At these locations, communication links with the CONUS and overseas locations are being established.

International Cooperation.—The United States has negotiated agreements with the United Kingdom and NATO whereby we will develop, procure, and launch advanced communications satellites for their use. Two satellites each were procured on a reimbursement basis for the United Kingdom and NATO. The spacecraft are nearly identical except that the NATO version has a squinted antenna to focus more output power in the NATO area of interest while the United Kingdom satellites have full earth coverage antennas to provide service from the United Kingdom as far away as Singapore. Both satellite systems are useable with the DSCS and, if required, the United States, United Kingdom, and NATO could supplement each other's individual capability.

The first United Kingdom SKYNET satellite was launched late in 1969. Tests have been conducted since that time aimed at the operational implementation of the full SKYNET space and ground system. The second SKYNET satellite was launched in August 1970, but failed to achieve orbit. A new Memorandum of Understanding covering the implementation of the next generation SKYNET II system was signed by the United States and the United Kingdom in April 1970. Under this Memorandum of Understanding the follow-on satellites will be produced by the United Kingdom with the assistance of the United States. The satellites will be launched by the United States, with the first launch expected in 1972.

The first NATO communications satellite was successfully launched by the United States in March 1970. The NATO ground system is being produced and the initial system operation is expected early in 1971. The second NATO satellite is due to be launched early in 1971. Planning is proceeding within NATO on a follow-on satellite communication program which will be required by 1975.

The DOD continued its participation in the North Atlantic Treaty Organization's cooperative tactical satellite communications test program, using the synchronous LES–6 satellite and a network of small, tactical terminals built and operated by the program participants Belgium, Canada, the Federal Republic of Germany, Italy, the Netherlands, Norway, the United Kingdom, the United States, and the Technical Centre, Supreme Headquarters, Allied Powers Europe.

Spaceborne Nuclear Detection (Vela).—Two new Vela satellites were launched by means of a Titan IIIC launch vehicle into circular orbits at approximately 18 earth radii in April of 1970. The new Vela satellites were the sixth pair in a series that began in 1963 and included launches in 1964, 1965, 1967, and 1969.

The Vela satellite program is a joint responsibility of the Department of Defense and the Atomic Energy Commission and is managed by the Advanced Research Projects Agency (ARPA). The purpose of the program is to demonstrate the feasibility of using satellite-borne sensors to detect nuclear explosions in the atmosphere and in space.

Vela satellites also carry sensors that monitor the radiation background at their altitudes. Data on the radiation background is used by Department of Defense and civilian meteorologists in preparing space radiation forecasts; NASA has used the data during Apollo flights.

Titan III Space Booster.—The Titan III family of launch vehicles continues to be used extensively for DOD payloads. A common buy of the Titan III B, C, and D configuration vehicles, made this year, included for the first time three vehicles for NASA use in launching their future application and scientific satellites. To date 48 Titan III launches have been made, 25 vehicles are now in production and 22 additional vehicles have been approved for follow-on production.

Geodetic Satellites.—DOD completed the observational phase of the DOD Geodetic Satellite Program during 1970. Data reduction and the integration of the results obtained from the four systems used in the program, i.e. the BC–4 Camera, the PC–1,000 Camera system, and the SECOR and Doppler systems, are planned for completion by June 1972. The goal of the DOD Geodetic Satellite Program is to define more precisely the earth's size, shape, and gravity field, in addition to providing geodetic positions for points on the earth's surface. DOD has phased out the BC–4 Camera system, the PC–1,000 Camera system, and the SECOR

electronic system. The Doppler system, using the Navy navigational satellites as well as geodetic doppler satellites, has been selected as the single system for continued DOD efforts in the geodetic satellite area. Geodetic satellite activities will be directed toward meeting special requirements for worldwide geodetic positioning and for additional defining and verifying of the results obtained to date. In 1970, the Air Force continued the South American geodetic net densification program in support of mapping and charting efforts in South America. The Army Corps of Engineers completed the remainder of the SECOR equatorial network in 1970. The observational data is now being reduced and analyzed. The PAGEOS program utilizing the BC–4 Camera system was also completed in 1970 and data reduction and analysis is now underway. DOD efforts in the geodetic satellite area will be directed to specific positioning requirements using the commercial type geodetic receiver doppler system (Geoceivers) now available and in use. A joint Army and Marine test program using Navy developed doppler backpack ground equipment was initiated during 1970 to continue the investigation of the potential application of satellite systems to tactical positioning requirements of the services. During 1970 the Navy Doppler Tracking Network (TRANET) tracked the Transit satellites from 13 permanent stations and 8 mobile vans to improve the earth's gravity model and center of mass coordinates. The satellite geodesy program has now determined the harmonic coefficients of the gravity model to the equivalent of the 14th degree and order and selected higher terms. In addition, the positions of nine global sites were determined this past year.

Navigation Satellite Activity.—The Navy navigation satellite system (Transit), which became fully operational in 1968, continued its operation during the year in support of the fleet. In addition, studies and limited experiments have been conducted to help define the next generation of defense navigation satellite system. Initial results indicate that a precision, three-dimension spaceborne position-fixing and navigation system should be feasible. Application analysis and cost effectiveness studies will continue before a decision is made on the next generation navigation satellite system.

Space Ground Support

DOD National Range and Tracking Facilities.—Department of Defense space activities are principally supported by the Air Force Eastern Test Range, the Space and Missile Test Center (which includes the Air Force Western Test Range), the Air Force Satellite Control Facility, the Navy Pacific Missile Range, and the Army White Sands Missile Range. Each is available to any Government user who may require its support.

Eastern Test Range.—During the past year the Eastern Test Range (ETR) continued its resizing to a posture for support of the primary DOD mission workload. As a result of this action the ETR is expected to evolve into a modest, but modern and efficient ballistic missile and space launch support facility capable of expansion if necessary. Support to other agencies such as NASA continues, but all additive costs to the ETR (those costs over the costs of supporting the primary DOD mission workload) in providing this support are reimbursable.

A joint DOD and NASA study concerning consolidation of common support services at the ETR and the NASA Kennedy Space Center (KSC) was also conducted during the year. As a result, actions are currently underway at the ETR and KSC to consolidate eight support services by fiscal year 1972. Five services will be consolidated under KSC and three under the ETR. After implementation, this consolidation is expected to save the Government over $1 million per year in the operation of these two facilities.

Western Test Range.—In April 1970 the Air Force organized the Space and Missile Test Center (SAMTEC). SAMTEC operates the Western Test Range and the Aerospace Test Wing launch organizations at both Patrick AFB, Fla., and Vandenberg AFB, Calif.

During 1970 several changes were made to SAMTEC's range capability. The range instrumentation ship fleet has continued to be reduced with the transfer of the one remaining Apollo ship, the USNS *Vanguard,* to full NASA control. The range has developed a new instrumented site in the Pacific for terminal support. During 1970, the Broad Ocean Scoring System (BOSS) installed on the range ship USNS *Watertown* was used for the first time. Under the redistribution of resources made available because of the cancellation of the Manned Orbiting Laboratory Program (MOL) the range acquired the MOL computerized aerospace ground equipment. This system used to display vehicle telemetry data during prelaunch and launch phases, is being phased into operation and will replace similar leased equipment.

Satellite Control Facility.—During 1970 satellite support activities showed no marked change from previous years. There were no major facility constructions at any of the stations. The Space Ground Link Subsystem and Univac 1230 computer installation was made at the Indian Ocean station, Seychelles Islands, thus completing the upgrading of all network stations. A major procurement action was initiated for three 46-foot antennas to replace the 14-foot antennas at the New Hampshire Station, Hawaii Tracking Station and

Vandenberg Tracking Station. Study and analysis continues in order to improve the reliability and responsiveness of the overall systems.

Aeronautics Activities

C–5 Heavy Logistics Transport Aircraft.—The C–5A is the product of a successful development and procurement program that has extended over several years. It will provide for the first time a capability to deploy 100 percent of the Army's outsize combat equipment by air. Because of its large payload capacity and unique flotation characteristic, the C–5A is capable of rapidly airlifting large quantities of equipment and combat personnel to meet worldwide contingencies.

The research, development, test, and evaluation phase of the C–5A program is nearing completion. Major static structural testing should be completed in May 1971 and flight demonstrations of 100 percent structural integrity will follow. Aircraft participating in the flight test program have accumulated over 5,132 hours of flying time as of October 31, 1970. Contractor and Air Force flight testing is scheduled for completion by the end of calendar year 1971 and using command operational suitability testing is already well underway.

Results of the flight test program indicate that the C–5A will meet or exceed all operational requirements. It has flown at a maximum gross takeoff weight of almost 400 tons—a world record, 17 tons in excess of its designed maximum takeoff weight. In addition, the C–5A has achieved a maximum speed of 0.89 Mach, a maximum altitude of 40,200 feet, a flight duration of 21 hours and has landed in less than 1,300 feet.

The first of six C–5A's was delivered to the MAC Transition Training Unit at Altus AFB on December 17, 1969. A total of 10 additional aircraft, delivered to operational units at Charleston AFB and Travis AFB are now flying regularly scheduled channel traffic missions to the Pacific and European theaters. Deliveries to operational units are scheduled to continue at a two-per-month rate and the last of the total planned procurement of 81 C–5A's will be delivered in February 1973.

The total cost of the C–5A program is currently estimated at $4.6 billion, including the cost of research and development, support equipment, and initial spares.

F/FB–111 Aircraft.—The F/FB–111 aircraft program is composed of various models which include four tactical versions, F–111A, F–111D, F–111E, and F–111F; one bomber, the FB–111; and one model designed for use by the Australian Air Force, the F–111C.

All F-111A's have been delivered. Production delivery of F-111E and FB-111 aircraft will be completed during 1971. Contractor and Air Force test efforts at Fort Worth, Tex., Eglin AFB, Fla. and Edwards AFB, Calif., are continuing in those areas which normally proceed throughout the production delivery phase. The bulk of this continuing work is in the areas of weapons clearances, static, and fatigue testing and performance parameters for altitude and airspeed.

Since the development and testing of the airframe and the airplane's general subsystems are essentially complete, development of advanced U.S. models of the F-111 has concentrated largely on the avionics system. The F-111D model which incorporates the expensive and more advanced Mark II avionics package is in production with delivery of the first aircraft scheduled for mid-1971. A less expensive and less advanced avionics system is being designed into the F-111F. This mission design series will not have the Mark II attack radar and integrated displays but will retain the Mark II inertial navigation set and digital computer system. In addition, the F-111F aircraft will have an improved propulsion system, utilizing new higher thrust TF-30-P-100 engines.

An F-111 accident in December 1969 resulted in the establishment of an extensive inspection program and a cold proof test of the airframe. This effort is proceeding as planned and a great deal of progress has been made. Considerable experience has been gained in the nondestructive inspection of critical parts and the cold proof test of the aircraft. Although some parts have been found to be in need of rework because of welding flaws and surface discontinuities due to tool marks, grinder burns, and corrosion pitting, no forging defects similar to the one which caused the December 1969 accident have been found. The first aircraft to complete the inspection program was returned to the using command in July 1970. Program completion is scheduled in July 1971.

The Tactical Air Command has resumed extensive combat crew training and operational mission qualification at Nellis AFB, Nev. The first deployment of F-111E aircraft to USAFE occurred in September 1970. Delivery of FB-111 aircraft to SAC at Carswell AFB, Tex., for use in the Combat Crew Training Wing was also resumed.

The first F-111C was accepted in September 1968. Subsequent acceptances were delayed because of modification work but are now anticipated after the modifications are satisfactorily completed.

F-14 Carrier-Based Tactical Fighter.—Engineering development of the F-14, a new advanced carrier-based tactical fighter, was initiated on February 3, 1969. The F-14A will utilize the TF30-P412 engine and the AWG-9 missile control system which will control Phoenix, Sparrow, and Sidewinder missiles and 20 mm. guns. The F-14A will have an improved area air defense capability and will be superior to the F-4 in other fighter roles. It will also have a significant air-to-ground capability. The development is on schedule. First flight of the F-14A occurred on December 21, 1970.

Engineering development of an advanced technology engine, sponsored jointly by the Navy and Air Force, was initiated early in 1970. This program will provide a very high thrust-to-weight ratio engine for the F-14B. The F-14B with its significantly improved performance will be capable of countering the predicted threats in the late 1970's and early 1980's.

F-15 Advanced Tactical Fighter.—The F-15 is a new twin-engine single place Air Force fighter, optimized for air superiority and designed to replace the F-4E as the Air Force's first line fighter in the mid-1970s. Air superiority design features emphasized in the F-15 include outstanding turn, climb, and acceleration characteristics and outstanding pilot visibility. The airframe development contract was awarded on December 31, 1969, after a 1-year contract definition competition among vying contractors. In March 1970 a contract was awarded for development of engines for both the F-15 and the Navy F-14B fighters. A contract for the F-15 radar was also awarded in September. The F-15 program is proceeding on schedule and successfully completed the first major review milestone in September 1970 which was the aircraft preliminary design review.

A-7 Attack Aircraft.—The joint Air Force-Navy development program has resulted in the operational deployment of the versatile A-7 light attack aircraft. Navy A7E's were employed in combat just 18 months after the first flight of the aircraft. Its performance in combat amply demonstrated the flexibility and capability that were design requirements. The Air Force A7D is being delivered to the Tactical Air Command, having completed the basic contractor and Air Force test programs with marked success. Pilot training is being conducted at Luke Air Force Base, and the first operational squadron at Myrtle Beach Air Force Base will soon reach a combat-ready status.

B-1 Bomber.—Engineering development of the basic B-1 airframe and engine was begun after contract award on June 5, 1970. The first development test is presently scheduled for late calendar year 1974. This date is subject to change if the planned funding profile is changed.

No production decision has been made. The present pace of the development program, however, is such as to permit achieving an initial operational capability in the late 1970's, if so desired.

Detailed design of the airframe and engine is now underway and has produced some configuration changes, particularly in the empennage and wing root areas. Cost versus performance tradeoffs have resulted in some modifications in the initial design concept without sacrifice of any significant performance characteristics.

The major improvements provided by the B–1 as compared to the characteristics of the B–52 are: greater low-level penetration speed; greater range vs. payload; reduced radar cross section and infrared signature; and an ability to operate from relatively short runways thereby permitting greater dispersal capability.

Carrier-Based Anti-Submarine Warfare Aircraft (S–3A).—The engineering development of the S–3A continued throughout 1970. The full system mockup review was held on schedule in March 1970. The TF–34 high bypass engine which is being designed specifically for the S–3A completed 4,000 hours of running time on the ground and is now ready in flight tests mounted on an engine test bed aircraft. Through the use of advanced ASW sensors and a digital computer, the S–3A will be able to provide significant improvement over the S–2 capability in searching large areas of the ocean, detecting modern nuclear submarines and in localizing and destroying submarines. Avionics subsystems including MAD, radar, and an infrared classification device progressed according to the planned development schedule with the fabrication of models for evaluation. The S–3A, with a four man crew, will operate in the 400-knot speed range at altitudes over 30,000 feet en route to operating areas and still be able to operate economically at the lower altitudes required during certain phases of antisubmarine operations.

E–2C Development.—The E–2C aircraft will provide carrier based airborne early warning (AEW) for air defense of the fleet and command and control of Navy aircraft in air-to-air combat, air-to-surface strikes, search and rescue operations, and general air traffic control.

Continued development and procurement of the E–2C, which is the latest of the E–2 family of AEW systems, will result in increased operational reliability and availability, improved radar performance (including an additional operational capability over and near land), and will alleviate quantitative AEW aircraft shortages.

EA–6B Development.—The EA–6B aircraft system development will be a tactical airborne electronic jammer aircraft which will provide support for carrier and advanced base strike aircraft. The EA–6B system will use the basic A–6 airframe, modified for a four-man crew, with new powerful jamming devices. The development is proceeding on schedule. Operational type testing conducted in 1970 has been very successful.

A–X Aircraft.—The Air Force is initiating development of the A–X, a new close air support aircraft optimized for effective support of friendly ground forces. The conceptual A–X, a single-place twin-engine aircraft providing STOL characteristics and excellent maneuverability, emphasizes long loiter, large payloads, and ease of maintenance. A Development Concept Paper was approved by the Deputy Secretary of Defense in April 1970 and request for proposals released to industry in May 1970. Six proposals, submitted in August 1970, have been evaluated and two contractors have been selected to build two prototype aircraft each for a competitive flyoff phase leading to the selection of the final contractor for full development and production.

Airborne Warning and Control System (AWACS).—In 1967 the Air Force completed the Overland Radar Technology program which demonstrated feasibility of the proposed radar techniques for AWACS. The Air Force completed a long lead radar component program in 1970 and recently selected a contractor for the AWACS program.

The AWACS will provide an airborne air surveillance capability and command, control, and communication functions in a military version of a subsonic commercial jet. The distinguishing technical feature of this weapon system will be the capability of its radar to detect and track aircraft operating at high or low altitudes over both land and water. The AWACS will provide command and control for interceptors and will control tactical air operations such as counter-air, interdiction, close air support, rescue, airlift, etc. The flexibility of the AWAC System will permit its employment at any level of military action ranging from show-of-force through general war, with capability to serve as an Airborne Command Post, Tactical Air Control Center, Airborne Direct Air Support Center, and Airborne Control and Reporting Center.

Helicopter Research.—Army has continued research to improve rotor craft capabilities. Progress has been made in providing rotor wing technology for future engineering development and in providing technology for specific helicopter concepts. A better understanding of the fundamental boundary layer flow over rotor blades has contributed to obtaining improved performance and control of helicopters. Advances have been made in basic air foil shapes that have provided new insight into the aerodynamics of rotor blades; the results permit improved payload performance. Contributions have also made to the understanding of the rotor dynamics and control of hingeless rotor systems.

On specific concepts, progress has been made in a compound helicopter research program. Various configurations were flight tested including teetering, servo-flap hingeless and flapping main rotors in conjunction with lifting wings and auxiliary power sources. Maximum speeds of 185 to 236 knots were demonstrated. Vibrational levels lower than those of conventional helicopters operating at the same air speeds were noted. The results showed that increased air speed and payload capabilities are possible with insignificant increases in vibration levels.

The Advance Research Projects Agency's Quiet Helicopter Program, which is under the technical direction of the Army, continues to make very satisfactory progress. The first phase of the program was completed early in 1970 and all technical objectives were either attained or exceeded.

The second and final phase of the Quiet Helicopter Program is in progress and is scheduled for completion early in 1971. It is expected that the noise level of the test vehicle, the OH–6 helicopter, will be reduced to less than 10 percent of its original level.

Heavy Lift Helicopter (HLH).—The Army is initiating a development program of full size critical helicopter components using competing concepts to establish a technology and cost base for future HLH aircraft. Typical components which might be selected for development include large rotors, propulsion and transmission drive systems, flight control systems, and load handling devices. The HLH is envisioned as a 110,000-pound gross weight tactical and logistics helicopter with a sea level payload capability of 22½ tons based on shipboard and standard C–5A pallet size loads. It would be able to transport virtually all of the Army and Marine tactical ground equipment. Recent test results using the largest available competing concepts in helicopters and standard military sea and ground vehicles confirmed the feasibility of using helicopters to unload large shipboard loads under adverse sea state during both day and night at a high productivity rate.

A Development Concept Paper was approved by the Deputy Secretary of Defense in September 1970 and requests for quotations were issued on November 14, 1970.

AH–56A Cheyenne.—The Cheyenne helicopter development program is nearing completion of the contractor phase of testing. Aimed at the Army's requirement for an advanced attack helicopter to seek out and destroy enemy armor by day, night or in adverse weather, the Cheyenne now offers great promise of fulfilling those objectives. In recent firing tests all Cheyenne weapons subsystems have demonstrated excellent accuracy. In flight tests its improved rotor control system has shown none of the technical problems which plagued earlier development efforts. The night vision system, while not yet flight tested, has demonstrated very sharp picture quality. Within the coming year the Army expects to be able to make a Cheyenne production recommendation based on successful demonstrated performance and cost-effectiveness.

AV–8A Harrier.—The Harrier is a single-seat, single fan jet transonic aircraft, manufactured in the United Kingdom. It is the operational version of the P–1127 Kestrel which was funded, developed, and evaluated by the United States, United Kingdom, and Federal Republic of Germany. The Royal Air Force has equipped two operating squadrons with the Harrier, and the U.S. Marine Corps and U.S. Air Force are actively participating in the British operational employment to take full advantage of their experience. During 1970 flight experience with Harrier passed the 7,000 hour mark. The U.S. Marine Corps will receive 12 AV–8A Harrier V/STOL aircraft commencing in 1971, for use in the close air support role. During 1970 detailed plans were formulated for a Navy-Marine Corps large scale investigation into the concept of V/STOL operations, and this investigation will commence in September 1971 utilizing the Harrier.

CX–84.—The Canadian Government was originally planning to fabricate and flight test three CX–84, tilt-wing aircraft. Flight testing was to be followed by military operational suitability testing. A shortage of program funds has forced the Canadians to reduce the program scope and they now plan to test and evaluate only one aircraft. This aircraft has been under contractor testing since its maiden flight in February 1970. Contractor testing will be completed in October 1971, and the Government operational suitability trials that follow will be completed in March 1972. The Army is monitoring the program.

Supporting Research and Technology

Continental United States Over-the-Horizon Radar System (CONUS OTH).—During 1970, the Air Force initiated program contract definition activities aimed at defining a CONUS OTH backscatter radar system for future development and deployment. This planned system will provide surveillance, detection, and early warning of a manned bomber attack against the CONUS. The radar system promises a significant increase in range and low altitude coverage in comparison to our present line-of-sight radar systems.

Advanced Liquid Rocket Technology.—In 1970, Air Force development of liquid rocket engine technology continued with emphasis upon demonstration of component performance critical to development of an engine for reusable space launch vehicle application. Specific task objectives of this project were continuously coordinated with NASA through the joint Advanced Chemical Rocket Engine (ACRE) working group to assure proper phasing of technology development. In August 1970, the Air Force project was concluded successfully, and the technology phased into the NASA space shuttle engine development program. This accomplishment by the Air Force has been a keystone in the implementation of the 1969 Space Task Group proposals to initiate development of a national reusable space transportation system, and provides confidence that the propulsion objectives for development of a reusable space launch vehicle can be met.

Upper Atmosphere Investigation.—The U.S. Army Ballistic Research Laboratory has been analyzing the data obtained during rocket firings conducted during 1969. From firings made in Alaska, electron density profiles have been obtained for those parts of the rocket flights where the ray paths did not pass through the barium clouds. From the cooperative polar-cap absorption data, electron density profiles have been constructed for the frequency pair 36 and 144 MHz, preliminary electron currents have been determined from the Langmuir probe observations, and preliminary absorption and absorption rate values have been obtained for the frequency pair 9 and 18 MHz. These results will contribute to the understanding of events occurring when radars look toward the polar horizon or when communications pass to or from the polar regions such that the signal passes through that part of the atmosphere where the aurora and polar cap absorption occurs.

Space Object Identification.—During 1970, ARPA continued to measure physical characteristics of objects in earth orbit. These measurements include radiation signatures in both the visible and infrared regions of the spectrum. This program is carried out at the ARPA Maui Optical Station, on Mount Haleakala in Maui.

Solar Radiation Monitoring Satellite Program (SOLRAD).—The Navy's SOLRAD program is an excellent example of a space science effort which has provided high operational utility. SOLRAD IX, launched in 1968, is continuing solar radiation monitoring to broaden knowledge of the physics of the sun and the mechanism of emission of solar particle, ultraviolet and X-ray radiation. This knowledge, in turn, will lead to development of techniques for predicting solar-induced disturbances affecting some electronic and space systems operations. During 1970 preparation continued to orbit SOLRAD X in January 1971, to further develop equipment and techniques for space

environment monitoring while providing data for research, development, and operating efforts. During 1970 SOLRAD provided solar activity information in direct support of Apollo activities.

Telemetered data received at the Navy research laboratory acquisition facility is relayed to the SOLRAD Data Operations Center at NRL. Real-time analog and stored digital telemetry data are converted to flux values. Daily pass-by-pass and flare profile messages are transmitted via the USAF operated Solar Observing and Forecasting Network for use by the National Oceanic and Atmospheric Administration Space Disturbance Forecast Center at Boulder, Colo., and the USAF Solar Forecast Center at the NORAD Cheyenne Mountain Complex, Colo. Predictions of periods of solar activity, which are likely to cause ionospheric disturbances, are transmitted to the Naval Communications Command for use in the formulation of Navy alerts to all communicators.

Advanced Satellite Secondary Propulsion Systems.—In 1970 the Air Force initiated development of an electric colloid thruster which will operate in the high micropound and low millipound thrust range to perform satellite attitude control and station keeping functions. The colloid thruster will have a specific impulse which is at least four times higher than current state-of-the-art thrusters, and will be designed to operate in the pulse and steady state modes. Design and fabrication of colloid thruster critical components are underway for integrated test and evaluation. Subsequent development phases provide for the fabrication of a prototype thruster, life testing, and space flight to demonstrate performance and compatibility of this advanced concept thruster in a satellite system.

Spacecraft Technology and Advanced Reentry Tests (START).—The Air Force's current efforts in developing technology for maneuverable reentry spacecraft consists of the PILOT (PIloted LOw-speed Tests) program and the Space Transportation System (STS) studies. PILOT was instituted to provide aerodynamic and stability and control data from Mach 2.0 to horizontal landing. It is a follow-on to the PRIME program which provided flight data from reentry conditions to approximately Mach 2. A total of 18 flights of the X–24A PILOT vehicle from 40,000 to 47,000 feet launch altitudes have been completed successfully. Eight were powered flights with the XLR–11 rocket engine and a supersonic speed of 1.15 Mach was achieved on October 14, 1970. Flow separation and stability characteristics of the X–24A vehicle at supersonic speed and during low-speed maneuvering are being investigated. A total of 30 X–24A flights are scheduled to be completed by the end of fiscal year 1971. The STS studies were undertaken by the Air Force to evaluate the capability of various system concepts, primarily developed under NASA Phase B studies, to meet Air Force mission requirements (payload, cross range, etc.). Follow-on studies and technology work in this area will depend on the results of the curent space shuttle effort.

Space Experiments Support Program.—The Air Force Space Experiments Support Program (SESP) provides spaceflights for proof tests of advanced technology applicable to new military space systems and for DOD research and development experiments. In 1970, an Army spacecraft to test a tactical positioning system rode into orbit as a secondary payload on the NASA launch of a weather satellite. Contracts were let for three launches for 1971 to orbit eight technological payloads and seven scientific experiments expected to provide demonstrations and data that will contribute to new or improved DOD systems.

Advanced Space Power Supply Technology.—Mission analyses show that next generation military satellite systems will need larger, longer life power supplies to attain mission performance and reliability requirements. To meet these requirements development efforts are underway to increase the power level and lifetime capabilities of spacecraft solar arrays and rechargeable battery systems. In 1970, development of a flexible, rollup type solar cell array has continued with emphasis on fabrication of a qualification model for ground test. In parallel with this test, fabrication of a flight model is proceeding on schedule for demonstration of this high performance array on a Space Experiments Support Program flight vehicle in late 1971. Successful demonstration of this technology will enable a 50-percent reduction in weight and volume over current solar cell array power systems in the 500 watts to 20 kilowatt power range.

Advanced Turbine Engine Gas Generator (ATEGG).—The ATEGG program is an Air Force advanced development program in which advanced state-of-the-art turbine engine components are assembled into demonstrator engines and tested. It is based on the fact that individual component operation in an isolated rig test environment is not completely representative of that component's operation when integrated into a high-performance engine and used in widely varying operational conditions.

The latest component technology and engine design philosophy for future weapon systems are demonstrated in these turbine engine demonstrators to provide an advanced realistic performance base from which to plan future weapon systems.

Over the past year, four participating engine contractors have demonstrated advances in thrust-to-weight ratio, overall efficiencies, smaller combustors and higher operating temperatures and pressure ratios. By including four participants, the Air Force achieves a secondary objective which is to maintain a broad, competitive industrial base from which to procure advanced engines for future weapon systems.

Advanced Propulsion Subsystem Integration (ASPI).—The ASPI program is an Air Force advanced development program for developing criteria, capability and techniques for integrating airframe and propulsion systems.

The goal of this program is to minimize engine-airframe interface problems. Starting with the forebody engine inlet and inlet interaction, all of the components through the engine and airframe back through the exhaust nozzle are analyzed.

The program has made significant contributions to the F–15 and B–1 system developments. As an example, one test effort in this program provided valuable data on airframe-inlet integration and inlet-engine interaction to each engine and airframe contractor involved in F–15 work. Efforts are also being conducted to improve the capability to correlate data between wind tunnel model testing and actual flight testing. Flight prediction techniques will be conducted during the same time period as the B–1 aircraft and engine development programs. This will provide a valuable tool in systems development and provide a data source for insuring the early resolution of integration problems.

This program also includes engine component development to adapt the advanced turbine engine gas generator cores to specific system requirements. Components in this program include a high tip-speed fan, composite material application to turbine engines, and a controlled output turbine for future turbine engines.

Turbine Engine Development.—The Army has conducted an advanced development program consisting of two 1,500 shaft horsepower demonstrator gas turbine engines to update helicopter propulsion system technology. Preliminary goals are 40 percent lower weight, 25 percent less fuel consumption, and significantly improved maintainability and reliability as compared to present day production engines.

The testing program to date has shown considerable promise of attaining these goals. Engineering development is planned to begin in fiscal year 1972.

Survivable Flight Control System Development Program (SFCS).—The SFCS advanced development progam was initiated by the Air Force Flight Dynamics Laboratory (AFFDL) in July 1969 with the award of a contract to an industrial contractor. The objective of this program is to develop technology to increase the tactical survivability of future aircraft through reduction in vulnerability of present complex hydromechanical flight control systems. This program will demonstrate by flight tests the principles of component separation, redundancy, and hardening as they are applied to the aircraft primary flight control system through use of an all-electronic control system and integrated hydraulic servo-actuator package techniques. This system will decrease vulnerability of the control linkages from the pilot's control stick to the surface actuators, and the integrated servo-actuator package will decrease vulnerability of the power source to the control actuators. The integration of both normal and backup operation into a single unit permits keeping the weight to a minimum while increasing survivability and reliability.

The first of a series of flight tests was made in April 1970 and demonstrated the integrated actuator package portion of the system which provides for emergency control for a "get-home-and-land" capability in the event normal hydraulic power to the stabilator is lost or rendered inoperative from battle damage.

In the flight tests the actuator exceeded performance expectations appreciably beyond the required emergency flight envelope. Flights have included speeds up to Mach 1.6 and 5g windup maneuvers.

Demonstration of this unit represents a significant step in the development of the complete fly-by-electrical-wire control system. Contracts for the complete control system have been awarded, and laboratory testing of the system is scheduled for November of 1971 with flight tests to begin early in 1972.

Seek Storm.—Project Seek Storm was established to provide an improved Air Force severe weather (hurricane, typhoon, extra tropical storm) reconnaissance capability. The project is designed to develop an improved weather radar which will provide military and civilian forecasters more precise intensity and location information on which to base storm path and strength predictions. The Air Force currently has two aircraft with experimental radar on board for hurricane reconnaissance. After sufficient data has been collected on radar characteristics, physical structure of storms, aircraft structural limitations, and potential antenna designs, the final development design of a new radar will begin in fiscal year 1972.

Medical Projects.—The Naval Aerospace Medical Institute at Pensacola, Fla., continued to conduct space-related medical tasks which includes: preflight aspects of long duration weightless flights with primates; hazards of proton radiation; techniques of in-flight electrocardiography; and effects of gravitational forces, inertial forces, and extended weightlessness upon man with particular emphasis on his vestibular system.

The School of Aerospace Medicine, San Antonio, Tex., has been studying the problems of the closed environment in terms of habitable atmospheres (carbon dioxide levels and partial pressures of oxygen) and in terms of the acute and chronic toxicological effects of trace contaminants.

Fluidics.—Application of fluidic technology to aeronautics was continued in several areas. Successful flight tests of a three-axis stability augmentation system (SAS) were accomplished on a UH–1 helicopter. An improved model of the fluidic turbine inlet temperature sensor was successfully tested in a T55 gas turbine engine. An application of fluidic devices to jet flaps on low-speed aircraft is being investigated at the Ames Research Center. In addition, the Army's Harry Diamond Laboratories is assigned a NASA effort to develop a fluidic shock wave control sensor. The device will sense and control the position of the shock wave in supersonic inlets on high-speed aircraft.

Relationship With Other Government Agencies

The Department of Defense continued close coordination and cooperation with other Government activities. There are presently six military officers assigned to the National Aeronautics and Space Council in the Executive Office of the President (three Air Force, two Navy, and one Army) and 208 military personnel assigned to NASA (131 Air Force, 24 Navy, 50 Army, and three Marine Corps). Described below are examples of types of cooperation and coordination.

Aeronautics and Astronautics Coordinating Board (AACB).—The AACB continues as the principal formal coordinating mechanism between DOD and NASA in the space and aeronautics areas. While a number of problems were considered by the Board, emphasis was placed on the Space Transportation System activity and on future large aeronautical facilities. The Board examined broadly the progress on the NASA Space Shuttle, the projected DOD use for the Shuttle, including considerations of possible impact on Shuttle design, and the interrelationship between the current launch vehicle families, their growth versions and the Space Shuttle launch program. In the area of large aeronautical facilities to meet future national needs, the Board determined that the large engine test facility and the large scale V/STOL wind tunnel were of highest priority and supported a limited effort to firm up facility designs. The Board will review the results of such study efforts prior to any decision to acquire such facilities.

Lunar and Planetary Activities.—The Corps of Engineers continued to assist NASA with large scale lunar topographic maps of scientific sites, photomaps, and landmark graphics for use in the Apollo program. Construction of a 1:2,000 scale relief model for Astronaut training for Apollo 13 was completed, and was used in the training simulator at the Manned Spacecraft Center in Houston, Texas. An investigation of the potential of automated photogrammetric equipment to reduce Lunar Orbiter photography more effectively and accurately than by present methods was completed. The Corps of Engineers continues to provide professional counsel and other technical assistance in support of extraterrestrial reseach.

Construction Support.—The U.S. Army Corps of Engineers continued to provide construction support of NASA at a reduced level during 1970. The work was accomplished on a reimbursable basis primarly at the Kennedy Space Center at a cost of $15 million. Cumulatively since 1961, the support provided totals $1.2 billion.

Aerospace Feeding Systems.—A sixth flexible-packaged, thermally processed, eat-with-a-spoon product—

meat balls and tomato sauce—was developed by the U.S. Army Natick Laboratories and used aboard Apollo 13. Five such items were developed earlier and used on previous Apollo flights. Flexibly packaged peanut butter and jelly, originally developed for a combat meal, were also used on Apollo 13. Storage tests for retention of nutritional quality and periodic evaluations for texture and flavor are in progress on a variety of dehydrated foods used aboard the different space flights. Exploratory studies during the past year have indicated the feasibility of heating prepackaged foods by microwave energy and simulated space flight conditions.

Apollo.—During 1970 the Army, Navy, and Air Force continued to provide fundamental support to NASA which is essential for manned space flight activities. These support services included: recovery ships, aircraft, and personnel; assistance with communications; SOLRAD solar activity data; and other supplementary forces.

Atomic Energy Commission

Introduction

Effort continued during 1970 on the development of nuclear power systems for future space applications—both for propulsion and for on-board electrical power. Highlight events include the following:

Nuclear Space Power.—The SNAP–19 and SNAP–27 radioisotope generators (RTG's) launched in 1969 both passed 1 year of continuous operation.

Disassembly of a flight type zirconium hydride reactor (S8DR) was completed after 7,000 hours of continuous testing.

Nuclear Rockets.—NERVA development activities concentrated on the definition and preliminary design of the flight rated NERVA engine.

A candidate fuel element for NERVA successfully completed 10 hours of electrical corrosion testing including 60 thermal cycles.

The Pewee–2 experimental reactor was fabricated and delivered for testing in early 1971.

Space Electric Power
Space Radioisotope Power Systems

SNAP–19 and SNAP–27.—Both the SNAP–27 and SNAP–19 systems which were launched during 1969 achieved 1 year of continuous operation during 1970. The SNAP–27 deployed on the moon in November 1969 has performed extremely well during its first year of operation and has been producing about 73 watts (higher than the mission requirement) since deployment on the moon. The stable operation of the SNAP–27 has enabled the ALSEP experiments to operate continuously during both the lunar day and lunar night and will allow for continued operation as long as the experiments themselves are functional. Important scientific data is being generated which will aid in understanding the structure, evolution, and history of the moon. An additional SNAP–27 unit was launched in 1970 aboard the Apollo 13 spacecraft but it returned to earth as a consequence of the subsequent aborting of that mission. Two units are scheduled for launch in 1971 with the Apollo 14 and 15 flights. An additional SNAP–27 has been ordered by NASA and it will be delivered in 1971. The SNAP–19 which provides supplementary power for the Nimbus spacecraft experiments is also performing well, though it has experienced some performance degradation because it is not a hermetically sealed unit.

Transit Generator.—Fabrication and testing of the 5-year life Transit generator for the Navy's advanced navigational satellite continued. The first complete electrically heated unit was fabricated and tested and will be delivered to the Navy for spacecraft integration efforts early in 1971. Fabrication of a nuclear fuel ground test unit was near completion—with testing scheduled to begin early in 1971. The Transit generator is the prime power source and will supply 30 watts of power to the Navy's advanced Transit navigational satellite.

Pioneer Generator.—The design of the modified SNAP–19 generator for application with NASA's Pioneer Jupiter probe missions was completed during 1970. Five electrically heated prototype generators were delivered to NASA and fabrication of four plutonium-238 fueled prototype generators for NASA spacecraft integration efforts was also near completion. These generators are scheduled for shipment early in 1971. Pioneer launches are scheduled in 1972 and 1973. Use of nuclear power on this mission reduces total power system weight and eliminates uncertainties concerning operation at extended distances from the sun which would be inherent with solar array systems. The reduced weight allows for including additional experiment packages which increases the total value of the mission.

Viking.—Early in 1970 the Viking program launch dates were deferred from 1973 to 1975. Consequently the Viking effort during this year was directed primarily towards spacecraft integration and study efforts using the SNAP–19 system.

Multi-Hundred Watt Generator Module.—Effort continued on development of a Multi-Hundred Watt (MHW) generator module which will form a basic building block for isotopic space power systems in the 100 to 1,000 electrical watt range. Specialized DOD satellites and NASA missions to the outer planets will require nuclear power systems and the projected power level requirements for these missions can be satisfied with the MHW system. Preliminary design studies were completed and fabrication of test components was initiated. The first converter should go on test in mid-1971. A fueled module demonstration is currently scheduled for the 1973–74 time period.

Isotope Brayton System.—NASA has given considerable emphasis to development of a plutonium-238 fueled radioisotope Brayton system for application in the electrical power range of a few kilowatts. The AEC has been pursuing the development of the fueled isotope capsule for application with this system. A nuclear safety feasibility study was conducted by the AEC with participation by both AEC and NASA laboratories.

Space Isotopic Fuel Development

Plutonium-238.—Plutonium-238 is currently the heat producing isotope being used or planned in all major space applications. Efforts continued towards development of improved cermet fuel forms and a plutonium molybdenum cermet fuel form was selected for use in the Pioneer, Transit, and Viking programs.

Curium-244.—A heat source loaded with Curium-244 successfully completed 1 year of test operation at the AEC's Oak Ridge National Laboratory. Curium-244 will be produced as a natural byproduct of the commercial reactors and has the potential of significantly reducing radioisotope fuel costs.

Space Reactor Power Systems

Zirconium-Hydride Reactor.—Disassembly of the second generation high power, high temperature uranium-zirconium hydride reactor (S8DR) was completed. Testing of the S8DR was begun in late 1968 and the reactor was shut down in late 1969 after about 7,000 hours of operation. Data collected during operation indicated that cracking of a number of fuel element claddings had occurred. Information obtained from the disassembly and detailed examination of this reactor is being incorporated into a planned core test which is to verify the adequacy of this reactor concept for long term (several years) operation. This test is currently scheduled to begin in 1973.

The zirconium-hydride reactor can be used with any of several conversion systems and the AEC is pursuing development of one of these: a compact thermoelectric conversion system. During 1970, thermal distortion of the thermoelectric converted module during operation was eliminated through the use of a refractory metal inner liner. The reactor-thermoelectric system will provide a power system of high reliability and simplicity from a few kilowatts up to around 35 kilowatts of electricity.

Thermionic Reactor.—A prime contractor was selected to continue the development of a thermionic fuel element and to construct an experimental reactor planned for operation in the mid-to-late 1970's. This reactor will be based on use of fuel elements which convert heat to electricity within the reactor core and which must be capable of long endurance operation at extremely high temperatures. Program emphasis is currently directed toward demonstration of a full length thermionic fuel element. In-pile partial length fuel elements achieved 5,000 hours of operation during 1970 and out-of-pile electrically heated diodes achieved 25,000 hours of operation.

Nuclear Rocket Program

The nuclear rocket program is a joint endeavor of the AEC and NASA aimed at providing a significant increase in propulsion capability for future space activities. The major program objective is to develop a 75,000-pound-thrust engine, called NERVA (Nuclear Engine for Rocket Vehicle Application) for space flight missions. The program includes a variety of advanced and supporting research and technology activities in which the aims are to extend the technology needed to improve nuclear rocket performance and to investigate advanced propulsion concepts.

NERVA Engine Development.—During 1970, the NERVA engine system development activities were concentrated on the completion of engine systems engineering analyses, the preparation of engine system specifications, and the conduct of detailed engine design. The work on the engine system and its related non-nuclear components (turbopumps, valves, nozzle) is described in the NASA section of this report. Activities related to development of the engine nuclear subsystem (the reactor) are described here.

Nuclear Subsystem Development.—Reactor systems engineering activities conducted during the past year were directed toward the selection, test, and evaluation of candidate materials and the evaluation of alternate component designs for incorporation in the referenced reactor design. Selection of the reference reactor design was accomplished through the examination of technology reactor systems tested earlier in the nuclear rocket program. From the analyses of these systems and their test data and the results from the systems engineering studies, system and component specifications were prepared and detailed reactor design was initiated.

The activities denoted above describe the iterative process which was applied to all reactor hardware to insure that the best design approaches and engineering procedures were being utilized to define the design of the NERVA flight reactor subsystem. These activities are now rapidly converging on a major milestone: the NERVA reactor preliminary design review (PDR). The purpose of this review will be to formally examine every aspect of the work that has been performed and to verify that the basic reactor design meets the performance and reliability requirements established for the NERVA engine system. Acceptance of the PDR results will be followed by the completion of the detailed design of reactor components and the fabrication of reactor hardware for development and qualification testing.

During the year, substantial progress was made on reactor fuel element research and development, the goals of which are to achieve a 10-hour operating duration and a recycling capability of up to 60 thermal cycles. As the nuclear fuel is the most critical part of the reactor subsystem, a rigorous fuel development program was pursued in several areas. The fuel element work is concentrated on two matrix materials: bead-loaded graphite and a graphite plus carbide composite. The former incorporates innovations in design and production processes reflecting the experience gained from laboratory evaluation and ground testing in prior reactors. The composite comprises a dispersion of the mixed carbide in a graphite matrix, which in laboratory studies to date has shown considerable promise for extended corrosion endurance under the cyclic operation required for the NERVA reactor. These composite fuel elements successfully completed 10 hours of electrical corrosion testing, including 60 thermal cycles. Fuel elements of both types were fabricated and a series of laboratory tests were conducted. Both types were fabricated for incorporation into a small experimental reactor called Pewee–2. The Pewee–2 reactor was assembled and shipped to the Nuclear Rocket Development Station for testing in early 1971. Performance data from this reactor will be used in making the selection of the optimum fuel element for the NERVA flight reactor series.

Advanced Research and Technology.—The program effort in advanced research and technology is directed toward improvement of the performance of nuclear rockets by increasing the operating time and operating temperature for solid-core reactors, and by investigation of advanced propulsion concepts. The major activities are the research, development, and laboratory evaluation of improved fuel elements and other special reactor materials, reactor fabrication and testing to evaluate both elements and reactor design features, and research and experimental effort in advanced fission and fusion propulsion concepts. This work is concentrated at the Agency's Los Alamos Scientific Laboratory in New Mexico.

In addition to the fuel element work described earlier, work also continued on the development of evaluation techniques for the composite and carbide fuel elements. The design of a nuclear furnace to be used for fuel element development and evaluation was completed, and fabrication of the parts for the first nuclear furnace test was initiated. Fabrication of the hardware for the modification of Test Cell "C" to test the furnace was also initiated. The furnace provides a fuel-element test bed to explore and simulate the necessary operating conditions of time, temperature, and cycles that the fuel experiences in a reactor but which are difficult to simulate in the existing electrically heated corrosion test furnace. The first nuclear furnace (Nuclear Furnace 1) test is scheduled for 1971.

Efforts also continued during the year to improve reactors and core designs to optimize the use of solid solution carbides.

In the area of advanced propulsion, fundamental research was conducted on plasma arc and other advanced concepts. In plasma arc research, substantial progress was made in experimentally producing a specific impulse of approximately two to three times that achieved in solid core rockets.

Satellite-Based Detection of Nuclear Explosions in Space and the Atmosphere

The AEC-instrumented Vela satellite program continued in 1970 with the sixth and final launch in six attempts. The sixth launch of twin spacecraft, Vela VB, was conducted by the Department of Defense on April 8, 1970, from Cape Kennedy, Fla., and utilized a Titan IIIC booster. The detector instrumentation on the 1970 satellites are performing well. The satellites are in near-circular orbits of approximately 65,000 nautical miles, comparable to the previously launched spacecraft. The complement of detectors on board includes those designed to record signals emanating from an atmospheric nuclear explosion and the X-rays, gamma rays, and neutrons generated by a high altitude or space nuclear explosion. The spacecraft on Launch I (1963), Launch II (1964), and Launch III (1965) were spin-stablized while those on Launch IV (1967), Launch V (1969), and Launch VB are attitude-controlled to point continuously toward the earth which substantially increases the capability of the downward-looking detector systems.

In addition to performing their primary functions as "watchdogs" for possible nuclear testing in the atmosphere and in space, the Vela satellites have provided invaluable data to scientists on the nature of solar X-rays, the solar wind, and other astrological phenomena. The satellites have also assisted in the manned spaceflight program.

Department of State

Introduction

The Department of State continued its efforts during 1970 to further the achievement of the objectives of the National Aeronautics and Space Act, particularly in terms of cooperation with other nations and groups of nations in the peaceful application of the results of aeronautical and space activities. Encouragement of greater international cooperation in space was an integral part of U.S. foreign policy and the conduct of our international relations during 1970.

Among the principal international developments in space affairs during 1970 were several new bilateral aeronautical and space cooperation agreements, discussions with foreign officials on participation in the post-Apollo program, expansion of possibilities for greater cooperation in space with the Soviet Union, further growth of international interest and cooperation in communication satellite systems, and increased interest in earth resources survey satellite programs.

Activities Within the United Nations.—The United Nations Committee on the Peaceful Uses of Outer Space and its Legal Subcommittee focused major efforts in 1970 on attempts to complete a draft convention on liability for damage caused by objects launched into outer space. The United States played an active role in these efforts as well as in the work of the Scientific and Technical Subcommittee and the Working Group on Direct Broadcast Satellites.

The Scientific and Technical Subcommittee meeting in April was marked by a cooperative approach to the promotion of the practical applications of space technology. Among proposals endorsed by the Subcommittee was a United States proposal that the new United Nations Expert on Space Applications assist in the creation of panels, including representatives from developing countries, to observe closely and report to the Outer Space Committee on such space application programs as the United States Earth Resources Survey program.

Meeting in May, the Working Group on Direct Broadcast Satellites considered further the social, cultural, legal, and other implications of satellite broadcasting. While agreeing on the promise of satellite broadcasting to contribute to economic, social, and cultural development in a context of international cooperation, the Working Group registered disagreement on the question of whether legal principles are needed to govern satellite broadcasting. The United States argued that adequate legal principles already exist in the Outer Space Treaty and other instruments.

In formal meetings and informal consultations during 1970, the Legal Subcommittee and the parent Outer Space Committee continued to seek agreement on provisions needed to complete the draft liability treaty. Agreement on the preamble and 13 articles was reached, but key questions on the settlement of disputed claims and the applicable law remained unresolved.

In January, at the invitation of the United States Ambassador to the United Nations, members of the Outer Space Committee and United Nations Secretariat officials visited NASA's Manned Spacecraft Center in Houston to hear briefings on NASA's Earth Resources Survey program and to view related facilities and equipment.

New Bilateral Agreements.—In March NASA signed an agreement with the Italian Space Commission (CNR) covering general arrangements for launching and associated services to be furnished by NASA to the Italian Space Commission for reimbursable launchings of Italian satellites on a case-by-case basis.

In May NASA and the Astronomical Netherlands Satellite (ANS) Program Authority concluded an agreement covering a cooperative project in which NASA will launch in 1974 or 1975 an astronomical satellite developed and constructed in The Netherlands which will explore stellar ultraviolet and X-ray radiations from a sun-synchronous orbit.

In November NASA and the British Science Research Council concluded an agreement for the launching of a fifth British scientific satellite by NASA in 1973 to study cosmic X-ray sources.

In December an existing agreement with Brazil for cooperative efforts on earth resources surveying experiments was being extended for an additional 2 years. This project, together with a similar cooperative effort with Mexico, has contributed valuable information to NASA's Earth Resources Survey program.

As the year closed, a new agreement was concluded with the Canadian Department of Industry, Trade, and Commerce for support of NASA sounding rockets and other scientific activities at the Churchill Research Range.

U.S.-Soviet Cooperation.—During 1970 the Department of State continued to support efforts to increase space cooperation with the Soviet Union. The most significant new development in 1970 was a meeting in Moscow in October in which Soviet and United States representatives discussed arrangements for compatible docking systems in future Soviet and NASA manned spacecraft. Agreement was reached on a series of further meetings and exchanges of technical information which could lead to compatible docking systems in future Soviet and NASA manned spaceflight programs.

Cooperative activities with the Soviet Union continued in the exchange of meteorological satellite data and aerospace biomedical information, and additional areas of possible cooperation are being explored.

Apollo Program Support.—During 1970 the Department of State and its overseas posts provided support for the Apollo 13 mission by arranging for basing of recovery forces at foreign installations and by coordinating offers of foreign assistance during the emergency return from the moon of the Apollo 13 astronauts. Cooperation on use of certain radio frequencies during the final phase of the Apollo 13 recovery operation was also sought and obtained from most nations in the world.

Post-Apollo.—Foreign interest in participation in NASA's post-Apollo program increased significantly during 1970. In September, the Chairman of the European Space Conference met with the Under Secretary for Political Affairs and other interested U.S. officials to discuss the political and economic aspects of possible European participation. The Department also supported NASA in obtaining European government assurances on protection of post-Apollo technical data that may be released by NASA.

Communications Satellites.—As stipulated in the Agreements of 1964 which created the International Telecommunications Satellite Consortium (Intelsat), the United States convened a conference in February 1969 to begin consideration of "definitive arrangements" for the global commercial communications system. The negotiations were continued by a Preparatory Committee which submitted its report to a resumed Plenipotentiary Conference in February 1970. The resumed Conference established an Intersessional Working Group to negotiate a single set of recommended texts of definitive arrangements. The United States served as host government for the Intersessional Working Group, which held three meetings (May, September, and November) in Washington and is expected to issue its report to a reconvened conference in 1971.

Intelsat added seven members in 1970, increasing its membership to 77 countries. Three Intelsat III satellites were launched in 1970, two of which were successfully placed in orbit and have been serving the Atlantic Region. This has increased significantly the volume and variety of global telecommunication services that have been made available to all continents of the world. The next series of satellites, Intelsat IV, the first of which is scheduled for launch in 1971, will further increase the capacity of the global system.

The total number of full-time circuits using Intelsat satellites at the end of 1970 represents an increase of about 34 percent over those in use at the end of 1969. Television transmission hours, all temporary service, increased in 1970 about 26 percent over 1969. Because many transmissions were to multiple earth stations simultaneously, the number of receive hours indicates a larger increase of about 32 percent over 1969.

Worldwide usage of the Intelsat system will be stimulated even more by a decision of the Interim Communications Satellite Committee, the governing body of Intelsat, to reduce by 25 percent the charge for full-time leasing of an Intelsat circuit, effective January 1, 1971.

During 1970 a significant effort was put forth to develop United States proposals for consideration at the World Administrative Radio Conference for Space Telecommunications, which is being convened by the International Telecommunication Union, a specialized agency of the United Nations, in Geneva in June 1971. The Conference is expected to make far-reaching decisions on technical and regulatory aspects of space telecommunications and is expected to allocate, for the first time, frequency bands for the broadcasting satellite service.

Earth Resources Survey Satellite Program.—During 1970 the United States continued to distribute to foreign governments and agencies information on United States activities concerning earth resources surveying. Planning was undertaken for an International Workshop on Earth Resources Survey Systems which the Department of State is cosponsoring with NASA and other Government agencies. Invitations to attend the Workshop, which is to be held in May 1971 at the University of Michigan, were extended in December to all United Nations Member States, a number of other nations and several international organizations.

Aeronautical Service Satellites.—The United States continued to work with ICAO during 1970 in considering requirements and characteristics for an Aeronautical Service Satellite system that would provide air traffic control services. Requirements for surveillance and navigation services are also being considered. The Department of State also participated with other United States Government agencies during 1970 in the formulation of policies and studies of the requirements and technical characteristics of such a satellite system.

Meteorological Satellites.—The United States continued to participate in planning activities of the World Meteorological Organization for the Global Atmospheric Research Program (GARP) to be undertaken in the mid-1970's. The satellite portion of GARP involves four meteorological satellites to be operated in conjunction with land- and sea-based facilities and balloon-borne instruments. Two of the satellites are to be launched by NASA and one by France. Japan is considering a commitment to launch the fourth satellite.

National Geodetic Satellite Program.—The National Geodetic Satellite Program (NGSP) was concluded in 1970 with 28 countries having been involved in its activities. The Department of State assisted the National Ocean Survey of the National Oceanic and Atmospheric Administration in making arrangements for movement of NGSP equipment and personnel and additional geodetic satellite survey activities in several foreign countries.

Sounding Rocket Activities.—The United States continued during 1970 an extensive program of sounding rocket launches from the United States and several foreign locations. New agreements covering arrangements for sounding rocket launches were signed during 1970 with the governments of Australia, India, Spain, Sweden, and France.

Tracking Networks.—In June an agreement with France was concluded to provide the general framework for mutual tracking support of satellite activities by France and NASA. During 1970 agreements with Australia and Malagasy for the operation of NASA tracking stations in those countries were extended. The Department of State also assisted NASA in making arrangements for ceasing operation of its tracking station at Guaymas, Mexico, and for the movement of equipment and personnel to the United States. The NASA tracking network also supported launches of the French-German DIAL satellite and the Japanese satellite OHSUMI in 1970.

Technology Transfer.—During 1970 the Department of State's Office of Munitions Control continued discussions with other U.S. Government agencies aimed at reducing the number of space-related items governed by export controls in the International Traffic in Arms Regulations. The Office of Munitions Control processed in 1970 an increased number of license requests for export of space-related hardware and technology to foreign space programs. Included were technical assistance and equipment for the Japanese Launch Vehicle and Satellite Development Program, the NASA-German HELIOS satellite, the Italian SIRIO satellite, the Astronomical Netherlands Satellite Program, the United Kingdom Defense Communication Satellite, and technical cooperation between several foreign industries and U.S. industry on study contracts in the NASA post-Apollo Space Transportation System program.

Cooperation with the Department of Defense.—The Department of State worked closely with the Department of Defense throughout 1970 on those space related activities of the DOD which were international in character or operationally involved other nations. The NATO Satellite Communications System and the cooperative program with the United Kingdom for the development of the SKYNET space communications system were two of the major programs carried out during the year. The first NATO communication satellite was launched from Cape Kennedy on March 20. Two earth terminals, one in Germany and the other in Italy are expected to be completed early in 1971. The terminal in Norfolk, Va. is scheduled for completion in June 1971. A second SKYNET satellite was launched in August but malfunctioned after reaching initial orbit. An agreement covering the second phase of the SKYNET satellite communication program was signed by the United States and the United Kingdom in April. A United States-United Kingdom combine is now under contract to design and construct the second generation SKYNET satellite.

Aeronautics.—In December an agreement was concluded with the Canadian Department of Industry, Trade, and Commerce covering arrangements for a joint project to design, develop, and test a new aircraft wing flap concept known as the Wing Augmentor System. The concept involves a wing trailing edge flap system based on jet nozzle thrust augumentation. Successful development of this system will significantly reduce landing and takeoff distance for jet aircraft, particularly large commercial transport aircraft.

The United States continued to work in ICAO to solve environmental problems arising from aircraft noise in the vicinity of airports and sonic boom in connection with the commercial introduction of supersonic aircraft. The first meeting of the ICAO Committee on Aircraft Noise, held in the fall of 1970, decided to recommend that new ICAO noise certification standards should be made applicable to airplanes of the 747-type for which a certificate of airworthiness is first issued on or after March 1, 1972. The Committee also established a working group to study the technical and cost/benefit aspects of noise certification modification requirements for existing subsonic turbojet aircraft.

The ICAO Sonic Boom Panel held its second meeting in October 1970. This panel has the task of developing proposals which will meet the objectives of a resolution of the ICAO Assembly. The resolution reaffirms the importance of not creating an unacceptable situation for the public through sonic boom of commercial supersonic transport aircraft (SST's), invites nations to furnish information concerning the operating characteristics of their SST's and the results of research into the effects of sonic boom as soon as available, instructs the ICAO Council to review ICAO documents to ensure they take account of the public problems of SST's and sonic boom, and invites manufacturing nations to furnish ICAO with proposals on the manner in which any specifications it might establish could be met.

Air terrorism and hijacking took on new and more severe forms in 1970 which posed serious threats to the safety of air transport. The Department of State pressed for additional adherence to the Tokyo Convention on prompt return of aircraft and passengers and for the completion of two new Conventions which would require States to extradite or prosecute hijackers and those intending to damage aircraft or vital aviation facilities. The proposed Convention on hijackers is the subject of a conference which began in The Hague in December. A fourth Convention was proposed by the United States in October to provide for possible sanctions against States not promptly returning aircraft and passengers or failing to take appropriate action in the case of hijackers who acted for international blackmail purposes. This last Convention is being considered by the ICAO Legal Committee.

Department of Transportation

Introduction

The Secretary of Transportation and his Department are charged with the preservation of the role of the United States as a leader in air transportation through, among other means, the application of pertinent research and development performed by DOT and other Government agencies and departments, as well as by industry.

Within the Department, the Assistant Secretary for Systems Development and Technology has the function of leading the research and development efforts of all DOT elements in addition to conducting a research program under his own direction. A Research and Development Management Council was established in 1970 to facilitate the coordination efforts between the organizational elements of DOT. Its role is to assure that the intermodal aspects of any research project are fully considered, that no unnecessary duplication exists, and that effective utilization is made of the Transportation Systems Center and other departmental research and development facilities.

Through such mechanisms, and by bringing the Secretary's broader perspective to bear on the Department's research and development budgets, significant improvements are underway in the management of all of DOT's research and development effort, including aeronautical R. & D.

The Department's Transportation Systems Center in Cambridge, Mass., was transferred to it from NASA on July 1, 1970. The new organization was reoriented, and has already begun to contribute to the Department's work, particularly in electronic techniques for controlling traffic, both in the air and on the surface. This transfer of function and research personnel was a significant step in the improvement of the research and development relationships between DOT and NASA because its work contributes heavily to the programs of both.

The Civil Aviation Research and Development (CARD) policy study is a significant example of DOT–NASA collaboration; it is designed to explore and define the significance of civil aviation to the Nation, to forecast the research effort that will be needed to enable the United States to maintain its position of leadership in aviation, and to develop alternatives for Government and industry financing of such development.

The two agencies also collaborate in applying satellite capabilities in traffic control—both transoceanic aeronautical control and marine traffic control. Advanced satellite technology will be used to support deployment of an initial experimental/preoperational satellite system for operational evaluation of voice and data communications and for experimentation in independent traffic surveillance. A separate, but related, study has attempted to analyze the benefits of space techniques for data relay from a large system of ocean buoys.

Recommendations made early this year by the DOT Air Traffic Control Advisory Committee underlie plans for air traffic system improvements being implemented by the Federal Aviation Administration (FAA). The Fourth Generation Air Traffic Capacity Study, a new long-range forecasting effort, was designed to identify technological advances needed to develop a control system that will allow efficient operation of air traffic and still be relatively insensitive to changing levels of demand on the system, while constantly improving safety.

A further extensive study seeks to quantify maritime-space radio communications requirements by synthesizing international merchant vessel population and oceanic distribution through 1980, projecting that population's message volume, and determining the radio frequency bandwidth that message traffic will need.

The U.S. Coast Guard Office of Research and Development has under development a self-contained system for the emergency unloading of stricken oil tankers. In the event of grounding, collision, or similar incident, the system allows the tanker to be unloaded or lightened sufficiently so that it may be refloated. This Air-Deliverable Anti-Pollution Transfer System (ADAPTS) will be capable of unloading 20,000 tons of liquid cargo within 24 hours of a reported ship pollution incident. The system which is packaged for air delivery includes transfer pumps, diesel engine pump prime movers, 500-ton rubber temporary storage containers and transfer hose.

The system is designed to perform in 40-m.p.h. winds and 12-foot seas with all components capable of being air delivered at the spill site within 4 hours of notification of an accident. The system is capable of deployment and initial operation without the use of surface craft and without support from the damaged ship. The first test of the entire system was conducted in February 1970. To date a total of four full system tests have been conducted, all under relatively calm conditions. Future tests of the system up to design environmental conditions are scheduled.

Aviation Safety Research and Development

En Route Operations.—The Department conducted significant research and development efforts during 1970 concerned with improving aviation safety in en route operations through the following typical programs:

(*a*) Aircraft wake turbulence.—A problem requiring a quick answer was addressed in February 1970: Whether the separation standard requiring following aircraft to stay at least 10 miles behind either of the two types of jumbo jets then in operation (747 and C–5A) should be retained or could be relaxed. The existing standard was based on theoretical calculations and early data. The conclusion—after FAA, the 747 manufacturer, NASA, and the U.S. Air Force had carried out a cooperative program that examined effects of wingtip vortexes generated not only by the jumbo jets but also by other types of jet aircraft—was that the longitudinal spacing behind the jumbo jets for following aircraft could safely be reduced to 5 miles, a spacing applying also to the wake of various other large jet aircraft. Further tests being conducted in this area will refine these results and determine more precise criteria of this kind for general aviation aircraft. Long-range work to characterize aircraft wake turbulence for any aircraft as a function of time and atmospheric variables is being continued in cooperation with the NASA vortex research program and others. Preliminary conclusions from these programs indicate that the extent of wingtip-generated vortex hazards can be reduced in various operational areas by: Air traffic control separation; flight procedures; improved vortex sensing, data processing, and pilot display; and improvements in airport taxiway and runway layout.

(*b*) Other air turbulence.—The FAA and the National Meteorological Center are cooperating in the work of forecasting clear air turbulence by combining probability analysis techniques developed for FAA with the Center's new model for forecasting winds and temperatures. The "unusual events recording systems," installed on three civil jet transports in previous years to obtain data on pilot and aircraft response to encounters with severe turbulence, recorded over 1,000 hours of inflight data without encountering any unusual event, which suggests that current flight procedures might be acceptable. The data obtained from this project will also be useful in other FAA programs.

(*c*) Flight characteristics criteria.—Two projects were completed and a third advanced during the year in this area, which serves aviation safety by developing and defining aircraft stability and control characteristics and the handling qualities of all forms of manned civil aircraft. This work, conducted in close coordination with the National Aeronautics and Space Administration and the Department of Defense, embraces both existing and new designs of aircraft, and is carried out by sponsoring analytical and experimental efforts with ground-based and inflight simulators for the wide range of civil aircraft and configurations involved. The program's objectives are to determine optimum characteristics of aircraft for use in system design and to promote the development of promising new aircraft control concepts. Achievements during 1970 applied to:

—Improving flight characteristics airworthiness requirements for certifying small general aviation aircraft.—The first phase of this project was carried out in 1967 under FAA sponsorship; the second—as part of a broader investigation jointly administered by NASA, the Naval Air Systems Command, and FAA—was conducted in 1968; and the final phase was completed in 1970 with the compilation of new stability and control data for designers and regulatory authorities.

—Establishing flight characteristics criteria for possible use in revising type certification standards for high performance business jets.—This two-phase project is jointly sponsored by the Air Force Flight Dynamics Laboratory and FAA. The first phase presented criteria for optimum lateral-directional handling qualities for cruising flight and minimum acceptable characteristics for setting airworthiness certification standards. The second phase determined lateral control requirements of executive jets and related military transport airplanes during landing approach in turbulence and crosswinds, as influenced by inertia, lateral directional coupling, and control-system characteristics.

—Investigating flight characteristics criteria for STOL (short takeoff and landing) transports.—This project uses a moving-base simulator to investigate flight characteristics of deflected jet and deflected slipstream STOL transports, and extends through three phases. The first phase, completed by an FAA contractor in 1970, was begun in July 1969 and carried out in close cooperation and coordination with the NASA Ames Research Center using the Ames moving-base simulator facilities.

The second phase will cover directional control and turn coordination criteria; the third, longitudinal dynamics and approach flight path control.

(d) Aircraft piracy and sabotage.—An antihijacking system was successfully field tested in 1969 and placed in limited airline use by the end of that year. This system consists of a weapon-detecting devise used in conjunction with a hijacker behavioral profile based on study of the personal characteristics of known hijackers. Greatly expanded use of the system occurred in July at New Orleans' Moisant International Airport, which became the first airport subjecting all passengers to screening by this system prior to boarding their planes. The main impetus to wider use of the system came from the unprecedented international hijacking events of September. A device called a Chemosensor has been developed as a possible solution to the aircraft sabotage problem. Its intended function is to detect the presence of a bomb anywhere within an aircraft. While evaluation of the Chemosensor revealed much merit, it requires further development to meet acceptable operational performance requirements.

(e) Midair collision hazard.—FAA participated in flight testing of a promising collision-avoidance system developed in previous years by a private contractor for the Air Transport Association. Earliest possible operational use of the system was considered to be at least 2 years away. The FAA also further tested, through simulation techniques, the effects of interaction between the collision-avoidance system and the air traffic control system. Since a collision-avoidance system is highly sophisticated technologically and expensive, it will be used mainly by airline and corporate aircraft. Several pilot-warning instrument system concepts, much simpler and less expensive, are undergoing R. & D. for general aviation aircraft by FAA, NASA, and industry.

(f) Other developments.—Other R. & D. efforts concerned with making aircraft safer in flight were concerned with the following:

—Stall-warning system.—Technical and operational criteria for improved stall-warning systems were determined in a two-phase effort. In the first phase, the most effective pilot-alerting method was found to be a control-wheel shaker, the second most effective an intermittent horn, the least effective a steady horn. The second phase tested a standard installation of a stall-warning system certificated in accordance with the Federal Aviation Regulations and an improved system using a lift transducer that detects the rate of change of the angle of attack.

—Stability augmentation.—Under an interagency agreement, the U.S. Air Force Flight Dynamics Laboratory completed flight testing of its automatic pilot-assisting equipment in a light, single-engine aircraft. The purpose was to assess the equipment's effectiveness in reducing accidents caused by pilot loss of control in bad weather.

—Improvement of static-pressure systems—Altimeter and airspeed systems reliability was tested and recommendations made to improve static-pressure systems of aircraft so that instruments would be more reliable while the aircraft are performing flight maneuvers or flying in bad weather.

—Inflight fire protection.—Criteria were distributed for installing and using equipment that records the concentration of fire-extinguishing agents in an aircraft's fire-extinguishing system. This equipment is the most reliable and feasible method of determining the effectiveness and performance of aircraft fire-extinguishing systems.

—General aviation exhaust system safety.—Accelerated procedures were developed for testing the airworthiness of general aviation aircraft exhaust systems. These procedures will preclude or significantly reduce the probability of carbon monoxide hazards resulting from high-temperature oxidizing or environment-caused corrosion of the exhaust system.

—Anti-icing wing-coating materials.—Although materials flight tested in 1970 were selected from materials tested previously in the icing research tunnel at NASA's Lewis Research Center, none was found to have effective anti-icing or de-icing properties.

Airport and Vicinity.—Significant efforts in this area were concerned with the following:

(a) Firefighting.—Basic data, usable for extrapolating fire-protection requirements for both smaller and larger aircraft, were obtained from full-scale fire tests performed at the Department's National Aviation Facilities Experimental Center, Atlantic City, N.J., with two obsolete U.S. Air Force B–47 Stratojet bombers. The data show requirements for type and number of firefighting vehicles, their strategic location around the aircraft, and type, quantity, and discharge rates of extinguishing agents.

(b) Runway friction.—Investigations of grooved runways yielded data on runway friction, environmental changes, and such effects on the using aircraft as vibrations induced in the airframe, wheel spin-up rates, and tire-chevron cutting. Investigations continue concerning seasonal environmental changes, wheel spin-up, and tire-chevron cutting.

Postcrash Safety.—Significant progress was made in the following areas:

(*a*) Gelled fuels.—Use of gelled fuels in aircraft has the potential for significantly reducing the hazard of fire following an aircraft crash. Chemical and physical research to improve gelled-fuel flow characteristics while maintaining their superior fire safety characteristics was performed after tests in a commercial jet transport fuel system had shown the most promising fuels developed from previous extensive research were too viscous. Two gelled fuels, however, were shown in short duration jet engine tests to be usable in modern jet engines without significant loss in engine efficiency. A study estimated that, over a 10-year period, industrywide use of gelled fuel would raise airline operating costs by 4 percent.

(*b*) Crash-resistant fuel system.—This system, utilizing strong bladder cells and a crash-operated valve system with interconnecting lanyards, was tested in actual impacts against pole-type obstacles at speeds up to 80 miles per hour. In all cases, the bladder tanks remained intact and the valves operated properly. Progress was achieved toward establishing criteria for carrying fuel in leading edges of aircraft wings, and evaluations of elastomer liners to improve crashworthiness of integral wing tanks were performed.

(*c*) Fire test of titanium SST fuselage.—The predicted greater ability of a titanium skin to protect against external fires was verified by a full-scale fuselage fire test, which also showed that obtaining full benefit from titanium's inherent fire resistance requires the use of high-temperature sealing materials.

(*d*) Aircraft cabin interior materials.—Several space program fire-resistant materials developed by NASA were evaluated at NAFEC for possible use in aircraft cabins. In the same area, the Department and the National Bureau of Standards established the accuracy of the latter's smoke test chamber and supported its recommendation to the American Society for Testing and Materials for use in a standard test method. This method will be specified in future FAA smoke-rule requirements for aircraft cabin interior materials.

(*e*) Aircraft cabin crash resistance.—The nature of structural failures in aircraft fuselages and in the seat- and cargo-restraining systems is being evaluated by comparing data from a full-scale crash test of a four-engine piston-powered airliner with design criteria, current airworthiness standards in the Federal Aviation regulations, and recently developed dynamic seat test criteria.

(*f*) Explosively created emergency exists.—The feasibility of opening emergency exits in the fuselage of a crashed airplane by linear-shaped explosives (two liquids separately inert but explosive when mixed) was demonstrated in scrap fuselage structure but, according to test indications, such a system must be incorporated in the aircraft design. The U.S. Army's Picatinny and Frankford Arsenals cooperated with FAA in accomplishing this project.

(*g*) Air-bag restraint system—The feasibility of using inflatable air bags to minimize impact effects on occupants of general aviation aircraft in crashes was determined, but adaptation of automotive air bags presently under development to current general aviation aircraft will require major modifications.

(*h*) Jumbo jet emergency evacuation simulator.— An emergency evacuation simulator capable of accommodating airline passengers in numbers representing a significant portion of jumbo jet capacity was being operated during the year by the Civil Aeromedical Institute at the Department's Aeronautical Center in Oklahoma City. The adjustable pitch, roll, and elevation of the simulator enable safety personnel to assess the effectiveness of escape equipment, ditching equipment, and escape procedures.

Air Traffic Control and Navigation System

FAA progressed during 1970 in its long-range plan to introduce automation in both terminal and en route traffic control. In addition, the Agency continued to develop area navigation routes to supplement conventional air routes for aircraft flying under instrument flight rules by developing area navigation routes, and to explore the potential uses of satellite technology in air navigation and communication.

Automated Radar Terminal System (ARTS) II.— This system is an experimental automation program for low- to medium-activity terminal areas. One candidate system is modular, can employ either numerics or alpha-numerics, and is programable. It can also use components of ARTS III (see below), thus simplifying logistics, maintenance, and training. Another candidate system, known as the AN/TPX–42, is the result of a joint FAA–USAF development program, and is being procured for low-density civil and military terminal areas.

FAA completed the first field test of a programable ARTS II, at Knoxville, Tenn., a low- to medium-density terminal area, following feasibility tests of the system at NAFEC before its installation at Knoxville. The 6-month field evaluation encompassed three separate test phases: (1) A numerics-only phase; (2) an alpha-numerics phase; and (3) a two-display configuration phase. The judgment at the end of the evaluation was that the system had performed effectively and had improved the handling of traffic in the Knoxville area. At year's end, ARTS II was operating full time as Knoxville's primary ATC facility. Work will continue in 1971 to explore beacon problems in greater depth and exploit the system's programable capabilities.

ARTS III.—By the end of 1970, the first ARTS III, FAA's automated system for high-density terminal areas, had been delivered to Chicago's O'Hare International Airport for operational use. FAA expects to deliver eight additional ARTS III's to high-density airports by the middle of 1971; FAA also expects ARTS III systems to be operational at 62 high-density airports in 1973.

In other ARTS III developments during calendar year 1970, FAA awarded a $500,000 contract for improving the tracking, air traffic control coverage, and computing capabilities of the system, and made an initial award on a contract to develop and implement an ARTS III computer progam for metering and spacing àir traffic.

NAS En Route Stage A.—FAA continued to install NAS En Route Stage A computers at air route traffic control centers (ARTCC's) for flight-data processing, the first step in automating en route air traffic control. At the end of the calendar year, such computers had been delivered to 15 centers. Five more centers are scheduled to receive this equipment. In addition, computer updating equipment for updating flight plans had been delivered to eight centers during 1970; three ARTCC's—Washington, Indianapolis, and Chicago—had put this equipment into operation by year's end.

Contracts awarded during the reporting period for NAS En Route Stage A equipment covered: Test consoles to house test equipment for computer display channels and computer updating equipment, two key elements of NAS En Route Stage A (March); design and development assistance, evaluation, and analysis (July); computers and computer components (June); a partial display channel processor (September); and modifying and expanding the en route operational air traffic control computer programs (November).

Aeronautical Satellites.—FAA continued to explore the potential usefulness of artificial satellites in aviation. This rapidly unfolding technology appears to be readily applicable to overwater surveillance and communication.

The increasing number and speed of air carrier aircraft flying international, overwater and polar routes has created problems in communication and surveillance. Because of fading, static, and other interference caused by natural phenomena, aircraft now flying such routes often lose radio contact with distant ground stations. Since this lack of reliable point-to-point communication makes air traffic surveillance over such aircraft impossible, flight separation requirements far exceeding those in use over land have been adopted for the safety of ocean-crossing aircraft. Air traffic capacity on these routes has thus been limited.

An aeronautical satellite system for transoceanic use could solve, or at least greatly ameliorate, these problems.

During 1970, FAA received proposals for launching a hybrid VHF/UHF satellite system for aeronautical use. One contractor proposed to conduct pre-operational tests with both frequencies and use the better testing one for the system's operational life. Another approach was to utilize the VHF portion of the system as an operational voice and data communication link, and the UHF portion for testing only.

Other ATC and Air Navigation Developments.—Among these were included the following:

(*a*) All-weather landing system.—This is a long-range undertaking involving the integration of a ground-based guidance system, an airborne system, and a lighting system. In 1970, NAFEC completed the evaluation of a ground-based guidance system—the STAN 37/38 ILS (instrument landing system)—borrowed from the United Kingdom. The purpose of the evaluation was to identify areas requiring further development. At year's end, the British-manufactured ILS was going through an airborne operational evaluation, scheduled for completion in August 1971. NAFEC had also completed flight testing of an airborne system capable of meeting category III weather minimums—that is weather conditions too poor for the pilot to: (1) Establish visual contact with the ground or runway before landing and (2) see along the runway beyond 1,200 feet.

(*b*) Area navigation.—FAA continued to pursue its long-range goal of developing area navigation routes for both en route and terminal IFR (instrument flight rules) traffic on a nationwide scale. Area navigation, by utilizing the full potential of VHF omnidirectional radio range/distance-measuring equipment (VOR/DME) navigation facilities, frees pilots from the need of flying a track to or from these facilities; this permits the establishment of new routes without installing ground-based navaids along each flight path. In June FAA established the first series of area navigation instrument approach procedures in the United States at six terminal areas—Longview, Tex., Kirksville, Mo., and Fullerton, Palm Springs, Lancaster, and Torrance, Calif. The new procedures permit pilots of aircraft equipped with area navigation equipment to make straight-in instrument approaches to runways without the use of runway-oriented electronic approach aids. This eliminates the need for pilots to conduct time-consuming procedure turns and circling maneuvers required by conventional IFR approaches. FAA also continued to test area navigation equipment. In March, NAFEC completed an evaluation of a private corporation's vector analog computer with the publication of a report describing the equipment's signal-processing techniques. In May the airborne computer was certified for use on a general aviation aircraft operated by the private corporation. In December, NAFEC completed an evaluation of an Avion roller map pictorial display.

Human Factors in Aviation

Pilots.—A study completed in 1970 in the area of airman standards, involving private and commercial pilots with flight experience ranging from 6 months to 9 years, showed a definite correlation between elapsed time from date of certification and loss of instrument proficiency.

Various pilot problems of a human-engineering type received attention in 1970. Examples are improvement of visual guidance by lights and paint patterns, effectiveness of cockpit instrument displays, collision-avoidance problems, visual illusions, and aircraft noise.

Air Traffic Controllers.—A study emphasizing human factors of equipment design, aiming to keep equipment-induced error to a minimum and to insure that controllers will be able to use with ease the new automated equipment being procured for towers and centers, will be made with a specialized radar display to be developed under a contract awarded in May 1970.

"Before and after" studies were underway during the year to determine quantitatively the effect on the controller's workload of introducing automation into the operational facilities.

An initial study of the accuracy of controllers in judging aircraft separation as represented on current analog radar displays showed nearly all estimates fell within 1.5 miles of the separation displayed. However, since the controllers were not burdened by the complete air traffic control job when making their estimates, these results were obtained under "best case" conditions; hence, further evidence will be required before serious consideration can be given to reducing the 3-mile separation standard for the terminal area.

Aviation and the Environment

FAA took a number of actions during 1970 addressed to maintaining or improving the quality of the environment. Among them were:

(*a*) Announcement, in October, of a program designed to reduce noise while increasing safety in the vicinity of airports serving jet aircraft.—Under the program, terminal air traffic controllers will delay the final landing descent of turbojets until these aircraft are relatively close to their destination airport; they will also instruct jet pilots taking off to climb out as rapidly as aircraft's performance capability and passenger comfort permit. Arriving jets will generally be kept at 10,000 feet or higher until they are approximately 30 miles from the airport. They will then be kept at least 5,000 feet above the ground until they reach the final descent area. Keeping the jets and hence their noise high enhances safety by minimizing the mix of jet and small general aviation traffic near the airport. The program is scheduled to be implemented at 119 terminal radar control facilities by February 1971; at 246 nonradar airports with towers by July 1971; at airports without radar or towers that serve scheduled air carrier turbojet flights by November 1971; at all remaining airports that serve turbojets by February 1972.

(*b*) Issuance of an advance notice of proposed rulemaking soliciting comments from the aviation community and the public at large on retrofitting existing jet aircraft with engine-noise-suppression devices, in November.—Recent research and development have demonstrated that devices capable of significantly reducing jet engine noise are within the state of the art. Still to be demonstrated, however, is the extent to which these devices may adversely affect aircraft airworthiness and whether they are economically feasible. This advance notice complements a December 1969 rule establishing allowable engine-noise levels for two classes of aircraft for which an application for a type certificate was made after January 1, 1967.

(*c*) Continuation of a project at the Civil Aeromedical Institute to determine the level of sonic booms tolerable to human sleep patterns by having instrumented subjects sleep in two specially installed sonic boom simulation rooms.

(*d*) Negotiation of an agreement with 31 airlines on the retrofit of JT8D engines with smoke-reducing combustors, in January.—These devices reduce the level of visible pollutants emitted by jet engines, but according to recent measurements do not help the problem of invisible pollutants. Under the retrofit plan, which was agreed to voluntarily by the airlines, combustors will be installed on some 3,000 engines on 737's, 727's, and DC–9's by late 1972. A public demonstration of the new combustor was conducted at Washington National Airport in September by a major air carrier with a combustor-equipped 727. The Department of Health, Education, and Welfare participated in negotiating the agreement.

(*e*) Awarding of a contract for the establishment of design criteria for the control and reduction of oxides of nitrogen (invisible pollutants) emitted by jet aircraft engines.—The study seeks to develop ways to reduce oxides of nitrogen without producing an increase in carbon monoxide, unburned hydrocarbons, and other jet engine emissions.

The Supersonic Transport

This has been another year of intense congressional interest in the supersonic transport program. House and Senate committees, in hearings on the fiscal year 1971 budget request for $290 million, considered in depth concerns expressed about noise, sonic booms, and other environmental impacts. The budget request was under consideration by a Conference Committee of the Congress in its session on the last day of the year.

In April 1970 the FAA issued a notice of proposed rulemaking formalizing the decision of the President that no supersonic transport may fly over U.S. territory at a speed that would cause a sonic boom to reach the ground.

Although present information indicates that projected SST operations will not cause significant climatic changes, the Department, in conjunction with the National Oceanic and Atmospheric Administration, NASA and other agencies, has described a Government environmental research program. It includes study of noise reduction. This research will provide data expected to increase confidence that large-scale SST operations will not significantly affect the environment.

Two interdisciplinary committees, the Environmental Advisory Committee and the Noise Advisory Committee, have been established. These are teams of scientists and experts with a variety of backgrounds and experience. They will monitor research programs where there is either uncertainty or lack of information.

After approval of the fiscal year 1970 budget on December 29, 1969, contractor manpower built up from an average of 3,400 in January 1970 to approximately 5,500 by the year's end. Work on both the airframe and engine proceeded on schedule throughout the year. The class II mockup structure was completed on schedule in June. The contractor awarded contracts to its major subcontractor teams in midyear, and they initiated fabrication of the prototype parts immediately thereafter. Having demonstrated the engine's world record thrust of approximately 69,000 pounds under static sea level conditions, the manufacturer continued testing the engines to increase their durability and reliability.

The contractors are working according to a schedule planned to achieve first flight in November 1972 and airplane certification by 1978.

Arms Control and Disarmament Agency

Introduction

Outer Space Treaty.—The first two objectives of the U.S. space program,

- —Continue to explore the moon;
- —Move ahead with bold exploration of the planets and the universe;

are moving forward on the legal highway provided by the Outer Space Treaty, which has now been subscribed to by 58 governments. It is reassuring that prior legal and intellectual concern insures that these new regions of exploration are closed to the arms race, and that these further space explorations can proceed within a peaceful, internationally controlled environment. ACDA is concerned, along with other agencies, in the necessary follow-on actions to insure that a proper liability convention is also brought into effect.

Success in banning weapons of mass destruction from outer space has shown that closing new environments to the arms race is an effective way of achieving international agreement on arms control. This success

pointed the way for a similar effort to ban such weapons from the seabed. The Conference of the Committee on Disarmament presented a draft treaty in this area to the U.N. General Assembly in September 1970, and that body passed a resolution supporting the treaty in December.

Space Cooperation.—The development of international cooperation in space activities can improve the political climate for a number of collateral goals, including arms control. The positive experiences of cooperative space program planning demonstrate ways in which countries can deal constructively with each other on technical problems. The experience of space cooperation and the manner in which it develops may also be a useful indicator as to the prospects for expanded cooperation in arms control, especially in the strategic area.

ACDA has continued its efforts to insure that space technology or equipment transferred by U.S. agencies or industries to other nations will be used solely for peaceful purposes. This procedure implements the U.S. policy of nonproliferation of missile and weapons technology.

Aerial and Space Systems in Support of Arms Control.—ACDA maintains an active interest in the improvement of technological and organizational capabilities for verifying arms control agreements. The space programs of other agencies are monitored for technological developments that can be adapted to arms control verification. Space-borne platforms with nonintrusive sensors, as well as data links and data processing systems, are of particular interest. Since confidence in future treaty arrangements will depend on how well the agreed provisions can be verified, ACDA devotes considerable effort to these activities. In addition, communication satellites can facilitate rapid exchange of information between governments during crisis situations. Such systems have enhanced reliability because they are not dependent on cooperation of other countries for passage of land lines.

Department of the Interior

Introduction

The U.S. Department of the Interior has long utilized aircraft in the performance of its missions for exploration, development, and management of the Nation's natural and cultural resources. Aircraft of several bureaus of the Department, contractor-owned aircraft, and other Federal agency-owned aircraft of all types are used operationally and experimentally. Experiments are conducted to test and develop improved capabilities that the aircraft themselves afford in support of Department programs and to test new ways in which use of airborne surveying and analytical instruments from cameras to radioactivity counters can improve the efficiency and effectiveness of departmental performance.

The Department has played an important role, also, throughout the past decade in support of the Nation's space exploration and lunar landing programs, and in support of the development of peaceful applications of space technology. Such support has included research of applications of satellites as unique platforms from which to make observations for research and monitoring of earth's environments and of remote sensing instruments to make the observations. Operational support has been provided to the NASA in lunar mapping, analysis of lunar materials, the development of lunar sampling programs and equipment, in the development of equipment and processes for life support systems in spacecraft, and in the calibration of equipment for the Earth Resources Technology Satellite (ERTS).

Aeronautics

During 1970, the Department employed fixed-wing aircraft and helicopters—its own, those of other agencies, and of private contractors—in support of both operations and research activities.

Operations.—Operational uses of aircraft and helicopters among bureaus of the Department have been as follows:

The Bonneville Power Administration.—For aerial patrol of power lines, transport of men, tools, and equipment to emergency spots to achieve rapid resumption of vital power service, and ferry of men to remote microwave stations.

The Bureau of Reclamation.—For reconnaissance of reclamation study areas and engineering sites, the acquisition of aerial photography for the planning of engineering works and alinements. Development of repair kits is under way at present, including lightweight aluminum towers, conductors, and accessories for the emergency repair of damaged 230- and 345-kilovolt power lines. These kits will be transported and erected by employment of helicopters. The Bureau also employed aircraft in the conduct of cloud seeding in its Atmospheric Water Resources Management Program and in support of the operations of the Bonneville Power Administration at Hungry Horse Basin, Idaho.

The Bureau of Mines.—To support mineral resource surveys in remote areas for the National Wilderness program.

The National Park Service.—For aerial photography and aerial visual observation in planning road alinements, site development, and engineering. It also used aircraft to obtain data for master plan development, vegetation mapping, fire patrol, archeological studies, and for survey of large mammal populations—moose, elk, bison, grizzly bear, and caribou—in large park areas such as Yellowstone, Glacier, Mount McKinley, and Katmai.

The Federal Water Quality Administration.—For detecting oil pollution, thermal loading and evaluating waste outfall characteristics in ocean waters.

The Geological Survey.—To obtain aerial photography for the national topographic mapping programs. In 1970, standard mapping photography was acquired for 227,000 square miles of the United States and high altitude aerial photography of more than 50,000 square miles was acquired, including 30,000 square miles in the Brooks Range and North Slope areas of Alaska. Aircraft were used also in the management of Federal Outer Continental Shelf mineral resources, to transport petroleum engineers and technicians to oil and gas drilling and producing operations, to perform inspection of such operations and search for the presence and sources of oil spills.

Research.—Research uses of aircraft involve their employment logistically in the movement of men and materials as discussed above, and as platforms for remote sensors—cameras, multiband scanning photometers, thermal infrared scanning radiometers, and radar mappers—to determine their applicability to the resources research and management functions of the several bureaus and offices of the Department of the Interior.

The Bonneville Power Administration is cooperating with the Bureau of Reclamation and the U.S. Corps of Engineers employing aircraft in conduct of a successful experiment in cloud seeding in the Hungry Horse Basin, Idaho.

The National Park Service is cooperating with Geological Survey, NASA, and other Federal, State, and municipal groups in remote sensing studies of Biscayne Bay and the Everglades National Park, Fla., the Hawaii Volcano, and the Grand Teton and Yellowstone National Parks. These studies are aimed at developing new methods for assessing both natural conditions of environments and the effects on them of natural hazards and the works of man.

The Geological Survey is cooperating with the NASA in conducting research of uses of special types and conditions of remote sensor data for conventional mapping and for new map products for topographic, geographic, geologic, and water resources surveys. It has instituted a program with New York State to use an airborne thermal infrared scanning radiometer to monitor the thermal effects on inland and estuary waters of urbanization and the ensuing natural and artificial discharge and circulation patterns. Studies in connection with the

Biscayne Bay and Everglades projects and with research in the Tampa sinkhole areas, in cooperation with the University of Michigan, have shown the feasibility of computer processing of airborne radiometer data for recognition and mapping of surface and shallow submarine biotic communities, and of an incipient sinkhole condition. High altitude aircraft data have been employed to prepare land use maps and data bases of selected 1970 Census cities, and both aircraft and Gemini and Apollo photography have been used to support analyses of the economic potential of an economically depressed area in southern Mississippi. Sidelooking airborne radar was employed to support geological research and mapping of the island of Hawaii, of Massachusetts, Connecticut, Rhode Island, and much of New York. Color and color infrared high altitude aerial photography are being used to study surface circulation patterns in San Francisco Bay, complex near-shore currents along the coast of Puerto Rico, sedimentation patterns along the south Texas coast and, with the Air Force Cambridge Research Laboratory, the sedimentary history of the Monomoy Point area of Massachusetts. Color, color infrared, and thermal infrared aerial data are providing bases for new studies of sedimentation and the effects of discharge of artificially heated water on the northern coast of Washington.

The Bureau of Mines, with the West Virginia Geological and Economic Survey, used NASA supplied radar data to develop a new understanding of regional structure and local oil producing area relationships in the Burning Springs, Va., area. Airborne thermal mapping surveys were conducted over burning culm banks in Pennsylvania and over areas of underground fire in the Eastern United States; they were also conducted in Colorado and Wyoming to determine usefulness of the systems in combating these very wasteful and hazardous conditions.

The Office of Water Resources Research supported research at the University of Rhode Island on aerial photography for remote sensing of pollution in Narragansett Bay; at the University of Montana on aerial photography and thermal infrared mapping to detect conditions of surface soil moisture before and after irrigation; at Cornell University on the use of aerial photography for prediction of water discharge for small watersheds; at the University of Wisconsin on the use of remote sensors for delineating flood plains in areas of deficient hydrologic data; and, at the University of Hawaii on the use of aeromagnetics and multiband photography for aid in the study of ground water resources.

The Federal Water Quality Administration funded research projects through grants and contracts at several universities and firms to develop remote sensing techniques for detecting and measuring agricultural pollution, pipeline leaks, and the discharge of pulp and paper mill effluents. An extensive evaluation is also under way on present aerial sensing techniques and their applicability to the detection and measurement of water characteristics.

Space

Research.—The Department of the Interior, through its Earth Resources Observation Systems (EROS) program, is cooperating with NASA, the Department of Defense, other Federal, State, and local governments, and educational and private research groups to develop useful applications of space and aeronautical remote sensing systems for resources exploration, analysis, and management. Research needs, projects, priorities, and support are defined and coordinated through working groups comprised of representatives of all Interior Bureaus and Offices. Working groups in Mineral and Land Resources, Water Resources, Human Resources and Activities, Marine Resources, and Mapping Requirements assure attention to all Department of the Interior areas of responsibility, balance among programs, and avoidance of duplicatory effort in a burgeoning and farflung field of activity.

Major efforts are going toward preparation to use data from ERTS–A scheduled for 1972 launching. Planning is underway for an EROS Data Center near Sioux Falls, S. Dak. The data center will have four major functions: (1) to process, disseminate, and store data from the ERTS satellites for the broad user community; (2) to extract generally useful resource information from the ERTS data and disseminate it for users; (3) to provide some facilities for user training and assistance in data use; and (4) to develop methods and produce resources maps and statistics from satellite and aerial data for basic research and planning and regularly updated information on changing conditions of environment for management.

In addition, the EROS program will conduct a large number of experiments with ERTS data to determine its usefulness in helping to fulfill the resource missions of the Department of the Interior.

The Bureau of Reclamation, the Geological Survey, and the Bonneville Power Administration are initiating a research program in the Stanford Research Institute to develop applications of satellite data to the systematic observation of snowfall, rainfall, and drought, their effects upon natural and artificial water catchment and distribution systems and the environment as a whole.

The Bureau of Mines is studying Gemini and Apollo photography to determine the applicability of space systems to analysis and prediction of regional effects of large scale mining operations, and surface effects of undeground fires.

The National Park Service is using Apollo 9 multiband photography of the barrier islands of the United States to aid in determination of management objectives there. It also uses Apollo 9 photography to enhance knowledge of the geology and topography of the Tucson-Phoenix area prior to the location of new roads and the realinement of old roads in the Saguarro National Monument. Gemini and Apollo photographs are used for in-service training programs for environment awareness.

The Geological Survey produced experimental photomaps of the Tucson, Arizona Quadrangle incorporating Apollo 9 photographs and the latest information obtainable by conventional mapping methods. It also supported the design of a computer program at the Ohio State University to locate photo coordinates on unrectified space photographs to make them immediately useful as working maps. Research is being conducted and facilities provided for enhancement of photographic data to enable correlation, combination, and selective separation for analysis of special information relative to depths of water and snow, types and condition of vegetation, works of man, and changes of these through time. Using Apollo 9 photographs, a photomosaic of the Southwest United States was developed for analysis of soil, rock, and vegetation relationships. From this, evidence was derived of recent arroyo formation and accelerated erosion in the desert as results of overgrazing and increasing aridity. One volcano in the Cascade Range was instrumented with temperature sensing devices and data are received from them eight times per week by relay through the Nimbus 4 satellite. A cooperative program is being developed with the Delaware River Basin Commission to design and implement a space data link through ERTS–A to provide simultaneous surface sensor and space observation data on the quality and movement of water. A Chesapeake Bay research project has been initiated involving Maryland, Delaware, and Virginia governmental agencies and universities and the U.S. Geological Survey geography, hydrology, geology, and cartography applications programs. Its goal is to develop a systematic and coordinated approach to the analysis and solution of regional environmental problems involving water resources, vegetation, the works of man, and the interactions among them. Supporting research at American University has indicated a very promising capability for relating marsh and estuarine vegetation to water conditions. In cooperation with the Geological Survey of Alabama, Apollo 9 photography was used to map hitherto undetermined shear zones, thereby demonstrating a value of space data for providing knowledge of great value to the study of water resources and the planning of dams and reservoirs. Supporting photometric research has shown a relationship between anomalous soil mineralization and vegetation conditions in a selected copper-molybdenum area in Maine, and radiometric research in a selected field area has distinguished limestone from dolomite. Research of passive microwave radiometer systems is being supported to determine their potential for measuring moisture content of snow fields to enable more accurate forecasting and more effective management of regional water resources. Programs were initiated using Gemini, Apollo, and high altitude aircraft multiband photography to develop methods of mapping land use and of monitoring and mapping environmental change. These methods will be incorporated into ERTS experiment and applications programs in 1972. Using Apollo and Gemini photographs, a map was prepared at 1:1,000,000 showing 11 categories of land use in the Southwestern United States. Research is being sponsored to develop the use of satellite and high altitude aircraft remote sensor data for archeological research and for analysis of the impact of urban development on local climates.

The Alaska Power Administration is examining the potential value of communications satellites for internal and external communications and for educational as well as standard television.

Operations.—The Geological Survey, in direct support of NASA, continued the analysis and mapping of the moon using Lunar Orbiter IV and Apollo 12 photographs. The potential values of radar for mapping lunar surface materials and of a lunar rover mounted magnetometer for analysis of rock types were demonstrated. Samples of the moon were analyzed and evidence was developed suggesting that the earth and the moon were formed about the same time, providing new support for a theory that the moon developed independently and had not spun-off from earth. The principal differences between lunar and earth materials compared to date appear to be in relative percentages of auxiliary minerals and in the effects of physical impact on rocks in the lunar environment. Support is being given to NASA in the calibration of return beam vidicon tubes being produced for ERTS–A. Through contract at the University of Illinois, studies are being made to determine the geometry of return beam vidicons and the systems and procedures to be employed to attain best possible geometry and fidelity in the data obtained by them. Administrative, review, and teaching support are being provided to the International Workshop on Remote Sensing to be presented at the University of Michigan May 3–14, 1971 under the sponsorship of NASA, the Departments of Agriculture, Interior and State, AID, and the Naval Oceanographic Office.

The Bureau of Mines conducted research on drilling, explosive, rock fracture, and materials handling processes in simulated lunar environment and performed analyses of mineral values of lunar rock samples.

The Office of Saline Water, jointly with NASA, funded research of the reverse osmosis process and of porous glass membranes for recovery of potable water from urine and wash water in closed systems. The development of a novel, lightweight, flexible, braided fiberglass support for the reverse osmosis process was an important result and will be the subject of continuing research.

International Cooperative Activities.—The Geological Survey and NASA are cooperating with Canada in connection with the International Field Year for the Great Lakes in the study of the applicability of air and spaceborne remote sensing systems for monitoring pollution and the natural and artificial processes of the Great Lakes. A study of geothermal conditions east of Lake Chapala, Mexico was conducted with NASA and Mexico. With the cooperation of the U.S.S.R., proton magnetometer measurements from Cosmos-49 were analyzed for application to the study of regional crustal conditions. Airborne and spaceborne remote sensor studies of Iceland's volcanic and geothermal fields were continued with the Air Force Cambridge Research Laboratory and Iceland's National Resource Council and National Energy Authority. In connection with these, a field study of the 1970 eruption of Hekla Volcano was made. In cooperation with the U.S. Department of State and the Government of Saudi Arabia, airborne magnetic, photographic, and radiometric surveys were made in support of geologic mapping to define the mineral resources base of Saudi Arabia. Similar work was conducted in cooperation with the Administration for International Development (AID) and the governments of Liberia and Indonesia. As a result of this work, several areas for oil exploration have been defined in Liberia. In Indonesia all resources are being studied, but special interest has been developed in potential geothermal power sources in central Java. Geological Survey support is being given to Brazil, Venezuela, Guyana, and other Latin American nations in the planning of projects to use airborne and spaceborne systems for resources analysis in both research and operations. Research of factors and effects of crater formation in natural crater areas and by artificial propagation was conducted cooperatively with the Department of Defense, the Geological Survey of Canada, and the Bureau of Mineral Resources of Australia. These studies are aimed at a better understanding of the geology of the moon.

The Bureau of Reclamation, with the cooperation of the Advanced Research Projects Agency, has begun research of remote sensor system applications to analyses of soil, drainage, water occurrence, and vegetation for reclamation planning in the United States AID-supported Pa Mong Project cooperative with the governments of Thailand and Laos.

Department of Agriculture

Introduction

The U.S. Department of Agriculture (USDA) continued its efforts in 1970 to develop applications of remote sensing and to improve its capability to collect and analyze the growing variety of earth resources data and information via remote sensing techniques. Its sensor-signature research extended from laboratories and field observations to aircraft and spacecraft platforms. Its objectives are to: (1) determine and evaluate the feasibilities and potentials for the improvement of agricultural, forestry, and range programs which depend upon the rapid accumulation, analysis, and application of information on crops, forests and wildlands, soils, and water conditions; (2) to assess the synoptic changes in man's nonurban environment; and (3) to identify in particular those applications where the benefits achieved would have a major impact on the national agricultural economy. The National Academy of Sciences has estimated that the losses incurred in agriculture in the United States due to insects, disease, and fire alone exceed $13 billion annually. A system of remote sensors that would be capable of early detection of these plant stress factors can have an immediate impact on control programs as well as the national economy. In order to provide optimum long-term benefits, the Department of Agriculture has initiated appropriate remote sensing research and development programs in the attempt to improve the ability and capability to obtain and analyze greater amounts of data of improved quality on a near realtime basis. It is believed that remote sensing techniques can add significant dimensions in the acquisition of both United States and world agricultural and wildland resources information. As one specific example, Forest Service Fire Research developed a new airborne thermal infrared system for both detection and mapping of forest fires. Operational tests in an 8,000 square mile forest area show that the system has outstanding efficiency. On a single night patrol flight, 59 new forest fires were rapidly detected following a dry lightning storm. In addition, during this critical fire season scores of spreading forest fires were mapped under conditions of dense smoke that prevented usual reconnaissance.

Cooperative Activities in Aerospace Programs

In recognizing the immediate need for a technically feasible and economically sound earth resources remote sensing program that can effectively utilize aerospace technology to collect near realtime data, the Department of Agriculture engaged in a number of Federal interagency activities.

In cooperation with NASA, USDA through its Agricultural Research Service and Forest Service continued its remote sensing research investigations pertinent to agricultural, forestry, and range problems. A large part of the research is being devoted to a better understanding of the interaction of radiant energy with plant tissues and soils. USDA continued to develop U.S. regional multidisciplinary experimental test sites for the future NASA high flight earth resources survey aircraft that would simulate the Earth Resources Technology Satellite (ERTS) overflights scheduled for orbit in 1972. In order to provide an adequate and effective data flow from ERTS to USDA, the Department also continued studies with NASA to assist in the development of a data network concept, including data acquisition, processing, reproduction, dissemination, analysis, evaluation, cataloging, storage, retrieval, and feedback.

Assistance was also provided NASA by USDA in the development of an International Workshop Program on remote sensing of earth resources scheduled for May 1971. USDA is expected to contribute 10 to 12 lecture topics.

USDA was a member of an interagency task group in a definitive policy study toward the establishment of a national earth resources survey program aimed at the full utilization of ground, aircraft, and satellite remote sensing data.

USDA was a member of a joint task force in which a study was made to determine the most effective and expeditious manner in which to monitor and evaluate national natural disasters and catastrophies via aerospace and other systems.

In order to determine the feasibility and potentiality of utilizing aerospace remote sensing technology for less developed countries USDA participated in an Agency for International Development symposium.

The interest of many countries has been aroused by USDA's remote sensing research activities. During 1970 visitors from Argentina, Australia, Belgium,

Brazil, Canada, England, France, Germany, India, Israel, Italy, Mexico, Netherlands, and South Africa came to the Department to be briefed. Briefings were also given to some 50 foreign agricultural counselors based at their Washington, D.C. embassies.

Remote Sensing Program

The Department, during 1970, recognized its need to continue its efforts to develop the capability to collect, analyze, and utilize the near realtime synoptic and sequential data to be obtained from remote sensing experimental satellites, in preparation for future operational satellite systems. It established an Earth Resources Survey Committee to aid in the coordination of effort and the formulation of guidelines for the Department's effective participation in a national earth resources program. It further assessed its in-house capabilities to handle the anticipated large quantities of data which will be acquired from the experimental Earth Resources Technology Satellites A and B, Skylab, and high flight aircraft systems proposed by NASA. Concomitantly, USDA further identified its data and information needs to effect the greater usage of aircraft and satellite systems of the future. It continued in the

attempt to acquire and properly equip a multi-instrumented remote sensing research aircraft in order to more effectively acquire, analyze, evaluate, and utilize data obtained on crops, forests, ranges, and on soils and water conditions in a more accurate, rapid, and timely manner. Possession of its own airborne remote sensing research platform will lessen considerably the Department's dependence upon others for the acquisition of data. Several approaches to the problem are being considered. An expanded effort was also made to apprise not only its agencies but also its 53 affiliated Federal and State experiment stations and 17 State schools of forestry, agribusinesses, and the agricultural community at large of the feasibility and the potential benefits to be derived from a remote sensing earth resources survey program. USDA, in cooperation with NASA and the National Academy of Sciences, published a 424-page treatise entitled "Remote Sensing—With Special Reference to Agriculture and Forestry." The purpose, in part, was to bridge the communications gap that exists among agricultural and forestry scientists, physical scientists, and data processing specialists. It also provides background information on the potential uses of remote sensing in agriculture and wildland resources and a technical appraisal of state-of-the-art sensors and discrimination techniques.

Department of Commerce

Introduction

The Department of Commerce has four major organizational units engaged in activities that contribute to the national aeronautics and space program. These are the National Oceanic and Atmospheric Administration, the National Bureau of Standards, the Maritime Administration, and the Office of Telecommunications. Other units of the Department contribute indirectly. The U.S. Patent Office, for example, issues patents on inventions with space applications, and the National Technical Information Service collects and distributes scientific and technical information produced under the aeronautics and space program.

National Oceanic and Atmospheric Administration

The National Oceanic and Atmospheric Administration (NOAA) was created within the U.S. Depart-

ment of Commerce on October 3, 1970, pursuant to Presidential Reorganization Plan No. 4 of 1970. The NOAA is composed of organizational entities from the Department of Commerce, the Department of the Interior, the Department of Transportation, the National Science Foundation, and the Department of Defense. The Environmental Science Services Administration (ESSA) of the Department of Commerce was abolished and its major units were incorporated into the NOAA. Current NOAA organizational elements and the organizations from which they were derived are shown below:

NOAA organizational elements	From
National Weather Service.	ESSA Weather Bureau.
National Marine Fisheries Service.	Bureau of Commercial Fisheries and the Marine Sport Fish Research Program, both from Department of the Interior.

NOAA organizational elements	*From*
Environmental Research Laboratories.	ESSA Research Laboratories.
National Ocean Survey	ESSA Coast and Geodetic Survey, and the U.S. Lake Survey from the U.S. Army Corps of Engineers.
National Environmental Satellite Service.	ESSA National Environmental Satellite Center.
Environmental Data Service.	ESSA Environmental Data Service, and the National Oceanographic Data Service from the U.S. Navy.
Office of Sea Grant	National Sea Grant Program of the National Science Foundation.
Data Buoy Project Office	National Data Buoy Project of the Coast Guard, Department of Transportation.
National Oceanographic Instrumentation Center.	Same name, U.S. Navy.
Marine Minerals Technology.	Same name, Department of the Interior.

The NOAA mission is to explore, map, and chart the global oceans, their basins, their geophysical forces and fields, and their biological and mineral resources. New physical and biological knowledge will be translated into systems to assess the sea's potential yield, and into techniques which the Nation and its industries can employ to manage, use, and conserve these animal and mineral resources. NOAA will monitor and predict the quickly changing elements of the physical environment in real time. The atmosphere, oceans, sun and the solid earth will be under constant surveillance. Predictions will be made of weather, tides, solar flares, and changes in gravity and geomagnetism. Warnings will be given on impending environmental hazards to ease the burden caused by hurricanes and floods, tornadoes, tidal waves, and other natural disaster conditions. NOAA also will monitor and predict the gradual and inexorable changes of climate, seismicity, marine-life distributions, earth tides, continental position, and the planet's internal circulations, and will note and examine the effects of civilization and industry on the environment and life. To accomplish these objectives, NOAA will draw upon the knowledge, talent, and experience of its personnel, and its wide range of facilities, and will strengthen the mutually important links between government, universities, and industry. NOAA and its institutional partners will develop technology and systems for more effective assessment of resources, utilization of environmental data, environmental monitoring and prediction, and possibly for environmental modification and control. Thus, the growing family of satellites, sensors, ships, data buoys, computers, and simulators, will be used to extend man's capability for observing his environment and to provide the technology for essential environmental services. In these ways NOAA will seek to improve the safety and the quality of life, and man's comprehension, use, and preservation of his home, the planet Earth.

Highlights of 1970.—On January 23, 1970, an Improved Tiros Operational Satellite, I–TOS 1, was successfully launched by NASA. This satellite is the operational prototype of the second generation of polar-orbiting operational environmental satellites. I–TOS 1 meets major National Operational Meteorological Satellite System (NOMSS) objectives in that it has the capability to obtain nighttime observations, temperature measurements of cloud tops and the earth's surface, and is equipped with a solar proton monitor.

ESSA–2, the first Automatic Picture Tansmission (APT) spacecraft of the Tiros Operational Satellite system was retired after almost 5 years of continuous service. This spacecraft was launched February 28, 1966, and was deactivated October 16, 1970, after 1,691 days in orbit.

The improved Satellite Infrared Spectrometer (SIRS–B) on Nimbus 4, launched April 8, 1970, obtains measurements of atmospheric water vapor content and vertical temperature profiles. SIRS–B also provides a more dense network of observations than did the earlier SIRS–A carried on Nimbus 3.

NOAA–1, designated I–TOS A prior to launch, was placed in orbit on December 11. This is the first operational satellite of the ITOS system.

Intensive, realtime operational experiments to use Applications Technology Satellite (ATS) pictures were conducted by the National Environmental Satellite Service, the National Severe Weather Warning Center, Kansas City, and the National Hurricane Center, Miami. The purpose was to test the utility of near-continuous cloud cover observations for severe weather warnings, and for hurricane surveillance, advisory, and warning operations.

NOAA and NASA initiated procurement for the Geostationary Operational Environmental Satellite (GOES) system. NASA will produce the operational prototype spacecraft in its Synchronous Meteorological Satellite (SMS) project.

Solar proton data, obtained in near real-time from the I–TOS 1 satellite, were used to support the Apollo 13 mission in the critical hours prior to reentry.

The National Marine Fisheries Service started investigations on the uses of aerospace sensors for charting the oceanic environment of marine life, and for locating and tracking fish stocks.

NOAA National Weather Service has furnished support, under the World Meteorological Organization Voluntary Assistance Program, for the installation in foreign countries of 10 ground stations for receiving data directly from U.S. environmental satellites.

National Weather Service

The National Weather Service (NWS) is involved in the aeronautics and space program in two ways. NWS furnishes weather support to the space program through its Space Operations Support Division and to civil and military aviation through its forecasting services and research programs. The NWS also is involved in determining the usefulness of space technology for its data gathering and dissemination systems, and the usefulness of space-acquired data for weather analysis and forecasting. During 1970 the National Weather Service has expanded its operational use of space technology using satellite-acquired data in its routine analysis and forecasting procedures, and satellite telemetry systems to relay information expeditiously. The NWS also provides meteorological guidance and support for space test facilities and operations.

Collection and Relay of Data by Satellites.—The Applications Technology Satellite ATS–1 has been used experimentally for the past 2 years to collect river stage and rainfall measurements from untended automatic stations and to relay these data to a central point for analysis. This successful experiment will become operational with the planned 1972 launch of the prototype GOES. These data will be used routinely in the preparation of flood forecasts, and for research into many water resources problems. The telemetry system will also be used to broadcast timely warnings of flood conditions. As the system develops, other hydrological sensor equipment will be added to the GOES data collection and relay system.

The ATS–3 satellite transponder is in use in a continuing operational experiment, testing an inexpensive shipboard data transmitter as part of the design of system for rapid collection of weather data from ships at sea.

Snow Mapping by Satellite.—Studies performed under contract for the National Environmental Satellite Service (NESS) and NWS have materially aided in providing a better understanding of the benefits and limitations of visual photographic mapping by satellite of snow-covered areas. Timely data on the areal extent and water equivalent of snowfields are required by hydrologists in the preparation of river and water supply forecasts for the nation. NWS River Forecast Centers are receiving satellite products for application to these operational problems.

Remote Sensing of the Water Equivalent of Snow.— Techniques are being tested for remote measurement of the water equivalent of snow cover from sensors aboard aircraft. Sensing techniques are based on the changes in attenuation of natural earth-emitted gamma radiation due to variations in the water equivalent of snow. The results of the first year of research are promising for future application of the method to operational river forecasting.

Cloud pictures collected routinely from the ATS satellites by NOAA's Wallops Station command and Data Acquisition Station are processed for retransmission by the ATS transponders to local Automatic Picture Transmission (APT) ground stations at Honolulu and San Francisco where they are used in the daily operations of the forecast offices.

Special receivers for ATS pictures were established at the National Severe Storm Forecast Center (NSSFC) at Kansas City and the National Hurricane Center (NHC) in Miami. The installations are complete, with high quality photographic recorders, special receiving equipment, and a complete photographic laboratory. In addition to photographic prints, 16-mm. movie loops are produced, by which the evolution and motion of the storms can be observed and studied. This represents a breakthrough for the field forecasters. It enabled the NHC to program reconnaissance flights more efficiently and the NSSFC to evaluate the radar weather data more effectively.

Digitized Cloud Mosaics.—Digitized mosaics of satellite cloud pictures are transmitted routinely from the National Meteorological Center to NWS forecast offices throughout the United States. The mosaics, now prepared and transmitted once a day, will be replaced with mosaics prepared and transmitted on an orbit-to-orbit basis (approximately once every 2 hours).

Automatic Picture Transmission.—Early in 1968 the National Weather Service began the transmission of raw APT signals in an existing central facsimile network. The APT data acquired at Wallops Station, Va., San Francisco, Calif., and Kunia, Hawaii, are transmitted to stations on the network within minutes after receipt from the satellite. Transmission of infrared nighttime imagery was added in November 1970. This operational network has been expanded to include a large number of Air Force and Navy installations in the conterminous United States. The number of APT stations needed for Government weather stations has decreased materially as a result of this network operation.

Under the voluntary assistance program the Weather Service has provided technical assistance and advice for installation of complete APT systems in 10 underdeveloped countries. More installations are planned.

Nimbus 4 Satellite Infrared Spectrometer.—The SIRS–B spectrometer, an improved version of the SIRS–A used on Nimbus 3, is furnishing global vertical temperature and moisture profiles daily. These data are used as experimental operational input to the numerical (computer) weather analysis programs, and are being evaluated for their accuracy. Availability of these data globally in realtime conceivably could lead not only to improvement in the computer forecasts but also to economic savings from reprogramming of the current ground-based upper-air observation network.

Meteorological Support to Space Operations and Test Facilities.—Through its Space Operations Support Division, NWS furnished the primary meteorological guidance for several NASA activities. NWS provided staff and local forecasting support for the Kennedy Space Center and the Manned Spacecraft Center, and forecasts of weather and sea conditions for the Apollo 13 flight.

After the Apollo 13 in-flight explosion, forecasts were required for many possible emergency landing areas in the Southern Hemisphere and finally for the actual landing some 500 miles south of the Samoan Islands. Weather satellites again provided a principal source of data on which these remote area forecasts were based. A new global prognosis chart prepared by the National Meteorological Center also was useful for the predictions in the Southern Hemisphere tropics.

At the NASA Mississippi Test Facility, the NWS team made weather observations and forecasts for the ground testing of the final nine Apollo-Saturn rocket engines scheduled at the facility.

At the NASA Wallops Stations, NWS provided weather support for the varied activities of that facility. In support of the scientific program conducted during the total solar eclipse on March 7, 1970, 24 rocket probes were fired, 13 in a 15-minute period. A vast number of surface and upper air weather observations were recorded before, during, and after the eclipse, in support of the rocket firings.

Utilization of Aircraft.—Meteorologist-pilots of the quality control staffs at NWS headquarters fly light, single or twin-engine aircraft (either rented or privately owned) in connection with quality control duties. These flights permit in-flight monitoring and evaluation of NWS-furnished aviation weather services; they also are used as a means of travel for station visits and on-station services evaluations.

In addition, aviation forecasters take familiarization trips as passengers in airline and other aircraft to become better acquainted with their areas of forecast responsibility and the use made of NWS products.

Services to Aviation.—Specialized weather information is provided to pilots, controllers, and aircraft operators to promote efficiency in aviation activities. This information is in the form of observations, forecasts, warnings, and pilot briefings.

Observations are made at 908 locations; many by other Government agencies, airlines, and airport personnel. Terminal forecasts are made for 425 airports, generally every 6 hours. Area forecasts and in-flight advisories are also provided. Forecasts for international aviation covering most of the Northern Hemisphere and part of the Southern Hemisphere are also provided in facsimile and digital forms, the latter being used extensively in computer flight planning by the airlines.

Pilot weather briefings are available through 248 National Weather Service offices, plus 334 FAA offices and 159 unmanned FAA facilities. About 2 million briefings are provided annually by the National Weather Service and about 13 million by the FAA.

National Marine Fisheries Service

The National Marine Fisheries Service (NMFS) plays a major role in the development and utilization of national fisheries resources. The NMFS mission is to discover, describe, develop, and conserve the living resources of the oceans, particularly those that affect the economy and food supplies of the United States. To this end the NMFS conducts biological and ecological research on fish and marine organisms, analyzes the economics of fishery operations and marketing, develops methods for improving catches, and conducts a voluntary grading and inspection program of fishery catches. The NMFS and the U.S. Coast Guard conduct joint enforcement and surveillance operations in territorial waters of the United States and on the high seas. Twenty-nine vessels, 30 laboratories, and 50 offices across the Nation are used to carry out the NMFS mission.

Aerospace Program for Remote Sensing.—Since the ocean environment determines the activity and movement of fishes and other marine life, it is necessary to study this environment in as much detail as possible. In the past such measurements were, of necessity, limited to those that could be acquired by ships and shore stations. Remote sensors, developed concurrently with aerospace technology, have great potential as means for acquiring detailed, timely measurements over large areas of the ocean. The NMFS signed an agreement with NASA on August 21, 1970, that initiated a program to assess the value of remote sensing to their mission. This is the National Marine Fisheries Aerospace Remote Sensing Program at NASA's Mississippi Test Facility. Sensors mounted on aircraft will be tested to determine their utility for measuring patterns of ocean surface temperature and for locating fish stocks. Instruments to be tested include low-light-level image intensifiers, lasers, aerial cameras, and spectrometers. As tests proceed, existing instruments may be modified and new instruments may be developed. In addition, observations of oceanic patterns over large areas will be studied by using measurements obtained from spacecraft sensors. The NASA is cooperating with and advising the NMFS in the development of instrumentation and sensor systems to gather data from spacecraft during the proposed Earth Resources Technology Satellite (ERTS) and Skylab programs. The NMFS has also started studies of the surface temperature patterns of the oceans using infrared data obtained by NOAA's Environmental Survey Satellites. These studies are part of a general program being developed by NMFS to relate space-acquired oceanic data to the NMFS mission requirement for assessing and monitoring living marine resources. The NMFS requirements for ocean surface data closely matches the requirements of the NWS and of the National Ocean Survey in that the data required in common are ocean surface temperatures, sea state (wave conditions), winds, sea currents, storm locations, salinity, and other phenomena.

Environmental Research Laboratories

The Environmental Research Laboratories (ERL), with headquarters in Boulder, Colo., conduct the fundamental investigations needed to improve man's understanding of the physical environment. Ten laboratories conduct research in the various scientific disciplines required in support of NOAA missions.

Office of the Director.—Two geophysical studies were conducted in support of systems design for geostationary satellites for aeronautical communications. One was to determine the effects of ionospheric irregularities in polar regions on S-band (1,700 MegaHertz) radio signals passing through the ionosphere. Transmissions received at Gilmore Creek, Alaska, from ESSA 8 and I–TOS 1 at both 1,700 MHz and 137 MHz were used to detect these effects (known as scintillations). Comparisons showed that scintillations at the higher frequency are considerably smaller than those at the lower frequencies usually used for satellite communications.

The second study was to determine what effects polar region solar proton events have on satellite signals. Although such events, known as polar cap absorption (PCA), are rare, they can absorb radio signals transmitted through the ionosphere. Such absorption can be considerable and can last many hours. Calculations of the effects of PCA on 137 MHz transmissions at the elevation angles to be used with geostationary satellites established the probable amount of such absorption and its geographical extent. Analysis of PCA events over the past 15 years also established the

probability of occurrence of various amounts of such absorption.

A cooperative program to study the interaction of mountain waves and clear air turbulence was undertaken by NOAA units, the National Center for Atmospheric Research (NCAR), the U.S. Air Force, and the Canadian Research Establishment. Aircraft used in the investigation included two USAF and one NOAA RB-57, NCAR's Saberliner and Buffalo, and the NOAA high-altitude glider. Measurements of turbulence and wind conditions in mountain waves were made at 25 levels, ranging from 13,000 to 65,000 feet, to obtain vertical profiles of these phenomena. Severe turbulence was encountered primarily at 60,000 feet, and wind direction reversals occurred in two cases. The new understanding of clear air turbulence gained from these investigations will be particularly useful to those flying high altitude and supersonic aircraft.

Atmospheric Physics and Chemistry Laboratory (Boulder).—In a program to study inadvertent weather modification caused by jet contrail "clouds," infrared radiometers carried aboard a NASA 990 aircraft were used to obtain thermal measurements. Immediately beneath the contrails, a decrease of about 7 percent in net incoming radiation was observed at the earth's surface. However, these effects were found to decrease rapidly as one moved 50 miles on either side of the jet corridor. A recent pilot program was conducted with a stratospheric jet aircraft carrying a down-looking spectrometer to measure atmospheric effects of infrared radiant emission from vapor trails. This experiment, conducted at 65,000 feet, showed essentially no effect at altitude and no effect at the earth's surface. These measurements are expected to be important in evaluating the effect of increasing jet aircraft traffic on local and worldwide climate.

Possibilities for eliminating the hazard to manned spacecraft launches caused by lightning discharges are being studied. One approach is to predict the possibility of natural electrical discharges, using measurements of electric field conditions in the launch area just prior to launch. The other approach is to discharge potential lightning by artificial means just prior to launch of a vehicle; this should greatly reduce the possibility of hazardous discharges during launch. Small rockets were launched into thunderclouds to test this idea. The rockets did trigger discharges, and aircraft measurements obtained in the cloud shortly after the rocket firings indicated a significant reduction in electrical field strengths.

Air Resources Laboratory (Washington, D.C.).—The laboratory and the FAA conducted studies on the effects of the sonic boom produced by supersonic aircraft. A study was done at Pendleton, Oreg., on the effect of sonic boom on the space-time variability of atmospheric parameters. A significant small-scale space variability in overpressure was detected.

A quantitative study was conducted on the geometry and intensity of wing tip vortices produced by heavy aircraft such as the 747 and C–5A flying at low altitudes. These measurements, gathered by sophisticated meteorological instruments mounted on low-flying aircraft, were used by the FAA for establishing regulations to guarantee safe distances between aircraft in flight.

ERL Research Flight Facility (Miami, Fla.).—The facility provided and operated aircraft in support of weather modification experiments, hurricane surveillance, and experiments requiring collection of data.

During the solar eclipse of March 7 RFF aircraft seeded stratiform clouds with dry ice in the vicinity of Langley AFB. The seeding was done to dissipate the cloud so the NASA facility could photograph the eclipse.

During the period April 15–May 31, RFF participated, with other research groups, in an experiment over south Florida using pyrotechnics to seed cumulus cloud with silver iodide. The objectives of the experiment were to repeat the single-cloud seeding experiment of May 1968 to obtain a statistically significant cloud sample (30 clouds) and to use massive silver iodide pyrotechnic seedings of individual cumulus clouds. The latter part of the experiment was to permit recognition and documentation of any changes in mesoscale structure and precipitation resulting from seeding.

Extensive reconnaissance and research was conducted on cyclogenesis on the Atlantic coast of the northeastern United States during the fall and winter of 1969. The main objective was to provide real-time data to the operational forecaster in an attempt to improve forecasts of coastal storms.

Aeronomy Laboratory (Boulder).—This laboratory studies the physical and chemical processes of the ionosphere, upper atmosphere, and exosphere of the earth and other planets.

One accomplishment of 1970 was the first completely successful rocket flight of an atomic-oxygen sensor for the upper atmosphere. Atomic oxygen is an important constituent of the atmosphere at altitudes above the stratopause; prior to the development of this new rocket-borne sensor, measurements of its concentration have not been obtainable. The new measurements will permit a definitive choice of a theory of the production and loss of atomic oxygen, thus promoting our understanding of the interaction between the upper and lower atmosphere.

A continuing extensive program of laboratory measurements of atmospheric ion-molecule reaction rates has resulted in major advances in understanding the importance of water vapor in the lower ionosphere and the role of carbon dioxide in the ionospheres of Mars and Venus.

Experimental studies in upper-atmosphere plasma physics are continuing. Under investigation is the structure of radio-frequency fields within the nonuniform plasma sheaths that surround spacecraft reentering the atmosphere.

Earth Sciences Laboratory (Boulder).—ESL conducts research in geomagnetism, seismology, geodesy, and related technologies.

Hydromagnetic wave emissions at 0.33 Hz were observed at the Dodge satellite as it drifted across the geomagnetic field line connecting Byrd (Antartica) and Great Whale River (Canada). These data are being used in studies of rapid variations in the geomagnetic field, and to test current theories on the origin of such emissions. The use of satellite observations will be increased as a result of the successful detection described above.

Space Disturbances Laboratory (Boulder).—This laboratory conducts research on solar-terrestrial physics, and develops techniques for accurate forecasting of solar disturbances, and their effects on the earth environment. SDL is the national and international focal point for current information on the solar-terrestrial environment; SDL disseminates this information and current forecasts to a wide variety of users.

Studies of solar physics are conducted to gain understanding of solar energy release mechanisms with the aim of improving forecasts of the times and locations of solar flares that can produce geophysical disturbances. Recent findings include:

—Analyses of high resolution magnetograms show that the magnetic field of the solar surface can be resolved into small elements with strengths of about 20 gauss.

—Periodic brightenings on the solar disc of hydrogen alpha mottles, with a period of about 5 minutes and phase coherence over regions 30,000 KM broad have been identified with solar acoustic-gravity waves.

—It has been found that energetic ultraviolet (EUV) radiation and hard X-ray bursts from solar flares are correlated. The energy of electrons required to produce hard X-rays appears sufficiently strong to account for the EUV, through ionization and subsequent radiative recombination in the lower chromosphere.

—The intensity variations of white light emission in some large flares were found to be well correlated with a strong flux of EUV at 10 to 1030 Angstroms, and that the flux increase in white light is approximately equal to that in the EUV range. This correlation is of interest since the occurrence of white-light flares seems to be directly connected with collisions between two sunspot groups.

Studies continue on the interactions between the magnetosphere and the solar wind, the transfer of energy from the solar wind into the earth's magnetosphere, and the behavior and transport of this energy within the magnetosphere ionosphere and upper atmosphere. Satellite measurements appear to confirm current theories on magnetosphere shock wave formation.

Experimental ground-based observation of interplanetary scintillations at 11.4-meter wavelengths yielded daily information from September 1969 through April 1970. This information on the velocity and small scale structure of the solar wind complements the suprathermal observations obtained by particle detectors aboard scientific satellites. These measurement techniques can be used to detect and fix the location of an interplanetary magnetic field sector boundary between the sun and the earth; such information could be used to predict when the boundary will sweep past the earth. If such observations became available routinely, they would be of great use in forecasting magnetic and ionospheric activity.

The SDL cooperated with a Canadian research group at York University in flying photometric sensors on two Black Brant III rockets. The start of an infrared aurora was measured by this instrumentation, yielding valuable information on the energy characteristics of a unique excited state of the oxygen molecule. This newly observed phenomenon suggests the existence of a source, other than particle precipitation, for infrared emissions. Auroral studies using rocket sensors are being planned with the University of Bergen and four launches are planned.

Data from the solar proton monitor aboard the I-TOS 1 were available for operational use during the Apollo 13 mission. Real-time data from this instrument are becoming available for routine use in space environment monitoring and forecasting. Solar proton and magnetic data, now available continuously from the ATS-1 and Pioneer satellites are particularly useful to the Space Disturbances Forecast Center for early detection and real-time analysis of solar proton events.

SDL assumed operation of the solar proton alert network (SPAN), under a contract with NASA. The SPAN network consists of four ground-based solar observation stations spaced to permit continuous observation of the sun with radio and optical telescopes. Data from this network are used to detect solar proton events. With the inclusion of this activity, the SDL has become a world data center for ground-observed solar data.

A new spectrohelioscope built and installed at SDL in 1970 permits routine observations of sunspot and plage magnetic polarities. This instrument has made possible the collection of a data base adequate for routine sunspot forecasting. It is now possible to predict the location of about 80 percent of all flares.

SDL is involved in determining specifications for a beacon to be flown on NASA's ATS F for use in studies of the magnetosphere and ionospheric electron densities. Signals from the beacon will be received by scientific groups in other nations; SDL is coordinating international scientific activities on the use of the signals.

SDL participates, under NASA contract, in the International Satellite for Ionospheric Studies (ISIS) program. The satellite data acquisition station at Boulder receives data from ISIS 1, and Alouette 1 and 2, and reduces the data to ionograms for dissemination to participating scientific groups.

Other ongoing programs of SDL include analysis of data from the Interplanetary Monitoring Platform (IMP) and Orbiting Geophysical Observatory (OGO) satellites, and support to NASA for the Apollo Telescope Mount program.

National Ocean Survey

The National Ocean Survey (NOS) continues to make steady progress in support of the aeronautical and space programs of the United States. The basic programs of the NOS in this area include the operational use of satellites for geodesy and precise navigation, research to determine the feasibility for using satellite techniques to perform assigned tasks, and operational aerial photography for charting. In addition, NOS provides seismic and geomagnetic support to space facilities and activities.

Aeronautical Charts.—Aeronautical charts published by NOS play a key role in the management and use of the national airspace. They are a means for implementing regulations and air traffic control procedures to make possible safe and efficient aerial navigation.

In 1970 considerable progress was made by NOS in converting all domestic aeronautical charts to specifications approved by the Inter-Agency Air Cartographic Committee. The specifications are designed to assure a single, uniform air cartographic product for use by both military and civil aviation.

Geometric Satellite Triangulation.—Data acquisition for the worldwide satellite triangulation network was completed during mid-November 1970. This program designed to establish a world data system connecting all of the continental data systems is based on the strictly geometric technique of photographing sun-reflective satellites against the star background. It began with the launch of PAGEOS in June 1966 as an integral part of the National Geodetic Satellite Program (NGSP), and will serve as the primary geometric framework for other phases of the program.

Forty-five stations in 23 countries have been established through the joint efforts of NASA, the U.S. Departments of Commerce and Defense, and the 23 host countries. This national program, under the technical direction of NOS will provide a unified three-dimensional framework encircling the earth and connecting all major land masses of the world within the extremely close tolerances in all three positional components.

NASA has overall management responsibility for the NGSP; they designed and launched the PAGEOS satellite and furnised orbital elements for computation of observation predictions. The Topographic Command (TOPOCOM) of the U.S. Army Corps of Engineers, has the primary responsibility for logistics. They furnished four field observation teams and equipment. NOS has the technical responsibility for data acquisition, reduction, analysis, and intial publication of results. NOS provided for personnel training and furnished operation manuals and up to 10 field observation teams at a time.

International cooperation has been generous and substantial, indicating the interest in and the recognized need for an accurate, three-dimensional worldwide geodetic control network. The following nations participated by permitting the establishment of from one to seven camera stations within the country or its territories: Argentina, Australia, Brazil, Chad, Chile, Denmark, Ecuador, Ethiopia, Federal Republic of Germany, Iran, Italy, Japan, Mascarene Islands, Mexico, New Zealand, Norway, the Philippines, Portugal, Senegal, South Africa, Surinam, Thailand, the United Kingdom, and the United States.

During the program, the Federal Republic of Germany furnished two camera teams and two observation systems. The United Kingdom supplied a field team. The Republic of South Africa, Australia, and Mexico furnished observation teams during operations in their countries. In addition, Australia provided complete logistic support for two stations at their Antarctic bases.

To scale the satellite triangulation properly, at least four base lines spaced around the world were essential to meet NGSP accuracy requirements. In the U.S. work continued on the measurement of a precise geodimeter traverse network with connections to two of the worldwide network stations and to several of the supplemental network stations. Geodetic organizations in Norway, Sweden, Denmark, Federal Republic of Germany, Austria, Italy, Australia, Nigeria, and France cooperated by measuring the required scale lines.

The PAGEOS and Echo II satellites were utilized as observational targets for all data acquisition. Of the almost 10,000 simultaneous photographic observations scheduled during the program, almost 1,500 were successful, resulting in about 3,000 useful plates. Photogrammetric processing during 1970 included 192 new plates measured, 427 old plates remeasured to conform to new criteria, and 256 plates processed through anaylsis and computation. To date in the program, a total of 1,550 plates has been measured and processed through analysis and computation. New computer programed data reduction and analysis methods have been introduced to provide a final accuracy of at least one part per million in terms of earth dimensions.

The measuring and processing of photographic plates will continue as planned, with completion of data processing scheduled to occur during 1972.

Many developments and improvements in methods and equipment were adopted during the period 1967 to 1970. Precise transfer of epoch time was accomplished at first by use of portable crystal clocks and later replaced by portable cesium clocks. Transponders aboard geostationary satellites of the ATS type were utilized for time transfer to remote islands in the Atlantic and Pacific Oceans. A time reset capability using polar-orbiting doppler satellites was developed and successfully used at stations in the Antarctic. As Loran C chains became synchronized and available, they were used to provide time reset capabilities without the necessity for carrying portable clocks from station to station.

As data acquisition for the world net drew to a close in the fall of 1970, NOS continued the Cooperative Program of Satellite Triangulation Densification in North America which was established in 1963. TOPOCOM and Canadian interests furnished airlifts and observer personnel. The United Kingdom is continuing support by providing two observation teams.

Observations were conducted from July through September 1970 at five stations in the southern United States. Currently, field teams are on station in Alaska, Canada, and Greenland. Current plans call for the completion of the field work during 1972 and the computations during 1974.

Photogrammetric Applications.—In the area of aerial photography technical and theoretical assistance was provided in support of the NASA Apollo Program. A metric camera experiment was designed to determine geometric as well as gravimetric conditions on the moon.

NOS operates two aircraft to conduct aerial photographic missions required for NOAA progams. One aircraft is a Government-owned, twin-turboprop; the other is a leased, twin-engine aircraft. Both are manned by specially trained NOAA pilots and aerial photographers.

The aerial metric photography, in which panchromatic, infrared, and color film is used, supports aeronautical and nautical charting programs, seaward boundary surveys, and coastal inundation mapping. Photogrammetry is also used in surveys of areas devastated by earthquakes and hurricanes, surveys of estuarine and ocean currents, and for monitoring crustal movements in areas of high seismicity.

Seismological Activities.—Expansion of the Tsunami Warning System continued. The eventual goal is a network of 30 seismograph stations and 84 tsunami detectors (tide gage and wave sensors). It is planned that elements in the network will eventually telemeter actual recordings to an analysis center in Hawaii via a geostationary satellite. Automatic transmission—by triggering or on query from the satellite—automatic signal identification, and on-line earthquake hypocenter and tsunami arrival-time computations are being planned.

Seismic background characteristics were determined for the Goldstone, Calif., NASA facility where a proposed laser satellite communication installation would be located. Vibrations caused by local industrial sources were identified and documented, and an optimum location for the installation was selected on the basis of this information.

A site evaluation study was made at White Sands, N. Mex., using shallow seismic refraction techniques. NASA plans to use the selected site for a project to determine the feasibility of using energy from rocket thrust plumes as a seismic energy source for the moon.

Geomagnetism.—NOS continued its long-term cooperation with NASA in the development of geophysical instrumentation for space applications. A controlled magnetic environment test chamber, the NOS Fredericksburg Geomagnetic Center, is used in this work. NOS also provided facilities and technical assistance to the U.S. Naval Oceanographic Office for testing and calibrating instrumentation employed on Project Magnet, a worldwide, airborne geomagnetic survey.

In a joint effort with NASA, NOS is using computers to process geomagnetic analog records from some 50 worldwide magnetic observatories and geomagnetic data collected by satellite and space probes. These cooperative efforts have been in progress for the past 7 years.

NOS published a Technical Report (C. & G.S. 38) containing a description of a Fortran II computer program for deriving magnetic values at points near and above the earth's surface. The mathematical model is the International Geomagnetic Reference Field for 1965; this model is used as a common base by scientists around the world in studies of the earth's main magnetic field and in studies of related atmospheric, iono-

spheric, and outer space parameters. The report also includes tables of total magnetic intensity and annual change data on a worldwide grid, and small scale world charts of total magnetic intensity.

The 1970 issue of the *World Magnetic Charts* was published; for the first time analytical methods were used to describe secular change patterns as well as distribution of the magnetic field. Among other important uses, these charts provide basic magnetic data for worldwide nautical and aeronautical charts.

Use of Navigation Satellites.—Five NOAA survey vessels are equipped with satellite navigation systems to provide the accuracy in position fixing necessary for deep sea surveys.

Satellite Telemetry Applications.—The Coast Survey Marine Observation System is a stable, moored, subsurface platform from which oceanographic and atmospheric measurements can be collected. A surface float with attached telemetry antenna provides the capability for telemetering data in real time via the ATS–3 satellite. The telemetry package was provided through a cooperative agreement with NASA. The power source is a radioisotope thermoelectric generator provided through a cooperative agreement with the U.S. Navy. One of the first applications planned for the platform is its use as a tsunami detection station in the mid-Pacific Ocean.

Plans are being made for development of a system for telemetering geomagnetic data in real time via satellite from a network of magnetic observatories to a central receiving station in College, Alaska.

National Environmental Satellite Service

The National Environmental Satellite Service (NESS) plans and operates environmental satellite systems, gathers and analyzes satellite data, and develops new methods of using satellites to obtain environmental data. As environmental satellite technology matures, sensors will be added to measure additional atmospheric characteristics, and to provide data on solar, ionospheric, oceanographic, and other geophysical phenomena.

Environmental Satellites.—The operational environmental satellite system inaugurated the second generation operational spacecraft with the launch of the NASA-funded I–TOS 1 in January 1970. The Improved Tiros Operational Satellite (I–TOS) replaces both the Automatic Picture Transmission (APT) and Advanced Vidicon Camera System (AVCS) satellites of the first-generation Tiros Operational Satellite (TOS) system which have been used since 1966. NOAA 1 (I–TOS A), the first of the NOAA–funded second-generation satellites, was launched in December 1970.

The I–TOS satellites fulfill a major service objective—daily observation of global weather conditions, day and night.

Operations of NOAA Satellites.—At yearend, two of the first-generation TOS satellites—ESSA 8 (APT) and ESSA 9 (AVCS)—remain in operable condition: ESSA 8 is used regularly to supplement the direct readout service from I–TOS 1 and NOAA 1. ESSA 9 is held in standby status to supplement the global observing services of the I–TOS spacecraft if needed.

The I–TOS satellite provides both full global coverage and direct local readout services. Observations are provided twice daily at 12-hour intervals. In addition to vidicon camera systems of the type used in the earlier TOS satellites, the I–TOS satellite carries a two-channel scanning radiometer. This sensor provides daytime and nighttime (infrared) observations of the earth's cloud cover. In addition, the data from the infrared sensor can be converted to temperature; in cloudy areas this information provides a measure of cloud top height. In clear and partly cloudy areas, sea surface temperatures may be derived from the infrared observations for use by environmental service agencies.

Both global and direct readout services are provided by I–TOS. Observations by the vidicon camera system and/or the scanning radiometer are recorded as the satellite proceeds along its orbit. The stored data are transmitted to ground stations in Alaska and Virginia, relayed to a central processing unit at Suitland, Md., processed, and made available to environmental service agencies nationally and internationally.

Data from the APT camera and the scanning-radiometer are broadcast continuously for reception by simply equipped ground stations within a 2,000-mile range of the satellite. A given station can obtain observations from the satellite during a period centered on 3 p.m., local standard time, and again around 3 a.m., local standard time. These data are acquired and used daily at some 500 locations in over 50 countries around the world. The pictures are used as a basis for local, area, and air-route forecasts, to illustrate television weather programs and newspaper weather reporting, and to support a variety of operations. In addition to the imaging and temperature sensors, the I–TOS carries a solar proton monitor (SPM) as part of its complement of operational instruments. This sensor provides a measure of the solar proton flux in the polar regions. These measurements are used in providing support to telecommunications agencies. Data from SPM were used to support Apollo 13 during critical hours before reentry.

Applications Technology Satellites.—NOAA has cooperated with NASA to continue the experimental operation of ATS–1 and ATS–3. During this past year, intensive operational experiments have been conducted in the application of geostationary satellite observations to severe storm advisory services and to hurricane surveillance, advisory, and warning services. Results of these experiments demonstrate the utility of near continuous observations to vital public warning and advisory services. For example:

One—At the National Severe Storms Center, on July 14, 1970, a line of clouds of the type associated with the early stages of severe weather was observed in the ATS picture. These clouds were in an area known to have high potential for the development of severe weather, but were undetected in the conventional network at this time. This interpretation of the satellite pictures led to an early issuance of a severe weather watch for the area downstream from where the cloud line was located. It was some 4 hours later that radar detected the squall line. This early warning was of particular value to the public as 26 events of severe weather occurred in the forecast area later in the day.

Two—On August 13 and 14, 1970, a tropical disturbance moved across the Atlantic from off Africa to just north of Puerto Rico. As it moved toward the U.S. mainland, it was observed by both satellites and aircraft. This storm contained unusually strong easterly winds, which the aircraft measured, ranging between 50 and 70 miles per hour in local areas. Normally, whenever winds this strong are observed in a tropical disturbance, it is named and warnings are issued so that all interests in its path can take hurricane precautions. However, the satellite showed that this was not a rotating storm and, therefore, did not cause immediate danger. On the basis of these satellite observations the decision was made at the National Hurricane Center in Miami not to name the storm and not to forecast that it would become a hurricane. The storm subsequently broke up, reformed, broke up again, and finally passed into the U.S. mainland near Cape Hatteras without becoming a hurricane.

An operational version of these stationary satellites, the Geostationary Operational Environmental Satellite (GOES) is being developed in NASA's Synchronous Meteorological Satellite (SMS) program. Launch of the first GOES prototype, SMS–A, is planned for mid-1972.

Nimbus IV.—This NASA research and development satellite, launched April 8, 1970, carried an improved version (SIRS–B) of the Satellite Infrared Spectrometer (SIRS–A) first flown in 1969 on Nimbus III. SIRS–A provided measurements along the satellite track from which atmospheric temperature profiles could be derived. The SIRS–B provides measurements along and to either side of the satellite track, from which both atmospheric temperature profiles and atmospheric water vapor content can be calculated. Temperature soundings obtained routinely from SIRS–B are used daily in the numerical upper air analyses and forecasts prepared by the NWS. The SIRS soundings are now being disseminated for use by other national and international environmental service agencies.

Environmental Service Products.—The NESS has continued the daily production and distribution of global and sectional cloud cover mosaics for use by environmental service agencies. Production of the average brightness and minimum brightness charts has continued also. These show 5-, 10-, 30-, and 90-day average cloud cover conditions, and the extent of snow and ice fields, respectively.

During the past year, techniques have been developed for deriving sea surface temperature analyses, and depictions of vertical and horizontal cloud distribution from the I–TOS infrared measurements. Production and evaluation of these new environmental service products have begun on a trial basis.

Operational Applications.—Meteorologists continue to find the satellite photographs particularly useful for detecting and tracking weather systems over about 80 percent of the earth where conventional observations are not available. This worldwide weather surveillance continues to contribute to more reliable and timely environmental service—forecasts, advisories, warnings—to maritime operations and to communities located within and around the ocean basins. For example, the 45 named tropical cyclones that occurred in the Northern Hemisphere in 1970 were all detected and tracked by satellites. Advisories concerning these storms and a larger number of unnamed tropical storms in both hemispheres, were sent to U.S. installations and foreign meteorological services worldwide.

Winds derived routinely from cloud motions observed by ATS 1 and 3 are used daily in numerical weather analyses produced by the National Weather Service and by U.S. military weather services.

Solar proton observations are used by the Space Disturbance Forecast Center in Boulder to support telecommunications and space activities. The data also are distributed to other space environment service agencies.

Research and Development Programs of the National Environmental Satellite Service.—The NESS devotes its research and development efforts toward applications studies to increase the utility of satellite observations to environmental services and development of techniques and sensors for measuring environmental variables from a satellite platform.

Major emphasis during this past year has been placed on studies to develop and refine techniques for extracting and using quantitative data from satellite observations for weather, oceanography, and hydrology service programs.

Some progress has been made toward automating methods for extracting winds from cloud motions observed by ATS 1 and 3.

Techniques for deriving temperature and geopotential height fields from SIRS data have been refined to eliminate dependence on the short-term statistical history of conventional observations.

Techniques currently available for remote sensing of the earth's surface are ineffective when the earth is cloud-covered. Microwave technology shows some promise of reducing or removing this restriction. Basic microwave physics has been examined and microwave observations obtained from the NASA aircraft program have been analysed during 1970 as part of a program to evaluate the utility of microwave sensors for acquiring data to meet NOAA requirements.

Major effort has been devoted to the design and development of the Vertical Temperature Profile Radiometer (VTPR) and the Infrared Temperature Profile Radiometer (ITPR). The VTPR is scheduled to begin operation on I–TOS in 1972. The ITPR, an advanced version of the VTPR type atmospheric temperature sounder, has completed aircraft tests and is scheduled to fly on a NASA Nimbus satellite in 1972. A team of United States and British scientists, under the leadership of NESS, has begun preliminary studies to specify the next generation atmospheric sounder for operational use in the latter half of the 1970's.

International Cooperation.—Worldwide direct readout service via APT continued during 1970 and direct nighttime observations from the scanning radiometer were added. Some 50 countries own and operate ground stations to receive these satellite observations. Weather facsimile experiment transmissions through ATS 1 and 3 have continued on a semioperational basis providing APT ground stations with a variety of satellite products.

The NESS provided training and study facilities for WMO and AID Fellows from Turkey, Japan, Korea, Indonesia, Chile, Argentina, the Philippines, India, Poland, Vietnam, and Pakistan.

International Cooperation Plans.—The United States is cooperating with countries engaged in space activities, as well as with other countries of the world, in the application of satellites to meteorology. This cooperation presently manifests itself in two major international programs, the Global Atmospheric Research Program (GARP) and the World Weather Watch (WWW).

During March 1970, a planning conference on GARP was held in Brussels, Belgium, to review plans and to ascertain the possible national contributions to the experiments. Environmental data from satellites will play a major role in the data requirements for the experiments. At this conference the United States reported that present plans call for one geostationary environmental satellite to be launched in mid to late 1972, and possibly another by mid-1973. In addition to the plans for geostationary satellites, the program for the polar orbiting ITOS operational meteorological satellites will be continued.

The WWW plan for 1972–75 calls for two or three near-polar orbiting meteorological satellites in continuous operation during the period. The plan also includes four geostationary satellites to provide for reasonably complete near-global cloud coverage, and for wind determinations in the tropics from cloud displacement measurements. The United States has indicated that it will support this requirement in a fashion similar to that proposed for GARP. The plan also states that at least some of the near-polar orbiting satellites should be equipped with local direct readout of cloud images. The United States is the only country so far that has supported this requirement by equipping its satellites with direct readout sensors. The United States has assisted WMO members in the installation of direct readout stations in their countries, through support under the WMO Voluntary Assistance Program. Support for 10 direct readout stations has been provided to date. Internationally, this has been a very important program since it offers to developing countries the opportunity to obtain almost instantaneous information on the meteorological conditions affecting the climate of the country for a relatively small expenditure of equipment and personnel resources.

Washington-Moscow Data Exchange.—The United States and the U.S.S.R. have continued the exchange of satellite information over the Washington-Moscow data circuit throughout 1970. The Soviet Union has provided television and infrared information from four identical Meteor satellites (Nos. 3, 4, 5, 6), all launched this year. The primary application of data received from Moscow at the World Weather Center, Washington, has been for research purposes. The United States has transmitted to Moscow satellite photographs and cloud analyses derived from data from ESSA 8 and 9, and the Improved-TOS satellites; these data are used routinely in the analyses made at the World Weather Center, Moscow. Representatives from the two countries met in Washington in March to discuss the joint operation of the circuit. Emerging from this meeting were agreements on high-speed data exchange and a change of circuit routing within Europe to improve reception of information.

Environmental Data Service

The Environmental Data Service collects, processes, archives, publishes, and issues environmental data gathered on a global scale. The Service maintains data centers for geodetic, geomagnetic, seismological, meteorological, aeronomic, and oceanographic information, providing a single source of environmental data readily available to specialized and general user groups. It provides administrative support for the corresponding World Data Centers–A, which receive data from cooperative investigations and other international sources. It also sponsors and conducts research and development activities to improve these functions, and coordinates the international exchange of atmospheric and space data. These functions are exercised through the data centers and related research and information activities described below.

The National Climatic Center (NCC).—This center is at Asheville, N.C., and archives meteorological surface and upper air data and NOAA satellite data. Raw and processed data from the National Weather Service and its cooperators, the U.S. Air Force's Air Weather Service, the Naval Weather Service, and foreign meteorological services are archived at the NCC. The NCC provides data retrieval services for a variety of users such as aviation and space activities, research, commerce, industry, and individuals. Data users can purchase, at production cost, copies of data in manuscript, microfilm, photographic, or magnetic tape form, and data summaries prepared to user specifications. Catalogs of satellite data are published periodically by EDS. The NCC also conducts a referral service for satellite data archived elsewhere, and provides information and advice about pertinent meteorological data. Accomplishments at the NCC relating to aeronautics and space activities during 1970 include:

1. Glossy 8×10 prints of individual frames of satellite cloud photography are now available from the NCC for interested users. Satellite photographs were previously available only in film strips.

2. The first of four volumes on the Upper Air Climatology of the Southern Hemisphere was produced in cooperation with the Department of Defense and the National Center for Atmospheric Research.

3. In cooperation with the Naval Weather Service Command, the first of two volumes of an Upper Air Climatology of the Northern Hemisphere was published; the second volume is in process.

4. Data for the above six volumes are available from NCC on magnetic tape, microfilm, and microfiche. These data have been supplied to NASA for use in its space vehicle reentry studies.

5. Progress on the design of a Clear Air Turbulence Atlas was achieved through a contract. An extensive

bibliography on the subject was compiled at NCC to supplement the contractor's listing, and is available on microfilm.

6. Climatological summaries were prepared for 41 selected airports in the United States in cooperation with the Federal Aviation Administration. These summaries contain several bivariate tables computed from observations taken when ceilings were below 200 feet or visibilities were less than one-half mile. These summaries were published by the FAA.

7. Cloud analyses transmitted on the national facsimile circuit are being coded and punched into cards for use by NASA in cloud cover studies.

8. The NCC has accepted responsibility for the receipt, processing, publication, and distribution of the High Altitude Meteorological Data received from the Meteorological Rocket Network, the EXAMET Net, and participating foreign countries. The data are published for the World Data Center–A for Meteorology and Nuclear Radiation.

In addition to the above, satellite data provide a particularly important contribution to the global Basic Data Sets which are being assembled by NCC for research in the Global Atmospheric Research Program. It will be the most complete collection of meteorological data possible for one winter month (Nov. 1969) and for one summer month (June 1970). ATS cloud and wind data and the SIRS data included are unique and otherwise unobtainable over large ocean areas.

The Aeronomy and Space Data Center (ASDC) Boulder, Colo.—ASDC has assumed responsibility for part of a new contract program between the NASA Manned Spacecraft Center and the NOAA Research Laboratories Space Disturbances Laboratory. Under this program 24-hour-a-day optical and radio monitoring data of solar conditions are gathered at three sites: Boulder, Colo., Carnarvon, Australia, and the Canary Islands. The solar films and solar radio noise data obtained are sent to the ASDC for processing, scaling, and archiving, after which they are made available to other scientists. The program produces a set of quality-controlled, highly homogeneous data, using the system developed by NASA in 1966 for the detection of hazardous solar particles. The solar patrol films, and reduced solar flare and radio noise data from these earlier observations, made in support of the Apollo and other space missions, have been transferred to this data center, and also are available to users. The Aeronomy and Space Data Center also archives solar-terrestrial data recorded by satellites and space probes. In addition, it publishes data monthly on several solar parameters (protons, X-rays, and solar wind) measured by satellites and space probes, in *Solar Geophysical Data*. This provides the international scientific and technical community with data valuable for understanding many solar-terrestrial relationships. Analyses of satellite and space probe experiments, included in data compilations for special events are published in the World Data Center–A *Upper Atmosphere Geophysics Report* series.

The National Oceanographic Data Center.—Oceanographic observations acquired by aircraft and satellite are still in an early stage of development. The National Oceanographic Data Center (NODC) has been conducting pilot projects for processing, storage, and retrieval of such data. It has acquired and begun digitization of a small number of air expendable bathythermograms to develop a processing system for the large number of observations anticipated. NODC has also undertaken a study to determine optimum techniques for storage and retrieval of sea surface temperature measurements acquired by airborne radiation thermometry.

The Geomagnetic Data Center.—This center furnishes hundreds of copies of observatory data annually to space researchers throughout the world. These data, primarily magnetograms (analog records) and indices derived from them, are furnished on microfilm, magnetic tape, and hard copy. They are used for correlation with data obtained from satellites and for interdisciplinary space studies.

The EDS Laboratory for Environmental Data Research.—This EDS Laboratory is investigating the uses of meteorological satellite data for climatological analysis:

1. Cloud climatology studies, in cooperation with NASA's Goddard Space Flight Center are designed to compute the mean monthly cloud cover over the Pacific Ocean. Frequency distribution of cloud cover amounts have been computed from the 8 years of satellite cloud cover analysis available, and maps of specific cloud amount frequency are ready for publication.

2. Climatological analyses, derived from satellite data, of cloud cover amounts in the Pacific Ocean are being compared to those in the Atlantic and Indian Oceans in an effort to understand oscillations in the cloud cover.

3. The influence of orographic effects on cloud cover was investigated with satellite cloud maps. It was found that the relative humidity at or near the surface is an important factor controlling the amount of orographically produced clouds.

4. Estimates were made of the energy associated with the large scale buoyant lifting of air masses over tropical oceans, using cloud top height data derived from satellite measurements. The estimates based on satellite data were within 10 percent of those based on surface observations.

5. The relationship between the scales of satellite observed patterns and of sea-water temperature dis-

tributions derived from satellite data are currently being studied by EDS, NASA, and the Naval Oceanographic Office.

National Bureau of Standards

The goal of NBS is to strengthen and advance the Nation's science and technology and to facilitate their effective application for public benefit. In working toward this goal, the Bureau pursues a wide range of activities, including many projects in space and aeronautics, in its three major institutes: the Institute for Basic Standards, the Institute for Materials Research, and the Institute for Applied Technology.

Institute for Basic Standards

Source for High Energy Photon Calibrations.—With the support of the Goddard Space Flight Center a source of monoenergetic photons is being developed that will be used in calibrating high energy photon detectors for use in satellites, rockets, and balloons. The NBS 180-million electron volt (MeV.) synchrotron will be used to produce a low flux of monochromatic photons in the 10-MeV. to 180-MeV. energy range by in-flight annihilation of positrons. This source will be in operation this year and may be used by many groups through the country.

Studies of the Penetration of High-Energy Radiation Through Matter.—The National Bureau of Standards is engaged in a long-range program for studying the interactions of fast charged particles and photons with matter. A part of this program, slanted towards problems and applications in space technology and science, is supported by a contract with NASA.

Computer programs have been written for calculating the penetration and diffusion of high-energy radiation through extended media. Their reliability has been established through an extensive series of comparisons with experimental data, and these programs are now beginning to pass from the development phase to the production phase. Many applications have been made to problems arising in a variety of space-related fields. Typical examples are: the interpretation of cavity chamber measurements in water media irradiated with high-energy electron beams, in order to establish the relation between the measured ionization in air and the corresponding absorbed dose in water; the determination of the response function of silicon, germanium and sodium iodide detectors, that is, the statistical relation between observed pulse height distributions and the actual photon or electron energy spectra; the calculation of the flux of auroral electrons incident onto the earth's atmosphere from the knowledge of the secondary x-rays observed in balloon experiments at heights of 30–40 km.; and the prediction of three-dimensional auroral ionization and luminosity patterns.

Low Gravity Thermometry.—NBS has developed an instrumentation system to detect the presence of liquid or gaseous phases as well as the temperature of hydrogen in a spacecraft cryogenic propellant tank under near-zero gravity conditions. The measurement system employs a thin-film carbon sensor that provides a relatively high-voltage signal for temperature measurement. Favorable heat-transfer characteristics allow the same sensor surface to discriminate between liquid and saturated vapor.

Apollo–13 Investigation.—Two members of the NBS Cryogenics Division worked as part of a six-man Board of Consultants to help establish the sequence of events leading to the Apollo–13 in-flight explosion. They were asked to assist NASA's investigating team to ensure scientific objectivity, critically review the analyses made by NASA personnel, and contribute their own expertise in the field of cryogenics. The carefully determined data on oxygen properties generated and supplied by the Cryogenics Division enabled the investigators to identify the most probable cause of failure and to establish a basis for redesign.

Comparison of Near- and Far-Field Determination of Antenna Patterns.—To support the deep space program as well as lunar missions, NASA's Jet Propulsion Laboratory required an accurate calibration of standard-gain horns to be used with their 210-foot dish antenna at Goldstone, Calif.

The approach NBS used to calibrate these horns was the measurement of the near-field distribution of radiation in a plane area in front of the horns. The data was then mathematically transformed to arrive at far-field antenna-gain patterns of high accuracy and great detail. The end result was a superior measurement at low cost.

Time and Frequency Signals Useful to NASA Sites.—The NBS standard frequency radio stations provide NASA tracking stations with high-frequency timing signals accurate to within milliseconds. The transmitter in Hawaii (WWVH) has been relocated and equipment and antennas improved, which will significantly improve services in the far Pacific areas. Where a more precise and stable frequency reference is required, the very low frequency transmissions of WWVL in Fort Collins, Colo., are widely used by NASA sites. Where ultraprecision timing applications exist in the United States, NASA's Goddard Space Flight Center is considering using a new TV timing system developed by NBS which is accurate to nanoseconds.

NASA has also contracted with NBS to theoretically predict amplitude and phase for various VLF transmissions under varying propagation conditions. Paths considered are between several VLF stations such as WWVL, and nine NASA tracking stations throughout the world. The VLF signals are used for calibrating the station frequency standards.

Photo Absorption and Ionization Data for NASA.—During the past year NBS has begun a collaborative program with the Manned Spacecraft Center, NASA, to compile and critically evaluate photo absorption and photo ionization cross-section data for atoms and simple molecules. These data are of critical importance in interpreting satellite, rocket and ground observation of radiation from planetary atmospheres and other hot radiating astrophysical objects.

A New Transition Probability Scale for Iron.—Astronomers are dependent upon laboratory values of atomic transition probabilities for their determination of the abundances of elements in the sun and stars. Measurements of many neutral iron transition probabilities have been performed at NBS with a wall-stabilized arc and a delayed coincidence lifetime apparatus, leading to a new set of data consistent with all other recent measurements. This set ties together these previously unrelated measurements, and differs from the older, widely used data by factors up to 30. On the basis of these new results, astronomers now believe that there is about 10 times more iron in the sun than previously assumed. The new values for the iron transition probabilities also resolve a long-standing inconsistency between the iron abundance in the corona and the photosphere.

Microwave Spectra of Molecules with Astrophysical Significance.—Radio astronomers have observed microwaves emitted from water vapor from several sources in the galaxy. This radiation corresponds to a vibrational-rotational transition in the ground electronic state of the water molecule. Detection of the corresponding radiation from water molecules containing a different isotope of oxygen (mass 18 instead of mass 16) would confirm the original assignment as well as provide information on the relative galactic abundance of these two oxygen isotopes and the emission excitation mechanism in the water molecule. Before an astronomical search can be made, it is necessary to have a laboratory measurement of the transition. This measurement has been made by NBS, the result being 5625.147 ± 0.015 MHz. for the appropriate transition frequency in water containing oxygen of mass 18.

Since absorption by the formaldehyde molecule in the galaxy has been detected, speculation exists about the occurrence of similar molecules. The new species thioformaldehyde, H_2CS, has been generated and its

microwave spectrum observed. A prediction of the appropriate frequency of the vibrational-rotational transitions (1046.48 ± 0.02 MHz.) has been made with precision sufficient for an astronomical search.

Thermodynamic Measurements on Gaseous and Liquid Fluorine.—Fluorine is one of the most reactive oxidizers known and its use with hydrogen provides the highest specific impulse of any stable oxidizer-fuel combination. Accurate thermodynamic-property data on both substances are required for the design of efficient rocket-propulsion systems, but few physical-property measurements have previously been made on compressed fluorine because of its extreme reactivity and toxicity. After solving the compatibility problems associated with handling this substance, accurate vapor pressures, densities and specific heats were measured at temperatures down to the triple point ($53.5°$ K.) and pressures to 21 meganewtons per square meter (equivalent to 3,100 p.s.i.). The volumetric and thermal measurements are being used with ideal gas-spectroscopic measurements to provide the most accurate and extensive thermodynamic-property data in existence for this substance.

Advances in Radiative Transfer.—The primary means of deriving the physical properties of the atmospheres of stars, including the sun, is by understanding the radiation they emit. In general the radiation is not formed under thermodynamic equilibrium conditions. Some accomplishments at NBS in the theory of radioactive transfer directed towards this goal include: a means of solving the general noncoherent scattering problem; investigation of the transfer of radiation in a stellar atmosphere in which electron scattering is important; and solutions of the radiation field in very extended spherical atmospheres.

Downed-Aircraft Emergency Locator Beacon.—The FAA has engaged NBS to assist them in determining acceptable performance standards for an emergency locator beacon for downed aircraft. The NBS is determining the minimum radiated power from an emergency locator transmitter (ELT); developing a measurement technique to permit the FAA to evaluate commercial ELT's at their facilities; determining the environmental effects of terrain, metal, weather, etc. on the ELT; and investigating a means of transferring an approved standard ELT to production line testing.

Use of the Moon as an Absolute Flux Calibration Source at Far Infrared and Microwave Wavelengths.—NBS has carried out calculations of the brightness temperature at the subsolar point on the moon in the spectral region between 5 microns and 10 centimeters wavelength. These calculations used thermal properties and opacities of the lunar soil which were determined from samples returned from the moon by the Apollo missions. The lunar source will be useful for calibrating observations of the sun, planets and other astronomical objects. This is especially important since the use of an extraterrestrial standard calibrates the atmospheric transmission as well as the instruments employed.

Observations of the Solar Chromosphere.—NBS scientists have made observations of the resonance multiplet and three infrared subordinate lines of singly ionized calcium. These observations were made at Kitt Peak National Observatory and Sacramento Peak Observatory and analysis of the data is underway. Theoretical calculations have been completed of the density and temperature dependence of the intensity ratios of these lines. The observational data will be combined with the calculations to make improved models of the solar chromosphere and to investigate such structures as plages, sunspots, the chromospheric network, and supergranule cells.

Apollo Lunar Ranging Experiment.—During 1970 the McDonald Observatory, in cooperation with the Lunar Ranging Experiment Team, has carried out laser range measurements from the earth to the moon using the Apollo 11 retroreflector package on the moon. The number of successful measurements per month has increased rapidly during the year, with results being obtained for most observing periods in the latter part of the year. NBS has participated in the work of the Lunar Ranging Experiment Team during the year and is working jointly with the Jet Propulsion Laboratory and the University of Maryland in the early analysis of the results. Substantial corrections are already indicated to the eccentricity of the lunar orbit and to the mean distance from the earth to the reflectors.

Institute for Materials Research

Planetary Atmospheres.—Theoretical calculations of radiative absorption cross sections for carbon dioxide and formaldehyde have been made by NBS in collaboration with NASA–Goddard. These cross sections are required to model the equilibrium behavior of a carbon dioxide atmosphere (e.g., Mars and Venus).

Simulated Lunar Samples.—The Bureau of Standards produces a wide range of materials of certified composition that can be used to calibrate analytical instruments and determine the accuracy of techniques of chemical analysis. A series of eight trace elements in glass Standard Reference Materials (SRM's) has recently been produced and certified for trace elements at four concentration levels (500, 50, 1, and 0.02 parts

per million). These SRM's will be of value in establishing the accuracy of methods used in geology and geochemistry and their application to lunar and other "space samples". The standards will be used to calibrate a wide variety of techniques including emission spectroscopy, nuclear methods of analysis, mass spectroscopy, polarography, and spectrophotometry.

Microprobe Standard Reference Materials (SRM's).—These standards were produced and certified to provide a highly homogeneous material at about the micrometer of spatial resolution. They are intended primarily for use in calibration of quantitative electron microprobe analytical techniques that are widely used for the chemical analysis of lunar materials. Twelve different metallic SRM's in the form of coated wires are offered for sale.

Thermodynamic Data of CHNOPS Compounds.—The Chemical Thermodynamics Data Center has completed a handbook of thermodynamic data of the compounds of the elements carbon, hydrogen, nitrogen, oxygen, phosphorus, and sulfur. This work was supported by NASA and is in support of their Exobiology Program.

Thermodynamics of Fluoride Compounds.—NBS has made an investigation of the thermodynamic properties of trifluoride and pentafluoride of chlorine which are of interest as oxidants for rocket propellants. The thermodynamic properties of fluorides and oxyfluorides of molybdenum are also being investigated because of their importance in evaluating the performance of molybdenum as a rocket structural material in a high temperature environment containing fluorine or fluorine containing compounds.

Analysis of Apollo Lunar Samples.—Analysis of lunar soil samples was carried out at NBS by scientists from other institutions. NBS has developed a new electron microprobe multiple detector system that allows the simultaneous investigation of seven elements on a given scan. Investigation of Apollo 11 samples with this instrument was done at the request of NASA.

Institute for Applied Technology

Tape Head Sticking.—NBS has carried out a study for NASA to determine the cause of failure in satellite tape recorders due to tape head sticking. A material was found in the tape backing film which produces a large increase in the coefficient of friction and which may be the cause of recorder failure.

Sterilizable Magnetic Tape.—A program sponsored by NASA, managed by NBS, and carried out at Battelle Memorial Institute produced a prototype magnetic tape that is stable when subjected to sterilization by heat, high energy radiation, or chemicals. The tape is needed for spacecraft designed to explore other planets without contaminating them.

Thermal Properties of Transistors.—Reliability of electronic systems used in space and aeronautics depends in large measure on the properties of the semiconductor devices used in their construction. An abrupt change in current-gain of a power transistor was correlated with the onset of current crowding in its operation and the formation of a hot-spot. This parameter is much easier to measure than thermal resistance which has been used to detect such instabilities in the past. This observation is expected to have great applicability in screening devices for defective constructions which might lead to burn-out of the device under operating conditions. It was also found that after a hot spot is formed in many transistors, it cannot always be eliminated by a reduction of the collector-emitter voltage to an operating condition normally free of hot spots. This "thermal hysteresis" effect reduces the maximum safe operating range of some transistors.

Wire Bond Evaluation.—NBS continued work on methods for the evaluation of wire bonds used in connecting semiconductor chips to external leads. Bond failure is a dominant cause of device failure in missile, spacecraft, and aircraft systems in both radiation and nonradiation environments. Techniques to establish uniform and reproducible bonding conditions have been developed for ultrasonic wire bonding machines. These involve direct measurement of the vibration amplitude of the bonding tool tip with a capacitor microphone or a magnetic detector. These observations have demonstrated that the vibration amplitude may be quite different for two or more operating conditions which have the same values of the parameters usually controlled. This appears to be a significant source of bond variability which can be avoided by use of the new techniques.

Microwave Semiconductor Devices.—NBS has undertaken a new project to provide improved measurement methods for microwave diodes. These diodes are critical elements in civilian and military satellite and ground communication links and in radar systems in which the sensitivity and range, and the reliability of the sets, depend substantially on the quality of the diodes. Serious trouble has been encountered in government procurement of these diodes because of the inadequacy of measurement methods currently in use to demonstrate conformance to performance specifications. Work has begun on measurements for properties such as noise figure, conversion loss, and impedance of mixer diodes.

Aircraft Tire Wear.—A program funded by the Air Force Flight Dynamics Laboratory is being conducted by NBS to develop a mathematical model of aircraft tire wear. Other work on aircraft tires includes a study of the internal stress in statically deformed pneumatic tires, computer simulation of skidding, modes of failure and impact performance, wave geometry, and development of nondestructive testing instruments and methods of measuring tread wear.

Wind Speed and Direction Indicators.—NBS has worked to improve instrumentation for measuring wind speed and direction. This work was supported by the Naval Air Systems Command and is important in carrier launches.

Analysis of a Capacity Concept for Runway and Final Approach Path Airspace.—The present measure of such capacity is that embodied in the "Airport Capacity Handbook" and based on a "tolerable average delay level" plus an assumption of highly random arrival times for aircraft. In an FAA-requested study, NBS has developed an alternative "maximum throughput rate" capacity concept, and rigorously established its representability by a simple mathematical formula. Because the formula explicitly combines the various parameters influencing capacity (e.g. traffic mix of aircraft types, runway occupancy time for each type, in-air separation standards), it is useful for studying "what if?" questions concerning capacity, such as the effect of a shift toward more use by large fast planes, as well as in analyzing the relative effectiveness for capacity enlargement of runway improvements versus improvements permitting smaller in-air separations.

Performance of High Temperature Thermocouples.—NBS investigation has shown that significant errors can be introduced when making temperature measurements with noble metal thermocouples in environments found in advanced aircraft propulsion systems. Further investigation is proceeding to determine the ranges of flow velocity and temperature in which such errors are important when noble metal thermocouples are used to monitor and adjust the performance of such systems. Development of means to minimize catalytic errors has begun.

Maritime Administration

The Maritime Administration is continuing its investigations into the commercial applications of existing satellite systems for both communications and navigation.

It is evident from trade and traffic density forecasts that the marine industry will require new or additional radio frequency allocations. An experiment is underway to evaluate UHF communications (L-band) using the ATS–5 satellite. If this project is successful, a new bank of radio frequencies will become available at a user cost comparable to or lower than VHF systems. Additionally, data transmission for marine traffic control (improved safety) could become a practical reality through a shoreside data-control center.

Satellite navigation systems offer significant potential from both economic and safety standpoints. The Maritime Administration is sponsoring shipboard tests of such systems (synchronous and orbiting) to determine relative reliability and reduce hardware costs.

Office of Telecommunications

The Office of Telecommunications of the Department of Commerce was reorganized in September to undertake a larger role in guiding the development of the Nation's telecommunications. The reorganization was accomplished by the Secretary in response to the President's Reorganization Plan No. 1 of 1970. The Office of Telecommunications is responsible for an extensive program of telecommunication services, economic and policy analyses, and technical and analytic support for the new Office of Telecommunications Policy in the Executive Office of the President. The Institute for Telecommunication Sciences was transferred from ESSA. The reorganized Office of Telecommunications operates as a primary unit in the Office of Assistant Secretary of Commerce for Science and Technology.

Office of Telecommunications studies have practical applications to aeronautic and space technology in areas of navigation, communication, remote sensing, and technical input to support policy considerations in frequency assignments. Work during 1970 included:

1. Radio propagation studies to improve the accuracy of long range radio-navigation systems used in aeronautical (as well as other) navigation. Results of the study now permit predictions and corrections for the effect of irregular and inhomogeneous terrain on the accuracy of Loran C radio-navigation positioning.

2. Studies were conducted on the effective use of the radio frequency spectrum assigned to space and aeronautic activities. Reports were prepared on "Electrospace Planning and Engineering for the Air Traffic Environment," and "Interference Predictions for VHF/UHF Air Navigation Aids." The "Electrospace" report deals with service limitations imposed upon VHF/UHF/SHF radio communication links by cochannel and adjacent-channel interference, and summarizes

methods that can be used for predicting available desired-to-undesired signal ratios (protection ratios) and determining the required protection ratios. The "navigation aid" report contains service range information relevant to distance measuring equipment (DME), instrument landing system (ILS), tactical air navigation (TACAN), and VHF omnirange (VOR).

3. Forecasts were made of radio propagation conditions for high frequency circuits used in the NASA Ground Communications Network. Operations included the issuance of "Special Disturbance Warnings" to the network and 24-hour to 6-hour forecasts for specific circuits of the networks during the Apollo 13 missions.

4. A method was proposed and developed to use satellite relays to synchronize a network of stations for use in worldwide navigation of air and space vehicles. Field measurement data showed that widely separated oscillators could be maintained within a synchronization of 1 percent of a cycle at 10 GHz. for an indefinite time as far as atmospheric transmission delays are concerned.

5. Laboratory and field measurement programs were conducted on the simulated and observed characteristics of microwave signals passing through the troposphere. The variations in amplitude and time delay of such signals are important in proposed techniques for using satellites to study global atmospheric structure. Other applications include communication between high-flying aircraft, orbiting satellites, and any elevated vehicle communicating with ground stations over paths with low elevation angles. Results to date indicate that signal fading of greater than 40 decibels occurs frequently. Horizontal space diversity can provide significantly improved system reliability.

6. A field measurement and analysis program in Radio Frequency Interference between satellite and ground stations is underway. The principal objective of the study is to determine the possibility and feasibility of alternatives to the present criteria specified for frequency sharing of satellite-ground terminals.

7. The staff participated on U.S. National Committees to the International Consultative Radio Committee (CCIR). Contributions made through the State Department provide, in part, the basis of U.S. positions relative to CCIR planning for the forthcoming World Administrative Radio Conference on Space Telecommunications scheduled for June 1971, in Geneva.

United States Information Agency

Introduction

In the year following the first moon landing the U.S. Information Agency brought some of the experience of that event to the home ground of millions. Pieces of the moon—lunar rocks returned by the Apollo 11 and 12 astronauts—were exhibited by the U.S. Information Service in virtually all the capital cities of the five continents, and many provincial cities as well.

At Osaka, Japan, an extra large lunar specimen, accompanied by the Apollo 8 spacecraft and a full-scale simulation of Apollo 11's landing site, was the center piece of the American Pavilion and was regarded as the greatest attraction at Expo '70. Over 18 million visitors filed by the lunar exhibit during 6 months, or at the rate of 100,000 a day.

The Agency's own feature film on the first moon landing, "The Infinite Journey," a 90-minute color documentary was shown in 132 countries. Many posts held VIP premieres of the film on the July 21 first anniversary.

The Agency employed all its media to tell the story of the mishap-laden journey of Apollo 13 and its final safe recovery. Later the Agency, and its posts abroad, assisted in the world tours of the Apollo 12 and Apollo 13 crews to many countries abroad. Through photos, films, wireless file, books, posters, and other media, the Agency and its 190 posts continued to explain the American space program to world audiences.

Guidelines

These guidelines were used in treatment of space developments:

(*a*) The moon landings under Apollo represent an extension of man's need to explore the unknown, the application of man's most advanced tools to unlocking the secrets of earth's nearest neighbor, and the intention to use both space knowledge and technological know-how for man's immediate benefit on earth.

(*b*) Looking beyond Apollo into the seventies, the American space program promises to be bold, diversified, and wide ranging. Its objectives are that the United States should continue lunar exploration; explore further the near planets and initially survey the outer planets; work to substantially cut costs by developing reusable space vehicles; seek to extend man's living and working capability in space; expand the practical applications of space technology, and encourage greater international cooperation in space.

(*c*) The United States encourages the participation of other countries in major aspects of its post-Apollo programs, and welcomes the agreement with the Soviet Union for development of mutually compatible docking arrangements as an instance of significant mutual endeavor in space.

(*d*) The American space program values automatic machines and uses them, but regards the role of man in space as established and invaluable. Either or both may be required, depending upon the objective.

(*e*) In fact the automatic instruments left on the moon by the Apollo 12 crew had been there 1 year to the day when the Soviets landed their robot vehicle, Lunokhod, on the moon. At the end of its first year the U.S. robot science station had produced valuable scientific findings on the nature and character of the moon, and showed every expectation of operating for still another year.

(*f*) No automatic machine, however, can be regarded as the equal of the astronaut, whose superior mobility and carrying capacity, together with his ability to exercise experience and judgment, make him a superior instrument for either close-up or wide-ranging exploration.

Treatment

Radio.—The crisis-ridden Apollo 13 mission was probably the most massive broadcasting effort of the year for the Voice of America. A look at Voice coverage, however, shows broad and detailed treatment of many space events.

Highlights show news carrying full reports on Skylab, the proposed space shuttle, the space ferry, further unmanned missions to Mars and Venus, and other space ventures proposed for the 1970's.

Voice broadcasts reported fully, for instance, on the Soviet's Luna 16 and 17, broadcasting Western reaction, scientific analyses, and congratulatory messages from NASA officials. Russian and most other services carried coverage of the first lunar rock conference at Houston where 200 United States and foreign scientists appraised the initial lunar soil and rock experiments.

The Italian Service interviewed a NASA scientist on medical applications of space research, while an

Estonian-language broadcast featured a discussion with an American astronomer on the subject of the moon structure. Hindi and Tamil shows promoted the moon rock as its exhibit moved through India. An hour-long Hindi broadcast interviewed India's leading meteorologist on weather satellites, analyzed the U.S. space program for the 1970's, and carried the NASA Administrator's statement on the desirability of United States-Soviet space cooperation.

All VOA airshows commemorated the moon-landing anniversary, including a documentary that featured Neil Armstrong's press interview.

When word first came that trouble had developed aboard the Apollo 13 spacecraft, VOA was on top of the story with calm, factual coverage, staying with it around the clock until after recovery. Prerecorded features were canceled for live reports from three Voice correspondents from Houston. In Latin America alone an estimated 108 million listeners heard Voice of America Spanish, Portuguese, and English broadcasts relayed by more than 1,400 stations.

Press and Publications.—The year saw no diminution of the demand from overseas for publishable material on the space program, so output of the Press and Publications Service continued at the high volume level of the year before.

The magazine effort was particularly comprehensive. America Illustrated, the Agency's magazine for the Soviet Union and Poland, devoted the whole of its April issue to space—16 in-depth articles on all major aspects of the program. This material was in large part picked up by other Agency magazines.

By the end of this year, editorial and art work had been completed on another special issue of America Illustrated, to be produced in February, to coincide with Apollo 14. This material will also be printed at approximately the same time in Panorama (Pakistan), Marzhaye Now (Iran), Pregled (Yugoslavia), Span (India), and the two Far Eastern magazines World Today and Horizons.

The extensive wireless and mailed feature output covered the entire spectrum of the space program, with emphasis on such aspects as additions to the body of scientific knowledge from moon exploration, spinoff values (sample titles: Space Research Produces Fire Protection Chemical, Space Medicine to Help Solve Problems on Earth), and U.S. efforts toward international cooperation.

In news terms, the dramatic return of the crippled Apollo 13 was thoroughly reported, after which attention was turned to the 1971 mission of Apollo 14.

During the year, as the moon specimens continued their travels, literally millions of copies of a simple two-fold leaflet entitled "A Lunar Sample," were printed in various languages for distribution to audiences viewing the rocks.

Photo output was varied. There were three picture stories, on special-issue stamps commemorating the moon landing, "An Artist Among the Astronauts," and "True Face of the Earth" on aerial photography which include three pictures from Apollo missions.

A special feature package on Apollo 13: 14 articles, five fact sheets, and an illustration of the mission's target point on the moon was in the hands of press and other media correspondents abroad weeks before lift-off. This was designed to inform foreign correspondents on salient aspects of the mission well in advance of launch. Providing full technical, biographical, and scientific details on the mission, the usefulness of the advance press kits has been widely acknowledged by the foreign press. The advance packet for Apollo 14 was produced and transmitted to the field in the late summer, and is being updated as new material develops.

Motion Pictures and Television.—The Agency gave its usual full coverage to Apollo 12, sending out a preflight filmed interview with the Astronaut Training Chief and, following the mission, 784 prints of "Apollo 12: Pinpoint for Science" to 129 countries in 26 languages.

Premission and postmission filmed reports on Apollo 13 were also distributed, as well as a moon-landing anniversary interview with Astronaut Armstrong. Reports on the 1970 eclipse of the sun, tracing of the weather via satellite, and a half-dozen other subjects appeared in Science Report, a half-hour monthly show distributed in, and telecasted regularly in 83 countries. In addition a considerable variety of film footage on space was distributed abroad in answer to requests by commercial film and television producers.

Newsclips sent worldwide to posts included the Saturn 5 roll-out for Apollo 13, the visit to Cape Kennedy of the President of the Congo, and the first press conference of the Apollo 14 crew. A half-hour production on astronaut training, "Moonlanding: Step 2," was sent to 126 countries for a total of 427 prints.

It is interesting that the Agency itself used space for transmission of its programs abroad fully 16 times during the year. This is more than communications satellites had been used previously since the Agency began using them in 1964.

But it was the feature film on the first moon landing that was the Agency's major space film effort of the year. In production for a year, "The Infinite Journey" led the viewer through man's agelong quest for discovery and, through the evolving Apollo program, to the moon. The film is expected to continue to have use through coming years.

Information Centers and Exhibits.—The exhibiting of historic space artifacts and lunar rocks to foreign audiences was of major significance in its relation to the American posture abroad.

In Eastern Europe, where audiences identify deeply with space, the Apollo 10 spacecraft was viewed by a million at the Budapest International Trade Fair, and became "the darling of the Fair" at the Poznan Trade Fair in Poland where close to a half million viewed it. After showings in Yugoslavia and Bulgaria, the spacecraft was the center piece of "Research and Development: U.S.A" at the Bucharest International Fair. The Apollo 10, a lunar rock and various accompanying space artifacts caused near chaos in the Fair's traffic flow, and drew an estimated 300,000 Rumanians.

Transported on a specially designed flatbed truck, Apollo 10 had been viewed by 2.5 million Europeans close to the end of the year. In Western Europe it was shown in the Scandinavian countries (Norway's largest newspaper called it "a small piece of human triumph that will adorn Oslo in the days ahead"), Vienna, and West German cities.

In November 1969 NASA made six pieces of moon rock available to USIA for world showing. These, scheduled and exhibited on all continents during the past year, are still greatly in demand. Showings are scheduled well into 1971.

In the first 6 months of 1970 the samples had been scrutinized by 8,370,513 persons, with millions more having seen them on television. Perhaps that many people again viewed the lunar rocks in the second half of the year.

In an eight-city tour of France, a moon rock called on the hometowns of one quarter of the French people, with 30 million more Frenchmen viewing it on television. Through television also, roughly half the population of metropolitan Portugal saw a lunar rock. In Ethiopia the moon rock was said to have marked the beginning of a wider acceptance of science. The Dean of Trinity Cathedral of Addis Ababa declared: "The American people have given us a scientific method for religion—to know how God had created unknown worlds. Thank God for giving us a chance to see this stone from the moon." In Singapore citizens of every age and race stood in block-long queues under a pitiless tropical sun waiting for a look at the rock. The exhibiting of the rock was in fact unique in its effect and immediate impact. In Moscow viewers nearly burst the walls of a moon rock exhibit that had not even been advertised.

To satisfy the demand for books on space, some 1,000 newly published books on Apollo and other aspects of space were shipped to post libraries. Under the Agency's book publishing programs, 17 titles on space exploration were produced in Chinese, Burmese, Thai, and Bengali, among other languages.

To inform audiences on the benefits of space exploration 106 sets of a slide lecture on this subject were sent out; so was a space science reader, "Footprints on the Moon: The Apollo Story," for English lessons.

National Science Foundation

Introduction

The National Science Foundation was established by Congress in 1950 as an independent agency to promote the progress of science. The Foundation supports scientific research and programs to strengthen research potential in all fields of science, and in 1970, contributed to the support of the aeronautic and space sciences through a number of its programs. Most of the research project support is provided to investigators who are sponsored by colleges and universities. The Foundation also supports and administers a number of national programs and national research centers which in turn provide significant support to investigators in the aeronautic and space sciences throughout the country. Through these organizational mechanisms the Foundation makes available radio and optical telescopes, scientific balloon services, and the unique facilities of the Antarctic continent.

Astronomy.—There has been a high rate of discovery of interstellar molecules in space just in the past 2 years. The identification of molecules of the OH radical, water, and ammonia have led to the discovery of more complex and unexpected molecules in space including formic acid, methyl alcohol, formaldehyde, carbon monoxide, and cyanoacetylene. All of the discoveries to date have been made at facilities in the

United States and many of them through the use of instruments at the National Radio Astronomy Observatory. The continuing discoveries by radio astronomers of these interstellar molecules should provide new knowledge of the formation of organic molecules in the universe.

The new detectors used for infrared astronomy for both ground-based and flight instruments have enabled astronomers to look at stars and galaxies in a spectral region which was not accessible in the past. The galactic center has proven to be an intense source of infrared waves, and many young stars also give off large amounts of infrared. Some of the sources suggest that stars are surrounded by large quantities of dust.

The Stratoscope Telescope was carried to a 15-mile altitude by a 5.5-million-cubic-foot helium balloon in the late spring of 1970. The 36-inch telescope was operated by ground command and produced pictures of unprecedented sharpness. The resolution of the telescope was five to 10 times better than ground-based installations which must peer through the earth's perturbing atmosphere. Photographs of Uranus showed a slightly flattened disk with distinct limb darkening from which it may be possible to learn more about the nature of the atmosphere. High quality pictures of Jupiter are undergoing further study. The nucleus of one of the Seyfert galaxies also was photographed and found to be about half the expected size. This discovery indicates that the approximately 10 billion stars in each Seyfert-like galaxy must be moving at an unusually high speed to avoid collapse into the center of the nucleus.

The positions of intense radio sources, which could conceivably be utilized as new navigational beacons, are now being measured with high accuracy by very long baseline techniques. These techniques involve the simultaneous observations of an object in space from two or more widely separated instruments and can be extended for use with earth satellites and lunar stations to provide longer baselines. The long baselines are made possible by the use of accurate clocks and recorders at different sites.

National Radio Astronomy Observatory (West Virginia and Arizona).

—The National Radio Astronomy Observatory (NRAO) maintains three major radio telescope facilities at Green Bank, W. Va. These include a three-element array of 85-foot diameter telescopes used as an interferometer; a 140-foot diameter fully steerable telescope; and a 300-foot diameter transit telescope. A 36-foot diameter millimeter-wavelength telescope is maintained at Kitt Peak, Ariz. All facilities are used at maximum capacity with observing time demands backlogged several months. Astronomers use NRAO instruments in very long baseline experiments to study celestial radio sources. Studies of their angular diameters, fine structure, and intensity variations have led to new theories of the formation of stars and galaxies. In another area of investigation at NRAO, new information concerning the distribution of molecules in the interstellar medium has opened new fields for astrophysical research.

Kitt Peak National Observatory (Arizona).

—Research is carried on in three principal fields—solar, stellar, and planetary sciences. In addition, major efforts are directed towards the design and construction of auxiliary instrumentation for use on telescopes and rockets. The observatory maintains seven telescopes for use of resident staff and visiting scientists: an 84-inch diameter general-purpose telescope; a remote control 50-inch telescope used mostly for photometric observations; two 36-inch photometric and spectroscopic telescopes; two 16-inch photometric telescopes; and the world's most powerful and versatile instrument for the study of the sun's surface and atmosphere—a 63-inch aperture solar telescope. A new, 150-inch telescope is expected to be in operation in 1972. Instruments at both Kitt Peak and its sister observatory in the Southern Hemisphere on Cerro Tololo are used to study the composition and characteristics of stars within our own galaxy as well as of distant galaxies and objects in remote regions of the observable universe. The unique solar telescope facility has been particularly useful in the study of physics of the outer layer of the nearest star, our sun, and has resulted in a better understanding of solar-terrestrial relationships. The rocket program has contributed to the solution of important problems concerning the chemistry and dynamics of planetary atmospheres and stellar X-ray sources.

Cerro Tololo Inter-American Observatory (Chile).

—Six telescopes were in operation during the year and available to scientists and students with observing programs, with the largest a 60-inch reflector used in a wide variety of investigations including low- and high-dispersion spectroscopy, photometry, and wide-field photography. A 150-inch telescope is under construction and should be ready for use in 1973. This instrument is similar to the one under construction at Kitt Peak and is being jointly funded by the National Science Foundation and the Ford Foundation. Visitors and staff are conducting programs of research in photometric, spectroscopic, and photographic observations of the moon, planets, asteroids, stars, pulsars, gaseous nebulae, clusters, quasars, and galaxies, many of which are visible only from the Southern Hemisphere. Studies of the rich star fields of the southern Milky Way and the Magellanic Clouds which are our nearest galactic neighbors have contributed significantly to our knowledge of the universe. Extensive surveys of stellar objects in the southern skies from this observatory have also enabled us to construct improved models of our own galaxy.

Arecibo Observatory (Puerto Rico).—The Arecibo Observatory was officially designated as a national center on October 1, 1969, and the 1,000-foot diameter telescope is now available to scientists and students throughout the United States. The unique facility consists of a fixed horizontal spherical antenna with an antenna beam that can be moved to angles of 20° in any direction. Radar research at the Arecibo Observatory has provided high spatial resolution maps of the Moon, Mercury, and Venus which are of great importance to space missions. Radar investigations have also yielded new information on the rotational characteristics of Venus and Mercury and, closer to earth, on the structure, dynamics, and chemistry of the ionosphere.

Meteorology Program.—The meteorology program supports a number of research programs which relate to aeronautics and space activities at various universities. These include studies of the large scale dynamics of the atmospheres of the earth and other planets. In the earth's atmosphere, there are several investigations underway to study clear air turbulence, the constituents and energetics of the stratosphere, atmospheric electricity, and remote-sensing techniques for constituents and atmospheric motions. An increasing use of satellite data is evident in such studies. Examples of this work include a study of the physical and statistical aspects of clear air turbulence, a study of the dynamics of the atmospheres of Mars, Venus, and Jupiter by means of both numerical experiments and analytic work, and a study of the distribution of atmospheric ozone and the energetics of the upper atmosphere to determine the radiation heating in the stratosphere.

Studies of atmospheric motions on all scales form the basis of dynamical meteorology and a considerable effort across the Nation in many universities results in analytic studies and numerical simulations of atmospheric dynamics. These range from studies of global dynamics to studies of boundary layer fluctuations at the earth's surface.

Remote sensing of the atmosphere represents one of the great advances in meteorology. Radar investigations, lidar and other optical techniques, and satellite soundings and photographs form the basis of a number of meteorological investigations supported by the National Science Foundation. These techniques yield information on severe storms, atmospheric motions and energetics, the motions of particulates within the atmosphere, radiation balances, and concentration of chemical species.

Solar-Terrestrial Program.—The earth's ionized outer atmosphere is influenced primarily by energetic particles and radiation from the sun and by interaction with the neutral atmosphere below. In 1970 a wide variety of outer-atmosphere phenomena were studied under the sponsorship of the National Science Foundation.

The sun, as the source of energy, was studied with particular emphasis on the dynamics of the outer regions of the solar atmosphere. The energetic plasma ejected continuously from these regions (the solar wind) was also studied, with model studies of the interaction of the solar wind and the terrestrial magnetic field. Structure in the solar wind and the interplanetary medium was examined through measurements of scattered light in the night sky and effects on cosmic rays reaching the earth.

Energy from the solar wind is injected into the magnetosphere where it is stored temporarily as an increase in magnetic energy in the tail of the magnetosphere. It is subsequently released spasmodically in bursts called "magnetospheric substorms," which are associated with disturbances in virtually all outer atmosphere phenomena in many different regions of the magnetosphere. Research supported in this area is providing a comprehensive view of the morphology of these disturbances and has produced a suggested way in which they might be modified or controlled; that is, through the use of a satellite to inject a low temperature plasma into a critical location. This has major significance in problems related to radio communications blackouts and to augmentation of surveillance radar clutter, both of which are associated with substorms.

In studies of the ionosphere, the dominant trend is the continued development of incoherent scatter radar techniques. There is a large and growing demand to study the ionosphere using the national facility at Arecibo and strong interest in the Millstone Hill facility near Boston.

A highlight of the year was the spectacular eclipse of the sun seen by millions of viewers near the U.S. eastern seaboard and by many millions more on television. Coordination of the many research teams observing the eclipse in the United States and Mexico was provided by the National Science Foundation.

National Center for Atmospheric Research (Colorado).—During 1970 the National Center for Atmospheric Research continued its studies of the sun, the interplanetary medium, and the earth's atmosphere. A major portion of its observing resources are devoted to measurement of solar prominence magnetic fields, which clearly are important to all forms of solar activity. Increasingly sophisticated models were developed and used to investigate the circulation of matter in the solar interior and its effects on the solar atmosphere. Present models of interactions between the solar corona and its magnetic fields reveal a discrepancy between observed and calculated coronal densities during the supersonic expansion of the solar corona which produces the solar wind. Attempts continue to resolve this discrepancy, which also bears on coronal heating. In solar-terrestrial physics, high altitude tidal winds, and their interactions with the earth's magnetic field were extensively studied.

An improved rocket-borne sampler, using liquid neon rather than liquid hydrogen, which can withstand pre-flight heat for decontamination at 840° F., was built and tested for launching in 1970. The use of constant-level superpressure balloons carrying lightweight electronics packages to track global horizontal air movements has continued. Test flights from New Zealand have demonstrated that above 53,000 feet balloons stay aloft an average of over 6 months and circle the globe many times. In the past year development was started on a concept for obtaining tropospheric wind data by releasing dropsondes from a balloon in the stratosphere.

In a related program, a series of superpressure balloons were launched from Ascension Island to investigate the so-called 26-month equatorial wind oscillation. These balloons are interrogated by the Nimbus 4 weather satellite, which obtains their positions and the atmospheric pressures and temperatures at the balloon float altitudes (67,000 or 77,000 feet).

During February and March of 1970 the Colorado Lee Wave Experiment was carried out in the Boulder area. Simultaneous observations were made at altitudes up to 65,000 feet of lee wave profiles, the growth and decay of clear and rotor cloud turbulence, and the characteristics of downslope windstorms. The study linked mountain-wave turbulence with Kelvin-Helmholtz waves and was a step toward learning to predict and detect atmospheric turbulence—a topic of great concern to commercial aviation.

Engineering.—The Engineering Division supports a number of research programs related to aeronautics and space activities. In general, the support provided is oriented toward earth-based problems such as wind flow over urban areas, wind effects on structures, dispersion of contaminants in the earth's boundary layer, application of aeronautical knowledge to biomechanics problems, aerodynamics of tube and air cushion vehicles, and a broad program of basic fluid mechanics and heat transfer research.. Particular emphasis is being given to societal related problems, to technology transfer, and to directing aeronautical researchers into new activities such as biomechanics.

Fundamental areas of research supported include the effects of adverse pressure gradient on turbulent boundary-layers, hypersonic rarified gas dynamics, and variational approaches in fluid mechanics, to name but a few. Research in specific engineering problem areas is supported by grants such as cavitation scale effects

for generalized value shapes, aerodynamic performance of gravity vacuum tube vehicles and dispersion of pollutants from tall chimneys. Support for research on the aerodynamics of insect flight is another interesting area of research where the results will be of interest to life scientists and possibly aid in the control of insect populations.

Experimental studies are underway to investigate plume dispersion from a tall stack under the meteorological conditions which cause fumigation—a condition where relatively high concentrations of pollutants are brought close to ground level. Once this process is better understood, appropriate action can be taken to alleviate the pollution potential.

Mathematics.—The Mathematics Section supports a wide range of research which directly and indirectly supports the space and aeronautics activities. The development of structure and methodology for solutions of integral and differential equations provides a basis for solutions of particular problems in these areas. Studies in celestial mechanics are underway. A program on convergence procedures in orbit calculations is being conducted at one university. In another example, difficulties which arise in the energy and momentum calculations associated with the problem are under investigation. In the area of stellar dynamics investigations are underway on the motion of a star in a galactic potential, on dynamics of large scale astrophysical phenomena, on the interstellar medium, and on bar-shaped galaxies.

U.S. Antarctic Research Program.—Many Antarctic studies relate directly or indirectly to the space program. Informal consultations on mutual problems are frequent between NSF and NASA, and a NASA official presently serves in an advisory capacity to the U.S. Antarctic Research Program.

Space program officials have shown particular interest in the management of the Antarctic program, as its operation at the end of a long logistic line bears some resemblance to the lunar exploration program. There are parallels, as well, between the Antarctic environment and those that may be encountered on other planets. For this reason, soil microbiological studies have been carried out in Antarctica for several years.

Because of the ease with which low-energy phenomena can manifest themselves at high geomagnetic latitudes, the polar regions are especially productive regions from which to perform investigations of the ionosphere and magnetosphere. Correct interpretation of the measurements leads to a better understanding of how the sun affects and controls the earth's environment. The measurements are made from ground level and from balloons, rockets, and satellites; they are made of events of opportunity as well as on a synoptic basis.

Education Activities.—In fiscal year 1970 approximately $2.4 million was obligated by the Foundation's three education divisions for activities which were, either in whole or in part, related to the aeronautic and space sciences. Since some of these awards were multidiscipline in nature—e.g., a project which provided training in several different disciplines for a group of high school teachers of science—it is therefore estimated that approximately $2.16 million was awarded in fiscal year 1970 for education in the aeronautic and space science per se.

The greatest proportion of these funds supported graduate fellowships and traineeships. These funds also provided for upgrading the subject matter background of teachers of science and mathematics in secondary schools, colleges, and universities, unusual independent study and research experiences for students and the improvement of instructional programs in aeronautic and space science in colleges and universities.

More than 1,450 individuals received training in the aeronautic and space sciences in projects supported by the three education divisions in fiscal year 1970. The majority of these individuals were junior and senior high school teachers of science and mathematics. Of the $2.16 million obligated by the Foundation for education programs in the aeronautics and space sciences in fiscal year 1970, 76 percent was for graduate education, 8 percent for undergraduate education and 16 percent for pre-college education programs.

National Academy of Sciences
National Academy of Engineering
National Research Council

Introduction

The National Academy of Sciences and the National Academy of Engineering are private organizations of scientists and engineers that serve as official advisers to the Federal Government under a congressional act of incorporation. These advisory services are carried out largely by the National Research Council, which was established by the Academy to act as an operating agency.

Highlights of the work of the Academies-Research Council in aeronautics and space during 1970 include the Space Science Board's study on priorities in space science and earth observations for the next decade and its review of the NASA life sciences programs; the Aeronautics and Space Engineering Board's counseling on civil aviation R. & D. policy and on the space shuttle; studies on development and applications of aerospace materials by the National Materials Advisory Board; the Committee on Atmospheric Sciences' Friday Harbor study on physical problems of the atmosphere; administration of NASA fellowships; and a wide range of advisory and review work in aeronautics, space applications, and physical life sciences· space programs.

Space Science Board

The Space Science Board is the National Academy of Sciences' principal advisory group on scientific direction of the U.S. space program and acts as Academy representative to the Committee on Space Research (COSPAR) of the International Council of Scientific Unions (ICSU). At Board meetings, space research and related topics are discussed with the senior staff of interested Federal agencies. During 1970, as is customary, sessions were scheduled to take into account critical times in budget planning and formulation; thus the Board's views have been made available to program planners for consideration. The Board, and several individual members, responded to requests from the Senate and House space committees for views on aspects of the space program in the form of testimony and statements on specific topics.

Priorities in Space Science and Earth Observations.—A Study on Priorities in Space Science and Earth Observations was convened by the Board at Woods Hole, Mass., from July 27 to August 15, 1970, with the participation of more than 90 scientists. Undertaken at the request of the National Aeronautics and Space Administration, the study was asked to determine criteria for relative priorities and to recommend levels of effort and support to be allocated to NASA programs in planetary exploration, lunar exploration, astronomy, fundamental and solar-terrestrial physics, the environmental sciences portion of space applications, and the life sciences, during the period 1971–80, based on likely contributions to basic knowledge and social benefit and on estimated total funding to be available.

The Study developed sets of priorities at three levels of funding. Evaluation of new starts during the coming decade was emphasized. The recommended programs and priorities were presented to NASA management at the conclusion of the study and are contained in the study's report, in press.

Review of NASA Life Sciences Programs.—A special study was conducted in the spring and summer of 1970 in response to a NASA request for a study of its objectives, programs, and procedures in the life sciences. The Study was to develop general guidelines for the organization and conduct of the life sciences activities within NASA. In its report, "Life Sciences in Space" (1970), the study calls for central direction of the NASA life sciences, with functional reorganization along disciplinary lines, and makes specific recommendations concerning the advisory structure, experiment selection, and personnel recruitment. It emphasizes the importance of international cooperation in space biological and medical programs. Exobiology—the search for extraterrestrial life and for deeper understanding of the origin of life—should remain the prime scientific priority in NASA life sciences, and, if manned spaceflight is to continue, a far broader program of space biomedicine and human biology should be undertaken to insure man's safety and efficiency and to qualify him for space. Finally, the study stresses the importance of ground-based research preparatory to and in support of space experiments.

Exploration of Venus.—The capability of relatively small spacecraft to answer fundamental questions about the planet Venus was assessed at a June 1970 study. The report, "Venus: Strategy for Exploration" (1970), concludes that scientific investigation of Venus is one of the most important objectives for planetary exploration in the 1970's and 1980's. It recommends that the Delta-launched, spin-stabilized, planetary Explorer be the prime vehicle for unmanned study of the planet by orbiters, atmospheric probes, and landers. The report recommends a mission strategy and, in the interest of maintaining minimal costs, emphasizes simplicity of operation on early lander missions and suggests that NASA be prepared to accept somewhat higher risk of mission failure if substantial over-all cost savings can be achieved.

Other Special Studies.—Possible contamination of Mars by spacecraft was the topic of two conferences held in July. The first, undertaken by the Board at the request of NASA's Bioscience Programs Office, reviewed and re-evaluated the probability of growth and spread of terrestrial organisms released from spacecraft which might crash land on the Martian surface. The practical importance of the question lies in the fact that significant planetary contamination would confuse the readings of instruments seeking to detect evidence of life on Mars, and that the greater the probability of growth of terrestrial organisms, the more strict must be the standards for sterilization of the spacecraft. On the basis of information obtained since the last review in 1967, the review group felt confident in recommending a reduction from the current value of the probability of growth from one in a thousand to one in 10,000. The second meeting was held by the Board's Committee on Potential Contamination and Interference from Space Experiments at the request of the Science Adviser to the President. It considered the potential contamination risks incurred with use of radioisotope thermoelectric generators (RTG) as power supply for the unmanned Viking 1975 mission to Mars. Concluding that the advantages of the RTG are considerable and the risk of compromising future experiments small, the Committee saw no objection to use of the RTG on this mission.

The Division of Physical Sciences' Solid State Sciences Panel and a Space Science Board group conducted a joint study for NASA's Office of Advanced Research and Technology on the possibilities of increased solar cell efficiency.

Space Medicine and Biology.—Review of individual NASA research projects and flight experiment proposals was a central activity of the Board's Committee on Space Medicine and its panels during 1970. These evaluations, made at the request of NASA, covered a wide range of disciplines in the life sciences; programs in cardiovascular physiology, calcium dynamics, and microbiology were given particular attention. The Radiobiological Advisory Panel issued its report, "Radiation Protection Guides and Constraints for Space Mission and Vehicle Design Studies Involving Nuclear Systems," in November 1970. Also published was "Space Biology," the report of the special Board study at the University of California, Santa Cruz, in July 1969, concerned with biological studies in the space environment.

International Relations.—The formal international activities of the Space Science Board are centered in the Committee on Space Research (COSPAR). COSPAR, as an Inter-Union organization of ICSU, fosters fundamental research in space science through the use of rockets, satellites, and deep-space probes. Data and significant results are exchanged on a cooperative basis through the World Data Center system. The 13th annual meeting of Cospar took place in Leningrad, U.S.S.R., May 20–24, 1970, immediately following the Inter-Union Commission on Solar-Terrestrial Physic's symposium. One major symposium was held during the COSPAR meeting—Remote Sounding of the Atmosphere. Reorganization of the COSPAR working group structure was augmented by the appointment of permanent chairmen and assignment of membership in the working groups. As in past years, the Board Committee on International Relations organized the U.S. participation in the COSPAR meeting, reviewed U.S. contributed papers, and prepared the annual report to COSPAR on U.S. space research during 1969.

COSPAR accepted the invitation of the U.S. National Academy of Sciences to host the 1971 annual meeting in Seattle, Wash., June 21–July 2. Symposia proposed for 1971 include: Results From the Recent Total Solar Eclipse, High Resolution Astronomical Observations From Space, Movements of the Neutral and Ionized Components of the Atmosphere Above 120 km., and Global Biophysics.

Aeronautics and Space Engineering Board

The Aeronautics and Space Engineering Board (ASEB) of the National Academy of Engineering provides advisory services to the Government in the areas of aeronautics and space engineering by focusing capabilities available within the Nation's engineering community on significant issues involving aerospace policies and programs. It recommends priorities to be assigned to engineering objectives, proposes ways to apply engineering competence to aerospace problems of national importance, and recommends methods of improving education in aerospace engineering and related disciplines.

During October–December 1969, the Board formed the ad hoc Study Advisory Committee on Aeronautics (SACA) to provide expert and broad advice and counsel to NASA and the DOT in their joint study of civil aviation R. & D. policy. The SACA met once in 1969 and four times in 1970 to offer comments on direction of the study, review its progress, and critique drafts of its report. Upon conclusion of each meeting a summary of comments was submitted to the study's director.

Since mid-1969, the ASEB has examined: (1) engineering approaches and concepts considered for the space shuttle, concentrating on sizing of the shuttle booster and orbiter, and (2) the overall program balance and timing for the various phases of development. The Board held a series of meetings at the NASA centers engaged in the space shuttle program and has submitted informal comments on the program's progress and direction to the NASA Administrator. NASA has strongly endorsed the Board's plan to continue following that program and to offer periodic advice on problem areas and critical decision points. This review is expected to continue into 1971.

The Board intends to continue its study and evaluation activities both in aeronautical and space transportation systems throughout 1971. The latter, in particular, may be expected to include increased consideration of international cooperation in space and space station utilization.

Division of Behavioral Sciences

Committee on Hearing, Bioacoustics, and Biomechanics (CHABA).—CHABA sponsored two aerospace meetings: the Fifth Annual Meeting on Vestibular Functions as Related to Space Travel, in Pensacola, Fla., and a Symposium on Biodynamic Models and Their Applications, in Dayton, Ohio. CHABA is cooperating with the International Civil Aeronautics Organization and the Organization of Cultural and Economic Development in setting international criteria for sonic boom. Another working group is establishing criteria for noise and vibration levels in aircraft. A report was published on the detection of submarines by means of sonar in helicopters. A revision of the Bioastronautics Data Book is nearing completion.

Committee on Vision.—At the request of NASA, a working group has been formed to advise the agency on its program to develop certification requirements for simulation of the aviator's visual environment. The NASA program to develop a device for testing visual functions during spaceflight has been reviewed. The chairman of the Committee's Executive Council debriefed the Apollo 11 commander on visual problems encountered in lunar exploration.

A working group continues to advise the FAA on its program to develop proximity warning indicators (PWI) for general aviation aircraft. Suggestions for research have been reviewed, and information on related programs in the Army, Navy, Air Force, and NASA is being collected. Any recommendations for specifications will be sent to the Aircrew Station Standardization Panel and to the FAA.

At the request of the Air Force and the Army, a working group has been formed to study the levels and effects of microwave radiation in aircraft and in radar installations.

Division of Earth Sciences

Committee on Space Programs for Earth Observations, Advisory to the Department of Interior.—The Advisory Committee has continued to prepare memoranda for the Department of Interior advising on various aspects of remote sensor programs in the discipline areas of geography, cartography, geology, hydrology, and oceanography. Meetings of specialized panels in these fields, as well as of a parent committee, addressed problems and opportunities arising in connection with the Department's Earth Resources Observation Systems (EROS) program. Committee investigations have included such tasks as the development of sensor technology, the evaluation of in-house and contract research proposals, the application of data to the tasks of the Department of Interior, and design and use of optimum equipment to be used in future earth resources survey aircraft, spacecraft, and processing centers.

Division of Engineering

National Materials Advisory Board (NMAB).—The general purpose of the NMAB is the advancement of materials science and engineering in the national interest. It undertakes to define technical problems, potential approaches, and new opportunities of national concern and relevance to Government, industry, or academia, attempting thereby to stimulate appropriate action.

Aeronautical and space materials and their applications continue to represent an area of problems that challenge the most advanced capabilities of materials technology. These difficulties derive from the extreme environmental conditions imposed on the materials used in aeronautical and space operations and the inherent necessity for minimum structural weight. A large part of the Board's attention and effort is devoted to advising the Government on its programs of aerospace materials research and development.

Beryllium, because of its light weight, strength, stiffness, and other unique properties, is being used to advantage in certain aerospace applications. However, problems relating to brittleness and inherent anisotropy remain. At the Government's request, the Board arranged and held a 3-day conference in March to review a large variety of applications of beryllium in aerospace hardware during the past 5 to 10 years and to discuss problems and opportunities. The Conference Proceedings were published in Report NMAB–272. In addition, an NMAB study is being conducted by the ad hoc Committee on Beryllium to recommend policy options relative to the future Government role in advancing beryllium technology.

A number of other NMAB ad hoc committee studies now under way concern the development and application of aerospace materials. Noteworthy among these are: A study to identify the factors that promote or inhibit the use of advanced materials, to evaluate the influence of these factors, and to recommend measures to encourage prompt utilization; a study of testing methods useful in predicting material performance in structures and components; a study of practices in aircraft design and materials selection, materials behavior, fabrication processes, and inspection techniques, to guide and foster optimal fracture-prevention practice in aircraft; and a study to define problems of producing high-performance castings (metal) and to plan a program for upgrading the technology.

Division of Physical Sciences

Committee on Atmospheric Sciences.—The Committee on Atmospheric Sciences is presently engaged in two studies involving research and technological development and application for observing and measuring the terrestrial atmosphere. A wide variety of physical problems dealing with the atmosphere were discussed and evaluated during a summer study held at Friday Harbor Laboratories of the University of Washington during June 1970. Scientific and technical issues pertaining to requirements necessary for advances in understanding atmospheric dynamics, chemistry, climate, and modifications—both intentional and inadvertent—were identified. The second study, nearing completion, concerns weather modifications and has elements in common with the first. Many of the specific measurements that have been identified as necessary to understand the dynamics of climate also pertain to the determination of ability to modify weather.

Among the principal conclusions of the studies are the following:

—The monitoring and measurements from space platforms should be coupled during the developmental stage with data obtained from ground-based sensing as well as from aircraft.

—The concerns of the public, the Government, and scientists have focused upon a major need to obtain reliable and continuing data on the particulate and gaseous composition of the atmosphere, particularly in light of the effects that man's activities may be having on the global change of climate. Local and regional aspects of man's interference with natural atmospheric processes are also very important. Global aspects are those to which the satellite is most obviously a key element. Measurements of the cloud populations of the globe have been continuing for a number of years. It is now important that measurements crucial to the radiative and heat budgets be made. Such measurements will include secular changes in global albedo and will require monitoring global and regional changes in cloud cover as well as the thermal characteristics of the atmosphere-ocean-land complex.

—The role of man in contributing large quantities of carbon dioxide and sulfur dioxide to the atmosphere may now be sufficiently great to alter the radiative and chemical characteristics of the atmosphere which are important in bringing about long-term changes in the global climate. It seems therefore prudent and wise to plan for an integrated system of monitoring from the earth's surface as well as from space which will confirm the existence, location, and time-variation of constituents, both gaseous and particulate, of natural or man-devised origin.

—The relative importance of various atmospheric constituents in effecting climatic change must also be tested through the use of existing numerical atmospheric models and models specifically developed to study long-term climatic changes. Computer developments that will permit testing of experimental models should be utilized to the fullest extent possible.

U.S. Committee for the Global Atmospheric Research Program.—The Global Atmospheric Research Program (GARP), a major international program established to improve our knowledge of the dynamics of the general circulation of the global atmosphere, has the ultimate goal to develop the physical and mathematical basis for extended predictions of the planetary circulation. The U.S. Committee for the GARP (USC–GARP) has worked closely with Federal agencies in developing the scientific objectives and is continuing to establish observational and technological requirements through its working groups that are considering specific scientific problems and planned field programs to deal with them. The USC–GARP is also serving as the focal point for coordination and communication between the scientific community and the Government, and will continue to assist in developing international planning for the scientific activities.

During the International Planning Conference on GARP, held in Brussels in March 1970, 25 nations agreed to move toward the implementation of the proposed observational experiments, in particular a tropical experiment to be conducted in the Atlantic during 1974, and a first global experiment to be undertaken a few years later. Space-based observation systems are crucial to both experiments for the identified remote measurements, data collection, platform tracking, and communications. GARP requirements have already been incorporated into the U.S. operational meteorological satellite system planned for that period, and several other nations, notably France, Germany, Japan, the United Kingdom, and the U.S.S.R. have indicated their intention to contribute space platforms. The USC–GARP will continue to participate in both national and international planning and coordination of these particular activities.

Office of Scientific Personnel

The NASA International University Fellowships in Space Science and the NASA Postdoctoral and Senior Postdoctoral Resident Research Associateship Programs, which are administered for NASA by the Office of Scientific Personnel, continue to have a strong attraction for scientists and engineers. The NASA International University Fellowships Program, jointly financed by NASA and participating space agencies of other countries, was completely subscribed, with 52 full-year fellowships, both in 1969 and 1970. A total of 282 fellowships have been awarded from the beginning of the program in 1961 to December 1970.

The number of applications for the Resident Research Associateship Program continues to exceed by a wide margin the number of appointments which are available. On August 30, 1970, there were 192 associates on tenure.

The associateship program, initiated in 1959, provides an opportunity for investigators of unusual ability to conduct research in NASA centers. In the fellowship program young scientists from other countries study and participate in space research at leading universities in the United States.

Committee on SST–Sonic Boom

The Committee on SST–Sonic Boom, through its subcommittee structure, met as necessary during the year to determine what additional sonic boom research is needed to better understand the impact of the boom on people, animals, and structures. Deliberations were based on a review of ongoing sonic boom research, within the guidelines of Presidential directives.

One of the areas of sonic boom generation and propagation research in which little work has been done and which the Committee currently considers important is the careful field measurement and subsequent analysis of shockwave phenomena produced by an aircraft in the Mach 1.0–1.2 range. During the year, a team from NASA's Langley Research Center planned such a field test centered on the 1,527-foot Bren Tower located on Jackass Flats at the AEC Nevada Proving Ground. The tower serves as the focal point for instrumentation to measure air mass and shockwave characteristics. The data obtained from this test will be of particular value as a check on sonic boom theory now in process of formulation and refinement in this speed regime. These theoretical efforts are under way partially as the result of earlier Committee interest and support of such work. The Committee cooperated with NASA on the Bren Tower project and continued its policy of close collaboration with other organizations sponsoring sonic boom research work in other areas.

The Smithsonian Institution

Introduction

The Smithsonian Institution has been concerned with aeronautics and space sciences for nearly a century, since its second Secretary conducted his pioneering research in the dynamics of manned flight.

Today, the Smithsonian Institution continues its contributing role in this Nation's aeronautics and space programs. The Institution's research programs in these disciplines are coordinated through the Office of the Assistant Secretary for Science. Aeronautics- and space-related activities are conducted by the Smithsonian Astrophysical Observatory (SAO), the Office of Environmental Sciences, the National Museum of Natural History, the Center for Short-Lived Phenomena (CSLP), and the National Air and Space Museum.

Recognizing the new tools and methodologies that are emerging with the development of satellites and space technology, the Smithsonian Institution is exploring the possibilities of their applications to biological and ecological problems requiring wide-range and long term surveillance. Observations of climatic changes on earth as reflections of a variety of cyclical fluctuations help to establish a baseline for the study of the world ecosystem.

The responses of animals to the environment can also be monitored and a test for a system for tracking migrating animals is currently underway. The Institution was cosponsor with NASA for a Symposium on Animal Orientation and Navigation which took place at Wallops Island, Va., on September 9–13, 1970.

The support of the public for the U.S. activities in space is largely dependent on the extent to which the man on the street understands its purposes. The exhibits in the National Air and Space Museum are designed to educate its visitors and to stimulate their interest. The great number of people visiting the museum daily attest to our success in this respect.

Smithsonian Astrophysical Observatory

The Smithsonian Astrophysical Observatory (SAO) has attempted to follow the tradition of its founder through a dynamic program of astrophysics and space sciences contributing to both the specific goals of the national space program and the broader goals of pure discovery.

During the past year, SAO researchers have made significant advances in the understanding of the nature and evolution of the solar system through the analyses of lunar and meteoritical samples; of the energetic processes in the universe through the observation of high-energy sources of radio, infrared, and gamma ray emissions; and of earth itself through an extensive program of geoastronomy that has helped establish basic models for the earth's size, shape, atmosphere, and gravitational field. Throughout all this research SAO has fostered international cooperation and whenever possible has as actively contributed to those worldwide efforts complementing national goals.

Earth Physics.—In ranging experiments utilizing satellites equipped with retroreflectors, the current laser systems developed by SAO have proven about 20 times more accurate than the Baker-Nunn camera used at the satellite tracking stations. Continued development of these systems may produce precision further improved by a factor of 10. Eventually, the laser should permit the measuring of the distances between ground stations to an accuracy of 1 inch. Obviously, such a capability would offer many new scientific possibilities, such as the direct measurement of continental drift, the solid-earth tides, the rotation of the poles, the spreading of the seabeds, ocean-level profiles, and large-scale crustal shifts.

Spacecraft-tracking data obtained by this network of cameras and lasers have contributed much to earth physics, specifically in SAO's research on atmospheric density variations, the gravitational field, and the geometry of the earth.

For example, much of what is known about the earth's atmosphere above 200 km. is based on SAO analysis of satellite orbital data gathered over the past decade. By a long-term study of the correlation between satellite drag and solar activity, SAO scientists last year generated the bulk of the data for an "International Reference Atmosphere." This tabulates the mean temperature and density variations of the atmosphere at any position for any period of the day and for varying solar and geophysical circumstances.

Similarly, the "Smithsonian Standard Earth" provides the most accurate representation yet produced of the earth's size, shape, and gravitational field. The 1970 edition was improved both by the addition of new laser data and by the contribution of data from a score of international sources, including the U.S.S.R.

International Scientific Cooperation.—Since its inception, the SAO spacecraft-tracking activity has fostered a high level of international cooperation, both through the operation of stations in foreign countries and through the active participation of foreign scientists in SAO research programs.

In addition, SAO has organized cooperative tracking programs for earth-science purposes, drawing on the resources of other agencies both at home and abroad. Such a joint campaign is now being implemented with overall coordination by the Centre National D'Etudes Spatiales of France and with SAO serving as one of the four major "subcenters." This program, known as the International Satellite Geodesy Experiment or ISAGEX, will be conducted from January to June 1971 and will emphasize laser tracking. Some 20 countries will participate. The observational data from this ambitious joint venture should permit significant advances in earth physics.

Analysis of Meteoritical and Lunar Samples.—On January 9, 1970, near Lost City, Okla., the field manager of SAO's Prairie Network recovered a 22-pound fragment of a meteorite photographed falling to earth 6 nights earlier. Within the next 4 months, three more fragments of the same fall were recovered in this area. This marked only the second time in history—and the first time, intentionally—that a meteorite photographed entering the earth's atmosphere had been recovered.

The rapid recovery of the Lost City Meteorite allowed almost immediate analysis of its short-lived radioisotopes created by cosmic-ray bombardment in space. More important, the photographic record of the fall provided information on the meteorite's origin (from the asteroid belt beyond the orbit of Mars) and its loss of mass in flight. Because the meteorite proved to be a bronzite chondrite, a type accounting for 35 percent of all falls, Lost City provides a standard reference model for many objects recovered in the past. Moreover, the photographic data can be used to calibrate information gathered on thousands of bright meteors photographed by the Prairie Network in the past 5 years.

Because of SAO's extensive experience with the analysis of recovered meteoritical material, three separate research groups were selected by NASA as principal investigators of lunar material returned by the Apollo astronauts.

One group, engaged in the mineralogical and petrological studies of samples through X-ray diffraction and electron-microprobe techniques, found an unexpected amount of gabbroic anorthosite in Apollo 11 samples. This anorthosite material matched the chemical composition of materials in the lunar highlands as revealed by earlier Surveyor landings, thus suggesting that the anorthosites might be mountain fragments tossed into the Mare Tranquillitatis (Apollo 11 landing site) by cratering impacts. The unusual anorthosite content of the lunar highlands has led to the suggestion that this material may have formed in the early evolution of the moon when it floated to the top of the molten matrix as a sort of geological scum, thereby forming the first part of the moon's crust. This theory has led, in turn, to a search of earth itself for similar outcroppings of anorthosite as examples of this planet's own primordial crust. A new view of the earth's evolution may result from this research on the lunar samples.

Another group has been conducting radioisotopic analyses of Apollo 11 and 12 samples to find traces of argon-37 and tritium, radioactive isotopes created by cosmic-ray exposure. This research reveals information concerning both radiation levels on the moon and exposure ages of the samples themselves. In related research, a third group is using a small, tabletop laser to free the radioactive gases in the lunar samples for mass-spectrometer analysis.

Energetic Processes in the Universe.—The past several years have witnessed an explosion of new astronomical discoveries, many of which may have consequences for mankind beyond our imagination. For example, at the edge of the known universe, powerful quasars are observed receding at nearly the velocity of light. The regular, rapid flashes of pulsars indicate the presence of matter so compressed it might be comparable to squeezing all the world's automobiles into a thimble. Intense sources of infrared radiation are detected at the core of several galaxies, including our own Milky Way. A host of molecules, many representing organic chemicals basic to the chain of life on earth, have been discovered in interstellar space, and a uniform microwave background seems to engulf the entire sky, indicating to some astronomers that they might be receiving the left-over radiation from the primordial explosion that created the universe.

To understand these and other problems associated with the creation and evolution of the universe, SAO scientists are conducting intensive research programs utilizing new instrumentation capable of observing longwave radio radiation, infrared and ultraviolet light, and very shortwave gamma rays.

SAO prepared and operated aboard the OAO–A2 an experiment called Celescope. It consisted of four astronomical telescopes mated with special television cameras designed to photograph star fields in four different wavelengths of ultraviolet light.

During more than 16 months of operation that ended in late April 1970, the Celescope experiment observed 3,000 star fields, taking 8,700 photographs that covered about 10 percent of the sky, including about 20 percent of the region near the Milky Way containing the majority of ultraviolet objects.

The photographs provide data for more than 25,000 stars in four ultraviolet regions of the spectrum. The experiment also observed the Moon, Comet Tago-Sato-Kosaka, and the planets Mars and Jupiter in ultraviolet light.

Smithsonian scientists are now compiling and analyzing the data in preparation for making a detailed comparison of the actual observations with theoretical stellar models developed at SAO. Complete analysis is expected to take several years, culminating in a catalog of ultraviolet star brightnesses and an interpretation of the material that will enable astronomers to refine their theories of the evolution of young or "hot" stars.

Observing the universe at radio wavelengths with both an 85-foot antenna operated jointly with Harvard University and a 140-foot antenna maintained by the National Radio Astronomy Observatory at Green Bank, W. Va., Smithsonian astronomers have discovered two new important constituents of interstellar gas—formic acid and methyl alcohol.

The search for these and other molecules in space is aided by the accurate determination in the laboratory of a particular molecule's radio wavelength frequency. These same laboratory experiments have also provided a possible explanation for the process by which infrared energy is converted to the microwave radiation observed from the water and hydroxyl molecules in space.

One of the most challenging fields of research at SAO involves gamma-ray astronomy. Theoretical studies indicate that some celestial objects should be emitting gamma rays. This ultra-high energy radiation may provide the key to understanding many phenomena, including magnetic fields, the density of matter, high-energy particles in intergalactic space, radio sources, and the pulsars. Indeed, gamma-ray studies may even provide answers to basic questions concerning the creation of matter and antimatter in the universe.

The search for gamma-ray sources is being conducted at SAO's Mount Hopkins Observatory with a 10-meter optical reflector and with balloon-borne detectors launched from Texas and India. The observations at Mount Hopkins represent one of the most sensitive ground-based searches ever conducted. One of the major suspected sources now under investigation is the pulsar at the center of the Crab Nebula.

Man in Space.—During the past year, SAO scientists also contributed to the growing body of information concerning the effects of the outer space environment on man.

Several theories have been suggested to explain the mysterious light flashes reported by Apollo astronauts. One investigator has theorized that the flashes may be Cherenkov light created inside their eyeballs. He suggests that when the charged particles, known as cosmic rays, penetrate the spacecraft walls and the helmets of the astronauts, they pass into the vitreous humor of the eyeball and produce extremely brief bursts of light. In short, the astronauts' eyeballs may be acting as small Cherenkov radiation counters. The theory was tested on the Apollo 13 flight, when the astronauts made careful observations of the flashes in a darkened cabin both with their eyes open and with them covered by a light-tight mask. On a future flight, they will attempt similar observations when in lunar orbit to see if the moon serves as a barrier against such radiation.

The Office of Environmental Sciences

Satellite tracking of animals, together with the monitoring of physiological factors simultaneously with conditions of the environment provides unique opportunities for investigating a vast array of important biological questions—such as the migratory movements and navigational guidance mechanisms of animals, patterns of dispersal, and concentration associated with feeding and/or reproduction, the entrainment of physiological cycles by environmental parameters, and patterns of the vector transmission of disease by migratory or nomadic animals.

As an initial step in this direction, a wild free-roaming elk was tracked and monitored on the National Elk Refuge during the month of April 1970, demonstrating the practicability of tracking animals on the surface of the earth by satellite. The experiment so far has been a qualified success, and the study will be continued with an improved instrument collar through an entire migratory cycle to correlate behavioral activities with tracking and simultaneous monitoring of physiological and environmental parameters.

National Museum of Natural History

The past year has been unique in the association of the National Museum of Natural History (NMNH) with the space program. After many years of collection and research on randomly acquired extraterrestrial rocks—meteorites—scientists at NMNH have been privileged to examine the lunar rocks purposefully collected by the Apollo missions. Thus the preceding man-years of thought, training, and experimentation were put to the ultimate challenge of elucidating the history.and evolution of the moon from these samples.

Samples of the Apollo 11 collections were received at the Museum in mid-September 1969, and since then virtually everyone in the Department of Mineral Sciences has been actively involved in a coordinated research effort on them, and on samples from the Apollo 12 mission. NMNH has been able to plan and execute a truly comprehensive investigation of the lunar materials—their chemical and mineralogical composition, and the interpretation of these data to provide a tentative account of their petrologic history and evolution. Although the samples received were small (totaling less than an ounce), it was possible to extract from them a remarkable variety of rock and mineral fragments. Among these was a unique object, a small metallic spheroid 4 millimeters in diameter. It evidently formed as a droplet of nickel-iron from a metallic meteorite which crashed on the moon. The surface of this spheroid is spotted with small craters, the product of impacts of lunar particles traveling at supersonic velocities. In its shape and surface features it mimics the moon itself.

Center for Short-Lived Phenomena

The Smithsonian Center for Short-lived Phenomena (CSLP) serves as an international early-alert system for the rapid receipt and dissemination of information concerning unpredictable and short-lived geophysical, biological, and astrophysical events of major scientific importance. During 1970, the CSLP participated in a number of activities related to the space sciences.

The Analysis of Extraterrestrial Materials.—The CSLP participated in the investigation of 13 major fireball events occurring in seven countries and six States during the year. These investigations included contact with event areas by telephone and cable, collecting eyewitness reports of magnitude, direction, duration, color, sound phenomena, and impact locations where they occurred. The reports were telephoned and cabled to interested scientists throughout the world who made on-the-spot investigations of the majority of the reports.

As a result of these investigations, the CSLP was responsible for the recovery and delivery to laboratories of four meteorite fragments from falls in Venezuela (January 18), Ethiopia (May 11), Sudan (August 15), and Swaziland (October 6). All four samples were subjected to extensive study, including radioisotopic analysis, in Smithsonian laboratories.

Man in Space.—Under contract to NASA, the CSLP continued its role in the attempts to determine the validity of the transient lunar phenomena—brightenings, colorations, etc.—supposedly observed in the moon's surface by ground-based observers.

During the Apollo 13 flight, the CSLP coordinated communications between 216 astronomical observers in 34 countries and the NASA Manned Spacecraft Center for the rapid relay of reports of transient lunar phenomena to the astronauts. The Apollo astronauts were unable to confirm any observations made from ground stations.

National Air and Space Museum

Under the terms of the space artifacts agreement with NASA, the National Air and Space Museum continued to receive rocket engines, manned spacecraft, scientific satellites, spacesuits, etc. All such material in exhibitable condition is placed on display at the Smithsonian or loaned to NASA centers, museums and other appropriate organizations in the United States and abroad. Overseas loans are coordinated with the U.S. Information Agency and the Department of Commerce. During 1970 major overseas exhibits of spacecraft were displayed at Expo 70 in Japan, and in western and eastern Europe. They were viewed by millions of visitors.

At the Smithsonian Institution in Washington, several newly displayed aircraft include an RAF Hurricane and the "Polar Star" of Antarctic fame. Charles Lindbergh's Tingmissartoq was displayed at Expo 70.

Other new exhibits at the museum were the communications satellite Early Bird, and Astronaut Armstrong's Apollo 11 lunar visor. An outstanding and complete library of oral history of space flight was received from a private donor.

Federal Communications Commission

Introduction

The major responsibilities of the Federal Communications Commission in aeronautics and space include the following:

1. Specific responsibilities in the communications satellite field such as authorizing Comsat's participation in the ownership and operation of satellites for use in the global communications satellite system and authorizing the construction and operation of U.S. non-Government earth stations.

2. Participation in national and international groups and organizations concerned with satellite communications for general use, as well as specialized uses by the aviation, marine, and amateur radio services.

3. Administration of domestic rules and regulations applicable to non-Government radiocommunications.

4. Participation in national and international development of frequency allocations and solutions to technical, operational, and policy problems regarding aeronautical communications, space satellites, and radio astronomy, as well as the coordination of international notification of specific frequency assignments and use.

Communication Satellites

International satellite communications have continued to grow at a rapid rate, so that at the end of the year the Intelsat system was using 2,126 circuits, an increase of 710 circuits over the number in operation at year-end 1969. Membership in the International Telecommunications Satellite Consortium (Intelsat) increased by an additional seven countries, as of December 31, 1970. The Global Satellite System now has 43 earth stations with 51 antennas in operation in 30 different countries.

Two additional satellites in the Intelsat III series were successfully launched and placed in service over the Atlantic Ocean. The configuration of the space portion of the Global System now consists of the two Intelsat III satellites serving the Atlantic region, one Intelsat III satellite serving the Pacific region, and one Intelsat III satellite serving the Indian Ocean region. An Intelsat II series satellite is providing service between the mainland and Hawaii. A sixth satellite,

also of the Intelsat II series, is available for service in the Atlantic region on a contingency basis.

The first commercial satellite, Early Bird, launched April 24, 1965, designed with a useful lifetime expectation of 18 months, has now lost its stationkeeping capability after five years of operation and is drifting westward. It could be used in emergency for communications between the U.S. earth stations on the west coast and the Hawaii earth station.

The Intelsat III F–2 satellite launched December 18, 1968, for service over the Atlantic experienced difficulties requiring its replacement, and the Intelsat III F–8 satellite, launched July 23, 1970, never achieved proper orbit due to an apparent malfunction of the satellite apogee motor.

The first satellite of the Intelsat IV series now under construction is scheduled for launch and placement over the Atlantic Ocean in early 1971.

The earth station in Alaska became operational in July 1970 with 80 circuits authorized for service to the U.S. mainland. The Guam earth station also became fully operational, bringing the total number of U.S. earth stations now operating in the Intelsat system to eight. Construction has been authorized and is now underway for a new replacement antenna at the Andover, Maine, earth station.

International Radio Consultative Committee

A Plenary meeting of all the study groups of the International Radio Consultative Committee (CCIR), including Study Group IV (Space Systems), was convened in February 1970 at New Delhi. The CCIR, encompassing 14 study groups, serves as an adviser to the International Telecommunication Union (ITU) on technical matters involving the use of radio. Five FCC members attended the plenary, one of them as vice chairman of the U.S. delegation and another as a major working group leader for Study Group IV. The plenary approved documents prepared by Study Group IV at the final CCIR meeting of September 1969 in Geneva with only minor changes. At the plenary continuation of an International Working Party (IWP) of Study Group IV on Efficient Use of the Geo-Stationary Orbit and an IWP of Study Group V on Propagation for Space Telecommunications was approved. An FCC representative serves on both IWP's. The IWP of Study Group IV met in London during the week of October 19 and the IWP of Study Group V met in Nice during the week of November 30 with the FCC member attending both meetings.

At the plenary a special joint study group meeting preceding the Space Conference, 1971, was set for February 1971. FCC members have been heavily involved in the preparation of over 100 technical documents for this special meeting, including documents on feasibility of satellite broadcasting on several frequency bands, criteria for sharing of frequencies between Comsat and terrestrial radio systems at frequencies above 1 GHz, discussion and proposals for the escalation of power flux densities from satellites with angle of arrival in bands shared with radio relay systems, and other similar documents.

The Commission will provide participation by about four of its members to the special joint study group meeting in February 1971. The intensive preparation for this meeting is responsive to the needs of the World Administrative Radio Conference (WARC) on Space in June 1971.

Radio Astronomy and Space Services

The Commission has been in continuing consultation with the Office of Telecommunications Policy and the Department of State in the preparatory work for the forthcoming WARC on matters pertaining to radio-astronomy and the space services. The ITU Administrative Council adopted a resolution in 1968 calling for such a conference and set forth a tentative agenda for comments. The date on which it will convene has now been set for June 7, 1971, and will run for 6 weeks. In response to the resolution, the FCC initiated an inquiry (docket No. 18294) in August 1968 for the purpose of developing proposals to that conference which would be responsive to the needs of its licensees. This preparatory work, conducted in consultation with the Office of Telecommunications Management and its successor, the Office of Telecommunications Policy (OTP), evolved through a series of seven notices of inquiry into a document entitled "Draft Proposals of the United States of America for the World Administrative Radio Conference for Space Telecommunications (Geneva, 1971)." The latter document was also transmitted abroad in August 1970, by the Department of State, to elicit the comments and reactions of other member countries of the ITU. The formal proposals of the United States to the Conference will be based on these draft proposals, as modified to take into account the national and international comments.

Aeronautical Services

Commission staff representatives have continued working nationally with other Government agencies and the aviation industry, and internationally with the International Civil Aviation Organization (ICAO) and the CCIR, toward development of system parameters and the application of space radio communication techniques to help satisfy the communication and navigation requirements of domestic and international civil aviation. During 1970 various tests and study programs previously established, as well as new programs, have been pursued. New authorizations or renewals have been granted where required.

The air transport industry, under the authorization of the Commission, continued tests which were begun in 1966 to assess the relative merits of emission techniques and normal power versus substantially higher power abroad aircraft as elements between a communication aeronautical station and aircraft via satellites. The Commission staff continued study of the results of those tests as well as the results of studies such as the previously contracted industry report of the program in order to determine the most suitable techniques to be used in aeronautical satellite systems. Such information assisted the Commission in developing preliminary views transmitted internationally for coordination prior to the forthcoming WARC.

The Commission, in discharging its statutory responsibilities with respect to nongovernment uses of radio for aviation, prescribes the manner and conditions under which frequencies may be assigned for aeronautical telecommunications. In addition the Commission assigns frequencies to aircraft radio stations, aeronautical en route, radionavigation, aeronautical advisory, and other stations comprising the aviation radio services.

The Commission continued to authorize various scheduled airlines to participate in tests using NASA's Applications Technology Satellites (ATS). Tests using ATS are presently continuing over both the Atlantic and the Pacific between ground terminals and aircraft. Continued analysis of the results is in progress with particular emphasis on the potential effect of satellite systems on the existing aeronautical radio communications systems. Further test programs, particularly in regard to UHF usage and technology are being prepared. Actions within the Commission are being taken to provide for the capability of collision-avoidance systems. The possibility of simplified and inexpensive equipment to provide pilot warning, in addition to the more complex and expensive collision-avoidance systems is being studied.

Commission staff representatives have participated in the preparation of guidance material for the use of U.S. representaitves to international conferences including those of the CCIR and the ICAO. Members of the staff again served on the U.S. delegation to the CCIR interim meeting at Geneva this year which treated, inter alia, aeronautical satellites. The staff is preparing documentation for the forthcoming WARC. This is particularly important because presently the ITU rules provide only a portion of the frequency requirements to satisfy the aeronautical requirements foreseen for the near future. Staff emphasis will be on the required changes to satisfy aeronautical requirements through the time period present to 1980.

Maritime Mobile Service

The ITU World Administration (Maritime) Radio Conference held in Geneva in September–November 1967 adopted recommendation No. MAR 3 relating to the utilization of space communication techniques in the maritime mobile service. The recommendation invited administrations, IMCO, and the CCIR, respectively, to undertake a study of maritime operational requirements for a safety and navigation radio communications system via satellite and the technical aspects of such systems. In 1970, the Commission, working with the Intergovernmental Maritime Consultative Organization (IMCO) Subcommittee on Radiocommunications, CCIR, the Radio Technical Commission for Marine Services (RTCM), industry, and other Government agencies, is continuing to study the potential value of adapting satellite relay techniques to the communications requirements of the marine mobile service.

The RTCM, an organization established by the FCC in which Government and industry, cooperate in studies of existing and proposed systems of maritime communications, previously established a special committee SC–57, Maritime Mobile Satellite Communications, to investigate the possibilities of utilizing satellites for marine communications and navigation. A test program was developed which was subsequently adopted by the Maritime Administration as a basis for tests conducted during early 1968 in which VHF communications were relayed via NASA's ATS–1 and ATS–3 satellites between U.S. ground terminals and the merchant ship S.S. *Santa Lucia* en route from Port Newark, N.J., through the Panama Canal to Valparaiso, Chile, and return. These tests together with those performed during 1967 through 1968 by the U.S. Coast Guard from the cutters USCGC *Klamath, Staten Island, Glacier,* and *Casco* have demonstrated the feasibility of communicating with ships at sea via satellite. This was a basic and vital first step.

The Commission is continually analyzing the results of these and other test programs and study reports to determine their validity and potential for satisfaction of maritime communications requirements and to establish the parameters for the additional test and study

programs that may be required. Additionally, working with the RTCM, the staff is developing a program plan for the evolutionary development and implementation of marine communication systems using space techniques. In 1970 it was determined that further information was required before a program plan can be finalized.

A Government-industry program has resulted in the establishment and documentation of a comprehensive statement of operational requirements which is being used as guidance in the development of the evolutionary program plan. Updating from newly received information was accomplished.

A detailed study generated by the RTCM SC–57 in 1970 and funded by governmental agencies, has been performed for the purpose of determining the required scope of a satellite system to satisfy maritime mobile requirements, on a worldwide basis, in the present to 1980 time frame. This study, as well as the test programs previously mentioned are being analyzed to determine specific existing and foreseen problems in order that feasible solutions can be promulgated.

Present efforts are directed, in particular, to the problem of feasibility of the sharing of systems or subsystems between aviation and marine services; feasibility of sharing of frequency bands for commonality (particularly for search and rescue); problems of terrestrial and space systems sharing frequencies; and preparation of documentation in advance of the forthcoming ITU Space WARC. Preconference coordination with other administrations is in progress.

The Commission, in reviewing responses to the seven notices of inquiry in docket No. 18294, is developing the U.S. position concerning maritime communication needs using satellite techniques. The ITU radio regulations (pars. 273A and 352B, EARC for Space, Geneva, 1963) presently contain authority for the aeronautical mobile service to use space communication techniques whereas no provisions exist for the maritime mobile service. The major efforts involved presently are directed specifically toward the analysis of all information now available in order to establish a viable U.S. position for the 1971 WARC.

Amateur Radio Service

The Radio Amateur Satellite Corp. (Amsat) satellite, Australis-Oscar (AO–5), carrying telemetry beacons, was launched January 23 and functioned 23 days on 144 MHz and 46 days on 29 MHz before the batteries were depleted. The command system for the 29-MHz beacon functioned reliably; the passive attitude-stabilization system proved to be excellent for the low polar orbit. Reception of the 29-MHz beacon indicated more experiments would be highly desirable at this order of frequency. The method of thermal control and the simplified multiple-parameter telemetry system proved to be practical and useful.

The same group is seeking NASA approval of a satellite proposal calling for the launch of a small communication relay satellite, Amsat-Oscar B(AO–B), operating in the 144- and 432-MHz amateur bands as a secondary payload on an unspecified NASA launch late in 1971. It would be used in the conduct of an experimental multiple-access communications program involving small, low-powered ground terminals operated by the amateur service.

Broadcasting Policy Coordination

The Commission furnished a member of the U.S. delegation to the UNESCO meeting of governmental experts on international arrangements in the space communication field which was held in Paris in December 1969. This meeting examined the problems involved in the use of space communication for the free flow of information, the rapid spread of education and greater cultural exchange. The meeting advised on a possible convention to insure legal protection of satellite television transmission against uses not authorized by the originating body; defined the studies which might be prepared by UNESCO on space communication; assessed the requirements of education, science, and culture in the allocation of frequencies for space communication; and discussed a draft declaration on the guiding principles which might govern the use of space communication for the furtherance of UNESCO's aims.

The Commission was represented on the U.S. delegation to the third session of the working group on direct broadcast satellites of the U.N. Committee on the Peaceful Uses of Outer Space at New York in May 1970. This group further studied satellite broadcasting with particular regard to international cooperation and the legal questions raised by broadcasting via satellite.

The Commission also participated in the work of Panel 1, Ad Hoc Intragovernmental Communication Satellite Policy Coordinating Committee, under the direction of the Office of Telecommunications Management (now Office of Telecommunications Policy). The Panel studied national policies relating to the use of satellites for international broadcasting, including general consideration of the technical, economic, legal, political, and other aspects of such broadcasting. Panel 1 issued its report on July 15, 1970.

SOURCE: National Aeronautics and Space Council, "Aeronautics and Space Report of the President," 1971.

Appendix C

Guide to NASA Policies and Procedures for Sponsored Research

NASA Objectives

NASA's long-range objectives were established by the National Aeronautics and Space Act of 1958. It provides that NASA conduct aeronautical and space activities in such a way as to contribute to:

—the expansion of human knowledge of phenomena in the atmosphere and space;

—the improvement of the usefulness, performance, speed, safety, and efficiency of aeronautical and space vehicles;

—the development and operation of vehicles capable of carrying instruments, equipment, supplies, and living organisms through space;

—the establishment of long-range studies of the potential benefits to be gained from, the opportunities for, and the problems involved in the utilization of aeronautical and space activities for peaceful and scientific purposes;

—the preservation of the role of the United States as a leader in aeronautical and space science and technology and in the application thereof to the conduct of peaceful activities within and outside the atmosphere;

—the most effective utilization of the scientific and engineering resources of the United States, with close cooperation among all interested agencies of the United States, in order to avoid unnecessary duplication of effort, facilities, and equipment.

University Relationships—Basic Policy

Universities are considered as partners with government and industry in the nation's aerospace program, and are encouraged to participate to the maximum extent practicable. University activities supported by NASA must be relevant to NASA's mission and contribute to the solution of problems facing the agency, and at the same time be compatible with the interests, activities and capabilities of the university. NASA believes that the objectives of these activities should be defined cooperatively, and that the support should be administered and the activity conducted in ways that ensure mutuality of benefits. Informal discussion between NASA and university scientists, engineers and administrators is encouraged as a means of exchanging information on needs, interests and methods of operation. Participation by students and teaching faculty in sponsored research is encouraged.

Types of University Relationships

NASA installations are encouraged to develop innovative and flexible working relationships with universities, that will facilitate fulfillment of NASA's mission and at the same time strengthen the research and instructional capabilities of the universities. The following relationships are typical. University faculty or other officials who believe that another mechanism will accomplish these ends better than the conventional research grant or contract method are invited to initiate discussions with officials of a NASA field installation or of the Headquarters Office of University Affairs.

Sponsored Research

The principal-and most visible-direct interaction between NASA and the university community is via the support of university research through the medium of grants and contracts.

Other forms of interaction are, however, possible under existing NASA policy. Such interaction would normally be undertaken pursuant to some form of cooperative agreement. Such agreements normally do not involve the exchange of any significant financial support. They do, however, generally involve some use of NASA facilities, equipment or services in exchange for use by NASA of university facilities, equipment, personnel, services or other consideration. The selection of appropriate subject matter for such agreements is, of course, subject to some constraints, such as availability of the NASA resources and the priority relationship of such subject matter to the NASA mission. Proposals for areas of cooperation should be addressed to the Director of the NASA field installation with which such cooperation is desired.

Other Relationships

Limited numbers of university scientists and engineers may be hired on a temporary basis (e.g., during a summer) to conduct special studies at NASA installations, and NASA staff may be granted special leave for extended periods to take courses of advanced study or to serve as instructors in universities.

University scientists may be invited to serve, on the basis of personal expertise and with minimum institutional involvement, as NASA consultants or members of technical advisory committees.

NASA's Research Interests

NASA is interested in and sponsors a wide range of research activities in universities, nonprofit institutions, industrial laboratories and other Government agencies, as well as in its own field installations. Projects range from very specifically defined investigations to broad multidisciplinary enterprises, and may be theoretical, experimental or both.

Much of NASA's sponsored research involves satellites, space probes, and manned aircraft and spacecraft. These investigations are subject to special constraints and demands, described in NHB 8030.1A, related to flight vehicle, environment and compatibility with other experiments, as well as the requirement for relevance to the purposes of particular flights

Most of NASA's sponsored research, however, is ground-based. Some of it may involve studies, research and technological advancement preliminary to undertaking a flight experiment, but the greater part is made up of basic and applied research related in some way to the improvement or exploitation of flight capabilities. Subject matter ranges from physical, mathematical, biological and medi-

cal sciences, through engineering sciences and their applications to aeronautics, space vehicles and propulsion, to socio-economic and management studies and the beneficial application of aerospace research and development. A complete listing of sub-areas of research is not feasible, but some insight into NASA's specific current and anticipated research needs can be gained from several sources: discussions with NASA scientists, public announcements of research needs of more than usual interest, related work published in the open literature, and various Government publications, including the authorization and appropriation acts of the Congress and the related hearings reports.

Relevance to NASA objectives is a primary requirement for sponsored research.

Unsolicited Proposals—General

The unsolicited proposal is the principal means for organizations to bring their research ideas and abilities to NASA's attention. Through this process institutions of higher education, other nonprofit scientific research organizations, and industry, propose research projects that they believe will help meet NASA's current and long-range program requirements.

Proposals for Flight Experiments

Proposals for flight experiments to be carried on earth satellites or spacecraft present special problems of coordination, evaluation, and selection, and are the subject of a separate NASA publication NHB 8030.1A, "Opportunities for Participation in Space Flight Investigations." Copies may be obtained from the Office of Space Science and Applications, Code SS, National Aeronautics and Space Administration, Washington, D. C. 20546. Proposals submitted in response to the above publication have not been considered as unsolicited proposals for statutory cost sharing purposes.

Proposals from Foreign Sources

As a general rule, NASA does not directly contract with, or award grants to, foreign organizations except where the requirements cannot, as a practical matter, be met within the United States.

Subject to the above policy constraints, there are several avenues for foreign participation in NASA's research programs. The first, and probably most important, is through support which the foreign organization may be able to obtain from its own government or from regional space organizations. The second is through a subcontract from a United States organization having a prime contract with NASA, on the basis of normal competitive practice. Finally, NASA directly supports a small amount of research in foreign countries based on unsolicited proposals (but such foreign projects are more frequently undertaken on a cooperative basis, wherein there is no exchange of funds).

Proposals from foreign sources, requesting financial support, should be addressed to the Proposal Control Officer, Code Y, National Aeronautics and Space Administration, Washington, D. C. 20546, in the same manner as domestic proposals. Foreign proposals for a cooperative undertaking should be submitted through the proposer's official national space agency to the NASA Office of International Affairs.

Where to Send Proposals

Universities and nonprofit organizations affiliated with universities should submit unsolicited proposals to: Proposal Control Officer, Code Y, National Aeronautics and Space Administration, Washington, D. C. 20546.

Other types of organizations may submit unsolicited proposals for research to either the above address or to a particular NASA field center known to have an interest in the subject.

Proposals submitted to the Proposal Control Officer will be assigned a NASA identification number and acknowledged. The number appears in the acknowledgment letter and should be referenced in all subsequent communications pertaining to that proposal.

Number of Copies

For evaluation, NASA requires ten copies of new proposals, and five copies of proposals for continu-

ation of a grant or research contract. Exception: fifteen copies are required of either new or renewal proposals for bioscience research. Processing of a proposal may be delayed if NASA receives less than the required number of copies.

When to Submit

There are no specific dates for the submission of unsolicited proposals. However, all proposals should be submitted at least 4 months in advance of the desired beginning of support.

What a New Proposal Should Include

When technical discussions between the proposer and NASA personnel have occurred the names and addresses of those involved should be included in the proposal transmittal letter.

Abbreviated drafts or preliminary proposals are generally of little value. They rarely contain sufficient information to permit full and considered review. Similarly, unsolicited proposals without cost estimates are regarded as incomplete proposals. If more information about NASA interest in a specific problem area is needed, it should be obtained by writing to or visiting the individual or office within NASA directly concerned with the research. The Proposal Control Officer can often identify such technical contacts in NASA Headquarters in Washington, and an inquiry to a field installation regarding its interest in a particular research area will normally be routed to the appropriate office.

NASA generally does not return proposals; therefore, they should not include "one-of-a-kind" documents, samples, slides, or movies. If such materials are essential to the proposal, they should be summarized for the evaluator.

Except for certain flight proposals submitted in accordance with NHB 8030.1A (See page 440), NASA does not usually require a prescribed format. However, all proposals should be specific and, where applicable, include these items:

1. *Institutional Data*

    Show the legal name, address, and type of organization submitting the proposal. Proposals should be signed by the principal investigator and by the administrative or business official authorized to sign for the institution. (NASA may not make a grant to an individual, and ordinarily does not contract with individuals for research. Also, if the proposing organization is part of a university system, the proposal should identify the campus which is to be the principal in the research effort.)

2. Abstract

In every proposal there should be an abstract describing the objective of the proposed research and the method of approach.

3. Schedule

State the proposed starting and completion dates for the research, making allowance for adequate proposal review and evaluation time in NASA. (See "When to Submit.")

4. Description of Proposed Research

The description should be a full statement of the research proposed, identifying and relating the key elements. Give attention to the nature and amount of experimental data to be collected; describe the methods or approaches to be used; and establish the criticalness of the theoretical approach or the crucial experiments.

When it is expected that the research will require more than one year for completion, the proposal should cover the complete project to the extent that it can be reasonably anticipated. Principal emphasis should, of course, be on the first year of work, and the description should distinguish clearly between the first year's work and that planned for subsequent years.

5. Facilities

Describe available facilities and major items of equipment especially adapted or suited to the proposed research, and any additional major equipment that will be required.

6. Personnel

The principal investigator is responsible for direct supervision of the work and usually participates in the conduct of the research regardless of whether he is to receive compensation from the grant or contract funds.

Include a short biographical sketch of the principal investigator, and a list of his principal publications. Give similar biographical information on other senior professional personnel who will be directly associated with the project. If applicable, list the number of students or other assistants, together with information as to their level of academic attainment. Show the names and titles of any other scientific and technical personnel associated substantially with the project in an advisory capacity.

7. Budget and Allowable Costs

Proposals should contain cost and technical parts in one volume. Include separate cost estimates for salaries and wages, equipment, expendable supplies, services, travel, subcontracts, publication, other miscellaneous direct costs that can be identified, and overhead. Categorize salaries and wages by principal investigator, other scientific and engineering professionals, graduate research assistants, and technicians and other nonprofessional personnel. Estimate all manpower data in terms of man-months or fractions of full-time. Explanatory notes should accompany the budget to provide identification and estimated cost of major capital equipment items to be acquired, justification of extraordinary travel costs, basis of overhead computation, and clarification of other items in the budget that are not self-evident. List estimated expenses as yearly requirements by major work phases. (Clarity on this point is vital. A grant or contract for two years of research with a one year budget can lead to severe difficulties!) The cost principles set forth in Exhibit B of the NASA Research Grant Handbook (NHB 5800.1) and Part 15 of the NASA Procurement Regulation (NPC 400) govern, respectively, the allowable costs of research on NASA grants and contracts. These principles, insofar as they pertain to educational institutions, are based on the requirements of Office of Management and Budget Circular A–21.

8. *Cost Sharing*

Appropriation acts governing NASA have, from time to time, required certain grantees and contractors to share in research project costs.

It is important that unsolicited research proposals identify the extent and nature of the proposed cost sharing contribution.

9. *Security*

If the proposed research requires access to or may generate classified information, the grantee or contractor will be required to comply with applicable Government security regulations. However, access to classified information will not be allowed unless the proposal clearly establishes that such access is essential to the proposed research. Under these conditions, the proposal should show the classification of the organization and the major investigators, and identify the cognizant security office.

10. *Disclosure of Technical Data*

It is NASA's policy not to use or disclose technical data included in unsolicited proposals for any purpose other than evaluation. However, the Agency cannot assume responsibility for improper disclosure or use of such data unless the proposer specifically identifies it by placing the following restrictive legend on the proposal cover:

"Technical data contained in pages _____ of this proposal shall not be used or disclosed, except for evaluation purposes, provided that if a contract or grant is awarded to this submitter as a result of or in connection with the submission of this proposal, the Government shall have the right to use or disclose this technical data to the extent provided in the contract or grant. This restriction does not limit the Government's right to use or disclose technical data obtained from another source without restriction."

If an unsolicited proposal is received with more restrictive disclosure conditions than are contained in the above legend, NASA may be unable to consider the proposal, in which case the proposer will be so advised.

Proposals for Continued Support

NASA considers requests for continuation of grants or contracts in much the same manner as proposals for new endeavors. However, it is not necessary that a renewal proposal repeat all of the information that was in the proposal upon which the current support was based. The renewal proposal should refer to its predecessor, update the parts that are no longer current, and indicate what elements of the research are expected to be covered during the period for which extended support is desired. A decription of any significant research finding since the most recent progress report would also be useful. The renewal proposal should treat in reasonable detail the research plans for the next period of support that were not covered adequately in the earlier proposal, and a cost estimate for the additional work must be included. The detail in the cost estimate should be similar to that in a new proposal. Also, see "When to Submit."

Additional Information or Revised Proposals

In order to facilitate its evaluation of a proposal, NASA may request additional technical or institutional information from the proposer. A proposer may also furnish additional material to NASA at any time, if, in his judgment, it would beneficially affect the consideration of the proposal. Any revised proposal must clearly show the NASA reference number assigned to its predecessor.

Submission to Other Agencies

NASA has no objection to simultaneous submission of a proposal to a number of Federal agencies, but must be notified when it is submitted to others or is funded by another agency.

Withdrawal

If a proposer wishes to have a submitted proposal withdrawn from consideration, he should promptly notify NASA.

Evaluation of Unsolicited Proposals

NASA's organization reflects its mission requirements rather than a division according to the classical scientific or engineering disciplines. Although the fundamental components of the sponsored research program are less visible under this arrangement, they constitute substantial and highly significant elements. For example, although there is no physics program per se, the materials program includes solid state physics. Similarly, atmospheric physics, solar physics, and cosmic radiation are parts of the space science program. As a result, a proposal may be a potential candidate for support by more than one Program Office or Center, each having responsibility for research in particular problem areas.

The Proposal Control Officer is familiar with the areas of interest of the technical programming group in NASA Headquarters and tries to ensure that each research proposal is sent to all potentially interested groups. Each group makes an independent evaluation of the proposal and often refers it to a NASA field installation for evaluation and possible support. Any reviewing group that has funding authority may accept and support a proposal that meets its program needs, even though other groups decline. When deemed necessary, NASA may utilize supplemental reviews by outside scientists or scientific panels for proposal evaluation. The decision to support a proposal is not by majority vote of all reviewers, but by evaluation of the potential contribution of the research to the objectives of the individual program under which it will be funded.

The principal elements considered in evaluating a proposal are its technical and programmatic relevance to NASA's objectives, the scientific or engineering merit of the proposal, the qualification of the principal investigator and his institution, and the cost of the project.

Types of Research Agreements

NASA generally uses five types of instrument to support research and related activities: grants, fixed-price contracts, cost-reimbursement type contracts, cooperative agreements and interagency fund transfers. NASA selects the type of instrument after considering the nature of the project to be supported, the performing organization, and pertinent administrative factors.

Grants

The grant is NASA's preferred instrument for support of basic research with appropriate institutions. NASA's grant authority is limited by statute to nonprofit institutions of higher education and nonprofit organizations whose primary purpose is the conduct of scientific research. A grant is an agreement by NASA to award, and by the grantee to accept and use, funds to support an identified activity. Ordinarily, this agreement is based on the grantee's proposal and contains a minimum of express conditions binding the grantee.

NASA addresses the grant and administrative correspondence thereunder to the business office of the grantee. Similarly, the grantee should channel grant administration correspondence through its business office. However, the Principal Investigator is encouraged to communicate directly with the cognizant NASA Technical Officer on research matters within the scope of the grant. Such informal technical exchange, coupled with the inherent flexibility of the grant agreement, enables the research to be pursued in directions of maximum mutual interest and benefit, with a minimum of formal documentation.

NASA grants usually are made for initial periods of one to three years, but may be made for other periods and may be extended for additional periods. Grants may be revoked in whole or in part, at any time, after consultation with the grantee.

Contracts

NASA generally uses the cost-reimbursement type when a contract is the instrument selected to support research. In appropriate cases, however, a fixed-price or other type of contract may be negotiated.

Cooperative Agreements

These express the terms and conditions of an agreement involving mutual benefits, and might involve use of NASA services, equipment or facilities.

Interagency Orders

Under special circumstances, NASA may contribute to the support of a research contract or grant issued by another Government agency. Such support, including support of research conducted for NASA by another Government agency, is furnished by a transfer of funds to that agency.

Step Funding

For long-term stability of research projects which are supported by grants, a technique known as step funding may be used. In this plan, a project begins with an obligation for full support for the first year, approximately two-thirds of full support for the second year, and one-third for the third year. At the end of the first year, if the grant is renewed, additional money is obligated to raise the second year's funding to full level, the third year to two-thirds, and another year is added at one-third level. The process is iterative. If NASA discontinues support, the institution is assured of funds for an orderly termination of the project over a two-year period.

Continuation proposals for step funded grants are required each year and it is important that they be submitted 4 months or longer before the grant is scheduled to drop to the two-thirds support level.

Administration of Grants and Research Contracts

Status Reports

NASA requires brief, informal semiannual status reports containing concise reviews of the progress of the work under research grants, and quarterly status reports are usually required under research contracts. These are minimum requirements, however, and sponsored investigators are encouraged to

communicate with their respective NASA Technical Officers at any time.

Technical Reports

Technical reports should describe results of research in sufficient detail to be suitable for publication in the open literature. They are generally not required on a regular schedule, but should be submitted whenever warranted by the progress of the research, or as otherwise provided if a contract is the selected vehicle.

NASA desires that all significant research results be published in some form. To obtain widest appropriate dissemination of the results of sponsored research, NASA encourages investigators to publish all useful research results in scientific or technical journals or as NASA publications. Published papers should acknowledge NASA's sponsorship. Copies of manuscripts to be submitted to journals should be furnished simultaneously to NASA and reprints should be provided after publication.

NASA does not require that manuscripts sent to outside journals be in any special format other than that prescribed by the journal, but papers to be published by NASA must meet the Agency's requirements for publication. The NASA address for obtaining information about technical reports is shown on page 447.

NASA provides its unclassified publications to the Clearinghouse for Federal Scientific and Technical Information, U.S. Department of Commerce, Springfield, Virginia 22151, for sale to the general public. Selected NASA publications are also sold by the Superintendent of Documents, Government Printing Office, Washington, D.C. 20402.

Financial Reports and Payment Policies

NASA makes first payments under grants in such amounts as may be agreed upon during negotiation. Subsequent payments are made in accordance with the grantee's quarterly cash requirement report (NASA Form 1031) which sets forth his estimated needs for the following quarter.

Funds received by a grantee and not expended or committed prior to conclusion of the research, or within 30 days following the termination date of the grant, must be refunded to NASA. However, when the rate of research effort has been less than anticipated and it appears that not all of the granted funds will be expended by the termination date, an extension of time for performance to a new termination date may be requested. Although such no-cost extensions usually are allowed, the request should be submitted well before the termination date to allow action to be completed without hiatus in coverage.

Payments under research contracts are made on the basis of vouchers submitted by the contractor. All payments are contingent upon satisfactory performance, including submission of progress, technical, financial management (NASA Form 533), Government property (NASA Form 1018) or other reports specified in the contract. In the case of cost-reimbursement contracts, provisional payments are subject to adjustment which may result from subsequent audit.

Payments under both grants and research contracts are made either by Treasury Department check or under the Treasury Department Letter of Credit System. (The latter is an advance funding technique whereby letters of credit in favor of the recipient organization are issued to the Federal Reserve Bank or Branch in the organization's area, to be drawn upon as needed to meet the actual cash requirements of carrying out the organization's NASA grants and contracts. Eligibility for this procedure is limited to nonprofit institutions with which NASA anticipates a continuing relationship of one year or longer, and whose aggregate annual volume of business with NASA equals or exceeds $250,000.)

Foreign and Domestic Travel

The proposal budget should include and separately identify the cost of all necessary travel, domestic and foreign. After award of a grant or contract, specific authorization for domestic travel is not required.

Foreign travel, however, even when the investigator considers it essential to the research effort, must be approved on an individual trip basis by the cognizant NASA Contracting or Grants Officer

before the trip is made. Evaluation of foreign travel requests requires intra-NASA and sometimes international coordination, and may involve further correspondence with the applicant. It is necessary, therefore, that foreign travel authorization be requested from the Grants or Contracting Officer as soon as the possibility of such travel arises. Costs of unauthorized travel may be disallowed.

Subcontracts

NASA does not encourage subcontracting of any part of the actual research under grants or contracts. Subcontracting for purposes other than purchase of standard equipment, supplies, or services, requires advance approval by the Grants or Contracting Officer.

Equipment

Performance of research under NASA grants and contracts frequently necessitates the acquisition of equipment. Title to equipment purchased with grant funds generally vests in the grantee subject to a time-limited option retained by NASA to acquire title to items costing in excess of $1000. Office furnishings or equipment or other items of a nontechnical nature may not be purchased with grant or contract funds unless they are essential to the research effort and approved in advance by the Grants or Contracting Officer. Title to equipment purchased with contract funds, and to any Government equipment furnished under a grant or contract, vests in the Government unless otherwise provided in the agreement.

Patents

NASA's enabling legislation requires that the Government assume title to any invention resulting from research sponsored by NASA. The Administrator of NASA may waive title to the grantee or contractor if it is determined to be in the public interest to do so, subject to the reservation of a royalty-free license to the Government. This requirement does not apply to any invention conceived and actually reduced to practice before the execution of the research agreement with NASA.

Each research grant and contract contains a clause requiring the furnishing to NASA of a written report covering any invention made during the performance of the research. These invention reports are separate from the status and technical reports required elsewhere.

Equal Employment and Civil Rights

NASA's sponsored research programs are subject to the Civil Rights Act of 1964, NASA's implementing regulations thereunder (14 CFR 1250) and Executive Order 11246, September 24, 1965 as amended by Executive Order 11375, October 13, 1967, relating to and prohibiting discrimination on grounds of race, color, religion, sex or national origin.

Accounting and Audit

Each grantee and contractor is expected to keep records in accordance with generally accepted accounting practice, consistently applied. These records must be adequate to allow the preparation of required reports and must show that payments received were used for the designated purpose. All records relating to expenditures under NASA contracts and grants are subject to audit by the Government.

Business Correspondence

Correspondence on business matters under a grant or contract should be signed or endorsed by an official authorized to bind the organization or institution.

Special Matters

Grants and contracts are subject to special conditions which may be required from time to time by NASA's annual Appropriations or Authorization Acts, other legislation or regulatory action. For example, NASA is currently prohibited from using appropriated funds for grants to educational institutions which are barring recruiting personnel of any of the Armed Forces of the United States from their premises or property at the time of the grant.

SOURCE: NASA, "A Guide to Policies and Procedures for Sponsored Research."

Addresses for Reference

Overall NASA relations with universities	NASA Office of University Affairs, Code Y Washington, D. C. 20546
All unsolicited proposals from universities; other unsolicited proposals not specifically for NASA field installations	NASA Proposal Control Officer, Code Y Washington, D. C. 20546
Inquiries about industrial proposals to field installations	The field installation to which addressed
Policies, procedures and regulations on the business administration of grants and research contracts	NASA Office of Industry Affairs and Technology Utilization Procurement Office Policy and Regulations Division, Code KDP-1 Washington, D. C. 20546
Inquiries about existing grants or research contracts	NASA Headquarters or field installation contracting office that issued the grant or contract
Information regarding support of research abroad	NASA Office of International Affairs, Code I Washington, D. C. 20546
Policies and procedures for, and announcements and distribution of, contractor and grantee technical reports	NASA Scientific & Technical Information Office Office of Industry Affairs and and Technology Utilization, Code KS Washington, D. C. 20546
Unclassified NASA technical publications	National Technical Information Service Springfield, Virginia 22151
Selected NASA publications	Superintendent of Documents Government Printing Office Washington, D. C. 20402
Information regarding patents, inventions, rights to inventions, and copyrights	NASA Assistant General Counsel for Patent Matters, Code GP Washington, D. C. 20546

INDEX

INVENTORY 74

COMPLETED

INVENTORY 1983